The War Against Japan, 1941–1945

WARS OF THE UNITED STATES
(Vol. 10)

GARLAND REFERENCE LIBRARY
OF SOCIAL SCIENCE
(Vol. 258)

WARS OF THE UNITED STATES
(Richard L. Blanco, General Editor)

The War Against Japan, 1941–1945
An Annotated Bibliography

John J. Sbrega

Garland Publishing, Inc. • New York and London
1989

Library of Congress Cataloging-in-Publication Data

Sbrega, John J. (John Joseph), 1941–
    The war against Japan, 1941–1945 : an annotated bibliography /
John J. Sbrega.
        p. cm. — (Wars of the United States ; vol. 10) (Garland
reference library of social science ; vol. 258)
        Includes indexes.
        ISBN 0-8240-8940-5 (alk. paper)
        1. World War, 1939–1945—Campaigns—Pacific Area—Bibliography.
2. Pacific Area—History—Bibliography.   3. World War, 1939–1945—
Bibliography.   I. Title.   II. Series: Wars of the United States ;
v. 10.   III. Series: Garland reference library of social science ;
v. 258.
Z6207.W8S29   1989
[D767.9]
016.94054'26—dc19   88-36535
                                                                  CIP

Printed on acid-free, 250-year-life paper
Manufactured in the United States of America

To Jo-Anne, with love and admiration

CONTENTS

PREFACE

Dr. John J. Sbrega, a Professor of History at the Community
College of Rhode Island, has written a unique reference work about
the struggle that the United States waged against a defiant enemy
over four decades ago. His THE WAR AGAINST JAPAN, 1941-1945: AN
ANNOTATED BIBLIOGRAPHY is a remarkable achievement. Professor
Sbrega has amassed material from a wide array of sources in order
to provide the researcher with the best literature about this protracted fight by our nation against a powerful foe. Judging by the
burgeoning output of films and publications about this era, interest
about the war in the Pacific remains high.

The author should be commended not only for the quantity of
material that he lists--over 5,200 entries--but also for the fact
that he cites books, articles, documents, novels, etc., published
on the subject up to December 1987. The organization of the volume
is very useful. Dr. Sbrega presents his subject matter in six broad
categories. His coverage of reference works, diplomatic political
aspects of the war, economic-legal features, military-naval-air
power operations, religious discussions related to the struggle, and
the social-cultural characteristics of the war related to the fighting in the Pacific all help to provide a convenient method of selecting the precise topics for which readers need dependable
references.

Due to the fact that Professor Sbrega studied innumerable declassified documents, one can obtain a unique perspective of the
war from the level of our policymakers of the era. Because the
plight of Japanese-Americans who were confined in military encamp-
ments is still a controversial matter that sears the conscience,
Sbrega cites ample material on this sensitive issue. There is also
ample material here--to mention but a few of the subjects--on the
efforts of the Allies for the United States in the Pacific, the ju-
dicial trials of Japanese commanders in postwar years for war crimes,
coverage of the lesser-known but fascinating campaigns in Southeast
Asia, and ample citations about the incredible adventures and hardships of those fighting men who participated in amphibious warfare.

This study is the tenth volume of annotated bibliographies
in the series Wars of the United States. It is an essential reference tool written by a respected scholar who is the author of many
articles about World War II. Dr. Sbrega merits praise not only for
the methodology of his organization and for his thoughtful coverage
of diverse topics but he especially deserves to be commended for
his writing ability. The writer possesses the talent of being able
to compress the essence of a book or article into a few terse,
well-chosen sentences. This book may be the definitive reference
work about our country's struggle against the Japanese in World
War II.

Richard L. Blanco
General Editor

INTRODUCTION

This annotated bibliography offers over 5,200 entries drawn from books, journals, magazines, and official documents related to the participation of the United States in the war against Japan, 1941-1945. The "cut-off" date for these selections--all published in English--is December 31, 1987. First a few words about what is not in this bibliography. Regularly published (e.g., weekly) news magazines, surveys, bulletins, reprinted speeches, and United Nations reviews have been excluded as have wartime works offering prescriptions on how to prevent World War III. In addition, under the guidance of the general editor of this bibliographic series on the wars of the United States, I eliminated references to the conflicting interpretations of various historiographical "schools." (See Richard L. Blanco, THE WAR OF THE AMERICAN REVOLUTION, New York: Garland Publishing, 1984, pp. xiii-xiv.) Thus, readers will find few direct references to historiographical debates such as the origins of the Cold War, who "lost" China, and atomic diplomacy. Nor have I exhausted the sources available on related topics (e.g., the Occupation of Japan, Asian histories, and biographies of prominent persons).

This book, however, does incorporate some unusual features. For instance, I have included official military reports that have been declassified and published in order to provide authoritative perspectives on the progress of the war. Similarly, material on the plight of the Japanese minority population in the United States (as well as the Japanese populations in Hawaii, Canada, and Peru) has been added not only as an important dimension of the war against Japan but also because of continuing public interest in the topic. As I write this introduction, for example, the question of compensation by the government to Japanese-American evacuees ($20,000 to each one?) remains under public discussion, and the 1988 presidential campaign has focused some attention on the American Civil Liberties Union. Another unique feature of this bibliographic guide is its citations on the scientific development of the atomic bomb and the postwar medical reports on the effects of the two atomic bombings. These two categories complement the entries on the decision to use the atomic bomb and the actual bombing missions against Hiroshima and Nagasaki. Readers are also invited to review the relatively new sources presented here on special weapons (including Japanese innovations) and biological/chemical warfare.

The organization of the book relies heavily on the Library of Congress classifications. Of course, readers may differ about the most appropriate category for a particular selection. For example, sources about the president's policies and attitudes on the eve of

the Japanese attack at Pearl Harbor appear in the section on the
origins of the war rather than the biographical category for
Roosevelt.
    For the convenience of American readers, I have inverted
Japanese proper names. Also, I am presenting Chinese names in the
form used during the war years rather than the newer Ying Ping
style; the traditional English representations are, after all, how
these Chinese people became known to wartime America. Note, too,
that no diacritic marks are used in order to simplify the spelling
of non-English names; these marks carry little meaning for American
readers.
    To avoid needless or repetitive statements, the reader
should consider each annotation within the context of the title
and/or topic. Moreover, I have avoided repeating information in an
annotation that is obvious. Unless otherwise specified, for
example, the phrase "during the war against Japan" is always
understood.
    Another technique I have used in the interest of efficiency is
to give only the last names of prominent persons. Some other of my
short-hand practices include the following: "this guide" means this
annotated bibliography, not the work being discussed; "interviews"
in the research of a work means that the author spoke with
participants or observers; "global" refers to all theaters of the
Second World War; "prewar," unless otherwise indicated, means
before December 7, 1941; within context, battles are occasionally
identified only by location (e.g., "Pearl Harbor" and "Hiroshima");
"contemporary" means the war years, 1941-1945; a "popular" or
"general" account describes a source geared to the general public
rather than an audience of scholarly specialists; and adjectives
not widely welcomed in scholarly reviews (e.g., "good,"
"interesting," even "very," etc.) are used here with the intention
of providing some abbreviated qualitative assessments for the
reader's benefit. No annotations are offered for the fictional
(and poetic) accounts cited; the value of such works often
transcends matters of historical accuracy and/or broadly based
research. To my frustration, I simply could not gain access to
some works because of constraints on my time and resources even
though I had managed to identify all or at least parts of the
citations. These works have not been evaluated ("NE") but are
included nevertheless within the most likely topical grouping.
Where appropriate, I have added comments about the "NE" listings
(e.g., "Forthcoming" to designate works scheduled for publication
after December 31, 1987, general information about the author
and/or subject matter, etc.). Rather than annotations, however,
these comments should be considered supplements to the "NE"
citations, which have been included in the interest of promoting
scholarly inquiry.
    Throughout this project, I felt at times like either a theater
critic ("I laughed, I cried") or a capsule writer for a television
guide ("Join the Beaver and his friends in their madcap

adventures"). No one is more aware than I of the pitfalls and shortcomings involved in concocting abbreviated analyses of complex and creative works. Abbreviation, by its very nature, leads to distortion. Sentences in my annotations cry out for an ending (i.e., period) but earn instead only a colon and a lengthy appendage in my efforts to cram as much information as possible into a brief critique. Yet few tasks are as rewarding as undertaking the systematic review of the literature directly associated with one's professional and intellectual (vocational as well as avocational) commitment. I should like to conclude this section by expressing my admiration for the general quality of historical writing on the war against Japan. The scholarship of the authors involved inspires awe and appreciation. It is a pleasure to be associated with these people and to be able to call them (however indirectly or presumptuously) "colleagues."

ORGANIZATION

The book is organized in six main sections. Part I presents reference works, including encyclopedias, pictorial accounts, and general works on the Second World War.

Part II deals with the diplomatic-political aspects of the war against Japan. These sources cover a broad range of topics. For example, the subsection on the origins of the war includes material on the continuing historiographical debate over whether or not Roosevelt maneuvered the United States into the war. The subsection on wartime diplomatic and political affairs examines subjects such as the wartime conferences, the entry of the Soviet Union in the war against Japan, Western colonialism, war aims, and the situation in China. Sources on the Occupation of Japan (sometimes referred to in this guide just as the Occupation--and always capitalized) appear in the subsection on postwar affairs. Readers are cautioned, however, that a detailed bibliographical appraisal of events in Japan from the 1945 surrender to the 1951 peace treaty falls beyond the scope of this guide.

The third main section contains sources on the economic and legal aspects of the war against Japan. Some of the subjects addressed include economic affairs within the United Nations coalition, Japan's Greater East Asia Co-Prosperity Sphere, Lend-Lease, and the economic situation in China. See also the legal subsection on the war crimes and war crimes trials.

Part IV presents sources on the military aspects of the war against Japan. The term "military" is used in this guide to embrace land, air, and sea forces. Readers looking for sources on the long range penetration groups (LRPGs) and the Burma Road are referred to the subsection on Burma (Land). Similarly, for material concerning Soviet combat operations and the Sino-Japanese

War, see the subsection on China/Manchuria/Korea (Land). As a
general rule, sources on air operations (e.g., close air support)
that are directly associated with a land engagement are grouped
under the "Land" subsection for that engagement. Note that items
on Marine and naval aviation appear in subsection IV.D.3.d.
Annotations for Unit histories (IV.E.) are not provided because of
the special nature of these works. That is, they rarely strive for
balance; moreover, nearly every activity of the unit is described
as a "good show." For sources and annotations dealing with the
atomic bomb, including its scientific development and the decision
to use the weapon, consult subsections IV.J.2.a-b.

Religious aspects of the war are contained in Part V, while
Part VI covers the social and cultural aspects. In the latter, see
especially the subsections on the treatment of Japanese minority
groups in the United States, Hawaii, Canada, and Peru (VI.G.1.a-c).
Also in Part VI, note that personal accounts by uniformed prisoners
of war and civilian internees are grouped separately.

ACKNOWLEDGMENTS

A project of this magnitude attracts many debts. (Consider,
for example, the security guard who came to my rescue after I had
inadvertently been locked inside the library at the University of
Rhode Island. Also, would readers consider it a favor--as I
do--when the librarian at Mount Holyoke College allowed me to
continue my research even though the non-air-conditioned building
was closed because of the supposedly unbearable heat?) Throughout
my travels, I have been deeply impressed with the competence,
professionalism, and cooperative attitude of librarians and
archivists who have rendered assistance to me. Without their help,
this project would never have come to fruition. In particular, I
want to acknowledge the assistance provided by administrators and
staff members at the following:

    Amherst College
    Armed Forces Staff College
    Army Military Institute (Carlisle Barracks, PA)
    Brown University
    Bryant College
    Community College of Rhode Island
    Georgetown University
    Library of Congress
    MacArthur Memorial Archives
    Marine Corps Historical Center
    Maxwell AFB, Alabama (Air University and Historical Research
        Center)

Mount Holyoke College
Naval Historical Center
Naval War College
New York Public Library
Office of Air Force History
Office of the Chief of Military History
Old Dominion University
Providence College
Rhode Island College
Smith College
Temple University
Tidewater Community College
University of Massachusetts, Amherst
University of Rhode Island
University of Virginia
Yale University

Special mention goes to the individuals who provided heroic
service either guiding me through the collections at their
institutions or ferreting out sources that were otherwise
impossible for me to access. For their patience and perseverance,
I am especially indebted to the following:

Armed Forces Staff College: Maj. Gen. Kenneth A. Jolemore
    (U.S.A.), Margaret Martin, and Mary Louise O'Brien;
Community College of Rhode Island: Nancy Blake, Elin Crowley,
    Charles D'Arezzo, James Frechette, Michael Friel, Betty
    McCool, Sylvia Mercier, Mark Murray, and Frank St.
    Pierre:
MacArthur Memorial Archives: Edward J. Boone, Jr., Lyman H.
    Hammond, Jr., Joseph M. Judge, and John Leeds;
Naval War College: Murray Bradley; and
Tidewater Community College: Anne K. Davis.

Throughout this project, I have benefitted from the advice and
support of many people. Professional colleagues, for example, like
Constance M. Jones, Wayne Knight, and Derris L. Raper have provided
endless hours of discussion and intellectual stimulation. I am
proud to have them for friends as well as professional colleagues.
The general editor of this project, Richard L. Blanco, patiently
received all my excuses about why deadlines kept shifting, and his
kind, but firm, presence provided just the guidance required to
bring this adventure to a close. At Garland Publishing, Paula
Ladenburg and her predecessor, Pam Chergotis, offered technical
expertise and encouragement that kept me on track. Ann Bradshaw,
Mary Elle, and Mary Jones cheerfully managed the technical
production of the manuscript, and without their considerable
abilities and unflagging good humor 5,259 items would still be
hopelessly lost in the bowels of the computer. ("What a great
system!") Also, for their support and personal interest in my

project as well as for their efforts in setting a nurturing
environment for scholarly pursuits at the Community College of
Rhode Island, I am indebted to Deans Judeth Crowley and John J.
Sousa ("Jack I"), Vice President for Academic Affairs Robert A.
Silvestre, and President Edward J. Liston.

My indebtedness extends to a number of proofreaders who gave
the manuscript in various draft stages such close attention.
Bibliographies, of course, present great challenges to
proofreaders, and I appreciate their meticulous work. The
manuscript has been stripped of many errors because of their work.
The proofreaders are Jose Aranda, Mark Gaipa, Steven McKenna, and
Robyn Younkin.

Similarly, I wish to acknowledge--and applaud--the excellent
work of the typists. Their performance in deciphering
near-illegible handwriting and their persistence in enduring what
must have seemed an interminable project merit special recognition.
The typists are Ann Bradshaw, Kathy Ciffo, Marcella L. Correy,
Marilyn Costa, Melissa DelGuidace, Mary Elle, Susan M. Gravel, Mary
Jones, Caren S. Neville, and Christine A. Villanova.

Friends and family rendered invaluable assistance throughout
this seven-year project. In particular, Jack and Janet Pyne
contributed selflessly and cheerfully (e.g., babysitting to release
me for research, reviewing the seemingly endless number of computer
printout sheets, and encouraging my endeavors) in seeing the
project through to its conclusion. My brother Dennis used his
legal expertise to obtain law review articles that I had difficulty
locating; my other brother, Bill, only had to be himself to offer
unlimited amounts of support and spirit-raising good cheer. My
in-laws, Ann and Edward J. Manijak, responded with love and
understanding to the needs--seemingly insatiable at times--of this
project.

A special place belongs to my mother, Rita A. (Counter)
Sbrega and my late father, John B. Sbrega. For instilling within
me the sense of purpose and discipline required to meet the
exacting demands of a project such as this (not to mention the many
other interesting challenges associated with a rich and rewarding
life) and for bolstering me with boundless love and support, I
shall always be grateful.

Two remarkable children deserve special mention. Daniel and
Christianne have displayed extraordinary patience and understanding
about the fact that for some reason Dad derived great satisfaction
from burying himself in notecards every night and every weekend.
Although it remained a mystery to them why Dad did not do the
things that other "normal" fathers did, Dan and Christi not only
tolerated this aberrant behavior but also acquiesced in the weird
rites associated with the research and writing of a book. ("Where
am I going? What am I going to do?") I hope that they draw useful
(including what I consider the "right") lessons from this
experience, but, in any event, I want to thank them for their
indulgence and their good humor. Neither will ever really know the

ACKNOWLEDGMENTS xxv

depth of the support the two of them provided in sustaining my
efforts.

It is traditional to reserve the final place for the most
important person. Without question, my biggest debt is owed to my
wife Jo-Anne. For her loving support and cheerful willingness to
help in any way--whether proofreading, preparing the indices, or
serving (too often) as a single parent--I am grateful beyond words.
(I must admit, however, that the whirring of her lawnmower and the
scraping of her snow shovel outside my window proved distracting at
times.) Indeed, it is in token recognition, wholly inadequate for
the measure of her valuable contribution, that this book is
dedicated to her with love and admiration.

North Kingstown, RI
June 16, 1988

The War Against Japan, 1941–1945

I. GENERAL WORKS

A. REFERENCE WORKS

1. ATLASES

1. Brown, E. Francis. THE WAR IN MAPS: AN ATLAS OF THE NEW
    YORK TIMES MAPS. New York: Oxford University Press,
    1946. 197 pp.

    Following the format of earlier editions, this book
    presents maps of the war as they appeared in the newspaper.
    The atlas covers prewar events and all theaters of the war.
    Selected topics extend beyond the military fronts to
    include political, strategic industrial areas, and
    communications systems.

2. Foreign Policy Association. TWELVE MAPS SHOWING THE UNITED
    STATES IN A GLOBAL WAR. New York: Foreign Policy
    Association, 1942.

    This slim volume is a useful contemporary reference;
    however, subsequent events in the course of the war against
    Japan would reveal some glaring omissions in this 1942
    perspective.

3. Fry, Varian, comp. WAR ATLAS: A HANDBOOK OF MAPS
    AND FACTS. New York: The Foreign Policy Association,
    1942.

    With text written by Francis Brown and maps prepared by
    Emil Herlin, this atlas is a valuable introduction to the
    regional situations at the start of the war.

4. Goodenough, Simon. WAR MAPS: WORLD WAR II FROM SEPTEMBER
    1939 TO AUGUST 1945, AIR, SEA, AND LAND, BATTLE BY
    BATTLE. New York: St. Martin's Press, 1982. 192 pp.

    A narrative accompanies the excellent maps, displays,
    and photographs. About 150 pages are devoted to "The War
    in the Orient."

5. Horrabin, James F. AN ATLAS-HISTORY OF THE SECOND GREAT
    WAR. London: T. Nelson, 1940-1946. 10 vols.

Here is an exhaustive collection of maps and diagrams for all theaters.

6. Modley, Rudolph. A HISTORY OF THE WAR IN MAPS, IN PHOTOGRAPHS, IN WORDS. New York: Penguin Books, 1943.

Here is a general reference which attracted much contemporary attention.

7. Mowrer, Edgar A. and Marthe Rajchman, comps. GLOBAL WAR: AN ATLAS OF WORLD STRATEGY. New York: William Morrow, 1943. 128 pp.

Mowrer provided the text, Rajchman prepared the maps and charts (about 70 in all). The book is divided into topical sections: Some Characteristics of the Great Powers (food, space, raw materials, manpower, gold reserves), World Communications, Natural Routes of Invasion, and Revolution in Warfare.

8. Stembridge, Jasper H., comp. THE OXFORD WAR ATLAS. London: Oxford University Press, 1942-1946. 5 vols.

Each of the volumes covers roughly one year of the war. The maps are arranged by theater and portray political events as well as military affairs.

9. United States. Department of the Army. Map Service. ATLAS OF THE WORLD BATTLE FRONTS IN SEMIMONTHLY PHASES TO AUGUST 15, 1945. Washington, D.C.: GPO, 1945. 101 pp.

This official atlas serves as a supplement to the Army's chief of staff war report to the Secretary of War (1943-1945). The displays highlight territories held and lost by Japanese forces.

10. WAR ATLAS FOR AMERICANS, New York: Simon and Schuster, 1944. 86 pp.

This contemporary reference was intended to assist the American public following the combat action in all theaters. The publisher benefitted from the assistance of consultants from OWI. There are over 80 maps and an accompanying narrative.

11. Young, Peter. ATLAS OF THE SECOND WORLD WAR. London: Weidenfeld and Nicolson, 1973. 288 pp.

The collection is divided into geographical regions and campaign boundaries. Photographs and brief narratives accompany the maps. The major emphasis is on the European Theater.

I.A.2. DICTIONARIES/LINGUISTICS

12. Berton, Peter A. M. NEW JAPANESE-ENGLISH DICTIONARY OF WARTIME CONTRIBUTIONS TO THE JAPANESE LANGUAGE. Tokyo: 1946.

    NE

13. Findling, John E., ed. DICTIONARY OF AMERICAN DIPLOMATIC HISTORY. Westport, CT: Greenwood Press, 1980.

    This reference work covers the period 1776-1978 and has a separate section on the war.

14. Greet, William C. WAR WORDS: RECOMMENDED PRONUNCIATIONS. New York: Columbia University Press, for CBS, 1943. 137 pp.

    This guide is a much-needed reference for research on the war in Asia. Place-names and personal names as well as battles are carefully presented. (A much more comprehensive second revised edition, with 608 pages, appeared in 1948.) Three columns for each word provide (a) the word, (b) the simplified Webster alphabet, and (c) phonetic respelling. With the wide choice of pronunciations available for Chinese words, Greet gratefully accepts the English-language versions (even though some, he acknowledges, are wildly "off").

15. Herzber, Max J. THE WAR AND LANGUAGE: A SYMPOSIUM ON THE EFFECTS OF WORLD WAR II UPON THE ENGLISH LANGUAGE. Springfield, MA: G & C Merriam Co., 1943. 8 pp.

    This brief, contemporary discussion opens a fascinating topic that deserves careful attention.

16. Kendall, Park. DICTIONARY OF SERVICE SLANG. New York: M. S. Mill, 1944. 64 pp.

    Here is a brief study of the changes—for better or worse—to the English language wrought by the war. If you don't like them, "tell it to the chaplain"!

17. Partrige, Eric, ed. A DICTIONARY OF FORCES' SLANG,

1939-1945. Freeport, NY: Books for Libraries Press,
1970. 212 pp.

The collection is divided into three parts: air force
(compiled by Partridge), navy (Wilfred Granville), and army
(Frank Roberts).

18. Richard, Dorothy E. GLOSSARY OF U.S. NAVAL CODE WORDS.
        Washington, D.C.: GPO, 1948. 33 pp.

     NE

19. Ruffner, Frederick G. and Robert C. Thomas, eds. CODE
        NAMES DICTIONARY. Detroit, MI: Gale Research, 1963.
        555 pp.

     Here is a detailed reference that contains the code
     names used in the war arranged in alphabetical order.
     Ruffner also includes popular terms and nicknames as well
     as what he calls "journalese" references.

20. Spiller, Roger J. DICTIONARY OF AMERICAN MILITARY
        BIOGRAPHY. Westport, CT: Greenwood, 1984, 3 vols.

     This comprehensive work should not be viewed as a random
     collection. Instead, Spiller, with his careful editing and
     cross-referencing, has put together what he calls "cohesive
     sets" of essays. Thus, the reader easily identifies the
     "set" on the war against Japan. For the most part the
     essays are well written, well researched, and balanced in
     interpretation.

21. Taylor, A. Marjorie, comp. THE LANGUAGE OF WORLD WAR II.
        New York: H.W. Wilson Co., 1944. 94 pp.

     Taylor arranges her references in alphabetical order.
     There are abbreviations, captions, quotations, slogans,
     titles, nicknames, and phrases. She avoids slang. Here is
     an excellent contemporary reference. A lengthier, revised
     edition (265 pp.) appeared in 1948.

22. Tunney, Christopher. A BIOGRAPHICAL DICTIONARY OF WORLD
        WAR II. New York: St. Martin's Press, 1972. 216 pp.

     Tunney provides profiles of over 400 figures who made
     noteworthy contributions to the war effort for their side.
     Entertainers, journalists, and poets are included as well
     as soldiers and statesmen. The narratives are deliberately
     kept on a factual basis and confined strictly to the war

years.

23. Young, Peter. A DICTIONARY OF BATTLES, 1816-1976. London:
     New English Library, 1977. 606 pp.

     A separate section on the war covers about 140 pages
     (including a few maps). A select bibliography appears at
     the end of the book and does little more than provide an
     introduction to the leading literature. One strength of
     the brief but fairly detailed summaries is that Young
     incorporates a sense of the overall significance of each
     battle.

24. Zandvoort, R.W. WARTIME ENGLISH: MATERIALS FOR A
     LINGUISTIC HISTORY OF WORLD WAR II. Westpoint, CT:
     Greenwood Press, 1974.

     This version is a reprint of the 1957 edition. The
     author feels that enough material exists from the war to
     fashion a separate (though limited) branch of linguistic
     history.

I.A.3. ENCYCLOPEDIA/ALMANACS/STATISTICS

25. Angelucci, Enzo. THE RAND-MCNALLY ENCYCLOPEDIA OF MILITARY
     AIRCRAFT, 1914-1980. Chicago: Military Press, 1983.
     546 pp.

     Here is a well-prepared, well-presented reference. The
     book includes many illustrations and over 250 photos in
     describing over 800 types of aircraft.

26. Baudot, Marcel, Henri Bernard, Hendrik Brugmans, Michael R.
     D. Foot, and Hans-Adolph Jacobsen, eds. THE HISTORICAL
     ENCYCLOPEDIA OF WORLD WAR II. New York: Facts on File,
     1980. 549 pp.

     Translated by Jesse Dilson, this book, originally
     published in 1977, contains some additional material
     prepared by Alvin D. Coox and Thomas R. H. Havens. The
     editors also have provided an introductory summary of
     events leading directly to the outbreak of the war. Each
     entry is informative and clearly written. This work lives
     up to its ambitious title. There is an easy-to-use system
     of cross-referencing.

27. Chant, Christopher. THE ENCYCLOPEDIA OF CODENAMES OF WORLD
     WAR II. London: Routledge and Kegan Paul, 1986. 344
     pp.

Here is a useful guide through the bewildering array of
military campaigns, secret operations, and special people.

28.   Cleveland, Reginald M. and Frederick P. Graham, eds. THE
        AVIATION ANNUAL OF 1945. Garden City, NY: Doubleday,
        Doran, 1944. 205 pp.

Here is an authoritative collection of reports on the
air war, including predictions for 1945. See especially
the views of H. H. Arnold and Ernest J. King.

29.   Cleveland, Reginald M. and Frederick P. Graham, eds. THE
        AVIATION ANNUAL OF 1944. Garden City, NY: Doubleday,
        Doran, 1943. 224 pp.

This collection is written by knowledgeable airmen and
leading officers, such as H. H. Arnold, Vice-Adm. John S.
McCain (Deputy CNO, Air), and Maj. Gen. Harold L. George
(head of Air Transport Command). The reports look ahead to
1944 as well as reflecting on the actual events of the air
war--taken in the most general sense--to date.

30.   Dupuy, R. Ernest and Trevor N. Dupuy. THE ENCYCLOPEDIA
        OF MILITARY HISTORY FROM 3,500 B.C. TO THE PRESENT.
        New York: Harper and Row, 1977. 1406 pp.

This valuable reference tool is divided chronologically
by general topics and sub-topics.

31.   Goralski, Robert. WORLD WAR II ALMANAC, 1931-1945: A
        POLITICAL AND MILITARY RECORD. New York: Putnam, 1981.
        486 pp.

This chronological record includes the trivial as well
as the significant. Many photographs bolster this
reference work.

32.   JAPANESE ARMED FORCES ORDER OF BATTLE, 1937-1945.
        Allentown, PA: Game Marketing Co., 1981. 2 vols.

This detailed reference includes organizational
information down to regimental level. Of interest is the
description of the Japanese replacement system.

33.   Keegan, John, ed. THE RAND-MCNALLY ENCYCLOPEDIA OF WORLD
        WAR II. Chicago: Rand-McNally, 1977. 256 pp.

Keegan sets out to offer the "many sided history" of the

war "arranged in encyclopedic form." The thousand-plus
articles touch on virtually every aspect of the war. The
color plates add a striking dimension.

34. Keegan, John, ed. WHO WAS WHO IN WORLD WAR II. New York:
     Thomas Y. Crowell, 1978.

     Keegan tailors the profiles to wartime events. In
     addition, he offers information on many of the lesser known
     figures in the war. Some photos are included.

35. Mason, David. WHO'S WHO IN WORLD WAR II. London:
     Weidenfeld and Nicolson, 1978. 363 pp.

     Here are biographical sketches of about 350 of the
     leading personalities of the war.

36. Parrish, Thomas, ed. THE SIMON AND SCHUSTER ENCYCLOPEDIA
     OF WORLD WAR II. New York: Simon and Schuster, 1978.
     767 pp.

     This comprehensive reference stands out among works of
     its kind. With about 4,000 entries, maps, photos, and
     expert advisers, Parrish has assembled a remarkable
     resource.

37. Snyder, Louis L. LOUIS L. SNYDER'S HISTORICAL GUIDE TO
     WORLD WAR II. Westport, CT: Greenwood Press, 1982.
     838 pp.

     Taking on a heroic task, Snyder organizes his
     encyclopedic guide in alphabetical order with much cross-
     referencing. A brief bibliography follows most of the
     entries. His emphasis is on political-economic-social
     affairs rather than military events.

38. Stanton, Shelby L. ORDER OF BATTLE, U.S. ARMY, WORLD WAR
     II. Novato, CA: Presidio, 1984. 620 pp.

     Here is an authoritative reference source. Stanton
     provides information on weapons, vehicles, and unit
     strengths, as well as organizational charts. Russell
     Weigley wrote the Foreword.

39. United States. Army Air Forces. ARMY AIR FORCES
     STATISTICAL DATA: WORLD WAR II. Washington, D.C.:
     GPO, 1945. 313 pp.

     Here is an official reference which indicates the

dimensions of the global air effort. The USAAF Office of
Statistical Control prepared the digest.

40. United States. Department of the Army. ORDER OF BATTLE OF
     THE UNITED STATES ARMY GROUND FORCES IN WORLD WAR II:
     PACIFIC THEATER OF OPERATIONS. Washington, D.C.:
     Office of the Chief of Military History, 1959. 697 pp.

     The data covers the period from December 7, 1941, to
     August 15, 1945. The book furnishes information on
     activations-dissolutions, reorganizations, location of
     units, missions, operations, and commanders. Each command
     is treated in the same fashion. Designed as a reference
     work, there is no evaluation of performance or analysis of
     factors that shaped the size or organization of Army
     forces.

41. United States. Department of the Army. Adjutant General.
     ARMY BATTLE CASUALTIES AND NONBATTLE DEATHS IN WORLD WAR
     II: FINAL REPORT, 7 DECEMBER 1941 - 31 DECEMBER 1946.
     Washington, D.C.: Dept. of the Army, 1947. 118 pp.

     The official statistics were compiled by the Casualties
     Branch of the Adjutant General's office, the official
     casualty recording and notification agency for the War
     Department.

42. THE WORLD ALMANAC BOOK OF WORLD WAR II. Englewood Cliffs,
     NJ: Prentice-Hall, 1981. 613 pp.

     Here is an extensive record of the events of the war in
     all theaters. The chronological presentations are
     sub-divided by geographical location.

43. Young, Peter, ed. THE MARSHALL CAVENDISH ILLUSTRATED
     ENCYCLOPEDIA OF WORLD WAR II: AN OBJECTIVE,
     CHRONOLOGICAL, AND COMPREHENSIVE HISTORY OF THE SECOND
     WORLD WAR. Freeport, NY: Marshall Cavendish, 1981. 11
     vols.

     Here is a massive narrative of the war, much of which
     was written by the Swiss historian, Eddy Bauer. As
     advertised, the account consistently strives for
     objectivity.

44. Young, Peter, ed. THE WORLD ALMANAC BOOK OF WORLD WAR II.
     New York: Ballantine Books, 1986. rev ed. 613 pp.

This well-illustrated reference centers on a detailed
chronology and biographical profiles of political-military
leaders. Young also provides information on air, land, and
sea weapons.

I.A.4. BIBLIOGRAPHIES/HISTORIOGRAPHIES

45. ABC-CLIO. WORLD WAR II FROM AN AMERICAN PERSPECTIVE: AN
    ANNOTATED BIBLIOGRAPHY. Santa Barbara, CA: ABC-CLIO,
    1982. 448 pp.

    Here are abstracts of over one thousand articles which
    appeared between 1971 and 1981.

46. Anderson, George L., ed. ISSUES AND CONFLICTS: STUDIES IN
    TWENTIETH-CENTURY AMERICAN DIPLOMACY. Lawrence, KS:
    University of Kansas Press, 1959. 374pp.

    In this collection, see especially Louis Sears,
    "Historical Revisionism Following the Two World Wars," pp.
    127-146.

48. Baylis, Gwyn M. BIBLIOGRAPHIC GUIDE TO THE TWO WORLD WARS:
    AN ANNOTATED SURVEY OF ENGLISH-LANGUAGE REFERENCE
    MATERIALS. London: Bowker, 1977. 578 pp.

    The author, who is with the Imperial War Museum,
    provides over 2,400. citations. The entries include
    scholarly evaluations. The book is divided into general
    topics rather than numerous sub-headings.

49. Bernard, Roy S., William Burns, and Duane Ryan, comps. THE
    ERA OF WORLD WAR II: GENERAL REFERENCE WORKS, BIOGRAPHY.
    Carlisle Barracks, PA: Dept. of the Army, 1977. 185 pp.

    This reference source provides citations for many
    leaders in the armed services. See especially the
    citations for field commanders in the Pacific at various
    levels.

50. Bloomberg, Marty and Hans H. Weber, comps. WORLD WAR II
    AND ITS ORIGINS: A SELECTED ANNOTATED BIBLIOGRAPHY OF
    BOOKS IN ENGLISH. Littleton, CO: Libraries Unlimited,
    1975. 311 pp.

    With over sixteen hundred entries, this volume carries
    special emphasis on military affairs. The annotations are
    interesting and informative.

51. Blumenson, Martin. "Can Official History Be Honest
    History?" MIL AFFS, 26 (Fall 1962), 153-161.

    Perhaps Blumenson intends his question to be rhetorical.
    He cites the U. S. Army in World War II series and notes
    the rigorous internal mechanisms designed to ensure
    accuracy. The view tilts to the rosy side of a
    controversial subject.

52. Burns, Richard Dean, ed. GUIDE TO AMERICAN FOREIGN
    RELATIONS SINCE 1700. Santa Barbara, CA: ABC-CLIO,
    1983. 1311 pp.

    This monumental work supersedes the Bemis-Griffin GUIDE
    (1935). With subject and author indexes, a dual-style
    table of contents, thousands of annotations (for sources up
    to 1981), and introductory essays for each main section,
    the volume is a valuable reference tool. The section on
    World War II serves as a convenient springboard for
    scholarly inquiry.

53. Burns, Richard Dean and Milton Leitenberg, eds. THE
    INDOCHINA WARS, 1941-1982. Santa Barbara, CA:
    ABC-CLIO, 1983. 290 pp.

    The bibliography includes sections on World War II and
    the First Indochina War that are useful for the purposes of
    this guide.

54. Coletta, Paolo E., comp. A BIBLIOGRAPHY OF AMERICAN NAVAL
    HISTORY. Annapolis, MD: Naval Institute Press, 1981.
    453 pp.

    Here is a first-rate reference, which includes
    comprehensive coverage of the era of the Second World War.
    Only a relatively few annotations are provided.

55. Doenecke, Justus D. "Beyond Polemics: An Historio-
    graphical Re-Appraisal of American Entry into World War
    II." HIST TEACHER, 12 (February 1979), 217-251.

    In this extensive historiographical essay, which
    incorporates 156 notes (many of which contain multiple
    citations), Doenecke treads with assurance among the various
    schools and interpretations of the war.

56. Doenecke, Justus D. "Harry Elmer Barnes." WISC MAG HIST,
    56 (Summer 1973), 311-323.

The author laments the exclusion of Barnes from the dialogue in "correct publications" because of Barnes' orientation. Doenecke warns that a similar fate could befall any of us. For Barnes, the attack at Pearl Harbor was the most fateful event of the twentieth century, and the bulk of his subsequent professional activities reflected that view.

57. Dornbusch, Charles E., ed. HISTORIES OF AMERICAN ARMY UNITS, WORLD WARS I AND II AND KOREAN CONFLICT. Washington, D. C.: Dept. of the Army, 1956. 310 pp.

    Here is a comprehensive bibliography highly regarded. Dornbusch has no equal in this field.

58. Dornbusch, Charles E., ed. HISTORIES, PERSONAL NARRATIVES, UNITED STATES ARMY: A CHECKLIST. Cornwallville, NY: Hope Farm Press, 1967. 400 pp.

    With 2,742 numbered items, this volume is a valuable research aid. Most of the descriptive information indicates where the unit has served.

59. Dornbusch, Charles E., ed. UNIT HISTORIES OF THE UNITED STATES AIR FORCES, INCLUDING PRIVATELY PRINTED PERSONAL NARRATIVES. Hampton Bays, NY: Hampton Books, 1958. 56 pp.

    This collection includes units serving in all theaters during the war. These items are not annotated.

60. Enser, A.G.S., ed. A SUBJECT BIBLIOGRAPHY OF THE SECOND WORLD WAR: BOOKS IN ENGLISH, 1939-1974. Boulder, CO: Westview Press, 1977. 592 pp.

    Despite the absence of annotations and the numbering of each citation, the book is a useful reference. Enser not only covers the important contemporary period but also divides the collection into sub-categories for easy reference to every theater.

61. Fowler, Wilton B., ed. AMERICAN DIPLOMATIC HISTORY SINCE 1890. Northbrook, IL: AHM, 1975.

    This bibliography is extensive and uncluttered by excessive sub-classifications. The entries are readily accessible. There are no annotations.

62. Funk, Arthur L., comp. THE SECOND WORLD WAR: A SELECT

BIBLIOGRAPHY OF BOOKS IN ENGLISH SINCE 1975. Claremont,
CA: Regina Books, 1985. 210 pp.

Funk, head of the American Committee on the History of
the Second World War (ACHSWW), acknowledges the existence
of "such a multitude of works" that it is impossible to
list everything. His compilation, which fills a gap
between the bibliography by Ziegler (up to 1965) and the
ACHSWW (Funk) bibliography (1966-1975), numbers over 2,100
unannotated citations.

63. Funk, Arthur L., comp. A SELECT BIBLIOGRAPHY OF BOOKS
     ON THE SECOND WORLD WAR, IN ENGLISH, PUBLISHED IN THE
     UNITED STATES, 1966-1975. Manhattan, KS: MA/AH
     Publishing, 1975. 34 pp.

     Here is an important bibliographical resource. The
     books published between 1966 andd 1975 began to make use
     of newly opened archival materials--in the United
     Kingdom as well as in the United States.

64. Goldman, Jack B., comp. NAVAL OPERATIONS IN WORLD WAR II,
     1939-1945: 100 TITLES FOR THE LARGE PUBLIC OF [SIC]
     ACADEMIC LIBRARY. n.p.: U.S. Naval School, 1956. 7 pp.

     This slim bibliography is sponsored by the Military
     Libraries Division of the Special Libraries Association.

65. Gorn, Michael and Charles Gross. "Published Air Force
     History: Still on the Runway." AEROSPACE H, 31
     (Spring, March 1984), 30-37.

     The article contains valuable bibliographic information
     on World War II as well as other American wars.

66. Hathaway, Milton G. "The Second World War." SCHOOL LIB J,
     30 (February 1984), 36-37.

     The author, an audiovisual librarian for the South
     Indiana Conference (United Methodist Church, Bloomington,
     IN), provides an annotated list of works of fiction. Most
     are written for juveniles and pertain to the war in Europe.
     In this guide, see the works of Jean Houston and Toshi
     Maruki.

67. Heimdahl, William C. and Edward J. Marolda, comps. GUIDE
     TO UNITED STATES NAVAL ADMINISTRATIVE HISTORIES OF WORLD
     WAR II. Washington, D.C.: Naval History Division, Dept.
     of the Navy, 1976. 219 pp.

The guide describes almost two hundred of these unpublished administrative histories. Some deal directly and many deal indirectly with Pacific operations. The narrative descriptions are well written.

68. Hess, Gary R. "Historiographical Essay: Global Expansion and Regional Balances: The Emerging Scholarship on United State Relations With India and Pakistan." PAC HR, 56 (May 1987), 259-295.

Hess exhibits excellent control of the literature in this valuable survey. See especially the section entitled "United States and Indian Nationalism, 1941-1947."

69. Higham, Robin, ed. A GUIDE TO THE SOURCES OF UNITED STATES MILITARY HISTORY. Hamden, CT: Archon Books, 1975. 559 pp.

The sections on World War II are particularly helpful. Each major subject heading (e.g., World War II) contains a bibliographic report as well as a listing of sources. Where applicable, directions are provided for prospective researchers to gain permission to use certain collections. A revised edition appeared in 1981.

70. Higham, Robin, ed. OFFICIAL HISTORIES: ESSAYS AND BIBLIOGRAPHIES FROM AROUND THE WORLD. Manhattan, KS: Kansas State University Press, 1970. 644 pp.

Here is a compendium of official military histories from the international community. Many of the citations deal with some aspect of the war.

71. Hsueh, Chun-tu, comp. THE CHINESE COMMUNIST MOVEMENT, 1937-1949: AN ANNOTATED BIBLIOGRAPHY OF SELECTED MATERIALS IN THE CHINESE COLLECTION OF THE HOOVER INSTITUTION ON WAR, REVOLUTION, AND PEACE. Stanford, CA: Hoover Institution, 1962. 312 pp.

The compiler presents 863 items, many of which bear Chinese titles. The annotations are in English. Much of the material is on the war against Japan. The collection includes works by Chinese Nationalists as well as communists. This is the second volume in the series. (The first volume appeared in 1960 and covered the period 1921-1937.)

72. International Commission for the Teaching of History. THE

TWO WORLD WARS: A SELECT BIBLIOGRAPHY. New York:
Pergammon Press, 1964.

Here is a convenient reference of the traditional
citations available at the time.

73. Iriye, Akira. "Contemporary History as History: American
     Expansionism into the Pacific Since 1941." PAC HR, 53
     (May 1984), 191-212.

     Here is a historiographical essay by an expert.
     Chronological sub-topics assist the reader.

74. London. Imperial War Museum. SECOND WORLD WAR: PACIFIC
     THEATRE: MILITARY PREPARATIONS. London: Imperial War
     Museum, 1953. 11 pp.

     This bibliography provides a good introduction to a
     theater which the British usually neglect.

75. London. Imperial War Museum. THE WOMEN'S PART IN THE
     SECOND WORLD WAR: A SELECTION OF REFERENCES. London:
     Imperial War Musuem, 1956. 25 pp.

     Although interesting, there is little (even indirectly)
     on the war against Japan.

76. Maurer, Maurer, ed. AIR FORCE COMBAT UNITS OF WORLD WAR
     II. Washington, D.C.: GOP, 1961. 506 pp.

     Nearly all of the units fit into four categories:
     bombardment, fighter, reconnaissance, and troop carrier.
     Maurer includes both foreign and domestic units. He traces
     the origins of each outfit and carries the story of most of
     them forward to 1956. The description of each carries
     information about insignia, decorations, campaigns, and
     commanders.

77. Maurer, Maurer, ed. COMBAT SQUADRONS OF THE AIR FORCE:
     WORLD WAR II. Washington, D.C.: Office of Air Force
     History, 1982. 841 pp.

     Originally published for the Air Force in 1969, this
     encyclopedic collection provides descriptive information
     such as assignments, stations, aircraft, and decorations.
     This valuable reference tool has a thorough index.

78. May, Ernest R. AMERICAN INTERVENTION: 1917 AND 1941.
     Washington, D.C.: Service Center for Teachers of

History, 1969.   26 pp.

Here is an authoritative survey of the literature.

79. Miller, Samuel D., comp. AN AEROSPACE BIBLIOGRAPHY.
     Washington, D.C.: Office of Air Force History, 1978.
     rev. ed.   341 pp.

     Originally produced in 1971, this updated version
     contains a valuable section on the air war.

80. Morton, Louis. "World War II: A Survey of Recent
     Writings." AMER HR, 75 (December 1970), 1987-2008.

     This historiographical essay has a separate section for
     the war against Japan. Also of special interest is the
     material on grand strategy.

81. Morton, Louis. WRITINGS ON WORLD WAR II. Washington,
     D.C.: Service Center for Teachers of History, 1967.   54
     pp.

     Morton assembles a brief bibliography of the war which
     is intended for courses at the undergraduate and secondary
     school levels. The collection amounts to a useful
     introduction to the study of the war.

82. Neumann, William L. "Allied Diplomacy in World War II: A
     Bibliographical Survey." USNIP, 81 (July 1955),
     829-834.

     Neumann offers a critical survey of available materials,
     especially documents, memoirs, and general histories.

83. New York Public Library. SUBJECT CATALOG OF THE WORLD WAR
     II COLLECTION. Boston: G.K. Hall, 1977. 3 vols.

     The library has an extensive collection of over 43,000
     items in several languages directly touching on the war and
     many more on related subjects. There are reproductions of
     reference entries, some are handwritten, and not all are
     legible. The New York Public Library subject headings are
     linked with those of the Library of Congress.

84. Nishiura, Susumu. "Japanese War History." AIR U REV, 16
     (March-April 1965), 90-93.

     Here is an excellent appraisal of Japanese
     historiography of the war.

85. Pappas, George S., comp. UNITED STATES ARMY UNIT
    HISTORIES. Carlisle Barracks, PA: U.S. Army Military
    History Institute, 1978. 2 vols.

    Here is an exhaustive list of unit histories which are
    housed at the Institute in Carlisle.

86. Perusse, Roland I. BIBLIOGRAPHY ON INTERNATIONAL
    PROPAGANDA: AN ANNOTATED LIST OF SECRET RECENT TITLES,
    TO INCLUDE PERTINENT ASPECTS OF INTERNATIONAL
    INFORMATION, INTERNATIONAL COMMUNICATION AND
    PSYCHOLOGICAL WARFARE. Washington, D.C. 31 L.

    NE

87. Phillips, Jill M., comp. THE STERILE PROMONTORY: THE
    SECOND WORLD WAR IN HISTORY, BIOGRAPHY, DIARY, POETRY,
    LITERATURE, AND FILM. New York: Gordon, 1985.

    Phillips has put together a broadly based
    bibliographical reference. The works are arranged by
    category.

88. "Plans for the Historiography of the United States in World
    War II." AMER HR, 49 (January 1944), 243-252.

    Here is a survey of the provisions made by the U.S.
    government for the systematic documentation of the war
    (civilian and military). A list of the chief historical
    officers in government agencies is appended.

89. Quinlivan, Michael and Jack B. Hilliard, eds. AN ANNOTATED
    BIBLIOGRAPHY OF THE UNITED STATES MARINE CORPS IN THE
    SECOND WORLD WAR. Washington, D.C.: USMC, 1965.
    44 pp.

    Here is a comprehensive reference on the subject which
    includes several unit histories. See especially the
    material on amphibious warfare.

90. Ryan, Duane, ed. THE WAR IN THE PACIFIC: GENERAL
    REFERENCE WORKS. Carlisle Barracks, PA: Army Military
    History Institute, 1978. 81 pp.

    This sharply focused bibliography is exhaustive and
    presents a valuable reference tool.

91. SELECT BIBLIOGRAPHY OF REVISIONIST BOOKS DEALING WITH THE

TWO WORLD WARS AND THEIR AFTERMATH. Oxnard, CA: Oxnard Press-Courier, 1958. 30 pp.

The limited listings for the war against Japan deal mainly with the controversial origins of the war.

92. Smith, Myron J., Jr., comp. AIR WAR BIBLIOGRAPHY, 1939-1945: ENGLISH-LANGUAGE SOURCES. Manhattan, KS: MA/AH Publishing, 1977-1982. 5 vols.

Smith compiles a major reference work. See the entries for the Pacific Theater in Volume II. For purposes of this guide, see also the sections on Strategy, Tactics, Escape, and POW Experiences. The entries are not annotated.

93. Smith, Myron, J., Jr., ed. THE SECRET WARS: A GUIDE TO SOURCES IN ENGLISH. Santa Barbara, CA: ABC-CLIO, 1980. 3 vols.

The first volume contains the entries for the Second World War. The collection is arranged by topic within geographical location. Topics covered include intelligence, propaganda, resistance movements, and secret operations. There are over 2,500 citations.

94. Smith, Mryon J., Jr., ed. WORLD WAR II AT SEA: A BIBLIOGRAPHY OF SOURCES IN ENGLISH. Metuchen, NJ: The Scarecrow Press, 1976. 3 vols.

Volume II covers the Pacific Theater. The entries in the volume, over 3,200 in all, are arranged chronologically within each region. Smith includes the navies and merchant marines of all major belligerents. Some annotations are provided. There are more than 10,000 entries in the full set.

95. Spier, Henry O., comp. WORLD WAR II IN OUR MAGAZINES AND BOOKS, SEPTEMBER 1939 TO SEPTEMBER 1945: A BIBLIOGRAPHY. New York: Stuyvesant Press, 1945. 96 pp.

This contemporary bibliography offers over 1,500 wartime citations. There are no annotations.

96. United States. Air Force. Air Force Academy Library. AIR POWER AND WARFARE. Colorado Springs, CO: USAFA, 1978. 101 pp.

This general bibliographic guide is a particularly

valuable reference on strategic bombing.

97. United States. Library of Congress. Legislative Reference
     Service. THE CONDUCT OF THE WAR: APRIL 1941-MAY 1943.
     Washington, D.C.: GPO, 1942-1943. 3 vols.

     This contemporary bibliography provides annotations for
     over 4,200 books and articles.

98. United States. Military History Institute. THE ERA OF
     WORLD WAR II. Washington, D.C.: GPO, 1977-1978. 4
     vols.

     NE

99. United States. Navy Department. Naval History Division.
     WORLD WAR II HISTORIES AND HISTORICAL REPORTS IN THE
     U.S. NAVAL HISTORY DIVISON. Washington, D.C.: Navy
     Dept., 1973. 226 pp.

     All the entries in this partial checklist are annotated,
     but not all the holdings of the Naval History Division on
     World War II are included. There are numerous
     administrative histories as well as the histories of ships
     and aviation units.

100. WORLD WAR II FROM AN AMERICAN PERSPECTIVE: AN ANNOTATED
     BIBLIOGRAPHY. Santa Barbara, CA: ABC-CLIO, 1983.
     277 pp.

     There are 1,107 citations--all annotated--taken from
     journals and magazines. The selected articles are
     contained in the data base of the American Bibliographical
     Center and appeared in periodicals during the period
     1971-1981.

101. Ziegler, Janet. WORLD WAR II: BOOKS IN ENGLISH,
     1945-1965. Stanford, CA: Hoover Institution Press,
     1971. 223 pp.

     Here is an indispensable reference tool for the study of
     the war. Ziegler presents 4,519 items, without
     annotations, that appeared during the first two decades
     after the war. See especially her introductory essay.

I.A.5. CHRONOLOGIES

102. "An Airpower Chronology: From Pearl Harbor to V-J Day."
     AF MAG, 68 (September 1985), 193-198.

Here is a chronology, prepared by the magazine's editors, of the significant events in the air war.

103. Argyle, Christopher J., comp. CHRONOLOGY OF WORLD WAR II: THE DAY-BY-DAY ILLUSTRATED RECORD, 1939-1949. Freeport, NY: Marshall Cavendish, 1981. 200 pp.

This valuable reference work includes summaries on virtually a daily basis. Its coverage of postwar (related) events, while not as comprehensive as the war years, sets it apart from most of the war chronologies.

104. Bates, F.E., comp. CHRONOLOGY OF WORLD WAR II. Maxwell AFB, AL: Air War College, 1947. 106 pp.

Here is a useful reference which focuses primarily on the air war in all theaters.

105. Carter, Kit C. and Robert Mueller, comps. THE ARMY AIR FORCES IN WORLD WAR II: COMBAT CHRONOLOGY, 1941-1945. Washington, D.C.: G.P.O., 1975. 992 pp.

This valuable reference work complements the seven-volume official history of the AAF in the war. It includes glossaries of code names, terms, and abbreviations.

106. Chamberlain, Waldo, Thomas Hovet, Jr., and Richard N. Swift, comps. A CHRONOLOGY OF THE UNITED NATIONS, 1941-1958. New York: Oceana Publishers, 1959. 48 pp.

Although useful for the general subject, the reference is disappointingly sparse for the war years.

107. "The Closing Days of the War Against Japan." ARMY INFO DIGEST, 5 (September 1950), 14-15.

In outline form, here is a chronology of the period July 16-September 2, 1945.

108. Detroit News. WAR . . . IN HEADLINES FROM THE DETROIT NEWS, 1939-1945. Detroit, MI: Detroit News, 1945. 104 pp.

The collection serves as a useful chronology.

109. Domei Tsushin Sha. WAR CHRONOLOGY GREATER EAST ASIA WAR. Shanghai: Shanghai Evening Post, 1943.

This chronology, compiled by the Domei News Agency, covers the period December 8, 1941 - December 8, 1942. Japanese successes earn special attention.

110. Dupuy, Trevor N., comp. CHRONOLOGICAL MILITARY HISTORY OF WORLD WAR II. New York: Franklin Watts, 1967. 84 pp.

The chronology covers all theaters in some detail.

111. EVENING BULLETIN, Philadelphia. WORLD WAR II IN HEADLINES AND PICTURES. Philadelphia, PA: EVENING BULLETIN, 112 pp.

The collection duplicates 56 front pages of the newspaper and over 150 action photographs.

112. Fortune, Charles H. THE WAR IN RETROSPECT: A DAY-TO-DAY RECORD OF WORLD WAR II. Dunedin, NZ: Evening Star, 1945. 2 vols.

Here is a detailed chronology of the war which goes beyond the "headline" events.

113. "From Pearl Harbor to V-J Day." AF MAG, 68 (September 1985), 193-198.

Forty years after the war, here is a chronology of aviation affairs in all theaters.

114. Great Britain. Ministry of Information. THE WAR IN THE FAR EAST: A CHRONOLOGY. London: HMSO, 1945. 33 pp.

The chronology selectively highlights the British performance. A list of commanders is appended.

115. Hopkins, John A.H., comp. DIARY OF WORLD EVENTS. Baltimore, MD: National Advertising Co., 1942-1948. 54 vols.

Hopkins served in the National Bureau of Information and Education. This chronological record of the war is photographically reproduced from U. S. and foreign newspapers. The selections include maps, photos, cartoons, anecdotes, official statements, and congressional acts. There is an idiosyncratic system of indexing.

116. Hovet, Thomas, Jr. and Erica Hovet, comps. ANNUAL REVIEW OF UNITED NATIONS AFFAIRS: A CHRONOLOGY AND FACT BOOK OF THE UNITED NATIONS, 1941-1979. Dobbs Ferry, NY:

Oceana Publications, 1979. 6th ed. 304 pp.

In addition to a chronology, the volume has a list of
personnel, tables, and texts of documents. A topical
cross-index (e.g., trusteeship) facilitates reference.

117. Kinnaird, Clark, ed. IT HAPPENED IN 1945. New York:
        Duell, Sloan and Pearce, 1946. 464 pp.

Kinnaird assembles a detailed chronology of the final
months.

118. Lambert, R.E., comp. VICTORY SOURCEBOOK. Freeport, NY:
        Readers' Reference and Research Bureau, 1941-1942.
        2 vols.

Lambert (U.S.N.R.) compiles a contemporary chronology of
events in 1941 and 1942.

119. Leonard, Thomas N., comp. DAY-BY-DAY: THE FORTIES. New
        York: Facts on File, 1977. 1,051 pp.

The chronology covers all theaters and devotes much
attention to the home front.

120. Library of Congress. Legislative Reference Service.
        EVENTS LEADNG UP TO WORLD WAR II: CHRONOLOGICAL HISTORY
        OF CERTAIN MAJOR INTERNATIONAL EVENTS LEADING UP TO AND
        DURING WORLD WAR II WITH THE OSTENSIBLE REASONS ADVANCED
        FOR THEIR OCCURRENCE, 1931-44. Washington, DC: GPO,
        1944.

This chronology highlights events in Europe and the Far
East. The narrative portions reveal much about the
contemporary American perspective.

121. New York Herald Tribune. FRONT PAGE HISTORY OF THE SECOND
        WORLD WAR. New York: Duell, Sloan and Pearce, 1946.
        464 pp.

This montage of front pages comprises an effective
chronology of the war.

122. New York Times. WORLD WAR II: A CHRONOLOGY. New York:
        New York Times, 1945. 32 pp.

This chronological record presents certain coverage of
all theaters.

123. Richard, Dorothy E. THE U.S. NAVY IN WORLD WAR II: A
        CHRONOLOGY. Washington, D.C.: GPO, 1949. 2 vols.

        This detailed chronology incorporates extensive coverage
      of operations in the Pacific. Richard (USNR) provides
      information on battles, ships lost/damaged, and enemy ships
      destroyed.

124. Royal Institute of International Affairs, ed. CHRONOLOGY
        OF THE SECOND WORLD WAR. London: RIIA, 1947. 374 pp.

        Despite its emphasis on European affairs, this
      contemporary compilation offers useful information. At the
      beginning of each month, short summaries are provided for
      air operations.

125. St. Joseph News Press. THE HISTORY OF WORLD WAR II, AS
        TOLD IN THE HEADLINES, MAPS AND CARTOONS FROM THE ST.
        JOSEPH NEWS PRESS AND ST. JOSEPH GAZETTE. St. Joseph,
        MO: St. Joseph News Press, 1945. 264 pp.

        This contemporary chronology, which includes some
      interesting cartoons as well as detailed map sections,
      portrays the continuing progress of the Allies in the
      various campaigns.

126. Salmaggi, Cesare and Alfredo Pallavisini, comps. 2194 DAYS
        OF WAR: AN ILLUSTRATED CHRONOLOGY OF THE SECOND WORLD
        WAR. New York: Gallery Books, 1977. 752 pp.

        The volume covers the period September 1, 1939 -
      September 2, 1945. Each page presents a simultaneous
      report on every theater. There are theater subheadings
      beneath each daily heading. The compilers attempt to avoid
      interpretation in presenting this factual record. The book
      contains 620 illustrations and 84 maps.

127. Smith, Myron J., Jr., ed. AIR WAR CHRONOLOGY, 1939-1945.
        Manhattan, KS: MA/AH Publishing, 1977. 5 vols.

        This continuing project covers the air war into 1943.
      The entries are arranged geographically.

128. United States. Congress. House of Representatives.
        Committee on Foreign Affairs. EVENTS LEADING UP TO
        WORLD WAR II: CHRONOLOGICAL HISTORY, 1931-1944.
        Washington, D.C.: GPO, 1945. 421 pp.

        Presented in chronological fashion, the information

provided is accompanied with citations. There are no
subject categories or thematic subdivisions.

129. United States. Library of Congress. Legislative Reference
      Service. EVENTS LEADING UP TO WORLD WAR II.
      Washington, D.C.: GPO, 1944. 421 pp.

      This extensive chronology covers the period 1931-1941.
      The material also extends beyond the start of the war into
      early 1944.

130. Vromans, A.G. A LIST OF CHRONOLOGICAL SURVEYS OF WORLD WAR
      II. Amsterdam, Neth.: Netherlands State Institute for
      War Documentation, 1956. 7 pp.

      NE

131. Williams, Mary H., comp. CHRONOLOGY, 1941-1945.
      Washington, D.C.: Office of the Chief of Military
      History, Dept. of the Army, 1960. 660 pp.

      With meticulous detail, Williams sets forth the
      "tactical events" of the war. The book covers the period
      from December 7, 1941, to September 2, 1945. The
      chronology--there is a separate chapter for each
      year--arises from unit histories, after-action reports and
      published official histories. For many of the daily
      entries, Williams includes geographical divisions and
      comments on the international situation. In general, she
      reports the activities not only of U.S. land, sea, and air
      forces but also of foreign forces. The Appendix contains a
      list of code names and abbreviations.

I.A.6. UNIFORMS/INSIGNIA/MARKINGS

132. Brown, Paul. INSIGNIA OF THE SERVICES. New York:
      Scribner, 1943. rev. ed. 62 pp.

      This reference work includes the women's services and
      provides many colored pictures of the different U. S.
      uniforms as well as insignia.

133. Kahn, E.J., Jr. and Henry F. McLemore. FIGHTING DIVISIONS:
      HISTORIES OF EACH U. S. ARMY COMBAT DIVISION IN WORLD
      WAR II. Washington, D. C.: Infantry Journal Press,
      1945. 235 pp.

      This excellent reference work includes information on
      each unit, its insignia (many are shown in color), and its

campaigns (dates and locations).

134. Kerrigan, Evans E. AMERICAN BADGES AND INSIGNIA. New
     York: Viking Press, 1967. 286 pp.

     The book covers the period 1767-1967. The drawings and
     explanations (no photographs) by the author are carefully
     presented.

135. Kerrigan, Evans E. AMERICAN WAR MEDALS AND DECORATIONS.
     New York: Viking Press, 1964. 149 pp.

     With many color plates, and with a brief history of the
     medals and decorations, this book is a valuable reference
     tool for the period 1782-1963.

136. Mollo, Andrew. ARMED FORCES OF WORLD WAR II: UNIFORMS,
     INSIGNIA AND ORGANIZATION. New York: Crown Publishing,
     1981. 312 pp.

     With meticulous care and solid research, Mollo describes
     the paraphernalia of all the major powers. There are
     several illustrations and photos.

137. Mollo, Andrew and Malcolm McGregor. NAVAL, MARINE, AND AIR
     FORCE UNIFORMS OF WORLD WAR 2. New York: Macmillan,
     1976. 231 pp.

     Here is a report on all the major powers in the war.
     Several photos and illustrations complement the
     descriptions.

138. Rosignoli, Guido. AIR FORCE BADGES AND INSIGNIA OF WORLD
     WAR II. New York: Arco, 1977. 200 pp.

     Heavily illustrated, the book includes the markings for
     the air forces of the leading powers in all theaters.

139. Rosignoli, Guido. ARMY BADGES AND INSIGNIA OF WORLD WAR
     II. New York: Macmillan, 1972. 228 pp.

     Rosignoli presents the badges and insignia of the armies
     of all the major powers in the war.

140. Rosignoli, Guido. BADGES AND INSIGNIA OF WORLD WAR II:
     AIR FORCE, NAVAL, MARINE. London: Burke Peerage, 1981.
     363 pp.

     Amassing more than 25,000 photos and drawings, the

author offers brief histories of the badges and insignia of the leading adversaries in all theaters.

141. Ross, Mary Steele. AMERICAN WOMEN IN UNIFORM. Garden City, NY: Garden City Publishing, 1943. 71 pp.

This slim volume examines all the U.S. women's war organizations (27) as well as the uniforms and insignia of each.

142. Rust, Kenn C. "Bomber Markings of the Twentieth A.F." AMER AVN HSJ, Pt. I: 7 (Fall 1962), 165-179, 223; Pt. II: 7 (Winter 1962), 257-273.

Rust, a professional writer on aviation, provides great detail on all the basic markings of the command's B-29 aircraft. The article includes a list of most of the bombing missions and targets in Japan flown by the 73rd Wing (records for the 499th Group do not exist).

143. Rust, Kenn C. "Fighter Markings -- P.O.A. (Pacific Ocean Area)." AMER AVN HSJ, 8 (Winter 1963), 256-266.

Here is a detailed report on the markings (including changes made during the war) of the fighter aircraft. Many illustrations accompany the narrative.

144. Windrow, Martin C. WORLD WAR 2 COMBAT UNIFORMS AND INSIGNIA. Cambridge: Stephens, 1977. 104 pp.

Windrow presents the uniform and insignia of the armies of the major combatants. He includes over 150 photos.

145. Wright, Howard T. "Changing Insignias." AEROSPACE H, 27 (Summer, June 1980), 113-115.

The author, a second lt. pilot, almost shot down an American aircraft early in the war because the U. S. insignia (a white star within a red circle) resembled the Japanese insignia. His conversations with Generals Eaker and Arnold contributed to modification of the U.S. insignia.

I.B. GENERAL ACCOUNTS/ANTHOLOGIES OF WORLD WAR II

146. Adams, Henry H. 1942: THE YEAR THAT DOOMED THE AXIS. New York: David McKay Co., 1967. 522 pp.

147. _____. YEARS OF DEADLY PERIL, 1939-1941. New York:
     McKay, 1969. 559 pp.

148. _____. YEARS OF EXPECTATION, GUADALCANAL TO NORMANDY.
     New York: McKay, 1973. 430 pp.

149. _____. YEARS TO VICTORY. New York: McKay, 1973.
     507 pp.

     These four volumes, not published in exact chronological
sequence, comprise Adams' survey of the war. Without
exception, the volumes are well written, well researched,
and more attentive to European concerns than to the war in
the Pacific. The volume covering 1942 (written before the
others) is especially interesting, as Adams concentrates on
stories about people rather than events.

150. Afro-American Company. THIS IS OUR WAR. Baltimore:
     Afro-American Company, 1945. 216 pp.

     The book is comprised of essays by six Afro-American
correspondents on special assignment (1943-1944). The
reports on "Tan Yanks" are all positive with emphasis on
concepts such as democracy, integration, and equal
treatment. A "rumor of friction" back in the U. S. A. is
downplayed. Vincent Tubbs writes on the Southwest Pacific
and Herbert M. Frisby describes the Alaskan-Aleutian front
(where Lena Horne is the leading pin-up attraction).

151. ARMY-NAVY JOURNAL. THE UNITED STATES AT WAR. Washington,
     D. C.: Army-Navy Journal, 1942. 180 pp.

     The journal's editors have assembled writings by
prominent Americans (e.g., Marshall, King, Leahy) and
diplomats (from Australia, India, Philippines, China).

152. Arnold-Foster, Mark. THE WORLD AT WAR. New York: Stein
     and Day, 1973. 340 pp.

     This narrative forms the basis for the popular
television series.

153. Baldwin, Hanson W. BATTLES LOST AND WON. New York:
     Harper and Row, 1966. 532 pp.

     For the war against Japan, see Chapter 4, "'The Rock':
The Fall of Corregidor"; Chapter 7, "Tarawa: A Study in
Courage"; Chapter 9, "The Greatest Sea Fight--Leyte Gulf";
and Chapter 11, "The Greatest Sea-Air Battle in

History--Okinawa." Baldwin rejects MacArthur's view that
the Philippines could have been saved at the beginning of
the war. Each chapter has its own bibliography, and the
sources include Baldwin's correspondence with many of the
principal actors in these battles.

154. Baldwin, Hanson W. GREAT MISTAKES OF THE WAR. New York:
Harper and Row, 1950. 114 pp.

Baldwin, the noted military correspondent, argues that
mistakes stemmed from the "political immaturity" of the
United States. Among the mistakes in the war against
Japan, Baldwin identifies the Yalta decisions, policies
toward China, Stilwell's appointment, confusion over the
defense of the Philippines, some aspects of MacArthur's
leadership, and the use of the atomic bomb. Although many
of his points remain controversial, Baldwin's expertise in
the field commands attention to his views.

155. Bradley, John H. and Jack W. Dice. THE SECOND WORLD WAR:
ASIA AND THE PACIFIC. West Point, NY: U. S. Military
Academy, 1980. 495 pp.

This book, part of the West Point series in military
history, offers an exceptional amount of detailed information.

156. Brent, Rafer, ed. GREAT WAR STORIES: TRUE ADVENTURES OF
FIGHTING MEN IN TWO WORLD WARS. New York: Bartholomew
House, 1957. 188 pp.

Here are anecdotes which cover the spectrum from
silliness to heroism.

157. Brookhouser, Frank, ed. THIS WAS YOUR WAR: AN ANTHOLOGY
OF GREAT WRITINGS FROM WORLD WAR II. Garden City, NY:
Doubleday, 1960. 498 pp.

Here are over eighty works of fiction and fact about the
Second World War. Selections from the war against Japan
include the writings of Peter Bowman, Norman Mailer, Alan
Matthews, Eugene Brown, Anton Myrer, Thomas Heggen, Herman
Wouk, Gordon Cubbledick, Clark Lee, William L. Laurence,
and James A. Michener.

158. Brown, Ken. "The Last Just War: How Just was It?"
PROGRESSIVE, 46 (August 1982), 18-20.

Despite the image of the United Nations' cause in the

World War as a just war, the author argues that the Allies
lost their moral bearings, especially with the use of what
he calls terror bombing.

159. Bruun, Geoffrey and Dwight E. Lee. THE SECOND WORLD WAR
      AND AFTER. Boston: Houghton Mifflin, 1964. 200 pp.

In this survey of the war, the authors emphasize that
Japan emerged from the First World War harboring major
grievances and resentment. Bruun and Lee also show how
four factors influenced the course of war in the Pacific:
(1) Japanese prewar preparations, including the seizure of
a formidable defensive zone; (2) rising nationalism in
Southeast Asia; (3) Japanese wartime expansion throughout
the Pacific; and (4) air power.

160. Buchanan, A. Russell. THE UNITED STATES AND WORLD WAR II.
      New York: Harper and Row, 1964. 2 vols.

In this general history, Buchanan emphasizes political-
military-economic perspectives. He draws heavily from the
published official histories. The subsequent availability
of rich new sources have seriously weakened its usefulness.

161. Caldwell, Cyril C. AIR POWER AND TOTAL WAR. New York:
      Coward-McCann, 1943. 244 pp.

In this contemporary survey of the role of air power in
the war, Caldwell looks at all theaters. His discussion of
the war against Japan is balanced and well written.

162. Calvocoressi, Peter and Guy Wint. TOTAL WAR. New York:
      Pantheon Books, 1972. 959 pp.

Here is a well-written survey with a useful annotated
bibliography. The authors stress social and economic
developments as well as political-military events. Wint
wrote most of the material on the war against Japan.
Despite the bibliographic entries, the dearth of citations
for the narrative weakens the book's value.

163. Cant, Gilbert. AMERICA'S NAVY IN WORLD WAR II. New York:
      The John Day Company, 1943. 432 pp.

Cant offers a wartime account of naval operations. He
complains about the Navy's excessive restrictions on the
dissemination of information (even within Navy circles) and
traces that policy to the wishes of Admiral Ernest R. King.
Included in the appendices are medal winners, Navy warships

lost (up to 31 December 1942), and Japan's naval losses.

164.   Cave, Floyd A., ed. THE ORIGINS AND CONSEQUENCES OF WORLD
        WAR II. New York: The Dryden Press, 1948. 820 pp.

        This series of essays is intended to survey rather than
        analyze historical sequences. Sumner Welles provides the
        Introduction. See especially the excellent essays on
        East Asia by Cave and W. Leon Godshall.

165.   Churchill, Winston. THE SECOND WAR. Boston: Houghton
        Mifflin, 1948-1954. 6 vols.

        Recently released documents reveal that these volumes
        should be considered carefully—for what is omitted rather
        than their contents. Nevertheless, Churchill has created a
        magisterial survey which not only contains a treasure of
        information (from his unique perspective) but also
        illustrates his loving care for the English language. The
        six separate titles are: I: THE GATHERING STORM; II: THEIR
        FINEST HOUR; III: THE GRAND ALLIANCE; IV: THE HINGE OF
        FATE; V: CLOSING THE RING; AND VI: TRIUMPH AND TRAGEDY.

166.   Clark, Gregory, ed. WAR STORIES. Toronto: Ryerson Press,
        1968. 171 pp.

        Here is a collection of interesting anecdotes from all
        theaters.

167.   Clarke, George Herbert. THE NEW TREASURY OF WAR POETRY:
        POEMS OF THE SECOND WORLD WAR. Boston: Houghton
        Mifflin, 1943. 285 pp.

        This collection of about 150 poems ranges from light-
        hearted to deadly serious. Not many touch on the war
        against Japan. Of particular interest are the poems by
        Robert A. Nathan on Capt. Colin P. Kelly, Jr. (although
        Kelly did not plunge his aircraft into a Japanese ship);
        Amanda Benjamin Hall on Madame Chiang ("Moon to China's
        Sun"); and John Gillespie Magee, Jr. on the thrill of
        "High Flight."

168.   Cochran, Thomas C. THE GREAT DEPRESSION AND WORLD WAR II.
        Glenview, IL: Scott Foresman, 1968. 214 pp.

        Part of the "American History Series" under senior
        editors David M. Potter and Carl N. Degler, this volume
        surveys the war in a relatively few pages. Thus, the
        controversial issues are not treated in depth. Cochran

feels that Roosevelt considered the entry of the United
States into the war as the best of some bad alternatives.
Pictorial essays and bibliographic essays appear at the end
of each chapter. This is a solid introduction--as
intended--to the subject.

169.   Collier, Basil. THE SECOND WORLD WAR: A MILITARY HISTORY,
       FROM MUNICH TO HIROSHIMA. New York: William Morrow,
       1967. 640 pp.

       Collier, an expert on the subject, provides a readable,
authoritative general history of the war. His extensive
knowledge of the war against Japan puts this work above
many of the other surveys.

170.   Collier, Richard. THE FREEDOM ROAD: 1944-1945. New
       York: Atheneum, 1984. 342 pp.

       In this well-researched book, Collier collects a
treasury of interesting anecdotes and quotations taken
from all theaters during the final two years of the war.

171.   Commager, Henry Steele, ed. THE STORY OF THE SECOND WORLD
       WAR. Boston: Little, Brown and Company, 1945. 578 pp.

       Making no claims that this work is a comprehensive
history of the war, Commager, instead, has constructed a
series of stories and statements which are presented in an
uncritical narrative. Although overwhelmingly concerned with Europe, the book does offer some excellent
material on the war against Japan. (See, for example,
the report by a survivor from the REPULSE.)

172.   Craven, Wesley F. and James L. Cate, eds. THE ARMY
       AIR FORCES IN WORLD WAR II. Chicago: University of
       Chicago Press, 1948-1958. 7 vols.

       Using separate authors for various subjects, the editors
assemble an official report on the global activities of the
AAF. It is a majestic report based on solid scholarship
and straightforward prose. One noteworthy feature is
Richard L. Watson's careful investigation of the debacle at
Clark Field in the Philippines during the first hours of
the war in the Pacific. The entire series represents
official history at its best.

173.   Cronon, E. David and Theodore D. Rosenof, comps. THE
       SECOND WORLD WAR AND THE ATOMIC AGE, 1940-1973.
       Northbrook, IL: AHM, 1975. 146 pp.

This reference work is part of the respected Goldentree
Bibliography series. The compilers include dissertations
as well as books and articles. there are over 2,700
unannotated items.

174. Cunningham, William H. and Ruth M. Stauffer, eds. THEY
      TELL THEIR STORY: 23 EPISODES IN THE GLOBAL WAR. New
      York: Harcourt, Brace, 1943. 287 pp.

      The 23 stories comprise a small treasure of primary
      sources. See especially the story of Eunice C. Hatchitt,
      "Bataan Nurse." Recommendations for further reading appear
      at the end of each episode.

175. Davidman, Joy, ed. WAR POEMS OF THE UNITED NATIONS.
      New York: Dial Press, 1943. 395 pp.

      The collection includes 300 poems by 150 poets. Of
      the few items that touch on the war against Japan,
      see Norman Rosten on Corregidor and the translations
      of three Chinese battle songs.

176. Davis, Harry, ed. THIS IS IT. New York: Vanguard Press,
      1944. 224 pp.

      Davis presents twelve contemporary narratives by
      servicemen who participated or observed important events in
      the war. The selections are from all theaters, and each
      offers a unique view of combat action.

177. Davis, Kenneth S. EXPERIENCE OF WAR: THE UNITED STATES IN
      WORLD WAR II. Garden City, NY: Doubleday and Company,
      1965. 704 pp.

      Davis seeks to present a readable approach to the
      "experience" of the war rather than a formal history. He
      relies mainly on published sources.

178. Dennis, Geoffrey, ed. THE WORLD AT WAR. London: Caxton
      Publishing Company, 1951. 4 vols.

      The volumes comprise an operational military history
      without attempting to comment on other elements of the
      war (e.g., political, economic, home front). Here is a
      contemporary chronicle, written as the events were taking
      place.

179. Detzer, Karl., ed. THE ARMY READER. Indianapolis, IN:

Bobbs-Merrill, 1943. 469 pp.

This collection surveys Army operations in all theaters. These contemporary articles have been published previously.

180.   Detzer, Karl. THE MIGHTIEST ARMY. Pleasantville, NY: Reader's Digest Association, 1945. 168 pp.

With many excellent photographs, Detzer's book describes Army operations in all theaters. Of interest is the focus on special weapons and special leaders.

181.   Divine, Robert A., ed. CAUSES AND CONSEQUENCES OF WORLD WAR II. Chicago: Quadrangle Books, 1969. 375 pp.

The collection offers a cross-section of views concerning American diplomacy in the "origins, conduct, and legacy" of the war. In assembling these articles, Divine concentrated only on the United States perspective. Of special interest are the articles on Pearl Harbor and the use of the atomic bomb.

182.   Dupuy, R. Ernest. WORLD WAR II: A COMPACT HISTORY. New York: Hawthorn Books, 1969. 334 pp.

This concise book presents a straightforward account by a colonel in the U.S. Army. Of interest is his insistence that Kimmel and Short suffered a "grave injustice" by not being given a court martial--and the opportunity to present their cases.

183.   Eisinger, Chester E., ed. THE 1940s: PROFILE OF A NATION IN CRISIS. Garden City, NY: Anchor Books, 1969. 526 pp.

Eisinger labels the main theme of the 1940s as an assault upon the self. According to him, the decade saw the ascendancy of the scientist, the loss of U.S. innocence, and a shift to internationalism. The collection of 37 black-and-white plates provides an excellent cultural perspective. Some of the articles address the attack at Pearl Harbor, combat in the Pacific, and the decision to drop the atomic bomb.

184.   Ellis, Christopher. FAMOUS SHIPS OF WORLD WAR II IN COLOR. New York: Arco, 1977.

Ellis has assembled some beautiful color photos of ships that attracted much attention in the war.

185. Ellis, John. THE SHARP END: THE FIGHTING MEN IN WORLD
         WAR II. New York: Charles Scribner's Sons, 1980.
         396 pp.

         Ellis examines what it was like to be a fighting man in
      each of the theaters. His investigation incorporates
      common categories, such as physical setting, casualties,
      discipline, morale, relaxation, and attitudes.

186. ENCYCLOPEDIA BRITANNICA, Editors of. TEN EVENTFUL YEARS.
         Chicago: Encyclopedia, 1947. 4 vols.

         This survey, edited by Walter Yust, covers the ten-year
      period 1937-1946 (inclusive). The brief summaries/articles
      are complemented with chronologies and tables of
      statistics.

187. Ensor, Robert C.K. A MINIATURE HISTORY OF THE WAR. New
         York: Oxford University Press, 1945. 153 pp.

         What makes this otherwise unremarkable summary
      (1939-1944) worthy of note is the author's insistence that
      the war in the Pacific drained resources from Europe and
      thereby lengthened the war in all theaters.

188. Esposito, Vincent J., ed. A CONCISE HISTORY OF WORLD WAR
         II. New York: Frederick A. Praeger, 1964. 434 pp.

         Prepared by Encyclopedia Americana, this collection
      contains excellent sections by outstanding historians
      (e.g., Ernest May, John Snell, S. Woodburn Kirby, and
      Robert Futrell).

189. Falls, Cyril. THE SECOND WORLD WAR: A SHORT HISTORY.
         3d rev. ed. London: Methuen, 1950. 312 pp.

         This short, general account rests primarily on a
      narrative of military history. Falls, as an Oxford
      professor of the history of war and a contributer to the
      official British history of the First World War, lends a
      voice of authority to this British perspective of the
      Second World War.

190. Flower, Desmond and James Reeves, eds. THE TASTE OF
         COURAGE: THE WAR, 1939-1945. New York: Harper and
         Brothers, 1960. 1120 pp.

         Although this collection of accounts by eyewitnesses

and participants leans heavily toward the European
Theater, it contains some valuable sections on the war
against Japan, especially on the topics of Pearl Harbor
and Midway.

191.   Ford, Corey and Alastair MacBain. THE LAST TIME I SAW
       THEM. New York: Scribner, 1946. 244 pp.

       Both authors are U.S. Army Intelligence officers. Their
       global travels took them to many air bases, and they relate
       the war adventures of some of the airmen they interviewed.
       The range of experiences makes for delightful reading.

192.   Fuller, J.F.C. THE SECOND WORLD WAR, 1939-1945: A
       STRATEGICAL AND TACTICAL HISTORY. 3d rev. ed.
       New York: Duell, Sloan and Pearce, 1954. 431 pp.

       Fuller limits his inquiry to the strategy and tactics of
       the war. He omits the war in China as not "illuminating"
       to his purpose. His judgments come ringing through. For
       example, mass bombing is "morally wrong," and the decision
       to use the atomic bomb is called a "political blunder of
       unfathomable consequences." With regard to the U.S. Army
       Air Forces, Fuller believes their tactical assignments to
       cooperate with the U.S. fleet against the Japanese fleet
       succeeded superbly, but their strategic operations proved
       less successful because American airpower was dissipated
       against Japanese industries and cities.

193.   Gannett, Lewis, ed. I SAW IT HAPPEN: EYEWITNESS ACCOUNTS
       OF THE WAR. New York: Pocket Books, 1942. 431 pp.

           NE

194.   Gurney, Gene. FIVE DOWN AND GLORY: A HISTORY OF THE
       AMERICAN AIR ACE. New York: Putnam, 1958. 302 pp.

       Here are biographical profiles, edited by Mark P.
       Friedlander, Jr., of U.S. pilots who became "aces" by
       shooting down five enemy aircraft. Some of the aces in
       this general history fought in the war against Japan.

195.   Halter, Jon C. TOP SECRET PROJECTS OF WORLD WAR II. New
       York: Julian Messner, 1978. 192 pp.

       In addition to projects in other theaters, Halter
       summarizes secret activities by Allies and Axis powers that
       affected the war against Japan. These include the surprise
       attack at Pearl Harbor, the Doolittle Raid, Magic, and the

development of the atomic bomb.

196. Hammerton, Sir John A., ed. THE SECOND GREAT WAR: A
      STANDARD HISTORY. London: Waverly, 1944. 5 vols.

      This self-proclaimed first authoritative history of the
war offers a contemporary British summary of the chief
military, political, and economic occurrences.

197. Hayes, Grace P. THE HISTORY OF THE JOINT CHIEFS OF STAFF
      IN WORLD WAR II: THE WAR AGAINST JAPAN. Annapolis, MD:
      Naval Institute Press, 1982. 964 pp.

      Hayes, a naval officer, wrote this history in 1953.
Although the study is based on primary documents, it cannot
be described as an "official" history because the JCS never
gave their formal approval. Nevertheless, the text was
examined at the time of writing and approved by "officers
who had participated in the events." The author provides
an outstanding administrative and strategic history as well
as a guide to sources for further research. Classified
SECRET until 1971, this publication includes a preface
written in 1982. Dean Allard has written an excellent
bibliographic essay.

198. Heiferman, Ronald. WORLD WAR II. London: Octopus Books,
      1973. 256 pp.

      This British work amounts to an almanac illustrated with
many photographs and maps. Although devoted to all
theaters, the book contains excellent information about
lesser-known events in the war against Japan.

199. Hess, Gary R. THE UNITED STATES AT WAR, 1941-1945.
      Arlington Heights, IL: Harlan Davidson, 1986. 166 pp.

      Hess surveys the war, how it was fought, and American
perceptions. He credits Roosevelt, the "practical
idealist," for promoting self-determination. The tough
questions of the war receive careful treatment in this
synthesis. For example, he argues that (a) domestic and
foreign circumstances/pressures restrained Roosevelt's
maneuverability concerning the embargo, his meeting with
Konoye, and the modus vivendi; (b) the air losses in the
Philippines were inexcusable; and (c) complex issues
surround the decision to use the atomic bomb. Here is a
short, sweet--and scholarly--treatment of the war.

200. Hinton, Harold B. AIR VICTORY: THE MEN AND THE MACHINES.

New York: Harper, 1948. 428 pp.

This general history of U.S. air power (1909-1945) is
well researched. There is a separate section on the war
against Japan.

201. Hirsch, Phil, ed. GREAT UNTOLD STORIES OF WORLD WAR II.
      New York: Pyramid Books, 1963. 191 pp.

      Some of these stories touch on Pacific operations.

202. Holbrook, Stewart H. NONE MORE COURAGEOUS: AMERICAN WAR
      HEROES OF TODAY. New York: Macmillan, 1942. 245 pp.

      Holbrook presents the stories of twenty combat heroes.
      Many are taken from the war against Japan. The
      contemporary profiles seem designed to boost American
      morale.

203. Hough, Donald. DARLING, I AM HOME. New York: W.W. Norton,
      1946. 176 pp.

      Here is an open letter that reviews the war in the
      context of world history. Hough's insightful analysis
      raises some difficult questions.

204. Howe, Quincy. ASHES OF VICTORY: WORLD WAR II AND ITS
      AFTERMATH. New York: Simon and Schuster, 1972.
      544 pp.

      The book is well written, despite the annoying absence
      of footnotes. Howe draws masterful descriptions of the
      major personalities. Throughout his narrative, he points
      out the ironies, paradoxes, and contradictions of the war.

205. Hoyle, Martha Byrd. A WORLD IN FLAMES: A HISTORY OF WORLD
      WAR II. New York: Atheneum, 1970. 356 pp.

      This compact history not only describes the major
      military events of the war in all theaters but also sets
      the combat against the political-diplomatic backdrop. Her
      prime concern lies with the execution, not the evolution,
      of strategy. The bibliography, now somewhat outdated,
      remains useful.

206. Husted, H.H. THUMB-NAIL HISTORY OF WORLD WAR II. Boston:
      Humphries, 1949. 442 pp.

      Husted offers what is essentially a chronological report

on the war in all theaters. The emphasis is on military
and political events.

207. Huston, James A. OUT OF THE BLUE: U.S. ARMY AIRBORNE
      OPERATIONS IN WORLD WAR II. West Lafayette, IN: Purdue
      University Studies, 1972.

      Although concerned chiefly with other theaters, Huston
      does include some operations in the Pacific (e.g., Nadzab,
      New Guinea; Burma; and Corregidor). He is particularly
      good in analyzing how the 11th Airborne Division rescued
      the POW-interns in the Philippines. His mild
      conclusion--the experience of World War II is insufficient
      to furnish answers on the role parachute and glider troops
      can play in combat--may leave some readers wondering
      whether "Airborne" is worth the expense.

208. International Committee for the History of the Second World
      War. POLITICS AND STRATEGY IN THE SECOND WORLD WAR.
      Manhattan, KS: MA/AH Publishing, 1976. 112 pp.

      Here are papers presented at the 1975 international
      conference in San Francisco. See especially the material
      on Japan and the United States.

209. Kennett, Lee B. FOR THE DURATION: THE UNITED STATES GOES
      TO WAR, PEARL HARBOR--1942. New York: Charles
      Scribner's Sons, 1985. 243 pp.

      Rather than composing a comprehensive history, Kennett
      selects certain themes in this portrait of the first six
      months of the war. Offering quaint details as well as
      significant events, he has written a well-researched
      glimpse of the home front. See especially his treatment of
      the early WRA experience.

210. Kirk, John and Robert O. Young, Jr. GREAT WEAPONS OF WORLD
      WAR II. New York: Walker, 1961.

      With an introduction by Hanson W. Baldwin, this volume
      offers descriptions of many of the notable weapons of the
      war. The authors (Kirk is a naval intelligence officer;
      Young is a writer) maintain that it is nearly impossible to
      understand the war without some knowledge of the weapons
      with which it was fought. There are some omissions. The
      volume is divided into categories (e.g., Air, Ships, Tanks,
      Artillery, Small Arms, etc). See especially the discussion
      of the atomic bomb.

211. Kurtz, Michael L. THE CHALLENGING OF AMERICA, 1920-1945.
       Arlington Heights, IL: Forum Press, 1986. 205 pp.

       In this survey, Kurtz presents moderate, balanced
       interpretations of controversies such as Roosevelt and the
       coming of the war, Yalta, and the decision to drop the
       atomic bomb. The overview is very readable and well
       researched.

212. Leckie, Robert. DELIVERED FROM EVIL: THE SAGA OF WORLD WAR
       II. New York: Harper and Row, 1987. 998 pp.

       With his focus on the role of the United States, Leckie
       writes a one-volume history of the war. Although
       necessarily episodic and anecdotal, the narrative is
       well written. Perhaps because of Leckie's wartime
       experience, there is more attention on the war in the
       Pacific than is usually the case in a general history of
       the war.

213. Leopard, Donald W. WORLD WAR II: A CONCISE HISTORY.
       Prospect Heights, IL: Waveland Press, 1982. 155 pp.

       Here is a brief overview that does little more than
       point to the highlights.

214. Lewin, Ronald, ed. FREEDOM'S BATTLE: THE WAR ON LAND,
       1939-1945.

              NE

215. Liddell Hart, Basil H. HISTORY OF THE SECOND WORLD WAR.
       New York: G.P. Putnam's Sons, 1970. 768 pp.

       The book presents the astute observations of an expert.
       Little attention, however, is paid to the war against
       Japan. Of interest is Liddell Hart's belief that war with
       Japan was inevitable when the United States imposed the
       economic sanctions in July 1941. In fact, the author feels
       that the Allies were lucky to have the outbreak of
       hostilities delayed until December.

216. Lidz, Richard. MANY KINDS OF COURAGE: AN ORAL HISTORY OF
       WORLD WAR II. New York: G.P. Putnam's Sons, 1980. 266
       pp.

       Not all of the people were directly interviewed by Lidz;
       moreover, some of them choose to use pseudonyms. The
       introductions to each selection, which help to set the

general context and provide information about the person,
are of some help. On the war against Japan, see the
personal accounts by Charles Merdinger, aboard the ARIZONA
at Pearl Harbor; James Kazato and Roy Yano, Japanese-
American evacuees; and Art Rittenberg a Marine at Iwo
Jima. See also the two selections on: (a) Irving
Strobing, who sent the last radio message from Corregidor;
and (b) Miss Palchikoff, who survived the atomic bombing at
Hiroshima.

217. LOOK. MY FAVORITE WAR STORY. New York: Whittlesey House,
     1945. 155 pp.

     Here are over thirty tales which are told by servicemen
     and reporters in all theaters. The stories range from
     humor to tragedy.

218. McCloy, John J. "Turning Points of the War: The Great
     Military Decisions." FOR AFFS, 26 (October 1947),
     52-72.

     With regard to the war against Japan, the assistant
     secretary of war selects the decisions to fight at Bataan,
     to take the fight to the Japanese in New Guinea, and to cut
     directly across the Pacific. His wartime position and his
     straightforward prose enhances the article. Regrettably,
     McCloy avoids discussion of Yalta (which he calls a postwar
     affair) and the decision to use the atomic bomb (which he
     feels is sufficiently treated in Stimson's article).

219. MacDonald, John, ed. GREAT BATTLES OF WORLD WAR II. New
     York: Macmillan, 1986. 192 pp.

     MacDonald, a British editor and military historian,
     offers first-rate selections that include excellent
     illustrations. For purposes of this guide, see the reports
     on Midway, Guadalcanal, Okinawa, and Koshima.

220. McInnis, Edgar W. THE WAR. Oxford, Eng.: Oxford
     University Press, 1940-1947. 6 vols.

     This Canadian professor composed a contemporary
     narrative volume for each year of the war. The emphasis is
     on military events. Each appendix includes a detailed
     chronology.

221. Macksey, Kenneth J. MILITARY ERRORS OF WORLD WAR II. Don
     Mills, Can.: Stoddart, 1987. 256 pp.

NE

222. Martin, Ralph G. THE GI WAR, 1941-1945. Boston: Little,
      Brown, 1967. 402 pp.

      The author, an Armed Forces correspondent (YANK, STARS
      AND STRIPES), bases his report on several interviews with
      combat veterans, private papers, and official records. Of
      special interest is the material gained in interviews with
      wounded and disabled servicemen.

223. Matloff, Maurice, ed. WORLD WAR II: A CONCISE MILITARY
      HISTORY OF AMERICA'S ALL-OUT, TWO-FRONT WAR. New York:
      David McKay, 1980.

      The collection, prepared in the Office of the Chief of
      Military History, includes articles by some of the top
      historians of the war. This is an excellent general
      introduction.

224. Maule, Henry. GREAT BATTLES OF WORLD WAR II. Chicago:
      Henry Regnery, 1973. 448 pp.

      Although this book addresses key engagements in all
      theaters, much of the material centers on the war against
      Japan. Each narrative includes an attempt to set the
      battle into context and to indicate its significance.

225. Meyer, Robert E., Jr., ed. THE STARS AND STRIPES STORY OF
      WORLD WAR II. New York: David McKay, 1960. 504 pp.

      Meyer presents an anthology from the newspaper which
      began publishing on April 18, 1942. The chapters are
      arranged chronologically. Here is an excellent
      contemporary view of the war. The emphasis is heavy on
      European affairs, but there is still much material on the
      Pacific.

226. Michel, Henri. THE SECOND WORLD WAR. New York: Praeger,
      1968. 947 pp.

      Despite the dominance of European affairs in this
      general history of the war, Michel does offer authoritative
      insights on the war in the Pacific. On separate tracks, he
      traces Japanese and American prewar policies. Of the
      American-Japanese negotiations, the author finds the
      diplomatic breakdown readily accepted by both sides. His
      analysis of the surprise attack at Pearl Harbor places
      responsibility with the top leaders. Thus, according to

Michel, Roosevelt did not take part in any conspiracy, but
he did subtly provoke the Japanese who then went too far in
response. See also the section entitled "Nature of the War
in the Pacific." Douglas Parmee translated the book from
the French.

227. Miller, Francis Trevelyan. HISTORY OF WORLD WAR II.
     Philadelphia, PA: Universal Book and Bible House, 1945.
     967 pp.

     In preparing this work, Miller received assistance from
     not only official representatives of 30 governments, but
     also a board of historical and military analysts (such as
     Victor H. Lawn in Far Eastern affairs). The book
     incorporates official photographs and documents which were
     available at the time. There are 102 chapters. Miller is
     decidedly pro-American in his analysis; he utilizes Japan's
     "treachery" to portray the United States as being drawn
     into war. There is no index, but Miller does append a
     lengthy chronology of the war.

228. Monaghan, Frank. WORLD WAR II: AN ILLUSTRATED HISTORY.
     Chicago: J.G. Ferguson, 1943. 530 pp.

     Monaghan, a Yale professor who entered active service
     after completing this manuscript, offers a contemporary
     view from the prewar era to the end of 1942. Many
     photographs, some paintings, and a lengthy chronology
     accompany the narrative.

229. Omitted.

230. NEW YORKER. THE NEW YORKER BOOK OF WAR PIECES. Freeport,
     NY: Books for Libraries Press, 1971. 562 pp.

     This collection of articles published during the war
     comprises an interesting anthology on a range of subjects,
     including a few from the war against Japan.

231. Oleck, Howard L., ed. EYE-WITNESS: WORLD WAR II BATTLES.
     New York: Belmont Books, 1963. 189 pp.

     This collection of reports, mainly by participants or
     correspondents on the scene, adds the flavor of
     authenticity. Few statements can attract more attention
     than those three little words: "I was there."

232. Oleck, Howard L. HEROIC BATTLES OF WORLD WAR II. New
     York: Belmont Books, 1962. 189 pp.

     Despite its emphasis on the war against Germany, the

book presents some interesting material on the Pacific war.

233. THE 100 BEST STORIES OF WORLD WAR II. New York: William
      H. Wise, 1945. 896 pp.

      This is an interesting collection which dwells on events
      and personalities in Europe. See the article by Charles A.
      Rawlings on the effort to resupply Bataan and on the
      heroics of the S.S. DONA NATI ("Ship of the Fighting
      Exiles") and that by Royal Arch Gunnison on the recovery of
      Leyte ("The Flag Goes Up Again").

234. O'Neill, H.C. A SHORT HISTORY OF THE SECOND WORLD WAR.
      New York: Frederick A. Praeger, 1950. 345 pp.

      O'Neill (who sometimes writes under the pseudonym
      "STRATEGICUS") does not hesitate to inject his opinions
      into this general history. Asserting that Japan was ready
      to surrender by May 1945, he argues that Konoye should have
      gone to the Soviet Union to accept any terms. Also, in his
      view, China was little more than "a broken reed." See,
      too, the opinionated finale entitled "Inquest."

235. Puleston, W.D. THE INFLUENCE OF SEA POWER IN WORLD WAR II.
      New Haven, CT: Yale University Press, 1947. 310 pp.

      The author, a retired Navy captain and a student of
      Mahan's writings, examines the strategies and objectives of
      the combatants. In this overview of the major sweeps of
      the war, Puleston, not surprisingly, asserts that sea power
      represented the key to victory. There is much material on
      campaigns in the Pacific.

236. Ramsey, Guy H.W., comp. EPIC STORIES OF THE SECOND WORLD
      WAR. London: Odhams Press, 1957. 318 pp.

      Here is an interesting collection which is taken from
      all theaters. Some of the stories are about familiar
      subjects.

237. Ready, J. Lee. FORGOTTEN ALLIES: THE MILITARY
      CONTRIBUTION OF THE COLONIES, EXILED GOVERNMENTS, AND
      LESSER POWERS IN THE ALLIED VICTORY IN WORLD WAR II.
      Jefferson, NC: McFarland, 1985. 2 vols.

      The second volume deals with the war against Japan. The
      author, a British historian, makes the telling point that
      one such group of forgotten allies was the element of the
      Japanese population that opposed warmongering. The war

efforts of designated units and component forces from
Australia, India, Burma, NEI, New Zealand, and the
Phillipines receive attention in this well-written
narrative.

238. Roskill, Stephen W. THE WAR AT SEA, 1939-1945. London:
      HMSO, 1954-1961. 3 vols.

      Capt. Roskill (RBN) is an acknowledged expert in naval
affairs. Much of his attention is on the war against
Germany and Italy, but his analysis is superb. His
narrative organizes Anglo-American activities through three
stages: defensive, equilibrium, and offensive.

239. Rothberg, Abraham, ed. EYEWITNESS HISTORY OF WORLD WAR II.
      New York: Bantam Books, 1962. 4 vols.

      The eyewitness reports are selected from all theaters.
The extent of the collection, as well as its quality,
separates it from other similar works.

240. SATURDAY EVENING POST. BATTLE: TRUE STORIES OF COMBAT IN
      WORLD WAR II FROM THE SATURDAY EVENING POST.   New York:
      Curtis Books, 1965. 310 pp.

      The collection is taken from all theaters. The articles
were published previously in the magazine.

241. Saundby, Sir Robert. AIR BOMBARDMENT: THE STORY OF ITS
      DEVELOPMENT. New York: Harper and Row, 1962. 259 pp.

      Saundby, a retired Royal Air Force Officer, extols
strategic bombing as the key to the Allied victory. He
notes, however, that in Washington and London political
leaders and commanding officers came to understand the
significance of strategic bombing only relatively late in
the war. There is much useful technical information in the
Appendix.

242. Schuon, Karl, ed. THE LEATHERNECKS: AN INFORMAL HISTORY
      OF THE U.S. MARINE CORPS. New York: Watts, 1964. 277
      pp.

      Here are personal accounts of Marines who participated
in various U.S. engagements, the bulk of which are taken
from the war against Japan. The articles first appeared in
LEATHERNECK.

243. Scoggin, Margaret C., comp. BATTLE STATIONS: TRUE STORIES

OF MEN IN WAR. New York: A.A. Knopf, 1953. 306 pp.

The anthology is taken from all theaters but not all service branches. For the war against Japan, see especially the articles by Carlos P. Rumulo and Edward L. Beach.

244. Scott, Jay. AMERICA'S WAR HEROES: DRAMATIC TRUE TALES OF COURAGEOUS MARINES, ARMY, AIR FORCE, AND NAVY MEN WHOSE EXPLOITS WON THEM THE CONGRESSIONAL MEDAL OF HONOR. Derby, CT: Monarch Books, 1961. 143 pp.

These brief summaries serve as little more than an introduction to these heroes.

245. Shugg, Roger W. and Harvey A. DeWeerd. WORLD WAR II: A CONCISE HISTORY. Washington, D.C.: Infantry Journal Press, 1947. 2d. ed. 548 pp.

Shugg, a history professor, and Lt. Col. DeWeerd (USA) compile a brief military history. Excellent maps supplement the readable text. The authors list the combat units and the order of battle.

246. Sill, Van R. AMERICAN MIRACLE: THE STORY OF WAR CONSTRUCTION AROUND THE WORLD. New York: Odyssey Press, 1947. 301 pp.

This general history incorporates a good deal of material on construction achievements in the Pacific.

247. Smith, Daniel M. and Joseph M. Siracusa. THE TESTING OF AMERICA: 1914-1945. St. Louis, MO: Forum Press, 1979. 256 pp.

After identifying the deep roots of U.S. non-interventionism/isolationism during the 1930s, the authors trace how America evolved, for good or ill, to a thorough internationalism by 1945. Of special interest are the conclusions by the authors that (1) Hull's note in November 1941 was merely a summary of the U.S. case for the historical record, not an ultimatum, and (2) the evacuation of Japanese-Americans was the most outrageous act of its kind in U.S. history. Curiously, the authors skirt the debate on the use of the atomic bomb. The book contains an excellent bibliographic essay.

248. Smith, Joseph R. GEOGRAPHY AND WORLD WAR II. Philadelphia, PA: The John C. Winston Co., 1943.

62 pp.

This popular contemporary introduction to the
geographical peculiarities of the various theaters is
especially useful for the many locations involved in the
war against Japan.

249. Snyder, Louis L., ed. MASTERPIECES OF WAR REPORTING: THE
      GREAT MOMENTS OF WORLD WAR II. New York: Julian
      Messner, 1962. 555 pp.

Snyder presents an interesting collection of first-hand
reports on famous battles and incidents in all theaters.
For the war against Japan, see especially Cecil Brown
aboard the REPULSE, Carlos P. Romulo at Corregidor, TIME
reporters at Pearl Harbor, a Japanese account of the
conquering of Singapore, and William E. Dyess on the Bataan
Death March. Some other reports of interest are by H.R.
Knickerbocker, Jack Belden, Eric Sevareid, William L.
Laurence, and Robert B. Cochrane.

250. Snyder, Louis L. THE WAR: A CONCISE HISTORY, 1939-1945.
      New York: Julian Messner, 1960. 579 pp.

Here is a well-written summary of the war, with most of
the emphasis on political/economic/military affairs.
Snyder seems more comfortable dealing with the war against
Germany. Eric Sevareid wrote the Foreword.

251. Sterling, Dorothy, ed. I HAVE SEEN WAR. New York: Hill
      and Wang, 1961. 273 pp.

Sterling presents 25 stories of the war, both fiction
and nonfiction, which are arranged chronologically. See
especially the articles on Pearl Harbor and the atomic
bombing of Nagasaki.

252. Stokesbury, James L. A SHORT HISTORY OF WORLD WAR II. New
      York: William Morrow, 1980. 352 pp.

Here is an outstanding survey of manageable proportions.
Stokesbury incorporates most of the latest research in
constructing this history of the war.

253. Sullivan, George. STRANGE BUT TRUE STORIES OF WORLD WAR
      II. New York: Walker, 1983. 128 pp.

Among the stories Sullivan presents for a general
audience, see his account of Japan's balloon bombs, the

radar pips near Kiska, Navajo communications, and the NISEI
in Europe.

254. Swing, Raymond Gram. PREVIEW OF HISTORY. Garden City, NY:
      Doubleday, Doran, 1943. 282 pp.

      The book is a collection of Swing's wartime broadcasts
      and speeches up to May 10, 1943. His observations are a
      good summary of the highlights of the war in all theaters.

255. Taylor, A.J.P., ed. HISTORY OF WORLD WAR II. London:
      Octopus Books, 1974. 285 pp.

      Taylor assembles a team of historians to present a
      general composite of the war. See especially the articles
      by A. Russell Buchanan on Pearl Harbor, Glen St. J. Barclay
      on Japan, and C.J.H. Watson on the use of the atomic bomb.

256. Terkel, Studs. THE GOOD WAR: AN ORAL HISTORY OF WORLD WAR
      II. New York: Pantheon Books, 1984. 589 pp.

      This collection of oral histories, arranged topically,
      offers a separate section on the war against Japan. The
      participants reaffirm the brutal nature of the combat in
      the Pacific. See, too, the contributions on the
      development and use of the atomic bomb, and the suffering
      associated with it; especially good is the statement by
      Philip Morrison.

257. TIME. TIME CAPSULE: HISTORY OF THE WAR YEARS, 1939-1945.
      New York: Bonanza Books, 1972. 7 vols.

      The seven volumes appear under one cover (1,650 pp.),
      but each volume covers a separate year with a separate
      index. The text condenses the actual contemporary
      narratives that appeared in TIME during each of the war
      years.

258. United Nations. Information Office. UNITED NATIONS
      CONTRIBUTIONS TO THE WAR. New York: U.N. Information
      Office, 1945. 43 pp.

      Here is a publicity pamphlet which praises all U.N.
      participants.

259. United States. War Department. General Staff. THE WORLD
      AT WAR, 1939-1944: A BRIEF HISTORY OF WORLD WAR II.
      Washington, D.C.: Infantry Journal Press, 1945.
      416 pp.

Here is a general account of the war on all fronts.
Though based on official reports, this authoritative
narrative was innocent enough to pass the wartime censor's
approval.

260. United States. War Department. MILITARY REPORTS ON THE
     UNITED NATIONS. Washington, D.C.: War Dept.,
     1942-1945. 2 vols.

     In this series of monthly reports, the War Department
     circulated information about war-related topics, such as
     tactical doctrine, organization, training methods,
     technical developments, and operations by the armies of the
     United Nations (excluding the U.S. Army).

261. United States. War Department. PRELUDE TO INVASION.
     Washington, D.C.: American Council on Public Affairs,
     1944. 332 pp.

     The narrative, based on official reports by Secretary of
     War Stimson, covers the period December 1941 to June 1944.
     With excellent photographs, the narrative summarizes events
     in all theaters.

262. Urquhart, Fred, ed. GREAT TRUE WAR ADVENTURES. London:
     Arco, 1957. 342 pp.

     NE

263. Van Sinderen, Adrian. THE STORY OF THE SIX YEARS OF TOTAL
     WAR. New York: Price, 1946. 393 pp.

     During the war, Van Sinderen kept a narrative account of
     the chief events in all theaters. In 1944 he published a
     short survey (206 pp.) that covered the period September
     1939-September 1943. This fuller version has as its chief
     value the reflection of the perceptive observer's
     contemporary views.

264. Weinberg, Gerhard L. WORLD IN THE BALANCE: BEHIND THE
     SCENES OF WORLD WAR II. Hanover, NH: University Press
     of New England, 1982.

     Here is a short synthesis which incorporates research
     from recently opened records. See especially the material
     based on the revelations of MAGIC.

265. Weyr, Thomas. WORLD WAR II. New York: Messner, 1970.

224 pp.

This highly readable survey concentrates on events in
Europe and the Mediterranean. Only in the final three
chapters does Weyr focus on the war against Japan. Of
special interest is the author's description of the
prominent personalities in the war.

266. Wilson, Theodore A., ed. WW2: READINGS ON CRITICAL ISSUES.
      New York: Charles Scribner's Sons, 1974. 515 pp.

      Here is an excellent, balanced collection that addresses
      important questions of the war. The book is highly
      recommended.

267. Woodward, David. SUNK! HOW THE GREAT BATTLESHIPS WERE
      LOST. Winchester, MA: Allen and Unwin, 1982. 153 pp.

      Here is a highly readable summary narrative of some of
      the interesting encounters in naval history. The material
      on World War II is taken from both major theaters.

268. Young, Peter, ed. DECISIVE BATTLES OF THE SECOND WORLD
      WAR: AN ANTHOLOGY. London: Barker, 1967. 439 pp.

      This collection emphasizes affairs in Europe and is
      written for a general audience.

269. Young, Peter. WORLD WAR, 1939-1945: A SHORT HISTORY. New
      York: Thomas Y. Crowell, 1966. 447 pp.

      Here is a useful one-volume survey of the war. Young
      writes well and with a certain authority (as a military
      historian and veteran of the European and Pacific
      Theaters).

I.B.1. PICTORIAL ACCOUNTS OF WORLD WAR II

270. Asahi Shimbun Publishing Company. VICTORY ON THE MARCH:
      A PICTORIAL RECORD OF THE WAR OF GREATER EAST ASIA.
      Tokyo: Asahi Shimbun Publishing Company, 1942. 111 pp.

      Here are Japanese photographs taken during their
      victorious operations early in the war.

271. Asahi Shimbun Publishing Company. WAR AND CONSTRUCTION.
      Tokyo: Asahi Shimbun Publishing Company, 1943.
      95 pp.

This collection of Japanese photographs focuses on operations during 1942.

272.   BATTLE STATIONS! New York: William H. Wise, 1946.
       402 pp.

Here are pictorial glimpses of the U.S. Navy's war at sea in all theaters. Some of the leading admirals of the war add brief comments.

273.   Caidin, Martin. AIR FORCE: A PICTORIAL HISTORY OF AMERICAN AIR POWER. New York: Rinehart, 1957. 232 pp.

This pictorial presentation addresses the period 1907 to 1957. Caidin took the selections from official and private collections.

274.   COLLIER'S PHOTOGRAPHIC HISTORY OF WORLD WAR II. New York: Collier, 1984. 270 pp.

This 9" X 12" volume includes many action photos from all theaters. The collection is arranged chronologically.

275.   Compton's Pictured Encyclopedia. SUMMARY OF THE SECOND WORLD WAR AND ITS CONSEQUENCES. Chicago: Compton, 1947. 134 pp.

Here is a reference of prominent personalities, places, events, scientific developments, and postwar plans.

276.   Davies, Al E. PICTORIAL HISTORY OF THE SECOND WORLD WAR. New York: William H. Wise, 1944. 2 vols.

The photos cover the period September 1939 to September 1943. A short narrative accompanies the pictures, which deal with all theaters of the war.

277.   Disabled American Veterans. LEST WE FORGET. Maplewood, NJ: Hammond, 1964. 80 pp.

Here is a pictorial sampling of action in all theaters.

278.   Dollinger, Hans. THE DECLINE AND FALL OF NAZI GERMANY AND IMPERIAL JAPAN: A PICTORIAL HISTORY OF THE FINAL DAYS OF WORLD WAR II. New York: Crown, 1968. 431 pp.

The accompanying narrative is translated from the German by Arnold Pomerans. With some detail, Dollinger presents a

summary of events from 1945. Of special interest is the
attention devoted to the ordeal of Japanese civilians.

279.   Grant, Ian. CAMERAMEN AT WAR. Cambridge: Stephens, 1980.

       NE

280.   Gurney, Gene. THE WAR IN THE AIR: A PICTORIAL HISTORY OF
       WORLD WAR II. New York: Crown Publishers, 1962.
       352 pp.

       Gurney arranges photos of the air war in all theaters.
       Many of the pictures are in color and show combat action.
       The collection is extensive, and Gurney admirably carries
       through his purpose.

281.   Henderson, Harry B. and Herman C. Morris. WAR IN OUR TIME.
       Garden City, NY: Doubleday, Doran, 1942. 416 pp.

       This pictorial history covers the period 1931-mid-1942.
       The accompanying text is self-proclaimed as analysis but
       can be more accurately characterized as narrative.

282.   Herridge, Charles. PICTORIAL HISTORY OF WORLD WAR II.
       London: Hamlyn, 1975.

       This British perspective presents some excellent photos,
       but the overwhelming interest is on the war against
       Germany.

283.   Hunter, Kenneth E. and Margaret E. Tackley, comps.
       PICTORIAL RECORD: THE WAR AGAINST JAPAN. Washington,
       D.C.: GPO, 1952. 471 pp.

       This pictorial account, edited by Mary Ann Bacon, is
       part of the official "U.S. Army in World War II" series.
       The collection is first-rate and offers glimpses of
       virtually every aspect of Army operations in the war
       against Japan.

284.   Hutchinson, Walter, ed. PICTORIAL HISTORY OF THE WAR.
       London: Hutchinson, 1939-1945. 26 vols.

       This excellent collection of photographs is supplemented
       with narrative sketches. The arrangement is chronological.

285.   Hyman, Nat, comp. EYES OF THE WAR: A PHOTOGRAPHIC REPORT
       OF WORLD WAR II. New York: Telepic, 1945. 2 vols.

Both volumes incorporate over one thousand photographs, most of which are first-rate. Volume II deals with the Pacific Theater.

286. THE ILLUSTRATED BOOK OF WORLD WAR II. New York: St. Martin's, 1972. 128 pp.

Taken from the pages of the British magazine ILLUSTRATED, this collection contains some of the best color photographs of the war. The book is divided by subject categories (e.g., Leaders, Weapons, Personnel, and Women at War).

287. Jablonski, Edward. A PICTORIAL HISTORY OF THE WORLD WAR II YEARS. Garden City, NY: Doubleday, 1979. 319 pp.

This is a distillation of Jablonski's four-volume AIR WAR. The stark black-and-white photos offer new and/or universal views of famous and notorious events.

288-297. Omitted.

298. LIFE. LIFE GOES TO WAR: A PICTURE HISTORY OF WORLD WAR II. Boston: Little, Brown, 1977. 303 pp.

Most of these excellent photographs appeared in contemporary issues of the magazine.

299. LIFE. LIFE'S PICTURE HISTORY OF WORLD WAR II. New York: Time, 1950. 368 pp.

The pictures are arranged chronologically and cover all theaters. There is some explanatory text. Most of the photos are in black and white.

301. LOOK. OUR AMERICAN HEROES: A PICTORIAL SAGA OF AMERICAN GALLANTRY ON ALL FIGHTING FRONTS OF THE WORLD. New York: Whittlesey House, 1943.

Here is a rousing pictorial collection that includes much combat action. The collection is taken from all theaters.

302. McCahill, William P., ed. HIT THE BEACH! YOUR MARINE CORPS IN ACTION. New York: William H. Wise, 1948. 386 pp.

The editor assembles an excellent photographic story, from the first to the last of the Marine operations in the Pacific.

303. Makanna, Philip. "Ghosts." AMER HIST ILLUS, 23 (May
     1988), 20-31.

     Here is a pictorial in color of Japan, Germany, Britain,
     and the United States at war.

304. Maloney, Tom, ed. U.S.A. AT WAR. New York: E. P. Dutton,
     1944. 304 pp.

     Here are about 160 photographs which give a stark,
     realistic glimpse of the war in all theaters.

305. Mayer, Sydney L. A PICTORIAL HISTORY OF WORLD WAR II.
     London: Octopus Books, 1976. 128 pp.

     The collection shows combat action in all theaters.

306. Maynard, Christopher and David Jeffries. AIR BATTLES: AIR
     COMBAT IN WORLD WAR II. New York: Franklin Watts, 1987.
     32 pp.

     Here is a pictorial summary aimed at the general public.

307. Meredith, Roy. THE AMERICAN WARS: A PICTORIAL HISTORY
     FROM QUEBEC TO KOREA, 1755-1953. Cleveland, OH: World
     Publishing, 1955.

     Less than one hundred pages (pp. 264-321) deal with the
     Second World War. See especially the work of the Marine
     Corps combat artists.

308. Morris, Herman C. and Harry R. Henderson, eds. WORLD WAR
     II IN PICTURES. New York: Journal of Living Publishing
     Corp., 1945. 3 vols.

     Here is an excellent contemporary selection of
     black-and-white photographs from all theaters.

309. OUR ARMY AT WAR. New York: Harper and Brothers, 1944.
     Unpaged.

     Here is a pictorial account, with official war
     department photographs, of the war in all theaters through
     1943. Gen. Marshall furnished the Introduction.

310. Pimlott, John. WORLD WAR II IN PHOTOGRAPHS. London:
     Orbis, 1984.

     The photographs are taken from all theaters. The

collection features combat action but also portrays support
services at work.

311. READER'S DIGEST. GREAT PHOTOGRAPHS OF WORLD WAR II.
      Pleasantville, NY: Reader's Digest Association, 1964.
      32 pp.

      This is a marvelous, moving collection of 40
      photographs. The sparse narrative serves to highlight the
      photos.

312. Salomon, Henry and Richard Hanser, eds. VICTORY AT SEA.
      Garden City, NY: Doubleday, 1960. 256 pp.

      Here is an excellent pictorial history of the war at
      sea. There are over 500 photographs portraying the action
      in all theaters.

313. Steichen, Edward, comp. U.S. NAVY WAR PHOTOS: PEARL
      HARBOR TO TOKYO BAY. New York: Crown Publishers, 1980.
      rev. ed.

      This all black-and-white collection is outstanding.
      There are some additions here to the original edition that
      appeared in 1956.

314. Stern, Robert C., comp. THE UNITED STATES NAVY IN WORLD
      WAR TWO, 1941-1942. New York: Sterling, 1987. 68 pp.

      Here is a pictorial collection that touches on all
      theaters. See especially the photos from Pearl Harbor.

315. Sulzberger, C.L. THE AMERICAN HERITAGE PICTURE HISTORY OF
      WORLD WAR II. New York: American Heritage Publishing
      Co., 1966. 640 pp.

      Here is one of the best pictorial accounts of the war,
      which Sulzberger calls a "vast, earth-convulsing
      revolution." With over 700 photographs and a crisp
      narrative, the book is highly recommended. An abridged
      version appeared in 1970 (386 pp.).

316. Taylor, A.J.P. THE SECOND WORLD WAR: AN ILLUSTRATED
      HISTORY. New York: G.P. Putnam's Sons, 1975. 234 pp.

      Despite its overemphasis on European affairs, this
      volume contains excellent photographs and a crisp
      narrative.

317. Topolski, Feliks. THREE CONTINENTS, 1944-1945. London:
      Methuen, 1946. 224 pp.

      Here is a pictorial report of the war on all fronts.
      See the material on CBI.

318. United States. Army Air Forces. BOMBS AWAY! New York:
      William H. Wise, 1947. 386 pp.

      Here is a pictorial account of the USAAF in the war.
      Some of the official photographs show unique views of the
      air war.

319. United States. Navy Department. UNITED STATES NAVY WAR
      PHOTOGRAPHS. New York: Crown Publishers, 1980.

      NE

320. United States. War Department. OUR ARMY AT WAR. New
      York: Harper and Brothers, 1944. 282 1.

      Here is the story of the leading campaign of the U.S.
      Army in the war as told in official War Department
      photographs. Gen. Marshall wrote the introduction. This
      is an excellent collection.

321. Veterans of Foreign Wars. PICTORIAL HISTORY OF THE SECOND
      WORLD WAR. New York: William H. Wise, 1948. 5 vols.

      The volumes are arranged chronologically, and the
      collection covers all theaters. Although some of the
      photographs are familiar, many are not. The photos of
      combat action in the Pacific, particularly the aerial
      encounters, are of special interest.

322. West, Levon. [pseud. Ivan Dmitri.] FLIGHT TO EVERYWHERE.
      New York: Whittlesey House, 1944. 240 pp.

      Here are over 400 photographs in color and
      black-and-white of the action in all theaters. West took
      as the focus of his long trip the work of the Army
      Transport Command.

323. Zich, Arthur. THE RISING SUN. Alexandria, VA: Time-Life
      Books, 1977. 208 pp.

      Here is a popular pictorial survey of the rise and fall
      of the Japanese empire. The focus is on Japanese
      society as opposed to events on the battlefield.

I.C. DOCUMENTS/RECORDS/ARCHIVAL COLLECTIONS/PRIVATE COLLECTIONS

324. Bevans, Charles I., comp. TREATIES AND OTHER INTERNATIONAL
      AGREEMENTS OF THE UNITED STATES OF AMERICA, 1776-1949.
      Washington, D.C.: GPO, 1968-. 12 vols.

      This authoritative collection includes wartime alliances
      and agreements for building a new international
      organization.

325. Boyd, Carl. "Recent Documentation for the Study of the
      Second World War." MICROFORM REV, 10 (Fall 1981),
      271-279.

      Here is a discreet survey of major documents and groups
      of records now available in microformat. Of particular
      interest for this guide are Boyd's descriptions of the
      records of Japanese embassies and consulates, war crimes
      and State Department files (especially Record Group 38, put
      together on direct request by Roosevelt for prewar
      information supplied by U.S. naval attaches).

326. Buchanan, A. Russell, ed. THE UNITED STATES AND WORLD WAR
      II: MILITARY AND DIPLOMATIC DOCUMENTS. Columbia, SC:
      University of South Carolina Press, 1972. 303 pp.

      Buchanan assembles a sampling rather than a
      comprehensive collection.

327. Bundy, Harvey. "Remembered Words." ATL MONTHLY, 199
      (March 1957), 56-57.

      Here is a series of quotations including wartime
      statements by Stimson and Churchill on the atomic bomb.

328. Detwiler, Donald S. and Charles B. Burdick, eds. WAR IN
      ASIA AND THE PACIFIC, 1937-1949: JAPANESE AND CHINESE
      STUDIES AND DOCUMENTS. New York: Garland, 1980.
      15 vols.

      This is a monumental collection that runs to almost
      8,500 pages. The first volume is an introduction and
      guide through the larger repository from which these
      studies are taken. Volumes two through twelve incorporate
      about 70 reports prepared by Japanese officials after the
      war. The final three volumes contain reports drawn up by
      Chinese Nationalists. This is a valuable resource that
      makes available important, otherwise hard-to-get-at

materials.

329. DOCUMENTS ON AMERICAN FOREIGN RELATIONS. Boston: World
      Peace Foundation, 1939-1948. 8 vols.

      The collection comprises a useful contemporary reference
      source. All of the important wartime conferences are
      included.

330. Eilcox, Francis O. and Thursten V. Kalijarvi, eds. RECENT
      AMERICAN FOREIGN POLICY: BASIC DOCUMENTS, 1941-1951.
      New York: Appleton-Century-Crofts, 1952. 927 pp.

      Despite the contemporary tune and the focus on Europe,
      this lengthy collection remains a useful reference source
      for the purposes of this guide.

331. Fishwick, Marshall W. "A Note on World War II Naval
      Records." AMER HR, 55 (October 1949), 82-85.

      Here is a summary of the locations of important naval
      war records. See especially Fishwick's explanation of the
      significant "Flag Files."

332. Gantenbein, James W., ed. DOCUMENTARY BACKGROUND OF WORLD
      WAR II, 1931-1941. New York: Columbia University
      Press, 1948. 1122 pp.

      This excellent collection outlines the foreign policies
      of the powers through the speeches and policies of their
      world leaders. International agreements and joint
      communiques are also included. There is a special section
      on American-Japanese relations and a chronology for the
      period 1938-1941. The reader could use more editorial
      guidance (e.g., introductory material, notes, etc.).

333. Great Britain. PUBLIC RECORD OFFICE. THE SECOND WORLD
      WAR: A GUIDE TO DOCUMENTS IN THE PUBLIC RECORD OFFICE.
      London: HMSO, 1972. 303 pp.

      Here is a valuable reference which is categorized by
      government department. L. Bell, Principal Assistant Keeper
      of Public Records, arranged the presentations. Appendices
      include operational code names, abbreviations, a list of
      War Cabinet committees, and citations for official
      histories. Although the book lacks adequate information
      about the complete filing numbers and the process of how to
      order specific documents, this is an indispensable source
      which should be digested before arriving at the P.R.O.

Much material on American participation in the war is
contained in these files; for the war against Japan, see
especially the little used records of the chiefs of staff
(CAB 79-80), the Far Eastern Committee (CAB 96), and the
miscellaneous CAB 21 file. [Editor's note: There has been
some controversy about the appropriate form for citing
references to the much used correspondence files of the
Foreign Office (FO 371). This 1972 guide is silent on the
subject. My correspondence with the P.R.O. confirms that
each citation should refer to both "file" and "piece"
numbers (e.g., FO 371/46210, F 2626/186/10).]

334. Hansen, Harold A., John G. Herndon, and William B.
        Langsdorf, eds. FIGHTING FOR FREEDOM: HISTORIC
        DOCUMENTS. Philadelphia, PA: John C. Winston, 1947.
        502 pp.

The collection contains selected speeches of wartime
leaders as well as public documents. The material is
arranged chronologically. Subject headings include the
United Nations charter and atomic energy.

335. Jacobsen, Hans-Adolph, and Arthur L. Smith, Jr., eds.
        WORLD WAR II: POLICY AND STRATEGY. Santa Barbara, CA:
        ABC-Clio, 1979. 505 pp.

The editors add commentary to the selected documents.
Among the collection are Japanese documents which are not
readily available. See also the "Victory Without Peace"
section on Indonesia, China and India. Photographs, maps,
glossary, and chronology enhance the volume.

336. Jones, Constance M., Derris L. Raper, and John J. Sbrega,
        eds. THE AMERICAN EXPERIENCE: DOCUMENTS AND NOTES.
        Dubuque, IA: Kendall/Hunt, 1987. 2d ed. 308 pp.

This general collection includes the texts of several
documents on the war. Headnotes set the context for each
document but avoid summarizing the content or distracting
the reader with patronizing questions. For some of the
documents on the war against Japan, see especially
Roosevelt's views on racial mixing, the Fulbright-Connally
resolutions, the Korematsu case, the decisions at Yalta,
and the decision to use the atomic bomb.

337. Langsam, Walter C., ed. HISTORIC DOCUMENTS OF WORLD WAR
        II. Princeton, NJ: Van Nostrand, 1958. 191 pp.

The documents touch on the prewar and postwar years as

well as the war. Langsam writes a brief introduction to
each document.

338. Mayer, Sydney L. and W. J. Koenig. THE TWO WORLD WARS: A
        GUIDE TO MANUSCRIPT COLLECTIONS IN THE UNITED KINGDOM.
        London: Bowker, 1976. 317 pp.

        The manuscript collections listed are all open to the
        general public. The arrangement is chronological within
        regional location. Mayer and Koenig choose not to include
        the holdings of the Public Record Office.

339. O'Neill, James E. and Robert W. Krauskopf, eds. WORLD WAR
        II: AN ACCOUNT OF ITS DOCUMENTS: CONFERENCE ON
        RESEARCH ON THE SECOND WORLD WAR. Washington, D.C.:
        Howard University Press, 1976. 269 pp.

        Here are eighteen papers presented at a 1971 conference
        which was sponsored by the National Archives and the
        American Committee on the History of the Second World War.
        For the war against Japan, see the essays about available
        documents by Louis Morton on the prologue to Pearl Harbor,
        Russell H. Fifield on U. S. policy toward Indochina,
        Barbara W. Tuchman on Stilwell, and W. Clayton James on
        MacArthur.

340. Royal Institute of International Affairs, ed. UNITED
        NATIONS DOCUMENTS, 1941-1945. London: RIIA, 1946. 271
        pp.

        The criterion for selection was whether a particular
        document addressed a "forward-looking" decision rather than
        the prosecution of the war. Most of the collection,
        however, is now fairly standard (e.g., conference
        communiques, U.N. Charter, Bretton Woods Agreement, UNESCO,
        etc.).

341. Schnapper, Morris B., ed. UNITED NATIONS AGREEMENTS.
        Washington, D.C.: American Council on Public Affairs,
        1944. 376 pp.

        Here are the texts of key documents from the period June
        12, 1941 to December 12, 1943. Many bilateral agreements
        reached by the United States are included. Schnapper
        points out that the documents demonstrate the increasing
        unity of the Allied coalition. There are separate indices
        by country and by subject.

342. Siracusa, Joseph M., ed. THE AMERICAN DIPLOMATIC

REVOLUTION: A DOCUMENTARY HISTORY OF THE COLD WAR, 1941-1947. New York: Holt, Rinehart and Winston, 1976. 263 pp.

Although this collection focuses mainly on Europe and the postwar years, Siracusa writes knowledgeably about wartime events in Asia.

343. Stacey, C.P. "War Diaries." CANADIAN ARMY J, 4 (Summer 1950), 17-24.

As an army historian, Stacey stresses the importance of maintaining official unit histories, or diaries. He lists some helpful guidelines.

344. United Nations. THE NATIONS HAVE DECLARED. Toronto: Canadian Institute of International Affairs, 1944. 3 vols.

This collection of documents includes the U.S. Charter as well as announcements from various Allied conferences.

345. United Nations. SURRENDER OF ITALY, GERMANY AND JAPAN. Washington, D.C.: GPO, 1946. 111 pp.

In addition to the instruments of surrender, this collection of documents includes papers and addresses by Truman and the supreme Allied commanders.

346. United Nations. UNITED NATIONS DOCUMENTS, 1941-1945. London: Royal Institute for International Affairs, 1946. 271 pp.

The collection touches on all U.N. wartime activities from Pearl Harbor up to and including the Moscow Foreign Ministers Conference in December 1945.

347. United States. Armed Forces Information School. PILLARS OF PEACE: DOCUMENTS PERTAINING TO AMERICAN INTEREST IN ESTABLISHING A LASTING WORLD PEACE, JANUARY 1941 TO FEBRUARY 1946. Carlisle Barracks, PA: Army Information School, 1946. 166 pp.

These wartime documents provide some insight into U.S. war aims by framing the general American vision of the postwar world. Not everything here arises out of naive idealism.

348. United States. Department of State. THE AXIS IN DEFEAT:

A COLLECTION OF DOCUMENTS ON AMERICAN POLICY TOWARD
GERMANY AND JAPAN. Washington, D.C.: GPO, 1945.
118 pp.

See in this valuable collection the material on the
results of key diplomatic conferences, the surrender of
Japan, and the occupation of Japan.

349. United States. Department of State. A DECADE OF AMERICAN
      FOREIGN POLICY: BASIC DOCUMENTS, 1941-1949.
      Washington, D.C.: GPO, 1985. 1,381 pp.

      Here is a revised edition of the 1950 volume prepared by
      the State Department's Historical Office and the Senate's
      Foreign Relations Committee. The revisions correct certain
      errors and omissions, reorganize the material, add some new
      documents (released at the time or shortly thereafter), and
      offer more expansive footnotes. Much of this useful
      collection deals with Asian affairs.

350. Vining, Donald, ed. AMERICAN DIARIES OF WORLD WAR II. New
      York: Pepys Press, 1982. 430 pp.

      These diary excerpts run the gamut of emotions and views
      of the war. Vining selects from all theaters. The
      excerpts narrate the human dimensions of the war.

351. Watts, Franklin, ed. VOICES OF HISTORY. Vol. I: New
      York: Franklin Watts, 1942. Vols. 2-4: New York:
      Gramercy, 1943-1945. 4 vols.

      Watts has gathered a detailed collection--the smallest
      volume exceeds 620 pages--of wartime speeches. The editor
      supposedly selected only important speeches, but, in fact,
      the volumes contain just about every planned public
      utterance of Allied leaders. A monthly chronology precedes
      each chapter.

352. Zobrist, Benedict K. "Resources of Presidential Libraries
      for the History of the Second World War." MIL AFFS, 39
      (April 1975), 82-85.

      Here is a valuable reference of materials in the
      libraries of Hoover, Roosevelt, Truman, Eisenhower, and
      Kennedy.

I.D. MILITARY HISTORIES (GENERAL)

353. Borowski, Harry R., ed. MILITARY PLANNING IN THE TWENTIETH

CENTURY. Washington, D.C.: Office of Air Force History, 1986. 464 pp.

Here are selections from the proceedings of the 1984 Military Symposium. See especially the papers by Alvin D. Coox on Japanese military education and planning prior to 1941 and Robert F. Futrell on Air Force planning after the war.

354. Dixon, Joe C., ed. THE AMERICAN MILITARY AND THE FAR EAST. Washington, D.C.: Office of Air Force History, 1980. 318 pp.

The ninth Military Symposium at the Air Force Academy in October 1980 attracted many "notables" in the field, such as Norman Graebner, Akira Iriye, Richard Stilwell, D. Clayton James, Allan Millett, Samuel Wells, and Joyce Lebra. These proceedings of the conference touch on (among other topics) the impact on Asian societies of American objectives and strategy.

355. Frankland, Noble and Christopher Dowling, eds. DECISIVE BATTLES OF THE TWENTIETH CENTURY. New York: David McKay, 1976. 348 pp.

For the war against Japan, see the excellent articles by Alvin D. Coox (Pearl Harbor), Peter Simkins (Midway), Sir Geoffry Evans (Imphal-Kohima), and Stanley L. Falk (Leyte Gulf). The editors append detailed maps which the reader will find useful.

356. Graebner, Norman A. THE AGE OF GLOBAL POWER: THE UNITED STATES SINCE 1939. New York: John Wiley & Sons, 1979. 345 pp.

In this authoritative analysis of the growth of the United States as a superpower, Graebner focuses on three elements: (1) the imperial presidency, (2) the military and bureaucratic directorships of American global defenses, and (3) the role of a scientific-economic-political elite in the United States. On the war in the Pacific, Graebner argues that the United States bears a certain responsibility along with Japan.

357. Gray, J. Glenn. THE WARRIORS: REFLECTIONS ON MEN IN BATTLE. New York: Harcourt Brace, 1959. 242 pp.

The author, a former G.I., describes men at war and their close association with death. Despite this world of violence, Gray's emphasis is on the human dimension.

358.   Hagan, Kenneth J. and William R. Roberts, eds. AGAINST ALL
       ENEMIES: INTERPRETATIONS OF AMERICAN MILITARY HISTORY
       FROM COLONIAL TIMES TO THE PRESENT. Westport, CT:
       Greenwood Press, 1986. 393 pp.

       In this wide-ranging collection, see Russell F. Weigley,
       "The Interwar Army, 1919-1941"; James L. Stokesbury, "The
       U.S. Army and Coalition Warfare, 1941-1945"; and Stephen E.
       Ambrose, "The Armed Services and American Strategy,
       1945-1953."

359.   Higham, Robin. AIR POWER: A CONCISE HISTORY. New York:
       St. Martin's Press, 1972. 282 pp.

       This scholarly overview contains little on the war in
       the Pacific. The balanced perspective, however, makes it
       useful to this project by indicating appropriate roles for
       air power in war. The bibliographic essay is a valuable
       reference.

360.   Higham, Robin, Abigail T. Siddall, and Carol Williams, eds.
       FLYING AIRCRAFT OF THE U.S.A.A.F.-U.S.A.F. Ames, IA and
       Manhattan, KS: Iowa State University Press and Sun-
       flower Books, 1975-1981. 3 vols.

       Experienced pilots describe the performance
       characteristics, operational use -- and idiosyncrasies --
       of each aircraft. Many photographs are interspersed among
       the volumes. The technical information and the first-hand
       reports give a "feel" for these aircraft. The material on
       the war against Japan is comprehensive.

361.   Hurley, Alfred F. and Robert C. Ehrhart, eds. AIR POWER
       AND WARFARE. Washington, D. C.: Office of Air Force
       History, 1979. 461 pp.

       Here are the proceedings of the 1978 Military History
       Symposium at the Air Force Academy. See especially the
       section entitled "World War II in the Air: Different
       National Experiences." Alvin D. Coox reports on the
       Japanese Air Force, and John Huston offers an analysis of
       Hap Arnold. See, too, the statements by Curtis LeMay and
       William I. Martin.

362.   Jessup, John E., Jr. and Robert W. Coakley, eds. A GUIDE
       TO THE STUDY AND USE OF MILITARY HISTORY. Washington,
       D. C.: Center of Military History, 1979.

These bibliographic essays cover a broad spectrum. For articles which touch on the war in the Pacific, see Jeffrey J. Clarke, "World Military History, 1786-1945"; and Charles B. MacDonald, "The United States and the Two World Wars."

363. Kennedy, Paul. THE RISE AND FALL OF THE GREAT POWERS. New York: Random House, 1987. 677 pp.

Kennedy, a historian, surveys the sweep of military history from 1500 to 2000. His narrative identifies the period 1919-1942 as the coming of the bipolar world (with "offstage superpowers"). After 1942, he traces the forces of stability and change in a bipolar world.

364. Leckie, Robert. THE WARS OF AMERICA. New York: Harper and Row, 1968.

In this general survey Leckie devotes a great deal of attention to the Second World War (pp. 657-832). He begins the section on the war with a description of the peace conference at Paris. Richard B. Morris wrote the Foreword.

365. Millett, Allen R. and Williamson Murray, eds. MILITARY EFFECTIVENESS. Winchester, MA: Unwin, Hyman, 1988. 3 vols.

NE

366. Quigley, Carroll. TRAGEDY AND HOPE: A HISTORY OF THE WORLD IN OUR TIME. New York: Macmillan, 1966. 1,348 pp.

In this masterful survey, Quigley offers some keen insights about the era of the Second World War. For example, the noted historian points out that Cordell Hull's deliberately ambiguous economic policy in 1939 was a mistake and helped promote the rise to power of the militarists in Japan. U.S. ambiguity, according to Quigley, fed Japanese fears of sanctions not yet imposed while simultaneously raising hopes in Japan about concessions not yet granted. In addition, Quigley identifies two U.S. errors in the prewar negotiations with Japan: (1) no correlation between U.S. demands on Japan and U.S power in the Pacific and (2) no correlation between strategic plans -- that is, "Europe First" -- and U.S. diplomacy. With regard to the Yalta meeting, Quigley reconstructs the contemporary situation ("cordial, cooperative, and optimistic") and downplays the idea of

paying a price to the Soviets to enter the war against
Japan. See, too, Quigley's authoritative handling of
scientific affairs, including valuable contributions to the
debate over the use of the atomic bomb. The appropriate
portions of this volume appeared in a separate book in 1968
entitled THE WORLD SINCE 1939: A HISTORY.

I.E. EAST ASIAN HISTORIES

367. Cohen, Warren I. THE CHINESE CONNECTION: ROGER S. GREEN,
     THOMAS W. LAMONT, GEORGE E. SOKOLSKY AND AMERICAN-EAST
     ASIAN RELATIONS. New York: Columbia University Press,
     1978. 322 pp.

     Here is a superb study of attempts by private citizens
     to influence international relations. The book is
     thoroughly researched and well written. Cohen points out
     the pitfalls of these private adventures as he analyzes
     U.S.-East Asian relations during the first half of the
     twentieth century.

368. Cohen, Warren I., ed. NEW FRONTIERS IN AMERICAN-EAST ASIAN
     RELATIONS: ESSAYS PRESENTED TO DOROTHY BORG. New York:
     Columbia University Press, 1983. 294 pp.

     Amidst a valuable collection which covers the broad
     sweep of American-East Asian relations, two outstanding
     essays touch upon the war against Japan. See the
     bibliographic surveys in Waldo Heinrichs, "The Middle
     Years, 1900-1945 and the Question of a Large U.S. Policy
     for East Asia" (pp. 77-106); and Ernest R. May, "Military
     and Naval Affairs since 1900" (pp. 107-127).

369. Davies, John Paton. "America and East Asia." FOR AFFS, 55
     (January 1977), 368-394.

     Here is an excellent survey of two hundred years of
     history by an expert in the field.

370. Griswold, A. Whitney. THE FAR EASTERN POLICY OF THE UNITED
     STATES. New York: Harcourt, Brace, 1938. 530 pp.

     Here is a classic history of the prewar situation.

371. Lowe, Peter. BRITAIN IN THE FAR EAST: A SURVEY FROM 1819
     TO THE PRESENT. London: Longman, 1981. 264 pp.

     This survey contains some excellent material on the
     prewar and wartime years.

372. Maki, John W., ed. CONFLICT AND TENSION IN THE FAR EAST:
      KEY DOCUMENTS 1894-1960. Seattle, WA: University of
      Washington Press, 1961. 245 pp.

      The section on World War II includes excellent Japanese
      primary sources.

373. May, Ernest R. and James C. Thompson, Jr., eds. AMERICAN-
      EAST ASIAN RELATIONS. Cambridge, MA: Harvard
      University Press, 1972.

      The collection spans the history of American-East Asian
      relations. Louis Morton's essay surveys the historiography
      of the period from 1937 to 1941.

374. Ness, Gayl D. and William Stahl. "Western Imperialist
      Armies in Asia." COMP STUD SOC HIST, 19 (January 1977),
      2-29.

      In this wide-ranging sweep of history, which includes
      little on World War II, the authors identify a fundamental
      cause of the Western conquests in Asia: "The social
      organization in which a military technology emerges and
      operates is decisive in determining how potent that
      technology will be." They also assert that when the West
      lost its destructive organizational superiority the age of
      Vasco Da Gama came to a close.

375. O'Connor, Richard. PACIFIC DESTINY: AN INFORMAL HISTORY
      OF THE U. S. IN THE FAR EAST: 1776-1968. Boston:
      Little, Brown, 1969. 505 pp.

      O'Connor's perspective emphasizes the evolution of the
      United States as a Pacific power. There is very little
      material on the war.

II. DIPLOMATIC AND POLITICAL ASPECTS OF THE WAR AGAINST JAPAN

A. ORIGINS OF THE WAR

1. GENERAL ACCOUNTS OF THE ORIGINS OF WORLD WAR II (PREWAR UNITED STATES)

376. Adamthwaite, Anthony P. THE MAKING OF THE SECOND WORLD WAR. Winchester, MA: Allen and Unwin, 1977. 2d ed. 235 pp.

Despite the overriding emphasis on events in Europe, this book gives a useful narrative on the origins of the war. The author includes a valuable collection of documents.

377. Ascoli, Max. "War Aims and America's Aims." SOCIAL RESEARCH, 8 (September 1941), 267-282.

Ascoli offers a prewar assessment of America's general interests. With an interventionist tone, Ascoli argues that the American dream must spread to all people if the United States is to remain safe.

378. Baldwin, Hanson W. THE CRUCIAL YEARS, 1939-1941: THE WORLD AT WAR. New York: Harper & Row, 1976. 499 pp.

The narrative concentrates on international leaders and ends with the surprise attack at Pearl Harbor.

379. Barron, Gloria J. LEADERSHIP IN CRISIS: FRANKLIN D. ROOSEVELT AND THE PATH TO INTERVENTION. Port Washington, NY: Kennikat Press, 1973. 145 pp.

Addressing the period 1939-1941, Barron feels that the president kept just in front of American public opinion in developing internationalist perspectives. The book is well researched, including many interviews, and the author is generally sympathetic to Roosevelt's efforts.

380. Baumont, Maurice. THE ORIGINS OF THE SECOND WORLD WAR. New Haven, CT: Yale University Press, 1978. 327 pp.

Despite the heavy emphasis on European affairs, there is some material on the Far Eastern crisis during the 1930s. The authoritative text is translated from the French by Simone de Courvreur Ferguson.

381. Beale, Howard K. SOME FALLACIES OF THE INTERVENTIONIST
      VIEW. Washington, D.C.: Author, 1941. 32 pp.

      Though not an isolationist, Beale nevertheless opposes
      the views of the so-called "internationalists" (or
      "interventionists") who, in his opinion, would drag
      the United States into the war.

382. Beattie, Edward W., Jr. FREELY TO PASS. New York:
      Crowell, 1942. 372 pp.

      Beattie, an American correspondent, travelled throughout
      the world in the years 1937-1941. The book is his report
      on these travels. Its chief value lies in having an
      eyewitness view on the eve of the United States' entry into
      the war.

383. Boyd, Carl. THE EXTRAORDINARY ENVOY: GENERAL HIROSHI
      OSHIMA AND DIPLOMACY IN THE THIRD REICH, 1934-1939.
      Lanham, MD: University Press of America, 1980. 246 pp.

      This well-researched and well-written book provides a
      unique perspective on the deteriorating international
      situation during the 1930s. By following the career of
      this Japanese general, Boyd traces events in both Europe
      and Asia during that fateful decade. The ups and downs of
      Oshima's career as Japan's ambassador to Germany add
      special flavor.

384. Brumback, Oscar. A MANUAL OF THE CITIZENS NO FOREIGN WAR
      COALITION. Washington, D. C.: The Citizen No Foreign
      War Coalition, 1941. 136 pp.

      The author, chairman of this noninterventionist group,
      charges that proponents of a "World Government" are
      scheming to involve the United States in a war with
      Japan--a war neither country wants.

385. Brune, Lester H. "United States Sea Power, Air Power and
      War Plans, 1919-1939." PROC CONF WAR DIP (The Citadel,
      1976), 37-43.

      Brune traces the differences among the Army, Navy, and
      State Department before the war, especially in East Asia.
      All three departments followed separate roads, according to
      the author, and the gap grew wider between war plans and
      foreign policies.

386. Buckley, Thomas H. and Edward B. Strong, Jr. AMERICAN

FOREIGN AND NATIONAL SECURITY POLICIES, 1914-1945.
Knoxville, TN: University of Tennessee Press, 1987.
210 pp.

The authors maintain that the connection between U.S.
foreign relations and U.S. military strategy, which is
taken for granted in the postwar era, is less appreciated
during the earlier years. Although they believe Roosevelt
engineered an effective propaganda campaign among the U.S.
public, especially in contending with pacifists,
isolationists, and Republicans, the authors question his
devious tactics, which, in part, stemmed from an
overestimation of the strength of isolationism in the
country. According to the authors, the "divorcement of
power and politics" began in the period 1914-1945, the same
years which witnessed the foundation laid for present-day
foreign policy and national security concerns. Despite the
title, much of the book tends toward historical survey.

387. Carlisle, Rodney. "The Foreign Policy Views of an
      Isolationist Press Lord: W. R. Hearst and the
      International Crisis, 1936-1941." J CONTEMP HIST, 9
      (July 1974), 217-227.

The author, the largest single editorial influence during
this period, warned that the real threat lay not in
Europe but across the Pacific in Japan. According to
the author, Hearst believed that the United States
should (a) do nothing to encourage the British or French,
(b) watch Japan and the Soviet Union, (c) establish a
credible military deterrence, and (d) avoid threatening
Germany or becoming involved with the League of Nations.
All of Hearst's opposition to the war vanished with the
attack on Pearl Harbor.

388. Carr, William. POLAND TO PEARL HARBOR. London: Edward
      Arnold, 1985. 183 pp.

Carr presents an interpretive essay which--lively if not
always persuasively--challenges some of the popular
generalizations about the war. His chief themes include
the transformation of the European war into a world war,
the collapse of the international order in the Far East,
the increasing militancy of Japanese policy, and the
American response to all of the above.

389. Chadwin, Mark Lincoln. THE HAWKS OF WORLD WAR II. Chapel
      Hill, NC: University of North Carolina Press, 1968.
      310 pp.

Chadwin traces the activities of the "Century Group" (later the Fight for Freedom Committee). Asian affairs occupied only a small place in these activities until November 1941. The author argues that the pressure of events, not the Century Group, led the United States into the war, but the group did make it somewhat easier for Roosevelt to take increasingly belligerent action.

390. Chamberlain, William H. WORLD'S IRON AGE. New York: Macmillan, 1941. 402 pp.

Chamberlain, a foreign correspondent, critiques the "iron age" mentality, which he applies to Roosevelt and American advocates of interventionism.

391. Cole, Wayne S. AMERICA FIRST: THE BATTLE AGAINST INTERVENTION, 1940-1941. Madison, WI: University of Wisconsin Press, 1953. 305 pp.

Cole analyzes "the leading noninterventionist pressure group" and its partisan bases in the struggle against Roosevelt's foreign policies in 1940-1941. While barely attracted to events in Asia, the group opposed American involvement there too--primarily because of insufficient U.S. interests in the region and a lack of enthusiasm for extricating endangered British imperial chestnuts. America First converted to wholehearted support for the war--against Japan--after the attack at Pearl Harbor.

392. Cole, Wayne S. "America First and the South, 1940-1941." J SOUTH HIST, 22 (February 1956), 36-47.

According to Cole, the South was convinced more than any other section that U.S. security depended on the need for a British victory. Incorporating research through private collections, Cole describes the almost total failure of the America First movement to organize in the South. He cites some of the important reasons as: (1) pride in the military, (2) pro-British sentiment, (3) loyalty to the Democratic Party, (4) economic benefits of defense spending in the region, (5) the economic competition from Japan for foreign markets held by the South, and (6) the psychological-emotional appeal against the forces of evil.

393. Cole, Wayne S. "Franklin D. Roosevelt and the Isolationists, 1932-1945." PROC CONF WAR DIP (The Citadel, 1976), 1-11.

Although Roosevelt played a key role in orchestrating
the attack on isolationism, Cole indicates that changing
circumstances at home and abroad may have defeated the
isolationists even without the efforts of the president.
Maintaining that Roosevelt did not intend the U.S. to enter
the war, Cole notes the "happy coincidence" for the
president that foreign affairs took precedence just as
Roosevelt's domestic program was floundering.

394.   Cole, Wayne S. ROOSEVELT AND THE ISOLATIONISTS, 1932-1945.
       Lincoln, NB: University of Nebraska Press, 1983.
       698 pp.

       Here is a careful assessment of the leading so-called
"isolationists" who exerted a profound influence on U.S.
policies, both foreign and domestic, during the 1930s.
Moreover, as Cole points out, their influence did not
evaporate during the war years. Consequently, Roosevelt
maintained a healthy respect for their views. The study is
extensively researched, especially through private
collections.

395.   Collier, Richard. THE ROAD TO PEARL HARBOR: 1941.
       New York: Atheneum, 1981.   310 pp.

       Despite the title, this book concentrates mainly on
affairs in Europe. Collier draws on unremarkable sources
in his narrative list of many individuals.

396.   Cuff, Samuel H. THE FACE OF WAR, 1931-1942. New York:
       Julian Messner, 1942.   290 pp.

       In this contemporary record, Cuff surveys global events
during the decade which culminated in the outbreak of the
war.

397.   Davis, Forrest and Lindley, Ernest K. HOW WAR CAME.
       New York: Simon and Schuster, 1942.   344 pp.

       With limited sources available, this contemporary
account surveys world events from the fall of France
to the attack at Pearl Harbor. Davis and Lindley
unabashedly praise Roosevelt and the "consistency,
idealism, and strength of United States foreign policy."
With regard to Far Eastern affairs, the authors suggest
that a Roosevelt-Konoye meeting might have been a
historically important meeting. It might have devised
a "Pacific Charter."

398.   Divine, Robert A. "Franklin D. Roosevelt and Collective
        Security, 1933." MVHR, 48 (January 1962), 42-59.

        Divine, a noted historian, places his examination of
        Roosevelt's attitude in 1933 about collective security
        within the context of the historiographical controversy
        over the U.S. entry into World War II. According to the
        author, when Roosevelt became convinced in 1933 that even a
        small step toward a more active international policy was
        unattainable, the president chose not to deviate from that
        isolationist sentiment. In 1933, Roosevelt was not yet a
        firm believer in collective security.

399.   Doenecke, Justus D. "The Anti-Interventionist Tradition:
        Leadership and Perceptions." LIT LIBERTY REV CONTEMP
        THOUGHT, 4 (Summer 1981), 7-67.

            NE

400.   Doenecke, Justus D. "Isolationists of the 1930s and 1940s:
        A Historiographical Essay." W GA COLL STUD SOC SCI, 13
        (June 1974), 5-39.

            NE

401.   Doenecke, Justus D. "The Literature of Isolationism: A
        Bibliographic Guide." J LIBERTARIAN STUD, 7 (Spring
        1983), 157-184.

            NE

402.   Doenecke, Justus D. THE LITERATURE OF ISOLATIONISM: A
        GUIDE TO NON-INTERVENTIONIST SCHOLARSHIP, 1930-1972.
        Colorado Springs, CO: Ralph Myles, 1972.

        Doenecke offers a useful guide through what is often
        inaccurately referred to as "isolationism." His
        considerable research effort reveals the complex,
        many-sided nature of the non-interventionists.

403.   Doenecke, Justus D. "Non-Intervention of the Left: The
        Keep America Out of the War Congress, 1938-1941." J
        CONTEMP HIST, 12 (April 1977), 231-236.

        Incorporating research from the papers of the Socialist
        Party (which sponsored the Congress) and other unpublished
        sources, Doenecke describes the bright potential but
        eventual failure of the movement. His list of problems
        includes liberal defections as the threat of

totalitarianism became clearer by 1940, the lack of labor
and farm support, the attraction of support from only the
intellectuals, the decline of pacifism by 1941, and
weaknesses within the internal organization. Designed
specifically to oppose Roosevelt's overseas commitments,
the movement dissolved with the attack at Pearl Harbor.

404. Donovan, John C. "Congressional Isolationists and the
        Roosevelt Foreign Policy." WORLD POL, 3 (April 1951),
        299-316.

        Donovan feels that isolationists in Congress restricted
the formulation of American foreign policy in the decade
prior to the war. His assessment of Roosevelt is that the
president, despite being less than candid, mirrored the
views of the American people and travelled at their pace.
Donovan criticizes the neutrality laws, especially for
having diverted the attention of Congress from seeking
measures that would have prevented war.

405. Errico, Charles J. "The New Deal, Internationalism, and
        the New American Consensus, 1938-1940." MD HISTORIAN, 9
        (Spring 1978), 17-31.

        Researching through the collections in the Roosevelt
Library, Errico argues that a new American consensus
appeared by 1940--a consensus that embraced both the
domestic New Deal and an internationalist foreign policy.
He describes a troubled administration turning outward from
its domestic troubles.

406. Fehrenbach, T.R. FDR'S UNDECLARED WAR, 1939 TO 1941. New
        York: D. McKay, 1967. 344 pp.

        The author takes a favorable view of Roosevelt's
leadership and goals during this crucial prewar period.

407. Fleming, D. F. WHILE AMERICA SLEPT. New York:
        Abindon-Cokesbury Press, 1944. 269 pp.

        Fleming surveys contemporary American foreign policy by
reviewing events from the fall of France to the Japanese
attack at Pearl Harbor.

408. Garver, John W. "Chiang Kai-shek's Quest for Soviet Entry
        into the Sino-Japanese War." POL SCI Q, 102 (Summer
        1987), 295-316.

        Garver, a political scientist, researched through

Chinese archival sources and the generalissimo's personal
diaries to describe Chiang's hopes to attract Soviet aid,
such as outlined in the 1937 Sino-Soviet agreement, for
China. By 1938, however, it became clear to Chiang that
the Soviets would not enter the war against Japan. He then
began to shift China's policies.

409. Goldberg, Joyce S. "FDR, Elbert D. Thomas, and American
     Neutrality." MID-AMERICA, 68 (January 1986), 35-50.

     Here is a report that Thomas's liberal internationalism
     proved ineffective in helping Roosevelt modify or
     circumvent the neutrality laws. According to the author,
     this failure, including the rejection of the Thomas
     Amendment, reflected the inability or unwillingness of U.S.
     leaders to confront European or Asian aggressors in the
     1930s.

410. Greene, Fred. "The Military View of American National
     Policy." AMER HR, 66 (January 1961), 354-377.

     The author, a political scientist, notes that the Army
     and Navy complained about a lack of guidance from the White
     House and the State Department on U.S. national policy. By
     1939, Greene contends, military advisers adopted a passive
     posture after twenty years of the powerful domestic
     pressures of peace-pacifism and economic woes.
     Isolationism, he writes, died hard. His research includes
     pertinent military planning documents.

411. Goodman, Grant K. "'Anti-Communism' in Japanese-Philippine
     Relations During the 1930s." J SEA STUD, 9 (September
     1978), 219-233.

     Using research Washington, Manila, and Tokyo (especially
     in the Quezon papers and the archives of the Japanese
     Foreign Ministry), Goodman describes the appeal in the
     Philippines of Japan's anti-Communist (and largely
     economic) program. Quezon walked carefully between Japan
     and the United States.

412. Griswold, A. Whitney. "European Factors in Far Eastern
     Diplomacy." FOR AFFS, 19 (January 1941), 297-309.

     The noted historian writes that all of Europe and the
     United States treat the Far East as a sphere of interest
     and a diplomatic chip for bargaining about other, more
     important areas. On the eve of the war, Griswold feels
     that Europe had become America's front door -- not back

door -- to the Far East. Balance in the Far East,
according to the author, can only be achieved in Europe and
not by Americans acting alone.

413. Guinsburg, Thomas N. THE PURSUIT OF ISOLATIONISM IN THE
        UNITED STATES SENATE FROM VERSAILLES TO PEARL HARBOR.
        New York: Garland, 1982. 325 pp.

        For purposes of this guide, the immediate prewar era is
        of special interest. Using extensive research through
        private collections, Guinsburg analyzes the rise and
        virtual demise of isolationism/non-interventionism. He
        particularly focuses on the roles of individual senators as
        he traces regional, political, and intellectual influences
        on their views of foreign policy.

414. Gunther, John. "Our Pacific Frontiers." FOR AFFS, 18
        (July 1940), 583-600.

        Gunther outlines American interests in the Far East. He
        focuses on the need for an American two-ocean navy --
        especially if Britain and France are defeated in Europe --
        able to conduct independent operations in the Pacific and
        the Atlantic.

415. Hachey, Thomas E. "Anglophile Sentiments in American
        Catholicism in 1940: A British Official's Confident
        Assessment." RECORDS AMER CATHOLIC HIST SOC PHILAD, 85
        (March-June 1974) 48-58.

        Here is the text of a report on a meeting in 1940 of
        prominent American Catholics. The author of the report,
        Robert Wilberforce (British Library of Information in New
        York), remarks on the widespread support for the British
        cause among the participants.

416. Haines, C. Grove and Ross J.S. Hoffman. THE ORIGINS AND
        BACKGROUND OF THE SECOND WORLD WAR. New York: Oxford
        University Press, 1947. 2d ed. 729 pp.

        The two professors present a lengthy report on the
        origins of the world war. Beginning with "The Century
        Before 1914" and arriving some fifteen chapters later with
        the entry of the United States into the war, the book is a
        lengthy summary-narrative more than a detailed analysis.
        Much of the emphasis is on Europe. The book first appeared
        in 1943.

417. Harrison, Richard A. "Testing the War: A Secret Probe

Towards Anglo-American Military Cooperation in 1936."
INT HIST REV, 7 (May 1985), 214-234.

In 1936, Roosevelt came to believe that the British were
interested in military cooperation with the United States.
Liaison efforts with Canada, for example, seemed to be one
concrete sign of this warming trend. Although historians
have paid much attention to the work of Secretary of War
Harry Woodring in promoting closer Anglo-American ties, the
author feels that Roosevelt furnished the motivating force
in 1936.

418.   Hoehling. A.A.   AMERICA'S ROAD TO WAR, 1939-1941.   London:
       Abelard-Schuman, 1970.   178 pp.

       Here is a balanced assessment of the coming of the war
       for the United States. In general, the author seems
       sympathetic to Roosevelt's leadership.

419.   Jacob, Philip E.   "Influences of World Events on U.S.
       'Neutrality' Opinion."   PUB OPIN Q, 4 (March 1940),
       48-65.

       The survey identifies different kinds of neutrality
       (e.g., personal, commercial, military, and financial).
       Jacob also discovered a range of sentiment among the
       American people from confidence in U.S. security to support
       for the cause of democracies.

420.   Jonas, Manfred.   ISOLATIONISM IN AMERICA, 1935-1941.
       Ithaca, NY: Cornell University Press, 1966.   315 pp.

       Although concerned primarily with European affairs, this
       excellent study sheds light on the scope and depth of
       isolationism in prewar America. The research is solid
       (although now somewhat dated); the analysis is insightful.

421.   Jones, Alfred Haworth.   "The Making of an Interventionist
       on the Air: Elmer Davis and CBS News, 1939-1941."   PAC
       HR, 42 (February 1973), 74-93.

       Jones traces the evolution of Davis from noninterven-
       tionist to advocate of belligerency in all but name. The
       shift for Davis came about, according to Jones, principally
       because of the altered U.S. strategic position. The article
       is informed with the author's research through the Milo
       Ryan phonoarchive (KIRO-CBS collection).

422.   Kimball, Jeffrey.   "The Influence of Ideology on

Interpretive Disagreement: A Report on a Survey of
Diplomatic, Military and Peace Historians on the Causes
of 20th Century U.S. Wars." HIST TEACHER, 17 (May
1984), 355-384.

Kimball concludes that most historians think in
patterned ways which can be labeled ideological. His
survey enables him to accept ideology as a valid concept in
historical interpretation. (See his specific work on the
war against Japan.)

423.   Koenig, Louis W. THE PRESIDENCY AND THE CRISIS: POWERS OF
       THE OFFICE FROM THE INVASION OF POLAND TO PEARL HARBOR.
       New York: Columbia University Press, 1944. 166 pp.

       Koenig analyzes the constitutional conflict between the
       executive and legislative branches. His main point of
       reference is the White House and Roosevelt's perspective.

424.   Langenberg, Willliam H. "What Price Vigilence? The
       KORMORAN-SYDNEY Battle." NAV WAR COLL REV, 33
       (January-February 1980), 78-84.

       The author recounts this German-Australian battle in
       November 1941 near Australia in which both ships sank. The
       main lesson, according to the author, is the lax attitude
       of the SYDNEY.

425.   Langer, William L. and S. Everett Gleason. THE CHALLENGE
       TO ISOLATION. New York: Harper and Row, 1952. 2 vols.

       With permission to work through closed official files,
       the authors analyze the period 1937-1941. Their research
       generally supports both U. S. prewar policies and the
       actions of President Roosevelt. In the Pacific, the
       policies of Japanese expansionists, according to the
       authors, led to war with the United States. Although
       somewhat superseded by subsequent revelations, this study
       remains an important part of the historiography on the
       origins of the war.

426.   Leutze, James. BARGAINING FOR SUPREMACY: ANGLO-AMERICAN
       NAVAL COLLABORATION, 1937-1941. Chapel Hill, NC:
       University of North Carolina Press, 1977. 328 pp.

       The focus is on the development of U.S. naval strategy
       and its effect on the United States and Britain. Leutze
       maintains that American insistence on developing a
       two-ocean navy and British underestimation of Japan almost

predetermined U.S. advantages in the postwar era. The book
is well researched and well written.

427. MacLeish, Archibald. THE IRRESPONSIBLES. New York: Duell,
      Sloan and Pearce, 1940. 34 pp.

      The noted author addresses the contemporary
      reorientation taking place in the attitudes of U.S.
      intellectuals about foreign affairs.

428. Martin, James J. AMERICAN LIBERALISM AND WORLD POLITICS,
      1931-1941. New York: Devin-Adair, 1965. 2 vols.

      Martin presents an exhaustive examination of liberal
      leaders and press during the period from the Manchurian
      crisis to the attack at Pearl Harbor. His findings,
      however, are not as remarkable as his research. For
      example, the basic conclusion that liberal opinion about
      war switched during the 1930s confirms rather than alters
      traditional historical interpretations. Martin examined
      the writings and speeches of some 250 people (or journals
      and newspapers).

429. NEW YORK TIMES. DAYS OF DECISION. New York: Doubleday,
      Doran, 1941.

      Here are the collected editorials of the newspaper for
      the period September 8-December 12, 1941. Charles Merz
      wrote the Introduction.

430. O'Connor, Raymond G. "The American Navy, 1939-1941: The
      Enlisted Perspective." MIL AFFS, 50 (October 1986),
      173-178.

      Here is the personal account by the noted diplomatic
      historian of his experiences as a sailor. His report
      contrasts the life of officers and enlisted in the Navy.
      He served as a signalman attached to Submarine Squadron
      Four at Pearl Harbor.

431. Offner, Arnold A., ed. AMERICA AND THE ORIGINS OF WORLD
      WAR II. Boston: Houghton Mifflin, 1971. 229 pp.

      Offner assembles an excellent collection of articles,
      covering a range of viewpoints on the origins of the war.
      There is a helpful bibliography. Of interest to this
      guide, see the articles by Borg, Butow, Schroeder, Morton,
      and Esthus.

432. Offner, Arnold A. THE ORIGINS OF THE SECOND WORLD WAR:
      AMERICAN FOREIGN POLICY AND WORLD POLITICS, 1914-1941.
      New York: Holt, Rinehart and Winston, 1975. 268 pp.

      Offner describes President Roosevelt as cautious but
      active in the years prior to the war.

433. Papachristou, Judith. "An Exercise in Anti-Imperialism:
      The Thirties." AMER STUD, 15 (Spring 1974), 61-77.

      The author identifies a strain in American thought that
      she calls both important and overlooked. This movement,
      which she describes as unorganized anti-imperialists,
      criticized Roosevelt for protecting U.S. business interests
      abroad.

434. Pettenkofer, Anton. "Hitler Means to DESTROY Japan." ASIA
      & AMERICAS, 41 (November 1941), 653-660.

      Citing the Japanese illusion that Hitler will' share
      world power with them, the author argues that Hitler
      instead will exterminate them. This is already in the
      record, the author says, in Nazi writings about colored
      peoples.

435. Porter, David L. THE SEVENTY-SIXTH CONGRESS AND WORLD WAR
      II, 1939-1940. Columbia, MO: University of Missouri
      Press, 1979. 235 pp.

      Porter chronicles the shift to internationalism during
      this crucial period. In his use of case studies and analyses
      of roll call votes, Porter identifies two elements to
      congressional debates: isolationists-vs.-internationalists
      and internationalists-vs.-interventionists. There is an
      excellent bibliography on prewar isolationism in the United
      States.

436. Savage, Katharine. PEOPLE AND POWER: THE STORY OF THREE
      NATIONS. New York: H.Z. Walck, 1960. 250 pp.

      This popular account ranks only slightly above her book
      for a juvenile audience: THE STORY OF THE SECOND WORLD WAR
      (1958). In addressing the origins of the war, Savage
      offers a critical assessment of the policies of Germany,
      Japan, and the Soviet Union.

437. Small, Melvin. WAS WAR NECESSARY?: NATIONAL SECURITY AND
      THE UNITED STATES ENTRY INTO WAR. Beverly Hills, CA:
      Sage Publications, 1980. 311 pp.

Surveying America's wars from 1812 through Korea, Small
finds few that can be justified. In his opinion, the
Second World War was not one of them.

438. Sniegoski, Stephen J. "Unified Democracy: An Aspect of
      American World War II Interventionist Thought,
      1939-1941." MD HISTORIAN, 9 (Spring 1978), 33-48.

In a well-researched study, the author shows that the
concept of interventionism attracted a broad consensus
cutting across the political spectrum.

439. Steele, Richard W. "The Pulse of the People: Franklin D.
      Roosevelt and the Gauging of American Public Opinion."
      J CONTEMP HIST, 9 (October 1974), 195-216.

Drawing extensively from material in the F.D.R. Library,
Steele explores Roosevelt's concern in determining the
impact of public attitudes on national policy and politics.
The President viewed these attitudes as potential obstacles
for policies he had already determined, according to
Steele.

440. Stenehjem, Michele Flynn. AN AMERICAN FIRST: JOHN T.
      FLYNN AND THE AMERICA FIRST COMMITTEE. New Rochelle,
      NY: Arlington House, 1976. 250 pp.

The author researched extensively through published and
private sources to examine Flynn and the New York chapter
of the America First Committee. Here was an urban,
sophisticated group, not the knee-jerk isolationism of some
Midwestern conservatives. Flynn, a journalist and economic
analyst, led the charge against the so-called
interventionists and the tilting of constitutional balance.
The author describes Flynn's disillusion once war came and
his eventual support of the U.S. war effort. According to
the author, Flynn nevertheless remained convinced that his
prewar position had been correct.

441. Thompson, Dean K. "World War II, Interventionism, and
      Henry Pitney Van Dusen." J PRESBYTERIAN HIST, 55
      (Winter 1977), 327-345.

The author, a Presbyterian minister, extolls the
activities of Van Dusen, who vehemently criticized the
pacifist-isolationist strain in prewar America.

442. Thorne, Christopher. THE LIMITS OF FOREIGN POLICY: THE

WEST, THE LEAGUE, AND THE FAR EASTERN CRISIS OF
1931-1933. New York: G.P. Putnam's Sons, 1972.
442 pp.

This well-written, well-researched book is of interest
to this guide because of Thorne's questioning of the notion
that the Manchurian crisis marked the origins of World
War II.

443. Tuleja, Thaddeus V. STATESMEN AND ADMIRALS: QUEST FOR A
FAR EASTERN NAVAL POLICY. New York: W.W. Norton, 1963.
256 pp.

In this knowledgeable survey, Tuleja tells of the
uncertain quest to define (and defend) the U.S. position in
Asia. See especially his analysis of the Philippines,
where the United States kept a presence but failed to
provide adequate resources for the defense of the islands.

444. Tuttle, William M., Jr. "Aid to the Allies Short-of-War
versus American Intervention, 1940: A Reappraisal of
William Allen White's Leadership." J AMER HIST, 56
(October 1970), 840-858.

With extensive use of private collections, Tuttle
describes White as an invaluable asset in the U.S. movement
to aid the Allies. Divisions within the movement, however,
contributed to White's resignation in disillusion and
confusion from the chairmanship of the Committee to Defend
America By Aiding the Allies.

445. Walter, John C. "Congressman Carl Vinson and Franklin D.
Roosevelt: Naval Preparedness and the Coming of World
War II, 1932-40." GA HIST Q, 64 (Fall 1980), 294-305.

The author sympathizes with Vinson's position in arguing
with Roosevelt for a rapid naval buildup. The article is
well researched, but its narrow focus skips over the
presidential perspective.

446. Warburg, James P. OUR WAR AND OUR PEACE. New York:
Farrar, 1941. 227 pp.

The noted U.S. economist points out what he feels are
the illusions of American isolationists who hope to stay
out of the war.

447. Wiener, Frederick B. "Opening an American Base in a
British Colony Before Pearl Harbor." HISTORY, NUMBERS

AND WAR, I, Pt. I (Spring 1977), 53-67; Pt. II (Summer 1977), 126-139.

NE

448. Wright, Quincy. "Repeal of the Neutrality Act." AMER J INT LAW, 36 (January 1942), 8-23.

In this legal examination of the neutrality legislation, Wright notes the shrinking scope of neutrality in the modern world. Aggressors, he believes, need not be treated equally.

449. Wyckoff, Don. "The Way It Was--World War II Begins." MC GAZ, 65 (December 1981), 34-37.

Here is an account by a rifle squad leader of training in North Carolina which served as preparation for the war.

II.A.2. PRELUDE TO THE WAR AGAINST JAPAN

450. Abend, Hallett. RAMPARTS OF THE PACIFIC. Garden City, NY: DOUBLEDAY, DORAN, 1942. 322 pp.

The author has long experience reporting on Asia. After extensive travels during 1941, Abend discusses economic, military (defensive), and strategic affairs. This excellent, perceptive presentation is a convenient overview of conditions in Asia just before the attack at Pearl Harbor. Of special note is Admiral Helfrich's opinion that the benefits Japan derived from being entrenched in Indochina far overshadowed the hurried preparations made by the Americans in the Philippines, the British in Malaya-Singapore, and the Dutch in NEI.

451. Adams, Frederick C. "The Road to Pearl Harbor: A Reexamination of American Far Eastern Policy, July 1937-December 1938." J AMER HIST, 58 (June 1971), 73-92.

Arguing that U.S. policy began to crystallize by December 1938, Adams identifies a series of steps the Roosevelt administration took to safeguard U.S. interests. Moreover, Washington knew, according to Adams, that these steps, such as strengthening China through the Export-Import Bank and launching the tung oil project, could lead to war with Japan. The author emphasizes the role of the open door policy in the growing rift between the United States and Japan.

452. Albertini, Rudolf Von and Albert Wirz. EUROPEAN COLONIAL
      RULE, 1880-1940: THE IMPACT OF THE WEST ON INDIA,
      SOUTHEAST ASIA, AND AFRICA. Cambridge, Eng.: Cambridge
      University Press, 1982.

      Here is an excellent survey that sets forth the
      political situation in Asia on the eve of the war.
      Although not generally clear to contemporaries, the
      elements for the explosive nationalist movements after the
      war are clearly identified by the authors.

453. Anderson, Irvine H., Jr. "The 1941 De Facto Embargo on Oil
      to Japan: A Bureaucratic Reflex." PAC HR, 44 (May
      1975), 201-231.

      Anderson examines the manner in which the U.S.
      government reached the decision to terminate Japan's oil
      supplies. Using the records of Export Control and the
      Treasury, the author reports that Roosevelt and Hull
      finally ratified an unplanned, de facto embargo initiated
      by the bureaucracy at the State Department and Treasury.
      Anderson speculates on why the embargo took official hold.

454. Anderson, Irvine H. THE STANDARD-VACUUM OIL COMPANY AND
      U.S. ASIAN POLICY, 1933-1941. Princeton: Princeton
      University Press, 1975. 260 pp.

      Using exhaustive research, Anderson reveals the close
      association between the Standard-Vacuum Oil Company and the
      State Department. When the Japanese sought to obtain their
      own sources of oil, the company turned to Washington for
      protection. The author is among the first to present a
      documented argument that mid-level bureaucrats exceeded
      Roosevelt's intentions by imposing the 1941 embargo against
      Japan.

455. Baker, Leonard. ROOSEVELT AND PEARL HARBOR. New York:
      Macmillan, 1970. 356 pp.

      Here is a spirited defense of Roosevelt's policies from
      the presidential election of 1940 to the attack at Pearl
      Harbor. Arranging his case in chronological order,
      generally in the form of monthly summaries, Baker adds
      hardly anything new in his indictment of Japanese
      aggression.

456. Omitted.

457. Ballantine, Joseph W. "Mukden to Pearl Harbor: The
      Foreign Policies of Japan." FOR AFFS, 27 (July 1949),

651-664.

This State Department official rejects the thesis that
the United States forced Japan in 1941 either to accept an
inferior position or to resort to war. Arguing that
Japanese militarists imposed their will on an irresolute
nation, Ballantine believes that after the Manchurian
incident only force would have made the Japanese leaders
abandon their policies.

458. Barclay, Glen St. John. THEIR FINEST HOUR. London:
      Barker, 1977. 192 pp.

In this examination of British strategic views, Barclay
points out the considerable extent to which the Churchill
government relied on the United States "to keep the
Japanese dog quiet." In a shift not lost upon the
antipodean dominions, the United States, from 1940 to 1941
(and later), became primarily responsible for the defense
of the British Empire in Asia.

459. Barnes, Harry Elmer. THE COURT HISTORIANS VERSUS
      REVISIONISM. n.p.: n.p., n.d.

NE. See also the following pamphlets by Barnes: RAUCH
ON ROOSEVELT; THE STRUGGLE AGAINST THE HISTORICAL BLACKOUT;
and WAS ROOSEVELT PUSHED INTO WAR BY POPULAR DEMAND IN
1941? [All NE]

460. Barnes, Harry Elmer. PEARL HARBOR AFTER A QUARTER OF A
      CENTURY. New York: Arno Press, 1972. 132 pp.

This reprint of a 1968 article charges that
Roosevelt, through secret diplomacy, committed the
United States to war even before the attack on Pearl
Harbor. Barnes attributes most of the drastic changes in
American foreign and domestic policies in the postwar era
to the involvement of the United States in World War II.
His general approach--if you don't believe that, how about
this?--precludes any balanced assessment.

461. Barnes, Harry Elmer, ed. PERPETUAL WAR FOR PERPETUAL
      PEACE. Westport, CT: Greenwood Press, 1969. 679 pp.

This reprint of the 1953 edition contains eleven
revisionist essays (three by Barnes). Each criticizes
some aspect of American policies or behavior. One of the
best is William L. Neumann's article, "How American Policy
Toward Japan Contributed to War in the Pacific."

462. Barnes, Harry Elmer. REVISIONISM: A KEY TO PEACE AND
      OTHER ESSAYS. San Francisco: Cato Institute, 1980.
      181 pp.

      This book consists of three caustic articles on the
      topics of revisionism, the historical coverup of the
      United States entry into World War II, and "1984" trends
      in America.

463. Barnes, Harry Elmer. SELECTED REVISIONIST PAMPHLETS.
      New York: Arno Press, 1972. 317 pp.

      In eight articles (separately paged), Barnes rails
      against the "historical blackout," or efforts to suppress
      the "truth" about the reasons for the Second World War and
      about the United States entry into the war. He rejects the
      "Globaloney" of the internationalists and critiques in
      detail the work of more "orthodox" historians, such as
      Rauch, Feis, and Langer-Gleason.

464. Barnhart, Michael A. JAPAN PREPARES FOR TOTAL WAR: THE
      SEARCH FOR ECONOMIC SECURITY, 1919-1941. Ithaca, NY:
      Cornell University Press, 1987. 290 pp.

      In focusing on the Japanese perspective, Barnhart
      criticizes the narrow, self-serving purposes which
      motivated Japanese policies (especially the Greater East
      Asia Co-Prosperity Sphere). The author incorporates
      extensive research, including the work of revisionist
      historians, in reaching the conclusion that American
      leaders could do little during these years in deflecting
      Japan from the path that led to war. The book is
      especially effective in analyzing the various viewpoints of
      the competing domestic factions inside Japan.

465. Barnhart, Michael A. "Japan's Economic Security and the
      Origins of the Pacific War." J STRAT STUD, 4 (June
      1981), 105-124.

      The author suggests that Japan's course after the First
      World War can be characterized as a "quest for autarky."
      This description, according to Barnhart, fits the larger
      historical picture since the Meiji Restoration of both
      Japanese expansionism abroad and calls for political and
      economic reform at home. Thus, he opposes the view that
      irrational leaders or uncontrollable young hotheads steered
      Japan into war in 1941.

466. Bartlett, Bruce R. COVER-UP: THE POLITICS OF PEARL HARBOR,
      1941-1946. New Rochelle, NY: Arlington House, 1978.
      189 pp.

      Here is a skeptical view of both the various official
      investigations and their conclusions. Bartlett believes
      that the assessments of blame should have reached the
      highest levels in Washington.

467. Bartlett, Bruce B. "The Pearl Harbor Coverup." REASON
      (February 1976), 24-27.

           NE

468. Beard, Charles A. PRESIDENT ROOSEVELT AND THE COMING OF
      THE WAR, 1941: A STUDY IN APPEARANCES AND REALITIES.
      New Haven, CT: Yale University Press, 1948. 614 pp.

      Here is a devastating attack against Roosevelt and his
      internationalist (interventionist) views. Beard, a
      distinguished historian, argues vociferously that the
      United States need not have become entangled in European
      political squabbles--except for the maneuvering of the
      president. The author died shortly after writing this
      book, which should be viewed as the companion volume to
      his other anti-Roosevelt tract, AMERICAN FOREIGN POLICY,
      1932-1940 (1946, 336 pp.).

469. Bemis, Samuel Flagg. "The First Gun of a Revisionist
      Historiography for the Second World War." J MOD HIST,
      19 (March 1948), 55-59.

      Bemis assembles his formidable arsenal against the
      anti-Roosevelt revisionism of George Morgenstern.

470. Ben-Zvi, Abraham. "American Preconceptions and Policies
      Toward Japan, 1940-1941: A Case Study in
      Misperception." INT STUD Q, 19 (June 1975), 228-248.

      The author, a professor of international relations in
      Israel, categorizes American policy makers in this case
      study according to their patterns of perception and
      interpretation. He finds errors in the "rigid unexamined
      adherence" of U. S. leaders to principles not necessarily
      relevant to the Far Eastern situation   in 1940-1941. His
      categories (global-realists, global-idealists, and
      national-pragmatists) contribute to a better
      understanding of this complex subject. The political
      science jargon is not obtrusive--in this particular case.

471.   Ben-Zvi, Abraham. PRELUDE TO PEARL HARBOR: A STUDY OF
       AMERICAN IMAGES TOWARD JAPAN, 1940-1941. New York:
       Vantage Press, 1979. 168 pp.

       Seeking to move beyond the "crude dichotomies" that
       exist about Pearl Harbor, the author points out that the
       president was not the chief architect of Far Eastern
       policy prior to the war. Rather, according to Ben-Zvi,
       close advisers persuaded Roosevelt to abandon efforts to
       reach accommodation with the Japanese in favor of an
       uncompromising intransigence. Ben-Zvi's methodology
       applies the theoretical contributions (and jargon) of
       political-science hypotheses about the pre-existing
       perceptions of these advisers, whom he categorizes as
       "global idealists" (Hull), "global realists" (Stimson,
       Morgenthau, and Hornbeck), and "national pragmatists"
       (Grew and Roosevelt himself). The author concludes that
       those in the first two groups misperceived military-
       political realities and recommended policies that
       contributed to the war with Japan.

472.   Ben-Zvi, Abraham. THE ILLUSION OF DETERRENCE: THE
       ROOSEVELT PRESIDENCY AND THE ORIGINS OF THE PACIFIC WAR.
       Boulder, CO: Westview Press, 1987. 136 pp.

       The author examines the views of key U.S. policy makers
       and government officials in 1940-1941. Their differing
       images of the world, Ben-Zvi argues, led to incompatible
       policy recommendations. His analysis differentiates among
       the world views formulated by global-realists,
       global-idealists, and nationalist-pragmatists.

473.   Blumenson, Martin. "The Soviet Power Play at Changkufeng."
       WORLD POL, 12 (January 1960), 249-263.

       The author points out that the general notion of a
       Soviet victory at Changkufeng stemmed from the fact that
       only Soviet sources were available. Blumenson maintains
       that newly opened Japanese sources plausibly make a
       different case. That is, Japan won the military battle but
       lost on the political front. He believes that the Soviets
       almost certainly would have backed down if the Japanese had
       enlarged the action. For political reasons, however, both
       sides chose to limit the engagement.

474.   Boothe, Leon K. "Will the Real President Roosevelt Please
       Step Forward: Roosevelt and the Japanese Invasion of
       China, 1937." PROC CONF WAR DIP (1976), 29-36.

Boothe examines the historiographical theories of
Roosevelt's motives in delivering the Quarantine Speech.
The article criticizes Roosevelt for having only vague
ideas and no orderly plans.

475. Borg, Dorothy and Shumpei Okamoto. PEARL HARBOR AS
      HISTORY: JAPANESE-AMERICAN RELATIONS, 1931-1941. New
      York: Columbia University Press, 1973. 801 pp.

Here is a masterpiece--a brilliant collection of essays
by some of the foremost scholars of the war. The articles
emerge from the Lake Kawaguchi Conference, July 14-18,
1969, which attracted outstanding historians from both the
United States and Japan. Virtually every article
constitutes mandatory reading for any serious consideration
of the general subject.

476. Boyd, Carl. "The Berlin-Tokyo Axis and Japanese Military
      Initiative." MOD ASIAN STUD, 15 (April 1981), 311-338.

In this well-researched, well-written piece, Boyd
focuses on the key role of Oshima Hiroshi in
German-Japanese relations from 1934-1941.

477. Boyd, Carl. "The Role of Hiroshi Oshima in the Preparation
      of the Anti-Comintern Pact." J ASIAN HIST, II (No. 1,
      1977), 49-71.

Using German and Japanese language sources, interviews,
and many primary sources, Boyd examines Oshima's role in
promoting close German-Japanese relations.
According to Boyd, Oshima, indifferent to the Japanese
Foreign Ministry and friendly with Ribbentrop, lacked
authority to initiate and conduct political negotiations.

478. Boyle, John H. "The Drought-Walsh Mission to Japan." PAC
      HR, 34 (May 1965), 141-161.

Tracing the activities of the two priests, Boyle
emphasizes that the key to the whole episode was the
Japanese error in considering the mission to be official
rather than strictly personal. The author includes
research through Japanese-language sources.

479. Bratzell, John F. and Leslie Rout, Jr. "Once More: Pearl
      Harbor, Microdots, and J. Edgar Hoover." AMER HR, 88
      (October 1983), 953-960.

Here is a short collection of correspondence concerning
the prewar dissemination of intelligence gained from a
secret microdot. For example, an FBI official refutes
charges that the agency mishandled important information.
The authors, however, reaffirm these charges. In addition,
letters from the journal's editor and author John Toland
discuss the difficulties of obtaining research material
from the FBI.

480. Bratzell, John F. and Leslie B. Rout, Jr. "Pearl Harbor,
     Microdots, and J. Edgar Hoover." AMER HR, 87 (December
     1982), 1342-1351.

Here is a critical study of the FBI leader. Despite the
disclosure by TRICYCLE that he was carrying a secret
microdot (which contained specific requests from German
intelligence about Hawaii), Hoover chose to emphasize to
the president the FBI's vigilance in apprehending TRICYCLE
and in uncovering the microdot technique. In fact, the
authors claim, little information—and nothing about the
material on Hawaii—ever reached the president or army-navy
intelligence.

481. Breslin, Thomas A. "Mystifying the Past: Establishment
     Historians and the Origins of the Pacific War." BULL
     CON ASIAN SCHOL, 8 (Oct-Dec 1976), 18-36.

After appraising some of the historiography on the
origins of the war with Japan, Breslin comes down on the
side of the revisionists. He calls for new studies of U.S.
capitalist interests in the Pacific and South Asia.

482. Breslin, Thomas A. "Trouble Over Oil: America, Japan and
     the Oil Cartel 1934-1935." BULL CON ASIAN SCHOL, 7
     (July-September 1975), 41-50.

Breslin argues that American, British, and Dutch oil
interests, with encouragement from U.S. government
officials, secretly tried to prevent oil shipments to
Manchukuo and Japan. He remarks on the militancy of these
private oil interests in pursuit of their own benefits.
The article is based mainly on State Department files.

483. Bridges, Brian. "Britain and Japanese Espionage in Pre-War
     Malaya: The Shinozaki Case." J CONTEMP HIST, 21
     (January 1986), 23-35.

Incorporating extensive research from British records,
Japanese sources, some autobiographical material from

Shinozaki, and declassified reports of the Singapore
police, Bridges examines the arrest, trial, and
imprisonment of the Japanese press attache in Singapore in
late 1940. Arrested under the Official Secrets Ordinance,
Shinozaki does not appear to have been involved in
significant espionage activities, but he does seem to have
crossed over to the other side of the line. Bridges puts
the episode into the larger context of deteriorating
British-Japanese relations before the war. Victorious
Japanese troops released Shinozaki from the Singapore jail
in February 1942, and he worked in the new Japanese
administration there (Education and Welfare Departments).

484. Brownlow, Donald G. THE ACCUSED. New York: Vantage
        Press, 1968. 190 pp.

        Incorporating interviews and some new material, Brownlow
offers a vigorous defense of Rear Adm. Husband E. Kimmel.
The spotlight of responsibility is shifted from Hawaii to
Washington, D. C.

485. Brune, Lester H. "Considerations of Force in Cordell
        Hull's Diplomacy, July 26 to November 26, 1941."
        DIP HIST, 2 (Fall 1978), 389-405.

        In this well-written analysis, Brune asserts that Hull
should have prolonged his negotiations for the purpose
of gaining time for the military. Failing to seek advice
from the military (which badly needed more preparations),
Hull clung to his long-held view that diplomacy and
military action were mutually exclusive.

486. Burns, Richard Dean. "Inspection of the Mandates,
        1919-1941." PAC HR, 37 (November 1968), 445-462.

        Burns feels that Japan's compliance on pledges not to
fortify the islands remains a contentious point. Japan's
unilateral withdrawal from the League of Nations, he
writes, did not loosen the pledges. Of interest is his
report that on-site inspection would probably not have
settled the question.

487. Burns, Richard Dean and Edward M. Bennett, eds. DIPLOMATS
        IN CRISIS: US-CHINESE-JAPANESE RELATIONS, 1919-1941.
        Santa Barbara, CA: ABC-CLIO, 1974. 345 pp.

        The volume incorporates thirteen essays on diplomats of
the period, including Grew, Johnson, Hornbeck, Yosuke,

Nomura, Koo, and Shigematsu. Most of the essays integrate
private papers and archival materials. Norman A. Graebner
provides an excellent introductory essay.

488. Burtness, Paul S. and Warren V. Ober, eds. THE PUZZLE OF
      PEARL HARBOR. Evanston, IL: Row, Peterson and Company,
      1962. 244 pp.

      The book contains 76 documents on the controversy of the
      attack at Pearl Harbor. There is neither a general
      introduction nor an introduction to each selection.

489. Burtness, Paul S. and Warren U. Ober. "Research
      Methodology: Problem of Pearl Harbor Intelligence
      Reports." MIL AFFS, 25 (Fall 1961), 132-146.

      The authors point out inaccuracies and conflicting
      information in the report of a Japanese agent in
      Hawaii (Yokishikawa) about his previous activities.

490. Burtness, Paul S. and Warren U. Ober. "Secretary Stimson
      and the First Pearl Harbor Investigation." AUS J POL
      HIST, 14 (April 1968), 24-36.

      The authors examine the work of the Roberts Commission
      and find that the congressional group exaggerated and
      distorted the responsibility of local commanders for the
      disaster at Pearl Harbor. According to the authors,
      Stimson, who had immediately replaced Short and Martin (the
      air commander in Hawaii), acted to reduce the culpability
      of officials in Washington and the Army's high command.
      The article concludes by arguing that the Roberts
      Commission reestablished the nation's confidence in the
      government and the armed forces. Of note is the authors'
      assertion that the Roberts report inferred the existence of
      MAGIC.

491. Burtness, Paul S. and Warren U. Ober. "Comment: 'The
      Strange Assignment of USS Lanikai.'" USNIP, 89
      (October 1963), 125-129.

      The authors call attention to the IABEL, the only one of
      the "three little ships" which actually put out to sea
      on this controversial mission. Additional remarks by
      Tolley reaffirm his belief that Washington intended to
      sacrifice the ships.

492. Butow, Robert J.C. "Backdoor Diplomacy in the Pacific: The
      Proposal for a Konoye-Roosevelt Meeting, 1941." J AMER

HIST, 59 (June 1972), 48-72.

Using new sources, such as the James M. Drought Papers, Butow analyzes the role of the John Doe Association in proposing a meeting between the two political leaders. Although the "marathon diplomatic minuet" (which lasted six weeks) failed, Butow expresses doubt that such a meeting would have been harmful. In fact, he suggests that the high-level meeting might have taken place had the John Doe Association not disrupted regular diplomatic channels. With timing becoming an all-important factor in late 1941, the author feels that a temporary modus vivendi might have been reached, which in turn might have been an important step in U.S.-Japanese relations.

493.   Butow, Robert J.C. "The Hull-Nomura Conversations: A
         Fundamental Misconception." AMER HR, 65 (July 1965),
         822-836.

Writing about the Walsh-Drought affair, Butow points out that the Japanese officials in Washington misinterpreted unofficial second-hand reports as coming directly from Roosevelt. During 1941, the author writes, the Hull-Nomura conversations dragged on without the true intentions of either government ever coming to light. The article is marked by painstaking research, especially through Japanese sources.

494.   Butow, Robert J.C. THE JOHN DOE ASSOCIATES: BACKDOOR
         DIPLOMACY FOR PEACE, 1941. Stanford, CA: Stanford
         University Press, 1974. 480 pp.

Butow exerts his typically first-rate scholarship to analyze the secret and unfortunate activities of the John Doe Associates (an American priest, a Japanese banker, and a Japanese army colonel) to avert war in 1941. Butow concludes that the group damaged (unintentionally) the cause of peace. The "Note on Sources" outlines Butow's investigation of this episode.

495.   Butow, Robert J.C. TOJO AND THE COMING OF THE WAR.
         Princeton: Princeton University Press, 1961. 584 pp.

This excellent book offers an insightful account of the Japanese perspective in 1941. Butow masterfully underscores the influence of officials in Japan just below the highest levels. Tojo emerges in these pages as a competent administrator (not a radical expansionist) who had persuaded himself that the main reason for Japan's presence in China was self-defense.

496. Byas, Hugh. GOVERNMENT BY ASSASSINATION. New York: A. A.
      Knopf, 1942. 369 pp.

      Byas, a prewar correspondent in Tokyo, exposes the
      sensational plots and extremism in Japanese politics during
      the 1930s.

497. Bywater, Hector C. THE GREAT PACIFIC WAR. Boston:
      Houghton Mifflin, 1942. 321 pp.

      Writing in 1925 about a future war (circa 1931-1933) in
      the Pacific, the author forecasts a surprise Japanese
      attack, a series of early Japanese successes, and the
      determination of the United States to see the war through
      to victory. Bywater, a British correspondent who had
      died by the time this book was published, predicted that at
      the end of the war China would be independent, Sakhalin
      would be in Soviet hands, and Japan would be in ruin.

498. Carlson, Evans F. TWIN STARS OF CHINA. New York: Dodd,
      Mead, 1940. 331 pp.

      Carlson, an American Marine officer, lived in China
      (1937-1938) and filed secret reports to Roosevelt through
      Missy LeHand. His favorable view of the Chinese Communists
      reflected his belief that they were not "true" communists.
      Also, he applauded their attempts to form a united front
      with Chiang Kai-shek in order to resist the Japanese
      aggressors.

499. Castle, Alfred L. "William R. Castle and Opposition to
      U.S. Involvement in an Asian War, 1939-1941." PAC HR,
      54 (August 1985), 337-351.

      Though not a pacifist, William Castle, Hoover's under
      secretary of state, nonetheless believed (in the opinion of
      the author) that war was no way to decide international
      affairs. This article shows how William Castle formulated
      a contemporary critique of Roosevelt that anticipated
      issues raised later by revisionist historians.

500. Chalufour, Aline. "Indo-China: Tragedy of Errors." ASIA &
      AMERICAS, 41 (December 1941), 703-706.

      The author, a French lawyer who taught for three years
      in Indochina, describes the circumstances there in 1940
      when, with Japan in control, French administrators made a

grievous error in not joining the Free French (and thereby
receiving British assistance).

501.   Chamberlain, William Henry. AMERICA'S SECOND CRUSADE.
       Chicago: Henry Regnery Company, 1950. 372 pp.

       Chamberlain believes that American involvement in the
       war--a "second crusade"--was a product of bankrupt
       illusions. His revisionist thesis carries a consistently
       critical tone against Roosevelt and his advisers,
       especially Hull.

502.   Chula, Prince. "Thailand." CONTEMP REV, 160 (November
       1941), 303-309.

       This royal Thai official explains the situation in
       Thailand and offers the Thai version of difficulties with
       both the French and British. Of interest is his country's
       rejection in 1939 of "Siam" as a name given by foreigners.

503.   Claus, Errol M. "The Roosevelt Administration and
       Manchukuo, 1933-1941." HISTORIAN, 32 (August 1970),
       595-611.

       The author, a history professor, describes Roosevelt's
       response to Manchukuo as a confused mix of moralism,
       legalism, and pragmatism. Principle, the author notes, was
       not permitted to override U.S. commercial interests.

504.   Clifford, Nicholas R.   RETREAT FROM CHINA: BRITISH POLICY
       IN THE FAR EAST, 1937-1941. Seattle, WA: University of
       Washington Press, 1967.

       Here is a critical analysis of British policy before the
       war. Clifford folds the developing Far Eastern crisis into
       the deteriorating global context which confronted British
       leaders at this time. The wealth of primary sources that
       emerged a few years after this book was published serves to
       reinforce many of Clifford's views.

505.   Cole, Wayne S. "American Entry into World War II: A
       Historiographical Appraisal." MVHR, 43 (March 1957),
       595-617.

       In this seminal article, Cole points out that the
       historiographical debate (up to 1957) mirrors the prewar
       debates about U.S. involvement in the war. While also
       examining the specific circumstances of the U.S. entry,
       Cole criticizes historians for not placing the decisions

and policies which led to Pearl Harbor into the context of
the First World War and the inter-war years. While
indicating areas for further study, the author warns that
polemics must be avoided. The historiographical
controversy, Cole notes, is hottest over what can least be
proved and doesn't warrant such dogmatism.

506.   Conroy, Hilary. "Government versus 'Patriot': The
        Background of Japan's Asiatic Expansion." PAC HR, 20
        (February 1951), 31-42.

        Conroy suggests that Japan's policy of continental
expansion had two broad patterns: a cautious government
policy and a third party movement, which had advocated
expansion for fifty years prior to the 1931 Manchurian
crisis. During the 1920s and 1930s, she writes, the third
party movement became associated with internal renovation
schemes to free the emperor from the grasp of the
conservatives.

507.   Conroy, Hilary. "Japanese Nationalism and Expansionism."
        AMER HR, 60 (July 1955), 818-829.

        Noting the controversial nature of the literature about
nationalism, Conroy seeks points of agreement that can
serve as a frame of reference for the study of nationalism.
For prewar Japan, the author writes, the character of
nationalism was shaped by expansionism and Kokka (state)
nationalism.

508.   Conroy, Hilary. "The Strange Diplomacy of Admiral Nomura."
        PROC AMER PHILOS SOC, 114 (June 18, 1970), 205-216.

        Incorporating valuable primary materials, including
Japanese sources, Conroy develops a balanced assessment of
Nomura's efforts.

509.   Coox, Alvin D. THE ANATOMY OF A SMALL WAR: THE SOVIET -
        JAPANESE STRUGGLE FOR CHANGKUFENG/KHASAN, 1938.
        Westport, CT: Greenwood Press, 1977. 409 pp.

        With extensive research, especially through Japanese
sources, Coox analyzes the border clash which held lessons
for both sides. Japanese restraint in the face of Soviet
intrusion provides the general context for this study.
Coox carefully explains the actions and decisions taken in
Tokyo during the episode. The study is masterful, but, as
always when dealing with the enigmatic Soviets, the
unavailability of Russian sources prevents a balanced

perspective. Notwithstanding this caveat, the Bibliography
of available sources is substantial.

510. Coox, Alvin D. "High Command and Field Army: The Kwantung
      Army and the Nomonhan Incident." MIL AFFS, 33 (October
      1969), 302-312.

      This article is marked by thorough research, including
      Japanese sources, and analysis. Coox describes how the
      field army, unknown to the Japanese High Command, crossed
      the Soviet boundary in April 1939. The resulting defeat by
      the Soviets had brought Japan to the brink of disaster.

511. Coox, Alvin D. NOMONHAN: JAPAN AGAINST RUSSIA, 1939.
      Stanford, CA: Stanford University Press, 1985. 2 vols.

      This study of over twelve-hundred pages examines the
      four-month clash in 1939 along the Halha River. Coox has
      conducted his research with meticulous care among the
      available sources. (The Soviets have refused to make
      available their archival materials.) Of special interest
      is his discovery of an official Japanese history of the
      Kwantung Army. Coox identifies this prolonged battle as a
      turning point--primarily because after the Soviet victory,
      the Japanese turned their attention southward. Also, he
      points out that U.S. intelligence fumbled an opportunity to
      gauge the Japanese military in action. A valuable
      "Afterthoughts" section is appended to this masterful
      study.

512. Coox, Alvin D. "Repulsing the Pearl Harbor Revisionists:
      The State of Present Literature on the Debacle." MIL
      AFFS, 50 (January 1986), 29-31.

      The author maintains that the critiques of the
      revisionists are not credible, especially the so-called
      "Devil Theory." Coox levels a devastating attack against
      Toland's INFAMY.

513. Costello, John E. "Remember Pearl Harbor." USNIP, 109
      (September 1983), 52-62.

      Costello focuses on the effective Japanese diplomacy
      before the war, especially in using secret intelligence and
      manipulating the John Doe Associates. He particularly
      criticizes the so-called deterrence of the B-17 force in
      the Philippines and MacArthur's mishandling of his air
      resources.

514. Craigie, Sir Robert Leslie. BEHIND THE JAPANESE MASK.
         London: Hutchinson and Company, 1945. 172 pp.

         Craigie describes his experience as British ambassador
      in Tokyo from 1938 to the outbreak of war. The memoirs
      avoid controversy. Craigie fails to address either the
      charges against him of being too "pro-Japanese" during his
      ambassadorship or his final report, which became a cause
      celebre within the Foreign Office because of his criticism
      of prewar British policies.

515. Croizat, Victor J. "Japan Drives Southwest." ARMY, 17
         (June 1967), 65-73.

         The ambitious Japanese vision of dominating the Far East
      spawned the decision to strike south. Rather than enter a
      protracted and costly struggle with the Soviet Union,
      Japanese leaders came to believe that all their goals could
      be attained within one year. Buna would serve as the
      western anchor of a far-flung "defense" perimeter.

516. Crowley, James B. JAPAN'S QUEST FOR AUTONOMY: NATIONAL
         SECURITY AND FOREIGN POLICY, 1930-1938. Princeton, NJ:
         Princeton University Press, 1966.

         Crowley integrates extensive research, including many
      Japanese sources, in this study of the motives behind
      Japanese expansionism. His conclusions criticize Japan for
      seeking hegemony in East Asia--a hegemony ill-concealed
      under the guise of the "Greater East Asia Co-Prosperity
      Sphere."

517. Crowley, James E., ed. MODERN EAST ASIA: ESSAYS IN
         INTERPRETATION. New York: Harcourt Brace, 1970.
         428 pp.

         In this commendable collection, see especially Crowley's
      essay, "A New Deal for Japan and Asia: One Road to Pearl
      Harbor." Few American historians can equal his command of
      the material.

518. Crowley, James B. "A Reconsideration of the Marco Polo
         Bridge Incident." J ASIAN STUD, 22 (May 1963), 277-291.

         In this well-researched article, Crowley--no apologist
      for Japan--argues that the Nanking government technically
      provoked this incident as part of a gamble to thwart
      continuing Japanese pressures. Crowley's research
      incorporates Japanese sources (including interviews) and he

calls for research through Chinese sources pertaining to
the episode. Of interest is his observation that the field
armies of both countries behaved more responsibly than
their governments.

519.   Current, Richard N. "How Stimson Meant to 'Maneuver' the
       Japanese." MVHR, 40 (June 1953), 67-74.

       This article centers on the famous Stimson diary entry
       for November 25, 1941. The author credits Walter Millis
       (THIS IS PEARL!, 1947) for pointing in the direction of the
       correct explanation. Taking note of Stimson's thinking and
       assumptions, Current argues that Stimson meant "our side"
       when he used the word "we" -- not just the United States.
       The secretary of war expected the attack to come against
       Thailand or the British Empire but certainly not against
       American soil (including the PI, Guam, or Hawaii).
       According to Current, Stimson saw the political problem for
       the Roosevelt administration as having to go to war
       suddenly on the basis of a Japanese move not clearly made
       against the United States.

520.   Daita, Kitaide. "The Last Flying Boat to Japan." RAF
       FLYING REV, 15 (September 1960), 16-17.

           NE

521.   Dingman, Roger. "Farewell to Friendship: The USS
       ASTORIA's Visit to Japan, April 1939." DIP HIST, 10
       (Spring 1986), 121-139.

       Illustrating how good intentions can go awry, Dingman
       describes the visit to Japan of the ASTORIA (carrying home
       the remains of former ambassador Saito Hiroshi) as a
       gesture that could not gloss over fundamental differences
       between the two countries.

522.   Divine, Robert A. THE RELUCTANT BELLIGERENT. New York:
       John Wiley, 1965. 172 pp.

       In this excellent synthesis about America on the edge of
       war, Divine portrays Roosevelt as a skillful leader who was
       sensitive to public attitudes. There is a valuable summary
       of the Hull-Nomura conversations. Divine includes a useful
       bibliographic essay.

523.   Doyle, Michael K. "The U.S. Navy and War Plan Orange,
       1933-1940: Making Necessity a Virtue." NAVAL WAR COLL
       REV, 33 (May-June 1980), 49-63.

With penetrating insight, Doyle examines the broad
context for the development of War Plan Orange. He argues
that the plan gained impetus during the late 1930s from two
factors: the conviction of strategic planners that the
United States would never abandon its interests in the
Pacific and the growing area of common Anglo-American
concerns in the Pacific.

524. Dreifort, John E. "Japan's Advance into Indochina, 1940:
      The French Response." J SEA STUD, 13 (September 1982),
      279-295.

      With the fall of France, the French administration in
Indochina had little hope for help from the British or
Americans. According to the author, British policy in
1940-1941 was not to give Japan an excuse for further
expansion. Dreifort argues that the French in Indochina
could hardly do more than offer ineffectual concessions.

525. Drummond, Donald F. THE PASSING OF AMERICAN NEUTRALITY,
      1937-1941. Ann Arbor, MI: University of Michigan Press,
      1955. 409 pp.

      Essentially, Drummond defends the policies and actions
of the Roosevelt administration in the prewar period. The
onus for the war is clearly on Japan, according to the
author.

526. Dunnigan, James F. and William Martel. HOW TO STOP A WAR.
      New York: Doubleday, 1987. 298 pp.

      In the section touching on the Pacific war, the authors
warn against underestimating a cornered (potential)
adversary. Of special interest is their opinion that the
war against Japan could have been avoided.

527. Dupuy, Trevor N. "Pearl Harbor: Who Blundered?" AMER
      HERITAGE, 13 (February 1962), 64-81.

      By pressing the question of whether a wiser diplomacy
might have avoided war with Japan, Col. Dupuy argues that
American civilians had every right to expect their armed
forces to be prepared for war. In this day-by-day look at
the period 25 November to 7 December 1941, the author
criticizes Marshall and Stark for not making the necessary
preparations. With great irony, Dupuy notes that Marshall
has received much credit for reorganizing the Army within
six months after the Japanese surprise attack.

528. Duus, Peter and Daniel I. Okimoto. "Fascism and the
          History of Pre-War Japan: The Failure of a Concept." J
          ASIAN STUD, 39 (November 1979), 65-76.

          The author debunks the concept of fascism in pre-war
      Japan. Despite the presence of some fascists and fascist
      ideas in Japan, Duus maintains that their numbers were too
      small to constitute a paradigm.

529. Eckstein, Gustav. IN PEACE JAPAN BREEDS WAR. New York:
          Harper and Brothers, 1943 rev. ed.   326 pp.

          With vignettes and capsule profiles of people he met in
      his travels, Eckstein makes an effort to understand the
      Japanese. The book was originally published in 1927. In
      this revised edition, Eckstein describes Yamagata, who
      constantly preached that in peace Japan should prepare for
      war, as the one man most responsible for the war in the
      Pacific--even though Yamagata died some 20 years before the
      attack at Pearl Harbor.

530. Eismeier, Dana L. "U.S. Oil Policy, Japan, and the Coming
          of the War in the Pacific, 1940-1941." MICH
          ACADEMICIAN, 14 (Spring 1982), 359-367.

          Here is a defense of American oil policy, which the
      author believes postponed a disastrous war in 1940 and
      almost all of 1941 for the ill-prepared United States.
      Eismeier calls attention to the role played by Morgenthau
      and Acheson, whom he refers to as "ideological allies."
      Both men held unusual leverage, Eismeier points out,
      because of the bureaucratic requirement that each
      transaction must have two export licenses: one from the
      Treasury (ensuring that all financial aspects were in
      order), the other from the State Department (granting
      physical export clearance).

531. Eller, Ernest M. "Pearl Harbor: Forty Years Later." SEA
          POWER, 24 (December 1981), 49-54.

          The author argues that the disaster at Pearl Harbor
      could have been avoided if, during the interwar years, the
      U.S. government had paid more attention to its navy and had
      taken a firm stand against the Japanese in Manchuria.
      Eller, however, praises the foresightedness of the
      president and Carl Vinson.

532. Emerson, Rupert. "The Dutch East Indies Adrift." FOR

AFFS, 18 (July 1940), 735-741.

Emerson, an expert on Southeast Asian affairs, warns
that the U.S. can not be indifferent to the fate of NEI.
Taking note of Japanese assurances in 1940 to NEI of
goodwill and disinterestedness, he believes such statements
are harbingers of imminent "protection" by the Japanese.
His report, however, stops short of gauging the reaction of
the people in the NEI, where there was much nationalist
spirit and little love for the Chinese or the Dutch.

533.   Emmerson, John K. "Tokyo 1941." FOR SERV J, Part I: 53
          (April 1976), 10-14, 25; Part II: 53 (May 1976), 5-9,
          26.

As a member of the U.S. Embassy in Tokyo during 1941,
Emmerson provides a unique view of the deterioration of
American-Japanese relations. He asserts that the Embassy
had become an in-grown society by late 1941 and that Grew
remained convinced that war with Japan was unnecessary.

534.   Esthus, Raymond A. "President Roosevelt's Commitment to
          Britain to Intervene in a Pacific War." MVHR, 50 (June
          1963), 28-38.

Esthus writes that the sum of evidence justifies the
conclusion that Roosevelt gave Britain a commitment of
armed U.S. support if Japan attacked British or Dutch
possessions. But in this article, he shows how confusion
persisted about whether that commitment covered certain
hypothetical situations. Esthus argues that Roosevelt
seemed intent on putting the question of war directly
before Congress. The British, however, did not doubt that
the president would use his leadership to have the United
States enter the war if Japan attacked British territory.

535.   Eyre, James K. "The Background to Japanese Naval Treachery
          in the Pacific. "USNIP, 70 (July 1944), 875-885.

Eyre, an American adviser to Osmena, traces Japanese
prewar treachery to practices (hardly startling in
retrospect) such as stealing ideas from the West, using the
Japanese populations abroad in an intelligence network, and
feeding misinformation to the West about Japanese
inferiority.

536.   Farley, Miriam S. "Strategic Imports From Southeast Asia."
          FE SURVEY, 11 (January 12, 1942), 12-16.

Farley provides useful reference information (e.g.,
statistics and tables) on the prewar U.S.-SEA economic
relationship.

537.   Feis, Herbert. THE ROAD TO PEARL HARBOR. Princeton, NJ:
       Princeton University Press, 1950. 356 pp.

With special access to restricted materials, Feis
focuses on American-Japanese relations leading to the war.
His conclusions criticize Japan expansionist policies and
exonerate American policies, which, he feels, were neither
unsound nor provocative. For the author, timing was
crucial: Japan could not wait, and the United States
wanted delay. Of special interest is Feis's explanation of
the prior knowledge the U. S. Army and Navy had about the
embargo in July 1941.

538.   Feis, Herbert. "War Came at Pearl Harbor: Suspicions
       Considered." YALE REV, 45 (March 1956), 378-390.

Here is a spirited defense of U.S. prewar policies. The
final American note (November 26, 1941), says Feis, was not
an ultimatum; it merely left the Japanese in their existing
state of distress. Feis has been criticized for being a
"court historian."

539.   Ferrell, Robert H. "Pearl Harbor and the Revisionists."
       HISTORIAN, 17 (Spring 1955), 215-233.

Ferrell rebukes the revisionists for their
"impressionistic and occasionally tautological arguments"
that Roosevelt deliberately goaded the Japanese into firing
the first shot against the United States. In Ferrell's
view, the disaster at Pearl Harbor revealed military errors
but not diplomatic intrigue.

540.   Fleisher, Wilfrid. OUR ENEMY JAPAN. Garden City, NY:
       Doubleday Doran, 1942. 236 pp.

Fleisher, a correspondent with extensive experience in
Asia, gives a background of the war by surveying prewar
relations between the United States and Japan. Much of his
focus is on the 1941 diplomatic negotiations.

541.   Fleisher, Wilfrid. VOLCANIC ISLE. New York: Doubleday
       Doran, 1941. 345 pp.

Fleisher provides his first-hand observations of the
political situation in Tokyo and the diplomatic

maneuverings of the Japanese in aligning with the Axis
Powers. His report includes assessments of the Japanese
political leaders.

542. Fletcher, William Miles. THE SEARCH FOR A NEW ORDER:
      INTELLECTUALS AND FASCISM IN PREWAR JAPAN. Chapel Hill,
      NC: University of North Carolina Press, 1983. 226 pp.

      Fletcher finds that Japan's abandonment of liberalism
was not a sudden or coerced process and that fascism was
seen by the Japanese as the solution to political-economic
ills. In following this shift, Fletcher traces the
contemporary ideas of three prominent intellectuals from
the Showa Research Association: Royama Masamichi, Ryu
Shintaro, and Miki Kiyoshi.

543. Flynn, John T. THE FINAL SECRET. New York: Author, 1945.
      2d rev. ed. 15 pp.

      Here is a devastating attack on Roosevelt who, in the
author's unsubstantiated opinion, actually sought--and
succeeded in arranging--U.S. involvement in the war.

544. Flynn, John T. THE FINAL SECRET OF PEARL HARBOR. New
      York: Devon-Adair, 1945.

      This book supplements Flynn's 1944 book, THE TRUTH ABOUT
PEARL HARBOR. Both works take a strong revisionist posture
in criticizing Roosevelt for conducting secret diplomacy
and for arranging the U.S. entry into the war.

545. Flynn, John T. THE ROOSEVELT MYTH. New York:
      Devin-Adair, 1948.

      Here is an anti-Roosevelt diatribe. The author argues
that Roosevelt actually maneuvered the country into the war
to salvage his waning political career.

546. Flynn, John T. THE TRUTH ABOUT PEARL HARBOR. New York:
      Author, 1944. 32 pp.

      Flynn launches a bitter attack against Roosevelt.
According to Flynn, the president maneuvered the country
into war and should bear moral responsibility for deceiving
the American people.

547. Frechtling, Louis E. "Japan's Oil Supplies." AMERASIA, 5
      (July 1941), 197-201.

The author points to the glaring inconsistency of the
democracies in denouncing Japanese aggression but
continuing to supply Japan. In analyzing Japan's oil
supplies (ninety percent of which came from imports),
Frechtling believes that, because of huge oil storages, any
foreign oil embargo would have little immediate effect.
Note that the publication of this article coincided with
Roosevelt's freeze order.

548. Friedman, Donald J. THE ROAD FROM ISOLATION: THE CAMPAIGN
      OF THE AMERICAN COMMITTEE FOR NON-PARTICIPATION IN
      JAPANESE AGGRESSION, 1938-1941. Cambridge, MA: Harvard
      University Press, 1968. 122 pp.

      This well-researched study calls attention to a group
      which battled against the strong isolationist impulse in
      prewar U.S. society in order to oppose Japanese expansion.

549. Fukuda, Teizaburo. "A Mistaken War." USNIP, 94 (December
      1968), 42-47.

      Rear Admiral Fukuda discloses that key Japanese naval
      leaders (and junior officers too) opposed going to war
      against the United States--a war that army leaders and
      diplomats supported.

550. Gayn, Mark J. THE FIGHT FOR THE PACIFIC. New York:
      William Morrow, 1941. 378 pp.

      Gayn reports on Japanese expansion and aggression in
      Asia. Claiming that Japan is threatening U.S. interests,
      he calls for Americans to wake up and confront the
      Japanese. In contrast to contemporary American attitudes,
      the author praises the realistic assessment of Stimson in
      1931.

551. Gilbert, Dan. WHAT REALLY HAPPENED AT PEARL HARBOR. Grand
      Rapids, MI: Zondervan Publishing House, 1943. 48 pp.

      NE

552. Gilchrist, Andrew. "Diplomacy and Disaster: Thailand and
      the British Empire in 1941." ASIAN AFFS, 13 (October
      1982), 249-264.

      Here is the memoir of a foreign service officer in
      Thailand on the eve of the war--a time when, according to
      the author, the British position was nearly hopeless. The
      memoir is strengthened by Gilchrist's frank observations

about his contemporaries (e.g., favorable on Pibul, mostly
favorable on Crosby, and not-so-favorable on Brooke-Popham).
In an extraneous aside, Gilchrist proudly announces that the
prewar bite he suffered from a mad dog came to the attention
of Noel Coward and did indeed inspire the famous
commemorative song.

553.   Grace, Richard J. "Whitehall and the Ghost of Appeasement:
       November 1941." DIP HIST, 3 (Spring 1979), 173-191.

       When Cordell Hull decided to drop his proposed modus
vivendi in late November 1941, he threw the bulk of the
blame on the attitude of the British. Grace argues that,
even though the British had plenty of sound reasons for
postponing a war with Japan, the ghost of appeasement
obscured the British vision. "Munich" dominated the frame
of reference for all proposals of diplomatic compromise.

554.   Greater East Asia War Inquiry Commission. THE
       AMERICAN-BRITISH CHALLENGE DIRECTED AGAINST NIPPON.
       Osaka, Japan: Mainichi, 1943. 128 pp.

       This propaganda effort condemns the Western democracies
for aggression against Japan and for crimes inflicted on
the people of Asia. For effect, some members of this
commission were carefully selected from countries other
than Japan.

555.   Greaves, Percy L. "FDR's Watergate: Pearl Harbor." REASON
       (February 1976), 16-23.

       NE

556.   Grew, Joseph C. REPORT FROM TOKYO. New York: Simon and
       Schuster, 1942. 88 pp.

       Grew offers a collection of ten speeches in which he
explains the situation in Japan to the American people.
With an authoritative tone, he describes the rise to power
of Japanese militarists and their design for conquest.

557.   Haggie, Paul. BRITANNIA AT BAY: THE DEFENSE OF THE
       BRITISH EMPIRE AGAINST JAPAN, 1931-1941. New York:
       Oxford University Press, 1981.

       Here is a well-researched analysis of British
perspectives on the coming of the war against Japan.
American attitudes and policies wielded uneven influences
in London throughout the decade.

558.   Haight, John McVickar, Jr.   "FDR's 'Big Stick.'"   USNIP,
       106 (July 1980), 68-73.

       During 1937-1938, Roosevelt sought cooperation with the
       British to draw the line against Japanese expansion. He
       secretly exchanged information with the British, sent
       Ingersoll to London, and even considered a blockade against
       the Japanese. But Chamberlain scuttled the president's
       projects which required the cooperation of the British
       Navy.

559.   Haight, John McVickar, Jr.   "Franklin D. Roosevelt and a
       Naval Quarantine of Japan."   PAC HR, 40 (May 1971),
       203-226.

       According to Haight, the president began formulating a
       plan in 1937 for a naval blockade of Japan. The author
       emphasizes the importance of Eden's 1938 resignation in
       ending the blockade scheme. Haight, however, argues that
       Roosevelt did not withdraw into isolation after the
       Quarantine speech but continued to believe that the United
       States, Britain, and France would have to stop Germany,
       Italy, and Japan.

560.   Haines, Gerald K.   "American Myopia and the Japanese Monroe
       Doctrine, 1931-41."   PROLOGUE, 13 (Summer 1981),
       101-114.

       The author, an archivist in the diplomatic branch of the
       National Archives, describes the close resemblance between
       the U.S. Monroe Doctrine and Japan's regional policies in
       East Asia. According to Haines, for instance, each sought
       to erect ideological barriers between the old and the new.
       The article is well researched and offers thought-provoking
       ideas.

561.   Harrison, Richard A.   "A Neutralization Plan for the
       Pacific: Roosevelt and Anglo-American Cooperation,
       1934-1937."   PAC HR, 57 (February 1988), 47-72.

       Harrison points out that, although the scheme of
       neutralizing the Western Pacific was unlikely, the idea did
       generate Anglo-American talks about collaboration. In the
       background was the idea that Anglo-American cooperation in
       the Pacific might lead to cooperation in Europe. Harrison
       sees a constant striving during the 1930s for an
       Anglo-American connection--despite all the apparent
       inconsistencies, changes of direction, uncertainty, and

ideas left undeveloped.

562. Hashimot, Tetsuma. THE UNTOLD STORY OF JAPANESE-AMERICAN
        NEGOTIATIONS. Tokyo: Shiunso, 1947. 130 pp.

        The author was the anonymous "Mr. Y." who served as an
        intermediary to American and British diplomats in Tokyo for
        the Japanese Cabinet. In 1941, Mr. Y went to Washington--
        even U.S. Ambassador Grew agreed that his presence there
        might be useful--but was not able to achieve a diplomatic
        breakthrough. After his return to Tokyo, he was arrested
        as a spy. The intervention of influential friends,
        however, helped resolve the matter.

563. Haven, Violet Sweet. GENTLEMEN OF JAPAN: A STUDY IN
        RAPIST DIPLOMACY. Chicago: Ziff-Davis, 1944. 321 pp.

        Haven, a reporter and teacher, travelled throughout the
        Far East prior to December 1941. She notes in particular
        certain activities of the Japanese, activities which made
        clear to her that Japan was preparing for war. In
        discussing the existence of a pro-Japanese Fifth Column,
        Haven critiques the Japanese-American population in Hawaii.

564. Herzberg, James R. A BROKEN BOND: AMERICAN ECONOMIC
        POLICIES TOWARD JAPAN, 1931-1941. New York: Garland,
        1988.

        Herzberg maintains that the U.S. embargo greatly
        enhanced the likelihood of war with Japan. During the
        1930s, trade between the two countries had been strong.
        With solid research and carefully stated positions, the
        author looks at the policies and misconceptions of the two
        powers.

565. Herzog, James H. CLOSING THE OPEN DOOR: AMERICAN-
        JAPANESE DIPLOMATIC NEGOTIATIONS, 1936-1941. Annapolis,
        MD: Naval Institute Press, 1973. 295 pp.

        Though written on the eve of the appearance of newly
        declassified materials, this study, nevertheless, analyzes
        soundly the final diplomatic encounters of the two powers
        before the war. Herzog pays particular attention to the
        influence of naval developments in shaping the perspectives
        and the policies forged in Washington and Tokyo.

566. Herzog, James H. "Influence of the United States Navy in
        the Embargo of Oil to Japan, 1940-1941." PAC HR, 35
        (August 1966), 317-328.

Cmdr. Herzog (USN) reports that top-level naval leaders, especially Admirals Turner and Stark, opposed an oil embargo against Japan. On the other hand, he describes Roosevelt's feeling that Japan would not take on both the British and Americans. Of interest is Herzog's finding that the secretary of the navy and second echelon naval officers supported the embargo.

567. Herzog, James H. "Oil to Japan." MIL REV, 45 (October 1965), 68-76.

According to Herzog, the decision to impose an embargo on oil against Japan divided Roosevelt's military advisors, especially the Navy. The author reports that the secretary of the navy and lower-level admirals favored the embargo, but the senior admirals, including the Chief of Naval Operations (Stark), opposed any action that would bring war with Japan. Stark particularly worried about the effect deteriorating relations with Japan would have on the situation in Europe.

568. Higgins, Trumbull. "East Wind Rain." USNIP, 81 (November 1955), 1198. (See also the comment by Louis Morton in ibid.), 82 (February 1956), 1198-1203.

Concerned primarily with the European perspective, Higgins sharply criticizes Japan's "imbecilic" policy in the Pacific before December 1941. He especially vilifies the Japanese decision to move south instead of northward against the Soviet Union--the last Axis chance for victory.
Morton, however, takes issue with the article by Higgins. Pointing out that Japan badly needed certain vital resources, Morton reminds Higgins that these resources were available only to the south.

569. Hiles, Charles C. A CRITIQUE OF ROBERTA WOHLSTETTER'S PEARL HARBOR: WARNING AND DECISION. New York: Revisionist Press, 1979.

Hiles upholds the general revisionist approach to the origins of U.S. involvement in the war. Wohlstetter's conclusions--judicious, sound, and well-received--run counter to his perspective.

570. Hill, Norman. "Was there an Ultimatum Before Pearl Harbor?" AMER J INT LAW, 42 (April 1948), 355-367.

Hill, a political scientist, closely examines both the

Japanese note of November 20, 1941, and the American note
of November 26, 1941. In a highly legalistic analysis, he
concludes that neither note constituted a "bona fide
ultimatum" which threatened war. This technical conclusion
will hardly satisfy critics who feel the American note had
pushed Japan to the wall. Of interest is Hill's
observation that the Japanese note fulfilled most of the
conditions of an ultimatum but gave no warning (which a
technically pure ultimatum should provide).

571. Hoehling, A.A. THE WEEK BEFORE PEARL HARBOR. New York:
     W.W. Norton, 1963. 238 pp.

     The author, a Navy ensign in the public information
     section in Washington, speaks of the "befogged canvas" in
     that city during this critical period. The book is
     especially good in outlining the complex interplay of
     personalities and their differing perspectives. In
     Hoehling's opinion, distinctions are blurred between
     heroism and villainy.

572. Hoffer, Peter C. "American Businessmen and the Japan
     Trade, 1931-1941: A Case Study of Attitude Formation."
     PAC HR, 41 (May 1972), 189-205.

     The author, a historian, finds that U.S. businessmen,
     during the period 1931-1941, maintained and stoutly
     defended their trade with Japan. The article integrates
     social and psychological dimensions of the topic as well as
     economic factors.

573. Holmes, Wilfred J. "Pearl Harbor Aftermath." USNIP, 104
     (Demcember 1978), 68-75.

     This intelligence expert gives his knowledgeable
     opinions about the attack at Pearl Harbor. Holmes feels
     that Admiral Kimmel was used as a scapegoat for the
     debacle.

574. Hooper, Paul F. "A Footnote on the Pacific War." HAWAIIAN
     J HIST, 9 (1975), 121-127.

     Here is an account of the efforts in 1940-1941 of David
     L. Crawford, president of the University of Hawaii, to
     arrange a treaty of friendship (peace) between the United
     States and Japan.

575. Hosoya, Chihiro. "Japanese-American Relations." PAC
     HISTORIAN, 23 (Winter 1979), 9-27.

By late 1941, Konoye had put all his hopes in arranging
a meeting with Roosevelt. Matsuoka, however, wanted to
handle Roosevelt in his own way--by being firm rather than
servile (as Konoye seemed to be). The author describes a
misunderstanding during Konoye's visit to the United States
in 1934 which reinforced Hornbeck's negative opinion about
a Konoye-Roosevelt meeting in 1941. The article concludes
with the author, a noted Japanese historian, speculating on
whether such a meeting would have been fruitful.

576.   Hosoya, Chihiro. "Miscalculations in Deterrent Policy:
        Japanese-U.S. Relations, 1938-1941." J PEACE RES (No.
        2, 1962), 97-115.

        The author, a noted historian, describes the period as a
        process of action and reaction. He argues that deterrence
        policy broke down because American hard-line factions
        misunderstood Japanese psychology and decision-making.
        According to the author, U.S. economic sanctions had
        exactly the opposite effect intended. Here is an example
        of hard liners' deterrent policy leading to miscalculations
        that exacerbated international tensions.

577.   Hoston, Germaine A. "Emperor, Nation, and the
        Transformation of Marxism to National Socialism in
        Prewar Japan: The Case of Sano Manabu." STUD COMP
        COMMUNISM, 18 (Spring 1985), 25-47.

        In prewar Japan, the fusion of Marxism and nationalistic
        elements produced a "chauvinistic brand of national
        socialism" similar to that of prewar Germany and Italy.
        For Hoston, a crucial condition was the existence of
        capitalism and imperialism in Japan at the time the
        Japanese Communist Party (JCP) was founded. The author
        incorporates research of Japanese sources to demonstrate
        this pattern of development in Japan through the career of
        JCP leader, Sano Manabu.

578.   Howard, Harry Paxton. "U.S. Treasury and the Far East."
        AMERASIA, 5 (November 1941), 399-414.

        Analyzing US-Chinese and US-Japanese financial relations
        during the 1930s, the author concludes that American
        policies reduced Free China to a state of financial
        dependence on the United States. He also feels that,
        despite the oil embargo, American policies facilitated
        Japanese aggression and that determined economic action by
        the United States in 1937 would have paralyzed Japan (at

the outset of the Sino-Japanese war).

579. Hoyt, Frederick B. "George Bronson Rea: From Old China
Hand to Apologist for Japan." PAC N W Q, 69 (April
1978), 61-70.

Using primary sources (especially State Department
files), Hoyt describes the prewar efforts of Rea, who
served as counselor to the Ministry of Foreign Affairs in
Manchukuo, to persuade the United States to accept Japan as
predominant in Asia. According to Hoyt, Rea sought to
avoid tragedy in American diplomacy by trying to unravel
the American insistence on preserving the Open Door policy
in China. Rea died in 1936.

580. Hsu, Immanuel C.Y. "Kurusu's Mission to the United States
and the Abortive MODUS VIVENDI." J MOD HIST, 24
(September 1952), 301-307.

Hsu interviewed or corresponded with both Kurusu and
Nomura in researching this article. Analyzing the
withdrawal of the proposed agreement--which earned only
superficial approval from the British and Dutch as well as
intensive opposition from the Chinese--Hsu argues that the
MODUS VIVENDI might have changed world history. A delay to
February 1942, he writes, would have revealed the tenuous
German position on the Russian front, and may well have
given pause to the potential adversaries in the Far East.
Instead, Japan regarded the substitute U.S. response as an
ultimatum. Of interest is Hsu's report that the two
principal Japanese diplomats in Washington knew nothing
about the plans to attack Pearl Harbor.

581. Ickle, Frank W. GERMAN-JAPANESE RELATIONSHIPS, 1936-1940.
New York: Bookman, 1956. 243 pp.

Ickle's analysis reveals the tenuous nature of this
partnership.

582. Iriye, Akira. "Japanese Imperialism and Aggression:
Reconsiderations." J ASIAN STUD, 23 (November 1963),
103-113.

Here is an important review of the work of Japanese
historians on the origins of the war. Iriye raises
questions about traditional Western theories of prewar
Japanese foreign policies.

583. Iriye, Akira. "Japan's Foreign Policies Between World

Wars--Sources and Interpretations." J ASIAN STUD, 26
(August 1967), 677-682.

Reviewing published Japanese source materials for the
period 1931-1941, Iriye points out that Japanese leaders
did not visualize actual conflict with the United States
until 1940. He also notes that the Japanese separated the
prewar issues of China and Southeast Asia. The article
offers a valuable survey of the coming of the war from the
Japanese perspective.

584. Iriye, Akira. THE ORIGINS OF THE SECOND WORLD WAR IN ASIA
      AND THE PACIFIC. London and New York: Longman, 1987.
      202 pp.

      Iriye offers an "international history of the prewar
      period." His analysis centers on Japan becoming isolated
      and embarking on a gamble to create a new international--
      anti-democratic--system. Of interest is Iriye's suggestion
      that the United States may have blundered by rejecting a
      meeting with Konoye. The opportunity might have led to
      some ambiguous agreement, according to the author, which,
      in turn, might have gained valuable time in postponing the
      war. The book is marked by extensive "international"
      research and the author's mastery of the material.

585. Janeway, Eliot. "U.S. Oil and Japan." ASIA & AMERICAS, 41
      (August 1941), 400.

      Here is a brief contemporary report on the U.S. debate
      over oil shipments to Japan. The author notes the efforts
      of Ickes to halt the shipments and (of special interest)
      the testimony of Acheson that Japan would move into the NEI
      if the U.S. cut the oil shipments. Janeway argues in favor
      of halting the shipments (and making Japan "choose between
      life and death").

586. Janis, Irving L. VICTIMS OF GROUPTHINK: A PSYCHOLOGICAL
      STUDY OF FOREIGN-POLICY DECISIONS AND FIASCOES. Boston:
      Houghton Mifflin, 1972. 276 pp.

      Relying on published sources, the author presents
      articles which blend social psychology, political science,
      and history. Janis, a professor of psychology, takes as
      his central theme the psychological drive for consensus at
      any cost--a drive that suppresses either dissent or the
      consideration of any alternatives. In his essay, "Pearl
      Harbor Revisited, or Why the Fortress Slept" (pp. 75-100),
      Janis looks at three groups: (a) the Navy leaders in

Hawaii; (b) the Army leaders in Hawaii; and (c) the
President's war council in Washington. His analysis
reveals how the illusion of invulnerability led to a
reassuring peace of mind. According to Janis, the three
groups mutually reinforced their lack of vigilence. The
book's tentative conclusions focus on methods of preventing
this so-called "Groupthink."

587. Kawakami, K.K. "Far Eastern Triangle." FOR AFFS, 18 (July
      1940), 632-645.

The impact of the war in Europe, the author writes, is
bringing about not only Anglo-Japanese reconciliation but
also an Anglo-American convergence of policy in China. The
article suggests that, for economic reasons, Japan prefers
accommodation with the United States--over Britain, if
necessary.

588. Kerr, George. "KODAMA Report: Plan for Conquest." FE
      SURVEY, 14 (July 18, 1945), 185-190.

Here is a report on the then-newly revealed document
from 1902 which outlined a plan for Japanese expansion.
Kerr says the West has always underestimated Japan.

589. Kimmel, Husband E. ADMIRAL KIMMEL'S STORY. Chicago:
      Henry Regnery, 1955. 206 pp.

The admiral sets his defenses against the criticisms
brought upon him since the attack at Pearl Harbor.
Considering the significance of the charges and the depth
of his bitterness, the book is surprisingly slim. Clearly,
he feels betrayed by naval and political leaders in
Washington. His basic complaint is that Washington kept
him in the dark about deteriorating U.S. relations with
Japan, especially because he never knew about either MAGIC
or its revelations. In his estimation, Kimmel was made a
scapegoat for malfeasance in Washington. The book is
crucial for studying the origins of the war with Japan;
Kimmel's arguments must be considered.

590. Kittredge, Tracy B. "United States Defense Policy and
      Strategy, 1941." US NEWS WORLD REP, 37 (December 3,
      1954), 52-63, 110-139.

Capt. Kittredge (USN) presents his views that are
described as representing those of Marshall and Stark.
Taking issue with revisionists like Theobald, the author
argues that the Army and Navy local commanders in Hawaii

were kept adequately informed--and warned. If actual
sightings of Japanese aircraft and submarines failed to
arouse alarm in Hawaii, he asks, would one more message
from Washington have done so? Of interest is his report
that the Army and Navy only learned accidentally of Hull's
harsh final note of November 26, 1941.

591. Koginos, Manny. THE PANAY INCIDENT: PRELUDE TO WAR.
      LaFayette, IND: Purdue University Press, 1967. 154 pp.

      Here is an excellent account of the prewar episode--
      well researched through sources available at the time.

592. Korotkov, G. "Pearl Harbor." SOVIET MIL REV (November
      1971), 42-45.

      The Soviet colonel emphasizes that, despite adequate
      warning, Americans were surprised at Pearl Harbor. His
      account denounces U.S. imperialism for fostering through
      appeasement two hotbeds of war in Europe and Asia.

593. Kubek, Anthony. HOW THE FAR EAST WAS LOST: AMERICAN
      POLICY AND THE CREATION OF COMMUNIST CHINA. Chicago:
      Henry Regnery, 1963.

      Kubek, a political scientist, feels that the United
      States deliberately provoked Japan into war. Concocting an
      elaborate scenario that has strong ideological overtones,
      Kubek works backwards from the "gain" of China by the
      communists. His case links the benefits for Moscow of
      China becoming communist, the alleged Soviet objective of
      contriving a U.S.-Japanese war, Harry Dexter White (the man
      who, according to Kubek, torpedoed a promising modus
      vivendi with Japan and replaced it with a virtual
      ultimatum) being a Soviet agent, the activities of Hull and
      Roosevelt in maneuvering Japan into firing the first shot,
      and finally, communists in the U. S. government. This
      prosecutor needs more evidence.

594. Kurusu, Saburo. TREACHEROUS AMERICA. Tokyo: Japan Times,
      1942. 56 pp.

      Ambassador Kurusu delivers a speech on the first
      anniversary of the proposed U.S. modus vivendi (which he
      refers to as a virtual ultimatum). The speech accuses the
      United States of pushing Japan into war.

595. Kutakov, L.N. JAPANESE FOREIGN POLICY ON THE EVE OF THE
      PACIFIC WAR: A SOVIET VIEW. Tallahassee, FL: Diplomatic

Press, 1972. 241 pp.

The Soviet view--a retrospective view--denounces the deception and trickery in the foreign policies conducted by Japan before the war. George A. Lensen edited this work.

596. Landon, Kenneth P. "The Thai Against the French," ASIA & AMERICA, 41 (March 1941), 172-174.

This authoritative report describes Thailand as a "question mark" in relations among the Japanese, French, British, and Americans.

597. LaPlant, John B. "The Evolution of Pacific Policy and Strategic Planning: June 1940-July 1941." NAV WAR COLL REV, 25 (May-June 1973), 57-72.

The author complains that military strategic planning and the conduit of foreign policy should have been better synchronized by 1941. He points out that, while the former took a global view, the latter tended to be compartmentalized among the various regions.

598. Lasswell, A. Bryan. "A Shanghai Incident." MC GAZ, 64 (September 1980), 54-57.

Here is the personal account of the arrest of sixteen Japanese gendarmes within the American zone at Shanghai in July 1940. Lasswell's knowledge of the Japanese language qualified him for this unusual assignment.

599. Lattimore, Owen. "Stalemate in China." FOR AFFS, 19 (April 1941), 621-632.

Pointing to Chinese resilience and Japanese flaws, Lattimore argues that the contemporary stalemate in China should not be viewed as permanent.

600. Lawry, John. "A catch in the boundary: Australia and the Free French Movement in 1940." J PAC HIST, 10 (No. 3, 1975), 64-82.

The author describes the background, including support from Australia, of the Gaullist bloodless coup in New Caledonia, September 19, 1940. His research incorporates material from Australian archives and French-language sources.

601. Leary, William M. "Assessing the Japanese Threat: Air

Intelligence Prior to Pearl Harbor." AEROSPACE HIST, 34
(Winter/December 1987), 272-277.

Although abundant technical data about Japan existed
before the war, Leary points out that very little analysis
was done by U.S. intelligence. Deeply engrained myths
about Japanese inferiority, he says, tended to override
intelligence information.

602. Lee, Bradford A. BRITAIN AND THE SINO-JAPANESE WAR,
      1937-1939. Stanford, CA: Stanford University Press,
      1973. 319 pp.

Here is a masterful, thoroughly researched history of a
critical period in the march to the Pacific war. Lee shows
that, contrary to popular historical opinion, the British
devoted a great deal of attention to the situation in the
Far East--and its implications for the embattled West.

603. Lee, Robert W. "Pearl Harbor." AMER OPINION, 24 (December
      1981), 19-24, 71-84.

The author, a businessman and writer, charges that
Roosevelt withheld information from the American people.
Outlining the revisionist writings, Lee makes clear that he
supports their arguments.

604. Leighton, Isabel, ed. THE ASPIRIN AGE: 1919-1941. New
      York: Simon and Schuster, 1949. 491 pp.

In this collection, see the article by Jonathan Daniels,
"Pearl Harbor Sunday: The End of an Era." Daniels, a
former adminstrative assistant to the president, defends
Roosevelt's actions and policies concerning Japan.

605. Leonard, Thomas M. "The Magic Messages and Pearl Harbor
      Revisited." PROC CONF WAR DIP (The Citadel, 1976),
      95-101.

Despite the claim by Adm. Kimmel, Leonard argues that
the presently available messages intercepted through MAGIC
do not indicate that Japan would attack Hawaii.

606. Leonard, Thomas M. "Stanley K. Hornbeck: Major Deterrent
      to American-Japanese Summitry, 1941." TOWSAN STATE J, 8
      (No. 2, 1974), 113-121.

      NE

607. Libby, Justin H. "American-Japanese Relations and the
          Coming War in the Pacific: A Congressional View." PAC
          HISTORIAN, 22 (Winter 1978), 379-390.

          Libby deals almost exclusively with congressional
      opinion toward Japan during the final months of the peace.
      Focusing on many leading congressional figures, he
      concludes that during 1941 Congress had reached a consensus
      on the need to contain Japan.

608. Libby, Justin H. "The Irreconcilable Conflict: Key Pittman
          and Japan During the Interwar Years." NEVADA HIST SOC
          Q, 18 (No. 3, 1975), 128-139.

          NE

609. Libby, Justin H. "Senators King and Thomas and the Coming
          War With Japan." UTAH H Q, 42 (Fall 1974), 370-380.

          Both Utah senators served on the Senate Foreign
      Relations Committee, and both reflected the confusion and
      uncertainty of the prewar times. Early on, King became
      determined to stop Japan, but Thomas only came to that
      position at the last minute.

610. Lin, H. Hsitien, comp. AMERICAN PRESS OPINION ON THE
          SINO-JAPANESE CONFLICT. New York: Chinese Cultural
          Society, 1937. 36 pp.

          After claiming to have read over 5,000 U.S. editorials,
      Lin presents a selected collection of 39 that
      overwhelmingly treats Japan as the aggressor and China as
      the victim. But the editorials also reveal a mixture of
      isolationist and interventionist attitudes.

611. Lowe, Peter. GREAT BRITAIN AND THE ORIGINS OF THE PACIFIC
          WAR. Oxford, Eng.: Clarendon Press, 1977. 318 pp.

          In this examination of the period 1937-1941, Lowe
      concludes that Japan bears the major responsibility for the
      outbreak of the war. He does, however, point out errors,
      omissions, misunderstandings, and sheer stupidity on the
      part of British and American officials--all of which
      contributed in some measure to the descent into war. The
      book is solidly researched through relatively new primary
      sources.

612. Lowenthal, Mark W. "Roosevelt and the Coming of the War:
          The Search for United States Policy 1937-42." J CONTEMP

HIST, 16 (July 1981), 413-440.

Incorporating extensive research through British and
American archival sources as well as published works,
Lowenthal offers a compromise between the views of
Roosevelt as either schemer or wise leader. This third
interpretation holds that Roosevelt knew generally what he
wanted as he went through a series of fits and starts.

613. Lu, David J. FROM THE MARCO POLO BRIDGE TO PEARL HARBOR.
       Washington, D.C.: Public Affairs Press, 1961. 274 pp.

Incorporating research through Japanese archival
materials, Lu traces the steps in the road to war between
Japan and the United States. His analysis sympathizes with
Matsuoka. According to Lu, Japanese leaders considered
their many peace proposals to China between 1937 and 1941
to be fair. He sees two causes of the war in 1941: (1)
Japan's refusal, especially at the insistence of the Army,
to retreat from China and (2) the American refusal to sell
oil and other materials to Japan. With the imposition of
the U.S. embargo, Lu says, Japanese naval leaders grew more
inclined to go to war. Of interest is the way Lu
downplays the importance of the Tripartite Pact.

614. McKechney, John. "The Pearl Harbor Controversy: A Debate
       Among Historians." MONUMENTA NIPPONICA, 18 (No. 1,
       1963), 45-87.

The author sides with the "Internationalist" historians
over the "Isolationists." Acknowledging that the Japanese
attack provided Roosevelt a "heaven sent" opportunity,
McKechney feels that the criticisms of U.S. treason and
stupidity are unwarranted. Rather, he says, Japan should
keep the credit for a daring attack.

615. Maddox, W. P. "America and Japan." ANNALS AMER ACAD POL
       SOC SCI, 215 (May 1941), 1-215.

The entire issue is devoted to an examination of
Japanese-American relations. Various subtopics include
Japan's East Asian policies, U.S. policies, cultural
divergence, and the immediate future. Here is a good
contemporary analysis of relations between the two
countries just prior to their going to war.

616. Marks, Frederick W., III. "Facade and Failure: The
       Hull-Nomura Talks of 1941." PRES STUD Q, 15 (Winter
       1985), 99-112.

With his usual fluid prose, Marks severely criticizes
Roosevelt and Hull for mishandling relations with Japan up
to December 7, 1941.

617. Marks Frederick W., III. "The Origins of FDR's Promise to
      Support Britain Militarily in the Far East--A New Look."
      PAC HR, 53 (November 1984), 447-462.

      Marks argues that the essence of Roosevelt's guarantee
      to Britain in early December 1941 not only surfaced in the
      fall of 1940 but also came within the context of generally
      the same pledges made often during the year preceding the
      attack at Pearl harbor. His article--well researched and
      grounded in conventional rather than startlingly new
      sources--raises new questions about U.S. prewar policies in
      Asia.

618. Masland, John. "Commercial Influences Upon American Far
      Eastern Policy, 1937-1941." PAC HR, 11 (September
      1942), 281-299.

      Masland argues that the United States was not led
      blindly by commercial interests. According to him, the
      American refusal to give up firmly established principles
      led to the collision with Japan. Of interest is his report
      that U.S. commercial interests did not want the freeze or
      other economic restrictions against Japan.

619. Maurer, Maurer. "A Delicate Mission: Aerial
      Reconnaissance of Japanese Islands Before World War II."
      MIL AFFS, 26 (Summer 1962), 66-75.

      In late November 1941, the AAF ordered two B-24s
      (non-combat ready) from the continental United States to
      report any Japanese buildups among the Pacific islands.
      Despite the top-level orders, long delays plagued the
      mission, largely because of a lack of coordination. The
      enterprise failed with one aircraft stuck on the West Coast
      awaiting repairs and the other destroyed in the Japanese
      attack at Pearl Harbor.

620. Megaw, M. Ruth. "The Scramble for the Pacific:
      Anglo-United States Rivalry in the 1930s." HIS STUD, 17
      (October 1977), 458-473.

      With extensive use of primary sources, Megaw analyzes
      the prewar commercial rivalry that extended to uninhabited
      coral atolls (for civil air bases in the Pacific).

Ironically, the British were alienating the Americans during the time when London wanted to cultivate a close relationship with Washington. Megaw presents the British perspective to this story of U. S. economic expansionism.

621. Meigs, Montgomery C. "This Must Mean the Philippines!" USNIP, 111 (August 1985), 72-78.

Arguing that Washington was preoccupied with the possibility of a Japanese attack against the Philippines, the author criticizes Roosevelt for failing to give firm direction to the development of strategic policy.

622. Melosi, Martin V. "National Security Misused: The Aftermath of Pearl Harbor." PROLOGUE, 9 (Summer 1977), 75-89.

Melosi offers a lesson in misapplied secrecy in setting national policy. He criticizes the Roosevelt administration for invoking secrecy as a justification to restrict blame for the debacle at Pearl Harbor to the two local commanders.

623. Melosi, Martin V. "Political Tremors From a Military Disaster: 'Pearl Harbor' and the Election of 1944." DIP HIST, 1 (Winter 1977), 79-95.

Surveying the differences between Roosevelt and the Republicans about Pearl Harbor, Melosi contends that as long as the question remained "political" there would be no national consensus.

624. Melosi, Martin V. THE SHADOW OF PEARL HARBOR: POLITICAL CONTROVERSY OVER THE SURPRISE ATTACK, 1941-1946. College Station, TX: Texas A & M University Press, 1977. 183 pp.

The controversy over responsibility for the surprise attack became a partisan political issue. Melosi focuses on the extent Roosevelt and high officials succeeded or failed in minimizing the domestic impact of Pearl Habor in keeping the blame away from themselves. According to the author, the actions of the administration immediately after the attack, such as relieving Kimmel and Short, led to charges of a coverup. Melosi argues that the administration paid disproportionate attention to personal culpability and overreacted in the concern that critics would make too much out of the available information.

625. Meyer, Richard J. "Instantaneous Communications." SIGNAL,
        12 (February 1968), 13-14.

        Maj. Gen. Meyer (USA) reports on the communications
      delay December 7, 1941.

626. Miles, Sherman. "Pearl Harbor in Retrospect." ATLANTIC
        MON, 182 (July 1948), 65-72.

        The author served as assistant chief of the Intelligence
      Division in the War Department. Although he admits that
      U.S. intelligence underestimated the Japanese, Miles does
      insist that Washington sent clear warnings to the two
      Hawaiian commanders.

627. Millis, Walter. THIS IS PEARL: THE UNITED STATES AND
        JAPAN--1941. New York: William Morrow, 1947. 384 pp.

        In this analysis of prewar American-Japanese relations,
      Millis generally defends the policies and actions of
      President Roosevelt. Primary responsibility for the
      disaster, according to the author, rests with the
      commanders in Hawaii, Kimmel and Short. The narrative is
      critical of MacArthur's leadership and the lack of
      preparations in the Philippines.

628. Mintz, Frank Paul. REVISIONISM AND THE ORIGINS OF PEARL
        HARBOR. Lanham, MD: University Press of America, 1985.
        156 pp.

        In this historiographical study, Mintz focuses on the
      question of what Roosevelt knew, or intended, in the months
      preceding December 7, 1941. Although Mintz doubts that a
      deep, dark conspiracy existed, he feels that Roosevelt's
      private commitments went far beyond his public position and
      that the president kept the commanders in Hawaii "in the
      dark" to enable Japan to achieve the advantage of surprise.
      According to the author, U.S. leaders believed that
      sanctions would persuade Japan to back down, especially
      after Germany attacked the Soviet Union.

629. Morgenstern, George. PEARL HARBOR: THE STORY OF THE
        SECRET WAR. New York: Devin-Adair, 1947. 425 pp.

        Newspaperman Morgenstern takes a critical view of
      Roosevelt's prewar leadership. The author is among the
      first revisionists to incorporate research from captured
      enemy records and the special Joint Investigating Committee

of Congress. Here is a tendentious book.

630. Moore, Jamie W. "Economic Interests and American-Japanese
      Relations: The Petroleum Monopoly Company." HISTORIAN,
      35 (August 1973), 551-567.

      During the 1930s, Japan set up an oil monopoly which was
      poorly organized and administered in confusion. Moore
      portrays this controversy as part of the larger struggle
      between Japan and the United States.

631. Morison, Samuel Eliot. "Did Roosevelt Start the War --
      History Through a Beard." ATLANTIC MON, 182 (August
      1948), 91-97.

      Here is a severely critical appraisal of the views of
      Charles Beard about U.S. entry into the war.

632. Morley, James W. THE DILEMMAS OF GROWTH IN PREWAR JAPAN.
      Princeton, NJ: Princeton University Press, 1971. 527
      pp.

      This is a collection of papers from the sixth seminar at
      Puerto Rico on modern Japan.

633-7. Morley, James W., ed. JAPAN'S ROAD TO THE PACIFIC WAR.
      New York: Columbia University Press, 1976-1985. 5
      vols.

      The volumes translate and condense a seven-volume study
      by Japanese historians in 1962-1963 (entitled TAIHEIYO
      SENSO E NO MICHI KAISEN GAIKO SHI). This is a most
      important series; it is essential to have this
      retrospective perspective from Japan. In chronological
      order, Morley's volumes are as follows (each carries the
      same main title as given above):

633. JAPAN ERUPTS: THE LONDON NAVAL CONFERENCE AND THE
      MANCHURIAN INCIDENT, 1928-1932 (1984, 410 pp.). See the
      essays by Kobayashi Tatsuo "The London Naval Treaty, 1930";
      Seki Hiroharu, "The Manchurian Incident, 1931"; and Shimada
      Toshihiku, "The Extension of Hostilities, 1931-1932."

634. THE CHINA QUAGMIRE: JAPAN'S EXPANSION ON THE ASIAN
      CONTINENT, 1933-1941 (1983, 508 pp.). Of interest is
      Japan's inability to extricate itself from a deepening
      involvement in China.

635. DETERRENT DIPLOMACY: JAPAN, GERMANY AND THE U.S.S.R.,

1935-1940 (1976, 363 pp.). Here is a close examination of
Japan's diplomatic relations with the two continental
powers.

636. THE FATEFUL CHOICE: JAPAN'S ADVANCE INTO SOUTHEAST ASIA,
1939-1941 (1980, 366 pp.). Of interest is the rationale
advanced for the move southward as an encirclement of
China.

637. THE FINAL CONFRONTATION: JAPAN'S NEGOTIATIONS WITH THE
UNITED STATES, 1941. Criticism continues against the
hard-line position of the United States.

638. Morley, James W. JAPAN'S FOREIGN POLICY, 1869-1941. New
York: Columbia University Press, 1974.

Morley expertly surveys Japanese foreign policy in the
period. The research is first-rate, and the narrative is
well written. His analysis rejects any idea of one
gigantic prelude to Pearl Harbor.

639. Morton, Louis. "The Japanese Decision for War." USNIP, 80
(December 1954), 1324-1335.

According to Morton, the Japanese decision for war
represented a gamble based on the hope that the European
situation would dominate U. S. attention. For the Japanese
leaders, the price of maintaining the peace had become too
high--tantamount to ignominious surrender in their eyes.
Morton points out that the Japanese underestimated the
U. S. reaction to the attack at Pearl Harbor.

640. Morton, Louis. "War Plan Orange: Evolution of a
Strategy." WORLD POL, 11 (January 1959), 221-250.

Pointing to the wide gap between means and ends in the
evolution of Pacific military policies from 1900 to 1941,
Morton focuses in particular on the continuing debate about
whether or not the Philippines were defensible. The 1938
Orange Plan, therefore, represented a compromise between
offensive and defensive strategy. Morton, however,
emphasizes that the U.S. failed either to reinforce the
Philippines and Guam.

641. Murata, Kiyoaki. "'Treachery' of Pearl Harbor." USNIP, 82
(August 1956), 904-906.

The author tries to minimize the "treachery" of Japanese
actions by focusing on the reasons for the delay in

delivering the fourteen-part message.

642. Myers, Albert. "KHALKIN GOL: Stalin's Battle to Stabilize
      the Soviet Far East." MIL REV, 63 (April 1983), 60-65.

      In reviewing the Soviet-Japanese clash near the Khalkin
      Gol River in August 1939, Myers calls the action a preview
      of tactics used in World War II.

643. Najita, Tetsuo. "Inukai Tsuyoshi: Some Dilemmas in Party
      Development in Pre-World War II Japan." AMER HR, 74
      (January 1969), 492-510.

      Najita examines the growing separation between organized
      political activities and other fields of action in Japan as
      illustrated in Tsuyoshi's career. How, the author asks,
      does a politician function in the pragmatic world of
      politics yet retain an image of ethical integrity?

644. Neidpath, James. THE SINGAPORE NAVAL BASE AND THE DEFENSE
      OF BRITAIN'S EASTERN EMPIRE, 1919-1941. Oxford, Eng.:
      Oxford University Press, 1981. 296 pp.

      Neidpath is critical of shifting British perceptions
      about the supposed "Fortress"--perceptions that were far
      from reality by 1941.

645. Neu, Charles E. THE TROUBLED ENCOUNTER: THE UNITED STATES
      AND JAPAN. New York: John Wiley, 1975.

      Here is a first-rate survey, well-researched and
      well-written, of U.S.-Japanese relations. See especially
      his excellent anlaysis of the prewar negotiations. Neu's
      control of the material and his wide-ranging scholarship
      combine to make this an important contribution.

646. Neumann, William L. "Ambiguity and Ambivalence in Ideas of
      National Interest in Asia." In: Alexander DeConde, ed.
      ISOLATION AND SECURITY. Durham, NC: Duke University
      Press, 1957. 204 pp.

      Neumann emphasizes the stark differences between
      rhetoric and action in U.S. perceptions of Asia. Despite
      tough talk, according to the author, Washington was
      unwilling to make the commitments necessary to support
      expanded versions of U.S. interests in that region.

647. Neumann, William L. AMERICA ENCOUNTERS JAPAN: FROM PERRY
      TO MACARTHUR. Baltimore, MD: The Johns Hopkins

University Press, 1963. 353 pp.

Neumann explores the ideas and attitudes which shaped
U.S. foreign policy and relations with Japan. Focusing on
certain prewar issues that broadened U.S.-Japanese friction
--Indochina, the Tri-partite Pact, the U.S. economic
freeze--Neumann maintains that Japan genuinely wanted to
avoid war during the 1941 negotiations. The study is
well-grounded in its research, and Neumann does not shrink
from controversial interpretations.

648. Neumann, William L. "Franklin D. Roosevelt and Japan,
      1913-1933." PAC HR, 22 (May 1953), 143-153.

Tracing Roosevelt's evolving views, Neumann identifies
three major stages: (1) 1913-1921, Japan could be a
potential enemy; (2) 1921-1933, enthusiasm for the
Washington Conference system; and (3) 1931-1933, new
diplomatic tensions created by the Manchurian crisis.

649. Nish, Ian, ed. SOME ASPECTS OF SOVIET-JAPANESE RELATIONS
      IN THE 1930s. London: London School of Economics and
      Political Science, 1982. 87 pp.

Nish presents the texts of three lectures: Akira Iriye
on the ideological background of the war; Brian Bridges on
Mongolia; and Jonathan Haslam on Soviet aid to China and
Japan. See especially Iriye's contention that the
increasingly isolated Japanese lacked a clear perception of
their culture. See, too, the comments by Ambassador H.
Nishi and P.J.W. Chapman.

650. Nobutaka Ike, ed. JAPAN'S DECISION FOR WAR: RECORDS OF
      THE 1941 POLICY CONFERENCES. Stanford, CA: Stanford
      Unviersity Press, 1967. 306 pp.

Ike translated as well as edited the Japanese documents.
The records for the liaision conferences are not official
minutes; rather they are the notes taken by a
representative of the Army's chief of staff. Here is an
indispensable source in gaining the Japanese perspective
and the decision-making process during the crisis year of
1941. Many of the documents are quoted entirely.

651. Nomura, Kichisaburo. "Stepping-Stones to War." USNIP, 77
      (September 1951), 927-931.

Admiral Nomura provides his impressions of the march to
war. He says that Konoye was short sighted in expecting to

maintain ties with both the United States and the Axis. Of
interest is Nomura's report of Togo telling him, even
before taking office as foreign minister, that the
foundation stones for war with the United States were
already in place.

652. Peffer, Nathaniel. "Omens in the Far East." FOR AFFS, 20
      (October 1941), 49-60.

      The author argues that, with the weakening of Japanese
      ability to control China, the attenuation of Japanese power
      into the South China Sea, the deflection of Soviet power to
      Europe, and the strengthening of Western colonies in
      Southeast Asia, the Far East is nearer to lasting peace
      than one year ago, or five years ago. His confidence that
      the omens are "propitious" in the Far East emerges just
      weeks before the outbreak of the war against Japan.

653. Pelz, Stephen E. RACE TO PEARL HARBOR: THE FAILURE OF THE
      SECOND LONDON NAVAL CONFERENCE AND THE ONSET OF WORLD
      WAR II. Cambridge, MA: Harvard University Press, 1974.
      268 pp.

      Pelz views the Imperial Japanese Navy as playing an
      influential part in building Japan's aggressive policies
      before the war. For navalists in Japan, Pelz believes,
      competition with the United States became a major cause of
      the war. Despite the grandiose title, which implies a
      causal connection between the conference and the war, the
      book is well researched and sheds light on the prewar
      years.

654. Perkins, Dexter. "Was Roosevelt Wrong?" VA Q REV, 30
      (Summer 1954), 355-372.

      Criticizing revisionism as history by hypothesis,
      Perkins notes the passions and prejudices of the critics of
      Roosevelt. He warns against underestimating the role of
      public sentiment; Roosevelt could not act simply as he
      chose.

655. Perry, Hamilton Darby. THE PANAY INCIDENT: PRELUDE TO
      PEARL HARBOR. New York: Macmillan, 1969.

      Here is a report, drawn from sources available at the
      time, on the Japanese air attack in 1937. Luigi Barzini,
      who survived the attack aboard the PANAY, wrote the
      Foreword.

656. Perry, Darby. "Rehearsal for World War II." AMER
      HERITAGE, 18 (April 1967), 40-45, 76-81.

      In his research of the attack on the PANAY, Perry
      interviewed and corresponded with American and Japanese
      participants. The article also includes still pictures
      from a movie filmed during the attack (which, incidentally,
      shows the excellent visibility on this clear day). Perry
      provides a solid, balanced report. Twelve U. S. survivors
      of the PANAY were at Pearl Harbor on December 7, 1941.

657. Pollard, Robert T. "Dynamics of Japanese Imperialism."
      PAC HR, 8 (March 1939), 5-35.

      Here is an examination of the social-political-economic
      conditions in Japan which promoted expansionism.

658. Prange, Gordon W. AT DAWN WE SLEPT: THE UNTOLD STORY OF
      PEARL HARBOR. New York: McGraw-Hill, 1981. 873 pp.

      This volume, published posthumously, represents the
      culmination of 37 years of research by Prange, who served
      as chief of the historical section in Japan under
      MacArthur. With exhaustive research through American and
      Japanese sources, including extensive interviews, Prange
      has produced a masterful study. He singles out Gen. Short
      for a good deal of criticism, but Prange also finds fault
      with Kimmel's performance, especially in not conducting
      long-range reconnaissance missions. In a separate section
      on revisiting the revisionists, Prange, no idolizer of
      Roosevelt, feels that the president's critics through the
      years have not substantiated their allegations. Donald M.
      Goldstein and Katherine V. Dillon collaborated with Prange
      and supervised the completion of the book. No study of
      Pearl Harbor is complete without taking this book into
      account.

659. Prange, Gordon W., Donald M. Goldstein, and Katherine V.
      Dillon. PEARL HARBOR: THE VERDICT OF HISTORY. New
      York: McGraw-Hill, 1986. 699 pp.

      The authors offer an interpretive (speculative?) essay.
      They feel that this material is inappropriate for
      inclusion in their formal history of the attack at Pearl
      Harbor, AT DAWN WE SLEPT. For example, the revisionist
      historians (especially the allegations of John Toland), who
      have criticized Roosevelt's leadership, earn sharp rebuke.
      Other topics include the "winds" message (irrelevent to
      events at Pearl Harbor, say the authors); views on the

behavior and leadership of Marshall, Stark, and other
"Advisers, Planners, and Chiefs"; the Three Little Ships
(the authors claim Roosevelt was merely a busybody seeking
information); and MacArthur's mishandling of his air
resources. Whatever else, the book makes interesting
reading.

660. Pratt, Sir John T. BEFORE PEARL HARBOUR: A STUDY OF THE
      HISTORICAL BACKGROUND TO THE WAR IN THE PACIFIC.
      London: Caxton, 1944. 59 pp.

      This British official speculates on the steady
      deterioration of relations with Japan after the First World
      War.

661. Puleston, W.D. THE ARMED FORCES OF THE PACIFIC: A
      COMPARISON OF THE MILITARY AND NAVAL POWER OF THE UNITED
      STATES AND JAPAN. New Haven, CT: Yale University
      Press, 1941. 273 pp.

      This contemporary report, although avoiding the
      distortions of racism and chauvinism that often plague such
      assessments, comes out overly optimistic for the American
      case. Nevertheless, the thoughtful Puleston warns against
      taking Japan too lightly.

662. Rader, Frank J. "The Works Progress Administration and
      Hawaii Preparedness, 1935-1940." MIL AFFS, 43 (February
      1979), 12-17.

      Using WPA records, Rader argues that WPA practices
      produced a close working relationship between local
      civilian and military authorities. He portrays Roosevelt
      as arbitrarily extending military control over Hawaii.

663. Regnery, Henry. "Historical Revisionism and World War II."
      MOD AGE, Pt. I: 20 (Summer 1976), 254-265; Pt. II: 20
      (Fall 1976), 402-411.

      Here is a first-hand account of Regnery's support for
      revisionist writings about the war. For example, he
      published works by Morgenstern, Beard, Chamberlain,
      Tansill, Kimmel, and Barnes. Regnery explains his policy:
      "Truth is worthwhile for its own sake."

664. Richardson, James O. ON THE TREADMILL TO PEARL HARBOR:
      THE MEMOIRS OF ADMIRAL JAMES O. RICHARDSON. Washington,
      D.C.: Navy History Division, 1974.

In these memoirs, Richardson explains his view that
moving the fleet to Pearl Harbor from the West Coast was a
major mistake. His arguments in defense of that view
ultimately cost him his job. While not questioning
Roosevelt's motives or actions directly, the admiral's
criticism does raise some interesting points.

665. Robertson, E.M., ed. THE ORIGINS OF THE SECOND WORLD WAR:
      HISTORICAL INTERPRETATIONS. London: Macmillan, 1971.
      312 pp.

      The selections are from articles published previously.
On the origins of the war with Japan, see the essays by
Akira Iriye and Robert Ferrell. Iriye, in two articles,
reviews Japanese historiography of the war; Ferrell
criticizes attempts by revisionists to blame Roosevelt for
exposing the fleet in order to promote his political
ambitions.

666. Roth, Andrew. JAPAN STRIKES SOUTH. New York: American
      Council, Institute of Pacific Relations, 1941.

      This brief report, sponsored by the IPR, offers a
contemporary's immediate response to the outbreak of the
war. Roth condemns Japanese aggression.

667. Roberts, Martha Byrd. "Reluctant Belligerent: The United
      States Enters World War II." AMER HIST ILLUS, 17
      (November 1982), 20-29.

      Here is a narrative of events, including events in
Europe, which led to the attack at Pearl Harbor. The
author portrays the United States as a reluctant
belligerent and the president as seeking to avoid direct
U.S. involvement in the war.

668. Russett, Bruce M. NO CLEAR AND PRESENT DANGER: A
      SKEPTICAL VIEW OF THE UNITED STATES ENTRY INTO WORLD WAR
      II. New York: Harper and Row, 1972. 111 pp.

      Russett, a political scientist, takes as his theme the
view that the U.S. entry had little effect on the essential
structure (i.e., the balance of forces) of international
politics. He adds that the war did not increase U.S.
security or the material welfare of the American people.
Without a demonstrated need for U.S. national interests,
Russett argues, the entry into the war was a major error.

669. Russett, Bruce. "Pearl Harbor: Deterrence Theory and

Decision Theory." J PEACE RES (No. 1, 1967), 89-106.

Arguing that rationality or irrationality is not a
useful vehicle for analyzing the decision-making process
(such as the Japanese decision for war with the United
States), Russett suggests instead the examination of
certain components of each decision and alternatives.
Although cluttered with jargon and dependent upon an
alleged decision-theory model, the article reveals that,
far from being an irrational act, Japan's decision for war
emerged as one of the more attractive alternatives facing
the Japanese in 1941.

670. Ryan, Paul B. "How Young We Were." USNIP, 94 (December
      1968), 26-36.

      Capt. Ryan (U.S.N.) criticizes the leadership in
      Washington on the eve of the war. Too many Americans,
      according to Ryan, badly underestimated the Japanese,
      especially through unfortunate racial stereotyping and
      miscalculations about alleged Japanese inferiority.

671. Ryan, Paul B. "The Thunder of Silence: General Marshall's
      Moral Dilemma." ARMED FORCES J INTL, 120 (August 1983),
      59-62.

      Ryan calls into question Marshall's role leading up to
      the attack at Pearl Harbor. The author is especially
      critical of Marshall's "do/don't" message to Gen. Short.

672. Sagan, Scott D. "The Origins of the Pacific War." J
      INTERDISC HIST, 18 (Spring 1988), 893-922.

      The author, a political scientist, detects a flaw in the
      present-day theory of deterrence. One lesson of Pearl
      Harbor, he maintains, is that a nation, if provoked, may
      resort to war out of desperation.

673. Sanborn, Frederic R. DESIGN FOR WAR: A STUDY OF SECRET
      POWER POLITICS, 1937-1941. New York: Devin-Adair,
      1951. 607 pp.

      Sanborn, an expert in international law, examines
      Roosevelt's words and actions during the prewar period.
      This is a critical view of the president. Sanborn argues
      that Roosevelt should have consulted Congress before
      entering into foreign adventures and American commitments.

674. Sansom, Sir George. "Japan's Fatal Blunder." INTL AFFS,

24 (October 1948), 543-554.

Drawing heavily from the U. S. Strategic Bombing Survey
and postwar interrogations, Sansom analyzes Japan's
decision (blunder?) to go to war with the United States.
Having miscalculated the strength of their domestic economy
and underestimated the surprising sharp response of their
enemies, the Japanese entered what they expected to be a
limited war, according to Sansom. He adds some thoughts
about the Japanese surrender and concludes that no single
cause forced that decision. In fact, he says, not even the
combination of the atomic bombings and the Soviet entry
into the war induced the Japanese to quit. Rather, Sansom
concludes that the decision to surrender emerged from the
"slow and devious processes characteristic of Japanese
political life."

675. Sasso, Claude R. "Scapegoats or Culprits: Kimmel and
       Short at Pearl Harbor." MIL REV, 63 (December 1983),
       28-47.

Arguing that each of the commanders was both a scapegoat
and a culprit, Sasso feels, nevertheless, that the two
should have been permitted to make a contribution to the
war effort.

676. Sato, Kyozo. "Japan's Position Before the Outbreak of the
       European War in September 1939." MOD ASIAN STUD, 14
       (February 1980), 129-143.

Using Japanese sources as well as secondary works in
English, Sato feels that the war in Europe should have
enabled Japan to develop an effective defense policy, but,
instead, Japanese leaders squandered the opportunity.

677. Schlesinger, Arthur M., Jr. "Roosevelt and His
       Detractors." HARPER'S MAG, 200 (June 1950), 62-68.

Pointing out that wars invariably bring on an aftermath
of disillusion, the author takes a detached, surprisingly
tolerant view of Roosevelt's critics. The president was no
miracle worker, the noted historian writes, but Roosevelt
was hardly ineffective.

678. Schroeder, Paul W. THE AXIS ALLIANCE AND JAPANESE-AMERICAN
       RELATIONS, 1941. Ithaca, NY: Cornell University Press,
       1958. 246 pp.

In this analysis of the immediate prewar months,

Schroeder concentrates on U.S. foreign policy. Criticizing
what he feels is an excessive moral emphasis, especially on
the part of Hull, Schroeder argues that the war was both
avoidable and unnecessary. Despite excellent research in
some areas, the ambitious project, as indicated in the
title of the book, exceeds the total research effort. For
example, Schroeder does not seem to incorporate Japanese
sources in his study. Moreover, this is hardly a balanced
assessment, either in its international context or in its
assessment of American diplomacy.

679.   Schuler, Frank and Robin Moore. THE PEARL HARBOR COVER-UP.
        New York: Pinnacle Books, 1976.

        Schuler, a Foreign Service Officer (1930-1953), argues
        that a clique within the State Department acted to cover up
        their own errors and negligence concerning the origins of
        the war with Japan. The book contains explicit charges
        that Grew and his aides destroyed or removed State
        Department files of evidence pointing to their
        responsibility for Pearl Harbor.

680.   Shai, Aron. ORIGINS OF THE WAR IN THE EAST. London: Croom
        Held, 1976. 267 pp.

        Shai shows command of a broadly based research effort as
        he analyzes the coming of the war. The book examines the
        perspectives and policies of the Chinese, Japanese,
        American, and British governments.

681.   Shai, Aron. "Was There a Far Eastern Munich?" J CONTEMP
        HIST, 9 (July 1974), 161-170.

        Arguing that appeasement in the Far East gained strength
        without a Munich crisis as such, Shai feels that the
        British began accommodating Japan through a gradual erosion
        of principle in which London drew distinctions between
        Japanese demands on British interests and Japanese demands
        on China. The article incorporates extensive research
        from British archival material.

682.   Sheldon, Charles D. "Japanese Aggression and the Emperor,
        1931-1941." MOD ASIAN STUD, 10 (February 1976), 1-40.

        Using contemporary Japanese sources (especially the
        diaries of Kido and Harada-Saionjii), the author analyzes
        the role of the Emperor in several episodes during the
        period. Sheldon rejects the arguments of the emperor's
        critics and accepts the explanation given by Hirohito

himself: the emperor could not have prevented the war from
starting, but he did receive requests to end the war.

683. Shelton, Michael W. "Plan Orange Revisited." USNIP, 110
        (December 1984), 50-56.

        Concerned with nuclear build-up since WW II, Shelton
        compares the prewar naval plan of war with Japan to the
        postwar naval plans for war with the Soviet Union.

684. Slonim, Gilven M. "Have We Learned the Lesson of Pearl
        Harbor?" NAVY, 9 (December 1966), 12-15.

        On December 7, 1941, Slonim was serving at an intercept
        radio station on Oahu. He insists that we need to learn
        "the lesson" of Pearl Harbor, and he contends that Kimmel
        and Short were sacrificed to satisfy public outrage.

685. Smith, Geoffrey S. TO SAVE A NATION: AMERICAN
        COUNTERSUBVERSIVES, THE NEW DEAL AND THE COMING OF WORLD
        WAR II. New York: Basic Books, 1973. 244 pp.

        Here is a knowledgeable survey of the U.S. political
        landscape and the contemporary domestic perspective on the
        origins of the war.

686. Smith-Hutton, H.H. "Tokyo, December 1941." SHIPMATE, n.v.
        (December 1973), 9-17.

        The author, serving at the time as a naval attache (Lt.
        Cmdr.) to Ambassador Grew, describes his duties and life in
        Tokyo on the eve of the war. Of interest is his request to
        the Japanese Navy Department--after the attack at Pearl
        Harbor--if the United States could expect to receive a
        declaration of war from Japan.

687. Staley, Eugene. "Let Japan Choose." FOR AFFS, 20 (October
        1941), 61-72.

        On the eve of the war, Staley writes that Japan has
        crawled onto a limb by joining the Axis. His
        recommendation is that the Americans, Dutch, and British,
        as well as the Soviet government in Siberia, not saw off
        the limb but, rather, make a reasonable offer to negotiate
        backed by firmness and military preparations.

688. Stanley, Roy M., II. PRELUDE TO PEARL HARBOR. New York:
        Charles Scribner's Sons, 1982. 213 pp.

With over 250 photographs, Stanley, a photo intelligence expert, provides a pictorial essay on events in China before the entry of the United States. He points out that American intelligence underrated Japanese military power.

689. Storry, Richard. THE DOUBLE PATRIOTS: A STUDY OF JAPANESE NATIONALISM. Boston: Houghton Mifflin, 1957.

Perhaps with some exaggeration, Storry highlights the schemes of extreme nationalists to steer Japan toward war.

690. Sudo, Hajime. "I Flew in Japan's Secret Air Corps." RAF FLYING REV, 15 (November 1959), 37-38.

Cmdr. Sudo flew in secret photo reconnaissance missions of U.S. bases in the Pacific by the Third Air Corps some seven months prior to December 7, 1941. His aircraft, a Mitsubishi Type 96 land-based attack bomber, carried no markings. A Japanese naval auxiliary ship provided navigation assistance to the pilots. Unaware that the Americans had radar capabilities, the Japanese denied any knowledge of the high altitude flights when the U. S. protested against them.

691. Sufrin, Mark. "Undercover." WW II, 1 (September 1986), 8, 62-65.

This is the story of Marine Lt. Col. Earl Ellis. Convinced that the Japanese would launch a surprise attack against the U. S., he undertook a self-assigned reconnaissance mission in 1923. He died under curious circumstances in the Palau Islands.

692. Taniguchi, Masaru. THE SOLDIER'S LOG: 10,000 MILES OF BATTLE. Tokyo: Hokuseido Press, 1940. 176 pp.

NE

693. Tansill, Charles C. BACK DOOR TO WAR: THE ROOSEVELT FOREIGN POLICY, 1933-1941. Chicago: Henry Regnery, 1952. 690 pp.

The distinguished historian turns from his usual judicious methodology to deliver an emotional, uneven critique of Roosevelt. One of Tansill's basic views--and perhaps this accounts for his specific criticisms of U.S.-Japanese relations in 1941--is that U.S. policy in Asia throughout the Twentieth Century centered on China rather than Japan. The book sharply rebukes Roosevelt for

what Tansill feels is a high-handed, unconstitutional
usurpation of foreign policy decisions. For Tansill,
Roosevelt turned to foreign adventures to distract
attention from the failures of his domestic program.

694. Tarling, Nicholas. "'A Vital British Interest': Britain,
      Japan, and the Security of Netherlands India in the
      Inter-War Period." J SEA STUD, 9 (September 1978),
      180-218.

      With extensive archival research, Tarling sets forth the
      reasons for each of the three powers (Japan, Britain and
      Holland) adapting a restrained attitude in the Far East.

695. Taylor, Sandra C. ADVOCATE OF UNDERSTANDING: SIDNEY GULICK
      AND THE SEARCH FOR PEACE WITH JAPAN. Kent, OH: Kent
      State University Press, 1985. 260 pp.

      With excellent research and graceful style, Taylor tells
      of a missionary who worked for closer ties between the
      United States and Japan. Although not directly related to
      the war, the book serves as a useful introduction to
      American-Japanese relations on the eve of World War II.

696. Taylor, Sandra C. "The Ineffectual Voice: Japan,
      Missionaries and American Foreign Policy, 1870-1941."
      PAC HR, 53 (February 1984), 20-38.

      Taylor reports on the inability of American missionaries
      to counter the image in the United States of Japan as a
      militaristic, imperialist power. Her analysis identifies
      reasons for this negative image (e.g., the contrast with
      China, domestic racism in the United States, and Protestant
      missionaries' passivity in trying to enlist assistance from
      the State Department). According to the author, the
      inability of the American missionaries is particularly
      significant in light of the democratic tendencies in Japan
      during the 1920s.

697. Taylor, Sandra C. "Japan's Missionary to the Americans:
      Sidney L. Gulick and America's Interwar Relationship
      With the Japanese." DIP HIST, 4 (Fall 1980), 387-407.

      During the 1920s and 1930s, Taylor writes, Gulick raised
      some controversy with his views on immigration restriction,
      treatment of Japanese-Americans, and calls for tolerance of
      Japan's policy in Asia. With exhaustive research, Taylor
      sets her analysis within the context of Gulick's general
      goals of fair treatment and the avoidance of war.

698. Theobald, Robert A. THE FINAL SECRET OF PEARL HARBOR: THE
      WASHINGTON CONTRIBUTION TO THE JAPANESE ATTACK. New
      York: Devin-Adair Co., 1954. 202 pp.

      Rear Admiral Theobald boldly asserts that Roosevelt
      maneuvered the American people into war by exposing the
      fleet at Pearl Harbor. Moreover, the author argues, there
      would have been no Pearl Harbor if Roosevelt had not
      withheld MAGIC revelations from the two Hawaiian
      commanders. As part of Theobald's scenario, leaders in
      Washington decided to cover up Roosevelt's harsh handling
      of relations with Japan. Theobald was commanding the
      Destroyer Battle Force at Pearl Harbor when the attack
      came. He feels that Kimmel and Short were made scapegoats
      for mismanagement in Washington. The book lacks balance or
      a sense of even-handedness.

699. THE TIMES. London. FAR EAST CRISIS: DREAM AND REALITY.
      London: THE TIMES, 1941. 125 pp.

      The book reprints contemporary articles on Asia that
      appeared in the newspaper.

700. Tinch, Clark W. "Quasi-War Between Japan and the U. S. S.
      R., 1937-1939." WORLD POL, 3 (January 1951), 174-199.

      Tinch, using sources in Russian, claims that two Soviet
      victories (although, he says, the accounts of both sides on
      Nomonhan differ) contributed to a Russo-Japanese modus
      vivendi and eventually a 1941 neutrality pact.

701. Tokyo Press Club. JAPAN SURVEYS THE EUROPEAN WAR. Tokyo:
      Tokyo Press Club, 1940. 88 pp.

      The members of the Tokyo Press Club present the opinions
      of "leading Japanese thinkers and writers" on the war in
      Europe. The views are not uniform, but in general there is
      a perception of Anglo-American enmity towards Japan as well
      as skepticism about the intentions in Moscow (ostensibly
      supporting Germany). With regard to Asia, the consensus
      held that nationalists, especially in India and Indonesia,
      could become more prominent if the war in Europe were to be
      prolonged.

702. Toland, John. INFAMY: PEARL HARBOR AND ITS AFTERMATH.
      Garden City, NY: Doubleday, 1982. 366 pp.

      This book attracted much attention by using the term

"massive cover-up" and by asserting that Kimmel and Short
were falsely made into scapegoats. Asserting that the
previous nine official investigations have produced enough
information to disprove the "official" version (i.e., only
Kimmel and Short were to blame), Toland offers his own
"Tenth Investigation." Of interest is Toland's discussion
of the naval rivalries on the Second Deck (2nd Floor of
Navy Building) which extended to the battle scene,
especially the U.S. defeat at Savo and the Turner-vs.-Noyes
feud. Although he says there were no heroes or villains on
either side, the author, in his concluding section, is
particularly critical of U.S. leadership and not the
Japanese in the onset of the war. The comedy of errors on
December 6-7, Toland points out, only makes sense as part
of a charade or massive cover-up. Roosevelt and the inner
circle, he charges, knew in advance that Pearl Harbor would
be attacked. Of special note is Toland's dismissal of the
controversy over the "winds execute" message as quixotic
and his claim that Gen. Marshall attended a reunion of the
1st Infantry Company, ROTC (at the University Club on 16
Street, N.W. in Washington, D.C.) the night of December 6.

703. Tolischus, Otto D. TOKYO RECORD. New York: Reynal and
      Hitchcock, 1943. 462 pp.

      In January 1941, the author replaced Hugh Byas as a U.S.
correspondent in Japan for the NEW YORK TIMES and THE TIMES
of London. The book is based on his journal entries and
observations. Of interest is his view that Konoye was the
"only possible man" capable of keeping the conflicting
forces in Japan in balance. Arrested on December 8 for
conveying information to "foreign agents harmful to Japan,"
Tolischus, while in jail, realized the "savage element" and
"pre-Hellenic" character of the Japanese. He returned to
New York aboard the GRIPSHOLM.

704. Tolley, Kemp. "Admiral Ambassador Standley." SHIPMATE, 40
      (September 1977), 27-29.

      Tolley concocts a tenuous argument which tries to
connect Standley's alleged maverick behavior as a member of
the Roberts Commission with the admiral's subsequent
assignment to the Soviet Union. Both Standley and Stark
knew too much, the author states, and that is why both were
shipped out of Washington in 1942. Of interest are the
unproven charges and innuendoes about the circumstances
surrounding the U.S. entry into the war that Tolley says he
learned from Standley.

705. Tolley, Kemp. CRUISE OF THE LANIKAI: INCITEMENT TO WAR.
      Annapolis, MD: Naval Institute Press, 1973. 345 pp.

      The LANIKAI, a 67-ton auxiliary (two-masted) schooner,
was part of a small force Adm. Hart had left on Luzon
before moving the Asiatic Fleet to Java. Tolley, commander
of the LANIKAI, argues that on direct orders on December 1,
1941, from Roosevelt, his ship and two others were
deliberately set as trip-wires to provoke a Japanese
attack. Nothing came of the episode--the Lanikai never
made it past Corregidor--when the attack at Pearl Harbor
superseded the president's orders. The crew eventually
arrived safely in Australia.

706. Tolley, Kemp. "Pearl Harbor Revisited." SHIPMATE, 44
      (December 1981), 13-15.

      Tolley reviews the political-intelligence controversy
surrounding the origins of the war. Of interest is the
author's report, based on indirect evidence, that
Roosevelt, Hopkins, Marshall, Stark and Knox all met
secretly during the early hours of December 7, 1941.
Another hearsay account by the author has Kimmel saying
that, if he had known of the approaching Japanese naval
force, he would have dispersed the fleet to the south
rather than confront the attackers. Tolley makes clear his
acceptance of John Toland's claim that leaders in
Washington had foreknowledge of the Japanese force en route
to Hawaii.

707. Tolley, Kemp. "The Strange Assignment of USS LANIKAI."
      USNIP, 88 (September 1962), 70-83.

      Tolley raises questions about Roosevelt's order on
December 2, 1941, to dispatch three little ships (including
Tolley's LANIKAI) in harm's way. Was this an attempt to
rig a tripwire for war? Tolley includes an interesting
epilogue about the LANIKAI's perilous journey to Australia
after war had been declared.

708. Tolley, Kemp. "The Strange Mission of the LANIKAI." AMER
      HERITAGE, 24 (October 1973), 56-61, 93-95.

      The article includes photos of the ship and of Tolley in
1941. He calls his orders to sail the LANIKAI were "oral,
informal, and brief." En route to its precarious station
when the war began, the ship eventually ran the blockade at
Corregidor. Tolley believes the president was seeking to
provoke a Japanese attack on the LANIKAI.

709. Trefousse, Hans L., ed. PEARL HARBOR: THE CONTINUING
       CONTROVERSY. Malabar, FL: Kreiger, 1982. 215 pp.

       Here is an excellent starting point for the questions
       surrounding Pearl Harbor. Trefousse presents a
       knowledgeable introduction as he addresses the
       historiographical interest and presents pertinent
       documents.

710. Trefousse, Hans L., ed. WHAT HAPPENED AT PEARL HARBOR?
       DOCUMENTS PERTAINING TO THE JAPANESE ATTACK OF DECEMBER
       7, 1941, AND ITS BACKGROUND. New York: Twayne, 1958.
       324 pp.

       Trefousse offers an excellent, well-balanced
       introduction. The collection of documents is divided into
       five general parts: Hawaii, Washington, Tokyo, Berlin, and
       the final U.S.-Japanese diplomatic negotiations.

711. United States. Congress. Joint Committee on the
       Investigation of the Pearl Harbor Attack. PEARL HARBOR
       ATTACK: HEARINGS BEFORE THE JOINT COMMITTEE ON THE
       INVESTIGATION OF THE PEARL HARBOR ATTACK. Washington,
       D.C.: GPO, 1946. 39 vols.

712. United States Congress. REPORT OF THE JOINT COMMITTEE ON
       THE INVESTIGATION OF THE PEARL HARBOR ATTACK.
       Washington, D.C.: GPO, 1946. 580 pp.

       The vast amount of material obtained in the hearings
       remains the most comprehensive collection about the
       continuing controversy. Some of the information was
       declassified by the United States Government and Allied
       Governments especially for these hearings. The Report
       criticizes a broad segment in both the Army and Navy,
       including the commanders at Hawaii, the War Plans Division,
       and the collection-dissemination of intelligence. As
       corrective measures, the Report calls for unity of command,
       the integration of intelligence operations, and review of
       statutory restrictions (such as the Communications Act of
       1934) that may have inadvertently aided the enemy. See
       especially the additional view of Sen. Keefe and the
       minority views of Sens. Ferguson and Brewster.

713. United States. Department of State. PEACE AND WAR
       1931-1941. Washington, D.C.:" GPO, 1943.

       In this publication, the State Department intended to

resolve some of the controversy surrounding the Japanese
attack at Pearl Harbor. The narrative and supporting
documents are presented for the historical record in
defense of U.S. prewar policies. Questions and criticisms
about the U.S. government's policies and actions, however,
persisted even after this volume appeared. Despite some
omissions and distortions, the book provides a valuable
introduction to the origins of the war.

714. United States. Federal Communications Commission.
      TRANSCRIPTS OF SHORT WAVE BROADCASTS: TOKYO.
      Washington, D.C.: GPO, 1941.

      NE

715. United States. Office of Strategic Services. JAPANESE
      SEIZURE OF FRENCH INDOCHINA. Washington, D.C.: OSS,
      1945. 3 pp.

      This OSS report emphasizes the weakness of the French
colonial administration which was unable to resist the
increasing Japanese demands.

716. United States. War Department. Bureau of Public
      Relations. THE BACKGROUND OF OUR WAR. New York:
      Farrar and Rinehart, 1942. 279 pp.

      This narrative is drawn from special lectures prepared
early in the war for an orientation on the origins of the
war. Self-described as an "objective" summary, the book
emphasizes Japanese aggression since 1931 in forcing war
upon the United States.

717. Utley, Jonathan G. "Conflicting Policies Over the
      Sino-Japanese War: State, War, and Navy, 1937-1941."
      PROC CONF WAR DIP (The Citadel, 1976), 154-161.

      Incorporating archival materials, Utley examines the
"civil-military conflict" over foreign policy. The three
U.S. departments, he writes, rarely agreed on Asian policy;
moreover, Utley reports that Navy often ignored State and
Army often acquiesced in policies it considered untenable

718. Utley, Jonathan G. "Diplomacy in a Democracy: The United
      States and Japan, 1937-1941." WORLD AFFS, 139 (Fall
      1976), 130-140.

      Utley analyzes the friction in the United States
between professional diplomats and groups of private

citizens (especially so-called internationalists who
favored a U. S. embargo) about trading with Japan.

719.   Utley, Jonathan G.   GOING TO WAR WITH JAPAN, 1937-1941.
       KNOXVILLE, TN: University of Tennessee Press, 1985.
       238 pp.

       Utley undertakes the commendable task of trying to
understand how diplomacy failed to avoid war. Examining
the ideas influencing the decisions of foreign policy
leaders, the author takes as his focus the execution of
policy by lower and mid-level bureaucrats. A major premise
is that the U.S. government's actions did not always
reflect high-level policy decisions. For example, Utley
argues that the economic freeze against Japan in July 1941
exceeded Roosevelt's intentions--even though the president
never sought to reverse the course that lower-level
bureacrats, like Dean Acheson, had arranged. Secretary of
State Hull receives much attention in this book. Of
special interest is Utley's description of Hull as burned
out and tired of fighting the bureaucracy by November 1941.

720.   Utley, Jonathan G.   "Upstairs, Downstairs at Foggy Bottom:
       Oil Exports and Japan, 1940-41." PROLOGUE, 8 (Spring
       1976), 17-28.

       Arguing that the proliferation of independent
organizations decreased the power of policy makers, Utley
demonstrates how lower-level bureaucrats, such as the
Foreign Funds Central Committee, undermined the moderate
economic policy towards Japan preferred by Roosevelt and
Hull. The article incorporates extensive research from
archival records.

721.   Van Alstyne, Richard W.   "Myth Versus Reality in the Far
       Eastern Policies of the United States." INT AFFS
       (London), 32 (July 1956), 287-297.

       The noted historian concludes that it is not possible to
give intelligible definition to U.S. objectives in the Far
East. Roosevelt, according to the author, did not think
carefully through his "bright ideas."

722.   Van Dyke, Hartford. THE SKELETON IN UNCLE SAM'S CLOSET.
       Vancouver, WA: Van Dyke Publications, 1973. 112 pp.

       The author repeats the charge that Roosevelt maneuvered
the country into war so that he could salvage his political
career. No new sources or material provided.

723. Van Mook, H.J. NETHERLANDS INDIES AND JAPAN: BATTLE ON
      PAPER, 1940-1941. New York: W.W. Norton, 1944. 138
      pp.

      Here is an authoritative account of the Netherlands-
      Japanese relations just prior to the war. The author
      served as economic director for the NEI. His narrative
      emphasizes political-economic affairs.

724. Vinacke, Harold M. "The Roosevelt White Paper and the
      Tanaka Memorial." AMERASIA, 5 (January 1942), 473-481.

      The author criticizes both American and Japanese
      policies during the previous decade.

725. Waller, George M., ed. PEARL HARBOR: ROOSEVELT AND THE
      COMING OF THE WAR. Lexington, MA: D.C. Heath, 1976.
      247 pp.

      Waller presents a collection that, in sum, offers a
      balance of viewpoints between Roosevelt's critics (Beard,
      Chamberlain, Tansill, Barnes, and Flynn) and defenders
      (Rauch, Feis, Sherwood, Bailey, Schlesinger, Perkins, and
      Langer-Gleason). The bibliogrophic essay is a useful guide
      to the historiographical literature.

726. Welles, Sumner. "Roosevelt and the Far East." HARPER'S
      MAG, Pt. I: 202 (February 1951), 27-38; Pt. II: 202
      (March 1951), 70-80.

      Here is a review of Roosevelt's knowledge of diplomatic
      history, geography, and geo-politics. In 1937, according
      to the author, Roosevelt considered an embargo against
      Japan. Welles claims from 1937 to 1941 he opposed the
      cutoff of oil and scrap iron to Japan generally out of
      concern about angering a beserk nation.

727. Welles, Sumner. SEVEN DECISIONS THAT SHAPED HISTORY. New
      York: Harper and Brothers, 1951. 236 pp.

      Describing these seven fateful decisions, Welles
      explains that he took part in each one. See especially his
      description of "Far Eastern Policy Before Pearl Harbor"
      (Chapter 3). Of interest, too, are his ideas for the
      postwar world which are contained in the final chapter.

728. Wellings, Joseph H. "Pearl Harbor Lessons and Problems of
      Today." SHIPMATE, 37 (March 1974), 16-18.

R ADM Wellings (ret.) argues the need for a strong,
well-prepared defense.

729.   Wheeler, Gerald E. "Isolated Japan: Anglo-American
        Diplomatic Cooperation, 1927-1936." PAC HR, 30 (May
        1961), 165-178.

        According to Wheeler, the rise of totalitarian powers
        (1927-1936) stopped international progress toward arms
        limitation or disarmament. In a new departure for U.S.
        foreign policy, Wheeler says that London and Washington
        agreed on naval parity between themselves, but the two
        Western democracies offered no statement of hope on parity
        for Japan, especially on the Japanese demand for a common
        upper limit.

730.   Wheeler, Gerald E. PRELUDE TO PEARL HARBOR: THE UNITED
        STATES NAVY AND THE FAR EAST, 1921-1931. Columbia, MO:
        University of Missouri Press, 1963.

        Here is a sound analysis of the efforts by the U.S. Navy
        between the wars to remain strong in the Pacific,
        especially in the face of growing Japanese power. The
        narrative covers the period from the Washington Naval
        Conference to the Manchurian crisis. Despite the overdrawn
        title, Wheeler's excellent report does not venture into the
        inevitability of events a decade later.

731.   Wheeler, Gerald E. THE ROAD TO WAR: UNITED STATES AND
        JAPAN, 1931-1941. St. Louis, MO: Forum Press, 1977. 14
        pp.

        This brief summary presents the diplomatic highlights of
        prewar relations between the two countries. The
        Bibliography is helpful.

732.   White, John A. "As the Russians Saw Our China Policy." PAC
        HR, 26 (May 1957), 147-160.

        Using Russian-language sources, White surveys
        Sino-American relations after 1917. White finds that the
        Soviet criticism of appeasing Japan in China during the
        1930s is infused with Cold War rhetoric.

733.   Wilds, Thomas. "How Japan Fortified the Mandated Islands."
        USNIP, 81 (April 1955), 400-407.

Using evidence which emerged from the war crimes trials, Wilds explains how the Japanese developed bases in the Mandates, despite being bound by international agreements not to do so. Two tables in the article list detailed information about the Japanese buildup. In 1934 the Japanese started a construction program that led to four important bases (Saipan, Palaus, Truk, and Ponape), but Wilds points out that the Japanese began intensive efforts to fortify the islands only two years before the war--not as part of some long-range scheme.

734. Wohlstetter, Roberta. "Cuba and Pearl Harbor: Hindsight and Foresight." FOR AFFS, 43 (July 1965), 691-707.

Analyzing both disasters (Pearl Harbor and Bay of Pigs) for the United States, the author points out that abundant information was available beforehand in both cases. Calling attention to the vagaries of interpretation and the "cry wolf" phenomenon, she emphasizes that the problem of warning is inseparable from the problem of decision.

735. Wohlstetter, Roberta. PEARL HARBOR: WARNING AND DECISION. Stanford, CA: Stanford University Press, 1962. 426 pp.

Here is a classic in the literature. Reconstructing the events which led to Pearl Harbor, Wohlstetter concludes that the United States government failed to anticipate Pearl Harbor not for lack of relevant materials but because of a plethora of irrelevant ones. No one agency held all the intelligence information, she points out, and it simply was not practical to send all the material to all theaters. According to the author, U.S. intelligence failed to produce an accurate image of Japan's assessments and capabilities. Exploring the lessons of this intelligence failure, she warns that a measure of uncertainty must be accepted. Of note, too, is Wohlstetter's criticism that, despite the clutter of intelligence information, complacency plagued Army-Navy coordination, especially in Hawaii. This book remains indispensable to any serious study of the subject.

736. Wohlstetter, Roberta. "Sunday, December 7, 1941, and the Monday Morning Quarterbacks." AF & SPACE DIG, 49 (December 1966), 82-86.

Twenty-five years after the fact, the author insists that no single piece of evidence clearly shows that an attack was coming at Pearl Harbor (despite an "impressive array" of fragmentary evidence). Critical of the "amateur

evaluator," Wohestetter, an acknowledged expert, argues
persuasively that American officials failed to anticipate
the attack not for want of relevant materials but because
of a plethora of irrelevant materials which impeded
insightful analysis.

737.   Yoshikawa, Takeo and Norman Stanford. "Top Secret
        Assignment." USNIP, 86 (December 1960), 26-39.

        Here is an account of Yoshikawa's experiences as an
        intelligence officer at the Japanese consulate in Honolulu
        on the eve of the war.

738.   Young, A. Morgan. "Japan's Diversions." CONTEMP REV, 160
        (September 1941), 157-161.

        The author, ex-editor of THE JAPANESE CHRONICLE, argues
        that Japanese interference in Thai and Indochinese affairs
        is a diversion from their quaqmire in China.

739.   Young, A. Morgan. "Japan Negotiating for Victory."
        CONTEMP REV, 160 (December 1941), 342-347.

        The author praises China's steadfastness in resisting
        Japanese aggression. Japan, he notes, is negotiating in
        Washington for political gains in Asia, especially China.

II.B. DIPLOMACY OF THE WAR AGAINST JAPAN

1. UNITED NATIONS COALITION (AND FRIENDS)

740.   Adamic, Louis. DINNER AT THE WHITE HOUSE. New York:
        Harper, 1946. 276 pp.

        After writing a book which called for national groups in
        the United States to promote democracy abroad (TWO WAY
        MESSAGE, 1941), Adamic attracted Roosevelt's attention.
        The President wanted to arrange a meeting between Adamic
        and that unrepentant imperialist, Winston Churchill. Here
        is the story of that meeting. The affair turned out to be
        one of dubious significance, but the book does offer
        useful portraits of Franklin and Eleanor Roosevelt as well
        as Churchill.

741.   Barclay, Glen St. John. "Australia Looks to America: The
        Wartime Relationship, 1939-1942." PAC HR, 46 (May
        1977), 251-271.

        Barclay reports that Australians were surprised and

shocked to learn that massive U.S. aid would not be
immediately available after the Japanese attack at Pearl
Harbor. During these early years of the war, according to
Barclay, Australia felt unappreciated by London and
Washington. The article is well written and based on
solid research.

742. American Historical Association. OUR CHINESE ALLY.
      Madison, WI: U. S. Armed Forces Institute, 1944. 61
      pp.

      Here is a brief overview written at a time when China
      was being debunked in the United States.

743. Bartlett, C.J. "Inter-Allied Relations in the Second World
      War." HISTORY, 63 (October 1978), 390-395.

      Bartlett explores some strengths and weaknesses of the
      Anglo-American wartime alliance as reflected in the recent
      (circa 1978) historigraphy.

744. Beitzel, Robert. THE UNEASY ALLIANCE. New York: Knopf,
      1972. 404 pp.

      Beitzel produces a penetrating analysis of the Big Three
      diplomacy with emphasis on Europe. The useful study does,
      however, rely heavily on Churchill's volumes for the
      British point of view rather than on archival records
      (which were just being opened at the time of this book's
      publication).

745. Bell, Roger. "Australian-American Disagreement Over the
      Peace Settlement With Japan, 1944-46." AUS OUTLOOK, 30
      (February 1976), 238-262.

      With extensive research, Bell analyzes the differences
      between the two partners--and the ascendancy of American
      policy--about the projected peace terms for Japan.

746. Bell, Roger J. UNEQUAL ALLIES: AUSTRALIAN-AMERICAN
      RELATIONS AND THE PACIFIC WAR. Melbourne, Australia:
      Melbourne University Press, 1977. 278 pp.

      Basing his account on thorough research through newly
      opened archival materials in Australia and the United
      States, Bell analyzes the wartime evolution of relations
      between these two Pacific partners. In addition, he
      assesses the impact of the war on their postwar relation-
      ship. His arguments refute the notions that (1) Australia

severed the "umbilical cord" to the United Kingdom and
(2) Australian-American relations remained closely aligned
during and after the war.

747. Chan, K. C. "The Abrogation of British Extraterritori-
ality in China, 1942-1943: A Study of Anglo-
American-Chinese Relations." MOD ASIAN STUD, 11
(April 1977), 257-291.

Integrating primary and secondary sources, Chan argues
that the negotiations to end these treaty rights reflected the basic views of each party during the
Twentieth Century. The British (pragmatic about China),
the Americans (waves of idealism and romanticism), and the
Chinese (shrewd diplomacy) reached agreement in January
1943.

748. Chan, K.C. "Britain's Reaction to Chiang Kai-shek's
Visit to India, February 1942." AUSTRALIAN J POL
HIST, 21 (August 1975), 52-61.

In early 1942, the Generalissimo expected Burma to
fall and grew anxious about the position of India
(which held strategic importance for China). Thus, he
wanted to travel to India to persuade the leaders of the
Congress Party to enter the war. Using British archival
materials and some Chinese sources, the author describes
not only the British bureaucratic struggle to control the
movements of the Generalissimo and Madame Chiang but also
an account (indirectly via British intelligence reports) of
their meetings with the leaders of India.

749. Colville, John. THE FRINGES OF POWER. New York: W. W.
Norton, 1985. 796 pp.

Colville draws on his diaries from his years as a
private secretary to the British prime minister
(1939-1945). Here is an inside view of the higher
direction of the war from the British perspective. The
author includes "Biographical Notes," in which he offers
frank assessments of the great and not-so-great. Note
Churchill's request to Truman about the testing of the
atomic bomb: "Let me know whether it is a flop or a plop."

750. Cohen, Warren I. AN INTERPRETIVE HISTORY OF SINO-AMERICAN
RELATIONS. New York: John Wiley, 1971.

Here is a masterful survey particularly strong for the
prewar, war, and immediate postwar years. Cohen has built

upon careful, thorough research, and he does not fail to
divulge his frank assessments of key personalities and
events.

751. Confesor, Tomas. "To Leyte and Washington in 1944-5."
      BULL AMER HIST COLL (Manila), 10 (July-September 1982),
      63-85.

      NE

752. Darilek, Richard E. A LOYAL OPPOSITION IN TIME OF WAR.
      Westport, CT: Greenwood Press, 1976. 239 pp.

      Darilek offers a well-researched study of the Republican
      Party during the war. His focus is on the role of the
      minority party in the formulation of foreign policy. As
      Darilek points out, only gradually did the acceptance of a
      bipartisan foreign policy emerge. The main priority was
      keeping the party united.

753. Dennet, Raymond. "Isolationism is Dead." FE SURVEY, 13
      (July 26, 1944), 135-137.

      Dennet, editor of this journal, argues that the debate
      between isolationists and internationalists has ended. For
      him, the key postwar question is how far should the U.S.
      get involved in cooperative action?

754. Doenecke, Justus D. "The Strange Career of American
      Isolationism, 1944-1954." PEACE & CHANGE, 3 (Summer,
      Fall 1975), 79-83.

      Identifying two views--"hypocritical paranoids" and
      far-sighted statesmen-- of isolationists, Doenecke
      describes several strengths and weaknesses of the movement.
      His narrative incorporates a present-day context.

755. Donnison, F.S.V. BRITISH MILITARY ADMINISTRATION IN THE
      FAR EAST, 1943-46. London: H. M. S. O., 1956.
      483 pp.

      This book is part of an excellent series on British
      participation in the war under the general editorship
      of J. R. M. Butler. The author has a lengthy record of
      service in India and Burma. His book centers on the
      history of the military administration of occupied
      territories. In November 1942, the British government
      sought to end the confusing system of separate chains
      of command for military and civil affairs by conferring

military commissions on the civil administrators. Topics
covered in this thoroughly researched study include
finance, relief, trade, industry, refugees, law, and
labor. Donnison does first-rate work in describing
British (administrative) discomfort caused by the emerging
nationalist movements in Southeast Asia and in explaining
British problems with the Chinese over Hong Kong and
Burma.

756. Dorman-Smith, Sir Reginald. "Civil Government Under
     Invasion Conditions." UNITED SERV INSTITUTE INDIA J, 73
     (1943).

     NE

757. Edwards, P.G. "Evatt and the Americans." HIST STUD
     (Melbourne), 18 (October 1979), 546-560.

     NE

758. Eggleston, George T. ROOSEVELT, CHURCHILL AND THE WORLD
     WAR II OPPOSITION. Old Greenwich, CT: Devin-Adair,
     1979. 255 pp.

     This book amounts to an autobiography of someone who
     served on the editorial boards of LIFE, SCRIBNER'S
     COMMENTATOR, and READER'S DIGEST. Although a
     self-described isolationist, Eggleston did join the Navy
     after the attack at Pearl Harbor. His prewar criticisms of
     the Roosevelt administration exposed him, he feels, to
     harassment from high levels outside the Navy during his
     tour of duty in Washington. The author believes that
     Washington was riddled with communists during the war, and
     he expresses astonishment that Roosevelt's policy, stated
     by Secretary of the Navy Frank Knox, was not to oppose the
     Communist Party in the United States. Even more disturbing
     for Eggleston, the Roosevelt administration actually
     encouraged the hiring of communists. The book is weakest
     when the author relies on secondary works to "prove"
     Roosevelt's secret diplomacy.

759. Eliot, George Fielding. "Australia, Keystone of Far
     Eastern Strategy." FOR AFFS, 20 (April 1942), 402-409.

     Eliot maintains that Australia can be the key to victory
     over Japan by becoming the central base for military
     operations in the Pacific.

760. Emmerson, John K. "China-Burma-India." FOR SERV J, Part

I: 54 (October 1977), 8-12, 33-34; Part II: 54
(November 1977), 11-14, 33-34.

Emmerson recounts his fourteen-month tour in CBI for the
State Department (including some time as a uniformed
member, without rank, of Merrill's Marauders). Stilwell
dominates Emmerson's attention in this article, and the
author describes the extreme feelings throughout the
theater for and against the American commander. Emmerson
still believes that the lack of attention to his advice to
appeal directly to the Japanese people with some offer of
hope beyond unconditional surrender unnecessarily prolonged
the war.

761.   Esthus, Raymond A.   FROM ENMITY TO ALLIANCE: U.S.-
       AUSTRALIAN RELATIONS, 1931-1941. Seattle: WA:
       University of Washington Press, 1964. 180 pp.

       Here is an excellent analysis of American-Australian
       relations during the decade prior to the war, from their
       sharp differences over trade and shipping to their
       rapprochement. Esthus argues that each side only gradually
       perceived the common interests of the two countries and the
       need for mutual cooperation.

762.   Feis, Herbert. CHURCHILL, ROOSEVELT, STALIN: THE WAR THEY
       WAGED AND THE PEACE THEY SOUGHT. Princeton, NJ:
       Princeton University Press, 1957. 692 pp.

       Enjoying special research privileges (e.g., Truman's
       correspondence with Churchill and Stalin, State Department
       files, Army records), Feis presents what is essentially the
       official version of American perspectives on the breakup of
       the coalition and the onset of the Cold War. Stalin, Feis
       concludes, aggressively orchestrated the global expansion
       of communism and therefore undermined the alliance. Of
       interest is Feis's suggestion that Truman may have delayed
       the meeting at Potsdam to await the testing of the atomic
       bomb. Despite the passage of time and the new sources
       available since this book was written, Feis's work is still
       valuable and useful.

763.   FIRST LADY OF CHINA. New York: IBM, 1943. 204 pp.

       Here is an account of Madame Chiang Kai-shek's visit to
       the United States. Many photos accompany the narrative.

764.   Fischer, Louis. DAWN OF VICTORY. New York: Duell, Sloan
       and Pearce, 1942. 270 pp.

In this survey, Fischer looks at the U. S. role in the
war. His narrative includes a report on the colonial
problems facing the British.

765. Friedrich, Carl J., ed. AMERICAN EXPERIENCES IN MILITARY
       GOVERNMENT IN WORLD II. New York: Rinehart, 1948.
       436 pp.

       The authors contributing to this collection served as
       "occupationeers" at the staff and field levels. They do
       not hold back in their criticisms of the military
       government system. The articles from the Pacific Theater
       deal primarily with Guam, Korea, and Japan. Each
       addresses common areas of military/civil administration
       (e.g., health, education, and labor).

766. Friend, Theodore. BETWEEN TWO EMPIRES: THE ORDEAL OF THE
       PHILIPPINES, 1929-1946. New Haven: Yale University
       Press, 1965. 312 pp.

       Friend bases his tightly reasoned work on interviews and
       multi-archival, multi-lingual research. His detailed
       analysis includes an examination of the shifting relations
       between Quezon and MacArthur.

767. Glendevon, Lord. "Ghandi and Linlithgow: A Critical
       Commentary." INDO-BR R, 11 (December 1984), 15-27.

       NE

768. Gormly, James L. THE COLLAPSE OF THE GRAND ALLIANCE,
       1945-1948. Baton Rouge, LA: Louisiana State University
       Press, 1987.

       This well-researched analysis traces the disintegration
       of the coalition and the onset of the Cold War. Gormly
       identifies the main problems besetting the alliance even
       before the German surrender.

769. Grajdanzev, Andrew. "The Soviet Far East and the Pacific
       War." FE SURVEY, 11 (May 4, 1942), 105-111.

       The author describes the state of armed neutrality
       between the Soviet Union and Japan. These strained
       relations, he points out, are working in the best
       interest of the Allies.

770. Habibuddin, S.M. "American Response to the Emergence of

Pakistan, 1940-47." INDIAN J POL, 13 (April-August
1979), 47-62.

NE

771. Habibuddin, S.M. "American Response to the Indian National
Movement, 1941-1947: A Reassessment." ITIHAS, 3
(January-June 1975), 111-140.

NE

772. Harbutt, Fraser. "Churchill, Hopkins, and the 'Other'
Americans: An Alternative Perspective on Anglo-American
Relations, 1941-1945." INT HIST REV, 8 (May 1986),
236-262.

The author argues that Churchill developed a system of
communications with a few influential Americans (e.g.,
Hopkins and Harriman). The Prime Minister, according to
Harbutt, ignored the "Europe" and "Empire" options urged
upon him by Eden and Beaverbrook. There is little on
Pacific affairs here.

773. Hathaway, Robert M. AMBIGUOUS PARTNERSHIP: BRITAIN AND
AMERICA, 1944-1947. New York: Columbia University
Press, 1981. 410 pp.

The author focuses on the assumptions British and
Americans held about each other and the world. His
analysis incorporates discrete topics that touch on the war
against Japan (e.g., colonialism, international trade, and
the terms of the peace). Although he argues against the
concept of a "special relationship," Hathaway points out
that the label has been much abused. In addition, he feels
that fading British power by 1944 may have contributed to a
sense of intellectual superiority in London when dealing
with Americans. The research is thorough; the analysis is
thought-provoking.

774. Haycock, Ronald J. "The 'Myth' of Imperial Defense:
Australian-Canadian Bilateral Military Cooperation,
1942." WAR & SOC, 2 (May 1984), 65-84.

Haycock did extensive research through archival records
and private collections in Australia and Canada to test the
ideal theory of imperial defense policy. He finds the
theory wanting in his investigation of Australian-Canadian
relations in 1942. The government of Australia, facing a
crisis and fearing a Japanese invasion, sought assistance

from Canada. As Haycock shows, the effort proved fruitless
as the Canadian government furnished only vague responses
and, in the end, did nothing.

775. Hess, Gary R.   AMERICA ENCOUNTERS INDIA, 1941-1947.
     Baltimore, MD: The Johns Hopkins Press, 1971.

     With painstaking research, Hess analyzes U.S. reviews on
     the ascendancy of Indian nationalism. The author is
     particularly effective in delineating Roosevelt's dilemma
     about wartime India: sympathetic to the aspirations of the
     people and an opponent of colonialism; yet unwilling to
     pressure the unrepentant Churchill and jeopardize the unity
     of the Allied coalition. This is an excellent survey of a
     crucial period.

776. Hilliker, J.F.   "Distant Ally: Canadian Relations with
     Australia During the Second World War." J IMP COMM
     HIST, 13 (October 1984), 46-67.

     The author served in the Canadian Department of External
     Affairs. In this well-researched article, Hilliker argues
     that the war narrowed differences between the two countries
     and set the context for goodwill in their postwar
     relations. He emphasizes, however, that close cooperation
     did not exist between the two countries during the war.

777. Jauhri, R.C.   "Linlithgow to Wavell: A Study of the
     Succession of the Viceroyalty." J INDIAN HIST, 56
     (April 1978), 183-195.

     NE

778. Johnston, George H.   PACIFIC PARTNER.   New York: Duell,
     Sloan and Pearce, 1944. 227 pp.

     Johnston provides a clear picture of Australia's war
     effort. The author, an Australian correspondent, is
     writing specifically for the benefit of the U. S. public.
     This well-written report also serves as an introduction to
     life in Australia (e.g., currency, politics, leaders,
     social life, linguistic differences, etc.). Despite the
     disclaimers, the view is rosy.

779. Jones, F.C., Hugh Borton, and B.R. Pearn. SURVEY OF
     INTERNATIONAL AFFAIRS, 1939-1946: THE FAR EAST, 1942-
     1946. London: Oxford University Press, for Royal
     Institute for International Affairs, 1955. 589 pp.

This volume is a classic. Despite the relatively early
date, it remains essential reading for any serious study of
the war against Japan. The authors roam far beyond the
military fronts in their analysis. Special emphasis is
given to political affairs and postwar planning. The texts
of principal documents are contained in the Appendix.

780. Kimball, Warren F., ed. CHURCHILL AND ROOSEVELT: THE
        COMPLETE CORRESPONDENCE. Princeton, NJ: Princeton
        University Press, 1984. 3 vols.

        In a model of editorial work, Kimball assembles the
        complete correspondence between the two leaders. The
        Roosevelt-Churchill exchanges numbered almost 2,000 (1,161
        from Churchill; 788 from Roosevelt) items during a 5-1/2
        year period. Kimball's essays and notes provide helpful
        references without intruding on the main feature--this
        wide-ranging, historic interchange.

781. Kimball, Warren F. "Churchill and Roosevelt: The Personal
        Equation." PROLOGUE, 6 (Fall 1974), 169-182.

        Kimball identifies various stages of the unique
        relationship. During the final stage, Kimball essentially
        agrees with the disclosure that Roosevelt neither initiated
        nor even wrote to Churchill from February to April 1945.
        Here is an authoritative report.

782. Kirk, Grayson L. and Walter R. Sharp. UNITING TODAY FOR
        TOMORROW. New York: Foreign Policy Association, 1942.

        The authors describe the need for the United Nations to
        stay together and cooperate not only in the war but also in
        the postwar era.

783. Kitchen, Martin. "Winston Churchill and the Soviet Union
        During the Second World War." HIST J, 30 (June 1987),
        415-436.

        The author feels that Churchill seriously misjudged
        Stalin and imagined a personal friendship where none
        existed.

784. Kolko, Gabriel. THE POLITICS OF WAR: THE WORLD AND UNITED
        STATES FOREIGN POLICY, 1943-1945. New York: Vintage
        Book, 1968. 685 pp.

        In a heavily documented interpretation, Kolko goes
        beyond the combat to examine U. S. political and economic

goals. He calls attention to the limits of American
capabilities and ideology. His tone is sharply critical.
See especially his treatment of the decision to use the
atomic bomb, which emerges, he claims, from a wartime
context that had already brutalized U. S. leaders into
insensitivity by 1945.

785. Lash, Joseph P. ROOSEVELT AND CHURCHILL, 1939-1941: THE
      PARTNERSHIP THAT SAVED THE WORLD. New York: W.W.
      Norton, 1976. 528 pp.

      Lash writes in bold, confident tones about the dawning
      period of this partnership. Describing the similarities
      and differences of each leader, Lash emphasizes how each
      regarded--and used--power. The book is well researched and
      includes the personal involvement of the author.

786. Lattimore, Owen. AMERICA AND ASIA. Claremont, CA:
      Claremont Colleges, 1943. 52 pp.

      In the two contemporary lectures presented in this book,
      Lattimore discusses problems not only in winning the war
      but also in the postwar era.

787. Lewin, Ronald. "Leadership in Coalition Warfare: World War
      II: A Tangled Web." RUSI, 127 (December 1982), 16-20.

      Lewin critizes the British wartime view that the United
      States owed them a debt for standing alone against the
      enemy. Arguing that Washington had a clearer view of U.S.
      interests than London had of British interests, the noted
      historian believes that no "special relationship" with
      Britain existed in American minds. Of interest is his
      description of CBI as the "greatest theatre of illusion in
      the war." Slim's compaign in the Irrawaddy, for example,
      is dismissed as "wholly irrelevant."

788. Lindsell, Lt. Gen. Sir Wilfrid. "India's Wartime Effort."
      MIL REV, 33 (January 1954), 80-85.

      The author praises the "immense" contributions (e.g.,
      jute and textile industries, munitions, supplies, and
      equipment) made by India.

789. Loewenheim, Francis L., Harold D. Langley, and Manfred
      Jonas, eds. ROOSEVELT AND CHURCHILL: THEIR SECRET
      WARTIME CORRESPONDENCE. New York: E.P. Dutton, 1975.
      805 pp.

The editors offer the heart of the extensive
correspondence between the two leaders. The texts of
approximately 550 messages are included from a total of
what the editors say is about 1,700. There are many
background and expository notes as well as an excellent
introduction on the relationship between Churchill and
Roosevelt.

790. Louis, William Roger. IMPERIALISM AT BAY: THE UNITED
      STATES AND THE DECOLONIZATION OF THE BRITISH EMPIRE,
      1941-1945. New York: Oxford University Press, 1978.
      594 pp.

      Louis explores the rich themes in international
relations of power politics, humanitarian concerns, and
economic rivalries as he analyzes Anglo-American
development of trusteeship from 1941 to 1945. Combining
formidable research through primary sources and an
expertise in British imperialism (through extensive
publications), Louis has produced a scholarly masterpiece
and an eminently readable book.

791. Love, Peter. "Curtin, MacArthur and Conscription,
      1942-43." HIST STUD, 17 (October 1977), 505-511.

      Love maintains that MacArthur was behind Curtain's
proposal to deploy outside of Australia those who had been
compulsorily enlisted into the Citizen Military Force.
According to Love, while MacArthur was giving military
advice, Curtin was acting within the broader context of
securing more American aid.

792. McMahon, Robert J. "Anglo-American Diplomacy and the
      Reoccupation of the Netherlands East Indies." DIP HIST,
      2 (Winter 1978), 1-23.

      Both the native population and the Dutch sought U.S.
support for their postwar plans. With the Americans and
British pressing the Dutch to talk with the Indonesian
leaders, McMahon feels that this established an important
precedent for future mediation efforts by outside parties.

793. Mathews, Basil J. UNITED WE STAND: THE PEOPLES OF THE
      UNITED NATIONS. Boston: Little, Brown, 1943. 366 pp.

      Mathews presents a brief summary of each of the
thirty-two United Nations. Here is a quick, reliable
reference, which offers information such as population,
political-economic-social conditions, and historical

background.

794. May, Ernest R. "The Development of Political-Military
      Consultation in the United States." POL SCI Q, 70 (June
      1955), 161-180.

      Here is an excellent account of the wartime
      organizational relationship among the Army, Navy, and State
      Department. May points out that until late 1941 the State
      Department had been virtually excluded from Army-Navy
      contingency plans for war throughout U. S. history.
      Tracing the various steps from Roosevelt's personal
      arrangements to Hull's Standing Liaison Committee (1943) to
      SWNCC, May emphasizes the limited policy-making roles each
      inter-agency group played. SWNCC, for example, would only
      work on problems referred to it--none of which involved
      policy decisions. The postwar phase, the NSC, answered an
      enduring organizational need, according to May.

795. Ministry of Foreign Affairs of the U.S.S.R. CORRESPONDENCE
      BETWEEN THE CHAIRMAN OF THE COUNCIL OF MINISTERS OF THE
      U.S.S.R. AND THE PRESIDENTS OF THE U.S.A. AND THE PRIME
      MINISTERS OF GREAT BRITAIN DURING THE GREAT PATRIOTIC
      WAR OF 1941-1945. Moscow: Foreign Languages Publishing
      House, 1957. 2 vols.

      The material presented here appears to be authentic.
      There seems, however, to be some omissions.

796. Muir, Peter. THIS IS INDIA. New York: Doubleday, 1943.
      237 pp.

      Here are the contempary observations of an American
      reporter who travelled throughout India for almost 18
      months. He focuses on political-economic-social affairs.

797. Nash, Walter. NEW ZEALAND: AWAKENING DEMOCRACY. New
      York: Duell, Sloan and Pearce, 1943. 335 pp.

      First Minister of New Zealand to the United States, Nash
      describes his country's war effort. The propaganda motives
      are well disguised.

798. Neild, Eric. WITH PEGAEUS IN INDIA. Aldershot, Eng.:
      Col. F. G. Neild, 1970. 110 pp.

      NE

799. Neumann, William L. AFTER VICTORY: CHURCHILL, ROOSEVELT,

STALIN AND THE MAKING OF PEACE. New York: Harper and Row, 1967. 212 pp.

Here is an examination of the diplomacy of peace-making efforts by fallible men. Neuman is not unduly critical of the Yalta decisions, but he does fault Roosevelt for being willing to overpay for his objectives. In addition to discussing assessments of the three leaders, Neumann analyzes the Japanese treaty of 1951 in its international context.

800. Nicholas, H.G., ed. WASHINGTON DESPATCHES, 1941-1945: WEEKLY POLITICAL REPORTS FROM THE BRITISH EMBASSY. Chicago: University of Chicago Press, 1981. 700 pp.

Most of the reports were compiled by Isaiah Berlin. This is a goldmine of information about both the American political process and British perspectives of that process. The British were anxious that U.S. public opinion would force a shift of resources from the war against Germany to the war against Japan.

801. Pacy, James S. "British Views of American Diplomats in China." ASIAN AFFS, 8 (March-April 1981), 251-261.

Pacy, a professor of political science, gives brief sketches of the British assessments. See especially those entries for Johnson, Gauss, Hurley, and Stuart.

802. Parker, Harold T. "Reflections on Thucydides and Some Aspects of Modern Coalition War." S ATL Q, 78 (Winter 1979), 73-83.

Parker examines an ancient view of coalition warfare that remains useful. For example, Thucydides identifies general features of coalitions: (1) they form slowly, (2) leaders are torn by conflicting calculations which affect grand strategy, (3) each partner must contribute to a truly united effort if victory is to be attained, and (4) they always fall apart before the final peace is made.

803. Patterson, Ernest Minor, ed. "The United Nations and the Future." ANNALS AMER ACAD POL SOC SCI, 228 (July 1943), 1-107.

The United Nations is the theme of this issue. See especially the articles by Sergio Osmena ("The United Nations and the Philippines"), M. J. Bonn ("The Future of Imperialism"), and Ruth Benedict ("Recognition of Cultural

Diversities in the Postwar World").

804. Powell, Daniel, ed. IDEAS IN CONFLICT. Glenview, IL:
        Scott, Foresman, 1975. 176 pp.

        Among these selected readings, see especially the
        sections on the Japanese-Americans and on the atomic bomb.

805. Raman, T.A. REPORT ON INDIA. New York: Oxford University
        Press, 1943. 231 pp.

        The author, a reporter in India, describes the situation
        in his country and India's contribution to the war.

806. Raman, T.A. WHAT DOES GANDHI WANT? New York; Oxford
        University Press, 1942. 117 pp.

        Raman, a reporter and Indian nationalist, supports
        Gandhi's political program. There are extensive excerpts
        from the Indian leader's speeches and writings.

807. Reynolds, David. "Competitive Cooperation: Anglo-American
        Relations in World War II." HIST J, 23 (March 1980),
        233-245.

        Reynolds argues that "competitive cooperation" is the
        best description for Anglo-American wartime relations.
        Countervailing pressures kept the two allies together.
        While unusually close, the relationship should not be held
        to unreasonable standards by historians, according to
        Reynolds.

808. Reynolds, David. THE CREATION OF THE ANGLO-AMERICAN
        ALLIANCE, 1937-1941: A STUDY IN COMPETITIVE
        COOPERATION. Chapel Hill, NC: University of North
        Carolina Press, 1981. 397 pp.

        In this masterful account, Reynolds sets out two
        purposes: to analyze the creation of the wartime
        Anglo-American alliance and to analyze the nature of that
        alliance. The book divides the relationship into three
        parts: 1937-1940, when the British held the lead;
        1940-1941, a period of confused equilibrium; and 1941, when
        the United States self-consciously asserted its potential
        as a great power. Japan and Asia, according to Reynolds,
        formed an important part of this evolutionary process.
        Examining their areas of agreement and difference, Reynolds
        characterizes the relationship as "competitive
        cooperation." Of interest is Reynolds' integration of

domestic pressures and the cultural framework of each of
the democratic partners. Reynolds has control of his
extensive research; moreover, he writes clearly and
judiciously.

809.   Rizvi, Gowher.   "The Congress Revolt of 1942: A Historical
       Revision." INDO-BR R, 11 (June 1985), 62-71.

       NE

810.   Sbrega, John J.   ANGLO-AMERICAN RELATIONS AND COLONIALISM
       IN EAST ASIA, 1941-1945. New York: Garland, 1983.   332
       pp.

       Drawing upon research through a wide variety of public
       and private primary sources in the United States and the
       United Kingdom, the author highlights certain strengths and
       weaknesses of the Anglo-American alliance. Within the
       context of colonialism, Sbrega examines key issues such as
       the formulation of war (peace) aims, the controversy
       surrounding the outbreak of the war with Japan, Indochina,
       territorial trusteeship, the structure of Asia in the
       postwar era, and some unintended consequences of the
       decision to use the atomic bomb. Some uncommon documents
       are reproduced in the Appendix.

811.   Sbrega, John J.   "Anglo-American Relations and the
       Selection of Mountbatten as Supreme Allied Commander,
       South East Asia." MIL AFFS, 46 (October 1982), 139-145.

       In this prize-winning article, Sbrega analyzes the
       selection process in London and in Washington for someone
       to command the newly organized SEAC. Before the episode
       had ended with the consensus choice of Mountbatten, ten
       other names had been proposed and rejected by one side or
       the other. The author draws from public archives and
       private collections in both countries.

812.   Stephens, Ian.   MONSOON MORNING. Mystic, CT: Laurence
       Verry, 1967.   291 pp.

       Here is the personal account of the editor of a Calcutta
       newspaper who supported the British in the war. The book
       reveals his astute observations on the war and on political
       affairs in India.

813.   Thorne, Christopher.   ALLIES OF A KIND: THE UNITED STATES,
       BRITAIN, AND THE WAR AGAINST JAPAN, 1941-1945. New
       York: Oxford University Press, 1978.   772 pp.

Here is a masterpiece of historical research and
analysis. Thorne integrates multi-archival research,
private collections, interviews, and secondary literature
to offer a remarkable wartime survey of Anglo-American
relations in the war against Japan. The book deals with
areas of cooperation and conflict within the special
relationship--areas that include India, Southeast Asia,
Australia, China, postwar Japan, and colonialism. Also,
Thorne highlights certain shared racial assumptions of
these two allies of a kind. The material in the chapter
endnotes is almost as fascinating as the text itself. Of
special interest is Thorne's gift for providing
capsule--and revealing--comments about wartime figures,
great and small.

814.   Thorne, Christopher. THE ISSUE OF WAR: STATES, SOCIETIES,
       AND THE FAR EASTERN CONFLICT, 1941-1945. London: Oxford
       University Press, 1985. 364 pp.

       Thorne integrates the international context of the war
against Japan. His dual purpose is to analyze (a) the
impact of the war on the states involved; and (b) the
course of international relations, especially among the
Asian states, during the war. In his words, Thorne seeks
to "abrogate the boundaries between Western and non-Western
history." The book is a synthesis of a vast research
undertaking that cuts across international (archival)
boundaries.

815.   Thorne, Christopher. RACIAL ASPECTS OF THE FAR EASTERN WAR
       OF 1941-1945. London: Oxford University Press, 1982.
       377 pp.

       The book reproduces Thorne's Raleigh Lecture material
from 1980. The noted historian builds on some of the
themes he developed in ALLIES OF A KIND, but he raises new
issues for further study.

816.   United States. Congress. Senate. Committee on Armed
       Services and Committee on Foreign Relations. MILITARY
       SITUATION IN THE FAR EAST. Washington, D.C.: GPO,
       1951. 5 vols.

       The hearings (82nd Cong., 1st sess.) inquired into the
relief of MacArthur by Truman. This is, however, a rich
source of material on the war against Japan and the
immediate postwar years.

817. United States. Congress. Senate. Committee on the
        Judiciary. INSTITUTE OF PACIFIC RELATIONS. Washington,
        D.C.: GPO, 1952. 15 vols.

        Some of the political material that emerged during this
        inquiry pertains to the war. IPR conducted a series of
        international conferences during the war that produced a
        broad and varied body of information on the postwar era.

818. Varg, Paul. CLOSING THE OPEN DOOR: SINO-AMERICAN
        RELATIONS, 1936-1946. East Lansing, MI: Michigan State
        University Press, 1973. 300 pp.

        Here is an analysis of shifting perspectives and
        situations between the two countries. Varg focuses on the
        personal role Roosevelt played in shaping U.S. relations
        with China.

819. Williams, J.E. "Chiang Kai-Shek's Intervention in Indian
        Politics." INT RELATIONS, 5 (May 1977), 49-70.

        The author identifies two instances of Chinese meddling:
        the Generalissimo's visit to India with his wife and his
        letters of support to imprisoned Indian leaders. Both
        episodes are treated by Williams as part of Sino-British
        relations in 1942.

820. Woodward, Sir E. Llewelyn. BRITISH FOREIGN POLICY IN THE
        SECOND WORLD WAR. London: HMSO, 1970-1976. 5 vols.

        Here is the official history of British foreign policy
        during the war. Each volume reflects Woodward's exhaustive
        research and command of the sources. Of note is his care
        not to exaggerate Anglo-American areas of friction just
        because, as he says, "the documents pile up around them" --
        a warning that many historians have failed to heed! See
        especially his sections on China, postwar planning for the
        Far East, and the projected international organization.
        Despite his sometimes uncritical acceptance of official
        British views, this is an indispensable source in the study
        of the diplomacy of the war. His citations serve as an
        introduction to the sources in the Public Record Office for
        the Foreign Office and diplomatic missions abroad. A
        one-volume summary (actually a detailed outline of the
        five-volume study) appeared in 1962 (596 pp.).

821. Wright, Quincy. "The End of Extraterritoriality in China."
        AMER J INTL LAW, 37 (April 1943), 286-289.

Wright marks this decision as a morally important step--a landmark in progress toward a universal community of states.

II.B.1.a. Allied Conferences

822. Dean, Vera Micheles. FROM CASABLANCA TO TEHERAN--WITH TEXTS OF DOCUMENTS. New York: Foreign Policy Association, 1944. 312 pp.

Here is a thoughtful contemporary account of some wartime conferences. The texts of the documents serve as the basis for her analysis.

823. Edmonds, Robin. "Yalta and Potsdam: Forty Years Afterwards." INT AFFS (London), 62 (Spring 1986), 197-216.

The author served in the British Diplomatic Service. This article offers a number of his views on the two wartime conferences. For example, Edmonds feels that no mature consideration of the use of the atomic bomb took place in 1945. Also he reports that at Potsdam the Soviets never disclosed the existence of their own uranium project (which had been under way since 1942). The Soviet scientist Kurchatov had predicted in 1945 that the Soviet Union would develop an atomic bomb within five years; he took only four.

824. Neumann, William L. MAKING THE PEACE, 1941-1945: THE DIPLOMACY OF WARTIME CONFERENCES. Washington, D.C.: Foundation for Foreign Affairs, 1950. 101 pp.

Here is a convenient overview of the diplomatic conferences from Argentia through Yalta.

825. Sainsbury, Keith. THE TURNING POINT; ROOSEVELT, STALIN, CHURCHILL, AND CHIANG KAI-SHEK, 1943: THE MOSCOW, CAIRO AND TEHERAN CONFERENCES. New York: Oxford University Press, 1985. 373 pp.

In this interpretive history, well grounded in primary and secondary sources, Sainsbury emphasizes the significance of the Teheran Conference. Arguing that the 1943 meeting provided the framework for the Yalta decisions, the author is critical of the American approach to postwar questions.

826. United States. Congress. House of Representatives.

Committee on Foreign Affairs. WORLD WAR II
INTERNATIONAL AGREEMENTS AND UNDERSTANDING ENTERED INTO
DURING SECRET CONFERENCES CONCERNING OTHER PEOPLES.
Washington, D.C.: GPO, 1953. 138 pp.

Here is a summary of some secret decisions reached as
opposed to a detailed analysis. There are no startling
revelations.

827. United States. Department of State. AGREEMENTS REACHED AT
      THE CAIRO, TEHRAN, YALTA, AND POTSDAM CONFERENCES:
      IMPLEMENTATION AND UNITED STATES POLICY. Washington,
      D.C.: GPO, 1948. 51 pp.

The U.S. government sought to end speculation about
alleged secret deals and questionable diplomatic practices
during the war by issuing this summary. It remains useful
as an indication of some of the agreements reached at the
wartime conferences.

828. United States. Department of State. FOREIGN RELATIONS OF
      THE UNITED STATES (1939-1945). Washington, D.C.: GPO,
      1956-1969.

These volumes, arranged chronologically by geographical
location, are indispensable to the study of United States
wartime diplomacy. The comprehensiveness of the documents
(diplomatic messages, memoranda, etc.) and the explanatory
editorial notes combine to make this series a documentary
model. There are some important omissions, however,
because of contemporary classification, delays in the
declassification process, clearances not granted by other
U.S. governmental agencies or foreign governments, and the
sheer volume of the material. Citations for archival
locations are provided. See especially the separate
volumes within the series which deal with the various
wartime conferences. In addition to the proceedings of the
plenary and sub-committee meetings as well as the
conference agreements and commuiniques, these volumes
contain extensive material on the State Department's
preparation, particularly the briefing papers, for each
conference. Thus, the reader has access to convenient
summaries of the evolving U.S. position during the war in
most of the key questions. These special conference
volumes within the FOREIGN RELATIONS OF THE UNITED STATES
series are:

     (a) CONFERENCES AT WASHINGTON (1941-1942) AND
          CASABLANCA (1943). (1968).

      (b)   CONFERENCES AT WASHINGTON AND QUEBEC, 1943.
           (1961).

      (c)   CONFERENCES AT CAIRO AND TEHRAN, 1943. (1970).

      (d)   CONFERENCE AT QUEBEC, 1944. (1972).

      (e)   CONFERENCES AT MALTA AND YALTA, 1945. (1955).

      (f)   CONFERENCE AT BERLIN [POTSDAM], 1945. (1960,
           2 vols.).

829. United States. Office of War Information. UNITED NATIONS
      CONFERENCES: FROM THE ATLANTIC CHARTER TO SAN
      FRANCISCO. London: OWI, 1945.

      Here is a summary for the general public of the
conferences and some of the key decisions reached at each.
The OWI also provides the texts of some conference
communiques.

II.B.1.a.i. Teheran

830. Eubank, Keith. SUMMIT AT TEHERAN. New York: William
      Morrow, 1985. 528 pp.

      The author considers this 1943 summit the crucial
meeting of the war. Emphasizing Roosevelt's desire to meet
Stalin, Eubank states that the president deliberately
distanced himself from Churchill in order to improve his
appeal to the Soviet leader. Overall, Eubank criticizes
the American position and policies regarding this
conference.

831. Mayle, Paul D. EUREKA SUMMIT: AGREEMENT IN PRINCIPLE AND
      THE BIG THREE AT TEHRAN, 1943. Wilmington, DE:
      University of Delaware Press, 1987. 210 pp.

      Mayle gives a brief overview of the diplomatic
conference. Perhaps the key achievement of the meeting, he
suggests, is the strengthening of the coalition.

II.B.1.a.ii. Yalta

832. Buhite, Russell D. DECISIONS AT YALTA: AN APPRAISAL OF
      SUMMIT DIPLOMACY. Wilmington, DE: Scholarly Resources,
      1986. 176 pp.

Only a small portion of this study is devoted to Asian affairs. The author seems unconvinced of the efficacy of summitry. He is especially critical of an ill-prepared Roosevelt who, Buhite says, had no specific objectives. Consequently, the President granted too many concessions to Stalin to gain the entry of the Russians into the war against Japan--a war, Buhite feels, that Stalin would have entered in any event.

833. Bundy, McGeorge. "The Test of Yalta." FOR AFFS, 27 (July 1949), 618-629.

The After the election of February 1945 and Yalta, Bundy contends, U.S.-Soviet relations began to deteriorate. The author maintains that Roosevelt and Churchill never granted anything they could have withheld--except perhaps the Kuriles. The Russians, for Bundy, "contrived to lose friends and alienate people."

834. Clemens, Diane Shaver. YALTA. New York: Oxford University Press, 1970. 356 pp.

Clemens praises the "spirit of Yalta." On Far Eastern issues, she observes that "Allied amity reigned unimpaired."

835. Fenno, Richard F., Jr., ed. THE YALTA CONFERENCE. Boston: D. C. Heath, 1955. 112 pp.

The book is part of the Heath "Problems in American Civilization" series. Fenno arranges his selections to analyze the conference on three levels: (a) Roosevelt's decision-making procedures, (b) the problem of responsibility, and (c) substantive account of the decisions reached. The bibliographical essay is still of some use, though long outdated.

836. Glagolev, N. "Historic Example of Cooperation." SOVIET MIL REV, No. 1 (January 1980), 36-38.

On the thirty-fifth anniversary of the Yalta agreements, the author feels that a continuation of the spirit of that conference in the Crimea might have produced an alternative to the Cold War. According to the author, however, the United States embarked instead on policies of aggression and expansion.

837. Hammen, Oscar J. "The `Ashes' of Yalta." S ATL Q, 53 (October 1954), 477-484.

Hammen, a history professor, emphasizes Roosevelt's insistence at the Crimean conference that China play an important role in the postwar era. The president also believed, according to the author, that U.S. power would influence Soviet behavior.

838. Hudson, G.F. "The Lesson of Yalta." COMMENTARY, 17 (April 1954), 373-380.

The British author, a historian and political analyst, calls his article "the cost of by-passing the democratic process." He is astounded that Roosevelt not only excluded Secretary Stettinius but also ignored the "splendid" briefing studies in preparing for Yalta. Obsessed with preserving Big Three unity, Roosevelt, according to the author, ignored the weaker nations.

839. Leahy, William D. "Notes on the Yalta Conference." WISC MAG HIST, 38 (Winter 1954), 67-72, 110-113.

Leahy, a Wisconsin resident, dips into his contemporary notes to offer flashbacks to the Yalta Conference. These include his recollections that: the president's health showed no sign of deterioration; neither Stalin nor Churchill shared Roosevelt's optimisim about the international organization; Stalin said the Soviet Union would want no reparations from Japan and would support the KMT; and the UN coalition would keep the peace long into the postwar era. Leahy says he had no feeling at the time that Yalta was a betrayal or sellout.

840. Leffler, Melvyn P. "Adherence to Agreements: Yalta and the Experiences of the Early Cold War.: INT SECURITY, II (Summer 1986), 88-123.

Incorporating an intensive research effort, Leffler examines each of the five categories of decisions reached at Yalta. He finds that both the Soviet Union ("substantial shortcomings") and United States departed from the accords. In the Far East, the author observes, there was much room for postwar confusion as Truman hardly knew of the secret Yalta agreements.

841. Lyons, Eugene. "Appeasement in Yalta." AMER MERCURY, 60 (April 1945), 461-468.

Lyons feels that a corrupt bargain was struck at Yalta. Critical of the perceived contemporary need to placate the

Soviet Union, he asks, why rejoice because an ally decided
to behave like an ally?

842.   Rodine, Floyd H.   YALTA--RESPONSIBILITY AND RESPONSE,
       JANUARY-MARCH 1945. Lawrence, KS: Coronado Press,
       1974. 155 pp.

       Confining his analysis to the weeks immediately before
       and after the conference, Rodine examines governmental and
       public reaction in the United States and Britain to Yalta.
       His research relies on the study of parliamentary and
       congressional debates as well as press reactions.

843.   Pan, Stephen C.Y.   "Legal Aspects of the Yalta Agreements."
       INTL LAW, 46 (January 1952), 40-59.

       Here is a perilous exercise of doubtful value.

844.   Snell, John L., ed.   THE MEANING OF YALTA. Baton Rouge,
       LA: Louisiana State University Press,   1956. 239 pp.

       While not a faultless summit meeting, Snell argues, the
       failure to live up to the Yalta agreement, rather than the
       agreement itself, contributed to the postwar dissolution of
       the Allies. See especially in this collection the essay by
       George A. Lensen, "Yalta and the Far East." Emphasizing
       the importance of the October 1944 meeting between Stalin
       and Churchill in laying the foundation for Yalta decisions
       regarding the Far East, Lensen, in turn, highlights the
       roles in Moscow of Harriman and John Deane.

845.   Sontag, Raymond J.   "Reflections on the Yalta Papers." FOR
       AFFS, 33 (July 1955), 615-623.

       Sontag laments the emphasis on the minutes of the Yalta
       meetings. He feels that the U. S. world view, as reflected
       in the pre-conference briefing papers, represents a source
       of pride for all Americans. At the end of the conference,
       he reminds us, American officials rejoiced over the
       promises made by the Soviets. Sontag insists that the Cold
       War was not started by the United States.

846.   Stettinius, Edward R., Jr.   ROOSEVELT AND THE RUSSIANS.
       Garden City, NY: Doubleday, 1949. 367 pp.

       In this view of the Crimean Conference which he attended
       as secretary of state, Stettinius argues that postwar
       fiction arose not from Yalta but the "subsequent failures
       to adhere to the policies Yalta stood for" and the

inability to carry out the Yalta agreements. The book contains good information on the background papers and pre-conference planning for Yalta, especially on China and trusteeship. Of interest is his defense of Alger Hiss's loyalty.

847. Theoharis, Athan. "James F. Byrnes: Unwitting Yalta Myth-Maker." POL SCI Q, 81 (December 1966), 581-592.

According to Theoharis, Byrnes, who served as an adviser to Roosevelt at Yalta, later claimed to have no knowledge of the agreements between Stalin and the president on the Far East. By deliberately feigning ignorance, the author observes, Byrnes helped confirm the allegations of the critics of Yalta.

848. Theoharis, Athan. "Roosevelt and Truman on Yalta." POL SCI Q, 87 (June 1972), 210-241.

This article analyzes the tactics and personalities of the two presidents. According to the author, the United States was more responsible than the Soviets for the manner in which the Cold War developed. In his opinion, Yalta presented attractive opportunities for detente.

849. Theoharis, Athan. THE YALTA MYTHS: AN ISSUE IN U.S. POLITICS, 1945-1955. Columbia, MO: University of Missouri Press, 1970. 263 pp.

Theoharis traces the long shadow of the Yalta agreements--and misperceptions about those agreements--into the postwar era.

850. Warren, Sidney. THE PRESIDENT AS WORLD LEADER. Philadelphia, PA: J.B. Lippincott, 1964.

The book advances the argument that Roosevelt--a realist--did about the best he could do at Yalta.

851. Zacharias, Ellis M. "The Inside Story of Yalta." UN WORLD, 3 (January 1949), 12-16.

The author, a naval intelligence officer, focuses on the question of the entrance of the Soviet Union into the war against Japan. Criticizing the "blunder mongers" who fault U. S. leadership at Yalta, Zacharias claims that the key to understanding the Yalta agreements lies in the erroneous, inflated calculations of the Japanese Order of Battle.

II.B.1.a.iii. Potsdam

852. Bates, John L. "The 'EUREKA' Conference: A Busy Time in
        Teheran." MIL REV, 66 (October 1986), 74-82.

        Col. Bates (U.S.A.) served as liaison officer (and
        Russian-language interpreter) at the conference. His
        observations and the detailed preparations for this
        meeting form the bulk of this personal account.

853. Feis, Herbert. BETWEEN WAR AND PEACE: THE POTSDAM
        CONFERENCE. Princeton, NJ: Princeton University Press,
        1960. 367 pp.

        In this analysis of the Potsdam Conference, Feis traces
        the beginning of the end of the Big Three Alliance. The
        book is well written and thoroughly researched. Feis looks
        elsewhere than the West in seeking reponsibility for the
        deteriorating relations.

854. Mee, Charles L., Jr. MEETING AT POTSDAM. New York:
        M. Evans, 1975. 370 pp.

        Mee provides a detailed account of the proceedings of
        the Potsdam Conference in July 1945. He is at his best in
        turning phrases to describe events and personalities.

855. Paterson, Thomas G. "Potsdam, the Atomic Bomb, and the
        Cold War: A Discussion With James F. Byrnes." PAC HR,
        41 (May 1972), 225-230.

        Here is a report on a memorandum by Senator Warren A.
        Austin of a conversation with Byrnes on August 20, 1945.
        The document (taken from Austin's papers) reveals points of
        interest about the hard bargaining at Potsdam, the use of
        the atomic bomb not only to end the war but also to keep
        the Russians out, Stalin's apparent disinterest in the
        atomic bomb, and Stalin's disclosure to Byrnes that the
        Soviet Union could not enter the war against Japan before
        August 15, 1945.

II.B.1.b. Entry of the Soviet Union

856. Dubinskii, A.M. THE FAR EAST IN THE SECOND WORLD WAR.
        Moscow: Nauka Publishing House, Central Dept. of
        Oriental Literature, 1972. 457 pp.

        The central theme here is the national liberation
        struggle in East and Southeast Asia (with help from the

Soviet Union).

857. Hindus, Maurice G. RUSSIA AND JAPAN. Garden City, NY:
      Doubleday Doran, 1942. 254 pp.

      The author knows the Soviet Union and its vast
      potential. He predicts war between the two powers before
      the "present conflict is over."

858. Kutakov, L. "The Failure of Japan's Foreign Policy at the
      End of the Second World War." INTL AFFS (Moscow), 8
      (August 1985), 78-86.

      In this decidedly pro-Soviet piece, the author rebukes
      the Japanese for their mistakes until the Soviet victories
      in Manchuria compelled Tokyo to end the war. Of special
      interest is his report that at some time after September
      1943 the Japanese sought Swedish help in arranging a peace
      settlement with the British and Americans. Kutakov implies
      that this overture incorporated peace terms obtained
      through direct links to Chiang Kai-shek.

859. Lensen, George A. THE STRANGE NEUTRALITY: SOVIET-JAPANESE
      RELATIONS DURING THE SECOND WORLD WAR, 1941-1945.
      Tallahassee, FL: Diplomatic Press, 1972. 332 pp.

      Having written extensively in the history of
      Russo-Japanese relations, Lensen has done much research in
      the Soviet Union and Japan. (The sources are often
      contradictory.) Of interest is his observation that the
      news of the atomic bomb probably had no impact on Soviet
      plans to enter the war. Also, Lensen acknowledges the
      military role of the Soviets in Manchuria. The appended
      material is useful; see especially "Soviet Treatment of
      American Flyers."

860. May, Ernest R. "The United States, the Soviet Union, and
      the Far Eastern War, 1941-1945." PAC HR, 24 (May 1955),
      153-174.

      Here is a knowledgeable survey of U.S.-Soviet relations
      about the war against Japan. May traces U.S. views about
      the Soviet entry into the war and feels that it was
      mid-1944 before the Soviet Union held an important place in
      American planning for the Far East. By Potsdam, however,
      he concludes that the climate had changed to American
      disinterest in Soviet offers.

861. Morton, Louis. "Soviet Intervention in the War With

Japan." FOR AFFS, 40 (July 1962), 653-662.

Morton upholds the Soviet intervention as a clear
example of subordinating political to military
considerations.

862.   Pegov, N.M. "Stalin on War With Japan, October 1941."
       SOVIET STUD HIST, 24 (Winter 1985-86), 26-38.

       Pegov, who served in the Soviet Foreign Ministry (1st
       Secretary, Maritime Territory Committee), writes of his
       meeting in Moscow with Stalin on October 15, 1941. With
       the immediacy of the German threat, and with his baggage
       already on the train waiting to take him to Vladivostok,
       Stalin discussed the tactics of fighting a war against
       Japan (withdraw to the north, partisan warfare, and save
       the fleet from a confrontation with the stronger Japanese
       fleet). Pegov asserts that from 1941 to 1943, Japan
       "daily" presented the Soviet Union with armed provocations.

863.   Plotnikov, G. "The Far East: Liberation Mission." SOVIET
       MIL REV, n.v. (September 1978), 2-5.

       Despite the "complicated home policy atmosphere" in
       China, Col. Plotnikov states, the Soviet Union decided to
       enter the war and assist the Chinese people.
       Characterizing the use of the atomic bomb as a serious
       crime against humanity, the author also argues that the
       presence of Soviet forces strengthened the Chinese
       revolutionary forces--and those in Vietnam too.

864.   Plotnikov, G. "Liberation Mission in the East." SOVIET
       MIL REV (August 1980), 12-14.

       Citing the Soviet aid to China in 1937-1938, Col.
       Plotnikov tells of the Soviet entry in 1945 just as the
       Japanese were encircling the Chinese Communist 8th Army.

865.   Sternberg, Fritz. "If Russia Fights Japan." ASIA &
       AMERICAS, 45 (June 1945), 269-272.

       The author, a writer and research economist, argues
       that, although the Soviet entry will hasten the defeat of
       Japan, the Soviets will make many demands, especially for a
       buffer zone. He questions whether the United States and
       Britain will be able to cooperate with the Soviet Union for
       common postwar progressive purposes.

866.   United States. Department of Defense. THE ENTRY OF THE

SOVIET UNION INTO THE WAR AGAINST JAPAN, MILITARY PLANS, 1941-1945. Washington, D.C.: GPO, 1955. 107 pp.

Here is a convenient summary of exchanges between the United States and the Soviet Union on the topic. There is no doubt about the desirability of the Soviet entry from the U.S. point of view.

II.B.1.c. Postwar Planning

867. Borchard, Edwin. "Flaws in Post-War Peace Plans." AMER J INT LAW, 38 (April 1944), 284-289.

This contemporary study warns against chasing the rainbow of collective security in the postwar years. The author, an international legal expert, argues that postwar planners should postpone talk of political apparatus until cooperation in the international community has been established. For Borchard, the strengths of international law have been "persuasion and application in practice."

868. Chamberlain, William H. AMERICA: PARTNER IN WORLD RULE. New York: Vanguard Press, 1945. 318 pp.

Composed while the war was in progress, this study identifies some probable postwar problems. Predicting unsatisfactory peace terms (for international stability), Chamberlain is especially critical of U. S. foreign policy and skeptical of professed U. S. ideals. Part of his melancholy prediction, too, springs from his distrust of the Soviet Union.

869. Cundliffe, John B. AGENDA FOR A POSTWAR WORLD. New York: Norton, 1942. 232 pp.

Cundliffe is an economics professor who had worked for the League of Nations and IPR. This early look at the postwar structure calls attention to the need for cooperation within the international community.

870. De Roussy De Sales, Raoul J.J.F. THE MAKING OF TOMORROW. New York: Reynal and Hitchcock, 1942. 338 pp.

This volume attracted much contemporary notice. The author, a French correspondent in the United States, addresses the causes of the war as well as the leading role he expects the United States to play in the postwar era. The book's popular appeal proved short-lived.

871. Fairbank, John K. "William L. Holland and the IPR in
          Historical Perspective." PAC AFFS, 52 (Winter 1979-80),
          587-590.

          Fairbank praises Holland's work, especially in promoting
          the integration of ideas about Asia through the IPR
          conferences.

872. Grajdanzev, Andrew. "TIME, LIFE, and FORTUNE's Pacific
          Post-War Plan." AMERASIA, 6 (October 25, 1942),
          362-370.

          Some of the ingredients in this large plan are: a call
          for an end to imperialism, renunciation of the geopolitical
          balance-of-power thesis, creation of a Pacific Council as
          an adjunct of the United Nations coalition, the return of
          Hong Kong to China, and the stripping of colonies away from
          Japan. The author underscores, however, that the plan not
          only omits mention of the Soviet Union and India but also
          weakens the morale of America's allies by calling upon them
          to surrender their points of advantage.

873. Hoover, Herbert and Hugh Gibson. THE PROBLEMS OF LASTING
          PEACE. Garden City, NY: Doubleday, Doran, 1942. 295
          pp.

          The authors identify and discuss what they refer to as
          seven "dynamic forces" that make for peace and war
          (ideologies, economic pressures, nationalism, imperialism,
          militarism, the complexes of fear-hate-revenge, and the
          will to peace). In seeking the essential foundations for
          peace, the authors evaluate the strengths and weaknesses of
          various peace plans that have been proposed.

874. Institute of Pacific Relations. SECURITY IN THE PACIFIC:
          A PRELIMINARY REPORT OF THE NINTH CONFERENCE OF THE
          INSTITUTE OF PACIFIC RELATIONS, HOT SPRINGS, VIRGINA,
          JANUARY 6-17, 1945. New York: IPR, 1945. 174 pp.

          The conference discussed many of the questions which
          would affect the postwar Pacific community. See especially
          the material on dependent areas and the future of
          colonialism.

875. Institute of Pacific Relations. WAR AND PEACE IN THE
          PACIFIC: A PRELIMINARY REPORT OF THE EIGHTH CONFERENCE
          OF THE INSTITUTE OF PACIFIC RELATIONS, MT. TREMBLANT,
          QUEBEC, 1942.

The two-week conference addressed the central problem of committing a united, cooperative effort among the Allies not only during the war but also in the postwar era.

876. Johnsen, Julia E., comp. EIGHT POINTS OF POST-WAR WORLD
       REORGANIZATION. New York: H. W. Wilson, 1942. 126 pp.

       Part of the "Reference Shelf" series, this volume presents expert contemporary opinions and differing perspectives on a postwar international organization.

877. Johnstone, William C. "Hot Springs Conference." FE
       SURVEY, 14 (January 31, 1945), 16-22.

       Here's a report on the proceedings of the IPR's ninth international conference, January 6-17, 1945. The agenda included economic recovery, race relations, collective security, and the future of dependent areas. Johnstone reports on the widespread skepticism among the delegates that a world organization could act decisively.

878. Nelson, Anna Kasten. "President Truman and the Evolution
       of the National Security Council." J AMER HIST, 72
       (September 1985), 360-378.

       Nelson traces the wartime origins of this 1947 creation. As the NSC developed firmly under the president's control, the author emphasizes the desire to impose order where near-chaos had formerly existed.

879. Notter, Harley A. POST WAR FOREIGN POLICY PREPARATION.
       Washington, D. C.: GPO, 1949. 726 pp.

       Here is a premier study in postwar planning. Notter helped manage the State Department's efforts to shape the directions of U. S. foreign policy after the war. With government officials and other experts, the various sub-committees studied practically every conceivable postwar question in all parts of the world. The book distills almost three hundred boxes of correspondence, notes, minutes, and memoranda associated with this planning apparatus. See especially the material on Southeast Asian nationalism, regional schemes, international trusteeship for dependent peoples, and the U. S. services' desire to control certain strategic areas. The book is indispensable for the study of postwar planning.

880. Welles, Sumner, ed. THE INTELLIGENT AMERICAN'S GUIDE TO
       THE PEACE. New York: Dryden Press, 1945. 370 pp.

Here is an authoritative introduction for the general
public to postwar political-economic problems. Welles is
particularly effective in providing an overview of emerging
dependent people and the role they will play in the postwar
era.

881. Welles, Sumner. THE TIME FOR DECISION. New York: Harper
      and Brothers, 1944. 431 pp.

The book focuses on Welles' postwar ideas about a world
organization (built by a "patient, step-by-step" process)
and the role of the United States. He supports the
promotion of international trade, and he warns about
avoiding the forces of reaction. In the Pacific, Welles
argues that the United States should assist China and
monitor Japan (deprived of "stolen" territories and
disarmed). When he assesses the prewar situation, Welles
affirms that U.S. foreign policies were "neither logical
nor consistent" between the wars, but he maintains,
nevertheless, that Japan's warlike intentions stood in
contrast to the U.S. desire for peace.

882. Willkie, Wendell L. ONE WORLD. New York: Simon and
      Schuster, 1943. 206 pp.

After a global tour in 1942, Willkie issued this plea
for unity and cooperation within the world community. His
ideas and idealism--perhaps marshaled in this book as an
attack against the remaining isolationists/non-interven-
tionists--continue to stir controversy.

883. Wittner, Lawrence S. "When CIA Hearts Were Young and Gay:
      Planning the Cold War." PEACE & CHANGE, 5 (Fall 1978),
      70-76.

The author maintains that OSS analyses of U.S.-U.S.S.R.
relations, particularly a memo on April 2, 1945, shifted
from "fostering Allied cooperation to fomenting Cold War
belligerency." There is no attempt either to put his
arguments in context or to analyze the Soviet position.

II.B.1.c.i. Regional Arrangements

884. Chow, S.R. "The Pacific After the War." FOR AFFS, 21
      (October 1942), 71-86.

Chow speculates on the keys to a stable postwar world.
He especially argues that China should play an important

role in international affairs after the war.

885. Dennet, Raymond. "U.S. Navy and Dependent Areas." F E
         SURVEY, 14 (April 25, 1945), 93-95.

      Questioning the demands of naval leaders to acquire
      strategically important points in the Pacific, Dennet calls
      for mature consideration of postwar policies. He warns
      that other powers will be watching the actions of the
      United States.

886. Dennet, Tyler. SECURITY IN THE PACIFIC AND THE FAR EAST.
         New York: IPR, 1942. 2 pp.

      This short essay on the shape of the postwar structure
      in Asia served as a document for the 8th IPR conference in
      1942.

887. FORTUNE (Editors of). "The United States in a New World:
         Pacific Relations." FORTUNE, 26 (August 1942, Special
         Supplement), 1-33.

      Here is a detailed contemporary survey which, despite
      the early stage of the war, looks to the postwar era.
      Among the ideas presented, note especially the call for
      experimental statehood for Indonesian states, an
      international commission to assume administration of Burma
      and Indochina, the equal partnership of China with the
      U.S., an overall integrated scheme for defense, and a
      canvass of the Japanese people on the retention of the
      emperor system.

888. Johnsen, Julia E., comp. PLANS FOR A POST-WAR WORLD. New
         York: H. W. Wilson, 1942. 238 pp.

      Vice President Wallace, Clark M. Eichelberger, Michael
      Straight, Eugene Staley, D. F. Fleming, and Oswald Garrison
      Villard are some of the respected authors who have
      contributed to this collection. Regional problems,
      including a special bibliography, appear in a separate
      section. Johnsen also provides a list of contemporary
      organizations working on postwar plans. See especially the
      article by Norman Thomas on a postwar world federation.

889. Lattimore, Owen. "The Fight for Democracy in Asia." FOR
         AFFS, 20 (July 1942), 694-704.

      In this contemporary piece, Lattimore discusses the
      character of the war rather than war aims. Refusing to

defend past practices in Asia, he believes that democracy
will be the key to the future of Asia (especially in
China).

890.   Lattimore, Owen. SOLUTION IN ASIA. Washington, DC:
           Infantry Journal Press, 1945. 138 pp.

       The noted Asian scholar sets forth his ideas on the
structure of postwar Asia (particularly China).

891.   Lattimore, Owen. "Yunnan, Pivot of Southeast Asia." FOR
           AFFS, 21 (April 1943), 476-493.

       Lattimore feels that what happens in Yunnan will be
important to the future of Asia. Because Yunnan lies
alongside Burma and Indochina, and because China will
resist being surrounded by a ring of imperialism in the
postwar era, Lattimore argues that Yunnan is where the West
should begin to think about the future of Asia.

892.   Peffer, Nathaniel. BASIS FOR PEACE IN THE FAR EAST. New
           York: Harper and Brothers, 1942. 277 pp.

       In this excellent contemporary analysis, Peffer shows
his understanding of the chief issues which face the
postwar planners. To build a lasting peace, he argues, not
only must Japan be accorded a prominent position in
regional affairs, but also Western powers must realize that
the days   of special privilege in Asia are finished. In
addition, Peffer calls for self-government in Southeast
Asia and the political-economic development of China.

893.   Popper, David H. "America's Alternative to Imperialism."
           AMERASIA, 6 (July 1942), 225-232.

       Instead of a postwar return to imperialism, Popper
argues that Pan-Americanism serves as an excellent model
for systems of regional cooperation.

894.   Potter, Aimee de. SELECTED BIBLIOGRAPHY ON POST-WAR
           RECONSTRUCTION IN THE FAR EAST. New York: American
           Council, Institute of Pacific Relations, 1942.

       This contemporary collection reveals that much thought
had been given to postwar planning in Asia quite early in
the war. This paper was delivered to the 8th conference of
the IPR.

II.B.1.c.ii. Status of Postwar Japan (and Emperor)

895. American Historical Association. WHAT SHALL BE DONE ABOUT
     JAPAN AFTER VICTORY? Madison, WI: U. S. Armed Forces
     Institute, 1945. 62 pp.

     This brief treatment explores some options and handles
     particularly well the question of reparations.

896. Bates, M. Searle. "How Will the War End for Japan?" FE
     SURVEY, 11 (July 13, 1942), 155-158.

     In one of the first public discussions on the topic,
     Bates warns that, without fair postwar opportunities for
     trade and economic development, Japan might return to
     policies of aggression. He also advocates retaining the
     emperor system (with "sensible moderation") and
     implementing the Atlantic Charter.

897. Colegrove, Kenneth W. "What Shall We Do With the Japanese
     Empire?" AMERASIA, 6 (October 25, 1942), 376-381.

     Colegrove gives no clear answer to his question, but he
     warns that the lack of constructive leadership in Japan
     should make Americans pause before destroying Japanese
     institutions and traditions.

898. Fleisher, Wilfrid. WHAT TO DO WITH JAPAN. Garden City,
     NY: Doubleday, 1945. 178 pp.

     Written before the end of the war by a noted
     correspondent, this book calls for strict controls over
     Japan. Reflecting the racial assumptions held by many of
     his contemporaries, Fleisher describes the Japanese people
     as "fanatical," "vindictive," "inscrutable," and "probably
     already planning a war of revenge."

899. Fo, Sun. "The Mikado Must Go." FOR AFFS, 23 (October
     1944), 17-25.

     Sun Fo criticizes the imperial system as the center of
     Japanese aggression. Arguing that progressive and
     democratic elements exist in Japan, he warns that retention
     of the emperor would strengthen the position of Chinese
     reactionaries.

900. Holton, Daniel C. "Shinto in the Postwar World." FE
     SURVEY, 14 (February 14, 1945), 29-33.

     The author, a leading (non-Japanese) expert on Japan,

argues that the Japanese must make changes in their
educational methods and outlook after the war. It is
possible, he writes, to separate the emperor from the
Japanese militarist system.

901. Johnstone, William C. "Must We Keep Japan Strong?" FE
       SURVEY, 11 (November 2, 1942), 225-228.

       The author, a political scientist, reminds U.S. postwar
       planners that the practice of geopolitical power politics
       contains no assurances for stable peace. Americans, he
       points out, need to understand more about Asia.

902. Keesing, Felix M. "Former Japanese Mandated Islands." FE
       SURVEY, 14 (September 26, 1945), 269-271.

       The author, an anthropologist, provides information
       about these islands and discusses possible postwar
       dispositions of the islands.

903. Lin, Hu. "How to Deal With Japan." FOR AFFS, 24 (January
       1946), 253-261.

       The author argues for eradicating militarism in Japan
       and changing the Japanese pattern of thinking. He is
       confident that the Japanese people will repent.

904. Maki, John W. JAPANESE MILITARISM: ITS CAUSES AND CURE.
       New York: A. A. Knopf, 1945. 258 pp.

       Outlining an ambitious program of postwar
       reconstruction, the author argues that the victors should
       help Japan rebuild to a new way of life. Maki sets his
       postwar design within a sound analysis of Japanese history.

905. Molton, Harold G. and Louis Marlio. CONTROL OF GERMANY AND
       JAPAN. Washington, DC: Brookings Institute, 1944.
       116 pp.

       This study explores methods to prevent the
       remilitarization of the enemy and to build up the victim
       countries. Molton (president of Brookings) and Marlio (a
       French industrialist) try to avoid emotion and revanche as
       they concentrate on postwar international enemies.

906. Morita, Hideyuki. "Preliminary Planning in the State
       Department Relative to Post-War Policy Toward Japan."
       AMER REV, (Tokyo), 12 (1978), 209-211.

NE

907. Peffer, Nathaniel. "Occupy Japan?" HARPER'S MAG, 188
      (April 1944), 385-390.

          Peffer fears that through forced occupation, democracy
      will become associated in Japanese minds with the
      humiliation of defeat while militarism will connote the
      golden era. There is no need to occupy Japan, he argues.
      Instead, he wants to render the Japanese incapable of
      further aggression and then leave them alone. Moreover,
      Peffer feels that a modernized China and an industrialized
      Soviet Union would help keep Japan in check.

908. Stewart, John R. "Japan's Manchuria Base." FE SURVEY, 11
      (August 24, 1942), 180-186.

          Pointing out that Manchuria should be a source of
      foodstuffs and raw materials to support Japan's home
      industries, the author feels instead that Japanese economic
      activities there are instead being diverted into
      independent industrial schemes.

II.B.1.c.iii. Concept of Territorial Trusteeship

909. Fox, Annette B. THE DISPOSITION OF ENEMY DEPENDENT AREAS.
      New Haven, CT: Yale Institute of International Studies,
      1945. 19 pp.

          The pamphlet looks to territorial trusteeship, or
      international administration, of the dependent areas after
      the war.

910. Gillchrist, H. "The Japanese Islands: Annexation or
      Trusteeship?" FOR AFFS, 22 (July 1944), 635-642.

          The jurisdiction claimed by the U.S. Navy over captured
      Japanese islands, according to the author, seems to
      conflict with the Atlantic Charter, Cairo Declaration, and
      the Covenant of the League of Nations. After looking at
      some alternatives, Gillchrist argues in favor of a modified
      American mandate system which would not only guarantee
      American interests but also strengthen the principle of
      trusteeship.

911. Habibuddin, S.M. "Franklin D. Roosevelt's Anti-Colonial
      Policy Towards Asia: Its Implications for India,
      Indo-China, and Indonesia (1941-1945)." J INDIAN HIST,
      53 (December 1975), 497-522.

Relying almost entirely on published sources, the author
accepts the traditional view of Roosevelt vigorously and
persistently opposing colonialism. The narrative makes the
point that the West considered the President's views too
radical while the East saw his ideas--especially the
outmoded trusteeships scheme--as behind the times and
lacking an appreciation of the new nationalism.

912. Hall, H. Duncan. "The British Commonwealth and
        Trusteeship." INT AFFS (London), 22 (April 1946),
        199-213.

The article praises the concept of territorial
trusteeship for being at the forefront of human advance.
Identifying the British experience as a precedent for the
principles of trusteeship, Hall calls trusteeship the
"green leading shoots" from the (British) "giant redwood
tree."

913. Holland, Sir Robert. "Trusteeship Aspirations." FOR AFFS,
        25 (October 1946), 118-129.

Besides the welfare of the natives and prospects of
international peace, another goal that emerges under the
UN's international trusteeship system is to promote
independence. The author regrets this trend because he
considers the goal of independence impractical. Instead,
Holland advocates giving full play to democratic
institutions but "within the limits of managerial
requirements."

914. Jacobson, Harold K. "Our Colonial Problems in the
        Pacific." FOR AFFS, 39 (October 1960), 56-66.

Jacobson, a political scientist, calls for review of
American policies as one of the last trusteeship
administrative authorities under the United Nations. It
would be ironic, he warns, if the United States came under
criticism for suppressing dependent peoples.

915. Johnstone, William C. "Trusteeship For Whom?" FE SURVEY,
        14 (June 20, 1945), 156-159.

Describing the Anglo-American proposals to the
trusteeship commission at the San Francisco conference,
Johnstone warns that the success of any trusteeship plan
will depend on moral pressure and the force of world
opinion. The article carries a tone of skepticism.

916.   Kimball, Solon T. "The Crisis in Colonial Administration."
          APP ANTHROP, 5 (Spring 1946), 8-16.

          Kimball asserts that the nationalist uprisings at the
        end of the war carry anthropological significance because
        they represent disturbances in the equilibrium of the
        social system. Highlighting the NEI as a case study, he
        argues that colonial administrations need to employ the
        science of human relations and culture. Any system of
        trusteeship, according to Kimball, will require joint
        participation and responsibility.

917.   Louis, William Roger, ed. NATIONAL SECURITY AND
          INTERNATIONAL TRUSTEESHIP IN THE PACIFIC. Annapolis,
          MD: Naval Institute Press, 1972. 182 pp.

          This collection of articles by officers at the Naval War
        College reveals the tension between interests and the
        nationalist aspirations of the dependent peoples and U.S.
        security. Louis, an expert in the field, writes about the
        concept of "strategic trusteeship," which strikes the
        middle ground for some key geographic locations. See the
        article by Col. Paul B. Haigwood (USMC), "Japan and the
        Mandates." Although Japan did not technically or
        officially fortify the mandates during the prewar years,
        Haigwood points out that commercial contracts with the
        Nanyo Corporation served to meet the needs of the Japanese
        militarists.

918.   Pomeroy, Earl S. "American Policy Respecting the
          Marshalls, Carolines, and Marianas, 1898-1941." PAC HR,
          17 (February 1948), 43-53.

          In this historical survey, Pomeroy contrasts Japan's use
        of the mandated islands with America's failure to develop
        them.

919.   Sandelmann, John. SOME OBSERVATIONS ON THE PROBLEM OF
          SELF-GOVERNMENT IN THE TRUST TERRITORY OF THE PACIFIC
          ISLANDS. Honolulu, HI: Trust Territory Government,
          1953.

          Here is an excellent postwar analysis which serves as a
        practical follow-up to the wartime philosophical
        discussions about the future of dependent peoples.

920.   Sbrega, John J. "Determination versus Drift: The
          Anglo-American Debate Over the Trusteeship Issue,

1941-1945." PAC HR, 55 (May 1986), 256-280.

Relying on public and private collections in the United
States and United Kingdom, Sbrega analyzes Anglo-American
efforts to shape a general policy of trusteeship for
dependent peoples. Originally intended by Roosevelt to
replace prewar colonialism, the concept of trusteeship
underwent some radical changes by the end of the war. See
especially the views of U.S. military leaders about holding
certain strategic areas in the Pacific.

921. Useem, John. "Governing the Occupied Areas of the South
        Pacific: Wartime Lessons and Peacetime Proposals." APP
        ANTHROP, 4 (Summer 1945), 1-10.

Useem critiques the governing procedures of wartime
civil affairs administrators. His report praises the
community councils made up of native leaders and civil
affairs administrators in some parts of Micronesia.

II.B.1.c.iv. Colonialism

922. Buck, Pearl. "American Imperialism in the Making." ASIA &
        AMERICAS, 45 (August 1945), 365-368.

As the war became a bitter struggle for power, Buck
explains, millions of Asians lumped the United States with
the European imperialists. She asks, what will the U.S.
do?

923. Bunce, Arthur C. "The Future of Korea." FE SURVEY, Pt. I:
        13 (April 19, 1944), 67-70; Pt. II: 13 (May 17, 1944),
        85-88.

The author, a professor of economics who lived in Korea
(1928-1934), emphasizes the importance of economic factors
as a prerequisite for true independence (as foreseen in
wartime Allied declarations).

924. Chan, F. Gilbert, ed. NATIONALISM IN EAST ASIA: AN
        ANNOTATED BIBLIOGRAPHY OF SELECTED WORKS. New York:
        Garland, 1981. 170 pp.

Here is an excellent reference source that includes
citations by country for the crucial era at the end of and
immediately following the war.

925. Chan Lau Kit-Ching. "The Hong-Kong Question During the
        Pacific War." J IMP COMM HIST, 2 (October 1973), 56-78.

With research through British archival sources, Chan
examines Hong Kong as a diplomatic issue between the
British and Chinese. Of interest is the report that in
1942 the British seriously considered relinquishing their
claims to the colony.

926. Darby, Phillip. THREE FACES OF IMPERIALISM: BRITISH AND
     AMERICAN APPROACHES TO ASIA AND AFRICA, 1870-1970. New
     Haven, CT: Yale University Press, 1987. 224 pp.

     Darby offers a comparison of British and American views
     during the eras when each country was in what he calls
     "ascendancy." The American era begins at the end of World
     War II.

927. Field, Frederick V. "The Mont Tremblant Conference." FE
     SURVEY, 12 (January 11, 1943), 3-10.

     Here is an unofficial report by an observer on the
     topics discussed at this 1942 IPR conference. See
     especially the material on the future of dependent areas.

928. Frost, Richard A. "Reflections on British Colonial
     Policy." PAC AFFS, 18 (December 1945), 309-320.

     Here is a defense of the British colonial system by the
     secretary of the Royal Institute of International Affairs.
     He is willing, however, to accept a new "International
     Colonial Commission" (with a "peripatetic inspectorate")
     under the projected international organization which would
     report on each colonial administration.

929. Grattan, C. Hartley. "What Will Happen to the British
     Empire?" HARPER'S MAG, 189 (June 1944), 110-116.

     Maintaining that the political balance of power is
     shifting to the four Dominions, Grattan notes that London
     is now seeking support rather than extending it. The
     Dominions, he believes, are not only gaining autonomy but
     also moving closer to their geographical neighbors.

930. Grimal, Henri. DECOLONIZATION: THE BRITISH, FRENCH, DUTCH
     AND BELGIAN EMPIRES, 1919-1963. Boulder, CO: Westview
     Press, 1978. 443 pp.

     The author analyzes the principal stages in the complex
     process of decolonization (and its corollary: the emergence
     of the so-called Third World). Stephan De Vos translated

this 1965 work. Grimal identifies four steps in the
process: (a) preparation (1919-1939); (b) new
relationships (World War II); (c) Asia; and (d) Africa.
The second step seemed to accelerate the process of
divergence. Documents, tables, and maps complement the
narrative. A chronology and biographical profiles are
appended. Of interest is Grimal's treatment of the
influence Christianity and Marxism have upon colonized
peoples and his evaluation of the conflicting pressures
that shaped U.S. wartime attitudes about colonialism.

931. Habibuddin, S.M. "American Attitude to the Great Fast
      Undertaken by Mahatma Gandhi during February 10 to March
      3, 1943." A R HIST STUD, 16 (No. 2, 1976/77), 102-112.

      The author, an academician in India, points out that
      Gandhi did not decide to undertake the fast in Raste.
      Examining American attitudes as revealed in some U.S.
      contemporary journals, the author finds not only general
      disapproval of British policies but also the interest of
      leading officials--Roosevelt, Hull and William Phillips (in
      India)--to help break the deadlock. Unfortunately, as the
      article indicates, failure to reach agreement gave rise to
      some anti-American sentiment in India.

932. Hailey, Lord. THE FUTURE OF COLONIAL PEOPLES. Princeton,
      NJ: Princeton University Press, 1944.

      At the time of writing, Hailey was participating in an
      Anglo-American effort to develop a joint declaration
      concerning the future of dependent peoples. In the book,
      he publicly reveals his enlightened views on British
      colonial policies. He makes clear that British practices
      and objectives require no apologies. His defense includes
      making information available (but not reporting) to some
      international agency.

933. Hargreaves, Alec G. "European Identity and the Colonial
      Frontier." J. EUR STUD, 12 (September 1982), 166-179.

      Hargreaves explores general aspects of the imperial
      "notion." For example, he deals with perceptions of the
      natives as well as racial assumptions of the imperialists.
      The article is of general interest and not focused
      exclusively on Asia.

934. Johnsen, Julia E., comp. INDEPENDENCE FOR INDIA? New
      York: H. W. Wilson, 1943. 292 pp.

Johnsen arranges a well-balanced discussion of the
proposition about India. The collection presents arguments
for both sides. She includes a useful bibliography.

935. Kember, James. "India in International Affairs, 1944-1947:
The Prelude to Independence." INT STUD, 15
(July-September 1976), 365-391.

The author, executive secretary of the New Zealand
Institute of International Affairs, describes the period
when the Allies were planning for peace and India was
moving toward independence. He describes India's policies
and official attitudes, especially in opposing colonialism,
racial discrimination, and totalitarianism. Of note is the
bitterness in India over Churchill's denial that the
Atlantic Charter applied to India.

936. Lasker, Bruno. "A Labor Code for Dependent Peoples." FE
SURVEY, 13 (June 14, 1944), 103-110.

In this report of the discussion on social policy at the
ILO conference, Lasker calls for a postwar labor code for
dependent areas. He writes of labor's new attitude:
"Poverty anywhere constitutes a danger to prosperity everywhere."

937. Louis, William Roger. "American Anti-Colonialism and the
Dissolution of the British Empire." INT AFFS (London),
62 (Summer 1985) 395-420.

Rogers concentrates on America's motives, strength of
purpose, and relationship with Britain in this analysis of
why the United States did not replace Britain's prewar
global leadership. Examining case studies of Roosevelt
(India), Truman (Libya), and Eisenhower (Suez), the noted
historian finds the United States caught between supporting
nationalist aims and minimizing strain on U.S. relations
with the Western allies.

938. Shridharani, Krishnalal J. WARNING TO THE WEST. New York:
Duell, Sloan and Pearce, 1942. 274 pp.

The author, arguing against racism, warns of the
emerging nationalist movements in Asia which will become a
major force in the postwar era.

939. Smith, Tony. THE END OF THE EUROPEAN EMPIRE:
DECOLONIZATION AFTER WORLD WAR II. Lexington, MA: D.C.
Heath, 1975. 262 pp.

Smith points out that few contemporaries foresaw the
speed of the decolonization process when the war ended.
See especially the sections on the British in India and the
French in Indochina. In addition, Smith raises issues for
further study.

940. Thompson, Laura. "Guam: Study in Military Government."
      FE SURVEY, 13 (August 9, 1944), 149-154.

The author, an anthropologist, calls for consistent U.S.
colonial policies. Forty years of naval rule on Guam, she
states, are difficult to reconcile with the ideal of
promoting democratic civil government.

941. Venkataramani, M.S. and B.K. Shrivastava "America and the
      Indian Political Crisis, July-August 1942." INT STUD, 6
      (July 1964), 1-48.

Using published sources (little more was available at
the time), the authors charge that, in criticizing the Quit
India movement, the United States failed to note India's
assurances of continued support for the war effort. The
authors conclude that Roosevelt responded to the failure of
the Cripps Mission and Churchill's resolve by backing away
from the crisis (and taking China with him).

942. Venkataramani, M.S. and B.K. Shrivastava. "The President
      and the Mahatma: America's Response to Gandhi's Fast,
      February-March 1943." INT REV SOC HIST, 13 (pt. 2,
      1968), 141-173.

The authors, Indian professors, point to the irony of
Gandhi's fast coming at a time when the United Nations were
fighting to guarantee the Four Freedoms. According to the
authors, Roosevelt, with little knowledge of Gandhi or what
he stood for, saw India as a theater of war under British
control.

943. Venkataramani, M.S. and B.K. Shrivastava. Vol. I: QUIT
      INDIA. Vol. II: ROOSEVELT, GANDHI, CHURCHILL: AMERICA
      AND THE LAST PHASE OF INDIA'S FREEDOM STRUGGLE. New
      Delhi, India: Radiant Press, 1980-1983. 2 vols.

The first volume carries the story to 1942. The authors
make no efforts to disguise their pro-nationalist,
anti-colonial sentiments. In their opinion, the United
States offered no significant support to the Indian
nationalist movement.

944. Watt, D.C. "American Anti-Colonial Policies and the End of
        European Colonial Empires, 1941-1962." In: A.N. den
        Hollander, ed. COURAGEOUS CONFLICT. Leiden: Brill,
        1973.

        With characteristic insight, Watt points out failings in
        the idealistic American approach. The U.S. anti-colonial
        goals were not achieved, he argues, not because of a fear
        of communism and the consequent need to remain friendly
        with Western Europe, but simply because America's power to
        act proved "illusory." Even worse, from an American point
        of view, Watt contends that U.S. moral (not economic)
        imperialism led to an arrogance that actually served to
        loosen American-West European ties. Of interest is Watt's
        observation that Willkie's political pressure in 1941 on
        Roosevelt forced the president, in turn, to extend the
        principles of the Atlantic Charter to Asia. Churchill
        responded defiantly by rejecting the "liquidation of the
        British Empire."

945. Williams, J.E. "The Joint Declaration on the Colonies: An
        Issue in Anglo-American Relations, 1942-1944." J INTL
        STUD, 2 (October 1976), 267-292.

        With newly released documents, Williams tells of the
        various joint efforts to draft a declaration concerning
        dependent peoples. His story, unaccountably, does not
        include the significant events of 1945 (e.g., at Yalta and
        San Francisco)

II.B.1.c.v. Southeast Asia

946. Fifield, Russell H. AMERICANS IN SOUTHEAST ASIA: THE
        ROOTS OF COMMITMENT. New York: Thomas Y. Crowell,
        1973.

        This knowledgeable study contains some excellent
        material about U.S. involvement in the region during the
        war years.

947. Landon, Kenneth P. "Nationalism in Southeastern Asia."
        FE QTRLY, 2 (February 1943), 139-152.

        Landon, a State Department specialist on Southeast Asia,
        presents a contemporary overview of the situation in Burma,
        Thailand, Indochina, and Malaya. He warns of the "rising
        tide" of Asian nationalist movements.

948. Open University, War and Society Course Team. WORLD WAR II
      OUTSIDE EUROPE. Milton Keynes, Eng.: Open University
      Press, 1973. 35 pp.

      This course outline, prepared by D. C. Watt, examines
      non-European developments. See especially the thoughtful
      attention given to Southeast Asia and emerging nationalist
      movements during the war.

949. Pannikar, Kavalam Madhava. THE FUTURE OF SOUTH-EAST ASIA.
      New York: Macmillan, 1944. 126 pp.

      Traversing the political landscape of the region,
      Pannikar expresses his opinion that, after the war, the
      Southeast Asians should be guided by the newly independent
      India. Here is a useful description of regional affairs,
      especially the question of colonialism.

950. Seabridge, G. W. "Some Problems of the White Man's Return
      to South-East Asia." INTL AFFS, 21 (April 1945),
      196-205.

      The author warns that the Western imperial powers should
      not expect an easy return to their prewar Asian colonies.
      Severe postwar obstacles face the white man in Southeast
      Asia--obstacles such as indigenous aspirations, food
      shortages, the political atmosphere, the role of China, and
      the effects of Japanese propaganda.

951. Tarling, Nicholas. "'Some Rather Nebulous Capacity': Lord
      Killearn's Appointment in Southeast Asia." MOD ASIAN
      STUD, 20 (July 1986), 559-600.

      Killearn received an appointment as a coordinator
      (without authority) to work on the postwar food crisis in
      Southeast Asia. The author faults the British for
      unrealistically planning their return to the Southeast
      Asian colonies.

952. Thorne, Christopher. "After the Europeans: American
      Designs for the Remaking of Southeast Asia." DIP HIST,
      12 (Spring 1988), 201-208.

      Although primarily a review article, Thorne provides a
      broad analysis of the general topic. Of special interest
      is his stinging rebuke to the Society for Historians of
      American Foreign Relations and its "national, cultural, and
      disciplinary parochialism" in the study of diplomatic
      history.

BURMA

953. Tarling, Nicholas. Pt. I: "'A New and a Better Cunning':
      British Wartime Planning for Post-War Burma, 1942-43."
      J SEA STUD, 13 (March 1982), 33-59. Pt. II: "'An
      Empire Gem': British Wartime Planning for Post-War
      Burma, 1943-44." J SEA STUD, 13 (September 1982),
      310-342.

      In a deeply researched analysis, Tarling highlights the
      role of Sir Reginald Dorman-Smith, head of the
      government-in-exile for Burma at Simla. The thread
      throughout both parts is the British determination to
      return and to leave a monument to their high purpose.

954. Tinker, Hugh and Andrew Griffin, eds. BURMA: THE STRUGGLE
      FOR INDEPENDENCE, 1944-1948. London: HMSO, 1983. 2
      vols.

      This extensive collection traces the thorny political
      questions associated with the Burmese quest. Of interest
      is the material on the war years, when political and
      military affairs intertwined.

INDOCHINA

955. Brown, Macalister and Joseph L. Zasloff. APPRENTICE
      REVOLUTIONARIES: THE COMMUNIST MOVEMENT IN LAOS,
      1930-1985. Stanford, CA: Hoover Institution, 1985. 463
      pp.

      The authors are experienced in Laotian affairs, but they
      list few sources--and fewer still that are reliable. See
      the chapters on the 1930s, the war, and the immediate
      postwar years, when the authors shift their focus to the
      emerging "nation."

956. Chandler, David P. "The Kingdom of Kampuchea,
      March-October, 1945: Japanese-Sponsored Independence in
      Cambodia." J SEA STUD, 17 (March 1986), 80-93.

      Incorporating new and interesting sources as well as
      interviews, Chandler concentrates on a key period--the
      interregnum--which set forces in motion in Cambodia for
      years to come. Identifying the rise of party politics in
      Cambodia, Chandler describes how King Sihanouk did not

remain acquiescent to France and how the French were never
able to regain the reformist momentum of the 1930s.

957. de la Roche, Jean. "Indo-China in the New French Colonial
      Framework." PAC AFFS, 18 (March 1945), 62-75.

      In this paper, which the author presented at the Hot
      Springs IPR Conference, de la Roche sets forth proposals
      for the postwar empire of France. With regard to
      Indochina, he says that France promises reforms designed
      for "true incorporation" in the French community within the
      spirit of the "traditional generosity which has always
      characterized French policy."

958. Dreifort, John E. "Indochina in Allied Wartime Diplomacy:
      The French Perspective." RES STUD, 48 (No. 1, 1980),
      25-39.

          NE

959. Grobb, Lorna B. "Annam Wants Its Freedom." ASIA &
      AMERICAS, 46 (October 1946), 441-444.

      With fifteen years of experience as a missionary in
      French Indochina, Grobb says that the Annamites--who lack
      discipline, experience with democracy, and an army--will
      need outside help, especially from the French, to achieve
      their political goals. Of interest is the author's
      descriptions of Ho Chi Minh (the "man with twenty names")
      and the Viet Minh (an amalgamation of caudaists, the Youth
      Movement, and Communists).

960. Herring, George C. "The Truman Administration and the
      Restoration of French Sovereignty in Indochina." DIP
      HIST, I (Spring 1977), 97-117.

      According to this article, the restoration of French
      sovereignty was no accident or inadvertence but, instead,
      the product of a deliberate design by top State Department
      officials. With extensive research, Herring argues that
      the Truman administration "squandered" whatever influence
      it may have held by acquiescing to France's return and by
      adopting a policy of non-involvement in Indochina. Of
      special interest is Herring's report of the compromise
      within a divided State Department that emerged in a policy
      paper on June 22, 1945.

961. Hess, Gary R. "Franklin Roosevelt and Indochina." J AMER
      HIST, 59 (September 1972), 353-368.

Rather than devoting careful consideration to thorny issues, Roosevelt, according to Hess, inclined toward simple answers. Hess criticizes the president for being too careful with his Allies and for not making full use of his military-diplomatic leverage. The author finds a specific example of this general pattern in the matter of Indochina. Roosevelt seized on the concept of territorial trusteeship for Indochina after the war, but, writes Hess, the President did not follow through on his ideas and the trusteeship scheme died with him. While no panacea, the author suggests that trusteeship merited more attention that it received. The article benefits from research through archival resources available at the time in the United States. Interestingly, government documents subsequently declassified in the U.S. and in Britain reinforce the general thrust of this article.

962. Khanh, Huynh Kim. "The Vietnamese August Revolution Reinterpreted." J ASIAN STUD, 30 (August 1971), 761-782.

The author, a political scientist, uses French archival sources, Vietnamese sources, and interviews to analyze the 1945 revolution. He points out the various results of the episode as a significant turning point in Vietnamese history.

963. LaFeber, Walter. "Roosevelt, Churchill, and Indochina, 1942-1945." AMER HR, 80 (December 1975), 1277-1295.

LaFeber argues that Roosevelt reversed course from his original determination to arrange an international trusteeship for postwar Indochina. Thus, the author writes, Truman's policies represented a continuation of Roosevelt's acquiescence to the return of the French colonial administration. Churchill, while avoiding a direct approach to the president, encouraged Britain's common colonial interests with the French. Of interest is LaFeber's contention that America's supposed idealism blended with U.S. self-interest. The article is well researched through U.S. and British archival sources.

964. Mahmood, Khalid. "French and American Attitudes Toward Vietnamese Independence." PAK HORIZON, 38, Pt. I: (No. 2, 1985), 59-83; Pt. II: (No. 3, 1985), 46-74.

The author argues that in 1945 the United States had been too ambivalent, only having half-heartedly recognized

the French. He makes the point that U.S. support for
nationalist movements would go far in thwarting the
communists.

965. Malay, A.S. "Bolshevism in the Colonies: Indochina and
      the 'Philippine Example.'" ASIAN STUD, 19
      (April-December 1981), 16-36.

      Based on French archival materials, this article shows
      how prewar French bureaucrats overstated the communist
      threat in the Philippines. In their reaction to avoid the
      influence in Indochina of both the communists and the
      Japanese, the French, according to Malay, mishandled the
      situation. There was little knowledge in Indochina about
      events in the Philippines.

966. Marr, David G. "Vietnam 1945: Some Questions." VIET
      FORUM, 6 (Summer-Fall 1985), 155-193.

      Using multi-archival materials and Vietnamese-language
      sources, Marr analyzes Vietnamese turmoil in 1945. Raising
      a series of questions, he argues that the DRV survived the
      trials through decisive action in creating the context for
      independence.

967. Marvel, W. Macy. "Drift and Intrigue: United States
      Relations with the Viet-Minh, 1945." MILLENNIUM, 4
      (Spring 1975), 10-27.

      Relying almost entirely on published sources, Marvel
      looks at three specific questions on Indochina: (1) the
      modification of Roosevelt's policies, (2) OSS aid to the
      Viet Minh, and (3) ambiguous U.S. policies about both
      France and colonial restoration.

968. Rice, Maximin, Edward. "The French Communists and the
      First Indochinese War, 1945-1954." CONTEMP FRENCH CIV,
      2 (Spring 1978), 359-378.

      The author concludes that the French communists compiled
      a mixed record concerning Indochina. Elements which
      contributed to the communists' vigorous opposition to the
      colonial war reflect nationalist considerations in France
      and Soviet foreign policy but reach back, too, to the
      Popular Front attitudes of the 1930s.

969. Rice-Maximin, Edward. "The United States, France and
      Vietnam, 1945-1950: The View From the State Department."
      CONTEMP FRENCH CIV, 7 (Fall 1982), 20-40.

Relying chiefly on published sources, the author argues
that Western European affairs dominated the State
Department's attention. Of interest is the report that the
so-called "Bao Dai solution" was not taken seriously in
France.

970. Rueff, Gaston. "The Future of French Indo-China." FOR
      AFFS, 23 (October 1944), 140-146.

This contemporary report reflects the French perspective
on Indochina. Praising the French forces and natives for
their resistance to the Japanese, Rueff looks ahead to
continuing the French imperial connection with Indochina
after the war (with perhaps an international system to
smooth some of the rough edges of the old form of
imperialism).

971. Rueff, Gaston. "Postwar Problems of French Indo-China:
      Economic Aspects." PAC AFFS, 18 (June 1945), 137-155.

Rueff presented this paper to the IPR conference at Hot
Springs, Virginia. He outlines the plans—and problems
—of improving the standard of living in Indochina through
postwar industrialization. There is much emphasis on
public works and loans.

972. Rueff, Gaston. "Postwar Problems of French Indo-China:
      Social and Political Aspects." PAC AFFS, 18 (September
      1945), 229-245.

Rueff describes some postwar plans which envision
widesweeping political reforms in Indochina (e.g.,
decentralization of political power, separation of
legislative and executive functions, nations sharing power,
etc.) and marked improvements in such areas as health,
housing, labor, and education.

973. Sbrega, John J. "'First catch your hare': Anglo-American
      Perspectives in Indochina During the Second World War."
      J SEA STUD, 14 (March 1983), 63-78.

This article incorporates extensive research through
archival materials and private collections to focus on two
themes: (1) the postwar status of the French colony and (2)
the larger question of France's future role in any
international security system. During these debates,
according to the author, British and American assessments
did not follow consistent courses; they not only diverged

from one another but also were internally inconsistent.

974.   Sbrega, John J. "Franco-American Relations and Indochina,
            1940-1945." PROC FREN COL HS (1980), 98-112.

        The author reports on the wartime tensions between the
        Free French and Americans over the postwar status of
        Indochina. Contrary to the intention of the president and
        some of his advisers (both in and out of the State
        Department), the French returned to colonial control of
        Indochina after the war. Sbrega analyzes some of the
        reasons for this political occurrence.

975.   Schlesinger, Arthur M., Jr. THE BITTER HERITAGE: VIETNAM
            AND THE AMERICAN DREAM, 1941-1946. Boston: Houghton
            Mifflin, 1966. 126 pp.

        Although the essay addresses certain concerns of the
        mid-1960s, Schlesinger includes a useful summary, from
        sources available at the time, of Roosevelt's trusteeship
        scheme for Indochina.

976.   Sheldon, George. "Status of the Viet Nam." FE SURVEY, 15
            (December 18, 1946), 373-377.

        The author reports his wartime observations while
        serving with the U.S. Army in Indochina. The Vietnamese,
        he says, offered the only overt resistance to the Japanese.
        Of interest is his statement that French guards killed
        Annamite political prisoners at two garrisons (Yen-Bay and
        Lao-Bang) before fleeing the Japanese coup in March 1945.
        Sheldon suggests reforms that will be required after the
        war.

977.   Smith, R.B. "The Work of the Provisional Government of
            Vietnam, August-December 1945." MOD ASIAN STUD, 12
            (October 1978), 571-609.

        The author consulted sources in the Vietnamese
        language--especially a new source, the decree book
        (official gazette) of the Provisional Government--to gain
        perspective on the aborted revolutionary government in late
        1945.

979.   Thorne, Christopher. "Indochina and Anglo-American
            Relations, 1942-1945." PAC HR, 45, (February 1976),
            73-96.

        Integrating international research through archival

materials and private collections, Thorne compares U.S.
criticism and British praise of the French colonial record
in Indochina. The article particularly focuses on the
personalities of Roosevelt and Churchill.

980. Tonnesson, Stein. "The Longest Wars: Indochina,
        1945-1975." J PEACE RES, 22 (No. 1, 1985), 9-29.

      Researching the Indochina files in French archives, the
author, an associate at the International Peace Research
Institute in Oslo, emphasizes the significance of the
Japanese coup of March 9, 1945. Of special note is his use
of previously unpublished material to identify French
provocations under the government of Georges Bidault.

981. United States. Congress. Senate. Committee on Foreign
        Relations. CAUSES, ORIGINS, CONSEQUENCES OF THE VIETNAM
        WAR. Washington, D.C.: GPO, 1972.

      The hearings in May 1972 uncovered some material
pertaining to World War II. See especially the testimony
of Abbot Low Moffat, who gives first-hand evidence of the
split within the State Department over the merging
nationalist movements in Asia at the end of the war.

982. Vu Nu Chieu. "The Other Side of the 1945 Vietnamese
        Revolution: The Empire of Viet-Nam (March-August
        1945)." J ASIAN STUD, 45 (February 1986), 293-328.

      Vu integrates research through new French archival
materials, Indochinese and Japanese periodicals,
Vietnamese-language sources, and published accounts by
Japanese officers. He focuses on the achievements of Tran
Trong Kim, head of the Vietnamese government. Denying that
this was a "token" government, Vu characterizes Kim's
activities as important first steps toward Vietnamese
independence.

MALAYA

983. Cheah Boon Kheng. "Sino-Malay Conflicts in Malaya,
        1945-1946: Communist Vendetta and Islamic Resistance."
        J SEA STUD, 12 (March 1981), 108-117.

      Here is a knowledgeable account of Chinese-Malay
relations. Drawing on British archival records and Malay
sources, Cheah describes how Malay Islamic leaders insisted
that the communists were a threat and how the Chinese and

the communists gradually became synonymous for the Islamic.
Of interest is the author's analysis of how the Japanese
occupation discredited the Chinese elite class.

984.   Cheah Boon Kheng. "Some Aspects of the Interregnum in
         Malaya (14 August - 3 September 1945)." J SEA STUD, 8
         (March 1977), 48-74.

         The focus here is on the relatively short interval when
         no formal government existed in Malaya. Cheah offers an
         excellent analysis of the political-military situation and
         the interaction of the various players: Force 136, MPAJA,
         Mountbatten, Chiang Kai-shek, the overseas Chinese, and the
         Japanese forces acting as police.

985.   Stockwell, A.J. "British Imperial Policy and
         Decolonization in Malaya, 1945-1952." J IMP COMM HIST,
         13 (October 1984), 68-87.

         The article surveys British planning for Malaya.
         Although British planners generally aimed at the eventual
         goal of self-government for most colonies, the ethnic
         divisions which wracked pre-war Malaya hindered that goal.
         Plans that did emerge from the war looked to a Malayan
         Union but were disrupted by postwar events.

NETHERLANDS EAST INDIES

986.   Anderson, Benedict R. O'G. JAVA IN A TIME OF REVOLUTION:
         OCCUPATION AND RESISTANCE, 1944-1946. Ithaca, NY:
         Cornell University Press, 1972. 494 pp.

         Here is a knowledgeable political history of transition
         from Dutch colony to Japan's occupation to MERDEKA.
         Anderson pays special attention to the emergence of
         indigenous political leaders. His research incorporates
         field work as well as Indonesian-language sources.

987.   Homan, Gerlof. "The United States and the Netherlands East
         Indies: The Evolution of American Anticolonialism."
         PAC HR, 53 (November 1984), 423-446.

         With extensive research, including Dutch-language
         sources, Homan traces U.S. difficulties in identifying with
         emerging nationalist movements in Asia, especially in the
         NEI.

988.   Kahin, George Mct. NATIONALISM AND REVOLUTION IN

INDONESIA. Ithaca, NY: Cornell University Press, 1952. 490 pp.

Here is a first-rate analysis of the emergence of Indonesian nationalism toward the end of the war--and beyond. Kahin's work has become a classic, indispensable to the study of this subject.

989. Kleffens, Eelco N. van. "The Democratic Future of the Netherlands Indies." FOR AFFS, 21 (October 1942), 87-102.

After reviewing the Dutch colonial record in the NEI before the war, the author looks forward to a pleasant resumption of the colonial connection after the war.

990. United States. Office of Strategic Services. PRE-LIBERATION DEVELOPMENTS IN THE NETHERLANDS EAST INDIES. Washington, D.C.: OSS, 1945. 4 1.

The OSS recognizes the growing influence of the nationalist movement in NEI. According to this report, the Dutch will face a difficult challenge in seeking to restore prewar colonial controls.

PHILIPPINE ISLANDS

991. Mills, Lennox A., ed. "Southeastern Asia and the Philippines." ANNALS AMER ACAD POL SOC SCI, 226 (March 1943), 1-150.

The entire issue is devoted to the topic. Many authorities contributed to these contemporary regional studies.

THAILAND (SIAM)

992. Peterson, A. "Britain and Siam: The Latest Phase." PAC AFFS, 19 (December 1946), 364-372.

The author served in SEAC psychological warfare and was a member of Force 136. His report tells of the British arranging to parachute Siamese students (trained by the British) into Siam in 1944 to make contact with the resistance. Of interest is the text of the British demands on Siam. Peterson, however, voices optimism about postwar Anglo-American-Thai relations.

993. Tarling, Nicholas. "Atonement Before Absolutism: British
      Policy Towards Thailand During World War II." J SIAM
      SOC, 66 (January 1978), 22–65.

      In an exhaustive research effort, Tarling finds no
      surprise that, in the Anglo-American friction over
      Thailand, the position of the more powerful United States
      prevailed. Of interest, too, are his points about Thais
      playing off the Anglo-American differences and the schisms
      within the British Foreign Office.

II.B.1.c.vi. Korea

994. Cumings, Bruce, ed. CHILD OF CONFLICT: THE
      KOREAN-AMERICAN RELATIONSHIP, 1943-1953. Seattle WA:
      University of Washington Press, 1983. 335 pp.

      For purposes of this guide, there is material in some of
      these essays which treats the colonial issue, the problem
      of dependent areas, and postwar planning. One of the
      attractive features of this collection is the long
      introductory essay by Cumings.

995. Cumings, Bruce. THE ORIGINS OF THE KOREAN WAR: LIBERATION
      AND THE EMERGENCE OF SEPARATE REGIMES, 1945-1947.
      Princeton, NJ: Princeton University Press, 1981.
      552 pp.

      This is the first of a two-volume study. Cumings takes
      a revisionist position in analyzing the immediate postwar
      situation in Korea. His assessment includes not only a
      focus on internal developments in Korea but also a
      description of Korea as a pawn in relations between the two
      great powers. The book is marked by its extensive research
      and its controversial conclusions.

996. Dennet, Tyler. "In Due Course." FE SURVEY, 14 (January
      17, 1945), 1-4.

      The author asserts that decisions about the future of
      Korea promise to constitute a test case of international
      cooperation and goodwill.

997. Dobbs, Charles M. THE UNWANTED SYMBOL: AMERICAN FOREIGN
      POLICY, THE COLD WAR, AND KOREA, 1945-1950. Kent, OH:
      Kent State University Press, 1981. 239 pp.

      Much of the book is concerned with the origins of the
      Korean War. Dobbs makes the point that, once Americans saw

little chance of cooperation from the Soviet Union in the
postwar era, they sought to disengage from the Korean
peninsula.

998. Grajdanzev, Andrew. "Korea in the Postwar World." FOR
        AFFS, 22 (April 1944), 479-483.

        The author argues that Koreans should be left alone "at
        once"--not at some future time--to develop their political
        and economic resources. The industrialization of the
        country eventually will occur. In the meantime, the Great
        Powers should guarantee Korea's independence and
        territorial integrity.

999. Keeton, George W. "Korea and the Future." CONTEMP REV,
        161 (June 1942), 354-358.

        Labelling Korea the "weakest spot" in Japan's "slave
        empire," the author describes Japanese rule in Korea as an
        "unredeemed failure." He urges the Allies to publicize
        independence for Korea as a war aim.

1000. Key, S. Ryang. "America's Historical Perception of Korea,
        1900-1945." J MOD KOREAN STUD, 2 (December 1985), 1-14.

        NE

1001. Matray, James I. "Captive of the Cold War: The Decision
        to Divide Korea at the 38th Parallel." PAC HR, 50 (May
        1981), 145-168.

        Portraying Korea as a captive of the Cold War, Matray
        maintains that Truman was pleased to stop the Soviets from
        taking all of Korea. According to Matray, Truman's refusal
        to negotiate once Korea had been partitioned guaranteed the
        division of that country.

1002. Matray, James I. "An End to Indifference: America's
        Korean Policy During World War II." DIP HIST, 2 (Spring
        1978), 181-196.

        The author finds little to fault in the Yalta agreement
        on Korea which called for a four-power trusteeship after
        the war. According to Matray, the concept of territorial
        trusteeship was a realistic policy for U. S. strategic
        considerations and avoided the dangers and instability of
        premature independence.

II.B.1.c.vii. INTERNATIONAL ORGANIZATION

1003. Arne, Sigrid. UNITED NATIONS PRIMER: THE KEY TO THE
       CONFERENCES. New York: Farrar, 1945. 156 pp.

       The author provides a lengthy discussion of key
       documents in the development of the United Nations
       Organization.

1004. Bentwich, Norman de M. FROM GENEVA TO SAN FRANCISCO.
       London: Gollancz, 1946. 111 pp.

       Here is a contemporary account of the development of the
       United Nations Organization.

1005. Divine, Robert A. SECOND CHANCE: THE TRIUMPH OF
       INTERNATIONALISM IN AMERICA DURING WORLD WAR II. New
       York: Atheneum, 1967. 371 pp.

       The noted historian analyzes the shift of the American
       people to an acceptance of internationalism, including U.S.
       membership in an international organization. His emphasis
       is on the three chief influences for this shift: pressure
       groups, political leaders, and intellectuals. Here is a
       well-written contribution amidst the ever-thorny subject of
       analyzing public opinion.

1006. Fox, William T.R. "The Super-Powers at San Francisco."
       REV POL, 8 (January 1946), 115-127.

       In this report on the San Francisco Conference, Fox
       indicates that the lesser powers sometimes had their
       say--and got their way.

1007. Institute on World Organization. WORLD ORGANIZATION.
       Washington, D.C.: American Council on Public Affairs,
       1943. 426 pp.

       Here is a collection of papers on both the League of
       Nations (its strengths and weaknesses) and the prospects of
       a postwar world organization. Some of the authors had
       served in the League of Nations' Secretariat.

1008. Johnstone, William C. "The San Francisco Conference." PAC
       AFFS, 18 (September 1945), 213-228.

       The author, an IPR representative at the conference,
       explains the machinery of the new world organization.
       Focusing particularly on Asia, Johnstone hints at postwar

friction arising among the Big Five because each had
important interests in that region.

1009. Mazuzan, George T. "America's U.N. Commitment, 1945-1953."
        HISTORIAN, 40 (February 1978), 309-330.

        The author maintains that Americans worked hard for the
        success of the U.N. As a case study, this article examines
        the career of Warren R. Austin, who managed to reconcile
        his personal views on U.S. foreign policy with the
        realities of the postwar world.

1010. Russell, Ruth B. A HISTORY OF THE UNITED NATIONS CHARTER:
        THE ROLE OF THE UNITED STATES, 1940-1945. Washington,
        D.C.: Brookings Institute, 1958. 1,140 pp.

        Incorporating extensive research through State
        Department files, Russell traces the development of the
        international organization as an influence on U.S. foreign
        policy. Much of this excellent study is devoted to the
        1945 conference at San Francisco. Jeannette E. Muther
        assisted Russell.

1011. United States. Congress. House of Representatives.
        Committee on International Relations. PROBLEMS OF WORLD
        WAR II AND ITS AFTERMATH. Washington, D.C.: GPO, 1976.
        2 vols.

        Here are selections from the committee's hearings in
        executive sessions during the period 1943-1950. Volume I
        contains material on the projected International
        Organization. See especially the statements by Fulbright
        (1943), Acheson (1945), and Pasvolsky (1945). See, too,
        the background material on postwar organizations that
        appears in Appendix I.

1012. World Peace Foundation. THE UNITED NATIONS IN THE MAKING:
        BASIC DOCUMENTS. Boston: World Peace Foundation, 1945.
        136 pp.

        The documents offer a wartime glimpse at the formation
        of the victorious coalition as well as the development of
        the international organization.

II.B.2. JAPAN AND FRIENDS/JAPANESE-OCCUPIED TERRITORIES

1013. Agoncillo, Teodoro A. THE FATEFUL YEARS: JAPAN'S
        ADVENTURE IN THE PHILIPPINES, 1941-1945. Quezon City,
        PI: Garcia, 1965. 551 pp.

This survey gives special emphasis to political and
social events as well as military affairs. The Japanese
commander, Yamashita, is portrayed to some extent as a
victim of circumstances beyond his control.

1014. Alvarez, David J. "The Vatican and the War in the Far
       East, 1941-1943." HISTORIAN, 40 (May 1978), 508-523.

This political scientist examines not only diplomatic
relations between the Vatican and Japan but also
Anglo-American reactions to this interchange. In the Far
East, according to Alvarez, Vatican interests outdistanced
its influence. Prior to the war, the Vatican emphasized
missionary work and education in the Orient while under the
protection of the European powers. The author feels that
after the war began, however, Vatican efforts to play a
diplomatic role in the region met with uneven results. The
article is marked by its solid research in English-,
French-, and Italian-language sources.

1015. Anderson, Benedict R. O'G. SOME ASPECTS OF INDONESIAN
       POLITICS UNDER THE JAPANESE OCCUPATION, 1944-1945.
       Ithaca, NY: Cornell Modern Indonesia Project, 1961. 126
       pp.

Here is a well-researched, well-written report on the
Japanese occupation. Anderson is particularly effective in
pointing out the emergence of Indonesian leaders and the
shifting perspectives (policies) of the Japanese.

1016. Bain, H. Foster. "Japan's Power of Resistance." FOR AFFS,
       22 (April 1944), 424-432.

Confessing difficulty in measuring the "mental and
material resources" available to Japan, Bain emphasizes the
importance of time for the Allies. According to Bain, the
Allies must win before (a) the people in occupied lands
give up hope and begin collaborating and (b) the Japanese
reverse their propaganda failures and start obtaining the
full resources of the conquered lands.

1017. Benda, Harry J. THE CRESCENT AND THE RISING SUN:
       INDONESIAN ISLAM UNDER THE JAPANESE OCCUPATION,
       1942-1945. The Hague: W. Van Hoeve, 1958. 320 pp.

Here is one of the best studies of its kind. The
extensive research, multi-archival and in multiple
languages, serves as a model; the insightful analysis

uncovers an important subject.

1018. Benda, Harry J., James K. Irikura, and Koichi Kishi, eds.
        JAPANESE MILITARY ADMINISTRATION IN INDONESIA: SELECTED
        DOCUMENTS. New Haven, CT: Yale University, Southeast
        Asian Studies, 1965. 279 pp.

        The collection, which includes Japanese and Dutch
        sources, greatly informs the study of this topic.

1019. Bergamini, David. JAPAN'S IMPERIAL CONSPIRACY. New York:
        William Morrow and Company, 1971. 1239 pp.

        There is no mistaking the author's firm conviction that
        the emperor bore responsibility for Japan's aggression.
        ("There was a great disparity between the deeds of Emperor
        Hirohito and the words which were said about him in later
        years.") Bergamini, born in Japan and a POW in the
        Philippines during the war, presents a forceful, but
        unbalanced, case.

1020. Berger, Gordon M. "The Three Dimensional Empire: Japanese
        Attitudes and the New Order in Asia, 1937-1945." JAPAN
        INTERPRETER, 12 (Summer 1978), 355-382.

        Berger assesses the attitudes and conceptions held by
        Japanese leaders in the 1930s and early 1940s about Japan's
        place in the world order. At the end of the war, Japan's
        willingness to grant true independence represented the
        bankruptcy, according to the author, of the original dream
        for a regional hierarchy led by Japan. The article
        incorporates Japanese sources and helps to define the
        Greater East Asia Co-Prosperity Sphere. Berger presents
        the three dimensions: (1) "Asian-ness"--to harmonize Asian
        identity, (2) "Western-ness"--to adhere to an international
        order defined by the West, and (3) "Japanese-ness"--to
        reflect Japan's unique historical experience.

1021. Borton, Hugh. "The Administration and Structure of
        Japanese Government." DEPT STATE BULL, 11 (December 24,
        1944), 817-833.

        Here is an authoritative account by a recognized expert
        on Japan. He explains the role of the emperor ("sacred and
        inviolable"), the control of the government by the military
        (complete and direct), and the efficiency of governmental
        and imperial machinery. At the time, Borton's title in the
        State Department was Country Specialist, Division of
        Territorial Studies, Office of Special Political Affairs.

1022. Browne, Courtney. TOJO: THE LAST BANZAI. Sydney, Aus.:
       Angus and Robertson, 1967. 245 pp.

       The author presents a sympathetic assessment of Tojo but
       does attempt to strike a balance. By arguing subtly in
       behalf of the thesis that Emperor Hirohito should have
       carried more responsibility for Japan's policies of
       aggression, Browne does project a more favorable light on
       Tojo. The book includes some excellent photographs from
       the personal collection of Tojo's widow.

1023. Buencamino, Victor. "Manila Under Japanese Occupation."
       BULL AMER HIST COLL, (Manila), Pt. I: 7 (July–September
       1979), 7–29; Pt. II: 8 (April–June 1980), 16–30.

       NE

1024. Chaya, Prem and Althea Chaya. THE PASSING HOURS: A RECORD
       OF FIVE AMAZING YEARS. Bangkok: Chatra Books, 1945.
       95 pp.

       Here is the personal account of a Thai couple about
       their experiences during the war.

1025. Coox, Alvin D. TOJO. New York: Ballantine Books, 1975.
       160 pp.

       Part of Ballantine's "War Leader" series, this slim
       volume offers a balanced, not unsympathetic profile of a
       much misunderstood man. The author is a well-respected
       scholar.

1026. Craig, William. THE FALL OF JAPAN. New York: Dial Press,
       1967. 368 pp.

       Here is a fine synthesis of events in Japan from the
       1944 resignation of Tojo to the end of the war. Those
       interested in the justification given for the decision to
       drop the atomic bombs will want to examine Ketsu-Go,
       Japan's operational defense plan to thwart any attempted
       invasion. Craig has selected some excellent photographs,
       and many interviews enabled him to incorporate the human
       dimension. Lt. Marcus McDilda, for instance, saved his
       life by considerably exaggerating his knowledge about the
       new atomic weapon.

1027. De Asis, Leocadio. FROM BATAAN TO TOKYO: DIARY OF A
       FILIPINO STUDENT IN WARTIME JAPAN, 1943–1944. Lawrence,

KS: University of Kansas Press, 1979.   231 pp.

The diarist, a law school graduate, was serving with the 2d Division, USAFEE, when he fell captive to the Japanese at Bataan. The Japanese selected him for special police training, including study in Tokyo, and he worked in the Ministry of Justice (Philippines). De Asis eventually escaped and rejoined the American forces. Grant K. Goodman edited the diary, which covers the period June 1943 to October 1944.

1028.   De Mendelssohn, Peter. JAPAN'S POLITICAL WARFARE. New York: Arno Press, 1972. 192 pp. [Reprint.]

NE

1029.   Direck Jayanama. SIAM AND WORLD WAR II. Bangkok: Social Science Association of Thailand Press, 1978. 358 pp.

Using Thai sources, Direck analyzes the unusual circumstances the war brought to Thailand. He explains in detail not only Thai relations with the Japanese but also Thailand as a cause of some Anglo-American friction.

1030.   Dower, John W. EMPIRE AND AFTERMATH: YOSHIDA SHIGERU AND THE JAPANESE EXPERIENCE, 1878-1954, Cambridge, MA: Harvard University Press, 1979. 618 pp.

Dower portrays Yoshida as a moderating force in Japanese diplomacy. Yoshida saw the war as an aberration (a "historic stumble") which might bring revolutionary changes to Japan. Dower explains Yoshida's role in helping draft the Konoye Memorial in February 1945. This is a valuable study on wartime Japanese politics.

1031.   Drachman, Edward R. UNITED STATES POLICY TOWARD VIETNAM, 1940-1945. Rutherford, NJ: Farleigh Dickinson University Press, 1970. 186 pp.

Although not well grounded in archival material, this book presents a useful analysis of early American involvement--such as it was--in Indochina.

1032.   Edmonds, I.G. THE RISE AND FALL OF THE JAPANESE EMPIRE. Derby, CT: Monarch Books, 1962. 236 pp.

Here is a critical summary which is aimed at the general public.

1033.   Elsbree, Willard H.   JAPAN'S ROLE IN SOUTHEAST ASIAN
          NATIONALIST MOVEMENTS, 1940-1945.   Cambridge, MA:
          Harvard University Press, 1953.   182 pp.

          Here is a first-rate study that remains useful.   The
          subsequent availability of sources after this book appeared
          tends to confirm many of Elsbree's conclusions.

1034.   Fishel, Wesley R.   "A Japanese Peace Maneuver in 1944."   FE
          QTRLY, 8 (August 1949), 387-397.

          Here is an account of secret negotiations in 1944 by a
          Chinese general and Japanese Baron Miyagawa Tadamaro
          (younger brother of Prince Konoye).   Basing his report on
          interviews with some of the participants (staff aides),
          Fishel maintains that the Japanese proposal and the Chinese
          counterproject should have been followed up, but the
          British and Americans were never told.   Chinese
          factionalism prevented decisive action.

1035.   Gibney, Frank.   FIVE GENTLEMEN OF JAPAN.   New York: Farrar
          Strauss & Young, 1953.   373 pp.

          Addressing the immediate aftermath of the war, Gibney
          calls attention to five Japanese leaders who, for him,
          represent the nation's character.   The five, including
          Emperor Hirohito, lead the effort in Japan's proud
          determination to rebuild.

1036.   Hahn, Emily.   HONG KONG HOLIDAY.   Garden City, NY:
          Doubleday, 1946.   305 pp.

          Hahn describes life in Hong Kong under the Japanese.
          She and her little daughter were kept under the watchful
          eye of the Japanese—a supervision that Hahn was able to
          breach on occasion—before being evacuated aboard the
          GRIPSHOLM.

1037.   Hankey, Lord.   POLITICS TRIALS AND ERRORS.   Chicago: Henry
          Regnery, 1950.   150 pp.

          During the war, Hankey maintained parts of his long and
          close association with Japan.   The distinguished British
          official gives a spirited defense of Shigemitsu, his friend
          for many years.

1038.   Ienaga, Saburo.   THE PACIFIC WAR: WORLD WAR II AND THE
          JAPANESE, 1931-1945.   NEW YORK: PANTHEON BOKS, 1978.
          316 pp.

Ienaga is a Japanese professor who hopes to use the war experience to stimulate a spirit of self-criticism among the Japanese people. He fears that Japan has become a "puppet" of the United States in the postwar era. In highly charged rhetoric (translated unsparingly by Frank Baldwin), the author heaps blame upon the Japanese leadership and imperial ideology which swept Japan into a war of certain defeat. (Japan's Ministry of Education has suppressed the author's textbooks for being excessively critical of Japan.)

1039.   Irie, Sukemasa. "My 50 Years With the Emperor." JAPAN Q,
        30 (January-March 1983), 39-43.

The author first began his service as imperial chamberlain in 1934. Emperor Hirohito believed that he overstepped his bounds as constitutional monarch, according to Irie, on two occasions: (1) the 1936 coup, when he labeled the troops "insurgents"; and (2) the decision for peace in August 1945. Irie denies that the emperor could have prevented the decision for war under the circumstances in 1941.

1040.   Jacobs, G.F. PRELUDE TO THE MONSOON: ASSIGNMENT IN
        SUMATRA. Philadelphia, PA: University of Pennsylvania
        Press, 1982. 249 pp.

Here is an eyewitness report by a South African (a major in the British Royal Marines) on events in Sumatra immediately after the Japanese surrender. Jacobs describes one aspect of the interregnum (August-October 1945) which saw significant political developments through most of Asia.

1041.   James, David H. THE RISE AND FALL OF THE JAPANESE EMPIRE.
        London: Allen and Unwin, 1951. 409 pp.

James, a British intelligence officer in Malaya and ex-POW, undertakes an ambitious project in this one-volume study. (The introduction treats all of Japanese history prior to World War II.) The narrative is readable; the author is knowledgeable--in certain areas.

1042.   Jones, F.C. JAPAN'S NEW ORDER IN EAST ASIA: ITS RISE AND
        FALL, 1937-1945. London: Oxford University Press,
        1954. 498 pp.

The British historian writes authoritatively about

wartime Japan. His analysis strips off the veneer of the
Greater East Asia Co-Prosperity Sphere.

1043. Kase, Toshikazu. JOURNEY TO THE MISSOURI. New Haven, CT:
       Yale University Press, 1950. 282 pp.

       Here is an illuminating description of Japan's march to
war--and ruin--by a leading expert in foreign policy. Kase
states his opinions frankly, with no effort to shield his
colleagues and other contemporaries. This important
historical account is edited by David Nelson Rowe, who also
wrote the Foreword.

1044. Kodama, Yoshio. SUGAMO DIARY. Tokyo: 1960. 275 pp.

       NE

1045. Korea. Ministry of Foreign Affairs. MEMORANDUM: KOREA'S
       ROLE IN THE ANTI-AXIS WAR. Chungking: 1944. 5 pp.

       The Korean provisional government in Chungking sets
forth its contribution and the service of the Korean people
in the war against Japan.

1046. Landon, Kenneth P. "Thailand's Struggle for National
       Security." FE QTRLY, 4 (November 1944), 5-26.

       This State Department official summarizes his
investigation of contemporary international newspapers for
information about Thai-Japanese relations. He describes
Thailand's steady drift towards Japan since 1933 as a
pragmatic response to Japanese power in Southeast Asia.

1047. Lebra, Joyce. "The INA and Japanese-Trained Armies in
       Southeast Asia: A Comparison." ORACLE, 1 (January
       1979), 28-37.

       NE

1048. Lebra, Joyce C. "The Significance of the Japanese Military
       Model for Southeast Asia." PAC AFFS, 48 (Summer 1975),
       215-229.

       With solid research, Lebra states that Japanese training
schools affected a generation of military-political
leadership in Southeast Asia. She characterizes the
Japanese occupation in the region as both positive (in its
modernizing and creative aspects) and negative (in its
repressive features).

1049.   Lieberman, Victor B.   "Reinterpreting Burmese History."
        COMP STUD SOC HIST, 29 (January 1987), 162-194.

        With his focus on state formation and centralization,
        the author stresses continuity in Burma politics from the
        precolonial era to the present day. His research includes
        Burmese-language sources.

1050.   Livingston, Jon, Joe Moore, and Felicia Oldfather, eds.
        THE JAPAN READER: IMPERIAL JAPAN, 1800-1945. New York:
        Pantheon Books, 197. 517 pp.

        This useful collection sheds much light on Japan and
        aspects of Japanese life. There is little, however, on
        foreign relations or the international context.

1051.   McKale, Donald M.   "The Nazi Party and the Far East,
        1931-1945." J CONTEMP HIST, 12 (April 1977), 291-311.

        With detailed research, McKale describes the efforts of
        German citizens in the Far East to recruit new members for
        the Nazi Party. He concludes that the Nazis had a negative
        impact on the Japanese cause.

1052.   McKinney, John B.   "I Remember V-J Day--Vividly." SIGNAL,
        21 (August 1967), 30-33, 65.

        The author gives a personal account of going to Japan to
        set up a communications system for MacArthur immediately
        after the surrender announcement from Tokyo.

1053.   Marr, David G.   VIETNAMESE TRADITION ON TRIAL, 1920-1945.
        Berkeley, CA: University of California, 1981.

        Here is an analysis of the Vietnamese people and their
        culture that is unequaled by any foreign (i.e.,
        non-Vietnamese) scholar. His research (including
        multi-language sources) and control of the material combine
        to produce a masterful book.

1054.   Martin, James V., Jr.   "Thai-American Relations in World
        War II." J ASIAN STUD, 22 (August 1963), 451-467.

        The author provides a summary based on archival
        research. There is little, however, on either the Free
        Thai Movement or Anglo-American friction over Thailand.

1055.   Maxon, Yale C.   CONTROL OF JAPANESE FOREIGN POLICY: A

STUDY OF CIVIL-MILITARY RIVALRY, 1930-1945. Berkeley,
CA: University of California Press, 1957. 286 pp.

Of interest in this study of the competition for power
is Maxon's detailed treatment of the schemes devised by
extremists to commit Japan to war. See also his analysis
of the concept of GEKOKUJO ("lower overbearing the higher"
or "government from below").

1056. Misselwitz, Henry F. JAPAN COMMITS HARA-KIRI: A
        SKETCHBOOK. San Mateo, CA: D.M. Paulson, 1945. 151
        pp.

Here are glimpses of events which marked the decline of
the Japanese Empire.

1057. Mosley, Leonard. HIROHITO: EMPEROR OF JAPAN. Englewood
        Cliffs, NJ: Prentice-Hall, 1966. 371 pp.

In preparing this biography, Mosley visited Japan and
conducted many interviews. Some important points in the
narrative include (a) Hirohito expressing regret, according
to the author, not only for failing to intervene against
the Tripartite Pact but also for not preventing the
Japanese move into Indochina ("like a thief at a fire") and
(b) the influence of Marquis Kido upon the Emperor. Also
of interest is Mosley's contention that Hull became more
willing to have a showdown with Japan (since Japan as enemy
might be less trouble for the United States than Japan
aiding Germany and Italy).

1058. Mote, Fredrick W., comp. JAPANESE-SPONSORED GOVERNMENTS IN
        CHINA, 1937-1945: AN ANNOTATED BIBLIOGRAPHY COMPILED
        FROM MATERIALS IN THE CHINESE COLLECTION OF THE HOOVER
        LIBRARY. Stanford, CA: Hoover Institution, Stanford
        University Press, 1954. 68 pp.

This bibliography contains about 350 entries (including
Chinese-language materials) and extensive annotations (all
in English). These puppet governments are being forgotten
in the history of the war, Mote says, but they controlled
about one-half of China's territory, population, and
resources. The entries include reference works, official
and unofficial publications from inside the
Japanese-controlled areas, serials, newspapers, and even
some resistance (or non-Japanese-controlled) materials. Of
interest are the reports of anti-Semitism inside these
puppet governments (see item #98) and Japanese violence in
occupied areas (item #129).

1059. Murray, Mary. ESCAPE: A THOUSAND MILES TO FREEDOM.
       Adelaide, Aus.: Rigby, 1965. 260 pp.

       Murray tells the story of the escape she led with
       sixteen others from Japanese-occupied New Ireland. Of
       interest is how some planters decided to remain on the
       island in expectations of a benign Japanese administration.

1060. Myers, Ramon H. and Mark R. Peattie, eds. THE JAPANESE
       COLONIAL EMPIRE, 1895-1945. Princeton, NJ: Princeton
       University Press, 1984. 544 pp.

       Here is an excellent collection that covers a wide range
       of perspectives.

1061. Newell, William H., ed. JAPAN IN ASIA, 1942-1945.
       Singapore: Singapore University Press, 1981.

       Here is an extensive collection which covers various
       aspects of the Japanese wartime experience in Asia. See
       especially the material on Japanese involvement with the
       nationalist movements.

1062. Nitz, Kiyoko Kurusu. "Independence Without Nationalists:
       The Japanese and Vietnamese Nationalism, 1940-1945." J
       SEA STUD, 15 (March 1984), 108-133.

       The author concludes that there were closer ties than
       previously thought between the Japanese and Vietnamese
       nationalists. For Nitz, a key episode came in the Japanese
       decision not to intervene in the August 1945 revolution.

1063. Nitz, Kiyoko Kurusu. "Japanese Policy Towards French
       Indochina During the Second World War: The Road to
       MEIGO SAKUSEN (9 March 1945)." J SEA STUD, 14
       (September 1983), 328-353.

       The author asks why did Japan decide to stage the 1945
       coup in Indochina? His conclusion is that the war
       situation forced Japan's hand. Nitz argues that the coup
       did bind together Japanese military and diplomatic leaders
       in an effort to save the Japanese empire and to liberate
       the people of Indochina.

1064. Nu, U. BURMA UNDER THE JAPANESE. London: Macmillan,
       1954. 132 pp.

       The author is a former Prime Minister of Burma. He

gives a personal account of the war years and the Japanese
occupation of his country. Of interest is Nu's analysis of
the rift inside Burma among nationalists, pro-British
sympathizers, and pro-Japanese collaborators. J.S.
Furnivall edited the book.

1065.   Numnonda, Thamsook. "Pibulsongkram's Thai Nation-Building
        Programme During the Japanese Military Presence,
        1941-1945." J SEA STUD, 9 (September 1978), 234-247.

        According to the author, Pibul's most important
        objective was to promote a cultural revolution, one that
        would continue modernization and the civilizing ways yet
        prevent intervention by the imperial powers. In 1942,
        Pibul turned to closer association with Japan. The article
        praises Pibul's cultural and political efforts.

1066.   Ogawa, Tetsuro. TERRACED HELL: A JAPANESE MEMOIR OF
        DEFEAT AND DEATH IN NORTHERN LUZON, PHILIPPINES.
        Rutland, VT: C. E. Tuttle, 1972. 222 pp.

        Here is the personal account of the hardships
        experienced by a teacher in the area near Baguio.

1067.   Pe, U Hla. NARRATIVE OF THE JAPANESE OCCUPATION. Ithaca,
        NY: Cornell University, SEA Program, 1961.

        Pe was an aide to Dr. Ba Maw, the director of Press and
        Publicity. The author's narrative is recorded by a friend,
        U Khin. Despite some lapses of memory and the inevitable
        cloudiness of retrospective recall, the book offers a
        useful view of wartime Burma and life under the Japanese
        occupation.

1068.   Phillips, R.T. "The Japanese Occupation of Hainan." MOD
        ASIAN STUD, 14 (February 1980), 93-109.

        Phillips relies on primary Japanese sources to analyze
        this operation, which had twin goals of (1) bolstering the
        Japanese economy (resources and products) and (2) providing
        an important naval base. The author describes the
        reluctance of the Japanese army but the insistence of the
        navy to undertake the operation. U.S. bombing of Japanese
        shipping eventually rendered Hainan an isolated outpost.

1069.   Porter, Catherine L. CRISIS IN THE PHILIPPINES. New York:
        A.A. Knopf, 1942. 162 pp.

        The book, spawned by the IPR, provides a ready reference

for economic and other statistical data on the Philippines.
Most of the narrative, however, is derived from published
secondary sources, especially newspapers.

1070.   Pramoj, M.R. Seni. "Thailand and Japan."   FE SURVEY, 12
        (October 12, 1943), 204-208.

        The author, Free Thai minister to the United States,
        promises that the captive Thai people will resist their
        Japanese conquerors.

1071.   Pramoj, M.R. Seni and Luang Vichit Vathakarn. PAPERS ON
        WORLD WAR II. Bangkok: 1967. 75 1.

        Pramoj, the wartime leader of the Free Thai Movement,
        adds an important perspective to the study of the war
        against Japan. After the war, he served as premier. The
        papers include information about the Thai declaration of
        war against the Allies, a summary of wartime U.S.-Thai
        relations, and a report on the difficult negotiations
        leading to the cessation of war with Great Britain. Pramoj
        authoritatively explains the complicated situation of
        Thailand's relations with the Allies.

1072.   Pusat, Tenega R. THE PUTERA REPORTS: PROBLEMS IN
        INDONESIAN-JAPANESE WARTIME COOPERATION. Ithaca, NY:
        Cornell University Press, 1971. 114 pp.

        This work, translated by William H. Frederick, provides
        a useful account of the Japanese occupation of the
        Netherlands East Indies.   See especially the material on
        emerging Indonesian nationalism.

1073.   Reid, Anthony. "The Japanese Occupation and Rival
        Indonesian Elites: Northern Sumatra in 1942."   J ASIAN
        STUD, 35 (November 1975), 49-61.

        Reid contends that the Japanese never felt threatened by
        any of the three rival elites: secular nationalists,
        Islamic leaders, and Pamong-Praja (aristocracy in
        transition to a bureaucracy). Prewar Dutch rule had
        polarized the Indonesians, Reid argues, and Japanese
        wartime occupation policy was to make use of all the rival
        Indonesian groups. According to the author, the violence
        that erupted in 1942 (and again in the postwar era) is
        attributable to rival Indonesian factions.

1074.   Reid, Anthony and Shiraishi Saya. "Rural Unrest in
        Sumatra, 1942: A Japanese Report."   INDONESIA, 21

(April 1976), 115-133.

Using newly discovered Japanese reports from the police
division of the 25th Army Military Administration
Headquarters, the authors describe the unrest and tension
in rural areas which arose under the Dutch regime on the
eve of the war. The report documents the harsh methods
used by a Capt. Inoue in suppressing the Aron movement.

1075. Shigemitsu, Mamoru. JAPAN AND HER DESTINY. London:
       Hutchinson, 1958. 392 pp.

       Shigemitsu remained active or closely in touch with
Japanese politics for about forty years. Here is an
authoritative survey of politics in Japan during the first
half of the 20th Century. Oswald White translated the
work.

1076. Shillony, Ben-Ami. POLITICS AND CULTURE IN WARTIME JAPAN.
       Oxford, Eng.: Clarendon Press, 1981. 238 pp.

       Here is a knowledgeable account of life in wartime
Japan. The author downplays the traditional view of Japan
as a totalitarian dictatorship.

1077. Silverstein, Josef, ed. SOUTHEAST ASIA IN WORLD WAR II:
       FOUR ESSAYS. New Haven, CT: Yale University Press,
       1966. 86 pp.

       In his overview of the Japanese occupation in SEA,
Silverstein points out five themes that dominate the
literature: (1) Japanese victories destroyed the myth of
white supremacy and guardianship, (2) natives initially
extended goodwill to the Japanese but became hostile in the
face of Japanese occupation policies and neo-colonialism,
(3) nationalism flourished under the Japanese, (4)
evolutionary social change was transformed into
revolutionary upheaval, and (5) local populations gained
experience--and confidence--in self-government.
Silverstein stresses that these five themes are generally
true of the region but not for each SEA country. In the
other essays, B.R.O'G. Anderson describes the psychological
and cultural ties between the Japanese and certain
Indonesian youth groups; Dorothy Guyot traces the emergence
of the Burmese Independence Army as a new elite group after
the war; and David Steinberg examines the complexities
surrounding the concept of collaboration in the
Philippines. The four authors write authoritatively and
offer valuable insights.

1078.   Spinks, Charles Nelson. "The Puppets of East Asia." ASIA
        & AMERICAS, 44 (May 1944), 212-215.

        Identifying six major puppet states of Japan (occupied
        China, Manchukuo, Thailand, Philippines, Burma and Free
        India), the author observes that the intricate
        administrative machinery was the product of long planning
        in Japan. He describes the puppet leaders as political
        malcontents, desperate nationalists, or products of earlier
        Japanese education/indoctrination.

1079.   Thompson, Virginia. POST MORTEM ON MALAYA. New York:
        Macmillan, 1943. 323 pp.

        In this contemporary report, Thompson stresses
        social/political/economic conditions in Malaya. Of
        interest is her analysis of the importance of tin and
        rubber--not only to Malaya but also to the world community.
        Thompson points to a number of potential postwar problems.

1080.   Thompson, Virginia. SIAM AND THE GREAT POWERS. New York:
        Foreign Policy Association, 1946. 331 pp.

        Here is a knowledgeable report on the awkward
        international position of Siam (Thailand). The author
        traces Siam's wartime relations with Japan as well as the
        ongoing postwar situation--problems with the British,
        friendship with the Americans.

1081.   Titarenko, M. "The Route of Japanese Militarism as a
        Factor That Promoted Popular Revolutions." FE AFFS
        (Moscow), (No. 1, 1986), 26-36.

        NE

1082.   Tokayer, Marvin and Mary Swartz. THE FUGU PLAN: THE UNTOLD
        STORY OF THE JAPANESE AND THE JEWS DURING WORLD WAR II.
        New York: Paddington, 1979. 287 pp.

        The authors focus on the harsh treatment visited upon
        the Jewish community in Shanghai by the Japanese.

1083.   Tolischus, Otto D. THROUGH JAPANESE EYES. New York:
        Reynal and Hitchcock, 1945. 182 pp.

        With excerpts from Japanese books, press, and
        broadcasts, the author offers Japanese views of such topics
        as war aims, the role of the emperor, Japanese history,

Japanese diplomacy, and Japanese militarism.

1084. Trager, Frank N. BURMA: JAPANESE MILITARY ADMINISTRATION.
       Philadelphia, PA: University of Pennsylvania Press,
       1971. 279 pp.

       Here are selected documents which have been translated
       by Won Zoon Yoon. See the helpful Introduction by Trager.

1085. Tsurumi, E. Patricia. "Education and Assimilation in
       Taiwan Under Japanese Rule, 1895-1945." MOD ASIAN STUD,
       13 (No. 4, 1979), 617-641.

       The author, a Canadian professor, observes that the
       Japanese used the educational system as a means toward
       their goal of assimilating the Taiwanese. The results
       appear mixed, but she calls for more study.

1086. United States. Department of State. SUMMARY OF JAPANESE
       POLICIES IN OCCUPIED AREAS. Washington, D.C.: GPO,
       1945. 2 1.

       This brief summary indicates some of the strengths and
       weaknesses of Japan's occupation policies. After a slow
       and uneven beginning, the Japanese quickly learned some
       effective techniques of propaganda and psychological
       warfare.

1087. United States. Office of Strategic Services. DEVELOPMENTS
       IN THAILAND CONNECTED WITH THE JAPANESE SURRENDER.
       Washington, D.C.: OSS, 1945. 4 1.

       The OSS analysts believe that Thai leaders, unburdened
       by Japanese domination, are moving to assert independent
       foreign policies--policies that will bring friendly postwar
       relations with the United States.

1088. United States. Office of Strategic Services. JAPANESE
       DOMINATION OF THAILAND. Washington, D.C.: OSS, 1944.
       63 pp.

       Here is a detailed chronological review of Japanese
       pressures which forced Thailand to provide assistance in
       the struggle against the Allies.

1089. United States. Office of Strategic Services. THE JAPANESE
       OCCUPATION OF THE SOUTHEAST CHINA COAST. Washington,
       D.C.: OSS, 1945. 7 pp.

Here is a brief summary of the Japanese occupation. See especially the description of conditions in Canton and Liuchow.

1090. United States. Office of Strategic Services. PROGRAM OF JAPAN IN CHINA. Washington, D.C. and Honolulu, HI: OSS, 1945. 3 vols.

This OSS study examines Japanese occupation policies in the coastal regions of China. Each volume covers a separate region: central in Volume I (223 pp.), southern in Volume II (262 pp.), and northern in Volume III (262 pp.).

1091. United States. Office of Strategic Services. PROGRAMS OF JAPAN IN MANCHUKUO, WITH BIOGRAPHIES. Washington, D.C.: OSS, 1943. 2 vols.

This extended study provides a close examination of conditions in Manchukuo. Of special interest are the biographical profiles of key leaders in the puppet government.

1092. United States. Office of Strategic Services. THAILAND UNDERTAKES TO WORK HER PASSAGE BACK. Washington, D.C.: OSS, 1945. 3 l.

The enigmatic title refers to Britain's hard-line view of Siam's duplicitous wartime policies. According to this OSS report, however, the Thais had been pressured by Japan during the war and were now moving toward a more natural position of friendship with the West (or at least the United States).

1093. United States. Office of the Strategic Services. THAILAND'S FOREIGN RELATIONS AFFECTED BY THE SURRENDER OF THE JAPANESE. Washington, D.C.: OSS, 1945. 5 l.

The view is expressed that Thailand, freed of Japanese influence, will move toward closer relations with the West in the postwar era.

1094. Ward, Robert S. ASIA FOR THE ASIATICS? THE TECHNIQUES OF JAPANESE OCCUPATION. Chicago: University of Chicago Press, 1945. 204 pp.

The author was in the Foreign Service at Hong Kong when the war began. The Japanese detained him for six months before he returned to the United States. Most of his

observations about the occupation policies of the Japanese
are based on his experience in Hong Kong. Laurence
Salisbury wrote the Introduction.

1095. Williams, J.E. "Siam: A Bone of Contention Between
        Britain and the United States, 1942-46." R INTL STUD, 8
        (July 1982), 187-202.

        The article demonstrates both the difficulties of
        arranging Anglo-American cooperation in Southeast Asia
        (especially when Britain remained a colonial power) and the
        adroitness of Siamese diplomacy.

1096. Yano, Toru. "Reflections on Japan's Southeast Asian
        Policy: Postwar Structure of 'NANSHIN.'" JAPAN ECHO, 1
        (No. 1, 1974), 36-45.

        With emphasis on the present day, Yano describes Japan's
        southward drive (NANSHIN) before, during, and after the
        war.

1097. Yoon, Won Z. "Military Expediency: A Determining Factor
        in the Japanese Policy Regarding Burmese Independence."
        J SEA STUD, 9 (September 1978), 248-267.

        With research through Japanese sources, Yoon traces
        Japanese wartime policies in Burma. By dissolving the
        Burmese government and creating a military administration,
        the local Japanese commander contributed to a Burmese
        uprising (the Anti-Fascist People's Freedom League). The
        sudden Japanese decision to grant independence--an
        independence without sovereignty--came too late. According
        to the author, Japan probably could have retained Burmese
        support if independence had been granted in March 1942.

1098. Yoshida, Shigeru. THE YOSHIDA MEMOIRS: THE STORY OF JAPAN
        IN CRISIS. Boston: Houghton Mifflin, 1962. 305 pp.

        These memoirs tell much about the swings in Japanese
        politics. In 1936, Yoshida writes, Gen. Terauchi and
        others on the Army General Staff opposed Yoshida (and his
        allies) for being too liberal and too favorable towards the
        British and Americans. Named ambassador to Britain,
        Yoshida felt he had to resign in the controversy over the
        Anti-Comintern Pact. From 1939 to 1945, he held no office
        until being appointed foreign minister at the end of the
        war. Of interest is his view that Hull's final note in
        November 1941 was no ultimatum. Yoshida praises the
        efforts of Grew and Craigie to preserve the peace. Much of

the book is devoted to postwar affairs. In one telling
anecdote from the prewar years, Yoshida describes the talk
of the army generals as reminiscent of American Indians
discussing how to get rid of the white man.

II.B.2.A. SURRENDER OF JAPAN

1099. Amrine, Michael. "A Rain of Ruin." AIR FORCE, 42 (April
1959), 189-197.

Amrine traces the events in Japan--"the calculated
ambiguity"--which led to the decision to surrender.

1100. "Atsugi Landing." AEROSP H, 27 (Winter, December, 1980),
262-263.

Here is a brief description of the arrival in Japan of
an advanced echelon of communications specialists on August
28, 1945 (two days before MacArthur).

1101. Bernstein, Barton J. "The Perils and Politics of
Surrender: Ending the War with Japan and Avoiding the
Third Atomic Bomb." PAC HR, 46 (February 1977), 1-27.

In this tale of "missed opportunities and narrowly
averted disasters," Bernstein analyzes the high-level
debate (August 10-14, 1945) inside the Truman
administration concerning the Japanese offer to surrender.
The U.S. response on August 11, 1945, was deliberately
vague, and, according to the author, not only prolonged the
war but also nearly allowed the militarists to triumph in
the debate within the Japanese government. Thus, the
prevailing Truman-Byrnes strategy was highly dangerous. Of
special interest is Bernstein's report on the conventional
bombing which continued even though the atomic bombing had
been stopped.

1102. Bisson, T.A. "Japan Prepares for Peace Offensive." FE
SURVEY, 13 (August 9, 1944), 145-148.

With the dissolution of Tojo's cabinet, Bisson believes
the new government in Japan will move toward a compromise
peace offer. Although the offer, in Bisson's view, will be
attractive and carefully timed--perhaps leaving Japan's
leadership intact and leaving Japan in control of important
raw materials--the author argues that any peace offer less
than unconditional surrender should be rejected.

1103. Brailey, Nigel J. THAILAND AND THE FALL OF SINGAPORE: A

FRUSTRATED REVOLUTION. Boulder, CO: Westview Press, 1986. 288 pp.

Brailey, a British professor of history, maintains that Thailand tried to stay out of the war but was dragged in by the Japanese. The fall of Singapore virtually decided the Thai entry, according to the author. This well-researched book covers the period 1932-1965 and is especially effective in explaining the Japanese role in Thailand before the war. Brailey feels not only that involvement in the war set back the Thai revolution some twenty-five years but also that subsequent British and American interference in Thai affairs continues to obstruct Thai development.

1104. Brooks, Lester. BEHIND JAPAN'S SURRENDER: THE SECRET STRUGGLE THAT ENDED AN EMPIRE. New York: McGraw-Hill, 1967. 428 pp.

Brooks describes the events leading to the narrow decision by the Japanese government to end the war. His narrative, which relies heavily on personal interviews, emphasizes the key role of certain Japanese leaders in influencing that decision. Brooks, who served at SCAP GHQ, concludes with an interesting section on "survivors": wartime Japanese leaders who remained influential in the postwar era.

1105. Butow, Robert J.C. JAPAN'S DECISION TO SURRENDER. Stanford: Stanford University Press, 1954. 259 pp.

In this superb work, Butow analyzes the interaction of the Allies' announced policy of unconditional surrender and the Japanese determination to preserve the status of the emperor. Hirohito intervened to insist on the surrender in 1945 because of the unusual conditions created by the use of the atomic bombs.

1106. Butow, Robert J.C. "The Surrender of Japan." USNIP, 81 (August 1955), 853-865.

Butow has done extensive research for this article. His sources include the International Military Tribunal, Far East, records; captured files of the Japanese ministry of Foreign Affairs; his interrogations of Japanese officials after the war; and Japanese-languages sources. Rather than portraying their capitulation as a hasty reaction to either the atomic bombings or the entry of the Soviet Union into the war, Butow suggests that the Japanese decision to surrender had origins as early as 1941. In that first

year, however, doubters of the cause were disinclined to
voice their views, especially in light of the early
Japanese military victories. This tightly reasoned,
carefully drawn article analyzes the gradual undermining of
support in Japan for the militarists.

1107. Carney, Robert B. "Under the Cold Gaze of the Victorious."
      USNIP, 109 (December 1983), 41-50.

      The article is the text of Carney's diary/memorandum on
      September 2, 1945, in his capacity as Halsey's chief of
      staff. For him, the surrender proceedings aboard the
      MISSOURI were "deeply soul satisfying."

1108. Coox, Alvin D. JAPAN: THE FINAL AGONY. New York:
      Ballantine Books, 1970. 159 pp.

      Here is a brief, but reliable, account of the last stage
      of the war. Drawing from several interviews, Coox traces
      the events and personalities that contributed to Japan's
      decision to surrender.

1109. Coughlin, William J. "The Great 'MOKUSATSU' Mistake: Was
      This the Deadliest Error of Our Time?" HARPER'S MAG,
      206 (March 1953), 31-40.

      This UP correspondent suggests that the truth behind
      Japan's rejection of the Potsdam terms "may" be grounded in
      a misunderstanding over one word. Coughlin points out that
      the official Japanese reply used the term MOKUSATSU which
      could mean "no comment" or a decision to "ignore" the
      terms. The Japanese government apparently intended the
      former, but the English translation stated the latter
      (which implied rejection and contributed to the decision to
      use the atomic bomb).

1110. CRIES FOR PEACE. Tokyo: Japan Times, 1978. 234 pp.

      NE

1111. Gallicchio, Marc S. THE COLD WAR BEGINS IN ASIA: AMERICAN
      EAST ASIAN POLICY AND THE FALL OF THE JAPANESE EMPIRE.
      New York: Columbia University Press, 1988. 187 pp.

      Gallicchio examines how Japan's surrender affected
      American postwar plans for East Asia, especially in China,
      Korea, Indochina, and Hong Kong. His well-researched
      analysis traces the effects of the important changes in
      leadership in the White House and State Department as

regards to American postwar planning for Asia. Of interest
is the author's description of how the Truman
administration's call for a significant U.S. presence on
the Asian mainland ran against the conviction of the JCS
that control of Japan should entail American security in
the Pacific without becoming mired on the mainland. The
unexpected surrender of Japan, Gallicchio explains,
encouraged the JCS to support the administration's policy
of limited intervention in north China--and Chinese
politics.

1112.   Ho, Ying-Chin. "Report on the Acceptance of the Japanese
          Surrender." CHINA MAG, 16 (July-August 1946), 25-31.

        Gen. Ho sets forth the details of China's
responsibilities in accepting the surrender of some 1.3
million Japanese troops. His narrative includes reports on
the various Chinese commanders involved and their specific
duties (e.g., disarming the enemy; arranging for
repatriation; identifying war criminals, traitors, and
collaborators).

1113.   Kalisch, Bertram. "Photographing the Surrender Aboard the
          USS MISSOURI." USNIP, 81 (August 1955), 866-873.

        Col. Kalisch (USA), a photography officer from GHQ, was
among the first Americans to enter Japan at the end of the
war. With one deputy from each of the three services, he
received orders to direct the U.S. pictorial coverage of
the surrender ceremony. His account describes the
preparation and the coverage.

1114.   Kawai Kazuo. "MOKUSATSU, Japan's Response to the Potsdam
          Declaration." PAC HR, 19 (November 1950), 409-414.

        The author, a professor at Stanford University, was
editor of the NIPPON TIMES during the war. Relying on his
notes and diary, the author points out that the Japanese
response to the declaration was misinterpreted by the
Allies. By using the term MOKUSATSU, he says, Japan meant
merely to withhold comment, but the outside world
understood the response to be a rejection. He emphasizes
that the Russians could have easily cleared up the
confusion.

1115.   Kawai Kazuo. "Militarist Activity Between Japan's Two
          Surrender Decisions." PAC HR, 22 (November 1953),
          383-389.

Here is an authoritative report on the efforts of
die-hard militarists in Japan to thwart the emperor's
decision for peace. The original decision, reached during
the night of August 9-10, had to be reaffirmed by the
emperor--principally through the efforts of Prime Minister
Suzuki--because of the agitation of younger officers.

1116. Mikesh, Robert C. "The Emperor's Courier." AIRMAN, 10
          (August 1966), 16-18.

Arrangements for the surrender led to a small
U.S.-Japanese "Green Cross" airline for about one month.
Ie Shima and Manila were key points in this "peace-courier"
process.

1117. Mikesh, Robert C. "The Emperor's Envoys." AF MAG, 58
          (August 1975), 62-67.

The author interviews two of the Japanese delegates to
MacArthur's Manila headquarters in August 1945 to make the
arrangements for the surrender. Oddly, in returning to
Japan with the specific terms, their aircraft crash-landed
in the surf just off the coast of Japan.

1118. Morison, Samuel Eliot. "Why Japan Surrendered." ATLANTIC
          MON, 206 (October 1960), 41-47.

The author feels that the Potsdam Declaration (Paragraph
7), by mentioning the withdrawal of occupation forces,
indicated to the Japanese--and reassured them--that the
emperor would be retained. Of interest is Morison's
description of the atomic bomb as the "keystone of a very
fragile arch" in Japan's decision to surrender.

1119. Pacific War Research Society. JAPAN'S LONGEST DAY. Tokyo:
          Kodansha International, 1969. 339 pp.

Written collaboratively by members of the society, this
work gives a close (virtually hourly) report of events in
Japan from noon, August 14, 1945, to noon the following
day. The group interviewed more than 75 people who
participated or observed in some way the process leading
to the decision to surrender. Here is a useful record of
a brief but crucial period in the war and in Japanese
history.

1120. Petrov, V. "Military-Political Lessons of the Defeat of
          Japanese Militarism." INT AFFS (Moscow), No. 9
          (September 1985), 3-12.

Marshal Petrov reports that the Soviet military
victories forced Japan to surrender, and the Soviet
assistance to the Chinese Communists in setting up a
revolutionary base foiled Chiang Kai-shek's political
goals. Therefore, the Marshal concludes, the Soviet Union
fulfilled its internationalist duties.

1121. Rzheshevskii, O.A. "Bourgeois Assessments of the Soviet
       Victory Over Japan." SOVIET STUD HIST, 24 (Winter
       1985-86), 69-79.

       The author takes issue with American historians who
       slight the Soviet role in the war against Japan. He
       reserves special scorn for those who write that the two
       atomic bombings forced Japan to surrender. His conclusion:
       "History, however, is merciless to falsifiers of any rank."

1122. Sigal, Leon V. FIGHTING TO A FINISH: THE POLITICS OF WAR
       TERMINATION IN THE UNITED STATES AND JAPAN, 1945.
       Ithaca, NY: Cornell University Press, 1988. 360 pp.

       NE (Forthcoming). Sigal takes as his focus the role of
       domestic bureaucratic politics in each country. He
       analyzes a series of important questions: Why the delays in
       ending a war both sides wanted ended? Why did Americans
       continue to insist on unconditional surrender? Why did the
       Japanese insist on retaining the emperor-system but
       surrendered without such guarantees? Why did the Truman
       administration decide to use the atomic bomb?

1123. Squires, Vernon C. "Landing at Tokyo Bay." AMER HERITAGE,
       36 (August/September 1985), 24-33.

       Here is the text of two letters written on September 4
       and 9, 1945, by Lt. Squires (U.S.N.) aboard the IOWA at
       Yokosuka, Japan. He gives an interesting description of
       this unique time and place, including American
       mine-sweeping activities, security precautions,
       preparations for the surrender ceremony, and personal
       adventures in Tokyo.

1124. Stephan, John J., ed. "The USSR and the Defeat of Imperial
       Japan, 1945." SOVIET STUD HIST, 24 (Winter 1985-86),
       3-25.

       Obviously familiar with the relevant sources (some of
       which he translated from Russian), Stephan provides a

valuable overview of the historiographical schools on
Soviet participation in the war against Japan.

125.   United States. Office of Strategic Services. DEVELOPMENTS
       IN JAPANESE REACTIONS TO SURRENDER. Washington, D.C.:
       OSS, 1945. 4 l.

       For the most part, according to this unscientific OSS
       survey, the Japanese people are accepting the wishes of the
       emperor.

126.   United States. Office of Strategic Services. JAPANESE
       ANALYSES OF THE CAUSES OF DEFEAT. Washington, D.C.:
       OSS, 1945. 6 l.

       Based on interrogations of some Japanese officers, this
       report is more a review of possible causes than a close
       analysis.

127.   Wheeler, Keith. THE FALL OF JAPAN. Alexandria, VA:
       Time-Life Books, 1983. 207 pp.

       Wheeler describes the final moments of the Japanese
       Empire. His narrative is geared to the general public.

128.   Wilds, Walter, ed. JAPAN'S STRUGGLE TO SURRENDER.
       Washington, D.C.: GPO, 1946.

       This contemporary collection of documents explores some
       of the dimensions of the complicated process of ending the
       war against Japan. Of interest is the report by the U.S.
       Strategic Bombing Survey, "The Political Target Under
       Assault," that Japan would have surrendered by November 1
       to December 1, 1945, even if there had been no atomic bomb,
       no entry of the Soviet Union, and no invasion of the home
       islands.

129.   Zacharias, Ellis M. "Eighteen Words That Bugged Japan."
       READER'S DIG, 47 (December 1945), 93-98.

       Here is a personal account by a naval intelligence
       officer on the importance of psychological warfare.
       Knowing that the Japanese wanted peace but were anxious
       about Allied policies regarding the emperor and
       unconditional surrender, the U.S., through Zacharias,
       arranged a Japanese-language broadcast in which Zacharias
       reassured the Japanese that the Atlantic Charter and the
       Cairo Declaration were the sources of American policy.

II.B.3. WAR AIMS

1130. Abend, Hallett. PACIFIC CHARTER: OUR DESTINY IN ASIA.
        Garden City, NY: Doubleday, Doran, 1943. 302 pp.

        This long-time correspondent argues that the United
        States should make clear its war and postwar aims. Echoing
        contemporary calls for a "Pacific Charter" to complement
        the Atlantic Charter, Abend feels that Japan should not be
        offered a "soft peace."

1131. Ascoli, Max. WAR AIMS AND AMERICA'S AIMS. New York: New
        School for Social Research, 1941.

        Here is a contemporary analysis of the Atlantic Charter.

1132. Carr, Edward H. CONDITIONS OF PEACE. London: Macmillan,
        1942.

        Carr provides a noteworthy contemporary statement of
        Allied war aims from the British perspective.

1133. Chase, John L. "Unconditional Surrender Reconsidered."
        POL S Q, 70 (June 1955), 258-279.

        In this spirited defense, Chase argues that the policy
        of unconditional surrender was one of the most effective
        achievements of American wartime statesmanship. The
        policy, according to Chase, served both tactical and
        strategic purposes.

1134. Domei Tsushin Sha. THE GREATER EAST ASIAN WAR: ITS CAUSES
        AND AIMS. Shanghai: Domei News Agency, 1942. 60 pp.

        This propaganda piece presents the Japanese perspective
        in the most favorable light.

1135. Dower, John W. "Rethinking World War II in Asia." REVS
        AMER HIST, 12 (June 1984), 155-169.

        Dower analyzes the trend in recent appraisals of the war
        against Japan that gives greater recognition to the
        similarities between the adversaries than to their
        differences.

1136. Elizalde, Joaquin M. "The Meaning of a Pacific Charter."
        AMERASIA, 6 (April 1942), 83-85.

        Contrasting the Filipinos' fighting spirit with the

lackluster performance of the natives of other Western
colonies, the author calls for a Pacific Charter which
promises the extension of liberal, progressive, free
democracy to Asia. Such a document, Elizalde maintains,
would bring a marked change in the war effort against
Japan.

1137. Hankey, Lord. "Unconditional Surrender." CONTEMP REV, 176
        (October 1949), 193-198.

        Here is a critical review of the policy. Hankey argues
that because Japan was offered no means of saving face, the
war was prolonged. His conclusion is that only the Soviet
Union gained from the policy.

1138. Holborn, Louise W., ed. WAR AND PEACE AIMS OF THE UNITED
        NATIONS. Boston: World Peace Foundation, 1943-1948. 2
        vols.

        Holborn offers a compilation of statements on war and
peace aims by the governments of the Allies. She provides
information on the development of these aims and on public
attitudes in each country. There are separate sections on
organized religions and political parties. Volume I
includes the period September 1, 1939 to December 31, 1942;
Volume II continues to the end of the war.

1139. Inter-Allied Review. WAR AND PEACE AIMS. New York: U.N.
        Information Office, 1945. 2 vols.

        This collection of documents surveys the announced
objectives of each Allied country. The book is a separate
publication of a special supplement from the journal,
Inter-Allied Review.

1140. Iokibe, Makoto. "American Policy Towards Japan's
        'Unconditional Surrender.'" JAPANESE J AMER STUD (No.
        1, 1981), 19-53.

        NE

1141. Iriye, Akira. POWER AND CULTURE: THE JAPANESE-AMERICAN
        WAR, 1941-1945. Cambridge, MA: Harvard University
        Press, 1981. 304 pp.

        In this controversial work, Iriye examines the meaning
of the Pacific war for Japanese and Americans. With regard
to war aims and peace objectives, the author argues that
the two adversaries had much in common. Though both sides

insisted on exaggerating their differences, the legacy of
American-Japanese interdependence has outlasted the tenuous
pan-Asianism that had divided the two countries. By
focusing on "culture," Iriye maintains that new emphasis
should be accorded American-Japanese similarities during
the war, especially in their visions of the postwar world.

1142. Kecskemeti, Paul. STRATEGIC SURRENDER: THE POLITICS OF
       VICTORY AND DEFEAT. Stanford, CA: Stanford University
       Press, 1958. 287 pp.

       The author examines the policy of unconditional
       surrender. The section on Japan focuses on (a) attracting
       a consensus within Japan to acknowledge defeat and (b)
       ensuring that the announced Allied aims did not jeopardize
       the status of the emperor. After a close analysis,
       Kecskemeti criticizes the policy. The book is a
       significant feature in the continuing historical debate
       over unconditional surrender.

1143. Lippmann, Walter. U.S. FOREIGN POLICY: SHIELD OF THE
       REPUBLIC. Boston, MA: Little, Brown, 1943. 177 pp.

       Lippmann looks to the postwar era and argues in part
       that the United States should continue to cooperate with
       Britain and must obtain a string of bases across the
       Pacific. The anchor to this string, in Lippmann's opinion,
       should be China--an independent, viable power. His central
       thesis, which is argued persuasively, calls for matching
       U.S. commitments to the resources available. This
       speculative book, however, says little about the means
       required to build this foreign policy shield.

1144. Lippmann, Walter. U.S. WAR AIMS. Boston, MA: Little,
       Brown, 1944. 235 pp.

       After examining the origins of the war, Lippmann shows
       how the fortunes of war are shaping the structure of the
       peace. As he describes U.S. war aims, Lippmann devotes
       much attention to the development of international
       machinery.

1145. Loebl, Eugen. "Moral Values and U.S. Policy: An End to
       the Age of Hypocrisy?" STRATEGIC REV, 14 (Spring 1986),
       27-35.

       Arguing that the United States must rebuild a democratic
       consensus, the author (a member of the wartime

Czechoslovakian Government-in-Exile) charges that Roosevelt
and Churchill's violation of the principles of the Atlantic
Charter—described as the "transcending tragedy of our
time"—set the stage for an Age of Hypocrisy over the next
four decades.

1146.   Lorwin, Lewis L. POSTWAR PLANS OF THE UNITED NATIONS. New
        York: Twentieth Century Fund, 1943. 307 pp.

        Lorwin describes the postwar plans being considered by
        each of the thirty-three nations comprising the United
        Nations coalition. In addition, he includes the views of
        American religious organizations. In presenting these
        plans, which he does not critique, Lorwin hopes to promote
        discussion of the postwar questions.

1147.   O'Connor, Raymond G. DIPLOMACY FOR VICTORY: FDR AND
        UNCONDITIONAL SURRENDER. New York: W. W. Norton, 1971.
        143 pp.

        O'Connor characterizes the controversial policy of
        unconditional surrender as a great success for Roosevelt.
        The president, while untroubled by distinctions between a
        treaty and an executive agreement, understood wartime
        objectives, and, according to the author, Roosevelt helped
        keep the coalition together by eliminating preconditions
        (at least theoretically) for a negotiated settlement. For
        O'Connor, unconditional surrender aided the president in
        achieving his two principal war aims: victory and an
        international organization.

1148.   Perry, Ralph Barton. OUR SIDE IS RIGHT. Cambridge, MA:
        Harvard University Press, 1942. 153 pp.

        Here is a scholarly exploration of U.S war aims. The
        title gives away the plot!

1149.   Sbrega, John J. "Anglo-American War Aims in World War II."
        VA SOC SCI J, 14 (November 1979), 67-78.

        In surveying Anglo-American war aims, Sbrega focuses on
        the principles of the Atlantic Charter and the policy of
        unconditional surrender. He notes the ironic consequence
        that noble ideals not only encouraged principled altruism
        but also camouflaged crass self-interest.

1150.   Spykman, Nicholas. AMERICA'S STRATEGY IN WORLD POLITICS:
        THE UNITED STATES AND THE BALANCE OF POWER. New York:
        Harcourt Brace, 1942. 500 pp.

Spykman, a Yale professor, warns that the annihilation
of Germany and Japan would only open the way for the
Russian Empire. That result, he says, would be at least as
bad as the contemporary fascist-totalitarian threat.

1151.   Stephan, John J. HAWAII UNDER THE RISING SUN. Honolulu,
        HI: University of Hawaii Press, 1984. 228 pp.

Stephan maintains that victory in Hawaii occupied a
prominent position in Japan's wartime strategy. Midway,
according to the author--who researched through Japanese
documents and conducted several interviews--was the first
step in the intended seizing of Hawaii. Stephan describes
the Japanese agenda for Hawaii as including land
redistribution, the dissolution of the Big 5 corporations,
revival of the Hawaiian monarchy, and the re-education of
the NISEI.

1152.   Timperley, Harold J. JAPAN: A WORLD PROBLEM. New York:
        John Day, 1942. 150 pp.

Accepting the premise that Japan harbored ambitions for
world domination, Timperley identifies historical and
psychological reasons for those ambitions--as opposed to
alleged economic motives. The book is an example of
contemporary speculation about the war.

1153.   United Nations. Information Office. "War and Peace Aims."
        UN REV, Special Supplements Nos. 1-7 (December 6,
        1942-February 15, 1946).

Here are extracts of official statements by Allied
governments. The collection makes a convenient reference,
and each of the supplements is a substantial volume (#1, 6
Dec 42, 136 pp.; #2, 7 July 43, 118 pp.; #3, 1 Jan 44, 127
pp.; #4, 15 Jul 44, 124 pp.; #5, 15 Jan 45, 112 pp.; #6, 15
Oct 45, 192 pp.; and #7, 15 Feb 46, 176 pp.).

1154.   United States. Office of War Information. ENEMY JAPAN.
        Washington, D.C.: Public Affairs Press, 1945.

This OWI publication reaffirms the war aim of
unconditional surrender and, despite its year of
publication, warns that a long war still looms ahead.
Intended for public consumption, the report's strenuous
reassertions against a negotiated settlement belie
differences of opinion within the United Nations coalition
on the subject.

1155. Villa, Brian L. "The U.S. Army, Unconditional Surrender,
       and the Potsdam Declaration." J AMER HIST, 63 (June
       1976), 66-92.

       With extensive research through government records,
       private collections, and interviews, the author argues that
       the policy of unconditional surrender (vigorously defended
       by the State Department) and the reluctance of Marshall and
       Grew to press their views for moderate terms to Japan
       combined to delay the peace.

1156. Wallace, Henry A. THE PRICE OF FREE WORLD VICTORY. New
       York: L.B. Fischer 1942. 37 pp.

       The Vice President gives a clear, concise statement of
       U.S. war aims. In this speech to the Free World
       Association on May 8, 1942, Wallace proclaimed the "century
       of the common man."

1157. Wright, Quincy. "Essential Human Rights and East Asia."
       FE SURVEY, 14 (March 14, 1945), 53-55.

       Wright reports that a committee of the American Law
       Institute drafted a statement of essential human rights and
       called for an international charter. These rights include
       an end to discriminatory treatment such as extra-
       territoriality and the exploitation of labor and
       immigrants.

1158. Ziff, William B. THE GENTLEMEN TALK OF PEACE. Chicago,
       IL: Ziff-Davis, 1944. 530 pp.

            NE

II.B.4. PROPAGANDA/PSYCHOLOGICAL WARFARE

1159. Ceylon, Department of Information. WHAT THE JAPANESE ARE
       SAYING. Colombo: Ceylon Government Press, 1944. 14
       pp.

       Here is an attempt to expose Japanese propaganda
       tactics.

1160. Crawford, Anthony R. "'Your Country Needs You': Posters
       From Two World Wars." GATEWAY HERITAGE, I (Spring
       1981), 32-41.

            NE

1161.   Darracott, Joseph, comp.   SECOND WORLD WAR POSTERS.
        London: Imperial War Museum, 1972.   72 pp.

        Here is a sampling of the art-propaganda weapon, the
        public poster. Most are in color; all are interesting.

1162.   George C. Marshall Research Foundation.   POSTERS OF WORLD
        WAR I AND WORLD WAR II IN THE GEORGE C. MARSHALL
        RESEARCH FOUNDATION.   Charlottesville, VA: University
        Press of Virginia, 1979.   127 pp.

        The collection, largely reproductions, includes samples
        of enemy as well as Allied (or "Associated Power")
        propaganda efforts.

1163.   Great Britain.   Information Services.   BRITAIN VERSUS
        JAPAN.   New York: British Information Services, 1944.
        31 pp.

        Here is a propaganda-narrative to remind Americans that
        the British, too, were participating in the war against
        Japan.

1164.   Judd, Denis, ed.   POSTERS OF WORLD WAR TWO.   New York:
        St. Martin's Press, 1973.   160 pp.

        This book has a distinct international flavor, with
        posters drawn from countries on both sides in all theaters.
        Translations are given for slogans in foreign languages.
        Organized by subject/themes (e.g., recruitment, women in
        wartime, the enemy, etc.), the selected posters demonstrate
        the persuasive power of this form of propaganda. Judd's
        accompanying text points out parallels and contrasts.

1165.   Lasker, Bruno and Agnes Roman.   PROPAGANDA FROM CHINA AND
        JAPAN.   Washington, DC: IPR, 1938.   120 pp.

        The authors build a case study in the recognition and
        use of propaganda. The focus of the work is the
        conflicting testimony about events in the Sino-Japanese
        war.

1166.   Margolin, Leo J.   PAPER BULLETS: A BRIEF HISTORY OF
        PSYCHOLOGICAL WARFARE IN WORLD WAR II.   New York:
        Froben Press, 1946.   149 pp.

        The author, an editor with the U.S. Army's Psychological
        Warfare Branch, discusses some successes and failures in

the war to win hearts and minds. He includes propaganda
techniques employed by both the Japanese and the Americans.
Contrary to popular opinion, he notes that Japanese
soldiers did surrender, and he credits some of this to
effective U.S. psychological tactics. On the other hand,
Margolin points out (with professional admiration?) the
double-barreled propaganda effort by the Japanese (a)
toward attracting colonial peoples and (b) toward
neutralizing U.S. public opinion before the war. His
conclusion warns of the need to remain vigilant to thwart
any Japanese (and German) attempts to gain revenge.

1167.   Menefee, Seldon C. "Japan's Propaganda War." ASIA &
          AMERICAS, 43 (March 1943), 167-169.

        The author, a sociologist, points to the clever
propaganda efforts of the enemy. His report identifies the
Japanese ploys that are difficult to combat: appeals to
nationalism, respect for religious beliefs, and
anti-(Western) imperialism.

1168.   Meo, Lucy D. JAPAN'S RADIO WAR ON AUSTRALIA, 1941-1945.
          New York: Cambridge University Press, 1968. 300 pp.

        This Australian author bases her report on the actual
Japanese wartime broadcasts. Her emphasis lies in the
Japanese propaganda descriptions of the benefits of the
Greater East Asia Co-Prosperity Sphere.

1169.   Paddock, Alfred H., Jr. U.S. ARMY SPECIAL WARFARE, ITS
          ORIGINS: PSYCHOLOGICAL AND UNCONVENTIONAL WARFARE,
          1941-1962. Washington, D.C.: National Defense
          University Press, 1982. 221 pp.

        This study includes material on guerrilla warfare.
Paddock finds that the war wielded a significant influence
in the development of the Army's Special Warfare doctrine,
especially in psychological-propaganda warfare.

1170.   Padover, Saul K. "Japanese Race Propaganda." PUB OPINION
          Q, 7 (Summer 1943), 191-204.

        The author asserts that Japan borrowed German tactics in
taking advantage of racial divisions. The answer, he says,
lies in the West's willingness to solve problems of the
second class citizens of the world.

1171. PAPER BULLETS: GREAT PROPAGANDA POSTERS: AXIS AND ALLIED
          COUNTRIES, WWII. New York: Chelsea House, 1977. 64 1.

Here are 28 posters from various countries on both sides
(translations are provided). See, too, the essay by Daniel
Lerner on psychological warfare.

1172. Rhodes, Anthony R.E. PROPAGANDA: THE ART OF PERSUASION IN
       WORLD WAR II. New York: Chelsea House, 1976. 319 pp.

The book contains over 600 illustrations in portraying
the various types of propaganda. These include cartoons,
movies, photographs, and newspapers. See the special essay
by Rhodes on psychological warfare.

1173. Schofield, William G. TREASON TRAIL. Chicago, IL:
       Rand-McNally, 1964. 266 pp.

Schofield, a reporter, looks only at Americans who
broadcast on enemy radio--what he calls the new "treason by
radio." His objective is to discover the motives of these
Americans. Only one of his subjects, Iva Toguri ("Tokyo
Rose"), is taken from the war against Japan. Although he
observes that Toguri's efforts probably helped the morale
of U.S. servicemen more than any entertainer had done,
Schofield argues that the intent, not necessarily the
result, of her actions was treasonous.

1174. United States. Office of War Information. VICTORY
       SPEAKER: AN ARSENAL OF INFORMATION FOR SPEAKERS.
       Washington, D.C.: GPO, 1942-1943. 5 portfolios.

The OWI furnished a total of five issues under this
title between December 18, 1942, and April 30, 1943. The
information is of a general nature; most of it dissolves
into public relations platitudes.

1175. Winkler, Allan M. THE POLITICS OF PROPAGANDA: THE OFFICE
       OF WAR INFORMATION, 1942-1945. New Haven, CT: Yale
       University Press, 1978. 230 pp.

In a well-written account, Winkler differentiates
between the objectives of Roosevelt and those of OWI. The
president and his close advisers (such as Hull and Stimson)
focused almost entirely on military victory. On the other
hand, OWI officials sought to shape propaganda efforts to
emphasize democratic values and human freedom.

1176. Zeman, Abynek. SELLING THE WAR: ART AND PROPAGANDA IN
       WORLD WAR II. London: Orbis Books, 1978. 120 pp.

NE

II.B.5. POLITICAL AFFAIRS IN CHINA

1177. Baker, Gilbert. THE CHANGING SCENE IN CHINA. New York:
       Friendship Press, 1948. 152 pp.

       Originally published in England at the close of the war
       (1946), the book concentrates primarily on the internal
       turmoil of Chinese politics. It does, however, include
       useful material on the effect of the war and the Japanese
       occupation.

1178. Band, Claire and William Band. TWO YEARS WITH THE CHINESE
       COMMUNISTS. New Haven, CT: Yale University Press,
       1948. 347 pp.

       William Band was teaching physics at Yenching University
       when the United States entered the war. The British couple
       escaped and found refuge with the Chinese Communists. The
       authors try to dispel any notion that these Chinese were
       not true communists.

1179. Barrett, David D. DIXIE MISSION: THE UNITED STATES ARMY
       OBSERVER GROUP IN YENAN, 1944. Berkely, CA: Center for
       Chinese Studies, University of California, 1970. 96 pp.

       Here is a report by the leader of the Dixie Mission.
       Col. Barrett and his associates gained a first-hand glimpse
       of life among the Chinese Communists. Their findings
       contrasted starkly with conditions under the Nationalists.

1180. Bisson, T.A. "China's Part in a Coalition War." FE SURVEY,
       12 (July 14, 1943), 135-140.

       In identifying many problems within China, particularly
       the need to strengthen democratic processes, this article
       by an experienced reporter-observer created a storm of
       controversy. Bisson described the contrast between the
       activities and military contribution of the Chinese
       Communists and the ineptness of the Kuomintang. Bisson's
       reports contributed to the debunking of China that swept
       the United States in 1943.

1181. Boyle, John Hunter. CHINA AND JAPAN AT WAR, 1937-1945:
       THE POLITICS OF COLLABORATION. Stanford, CA: Stanford
       University Press, 1972. 430 pp.

       Arguing that the issue of collaboration has been

submerged in the turmoil of China's revolution, Boyle
examines relations between the Japanese and their Chinese
collaborators. He warns that there were few actual
"puppets" (in the sense of "spiritless dummies") and that
the term puppet should be used with care. There is an
excellent bibliographic essay, which incorporates
unpublished Japanese and Chinese sources.

1182. Boyle, John Hunter. "The Japanese as a Disease of the
        Skin." FOR SERVICE J, 56 (November 1979), 27-29, 45.

        The author believes that Chiang Kai-shek resorted to
        "crisis tactics" in efforts to obtain more assistance from
        his Western allies and to avert attention from "internal
        corruption, malaise, and lost opportunities."

1183. Bunker, Gerald E. PEACE CONSPIRACY: WANG CHING-WEI AND THE
        CHINA WAR, 1937-1941. Cambridge, MA: Harvard University
        Press, 1972. 327 pp.

        Bunker deals with Wang's break with Chiang Kai-shek and
        the KMT's attempt to set up a puppet government in 1940.
        Wang had been a major disciple of Sun Yat-sen. The book
        incorporates Chinese and Japanese sources.

1184. Chen, Yung-Fa. MAKING REVOLUTION: THE COMMUNIST MOVEMENT
        IN EASTERN AND CENTRAL CHINA, 1937-1945. Berkeley, CA:
        University of California Press, 1986. 690 pp.

        The book focuses on wartime relations between the
        communists and the rural population, especially in Kiangsi
        and An Hwei Provinces. Relying on primary sources,
        including CCP documents, Chen says that there were many
        reasons for the success of the communists, but one of the
        most important was effective organization.

1184a. Chi, Hsi-sheng. NATIONALIST CHINA AT WAR: MILITARY
        DEFEATS AND POLITICAL COLLAPSE, 1937-1945. Ann Arbor,
        MI: University of Michigan Press, 1982. 309 pp.

        The underlying cause of China's woes in this period,
        according to the author, was the militarization of the
        country by Chiang Kai-shek. The authoritarian policies of
        the Nationalist Government, Chi feels, set the general
        climate that would lead to military and political disaster.

1185. Chiang Mei-ling (Soong). WE CHINESE WOMEN. New York:
        The John Day Company, 1943. 53 pp.

The title is taken from one of the entries in this collection of 1942 speeches by Madame Chiang.

1186. Clubb, O. Edmund. THE WITNESS AND I. New York: Columbia University Press, 1974. 314 pp.

Clubb offers a report on his experiences as a Foreign Service Officer. Many of the sins of the McCarthy Era trace back to the diplomatic-political reporting from wartime China.

1187. Coble, Parks M., Jr. "Chiang Kai-shek and the Anti-Japanese Movement in China: Zou Tao-fen and the National Salvation Association, 1931-1937." J ASIAN STUD, 44 (February 1985), 293-310.

Coble contrasts the Generalissimo's unpopular appeasement of the Japanese during the 1930s (in order to gain time for China) with the anti-Japanese, radical social reform positions of the National Salvation Association. The research is excellent.

1188. Cohen, Warren I. "The Development of Chinese Communist Policy Toward the United States, 1934-1945." ORBIS, 11 (Summer 1967), 551-569.

Despite a heritage of animosity toward the United States, Cohen says that the Chinese Communists became more friendly to Americans in the years 1937 to 1939. Though a spirit of wartime cooperation continued through 1944 (when the communists favored Roosevelt's fourth term over the "reactionary" Republicans), the following year, however, the Chinese Communists adopted a more critical view of the U.S. as a result of Hurley's announcement of support for only the KMT, Roosevelt's death, and Stalin's signalling of the end of wartime cooperation. By 1946, the communists launched an anti-U.S. campaign that lasted more than 20 years. In this excellent analytical survey, Cohen integrates research through Chinese sources. Of interest is his report on relations between Mao and Stalin.

1189. Edgerton, F. Van. "The Carlson Intelligence Mission to China." MICH ACADEMICIAN, 9 (Spring 1977), 419-432.

Here is an analysis of the mission of Capt. Evans C. Carlson (USMC) in 1937-1938. Roosevelt had Carlson send his frank assessments through the president's secretary, Missy LeHand. Carlson wrote favorable reports about the Chinese Communists. Feeling that he was being censored,

Carlson resigned so that he could write and lecture in China. The author believes that Carlson was out of his element in trying to assess the communists. In 1941 Carlson was recommissioned and took part in the famous raid that bears his name.

1190. Emmerson, John K. A VIEW FROM YENAN. Washington, D.C.: School of Foreign Service, Georgetown University, 1979. 15 pp.

In these wartime dispatches, Emmerson, a Foreign Service Officer and Japanese-language specialist, describes Japanese attitudes about the war. Part of his responsibility was to interrogate Japanese POWs. Of particular interest is his analysis of the Chinese Communists.

1191. Esherick, Joseph W., ed. LOST CHANCE IN CHINA: THE WORLD WAR II DISPATCHES OF JOHN S. SERVICE. New York: Random House, 1974. 409 pp.

The collection presents an honest, thoughtful analysis of the war situation in China by a talented Foreign Service Officer. The views expressed by Service, especially about the Chinese Communists, aroused political controversy that curtailed his promising career.

1192. Fairbank, John K. "Dilemmas of American Far Eastern Policy." PAC AFFS, 36 (Winter 1963-64), 430-437.

This is a review article but presents a vehicle for shedding light on the domestic situation in wartime China.

1193. Feis, Herbert. THE CHINA TANGLE. Princeton, NJ: Princeton University Press. 445 pp.

Feis, often criticized as a "court historian," examines the American experience in China during the war and immediately thereafter. U.S. support to China included war material and political-economic assistance, but, according to Feis, conditions and personalities in that country contributed to a logjam that could not be untangled. Short of all-out military intervention by the United States, which Feis does not advocate, he feels that Americans could do little more than they did in trying to resolve the situation in China.

1194. Fetzer, James. "The Case of John Paton Davies, Jr." FOR SERV J, 54 (November 1977), 15-22, 31-32.

Fetzer describes the circumstances which led to Davies'
dismissal from the Foreign Service in 1954. Of special
interest is Fetzer's account of a memorandum written by
Davies in 1949 which advocated the study of selective U.S.
bombing attacks against the Chinese Communists.

1195. Fitch, Geraldine. FORMOSA BEACHEAD. Chicago: Henry
        Regnery, 1953.

Fitch sharply criticizes the reports of the
controversial Foreign Service officers in China during the
war.

1196. Fleming, Denna F. CAN WE WIN THE PEACE? Nashville, TN:
        Broadman Press, 1944. 112 pp.

In these lectures to a Southern Baptist theological
seminary, Fleming describes his vision of a stable postwar
order. For him, China will be a key to international
stability.

1197. Forman, Harrison. REPORT FROM RED CHINA. New York: Henry
        Holt, 1945. 250 pp.

This reporter's account of his observations and
experiences highly favors the Chinese Communists over the
Chinese Nationalists. Forman particularly praises the
fighting abilities and campaigning efforts of the Communist
forces.

1198. Gelder, Stuart, ed. THE CHINESE COMMUNISTS. Westport, CT:
        Hyperion Press, 1975. 290 pp.

This publication is a reprint of the original edition
which appeared in 1946. Gelder, a war correspondent in
C-B-I, presents articles written by correspondents and
Chinese Communists during the war. See especially the
sections on the general military sitution in China and on
the anti-Japanese bases in North China.

1199. Gordon, Leonard. "American Planning for Taiwan,
        1942-1945." PAC HR, 37 (May 1968), 201-228.

Gordon, using U.S. archival sources, traces the wartime
planning for Taiwan. His narrative describes the effect on
the planning process of reports that showed declining
American confidence in China. Of interest is his argument
that the planners upheld the goal of the Open Door and

never contemplated either pressing the Chinese for base
rights or seizing Taiwan.

1200. Han Suyin. [pseud.] BRIDELESS SUMMER. New York: G.P.
       Putnam's Sons, 1968. 347 pp.

       Here is a view of the war from Chungking—memoirs
written by the wife of a KMT official.

1201. Hsueh, Chun-tu, comp. THE CHINESE COMMUNIST MOVEMENT,
       1937-1949: AN ANNOTATED BIBLIOGRAPHY OF SELECTED
       MATERIALS IN THE CHINESE COLLECTION OF THE HOOVER
       INSTITUTION ON WAR, REVOLUTION, AND PEACE. Stanford,
       CA: Hoover Institution, 1962. 312 pp.

       The compiler presents 863 items, many of which bear
Chinese titles. The annotations are in English. Much of
the material is on the war against Japan. The collection
includes works by Chinese Nationalists as well as Chinese
Communists. This is the second volume in the series. (The
first volume appeared in 1960 and covered the period
1921-1937.)

1202. Jiang, Arnold Xiangze. THE UNITED STATES AND CHINA.
       Chicago, IL: University of Chicago Press, 1988. 208 pp.

       Here is a broad view of Sino-American relations as seen
from the Chinese perspective.

1203. Johnson, Chalmers. PEASANT NATIONALISM AND COMMUNIST
       POWER: THE EMERGENCE OF REVOLUTIONARY CHINA, 1937-1945.
       Stanford, CA: Stanford University Press, 1962. 256 pp.

       Using the files of the Japanese Army in China and the
Asian Development Board, Johnson argues that important
links between the Chinese Communists and the peasantry were
forged during the war. According to Johnson, the peasants
rallied to the forces that would fight the Japanese; the
communists looked good in comparison to the Kuomintang.

1204. Kahn, E.J., Jr. THE CHINA HANDS. New York: Viking Press,
       1975. 337 pp.

       In this examination of certain Foreign Service officers,
Kahn looks at their backgrounds and activities, especially
their wartime reports. Some of these officers—John S.
Service; John Paton Davies, Jr.; and John Carter Vincent—
saw their careers ruined or damaged in the controversy. As
Vincent has protested, loyalty to Chiang Kai-shek turned

into a test case of loyalty to the United States.
Similarly, the sympathetic Kahn criticizes the critics who
had difficulty understanding the difference between
predicting the defeat of the Nationalists and preferring
it.

1205. Lattimore, Owen. "America Has Not Time to Lose." ASIA &
        AMERICAS, 41 (April 1941), 159-163.

        The author urges the United States not to abandon China
        (after years of aimless policies in Asia). America should
        not only defend democracy, he says, but also extend it.

1206. Lauren, Paul Gordon, ed. THE CHINA HANDS' LEGACY.
        Boulder, Co: Westview Press, 1986. 208 pp.

        Contemporary Foreign Service officers and journalists
        convene some forty years later to relect on wartime China.
        The collection also incorporates essays by noted historians
        (e.g., Akira Iriye, Immanuel C.Y. Hsu, and Ernest R. May)
        who present their views on the subject. See especially the
        article by John Paton Davies.

1207. Lawrence, H.P. "The Conquest of China." RUSI, 95 (May
        1950), 268-278.

        The author summarizes events in China up to the takeover
        of the Chinese Communists.

1208. Lee, Chong-Sik. REVOLUTIONARY STRUGGLE IN MANCHURIA:
        CHINESE COMMUNISM AND SOVIET INTEREST, 1922-1945.
        Berkely, CA: University of California Press, 1983.
        366 pp.

        This well-researched study (it includes Chinese-language
        sources) reveals the persistent communist interest in
        Manchuria. See especially the events of 1945, when Soviet
        armed forces rolled into the region.

1209. Levine, Steven I. ANVIL OF VICTORY: THE COMMUNIST
        REVOLUTION IN MANCHURIA, 1945-1948. New York: Columbia
        University Press, 1987. 314 pp.

        Levine addresses the questions of how and why the
        communists won. U.S. aid to the Nationalists, he says, was
        roughly equivalent to the help given to communists by
        Stalin. Communist strategy, especially in the northeast
        region, combined the urban-based organizations with
        "induced" peasant revolutions in rural areas. According to

the author, Japanese weapons (given to the communists by
the Red Army) and time (to enable the superior communist
organization to take effect) were key elements in the
victory.

1210.   Lin, Yu-T'ang. BETWEEN TEARS AND LAUGHTER. New York: John
        Day, 1943. 216 pp.

        Here is an authoritative view of the contemporary
        political scene in China. Lin wrote the book after his
        first wartime visit (return) to China.

1211.   Lin, Yu-T'ang. VIGIL OF A NATION. New York: John Day,
        1945. 262 pp.

        Lin made two wartime visits to China. His comments
        about his native land are a mixture of first-hand reports
        and philosophic musings.

1212.   Llewellyn, Bernard. I LEFT MY ROOTS IN CHINA. New York:
        Oxford University Press, 1953. 175 pp.

        The author travelled extensively in China and describes
        conditions in the country during the war.

1213.   MacKinnon, Stephen R. and Oris Friesen. CHINA REPORTING:
        AN ORAL HISTORY OF AMERICAN JOURNALISM IN THE 1930s AND
        1940s. Berkeley, CA: University of California Press,
        1987. 230 pp.

        Here is a valuable collection of reports by people who
        witnessed the events in China that they describe. Some
        common themes surface: a love for China and the people
        (although not the government) and a sense of frustration at
        the way things unfolded.

1214.   McLane, Charles B. SOVIET POLICY AND THE CHINESE
        COMMUNISTS, 1931-1946. New York: Columbia University
        Press, 1958. 310 pp.

        McLane's analysis is well researched and incorporates
        Russian-language sources. See especially his emphasis that
        the Chinese Communist leadership should not have been
        surprised by the 1945 Sino-Soviet treaty.

1215.   May, Gary. CHINA SCAPEGOAT: THE DIPLOMATIC ORDEAL OF JOHN
        CARTER VINCENT. Washington, D.C.: New Republic Books,
        1979. 370 pp.

Here is a well-researched scholarly assessment of the
controversial Foreign Service officer. Controversy,
however, is hardly what Vincent sought or desired.
According to May, the reports from China stemmed from
Vincent's efforts to portray accurately the wartime
situation there.

1216. Melby, John F. THE MANDATE OF HEAVEN. Toronto: University
       of Toronto Press, 1968. 313 pp.

Here is the view by a Foreign Service Officer--as an
"Old China Hand"--of the civil war in China after Japan's
surrender.

1217. Meng, C.Y.W. "Representative Government Emerges in China."
       FOR AFFS, 22 (April 1944), 484-488.

Maintaining that Japanese blows drove the Chinese people
together, the author, a Chinese bank officer, describes the
growing democracy in China, especially a developing sense
of "constitutional morality."

1218. Meskill, Johanna M. HITLER AND JAPAN: THE HOLLOW
       ALLIANCE. New York: Atherton, 1966. 245 pp.

The narrative reveals that Tokyo and Berlin failed to
cooperate largely because of different goals the two
countries had and their mutual mistrust. The author has
managed exhaustive research as she carries her story to the
end of the war.

1219. National Planning Association. CHINA'S RELIEF NEEDS.
       Washington, D.C.: NPA, 1945. 52 pp.

By providing this report, the NPA gives a good
indication of the magnitude of the postwar problems facing
the Chinese.

1220. Ng-Quinn, Michael. "Ideology and the Origins of Mutual
       Hostility in U.S.-China Relations: The 1940s in
       Retrospect." ASIAN THOUGHT & SOC, 10 (November 1985),
       165-178.

Ideology, while important, is not the most significant
factor in Sino-American relations, according to the author.
He seeks a fuller explanation of the mutual hostility
during the 1940s.

1221. Peck, Graham. TWO KINDS OF TIME. Boston: Houghton

Mifflin, 1950. 725 pp.

After spending more than five years in China, the author
cannot conceal his anti-government views. As a
correspondent and artist (he includes some of his
sketches), Graham provides a knowledgeable report on life
in China and the war with Japan. A shorter version of this
book appeared in 1967 (353 pp.).

1222. Powell, John B. MY TWENTY-FIVE YEARS IN CHINA. New York:
       Macmillan, 1945. 436 pp.

Powell, a reporter and editor, provides a knowledgeable
narrative about life in China, both before and during the
war. Imprisoned for a time by the Japanese, he proves a
keen observer--and reporter.

1223. Readon-Anderson, James. YENAN AND THE GREAT POWERS: THE
       ORIGINS OF CHINESE COMMUNIST FOREIGN POLICY, 1944-1946.
       New York: Columbia University Press, 1980. 216 pp.

The author incorporates extensive research in this
analysis of the Chinese Communists. Although the book
portrays the communists' goals, Reardon-Anderson takes a
balanced, scholarly approach.

1224. Rosinger, Lawrence K. CHINA'S CRISIS. New York: A.A.
       Knopf, 1945. 259 pp.

Here is an excellent analysis of China at war. Rosinger
assesses the domestic situation as well as China's place
within the Allied coalition.

1225. Rosinger, Lawrence K. CHINA'S WARTIME POLITICS.
       Princeton, NJ: Princeton University Press, 1944. 133
       pp.

In this balanced account, which was sponsored by the
IPR, Rosinger portrays China at war. About one-half the
book comprises documents and public statements.

1226. Rosinger, Lawrence K. CHINA'S WARTIME POLITICS, 1937-1944.
       Princeton, NJ: Princeton University Press, 1944.
       133 pp.

The author, an expert in Asian affairs, examines the
political development of China within the context of the
postwar need for China to become a member of the Big 5.
Rosinger reports that, to the relief of Americans, China is

moving toward constitutional government. There is little
on regional/local politics or relations with the Allies.
About one-half the book is devoted to reproducing Chinese
political documents.

1227.   Schaller, Michael. THE UNITED STATES AND CHINA IN THE
        TWENTIETH CENTURY.   New York: Oxford University Press,
        1979. 199 pp.

        Much of this excellent synthesis is devoted to the World
War II era. Not sparing in his interpretations, Schaller
argues that Roosevelt never fully realized he had linked
the United States to a decaying government, despite massive
infusions of aid. The author points out that the Chinese
Communists never received a full hearing in the United
States.

1228.   Schaller, Michael. THE U.S. CRUSADE IN CHINA, 1938-1945.
        New York: Columbia University Press, 1979. 364 pp.

        In this excellent survey of Sino-American relations
during the World War II era, Schaller argues that Americans
poorly understood Chinese politics (and especially the
Kuomintang). The author singles out the U.S. loan to China
in 1938 as a major change in American policies and
attitudes; henceforth, according to Schaller, the United
States hoped to use China to contain Japan. Schaller
provides a balanced assessment of the controversial
Stilwell. In addition, the author carefully treats the
U.S. spurning of the Chinese Communists and the secret role
of SACO.

1229.   Seagrave, Sterling. THE SOONG DYNASTY. New York: Harper
        and Row, 1985. 532 pp.

        Here is a devastating attack on the Soong family.
Seagrave (son of the Burma Surgeon) concludes that the six
children of the Charles Soong family--really named Han, not
Soong--with the exception of Dr. Sun's widow, Ching-Ling,
"passed through life like a team of pickpockets through a
carnival crowd." Of interest is Seagrave's discovery of a
British copy of Chiang Kai-shek's police record.

1230.   Selden, Mark. THE YENAN WAY IN REVOLUTIONARY CHINA.
        Cambridge, MA: Harvard University Press, 1971. 311 pp.

        With a considerable research effort, Selden analyzes the
social, political, economic, and military systems developed
by the Chinese Communists in the Shensi-Kansu-Ninghua

border region. According to the author, the communists
attracted support from the peasants by involving the people
in egalitarian reform programs.

1231.   Service, John. S. THE AMERASIA PAPERS: SOME PROBLEMS IN
        THE HISTORY OF U.S.-CHINA RELATIONS. Berkeley, CA:
        University of California Press, 1971. 220 pp.

        The Foreign Service Officer offers an explanation of his
role in the notorious AMERASIA case. Of interest is
Service's view that U.S. relations with the Nationalists
and the Communists in China might have been resolved.
Hurley comes in for special criticism.

1232.   Service, John S. LOST CHANCE IN CHINA: THE WORLD WAR II
        DISPATCHES OF JOHN S. SERVICE. New York: Random House,
        1974. 409 pp.

        Service, condemned in some influential quarters for
allegedly writing a pro-communist bias into his dispatches
from China, suffered in his Foreign Service career because
of the charges. The clear intention of this book is to
demonstrate that his contemporary reports were merely
objective evaluations. In comparison with the multiple
problems of the Nationalist Government, the Chinese
Communists had a certain appeal to contemporary observers.
J.W. Esherick edited the book.

1233.   Shai, Aron. "Britain, China and the End of Empire." J
        CONTEMP HIST, 15 (April 1980), 287-298.

        Incorporating British archival sources, Shai argues that
Britain will not return to a position of privilege in
China. The Chinese philosophy about reconstruction is to
accept help only on certain conditions, he says, and, in
any event, the project will be much too large for postwar
British resources.

1234.   Sheean, Vincent. BETWEEN THE THUNDER AND THE SUN. New
        York: Random House, 1943. 428 pp.

        This book gained a certain notoriety as one of the first
public accounts criticizing the situation in China. Sheean
offers his candid assessments both of the indifferent
manner in which the Chinese opposed the Japanese and of the
internal repression of Chiang Kai-shek's regime.

1235.   Shewmaker, Kenneth E. "The American Liberal Dream: Evans
        F. Carlson and the Chinese Communists, 1937-1947." PAC

HR, 38 (May 1969), 207-216.

The article describes Carlson's projection of the American liberal dream onto the Chinese Communists. Revealing typical U.S. pragmatism, Carlson, according to Shewmaker, did not think in structured ideological terms and was unable to see the Communists as revolutionaries.

1236. Shewmaker, Kenneth E. "The Mandate of Heaven vs. U.S. Newsmen in China." JOURNALISM Q, 46 (Summer 1969), 274-280.

Here is an outline of the cyclical relationship between the Chinese government and U.S. newsmen. If Chinese officials had little regard for free speech (a Western concept), the author writes, the newsmen had little understanding of the Asian concept of "face."

1237. Smedley, Agnes. BATTLE HYMN OF CHINA. New York: A.A. Knopf, 1943. 544 pp.

The author describes the situation in China during her long stay (1929-1941). In telling of the suffering and damage of the war in China, Smedley concentrates on the exploits of the common citizens. She particularly praises the accomplishments and aims of the Chinese Communists.

1238. Snow, Edgar. PEOPLE ON OUR SIDE. New York: Random House, 1944. 324 pp.

Snow, a correspondent for the SATURDAY EVENING POST, writes of his experiences in China as well as the Soviet Union and India. His narrative focuses on the daily life of the average citizens. Of interest is his description of the difficult obstacles that may block international cooperation and stability in the postwar era.

1239. Stein, Gunther. "The Other China." FOR AFFS, 24 (October 1945), 62-74.

Stein maintains that communism is so strong and so embedded in China that it could not be destroyed--even in a civil war.

1240. Sues, Ilona Ralf. SHARK'S FINS AND MILLET. Boston: Little, Brown, 1944. 331 pp.

The author left a position in the League of Nations Secretariat and went to China as a free-lance journalist.

She became associated with one of Madame Chiang's
reorganizational programs and worked with W.H. Donald. The
title comes from the shark fin being a delicacy of the rich
and millet a staple of the poor; Sues refers to the book as
a "medley" of the complexities of wartime China. Of
interest is her visit with the Chinese Communists.

1241. Sutter, Robert G. CHINA-WATCH: TOWARD SINO-AMERICAN
      RECONCILIATION. Baltimore, MD: Johns Hopkins
      University Press, 1978. 155 pp.

      The first part of the book deals with the years of World
War II. The author is an expert on Asian affairs and a
former CIA analyst in China. His narrative incorporates
research through newly opened U.S. reports on the People's
Republic of China. In these early years, Sutter criticizes
U.S. policy towards the Chinese Communists.

1242. Tang Tsou. AMERICA'S FAILURE IN CHINA, 1941-50. Chicago:
      University of Chicago Press, 1963. 614 pp.

      The author, a political scientist, concentrates on the
discrepancy between U.S. professed objectives in China,
such as the Open Door, and U.S. unwillingness to go to war
for those objectives. This discrepancy, says Tsou, led to
wishful thinking by American leaders—about the KMT, the
Chinese Communists, and cooperation between the competing
Chinese groups. According to the author, American wartime
views of China lay squarely in the American political
tradition—depreciating ideology and emphasizing economic
power. This is a thought-provoking analysis which focuses
on the importance of ideas underlying diplomacy. ("All
nations live by myths," observes Tsou.)

1243. Tipton, Laurence. CHINESE ESCAPADE. New York: Macmillan,
      1949. 247 pp.

      In this personal account, Tipton, a British businessman
in China, tells of his arrest and escape. Once free, he
joined a band of Chinese guerrillas. The book gives a good
description of domestic politics and conditions in China.

1244. Tong, Hollington K. DATELINE: CHINA. New York: Rockport
      Press, 1950. 269 pp.

      Tong, a graduate of the first class of the Pulitzer
School of Journalism at Columbia University, reports on
what he feels is the beginning of China's press relations
with the world. From 1937 to 1945, Tong held a twofold

position: (1) Vice Minister of Information with
responsibility for China's overseas publications and (2)
chief censor of outgoing foreign news dispatches. For him,
the lesson of World War II was the "expert mobilization of
total public opinion." Points of interest in the book
include Tong's profiles of foreign reporters (W.A. Farmer,
T.H. White, M. Votaw, and V. Sheean), his defense of Gen.
Tai Li, and his account of the differences between the
reactions of Chinese and foreign journalists during the
visit to Yenan. The author admits that he was told to
monitor the reporting of foreign correspondents on certain
topics, including inflation, the communists, and internal
KMT affairs.

1245. Tozer, Warren W. "The Foreign Correspondents' Visit to
        Yenan in 1944: A Reassessment." PAC HR, 41 (May 1972),
        207-224.

        Although some historians and contemporary critics
        charged that the reports of eight correspondents who
        visited Yenan in 1944 were biased, Tozer argues that their
        dispatches presented reasonable assessments of the
        situation. He feels, however, that the dispatches had
        little effect on U.S. policy.

1246. Tsuji, Masanoba. UNDERGROUND ESCAPE. Tokyo: R. Booth and
        T. Fukuda, 1952. 298 pp.

        NE

1247. Tuchman, Barbara. "If Mao Had Come to Washington: An
        Essay in Alternatives." FOR AFFS, 51 (October 1972),
        44-64.

        In January 1945, Mao requested a meeting with Roosevelt.
        Describing the Chinese Communists as pragmatic (above all
        else), Tuchman feels that Patrick J. Hurley was the key to
        the situation. The ambassador persisted--and the president
        agreed--that the U.S. should deal only with Chiang
        Kai-shek. Thus, with the American course in China set,
        Tuchman criticizes Washington for not having the moral
        courage to terminate a mistaken policy.

1248. Van Slyke, Lyman P., ed. THE CHINESE COMMUNIST MOVEMENT.
        Stanford, CA: Stanford University Press, 1968. 274 pp.

        Here is the text of a War Department report written in
        July 1945. The document was originally published in 1952,
        after the 1951 senate hearings on the Institute of Pacific

Relations. Van Slyke offers a useful Introduction.

1249. Wei, William. "The Guomindang's Three Parts Military and
        Seven Parts Politics Policy." ASIAN PROFILE, 10 (April
        1982), 111-127.

        This policy, introduced on June 19, 1932, stressed
        politics over socio-economic programs. According to the
        author, the policy failed but did extend the government's
        influence into the provinces. There is an extensive
        bibliography for this article.

1250. Wei-Kuo, Chiang. "How the Chinese Won the Eight-Year
        Sino-Japanese War, 1937-1945." CHINESE CULT, 17 (No. 2,
        June 1976), 1-26.

        Here is a soaring tribute to Chiang Kai-shek and the
        Nationalist Government.

1251. White, Theodore H. and Annalee Jacoby. THUNDER OUT OF
        CHINA. New York: William Sloane Associates, 1946.   331
        pp.

        The two TIME reporters tell the story of the war in
        China and what they call the tragedy of Chiang Kai-Shek.
        The Chinese Communists, on the other hand (according to the
        authors), know what the people want and are giving it to
        them. The book is marked by the authors' frank appraisals.
        For example, they condemn the considerable effort by
        Chiang's forces to contain the Communists. Also, Stilwell
        earns high praise, and after the general's departure, the
        authors say, U.S. concern for China turned from the
        military to the political (postwar) sphere. Of interest is
        the authors' view that U.S. servicemen should be educated
        to draw distinctions between the (good) Chinese people and
        the (bad) Chinese government. Both authors have extensive
        experience in China, and their views compel attention.

1252. Yin, Ching-Yao. "The Bitter Struggle Between the KMT and
        the CCP." ASIAN SURVEY, 11 (June 1981), 622-631.

        The author, a research fellow in Taiwan, praises the
        development of the Republic of China, especially in
        comparison with that of Communist China. Using
        Chinese-language sources, Yin claims that Mao committed
        only one-tenth of CCP resources to fight the Japanese (20%
        deployed against the KMT and 70% helped nurture the growth
        of the CCP) and did little or no fighting (except at the
        Battle of Pinghsingkwan).

1253. Zhelokhovtsev, A. "The Chinese Assessment of World War
        Two." FE AFFS (Moscow), (No. 2, 1985), 17-29.

        NE

II.C. POSTWAR AFFAIRS (SELECTED TOPICS)

1. OCCUPATION OF JAPAN

1254. Almond, Edward M. THE HISTORICAL MEMORIES OF EDWARD M.
        ALMOND, LT. GEN., USA (RET.). Carlisle Barracks, PA:
        U.S. Military Institute, 1975.

        Here are the memoirs of an officer who joined
        MacArthur's GHQ (G-1) in 1946 and later became Deputy Chief
        of Staff and Chief of Staff.

1255. Bloch, Henry S. and B.F. Hoselitz. ECONOMICS OF MILITARY
        OCCUPATION. Chicago, IL: Foundation Press, 1944. 141
        pp.

        The authors examine selected problems which will beset
        any military occupation. Some examples of these problems
        are military currency, taxation, price controls, and
        rationing. Of special interest is the discussion of how
        the Germans and Japanese handled their occupation
        responsibilities.

1256. Brands, H.W., Jr. "The United States and the Reemergence
        of Independent Japan." PAC AFFS, 59 (Fall 1986),
        387-401.

        Here is a review of the Occupation with special emphasis
        on economic developments. Brands also describes the
        pressures for rearming Japan.

1257. Buckley, Roger J. OCCUPATION DIPLOMACY: BRITAIN, THE
        UNITED STATES AND JAPAN, 1945-52. Cambridge, England:
        Cambridge University Press, 1982. 294 pp.

        Buckley integrates multi-archival research in revealing
        the British contribution to the "American" occupation of
        Japan. This excellent study also traces the growing Anglo-
        American rivalry in the economic sphere.

1258. Burkman, Thomas W., ed. THE OCCUPATION OF JAPAN: THE
        INTERNATIONALIST CONTEXT. Norfolk, VA: MacArthur
        Foundation, 1984. 299 pp.

Here are the proceedings of a symposium sponsored by the MacArthur Foundation in October 1982. The participants included international scholars, former "Occupationeers" and diplomats. In addition to his first-rate editorial work, Burkman provides a valuable introductory essay which warns against an oversimplistic bilateral context for the history of the occupation of Japan. The volume incorporates excellent photographs from the archives at the MacArthur Memorial.

1259.   Cohen, Theodore. REMAKING JAPAN: THE AMERICAN OCCUPATION AS NEW DEAL. New York: Free Press, 1987. 533 pp.

Cohen served in the Occupation, first as chief of the Labor Division, then as advisor to Gen. Marquat. As a graduate student, he had specialized in Japanese labor. He expresses pride in arranging the 1945 Trade Union Law, the 1946 Labor Relations Adjustment Act, and the 1947 Labor Standards Law. His narrative praises the work of MacArthur and the accomplishments of the Occupation. Herbert Passin edited the posthumous English version of Cohen's memoirs.

1260.   Colville, John. "How the West Lost the Peace." COMMENTARY, 80 (September 1985), 41-48.

The private secretary to Churchill reflects the disillusion of the postwar era.

1261.   Dower, John W. "Occupied Japan as History and Occupation History as Politics." J ASIAN STUD, 34 (February 1975), 485-504.

Here is a historiographical survey of the Occupation. In his call for more studies, Dower reminds readers of the involvement of the British and other Allies.

1262.   Embree, John F. "Military Occupation of Japan." FE SURVEY, 13 (September 20, 1944), 173-176.

Looking ahead to the Allied occupation of Japan after the war, Embree recommends that all military administrators must understand the Japanese culture. What the United States does in occupied Asia, Embree writes, may decide who wins the peace. Of interest is his argument against any attempt to overthrow the emperor.

1263.   Feis, Herbert. CONTEST OVER JAPAN. New York: W.W. Norton, 1967. 187 pp.

For Feis, the contest was between the Soviets and
Americans for the right to direct the policies of the
occupation of Japan. Truman would not permit any joint
system of control, and Feis reports the resolution of the
matter as a clear-cut victory for the United States. The
book includes the texts of seven key documents.

1264.   Feis, Herbert. FROM TRUST TO TERROR: THE ONSET OF THE
        COLD WAR. New York: W. W. Norton, 1970. 428 pp.

        In forming an explanation of the origins of the Cold
War, Feis follows a traditional historiographical path.
Despite allegations to the contrary, Feis believes that
Truman did not alter Roosevelt's basic policies. Demands
from the Russians, not the Americans, split the alliance,
according to Feis. He points out that U.S. policies in
1945 were set by people who did not know that the atomic
bomb was being developed.

1265.   Gayn, Mark J. JAPAN DIARY. New York: W. Sloane
        Associates, 1948. 517 pp.

        Gayn, foreign correspondent in postwar Japan for the
CHICAGO SUN, presents his diary account of events during
the Occupation of Japan. His report takes a critical tone
as he feels too much attention is being paid to U.S.
foreign policy objectives and not enough to the people of
Japan.

1266.   Gilmartin, William M. and W.I. Ladejinsky. "The Japanese
        Problem: The Promise of Agrarian Reform in Japan." FOR
        AFFS, 26 (January 1948), 312-324.

        Holding that sound economic and social conditions in
Japan are impossible with the institutional exploitation of
tenants by landlords, the authors identify land reform as
the key to a new agrarian order not only in Japan but also
throughout Asia.

1267.   Goodman, Grant K. "MacArthur and Japan: A Revisionist
        View." BULL AMER HIST COLL, (Manila), 10
        (October-December 1982), 68-75.

        NE

1268.   Harries, Meirion and Susie Harries. SHEATHING THE SWORD:
        THE DEMILITARIZATION OF JAPAN. New York: Macmillan,
        1987. 364 pp.

NE

1269. Knutson, Andie L. "Japanese Opinion Surveys: The Special
       Need and the Special Difficulties." PUB OPINION Q, 9
       (Fall 1945), 313-319.

       Dwelling on the problems involved (e.g., social and
       linguistic) in opinion analysis from Japan, the author says
       that, nevertheless, the potential political and universal
       benefits make the effort worthwhile.

1270. Ladejinsky, W. I. "Trial Balance in Japan." FOR AFFS, 27
       (October 1948), 104-116.

       The author recommends that the Occupation emphasize
       training in leadership for the newly established
       institutions in Japan.

1271. Lewe Van Advard, Baron E.J. JAPAN: FROM SURRENDER TO
       PEACE. New York; Frederick A. Praeger, 1952. 351 pp.

       This Dutch Foreign Service officer gives a highly
       favorable view of MacArthur and the occupation.

1272. MacArthur Memorial. THE OCCUPATION OF JAPAN: ECONOMIC
       POLICY AND REFORM. Norfolk, VA: City of Norfolk, 1980.
       382 pp.

       This conference took place April 13-15, 1978. One of
       the highlights was the speech by Cornelius K. Iida of the
       Department of Commerce. Iida grew up in Japan during the
       occupation. The Appendix includes information compiled by
       Frank Joseph Shulman about both the Gordon W. Prange
       collection at the University of Maryland and doctoral
       dissertations on the Occupation of Japan. L.H. Redford
       edited the proceedings.

1273. MacArthur Memorial. THE OCCUPATION OF JAPAN: EDUCATIONAL
       AND SOCIAL REFORM. Norfolk, VA: City of Norfolk, 1982.
       529 pp.

       Here are the proceedings of a conference (October 16-18,
       1980) which included both historians and "Occupationeers."
       Thomas W. Burkman edited the text. Elizabeth Gray Vining
       was a featured speaker, and Frank J. Sackton delivered the
       keynote address.

1274. MacArthur Memorial. THE OCCUPATION OF JAPAN: IMPACT OF

LEGAL REFORM. Norfolk, VA: City of Norfolk, 1978. 212 pp.

L.H. Redford edited the proceedings of this 1977 conference.

1275. MacArthur Memorial. THE OCCUPATION OF JAPAN: THE INTERNATIONAL CONTEXT. Norfolk, VA: MacArthur Memorial Foundation, 1984. 299 pp.

Thomas W. Burkman edited the proceedings of this conference which took place at Old Dominion University (October 21-22, 1982). The meeting attracted international scholars, diplomats, and "Occupationeers." The Appendix contains a summary by Robert A. Fearey of the negotiations leading to the 1951 peace treaty. Fearey's report was read and approved by John Foster Dulles.

1276. MacArthur Memorial. THE OCCUPATION OF JAPAN: THE PROCEEDINGS OF A SEMINAR ON THE OCCUPATION OF JAPAN AND ITS LEGACY TO THE POSTWAR WORLD. Norfolk, VA: City of Norfolk, 1976. 158 pp.

L.H. Redford edited the proceedings of this seminar, which met November 6-7, 1975. The sessions covered a variety of topics. See especially the remarks of D. Clayton James and Rinjiro Sodei.

1277. Moore, Ray A. "Reflections on the Occupation of Japan." J ASIAN STUD, 38 (August 1979), 721-734.

Here is a good overview of the work either already done or in progress about the Occupation. Moore points out some areas for further study.

1278. Morley, James W. "The First Seven Weeks." JAPAN INTERPRETER, 6 (Summer 1970), 151-164.

Using Japanese sources and the records of SCAP, Morley examines the attitudes, purposes, and actions of the men who led Japan during the first two months of the Occupation. Special attention is given to Prince Konoye.

1279. Nish, Ian, ed. THE BRITISH COMMONWEALTH AND THE OCCUPATION OF JAPAN. London: London School of Economics and Political Science, 1983. 90 pp.

Here is a collection of papers arranged by the noted scholar on Japan which were presented to the International

Center for Economics and Related Disciplines. The authors review the war contributions of the various members of the Commonwealth.

1280.   Nishi, Toshio. UNCONDITIONAL DEMOCRACY: EDUCATION AND POLITICS IN OCCUPIED JAPAN, 1945-1952. Stanford, CA: Hoover Institution, 1982. 367 pp.

According to the author, MacArthur used education during the Occupation to influence the political orientation of Japan. At first, Nishi says, leftists and intellectuals received encouragement, but with the hardening of the Cold War, U.S. attention shifted to ultra nationalists in Japan. The author was born in Japan in December 1941 and experienced the Occupation.

1281.   Oppler, Alfred C. LEGAL REFORM IN OCCUPIED JAPAN: A PARTICIPANT LOOKS BACK. Princeton, NJ: Princeton University Press, 1976. 345 pp.

Oppler, a German-born jurist who came to the United States in 1939, received an invitation in 1946 to join the Occupation staff. He describes his role and SCAP's authority in reforming the Japanese legal order so as to implement the new constitution.

1282.   Reischauer, Edwin O. THE UNITED STATES AND JAPAN. New York: Viking, 1965. 3d ed. 394 pp.

Here is an expert's analysis of the national character of Japan and the internal tensions with the concept of Westernization. Objective about MacArthur's performance, and optimistic about U.S.-Japanese postwar relations, Reischauer awards generally good marks to the Occupation. The first edition appeared in 1950.

1283.   Sansom, Sir George. "Conflicting Purposes in Japan." FOR AFFS, 26 (January 1948), 302-311.

The author, a British diplomat and an expert on Japan, points out that most Japanese people blame their government not for making war but for entering a war that could not be won. Forecasting a short period of tutelage for Japan, Sansom does not rule out the possibility of a reconstructed Japan dominating Asia economically.

1284.   Schaller, Michael. THE AMERICAN OCCUPATION OF JAPAN: THE ORIGINS OF THE COLD WAR IN ASIA. New York: Oxford University press, 1985. 384 pp.

Schaller's well-researched, well-written account sheds light on the postwar structure of Asia. The United States, according to Schaller, viewed Japan as both a showcase model in capitalism for Asia and a regional bulwark against communism. Of interest is Schaller's inclination to minimize the internal reform of Japan as a dominant concern for American leaders (especially after 1947).

1285.   Schaller, Michael. "MacArthur's Japan: The View From Washington." DIP HIST 10 (Winter 1986), 1-23.

In this well-researched study, Schaller re-focuses attention on the role of MacArthur. The general, according to Schaller, seemed to be losing interest in the details of the Occupation and turning to other issues in East Asia, especially Taiwan.

1286.   Shaw, Henry I., Jr. THE UNITED STATES MARINES IN THE OCCUPATION OF JAPAN. Washington, D.C.: USMC, 1961. 29 pp.

Here is an officially approved account of the Occupation of Japan. Shaw provides an excellent summary which is well documented. The book was reprinted in 1969.

1287.   Smitham, David. "The Reform of Japanese Broadcasting, 1945-1952." HIST J FILM RADIO TV, 6 (No. 1, 1986), 65-84.

NE

1288.   Supreme Commander for the Allied Powers. Civil Information and Education Section. LIST OF STRUCTURES DESIGNATED AS NATIONAL TREASURES. Tokyo: SCAP, 1946. 175 pp.

The compilation of these listings arose as part of the Occupation devoted to civil affairs and education.

1289.   Supreme Commander for the Allied Powers. Natural Resources Center. POSSIBILITY OF REPARATIONS FROM JAPAN'S NATURAL RESOURCES. Tokyo: SCAP, 1945. 42 pp.

The memorandum offers a useful survey of the value of Japan's natural resources at the end of the war.

1290.   Trainor, Joseph C. EDUCATIONAL REFORM IN OCCUPATIONAL JAPAN. Tokyo: Meisei University Press, 1983. 427 pp.

Trainor recounts his experiences with the Education
Division of SCAP, from 1945 to 1952.

1291. United States. Department of State. CONTROL OF INFLATION
        IN JAPAN. Washington, D.C.: GPO, 1945. 40 pp.

        Here is a brief report on the state of the Japanese
        economy. The State Department expressed concern over the
        possibility of a ruinous inflationary spiral on postwar
        Japan because of economic dislocations brought on by the
        war.

1292. United States. Department of State. OCCUPATION OF JAPAN.
        Washington, D.C.: GPO, 1946. 173 pp.

        Here is a report, including the text of supporting
        documents, on the origins and framework of the Occupation.
        See especially the material which defines MacArthur's
        authorority through the Allied Powers. Topics covered
        include education, economics, war, industry, labor, and
        international trade.

1293. United States. Office of Strategic Services. FOOD
        SITUATION IN JAPAN. Washington, D.C.: OSS, 1945. 5 l.

        Written at the close of the war, this OSS report
        expresses concern about impending food shortages in Japan.
        This problem, according to the OSS, could be a major
        challenge for the occupation.

1294. Vincent, J.C., John H. Hilldring, and R.L. Dennison. "Our
        Occupation Policy for Japan." DEPT STATE BULL, 13
        (October 7, 1945), 538-545.

        The article is the text of a radio forum involving State
        Department officers which dealt with how the Occupation is
        being carried out and how the Japanese people are reacting.

1295. Vining, Elizabeth Gray. WINDOWS FOR THE CROWN PRINCE.
        Philadelphia, PA: Lippincott, 1952. 320 pp.

        Vining served as tutor for Crown Prince Akihito.
        Associated with her story is descriptive material on
        Japanese social life and customs just after the war. See
        especially the views of the Crown Prince about the atomic
        bomb.

1296. Ward, Robert E. and Frank Joseph Shulman, eds. THE ALLIED
        OCCUPATION OF JAPAN, 1945-1952: AN ANNOTATED

BIBLIOGRAPHY OF WESTERN LANGUAGE MATERIALS. Chicago: American Library Association, 1974. 887 pp.

Here is an admirable piece of work. The editors, with the assistance of Masashi Nishihara and Mary Tobin Espey, provide excellent annotations in this exhaustive reference source.

1297. Williams, Justin, Sr. "Completing Japan's Political Reorientation, 1947-1952: A Crucial Phase of the Allied Occupation." AMER HR, 73 (June 1968), 1454-1469.

The author, chief of the Government Section's Legislature Division in the Occupation, emphasizes Japan's progress toward democracy (especially after the May 1947 constitution). His intention, however, is to correct the "erroneous impression" that during the first two years of the Occupation "the peaceful and responsible government" envisioned at Potsdam for Japan had been established.

1298. Williams, Justin, Sr. "From Charlottesville to Tokyo: Military Government Training and Democratic Reforms in Occupied Japan." PAC HR, 51 (November 1982), 407-422.

Williams, chief of the Parliamentary and Political Division at SCAP HQ (1946-52), looks at the character of indoctrination that groomed military government personnel for service with SCAP. The key to success, for Williams, was that the administrators were trained and ready to go to Japan as soon as the war ended.

1299. Williams, Justin, Sr. JAPAN'S POLITICAL REVOLUTION UNDER MACARTHUR: A PARTICIPANT'S ACCOUNT. Tokyo: University of Tokyo Press, 1979. 305 pp.

This memoir by an "Occupationeer" emphasizes the political reforms and constitutional development. There is much praise for MacArthur and much pride in the accomplishments of the Occupation.

1300. Wittner, Lawrence S. "MacArthur and the Missionaries: God and Man in Occupied Japan." PAC HR, 40 (February 1971), 77-98.

According to Wittner, U.S. efforts to create a Christian Japan failed principally because of the firm base of Buddhist and Shinto religions in Japan. The article, well researched, especially through private collections, cites other reasons, such as the poor example of some U.S.

Christian G.I.s, Ridgway's low-key attitude after
succeeding MacArthur, and the superficial signs of
conversion that fooled the missionaries.

1301.   Wolfe, Robert, ed. AMERICANS AS PROCONSULS: UNITED STATES
        MILITARY GOVERNMENT IN GERMANY AND JAPAN, 1944-1952.
        Carbondale, IL: Southern Illinois University Press,
        1984.

        Here are the proceedings of a 1977 conference in
        Washington which was sponsored by the American Committee on
        the History of the Second World War. The papers include a
        blend of historians and "occupationeers." Forrest C. Pogue
        wrote the Foreword.

1302.   Woodard, William B. THE ALLIED OCCUPATION OF JAPAN,
        1945-1952, AND JAPANESE RELIGIONS. Leiden: Brill, 1972.
        393 pp.

        Here is a memoir that emphasizes the religious aspects
        of the Occupation. Woodard helped instill reforms that
        eased the rigid, militaristic religions of prewar Japan.

1303.   Zylstra, Henry. LETTERS FROM OCCUPIED JAPAN, SEPTEMBER TO
        DECEMBER, 1945. Orange City, IA: Middleburg Press,
        1982.

        In this personal perspective, "Occupationeer" Zylstra
        offers a valuable description of parts of Japanese society
        at war's end.

II.C.2. PHILIPPINE ISLANDS

1303a. Catapusan, Benicio T. "Filipino Attitudes Toward G.I.
        Joe." SOCIOLOGY SOC RES, 30 (July-August 1946),
        466-475.

        The author served in the Department of Public
        Instruction in Manila. His report indicates that Filipino
        attitudes are shaped by several factors: expectations,
        gratitude, sympathy, jealousy, resentment at being
        discriminated against, and antagonism. Writing in 1946,
        the author believes that the accommodation stage is just
        beginning.

1304.   Crippen, Harlan R. "American Imperialism and Philippine
        Independence." SCIENCE & SOC, 11 (Spring 1947), 97-126.

        The author criticizes U.S. imperialism and a reactionary
        foreign policy that chose the "near fascism" of Roxas over

the moderation of Osmena.

1305. Golay, Frank H., ed. THE UNITED STATES AND THE
       PHILIPPINES. Englewood Cliffs, NJ: Prentice-Hall,
       1966. 179 pp.

       This collection of articles by American and Filipino
       writers is designed for the general public. See especially
       the article by David Wurfel, "Problems of Decolonization"
       (pp. 149-173).

1306. Netzorg, Morton J. THE PHILIPPINES IN WORLD WAR II AND TO
       INDEPENDENCE, DECEMBER 8, 1941-JULY 4, 1946: AN
       ANNOTATED BIBLIOGRAPHY. Ithaca, NY: SEA Program,
       Cornell University, 1977.

       The bibliography includes some extensive annotations.
       See especially the material on guerrilla operations.

1307. Pink, Louis H. "Unfinished Business in the Philippines."
       FOR AFFS, 25 (January 1947), 263-274.

       This article indicates that the United States could be
       more helpful in promoting the independence of the
       Philippine Islands (especially through economic
       assistance).

1308. Robinson, Cedric J. "The American Press and the Repairing
       of the Philippines." RACE & CLASS, 28 (Autumn 1986),
       31-44.

       The author describes the concept of "repair" and notes
       that journalists, like politicians, work out of their basic
       assumptions about the bounds of social and political
       normalcy. Thus, journalists construct, or refigure, the
       news. Within the context of the Philippines, Robinson
       links both MacArthur's repression of the Huks and his
       rehabilitation of Filipino oligarchs with the importance of
       the Philippines as a site for launching covert operations
       and funneling American spies throughout Asia.

1309. Romulo, Carlos P. I SEE THE PHILIPPINES RISE. Garden
       City, NY: Doubleday, Doran, 1946. 273 pp.

       Romulo gives a personal account of his service as well
       as a report on the war in the Philippines. While friendly
       to the United States, the author seeks recognition for the
       Filipino war effort.

1310. Salamanca, Bonifacio S. THE NEGOTIATION AND DISPOSITION OF
       THE PHILIPPINE WAR DAMAGE CLAIMS: A STUDY IN PHILIPPINE
       -AMERICAN DIPLOMACY. Cambridge, MA: Harvard University
       Press, 1984.

       Here is an exhaustive study of the legalities and
       diplomacy of the claims. Salamanca traces the story to
       completion in 1972.

1311. Shalom, Stephen Rosskamm, ed. THE UNITED STATES AND THE
       PHILIPPINES: A STUDY OF NEOCOLONIALISM. Philadelphia,
       PA: Institute for the Study of Human Issues, 1981. 302
       pp.

       This collection, which concentrates on postwar U.S.-
       Filipino relations, is long on emotion and critical of
       American policies. In addition to the editor's article,
       see, for example, the articles by Alejandro Lichauco and
       William J. Pomeroy.

II.C.3. CHINA

1312. Buhite, Russell D. "'Major Interests': American Policy
       Toward China, Taiwan, and Korea, 1945-1950." PAC HR, 47
       (August 1978), 425-451.

       Buhite argues that, in dealing with Asia, U.S. officials
       created a mid-way category of "major" interests as a link
       between "vital" and "peripheral" national interests.
       Pointing out that "major" interests required substantial
       resources, the author identifies the three countries as
       "major" American interests--both to preserve U.S.
       credibility and to prevent a single power from dominating
       Asia.

1313. Chiang Kai-shek. CHINA'S DESTINY AND CHINESE ECONOMIC
       THEORY. New York: Roy Publishers, 1947. 347 pp.

       Philip J. Jaffe translated and edited this work. It
       should be read with care since the original version set out
       a much more ambitious "destiny" than was deemed appropriate
       for Western readers.

1314. Cohen, Warren I. "American Observers and the Sino-Soviet
       Friendship Treaty of August, 1945." PAC HR, 35 (August
       1966), 347-349.

       Cohen cites a document in the Republic of China archives
       that confirms the observations of U.S. personnel in China

at the time. They reported in 1945 that the Chinese
Communists were surprised and disappointed that Moscow had
reached agreement with the Nationalists.

1315.   Congressional Quarterly Service.   CHINA AND U.S. FAR EAST
        POLICY, 1945-1966.   Washington, D.C.:   Congressional
        Quarterly Service, 1967.   348 pp.

        This survey of the postwar era marks the dramatic change
        in Sino-American relations from allies to adversaries.   The
        book includes a chronology, brief profiles of Chinese
        leaders, and the text of important documents.   Most of the
        material is concerned with the post-1949 years.

1316.   Head, William P.   AMERICA'S CHINA SOJOURN: AMERICA'S
        FOREIGN POLICY AND ITS EFFECTS ON SINO-AMERICAN
        RELATIONS, 1942-1948.   Lanham, MD: University Press of
        America, 1983.   366 pp.

        This well-written political history examines an
        important period in Sino-American relations.   With solid
        research and a balanced perspective, Head surveys the
        shaping of U.S. foreign policy.   He finds that American
        attention was fixed on Europe and that Washington
        underestimated Asian nationalist movements.

1317.   Koen, Ross Y.   THE CHINA LOBBY IN AMERICAN POLITICS.   New
        York: Harper and Row, 1974.   279 pp.

        Although this study gives relatively small attention to
        the war years, Koen does generally indicate the dimension
        and influence of the China lobby in the United States.

1318.   May, Gary.   "The New China Hands: John Carter Vincent and
        the American Foreign Service in China, 1941-1947."   PROC
        CONF WAR DIP (The Citadel, 1977), 102-105.

        May describes the belief of the new China Hands that the
        United States should use its influence (including financial
        leverage) to bring about a liberal ascendancy in China.

1319.   Pepper, Suzanne.   CIVIL WAR IN CHINA: THE POLITICAL
        STRUGGLE, 1945-1949.   Berkeley, CA: University of
        California Press, 1978.   472 pp.

        Here is an outstanding contribution to the literature on
        the situation in China, both during and immediately after
        the war.   With meticulous research, Pepper analyzes the
        strengths and weaknesses of both sides.

1320.   Shai, Aron. BRITAIN AND CHINA, 1941-47: IMPERIAL
        MOMENTUM. New York: St. Martin's Press, 1984. 190 pp.

        By "imperial momentum," Shai means British attempts to
        restore prewar relations with China. He takes as a working
        premise that China formed part of the British informal
        empire. Tracing the decline of British influence in China
        at the time U.S. influence was rising, Shai argues that
        1947, not 1945, marks the end of this story. The author
        highlights the Hooper memorandum (August 7, 1947) and the
        British decision to halt trade with China while conditions
        remained unsettled in that country.

1321.   Shewmaker, Kenneth E. "The Agrarian Reformer Myth." CHINA
        Q, 34 (April-June 1968), 66-81.

        The author, a history professor, criticizes the
        "nonsense" written by critics of the so-called myth.
        Arguing that communism was not immediately relevant in
        China, Shewmaker points out that observers (e.g., Freda
        Utley, Evans Carlson, Harrison Forman, etc.) minimized the
        importance of communism in their writings. The Chinese
        Communists, the author notes, have always followed an
        independent course from Moscow.

1322.   Shewmaker, Kenneth. AMERICANS AND THE CHINESE COMMUNISTS,
        1927-1945. Ithaca, NY: Cornell University Press, 1971.

        Here is an excellent account of the uncertain
        relationship between Americans and the Chinese Communists.
        See especially Shewmaker's report on the views of U.S.
        correspondents about the communists during the war.

1323.   United States. Department of State. THE CHINA WHITE
        PAPER, AUGUST 1949. Stanford, CA: Stanford University
        Press, 1967. 1,079 pp.

        Originally issued in 1949 under the title UNITED STATES
        RELATIONS WITH CHINA, this volume devotes special attention
        to the period 1944-1949. There are roughly 400 pages of
        narrative/summary and 600 pages of documents. The United
        States was not a detached observer of events in China
        during this period; there are some omissions and
        distortions. Contemporary critics denounced the timing of
        the original publication of the volume. See the letter of
        transmittal from Secretary of State Acheson to President
        Truman, July 30, 1949.

1324.   United States. Department of State.   CLAIMS RESULTING FROM
        THE ACTIVITIES OF UNITED STATES MILITARY FORCES IN
        CHINA. Washington, D.C.:   GPO, 1948.   10 pp.

        NE

1325.   Utley, Freda.   THE CHINA STORY.   Chicago: Henry Regnery,
        1951.

        This critical narrative includes some wartime
        descriptions of China, but Utley mainly focuses on postwar
        affairs. Moreover, her tone indicates that she confidently
        knows the answer to the question: Who lost China?   She
        looks to Washington. As a reporter with long experience in
        Asia, Utley particularly criticizes the liberal Foreign
        Service Officers and State Department Officials. For her,
        the wartime Foreign Service Officers in China undermined
        the Nationalists and preferred the communists.

1326.   White, John A.   THE UNITED STATES MARINES IN NORTH CHINA.
        Millbrae, CA: Author, 1974.   217 pp.

        In this personal account by the former Marine, White
        describes how he and his fellow Marines became enmeshed in
        Chinese politics. Despite avowed U.S. neutrality, White
        indicates the efforts of the Marines in supporting the
        Nationalists against the Chinese Communists.

II.C.4. PEACE SETTLEMENTS

1327.   Cohen, Bernard C.   POLITICAL PROCESS AND FOREIGN POLICY:
        THE MAKING OF THE JAPANESE PEACE SETTLEMENT. Princeton,
        NJ: Princeton University Press, 1957.   293 pp.

        In this wide-ranging analysis, Cohen examines the
        domestic pressures that faced U.S. leaders while working
        out the terms of peace with Japan.

1328.   Colville, John.   "How the West Lost the Peace in 1945."
        COMMENTARY, 80 (September 1985), 41-47.

        Colville served as private secretary to Churchill and
        Attlee during the war. He feels that Roosevelt's illness
        prevented forceful action at a crucial time. Truman,
        according to the author, arrived too late but did all he
        could to remedy the situation.

1329.   Conference for Conclusion and Signature of Treaty of Peace
        With Japan. JAPAN PEACE CONFERENCE, August 8 -

September 9, 1951. Washington, D.C.: GPO, 1952. 2
vols.

Here is a collection of documents on the final peace
treaty. The volumes include a report on the proceedings of
the conference in San Francisco (468 pp.) and the text of
the treaty (25 pp.).

1330. Dulles, John Foster. ESSENTIALS OF A PEACE WITH JAPAN.
       Washington, D. C.: Dept. of State, 1951. 11 pp.

       In this brief report, Dulles explains the final
arrangements in the peace treaty with Japan.

1331. Dunn, Frederick S. PEACE-MAKING AND THE SETTLEMENT WITH
       JAPAN. Princeton, NJ: Princeton University Press,
       1963. 210 pp.

       Using the limited sources available at the time, Dunn
shows how planning peace with Japan became subordinate
to Soviet-American relations in the Cold War.

1332. Fine, Herbert A. "The Liquidation of World War II in
       Thailand." PAC HR, 34 (February 1965), 65-82.

       The author, a historian at the State Department, traces
the American role in the British-Thai negotiations to end
the war. Refusing to acquiesce to a harsh victor's peace,
the United States, according to the author, succeeded in
softening British terms. The article incorporates thorough
research through State Department files.

1333. Foran, Songsri. THAI-BRITISH-AMERICAN RELATIONS DURING
       WORLD WAR II AND THE IMMEDIATE POSTWAR PERIOD,
       1940-1946. Bangkok, Thai.: Thai Khadi Research
       Institute, 1981. 335 pp.

       Professor Soran presents a solidly researched analysis
of this complex diplomatic triangle. Thai sources add to
traditional Western interpretations. Of interest is his
treatment of both the territorial disputes with Indochina
and the negotiations leading to the postwar Thai-British
Agreement.

1334. Liang, Chin-Tung. "The Sino-Soviet Treaty of Friendship
       and Alliance of 1945: The Inside Story." CHINESE CULT,
       17 (September 1976), 1-26.

       Relying almost entirely on published sources, the author

examines what he calls the "failure" of the treaty.

1335.   Tarling, Nicholas. "Rice and Reconciliation: The
        Anglo-Thai Peace Negotiations of 1945." J SIAM SOC, 66
        (July 1978), 59-111.

        Here is a detailed report on the three-way negotiations
        leading to the treaty of January 1, 1946. With careful,
        patient analysis and solid research (although U.S. archival
        sources seem omitted), Tarling also traces the importance
        of the previous Thai rice supply at a time when areas of
        SEA faced starvation.

1336.   United States. Congress. Senate. Committee on Foreign
        Relations. JAPANESE PEACE TREATY AND OTHER TREATIES
        RELATING TO SECURITY IN THE PACIFIC . . . JANUARY 21,
        22, 23, and 25, 1952. Washington, D.C.: GPO, 1952.
        182 pp.

        Secretary of State Dean Acheson presented four treaties
        for senatorial advice and consent: Treaty of Peace of
        Japan, Security Treaty with Japan, Mutual Defense Treaty
        with the Philippines, and Security Treaty with Australia
        and New Zealand. Although there is a strong Cold War
        flavor here, especially an overriding concern with
        communist aggression in the Far East, the material may also
        be viewed from the perspective of the ending of World War
        II.

1337.   Wheeler-Bennett, Sir John and Anthony Nicholls. THE
        SEMBLANCE OF PEACE. London: Macmillan, 1972. 878 pp.

        Here is a scholarly analysis of the peace settlement and
        political aftermath of the war.

1338.   Yoshitsu, Michael M. JAPAN AND THE SAN FRANCISCO PEACE
        SETTLEMENT. New York: Columbia University Press, 1983.
        120 pp.

        NE

II.D. POSTWAR AFFAIRS IN ASIA

1339.   Arnold, Edwin G. "Self-Government in U.S. Territories."
        FOR AFFS, 25 (July 1947), 655-666.

        Arnold gives a postwar report on the progress in U.S.
        trust territories.

1340.   Bell, Roger. "Australian-American Discord: Negotiations
        for Post-War Base and Security Arrangements in the
        Pacific, 1944-46." AUS OUTLOOK, 27 (April 1973), 12-33.

        With thorough research through primary sources in both
        countries, Bell examines the friction between the United
        States and Australia over the issue of postwar security
        arrangements. The Australian government (perhaps with the
        exception of Evatt) wanted reciprocal base rights and a
        regional defense scheme rather than passively accepting
        unilateral American expansion. Bell feels that the trouble
        first appeared during the negotiations in late 1943.

1341.   Benda, Harry J. "Decolonization in Indonesia." AMER HR,
        70 (July 1965), 1058-1073.

        Incorporating excellent research, Benda, an acknowledged
        expert on the subject, traces a major theme of continuity
        and change in Indonesia. Seeking to reintegrate
        present-day Indonesia with Indonesian history, he explains
        the difficult adjustment of Indonesia to its own identity.

1342.   Bergbauer, Harry W., Jr. "A Review of the Political Status
        of the Trust Territory of the Pacific." NAV WAR COLL
        REV, 22 (March 1970), 43-51.

        The author provides a brief summary of the strategic
        trusteeship of Micronesia.

1343.   Bisson, T. A. AMERICA'S FAR EASTERN POLICY. New York:
        Macmillan, 1945. 235 pp.

        Offering useful background information, Bisson places
        Far Eastern events into the global context for American
        foreign policy. He includes the texts of key (public)
        documents. His report anticipates political-economic-
        social issues that will dominate the postwar era.

1344.   Buhite, Russell D. SOVIET-AMERICAN RELATIONS IN ASIA,
        1945-1954. Norman, OK: University of Oklahoma Press,
        1981. 254 pp.

        For purposes of this bibliography, only the very
        beginning of this book is useful. Buhite incorporates a
        critical evaluation of the vitally important months of 1945
        and early 1946.

1345.   Bunin, V. "The Defeat of Japanese Militarism: Lessons for
        Our Time." FE AFFS (Moscow), (No. 3, 1985), 25-35.

NE

1346.   Burton, Wilbur. "American Blunders in Far Southern Asia."
        AMER PERSPECTIVES, 4 (Summer 1950), 305-318.

        Concentrating on Indochina, the author asserts that
        Washington should have supported the cause of Ho Chi Minh,
        whom Burton describes as nobody's puppet.

1347.   Cribb, Robert. "The Revolution Delayed: The Indonesian
        Republic and the Netherlands Indies, August-November
        1945." AUS J POL HIST, 32 (No. 1, 1986), 72-85.

        Cribb seeks to explain the delay in 1945 in the
        effective start of the war for independence. His
        conclusion is that both sides were weak and ill-prepared.
        The article incorporates interviews as well as British and
        Dutch sources.

1348.   Dingman, Roger. "Strategic Planning and the Policy
        Process: American Plans for War in East Asia, 1945-
        1950." NAVAL WAR COLL REV, 32 (November-December
        1979), 4-21.

        Dingman analyzes the complex process of strategic
        planning. He identifies the central feature of the process
        as being able to balance imperatives; he also claims that
        the planning for war specifically in East Asia can serve as
        a general model for strategic planning elsewhere.

1349.   Dobbs, Charles M. THE UNWANTED SYMBOL: AMERICAN FOREIGN
        POLICY, THE COLD WAR AND KOREA, 1945-1950. Kent, OH:
        Kent State University Press, 1981.

        Here is a "Cold War" account that covers the immediate
        postwar years. Dobbs portrays Korea as a pawn in the U.S.
        -U.S.S.R. rivalry.

1350.   Ellis, Albert F. MID-PACIFIC OUTPOSTS. Auckland, Aus.:
        Brown and Stewart, 1946. 303 pp.

        NE

1351.   Embree, John F. "Micronesia: The Navy and Democracy." FE
        SURVEY, 15 (June 5, 1946), 161-164.

        In this report on postwar U.S. Navy administrations
        within the Marshalls, Carolines, and Marianas, Embree

describes some of the economic and political problems. But
he is particularly critical of "confidential government,"
in which all Navy administrative reports are classified and
closed from public access.

1352.   Emerson, Rupert. "An Analysis of Nationalism in Southeast
        Asia." FE QTRLY, 5 (February 1946), 208-215.

        Here is an objective assessment from an expert in State
Department wartime planning on the subject. Acknowledging
that further splintering of the nationalist governments
might occur after the imperial powers depart, Emerson
suggests a regional federation in Southeast Asia as one
possible solution.

1353.   Emerson, Rupert. FROM EMPIRE TO NATION. Cambridge, MA:
        Harvard University Press, 1960. 466 pp.

        Emerson, a State Department specialist on dependent
areas, addresses the rise of nationalist movements and the
decline of Western imperialism in Asia and Africa. As
dependent peoples asserted their aspirations, especially at
the end of the war, the Western powers found it
increasingly difficult to reassemble their prewar colonial
structures. Emerson avoids the easy stereotypes in this
thoughtful approach to complex questions.

1354.   Evers, Hans-Dieter. "The Bureaucratization of Southeast
        Asia." COMP STUD SOC HIST, 29 (October 1987), 666-685.

        Evers examines the "rapid breathtaking" increase in the
number of government servants throughout Southeast Asia
during the transition from colonial dependency to
independence. According to the author, Malaysia,
Indonesia, and Vietnam are the leaders in this field.

1355.   Furnivall, John S. COLONIAL POLICY AND PRACTICE: A
        COMPARATIVE STUDY OF BURMA AND NETHERLANDS INDIES.
        Cambridge, Eng.: Cambridge University Press, 1948.

        The British author offers a comparison that raises the
thorny questions about the ultimate aims of colonialism and
the aspirations of dependent peoples.

1356.   Grajdanzev, Andrew. "Korea Divided." FE SURVEY, 14
        (October 10, 1945), 281-283.

        Here is a warning that the artificial division of Korea
will create problems. The author notes that social

conditions differ markedly in the American and Soviet
spheres.

1357. Great Britain. Secretary of State for Foreign Affairs.
       DOCUMENTS RELATING TO BRITISH INVOLVEMENT IN THE
       CONFLICT IN INDO-CHINA, 1945-1965. London: HMSO, 1965.

       Although most of the attention is on the latter part of
       the period, this collection does offer some useful
       information on the immediate postwar era. The documents
       selected--as well as those omitted--must be carefully
       considered.

1358. Hess, Gary R. THE UNITED STATES' EMERGENCE AS A SOUTHEAST
       ASIAN POWER, 1940-1950. New York: Columbia University
       Press, 1987. 448 pp.

       In a well-researched, well-written study, Hess analyzes
       the origins of the U.S. response to Japanese aggression,
       emerging nationalist movements in the region, and the
       growth of Asian communism. The time frame for some of
       these issues does not coincide with the war years, and Hess
       wisely selects a broader period. Of special interest is
       his careful handling of a delicate dilemma for U.S.
       leaders, namely, how to encourage indigenous aspirations in
       Southeast Asia for self-government yet maintain close
       working relationships with the European imperial powers.
       The excellent bibliography is a useful guide to further
       research.

1359. Hess, Gary R. "United States Policy and the Origins of the
       French-Vietminh War, 1945-46." PEACE & CHANGE, 3 (No.
       2, 1975), 21-33.

       Examining a key period that has received little
       attention, Hess emphasizes the Cold War (European) context
       that shaped U.S. policy in Indochina. This period may have
       been a "lost opportunity" for American leaders, according
       to Hess.

1360. Hitch, Thomas K. "Administration of America's Pacific
       Islands." POL SCI Q, 61 (September 1946), 384-407.

       Although admitting that the Navy has done excellent work
       in administering U.S. possessions in the Pacific, Hitch
       feels that it can not continue to do so without adhering to
       high standards of training. He warns that the duties of
       administration could easily fall again into low repute
       within the Navy.

1361.   Iriye, Akira. THE COLD WAR IN ASIA: A HISTORICAL
            INTRODUCTION. Englewood Cliffs, NJ: Prentice-Hall,
            1974. 214 pp.

        This interpretive and speculative history concentrates
        on American-Asian relations during the 1940s. The end of
        the war brought the emergence of a "Yalta System," which
        Iriye describes as essentially a U.S.-Soviet definition of
        world politics. The author argues that, with the onset of
        the civil war in China, the specific arrangements of the
        Yalta system disintegrated. The universalistic dual blocs
        of the Cold War replaced the Yalta compromises. Iriye
        includes an excellent bibliographic essay.

1362.   Jeffrey, Robin, ed. ASIA--THE WINNING OF INDEPENDENCE:
            THE PHILIPPINES, INDIA, INDONESIA, VIETNAM, MALAYA. New
            York: St. Martin's Press, 1981. 337 pp.

        Noted authors on each country review their studies on
        the end of colonialism and the postwar transition. The
        authors (in the order given in the title) are Alfred W.
        McCoy, Robin Jeffrey, Anthony Reid, David Marr, and Lee Kam
        Hing.

1363.   Johnstone, William C. "Regionalism in the Pacific." FE
            SURVEY, 14 (July 4, 1945), 169-171.

        The author writes of the uncertainty that remains after
        the San Francisco Conference (which he attended) about
        regional machinery. His report calls for all of the Big
        Five to take part in Pacific postwar affairs.

1364.   Lattimore, Owen. "The Outer Mongolian Horizon." FOR AFFS,
            24 (July 1946), 648-660.

        Lattimore describes the history of Outer Mongolia and
        its key geo-political position in the strategic chain that
        runs from Korea to Turkey.

1365.   Lee, Clark G. ONE LAST LOOK AROUND. New York: Duell,
            Sloan and Pearce, 1947. 308 pp.

        Here is a useful review of the immediate postwar
        situation in Asia, as seen by a perceptive U.S.
        correspondent.

1366.   Mansvetov, Fedor S. "Russia and China in Outer Mongolia."
            FOR AFFS, 24 (October 1945), 143-152.

Here is a statement on the need to clarify the status of
the Mongolian People's Republic. The author believes that
the people want to avoid colonization by either the Soviets
or the Chinese.

1367. Nish, Ian, ed. SOME ASPECTS OF SOVIET-JAPANESE RELATIONS
      IN THE 1930S. London: London School of Economics and
      Political Science, 1982. 87 pp.

      Nish presents three lectures by international scholars
      to the International Center for Economics and Related
      Disciplines. The authors are Akira Iriye, on the
      ideological background to Japan's war against Asia and the
      West; Brian Bridges, on the role of Mongolia; and Jonathan
      Haslam, on Soviet aid to China and Japan. See, too, the
      comments by P.J.W. Chapman and Ambassador H. Nishi.

1368. Patti, Archimedes L.A. WHY VIETNAM? PRELUDE TO AMERICA'S
      ALBATROSS. Berkeley, CA: University of California
      Press, 1983.

      Patti was involved in U.S. national security affairs
      from 1942 to 1971. Although primarily concerned with
      recent history, his account incorporates a useful
      description of events and personalities in Indochina during
      the Second World War and in the immediate postwar era.

1369. Reischauer, Edwin O. "The Real Meaning of Pearl Harbor."
      AMER HERITAGE, 33 (December 1981), 104-105.

      Looking at the impact of Pearl Harbor (and the U.S.
      entry into the war) on history, Reischauer examines the
      changes exerted by the war on the international role of the
      United States and the disassembling of the Japanese Empire.
      He also briefly surveys changes in the international
      community during the immediate postwar era.

1370. Richard, Dorothy E. U.S. NAVAL ADMINISTRATION OF THE TRUST
      TERRITORY OF THE PACIFIC ISLANDS. Washington, D.C.:
      Office of the Chief of Naval Operations, 1957. 3 vols.

      This lengthy report may be viewed as the epilogue to the
      wartime discussions about the future of dependent peoples
      and Roosevelt's ideas on territorial trusteeship.

1371. Rivlin, Benjamin. "Self Determination and Colonial Areas."
      INTL CONCILIATION, No. 501 (January 1955), 195-271.

Rivlin, a political scientist, served on the United
Nations staff working on territorial trusteeship. He
adopts a conciliatory tone in tracing the development of
trusteeship. Denying the criticism that the UN is
distorting the right of self-determination, Rivlin admits
that certain maladjustments exist which require immediate
attention.

1372.   Rose, Lisle A.   AFTER YALTA.   New York: Charles Scribner's
        Sons, 1973.   216 pp.

In this thoughtful analysis of political-diplomatic
questions that emerged from the war, Rose describes
domestic turmoil and "dubious" U.S. military ventures in
Asia. He concludes that many postwar problems for
Americans sprang from the "tragic delusions of a divided
people" rather than from any deliberate design. See
especially his discussion of postwar atomic diplomacy by
both sides. According to Rose, the ingredients of the Cold
War were in place by mid-1946.

1373.   Rose, Lisle A.   DUBIOUS VICTORY.   Kent, OH: Kent State
        University Press, 1973.   392 pp.

Rose analyzes the postwar questions, mainly problems,
that have plagued the United States. His thought-provoking
narrative emphasizes Asian affairs.

1374.   Rose, Lisle A.   THE LONG SHADOW: REFLECTIONS ON THE SECOND
        WORLD WAR ERA.   Westport, CT: Greenwood Press, 1978.
        224 pp.

Rose maintains that much of U.S. policy toward East Asia
and Southeast Asia after 1945 developed from the tragic
legacy of prewar isolationism. The narrative repeatedly
reminds readers of the "naive and benign perceptions"
Americans held about Asia. See the interesing, speculative
chapter on "The Victims" of the war. Of special interest,
too, is the way Rose characterizes the ill-considered
"pencil-like thrust" at Iwo Jima and the Philippines as the
"cornerstone" of U.S. planning in the Pacific.

1375.   Sayre, Francis B.   "Legal Problems Arising From the United
        Nations Trusteeship System."   AMER J INT LAW, 42, (April
        1948), 263-298.

The author, U.S. representative to the U.N. Trusteeship
Council and former U.S. High Commissioner in the
Philippines, points to some of the major problems in the

postwar system of trusteeship. These include questions of
sovereignty, optional or obligatory participation,
termination of the process, vaguely defined terms, and the
role of the Security Council.

1376. Sayre, Francis B. "Trust Territories' Progress Towards
       Self-Government." DEPT STATE BULL, 25 (December 24,
       1951), 1024-1027.

       Here is the text of a statement by Sayre to Committee IV
       (Trusteeship) of the U.N. In his progress report, Sayre
       observed, "The old conception of colonialism is dead or is
       dying fast."

1377. Silverstein, Josef. "The Other Side of Burma's Struggle
       for Independence." PAC AFFS, 58 (Spring 1985), 98-108.

       Here is a review of the official British history on the
       topic. Silverstein sets the chief perspectives (and
       personalities) in London and in the various regions of
       Burma.

1378. Siracusa, Joseph M. and Glen St. John Barclay, eds. THE
       IMPACT OF THE COLD WAR: RECONSIDERATIONS. Port
       Washington, NY: Kennikat, 1977.

       The collection includes much valuable material on Asian
       affairs. See especially Siracusa's essay on Roosevelt,
       Truman and Indochina.

1379. Thomas, Norman. APPEAL TO THE NATIONS. New York: Henry
       Holt, 1947. 175 pp.

       In this description of his vision of the postwar world,
       Thomas calls for international cooperation. Although he
       does not offer specific details, Thomas builds a general
       framework for enduring world stability and peace.

1380. Thorne, Christopher. AMERICAN POLITICAL CULTURE AND THE
       ASIAN FRONTIER, 1943-1973.

       NE (Forthcoming).

1381. Tinker, Hugh. "The Contraction of Empire in Asia, 1945-48:
       The Military Dimension." J IMP COMM HIST, 16 (January
       1988), 218-233.

       Relying on British archival sources, Tinker argues that
       only the illusion of power remained in Asia for the British

Empire. Neither political party, when in power, he
maintains, grasped the changing circumstances.

1382. Vandenbosch, Amry. "Regionalism in Southeast Asia." F E
        QTRLY, 5 (August 1946), 426-438.

        Here is a contemporary case by a postwar planning
official for a regional consultative commission under the
United Nations. Vandenbosch and others presented similar
arguments to Harley A. Notter's wartime committee. The
author calls attention to important sub-topics of regional
concern, such as geography, climate, culture, minority
groups, religion, trade, security, and socio-economic
conditions.

1383. Van Mook, H.F. "Indonesia and the Problems of Southeast
        Asia." FOR AFFS, 27 (July 1949), 561-575.

        The author, a Dutch official, analyzes the problems
facing semi-dependent areas in transition to nationhood.
He defends Dutch policies and predicts the emergence of a
United States of Indonesia which will be closely allied to
the Netherlands.

1384. Williams, J.E. "A Postscript to Empire: Britain's
        Military Posture in Southern Asia, 1945-48." ARMY Q,
        104 (October 1974), 596-611.

        Williams argues that the turning point for British
colonialism in Asia occurred not in the war but in
1947-1948 with the refusal of the new governments in New
Delhi and Karachi to join in the defense of the
Commonwealth and with the emergency in Malaya. The article
is particularly effective in emphasizing the importance of
the period immediately following the Japanese surrender and
the pressures for demobilization.

1385. Yonosuke, Nagai and Akira Iriye, eds. THE ORIGINS OF THE
        COLD WAR IN ASIA. New York: Columbia University Press,
        1977.

        Here is a valuable collection of essays by British,
American, and Japanese scholars on the aftermath of the war
in Asia. The articles incorporate newly declassified
documents.

II.E. MEMOIRS AND BIOGRAPHIES

1. COLLECTIVE ACCOUNTS

1386. Dallek, Robert et al. "World War II: 30 Years After."
       SURVEY, 21 (Winter-Spring 1975), 1-42.

       This 1974 symposium, sponsored by the Organization of
       American Historians, included papers by Dallek on
       Roosevelt, Alexander Dallin on Stalin, and David Dilks on
       Churchill. See, too, the related comments of Hugh
       Seton-Watson and the critique by George Kennan. Of
       interest is Dallek's description of Roosevelt as a cautious
       politician and Kennan's use of the word "dilettantish" to
       characterize the president.

1387. Feis, Herbert. "The Three Who Led." FOR AFFS, 37 (January
       1959), 282-292.

       Feis provides authoritative assessments of the wartime
       leadership of the Big Three--Roosevelt, Churchill, and
       Stalin.

1388. Taylor, A.J.P. THE WAR LORDS. New York: Atheneum, 1978.
       189 pp.

       The book presents six of Taylor's lectures for the BBC.
       As always, Taylor is provocative and interesting. Each of
       the first five programs analyzes a war leader--Roosevelt,
       Churchill, Hitler, Stalin, and Mussolini. The sixth,
       however, is of particular interest to this guide. Taylor
       explains why no such "war lord" existed in Japan and,
       indeed, why there seemed to be no supreme direction at all
       in Japan.

II.E.2. SELECTED INDIVIDUALS

CHIANG KAI-SHEK

1389. Chiang Kai-shek. ALL WE ARE AND ALL WE HAVE. New York:
       The John Day Company, 1943. 61 pp.

       The Chinese leader sets forth his war aims and calls for
       a united, wholehearted war effort ("Patriotism Is Not
       Enough"). In view of China's dire circumstances, it is
       interesting to note Chiang's claim that on the day
       after Pearl Harbor, he offered all possible assistance to
       the United States.

1390. Chiang Kai-shek. BEFORE FINAL VICTORY. New York: Chinese
       News Service, 1945. 80 pp.

Among these 18 speeches by the Generalissimo during 1943-1944, see especially "The Turning Point of the War," "Before Final Victory," and his remarks on the surrender of extraterritoriality privileges in China by the Americans and British.

1391. Chiang Kai-shek. THE COLLECTED WARTIME MESSAGES OF GENERALISSIMO CHIANG KAI-SHEK, 1937-1945. New York: The John Day Company, 1946. 2 vols.

This collection offers a convenient springboard for inquiring into both the public side of Chiang and China's war effort.

1392. Chiang Kai-shek. RESISTANCE AND RECONSTRUCTION. Freeport, NY: Books for Libraries Press, 1970. 322 pp.

Here are wartime messages by Chiang which include postwar plans.

1393. Chiang, Kai-shek, Madame. SELECTED SPEECHES BY MADAME CHIANG KAI-SHEK. Taipei: Government Information Office, 1957. 73 pp.

The volume begins with her speeches in 1943 and continues beyond the years of World War II.

1393a. Chiang Wei-kuo. HOW GENERALISSIMO CHIANG KAI-SHEK WON THE EIGHT-YEAR SINO-JAPANESE WAR, 1937-1945. Taipei, Taiwan: Republic of China Li Ming Culture Enterprise Company, 1979. 374 pp.

Using archival materials of the Republic of China, the author assembles a highly sympathetic account.

1394. Chiang Wei-Kuo. "How the Chinese Won the Eight-Year Sino-Japanese War, 1937-1945." CHINESE CULT, 17 (June 1976), 1-26.

Here is fulsome praise for the "great and judicious leader," the generalissimo.

WINSTON S. CHURCHILL

1395. Cohen, Eliot A. "Churchill at War." COMMENTARY, 83 (May 1987), 40-49.

Cohen praises his subject without lapsing into hagiography. The narrative dwells on the elements of

Churchill's strategic vision.

1396.   Gilbert, Martin. ROAD TO VICTORY: WINSTON S. CHURCHILL,
        1941-5. London: Heinemann, 1986. 1417 pp.

        Here is the latest volume in what has become a classic
        biographical study. The research, the writing, the
        analysis are all first rate. There is, however, no
        mistaking the heavy emphasis on things European.

1397.   Moran, Lord. CHURCHILL: TAKEN FROM THE DIARIES OF LORD
        MORAN. Boston: Houghton Mifflin, 1966. 877 pp.

        This remarkably revealing portrait of Churchill comes
        from the diary of his physician. The frank confidences and
        the unguarded moments make compelling reading. Although
        the book stirred controversy, it offers a well-rounded
        picture of the war leader—in doubt and in courage. Of
        interest is the material on Churchill's determination to
        resist Roosevelt's encroachments against colonialism.

1398.   Rickert, William E. "Winston Churchill's Archetypal
        Metaphors: A Mythopoetic Translation of World War II."
        CENTRAL STATES SPEECH J, 28 (Summer 1977), 106-112.

        Rickert, a professor of communication, believes that
        Churchill not only described the war but also translated it
        for the British people. According to the author,
        Churchill's wartime rhetoric made extensive use of
        metaphors to create a mythopoetic tale that began in the
        1930s and promised perseverance to the final triumph.

JOSEPH C. GREW

1399.   Grew, Joseph C. TEN YEARS IN JAPAN. New York: Simon and
        Schuster, 1944. 554 pp.

        Based on his diary, Grew recounts his life in Japan
        before the war. This is a valuable contemporary source.
        The U.S. ambassador to Japan speaks knowledgeably about
        prewar Japanese diplomacy. See especially his reports of
        rumors of plans for a surprise attack on Pearl Harbor
        (January 27, 1941) and the possibility of a Japanese move
        "with dangerous and dramatic suddenness" (November 3,
        1941). For a time Grew seemed tainted, perceived (perhaps
        for good reason) in Washington as an appeaser, and he
        argued somewhat tortuously about the benefits of his
        policy of "constructive conciliation" (September 30, 1941).

1400.   Grew, Joseph C. TURBULENT ERA: A DIPLOMATIC RECORD OF
        FORTY YEARS, 1904-1945. Boston: Houghton Mifflin,
        1952. 2 vols.

        The volumes, edited by Walter Johnson, highlight Grew's
        long career. His tenure as prewar U.S. ambassador to Japan
        reveals the difficult challenges he faced. Advantages of
        hindsight seem to color some of his observations about
        prewar Japan. Of interest is Grew's advice to President
        Truman at the time of Germany's surrender that Japan might
        be prepared to accept a negotiated settlement.

1401.   Heinrichs, Waldo H., Jr. AMERICAN AMBASSADOR: JOSEPH C.
        GREW AND THE DEVELOPMENT OF THE UNITED STATES DIPLOMATIC
        TRADITION. Boston: Little, Brown, 1966.

        In this excellent account, Heinrichs not only analyzes
        Grew's performance as an ambassador (Turkey, 1927-1932;
        Japan, 1932-1941) but also assesses the U.S. Foreign
        Service. Heinrichs is particularly effective in dealing
        with the domestic factions in Japan during the 1930s' and
        Grew's reporting of shifting circumstances. The complexity
        of the situation in 1941 put Grew to the test. The book is
        well written, and Heinrichs provides a valuable
        bibliography.

HARRY HOPKINS

1402.   McJimsey, George. HARRY HOPKINS: ALLY OF THE POOR AND
        DEFENDER OF DEMOCRACY. Cambridge, MA: Harvard
        University Press, 1987. 474 pp.

        The book takes advantage of about forty years of
        revelations from one source or another to update the
        standard comtemporary interpretation by Sherwood. In this
        balanced, well-researched assessment, McJimsey captures
        Hopkins' prime motivation: to serve.

1403.   Sherwood, Robert E. ROOSEVELT AND HOPKINS: AN INTIMATE
        HISTORY. New York: Harper and Brothers, 1948. 979 pp.

        Here is an excellent study, written by a friend of both
        the president and his long-time aide. The Roosevelt-
        Hopkins relationship was a key ingredient in forging not
        only the United States war effort but also the victorious
        United Nations coalition. Sherwood is masterful in his
        analysis and his writing. He writes of the "heavily
        forested interior" of Roosevelt's complex mind and of the
        "common-law alliance" between the United States and Great

Britain. Despite his extraordinary contributions during
the war, Hopkins at the end of his life held great
misgivings about the future of the world, according to
Sherwood.

PATRICK J. HURLEY

1404. Buhite, Russell D. PATRICK J. HURLEY AND AMERICAN FOREIGN
       POLICY. Ithaca, NY: Cornell University Press, 1972.
       342 pp.

       This is a well-researched and well-written biography.
       Buhite does not fail either to come down hard or to praise
       his subject--as the evidence warrants.

1405. Buhite, Russell D. "Patrick J. Hurley and the Yalta Far
       Eastern Agreement." PAC HR, 37 (August 1968), 343-352.

       According to the author, Hurley, in 1951, interpreted
       the Yalta agreements as a cowardly surrender led by a
       president who did not realize the implications of the
       deals. In 1945, however, as Buhite points out, Hurley
       accepted the Yalta accords as the necessary price for the
       entry of the Soviet Union in the war against Japan. In
       fact, Buhite believes that Hurley compiled a good record in
       China and did as he was directed. It would have been
       wiser, Buhite feels, for Hurley not to have made many of
       his postwar statements.

1406. Liang, Chin-tung. "Patrick Hurley, the China Mediator."
       BULL INST MOD HIST ACAD SINICA, 6 (June 1977), 329-354.

       NE

1407. Lohbeck, Don. PATRICK J. HURLEY. Chicago, IL: Henry
       Regnery, 1956. 513 pp.

       Here is a sympathetic treatment of a controversial
       figure. In China, Hurley essentially adopted the viewpoint
       of Chiang Kai-shek. Lohbeck seems to share some of these
       same views, especially with regard to Stilwell. Of
       interest is Hurley's involvement in U.S. attempts to crack
       the Japanese blockade and reach Bataan during early 1942.
       Lohbeck enjoyed certain research privileges in this
       authorized biography.

LORD LOTHIAN

1408. Jeffries-Jones, Rhodri. "Lord Lothian and American

Democracy: An Illusion in Pursuit of an Illusion."
CANADIAN REV AMER STUD, 17 (Winter 1986), 411-422.

The author, a history professor, notes that the British
ambassador had extensive knowledge of the United States,
but other factors accounted for his diplomatic successes
(e.g., diplomatic skills, crucial intermediary role
between Roosevelt and Churchill, contrast with the
weaknesses of Joseph Kennedy, and the subject of a
flattering British propaganda campaign.)

1409.   Reynolds, David.   "Lord Lothian and Anglo-American
        Relations, 1939-1940."   AMER PHILOS SOC TRANS, 73 (Pt.
        2, 1983), 1-65.

Here is a knowledgeable, balanced assessment.   On the
whole, Reynolds feels that Lothian's diplomatic successes
far outweigh his failures during this critical juncture in
Anglo-American relations.

WILLIAM PHILLPS

1410.   Clymer, Kenton J.   "The Education of William Phillips:
        Self-Determination and American Policy Toward India,
        1942-1945."   DIP HIST, 8 (Winter 1984), 13-35.

Clymer analyzes the Indian interlude of the diplomatic
career of Phillips, who was caught in the tension between
ideological commitment and the practical need to cooperate
with the colonial powers.   According to the author,
Phillips, while not fully trusting Roosevelt, remained
deeply committed to the principle of self-determination.

1411.   Phillips, William.   VENTURES IN DIPLOMACY.   Boston: Beacon
        Press, 1952.

Amidst these memories, Phillips describes his service as
Roosevelt's personal representative to India in 1943.   The
author has some insights about British colonialism and the
postwar structure of Asia.

FRANKLIN D. ROOSEVELT

1412.   Bateman, Herman E.   "Observations on President's
        Roosevelt's Health During World War II."   MVHR, 43 (June
        1956), 82-102.

Bateman points out that virtually no writer expressed
serious concern over Roosevelt's health at the time.   In

fact, the president's physician, Ross T. McIntire, asserted
that Roosevelt was in good health for his age (62) during
late 1944 and early 1945. The author concludes that clear
evidence is not available, but in all probability no one
could have forecast the sudden end.

1414. Burns, James MacGregor. ROOSEVELT: THE SOLDIER OF
        FREEDOM, 1940-1945. New York: Harcourt, Brace
        Jovanovich, 1970. 722 pp.

        In the second volume of his biography, Burns portrays
Roosevelt as both a man of principle and a man of
REALPOLITIK. For Burns, many of the contradictions in
Roosevelt's policies stemmed from the president acting not
only as a soldier but also as an ideologue (who had picked
up Wilson's fallen banner). Sub-topics in this study
include the origins of the Cold War, the transformation of
the presidency, and the alteration of American society.
New source materials (since 1970) have weakened but not
seriously damaged the usefulness of this book--primarily
because of its interpretive, suggestive nature.

1415. Dallek, Robert. FRANKLIN D. ROOSEVELT AND AMERICAN FOREIGN
        POLICY, 1932-1945. New York: Oxford University Press,
        1979. 657 pp.

        Dallek respects Roosevelt's political skills--aware of
how far he could go as President and pragmatic in
responding to domestic pressures. During the prewar years,
according to the author, Roosevelt created precedents for
the manipulation of public opinion in support of a good
cause. Of special interest is Dallek's treatment of
Roosevelt's decision not to meet with Konoye without prior
guarantees.

1416. Dallek, Robert, ed. THE ROOSEVELT DIPLOMACY AND WORLD WAR
        II. New York: Holt, Rinehart and Winston, 1970. 125
        pp.

        Part of the "American Problems Studies" series, this
collection encompasses opposing interpretations by
respected scholars. Dallek includes an excellent
bibliographic essay.

1417. Divine, Robert A. ROOSEVELT AND WORLD WAR II. Baltimore,
        MD: Penquin Books, 1969. 107 pp.

        This slim volume offers four lectures by Divine. He
portrays the president as a succcessful politican but not a

great statesman. Concentrating on Roosevelt's distinctive
role, two of the lectures treat the prewar years and
describe a leader earnestly seeking to keep his country out
of the war. Divine carefully refutes the stereotypes that
surround Roosevelt. Of special interest are the author's
views on the type of leader that the political system in
the United States produces.

1418. Dulles, Foster Rhea and Gerald E. Ridinger. "The
        Anti-Colonial Policies of Franklin D. Roosevelt." POL SCI
        Q, 70 (March 1955), 1-18.

        Limited to published sources—about all that was
        available at the time—the authors describe Roosevelt's
        "vigorous and persistent opposition to colonialism."
        According to the authors, the president believed that the
        future peace of the world depended on the recognition by
        the powers of the legitimate aspirations of colonial
        peoples. Recently declassified materials, while
        re-affirming Roosevelt's anti-colonial views, have brought
        into question just how vigorously and how persistently he
        pursued them.

1419. Eliasberg, W.G. "How Long Was Roosevelt Ill Before His
        Death?" DISEASES NERVOUS SYSTEM, 14 (November 1953),
        323-328.

        NE

1420. Emerson, William. "Franklin Roosevelt as
        Commander-in-Chief in World War II." MIL AFFS, 22
        (Winter 1958-59), 181-207.

        Emerson argues that the president, far more than is
        generally realized, remained sensitive to political aspects
        of the war. Also, despite the impression (which Roosevelt
        nurtured) that he relied on the joint chiefs of staff,
        Emerson feels that the president often went his own way in
        military matters.

1421. "FDR: The Last Photo." AMER HERITAGE, 38 (July-August
        1987), 102-103.

        Elizabeth Shoumatoff, commissioned to paint the
        president's portrait, took this photograph of Roosevelt on
        April 11, 1945. The next day, she was present when he
        died. Shoumatoff passed away in 1980 and left a short
        memoir. Of interest is her statement that she never heard
        Roosevelt say anything about a headache in his last moments

as has been so often reported. This photo will remain of
continuing historical interest.

1422.   Field, Henry. "How FDR Did His Homework." SAT REV, 44
        (July 8, 1961), 8-10, 46.

        The author describes Roosevelt's "painstaking precision"
in preparing for the wartime conferences. Field, an
anthropologist at the Library of Congress, prepared special
reports for the president's eyes only.

1423.   Fish, Hamilton. FDR: THE OTHER SIDE OF THE COIN. New
        York: Vantage Press, 1976. 255 pp.

        Reappraising his original position, the author, a
distinguished Republican congressman during the war, now
feels that Roosevelt (with the support of Hull and Stimson)
deliberately provoked the Japanese into war.

1424.   Graham, Otis L., Jr. and Meghan R. Wander, eds. FRANKLIN
        D. ROOSEVELT: HIS LIFE AND TIME: AN ENCYCLOPEDIC VIEW.
        Boston: G.K. Hall, 1985. 483 pp.

        An impressive array of contributors provides facts and
anecdotes about Roosevelt. The encyclopedic format
includes an extensive index.

1425.   Hassett, William D. OFF THE RECORD WITH FDR, 1942-1945.
        New Brunswick, NJ: Rutgers University Press, 1958. 366
        pp.

        The author was confidential secretary in the White House
under Roosevelt. The personal diary he kept reveals frank
opinions about events and personalities. There is no
effort to disguise his affection and loyalty to Roosevelt.
The book is a good source for the period.

1426.   Heinrichs, Waldo. THRESHOLD OF WAR: FRANKLIN D. ROOSEVELT
        AND AMERICA'S ENTRY INTO WORLD WAR II. New York:
        Oxford University Press, 1988. 280 pp.

        Here is a comprehensive study of the U.S. entry, but
Heinrichs deals concurrently with the European and East
Asian dimensions. Thus, his analysis of the international
context avoids the compartmentalization that weakens other
studies of the origins of the war. The work is well
written, and his research goes more deeply than other
accounts into military (naval) operational sources and
intelligence material. General to Heinrichs' thesis is

Roosevelt's developing interest not only in sustaining the U.S.S.R. as the central feature in his global policies but also in containing Japan.

1427.   Kimball, Warren F., ed. FRANKLIN D. ROOSEVELT AND THE WORLD CRISIS, 1937-1945. Lexington, MA: D. C. Heath, 1973. 297 pp.

This valuable collection offers a rich variety of views on Roosevelt. The perspective of each author is given its due in Kimball's trenchant introductions. Kimball also presents an authoritative bibliographic essay which is a helpful guide to anyone trying to wade through the massive bulk of literature on the president.

1428.   Kinsella, William E. LEADERSHIP IN ISOLATION. Boston: G. K. Hall, 1978. 282 pp.

Here is an analysis not only of Roosevelt's leadership as the United States moved into the war but also of the broad context of contemporary American society. Kinsella shows how the president both mirrored and molded that society.

1429.   McIntire, Ross T. WHITE HOUSE PHYSICIAN. New York: G. P. Putnam's Sons, 1946. 244 pp.

In collaboration with George Creel, McIntire recounts his experiences as Roosevelt's doctor (1933-1945). The doctor stands by his original judgment that Roosevelt was in excellent health "for a man of his age." Writing that the President showed none of the usual signs of cerebral hemorrhage (e.g., high blood pressure, arteriosclerosis, and liver or kidney problems), McIntire reports on his phone conversations during the President's final moments. Of interest is his observation that Roosevelt appreciated MacArthur's military genius. Also (for those interested in such things), McIntire's account of those present at the house in Warm Springs on April 12 has one glaring omission, Lucy Rutherford.

1430.   Marks, Frederick W. WIND OVER SAND: THE DIPLOMACY OF FRANKLIN ROOSEVELT. Athens, GA: University of Georgia Press, 1988. 472 pp.

Here is an exceptionally well-written study that is carefully researched. Marks covers the period 1933-1945. He finds the president's rhetoric at odds with concrete action. Of special interest is Marks' criticism of

Roosevelt's actions and policies on the eve of war which, Marks feels, virtually pushed Japan into war.

1431. Miller, Nathan. F.D.R.: AN INTIMATE HISTORY. Garden City, NY: Doubleday, 1983. 563 pp.

Here is a gracefully written, even elegant, portrayal. Miller, an associate of the Roosevelt family, describes a "prismatic" president who "collected ideas the way he collected stamps." The narrative carefully approaches Roosevelt's personal relationships and the secret tapings of conversations in the Oval Office.

1432. Morgan, Ted. FRANKLIN D. ROOSEVELT: A BIOGRAPHY. New York: Simon and Schuster, 1985. 830 pp.

Morgan's one-volume study is a useful popular account.

1433. Neumann, William L. "Roosevelt's Foreign Policy Decisions, 1940-1945." MOD AGE, 19 (Summer 1975), 272-284.

Neumann writes that Roosevelt's wartime pattern was to avoid lengthy debates or quarrels--even if the President had to lie to do so. Roosevelt earns criticism in this article for his stalling and his failure to do the hard thinking/decision-making that was required.

1434. Polenberg, Richard. "Historians and the Liberal Presidency: Recent Appraisals of Roosevelt and Truman." S ATL Q, 75 (Winter 1976), 20-35.

Noting the value-laden judgments in these recent appraisals (especially the critiques of revisionist historians), Polenberg believes that no historical consensus will emerge until historians distinguish between what happened and what they wish had happened.

1435. Range, Willard. FRANKLIN D. ROOSEVELT'S WORLD ORDER. Athens, GA: University of Georgia Press, 1959.

Although not a study in blind praise, Range generally applauds Roosevelt's foreign policies. The author, a political scientist, identifies the thread of Wilsonian internationalism running through the actions, words, and intentions of the pragmatic president. With regard to the breakdown of negotiations with Japan, Range defends the U.S. position.

1436. Roosevelt, Elliott. AS HE SAW IT. New York: Duell, Sloan

and Pearce, 1946.   270 pp.

It has become standard practice for historians to warn
that this book must be read cautiously--and then to cite it
regularly. Most of Elliott's descriptions of his father's
attitudes and ideas can be cross-checked in the literature
and are reliable, but perhaps not in the precise details
presented. His reconstruction of direct conversations, for
example, seems contrived. Nevertheless, the author did
accompany his father to important meetings and was privy
to confidential discussions (either in small groups or
alone with the president). The book is especially valuable
for material on the underlying friction between the
president and Churchill over colonialism.

1437. Roosevelt, Elliott and James Brough. A RENDEZVOUS WITH
        DESTINY. New York: G.P. Putnam's Sons, 1975. 446 pp.

Drawing heavily from his earlier book, AS HE SAW IT,
Roosevelt reveals some of his confidential conversations
with his father as well as some frank observations about--
and by--other leading figures during the war. The book is
useful in recapturing some of the flavor of the president's
sentiments.

1438. Rosenbaum, Herbert D. and Elizabeth Bartelme, eds.
        FRANKLIN D. ROOSEVELT: THE MAN, THE MYTH, THE ERA,
        1882-1945. Westport, CT: Greenwood Press, 1987.
        411 pp.

This collection formed part of the papers presented at
Hofstra University in honor of the centennial of
Roosevelt's birth. See especially the introduction by
Frank Freidel on Roosevelt's legacy. The only essay which
deals directly with the war against Japan is John Sbrega's
analysis of the president's anticolonial views on
Indochina.

1439. Sbrega, John J. "The Anticolonial Policies of Franklin D.
        Roosevelt: A Reappraisal." POL SCI Q, 101 (May 1986),
        65-84.

Here is a critical view of Roosevelt's vaguely defined
ideas. Using Indochina as a test case, Sbrega argues that
the president failed either to follow through on his
concept of trusteeship or to use his influence with the
Allies in seeking postwar improvements for dependent
peoples. Among the obstacles identified in thwarting
Roosevelt's goals was the need to cooperate with the Allies

during and after the war.

440. Steele, Richard W. "Franklin D. Roosevelt and His Foreign
      Policy Critics." POL SCI Q, 94 (Spring 1979), 15-32.

      In this critical appraisal, Steele especially faults
      Roosevelt's disposition to view dissidence as disloyalty.
      But see the rejoinder by Arthur M. Schlessinger, Jr. (pp.
      33-35).

441. Steele, Richard W. "The Great Debate: Roosevelt, the
      Media and the Coming of the War, 1940-1941." J. AMER
      HIST, 71 (June 1984), 69-92.

      During the eighteen months before Pearl Harbor, Steele
      argues, Roosevelt sought to avoid controversy and stifle
      national public debate. In this effort the president
      obtained the collaboration of the mass media, according to
      the author.

442. Young, Lowell T. "Franklin D. Roosevelt and America's
      Islets: Acquisition of Territory in the Caribbean and
      in the Pacific." HISTORIAN, 35 (February 1973),
      205-220.

      Although the United States planned to give up the
      Philippines, the author asserts that Roosevelt did not
      contemplate a reduction in U.S. power. Young maintains
      that Roosevelt, while an "ardent anti-colonialist," wanted
      to expand U.S. power by acquiring strategic islets (some of
      which were uninhabited).

JOHN LEIGHTON STUART

443. Rea, Kenneth W. and John C. Brewer, eds. THE FORGOTTEN
      AMBASSADOR: THE REPORTS OF JOHN LEIGHTON STUART,
      1946-1949. Boulder, CO: Westview Press, 1981. 345 pp.

      These postwar ambassadorial dispatches are of interest
      to this guide primarily because of the descriptions of the
      situation in China in the aftermath of Japan's surrender.
      U.S. forces became entangled in the domestic turmoil.
      Stuart, of course, had to walk a fine line.

444. Smylie, Robert F. "John Leighton Stuart: A Missionary in
      the Sino-Japanese Conflict, 1937-1941." J PRESBYTERIAN
      HIST 53 (Fall 1975), 256-276.

      The author, a United Presbyterian minister, writes that

Stuart advocated countering Japanese militarism in China
through increased U.S. aid and a stringent blockade.
Stuart, who served as president of Yenching University,
earned widespread respect in China, but, not being a
professional diplomat, he received scant attention from
Roosevelt.

1445.   Stuart, John Leighton. FIFTY YEARS IN CHINA: THE MEMOIRS
         OF JOHN LEIGHTON STUART, MISSIONARY AND AMBASSADOR. New
         York: Random House, 1954. 346 pp.

A significant period of Chinese history is presented
through Stuart's eyes. The years of his ambassadorship
(1946-1949) marked a particularly critical time, and his
narrative makes clear his awkward position during these
years.

HARRY S. TRUMAN

1446.   Ferrell, Robert H. HARRY S. TRUMAN AND THE MODERN AMERICAN
         PRESIDENCY. Boston: Little,Brown, 1983. 220 pp.

Of interest in this excellent biography is Ferrell's
treatment of the early months of the Truman presidency. At
first, the author argues, Truman tried to do what Roosevelt
would have done, but gradually the new President began to
show his "natural independence." Nevertheless, Ferrell
points out that Truman usually acted only after consulting
his advisers. Also of interest is Ferrell's revelation
that, despite Truman's public show of confidence about the
use of the atomic bomb, in private the President remained
doubtful about the wisdom of that decision.

1447.   Haynes, Richard F. THE AWESOME POWER: HARRY S. TRUMAN AS
         COMMANDER IN CHIEF. Baton Rouge, LA: Louisiana State
         University Press, 1973. 359 pp.

This study describes how Truman expanded the powers of
the presidency and upheld the principle of civilian control
of the military. Of interest is the author's rejection of
Truman's reasons for using the atomic bomb; Haynes feels
that the only purpose served in that decision was to reveal
that atomic weapons should never be used in the future.

1448.   Maddox, Robert J. FROM WAR TO COLD WAR: THE EDUCATION OF
         HARRY S. TRUMAN. Boulder, CO: Westview Press, 1987.
         192 pp.

According to Maddox, Truman did not undermine the

cooperative policies of his predecessor. In fact, the
author argues that Truman, before Potsdam, was inclined to
work with Stalin as opposed to Roosevelt who was moving
toward a much firmer stance against the Soviets just before
his death. It was only after Potsdam, Maddox says, when
sharp differences arose with the Soviets, that Truman moved
to a hard-line attitude.

1449.   Mark, Eduard. "'Today Has Been a Historical One': Harry
        S. Truman's Diary of the Potsdam Conference." DIP HIST,
        4 (Summer 1980), 317-326.

        Mark presents a newly discovered conference diary kept
        by Truman (July 16-30, 1945). See especially the
        president's writings on the atomic bomb (a "terrible
        bomb"): "It may be the fire destruction prophesized in the
        Euphrates River Valley Era after Noah and his fabulous
        Ark."

1450.   Truman, Harry S. MEMOIRS BY HARRY S. TRUMAN: VOL. I:
        YEAR OF DECISIONS, 1945. VOL. II: YEARS OF TRIAL AND
        HOPE, 1946-1952. Garden City, NY: Doubleday, 1956. 2
        vols.

        Truman describes Roosevelt's hopes for China and the
        postwar world--a China that Truman felt was little more
        than a geographical expression. Of special interest is
        Truman's views on the decision to use the atomic bomb.
        Historians continue to debate Truman's insistence that he
        sought only to follow Roosevelt's policies.

II.E.3. OTHERS

1451.   Allison, John M. AMBASSADOR FROM THE PRAIRIE, OR ALLISON
        WONDERLAND. Boston: Houghton Mifflin, 1973. 400 pp.

        As a Foreign Service Officer, Allison served in China
        and Japan before the war. In this light-hearted report, he
        tells of his experiences as an internee in Japan, a U.N.
        representative in London, and his role in the negotiations
        for the 1951 peace treaty with Japan. See especially his
        anecdotes about MacArthur, John Foster Dulles, and Patrick
        J. Hurley.

1452.   Borra, Ranjan. "The Image of Subhas Chandra Bose in
        American Journals During World War II." ORACLE, 2
        (April 1980), 33-48.

        NE

1453.   Buhite, Russell D. NELSON T. JOHNSON AND AMERICAN POLICY
        TOWARD CHINA, 1925-1941. East Lansing, MI: Michigan
        State University Press, 1968. 163 pp.

        This biographical study concentrates on the years 1925-
        1941, when Johnson, as both a state department official and
        an ambassador to China, affected American policy decisions
        regarding China.

1454.   Caidin, Martin and Edward Hymoff. THE MISSION.
        Philadelphia, PA: J. B. Lippincott, 1964. 208 pp.

        Early in the war, Roosevelt selected Congressman Lyndon
        B. Johnson to report on the situation in the Southwest
        Pacific. Johnson criticized the poor communications and
        transportation systems in the theater as well as the
        inter-service rivalries. His sketch of MacArthur is not
        flattering. This book appeared in the midst of a
        presidential campaign which involved Johnson.

1455.   Davies, John Paton, Jr. DRAGON BY THE TAIL. New York: W.
        W. Norton, 1972. 448 pp.

        Foreign Service Officer Davies analyzes the experiences
        of Americans, British, Japanese, and Russians in China.
        Due to his expertise on the subject, which in part derives
        from a personally painful tour of duty in China, Davies
        gives an authoritative account. At the end of the war and
        in the postwar years, he became enmeshed in the controversy
        over the Chinese Communists which wracked the State
        Department. The controversy tarnished Davies' promising
        career by calling into question his loyalty to the United
        States. The book serves as both a memoir (astonishingly
        restrained) and a diplomatic history.

1456.   Eden, Anthony. THE MEMOIRS OF ANTHONY EDEN, EARL OF AVON:
        THE RECKONING. Boston: Houghton Mifflin, 1965. 623
        pp.

        The British Foreign Secretary under Churchill served in
        a unique position to participate in momentous diplomatic
        decisions. Although he was instrumental in efforts to
        develop a joint Anglo-American policy on the postwar status
        of dependent peoples and trusteeship, Eden's memoirs say
        disappointingly little on the subject. His observations on
        world leaders and diplomatic events during the war are
        frankly stated. Regarding Roosevelt's reluctance to
        restore prewar colonial regimes, Eden feels the President

did not fully understand the question and was juggling
balls of dynamite.

1457. Emmerson, John K. THE JAPANESE THREAD: A LIFE IN THE
       UNITED STATES FOREIGN SERVICE. New York: Holt,
       Rinehart and Winston, 1978. 465 pp.

       These memoirs are exceptionally well written.
       Emmerson's career enabled him to observe and participate in
       crucial decisions which affected Asian-American affairs.
       His association with the Chinese Communists became a point
       of much controversy.

1458. Fischer, Louis. A WEEK WITH GANDHI. New York: Duell,
       Sloan and Pearce, 1942. 122 pp.

       Fischer's extended interview highlights the situation in
       India. The book provides a contemporary glimpse of this
       interesting and complex leader.

1459. Hull, Cordell. THE MEMOIRS OF CORDELL HULL. New York:
       Macmillan, 1948. 2 vols.

       The memoirs of the secretary of state provide much
       information on a variety of wartime political-diplomatic-
       economic subjects. Of special interest is Hull's view
       about the postwar status of dependent peoples. He
       understood the complex nature of this dilemma, saying that
       the U.S. could not hope to work with the Western imperial
       powers after the war in Europe while it sought to strip
       away their colonial empires elsewhere.

1460. Kido, Koichi. THE DIARY OF MARQUIS KIDO, 1931-1945.
       Frederick, MD: University Publications of America,
       1984.

       The English-language publication of this document is
       long overdue. Kido occupied a privileged position in the
       crucial period before and during the war. His diary makes
       an important contribution.

1461. Lindbergh, Charles A. THE WARTIME JOURNALS OF CHARLES A
       LINDBERGH. New York: Harcourt, Brace and Jovanovich,
       1970. 1,038 pp.

       The journal covers the years 1937-1945. Its frank,
       honest--sometimes naive--opinions reveal much about this
       American hero. Lindbergh's contributions to the war
       against Japan included a demonstration to MacArthur about

the air range to Hollandia and the shooting down of two
Japanese zeroes.

1462. Murphy, Robert D. DIPLOMAT AMONG WARRIORS. Garden City,
NY: Doubleday, 1964. 470 pp.

Although Murphy's wartime experience as an American
representative was in North African/European affairs, the
book contains important information which affected events
in Southeast Asia. Murphy, perhaps acting on direct orders
or perhaps displaying excessive exuberance, issued specific
guarantees to the Free French about the complete and
unconditional restoration of the French Empire as it
existed in 1939. Murphy and Washington (for there were
other similar pledges) undoubtedly sought to bolster the
flagging French morale, but the U.S. position caused
inter-Allied squabbling. Why, the British wanted to know,
did Americans provide such guarantees to France, which
dropped out of the war, and continue to make pointed
threats about the postwar breakup of the colonial
possessions of Britain, which had continued the
anti-totalitarian struggle? The American pledges, of
course, included Indochina, which had become virtually a
litmus test for Roosevelt's anticolonial intentions.
Murphy's enthusiasm landed him in hot water with the
president.

1463. Onorato, Michael P., ed. ORIGINS OF THE PHILIPPINE
REPUBLIC: EXTRACTS FROM THE DIARIES AND RECORDS OF
FRANCIS BURTON HARRISON. Ithaca, NY: Cornell
University Press, 1974. 258 pp.

An ex-governor general, Harrison served as an adviser to
Quezon. There is some useful material about the Filipino
president (1942-1944).

1464. Quezon, Manuel L. THE GOOD FIGHT. New York:
Appleton-Century, 1946. 335 pp.

This posthumously published autobiography of the
president of the Philippines contains information on the
situations before and during the war in that country. See
especially his explanation of the days immediately
following Pearl Harbor, when the president and his
government sought to develop an honorable course of action.
MacArthur has written an introduction to the book.

1465. Romulo, Carlos P. I WALKED WITH HEROES. New York: Holt,
Rinehart and Winston, 1961. 342 pp.

Here are first-hand views of some leading figures. Romulo singles out Quezon and MacArthur for special praise. Of interest is the author's description of Quezon's discussions with Osmena about declaring the Philippines neutral. Romulo worked as a wartime aide to MacArthur and does not conceal his admiration for the general.

1466. Sayre, Francis B. GLAD ADVENTURE. New York: Macmillan, 1957. 356 pp.

These memoirs are not particularly candid. There is little on either the 1941 "neutrality" scheme or Sayre's role (delay?) in evacuating U.S. citizens from the Philippines. The U.S. Commissioner does indicate that MacArthur seemed to be losing favor with President Quezon before the war. Of some interest, too, for this guide is Sayre's account of his postwar service on the territorial trusteeship council.

1467. Togo, Shigenori. THE CAUSE OF JAPAN. New York: Simon and Schuster, 1956. 372 pp.

The author, foreign ministry in Japan from 1941 to the end of the war, wrote this memoir while in prison after the war. While critical of American prewar inflexibility, Togo describes his struggles with Japanese militarists. His narrative offers some insights about the decision-making process in Japan. See, too, the valuable introduction by the book's translators, Togo Fumihiko and Ben Bruce Blackeney.

1468. Tong, Hollington K. "Pearl Harbor Prelude: Personal Reminiscences." SINO-AMER RELS, 2 (Winter 1976), 36-64.

NE

1469. Willoughby, Amea. I WAS ON CORREGIDOR. New York: Harper and Brothers, 1943. 249 pp.

The author's husband was an executive assistant to the U.S. High Commissioner in the Philippines, Francis B. Sayre. In a well-written, straightforward narrative, she tells of their move from Manila to Corregidor and their subsequent evacuation by submarine to Australia.

II.F. DIPLOMATIC HISTORIES OF THE WAR (GENERAL)

1470. Ambrose, Stephen E. RISE TO GLOBALISM: AMERICAN FOREIGN

POLICY, 1938-1970. Baltimore: Penguin Books, 1971.
352 pp.

This well-written survey offers interesting
interpretations of the war years.

1471. Graebner, Norman A., ed. STUDIES IN AMERICAN DIPLOMACY,
1865-1945, VOLUME VIII: AMERICAN VALUES PROJECTED
ABROAD. Lanham, MD: University Press of America, 1985.
190 pp.

In this excellent collection, see especially the essays
by Richard Dean Burns, "Cordell Hull and American Interwar
Internationalism" and Whittle Johnston, "Franklin D.
Roosevelt and the Wartime Strategy For Peace."

1472. Hohenberg, John. BETWEEN TWO WORLDS: POLICY, PRESS, AND
PUBLIC OPINION IN ASIA-AMERICAN RELATIONS. New York:
Praeger, 1967.

The author's analysis addresses the years from 1941 into
the 1960s. He explains the tensions between governments
and the foreign press. Primacy is given to political
affairs.

1473. Leonard, Thomas. "The United States and World War II:
Conflicting Views of American Diplomacy." TOWSAN STATE
J, 7 (No. 1, 1972), 25-30.

NE

1474. O'Connor, Raymond G. FORCE AND DIPLOMACY: ESSAYS MILITARY
AND DIPLOMATIC. Miami, FL: University of Miami Press,
1972. 167 pp.

In this collection of essays, see especially O'Connor's
analysis of prewar U.S. economic sanctions against Japan
and his reinterpretation of the Roosevelt-Churchill
diplomacy.

1475. Smith, Gaddis. AMERICAN DIPLOMACY DURING THE SECOND WORLD
WAR, 1941-1945. New York: John Wiley and Sons, 1985.
2d. ed. 201 pp.

This magnificient review of U.S. wartime diplomacy
continues to hold up--even with the opening of archival
records and other primary sources since its original
publication in 1965. Adopting the contemporary
perspective, Smith avoids the pitfalls of the "where we

went wrong" approach. See especially his critical analysis
of Roosevelt's assumptions about the postwar era (e.g.,
anticipating U.S. trouble with Britain; holding hope for
U.S.-Soviet relations). Smith's conclusion about the
decision to use the atomic bomb stands out in a body of
literature cluttered with alleged revisionism,
emotionalism, and presentism.

1476. Snell, John L. ILLUSION AND NECESSITY: THE DIPLOMACY OF
       GLOBAL WAR, 1939-1945. Boston, MA: Houghton Mifflin,
       1963. 229 pp.

       Here is a global perspective on the diplomacy of the
war. Snell weaves his narrative around the general theme
that wartime diplomatists suffered illusions and were
subjected to tragic necessities. His narrative generally
applauds U.S. diplomacy, especially the leadership and
vision of Roosevelt and Truman, and the author asserts that
Americans by far did not commit the worst foreign policy
mistakes in the war. Snell argues that the fundamental
different interests of the Big Three weakened the alliance
which shortly after the war slipped into a state of
suspicious animosity. He, nevertheless, feels that Soviet
actions were chiefly responsible for the winning coalition.

III. ECONOMIC AND LEGAL ASPECTS OF THE WAR AGAINST JAPAN

A. GENERAL ACCOUNTS

1477. Bundell, Walter, Jr. MILITARY MONEY: A FISCAL HISTORY OF
      THE U.S. ARMY OVERSEAS IN WORLD WAR II. College
      Station, TX: Texas A & M University Press, 1980.

      Although he sleights SWPA, Bundell does a good job of
      discussing problems of the army-navy mix in the Central
      Pacific. This is a unique study, and the author knows the
      material thoroughly.

1478. Diebold, William. NEW DIRECTIONS IN OUR TRADE POLICY.
      New York: Council on Foreign Relations, 1941. 174 pp.

      In this prewar piece, Diebold discusses the probable
      effects of the war on the U.S. economy and trade patterns.
      In considering the global context for U.S. trade, Diebold
      warns of the need to counter Japanese aggression in Asia.

1479. Korovin, Eugene A. "The Second World War and International
      Law." AMER J INT LAW, 40 (October 1946), 742-755.

      This Soviet law professor offers an analysis of the
      implications of national sovereignty in light of the
      lessons of the war.

1480. United States. Department of the Army. Service Forces. A
      GUIDE TO INTERNATIONAL SUPPLY. Washington, D.C.: War
      Dept. 1945. 156 pp.

      The International Division of the Army's Service Forces
      prepared this book to offer indoctrination and instruction
      in the planning and procedures of international supply in
      (1) Lend-Lease, (2) reciprocal aid, and (3) civilian
      supply. The first two categories contain material on our
      Pacific partners. See especially under reciprocal aid the
      discussion of U.S. economic relations with the British
      colonies.

III.B. UNITED NATIONS COALITION (AND FRIENDS)

1481. Bell, Roger. "Australian-American Relations and Reciprocal
       Wartime Economic Assistance, 1941-6: An Ambivalent
       Association." AUS ECON H REV, 16 (March 1976), 23-49.

       Using archival sources and private collections, Bell
       reveals that neither country was willing to compromise its
       economic interests and that each sought to exploit wartime
       economic arrangements for economic and trade benefits after
       the war. Despite the extensive amounts of reciprocal aid
       during the war, the two partners did not share postwar
       objectives.

1482. Bell, Roger. "Testing the Open Door Thesis in Australia,
       1941-1946." PAC HR, 51 (August 1982), 283-311.

       Denying that the U.S. policy of multilateralism was
       selfless, Bell integrates archival research to argue that
       Americans sought advantages from their dominant economic
       and military position.

1483. Broek, J.O.M. "The Future of Southeast Asia." FE SURVEY,
       12 (December 22, 1943), 243-247.

       Having his fill of abstract doctrines, Broek calls for
       regional teamwork to overcome concrete problems. He
       emphasizes the essential need for economic development in
       Southeast Asia.

1484. Chapman, Wilbert M. FISHING IN TROUBLED WATERS.
       Philadelphia: J. B. Lippincott, 1949. 256 pp.

       A professor of ichthyology, Chapman narrates his efforts
       to launch a commercial fishery in the Solomons in order to
       enrich the diet of the Americans. Despite formidable
       obstacles, his project largely succeeded. In this
       interesting account, the professor cannot resist describing
       the fascinating sea inhabitants.

1485. Day, David A. "P.G. Taylor and the Alternative Pacific
       Route, 1939-45." AUS J POL HIST, 32 (No. 1, 1986),
       6-19.

       Taylor, an Australian aviator, sought alternative
       Pacific-global air routes for Australia which would avoid
       an "all red" route (British) or a route through Hawaii
       (American). As Day points out, however, circumstances
       virtually forced Australia to accept the U.S. route through

Hawaii.

1486. Dobson, Alan P. "The Other Air Battle: The American
          Pursuit of Post-War Aviation Rights." HIST J, 28 (June
          1985), 429-439.

          Looking at the wartime discussions on civil aviation,
       Dobson points out that the American arguments for free
       enterprise reinforced U.S. interests.

1487. FORTUNE Magazine. JAPAN AND THE JAPANESE: A MILITARY
          POWER WE MUST DEFEAT: A PACIFIC PROBLEM WE MUST SOLVE.
          Washington, D.C.: Infantry Journal Press, 1944. 182 pp.

          This report by FORTUNE's editors delineates the economic
       as well as strategic aspects of the war in the Pacific.
       There are descriptions of the Japanese dismantling the
       economic resources of the occupied areas.

1488. Holbrook, Francis X. and John Nikol. "Harold Gatty and the
          Bridging of the Pacific." AEROSPACE H, 29 (Fall/
          September 1982), 176-182.

          The acquisition and control of Wake Island, the key
       between Midway and Guam, helped complete the American
       bridge across the Pacific. The authors highlight the role
       of Juan Terry Trippe, the head of Pan American Airways, and
       the efforts of Harold Gatty, who also arranged for a
       southwesterly route to Australia and New Zealand.

1489. Nelson, Donald M. ARSENAL OF DEMOCRACY: THE STORY OF
          AMERICAN WAR PRODUCTION. New York: Harcourt, Brace,
          1946. 439 pp.

          Nelson, head of the War Production Board, discusses the
       system and resources that enabled the United States to
       fulfill Roosevelt's pledge to become the "arsenal of
       democracy." Of interest is his report on producing
       material for China and Australia.

1490. Selle, Earl A. DONALD OF CHINA. New York: Harper, 1948.
          369 pp.

          Here is a sympathetic biography of William Henry Donald,
       financial adviser to Chiang Kai-shek.

1491. Sewall, Arthur F. "Key Pittman and the Quest for the China
          Market, 1933-1940." PAC HR, 44 (August 1975), 351-371.

Sewall writes that Pittman never embraced the thesis
that the search for overseas markets would lead to U.S.
economic recovery. For Pittman, the interests of Nevada
were foremost; an increase in the world price of silver,
however, would enable the Chinese to purchase more U.S.
goods.

1492. Venkataramani, M.S. "The Roosevelt Administration and the
       Great Indian Famine." INT STUD, 4 (January 1963),
       241-264.

       The author, head of the Department of American History
       and Institutions at India's School of International
       Studies, criticizes the Roosevelt administration for not
       doing enough to counter the 1943 famine. He questions
       Roosevelt's determination to end colonialism.

III.C. JAPAN AND FRIENDS

1493. Bisson, T.A. ASPECTS OF WARTIME ECONOMIC CONTROL IN JAPAN.
       New York: IPR, 1945. 108 pp.

       This report, based on Bisson's extensive research,
       served as a focus of discussion at the IPR conference in
       January 1945.

1494. Bisson, T.A. JAPAN'S WAR ECONOMY. New York: Macmillan,
       1945. 267 pp.

       This insightful report includes the texts of several key
       documents. Bisson admits that all the data are not yet
       present, but he offers an excellent appraisal. He is
       especially effective in describing the internal struggle
       for economic control in Japan between the Zaibatsu and the
       militarists (who, he says, are losing).

1495. Cohen, Jerome B. THE JAPANESE WAR ECONOMY, 1937-1945.
       Minneapolis, MN: University of Minnesota Press, 1949.
       545 pp.

       Here is a first-rate study by an American authority on
       the subject. Of special interest is the Foreword by a
       British expert on Japan, Sir George Sansom.

1496. Cohen, Jerome B. JAPAN'S ECONOMY IN WAR AND
       RECONSTRUCTION. New York: IPR, 1949. 545 pp.

       The author, a noted economist and a member of the U.S.
       Strategic Bombing Survey, feels that the Japanese defeat

was decided by the economic blockade. In this
authoritative analysis, Cohen evaluates Japan's economy
("frail and low level") during the 1930s and 1940s.

1497. Mitchell, Kate L. JAPAN'S INDUSTRIAL STRENGTH. New York:
        A.A. Knopf, 1942. 149 pp.

        In this IPR-sponsored project, Mitchell incorporates
        statistical material from the period 1931-1940 to offer a
        useful gauge on Japan's war economy. Of interest is her
        analysis of how Formosa, Korea, and Manchuria provided
        economic resources for the Japanese.

1498. Rice, Richard. "Economic Mobilization in Wartime Japan:
        Business, Bureaucracy, and Military in Conflict."
        J ASIAN STUD, 38 (August 1979), 689-706.

        According to Rice, conflict rather than cooperation
        dominated relations among these three groups. Obviously
        familiar with the subject, Rice incorporates Japanese
        sources in his analysis.

1499. Schumpeter, Elizabeth B., ed. THE INDUSTRIALIZATION OF
        JAPAN AND MANCHURIA, 1930-1940. Cambridge, MA:
        Harvard-Radcliffe Publications, 1941. 944 pp.

        This excellent collection comprises a professional
        analysis of prewar economic conditions in Japan and
        Manchuria. The book highlights Japanese economic
        development on the eve of Pearl Harbor.

1500. United States. Foreign Economic Administration. JAPAN'S
        WAR ECONOMY, 1943-1944. Washington, D.C.: FEA, 1943.
        283 pp.

        Here is a detailed report on the state of Japan's
        wartime economy as of 1943. Of interest is the forecast by
        FEA of a deteriorating situation for 1944.

1501. United States. Office of Coordinator of Information.
        EVIDENCES OF ECONOMIC PRESSURE IN JAPAN, DECEMBER 6,
        1941. Washington, D.C.: GPO, 1941. 6 pp.

        The date is the key to the significance of this brief
        report. Here is a contemporary account of the Japanese
        economy (literally) on the eve of the war.

1502. United States. Office of Strategic Services. COMMENTS ON
        ESTIMATES OF MINIMUM JAPANESE IMPORT REQUIREMENTS.

Washington, D.C.: OSS, 1944. 18 1.

This OSS analysis argues that Japan will be facing
increased shortages of food and other needed imports as
Allied economic warfare takes its toll.

1503. United States. Office of Strategic Services.
        GERMAN-JAPANESE BLOCKADE RUNNING. Washington, D.C.:
        OSS, 1942. 9 pp.

Here is the view that, despite some successes in evading
Allied blockades, the enemy is feeling the pinch.

1504. United States. Office of Strategic Services. JAPAN:
        WINTER, 1944-1945. Washington, D.C.: OSS, 1945. 3 1.

This brief report indicates the effectiveness of Allied
economic warfare. The widespread shortages in the Japanese
homeland are described in general terms.

1505. United States. Office of Strategic Services. SUGGESTED
        REVISIONS IN JIS REPORT ON ECONOMIC WARFARE AGAINST
        JAPAN. Washington, D.C.: OSS, 1945. 5 1.

This amendment to a key intelligence report calls for
more emphasis on disrupting the Japanese transportation
systems.

III.C.1. GREATER EAST ASIA CO-PROSPERITY SPHERE (INCLUDING JAPANESE-OCCUPIED TERRITORIES)

1506. Beasley, W.G. JAPANESE IMPERIALISM, 1894-1945. New York:
        Oxford University Press, 1987. 279 pp.

Beasley analyzes the development of Japanese imperialism
and the concept of the Greater East Asia Co-Prosperity
Sphere. Within the sphere, the author shows, not all
partners would be equal as the Japanese sought to control
all of Asia.

1507. Great Britain. Ministry of Information. ECONOMIC
        DEVELOPMENTS IN JAPAN AND JAPAN-CONTROLLED TERRITORY
        FROM SEPTEMBER 1944 TO THE TIME OF HER COLLAPSE.
        London: HMSO, 1945. 36 pp.

This economic survey seems designed not only to warn of
the dire economic situation that existed in the prewar
colonial areas (especially British imperial holdings) but
also to point out who was responsible. Food supplies, in

particular, were falling to alarming levels.

1508.   Lebra, Joyce C., ed. JAPAN'S GREATER EAST ASIA
        CO-PROSPERITY SPHERE IN WORLD WAR II: SELECTED READINGS
        AND DOCUMENTS. New York: Oxford University Press,
        1975.

        The selections focus particularly on China and southeast
        Asia. the Japanese rationale moved beyond the naked
        aggrandizement which Westerners tend to identify with the
        slogan.

1509.   Lebra, Joyce. JUNGLE ALLIANCE: JAPAN AND THE INDIAN
        NATIONAL ARMY. Singapore: Donald Moore for Asia
        Pacific Press, 1971. 255 pp.

        Here is a well researched study that intermingles
        political, economics and military affairs.

1510.   Liu, Daniel H. "Manchurian Booty and International Law."
        AMER J INTL LAW, 40 (July 1946), 584-591.

        The author, occasional secretary to China's ambassador
        in the United States, advances the Chinese contention that
        the Soviet Union is far exceeding the scope of war booty in
        claiming all Japanese enterprises in northeastern China.

1511.   Porter, Catherine. "Japan's Blueprint for the
        Philippines." FE SURVEY, 12 (May 31, 1943), 109-112.

        The author warns that Japan could gain many economic
        benefits before being driven out of the Philippines.

1512.   Spinks, Charles Nelson. "The Man Behind in Japan." ASIA &
        AMERICAS, 43 (April 1943), 218-221.

        Here is a brief profile of Naoki Hoshino, chief
        secretary of the cabinet and one of the architects of
        Japan's new order.

1513.   Sweeney, T.H. "The Nip and the Yen." ARMY Q, 15 (October
        1947), 80-88.

        Here is an account of the "financial fifth column" left
        in Southeast Asia by the Japanese. Immediately after the
        war, the author was responsible for all Japanese
        expenditures in Indochina. Recounting their poor fiscal
        record, Sweeny found that the Japanese handled all foreign
        currencies at the same rate (regardless of international

values).

1514. United States. Department of State. EFFECTS OF JAPANESE
       OCCUPATION OF NETHERLANDS EAST INDIES. Washington,
       D.C.: GPO, 1945. 3 l.

       Here is a brief summary of Japan's record in NEI. Of
       interest is the Japanese treatment of Indonesian
       nationalists.

1515. United States. Department of State. JAPANESE USE OF
       BURMESE INDUSTRY. Washington, D.C.: GPO, 1945. 65 pp.

       Prepared by the Interim Research and Intelligence
       Service of the State Department's Research and Analysis
       Branch, this report summarizes the Japanese takeover of
       industrial resources in Burma.

1516. United States. Foreign Economic Administration. ECONOMIC
       CHANGES IN THE PHILIPPINES DURING TWO YEARS OF JAPANESE
       OCCUPATION. Washington, D.C.: GPO, 1944. 36 pp.

       This FEA report summarized the policies and activities
       of the Japanese occupation of the Philippines. The brutal
       treatment of the people and the wholesale economic
       takeovers by the Japanese earned the undying enmity of the
       Filipinos.

1517. United States. Office of Strategic Services. ECONOMIC
       REORGANIZATION OF BURMA. Washington, D.C.: OSS, 1944.
       4 l.

       According to this report, the Japanese have dominated
       the economy and resources of Burma. This will present
       difficult challenges in the immediate postwar years.

1518. United States. Office of Strategic Services. JAPANESE
       ATTEMPTS AT INDOCTRINATION OF YOUTH IN OCCUPIED AREAS.
       Washington, D.C.: OSS, 1945. 7 l.

       Here is a brief but valuable examination of some
       effective Japanese propaganda techniques. Some youth
       movements in occupied areas have been expressing
       anti-Western, anti-colonial sentiments.

1519. United States. Office of Strategic Services. JAPANESE
       NEEDS FOR IMPORTS FROM OUTSIDE THE AREAS JAPAN CONTROLS.
       Washington, D.C.: OSS, 1944.

Here is a capsule analysis which, in effect, indicates the Allied progress in the war. The conclusions in this report describe the accelerating deterioration of the Japanese position. More and more goods are becoming less and less accessible to the Japanese.

1520.   United States. Office of Strategic Services. JAPANESE USE OF LAND TRANSPORT IN SOUTH EAST ASIA. Washington, D.C.: OSS, 1944. 29 pp.

Here is a brief study of overland routes (rails, roads, and rivers) among the Southeast Asian countries of Burma, Thailand, Indochina, and Malaya. See especially the descriptions of Japanese efforts for the control and redistribution of raw materials.

1521.   United States. Office of Strategic Services. PROGRAMS OF JAPAN IN THE CELEBES. Honolulu, HI: OSS, 1945. 92 pp.

Here is a study, based on reports from the NEI, of Japanese occupation policies.

III.D. LEND-LEASE

1522.   Kimball, Warren. "Lend-Lease and the Open Door: The Temptation of British Opulence, 1937-1942." POL SCI Q, 86 (June 1971), 232-259.

In a balanced, scholarly, and well-researched assessment, Kimball contrasts the realistic political appraisal that launched the original Lend-Lease act with the flawed American reasoning which shaped the Master Lend-Lease Agreement for the British. Perhaps symbolized by Hull displacing Morgenthau as the leading influence in foreign economic policy, the United States (unwisely), according to Kimball, set out to save Britain from herself.

1523.   Kimball, Warren F. THE MOST UNSORDID ACT: LEND-LEASE, 1939-1941. Baltimore, MD: The Johns Hopkins University Press, 1969. 281 pp.

Here is a classic study. Kimball, in this well-researched, well-written analysis, views Lend-Lease as a public announcement of the most productive and cooperative coalition of modern times.

1524.   Stettinius, Edward R., Jr. LEND-LEASE: WEAPON FOR VICTORY. New York: Macmillan, 1944. 358 pp.

Here are the views of the Lend-Lease administrator. In describing the global program, Stettinuis extols Lend-Lease achievements in China, India, Australia, and New Zealand. See his section entitled "Lend-Lease on the Roads to Tokyo."

1525. United States. War Department. LEND-LEASE SHIPMENTS: WORLD WAR II. Washington, D.C.: War Dept., 1946. 261 pp.

Here is a report on the "important items" which were furnished to foreign governments during the war. The first section describes the grand totals. See especially the section on China.

III.E. CHINA

1526. Behre, Charles H., Jr. and Kung-Ping Wang. "China's Mineral Wealth." FOR AFFS, 23 (October 1944), 130-139.

The two technical experts point out that the development of China's mineral resources would mean an increase in other imports from the United States, enhancement of the process of industrialization in China, and, ultimately, the growth of world trade.

1527. Brandfon, Robert Leon. "The Young Thesis, the Loss of China, and United States Gold Policy." INTL HR, 9 (May 1987), 227-249.

Newly opened military and treasury records reveal, according to Brandfon, the role of the treasury in shaping U.S. policy towards China. Arthur Young has written that shipments of U.S. gold, designed to help stabilize prices in China, were delayed, and this delay undermined the Nationalist government. Brandfon sheds new light on the reasons for not only the delay (stemming from U.S. domestic politics) but also Morgenthau's apparent reversal of attitude.

1528. Carlson, Evans F. "Economic Democracy in China." AMERASIA, 5 (March 1941), 5-10.

The author, a Marine officer, wrote this article shortly after returning from China. Concentrating on the need for economic development in China, Carlson praises not only the work of the Industrial Cooperative Movement but also the contributions of foreign advisers (e.g., R. Alley, Ralph Lapwood, George Hogg, Theodore Herman, and Van Ness).

1529.   Chang, Kia-Ngau. THE INFLATIONARY SPIRAL: THE EXPERIENCE
        IN CHINA, 1939-1950. New York: John Wiley, 1959. 394
        pp.

        In this detailed study of China's economy, Chang
        underscores the fiscal and monetary failures of the
        Kuomintang. He says that the Nationalist leaders never
        really attacked basic problems.

1530.   China, Ministry of Information. RELIEF AND REHABILITATION
        IN CHINA. Washington, D.C.: China News Service, 1944.
        37 pp.

        Here is the text of a report by the Nationalist
        Government on economic programs, both planned and in
        progress, in China. The document not only serves as good
        wartime propaganda but also makes a pitch for more American
        aid.

1531.   Ghosh, Partha S. "Sino-American Economic Relations,
        1929-1939." INT STUD, 15 (July-September, 1976),
        343-364.

        This article traces the decline of U.S. trade with China
        after 1929. Ghosh remarks on the wide gap between U.S.
        rhetoric and U.S. deeds. According to the author, the
        Chinese economy never received due consideration in the
        United States.

1532.   Judd, Walter H. "Understanding the Chinese." INFANTRY J,
        57 (August 1945), 46-48.

        Congressman Judd, a warm friend of the Chinese, calls
        for more efforts by the American people to understand the
        Chinese--and much more U.S. aid to China.

1532a. Kia-Ngau Chang. "China's Need for Transport: A Problem in
        Stability and Democracy." FOR AFFS, 23 (April 1975),
        465-475.

        The author outlines a comprehensive reconstruction plan
        for transport in China which could total $650 billion. He
        omits any discussion of how China will arrange financial
        support for the project.

1533.   Mallory, Walter H. "The Open Door in China: A
        Reappraisal." FOR AFFS, 26 (October 1947), 155-168.

In the postwar appraisal, Mallory defends traditional
U.S. policies toward China, especially the Open Door. He
counsels caution about offering any assistance before
conditions settle down in China, and he warns that the U.S.
is likely to regret either supporting the KMT completely or
switching to support the CCP. Anything having to do with
China, Mallory states, requires patience.

1534. Meng, C.Y.W. "Foreign Enterprise in Postwar China." FE
       SURVEY, 12 (November 3, 1943), 212-219.

       The author, an official with the Central Bank of China,
promises--and warns of--postwar readjustments of special
rights and privileges formerly enjoyed by foreigners in
China.

1535. Quigley, Harold S. CHINA TODAY. New York: Carnegie
       Endowment for International Peace, 1944. 663 pp.

       This contemporary report deals with semi-American
collaboration, especially in the economic field.

1536. Ray, J. Franklin. "Getting the Goods to China." FE
       SURVEY, 12 (March 8, 1943), 51-54.

       This encouraging report by the chief of the China Branch
in the Lend-Lease Administration indicates much improvement
in the system and continuing growth in the amount of
support for China.

1537. Steward, Maxwell S. WAR-TIME CHINA. New York: IPR, 1944.
       63 pp.

       This brief report, sponsored by the Institute of Pacific
Relations, calls attention to specific (non-military)
problems in the war-torn country. Economic development is
a consistent theme.

1538. Tong, Hollington K., ed. CHINA AFTER SEVEN YEARS OF WAR.
       New York: Macmillan, 1945. 246 pp.

       This collection of Chinese writings portrays life in
wartime China. Topics addressed include literature, women,
the military, and the economy. Readers will search in
vain, however, for information about the communists.

1539. United States. Congress. Senate. Committee on the
       Judiciary. MORGENTHAU DIARY (CHINA). Washington, D.C.:
       GPO, 1965. 2 vols.

At the special request of the committee, all the
material pertaining to China was extracted from the
secretary of the treasury's diary and published separately.
The collection offers valuable information on economic
affairs in China.

1540. United States. Office of Coordinator of Information.
      AMERICAN AID TO CHINA. Washington, D.C.: GPO, 1941.
      74 pp.

      The Far East Section of the Research and Analysis Branch
      compiled this summary narrative of American aid to China
      before the entry of the United States into the war.

1541. Young, Arthur N. CHINA AND THE HELPING HAND. Cambridge,
      MA: Harvard University Press, 1964. 502 pp.

      Young, a fiscal adviser in China from 1929 to 1947,
      discusses the strengths and weaknesses of the economic
      situation in China. Acknowledging the complexities of the
      problem, he argues that the United States partly
      contributed to the downfall of the Nationalists by not
      doing everything possible. The book draws on his
      experiences as well as many Chinese sources.

1542. Young, Arthur N. CHINA'S WARTIME FINANCE AND INFLATION,
      1937-1945. Cambridge, MA: Harvard University Press,
      1966. 421 pp.

      Here are the insightful views of a long-time economic
      adviser in China. Young analyzes the fiscal policies of
      the Nationalist government and the effects of the massive
      amount of foreign aid during the war. His narrative is
      especially effective in analyzing the ruinous impact of the
      raging inflation in China.

III.F. POSTWAR

1543. Chase, Stuart. PERSPECTIVES. New York: Post War World
      Council, 1943. 19 pp.

      Chase speculates on the economic structure of the post
      war world.

1544. Eckes, Alfred E., Jr. "Open Door Expansionism
      Reconsidered: The World War II Experience." J AMER
      HIST, 59 (March 1973), 909-924.

Eckes, a history professor, offers a critique of the New
Left. Countering the New Left's idea that open door
expansionism was an outgrowth of domestic conditions, Eckes
explains that the concept of broad international economic
cooperation for the postwar era earned applause from the
Allies. For Eckes, multilateralism represented not a
tragedy but a triumph of American diplomacy. The article
incorporates some new sources in economic history,
especially some of Morgenthau's "diaries."

1545. Kahin, George McT., Guy Pauker, and Lucien W. Pye.
"Comparative Politics of Non-Western Countries." AMER
POL SCI REV, 49 (December 1955), 1022-1041.

Noting fundamental differences in the political
processes between West and non-West, the authors show how
the timing and conditions of introducing Western ways can
vary among non-Western countries, depending on such factors
as the consensus about political activities, the rate of
recruitment of new supporters, quality of leadership,
defined roles, and formal organized interests.

1546. Kirk, Grayson. "Wings Over the Pacific." FOR AFFS, 20
(January 1942), 293-302.

Taking as his premise the "tremendous importance" of the
development of air power as a new force, Kirk calls
attention not only to the need to develop new civil air
routes in the Pacific but also to the fierce international
competition in civil aviation that will emerge in the
postwar era.

1547. Mitchell, Kate L. INDUSTRIALIZATION OF THE WESTERN
PACIFIC. Washington, D.C.: American Council on Public
Affairs, 1942. 322 pp.

Mitchell compiles a ready reference tool in this broad
economic survey, which was actually written on the eve of
the war. She looks at the extent and nature of industrial
development in East Asia and the South Pacific.

1548. "Pattern of Reconquest." AMERASIA, 9 (October 1945),
267-279.

As the U.S. looks to the free market in the postwar era,
fundamental conflicts will arise in Southeast Asia.
According to this article, such conflicts include
Anglo-American economic rivalry and the restoration of
colonial rule in Indochina and NEI.

1549. Phelan-Cressey, Harriet. "The Post-War Strategy of
          American Business." AMERASIA, 7 (October 25, 1943),
          347-353.

          The author calls for imaginative--and enlightened--views
          of U.S. businessmen beyond the nineteenth-century concept
          of capturing markets.

III.G. WAR CRIMES/TRIALS

1. GENERAL ACCOUNTS/REFERENCE WORKS

1550. Abrahams, Gerald. DAY OF RECKONING. London: W. H. Allen,
          1943.

          Here are allegations (and descriptions) of war
          atrocities which Abrahams ties to the announced intentions
          of the United Nations to conduct war crimes trials at the
          war's end.

1551. Allen, Lafe Franklin. "Japan's Militarists Face the
          Music." FOR SERVICE J, 24 (August 1947), 14-17, 41-44.

          Allen, an army military government officer in Japan,
          examines the process of the war crimes trials in the Far
          East. Although he reassures readers that each of the
          twenty-eight Japanese defendants will have a fair trial,
          Allen lambastes their "synthetic moral values."

1552. Anderson, C. Arnold. "The Utility of the Proposed Trial
          and Punishment of Enemy Leaders." AMER POL SCI REV, 37
          (December 1943), 1081-1100.

          Although this article concentrates on the situation in
          Germany, many of its general views also apply to Japan.
          Anderson asks whether punishing leaders would actually
          strengthen peace in the postwar era. He suggests that
          alleged war criminals should be tried by their own
          nationals. Anderson doubts that war crimes trials will
          have any deterrent effect in the future.

1553. Brackman, Arnold C. THE OTHER NUREMBERG: THE UNTOLD STORY
          OF THE TOKYO WAR CRIMES TRIALS. New York: William
          Morrow, 1987. 432 pp.

          Here is a popular account of the International Military
          Tribunal which tried 28 Japanese defendants between 1946
          and 1948. Brackman, a correspondent covering the

proceedings, integrates official transcripts and
interviews. His narrative graphically describes the crimes
that took place. There are no notes and the Bibliography
is surprisingly brief. Of interest is his report of the
internal divisions among the eleven Allied legal
representatives about the proceedings. Brackman died
before the book was published.

1553a. Brown, Brendan F. "Red China, the Tokyo Trial, and
       Aggressive War." LOUIS BAR ASSOC J, n.v. (January 3,
       1956), 145-159.

       Brown contends that the task of the United States is "to
       continue to humor those nations which have strayed from the
       path of sanity" (i.e., Red China and the Soviet Union).
       His argument relies on the international code of conduct
       established in the Tokyo war crimes trials.

1554. Brown, Delmer M. "Recent Japanese Political and Historical
      Materials." AMER POL SCI REV, 43 (October 1949),
      1010-1017.

       Brown researches the International Military Tribunal,
       Far East (IMTFE) records pertaining to the war crimes
       trials. According to him, about 50% of the 4,000 documents
       collected by the International Prosecution Section (IPS)
       were used at the trial--and most of these were only
       excerpted. The article examines the index categories of
       the IPS documents. The IMTFE records and files of the
       Japanese Navy and Army were the only two categories of
       documents open to private research at the time.

1555. Cowles, Willard B. "Trials of War Criminals." AMER J INT
      LAW, 42 (April 1948), 299-319.

       Cowles argues that trials for violating laws and customs
       of war are justified--and in doing so, he tries to dispel
       confusion over the lack of precedent.

1556. Dull, Paul S. and Michael Takaaki Umemura. THE TOKYO
      TRIALS: A FUNCTIONAL INDEX TO THE PROCEEDINGS OF THE
      INTERNATIONAL MILITARY TRIBUNAL FOR THE FAR EAST. Ann
      Arbor, MI: University of Michigan Press, 1957. 94 pp.

       This guide helps sort out the over 40,000 pages of the
       Tribunal's proceedings. It is a welcome reference help.

1557. Fixel, Rowland W. TRIAL OF JAPAN'S WAR LORDS. n.p.: 1959.
      249 l.

NE

1558. Freeman, Alwyn V. "War Crimes by Enemy Nationals
        Administering Justice in Occupied Territory." AMER J
        INT LAW, 41 (July 1947), 579-610.

        Freeman argues that people in this category should not
        be brought to trial just because they had been installed
        illegally. Rather, he says, the specific action of each of
        these courts should be scrutinized for statute violations
        or violations of fundamental principles of human justice
        (incorporated in The Hague Convention IV of 1907).

1559. Friedman, Leon, comp. THE LAW OF WAR: A DOCUMENTARY
        HISTORY. New York: Random House, 1972. 2 vols.

        Arranged chronologically within three broad categories
        (the Grotius code, international agreements, and war
        crimes), this collection draws from documentation in
        international law since 1600. See the work of the Far
        Eastern Tribunal, especially the material on war crimes in
        the Philippines.

1560. Hanayama, Shinsho. THE WAY OF DELIVERANCE. New York:
        Charles Scribner's Sons, 1950. 297 pp.

        The author spent three years ministering to the
        condemned Class A Japanese war criminals. Without breaking
        privileged confidentiality, he offers insightful
        observations on the general subjects of war and war crimes
        as well as on the specific people in his care. The book
        was originally translated by Hideo Suzuki, Eiichi Noda, and
        James K. Sasaki, and revised by Harrison Collins.

1561. Hessel, Eugene A. "Let the Judges Do the Hanging."
        CHRISTIAN CENT, 66 (August 24, 1949), 984-986.

        Hessel, a Presbyterian minister in Manila, held services
        for the Japanese prisoners. In this article, he raises
        several questions about the war crimes trials. If the
        judges were to view the executions, he suggests, maybe they
        would not be so quick to give out the death penalty.

1562. Hosoya, Chihiro, Nisuke Ando, and Yasuaki Onuma, eds. THE
        TOKYO WAR CRIMES TRIAL: AN INTERNATIONAL SYMPOSIUM.
        Tokyo: Kodansha International, 1986. 226 pp.

        The 1983 symposium explored historical and present-day

perspectives on the war crimes. Japanese historians noted
the differences between the German and Japanese trials. Of
special interest is the concern expressed about the dangers
of current revisionism, such as that promoted by the
ex-minister of education, Fujio Masayuki.

1563. Hsu, Shuhsi. A DIGEST OF JAPANESE WAR CONDUCT. Shanghai:
       Kelly & Walsh, 1939. 102 pp.

       The compilation lists alleged Japanese war crimes and
       misconduct during the early months of the Sino-Japanese
       war. Hsu is identified as an occasional adviser to the
       Chinese Ministry of Foreign Affairs.

1564. Iwamatsu, Shigetoshi. "A Perspective on the War Crimes."
       BULL ATOMIC SCI, 38 (February 1982), 29-33.

       The author, a survivor of the atomic bombing at
       Nagasaki, criticizes Japanese prewar and wartime policies,
       both foreign and domestic. His strongly stated position
       holds that Japanese must first examine their war crimes
       before criticizing the use of the atomic bomb.

1565. Kinnaird, Clark. THIS MUST NOT HAPPEN AGAIN. New York:
       Howell, Soskin, 1945. 157 pp.

       Here is a photographic account of atrocities committed
       by Germans and Japanese during the war. The accompanying
       narrative adds little to the horrors graphically portrayed.

1566. Lachs, Manfred. WAR CRIMES: AN ATTEMPT TO DEFINE THE
       ISSUES. London: Stevens, 1945. 108 pp.

       Here is a legalistic approach to an emotional question.

1567. Levy, Albert G.D. "The Law and Procedure of War Crimes
       Trials." AMER POL SCI REV, 37 (December 1943),
       1,052-1,081.

       Levy describes a new legal principle about to emerge
       from the war: individuals (not just nations) can be held
       responsible for crimes against humanity.

1568. Lewis, John R. A BIBLIOGRAPHY OF WAR CRIMES TRIALS:
       UNCERTAIN JUDGMENT. Santa Barbara, CA: ABC-CLIO, 1979.

       This is a useful guide. There is a good deal of
       information on the Far Eastern tribunal.

1569. Liu, James T.C. "The Tokyo Trials: Source Materials." FE
         SURVEY, 17 (July 28, 1948), 168-170.

         The author served as assistant to the Chinese
         prosecutor. He describes important Japanese sources that
         have been uncovered (e.g., prewar Imperial Conferences;
         Liaison Conferences; and memoirs by Kido, Saionji, Harrada,
         and Konoye) and recommends that SCAP not return them to the
         original owners.

1570. MacArthur, Douglas. "General Douglas MacArthur's Review of
         the War Crimes Sentences Issued on November 24, 1948."
         CONTEMP JAPAN, 17 (July/December 1948), 433-434.

         MacArthur, who called his duty to review the sentences
         "utterly repugnant to me," could find nothing to warrant
         his intervention. (For the text of the sentences of the
         International Military Tribunal for the Far East, see pp.
         416-433.)

1571. Minear, Richard H. VICTORS' JUSTICE: THE TOKYO WAR CRIMES
         TRIAL. Princeton, NJ: Princeton University Press,
         1971. 229 pp.

         Here is a partisan view, which is highly critical of the
         proceedings. Minear calls his initial effort at neutrality
         "fraudulent" and admits his scholarly pursuits turned in a
         political direction. His criticism of the trial, he makes
         clear, in no way offers judgments about the historical
         responsibility attached to Japanese policies. Minear warns
         against the quasi-imperial role of the United States in
         postwar Pacific affairs, and he dedicates the book to
         American opponents of the war in Vietnam.

1572. Pal, Radhabinod. INTERNATIONAL MILITARY TRIBUNAL FOR THE
         FAR EAST: DISSENTIENT JUDGMENT. Calcutta: Sanyal, 1953.
         70 l.

         The author, an Indian jurist, takes issue with the war
         crimes trials. Essentially, he feels that justice in these
         cases was merely in the eye of the victors.

1573. Piccigallo, Philip R. THE JAPANESE ON TRIAL: ALLIED WAR
         CRIMES OPERATIONS IN THE EAST, 1945-1951. Austin, TX:
         University of Texas Press, 1979. 292 pp.

         The author argues that the trials were made to fit the
         overall national and foreign policies of each of the
         Allies. Giving an overview of the almost 6,000 trials,

Piccigallo investigates the mechanics of the legal
operation, such as uncovering atrocities, gathering
evidence, and interviewing witnesses. His conclusion is
that, despite some flaws, the trials revealed a devotion to
justice. His case is unpersuasive, however, as he seeks to
align the principal policies (especially as the Cold War
began to develop) of each ally with the blind principles of
justice. The book is extremely well researched and
incorporates an extensive bibliography.

1574. Pritchard, R. John. "The Historical Experience of British
       War Crimes Courts in the Far East, 1946-1948." INT REL
       (London), 6 (May 1978), 310-326.

       The author, a history professor, contends that the
       professionalism of the British military tribunal in Asia
       stands in sharp contrast to the comportment of the other
       international, particularly U.S., tribunals. Many of the
       judgments, he feels, erred on the side of leniency.

1575. Pritchard, R. John and Sonia Maghanua Zaide, eds. THE
       TOKYO WAR CRIMES TRIALS: COMPLETE TRANSCRIPTS OF THE
       PROCEEDINGS OF THE INTERNATIONAL MILITARY TRIBUNAL FOR
       THE FAR EAST. New York: Garland, 1981. 22 vols.

       The editors include annotations to this complete record
       of the proceedings. The trials took place during the
       period 1946-1948. D.C. Watt served as project director for
       this vast undertaking.

1576. Quezon, Manuel L. "Japanese Atrocities." UN REV, 4
       (February 15, 1944), 78.

       This brief statement by the president of the Philippines
       expresses horror at Japanese war crimes in his country. He
       promises neither to forgive nor forget.

1577. Roling, B.V.A. and C.F. Ruter, eds. THE TOKYO JUDGMENT:
       THE INTERNATIONAL MILITARY TRIBUNAL FOR THE FAR EAST.
       Amsterdam, Neth.: APA-University Press, 1977.

       Here is the massive record of the proceedings of the
       IMTFE.

1578. Russell, Lord. THE KNIGHTS OF BUSHIDO: THE SHOCKING
       HISTORY OF JAPANESE WAR ATROCITIES. New York: E.P.
       Dutton, 1958. 334 pp.

       Russell incorporates the revelations from the

International Military Tribunal for the Far East not only
to describe the war crimes perpetrated by the Japanese but
also to analyze the rationale behind their shocking
behavior.

1579.   Scanlon, Helen L. WAR CRIMES: A SELECTED LIST OF BOOKS
        AND ARTICLES DEFINING WAR CRIMES UNDER INTERNATIONAL LAW
        AND DISCUSSING THEIR TRIAL AND PUNISHMENT, INCLUDING
        WORKS ON AN INTERNATIONAL CRIMINAL COURT. Washington,
        D.C.: Carnegie Endowment for International Peace
        Library, 1945.

        This bibliography was prepared to encourage discussion
of the handling of alleged war crimes in World War II.

1580.   Shigetoshi Iwamatsu. "A Perspective on the War Crimes."
        BULL ATOMIC SCI, 38 (February 1982), 29-32.

        The author, a survivor of the Nagasaki bombing,
criticizes both the United States (for using the atomic
bomb) and Japan (for war crimes). He believes that the
Soviet entry into the war--as a threat to the Tenno-Emperor
system--forced Japan to surrender.

1581.   Tomes, Jonathan P. "Indirect Responsibility for War
        Crimes." MIL REV, 66 (November 1966), 37-44.

        The author, an Army officer and instructor of military
law, concludes that Yamashita received a fair trial under
contemporary standards. Indirect responsibility is a basis
for criminal liability, he writes.

1582.   Tutorow, Norman E., comp. WAR CRIMES, WAR CRIMINALS, AND
        WAR CRIMES TRIALS: AN ANNOTATED BIBLIOGRAPHY AND SOURCE
        BOOK. New York: Garland, 1986. 548 pp.

        Aided by Karen Winnovich, Tutorow has accomplished a
monumental task. See especially the section on the
International Military Tribunal for the Far East. The
annotations provide helpful guides through the maze of
material.

1583.   United Nations. Communications and Records Division.
        Archives Section. GUIDE TO RECORDS OF THE UNITED
        NATIONS WAR CRIMES COMMISSION, LONDON, 1943-1948.
        London: HMSO, 1951.

        Here is a valuable reference and finding aid for the
proceedings of the war crimes trials.

1584. United Nations. Information Office. JAPAN'S RECORD AND
       WORLD SECURITY. New York: U.N. Information Office,
       1945. 40 pp.

       Here is a brief wartime summary of alleged atrocities
       and other war crimes committed by the Japanese and their
       allies.

1585. United Nations. Information Office. PUNISHMENT FOR WAR
       CRIMES. New York: U.N. Information Office, 1943.

       This pamphlet reproduces the Inter-Allied Declaration
       which was signed in London on January 13, 1942. The Allies
       pledge to punish (enemy) war criminals. Also included is a
       memorandum which alleges evidence already gathered of
       atrocities committed by the Japanese.

1586. United Nations. War Crimes Commission. HISTORY OF THE
       UNITED NATIONS WAR CRIMES COMMISSION AND THE DEVELOPMENT
       OF THE LAWS OF WAR. London: HMSO, 1948. 592 pp.

       Here is a detailed description of the work of the U.N.
       War Crimes Commission. There is a useful explanation of
       the development of international law regarding war crimes.

1587. United Nations. War Crimes Commission. LAW REPORTS OF
       TRIALS OF WAR CRIMINALS. London: HMSO, 1949. 15 vols.

       For each case, there is an outline of the trial
       proceedings, charges, facts bearing on the case, evidence
       presented, arguments for the defense, and special notes.
       See, for example, the report on the Yamashita trial, which
       is described as fair by contemporary standards. In
       rebutting the arguments of defense attorney Reel, the
       narrative states that a reading of the trial transcript
       reveals that Yamashita actually ordered certain atrocities.

1588. United States. Congress. House of Representatives.
       Committee on Foreign Affairs. PHILIPPINE WAR DAMAGE
       CLAIMS. Washington, D.C.: GPO, 1960. 93 pp.

       The summary report outlines claims, amounting to
       millions of dollars, put forward because of damage done
       during the war.

1589. United States. Congress. Senate. Committee on Military
       Affairs. THE SACK OF MANILA. Washington, D.C.: GPO,
       1945. 29 pp.

Here is a report on alleged atrocities committed by the Japanese. See the sworn statements by alleged victims and witnesses.

590. United States. Departments of the Army and Navy. JAPANESE ATROCITIES TO PRISONERS OF WAR. Washington, D.C.: GPO, 1944.

Here are the first public reports (with offical sanction) of the Bataan Death March and other atrocities committed by the Japanese. The book is based on the testimony of POWs who escaped from the Philippines in 1942. The armed services had been reluctant to make public these eyewitness accounts, given the unpredictability of the Japanese reaction.

591. United States. Department of State. "Japanese Atrocities: U.S. Representations of January 27, 1944 to Japan." DEPT STATE BULL, 10 (February 12, 1944), 168-175.

Here are the texts of two telegrams sent through the Swiss (protectors of U.S. interests in Japan) about the mistreatment of American nationals in Japanese hands throughout Asia and the Pacific.

592. United States. Navy Department. TRIAL OF JAPANESE WAR CRIMINALS. Washington, D.C.: GPO, 1946.

NE

593. Wright, Quincy. "War Criminals." AMER J INT LAW, 39 (January 1945), 257-285.

This article warns against trespassing important rights (which the Allies fought the war to defend). Wright feels that careful legal distinctions must be drawn before proceeding with war crimes trials.

II.G.2. MEMOIRS AND BIOGRAPHIES

594. Barker, A.J. YAMASHITA. New York: Ballantine Books, 1973. 159 pp.

The book is part of a series on war leaders. According to the author, MacArthur needed a scapegoat before implementing lenient occupation policies and found one in Yamashita. The biography is sympathetic in tone but not uncritical.

1595. Bartlett, Donald. "Vice Admiral Chuichi Hara--
       Unforgettable Foe." USNIP, 96 (October 1970), 49-55.

       Commander Bartlett (USN) served on the survey team at
       Truk in November 1945. He paints a sympathetic picture of
       the Japanese leader of the 4th Fleet who was tried and
       found guilty of maltreating POW's under his command.

1596. Blakeney, Ben Bruce. "International Military Tribunal:
       Arguments for Motions to Dismiss." AMER BAR ASSOC J, 32
       (August 1946), 475-477, 523.

       Maj. Blakeney (USAAF), counsel for Gen. Umerzo, advances
       the general argument for all defendants represented by
       American counselors that the tribunal lacked jurisdiction.
       The article addresses some of the broad principles involved
       in such trials. The tribunal over-ruled Blakeney's
       argument.

1597. Blewett, George F. "Victor's Justice: The Tokyo War
       Crimes Trial." AMER PERSPECTIVES, 4 (Summer 1950),
       282-292.

       Attorney Blewett defended Tojo in the Tokyo trial. He
       criticizes the theory and the practice of the proceedings,
       and he points out, in retrospect, that, despite rosy
       predictions at Tokyo, no "new morality" has arisen in
       international relations.

1598. Comyns-Carr, A.S. "The Judgment of the International
       Military Tribunal for the Far East." TRANS GROTIUS SOC,
       30 (November 1948), 141-151.

       The author served as a member of the British prosecution
       staff in this Tokyo Tribunal. Like Nuremberg, he writes,
       the Tokyo Tribunal (1) defined waging and conspiring to
       wage war as a war crime and (2) handed down no death
       penalties except for crimes against POWs or other illegal
       outrages. In a historical summary, Comyns-Carr traces how
       a grandiose plot in the minds of a few Japanese officers
       and civilians during the 1920s developed into the
       dominating purpose of the Japanese government by 1941. Of
       interest is his discussion of the language problems the
       Tokyo Tribunal encountered--especially the fierce dispute
       over the use of classical or colloquial Outer Mongolian!

1599. Comyns-Carr, A.S. "The Tokyo War Crimes Trial." FE
       SURVEY, 18 (May 18, 1949), 109-114.

From his perspective as a member of the prosecution staff at Tokyo, the author endorses the judgment as "massive and impressive." Contending that the historical evidence uncovered a grandiose plot which grew in Japan from the 1920s, he concludes that the planning and waging of aggressive war constitute criminal behavior.

600. Feldhaus, J. Gordon. "The Trial of Yamashita." CURRENT LEGAL THOUGHT, 13 (August 1947), 251-262.

Feldhaus served as a member of Yamashita's defense counsel. Of interest is the author's argument that the poor British military resistance inflated Yamashita's reputation, which, in turn, contributed to his standing trial after the war. In fact, Feldhaus argues that the British would have won in Malaya if they had put up a more determined fight. The article summarizes the proceedings of the trial.

601. Guy, George F. "The Defense of Yamashita." WYOMING LAW J, 4 (Fall 1949), 152-180.

The author, a major in the Judge Advocate Section, Headquarters Eighth Army, worked as one of the defense counsels for Yamashita. Guy contends that not one piece of evidence showed that the general ordered or condoned any war crime. The article underlines the human dimension of the proceedings.

602. Hart, Franklin A. "Yamashita, Nuremberg and Vietnam: Command Responsibility Reappraised." NAVAL WAR COLL REV, 25 (September-October 1972), 19-36.

The author draws upon evidence at Nuremberg and the Yamashita case to argue that a commander's guilt should arise only from personal negligence or misconduct. Explicitly refuting the broad interpretation of overall command responsibility put forward by Telford Taylor, Hart points out that Yamashita's conviction stemmed from specific personal knowledge of atrocities.

603. Horwitz, Solis. "The Tokyo Trial." INTL CONCILIATION, 465 (November 1950), 473-584.

Here is a particular perspective on the trials as described by a member of the prosecution. Of special interest are the details provided by Horwitz in this lengthy account.

1604.   Howard, J. Woodford. MR. JUSTICE MURPHY: A POLITICAL
             BIOGRAPHY. Princeton, NJ: Princeton University Press,
             1968. 585 pp.

        This political biography is pertinent to our guide
    because of Murphy's courageous protest against the conduct
    of the trials in Manila of the Japanese generals (Yamashita
    and Homma).

1605.   Japanese American Citizens League. IVA TOGURI: VICTIM OF
             A LEGEND. Salt Lake City, UT: JACL, 1975.

        Here is a sympathetic account of the trial of "Tokyo
    Rose."

1606.   Katona, Paul. "Japanese War Crimes Trials." FREE WORLD,
             12 (November 1946), 37-40.

        The author is a journalist and lawyer who served on the
    Judge Advocate's staff during Yamashita's trial. Katona
    believes that the misconduct of the Japanese troops was so
    widespread that Yamashita must have either known about or
    ordered the war crimes. Of interest is the author's point
    that, because Japan accepted the Potsdam Declaration (which
    called for "stern justice" to war criminals), the Tokyo
    trial was even more legal than the Nuremberg trial.

1607.   Keenan, Joseph B. "Observations and Lessons From
             International Criminal Trials." U KAN CITY LAW REV, 17
             (1949), 117-128.

        The author served as U.S. chief counsel for the
    prosecution in the trials of Japanese war criminals. The
    outstanding lesson of the trials, he says, is that peoples
    never want war and that the crime always belongs to
    leadership. For Keenan, the Tokyo trials provided a
    "wholesome example" of Anglo-Saxon justice.

1607a. Kenworthy, Aubrey Saint. THE TIGER OF MALAYA: THE INSIDE
             STORY OF THE JAPANESE ATROCITIES. New York: Exposition
             Press. 112 pp.

        Here is a unique view of the war crimes trial of
    Yamashita as seen by one of his American guards.

1608.   Kodama, Yoshio. SUGAMO DIARY. Tokyo: 1960. 275 pp.

        Here is a memoir of the Tokyo war crimes trials. Taro

Fukuda translated the work.

1609. Kutler, Sanley I. "Forging a Legend: The Treason of 'Tokyo
        Rose.'" WISC LAW REV, 1980 (No. 6, 1980), 1341-1382.

        Historian Kutler applies the distinguished scholarship
        on treason of Willard Hurst to the case of Tokyo Rose. In
        this case, the author argues, the maneuverings of
        bureaucrats, political ambition, and other personal goals
        of people (in and out of government)--all within the
        atmosphere of the Cold War in 1949--contributed to a
        judicial decision virtually disconnected from principles of
        law or justice. This well-researched study describes Tokyo
        Rose as "a pawn and nothing more" from 1941 to 1949.

1610. Lael, Richard R. THE YAMASHITA PRECEDENT. Wilmington, DE:
        Scholarly Resources, 1982. 165 pp.

        One of Lael's chief concerns is the limit of command
        responsibility. With thorough research, he points out
        flaws in Yamashita's trial and criticizes MacArthur for
        what Lael considers to be undue haste in expediting the
        proceedings. Of interest is Lael's description of changes
        made in international law on the subject of war crimes
        after this trial. He calls for clarification of the legal
        definition of war crimes and the scope of applicability.
        According to Lael, the Yamashita case is a poor precedent.

1611. Lipton, Dean. "Wayne M. Collins and the Case of 'Tokyo
        Rose.'" J CONTEMP STUD, 8 (Fall-Winter 1985), 25-41.

        Lipton calls attention to the work of attorney Collins
        in seeking legal relief for Iva Toguri.

1612. Lyman, Albert. "A Reviewer Reviews the Yokohama War Crimes
        Trials." J BAR ASSOC WASH D.C., 17 (June 1950),
        267-280.

        In 1948-1949, the author served as a civilian appellate
        reviewer for the war crimes trials at Yokohama. These
        trials were confined to CLASS B and C crimes. He believes
        that most of the sentences were proper and that the guilty
        verdicts generally rested on "competent evidence." Of
        interest are his explanations of two troublesome concepts:
        command responsibility and "contributing to the death of a
        decedent."

1613. Meek, Frank E. "Remarks in the War Crimes Trials in the

Pacific." IDAHO STATE BAR PROC, 21 (June 1947), 37-43.

Col. Meek (U.S.A.) was chief of prosecution in the
Pacific war crimes trials. After the Potsdam Declaration,
he says, the War Crimes Branch of General Headquarters was
set up to investigate allegations of war crimes in the
Pacific. He maintains that the law followed the flag and
that the trials were conducted fairly. Of interest are his
comments that Homma had attended two Geneva Conventions and
Mrs. Yamashita was a remarkable witness for the defense.

1614.   Okamura, Raymond. "Iva Toguri: Victim of an American
        Fantasy." In: COUNTERPOINT: PERSPECTIVES ON ASIAN
        AMERICANS. 1976.

        NE

1615.   Parks, William H. "Command Responsibility for War Crimes."
        MIL LAW REV, 62 (Fall 1973), 22-38.

        Based on the trial transcript, Parks believes that
        Yamashita received a fair trial. The author, an Army legal
        officer, asserts that the Japanese commander not only knew
        of atrocities but also ordered some.

1616.   Potter, John D. THE LIFE AND DEATH OF A JAPANESE GENERAL.
        New American Library, 1962. 199 pp.

        Here is a brief biography of Gen. Yamashita. The
        author, a correspondent, interviewed the Japanese leader
        just before Yamashita's execution as a war criminal. In
        sympathy for his subject, Potter quotes the dissenting
        opinion of Justice Frank Murphy who protested the judgment
        as "judicial lynching." A similar British version appeared
        in 1963 (210 pp.) under the title: A SOLDIER MUST HANG: A
        BIOGRAPHY OF AN ORIENTAL GENERAL.

1617.   Reel, A. Frank. THE CASE OF GENERAL YAMASHITA. Chicago:
        University of Chicago Press, 1949. 324 pp.

        Capt. Reel (USA) served on Yamashita's legal defense
        staff. Highly critical of the trial, Reel believes that
        the proceedings were a bad precedent, "unjust,
        hypocritical, and vindictive." Raising the moral issue of
        victor's justice, Reel believes that the concept of command
        responsibility has been construed too narrowly and does not
        make allowances for shifting situations on the battlefied.

1618.   Shiroyama, Saburo. WAR CRIMINAL: THE LIFE AND DEATH OF

HIROTA KOKI. Tokyo: Kodansha International, 1977.

In this work, translated by John Bester, Shiroyama
criticizes the proceedings of the trial of Hirota Koki, the
sole Japanese civilian executed as a war criminal.

1619. Sleeman, Colin. TRIAL OF CAPTAIN GOZAWA SADAICHI AND NINE
OTHERS. London: Hodge, 1948. 245 pp.

Here is a close account of the proceedings of the war
crimes trials.

1620. Spurlock, Paul E. "The Yokohama War Crimes Trials: The
Truth About a Misunderstood Subject." AMER BAR ASSOC J,
36 (May 1950), 387-389, 436-437.

Working for the 8th Army, the author served as a
civilian reviewer of the records from the Yokahama trials
and of sentences imposed on defendants convicted of war
crimes. His description of the complex process is intended
to reassure his fellow lawyers in the United States about
the integrity of the trials. Every conviction underwent
mandatory review at two or more higher levels. Of interest
is his report on some of the harsh sentences that were
reduced to more lenient terms.

1621. Stratton, Samuel S. "Tiger of Malaya." USNIP, 80
(February 1954), 136-143.

Naval officer (later congressman) Stratton was the first
American to interview Gen. Yamashita at length in Manila
during September 1945. This is an account of Stratton's
impressions of the "Tiger of Malaya."

1622. Supreme Commander for the Allied Powers. Government
Section. THE CASE OF GENERAL YAMASHITA: A MEMORANDUM.
Tokyo: SCAP, 1950. 82 pp.

This memorandum, written by Gen. Courtney Whitney,
reviews the evidence amassed against Yamashita and
generally affirms the guilty verdict.

1623. Sutton, David Nelson. "The Trial of Tojo: The Most
Important Trial in All History?" AMER BAR ASSOC J, 36
(February 1950), 93-96, 160-165.

The author, president of the Virginia State Bar
Association, served as associate counsel for the
prosecution before the International Military Tribunal for

the Far East. The article outlines Japanese aggression and
war crimes during the period 1928-1945. The trials, he
feels, were justified as an expression of international
will.

1624. Taylor, Lawrence. A TRIAL OF GENERALS. South Bend, IN:
        Icarus Press, 1981. 233 pp.

        The author, a criminal attorney, offers an emotional,
        undocumented case in support of Homma and Yamashita. In
        addition, Taylor presents an indictment of MacArthur for
        allowing the trials to proceed as they did. According to
        Taylor, the trials were a travesty of justice and helped
        establish a poor precedent.

1625. Uyeda, Clifford I. "The Pardoning of 'Tokyo Rose': A
        Report on the Restoration of American Citizenship to Iva
        Ikuko Toguri." AMERASIA J, 5 (Fall 1978), 69-93.

        On his last full day in office, President Ford granted a
        pardon to Toguri. The author worked with John Hada to
        undertake a program to change U.S. public opinion about
        her. Uyeda praises the contribution of Wayne M. Collins
        but feels the JACL did little.

1626. Ward, David A. "The Unending War of Iva Toguri D'Aquino:
        The Trial and Conviction of 'Tokyo Rose.'" AMERASIA, J,
        1 (July 1971), 26-35.

        Relying on published sources, Ward reviews the case and
        argues that the U.S. government should redress this
        grievance.

IV. MILITARY ASPECTS OF THE WAR AGAINST JAPAN

A. GENERAL ACCOUNTS

1627. Adams, Bruce and Robert Howlett. BATTLEGROUND SOUTH
      PACIFIC. Rutland, VT: Charles E. Tuttle, 1970. 233 pp.

      The writer of the text, Howlett, provides a
      straightforward narrative. The photographs by Adams, all
      from the present day, fit into the "revisited" genre.
      Special chapters are included on the coastwatchers.

1628. Allen, Louis. THE END OF THE WAR IN ASIA. London:
      Hart-Davis, MacGibbon, 1976. 306 pp.

      Allen examines the interplay in various Asian countries
      of Japanese occupation forces, native populations
      (especially nationalist movements and Japanese residents),
      and the United Nations forces (including the Western
      imperial powers seeking to reimpose their prewar colonial
      authority). His depth of research and interesting style of
      writing combine to produce an informed perspective on the
      crucial final stages of the war.

1629. Argyle, Christopher J. JAPAN AT WAR, 1937-1945. London:
      A. Barker, 1976. 224 pp.

      Here is a brief survey which examines the Japanese
      perspective.

1630. Bahrenburg, Bruce. THE PACIFIC: THEN AND NOW. New York:
      Putnam, 1971. 318 pp.

      Bahrenburg, a correspondent, reports on his visits to
      Pacific battlefields of the war. This "travelogue"
      approach carries limited value but does offer the reactions
      to the war of present-day inhabitants. The accompanying
      photographs are interesting.

1631.   Baldwin, Hanson W. "America at War: Victory in the
        Pacific." FOR AFFS, 24 (October 1945), 26-39.

        Here is a survey of military and diplomatic events by an
        expert reporter in military affairs. Baldwin includes a
        useful table of air, land, and sea commanders. Of special
        interest is his treatment of LeMay's announcements
        beforehand of the names of cities about to be bombed.

1632.   Bateson, Charles. THE WAR WITH JAPAN: A CONCISE HISTORY.
        Sydney, Aus.: Ure Smith, 1968. 417 pp.

        Although generally avoiding political issues in this
        straightforward narrative, Bateson feels that the war might
        have ended sooner if the United States had made clear that
        Japan's emperor system would be retained and that Emperor
        Hirohito would not be considered a war criminal. Under
        such circumstances, the author argues, there would have
        been no need for the atomic bombings. A few notes and some
        suggestions for further reading follow each chapter. The
        book contains some excellent photographs, particularly
        those selected from the Australian War Museum.

1633.   Bhargava, K.D. and K.N.V. Sastri. CAMPAIGNS IN SOUTH-EAST
        ASIA, 1941-1942. Bombay: Orient Longmans, 1960. 416
        pp.

        The authors use careful research to build this detailed
        overview of the Japanese successes early in the war.

1634.   Broek, J.O.M. "Weather and the War." FE SURVEY, 13 (March
        22, 1944), 49-52.

        Broek describes the continuing heat and high humidity
        that foster parasites and bacteria which, in turn, nurture
        diseases. He also points to problems that monsoons create
        for combat units.

1635.   California University, Southern Branch, Los Angeles.
        SOUTHWEST PACIFIC AND THE WAR. Berkeley, CA: University
        of California, 1944. 168 pp.

        Here is a collection of lectures by faculty at the
        University of California on the war against Japan. The
        various topics covered include geography, culture,
        diplomacy, and strategy.

1636.   Cant, Gilbert. THE GREAT PACIFIC VICTORY: FROM THE
        SOLOMONS TO TOKYO. New York: The John Day Company,

1945. 422 pp.

This is a well-written contemporary account, without
footnotes or a bibliography, which focuses primarily on
naval operations. Cant suggests that no language among the
peoples of the Pacific was stranger than the military
jargon ("agglutinative speech") spread by Americans there
during the war.

1637. Caporale, Louis G. "The Pacific War--1941-1945." MC GAZ,
       69 (November 1985), 46-57.

       Here is a sketchy outline of the major operations in the
       Pacific.

1638. Clausen, Walter B. BLOOD FOR THE EMPEROR: A NARRATIVE
       HISTORY OF THE HUMAN SIDE OF THE WAR IN THE PACIFIC.
       New York: D. Appleton-Century Company, 1943. 341 pp.

       The author, a war correspondent assigned to Nimitz's
       headquarters, tries to focus on the human side of the war.
       According to Clausen, the Japanese remained convinced of
       their destiny to rule the world.

1639. Coffey, Thomas M. IMPERIAL TRAGEDY: JAPAN IN WORLD WAR
       II: THE FIRST DAYS AND THE LAST. New York: The World
       Publishing Company, 1970. 531 pp.

       Coffey divides his work into two parts: December 1941
       and August 1945. Although it has no footnotes, the book is
       well written and presents the human side of the war.

1640. Collier, Basil. JAPAN AT WAR: AN ILLUSTRATED HISTORY OF
       THE WAR IN THE FAR EAST, 1931-1945. London: Sidgwick
       and Jackson, 1975. 192 pp.

       Here is a brief overview of the war which boasts a large
       number of excellent photographs. The coverage of the war
       in Southeast Asia is particularly good.

1641. Collier, Basil. THE WAR IN THE FAR EAST, 1941-1945: A
       MILITARY HISTORY. New York: William Morrow and
       Company, 1969. 539 pp.

       Collier contends that both sides erred during the war,
       but the Japanese committed the more grievous errors. The
       rapid-fire pace of the book does not prevent Collier from
       including his assessments, such as criticism of Nagumo at
       Pearl Harbor, MacArthur's misuse of air power, Fletcher's

failure to reinforce Wake Island, and Mountbatten's organizational structure in South East Asia Command.

1642. Cooper, Dennis Glen. "Tales of Gallantry in the Southwest Pacific, 1942." AEROSP H, 32 (Summer/June 1985), 107-116.

As Intelligence Officer of the 475 Fighter Group--the only one to be completely organized overseas (in Australia) --Cooper tells stories of the unit's heroic officers and enlisted men. He adds postwar updates about the heroes.

1643. Coox, Alvin D. "The Pacific War Revisited." PAC AFFS, 56 (Spring 1983), 106-112.

In this excellent review article of recent historiography, Coox measures judiciously his praise and criticism.

1644. Costello, John. THE PACIFIC WAR. New York: Rawson, Wade Publishers, 1981. 742 pp.

This account is well written and heavily documented. Costello criticizes MacArthur's misuse of air power in defending the Philippines and the decision to drop the atomic bombs (which he feels were unnecessary by mid-1945). The author claims that Roosevelt wanted the U.S. entry into the war and knew by November 1941 that war was coming. But Costello fails to discover the "smoking gun" that has eluded Roosevelt's critics ever since the attack at Pearl Harbor. One strength of this book is its emphasis on the roles of the British, Chinese, and Dutch during the diplomacy of the prewar era.

1645. Daniels, Gordon, ed. PROCEEDINGS OF THE BRITISH ASSOCIATION FOR JAPANESE STUDIES. Vol. III: 1978. PART I: HISTORY AND INTERNATIONAL RELATIONS. Sheffield, U.K.:   University of Sheffield Centre of Japanese Studies, 1978. 164 pp.

For essays on the war, see Ian Nish's analysis of Yoshida's early career (a liberal and a member of the Anglo-American group Ei-Beiha, but also an advocate for expansion in China), R. John Pritchard's reassessment of Changkufeng as a Japanese military victory, as well as the articles by Yuichi Inoue on the Arita-Craigie economic discussions and Michael P. Hayes on the Japanese press and the Emperor, 1945-1946.

1646. Daniels, Gordon, ed. PROCEEDINGS OF THE BRITISH

ASSOCIATION FOR JAPANESE STUDIES. Vol. IV: 1979. PART
I: HISTORY AND INTERNATIONAL RELATIONS. Sheffield,
U.K.: University of Sheffield Centre of Japanese
Studies, 1979. 171 pp.

John W. M. Chapman argues in his essay, "German Signals
Intelligence and the Pacific War," that no real trust
existed between the Japanese and German navies. Also, Ian
Nish offers some personal recollections of his experience
in the Combined Services Detailed Interrogation Center
during the early phase of the occupation of Japan.

1647. Day, David. "Anzacs on the Run: The View From Whitehall,
      1941-42." J IMP COMM HIST, 14 (May 1986), 187-202.

Focusing on the competition for British military
resources among the theaters, Day asks why the British
chose to ignore the Japanese. The answer, he feels, lies
partly in the British view of the collapse of Australia's
fighting reputation. Using thorough research through
British archival and private sources (but no Australian
sources), Day finds uncritical acceptance in Britain of
anti-Australian stories. Some of the reasons include
military events in Greece, Crete, and Libya; Menzies'
political challenge; the Curtin-Churchill feud; the fall of
Malaya and Singapore (where one British officer called the
Australians "undisciplined swine"); and Australian
rejection of the diversion of troops to Rangoon.

1648. DECISIVE BATTLES OF THE PACIFIC WAR. London: Hamlyn,
      1979.

      NE

1649. Driscoll, Joseph. PACIFIC VICTORY, 1945. Philadelphia,
      PA: J. B. Lippincott, 1944. 297 pp.

Here is a contemporary account which expects victory
over Japan in 1945--much sooner than most predictions.
Driscoll believes that by then the United States and
Britain will have won in Europe and will be able to direct
their combined strength against Japan.

1650. Floherty, John J. THE COURAGE AND THE GLORY.
      Philadelphia, PA: J. B. Lippincott, 1942. 189 pp.

The writing is blatant propaganda designed to stiffen
morale in the face of bleak war news. MacArthur and other
U.S. leaders appear larger than life.

1651.   Fooks, H.E. "The War in the Pacific." RUSI, Part I:
        "Guadalcanal to Leyte Gulf," 95 (August 1950), 448-458;
        Part II: "Guadalcanal to Leyte Gulf" [con't], 96
        (February 1951), 81-92; Part III: "Leyte Island to
        Mindoro," 96 (August 1951), 416-424; Part IV: "The
        Liberation of the Philippines," 97 (August 1952),
        392-401; Part V: "Towards Japan," 97 (November 1952),
        516-522; Part VI: "Conclusion: Okinawa," 98 (August
        1953), 389-400.

        These articles comprise a convenient--and
        expert--summary of the war against Japan. Appendixes and
        sketch maps enhance Fooks' analysis.

1652.   Frank, Benis M. and Henry I. Shaw, Jr. HISTORY OF U.S.
        MARINE CORPS OPERATIONS IN WORLD WAR II: VOL. V:
        VICTORY AND OCCUPATION. Washington, D.C.: G.P.O.,
        1968. 945 pp.

        Here is the official version of Marine Corps activities
        in the Okinawa campaign and the occupation of Japan and
        northern China. The authors enjoyed special access to
        official documents, including battle reports and
        correspondence. Of interest is the fate at the start of
        the war of the Marine embassy and legation guards, whom the
        Japanese refused to consider as part of the U.S. diplomatic
        corps. Rather than being repatriated, these Marines spent
        the duration of the war as POWs.

1653.   Garand, George W. and Truman R. Strobridge. HISTORY OF
        U.S. MARINE CORPS OPERATIONS IN WORLD WAR II: WESTERN
        PACIFIC OPERATIONS. Washington, D.C.: U. S. Marine
        Corps, 1971. 848 pp.

        This official volume covers the period from
        mid-September 1944 to late March 1945, which includes the
        bloody battles at Peleliu and Iwo Jima. The authors treat
        the use of artillery and air support as integral parts of
        each operation. Japanese defensive tactics seemed to
        become more effective with each U. S. amphibious assault in
        this period.

1654.   Hall, Basil. "Pacific Front Line." ARMY Q, 53 (October
        1946), 42-48.

        Hall, an officer in the Australian Intelligence Corps,
        describes the prewar miscalculations which led to the early
        string of Japanese successes. The article emphasizes the

value of American aid and Australian use of that aid as the
keys to the Allied victory.

1655. Harcourt-Smith, Simon. FIRE IN THE PACIFIC. New York:
       A.A. Knopf, 1942. 236 pp.

       The author is a British official in the Foreign Office
       who had diplomatic experience in the Far East before the
       war. In the survey of the period 1931-1942, Harcourt-Smith
       faults the lack of intelligence as a key to the succession
       of military defeats. He overlooks the racially-based
       arrogance and superiority exhibited so frequently in the
       West, perhaps because his writing reflects a similar
       attitude.

1656. Henderson, F.P. "NGF Support in the Solomons." MC GAZ,
       Part I: "Guadalcanal," 40 (March 1956), 44-51; Part II:
       "Central Solomons," 40 (June 1956), 36-40; Part III:
       "Bougainville and Kavieng," 40 (December 1956), 46-51.

       Naval gun fire during the early campaigns, according to
       the author, was not the smooth, coordinated instrument of
       destruction that it became later. Henderson draws valuable
       lessons from his survey of the gradual development of NGF.

1657. HISTORY OF THE HEADQUARTERS, 14TH ANTIAIRCRAFT COMMAND.
       APO San Francisco: Department of the Army, n.d. [1945?]
       268 pp.

       The unit came into existence in October 1943 to
       consolidate all antiaircraft units in the theater.
       Separate chapters deal with integral parts of the unit
       (e.g., intelligence, supply, plans, etc.), and each chapter
       has a concluding summary.

1658. Hodge, Clarence L. and Murray Befeler, eds. PEARL HARBOR
       TO TOKYO. Honolulu: Tongg, 1945. 156 pp.

       Here are pictorial highlights of the war against Japan.
       Many photos were shot in combat.

1659. Hough, Frank O. THE ISLAND WAR: THE UNITED STATES MARINE
       CORPS IN THE PACIFIC. Philadelphia, PA: J.B.
       Lippincott, 1947. 413 pp.

       Although this study is not an official history of Marine
       Corps operations, it is authoritative. Hough makes
       extensive use of official U.S. and Japanese sources.
       Particularly effective is his treatment of the close

coordination between Marine ground forces and air support.

1660.   Hough, Frank O., Verle E. Ludwig, and Henry I. Shaw, Jr.
        THE HISTORY OF THE U.S. MARINE CORPS IN WORLD WAR II:
        PEARL HARBOR TO GUADALCANAL. Washington, D.C.: U.S.
        Marine Corps, 1958. 449 pp.

        This official history makes use of Marine records,
        especially unit histories and after-battle reports. The
        subject material traces the prewar inception of the USMC
        amphibious mission through the Guadalcanal campaign. The
        Appendix includes unit commendations, casualties, and units
        involved in each combat operation.

1661.   Hough, Richard. THE LONGEST BATTLE: THE WAR AT SEA,
        1939-1945. New York: William Morrow, 1987. 371 pp.

        Hough presents a readable and well-researched survey.
        He integrates the first-hand accounts of many participants.
        In addition to covering the major naval encounters, Hough
        highlights the human side of the war at sea in all
        theaters. There are short biographies of over twenty naval
        leaders.

1662.   Howard, Clive and Joe Whitley. ONE DAMNED ISLAND AFTER
        ANOTHER. Chapel Hill, NC: University of North Carolina
        Press, 1946. 403 pp.

        In this view of the air war in the Pacific, which can
        also be seen as a contemporary combat history of the 7th
        Air Force, the authors blend in the human side of the
        story. There are no explanatory notes.

1662a. Byrd, Martha Hoyle. A WORLD IN FLAMES: A HISTORY OF WORLD
        WAR II. New York: Atheneum, 1970. 356 pp.

        This compact history not only describes the major
        military events of the war in all theaters but also sets
        the combat against the political-diplomatic backdrop. The
        author's prime concern lies with the execution, not the
        evolution, of strategy. The bibliography, now somewhat
        outdated, remains useful.

        [1663-1679.] Hoyt, Edwin P. The many books written by
        Hoyt yield to a few generalizations. Each is well
        written and solidly (if not exhaustively) researched.
        Hoyt blends into his narrative some vivid illustrations
        and astute observations which help explain the
        historical context of his subject. Although Hoyt

chooses not to adopt the apparatus of formal
scholarship, his books serve as useful introductions,
particularly for the general public, to various topics
in the war against Japan.

1663. THE BATTLE OF LEYTE GULF; THE DEATH KNELL OF THE JAPANESE
      FLEET. New York: McKay, 1972. 384 pp.

1664. BLUE SKIES AND BLOOD. New York: Paul S. Ericksson, 1975.
      217 pp.

1665. BOWFIN: THE STORY OF ONE OF AMERICA'S FABLED FLEET
      SUBMARINES IN WORLD WAR II. New York: Van Nostrand
      Reinhold, 1983.

1666. THE CARRIER WAR. New York: Lancer Books, 1972.

1667. CLOSING THE CIRCLE. New York: Van Nostrand Reinhold,
      1982. 240 pp.

1668. THE DESTROYER KILLER. Middlebury, VT., 1983.

1669. THE GLORY OF THE SOLOMONS. New York: Stein and Day, 1983.
      348 pp.

1669a. GUADALCANAL. New York: Stein and Day, 1982. 322 pp.

1670. HOW THEY WON THE WAR IN THE PACIFIC: NIMITZ AND HIS
      ADMIRALS. Weybright and Talley, 1971.

1671. JAPAN'S WAR: THE GREAT PACIFIC CONFLICT, 1853 to 1952.
      New York: McGraw-Hill, 1986. 514 pp.

1672. THE KAMIKAZES. New York: Arbor House, 1983. 334 pp.

1673. LEYTE GULF: THE DEATH OF THE PRINCETON. New York: Avon,
      1987. 160 pp.

1674. THE LONELY SHIPS: THE LIFE AND DEATH OF THE U.S. ASIATIC
      FLEET. New York: McKay, 1976. 338 pp.

1675. McCAMPBELL'S HEROES: THE STORY OF THE U.S. NAVY'S MOST
      CELEBRATED CARRIER FIGHTERS OF THE PACIFIC WAR. New
      York: Van Nostrand Reinhold, 1983.

1676. PACIFIC DESTINY. New York: Norton, 1981.

1677. STORM OVER THE GILBERTS: WAR IN THE CENTRAL PACIFIC, 1943.
      New York: Van Nostrand Reinhold, 1978. 192 pp.

1678. TO THE MARIANAS: WAR IN THE CENTRAL PACIFIC, 1944. New
       York: Van Nostrand Reinhold, 1980. 292 pp.

1679. WAR IN THE DEEP. New York: Putnam, 1978. 155 pp.

1680. Jones, James. WWII. New York: Grosset and Dunlap, 1975.
       272 pp.

       Jones combines his personal views and experiences with
       some historical research to create a fascinating, lively,
       but limited narrative of the war. The book contains an
       outstanding exhibit of war art.

1681. Kennedy, Paul. PACIFIC ONSLAUGHT, 7th DECEMBER 1941-7th
       FEBRUARY 1943. New York: Ballantine Books, 1972. 159
       pp.

       Kennedy authoritatively summarizes the full flush of
       Japan's early victories. The narrative identifies the
       reasons for Japan's successes, including considerable
       Allied shortcomings.

1682. Kirby, S. Woodburn, ed. THE WAR AGAINST JAPAN. London:
       HMSO, 1957-1969. 5 vols.

       Maj. Gen. Kirby has produced a magnificent survey in
       these official history volumes. The authors enjoyed access
       to British records and some U.S.-Japanese documents as well
       as the aid of excellent contributers (Capt. C. D. Addis,
       Col. J. F. Meikle John, Brig. M. R. Roberts, Col. G. T.
       Wards, and Air Vice Marshal W. L. Desoer). The separate
       volumes are:

              I.   THE LOSS OF SINGAPORE
             II.   INDIA'S MOST DANGEROUS HOUR
            III.   THE DECISIVE BATTLES
             IV.   THE RECONQUEST OF BURMA
              V.   THE SURRENDER OF JAPAN

1683. Krueger, Walter. FROM DOWN UNDER TO NIPPON: THE STORY OF
       THE SIXTH ARMY IN WORLD WAR II. Washington, D. C.:
       Combat Forces Press, 1953. 393 pp.

       Gen. Krueger describes the accomplishments of his Sixth
       Army. Relying on his official reports and studies by his
       staff, Krueger produces a significant part of the history
       of the war against Japan.

1684. Leckie, Robert. STRONG ARMED MEN: THE MARINES AGAINST

JAPAN. New York: Random House, 1963.   563 pp.

The author, himself a combat marine, describes the
exploits of the marines as they moved from Guadalcanal to
Okinawa. Incorporating U.S. and Japanese sources, Leckie
provides a detailed narrative of the fierce Pacific
encounters. There is a special segment devoted to those
who earned the Medal of Honor.

1685. Liddell Hart, Basil H. "The Second World War: A Summing
       Up: Key Factors and Turning Points." CANADIAN ARMY J,
       15 (Spring 1961), 82, 88-97.

Although this noted military historian faults the
British for neglecting Far Eastern defenses (especially in
light of the long-held British view that the Japanese would
fight for oil supplies), he argues that there was no real
turning point in the Pacific war--"only an incoming tide."
The author holds that air power defeated Japan (without the
atomic bomb) and that the policy of unconditional surrender
needlessly blocked the Allied cause.

1686. Love, Edmund G. WAR IS A PRIVATE AFFAIR. New York:
       Harcourt, Brace, 1959. 192 pp.

Love offers an interesting collection of anecdotes about
the war.

1687. Macintyre, Donald. THE BATTLE FOR THE PACIFIC. New York:
       W. W. Norton, 1966. 240 pp.

An accomplished writer, Macintyre is obviously
knowledgeable about naval history. This volume completes
his trilogy, which examines the naval war in each of the
three main theaters. The fast-paced narrative has some
gaps (submarine operations are seriously underplayed), but
the volume serves as a useful overview.

1688. McMillian, George, et al. UNCOMMON VALOR: MARINE
       DIVISIONS IN ACTION. Washington, D.C.:   Infantry
       Journal Press, 1946. 256 pp.

Here is a tribute to Marine combat units. Six Marine
correspondents report on the activities of the six Marine
divisions in the Pacific War. These are easily read,
knowledgeable summaries.

1689. Marshall, George C., Henry H. Arnold, and Ernest J. King.
       THE WAR REPORTS OF GENERAL OF THE ARMY GEORGE C.

MARSHALL, CHIEF OF STAFF, GENERAL OF THE ARMY H. H.
ARNOLD, COMMANDING GENERAL, ARMY AIR FORCES, AND FLEET
ADMIRAL ERNEST J. KING, COMMANDER-IN-CHIEF, UNITED
STATES FLEET AND CHIEF OF NAVAL OPERATIONS.
Philadelphia, PA: J. B. Lippincott, 1947. 801 pp.

Here are the wartime reports of the three service
leaders. Censorship--and tact--caused some
less-than-candid statements and some significant omissions.

1690. Martin, Ralph G. WORLD WAR II: A PHOTOGRAPHIC RECORD OF
THE WAR IN THE PACIFIC FROM PEARL HARBOR TO V-J DAY.
Greenwich, CT: Fawcett Publications, 1965. 224 pp.

This pictoral collection hardly amounts to a record of
the Pacific War, but it does offer some extraordinary views
of both combat and support teams in action. Martin has
done an exceptional job in compiling an exceptional
presentation.

1691. Mason, John T. THE PACIFIC WAR REMEMBERED. Annapolis, MD:
Naval Institute Press, 1986. 373 pp.

These recollections provide information about leaders,
major decisions, strategy, and tactics, as well as numerous
personal accounts. Mason collected these reminiscences
over a twenty-five year period from about thirty
participants. He includes a brief profile of each of the
participants.

1692. Mayer, Sydney L. THE JAPANESE WAR MACHINE. Feltham: Bison
Books, 1976. 255 pp.

Mayer, a military expert, offers a study of Japan's
equipment, supplies, and logistical arrangements.

1693. Metcalf, Clyde H., ed. MARINE CORPS READER. New York: G.
P. Putnam's sons, 1944. 600 pp.

Col. Metcalf (USMC) presents a collection of articles by
Marines about combat action in the Pacific. He includes a
list of personnel and units that earned distinguished
medals.

1694. Monks, John C., Jr. A RIBBON AND A STAR. New York: Henry
Holt, 1945. 242 pp.

Monks (co-author of BROTHER RAT) participated with the
3rd Marine Division in combat at Bougainville. Another

participant, John Falter, provided the illustrations. Here
is a tribute to the performance of the Marines.

1695. Morris, Richard B. and James Woodress, eds. GLOBAL
        CONFLICT: THE UNITED STATES IN WORLD WAR II, 1937-1946.
        New York: McGraw-Hill, 1962. 58 pp.

        Many of these selections have been previously published.
        There are eyewitness accounts of battles (e.g., Pearl
        Harbor, Midway, Los Negros, Kwajalein) and significant
        events (e.g., atomic bombings, V-J Day). See especially
        the report by British correspondent Colin McDonald, who was
        aboard the PANAY.

1696. Morton, Louis. "The Marianas." MIL REV, 47 (July 1967),
        71-82.

        Fighting two enemies--terrain as well as the Japanese--
        Americans seized Guam to mark the end of Nimitz's Marianas
        campaign (Saipan and Tinian). This penetration of the
        Japanese line of defense created turmoil in Japanese
        politics.

1697. Morton, Louis. "The North Pacific: 1941-1943." MIL REV,
        43 (January 1963), 34-47.

        Though offering the shortest route to Japan across the
        Pacific for Americans, the northern Pacific region proved
        inhospitable. According to Morton, U.S. plans to make use
        of the northern Pacific, which predated Pearl Harbor, were
        fruitless all through the war.

1698. Oppenheimer, Harold L. MARCH TO THE SOUND OF DRUMS.
        Danville, IL: Wabash Press, 1966. 333 pp.

        The author offers interesting anecdotes about the Marine
        Corps and action in the Pacific.

1699. PACIFIC THEATER (ARMY AND MARINE CORPS SUPPLEMENT).
        Allentown, PA: Valor Publishing Company, reprint.

        The book describes the Army and Marine command staff and
        support units in the Pacific, C-B-I, and Alaska.

1700. Peyton, Green. [pseud. Green Peyton Wertenbaker.] 5,000
        MILES TOWARDS TOKYO. Norman, OK: University of Oklahoma
        Press, 1945. 173 pp.

        Here is a brief report on the action in the Pacific

Theater.

1701.   Pfannes, Charles E. and Victor A. Salamone. THE GREAT
        BATTLES OF WORLD WAR II. VOL I: THE PACIFIC ISLANDS.
        New York: Kensington, 1985. 366 pp.

        The authors offer a popular account of some of the key
        battles. The writing is first rate, and the authors are
        knowledgeable.

1702.   Pratt, Fletcher. FLEET AGAINST JAPAN. New York: Harper
        and Brothers, 1946. 263 pp.

        Pratt provides highlights of the important battles and
        leaders in the Pacific war.

1703.   Pratt, Fletcher. THE MARINES' WAR. New York: William
        Sloane Associates, 1948. 456 pp.

        Using Japanese sources as well as special access to
        closed Marine and Navy records, Pratt analyzes the role of
        the Marine Corps in the Pacific war. Despite the offical
        support, he compiles a balanced assessment which does not
        hesitate to identify failings or errors.

1704.   Pratt Fletcher. THE NAVY'S WAR. New York: Harper and
        Brothers, 1944. 295 pp.

        Here is a knowledgeable, contemporary overview of the
        progress of the global war at sea. Pratt incorporates
        anecdotes and glimpses of personalities which give added
        flavor to his narrative.

1705.   Pratt, Fletcher. WAR FOR THE WORLD. New Haven, CT: Yale
        University Press, 1950. 364 pp.

        With special emphasis on the war at sea, Pratt offers an
        excellent summary of the war in all theaters.

1706.   Preston, Anthony, ed. DECISIVE BATTLES OF THE PACIFIC WAR.
        London: Hamlyn, 1979. 192 pp.

        The narrative highlights the key battles. Many maps and
        photographs are included.

1707.   Shane, Ted. HEROES OF THE PACIFIC. New York: Julian
        Messner, 1944. 373 pp.

        In a well-written contemporary assessment, Shane praises

the qualities (e.g., courage and humor) of the American
fighting men.

1708.   Shaw, Henry I., Jr., Bernard C. Nalty, and Edwin T.
        Turnbladh. HISTORY OF U.S. MARINE CORPS OPERATIONS IN
        WORLD WAR II: CENTRAL PACIFIC DRIVE. Washington, D.C.:
        USMC, 1966. 685 pp.

        In this excellent official history, the authors evaluate
        the USMC theory and practice of amphibious warfare. The
        narrative emphasizes the soundness of prewar doctrine and
        the wartime adjustments to that solid foundation.

1709.   Shaw, Henry I., Jr. and Douglas T. Kane. HISTORY OF U.S.
        MARINE CORPS OPERATIONS IN WORLD WAR II: ISOLATION OF
        RABAUL. Washington, D.C.: USMC, 1963. 632 pp.

        This official history is a well-documented account of a
        critical period in which the Marines shifted to the
        offensive. The authors stress that the Marine momentum
        began moving toward the vital center of the Japanese
        defensive perimeter. The operations and decisions are
        carefully explained.

1710.   Smith, Stanley E., ed. THE UNITED STATES MARINE CORPS IN
        WORLD WAR II. New York: Random House, 1969. 965 pp.

        Here is a collection of more than 100 articles which
        cover the entire war. Most of these articles have been
        previously published. See, for example, the entries by
        Devereux, Lee, Tregaskis, Leckie, Boyington, and
        Vandegrift.

1711.   Spector, Ronald H. EAGLE AGAINST THE SUN: THE AMERICAN
        WAR WITH JAPAN. New York: Free Press, 1985. 589 pp.

        Here is a first-rate history. Spector is especially
        effective in analyzing inter-service relations and
        rivalries. The Nimitz-MacArthur commands, for instance,
        were less a wise strategic decision, according to the
        author, and more a reflection of fierce rivalry. Specter,
        however, does point out how the service leaders ingeniously
        devised courses of action to prosecute the war without
        settling the differences among the services. For him, the
        superior strength and resources of the U.S. overcame the
        lack of overall strategy and divided command. Thus,
        defeating Japan became a matter of "breaking the logistical
        bottlenecks." Although offering balanced assessments of
        leading controversies of the war (e.g., the surprise at

Pearl Harbor, the use of the atomic bomb, and the
Halsey-Spruance debate), Spector is not reluctant to offer
frank criticsms (e.g., MacArthur being "unsuited by
temperament, character, and judgment" for command; the poor
use of codebreaking revelations at Papua and Leyte;
Japanese failures to follow-up advantages at Bougainville-
Empress Augusta Bay in 1943 or Biak in 1944). Spector has
done an excellent job in blending extensive research
through primary and secondary sources.

1712.   Stamps, T. Dodson and Vincent J. Esposito, eds. A MILITARY
        HISTORY OF WORLD WAR II WITH ATLAS: VOLUME II:
        OPERATIONS IN THE MEDITERRANEAN AND PACIFIC THEATERS.
        West Point, NY: U.S. Military Academy, 1956. 567 pp.

        This authoritative history emerged from the
        distinguished resources at West Point. The authors analyze
        the reasons for the successful holding-offensive action in
        the Pacific while the Allies pursued victory in Europe.
        These reasons included the great distances in the Pacific,
        MAGIC revelations, Japanese blunders in not concentrating
        on the Southwest Pacific (Australia might not have been
        saved, according to this account), disposal of Japanese
        forces, determined Japanese resistance on every piece of
        land, severe damage to Japanese shipping, and the
        development of logistical support (72 amphibious landings
        in less than 3 years).

1713.   Steinberg, Rafael. ISLAND FIGHTING. Alexandria, VA:
        Time-Life Books, 1978. 208 pp.

        Here is a popular account of the American march across
        the Pacific.

1714.   Taylor, Theodore. FIRE ON THE BEACHES. New York: W. W.
        Norton, 1958. 248 pp.

        Taylor describes the efforts of the U.S. merchant marine
        to elude German and Japanese submarines. Suffering heavy
        damage on both coasts early in the war, Americans developed
        protective escorts, convoy procedures, and other
        anti-submarine techniques.

1715.   Thompson, Paul W. et al. HOW THE JAP ARMY FIGHTS. New
        York: Penguin, 1943. 187 pp.

        This contemporary collection draws upon the early
        engagements to set a pattern of enemy behavior in the
        field. See especially the article by Milton A. Hill,

"Lessons of Bataan."

1716. TIME-LIFE, Editors of. WORLD WAR II: JAPAN AT WAR.
       Alexandria, VA: Time-Life Books, 1980. 208 pp.

       Using Japanese and American historians as consultants,
       this popular account surveys the war from the Japanese
       perspective. The book includes excellent pictorial essays.

1717. Toland, John. BUT NOT IN SHAME: THE SIX MONTHS AFTER
       PEARL HARBOR. New York: Random House, 1961. 427 pp.

       According to Toland, these six months were a key period
       in U.S. history. He incorporates several interviews and
       unpublished manuscripts by participants to describe the
       events of the war from Pearl Harbor to Midway. His
       narrative dwells on the human dimension. Here is one of
       the fine popular accounts of the fall of the Philippines.
       Toland is critical of Admiral Hart but has little to say
       about the destruction of MacArthur's air resources. See,
       too, his portrayal of the MacArthur-Wainwright
       relationship.

1718. Toland, John. GODS OF WAR. Garden City: Doubleday, 1985.
       598 pp.

       Toland turns to fiction in his continuing work on the
       war against Japan. Arguing that this novel retains the
       true spirit of history, Toland uses the endnotes to
       indicate the true accounts which inspired his fictional
       episodes. Thus, the reader learns Toland's views, for
       example, about the Philippine government's payments to
       MacArthur and three of his aides, the reason Marshall
       rejected Chennault's apparently valuable advice on how to
       overcome the Japanese Zeroes, and the racial violence among
       Americans on Guam.

1719. Toland, John. THE RISING SUN: THE DECLINE AND FALL OF THE
       JAPANESE EMPIRE, 1936-1945. New York: Random House,
       1970. 1,181 pp.

       Focusing on the Japanese perspective, Toland
       incorporates extensive research through interviews and
       private collections. His graceful prose is particularly
       effective in drawing out the human side--exposing both
       strengths and weaknesses--of the story.

1720. TRUE, Editors of. TRUE WAR STORIES: A CREST ANTHOLOGY,
       SELECTED BY BOB CONSIDINE FROM TRUE, THE MAN'S MAGAZINE.

Greenwich, CT: Fawcett Publishing, 1961.   239 pp.

The collection reflects the adventuresome spirit of the
popular magazine.

1721.   United States. Department of the Army. Far East Command.
HISTORY OF THE UNITED STATES ARMY FORCES IN THE FAR
EAST, 1943-1945. Tokyo: Far East Command, 1948.
256 pp.

Written by MacArthur's G-2 Historical Section, this Army
history is especially useful in clarifying the functions of
the three-part command structure in the South West Pacific
Area: (1) operations--General Headquarters, South West
Pacific Area; (2) administration--Headquarters, U.S. Army,
Far East; and (3) supply--Headquarters, U.S. Army, Services
of Supply.

1722.   United States. Department of the Army. Forces in the
Pacific. ENGINEERS OF THE SOUTHWEST PACIFIC, 1941-1945.
Washington, D.C.: GPO, 1947-1950.   8 vols.

This detailed account of the work of the Army engineers
confirms MacArthur's observation, "It was an Engineer's
war." See the final volume which explores the lessons
learned from all the operations against Japan.

1723.   United States. Department of the Army. Forces in the
Pacific Ocean Areas. PARTICIPATION IN THE WESTERN
CAROLINES AND CENTRAL PHILIPPINES OPERATIONS BY UNITED
STATES ARMY FORCES PACIFIC OCEAN AREAS, SEPTEMBER -
NOVEMBER 1944. Washington, D.C.: War Dept., 1945.   396
pp.

The study is based on the reports of various commanders
of Army units that particpated in these operations. The
information in the reports includes administration,
training, and logistic responsibilities--and even some
epidemiologic investigation.

1724.   United States. Department of the Army. Forces in the
Middle Pacific. 2605: THE LAST STEP. Washington,
D.C.: War Dept., 1945, 2 vols.

In this general history of Army operations against
Japan, the main theme is that in all 2605 years of Japanese
history (as of 1945), Japan had never been so humiliated.
The narrative focuses on the advance across the Pacific;
operations in Borneo, China, Manchuria, and SOWESPAC; and

the impact on Japan.

1725. United States. Army Air Forces. THE AAF IN AUSTRALIA: TO
       THE SUMMER OF 1942. Washington, D.C.: USAAF, 1944.
       215 pp.

       This study focuses primarily on administrative
developments--and problems encountered.

1726. United States. Army Air Forces. ARMY AIR FORCES IN THE
       WAR AGAINST JAPAN, 1941-1942. Washington, D.C.: GPO,
       1945. 171 pp.

       This factual account contains no attempt at analysis.
There are few explanations and very little criticism.

1727. United States. Department of Defense. SOME ASPECTS OF THE
       MILITARY HISTORY OF JAPAN AFTER WORLD WAR II. Tokyo:
       Japanese Military History Commission, 1978.

       Despite the title, the Japanese commissioners devoted
considerable attention to World War II.

1728. Wade, Garry H. "World War II Division Commanders." MIL
       REV, 66 (March 1986), 61-67.

       Lt. Col. Wade (USA) offers a study in how to become a
division commander. Looking at variable factors (e.g.,
age, promotions, duty assignments, performance), the author
finds that, while not every division commander in the war
was a superstar, every successful one was proficient in
military doctrine and held his unit together. Of interest
is that 46 of the 87 total U.S. divisions had the same
commander throughout the war, but most of the 46 had ten
months or less experience overseas during the war.

1729. Warner, Philip. JAPANESE ARMY OF WORLD WAR II. New York:
       Hippocrene Books, 1972. 40 pp.

       With color plates by Michael Youens, the book offers a
useful, if brief, introduction to the topic. Warner
discusses Japanese land tactics and describes many aspects
of the Imperial Japanese Army, including military drills,
combat weapons and equipment, tanks, and artillery. Of
interest is Warner's identification of the military
ranks--by their Japanese names--and the Army organizations.

1730. Weigley, Russell F. THE AMERICAN WAY OF WAR: A HISTORY OF
       UNITED STATES MILITARY STRATEGY AND POLICY. New York:

Macmillan, 1973. 590 pp.

Arguing that the American way of war is to destroy
totally the enemy, Weigley offers some interesting material
on the war against Japan. For instance, he includes a
section on the impact of Mahan upon operations in the
Pacific. Also, in discussing the role of air power in the
war, Weigley suggests that the strategic bombing effort to
destroy the enemy's society may be morally defensible as a
means to break a stalemate on the battlefield. The author,
a recognized authority in military history, provides an
excellent analysis on air and naval developments in the
Pacific between the wars.

1731. Weller, Donald. "Salvo--Splash! The Development of Naval
        Gunfire Support in World War II." USNIP, Pt. I: 80
        (August 1954), 839-849; Pt. II: 80 (September 1954),
        1010-1021.

        As a Marine staff officer at the time, Weller has
        intimate knowledge of the planning of pre-invasion naval
        fire support. His survey of Pacific operations points to
        the chief lesson learned at Tarawa: destroy enemy
        defenses, don't just neutralize them. Weller discusses the
        effectiveness of pre-D Day and D Day gunfire, and he
        presents a balanced view of the controversy about the
        length of pre-invasion naval bombardment at Iwo Jima.

1732. Wheeler, Keith. JAPAN AT WAR. Alexandria, VA: Time-Life
        Books, 1980. 208 pp.

        Wheeler presents the Japanese perspective of the causes
        and conduct of the war. This is a popular account.

1733. Wheeler, Keith. THE ROAD TO TOKYO. Alexandria, VA:
        Time-Life Books, 1979. 208 pp.

        Here is a brief, popular summary of the Allied march
        across the Pacific. The photos are excellent.

1734. Wheeler, Richard. A SPECIAL VALOR: THE U.S. MARINES IN
        THE PACIFIC WAR. New York: Harper and Row. 1983. 466
        pp.

        Wheeler, a Marine veteran of the war and later a
        correspondent, describes the activities and accomplishments
        of the Marines across the Pacific Theater. The "Semper Fi"
        spirit pervades the book. With the advantage of many
        interviews, Wheeler emphasizes the human dimension of

Marine operations. There are no notes and only a brief
bibliography.

1735. Wilkerson, Lawrence B. "Low Altitude Mass Tactical
       Operations." MIL REV, 61 (July 1981), 24-32.

       Discussing the advantages--and the present-day value--of
       low-altitude parachute drops in combat, Wilkerson includes
       descriptions of action at Nadzab airfield, Numfoor
       airfield, Tagaytay Ridge, Corregidor, and Los Banos.

1736. Williams, R.C., Jr. "Jap Mines." INFANTRY J, 56 (June
       1945), 11-14.

       With steady improvements in Japanese minefields,
       Williams looks at various Allied countering tactics.

1737. Wilson, Dick. WHEN TIGERS FIGHT: THE STORY OF THE
       SINO-JAPANESE WAR, 1937-1945. New York: Viking Press,
       1982. 269 pp.

       The author, a journalist and writer, maintains that,
       despite the extensive literature on political-diplomatic
       aspects of the war, not much has been written on the actual
       fighting. His narrative fills that gap. Wilson's
       description of the combat action is directed at a general
       audience.

1738. Winton, John. AIR POWER AT SEA, 1939-1945. New York:
       Thomas Y. Crowell, 1977. 187 pp.

       Winton provides a brief, knowledgeable summary of the
       air war at sea in all theaters. Of interest is his
       assessment of Japanese aircraft carrier operations.

1739. Winton, John. WAR IN THE PACIFIC: PEARL HARBOR TO TOKYO
       BAY. New York: Mayflower Books, 1978.

       Winton, a British military writer, surveys the Pacific
       war almost entirely from the point of view of the war at
       sea. He emphasizes the decisive role of the aircraft
       carrier for both sides. His narrative, moreover, serves as
       a reminder that the U.S. Navy did not act alone.

1740. Winton, John, ed. THE WAR AT SEA: THE BRITISH NAVY IN
       WORLD WAR II. New York: William Morrow, 1968. 416 pp.

       This anthology of personal accounts is arranged
       chronologically. Among the selections which deal with the

war against Japan, see the sinking of the HAGURO, the
kamikazes, the attack on Takao, and the parade at the
Changi jail on Armistice Day.

IV.A.1. PICTORIAL ACCOUNTS

1741. Adams, Bruce. RUST IN PEACE. Sydney, Aus.: Antipodean
        Publishers, 1975. 239 pp.

        Adams and his camera revisit battlegrounds in the South
        Pacific.

1742. Mydans, Carl. CARL MYDANS, PHOTO JOURNALIST. New York:
        Harry N. Abrams, 1985. 206 pp.

        Mydans presents his work as a photographer for LIFE.
        His collection, including some marvelous black-and-white
        shots, reveals the faces of war: prisoners, privates, and
        generals.

1743. New York Museum of Modern Art. POWER IN THE PACIFIC. New
        York: U.S. Camera, 1945. 144 pp.

        This pictorial collection highlights U.S. air and naval
        power in the Pacific. The museum prepared a special
        exhibit for these photos.

1744. Pappas, Sam. REMEMBER ... Chicago: author, 1946. 25
        plates.

        Here is a brief photographic report on some Pacific
        action.

1745. Steichen, Edward, comp. POWER IN THE PACIFIC. New York:
        U.S. Camera, 1945. 144 pp.

        Capt. Steichen (USN) presents a collection of official
        Navy, Marine, and Coast Guard photos that were exhibited at
        the Museum of Modern Art in New York City. The collection
        is devoted to the war against Japan.

IV.B. MEMOIRS/BIOGRAPHIES/CORRESPONDENCE/DIARIES

1. COLLECTIVE ACCOUNTS

1746. Berry, Henry, ed. SEMPER FI, MAC. New York: Arbor House,
        1982. 375 pp.

        Berry offers reports and personal accounts by Marines

who participated in famous battles of the war.

1747. Boswell, Rolfe. MEDALS FOR MARINES. New York: Crowell,
       1945. 211 pp.

       Boswell relates the heroism of Marines--individuals and
       units--in Pacific operations.

1748. Braun, Saul M. SEVEN HEROES: MEDAL OF HONOR STORIES OF
       THE WAR IN THE PACIFIC. New York: G. P. Putnam's Sons,
       1965. 224 pp.

       Although this book falls within the category of
       "Juvenile Literature," it is included here because of the
       special nature of the topic. The seven heroes are Henry
       Elrod, Mitchell Paige, Bruce McCandless, Robert Hanson,
       Arthur Murray Preston, Eugene Fluckey, and Joseph Timothy
       O'Callahan.

1749. Chamberlain, Thomas H. THE GENERALS AND THE ADMIRALS.
       New York: Devin-Adair Company, 1945. 62 pp.

       Here are brief biographies of thirty well-known
       commanders.

1750. Congdon, Don, ed. COMBAT WORLD WAR II: PACIFIC THEATER OF
       OPERATIONS. New York: Arbor House, 1983. 750 pp.

       Congdon edits and introduces first-hand accounts (by
       eyewitnesses and participants) of the war against Japan.
       This collection has over thirty reports which date from the
       fall of Singapore to the atomic bombings. A companion
       volume deals with the European Theater.

1751. Craf, John R. INVASION LEADERS. Philadelphia, PA:
       McKinley, 1944. 39 pp.

       This brief contemporary book glorifies, among others,
       the Pacific exploits of MacArthur, Doolittle, Somervell,
       and Chennault.

1752. Curtiss, Mina S., ed. LETTERS HOME. Boston: Little,
       Brown, 1944. 314 pp.

       Curtiss, a professor of English, presents letters
       written home by servicemen in all theaters. The hallmark
       of this contemporary collection is the honesty of the
       writers.

1753. DeWeerd, Harvey A. GREAT SOLDIERS OF WORLD WAR II. New
          York: W.W. Norton, 1944. 316 pp.

          This contemporary list of commanders contains only
          two from the war against Japan: MacArthur and Chiang
          Kai-shek. Both earn high praise from DeWeerd, an
          associate editor of INFANTRY JOURNAL.

1754. Geffen, William, ed. COMMAND AND COMMANDERS IN MODERN
          WARFARE. Washington, D. C.: Office of Air Force
          History, 1971. 340 pp.

          These proceedings of the 1968 Military History Symposium
          at the Air Force Academy include a section on U.S. naval
          leaders in the war. Conference participants, including E.
          B. Potter and Raymond G. O'Connor, analyze the combat
          performances of leaders such as (in the Pacific) Arleigh
          Burke, Harry H. Hill, and Robert B. Carney.

1755. Horner, D.M. CRISIS OF COMMAND: AUSTRALIAN GENERALSHIP
          AND THE JAPANESE THREAT, 1941-1943. Canberra, Aus.:
          Australian National University Press, 1978. 395 pp.

          In this study of leadership, Horner identifies and
          discusses certain qualities that make great generals.
          Concluding that Australia was well served by its generals,
          Horner sharply criticizes MacArthur for sacking and
          undercutting three Australian generals without
          understanding their circumstances.

1756. James, D. Clayton and Anne Sharp Wells. A TIME FOR GIANTS:
          POLITICS OF THE AMERICAN HIGH COMMAND IN WORLD WAR II.
          New York: Franklin Watts, 1987. 317 pp.

          Examining the rise to senior command positions of
          eighteen U.S. officers, the authors conclude that merit and
          military politics (especially family relations and
          intra-service rivalries among commanders) contributed to
          their ascendancy. See especially the material on Marshall,
          MacArthur, King, Nimitz, Halsey, and Stilwell.

1757. Larrabee, Eric. COMMANDER IN CHIEF: FRANKLIN D.
          ROOSEVELT, HIS LIEUTENANTS AND THEIR WAR. New York:
          Harper and Row, 1987. 723 pp.

          This reference work by a professional writer integrates
          broad research in presenting biographical profiles of US
          military-naval leaders. Soon after America entered the
          war, Larrabee argues, first-rate leaders emerged to direct

the country's fortunes in combat. Larrabee praises
Roosevelt and has kind words for most of the "lieutenants"
(including Marshall, Arnold, and Wedemeyer).

1758. Loomis, Robert D. GREAT AMERICAN FIGHTER PILOTS OF WORLD
        WAR II. New York: Random House, 1961. 208 pp.

        The book is slim and there are important omissions, but
this report by a knowledgeable author provides an excellent
introduction to the most glamorous part of the air war.
Loomis has a knack for capturing the "spirit" of each of
his subjects in a short profile.

1759. Lutz, Alma, ed. WITH LOVE, JANE. New York: John Day,
        1945. 199 pp.

        Here is a collection of wartime letters from American
women in various branches in the different theaters.

1760. Maule, Harry E., ed. BOOK OF WAR LETTERS. New York:
        Random House, 1943. 328 pp.

        Maule assembles letters from American men and women in
uniform in all theaters. The subjects cover a wide range
of topics, attitudes, and perspectives.

1761. Puryear, Edgar F. NINETEEN STARS. Washington, D.C.;
        Coiner Publications, 1971. 437 pp.

        The nineteen stars belong to Marshall, MacArthur,
Eisenhower, and Patton. Rather than an analysis of each
general, Puryear looks broadly at the qualities of
leadership. He picks out the strengths of each man but
pays little attention to their weaknesses.

1762. Smith, Stanley E., ed. THE UNITED STATES NAVY IN WORLD WAR
        II. New York: William Morrow, 1966. 1,049 pp.

        Smith presents personal accounts by participants and
correspondents as well as the writings of historians in
this comprehensive view of the war at sea. His
introductions and explanations give cohesion to the
anthology.

1763. Smyth, Sir John. LEADERSHIP IN WAR, 1939-1945; THE
        GENERALS IN VICTORY AND DEFEAT. New York: St. Martin's
        Press, 1974. 247 pp.

        Smyth, a British miltary expert, knew--and even worked

with or taught--many of the British top-level commanders.
There is a good amount of material on the war against
Japan; Smyth describes generals in defeat (Wavell Percival,
Chiang Kai-shek, and Alexander) and lavishes praise on
Slim. Of interest is Smyth's own involvement as commander
of the 17th Division in the debacle at Sittang.

1764. Tapert, Annette, ed. LINES OF BATTLE: LETTERS FROM
        AMERICAN SERVICEMEN, 1941-1945. Chicago: Times Books,
        1987. 297 pp.

        These letters to friends and relatives are arranged in
        chronological order. The collection is taken from all
        theaters, all services, and all ranks. Tapert also
        includes photographs of some of the authors.

1765. THESE ARE THE GENERALS. New York: A.A. Knopp, 1943.

        Among these brief profiles of U.S. leaders, see Claire
        Booth Luce on MacArthur and William Clemmens on Chennault.
        Walter Millis wrote the Foreword.

1766. Thomas, Lowell. THESE MEN SHALL NEVER DIE. Philadelphia,
        PA: John C. Winston, 1943. 308 pp.

        Thomas recounts the exploits of a selection of
        "representative men of valor" during the first year of the
        war. Several are taken from the Pacific, with the men of
        Bataan being prominent.

1767. Wise, James W., ed. VERY TRULY OURS: LETTERS FROM
        AMERICA'S FIGHTING MEN. New York: Dial Press, 1943.
        208 pp.

        As the product of a publicized call for contributions,
        the book presents a variety of letters from servicemen and
        seamen of all ranks in all branches from all theaters.

1768. Wolfe, Don M., ed. THE PURPLE TESTAMENT: LIFE STORIES BY
        DISABLED VETERANS. Harrisburg, PA: Stackpole, 1946.
        361 pp.

        Wolfe assembles over 50 personal accounts by a special
        group. One can not read these reports and remain unmoved.

IV.B.2. SELECTED INDIVIDUALS

HENRY H. ARNOLD

1769. Arnold, Henry H. GLOBAL MISSION. New York: Harper, 1949.
       626 pp.

       Here are the war memoirs of the commanding general of
       the Army Air Forces. Of particular importance is Arnold's
       description of the prewar indecision among strategists
       about the strategic need and/or the ability to defend the
       Philippine Islands.

1770. Coffey, Thomas M. HAP: THE STORY OF THE U.S. AIR FORCE
       AND THE MAN WHO BUILT IT, GENERAL HENRY H. "HAP" ARNOLD.
       New York: Viking, 1982. 415 pp.

       Using primary sources, including Arnold's papers and
       many interviews, Coffey offers a biography that appeals to
       the general public as well as scholars.

1771. Kuter, Laurence S. "The General vs the Establishment:
       General H. H. Arnold and the Air Staff." AEROSPACE H,
       21 (Winter, December 1974), 185-189.

       General Kuter, who served on Arnold's staff during the
       war, tells of Arnold's problems in setting up the AAF
       organization (including the advisory council).

1772. Kuter, Laurence S. "How Hap Arnold Built the AAF." AF
       MAG, 56 (September, 1973), 88-93.

       Kuter describes Arnold as a free wheeler who detested
       routine staff work. Arnold's unorthodox procedures usually
       produced good results, according to the author.

JOHN BIRCH

1773. Hefley, James C. and Marti Hefley. THE SECRET FILE ON JOHN
       BIRCH. Wheaton, IL: Tyndale House, 1980. 231 pp.

       Here is a story which addresses the war in China. The
       authors tell of spies and missionaries in addition to
       Birch.

1774. Lyons, S.C. HIS NAME WAS JOHN BIRCH. Dry Branch, GA:
       Author, 1968. 40 pp.

       Here is a brief account of the life and the
       circumstances surrounding the death of John Birch.

1775. Walsh, James P. "The Death of John Birch--Documented."
       WISC MAG HIST, 58 (Spring 1975), 209-218.

Capt. Birch (USA), who had done missionary work before the war and was in Army wartime intelligence, asked for detached service to the OSS at war's end. The author bases this article on new documentary evidence, including the first-hard report of Birch's death by a Chinese intelligence officer, Tung, who accompanied Birch. Tung, also left for dead with Birch by the Chinesse Communists, feels that Birch's hostile attitude provoked the communists.

1776.   Welch, Robert H.W., Jr. THE LIFE OF JOHN BIRCH. Boston: Western Islands Publishers, 1960. 135 pp.

This biography first appeared in 1954 (Regnery, 118 pp.). The purpose of the book, according to Welch, is to ensure that Birch did not die in vain. For the author, Birch's death exposed the creeping tentacles of the international communist conspiracy. Birch served with the OSS "on loan" from Chennault's command. Welch feels that the killing of Birch by the Chinese Communists was covered up by the U.S. government--itself heavily influenced by communism. Of interest is Birch's role in helping Jimmy Doolittle escape.

CLAIRE L. CHENNAULT

1777.   Ayling, Keith. OLD LEATHERFACE OF THE FLYING TIGERS. Indianapolis, IN: Bobbs-Merrill, 1945. 274 pp.

Written while the war against Japan was going on, Ayling praises the theory and tactics of Chennault. The narrative employs a journalistic style which leaves out footnotes and bibliography.

1778.   Byrd, Martha. CHENNAULT: GIVING WINGS TO THE TIGER. Tuscaloosa, AL: University of Alabama Press, 1987. 480 pp.

Here is a balanced assessment of a complex--and controversial--character. Whatever his failings, Chennault earned the love of Chinese people from the highest official to the common citizen, largely through what Byrd calls his "direct, elemental, simple" style. She has thoroughly researched her subject.

1779.   Chennault, Anna C. A THOUSAND SPRINGS: THE BIOGRAPHY OF A MARRIAGE. New York: Paul S. Eriksson, 1962. 318 pp.

Mrs. Chennault provides a narrative of her life with the controversial American. She first met him when she was a newspaperwoman, and the relationship grew into marriage. The photographs add to her story. The couple lived in interesting times!

1780.   Chennault, Claire L. WAY OF A FIGHTER. New York: G. P. Putnam's Sons, 1949. 375 pp.

This memoir elaborates Chennault's continuing support for Chiang Kai-shek and his attacks against Stilwell. Chennault says far too little about the aerial tactics he developed in China that proved successful in air-to-air encounters with technically superior Japanese aircraft. In retrospect, the author has little to add concerning the wartime controversy over air strategy in the theater. Writing in the disillusionment of the immediate postwar era, and watching events unfold in the Chinese civil war, Chennault is especially critical of U.S. policies.

1781.   Hibel, Franklin. "Chennault: From Maverick to Marvel." AF MAG, 57 (November 1974), 90-94.

This article provides a brief summary of Chennault's career, both during and after the war.

1782.   Peragallo, James L. "Chennault: Guerrilla of the Air." AEROSPACE H, 20 (Spring, March 1973), 1-6.

In this prize-winning essay, the author, a cadet at the Air Force Academy, portrays Chennault as a guerrilla of the air. Peragallo analyzes the reasons for Chennault's overall success--and unconventional tactics.

1783.   Scott, Robert L., Jr. FLYING TIGER: CHENNAULT OF CHINA. Garden City, NY: Doubleday, 1959. 285 pp.

Scott served under Chennault and makes no attempt to conceal his affection for his commander. Much of the book supports Chennault's side in his continuing struggle with Stilwell. There are no notes or bibliography.

ROBERT L. EICHELBERGER

1784.   Eichelberger, Robert L. OUR JUNGLE ROAD TO TOKYO. New York: Viking Press, 1950. 360 pp.

In collaboration with Milton Mackaye, General Eichelberger describes his experiences in the Pacific,

first as Commanding General, I Corps, and later as
commander of the 8th Army. One main feature of this book
is Eichelberger's restraint in revealing his usually frank
opinions about the Allies, his colleagues, and the higher
direction of the war. He was not known by contemporaries
for his tact. The book does, however, provide an excellent
view of the war through the eyes of a front-line general.

1785.   Luvaas, Jay, ed. DEAR MISS EM: GENERAL EICHELBERGER'S WAR
        IN THE PACIFIC, 1942-1945. Westport, CT: Greenwood,
        1972. 322 pp.

        This collection of letters from Eichelberger to his wife
        offers a marvelous glimpse of the war in the Pacific. The
        general wrote virtually every day with his candid
        observations. The humor, the petty wrangling, news about
        promotions (pending or denied), MacArthur's tight control
        of public relations, and even perhaps an occasional longing
        for an assignment to Europe (where his West Point
        classmate, George Patton, was earning fame)--all are
        included here. Luvaas has written an excellent
        introduction and has done an outstanding job in selecting
        and editing this small sampling of the total
        correspondence.

1786.   Shortal, John Francis. FORGED BY FIRE: ROBERT L.
        EICHELBERGER AND THE PACIFIC WAR. Columbia, SC:
        University of South Carolina Press, 1987. 154 pp.

        Relying on the general's private papers and "dictations"
        (1952-1960), Shortal traces Eichelberger's development as a
        combat commander. Despite saving stalled operations on at
        least four occasions for MacArthur, Eichelberger's
        relationship with his commander was strained. Shortal
        argues that MacArthur not only blocked Eichelberger's
        opportunities for professional advancement but also did not
        accord his "fireman" personal respect. Shortal
        characterizes Eichelberger as the most successful U.S.
        general in the war--the one who captured the most enemy
        territory in the shortest amount of time.

1787.   Shortal, John F. "MacArthur's Fireman: Robert L.
        Eichelberger." PARAMETERS, 16 (Autumn 1986), 58-68.

        Shortal focuses on three campaigns--Buna (1942), Biak
        (1944), and Manila (1945)--in which MacArthur's forces
        suffered initial setbacks and called Eichelberger to the
        rescue. Relying on Eichelberger's papers, the author
        identifies the field general's strengths: tactical

innovation, common sense, and personal leadership.

1788. Shortal, John F. "MacArthur's Top General." WW II, 2
        (July 1987), 12-17.

        Here is a tribute to Robert L. Eichelberger.

WILLIAM F. HALSEY

1789. Fleming, Thomas. "Personality." WW II, 1 (May 1986), 10,
        60-64.

        Fleming, a professional writer and Navy veteran, offers
a friendly profile of Halsey. Remarking on how much the
sailors loved him (and how much the admiral hated the name
"Bull"), Fleming describes Halsey's bulldog ferocity, luck,
diplomacy, and readiness to take losses to gain his
objective. The article skirts the controversies of Leyte
Gulf and the typhoon.

1790. Frank, Benis M. HALSEY. New York: Ballantine Books,
        1974. 160 pp.

        Frank includes some excellent photographs in this
solid biography which is addressed to a general audience.

1791. Halsey, William F. and J. Bryan III. ADMIRAL HALSEY'S
        STORY. New York: Whittlesey House, 1947. 310 pp.

        Less an autobiography than a report to the American
people, this book provides the viewpoint of the top naval
leadership in the war against Japan. All the important
naval engagements are summarized. The book is marked by
its vigorous defense of Kimmel and a detailed analysis of
events at the Battle of Leyte Gulf.

1792. Jordan, Ralph B. BORN TO FIGHT: THE LIFE OF ADMIRAL
        HALSEY. New York: David McKay, 1946. 208 pp.

        Here is a contemporary piece, designed for public
consumption.

1793. Potter, E.B. BULL HALSEY. Annapolis, MD: Naval Institute
        Press, 1985. 352 pp.

        With access to Halsey's unpublished memoirs and the
cooperation of the Halsey family, Potter presents a friendly
picture of the naval leader.

JOHN F. KENNEDY

1794.   Donovan, Robert J. PT 109: JOHN F. KENNEDY IN WORLD WAR
        II. New York: McGraw-Hill, 1961. 247 pp.

        Donovan enjoyed the full cooperation of President
        Kennedy in preparing this account. His research
        preparation also included interviews with Kennedy's fellow
        survivors, Japanese crewmen, native rescuers, and
        Coastwatcher Evans. The book covers other Kennedy
        experiences in the war but focuses on the ramming by the
        Japanese destroyer AMAGIRI in the Blackett Strait on August
        2, 1943. That Donovan believes the case that the ramming
        may have been accidental is difficult to sustain.

1795.   Hersey, John. "Survival." NEW YORKER, 20 (June 17, 1944),
        31-43.

        The noted writer bases his account of PT-109 being
        rammed by a Japanese destroyer in Blackett Strait on an
        interview with one of the survivors, John F. Kennedy.
        Coastwatcher Reg Evans is misidentified.

1796.   Whipple, Chandler. Lt. JOHN F. KENNEDY--EXPENDABLE! New
        York: Universal Publishing and Distributing Corp.,
        1962. 160 pp.

        The narrative is aimed at the general public, and
        perhaps some exaggeration creeps into the story.

GEORGE C. KENNEY

1797.   Falk, Stanley L. "General Kenney, the Indirect Approach
        and the B-29's." AEROSPACE H, 28 (Fall, September
        1981), 147-155.

        Falk shares the view of the U.S. Strategic Bombing
        Survey that the B-29s could have been effective in an
        indirect approach against economic targets. The author,
        however, stops short of asserting that the indirect
        approach would have shortened the war. Kenney supported
        MacArthur's strategic "indirect approach," but Arnold held
        differing views.

1798.   Kenney, George C. GENERAL KENNEY REPORTS: A PERSONAL
        HISTORY OF THE PACIFIC WAR. New York: Duell, Sloan and
        Pearce, 1949. 594 pp.

Kenney, commander of the Allied Air Forces in the
Southwest Pacific, offers a personal history, which, in
effect, is a history of the Fifth Air Force. His tenure
ran from 1942 to the end of the war. Here is a view of the
air war from the highest levels. Kenney gives his honest
and frank opinions about events and personalities--and
mistakes. For example, he gives an informative report on
an important conference at Pearl Harbor (January 23-28,
1944); describes Sutherland as someone hard to get along
with; and praises MacArthur. Also, in Kenney's opinion,
the Japanese failed to use air power to full advantage.

799.   Wolk, Herman S. "The Other Founding Father." AIR FORCE,
        70 (September 1987), 164-173.

This USAF historian offers a profile of George Kenney,
commander of 5th Air Force. According to Wolk, Kenney's
strengths included innovations (such as parachute
fragmentation bombs), his elimination of USAAF "deadwood,"
a cooperative personality, and his key role in the founding
of a separate air force.

800.   Wolk, Herman S. "A Wartime Leader." AIRMAN, 29 (July
        1985), 15-17.

Here is a brief report of the wartime contributions of
George Kenney, who, according to Wolk, sought new ways to
win the Pacific war on a shoestring.

ERNEST J. KING

801.   Buell, Thomas E. MASTER OF SEAPOWER. Boston: Little,
        Brown, 1980. 583 pp.

Here is a masterful--and long-needed--assessment of
Fleet Admiral Ernest J. King. On the whole, the biography
is sympathetic, but Buell, nonetheless, provides a balanced
perspective in this well-researched study.

802.   Goddard, Victor. "Fleet Admiral King's One Mistake."
        AEROSPACE H, 31 (June 1984), 101-106.

The author, an English officer, served as chief of the
New Zealand Air Staff in December 1941. King, a notorious
Anglophobe, mistakenly believed Goddard to be a New
Zealander. During their conversation about building up the
New Zealand air forces, King bluntly asked Goddard, "When
are you going to get your freedom?"

1803.   King, Ernest J. "Combat Operations, March 1944 to March
            1945." USNIP, 71 (March 1945), 598-643.

        Here is the text of King's report to the secretary of
        the navy. King warns that "a quick and easy Pacific
        victory cannot be taken for granted" even after the defeat
        of Germany.

1804.   King, Ernest J. and Walter Muir Whitehall. FLEET ADMIRAL
            KING: A NAVAL RECORD. New York: W. W. Norton, 1952.
            674 pp.

        King kept no diary or many personal papers on the war.
        By 1941, he had served forty-four years in the Navy. In
        this book, he explains policies and decisions from the
        wartime perspective—as matters seemed at the time. The
        narrative is particularly useful for information on some
        wartime conferences, but in this autobiography (at least of
        King's career) not everything could be included. Whitehall
        worked on King's support staff during the war.

1805.   Love, Robert William, Jr., ed. THE CHIEFS OF NAVAL
            OPERATIONS. Annapolis, MD: Naval Institute Press, 1980.
            448 pp.

        In this biographical collection, see Love's article on
        Adm. King.

1806.   Reynolds, Clark G. "Admiral Ernest J. King and the
            Strategy for Victory in the Pacific." NAV WAR COLL REV,
            28 (Winter 1976), 57-64.

        Here is a tribute to King (CNO and C-in-C U. S. Fleet).
        Reynolds recounts how King overcame obstacles to achieve
        victory in the Pacific. These obstacles included European
        requests for resources, MacArthur's personality, naval
        factions in Washington, British requests to participate in
        Pacific operations, and the Japanese Imperial Navy.

1807.   Sanders, H. "King of the Oceans." USNIP, 100 (August
            1974), 52-59.

        Here is a flattering portrait of Adm. King by one of his
        staff members

WILLIAM D. LEAHY

1808. Adams, Henry H. WITNESS TO POWER: THE LIFE OF FLEET
      ADMIRAL WILLIAM D. LEAHY. Annapolis: Naval
      InstitutePress, 1985. 391 pp.

      Basing his research on Leahy's papers and many
      interviews (with less attention to archival sources), Adams
      presents the first detailed biography of Leahy. Written by
      someone who is familiar with the subject, the book provides
      a valuable introduction to this complex war leader.

1809. Leahy, William D. I WAS THERE: THE PERSONAL STORY OF THE
      CHIEF OF STAFF TO PRESIDENTS ROOSEVELT AND TRUMAN, BASED
      ON HIS NOTES AND DIARIES MADE AT THE TIME. New York:
      Whittlesey House, 1950. 527 pp.

      This is an indispensable source for the study of the
      war. Leahy was involved, or knew about, virtually every
      aspect of American participation in the war. See
      especially his skepticism about both the development and
      the use of the atomic bomb. Truman wrote the Foreword.

CURTIS E. LEMAY

1810. Coffer, Thomas M. IRON EAGLE. New York: Crown Publishing,
      1986. 474 pp.

      Here is a biographical appraisal, generally favorable,
      of Curtis LeMay.

1811. LeMay, Curtis E. MISSION WITH LEMAY. Garden City, NY:
      Doubleday, 1965.

      In these memoirs, LeMay tells how his work with B-29
      strategic bombing led to his decision to switch to
      low-level, fire-bombing raids. This is a no-holds-barred
      report.

DOUGLAS MACARTHUR

1812. Archer, Jules. FRONT-LINE GENERAL: DOUGLAS MACARTHUR.
      New York: Julien Messner, 1963. 191 pp.

      The author served four years in the Pacific with the
      Army Air Forces and later as a freelance correspondent. He
      describes MacArthur's surprise at not finding a highly
      trained army waiting for him in Australia. ("It was the
      greatest shock and surprise of the whole war.") Archer
      provides a quick and uncomplicated account, nearly all of
      which praises MacArthur.

1813. ARMY TIMES. THE BANNERS AND THE GLORY: THE STORY OF
          GENERAL DOUGLAS MACARTHUR. New York: Putnam, 1965.
          284 pp.

       The editors have compiled an overview of the general's
    achievements in the war.

1814. Asbury, Herbert and Frank Gervasi. "MacArthur--the Story
          of a Great American Soldier." READER'S DIG, 48 (January
          1946), 21-28.

       Here is a flattering portrait, but the authors do
    debunk some of the myths surrounding the man, especially
    the charge that he needlessly exposed himself to enemy
    fire.

1815. Beck, John Jacob. MACARTHUR AND WAINWRIGHT. Albuquerque,
          NM: University of New Mexico Press, 1974. 302 pp.

       This well-researched work, while offering little that is
    new, remains a useful analysis of relations between the two
    generals. Lengthy quotations are designed to enable the
    participants to speak for themselves. The author includes
    a valuable annotated bibliography.

1816. Blair, Clay, Jr. MACARTHUR. New York: Pocket Books, 1977.
          375 pp.

       Relying on official histories and other traditional
    sources, Blair is often critical of the general.
    Codebreakers and submariners seem to be the author's
    favorites in this book. Blair feels that MacArthur's
    misuse of air power in trying to defend the Philippines
    compares with the gross errors attributed to the two
    commanders in Hawaii. General Sutherland is portrayed as
    someone who not only shielded MacArthur but also made
    decisions that MacArthur should have made.

1817. Coffman, Edward M. and Paul H. Hass, eds. "With MacArthur
          in the Pacific: A Memoir By Philip F. LaFollette." WISC
          MAG HIST, 64 (Winter 1980-81), 83-106.

       From October 1942 to June 1945, LaFollette served in
    MacArthur's public relations office and as an assistant to
    Sutherland. He writes that the only flaw the general had
    was a lack of humility (including a sense of humor).
    MacArthur's staff remained loyal not out of affection but
    from professional respect for his military capacities.

This military memoir was not included in LaFollette's posthumously-produced political memoir. Of special interest is LaFollette's report of Roosevelt saying that the U.S. could lick Japan with one hand tied.

1818. Considine, Bob. GENERAL DOUGLAS MACARTHUR. Greenwich, CT: Gold Medal Books, 1964. 126 pp.

The book is unexceptional and highly favorable to the general. Considine reports that MacArthur only learned of the existence of the atomic bomb in a report by Brig. Gen. Thomas Farrell in late July 1945.

1819. Considine, Bob. MACARTHUR THE MAGNIFICENT. London: Hutchinson, 1942. 183 pp.

Here is a powder-puff piece of propaganda.

1820. Danielson, Richard E. "Bradley and MacArthur." ATLANTIC MON, 188 (July 1951), 78-80.

Here is a survey of recent literature about the two generals.

1821. Dunn, William J. "MacArthur's Mansion and Other Myths." ARMY MAG, 23 (March 1973), 39-44.

Dunn, a CBS news correspondent, rejects certain stories critical of MacArthur, including his supposed lack of courage as "Dugout Doug" and his alleged luxurious living accommodations. He calls them "canards."

1822. Edgerton, Ronald K. "General Douglas MacArthur and the American Military Impact in the Philippines." PHILIPPINE STUD, 25 (No. 4, 1977), 420-440.

NE

1823. Egeberg, Roger Olaf. THE GENERAL; MACARTHUR AND THE MAN HE CALLED "DOC." New York: Hippocrene Books, 1983. 242 pp.

Egeberg served as MacArthur's physician in 1944-1945. Because of his access to the general, Egeberg acted as an unofficial conduit to get messages or hints through to MacArthur around the official channel which was controlled by Sutherland. In fact, one of his few criticisms of MacArthur is that the general limited his contacts with his generals and relied too heavily on Sutherland. The

author remains protective of his former patient but
provides an interesting ("intimate" is too strong a description for "The General") view of life inside the
court--whether it involved landing at Momatu Beach;
MacArthur's reasons for abstaining from alcohol or wearing
few medals; estimating that MacArthur paced 6-7 miles per
day in his office; Lindbergh personally proving the
feasibility of attacking Hollandia; unloading brooms and
mops as the first "weapons of war" at Morotai; or musing
about the purpose of the mysterious female "Captain Z." Of
particular interest is MacArthur's emphasis on loyalty,
courage, and intelligence as the three top criteria
leaders must demand of their staff members.

1824. Eyre, James K., Jr. THE ROOSEVELT-MACARTHUR CONFLICT.
      Chambersburg, PA: The Craft Press, 1950. 234 pp.

      The author advised President Osmena after the war, and
the book (apparently subsidized by the author) incorporates
statements by prominent Filipino officials which attest to
Eyre's qualifications. Some of the reasons given for
MacArthur having come to regard Roosevelt as an "arch-foe"
(Eyre's term) include the general's displeasure about (a)
Roosevelt's appointments in the higher echelons of the Army
once MacArthur left as Army Chief of Staff, (b) the lack of
U.S. support in preparing for the defense of the
Philippines, (c) Roosevelt's failure to understand the
circumstances confronting the Philippines and President
Quezon by February 1942, (d) Roosevelt's decisions during
the Bataan-Corregidor crises, and (e) the shock of not
finding any army waiting for him in Australia (as he felt
Roosevelt had promised). Eyre also describes the shifting
perspectives of Quezon in his dealings with Roosevelt and
MacArthur. In fact, much of the book focuses on Philippine
politics and the interaction among the Quezon-Osmena-Roxas
factions.

1825. Forbes, Joseph. "General Douglas MacArthur and the
      Implementation of American and Australian Civilian
      Policy Decisions in 1944 and 1945." MIL AFFS, 49
      (January 1985), 1-4.

      Forbes defends MacArthur against some of the criticisms
raised by certain historians who felt the general had
exceeded his authority. The author emphasizes that the
source of MacArthur's authority was Roosevelt, not the
joint chiefs of staff.

1826. Forrest, Jerome and Clark W. Kawakami. "General MacArthur

and His Vanishing War History." REPORTER, 7 (October
14, 1952), 20-25.

The authors are two historians who worked on the staff
of the Tokyo Historical Project for MacArthur. The secret
project began in 1946 under the general editorship of
Charles A. Willoughby. The staff numbered from twenty-five
to one hundred and included Japanese artists who were
especially commissioned to create accompanying
illustrations and detailed maps. The first product
encompassed three volumes: MacArthur's operations,
Japanese operations, and the occupation of
Japan.

1827. Gavin, James M. "Two Fighting Generals--Patton and
      MacArthur." ATLANTIC MON, 215 (February 1965), 55-61.

Gavin praises both generals (despite the tone of
infallibility in MacArthur's memoirs) and notes that both
prepared all their professional lives in case their country
ever became involved in war.

1828. Goodman, Henry C. with Cliff Dudley. SUPREME COMMANDER.
      Harrison, AR: New Leaf Press, 1980. 125 pp.

Perhaps the most interesting part of this book is
Goodman's description of the curious circumstances
surrounding his appointment and his dismissal as
MacArthur's personal pilot.

1829. Huff, Sid with Joe Alex Morris. MY FIFTEEN YEARS WITH
      GENERAL MACARTHUR. New York: Curtis Publishing, 1951.
      142 pp.

As a long-time aide-de-camp to MacArthur, Huff has many
stories to tell.

1830. Hunt, Frazier. MACARTHUR AND THE WAR AGAINST JAPAN. New
      York: Charles Scribner's Sons, 1944. 182 pp.

Hunt presents what is virtually an uncritical account of
MacArthur's performance.

1831. Hunt, Frazier. THE UNTOLD STORY OF DOUGLAS MACARTHUR. Old
      Greenwich, CT: Devin-Adair, 1954. 533 pp.

Correspondent Hunt sees his friend in the most favorable
light.

1832.   James, D. Clayton. "MacArthur's Lapses From An Envelopment
        Strategy in 1945." PARAMETERS, 10 (June 1980), 26-32.

        Challenging certain myths about MacArthur, James
        concludes that the general virtually ignored the wishes of
        the joint chiefs of staff. For example, James explains
        that MacArthur took all of the Philippines, contrary to the
        wishes of the JCS, who wanted only key areas seized. Also,
        while the JCS envisioned OLYMPIC as the next major
        operation (when the war ended), James reveals that
        MacArthur was planning an attack on Java.

1833.   James, D. Clayton. THE YEARS OF MACARTHUR. Boston:
        Houghton Mifflin, 1970-1985. 3 vols.

        Here is a masterful biography. James combines
        meticulous research, clear (and quotable) writing, and
        sound historical judgment to draw as complete a picture of
        MacArthur as we are ever likely to see. The strengths and
        weaknesses of this complex character stand in sharp detail.
        Volume II analyzes the Second World War. Of interest is
        the continuing (frustrating) uncertainty concerning
        responsibility for the 1941 debacle at Clark Field.

1834.   Kelley, Frank and Cornelius Ryan. MACARTHUR, MAN OF ACTION.
        New York: Lion Books, 1951. 154 pp.

        Here is a flattering account.

1835.   Kelley, William A. MACARTHUR: HERO OF DESTINY.
        Greenwich, CT: Fawcett, 1942. 66 pp.

        Capt. Kelley fought under MacArthur. His description of
        the general appears as told to Frederick C. Painton.

1836.   Kenney, George C. THE MACARTHUR I KNOW. New York: Duell,
        Sloan and Pearce, 1951. 264 pp.

        There is much praise here from the air leader for his
        commanding officer.

1837.   Lee, Clark and Richard Henschel. DOUGLAS MACARTHUR. New
        York: Henry Holt, 1952. 370 pp.

        This Cold War, pro-MacArthur view emphasizes the alleged
        thirty-year feud between MacArthur and Marshall. The
        authors hint at a deal in which Roosevelt approved the
        strategy of returning to the Philippines in 1944 and
        MacArthur issued optimistic (exaggerated?) war reports

during the final weeks of the 1944 presidential election.

1838. Long, Gavin. MACARTHUR AS MILITARY COMMANDER. London:
       Batsford, 1969. 254 pp.

       As part of a series on military commanders, the book
       offers a popular account of the general's long career.

1839. "The MacArthur Corridor." ASSEMBLY (December 1981), 16-17,
       40-41.

       NE

1840. MacArthur, Douglas. REMINISCENCES. New York:
       McGraw-Hill, 1964. 438 pp.

       The memoirs are extremely well written and provide a
       valuable component of the historiography of the war. See
       especially MacArthur's account of his preparations in the
       Philippines before the war and his postwar views on the
       collaborationist issue in the Philippines. Taken alone,
       his eloquence is persuasive; critics, however, have
       described the book as self-serving.

1841. MacArthur, Douglas. REPORT ON NATIONAL DEFENSES IN THE
       PHILIPPINES. Manila: Bureau of Printing, 1936. 52 pp.

       In his unique contemporary situation, MacArthur writes
       of his plans to build a citizens' army. He points to the
       resources, especially money, that need to be provided.

1842. MacArthur, Douglas. THE REPORTS OF GENERAL MACARTHUR.
       Washington, D.C.: G.P.O., 1966. 2 vols.

       The first volume describes MacArthur's compaign in the
       Pacific. Detailed maps enhance the narrative. Volume Two
       incorporates the records of the Japanese Demobilization
       Bureau and postwar interviews with Japanese officers to
       examine Japanese operations in the Southwest Pacific. Of
       special interest is the material on the prewar plans of the
       Japanese armed forces.

1843. MacArthur, Douglas. A SOLDIER SPEAKS: PUBLIC PAPERS AND
       SPEECHES OF GENERAL OF THE ARMY DOUGLAS MACARTHUR. New
       York: Praeger, 1965. 397 pp.

       Carlos Romulo wrote the Foreword, and Vorine Whan edited
       the collection. Here is a sampling of MacArthur's
       eloquence and power of persuasion.

1844.   Manchester, William. AMERICAN CAESAR: DOUGLAS MACARTHUR,
        1880-1964. Boston: Little, Brown, 1978.

        This portrait of the General, while always interesting
        reading, looks familiar. The book echoes previously
        published interpretations; there is little that is new.
        Nevertheless, the fluid prose and fascinating imagery
        attest to Manchester's prowess as a writer who can compel
        the reader's attention.

1845.   Mayer, Sydney L. MACARTHUR. New York: Ballantine Books,
        1971. 159 pp.

        Mayer's portrait is well balanced. He praises the
        General as a military strategist, but there is criticism as
        well. For example, Mayer feels that MacArthur showed poor
        judgment in arranging the Filipino training program and in
        allowing bombers to be caught on the ground at Clark Field.
        Mayer believes that MacArthur's command of the language
        probably saved his career in that the General should have
        been fired after the surrender at Bataan and Corregidor.

1846.   Miller, Francis Trevelyan. GENERAL DOUGLAS MACARTHUR:
        FIGHTER FOR FREEDOM. Philadelphia, PA: Winston, 1942.
        288 pp.

        This contemporary view praises the general for his wartime
        leadership. A later edition (1951) adds statesmanship to
        MacArthur's strengths.

1847.   Newton, Clarke. THE FIGHTING DOUGLAS MACARTHUR. New York:
        Dodd, Mead, 1965. 211 pp.

        Newton provides a popular account, without notes and
        with a skimpy bibliography, that takes a favorable view of
        the general's wartime performance.

1848.   Omitted.

1849.   Pearl, Jack. GENERAL DOUGLAS MACARTHUR. Derry, CT:
        Monarch Books, 1961.

        Here is a popular account that is full of praise for
        MacArthur.

1850.   Petillo, Carol M. "Douglas MacArthur and Manuel Quezon: A
        Note on an Imperial Bond." PAC HR, 48 (February 1979),
        107-117.

        Among archival records, Petillo finds Executive Order

#1, January 3, 1942, by Quezon which allocated $640,000
among MacArthur, Sutherland, R. Marshall, and Huff. She
speculates on the possible reasons for these unusual cash
awards.

1851. Petillo, Carol M. DOUGLAS MACARTHUR: THE PHILIPPINE
          YEARS. Bloomington, IN: Indiana University Press,
          1981. 301 pp.

     Incorporating psychoanalytic models, Petillo seeks to
open a new dimension in the existing scholarship on
MacArthur. One of the problems with this approach,
however, is the dearth of material recorded by the general
about his personal feelings. Petillo emphasizes
MacArthur's obsession with returning to the Philippines,
and she suggests that his personality and strong will
forced that strategic decision. Things get even murkier
when the author ventures the notion that MacArthur took a
wife (Jean) to replace his ailing mother. With regard to
the destruction of the bombers at Clark Field, the author
is silent. The book created a public sensation with its
revelation that MacArthur accepted a gift of $500,000 from
Quezon on January 3, 1942. Other cash awards went to
Sutherland ($75,000), Huff ($20,000), and R. Marshall
($45,000). In June 1942, Petillo reports, Eisenhower
turned down an offer of a cash gift from the grateful
Quezon. Petillo's important discovery underscores the need
for further study.

1852. Pontius, Dale. "MacArthur and the Filipinos." ASIA &
          AMERICAS, Pt. I: 46 (October 1946), 437-440; Pt. II:
          46 (November 1946), 509-512.

     The author, a political scientist who had served on
MacArthur's counter-intelligence staff, offers his views of
MacArthur. The general, he feels, seemed indifferent to
Osmena, ignored the Huks, and gave unqualified support to
Roxas -- perhaps unwisely, given the suspicions about Roxas
being a collaborator. Noting that some of MacArthur's
staff, like Parsons and Whitney, had close ties to Filipino
business circles, Pontius criticizes MacArthur for
disregarding democratic processes.

1853. Reynolds, Clark G. "MacArthur as Maritime Strategist."
          NAV WAR COLL REV, 33 (March-April 1980), 79-102.

     Reynolds applauds the "indirect approach" adapted by
MacArthur. Pointing out that maritime strategy is broader
than naval strategy, Reynolds praises MacArthur's use of

army, navy, and air force personnel in seaborne operations.
The article incorporates separate commentary by Stanley L.
Falk and Gerald L. Wheeler, who both criticize Reynolds'
assessment.

1854.   Rhoades, Weldon E. FLYING MACARTHUR TO VICTORY: College
        Station, TX: Texas A&M University Press, 1987. 563 pp.

        As MacArthur's personal pilot, "Dusty" Rhoades enjoyed a
        unique vantage point. His diary formed the basis for this
        book, and he describes the highlights--and some lowlights--
        in the war against Japan. By waiting this long to publish,
        Rhoades undoubtedly kept faith with a personal code;
        nevertheless, the book remains useful.

1855.   Roebling, Karl. GREAT MYTHS OF WORLD WAR II. Fern Park,
        FL: Paragon Press/Dynapress, 1985. 261 pp.

        Of the 14 myths considered, only one deals with the war
        against Japan. Roebling examines the circumstances
        surrounding MacArthur being awarded the Medal of Honor.
        Generally sympathetic to MacArthur, the author explains
        that the medal may be given for reasons other than an act
        of bravery.

1856.   Rogers, Paul P. "An Exchange of Opinion: MacArthur,
        Quezon, and Executive Order Number One--Another View."
        PAC HR, 52 (February 1983), 93-102.

        Rogers, a stenographer for MacArthur, affirms
        MacArthur's integrity throughout the episode (reported by
        Carol Petillo) in which Quezon authorized monetary awards
        to MacArthur and three other U.S. officers. Petillo offers
        a rejoinder.

1857.   Steinberg, Alfred. DOUGLAS MACARTHUR. New York: G.P.
        Putnam's Sons, 1961. 192 pp.

        This is a popular report which is geared to a younger
        audience. The book is part of the "Lives to Remember"
        series.

1858.   Supreme Commander for the Allied Powers. REPORTS OF
        GENERAL MACARTHUR. Washington, D.C.: GPO, 1966. 2
        vols.

        The reports were prepared by the general's staff in
        1950. MacArthur was unwilling to publish the documents

because he felt they needed further editing and
additions/corrections. The first volume provides a
detailed narrative of MacArthur's wartime leadership. Also
see the plans for the projected invasion of Japan.
Volume II concentrates on operations which were conducted
by the Japanese.

1859. Thorne, Christopher. "MacArthur, Australia and the
British, 1942-1943: The Secret Journal of MacArthur's
British Liaison Officer." AUS OUTLOOK, Pt. I: 29
(April 1975), 53-67; Pt. II: 29 (August 1975), 197-210.

In this controversial article, Thorne explores the
political and personal rivalries as revealed in the journal
of Col. Gerald Hugh Wilkinson. The British officer
described MacArthur's sentiments allegedly criticizing the
Australian war effort and distrusting Roosevelt and
Churchill.

1860. Whitney, Courtney. MACARTHUR: HIS RENDEZVOUS WITH
HISTORY. New York: A.A. Knopf, 1956. 560 pp.

Whitney constructs a flattering account of his
commanding officer. Of special interest is Whitney's
belief that the importance of the bombers lost at Clark
Field was much exaggerated.

1861. Willoughby, Charles A. and John Chamberlain. MACARTHUR,
1941-1951. New York: McGraw-Hill, 1954. 441 pp.

Gen. Willoughby, MacArthur's chief of intelligence,
concocts what might well be characterized as a court
history. MacArthur is presented in uncritical terms.

1862. Wittner, Lawrence S., ed. MACARTHUR. Englewood Cliffs,
NJ: Prentice-Hall, 1971. 192 pp.

The collection presents various political perspectives
on the general. Much of the material pertains to the
postwar years.

GEORGE C. MARSHALL

1863. Danchev, Alex. "A Special Relationship: Field Marshal Sir
John Dill and General George C. Marshall." RUSI, 130
(June 1985), 56-61.

The author sheds light on one of the most important--and
underrated--elements in Anglo-American relations during the

war.

1864. Marshall, George C. BIENNIAL REPORT OF THE CHIEF OF STAFF
       OF THE UNITED STATES ARMY, JULY 1, 1943 TO JUNE 30 1945,
       TO THE SECRETARY OF WAR. Washington, D. C.: Infantry
       Journal Press, 1946. 247 pp.

       This official report, purged of any secrets or
       controversies or mistakes, remains, nonetheless, an
       important primary source on the final two years of the war
       in all theaters.

1865. Mosely, Leonard. MARSHALL: HERO FOR OUR TIMES. San
       Francisco, CA: Hearst Books, 1982. 608 pp.

       This one-volume study is readable and generally
       favorable to its subject. Mosley does raise questions--
       and doubts--about Marshall's role in the circumstances
       leading to the debacle at Pearl Harbor.

1866. Pogue, Forrest C. GEORGE C. MARSHALL: ORDEAL AND HOPE,
       1939-1942. New York: Viking Press, 1966. 491 pp.

       Pogue presents a model of research and analysis in
       preparing this multi-volume biography. The narrative strikes
       a judicious assessment of the military leader who earned
       widespread respect. Pogue is critical of Marshall's
       performance in late 1941 and particularly takes the general
       to task for failing to reorganize the War Department in
       1940-1941. See, too, the interesting contrasts drawn by
       Pogue between Marshall and MacArthur.

1867. Pogue, Forrest C. GEORGE C. MARSHALL: ORGANIZER OF
       VICTORY, 1943-1945. New York: Viking Press, 1973. 683
       pp.

       With regard to the war against Japan, this volume
       describes the formation of South East Asia Command, the
       command appointment of Mountbatten, and the always sensitive
       relations between Washington and MacArthur. The work is
       somewhat disappointing in its hurried handling of the
       development and use of the atomic bomb.

1868. Sutherland, John P. "The Story General Marshall Told Me."
       US NEWS WORLD REP, 47 (November 2, 1959), 50-56.

       Drawing upon confidential interviews in 1954-1955
       granted by the general (on condition nothing be revealed
       until after his death), Sutherland provides information on

a range of topics. For example, Marshall felt certain that
he was at home with his recuperating wife the night of
December 6-7, 1941. Other items of interest include his
criticism of the revisionists (especially Theobald), his
feeling that the atomic bombings precipitated the Japanese
surrender "by months" (and that the situation had demanded
"shock action"), his uncertainty about the number of lives
an invasion of Japan would cost, his revelation that
invasion plans had called for a total of 9 atomic bombings
in 3 attacks (6 in the initial assault on September 23,
1945; 3 to hit Japanese reserves), his complaint of
"constant squabbling" among the services (e.g., the Navy
refused to train AAF B-26 crews in the Aleutians), his
hopes at Yalta to confirm the Soviet entry into the war
against Japan, and his disappointment at the lax security
in the White House (especially with MAGIC information).

1869. Watson, Mark S. CHIEF OF STAFF: PREWAR PLANS AND
        PREPARATIONS. Washington, D.C.: Office of the Chief of
        Military History, Dept. of the Army, 1950. 551 pp.

        The author concentrates on the role of Gen. Marshall
        from 1939 to 1941. Marshall recognized the pressing need
        to remedy the ill-prepared and ill-equipped U.S. Army.
        Also, the book indicates some outlines of U.S.-British
        clandestine cooperation in 1940-1941 (before Pearl Harbor).
        Pointing to a "fateful series of mischances" surrounding
        the Japanese attack at Pearl Harbor (e.g., the failures of:
        U.S. intelligence, Washington to understand Short's
        actions, Hawaii to understand the gravity of the situation,
        Army communications at a crucial time), Watson feels that
        the United States might have thwarted the surprise attack.

LORD MOUNTBATTEN

1870. Hough, Richard A. MOUNTBATTEN. New York: Random House,
        1981. 302 pp.

        Hough presents a sympathetic picture of his subject. Of
        special interest is the material on SEAC and postwar India.

1871. Mountbatten, Vice-Admiral the Lord Louis. POST-SURRENDER
        TASKS. London: HMSO, 1969. 42 PP.

        Here is an excerpt (Section E) from Mountbatten's
        official 1951 report as SACSEA. Of interest is his use of
        Japanese forces, as the only armed, organized units in some
        areas, to maintain law and order.

1872. Mountbatten, Vice-Admiral the Lord Louis. REPORT TO THE
       COMBINED CHIEFS OF STAFF BY THE SUPREME ALLIED
       COMMANDER, SOUTH-EAST ASIA, 1943-1945. London: HMSO,
       1951. 280 pp.

       Mountbatten describes the achievements of his SEAC
       forces and the formidable obstacles which had to be
       overcome ("Monsoon, Malaria, and Morale"). In view of the
       low priority his command held in the competition for Allied
       resources, Mountbatten may be forgiven a certain amount of
       exaggeration. Certainly SEAC did much for what little they
       had. Of special interest, in view of the controversy later
       in the war over theater boundaries, is Appendix D, notes by
       Lt. Gen. Brehon B. Somervell (USA) of a meeting between
       Mountbatten and Chiang Kai-Shek, in which decisions about
       whose theater would incorporate Indochina and Thailand were
       postponed.

1873. Mountbatten, Vice-Admiral the Lord Louis. THE STRATEGY OF
       THE SOUTH-EAST ASIAN CAMPAIGN. Ludhiana, India: Punjab
       Printing, 1946. 32 pp.

       Here is the text of a lecture by Mountbatten to the
       Royal United Services Institution. He provides a brief
       review of the highlights on the road to victory--only the
       good things.

1874. Swinson, Arthur. MOUNTBATTEN. New York: Ballantine Books,
       1971. 160 pp.

       Here is a brief, but knowledgeable, summary of
       Mountbatten's exciting career. Swinson effectively
       portrays his subject's frustrations in lacking resources
       for planned SEAC operations.

1875. Ziegler, Philip. MOUNTBATTEN. New York: Harper and Row,
       1985. 784 pp.

       Here is an authorized biography, which intertwines
       Mountbatten's personal and professional lives. Of special
       interest is the material on Mountbatten's appointment and
       contribution as Supreme Allied Commander, South East Asia.

CHESTER W. NIMITZ

1876. Driskill, Frank A. and Dede W. Casad. CHESTER W. NIMITZ:
       ADMIRAL OF THE HILLS. Austin, TX: Eakin Press, 1983.

NE

1877. Potter, E.B. NIMITZ. Annapolis, MD: Naval Institute
          Press, 1976. 507 pp.

          Potter, a professor of naval history, composes a
     knowledgeable biography. Some points of special interest
     about Nimitz include his careful handling of the relief of
     Ralph Smith, his retention of much of Kimmel's staff
     (especially Edwin T. Layton in intelligence), his patience
     during the Battle of Midway, and his attitude about women in
     the service (few women--excluding nurses--were stationed in
     Hawaii while Nimitz was there). There are no notes or
     citations, but the author's extensive research is evident.

1878. Weddle, Robert S. "Texas to Tokyo Bay: Admiral Chester W.
          Nimitz." AMER HIST ILLUS, 10 (August 1975), 4-9, 39-47.

          In this review of Nimitz's career, Weddle emphasizes the
     admiral's ability to raise morale after Pearl Habor. While
     others concentrated on American errors, Nimitz emphasized
     the mistakes Japan committed on December 7,1941 (e.g.,
     missing submarine pens, oil reserves, and the carriers).

FIELD MARSHAL SIR WILLIAM SLIM

1879. Calvert, Michael. SLIM. New York: Ballantine Books,
          1973. 160 pp.

          Part of the Ballantine series on war leaders, this book
     portrays Slim more as a practical campaigner than a grand
     strategist. Calvert asserts that no other British general
     could have matched Slim's achievements under the same
     conditions. His two greatest attributes, according to the
     author, were Slim's bulldog tenacity and his sharing the
     hardships of his men.

1880. Fergusson, Bernard. "Field-Marshal the Viscount Slim of
          Yarralumla and Bishopston." ARMY Q DEF J, 101 (No. 3,
          1971), 268-272.

          The author, who served in Burma, recounts some of his
     favorite stories about Slim.

1881. Lewin, Ronald. SLIM: THE STANDARD BEARER. Hamden, CT:
          Shoe String Press, 1976.

          Here is a first-rate biography. Lewin carefully details

the pivotal role of Slim in the reclaiming of Burno.

1882. Slim, Field-Marshal Sir William. DEFEAT INTO VICTORY.
        London: Cassell, 1956. 576 pp.

        The British leader's memoir offers the perspective of a
        corps commander. Slim bases his account on the
        contemporary "skeleton" diary he kept and other wartime
        papers. See Slim's interesting "After Thoughts."

1883. Slim, Field Marshal Sir William. UNOFFICIAL HISTORY. New
        York: D. McKay, 1962. 242 pp.

        Here is Slim's version of the history of the CBI
        Theater. Although he and his forces play a major role, the
        book is not limited to an autobiographical account.

RAYMOND A. SPRUANCE

1884. Buell, Thomas E. THE QUIET WARRIOR: A BIOGRAPHY OF
        ADMIRAL RAYMOND A. SPRUANCE. Boston: Little, Brown,
        1974. 544 pp.

        Buell offers a well-written, well-researched study
        which, at times, lapses from a critical perspective.

1885. Forrestal, E.P. ADMIRAL RAYMOND A. SPRUANCE, USN: A STUDY
        IN COMMAND. Washington, D. C.: Department of the Navy,
        1966. 275 pp.

        The author, a friend and associate of Admiral Spruance,
        provides a highly favorable--and persuasive--view of this
        outstanding naval leader.

1886. Spruance, Raymond A. "The Victory in the Pacific." UNITED
        SERV INSTITUTE INDIA J (November 1946).

            NE

JOSEPH W. STILWELL

1887. Anders, Leslie. THE LEDO ROAD: GENERAL JOSEPH W.
        STILWELL'S HIGHWAY TO CHINA. Norman, OK: University of
        Oklahoma Press, 1965. 255 pp.

        This defense of both the value of the project and its
        prime mover, Stilwell, incorporates Anders' interviews and
        correspondence with many of the participants. The author
        is a former historian in the Army's Office of the Chief of

Engineers.

1888. Beldon, Jack. RETREAT WITH STILWELL. New York: A. A.
        Knopf, 1943. 368 pp.

        Here is a reporter's account of the walkout from Burma.
        Here, too, is a portrait of Stilwell at his best: tough,
        strong, persistent.

1889. Dorn, Frank. WALKOUT WITH STILWELL IN BURMA. New York:
        Thomas Y. Crowell, 1971. 258 pp.

        Dorn writes of his challenging experiences in escaping
        from Burma after the defeat of the Allies. His eyewitness
        description of Stilwell reveals a hardened, self-reliant,
        determined commander who shared the burdens of his troops.
        Of great significance is Dorn's report of preparing plans
        to assassinate Chiang Kai-shek based on orders to Stilwell
        from "the very highest level." Dorn's daily log forms the
        basis for his narrative.

1890. Eldridge, Fred. WRATH IN BURMA ; THE UNCENSORED STORY OF
        GENERAL STILWELL AND INTERNATIONAL MANEUVERS IN THE
        FAR EAST. Garden City, NY: Doubleday, 1946. 320 pp.

        The "story" turns out to be the hero (Stilwell)
        battling the British, Chiang Kai-shek, and the alleged
        intrigues of Patrick J. Hurley.

1891. Liang, Chin Tung. GENERAL STILWELL IN CHINA, 1942-1944:
        THE FULL STORY. Jamaica, NY: St. John's University
        Press, 1972. 321 pp.

        With access to unpublished Chinese documents, Liang
        presents the Nationalist Chinese version of events in China
        during this period. He is critical of Stilwell, both as a
        leader and a strategist. Chiang Kai-Shek, on the other
        hand, earns high praise. Much of the fiction between the
        two men stemmed from the awkward postions assigned to
        Stilwell.

1892. Romanus, Charles F. and Riley Sunderland. STILWELL'S
        MISSION TO CHINA. Washington, D.C.: Office of the
        Chief of Military History, Dept. of the Army, 1953.
        441 pp.

1893. ------. STILWELL'S COMMAND PROBLEMS. Washington, D.C.:
        Office of the Chief of Military History, Dept. of the
        Army, 1956. 607 pp.

1894. ------. TIME RUNS OUT IN CBI. Washington, D.C.: Office
       of the Chief of Military History, Dept. of the Army,
       1959. 428 pp.

       Here is a magnificient effort. The authors meticulously
       research Stilwell's wartime adventures in CBI. The
       general's interaction--and friction--with Chinese leaders,
       especially Chiang Kai-shek, are described in detail. The
       three volumes remain a vital part of the literature on the
       subject.

1895. Romanus, Charles and Riley Sunderland, eds. STILWELL'S
       PERSONNEL FILE: CHINA, BURMA, INDIA, 1942-1944.
       Wilmington, DE: Scholarly Resources Press, 1976.
       5 vols.

       The collection reproduces many of the records of the
       general's tour of duty in CBI. The correspondence,
       memoranda, and minutes are taken from the Stilwell files
       deposited at the Washington National Records Center.
       (Suitland, MD).

1896. Rooney, Douglas D. STILWELL. New York: Ballantine Books,
       1971. 160 pp.

       The narrative reveals the rugged spirit of "Vinegar
       Joe." An excellent collection of photos complements this
       wartime biography.

1897. Schaller, Michael. "The Command Crisis in China, 1944: A
       Road Not Taken." DIP HIST, 4 (Summer 1980), 327-331.

       Here is the full text of a document unearthed by
       Schaller which resists Chinese arguments for the recall of
       Stilwell. The draft of a letter to Chiang Kai-shek,
       written for Roosevelt's signature by Marshall, was never
       sent.

1898. Shutt, Timothy Baker. "At War's Farthest End." MIL HIST,
       2 (June 1986), 40-47.

       Shutt bases the article on an interview with Marvin
       Walker who had served on Stilwell's staff in 1944. Walker
       describes Stilwell as a "3 star platoon leader" who lived
       like the lowest private in the command.

1899. Stilwell, Joseph W. THE STILWELL PAPERS. New York:
       William Sloane Associates, 1948. 357 pp.

Arranged and edited by Theodore H. White, the papers are
taken from Stilwell's personal command journal, his diary
and reflections, and his letters to Mrs. Stilwell. The
general's frank observations reveal much about CBI affairs.
Stilwell's strengths and weaknesses surface in these
pages. Editor White might have made a contribution by
injecting moderate tones of civility in Vinegar Joe's
writings (e.g., "What the general means is ....").

900.   Sunderland, Riley. "General Stilwell's Attempt to Save
       Burma." MIL REV, 29 (February 1950), 3-9.

       Sunderland, a widely recognized authority on the
       subject, traces the difficulties Stilwell encountered in
       1942.

901.   Tsou, Tang. "Stilwell and the Generalissimo." MIDWAY, No.
       17 (Winter 1964), 42-79.

       Tsou examines the discrepancy between the ambitious
       wartime plans for China and the scant resources actually
       allocated to that theater. Also, he looks at the use made
       of those resources. Addressing the recall of Stilwell,
       Tsou makes two key observations: (1) Chiang Kai-shek felt
       that the U. S. had to stay with him and (2) the U. S.,
       especially Roosevelt, grew (further?) disillusioned with
       China.

902.   Tuchman, Barbara W. STILWELL AND THE AMERICAN EXPERIENCE
       IN CHINA, 1911-1945. New York: Macmillan, 1970. 621
       pp.

       Tuchman, a gifted writer with first-hand experience in
       China, integrates her biographical material within the
       context of Chinese history. Stillwell first went to China
       in 1911 during the revolution. The book centers on the
       wartime relationship between Stilwell and Chiang Kai-shek.
       Although she does not lapse into stereotypes of main
       characters, such as Mountbatten, Nelson, Hurley and even
       Chiang Kai-shek, this is hardly a balanced effort. Was
       Stilwell's chief mission to fight the war independently or
       to get along with "Peanut" (his irreverent private nickname
       for the Generalissimo)? Moreover, Stilwell hardly inspired
       the confidence of Roosevelt. Yet, Tuchman knows her
       subject. Stilwell's considerable strengths are prominently
       displayed in these pages. See especially her careful
       treatment of the Chinese Communists.

1903.   White, Theodore H., ed. THE STILWELL PAPERS. New York:
              William Sloane Associates, 1948. 357 pp.

              Here are the private papers, correspondence, and journal
         jottings of the controversial general. The collection,
         which represents about one-half of the total of his private
         writings, covers the period from Pearl Harbor to Stilwell's
         recall in 1944. The collection offers little that is
         new--Vinegar Joe rarely left doubt about where he stood.
         White deletes none of the expletives. The editor does say,
         however, that the writings were for Stilwell's use only
         and, consequently, do not reflect the general's warmth and
         kindliness.

1904.   Young, Kenneth R. "The Stilwell Controversy: A
              Bibliographic Review." MIL AFFS, 39 (April 1975),
              66-68.

              Evaluating more than twenty sources, Young gives an
         even-handed account of the differing assessments of the
         controversial general.

JONATHAN M. WAINWRIGHT

1905.   Ancheta, Celedonio A., ed. THE WAINWRIGHT PAPERS: WITH
              NOTES AND COMMENTS. Quezon City, PI: New Day
              Publishers, 1980-1982. 4 vols.

              This collection incorporates reports of operations and
         activities of commands and units in the Philipines prepared
         by Wainwright and some of his commanders and staff. These
         reports emerged from notes they made during the war and
         from a special collective assignment to Fort Sam Houston,
         Texas on Wainwright's orders in 1946. In view of the
         circumstances, Wainwright concludes by calling his
         ill-fated command in the Philippines "a brilliant chapter
         in the annals of American Military History."

1906.   Schultz, Duane P. HERO OF BATAAN: THE STORY OF GENERAL
              JONATHAN M. WAINWRIGHT. New York: St. Martin's Press,
              1981. 479 pp.

              Much of the interest in this book focuses on the
         shifting relations between Wainwright and MacArthur. While
         their prewar relationship was cordial, Schultz states that
         the misunderstanding and ill-feeling which surrounded
         MacArthur's departure from the Philippines soured the
         friendship. MacArthur had opposed Roosevelt's rescinding
         of the order to Wainwright not to surrender. In addition,

Schultz writes, MacArthur blamed Wainwright to some degree
for the Death March because the commander had not carried
out MacArthur's orders to launch a broad offensive
campaign. The book is well researched and highly readable.

1907. Wainright, Jonathan M. "Five Years Ago." ARMY INFO
DIGEST, 5 (September 1950), 11-13.

Wainright recalls his liberation and participation in
the surrender ceremonies. He heaps praise on MacArthur.

1908. Wainwright, Jonathan M. GENERAL WAINWRIGHT'S STORY.
Garden City, NY: Doubleday, 1946. 314 pp.

Here is a factual, understated report by Wainwright
(with the editorial help of Bob Considine). The general
paints a grim picture of the prewar situation in the
Philippines. Ill-prepared forces, for instance, had no
unit training until mid 1941. Moreover, unaware of the
deterioration of diplomatic negotiations, MacArthur and
Wainwright anticipated no war until at least April 1942.
The two generals, Wainwright says, felt saddled with the
"defeatist" strategy of War Plan Orange-3 (to hold at
Bataan). The book provides authoritative information on
the fighting, surrender, and imprisonment of the Allied
forces. Wainwright makes clear that he had no
responsibility for the U.S. air resources. Of special
interest is his report of Japanese troops surrounded at
Quinauan Point and their refusal to surrender. Was this
the first such episode of determined Japanese resistance in
the war?

ALBERT C. WEDEMEYER

1909. Eiler, Keith E. "The Man Who Planned The Victory." AMER
HERITAGE, 34 (October 1983), 36-48.

The article is based on an interview with Gen.
Wedemeyer. The general praises Mountbatten and describes
their wartime cooperation--despite the writings of the
revisionists. Defending Chiang Kai-shek (his was a "tough
situation"), Wedemeyer makes clear his view that the
communists were not simply "agrarian reformers." Of
interest is the general's account of his trip to China in
1947 for President Truman.

1910. Eiler, Keith E. ed., WEDEMEYER ON WAR AND PEACE. Stanford,
CA: Hoover Institution Press, 1987. 245 pp.

Utilizing materials from the archives of the Hoover
Institution, the book offers a lesson in the principles of
military strategy.

1911. Johnson, Thomas M. and Gretta Palmer. "Wedemeyer's
        Outstretched Hand." READER'S DIG, 48 (October 1946),
        127-130.

        This article praises the U.S. general for his
        contribution in changing the climate in China towards
        Sino-American relations.

1912. Wedemeyer, Albert C. "Relations With Wartime China: A
        Reminiscence." ASIAN AFFS, 4 (January-February 1976),
        196-201.

        In this memoir-report, Gen. Wedemeyer discusses his role
        in China. Upon arriving in China, he says that he found
        poor relations between the Chinese and Americans. His
        praise of Chiang Kai-shek matches his criticism of the
        Chinese Communists.

1913. Wedemeyer, Albert C. WEDEMEYER REPORTS! New York: Henry
        Holt, 1958. 497 pp.

        Gen. Wedemeyer criticizes U.S. policies in Asia, which
        in his opinion have amounted to a postwar disaster. These
        memoirs are marked by the general's frank opinions,
        especially about prominent personalities in the war. For
        example, Roosevelt (for his prewar maneuvering, the policy
        of unconditional surrender, and his insistence that the
        Soviets enter the war against Japan) receives sharp
        criticism--as do Stilwell, Foreign Service officers in
        China (Davies, Servige, Emerson and Ludden), and even
        Hurley (for refusing to recognize he had been deceived).
        Wedemeyer maintains that Chiang Kai-shek was merely the
        head of a loose coalition and that the Nationlist
        Government, despite Stilwell's stories, fought the Japanese
        tenaciously.

ORDE C. WINGATE

1914. Bidwell, Shelford. "Wingate and the Official Historians."
        J CONTEMP HIST, 15 (April 1980), 245-256.

        The author responds to an article by Peter Mead about
        the harsh judgments of Wingate by Britain's official
        historians. Bidwell's balanced view is that Wingate holds
        an "honourable place" among military leaders of the war but

falls short of greatness.

915. Mead, Peter W. "Orde Wingate and the Official Historians."
        J CONTEMP HIST, 14 (January 1979), 55-82.

        Mead takes issue with "a particularly gross
        malassessment" of Wingate in the official British history
        of the war. In his defense of Wingate, Mead attacks the
        prejudices of the historians, especially Gen. Kirby and
        Brig. Roberts.

916. Mosley, Leonard. GIDEON GOES TO WAR. New York: Charles
        Scribner's Sons, 1955. 256 pp.

        Here is a well-written narrative on Orde Wingate and his
        campaigning in Burma.

917. Rossetto, L. MAJOR-GENERAL ORDE CHARLES WINGATE AND THE
        DEVELOPMENT OF LONG-RANGE PENETRATION. Manhattan, KS:
        MA/AH Publishing, 1982. 471 pp.

        Here is an excellent analysis of Wingate and the LRPGs.
        Rossetto offers a balanced assessment; he feels that the
        LRPGs represented a conceptual breakthrough but notes some
        crucial flaws in Wingate's operations.

918. Sykes, Christopher. ORDE WINGATE. Cleveland, OH: World
        Publishing, 1959. 575 pp.

        Sykes composes a knowledgeable, sympathetic view of the
        mystical British leader.

919. Tulloch, Derek. WINGATE: IN PEACE AND WAR. London:
        MacDonald, 1972. 300 pp.

        The author served as Wingate's chief of staff
        (1943-1944). He and Wingate had been young cadets
        together. The complex interplay of personalities (e.g.,
        Slim, Mountbatten, Giffard, Stilwell, Chennault) is given
        sensitive treatment by Tulloch. In his praise for Wingate,
        the author charges that official British military circles
        have sought to minimize Wingate's ideas and achievements
        because of his unorthodoxy. See especially Tulloch's
        description of the effect on Wingate of having to leave
        behind the sick and wounded in his long-range penetration
        groups.

IV.B.3. OTHERS

1920. Anders, Leslie. GENTLE KNIGHT: THE LIFE AND TIMES OF
        MAJOR GENERAL EDWIN FORREST HARDING. Kent, OH: Kent
        State University Press, 1985. 384 pp.

        Integrating archival sources with correspondence and
        interviews, Anders draws a sympathetic portrait of his
        subject. As commander of the Green Division, Harding
        received pressure from MacArthur (himself pressed by the
        Australians) for action, despite having inadequate
        resources. The author charges that MacArthur made Harding
        the scapegoat for the first failure to take Buna.

1921. Barker, Chris A. TOMORROW MAY NEVER COME. Independence,
        MO: Susquehanna Publishers, 1982. 415 pp.

        Here is a Marine's personal account of his love affair
        with the battleship COLORADO.

1922. Blank, Joseph P. "Lieutenant Holguin's Final Mission."
        READER'S DIG., 130 (April 1987), 83-88.

        Here is a description of the fortieth mission of Jose
        "Joe" Holguin, a B-17 pilot, over Rabaul. The plane was
        shot down on June 25, 1943, and Holguin survived. He later
        fell captive to the Japanese and remained a POW at Rabaul.
        Years later (1981-83), Holguin returned to the crash site
        and found the remains of five members of his crew. Four
        other crewmen are still missing.

1923. Blankfort, Michael. THE BIG YANKEE: THE LIFE OF CARLSON
        OF THE RAIDERS. Boston: Little, Brown and Company,
        1947. 380 pp.

        This book succeeds in restoring the human dimensions of
        the myth of Evans F. Carlson. As a biographer sympathetic
        to his subject, Blankfort characterizes Carlson as a
        progressive democrat and an intellectual.

1924. Bond, Brian, ed. CHIEF OF STAFF: THE DIARIES OF
        LIEUTENANT-GENERAL SIR HENRY POWNALL. Hamden, CT:
        Archon Books, 1974. 2 vols.

        Pownall went to the Far East in December 1941. In 1943,
        he became chief of staff in Mountbatten's new command until
        his departure in December 1944. Under Bond's able editing,
        the diaries reveal an inside look at Southeast Asia
        Command's operations and personalities.

1925. Brereton, Lewis H. THE BRERETON DIARIES: THE WAR IN THE

AIR IN THE PACIFIC, MIDDLE EAST AND EUROPE, 3 OCTOBER
1941 - 8 MAY 1945. New York: Morrow, 1946. 450 pp.

Brereton remained involved in operations in the Pacific
until June 1942. His diaries constitute not only a report
on the prewar preparations in the Philippines but also an
indictment of American leadership in Washington during the
hours of confusion which followed the attack at Pearl
Harbor.

1926. Brown, David T. LETTERS, 1941-45, OF DAVID TUCKER BROWN,
       JR., U. S. MARINE CORPS RESERVE, KILLED IN ACTION ON
       OKINAWA SHIMA, RYUKYU ISLANDS. n.p.: Author, 1946.
       105 pp.

This poignant collection, which amounts to a combat
Marine's posthumous memoir, was also published under the
title MARINE FROM VIRGINIA (Chapel Hill, NC: University
of North Carolina Press, 1947).

1927. Butcher, M.E. "Admiral Frank Jack Fletcher, Pioneer
       Warrior or Gross Sinner?" NAV WAR COLL REV, 40 (Winter
       1987), 69-79.

This well-researched article profiles Fletcher's record
as tactical commander at Coral Sea, Midway, and the Eastern
Solomons. These first three carrier battles represented
50% of the total such engagements ever fought. Butcher
offers some defense against Fletcher's critics, especially
for the episodes at Wake and Savo. But Butcher also points
out, that Fletcher was not an aviator, had little
experience in carrier operations, and failed to gain the
confidence of Adm. King.

1928. Butterfield, Roger. AL SCHMID, MARINE. New York: Norton,
       1944. 142 pp.

Here is a unique perspective on the action in the
Solomons as seen through the eyes of one of the
participants.

1929. Chase, William C. FRONT LINE GENERAL: THE COMMANDS OF
       WILLIAM C. CHASE: AN AUTOBIOGRAPHY. Houston, TX:
       Pacesetter Press, 1975. 228 pp.

Here is an interesting autobiography of a battlefield
leader involved in some of the heaviest fighting,
especially in the Admiralty Islands and the Philippines.
For example, Chase led not only the landing at Tacloban

(MacArthur's celebrated "return") but also the successful
campaign on Luzon to liberate the Santo Tomas Internment
Camp. Chase defends his decision to release the Japanese
guards at the camp who had taken hostages on the grounds
that he could save more lives among the interns--as
MacArthur had ordered. The book provides a valuable
glimpse of the life of a general leading combat units.

1930. Davis, Burke. MARINE! THE LIFE OF LT. GEN. LEWIS B.
        (CHESTY) PULLER, USMC (RET). Boston: Little, Brown and
        Company, 1962. 403 pp.

        This is an uncritical account of Puller's career,
        especially his service in the war against Japan.

1931. Davis, Russell G. MARINE AT WAR. Boston: Little, Brown,
        1961. 258 pp.

        Davis served as a Marine rifleman at Peleliu and
        Okinawa. He was wounded twice. His narrative is well
        written and provides a first-hand view of Pacific combat.

1932. Dye, John T. GOLDEN LEAVES. Los Angeles: Ward Ritchie
        Press, 1962. 227 pp.

        NE

1933. Dyer, George Carroll. THE AMPHIBIANS CAME TO CONQUER: THE
        STORY OF ADMIRAL RICHMOND KELLY TURNER. Washington,
        D.C.: Government Printing Office, 1969. 2 vols.

        This work is far too long. Rather than summarizing or
        selecting representative quotations of certain memoranda,
        Dyer frequently chooses to reprint the full texts. He also
        incorporates subheadings on virtually every page. It is
        enough to make von Ranke proud--and the reader wince.
        Moreover, does the author really believe that the term "a
        Chinese copy" (p. 362) represents an appropriate synonym
        for the term "duplicate"? Although Turner appears in the
        best light--as the "father of the Joint Chiefs of Staff"
        (because of his 1942 memorandum on organizational changes),
        and even the defeat at Savo Island is labeled a "valuable
        lesson" for the future--Dyer does gently rebuke Turner for
        not being clearer or more forceful in his warning messages
        from the Navy War Plans Division prior to Pearl Harbor.
        This is a soft view of "Terrible Turner."

1934. George, John B. SHOTS FIRED IN ANGER. Plantersville, SC:
        Small Arms Technical Publishing, 1947. 421 pp.

George tells of his experiences as a rifleman in Gen.
Patch's forces at Guadalcanal and as one of Merrill's
Marauders in Burma. The book was reprinted in 1981,
through the auspices of the National Rifle Association (535
pp.).

1935. Graham, Vickie M. "A Superior Private." AIRMAN, 31
       (December 1987), 27-29.

       Here is a brief profile of Joe Muratsuch, a U.S. citizen
       and Japanese-American, who was working in Japan as a
       bookkeeper when the war began. Despite his protests and
       the fact that he did not speak Japanese very well, Joe was
       drafted into the Japanese Army. As a truck driver in China
       he attained the rank of superior private. He is presently
       a historian at Hickam AFB, Hawaii.

1936. Hastings, Robert P. PRIVATEER IN THE COCONUT NAVY. LA:
       n.p., 1946. 105 pp.

       NE

1937. Hogan, John J. I AM NOT ALONE. Washington, D.C.:
       Mackinac Press, 1947. 132 pp.

       The book presents the letters of Hogan, an infantryman
       who was killed at Okinawa. The collection indicates his
       strong feelings about the need to strengthen moral fiber in
       the postwar era.

1938. Kodama, Yoshio. I WAS DEFEATED. Tokyo: Booth and Fukuda,
       1951. 223 pp.

       NE

1939. Laffin, John. RETURN TO GLORY. Sydney, Aus.: Angus and
       Robertson, 1956. 124 pp.

       Laffin is an Australian infantryman who participated in
       the Allied advance across the Southwest Pacific. This book
       reports on his return travels to those battlefields ten
       years after the war.

1940. Leckie, Robert. HELMET FOR MY PILLOW. New York: Random
       House, 1957. 311 pp.

       Here is the personal story of an enlisted marine in
       combat. Leckie served with the 1st Marine Division, 2nd

Battalion, at Guadalcanal and Pelelieu.

1941. Lee, Robert E. TO THE WAR. New York: A.A. Knopf, 1969.
       170 pp.

       Here is the personal account of a young junior officer
       in the naval reserves. He tells of his training and
       wartime experience in the Pacific. As a supervisor of
       maintenance and repair projects, Lee saw little front-line
       action.

1942. Leutze, James. A DIFFERENT KIND OF VICTORY: A BIOGRAPHY
       OF ADMIRAL THOMAS C. HART. Annapolis, MD: Naval
       Institute Press, 1981. 362 pp.

       Hart was at the head of the Asiatic Fleet when the war
       began. In the final days before the attack at Pearl
       Harbor, Hart believed that Roosevelt not only sought to
       provoke an incident with the order to dispatch the "three
       little ships" but also had committed the United States to
       go to war if British territory came under attack. Hart, in
       fact, sent Destroyer Division 57 on December 6 for service
       under the British naval commander at Singapore. Leutze
       describes the deteriorating relations in 1941 between Hart
       and MacArthur but argues unconvincingly that their
       differences remained purely professional. For example,
       Hart actually questioned MacArthur's sanity. The book also
       reveals the depths of the Navy's problem with faulty
       magnetic exploding devices on the torpedoes. After only
       one month as naval commander of ABDA (with all the
       attendant political problems), Hart left for reasons of
       "health."

1943. McMichael, Scott R. "Common Man, Uncommon Leadership."
       PARAMETERS, 16 (Summer 1986), 45-57.

       Here is a report on Capt. Charles N. Hunter, deputy
       commander of Merrill's Marauders. The author describes him
       as an ordinary officer with many faults who excelled in the
       performance of his duties. Critical of Stilwell and his
       staff, McMichael calls Merrill's unit perhaps the most
       badly handled U.S. force in the war.

1944. Manchester, William. GOODBYE, DARKNESS. Boston: Little
       Brown, 1980. 401 pp.

       In a personal and emotional narrative, the noted author
       recalls his part in the Pacific war. See especially his
       moving account of the first enemy soldier he killed.

1945.   Manchester, William. "The Man Who Could Speak Japanese."
        AMER HERITAGE, 27 (December 1975), 36-39, 91-95.

        Here is the story of Private Harold Dumas, a Marine who
        served with Manchester and exaggerated his credentials.
        For example, he was not a veteran of Guadalcanal, not the
        husband of a starlet, not a newspaperman, and not an
        officer -- all things he claimed to be. But above all,
        Dumas did not know Japanese even though he talked his way
        into an interpreter's position.

1946.   Manchester, William. "A Second Landing Finally Ends the
        War." LIFE, 2 (May 1979), 72-87.

        Manchester provides a memoir of his service in action at
        Okinawa. Despite incurring a "million dollar wound," he
        chose to return to battle where he suffered a more severe
        wound.

1947.   Maung Maung, U. TO A SOLDIER'S SON. Rangoon, Burma:
        Sarpay Beikman, 1974. 158 pp.

        NE

1948.   Potter, John D. YAMAMOTO: THE MAN WHO MENACED AMERICA.
        New York: Viking Press, 1965. 332 pp.

        In this biography, Potter succeeds in bringing out the
        personal--as opposed to the professional--qualities of the
        man. The book has general appeal and presents the Japanese
        perspective of the road to war with the United States.

1949.   St. George, Thomas R. PROCEED WITHOUT DELAY. New York:
        Thomas Crowell, 1945. 181 pp.

        Here is the personal account of an Army sergeant about
        his travels throughout the Pacific. St. George laces his
        report with humor and insight. The highly readable book
        ends with the U.S. return to the Philippines.

1950.   Schmid, Albert A. AL SCHMID, MARINE. New York: W.W.
        Norton, 1944. 142 pp.

        Here is a "folksy" memoir of the fighting in the South
        Pacific (as told to Roger Butterfield). Schmid suffered
        severe wounds during combat action in the Solomons.

1951.   Smith, Holland M. CORAL AND BRASS. New York: Charles

Scribner's Sons, 1949. 289 pp.

This personal account is written mainly from memory, without the advantage of a diary or other personal records. In general, Smith feels that the Navy could have provided more support to his Marines. Nor does the prickly Marine general spare his criticism of the Army. On the controversial relief of Ralph Smith, the author calls the episode a distraction from the war effort.

1952. Taylor, Theodore. THE MAGNIFICENT MITSCHER. New York: W.W. Norton, 1954. 364 pp.

In this biography of Adm. Marc A. Mitscher (Deputy Chief of Naval Operations for Air), Taylor emphasized the seminal role of naval air power in the defeat of Japan. The admiral commanded the HORNET (that launched the Doolittle Raid) and served as the first carrier task force commander under Spruance and Halsey. The absence of a diary or other personal papers hampers a historical appraisal of Mitscher.

1953. Trudeau, Arthur G. ENGINEER MEMOIRS. Washington, D.C.: U.S. Army Corps of Engineers, 1986. 419 pp.

The book is based on an oral history interview Lt. Gen. (ret.) Trudeau granted in 1971 at the Army War College. Chief of staff of the new Engineer Amphibian Command, he selected a site in Australia for assembling pre-fabricated landing craft. The creation of his unit was a response to MacArthur's appeal for engineer amphibian troops. Later, as commander of Base X in Manila, Trudeau helped re-equip and prepare the 6th and 8th Armies for the invasion of Japan. Of special interest is the author's service with the War Crimes Tribunal. He is troubled by his understanding of MacArthur's orders essentially to use hearsay and circumstantial evidence when the sound evidence was exhausted.

1954. Vandegrift, A.A. ONCE A MARINE; THE MEMOIRS OF GENERAL A. A. VANDEGRIFT, U.S.M.C. New York: W.W. Norton, 1964. 338 pp.

The author commanded the 1st Marine Division at Guadalacanal. Thereafter, he served as commandant of the Marine Corps for the rest of the war. His distinguished career spanned the period 1909-1949. This inside view appears as told to Robert B. Asprey.

1955. Whitney, Cornelius Vanderbilt. LONE AND LEVEL SANDS. New

York: Farrar, Strauss and Young, 1951. 314 pp.

Col. Whitney served as an intelligence officer in the
USAAF. His duty included tours in India and the Pacific.
This personal account is of special interest because of
Whitney's association with top-level officers.

1956. Wiart, Carton de. HAPPY ODYSSEY. London: Pan Books,
1955.

Here are the memoirs of Churchill's personal
representative to Chiang Kai-Shek. The general handled
political and military affairs for the British under a
unified system Chiang could not get the Americans to adopt.
Of interest is Gen. Wiart's combat experiences in Europe,
including the serious wounds that he suffered.

IV.C. GRAND STRATEGY AND HIGH COMMAND

1957. Baldwin, Hanson W. STRATEGY FOR VICTORY. New York: W. W.
Norton, 1942. 172 pp.

As a respected writer on military affairs, Baldwin airs
his views about how America's enemies can be defeated.

1958. Bauer, K. Jack and Alan C. Coox. "Olympic vs. Ketsu-Go."
MC GAZ, 49 (August 1965), 32-44.

Bauer presents the American plan to assault Kyushu in
the fall of 1945 (Olympic), and Coox [Alvin D.?] describes
the corresponding Japanese defensive plans (Ketsu-Go).
Fortunately for everyone, the fierce final phase of the
war, as foretold in these plans, never occurred.

959. Brandt, William. "Pacific Strategy in an Indivisible War."
AMERASIA, 5 (February 1942), 530-534.

Brandt criticizes the purely defensive strategy designed
for the Pacific Theater.

960. Brett, Homer. BLUEPRINT FOR VICTORY. New York: Appleton-
Century, 1943. 215 pp.

In this wartime statement, consular officer Brett argues
that the United States must destroy Japan quickly--before
the Japanese incorporate their new holdings. Arguing
directly against the Europe-first strategy, he recommends
the use of Alaskan and Aleutian bases to devastate Japan
through aerial attacks.

1961.   Brower, Charles F. "Assault or Siege: The Debate Over
        Final Strategy for the Defeat of Japan, 1943-1945."
        JOINT PERSP, 2 (Spring 1982), 72-83.

        In general, one's service affiliation determined one's
        position in this debate. The Army favored an assault;
        the Navy and AAF wanted a siege. Relying mainly on
        published sources, Brower feels that political con-
        siderations dominated this entire process.

1962.   Butler, James R.M., ed. GRAND STRATEGY. London: HMSO,
        1956-1976. 6 vols.

        With this official history, the British have produced a
        masterpiece. Notwithstanding the predominantly British
        perspective, these volumes are indispensable to any study
        of the war.

1963.   Canella, Charles J. " Study in Combined Command: China-
        Burma-India." MIL REV, 45 (July 1965), 55-71.

        Criticizing the lack of central direction, the confused
        organizational structure, and the fact that national
        considerations were kept from the component commanders,
        Canella charges that CBI-SEAC military operations violated
        the basic concepts of military management.

1964.   Cook, Charles O., Jr. "The Pacific Command Divided: The
        'Most Unexplainable' Decision." USNIP, 104 (September
        1978), 55-61.

        Cook, a retired Naval officer, explains the divided
        command structure (i.e. MacArthur-SWPA, Nimitz-POA)
        within the context of high-level political maneuvering.
        With Roosevelt torn between his reluctance to appoint
        MacArthur to overall command and his awareness of
        MacArthur's widespread popularity, the JCS, according to
        Cook, helped ease Roosevelt's dilemma by recommending a
        divided system to the president in March 1942.

1965.   Davis, Frank. "Operation OLYMPIC: The Invasion of Japan:
        November 1, 1945." STRATEGY & TACTICS, 45 (1974), 4-20.

        NE

1966.   Day, David. "Promise and Performance: Britain's Pacific
        Pledge, 1943-45." WAR & SOC, 4 (September 1986), 71-93.

Incorporating British archival documents and private collections (including the under-used Ismay Papers), Day analyzes the reasons for three years of temporizing by the British to fulfill their pledge to defeat Japan and restore the Far Eastern portions of the empire. Day concludes that "creature comforts" and civilian production took precedence over British rhetoric.

1967. Earle, Edward Mead, ed. MAKERS OF MODERN STRATEGY. Princeton, NJ: Princeton University Press, 1971. 553 pp.

In this excellent collection, compiled with the collaboration of Gordon A. Craig and Felix Gilbert, see especially the article by Alexander Kiralfy, "Japanese Naval Strategy." Kiralfy offers a balanced assessment without failing to measure out both praise and criticism.

1968. Funk, Arthur L., ed. POLITICS AND STRATEGY IN THE SECOND WORLD WAR. Manhattan, KS: MA/AH, 1976. 112 pp.

Here is a collection of papers which were presented at a 1975 conference in San Francisco. The International Committee for the History of the Second World War, headed by Henri Michel, sponsored the meeting.

1969. Goralski, Robert and Russell W. Freeburg. OIL AND WAR: HOW THE DEADLY STRUGGLE FOR FUEL IN WW II MEANT VICTORY OR DEFEAT. New York: William Morrow, 1987. 320 pp.

The authors focus on oil as the strategic key to the war. In fact, they explain the defeat of the Axis in terms of oil. Their account is geared to the general public.

1970. Fukudome, Shigeri. "Strategic Aspects of the Battle Off Formosa." USNIP, 78 (December 1952), 1285-1295.

Admiral Fukudome, commander of the 2d Air Fleet at Formosa, explains how the loss of the Marianas led to the four part SHO-GUN plan to defend the Philippines, Ryukyus, Hokkaido-Kuriles, and the home islands. His account reveals the poor state of Japanese combat aircraft and the low number of qualified pilots available to try to implement these difficult plans (which called for air combat operations at night and/or in bad weather).

1971. Greenfield, Kent Roberts. AMERICAN STRATEGY IN WORLD WAR II: A RECONSIDERATION. Baltimore, MD: The Johns Hopkins Press, 1963. 145 pp.

The book reproduces four J.P. Young Lectures which
Greenfield delivered in 1962. The material Greenfield
presented by the former Chief Historian of the Department
of the Army provides an excellent synthesis. He analyzes,
for example, the competing priorities among the theaters
(in late 1942 more U.S. troops were fighting Japanese than
Germans, despite the agreed "Germany-first" strategy), the
need to follow through on the victory at Midway, the
offensive drives of both MacArthur and Nimitz, LeMay's
demonstration of what independent air power could
accomplish, and the necessity for invading Japan had the
surrender not come when it did. See, too, the author's
evaluation of Roosevelt who, according to Greenfield, acted
independently or against the advice of the chiefs of staff
from 1939 to 1941 but who, after Pearl Harbor, generally
followed almost all their advice--despite more than just a
few exceptions.

1972.   Greenfield, Kent Roberts, ed. COMMAND DECISIONS. New
            York: Harcourt, Brace, 1959. 481 pp.

Greenfield arranges a collection of essays by historians
involved in the official history of the U.S. Army in World
War II series. Some twenty decisions are analyzed. See
especially the studies on the war against Japan by Louis
Morton ([a] Japan's decision for war, [b] the decision to
withdraw to Bataan, and [c] the decision to use the atomic
bomb), John Miller on MacArthur and the Admiralties, Robert
Ross Smith on the strategic debate of Luzon-vs.-Furmosa,
and Stetson Conn on the decision to evacuate Japanese-
Americans from the West Coast. Virtually every essay in
the collection is thoroughly researched, well presented,
and thought provoking.

1973.   Greenfield, Kent Roberts, Robert R. Palmer, and Bell I.
            Wiley.   THE ORGANIZATION OF GROUND COMBAT TROOPS.
            Washington, D.C.: Historical Division, Dept. of the
            Army, 1947. 540 pp.

Here is some excellent material on the size,
organization, and deployment of Army units during the war.

1974.   Grigg, John. 1943, THE VICTORY THAT NEVER WAS. New York:
            Hill and Wang, 1980. 254 pp.

Although this British argument concentrates entirely on
the Allied failure to launch a second front in Europe
during 1943, the book is of interest to this guide because

of Grigg's view that American insistence on expending
resources in the Pacific contributed to strategic confusion
and distractions.

1975.   Horner, D.M. "Australia and Allied Strategy in the
             Pacific, 1941-1945." DEFENSE FORCE J,
             (November/December 1981), 45-54.

        NE

1976.   Huie, William Bradford. THE CASE AGAINST THE ADMIRALS.
             New York: E.P. Dutton, 1946. 216 pp.

        Huie criticizes the Navy for opposing both a unified
        command structure and the development of air power.
        Although his case is mainly built against the Navy (and its
        top-level admirals), Huie also charges the Army with being
        uncooperative.

1977.   Jacobs, W.A. "Strategic Bombing and American National
             Strategy." MIL AFFS, 50 (July 1986), 133-139.

        Jacobs argues that the United States did not adhere to
        the agreed-upon strategy of "Europe first." Precious war
        resources sent to the Pacific, he feels, hampered the
        strategic bombing of Germany.

1978.   Jones, D.P. "The Case Against CINCSEA." AF SPACE DIG, 50
             (October 1967), 104-108.

        Written during the Vietnam War, this article criticizes
        the double unified command structure (such as operated in
        the Pacific during World War II). Jones reminds readers
        that Stratemeyer in C-B-I did not lack for people telling
        him what to do. The article provides a useful summary of
        command and control problems in Southeast Asia in the war
        against Japan.

1979.   Kerr, Clayton P. THE ORGANIZATION OF THE PACIFIC OCEAN
             AREAS AND OF THE SOUTHWEST PACIFIC AREA. Norfolk, VA:
             Army & Navy Staff College, 1945. 31 pp.

        Col. Kerr (U.S.A.) gives a brief but useful explanation
        of the various Pacific organizations. His narrative points
        out the influence on organizational structure of geography,
        the size of forces in each area, and the pre-existing
        framework before the war.

1980.   Kiralfy, Alexander. VICTORY IN THE PACIFIC: HOW WE MUST

DEFEAT JAPAN. New York: John Day, 1942. 283 pp.

The author maintains that the entire Japanese system of war is unsound. Far overextended through its initial victories, Japan, according to Kiralfy, will soon pay dearly. As a naval analyst, he feels that the Japanese have assembled only an average army and navy and that the Japanese navy will not risk an all-out decisive engagement. Of interest is Kiralfy's contemporary argument against a war of attrition in retracing Japan's victories in favor of striking directly against Japan either in the Kurile Islands or perhaps through a Vladivostok-Sakhalin front.

1981.   Lott, Arnold S. "Japan's Nightmare--Mine Blockade."
        USNIP, 85 (November 1959), 39-51.

        Lott emphasizes the importance of the mining of Japan's inner zone (Operation STARVATION). Submarines and B-29s carried out the mining operation.

1982.   Lowenthal, Mark M. LEADERSHIP AND INDECISION: AMERICAN
        WAR PLANNING AND POLICY PROCESS, 1937-1942. New York:
        Garland, 1987. 2 vols.

        In his analysis of the formation of U.S. military strategy and foreign policy, Lowenthal concentrates on the process rather than the product. The author, an analyst with the Department of State, traces the influence of the British in this period. See especially his treatment of the global crises in 1937.

1983.   MacCloskey, Monro. PLANNING FOR VICTORY--WORLD WAR II: A
        BEHIND THE SCENES ACCOUNT. New York: Richard Rosen
        Press, 1970.

        NE

1984.   McCloy, John. "The Great Military Decisions." FOR AFFS,
        26 (October 1947), 52-72.

        In discussing these decisions with regard to the war against Japan, McCloy emphasizes the heroic stand at Britaan, the offensive against New Guinea, the Guadalcanal landing, the naval concentration at Midway, and the effective use of both submarines and strategic bombers. He omits the two atomic bombings.

1985.   Matloff, Maurice. "The Evaluation of Strategic Thought."
        NAV WAR COLL FORUM, n.v. (Spring 1971), 69-81.

The chief historian in the Army's Office of the Chief of
Military History observes that World War II embraced every
conceivable principle of war. U.S. strategic planners, he
observes, had plenty of advance notice for this war—a war
of corporate leadership, with large planning staffs in
Washington and in the headquarters of every theater.

1986. Matloff, Maurice and Edwin M. Snell. STRATEGIC PLANNING
        FOR COALITION WARFARE, 1941-1944. Washington, D.C.:
        Office of the Chief of Military History, Dept. of the
        Army, 1953-1959. 2 vols.

        Here is an excellent account of wartime planning, from
        the eve of the war to the final stages. With access to
        Army documents and records, the authors compile a
        first-rate history.

1987. Morgan, H.G. PLANNING THE DEFEAT OF JAPAN. Washington,
        D.C.: Office of the Chief of Military History, Dept. of
        the Army, 1961. 197 l.

        This publication reproduces a typescript which deals
        with the overall strategy of the war. The analysis is
        based on close research through Army files.

1988. Morison, Samuel Eliot. "Pacific Strategy." MC GAZ, Pt.
        I: 46 (August 1962), 34-40; Pt. II: 46 (September
        1962), 34-39.

        Morison takes a broad brushstroke of history in
        presenting an analysis of the strategy of the war in the
        Pacific. His favorable treatment of U. S. strategy,
        including the compromise between MacArthur and the Navy,
        contrasts sharply with his criticism of the "stupidity" of
        Japanese strategy.

1989. Morison, Samuel Eliot. STRATEGY AND COMPROMISE. Boston:
        Little, Brown, 1958. 120 pp.

        This slim volume examines the overall strategy of the
        Allies. His criticism of the important compromises are
        thought-provoking. Of interest, too, is Morison's
        authoritative analysis of Japan's strategy, which, he says,
        was fundamentally unsound.

1990. Morton, Louis. "Command in the Pacific, 1941-1945." MIL
        REV, 41 (December 1961), 76-88.

Because of service interests/prestige, personality
roles, doctrinal differences, and service rivalries, Morton
reports that the command structure in the Pacific had
turned full circle by 1945. Unified commands had been
established in 1942, but the United States gradually
abandoned that system. Morton points out, though, that by
1945 Spaatz, MacArthur, and Nimitz all enjoyed virtually
equal status.

1991. Morton, Louis. "Crisis in the Pacific." MIL REV, 46
       (April 1966), 12-21.

Here is a knowledgeable account of the Japanese
perspective from late 1943 to mid-1944. Having established
an Absolute National Defensive Line, the Japanese worried
most during this period about Nimitz's intrusion into the
Gilberts.

1992. Morton, Louis. "Japanese Policy and Strategy in Mid-War."
       USNIP, 85 (February 1959), 52-64.

Morton refutes the notion of Japanese inflexibility and
rigidity during the war. He examines the full-scale review
of the war effort in September 1943 by Japanese leaders
(including the emperor) which led to the creation of the
Absolute National Defense Line.

1993. Morton, Louis. "The Long Road to Unity of Command." MIL
       REV, 39 (January 1960), 3-12.

Here is an account of the evolution of a universally
recognized principle for U.S. armed forces.

1994. Morton, Louis. PACIFIC COMMAND: A STUDY IN INTERSERVICE
       RELATIONS. Colorado Springs, CO: US Air Force Academy,
       1961. 33 pp.

Here is the text of the Harmon Memorial Lecture in
Military History at the USAF Academy. Morton maintains
that prewar efforts to establish unity of command for the
Far East foundered in the rivalry between the Army and
Navy. For similar reasons, he says, no single commander
was appointed during the war, and the war's end saw three
main commands in the Pacific: Army, Navy, and strategic
bombardment forces. He does make clear, however, that the
haggling existed only in the rear areas (Washington,
Hawaii, and Australia) and not in the field.

1995. Morton, Louis. STRATEGY AND COMMAND: THE FIRST TWO YEARS.

Washington, D.C.: Office of the Chief of Miliary
History, Dept. of the Army 1962. 783 pp.

Despite some early uncertainty, Morton concludes that
the first two years of the war saw the development of the
winning combination throughout the top Army echelons. The
book is an outstanding example of official history at its
best.

1996. Prados, John. "The War Against Japan, 1941-1945."
       STRATEGY & TACTICS, 65 (1977), 27-32.

       NE

1997. Price, Willard. "The Case for Island Hopping." ASIA &
       AMERICAS, 44 (February 1944), 63-67.

       Arguing that China represents the key to victory, the
       author believes that island-hopping will provide the
       quickest method for the Allies to reach China.

1998. Renner, George T. "How to Win in the Pacific." AMER MAG,
       135 (June 1943), 48-49, 103.

       Renner, an author-geographer, calls for an alliance with
       the Soviet Union against Japan. His argument stresses that
       Japan is located "around the corner" from Alaska not
       "across the Pacific" from Australia.

1999. Reynolds, Clark G. "Maritime Strategy of World War II:
       Some Implications?" NAV WAR COLL REV, 39 (May-June
       1986), 43-50.

       Citing the two parts of maritime Allied strategy of
       neutralizing and defeating the enemy at sea and in the air
       while striking the enemy's home armies, Reynolds argues
       that Americans and British embraced the same maritime
       strategy with difference of emphasis and detail. For
       Reynolds, the key elements of the war in the Pacific were
       control of sea lines of communication, the air-sea
       isolation of Japan, and the bombing of home islands.

2000. Robertson, John. "Australia and the 'Beat Hitler First'
       Strategy, 1941-42: A Problem in Wartime Consultation."
       J IMP COMM HIST, 11 (May 1983), 300-321.

       With excellent research through British and Australian
       archival sources, Robertson describes a breakdown of
       communications in Australia's government. H.V. Evatt was

surprised, according to the author, to learn in December
1941 that Roosevelt and Churchill had already agreed upon a
strategy of beating Germany first. In this narrative,
Robertson highlights the roles of Bruce and Paige as well
as the British concern for secrecy.

2001. Rosenfarb, Joseph. HIGHWAY TO TOKYO. Boston: Little,
       Brown, 1943. 117 pp.

       The author, an American lawyer without expertise or
       training on Asian affairs, analyzes various wartime routes
       to Japan and concludes that the best way to defeat the
       Japanese is to begin working northward from the South
       Pacific.

2002. Slonim, Gilven M. "A Flagship View of Command Decisions."
       USNIP, 84 (April 1958), 80-89.

       Stressing the need to consider "atmosphere" in
       decision-making, Slonim gives an account of his observation
       (and participation) in several Pacific operations.

2003. Stirling, Yates, Jr. WHY SEA POWER WILL WIN THE WAR. New
       York: Frederick Fell, 1944. 319 pp.

       Stirling, a retired admiral, revives some of his
       published newspaper articles to deliver homage to the
       general concept of sea power and the specific resources of
       the U.S. Navy. Of interest is Stirling's rejection of the
       notion of a separate American air force.

2004. Stoler, Mark A. "The 'Pacific First' Alternative in
       American World War II Strategy." INTL HIST REV, 2 (July
       1980), 432-452.

       Taking issue with the notion that the case for a
       "Pacific First" strategy was merely a ploy to bluff the
       British into launching a second front in Europe (as
       Roosevelt, Stimson, and Marshall all believed), Stoler says
       that the American proposals for concerted action in the
       Pacific during 1942 and 1943 were serious. Although Stoler
       concurs that an element of bluff did exist, he feels that
       the American pressures led to major modification of
       Anglo-American strategy for the rest of the war. As a
       result, Roosevelt was pleased that the modification led to
       an increased flow of men and material to the Pacific.

2005. Tolley, Kemp. "Divided We Fell." USNIP, 92 (October
       1966), 36-51.

Noting that the principle of unified command--widely
recognized today--was not readily accepted on the eve of
the war, Tolley describes the lack of rapport between Hart
and MacArthur and between Hart and Glassford. Each of
these problems might not have been significant by itself,
say Tolley, but each contributed to the U.S. humiliation at
the start of the war.

2006. Van Courtland Moon, John Ellis. CONFINES OF CONCEPT:
        AMERICAN STRATEGY IN WORLD WAR II. New York: Garland,
        1987. 2 vols.

Moon analyzes U.S. strategy within various categories of
concepts. His view of the war describes a blend of sound
strategy with the need to improvise. Of interest is his
criticism that postwar plans were not implemented.

2007. Willmott, H.P. THE BARRIER AND THE JAVELIN: JAPANESE AND
        ALLIED PACIFIC STRATEGIES, FEBRUARY TO JUNE 1942.
        Annapolis, MD: Naval Institute Press, 1983. 596 pp.

The book focuses on the naval battles at Coral Sea and
Midway. Willmott calls the Japanese losses a
"catastrophe." With encyclopedic detail, he surveys this
1942 period and contends that U.S. strategic assessments
(and forces) outmatched those of Japan. For Willmott
Japan's strategy was seriously flawed through ineffective
dispersal of forces and confused intentions. The research
is exhaustive.

2008. Willmott, H.P. EMPIRES IN THE BALANCE: JAPANESE AND
        ALLIED PACIFIC STRATEGIES TO APRIL 1942. Annapolis, MD:
        Naval Institute Press, 1982. 487 pp.

The noted British military historian uses a
multi-national perspective to balance what he calls
"ethnocentric" accounts of the initial stage of the war.
The book ends with an episode which the author says held
great psychological importance, the Doolittle raid.
Analyzing the origins of the war, Willmott concludes that
the foreign policy objectives of the West were out of
alignment with defensive capabilities. The Japanese, on
the other hand, had virtually locked themselves on a course
that could lead only to war. Ironically, according to
Willmott, the eventual defeat of the Japanese was taking
shape during the months of their greatest successes. Here
is a sound military analysis that does not fail to offer
criticism or praise. The bibliography virtually exhausts

the secondary literature.

IV.D. Campaigns/Operations/Battles

  1. **Land**

    a. **Alaska**

2009. Hays, Otis E., Jr. "White Star, Red Star." ALASKA J, 12
       (Summer 1982), 9-17.

       Hays discusses the Alaska-Siberian Air Ferry Route,
       which began in September 1942 and lasted to 1945. Soviet
       pilots in Fairbanks flew Lend-Lease planes to the Soviet
       Union (with the American white star painted red). The
       author states that the Soviet pilots stuffed the aircraft
       with candy and luxury items (e.g., perfume, lingerie, and
       soap). The goal of the project was to ferry 142 planes per
       month.

2010. Marston, Muktuk. MEN OF THE TUNDRA: ESKIMOS AT WAR. New
       York: October House, 1969. 227 pp.

       With the creation of the Alaska Territorial Guard,
       Marston recruited Eskimos for service in the unit. His
       travels and experiences make interesting reading. The
       author criticizes the bureaucratic problems that hindered
       his efforts. Of interest is his report on the
       racial-social divisions in Alaska.

2011. Mills, Stephen E. ARCTIC WAR BIRDS: ALASKA AVIATION OF
       WORLD WAR II. Seattle, WA: Superior, 1971. 191 pp.

       This pictorial report on bush flying includes some
       material on the Aleutian campaign.

2012. Naske, Claus-M. "The Battle of Alaska Has Ended... and the
       Japs Won It." MIL AFFS, 49 (July 1985), 144-151.

       The author examines the wartime role of Governor Ernest
       Gruening of Alaska. Gruening was particularly critical of
       the controversial retaking of Attu and Kiska.

2013. Paneth, Philip. ALASKAN BACKDOOR TO JAPAN. London:
       Alliance Press, 1943. 108 pp.

       Here is a contemporary argument that the path to victory
       leads through Alaska and the northern route.

2014. Pocock, Arthur F. RED FLANNELS AND GREEN ICE. New York:
       Random House, 1949. 272 pp.

       Pocock reports on wartime life with the Coast Guard
       during a cruise, which included a stopover in Alaska. It
       is interesting and funny reading. See especially his
       descriptions of the Eskimos.

2015. Potter, Jean. ALASKA UNDER ARMS. New York: Macmillan,
       1942. 200 pp.

       The author, a professional writer, travelled and
       researched widely in Alaska to prepare this contemporary
       description of Alaska at war.

IV.D.1.b. Buna

2016. Heller, Charles E. and William A. Stofft, eds. AMERICA'S
       FIRST BATTLES, 1776-1965. Lawrence, KS: University
       Press of Kansas, 1986. 416 pp.

       The theme of this interesting collection is that the
       first battles in a war have a certain distinctiveness that
       often becomes obscured in history. For the war against
       Japan, see the article by historian Jay Luvaas on Buna.
       Despite problems in U.S. field leadership and despite the
       poor application of training doctrine, he judges the
       encounter a success for U.S. forces.

2017. Mayo, Lida. BLOODY BUNA. Garden City, NY: Doubleday,
       1974. 222 pp.

       Mayo had served in the Office of Chief of Military
       History. The engagement at Buna in January 1943 was the
       first major land victory for the Allies against the
       Japanese. The battle became one of attrition, in which the
       Americans and Australians out-supplied and outlasted the
       enemy. The author points out that the unnecessary amount
       of bloodshed fostered the cry of "no more Bunas." For
       Mayo, the importance of the battle lies in thwarting a
       Japanese invasion of Australia.

2018. United States. War Department. PAPUAN CAMPAIGN: THE
       BUNA-SANANANDA OPERATION. Washington, D.C.: War Dept.,
       1944. 107 pp.

       Here are the highlights of the campaign from November
       16, 1942 to January 23, 1943. The account is geared
       specifically to "military personnel and primarily for

wounded in hospitals." The campaign is described as a
tactical offensive, which in a larger sense was really a
defensive operation.

IV.D.1.c. Burma

2019. Allen, Louis. BURMA: THE LONGEST WAR, 1941-1945.
       New York: St. Martin's, 1985. 686 pp.

       Allen, an intelligence officer during the war who is
       familiar with the language and culture of Japan, draws a
       magnificent synthesis based on prodigious multi-archival
       research. His balanced approach presents the perspectives
       of the combatants. His accounts of a Japanese colonel
       eating the liver of an American pilot to show disrespect
       for the enemy (hunger did not spawn all incidents of
       cannibalism) and his careful analysis of how the
       adversaries viewed each other ("sex, race, class and
       aesthetic response") are just two examples of a book
       replete with insight and scholarship.

2020. Baggaley, James. A CHINDIT STORY. London: Souvenir,
       1954. 163 pp.

       Here is a personal account of the exploits of Wingate's
       special forces in Burma.

2021. Baker, Alan D. MERRILL'S MARAUDERS. New York: Ballantine
       Books, 1972. 159 pp.

       A brief, popular account of part of the campaign in
       Burma. Although designed to appeal to the general public,
       the narrative is based on solid research.

2022. Barnett, Correlli. "The Impact of Surprise and Initiative
       in War." RUSI, 129 (June 1984), 20-26.

       Using examples of Slim's leadership in Burma (e.g., at
       Meiktila and crossing the Irrawaddy), this British military
       historian concludes that surprise and excellent leadership
       can triumph over a superior-sized force.

2023. Barrett, Neil H. CHINGHPAW. New York: Vantage, 1962.
       173 pp.

       A brief, popular account of the campaign in Burma.

2024. Beaumont, Winifred H. A DETAIL ON THE BURMA FRONT.
       London: British Broadcasting Corporation, 1977. 160

pp.

Beaumont gives her personal account as a nurse in Burma
of the work of the medical service.

2025.   Bidwell, Shelford. THE CHINDIT WAR: STILWELL, WINGATE,
        AND THE CAMPAIGN IN BURMA: 1944. New York: Macmillan,
        1979. 304 pp.

        Criticizing the campaign in Burma during 1944, Bidwell
        labels the whole exercise a waste of effort and sacrifice
        since the defeat of Japan came about in the Pacific. He
        particularly disparages the goals--the Stilwell Road is
        called "a monument to a monumental misjudgment"--and
        methods used in waging the campaign. One of the strengths
        of the book is the author's comparison of American and
        British views on war-making, which unfolds as part of his
        balanced evaluations of Stilwell and Wingate.

2026.   Boyle, Patrick R. JUNGLE, JUNGLE, LITTLE CHINDIT. London:
        Hollis and Carter, 1946. 97 pp.

        Here is a humorous glimpse of the guerrilla war in
        Burma. Major Boyle served in one of the long-range
        penetration groups.

2027.   Broderick, Alan H. BEYOND THE BURMA ROAD. London:
        Hutchison, 1944. 112 pp.

        Here is a British perspective on the war effort in
        Burma.

2028.   Burchett, Wilfred G. WINGATE'S PHANTOM ARMY. London:
        Muller, 1946. 195 pp.

        Here is a popular account by a British writer of the
        famed long-range penetration groups in Burma.

2029.   Callahan, Raymond. BURMA, 1942-1945. Newark, DE:
        University of Delaware Press, 1978. 190 pp.

        Callahan describes the Burma campaign as a "barren
        victory" which had no political goals. Slim earns the
        author's praise above all other commanders.

2030.   Calvert, Michael. CHINDITS--LONG RANGE PENETRATION. New
        York: Ballantine Books, 1973. 159 pp.

        Calvert discusses the origins and tactics of the long-

range penetration groups in Burma. His assessment of the
controversial Wingate is balanced and restrained.

2031. Campbell, Arthur. THE SEIGE: A STORY FROM KOHIMA. New
        York: Macmillan, 1956. 211 pp.

        In March 1944 the Japanese launched an assault in Burma
        that was intended to carry them into India. Major
        Campbell, a British combat veteran, describes the defensive
        action by the Royal West Kents at Kohima. The heroics of
        the badly outnumbered unit helped thwart the Japanese
        drive.

2032. Caulfield, D.C. "The Bright Flame." MC GAZ, 48
        (October 1964), 41-46.

        Wingate is "the bright flame," and the author feels that
        valuable lessons can still be learned from the experiences
        of the Long Range Penetration Groups in Burma.

2033. Collins, Maurice. LAST AND FIRST IN BURMA. New York:
        Macmillan, 1956. 303 pp.

        The book deals with the period 1941-1948 and has as a
        backdrop the emerging nationalist aspirations. Of special
        interest is the extensive treatment of the controversial
        British governor, Sir Reginald Dorman-Smith.

2034. Dar, E.H. "Armoured Operations During the Early Phases of
        the Reconquest of Burma." ARMY Q DEF J, 101 (April
        1971), 342-349.

        The author, a lieutenant colonel in the Pakistan Army,
        concentrates on the period from December 1944 to March
        1945. Describing the exploits of the 14th Army, he draws
        attention to the effectiveness of the Sherman tanks.

2035. Davies, H.L. "A Background to the First Burma Campaign,
        1941-2." ARMY Q, 71 (January 1956), 218-227.

        Maj. Gen. Davies expresses pride in the men involved in
        this difficult campaign. He offers some background
        information on some of the causes of the Japanese victory.

2036. Eilxo, W.A. CHINDIT COLUMN 76. London: Longmans, Green,
        1945. 137 pp.

        Here is a short report on the fierce combat and
        conditions encountered in Burma. The focus is one element

of the long-range penetration groups.

2037.   Evans, Geoffrey and Antony Brett-James. IMPHAL: A
        FLOWER ON LOFTY HEIGHTS. London: Macmillan, 1962.
        348 pp.

        Although the Japanese suffered the worst defeat on land
        in their history at Imphal, little is known about this
        1944 battle. Here is a knowledgeable account by authors
        who are familiar with the geographical area and the history
        of the campaign. They provide a separate index of the
        units involved.

2038.   Fellowes-Gordon, Ian. THE MAGIC WAR: THE BATTLE FOR NORTH
        BURMA. New York: Scribner, 1972. 180 pp.

        This description of the campaign in Upper Burma is given
        by a British officer who led native tribesmen (Kachin).
        The author explains not only the guerrilla war he waged but
        also the cooperation his unusual force gave to the
        Americans, British, and Chinese. Stilwell earns his
        praise.

2039.   Fergusson, Bernard E. BEYOND THE CHINDWIN. London:
        Collins, 1945. 255 pp.

        The author commanded the Number Five Column of the
        1943 Wingate expedition. Although the narrative dwells
        chiefly on the exploits of his group rather than the
        entire operation, and although he admits that the
        expedition failed to realize many tangible accomplishments,
        Fergusson does argue that the value of the long-range
        penetration adventure lay in (a) proving it was possible
        and (b) worrying the Japanese.

2040.   Geren, Paul F. BURMA DIARY, New York: Harper & Brothers,
        1944. 57 pp.

        Despite its brevity, this book offers an image of the
        horrors of war. The diary covers Geren's first six months
        of the war. Many of the diary entries reveal his innermost
        feelings and thoughts.

2041.   Great Britain. Central Office of Information. THE
        CAMPAIGN IN BURMA. London: HMSO, 1946. 175 pp.

        This officially sanctioned summary is particularly
        effective in describing the 1943 preparations for the new
        South East Asia Command. Lt. Col. Frank Owen, an

experienced British propagandist-publicist in the Burma
campaign, wrote most of the narrative.

2042. Halley, David. WITH WINGATE IN BURMA. London: William
       Hodge, 1945. 189 pp.

       Life with the long-range penetration groups in Burma is
       described by one of the participants. The challenges and
       tolls taken by non-combat-related factors severely affected
       the performance of these irregular forces.

2043. Heilbrun, Otto. "The Future of Deep Penetration." ARMY Q
       DEF J, 98 (July 1969), 197-204.

       Upon examining the lessons learned from Operation
       THURSDAY, the second Chindit expedition into Burma in 1944,
       the author feels that long-range penetration groups are of
       limited military value.

2044. Hendershot, Clarence. "Burma's Value to the Japanese." FE
       SURVEY, 11 (August 10, 1942), 176-178.

       The author sees the value as being threefold: ending a
       threat to the Japanese flank, providing access to raw
       materials (and denying these to the Allies), and serving as
       a base for Japanese offensive operations against China.

2045. Hilsman, Roger. "Burma Ambush!" MC GAZ, 46 (January
       1962), 12-13.

       Hilsman, who later served in the Kennedy administration,
       relates his experiences in Burma with an OSS guerrilla
       battalion consisting of about two hundred Burmese and four
       Americans.

2046. Hiroshi, Fuwa. "Japanese Operations in the Hukawng
       Valley." MIL REV, 42 (January 1962), 48-63.

       Here is the saga of the Japanese 18th Division under
       Lt. Gen. Shinichi Tanaka. Between December 1943 and July
       1944, the unit--with no air support, badly outnumbered (3
       to 1), and decimated by illness--delayed the Sino-American
       advance through this valley in northern Burma.

2047. Ho, Yung Chi. THE BIG CIRCLE. New York: Exposition
       Press, 1948. 152 pp.

       China's role throughout the campaign in Burma is
       summarized. Ho uses Chinese primary sources.

2048. Hunter, Charles N. GALAHAD. San Antonio, TX: Naylor,
          1963. 233 pp.

          Here is a report on the challenges of campaigning in
       Burma (1943-1944).

2049. Kadel, Robert J., ed. WHERE I CAME IN. Paducah, KY:
          Turner Publications, 1986. 384 pp.

          The C-B-I Veterans Association sponsored this collection
       of personal accounts of the war in that theater. Many are
       humorous.

2050. Lathrop, Alan K. "The Employment of Chinese Nationalist
          Troops in the First Burma Campaign." J SEA STUD, 12
          (September 1981), 403-432.

          The author traces the Chinese role in the poorly
       prepared effort of the Allies during the first Burma
       campaign. British hesitation to accept Chiang's offer of
       troops insulted the Chinese. The article describes the
       military defeat and details the heavy losses suffered by
       the Chinese.

2051. London. Imperial War Museum. THE SECOND WORLD WAR: THE
          BURMA CAMPAIGN: LIST OF SELECTED TITLES, BOOKS AND
          PAMPHLETS. London: Imperial War Museum, 1960.

          The citations indicate British perspectives on the
       campaign.

2052. Lunt, James. A HELL OF A LICKING: THE RETREAT FROM BURMA,
          1941-1942. London: Collins, 1986. 318 pp.

          NE

2053. Lunt, James. "A Hell of a Licking: Some Reflections on
          the Retreat From Burma, December 1941-May 1942." RUSI,
          130 (September 1985), 55-58.

          The author, a battalion commander in Burma, feels the
       Allies suffered a defeat because of a poor strategic
       appreciation, poor training, and poor leadership.

2054. McCann, John A. "Airpower and 'The Man.'" AIRPOWER H, 6
          (April 1959), 108-124.

          Here is the story of Orde Wingate and how Gen. Arnold,

upon meeting him, committed American air support to
Wingate.

2055. MacHorton, Ian. THE HUNDRED DAYS OF LT. MACHORTON. New
        York: David McKay Co., 1962. 224 pp.

        Lt. MacHorton, in collaboration with Henry Maule,
        chronicles his experience as a nineteen-year-old on the
        first long range penetration group in Burma. He shared the
        troops' widespread respect for Wingate. Wounded in action,
        MacHorton was left behind (standard operating procedure)
        and spent one hundred days on his own trying to reach
        safety. His odyssey included being nursed back to health
        by a band of Nepalese who lived in Burma, another wound and
        capture by the Japanese, escape, and--after swimming across
        the Chindwin--facing death at the hands of a group of
        traitorous Sikhs. Finally, he made it. The book
        reminisces about life and combat with the LRPG.

2056. MacHorton, Ian with Henry Maule. SAFER THAN A KNOWN WAY:
        ONE MAN'S EPIC STRUGGLE AGAINST JAPANESE AND JUNGLE.
        London: Odhams Press, 1958. 224 pp.

        NE

2057. McLintock, James D. THE MANIPUR ROAD: STORY OF THE
        MANDALAY CAMPAIGN. Westport, CT: Associated Bookseller,
        1959. 158 pp.

        Here is a brief account geared to the general public.

2058. McLean, Donald B. MERRILL'S MARAUDERS, FEBRUARY-MAY 1944.
        Forest Grove, OR: Normount Armament Co., 1968. 117 pp.

        Here is a summary of some of the special operations in
        Burma. McLean's authoritative knowledge of technical
        information on armaments highlights the narrative.

2059. Mains, Tony. THE RETREAT FROM BURMA: AN INTELLIGENCE
        OFFICER'S PERSONAL STORY. London: Foulsham, 1973.
        151 pp.

        Mains recounts his harrowing 1942 experiences in fleeing
        from the Japanese forces in Burma.

2060. Masters, John. THE CHINDIT WAR: STILWELL, WINGATE AND THE
        CAMPAIGN IN BURMA: 1944.

        NE

2061. Masters, John. THE ROAD PAST MANDALAY. New York: Harper
       and Row, 1961. 341 pp.

       The author, a British officer who served in the Indian
       Army, tells of his combat experience in Burma. He offers
       interesting stories about some of the leading Allied
       personalities in the theater.

2062. Mead, Peter W. "The Chindit Operations of 1944" RUSI, 100
       (May 1955), 250-262.

       Displaying detailed knowledge of the campaign, Mead
       covers its four phases. In addition, he voices his
       reservations about the tactical results being worth the
       high cost.

2063. Mitchelmore, G. "The 'first' First Air Commandos." AIRMAN,
       14 (February 1970), 63-64.

       Here is a brief summary of the 1st Air Commandos and
       their participation in Wingate's long-range penetration
       campaign. The unit's commander, Col. Philip G. Cochran,
       inspired the Flip Corkin character created by cartoonist
       Milton Caniff.

2064. "Mobility in the Jungle." AIR U Q REV, 7 (Winter 1954-55),
       33-42.

       Here is an examination of the techniques of airborne
       invasion which Wingate and Cochran employed in 1944.
       Although the campaign fell short of optimistic
       expectations, the authors feel that this airborne concept
       holds great promise for the future.

2065. Moser, Don. CHINA, BURMA, INDIA. Alexandria, VA:
       Time-Life Books, 1978. 208 pp.

       Moser provides a knowledgeable, popular account of
       action in CBI.

2066. Moxon, Oliver. THE LAST MONSOON. London: Robert Hale,
       1957.

       Although not a work of fiction, the author does
       introduce fictional characters in this account of the
       Battle of Kohima in 1944. He concentrates on the aerial
       operations there, especially the work of the "Mandrake"
       Squadron of the 3d Tactical Air Force with the 14th Army.

Moxon is particularly adept at revealing the human side of these airmen.

2067. Ogburn, Charlton, Jr. THE MARAUDERS. New York: Harper and Brothers, 1959. 307 pp.

Ogburn served with Merrill's Marauders in Burma (GALAHAD). Later, he entered diplomatic service in the State Department. The book gives his account of the combat action. These personal reports about the fighting in Burma are important because of the scarcity of surviving documents.

2068. Owen, Frank. THE CAMPAIGN IN BURMA. London: HMSO, 1946. 175 PP.

Owen has broad experience with SEAC. His report on operations and personalities is uncharacteristically bland--perhaps because of the book's "official" nature. Must everything be a good show? The photos are excellent.

2069. Paline, Taung. "Merrill's Marauders." GUARDIAN, 28 (February 1978), 35-39.

NE

2070. Perrett, Bryan. TANK TRACKS TO RANGOON. London: R. Hale, 1978. 255 pp.

Perrett writes on tank warfare in the Burma campaign.

2071. Roberts, M.R. "Brief Outline of the Burma Campaign of 1941-1945." ARMY Q, 68 (July 1954), 180-197.

Brig. Roberts offers a comprehensive outline of the various phases of the Burma campaign. He praises Slim and seems annoyed that Stilwell held so many responsibilities. An excellent sketch map accompanies the article.

2071a. Roberts, M.R. "The Campaign in Burma, 1943-1945." RUSI, Pt. I: "The Turn of the Tide and the Decisive Battles," 101 (May 1956), 235-251; Pt. II: "The Reconquest," 101 (August 1956), 412-426.

Roberts shows his expertise in this close, detailed account. The article lacks an overall summation.

2072. Rolo, Charles J. WINGATE'S RAIDERS. New York: Viking Press, 1944. 147 pp.

From extensive interviews with Wingate's officers, Rolo reports on the first Burma expedition: the famed long-range penetration group of 1943. The focus of the story is the complex personality of Wingate, whom contemporaries were describing as "the new Lawrence of Arabia."

2072a. Safrani, Abid Hasan. THE MEN FROM IMPHAL. Calcutta, India: Netaji Research Bureau, 1971. 103 pp.

NE

2073. Saunders, Hilary A. St. G. THE GREEN BERET: THE STORY OF THE COMMANDOES, 1940-1945. London: Joseph, 1949. 362 pp.

This general account includes some information on irregular operations in Burma. Mountbatten wrote the Introduction.

2074. Sewell, Horace S. "The Campaign in Burma." FOR AFFS, 23 (April 1945), 496-504.

This straightforward narrative praises the work of Mountbatten's forces and the leadership of Slim and Stilwell.

2075. Shaw, James. THE MARCH OUT. London: Hart-Davis, 1953. 206 pp.

Here is an account of the final adventure of the Chindits in Burma. Shaw reports on the accomplishments-- and the weaknesses--of the famed long-range penetration groups.

2076. Sinclair, William Boyd. CONFUSION BEYOND IMAGINATION. Coeur d'Alene, ID: Joe F. Whitley, 1986. 329 pp.

Here is the start of a remarkable personal undertaking. Col. Sinclair (USAF, ret.) served as associate editor of CBI ROUNDUP in 1944-1945. His project is planned for ten volumes (or books) and will uncover his personal history (not an autobiography) of events and personalities in CBI. The title, a play on CBI, springs from the traditional skepticism and irreverence in all wars at the footsoldier's level. Book I is subtitled JUNGLE PADDY AND MOUNTAIN HEROES, AWARDED AND UNREWARDED MUD, GRAVEL, RUTS, AND ROCKS. The work is filled with anecdotes, humor, tragedy,

rumors, gossip, colorful personalities--all filtered
through Sinclair's perspective. (Can you imagine the rage
of the Japanese soldier who could think of nothing worse to
shout than "Eleanor eats powdered eggs!") Sinclair's saucy
style occasionally lapses into the "wiseacre" category, but
this is a refreshingly fresh approach to a forsaken
theater. The photos are exceptional. Book II will examine
the air war.

2077.   Smith, E.D. BATTLE FOR BURMA. New York: Holmes and
          Meier, 1979. 190 pp.

          Smith incorporates a number of personal accounts by
participants in retelling some highlights of the campaign
in Burma.

2078.   Smith, Philip R., Jr. "Jungle Fighters." ARMY DIG, 26
          (May 1971), 10-13.

          Here is an account of the operations of Merrill's
Marauders (5307 Composite Unit--PROV), formed in late 1943.
Not many lived to see the final victory in North Burma.

2079.   Snelling, A.H.J. Pt. I: "Some Fourteenth Army
          Administrative Problems." ARMY Q, 53 (January 1947),
          219-230; Pt. II: "More Fourteenth Army Administrative
          Problems." ARMY Q, 54 (April 1947), 49-65.

          Maj. Gen. Snelling describes the nightmarish logistical
problems which hampered the Burma campaign. He says that
the Battle of Imphal Plain was the greatest defeat ever
inflicted upon the Japanese army, but administrative
problems, especially the setting of priorities within
seriously overloaded lines of communication, made it
difficult to follow through on the advantage. The article
contains helpful sketch maps as well as an interesting
section on the unit's duck breeding efforts.

2080.   Stone, James H. "The Marauders and the Microbes."
          INFANTRY J, 44 (March 1949), 4-11.

          The author describes the debilitating effects of
amoebas, bacteria, rickettsiae, and viruses on Merrill's
Mauraders. Intending no criticism of U.S. command, Stone
points out that the static defensive positions assigned to
the unit exacerbated the situation.

2081.   Swinson, Arthur. KOHIMA. London: Cassell, 1966. 275 pp.

The author served under Slim in this key battle which
turned the Allied fortunes of the war in Assam. Given the
difficult terrain, which all but precluded the maneuvering
movements of large formations, Swinson stresses the
importance of small units in the battle. Swinson sorts out
the controversy surrounding Grover's Second Division, and
the author carefully analyzes the decisions and ideas of
the four leading generals.

082. Tainsh, Alsadair R. AND SOME FELL BY THE WAYSIDE: AN
      ACCOUNT OF THE NORTH BURMA EVACUATION. Bombay, India:
      Orient Longmans, 1948. 175 pp.

      NE

083. Tan Pei-Ying. "How They Worked on the Burma Road." ASIA &
      AMERICAS, 45 (September 1945), 443-448.

      The author, a construction supervisor on the Burma Road,
      describes the perseverance of the workers, including women
      and children, throughout the ordeal.

084. Tan Pei-ying. THE BUILDING OF THE BURMA ROAD. New York:
      McGraw-Hill, 1945. 200 pp.

      Here is a contemporary account of the long, physical
      ordeal of carving out the famous land line.

085. Thomas, Lowell. BACK TO MANDALAY. New York: Greystone
      Press, 1951. 320 pp.

      Here is a narrative about Col. Phillips Cochrane and the
      American role in the operations of the Long Range
      Penetration Group led by Wingate. This adventure story is
      geared to a popular audience.

086. Tinker, Hugh. "A Forgotten Long March: The Indian Exodus
      From Burma, 1942." J SEA STUD, 6 (March 1975), 1-15.

      This tale of Indian inhabitants in Burma seeking refuge,
      Tinker admits, carries no significant historical lesson but
      does portray a record of human endurance. Despite the
      shortcomings of the Burma government and obvious British
      discrimination, the author argues that the British actually
      could exert very little control over these Indians.

087. Turnbull, Patrick. BATTLE OF THE BOX. London: I. Allen,
      1979. 144 pp.

Turnbull provides a well-researched account of the
campaigning in Burma. Of interest, too, is the material on
Japanese occupation policies and practices.

2088. United States. Department of the Army. Forces in the Far
       East. BURMA OPERATIONS RECORD. Washington, D.C.:
       Office of the Chief of Military History, 1958. 24 pp.

This monograph, revised from the 1952 version, describes
HA-GO operations by the 28th Japanese Army in the Akyab
area.

2089. United States. Department of the Army. Japan. BURMA
       OPERATIONS RECORD: 15TH ARMY OPERATIONS IN IMPHAL AREA
       AND WITHDRAWAL TO NORTHERN BURMA. Washington, D.C.:
       Office of the Chief of Military History, 1957. 189 pp.

Another in the series of Japanese monographs, this study
focuses on operations in Burma, especially Japanese
attempts to counter Wingate's long-range penetration
forces. The 1944 forray by Wingate upset Japanese plans to
complete the Imphal campaign. Of note is the "great
mistake" by the Japanese forces: the inability to disrupt
the Allied cooperation between ground and tactical air
forces.

2090. United States. Office of Strategic Services. FORCES OF
       OPPOSITION TO THE JAPANESE IN BURMA. Washington, D.C.:
       OSS, 1945. 4 l.

This report is compiled with an eye to postwar political
affairs in Burma.

2091. Vote, Robert. "Merrill's Marauders." AMER HIST ILLUS, 18
       (June 1983), 40-47.

Vote feels that the "Marauder" nickname is well
justified given a series of "off-duty offenses" by members
of the unit. His narrative highlights the role of NISEI
interpreter Sgt. Roy H. Matsumoto and the Allied victory at
Myitkyina. Describing the physical deterioration of the
unit, Vote reports that the Marauders trickled away and
ceased to exist.

IV.D.1.d. China/Manchuria/Korea

2092. Achkasov, V.I. and M.F. Iur'ev. "China's War of Liberation
       and the Defeat of Imperialist Japan: The Soviet Role."
       SOVIET STUD HIST, 24 (Winter 1985-86), 39-68.

The authors maintain that the entry of the Soviet Union into the war caused the Japanese to surrender. In praising the Soviet combat role in Manchuria, the authors insist that the Kwantung Army was not a weak force, as Western revisionists have argued. Of some interest in this article is the description of Soviet aid, especially arms and pilots, to China in the 1930's. The authors feel that the KMT, with its feudal-militaristic relationships, had the fundamental weakness of lacking a sense of unity with its soldiers.

2093.   Ammon, Georgy. "Tactical Amphibious Assaults." SOVIET MIL REV, No. 3 (March 1986), 55-56.

Capt. Ammon summarizes the major amphibious assaults by the Soviet Union. The first noteworthy assault by the Soviets in the Pacific War came against the Korean port of Seishin on August 13, 1945. The author provides some statistics on this three-day battle.

2094.   Betit, Eugene D. "The Soviet Manchurian Campaign, August 1945: Prototype for the Soviet Offensive." MIL REV, 56 (May 1976), 65-73.

Captain Betit (USA) summarizes the Soviet campaign in Manchuria which caught the Japanese unawares. Based on the possible lessons learned from the campaign, he cautions future planning about Soviet strategy and tactics.

2095.   Brugger, Bill. CHINA: LIBERATION AND TRANSFORMATION, 1942-1962. Totowa, NJ: Barnes-Noble, 1981. 288 pp.

Brugger, a professor in Australia, contrasts the wartime performances of the Chinese Communists and the Kuomintang. In his view, the former far outpaced the latter. Much of the book is devoted to postwar events in China.

2096.   Burr, Samuel E. CHINA A.P.O.: MORE THAN EXPERIENCE: A STORY OF THE CHINA THEATER, 1944-1945. Highstown, NJ: Burr Publishing, 1982. 209 pp.

In a light-hearted as well as serious vein, Burr provides an account of his experiences in China.

2097.   Buss, Claude A. WAR AND DIPLOMACY IN EASTERN ASIA. New York: Macmillan, 1941. 570 pp.

In this readable, balanced report, the author provides

an excellent overview of the Sino-Japanese War. Buss, a
political scientist, served at the time as an adviser to
the American high commissioner in the Philippines.

2098.   China, Ministry of Information. CHINA AFTER FIVE YEARS OF
        WAR. New York: Chinese News Service, 1942. 233 pp.

        This report covers the period July 1937 to June 1942.
        The articles are grouped into five categories: government,
        military affairs, economic efforts, administration, and
        education-society. Almost all the articles are written by
        staff members at the Ministry of Information. The quality
        of the writing is, at best, "uneven" and, to say the least,
        "sympathetic."

2099.   China, Ministry of Information. INSIDE WARTIME CHINA.
        Chungking: Prabasi Press, 1943. 100 pp.

        Here is a pictorial review--officially sanctioned--of
        the war in China.

2100.   Cohen, Warren I. "Who fought the Japanese in Hunan? Some
        Views of China's War Effort." J ASIAN STUD, 27
        (November 1967), 111-115.

        Using new documents released in 1962 (after being held
        for five years to avoid upsetting Taiwan), Cohen reports
        that the fierce fighting by the Chinese in Hunan was
        accomplished not by forces loyal to Chiang Kai-shek--as the
        Taiwan regime now claims--but by troops under the
        independent Gen. Hseuh Yueh. In fact, Cohen writes that
        the general's troops were supplied with U.S. arms over the
        objections of the KMT. Cohen finds no evidence to
        contradict the view that armies under Chiang had virtually
        stopped fighting in 1942.

2101.   Conroy, F. Hilary. "Japan's War in China: Historical
        Parallel to Vietnam?" PAC AFFS, 43 (1970), 61-72.

        Conroy maintains that Americans have paid little atten-
        tion to the rationale behind Japan's war in China.
        Through an excellent bibliographical survey of the
        Japanese presence in China, she tracks the changing
        Japanese rationale to its ultimate conclusion: self
        defense. There are chilling parallels between the
        internal debates in Japan during the 1930s and in the
        United States during the 1960s.

2102.   Conroy, F. Hilary. "Japan's War in China: An Ideological

Somersault." PAC H R, 21 (November 1952), 367-379.

Conroy's article shows that righteous conviction and
self-delusion are not always easily separated. When the
Japanese first intervened in China, Conroy points out, they
explained their action as being in the best interests of
Japan and China within the overall context of the revival
of Asia. For the Japanese, the initial resistance they
encountered in China was from extremists (like Chiang
Kai-shek and the KMT). The author, however, identifies the
ideological maneuverings of the Japanese as it shifted to
an announced goal of anti-communism and then linked the war
in China to an anti-West crusade.

2103. Coox, Alvin D. "The Myth of the Kwantung Army." MC GAZ,
        42 (July 1958), 36-43.

Coox dismisses this supposedly formidable force as "a
colossal bluff." Although the Kwantung Army deeply
influenced Americans and Russians in the war, Coox shows
how its strength had been drained almost entirely by 1945.
His solid research effort incorporates many interviews with
Japanese who are knowledgeable in the affairs of the
Kwantung Army.

2104. Dobbs, Charles M. "American Marines in North China,
        1945-1946." S ATL Q, 76 (SUMMER 1977), 318-331.

Based largely on published works, this article delves
into the experiences of the fifty thousand Marines sent to
North China ostensibly to accept the surrender of five
hundred thousand Japanese troops. The author believes that
the real reason for this assignment was to contain the
Chinese Communists. The Marines, despite some excesses,
tried to ease tensions in China, according to Dobbs, but
they became entangled with the two opposing forces and
withdrew in early 1947.

2105. Dorn, Frank. THE SINO-JAPANESE WAR, 1937-1941. New York:
        Macmillan, 1974. 477 pp.

Dorn, with extensive experience in China, writes
knowledgeably about this conflict. His account is
especially useful in setting the scene for active American
participation in the war. He describes the events and
personalities with an ease that few Americans can match.

2106. Dzirkals, Lilita. "LIGHTNING WAR" IN MANCHURIA. Santa
        Monica, CA: Rand Corp., 1976. 116 pp.

NE

2107.   Ekman, Michael E. "The 1945 Soviet Manchurian Campaign: A
        Model for Sino-Soviet WaR." NAVAL WAR COLL REV, 27
        (JULY-AUGUST 1974), 81-89.

        Based on the premise that a future Sino-Soviet war would
        "probably follow" the same pattern as in Manchuria in 1945,
        this article focuses on the Soviet campaign which brought
        victory in just over one hundred days.

2108.   Fontenot, Gregory. "The Promise of COBRA: The Reality of
        Manchuria." MIL REV, 65 (September 1985), 54-62.

        This article examines the operational style of the
        Soviet Union. Pointing out that the Soviets had learned
        much from the war in Europe, Major Fontenot (USA) is
        clearly impressed with the skill and sound doctrine--
        agility, initiative, depth, synchronization--of the Soviets
        in the Manchurian campaign. He compares the Soviet
        successes to the less favorable U.S. COBRA operation in the
        Norman bocage under Gen. Bradley.

2109.   Frost, Edwin C. "China Convoy." AEROSPACE H, 30 (Spring,
        March 1983), 15-23.

        Here is the personal account of an automotive mainten-
        ance officer who travelled with a convoy over the Stilwell
        Road in May-June 1945. Frost claims that no formal report
        exists on this particular operation.

2110.   Frolov, B. "The Final Blow." SOVIET MIL REV, No. 8
        (August 1985), 39-43.

        Arguing that the entry of the Soviet Union (not the
        atomic bombings) forced Japan to surrender, Frolov
        describes the Soviet victory over the Kwantung Army in
        Manchuria (600,000 POWs). In his view, this victory formed
        the premise for the end of Western imperialism and
        revolutions in China, North Korea, and Vietnam.

2111.   Garthoff, Raymond L. "Marshal Malinovsky's Manchurian
        Campaign." MIL REV, 46 (October 1966), 50-61.

        Between April and August 1945, the Soviet Union moved
        about 1.5 million troops to the east. Malinovsky directed
        one of the three fronts established by the special high
        command under Vasilevsky. The Soviet lightning strike

surprised and overwhelmed the Japanese.

2112. Garthoff, Raymond L. "Soviet Intervention in Manchuria,
       1945-1946." ORBIS, 10 (Summer 1966), 520-547.

       The author argues that the Soviets' decision to
       intervene in the war was advanced to an earlier date,
       prompted by the first atomic bombing. In describing the
       campaign in Manchuria, he carries the story forward to the
       triumph of the Chinese Communists because, for him, the two
       events are closely related. Of interest is his report of
       Soviet probes along the Manchurian border in July, August
       and December 1944. Garthoff notes that the Soviets gave up
       most of their special rights in Manchuria by 1955 and that
       even the Soviet Consulate there was closed in 1962.

2113. Garthoff, Raymond L. "The Soviet Manchurian Campaign,
       August 1945." MIL AFFS, 33 (October 1969), 312-336.

       The author, a counselor in the U.S. mission to NATO,
       describes the organization of the Soviet Special High
       Command in the Far East and what he calls the "remarkable
       achievement" of marshaling troops and resources after four
       difficult years of war in Europe. Of interest is his
       report that, of the 600,000 Japanese prisoners taken in
       Manchuria, over 513,000 had been repatriated by April 1950.

2114. Garthoff, Raymond L. "Soviet Operations in the War With
       Japan, August 1945." USNIP, 92 (May 1966), 50-63.

       Observing that the Soviet naval and landing operations
       have been neglected by military historians, Garthoff points
       out that Soviet amphibious operations were largely
       uncontested. Where opposition arose, however, such as at
       Chongjin and Shimushu, the Japanese defenders exposed
       shortcomings in Soviet planning and performance.

2115. Gayn, Mark J. and John C. Caldwell. AMERICAN AGENT. New
       York: Henry Holt, 1947. 220 pp.

       Caldwell ("as told to" Gayn) relates his experiences as
       the son of American missionaries in China and, later, as an
       OWI agent in Fukien Province. Most of his OWI work
       involved disseminating propaganda. Of interest is his
       interaction with the Chinese Communists. Here is a good
       picture of life in one part of wartime China.

2116. Glantz, David M. AUGUST STORM. Vol. I: THE SOVIET 1945
       STRATEGIC OFFENSIVE IN MANCHURIA; Vol. II: SOVIET

TACTICAL AND OPERATIONAL COMBAT IN MANCHURIA, 1945. Ft.
Leavenworth, KS: U. S. Army Command and General Staff
College, 1983. 448 pp.

Lt. Col. Glantz (USA), using Soviet sources and cross-
checking Japanese historical accounts, highlights the
techniques of the Soviets at various levels of command.
This was not an easy campaign, says the author, who argues
that the Kwantung Army, while not up to its effectiveness
in 1941, proved a difficult foe. Using eight case studies
to examine vital parts of the campaign, Glantz concludes
that the Soviets demonstrated both initiative and
flexibility in the execution of assignments and displayed
meticulous planning at all levels.

2117. Gorelov, G. "Rout of the Kwantung Army." SOVIET MIL REV,
No. 8 (August 1970), 36-39.

Describing the three-pronged Soviet offense
in Manchuria, the author emphasizes the decisive role of
that campaign in forcing Japan to surrender.

2118. Grayson, Benson Lee. "Soviet Military Operations in the
Far East--1945." MIL ENGR, 50 (January-February 1958),
41-45.

Grayson seems to question if any lessons can be drawn
from this campaign by the "free world." According to him,
the Japanese Kwantung Army was only a poor shadow in 1945,
so that the outcome of the military operation was never in
doubt.

2119. Great Britain. Ministry of Information. THE WAR IN CHINA.
London: HMSO, 1945. 9 pp.

This brief report does little more than give an official
outline of British participation in the war in China.

2120. Grimsdale, G.E. "War Against Japan in China." RUSI, 95
(May 1950), 260-267.

The author looks at the importance of the China Theater
to the United Nations. He criticizes Chiang Kai-shek's
dictatorial methods as well as Stilwell's stubborn
insistence on his "schemes" in Burma. Chennault's plans to
strengthen air power earn Grimsdale's approval. The
conclusion is hardly startling: it is difficult to wage
war while the personalities at the top clash.

121.   Harrison, John A. "The USSR, Japan and the End of the
            Great Pacific War." PARAMETERS, 14 (Summer 1984),
            76-87.

        Here is a scholarly account of the last months of the
        war against Japan. The main focus is on the deteriorating
        Soviet-Japanese diplomatic relations and the campaign in
        Manchuria.

122.   Hu, Pu-Yu. A BRIEF HISTORY OF THE SINO-JAPANESE WAR.
            Taipei, Taiwan: Chung Wu Publishing, 1974. 358 pp.

        Adopting the view that "he who is on the right road is
        helped," Hu extols the leadership of Chiang Kai-shek. The
        author argues that the Russians and Chinese Communists
        stole the fruits of the victory over Japan, and he calls
        for a return of the Nationalists to the mainland.

123.   Hutchings, Graham. "A Province at War: Guangxi During the
            Sino-Japanese Conflict, 1937-1945." CHINA Q, No. 108
            (December 1986), 652-679.

        With extensive research from Chinese sources, the author
        concludes that, despite the enormous sacrifices, the war
        resolved little in the strained relations between this
        province and the central government. The article offers a
        detailed examination of the various stages and the effects
        of the war on Guangxi.

124.   Ivanov, S. "Victory in the Far East." SOVIET MIL REV,
            n.v. (August 1975), 2-5.

        Gen. Ivanov served as chief of staff of the High Command
        for Soviet forces in the Far East under Vasilevsky. He
        describes the difficult but successful maneuvering of
        Soviet tanks in both mountainous (Gen. A. Kravchenko) and
        marshy (Marshal K. Meretskov) terrain. According to the
        author, the war would have lasted another 18 months without
        the Soviet entry, and Soviet forces faced Japanese forces
        numbering 1.2 million.

125.   Lindsay, Michael. THE UNKNOWN WAR: NORTH CHINA,
            1937-1945. London: Bergstrom and Boyle, 1975. 116 pp.

        Here is the only photographic record by a foreign
        observer of Chinese Communist activities from 1938 to 1944.
        Working with the communists, Linday provides a favorable,
        multi-faceted description. Of interest is Linday's reports
        that Patrick J. Hurley despised the Chinese as hopeless

people and that Mao offered concessions in late 1945 to
avoid civil war.

2126. Loo, Pin-fei. IT IS DARK UNDERGROUND. New York: G.P.
       Putnam's Sons, 1946. 200 pp.

       In this unusual story of the resistance, the author
       describes his work with Chinese youths (the FIRE GODS) in
       sabotage, assassinations, and other anti-Japanese
       activities. Even allowing for the exaggerations that
       inevitably creep into reports like these, the author and
       his fellow conspirators do seem to have made a
       contribution. Of interest is his admission that some
       (many?) Chinese youths refused to resist the Japanese.

2127. Mears, Helen. THE YEAR OF THE WILD BOAR. Philadelphia,
       PA: J. B. Lippincott, 1942.

       Mears writes of her experiences while living in Japan
       during the China Incident.

2128. Miller, John R. "The Chiang-Stilwell Conflict, 1942-1944."
       MIL AFFS, 43 (Spring, March 1979), 59-62.

       According to the author, Chiang could not suspend
       politics to fight the war. Thus, because of catering to
       certain narrow interests (e.g., CC Clique, Whampoa Clique),
       Chiang could not follow the military advice of Stilwell.

2129. Miller, J.G. "The Mad Monks." MC GAZ, 52 (November 1968),
       45-48.

       Here are some exploits of Unit One (SACO), which
       harassed Japanese occupation forces in the Shanghai-Nanking
       region. In trying to avoid reminders of the unequal
       treaties, Milton E. Miles wanted to keep "Old China Hands"
       out of SACO. The author maintains that Miles's
       organization had no ideological overtones.

2130. Nikolaev, Nikolai N. THIRTY YEARS SINCE THE VICTORY OVER
       MILITARIST JAPAN. Moscow: Novosti, 1975. 63 pp.

       The author recalls the role of the Soviet forces in
       causing the defeat of Japan. In his opinion, the West has
       slighted the contribution of the Red Army's campaign in
       Manchuria.

2131. Pan, Stephen Chao-Ying. CHINA FIGHTS ON. New York:
       Fleming H. Revell, 1945. 188 pp.

This account of China's war effort and inter-Allied relations stretches from 1931 to the Dumbarton Oaks conference (where the author served as a technical consultant for the Chinese delegation).

2132.   Payne, P.S.R. CHINESE DIARIES, 1941-1946. New York: Waybright and Talley, 1970. 403 pp.

This British correspondent reveals his private observations and ideas about China and the war.

2133.   Payne, P.S.R. FOREVER CHINA. New York: Dodd, Mead, 1945. 573 pp.

The diary entries of this British correspondent cover the period December 1941 to April 1944. Payne offers insightful views on the Chinese people and their wartime suffering.

2134.   Petukhov, V. "The U.S.S.R.: Korea's Liberator and Reliable Ally." FE AFFS (Moscow), (No. 3, 1985), 36-45.

NE

2135.   Plotnikov, G. "Liberation Mission in the East." SOVIET MIL REV, n.v. (August 1980), 12-14.

Col. Plotnikov extols the accomplishments of the Soviet military forces in Asia.

2136.   Pollock, John C. A FOREIGN DEVIL IN CHINA. Minneapolis, MN: World Wide Publishers, 1971. 251 pp.

Pollock writes about the experiences of L. Nelson Bell, a surgeon who lived in China until mid-1941. Here is a useful description of life in war-torn China.

2137.   Quigley, Harold S. FAR EASTERN WAR, 1937-1941. Boston: World Peace Foundation, 1942. 369 pp.

Here is a rich source of information on the war in China. Quigley includes the text of many public documents and statements to his summary-narrative. His report is strongest in economic affairs.

2138.   Rothwell, Richard B. "Shanghai Emergency." MC GAZ, 56 (November 1972), 45-53.

          In August 1937, American Marines in China labored to
     protect U.S. property without jeopardizing U.S. neutrality.
     Rothwell reports that not one American life was lost in an
     area where one million Japanese and Chinese soldiers
     battled each other.

2139. "Shanghai, 1937-1938: How Bittersweet It Was." USNIP, 100
          (November 1974), 79-91.

          This account provides pictures of the 4th Marines
     detachment and conditions at Shanghai during the Japanese
     occupation. The late Sgt. Major Albert C. Marts (U.S.M.C.)
     took the pictures which are presented here by Prof. Robert
     M. Leventhal.

2140. Shickin, Iosif. "The Last Chapter of the Second World
          War." SOC SCIENCES, I (January-March 1972).

          NE

2141. Sih, Paul K.T., ed. NATIONALIST CHINA DURING THE
          SINO-JAPANESE WAR, 1937-1945. Hicksville, NY:
          Exposition Press, 1977. 435 pp.

          Here is a collection of papers by Canadian, American,
     and Chinese (R.O.C.) scholars. Some of the topics
     addressed are the origins of the war, overall strategy,
     economic development, regional politics, and the
     Sino-Soviet treaty.

2142. Stratton, Roy. "Navy Guerrilla." USNIP, 89 (July 1963),
          83-87.

          Stratton profiles Capt. Milton E. Miles, the first
     director of the Far Eastern Branch of OSS.

2143. Sunderland, Riley. "The Secret Embargo." PAC HR, 29
          (February 1960), 75-80.

          The secret embargo was imposed by Chiang Kai-shek. He
     forbade arms shipments to Chinese forces defending
     airfields during the Japanese offensive in 1944. According
     to Sunderland, Stilwell probably saved the Sino-American
     alliance by concealing the embargo from Washington.

2144. "Two Battlefields in the War Against Japan." E HORIZON, 17
          (July 1978), 38-43.

          Here is the perspective of the Chinese Communists, which

contrasts the KMT front with the front of liberated areas.

2145.   Tsou, Tang. "The Historians and the Generals." PAC HR, 31
          (February 1962), 41-66.

          The author surveys the arguments for and against the use
        of the Chinese Communists in the war. Citing U.S.
        eagerness for military victory, Tsou believes that American
        calls for a coalition government in China and more vigorous
        persecution of the war stemmed from U.S. misjudgments about
        both postwar Soviet intentions and the commitment of the
        Chinese Communists to communism. Of interest is Tsou's
        charge that Wedemeyer, despite postwar disavowals,
        supported the idea of a coalition government.

2146.   United States. Department of the Army. Forces in the Far
          East. ARMOR OPERATIONS. Washington, D.C.: Office of
          the Chief of Military History, 1957. 154 pp.

          This work provides an authoritative version of the
        campaign in Manchuria by Japanese armored units.

2147.   United States. Department of the Army. Forces in the Far
          East. ARMY OPERATIONS IN CHINA. Washington, D.C.:
          Office of the Chief of Military History, 1956. 2 vols.

          Here is a detailed narrative of Japanese Army operations
        in China from 1937 to 1945. The authors are Japanese
        officers who participated in these operations.

2148.   United States. Department of the Army. Forces in the Far
          East. CHINA AREA OPERATIONS RECORD. Washington, D.C.:
          Office of the Chief of Military History, 1952. 126 pp.

          Here is a report on the logistical operations of the
        Sixth Area Army.

2149.   United States. Department of the Army. Forces in the Far
          East. CHINA AREA OPERATIONS RECORD: COMMAND OF THE
          CHINA EXPEDITIONARY ARMY. Washington, D.C.: Office of
          the Chief of Military History, 1952. 194 pp.

          The Japanese authors of this work served in China.
        Their report focuses on the command functions in China from
        August 1943 to the end of the war.

2150.   United States. Department of the Army. Forces in the Far
          East. JAPANESE PREPARATIONS FOR OPERATIONS IN
          MANCHURIA, JANUARY 1943-AUGUST 1945. Washington, D.C.:

Office of the Chief of Military History, 1953.   199 pp.

This authoritative account provides information on the
preparations of the Kwantung Army in Manchuria for
operations against the Soviet Union.

2151.   United States. Department of the Army. Forces in the Far
        East. OPERATIONS IN THE KUN-LUN-KUAN AREA. Washington,
        D.C.: Office of the Chief of Military History, 1952.

This Japanese report document efforts by the Japanese
Army to smash the supply line from Indochina to China.
These efforts were carried out from February through June
of 1938.

2152.   United States. Department of the Army. Forces in the Far
        East. RECORD OF OPERATIONS AGAINST SOVIET RUSSIA,
        EASTERN FRONT (AUGUST 1945). Washington, D.C.: Office
        of the Chief of Military History, 1954.   361 pp.

Here is an account of the Japanese Army's operations in
1945. The first chapter follows the Kwantung Army in
operations throughout Manchuria; the rest of the report
deals with the eastern front and the activities of the
First Area Army. The volume forms part of the Japanese
monograph series.

2153.   United States. Department of the Army. Forces in the Far
        East. RECORD OF OPERATIONS AGAINST SOVIET RUSSIA.
        Washington, D.C.: Office of the Chief of Military
        History, 1954.   296 pp.

This Japanese monograph covers the period January
1943-August 1945. The narrative reports on operations in
northern Korea as well as western and northern parts of
Manchuria.

2154.   United States. Department of the Army. Forces in the Far
        East. SEVENTEENTH AREA ARMY OPERATIONS, 1941-1945.
        Washington, D.C.: Office of the Chief of Military
        History, 1956.   46 pp.

This Japanese monograph describes the fighting in
Korea--considered part of the Japanese homeland.
Interviews with participating Japanese officers reveal the
situations in northern Korea at war's end, including the
Soviet invasion.

2155.   United States. Department of the Army. Forces in the Far

East. SOUTH CHINA AREA: OPERATIONS RECORD, 1937-1941.
Washington, D.C.: Office of the Chief of Military
History, 1956. 139 pp.

This report, by participating Japanese officers, takes
on added significance as a description of the increasing
Japanese frustration in vainly seeking to end the war in
China. This frustration helped influence Japan towards a
path which led to war with Western democracies.

2156. United States. Department of the Army. Japan. CHINA AREA
OPERATIONS RECORD: JULY 1937-NOVEMBER 1941.
Washington, D.C.: Office of the Chief of Military
History, 1957.

This Japanese monograph provides a general outline of
Japanese operations in China. See especially the material
on the China Incident.

2157. United States. Office of the Coordinator of Information.
OUR CHINESE ALLIES IN SOUTH EAST ASIA. Washington,
D.C.: GPO, 1942. 12 pp.

Here is a slim summary of Chinese influence and
activities in Southeast Asia prior to the United States
entry.

2158. United States. Office of Coordinator of Information.
RESULTS OF JAPAN'S CONQUEST OF BURMA. Washington, D.C.:
GPO, 1942. 7 1.

The Research and Analysis Branch presents a summary of
the Japanese victory.

2159. United States. Office of Strategic Services. THE
GUERRILLA FRONT IN NORTH CHINA. Washington, D.C.: OSS,
1943. 22 pp.

Here is one of the first reports based on fairly
reliable sources of the activities of the Chinese
Communists.

2160. Vasilevsky, Alexander M. "Rout of the Kwantung Army."
SOVIET MIL REV, Suppl. (August 1980), 1-9.

The author was commander-in-chief of the Soviet forces
in the Far East. Even during the most difficult days of
the war in Europe, he says, the Soviets kept 30-40
divisions in the Far East. Officially the Soviet campaign

lasted 24 days, but according to the author, it actually
took about twelve days. Some items of interest in the
article are: (1) Japan fired on Soviet merchant ships in
December 1941; (2) in April 1945, he began planning
operations against Japan; (3) on July 16, 1945 (the day of
the Trinity test), he received a call from Stalin in
Potsdam to advance the date of war with Japan by ten days;
(4) Gen. Yamada relates the story of the Kwantung Army's
surrender.

2161.   Vigor, Peter W. and Christopher Donnelly. "The Manchurian
        Campaign and Its Relevance to Modern Strategy." COMP
        STRATEGY, 2 (No. 2, 1980), 159-178.

        The authors, both at Sandhurst, argue that the Soviet
        operations in 1945 continue to be relevant to present-day
        planning.

2162.   Wilson, David. "Leathernecks in North China, 1945." BULL
        CON ASIAN SCHOL, 4 (Summer 1972), 33-37.

        Relying on published sources, Wilson criticizes the use
        of U.S. Marines and Japanese troops to fight Chinese
        Communists after the war. The author appears to
        oversimplify a complex situation.

2163.   Zakharov, M.V., ed. FINALE: A RETROSPECTIVE REVIEW OF
        IMPERIALIST JAPAN'S DEFEAT IN 1945. Moscow, U.S.S.R.:
        Progress Publishers, 1972. 247 pp.

        The collection, translated by David Skvirsky, generally
        praises the decisive role of the Soviet armed forces and
        condemns the aggression of Japan. See especially the
        article by R.Y. Malinovsky.

IV.D.1.e. Guadalcanal

2164.   Buell, Thomas B. "Guadalcanal: Neither Side Would
        Quit." USNIP, 106 (April 1980), 60-65.

        Buell reflects on Admiral King's preference for limited
        operations in the Pacific (against the Europe-firsters).
        The defeat at Savo Island stunned King, who then backed
        away from his emphasis on offensive operations. With
        meticulous research and focus on King, the author analyzes
        the six-month struggle of attrition at Guadalcanal.

2165.   Caporale, Louis G. "Remembering Guadalcanal." MC GAZ,
        66 (August 1982), 13-16.

Caporale reviews the campaign and highlights the participating Marine units and leaders.

2166. Carmichael, Thomas N. THE NINETY DAYS. New York: B. Geis Associates, 1971. 339 pp.

Here is an account of a brief but crucial portion of the campaign for Guadalcanal.

2167. Coggins, Jack. THE CAMPAIGN FOR GUADALCANAL. Garden City, NY: Doubleday, 1972. 208 pp.

Here is a solid account, well researched and well written, of the entire campaign.

2168. Cook, Charles. THE BATTLE OF CAPE ESPERANCE: ENCOUNTER AT GUADALCANAL. New York: Thomas Y. Crowell, 1968. 156 pp.

The author participated in this 1942 battle—the first night attack by the U.S. Navy in the South Pacific—while aboard the cruiser HELENA. His narrative stems mainly from his experience and several interviews. Once again we have a combat veteran from the winning side describing the confusion and errors which seem inherent in battle. Of special interest is Cook's report on the inability of the Navy to exploit the advantages of radar.

2169. Werstein, Irving. GUADALCANAL. New York: Thomas Y. Crowell, 1963. 186 pp.

Here is a popular account of the brutal battle.

2170. Fooks, H.E. "The Guadalcanal Campaign—1942–1943." RUSI, 94 (November 1949), 591–604.

Fooks examines the entire campaign for Guadalcanal. For example, he gives a knowledgeable report on the American defeat at Savo. At the start of the campaign, Americans encountered difficulty in finding accurate charts and maps, but later they obtained useful information from Australians who had lived on Guadalcanal.

2171. Foster, John. GUADALCANAL GENERAL: THE STORY OF A. A. VANDEGRIFT USMC. New York: William Morrow, 1966. 224 pp.

The author, a newspaperman, presents a straightforward,

uncritical account.

2172. Frank, Benis M. "Vandegrift's Guadalcanal Command." MC
       GAZ, 71 (August 1987), 56-59.

       Frank, an official USMC historian, gives details of the
       famous group photograph of the commanders and staff
       officers of the 1st Marine Division. Of the 40 people in
       the group, 25 went on to earn flag rank. Frank identifies
       the surviving members of the group.

2173. Gatchel, Theodore L. "Marines in Support of a Naval
       Campaign: Guadalcanal as a Prototype." M C GAZ, 70
       (January 1986), 40-52.

       This uncritical article reemphasizes the naval character
       of the Marine Corps.

2174. George, John B. SHOTS FIRED IN ANGER. Plantersville, SC:
       Small Arms Technical Publishing, 1947. 421 pp.

       The author gives his account as a rifleman at
       Guadalcanal. George served in the 132d Infantry of the
       Illinois National Guard in the Americal Division.

2175. Glasser, Arthur F. AND SOME BELIEVED. Chicago, IL: Moody
       Press, 1946. 208 pp.

       Here is the personal account by a Marine chaplain of his
       experiences at Guadalcanal.

2176. Grady, Thomas G. ON VALOR'S SIDE. Garden City, NY:
       Doubleday, 1963. 364 pp.

       Grady provides a detailed narrative of the fighting on
       Guadalcanal.

2177. Griffith, Samuel B., II. THE BATTLE FOR GUADALCANAL.
       Philadelphia, PA: J.B. Lippincott, 1963. 282 pp.

       Brig. Gen. Griffith (USMC) integrates American and
       Japanese sources--mainly documents--to give a detailed
       history of the campaign. His criticisms and praises fall
       where warranted. One strength of the book is the author's
       attention to the human dimension of war.

2178. Hammel, Eric. "Bogies at Angels Twelve." WWII, 1 (May
       1986), 34-41.

Here is an account of the epic aerial struggles at
Guadalcanal. Hammel describes the U.S. destruction of the
Japanese 25th Naval Air Flotilla (August 7-8, 1942).
Despite this victory, he notes, the campaign lingered
another six months.

2179.   Hammel, Eric M. GUADALCANAL: THE CARRIER BATTLES. New
York: Crown Publishers, 1987. 505 pp.

Hammel portrays the United States invasion of the
Eastern Solomons as an attempt to stop a renewed Japanese
drive towards New Hebrides. Of interest is his account of
the internal U.S. debate between those who favored an
immediate gamble and those who preferred to wait until
American resources would come into play. The issue,
according to Hammel, turned largely on the decisions of V.
Adm. Fletcher. Although the overall battle for the Eastern
Solomons was a draw, Hammel feels that the Japanese,
especially at Santa Cruz, lost talented airmen and with
them the last chance to win the war.

2180.   Hammel, Eric M. GUADALCANAL: DECISION AT SEA. New York:
Crown Publishers, 1988.

Hammel continues his focused analysis on the action at
Guadalcanal. This volume portrays the struggle for command
of the adjacent waters, which he integrates into the
overall campaign.

2181.   Hammel, Eric M. GUADALCANAL: STARVATION ISLAND. New York:
Crown Publishers, 1987. 478 pp.

Here is a well-researched, well-written account of the
bitter fighting which, according to Hammel, carried the
seeds of Japan's defeat--even this early in the war.

2182.   Hersey, John. INTO THE VALLEY. New York: A.A. Knopf,
1943. 138 pp.

In this microscopic view of war, Hersey tells the story
of one Marine rifle company at Guadalcanal. Capt. Charles
Rigaud and the men in his company H are the leading
characters as they participate in the 3rd Battle of the
Matanikau River. Hersey offers a detailed look at the
human side of war. This book may well be the best of its
kind.

2183.   Horton, D.C. NEW GEORGIA: PATTERN FOR VICTORY. New York:
Ballantine Books, 1971. 160 pp.

Horton contrasts the local commanders on both sides in
the campaign: the inflexible Japanese and the untrained
U.S. novitiates (longing for the luxuries of the base
camp). He effectively places the campaign in the broad
context of the war. There is an entire chapter on JFK and
PT 109.

2184. Hough, Frank O. and J.A. Crown. THE CAMPAIGN ON NEW
      BRITAIN. Washington, D. C.: U. S. Marine Corps, 1952.
      220 pp.

      Lt. Col. Hough and Maj. Crown write the official Marine
      history of the campaign. They describe the difficulties of
      moving the Marines from Australia to New Britain. Of value
      is their description of small unit tactics.

2185. Kent, Graeme. GUADALCANAL: ISLAND ORDEAL. New York:
      Ballantine Books, 1971. 158 pp.

      Kent offers a knowledgeable, brief summary of the
      difficult campaign.

2186. Kirland, Thomas V. "The Incredible Cactus Air Force." MC
      GAZ, 43 (May 1959), 42-46.

      Kirkland describes the joint "hybrid" air elements
      (Marine - Navy - AAF) in action at Guadalcanal. "Cactus"
      was the code name for Guadalcanal. Although the U.S.
      aircraft (P-400s and F-4Fs) did not measure up to the
      Japanese Zero, the author credits superior tactics,
      especially the two-plane section, for the American success.

2187. Leckie, Robert. CHALLENGE FOR THE PACIFIC:
      GUADALCANAL--THE TURNING POINT OF THE WAR. Garden City,
      NY: Doubleday, 1965. 372 pp.

      The narrative is well grounded in published sources.
      Despite the author having seen action as a Marine on
      Guadalcanal, there is little here that is new. The story,
      however, is well told.

2188. Lee, Robert E. VICTORY AT GUADALCANAL. Novato, CA:
      Presidio press, 1981. 260 pp.

      Lee imbues his narrative with imagined dialogue.
      Despite some errors (and an incomplete bibliography), the
      book gives a useful account of the campaign.

2189. McCandless, Bruce. "The SAN FRANCISCO Story." USNIP, 84
       (November 1958), 35-53.

       R. Adm. McCandless recounts his service aboard the SAN
       FRANCISCO during the battle for Guadalcanal.

2190. Merillat, Herbert C.L. GUADALCANAL REMEMBERED. New York:
       Dodd, Mead, 1982. 332 pp.

       Merillat relies on his contemporary diary entries and
       his memory to narrate this day-by-day account of the
       Marines in action at Guadalcanal. He observed the combat
       as a press officer who was attached to the First Marine
       Division.

2191. Merillat, Herbert C.L. THE ISLAND. Boston: Houghton
       Mifflin, 1944. 283 pp.

       Capt. Merillat (USMC) describes the actions of his unit,
       the First Marine Division, at Guadalcanal. He reports on·
       the daily activities of virtually every Marine Platoon
       during the period August 7-December 9, 1942.

2192. Miller, Thomas G. CACTUS AIR FORCE. New York: Harper and
       Row, 1969. 242 pp.

       Miller provides a well-written account of the airmen and
       the air war over Guadalcanal (code name CACTUS).

2193. Miller, John, Jr. GUADALCANAL: THE FIRST OFFENSIVE.
       Washington, DC.: Historical Division, Dept. of the
       Army, 1949. 413 pp.

       Miller highlights the Army's role in the first offensive
       campaign launched against the Japanese. Official Army
       records, including after-action reports and unit histories,
       form the basis of this excellent history.

2194. Mizrahi, Joseph V. "Fifty Bombers Headed Yours." WINGS,
       16 (August 1986), 10-54.

       Here is a report on the air battle for Henderson Field.
       The author concentrates on the contests between the Zero
       and the F4F Wildcat. Excellent photos accompany this
       well-written narrative.

2195. Patrick, Stephen B. "The Battle for Guadalcanal, 7 August
       1942-7 February 1943." STRATEGY & TACTICS, 39 (1973),
       23-38.

NE

2196. Sternlicht, Sanford V. "We Want the Big Ones." NAVY, 3
       (March 1960), 16-18.

       Here is a description of U.S. naval operations under
       Adm. Daniel J. Callaghan in November 1942. These
       operations protected (narrowly) the Marines on the beaches
       of Guadalcanal.

2197. Stevenson, Nikolai. "Four Months on the Front Line." AMER
       HERITAGE, 36 (October/November 1985), 49-56.

       Capt. Stevenson (USMC) tells of his experiences as a
       company commander at Guadalcanal. His narrative describes
       the confusion and the unshakable aftereffects of war.

2198. Tanaka, Raizo. "Japan's Losing Struggle for Guadalcanal."
       USNIP, Pt. I: 82 (July 1956), 687-699; Pt. II: 82
       (August 1956), 815-831.

       Here is a description by the commander of a Japanese
       destroyer squadron of his five-month effort to bring troops
       and supplies to Guadalcanal. His ordeal foreshadowed the
       growing disparities in strength (and planning) of the two
       sides. Roger Pineau translated and edited the account.

2199. Tregaskis, Richard. GUADALCANAL DIARY. Garden City, NY:
       Blue Ribbon books, 1943. 263 pp.

       Here is a "classic" of the war. Tregaskis presents a
       starkly realistic account of his experience as a
       correspondent with the Marines, July 26-September 26, 1942.
       This book captured contemporary public attention in a way
       that few such personal accounts have ever matched.

2200. Twining, Merrill B. "'Head for the Hills!'" MC GAZ, 71
       (August 1987), 46-55.

       Twining (then-Lt. Col., USMC) enjoyed a special
       relationship with Vandergrift. When Adm. Ghormley felt
       compelled to withdraw naval support from the Marines at
       Guadalcanal, the author took some unusual planning
       initiatives--initiatives which continue to make him
       uncomfortable.

2201. United States. Army Air Forces. GUADALCANAL AND THE
       ORIGINS OF THE THIRTEENTH AIR FORCE. Washington, D.C.:

Dept. of the Army, 1945. 282 pp.

This study looks at the Guadalcanal campaign and the
joint service efforts that stopped the Japanese. The AAF
played a secondary role in the encounter, according to this
study, because of priority requirements elsewhere.
Nevertheless, the effort literally wore out the aircraft
and demonstrated the need for something beyond the local
command structure that was in existence.

2202. Zimmerman, John L. THE GUADALCANAL CAMPAIGN. Washington,
       D.C.: USMC, 1949. 189 pp.

This operational monograph gives a complete and official
account of the campaign. The informative notes indicate
the extensive research incorporated by Zimmerman. Of
interest is his analysis of the first U.S. amphibious
operation of the war (August 1942).

IV.D.1.f. Guam

2203. Hammer, David H. LION SIX. Annapolis, MD: U.S. Naval
       Institute Press, 1947. 107 pp.

Hammer describes the naval operating base at Guam.

2204. Lademan, J.U., Jr. "USS GOLD STAR--Flagship of the Guam
       Navy." USNIP, 99 (December 1973), 67-79.

The Gold Star, a "miscellaneous auxiliary" vessel,
picked up supplies for Guam from various Pacific ports.
The day of the attack at Pearl Harbor found the ship in the
Philippines. The GOLD STAR and the crew (including the
author) sailed to Australia by way of Borneo.

2205. Lodge, O.R. THE RECAPTURE OF GUAM. Washington, D.C.:
       USMC, 1954. 214 pp.

This official Marine history includes excellent
illustrations and maps. Of interest is the way Japanese
island defenses and Marine tactics evolved with regard to
amphibious warfare.

2206. Maga, Timothy P. DEFENDING PARADISE. New York: Garland,
       1987. 233 pp.

Maga, integrating archival materials and new sources,
examines the relationship between the United States and
Guam from 1898 to 1950. Amidst his analysis of U. S. Naval

administration of the island and Guam's economic-political
development, Maga incorporates a report on the wartime
period of the Japanese occupation.

2207. Palomo, Tony. ISLAND IN AGONY. Washington, D.C.: Author,
1984. 261 pp.

Here is a personal account of the fighting at Guam.

2208. Tweed, George R. ROBINSON CRUSOE, U.S.N. New York:
Whittlesey House, 1945. 267 pp.

The author (RMIC) spent two and one-half years on Guam
after the Japanese occupied the island. His extraordinary
adventures, which include close relations with the friendly
natives and innovative survival techniques, are told to
Blake Clark.

2209. Umezawa, Haruo and Louis Metzger. "The Defense of Guam."
MC GAZ, 48 (August 1964), 36-43.

This article, based on an official report by the
Japanese Self Defense Force, reveals that Japanese units in
defense of Guam spread out too thinly, thus violating the
cardinal rule of defending a vital area.

2210. Wilds, Thomas. "The Japanese Seizure of Guam." MC GAZ, 39
(July 1955), 20-23.

Wilds describes the Japanese victory, especially the
activities of the Hayashi Detachment at Agana, on December
10, 1941.

IV.D.1.g. Hong Kong

2211. Brown, Wenzell. HONG KONG AFTERMATH. New York: Smith and
Durrell, 1943. 283 pp.

Here is a report on the surrender of Hong Kong and the
particularly brutal excesses inflicted on the POWs by the
Japanese at the Stanley prison camp.

2212. Carew, John M. [pseud. Tim Carew.] FALL OF HONG KONG.
London: Blond, 1960. 228 pp.

Carew narrates the unhappy story of this British defeat.
He criticizes the prewar preparations and attitudes of the
British.

2213.   Ferguson, Ted. DESPERATE SIEGE: THE BATTLE OF HONG KONG.
        Garden City, NY: Doubleday and Company, 1980. 252 pp.

        The author characterizes the defeat as a "shameful
        tragedy," in which the Canadian government mishandled
        the assignment of 2,000 Canadian soldiers to Hong Kong,
        and Churchill prematurely wrote off the defenders of the
        colony. Organizing his report around a detailed
        chronology, and incorporating extensive interviews,
        Ferguson includes some of the tragic aftermath of the
        episode by describing the experiences of those taken
        prisoner by the Japanese.

2214.   Lindsay, Oliver. AT THE GOING DOWN OF THE SUN. London:
        Hamish Hamilton, 1981. 258 pp.

        Here is a knowledgeable report on affairs in Hong Kong
        and Southeast Asia during the war. Lindsay is particularly
        well-versed in the history of Hong Kong.

2215.   Lindsay, Oliver. THE LASTING HONOUR. London: Hamish
        Hamilton, 1978. 226 pp.

        Lindsay writes of the fall of Hong Kong in December
        1941. Despite the inferior numbers of the Japanese,
        Lindsay maintains that the lack of adequate naval air
        support for British defenders made the colony's defeat a
        "foregone conclusion."

2216.   Luff, John. THE HIDDEN YEARS. Hong Kong: South China
        Morning Post, 1967. 234 pp.

        NE

2217.   Marsman, Jan H. I ESCAPED FROM HONG KONG. New York:
        Reynal, 1942. 249 pp.

        A U.S. citizen and businessman in Hong Kong before the
        war, Marsman tells of the horrors of the Japanese attack.
        The narrative recounts his experiences as a captive and his
        escape.

2218.   Stacey, C.P. "The Defence of Hong Kong." CANADIAN ARMY J,
        Pt. I: 4 (November 1950), 5-13; Pt. II: 4 (December
        1950), 18-31.

        Col. Stacey served as director of the army's historical
        section. In just over seventeen days of fighting, the
        Japanese inflicted heavy losses on the defenders at Hong

Kong. It is interesting to note that as early as 1939 the
War Office felt that the Japanese, secure on the China
mainland, might not attack Hong Kong by sea. Also,
Canadian troops manning battle stations on the island were
quartered on the mainland. With the resources at his
command, Stacey makes an important contribution with this
article.

IV.D.1.h. Indochina

2219. Smith, Ralph B. "The Japanese Period in Indochina and the
        Coup of 9 March 1945." J SEA STUD, 9 (September 1978),
        268-301.

        In a well-researched effort that integrates Japanese,
French, Vietnamese, and British primary sources, Smith
offers an explanation of the coup and its aftermath.

2220. Spector, Ronald. "Allied Intelligence and Indochina,
        1943-1945." PAC HR, 51 (February 1982), 23-50.

        Spector finds that the actions of Americans in Indochina
were out of phase with U.S. policies in Washington.
By cooperating in intelligence operations with the French
(and the Viet Minh), the local Americans, according to the
author, were violating the spirit if not the letter of
vague policy directives from Roosevelt.

2221. Spector, Ronald. "'What the Local Annamites Are Thinking':
        American Views of Vietnamese in China, 1942-1945." SEA:
        INT Q, 3 (Spring 1974), 741-751.

        Spector demonstrates that Americans had ample
information about the Viet Minh and Vietnamese nationalism
from Vietnamese leaders who fled to China after the failure
of their revolution in 1940-1941. This information,
however, was ignored or even unknown at the highest U.S.
levels, according to the author.

IV.D.1.i. Malaya

2222. Chapman, Frederick Spencer. THE JUNGLE IS NEUTRAL. New
        York: W.W. Norton, 1949. 384 pp.

        Lt. Col. Chapman lived and fought in the Malayan jungle
for three years. In his efforts to organize the
anti-Japanese resistance, he trained many Chinese (most of
whom were communists). His understated personal account
hardly does justice to the dangers and challenges he faced.

2223. Morton, E.V.B. "Operation Zipper: Personal Reminiscences
          of the Re-Occupation of Malaya in 1945." NAVAL REV, 72
          (October 1984), 329-335.

       Here are some lighter moments and reminiscences about
Malaya in 1945 by a medical officer aboard the HMS PURSUER.
Morton expresses gratitude for the atomic bombings and the
cancellation of Operation ZIPPER (which no longer required
his services).

2224. Robinson, A.O. "The Malayan Campaign in the Light of the
          Principles of War." RUSI, Pt. I: 109 (August 1964),
          224-232; Pt. II: 109 (November 1964), 325-337.

       The author participated in this campaign. His
retrospective recommendations--a clearly defined aim for
the British army, concentration of force, offensive action,
and adoption of other well-known principles of war
(surprise, mobility, economy of force, security,
cooperation, and pursuit)--would have brought victory in
Malaya. In the event, British forces were weak everywhere
and strong nowhere.

2225. Shorrick, N. "In Another Place." RAF Q, 10 (Winter 1970),
          299-305.

       Here is a tribute to the heroism of the RAF at Malaya
and Singapore. Shorrick claims that the air wing has borne
a disproportionate share of criticism for these defeats.

2226. Thatcher, Dorothy. PAI NAA. London: White Lion
          Publishers, 1974. 184 pp.

          NE

IV.D.1.j. **Netherlands East Indies**

2227. Hideaki, Inayama. "Battle Over Palembang." RAF FLYING
          REV, 15 (May 1960), 26-28.

          NE

2228. Houston, R.B. "What Happened in Java, 1945-46?" ARMY Q,
          55 (January 1948), 194-200.

       With the unavoidable hiatus after Tokyo's surrender
announcement, Mountbatten only reluctantly accepted

responsibility for Java. The author describes the turmoil intertwined with emerging nationalism in Java.

2229.   Hyland, John J. "Flying PBYs in World War II." USNIP, Suppl. (March 1985), 70-74.

The author was flying reconnaissance missions in the Philippines when the war began. He and the rest of Patrol Wing Ten moved to the Netherlands East Indies, where the unit undertook some disastrous offensive operations.

2230.   Johnsen, Lester J. "You Men on Java Are Not Forgotten." AF MAG, 63 (September 1980), 106-108.

Here is a personal account by a P-40 pilot in the 17th Provisional Pursuit Squadron which escorted A-24 and B-17 bombers. [In early March 1942, Johnsen and his unit had to relocate from Java to Australia.]

2231.   Miyamoto, Schizuo. THE SUPPLEMENT TO THE "DISPOSAL RECORD OF THE WAR'S END IN JAVA." Tokyo: 1974. 68 pp.

NE

2232.   Pelzer, Karl J. "Japan's Drive Against the Netherlands East Indies." FE SURVEY, 11 (February 9, 1942), 36-40.

With the NEI as a main Japanese objective, this article suggests that Java could be the place to launch an Allied counter-offensive.

2233.   Salo, Mauno A. "Java Sojourn." AMER AVN HSJ, 12 (Fall 1967), 190-192.

The article is based on an interview with a B-17 pilot, Harlan O. Bjerke, who flew operations out of Java from December 1941 to April 1942. The pilot praises the proficiency of the Japanese pilots and the capabilities of the famed Zero.

2234.   Van Der Grift, Cornelius and E.H. Lansing. ESCAPE FROM JAVA. New York: Thomas Crowell, 1943. 166 pp.

When the war began, Van Der Grift, a Dutch citizen and civilian, was working in Batavia. The book tells of his hazardous escape in a small vessel across the Indian Ocean.

2235.   Veth, K.L. "Shootout at Palembang: The 'Hellbinds' Mine the Moesi River." AMER AVN HSJ, 25 (Summer 1980),

72-74.

The author, a naval technical adviser, flew as an
observer on this mission, which Mountbatten had suggested.
The success of this low-level mining operation in Sumatra
by normally high-level bombers (B-29s) led to the mining of
rivers in Japan ("Operation STARVATION").

2236. United States. Department of the Army. Forces in the Far
East. BALIKPAPAN: INVASION OPERATIONS RECORD.
Washington, D.C.: Office of the Chief of Military
History, Dept. of the Army, 1953. 8 pp.

This Japanese history focuses on the invasion of
Balikpapan. The purpose of this invasion, which occured
January 21-26, 1942, was to seize the rich oil fields and
strategically important airfields of Balikpapan.

2237. United States. Department of the Army. Forces in the Far
East. THE INVASION OF THE NETHERLANDS EAST INDIES.
Washington, D.C.: Office of the Chief of Military
History, 1958. 66 pp.

Here is the story of the Japanese victory March 1-9,
1942. The Japanese authors are officers who participated
in the campaign. They reveal that operations orders for
preparing the attack were received on November 6, 1941, and
the Army forces left Japan on November 19.

2238. United States. Department of the Army. Forces in the Far
East. BANDJERMASIN INVASION: OPERATIONS RECORD.
Washington, D.C.: Office of the Chief of Military
History, 1953. 7 pp.

This brief Japanese monograph follows the movements of
the Sea Drive Unit and the Land Drive Unit against the
capital of Dutch Borneo (Jan-Feb 1942). This report claims
that 80% of the Land Drive Unit came down with malaria
during this campaign.

2239. United States. Department of the Army. Forces in the Far
East. PALEMBANG AND BANGKA ISLAND: OPERATIONS RECORD.
Washington, D.C.: Office of the Chief of Military
History, 1953. 16 pp.

This document summarizes the Japanese seizure of prize
resources in the Southern Area. Airborne Japanese troops
linked up with the 38th Division Advance Force for a
relatively quick and easy victory.

2240.   United States. Department of the Army. Forces in the Far
        East.   REPORT ON INSTALLATIONS AND CAPTURED WEAPONS,
        JAVA AND SINGAPORE. Washington, D.C.: Office of the
        Chief of Military History, 1958. 115 pp.

        Here is a report by two Japanese officers who conducted
        an inspection tour from March to May, 1942. Their report
        makes dull reading, with its long inventory lists of
        captured items.

2241.   United States. Department of the Army. Forces in the Far
        East. SUMATRA OPERATIONS RECORD. Washington, D.C.:
        Office of the Chief of Military History, 1953. 18 pp.

        This record provides an account of the Japanese 25th
        Army's invasion of northern and central Sumatra. Of
        interest is the first-hand descriptions of the war damage
        done to the oil refineries and storage areas during the
        campaign in March 1942. Most of the repairs were
        accomplished within six months, the Japanese authors say,
        and resources, such as oil-drilling equipment,
        transportation, and shipping facilities, were captured
        largely intact.

2242.   United States. Department of the Army. Forces in the Far
        East. TARAKAN INVASION: OPERATIONS RECORD.
        Washington, D.C.: Office of the Chief of Military
        History, 1952.

        This operation took less than three days in mid-January
        1942. The authors, Japanese officers who participated in
        the operation, describe the objective as the capture of the
        oil fields, oil refineries, and the airfield on the island.
        After the Army's victory, control was turned over to the
        Japanese Navy.

2243.   United States. Department of the Army. Japan. BORNEO
        OPERATIONS, 1941-1945. Tokyo: Dept. of the Army, 1957.
        101 pp.

        Here is the text of a Japanese monograph on the defense
        of British Borneo by the Japanese Army and the defense of
        Dutch Borneo by the Japanese Navy. Of interest is the
        Army's call for reinforcements when the Allied landings in
        the Philippines exposed the 37th Japanese Army in Northeast
        Borneo.

IV.D.l.k. New Guinea

2244. Arthur, Anthony. THE BUSHMASTERS: AMERICA'S JUNGLE
       WARRIORS OF WORLD WAR II. New York: St. Martin's Press,
       1987. 270 pp.

       The author, a historian, explores the activities of some
       members of the 158th Infantry Regiment in the jungles of
       New Guinea. The unit was made up of a broad ethnic mix
       (e.g., native Americans, Mexican-Americans, NISEI, and
       "Anglos," including a Polish-American prizefighter).
       Arthur concentrates on about a dozen personalities rather
       than trying to present a more formal unit history.

2245. Brown, G.M. "Attitudes to an Invasion of Australia in
       1942." RUSI, 122 (March 1977), 27-31.

       The author, a graduate student, questions the
       conventional wisdom that Japan planned to invade Australia.
       The New Guinea operations failed for Japan, Brown says,
       because the Japanese Army let itself be talked into over
       extending Army forces by the Japanese Navy. According to
       Brown, invasion is a persistent theme throughout Australian
       history.

2246. Cortesi, Lawrence. PACIFIC SIEGE. New York: Kensington
       Books, 1984. 384 pp.

       This book describes naval-air operations at New Guinea.

2247. Cortesi, Lawrence. PACIFIC STRIKE. New York: Kensington
       Books, 1982. 265 pp.

       Cortesi offers a well-written summary of the action at
       New Guinea.

2248. Deacon, Kenneth J. "Arara Beachhead." MIL ENGR, 59
       (March-April 1967), 120.

       Here is a report on the work of Tornado Task Force
       constructing an airfield and repelling enemy counterattacks
       in Dutch New Guinea.

2249. Deacon, Kenneth J. "Cave Warfare on Biak Island, 1944."
       MIL ENGR, 54 (January-February 1962), 4-6.

       The work of the Hurricane Task Force in the conquest of
       Biak demonstrated the limitations of caves and other
       systems of static defense.

2250. Deacon, Kenneth J. "They Held the Beachhead." MIL ENGR,
       52 (November-December), 467.

       Engineers in Mackechnie's unit not only established a
       forward base at Nassau Bay in New Guinea but also defended
       the base against Japanese assaults.

2251. Drea, Edward J. DEFENDING THE DRINIUMOR: COVERING FORCE
       OPERATIONS IN NEW GUINEA, 1944. Fort Leavenworth, KS:
       Combat Studies Institute, 1984. 182 pp.

       Drea attempts to correlate the ULTRA revelations with
       MacArthur's campaign in Aitape, New Guinea, which led to
       the destruction of the Imperial Japanese 18th Army.

2252. Hammel, Eric M. "Guadalcanal: 1st Battle of the Matanikau
       (River)." MC GAZ, 66 (August 1982), 48-54.

       The author provides details of events during the first
       real engagement with the Japanese. The Matanikau River was
       critical to the American position.

2253. Haugland, Vern. LETTER FROM NEW GUINEA. New York:
       Farrar, 1943. 148 pp.

       The correspondent's "letter" tells of his adventures in
       New Guinea. For seven weeks, he struggled to return to
       safety after surviving an airplane crash. The experience
       converted him to spritual faith.

2254. Holdsworth, David Keith. PAPUA NEW GUINEA BATTLEFIELDS.
       Adelaide, Aus: Rigby, 1974. 36pp.

       Holdsworth takes a present-day, pictorial look at the
       famous battlefield.

2255. Johnston, George H. NEW GUINEA DIARY. London: Gollancz,
       1944. 237 pp.

       Here are the observations of an astute reporter as
       recorded in his private journal. Johnston talks about
       personalities and events in the war.

2256. Johnston, George H. THE TOUGHEST FIGHTING IN THE WORLD.
       New York: Duell, Sloan, and Pearce, 1943. 240 pp.

       An Australian correspondent gives a first-hand view of
       the rugged fighting in New Guinea. See especially
       Johnston's description of the fighting at "Bloody Buna."

He explains the importance of Port Moresby to Australia and
the strategic significance of the New Guinea campaign.

257. Kahn, E.J., Jr. G.I. JUNGLE: AN AMERICAN SOLDIER IN
     AUSTRALIA AND NEW GUINEA. New York: Simon and
     Schuster, 1943. 150 pp.

     Kahn, a professional writer, spent some time in the
Army. He is a keen observer, but his descriptions deal
more with service life in general than with actual combat.

258. King, William M. WAR IN NEW GUINEA. Orlando, FL: Author,
     1944. 48 pp.

     This pictorial collection is described by King as
official war photographs of the battle for Australia.

259. Lawless, Roger E. "The Biak Operation." MIL REV, Part I:
     33 (May 1953), 53-62; Part II: 33 (June 1953), 48-62.

     Here is an account of the landing by the Hurricane Task
Force at Biak. Although the initial phase of the attack
achieved complete surprise, the operation bogged down
because of inadequate intelligence, a lack of coordination
among the task force units, and the fierce defense put up
by the Japanese.

260. McCarthy, Dudley. SOUTH-WEST PACIFIC AREA--FIRST YEAR:
     KOKOKA TO WAU. Canberra, Aus.: Australia War Memorial,
     1959. 656 pp.

     McCarthy provides an excellent analysis of the first
year of campaigning. The details of operations in New
Guinea highlight the volume.

261. Milner, Samuel. VICTORY IN PAPUA. Washington, DC: Office
     of the Chief of Military History, Dept. of the Army,
     1957. 409 pp.

     Here is the Army's official history of the key
encounter.

262. Moody, Dallas D. AERIAL GUNNER FROM VIRGINIA: THE LETTERS
     OF DON MOODY TO HIS FAMILY DURING 1944. Richmond, VA:
     Virginia State Library, 1950. 366 pp.

     Moody served as a tail gunner aboard a B-24 Liberator.
The 1944 correspondence describes his training and combat
duties in New Guinea. Moody died in October 1944 on his

third mission. William E. Hemphill edited the work.

2263.   Paull, Raymond. RETREAT FROM KOKODA. Melbourne, Aus.:
        Heinemann, 1958. 319 pp.

        NE

2264.   Riegelman, Harold. CAVES OF BIAK. New York: Dial Press,
        1955. 278 pp.

        This book is an Army officer's personal account of his
        duty in the South Pacific. Riegelman injects much humor in
        his memoir. Of interest are his detailed descriptions of
        his geographical surroundings.

2265.   Robinson, Pat. THE FIGHT FOR NEW GUINEA: GENERAL DOUGLAS
        MACARTHUR'S FIRST OFFENSIVE. New York: Random House,
        1943. 183 pp.

        MacArthur's first offensive thwarted the Japanese in
        their attempts to overrun New Guinea. Robinson, a
        correspondent, observed the fighting and reports the story.
        Robinson, in fact, had served two years in MacArthur's
        Rainbow Division during the First World War. The book
        presents a loose collection of war stories about U.S.
        participants.

2266.   Ryan, Peter. FEAR DRIVE MY FEET. Carlton, Aus.:
        Melbourne University Press, 1974. 251 pp.

        NE

2267.   Shortal, John F. "Hollandia: A Training Victory." MIL
        REV, 66 (May 1986), 40-48.

        Maj. Shortal (USA) identifies the key to this victory as
        the rigorous, realistic training programs and policies
        instituted by Eichelberger. The research includes use of
        the general's papers as well as unpublished military
        histories.

2268.   Smith, Robert Ross. THE APPROACH TO THE PHILIPPINES.
        Washington, D.C.: Office of the Chief of Military
        History, Dept. of the Army, 1953. 623 pp.

        Smith's expert analysis covers the Army's progress in
        the Southwest Pacific from April to October 1944.

2269.   Stockton, Frank J. "Southwest Pacific Alamo Scouts."

ARMORED CAV J, 56 (January-February 1947), 55-56.

Alamo scouts behind enemy lines effectively served the Sixth Army in operations near the Maori River in Dutch New Guinea during October 1944.

2270. ON TARGET: WITH THE AMERICAN AND AUSTRALIAN ANTI-AIRCRAFT BRIGADE IN NEW GUINEA. Sydney, Aus.: Angus and Robertson, 1943. 171 pp.

This book contains accounts written by American and Australian artillerymen about their combat duties.

2271. United States. Army Air Forces. AIR TRANSPORT OPERATIONS: THE BATTLE OF WAU. Australia: N.P., 1945. 24 pp.

This encounter provided the first oportunity for ATC to show its potential value to combat operations in the southwest Pacific. The rugged terrain dictated the use of airlifts for troop reinforcements and supplies.

2272. Vader, John. NEW GUINEA: THE TIDE IS STEMMED. New York: Ballantine Books, 1971. 159 pp.

Vader writes knowledgeably about the campaign that blunted the Japanese drive. The book describes the tactical decisions and techniques that enabled Allied forces to launch their own offensive operations.

IV.D.1.1. Philippine Islands

2273. Aluit, Alphonso J. CORREGIDOR. Manila, PI: Calleon Publications, 1977. 5th rev. ed. 128 pp.

Here is a classic treatment of this heroic episode. The Filipino role receives the attention it deserves.

2274. Ancheta, Celedonio A. "The Significance of October 20, 1944." PHILIPPINE HIST ASSOC: HIST BULL, 12 (Nos. 1-4, 1968), 216-233.

NE

2275. Appel, Benjamin. WE WERE THERE AT THE BATTLE FOR BATAAN. New York: Grosset and Dunlap, 1957. 189 pp.

Written for the general public with Courtney Whitney as a consultant, this book is part of the popular

"We Were There" series.

2276. "Army Nurses at Leyte." AMER J NURSING, 45 (January 1945),
       44.

       This brief report focuses on the return to Leyte of U.S.
       Army nurses, at least one of whom had evacuated Corregidor
       in 1942.

2277. Arthur, Anthony. DELIVERANCE AT LOS BANOS. New York: St.
       Martin's Press, 1985. 287 pp.

       Arthur's work gives a vivid account of life for the
       civilian internees at Los Banos, a former agricultural
       college in the Philippines. The internees represented
       several nationalities and classes. As MacArthur and his
       forces began operations to reclaim the Philippines, the
       author describes how the fear of execution exacerbated the
       poor living conditions. The daring operation on February
       23, 1945, succeeded in rescuing the internees without a
       single fatality.

2278. Babcock, C. Stanton. "Philippine Campaign." CAVALRY J,
       Part I: 52 (March-April 1943), 7-11. Part II: 52
       (May-June 1943), 28-35.

       The author, with the U. S. Embassy in Tokyo, wrote this
       account during his confinement at the start of the war. He
       used only Japanese sources.

2279. Bailey, Maxwell C. "Raid at Los Banos." MIL REV, 63 (May
       1983) 51-66.

       Bailey describes the careful coordination and execution
       (and luck?) behind the liberation of American prisoners at
       this camp in the Philippines.

2280. Baldwin, Hanson W. "The Fourth Marines at Corregidor."
       MC GAZ, Part I: 30 (November 1946), 13-18. Part II:
       30 (December 1946), 27-35. Part III: 31 (January
       1947), 23-29. Part IV: 31 (February 1947), 39-43.

       Here is an excellent account. The 4th Marine Regiment
       assumed responsibility for the beach defenses on
       Corregidor.

2281. Belote, James H. and William M. Belote. CORREGIDOR: THE
       SAGA OF A FORTRESS. New York: Harper and Row, 1967.
       273 pp.

The Belotes' book is an excellent, detailed narrative.
The authors base their account on many interviews, official
records, and unpublished diaries and papers. The book,
however, is weakened by the absence of footnotes.

282. Bogart, Charles H. "Corregidor, the Last Month of Peace:
        The Letters of Captain John D. Wood." VA MAG HIST &
        BIO, 93 (October 1985), 435-455.

        Wood went to the Philippines with his new bride in 1939.
        The War Department extended his two-year tour, and his wife
        returned home, as ordered, in early 1941. The letters, all
        written in 1941 (with the last on November 30), provide a
        valuable glimpse of life in a tense situation. After being
        taken prisoner on Corregidor, Wood died aboard a Japanese
        transport sunk by an American submarine in October 1944.

283. Boggs, Charles W., Jr. MARINE AVIATION IN THE PHILIPPINES.
        Washington, D. C.: U. S. Marine Corps Historical
        Division, 1951. 166 pp.

        This book, part of the official Marine Corps history
        series, is filled with details and statistics. Boggs
        incorporates the comments of several participants in the
        operations. His assessments of air/ground cooperation and
        of air support to the guerrillas are particularly
        illuminating.

284. Braly, William C. "Corregidor--A Name, a Symbol, a Tradi-
        tion." COAST ARTILL J, 90 (July-August 1947), 2-9,
        36-44.

        Braly commanded the harbor defenses of Manila and Subic
        Bay. His personal account relies on the Operations Office
        log and his diary as a POW. In retrospect, Braly wonders
        if a truly united effort among the services might have
        averted the fall of the Philippines.

285. Braly, William C. THE HARD WAY HOME. Washington, D. C.:
        Infantry Journal Press, 1947. 282 pp.

        Here is the landing officer's personal account of the
        landing officer at Manila Bay and Subic Bay. While serving
        with the coastal artillery-harbor defense forces, Braly was
        among those captured at Corregidor. In his detailed diary,
        he documents Japanese excesses and war crimes with
        meticulous care.

2286. Cannon, M. Hamlin. LEYTE: THE RETURN TO THE PHILIPPINES.
       Washington, D.C.: Department of the Army, Office of the
       Chief of Military History, 1954. 420 pp.

       This official history, sponsored by the U. S. Army, is
       meticulously researched. It remains required reading for
       any serious study of the subject.

2287. Case, Blair. "Clark Field: Air Defense Debacle in the
       Philippines." AIR DEF MAG, n.v. (July-September 1982),
       4-7.

       In this brief summary, Case points to the lack of air
       defense aircraft in the Philippines to complement the
       B-17s.

2288. Chandler, William E. "26th Cavalry (PS) Battles to Glory."
       ARMORED CAV J, PART I: 56 (March-April 1947), 10-16.
       Part II: 56 (May-June 1947), 7-15. Part III: 56
       (July-August 1947), 15-22.

       The author, S-3 officer in the 26th Cavalry Philippine
       Scouts, wrote this action report while a POW. It describes
       one part of the defense of the Philippines. Filipinos
       manned the unit which was led by American officers.

2289. Chynoweth, Bradford Grethen. BELLAMY PARK: MEMOIRS.
       Hicksville, NY: Exposition Press, 1975. 301 pp.

       Here is the personal account (to 1942) of the commander
       of Filipino-American forces in Visayas. MacArthur's Chief
       of Staff, Richard Sutherland, receives some sharp
       criticism.

2290. COMBAT OVER CORREGIDOR. n.p.: 503d Parachute Combat Team,
       1945. 131 pp.

       This unit history of the 503d Parachute Combat Team
       apparently was written by a "jump-qualified" medic. The
       narrative covers his memories (admittedly based also on
       false reports and rumors) of the operation to retake
       Corregidor.

2291. Conroy, Robert. THE BATTLE OF BATAAN. New York:
       Macmillan, 1969. 85 pp.

       This brief volume is geared for the general public.
       Conroy calls the episode "America's greatest defeat."

292. Cook, Charles O., Jr. "The Strange Case of Rainbow-5."
        USNIP, 104 (August 1978), 67-73.

        Cook believes that no responsible U. S. commander would
        admit that prewar planning (Rainbow-5) virtually dismissed
        the Philippines as unsalvable. Roosevelt never approved or
        disapproved of Rainbow-5. According to Cook, the losses at
        Pearl Harbor served as a false excuse for not getting
        supplies and reinforcements to the Philippines. He also
        charges MacArthur with conduct close to insubordination.

293. Cortesi, Lawrence. THE BATTLE FOR MANILA. New York:
        Kensington Books, 1984. 288 pp.

        Cortesi emphasizes the grueling fight for the Allied
        liberation of the capital.

294. Daiguio, Amador T. BATAAN HARVEST. Manila PI:
        Florintino, 1973.

        NE

295. Daugherty, William F. "Flying Columns." ARMOR, 76
        (March-April 1967), 18-23.

        Capt. Daugherty (USA) reports on the use of armor in the
        liberation of the prisoners at Santo Tomas in Manila,
        February 1-3, 1945.

296. Davis, Helen McLaughlin. "The Women of Bataan." THE
        WOMAN, (June 1943), 13-15.

        NE

297. Davison, T.W. "Notes on Japanese Preparations for the
        Philippine Conquest." USNIP, 72 (June 1946), 792-799.

        This article is based on the author's observations while
        in the Philippines (December 1939-May 1942). In
        retrospect, he tells of the "little Japan" colonies
        scattered throughout the Philippines, the camera-bearing
        Japanese tourists, and the observation of activities at
        U.S. airfields. Davison believes that the Japanese took
        great care and detail in their preparations.

298. Deacon, Kenneth J. "Assault Crossings on the Pasig River."
        MIL ENGR, 50 (January-February 1958), 8-10.

        Deacon describes the role of the engineers in supporting

the advance of large forces across the strongly fortified
river near Manila.

2299.   Deacon, Kenneth J.   "Cagayan Valley Operations, 1945."   MIL
            ENGR, 56 (May-April 1964), 122.

        In May-June 1945, the engineers helped the 37th Infantry
Division liberate the Cagayan Valley in the Philippines.

2300.   Deacon, Kenneth J.   "Capture of Baguio, 1945."   MIL ENGR,
            57 (May-June 1965), 168.

        Engineers (from portions of the 117th and 108th
Engineers) supported the drive on Baguio in the Philippines
by the 37th Infantry Divion.

2301.   Deacon, Kenneth J.   "Engineers in the Los Banos Raid."   MIL
            ENGR, 50 (March-April 1958), 99-101.

        A patrol of engineers gathered the technical
intelligence necessary for the airdrop and the landing of
amphibian tractors so that the 11th Airborne Division could
liberate the more than two thousand internees at Los Banos
in the Philippines.

2302.   Deacon, Kenneth J.   "Limay Ridge, 1942."   MIL ENGR, 58
            (July-August 1966), 274.

        Deacon describes the action which preceded the surrender
of Company C, 803d Engineer Aviation Battalion, at Bataan.

2303.   Deacon, Kenneth J.   "Los Negros Island, 1944."   MIL ENGR,
            58 (November-December 1966), 403.

        As part of the campaign for the Admiralty Islands,
engineers and Seabees prepared the bulkhead, beach, roads,
and depots at Los Negros, in what was mistakenly predicted
to be an easy victory.

2304.   Deacon, Kenneth J.   "Mine Warfare in Manila, 1945."   MIL
            ENGR, 57 (September-October 1965), 348.

        Elements of the 8th, 117th, and 127th Engineers served
with assault squads in reducing the fortifications of the
Japanese defenders at Manila.

2305.   Deacon, Kenneth J.   "Rescue at Wheeler Point."   MIL ENGR,
            52 (May-June 1960), 182.

During the action to clear Manila Bay, amphibian
engineers operated between Mariveles and Corregidor.

2306.   Deacon, Kenneth J. "Seizure of the Bauang Bridges." MIL
        ENGR, 52 (July-August 1960), 292-294.

        Deacon, an experienced military correspondent, labels
        this operation in the Philippines one of the most brilliant
        small unit actions of the war: a model of
        infantry-engineer teamwork in night attack operations.

2307.   Dickerson, G.W. "Defeat on Leyte." INFANTRY J, 65 (July
        1949), 30-33.

        Dickerson's solid analysis of the Japanese defeat
        incorporates a new and valuable source: a contemporary
        report by the chief of staff (Gen. Tomochika) of the
        defending Japanese 35th Army on Leyte.

2308.   Dorny, Louis B. "Patrol Wing Ten's Raid on Jolo." USNIP,
        suppl. vol. (March 1985), 72-77.

        In an effort to gain strategic advantages in the
        southern Philippines, Patrol Wing Ten attacked the island
        of Jolo. Dorny describes how Japanese defenses thwarted
        the attacking PBY aircraft.

2309.   Downey, Fairfax. "The Last Charge." BY VALOR AND ARMS, 2
        (No. 4, 1976), 41-43.

        NE

2310.   Drake, Charles C. "I Surrendered Corregidor." COLLIERS,
        123 (8 January 1949), 12-13, 64-66.

        Gen. Drake (USA) was third in command under Wainwright.
        When Wainwright, Beebe, and Moore left under a white flag,
        Drake remained as commander of the Malinta tunnel complex.
        Of interest is the role of Drake's chief of staff, Lt. Col.
        Ted Kalukuka. Kalukuka spoke five languages and used
        Russian to converse with a Japanese lieutenant in making
        the arrangements for the final surrender.

2311.   Edmonds, Walter D. THEY FOUGHT WITH WHAT THEY HAD.
        Boston: Little, Brown, 1951. 532 pp.

        Edmonds presents a detailed, practically hour-by-hour
        report on the Japanese invasion of the Philippines.
        He describes three major problems: poor intelligence,

inappropriate (and too few) aircraft, and the "niggardly
policy" of Congress regarding prewar defensive
preparations. The author presents evidence of friction
between GHQ and Army Air Forces HQ, but he generally
concludes that the defeat represented "just a dis-
organized business."

2312. Edmonds, Walter D. "What Happened at Clark Field?"
        ATLANTIC MON, 188 (July 1951), 19-33.

        Edmonds reviews the conflicting accounts concerning the
        mishandling of air resources, but he is unable to sort out
        the responsibility. The episode remains a mystery.

2313. Espinosa, Gregoria I. "Filipino Nurses in Bataan and
        Corregidor. " AMER J NURSING, 46 (February 1946),
        97-98.

        Espinosa worked with the U.S. Army Nurse Corps as a
        civilian nurse. Her description of the last days at
        Corregidor indicate the arduous conditions on "The Rock" at
        the time of the surrender.

2314. Falk, Stanley L. "The Bataan Death March Remembered."
        ARMY, 17 (April 1967), 44-53.

        On the twenty-fifth anniversary of the Death March, Falk
        recalls that, for the Japanese, the disposition of these
        prisoners was a relatively unimportant matter. He
        attributes the disaster to four key factors: the poor
        physical condition of the prisoners by the time they
        surrendered, the unpreparedness of the Japanese to receive
        so many prisoners, the cruelty of individual Japanese
        troops, and the failure of Japanese leadership.

2315. Falk, Stanley. BATAAN: THE MARCH OF DEATH. New York:
        Jove Publications, 1972. 256 pp.

        This excellent, balanced analysis rises out of the
        author's extensive interviews (with Japanese and American
        participants) and his obvious command of the literature
        (primary as well as secondary sources). Falk explains his
        belief that the Death March was neither planned nor
        deliberate. He does, however, sharply criticize barbaric
        episodes, such as the massacre of the 91st Philippines Army
        Division. His informed estimate of the deaths associated
        with the march (600-650 Americans; 5,000-10,000 Filipinos)
        fills a gap in the official history. The photographs are
        excellent, and the Appendix includes Japanese Army

regulations about prisoners of war.

2316. Falk, Stanley. DECISION AT LEYTE. New York: W. W.
        Norton, 1966. 330 pp.

        Falk offers a balanced, scholarly analysis of this
        campaign. Ironically, of all the activities that made up
        the Battle of Leyte Gulf, none was fought in that body of
        water. This is an excellent presentation.

2317. Falk, Stanley. LIBERATION OF THE PHILIPPINES. New York:
        Ballantine Books, 1971. 160 pp.

        This is a brief but authoritative account.

2318. Finn, John M. "Patrol Into Japland." INFANTRY J, 56 (June
        1945), 22-25.

        Finn, commander of the 32d Infantry, recalls his
        experience in late November 1944 on a patrol involved in
        the retaking of Leyte.

2319. Finn, John M. "Shoestring Ridge." INFANTRY J, Part I: 57
        (September 1945), 47-52; Part II: 57 (October 1945),
        49-53.

        Finn describes how the unit he commanded (32d Infantry)
        captured Ormoc, on the western edge of Leyte.

2320. "The Fire-Bombing of Clark Field." FATE, 36 (December
        1983), 76-80.

              NE

2321. Firth, Robert H. A MATTER OF TIME: WHY THE PHILIPPINES
        FELL. Walnut, CA: author, 1981. 139 pp.

              NE

2322. Flanagan, E.M., Jr. THE LOS BANOS RAID: THE ELEVENTH
        AIRBORNE JUMPS AT DAWN. Novalto, CA: Presidio, 1986.
        276 pp.

        Here is a detailed, well-researched account of the
        rescue of some civilian internees in the Philippines.
        Flanagan highlights the airborne role.

2323. Flanagan, Edward M. "The Raid On Los Banos." ARMY, 33

(June 1983), 64-69.

Lt. Gen. Flanagan (USA) provides the details of the raid
by the 11th Division at Los Banos on February 23, 1945.
The operation rescued over two thousand internees, many of
whom were civilians.

2324. Foss, Peter J. "'Angels' at Los Banos." INFANTRY, 55
       (May-June 1965), 52-55.

       Foss describes the rescue of 2,147 internees at Los
       Banos by the 11th Airborne Division. Some of the internees
       called their rescuers "angels," and thereafter that
       nickname became officially attached to the division.

2325. Futrell, Robert F. "Air Hostilities in the Philippines, 8
       December 1941." AIR U REV, 16 (January-February 1965),
       33-45.

       Cautioning that much evidence has been lost or
       destroyed, the author asserts that, on the basis of
       existing documentation, Brereton did request--and was
       denied--permission to launch a B-17 strike against Formosa
       on December 8, 1941. It remains unclear, according to
       Futrell, whether or not Brereton received orders prior to
       the war to remove all B-17s to Mindanao. His conclusions
       about the fatal delay in bombing Formosa make allowances
       for (1) the long period of thinking only defensively, (2)
       unfamiliarity with strategic air capabilities, and (3)
       uncertainty about the directive that Japan must attack
       first (was the attack at Pearl Harbor to be considered an
       attack on the Philippines?). Here is a judicious inquiry
       and a valuable contribution to this controversial subject.

2326. Gordon, John, IV. "Among the Best: The Philippine
       Scouts." MIL REV, (67 September 1987), 69-79.

       Capt. Gordon (USA) praises the combat record of the
       Scouts. He emphasizes the significant role of the Scout
       NCOs as leaders and trainers.

2327. Gordon, John. "The Best Arm We Had." FIELD ARTILLERY J,
       (November-December 1984), 26-31.

       Capt. Gordon (USA) reports that American and Filipino
       gunners played a key role in holding Wainwright's defensive
       lines (December 24, 1941-January 5, 1942). MacArthur
       referred to the field artillery as "the best arm" he had.

2328. Gordon, John, IV. "The Navy's Infantry at Bataan." USNIP,
       SUPPL. (March 1985), 64-69.

       Of the available manpower at Bataan (about 500 men), the
       U. S. Navy formed a special battalion. The unit included
       some Marines, and the Navy men were told to do as the
       Marines did. In severe fighting, the special battalion
       acquitted itself well.

2329. Gumban, Edgardo T. BATAAN COMPANY COMMANDER. N. P.
       [Philippines]: published by author, n.d. [1976?]   125
       pp.

       This is the diary of a Filipino company commander.

2330. Heller, Charles E. "Corregidor--An Airborne Assault."
       INFANTRY, 72 (January-February 1982), 22-25.

       NE

2331. Hernandez, Al. BAHALA NA, COME WHAT MAY: THE STORY OF
       MISSION ISRM (I SHALL RETURN MACARTHUR), AN ARMY-NAVY
       INTELLIGENCE MISSION IN THE PACIFIC. AS TOLD TO DIXON
       EARLE. Berkeley, CA: Howell-North, 1961.   351 pp.

       NE

2332. Hersey, John. MEN ON BATAAN. New York: A.A. Knopf, 1942.
       313 pp.

       Hersey offers contemporary praise for MacArthur. The
       defeats in the Philippines are told by piecing together the
       scant sources available. The book ends with MacArthur
       safely in Australia.

2333. Hewlett, Frank. "Quartermasters on Bataan." QUARTERMASTER
       REV (May-June 1942).

       NE

2334. Hogaboom, William F. "Action Report: Bataan." MC GAZ, 30
       (April 1946), 25-33.

       Hogaboom's book tells of a Marine platoon which held out
       against the Japanese until the surrender at Bataan. The
       unhappy epilogue underlines the illogical, unjust nature of
       war.

2335. Ind, Allison. BATAAN: THE JUDGMENT SEAT. New York:

Macmillan, 1944.   395 pp.

Here is a first-hand report on the experiences of the
U.S. Army Philippine Command, May 1941 - May 1942. Lt.
Col. Ind (G-2) arrived in Manila in mid-1941, a time, he
says, that was too late to prepare adequately for the
defense of the Philippines. His tone is critical not only
of the lack of preparations but also of the arrogance and
racism that led to a false sense of superiority among
Americans. Also, according to the author, Brereton
scrapped plans for a bombing attack on Formosa (no farther
than the 23d Parallel) until obtaining photographs of
prospective targets. Of interest is Ind's report that the
B-17 which evacuated him (and the USAAF records) from the
Philippines crash-landed in Australia after running out of
fuel.

2336. Irwin, C.L. "Corregidor in Action." COAST ARTIL J, 86
        (January-February 1943), 9-12.

Col. Irwin (USA) served as G-3 for MacArthur and
Wainwright until he evacuated Corregidor just before the
surrender. His narrative includes special commendation for
the work of the Philippine Scouts and calls attention to
the dire food shortages on Corregidor (where eight days'
worth of rations equalled merely one day's food requirement
at Bataan).

2337. Jacoby, Melville. "Corregidor Cable No. 79." FIELD
        ARTILLERY J, 32 (April 1942), 263-267.

This report of February 17, 1942, contains much human
interest material about the defenders at Corregidor.

2338. Johansen, Herbert O. "Bonzai at Burauren." AIR FORCE, 28
        (March 1945), 4-8.

The author describes the successful defense in early
December 1944 of the headquarters for the 5th Air Force at
Leyte against Japanese infiltrators and paratroopers.

2339. Johnson, Harold K. "Defense Along the Abucay Line." MIL
        REV, 28 (February 1949), 43-52.

The future head of the Joint Chiefs of Staff focuses on
the small unit action along the Abucay line at Bataan. The
Philippine Scouts of the 57th Infantry served with
distinction in holding this line January 7-23, 1942.

2340. Keene, J.W. "Corregidor." MC GAZ, 49 (November 1965),
      65-69.

      Keene gives a personal account of the surrender at
      Corregidor. He served with the 4th Marines at Cavite Navy
      Yard.

2341. Kennedy, Milly Wood. CORREGIDOR: GLORY...GHOSTS...AND
      GOLD. Fairbanks, SD: Author, 1971. 255 pp.

      This is a well-written account of the last days at
      Corregidor, but Kennedy offers little that is new. The
      book contains some excellent photographs.

2342. King, Michael J. RANGERS: SELECTED COMBAT OPERATIONS IN
      WORLD WAR II. Ft. Leavenworth, KS: Army Command &
      General Staff School, 1985. 89 pp.

      Of the five operations examined, only one occurred in
      the war against Japan. The episode involved the rescue of
      511 POWs at Cabanatuan by the 6th Ranger Battalion, Alamo
      Scouts, and Filipino guerrillas. Analyzing this victory,
      King calls it one of the Army's most complex operations in
      the war.

2343. Kirkpatrick, Charles E. "ADA in Bataan--A Retrograde
      Operation." AIR DEF ARTILLERY, n.v. (Spring 1985),
      40-45.

      The author credits the work of the 200th Coast Artillery
      and the 515th Coast Artillery in delaying the Japanese
      advance during the U.S.-Filipino retrograde operation in
      withdrawing to Bataan. According to the author, two
      important lessons emerged for artillery doctrine from the
      operation: (a) the return of AAA units to the division and
      (b) the shift from defense of critical assets to defense of
      maneuvering units.

2344. Kirkpatrick, Charles E. "Echoes of a Distant Battle--Air
      Defense Lessons of the Philippine Defense Campaign of
      1941-1942." AIR DEF ARTILLERY (Winter 1984), 4-6.

      Drawing lessons from the "first battle," Kirkpatrick
      outlines the operation of the 60th Coast Artillery in the
      defense of Manila Bay (December 8, 1941-May 6, 1942).

2345. Knox, Donald. DEATH MARCH: THE SURVIVORS OF BATAAN. New
      York: Harcourt, Brace, and Jovanovich, 1981. 482 pp.

Knox, a television producer, has assembled the forty-year-old recollections of sixty-eight survivors of the Bataan Death March. The book contains much valuable information--information that will take the reader through a wide range of emotions.

2346.   Leek, Jerome B. CORREGIDOR G.I. Culver City, CA: Highland Press, 1948. 335 pp.

Leek surrendered at Corregidor. His Japanese captors forced him to participate in the Manila "Gloat March," and he spent the rest of the war in a prison camp near Cabu in eastern Luzon. Leek reports on atrocities that General Homma witnessed, thereby calling into question the general's main line of defense at his war crimes trial.

2347.   McAnsh, A.T. "Incident on the Road to Baguio." INFANTRY J, 58 (March 1946), 29-31.

The author recounts the results of a Japanese ambush in northern Luzon against the 3d Battalion on April 14, 1945.

2348.   McCandlish, W.F. "How Explosives Went to War in the Philippines." EXPLOSIVES ENGR (September-October 1945), 198-211.

NE

2349.   McCutcheon, Keith B. "Close Air Support on Luzon." MC GAZ, 29 (September 1945), 38-39.

The author attests to the close coordination between air and ground forces in this Philippines campaign. The SBDs are especially singled out for his praise. Of interest is his observation that close air support had not previously been used to its fullest potential.

2350.   McGee, John H. RICE AND SALT: A HISTORY OF THE DEFENSE AND OCCUPATION OF MINDANAO DURING WORLD WAR II. San Antonio, TX: Naylor, 1962. 242 pp.

NE

2351.   McGurk, Anna. "Postmarked Manila." AIR POWER HIST, 6 (July 1959), 207-216.

From Manila, the author wrote a letter to her sister which describes the American reoccupation.

2352. Maddox, Robert J. "Bandits Over Clark Field." AMER HIST
      ILLUS, 9 (June 1974), 20-27.

      The author describes the confusion about U.S. air
      resources in the Philippines, the heavy damage inflicted by
      the Japanese, and the contrasting accounts by Brereton and
      MacArthur-Sunderland. Maddox does, however, downplay the
      significance of the episode.

2353. Mallonee, Richard C., II, ed. THE NAKED FLAGPOLE: BATTLE
      FOR BATAAN. Sam Rafael, CA: Presidio Press, 1980. 204
      pp.

      The editor presents the diary kept by his father, a
      colonel in the 21st Field Artillery Regiment, 21st
      Division, Philippine Army. The diary may be the only
      eyewitness account of the campaign in the Philippines which
      has survived the war. This is an excellent source on the
      defense of the Philippines. After the surrender, Mallonee
      writes of the Bataan Death March (with the chief horror
      being the poor physical condition of the captives) and his
      subsequent moves to Taiwan, Formosa, and Mukden. His POW
      pay amounted to 310 yen per month. Of interest is the
      description of the Japanese guards being amused at the
      inability of the bowlegged Gen. Wainwright to keep his
      knees together when standing at attention.

2354. Marquardt, Frederick S. BEFORE BATAAN AND AFTER: A
      PERSONALIZED HISTORY OF OUR PHILIPPINE EXPERIMENT.
      Indianapolis, IN: Bobbs-Merrill, 1943. 315 pp.

      Marquardt, a newspaper reporter in the Philippines,
      chronicles the events he witnessed. The book amounts to an
      excellent contemporary report on affairs in the
      Philippines.

2355. Mathews, Richard. "Further Escape Denied." WWII, 1 (July
      1986), 34-41.

      Here is a report on the 1945 activities of Maj. Robert
      V. Connally and his special task force in sealing off the
      Japanese forces under Yamashita in northern Luzon.

2356. Mellnik, Stephen M. "How the Japs Took Corregidor." COAST
      ARTILL J, 88 (March-April 1945), 2-11, 17.

      Col. Mellnik had been an artillery officer in the
      Philippines at the outbreak of the war. This report,
      written soon after his escape as a Japanese prisoner, could

not be published until after Corregidor had been retaken.
He says that the heavy Japanese bombings produced
surprisingly few casualties. Moreover, Mellnik feels that
even despite changing circumstances, local Japanese
military officers will continue to follow their original
tactical orders.

2357. Mellnick, Stephen M. "The Life and Death of the 200th
          Coast Artillery (AA)." COAST ARTILL J, 90 (March-April
          1947), 2-7.

          Here is a personal account of the activity and the
surrender of his unit on April 9, 1942, at Bataan.

2358. Miller, Ernest B. BATAAN UNCENSORED. Long Prairie, MN:
          Hart Publications, 1949. 409 pp.

          Miller commanded the 19th Tank Batallion, but spent most
of the war as a POW. His strong criticism of U.S.
defensive preparations in the Philippines extends to
MacArthur and Wainwright. He complains of excessive "red
tape" and "indecision." U.S. military leadership did not
impress Miller.

2359. Moriya, Tadashi. NO REQUIEM. Tokyo: Hokuseido Press,
          1968. 374 pp.

          Translated by Geoffrey S. Kishimoto, the book represents
the personal account of a Japanese soldier in the
Philippines.

2360. Morrill, John H. and Martin W. Thornton. SOUTH FROM
          CORREGIDOR. New York: Simon and Schuster, 1943.
          252 pp.

          Lt. Cmdr. Morrill (USN) served in the Philippines aboard
the mine-sweeping QUAIL. In this well-written account, he
describes the fighting at Corregidor. The book, however,
centers on Morrill's adventures during a 31-day
voyage-escape to Australia on a small (36-foot) boat with a
crew of 17.

2361. Morris, Eric. CORREGIDOR: THE END OF THE LINE. New York:
          Stein and Day, 1981. 528 pp.

          The author, a military teacher at Sandhurst, presents
not a formal history but an excellent portrayal of the
human experience during the ordeal at Corregidor. Morris's
narrative is intertwined with such vignettes. The book is

based almost entirely on interviews.

2362.   Morton, Louis, ed.   "Bataan Diary of Major Achille C.
        Tisdelle."   MIL AFFS, 11 (Fall 1947), 131-148.

        Tisdelle, an aide to Maj. Gen. King, became a POW in the
        Philippines. Because the diarist held a position with
        access to reliable information, Morton calls this diary
        (for the period February 1 - April 13, 1932) "the most
        valuable single document" about the surrender at Bataan.

2363.   Morton, Louis. THE FALL OF THE PHILIPPINES. Washington,
        D.C.: Office of the Chief of Military History, Dept. of
        the Army, 1953. 643 pp.

        Although Morton points out serious mistakes made by
        MacArthur in the defense of the Philippines, the general's
        reputation (according to Morton) will not be seriously
        affected. Noting the serious shortage of food and foreign
        support services, Morton labels Bataan a "medical defeat."
        He chooses to omit the Death March because it had no effect
        on the course of military operations.

2364.   Morton, Louis.   "The Philippine Army, 1935-1939:
        Eisenhower's Memorandum to Quezon."   MIL AFFS, 12
        (Summer 1948), 103-107.

        During the period 1935-1939, Eisenhower served in the
        Office of the Military Advisor in Manila, working to create
        a Filipino national army. Morton focuses on a memorandum
        Eisenhower wrote June 22, 1942, just prior to his departure
        for North Africa. The memo traces the origins of the
        Philippine army.

2365.   Palmer, Bruce, Jr.   "Covering the Withdrawal into Bataan."
        INFANTRY SCHOOL Q, 37 (July 1950), 42-65.

        In this examination of one of the few large-scale
        sustained movements to the rear by U. S. troops in the war,
        General Palmer (U.S.A.) reaffirms the soundness of
        fundamental Army doctrine. Palmer uses source material
        available only at the Infantry School.

2366.   Parker, T.C.   "The Epic of Corregidor-Bataan, December 24,
        1941-May 4, 1942."   USNIP, 69 (January 1943), 9-22.

        Parker served as naval aide to High Commissioner Sayre.
        In this contemporary account, Parker describes conditions
        in the final phase of the first battle for the Philippines,

including the destruction of remaining currency (lighting cigarettes with $100 bills); the earthquake at Corregidor on April 8, 1942; and the bogus Philippine money clearly marked "Printed in Japan."

2367. Parker, T.C. "Thirteen Women in a Submarine." USNIP, 76 (July 1950), 716-721.

The author left Corregidor by submarine on May 3, 1942. Also aboard were thirteen women. He describes the inconveniences for all hands and the humor associated with these circumstances during the seventeen-day voyage to Australia.

2368. Postlethwait, E.M. "Corregidor Coordination." INFANTRY J, 57 (August 1945), 16-19.

The author maintains that the campaign to retake Corregidor should serve as a model for coordination among the services. He especially applauds the performance of the support elements (air and naval bombardment).

2369. Prickett, William F. "Naval Battalion at Mariveles." MC GAZ, 34 (June 1950), 40-43.

Here is the story of a unit--neither purely "naval" nor a "battalion"--of a mixed group of unattached personnel (about two hundred total) who gathered at Mariveles, one of the last remaining naval facilities in the western Pacific by January 1942. The commander, "Fidgety Frank" Bridget, launched a mini-attack, not realizing that Japanese forces badly outnumbered his "battalion."

2370. Redmond, Juanita. I SERVED ON BATAAN. Philadelphia, PA: J.B. Lippincott, 1943. 167 pp.

Lt. Redmond (USA) describes her experiences as a nurse in Manila, Bataan, and Corregidor. It is a moving account.

2371. Ritt, Carl. "Filipino Nurses on Bataan." AMER J NURSING, 45 (May 1945), 346-347.

One doctor (G.M. Pablan) and two nurses (Carmen Lanot and Bruna R. Calvan) remained at Bataan after the surrender. Ritt tells how they treated not only Filipino civilians but also secretly cared for guerrillas.

2372-2373. Omitted.

2374. Romulo, Carlos P. I SAW THE FALL OF THE PHILIPPINES. Garden City, NY: Doubleday, Doran, 1942. 323 pp.

Romulo, a newspaper and radio owner in the Philippines, fought with MacArthur's forces at Bataan and Corregidor. His reports about the U.S.-Filipino defenses earned Romulo a Pulitzer Prize. He left with MacArthur and served as an aide to the general.

2375. Rutherford, Ward. FALL OF THE PHILIPPINES. New York: Ballantine Books, 1971. 159 pp.

In this highly readable, popular account, Rutherford criticizes MacArthur's leadership. According to the author, the loss of U.S. air resources not only demonstrated poor command judgment but also made improbable a successful defense of the Philippines.

2376. Sackton, Frank J. "Night Attacks in the Philippines." INF J, 57 (August 1945), 32-33.

The author recommends certain tactical steps to follow in these engagements.

2377. Savary, Gladys S. OUTSIDE THE WALLS. New York: Vantage Press, 1954. 206 pp.

Savary presents a well-written account of life under the Japanese occupation in the Philippines (Manila).

2378. Schirmer, Daniel B. and Stephen R. Shalom, eds. THE PHILIPPINE READER. Boston: South End Press, 1987. 425 pp.

The collections covers much of the U.S.-Philippines relationship. Some of the material touches on the war.

2379. Seay, Joseph B. "The 11th Airborne Division in the Leyte Mountain Operation." MIL REV, 29 (October 1949), 17-24.

For over one month, the unit faced--and solved--difficult problems of supply in an inhospitable region.

2380. Sharp, E.A. "Corregidor Revisited." BULL AMER HIST COLL (Manila), 6 (January-March 1978), 25-29.

NE

2381. Shimada, Koichi, "Japanese Naval Air Operations in the Philippines Invasion." USNIP, 81 (January 1955), 1-17.

The author, a navy officer who became a brigadier
general in the army, particpated in the attack against the
Philippines in December 1941. Relying on the famed "Zero"
--the "sword, shield and buckle" of the invasion--the
Japanese pilots were surprised to find U. S. aircraft
sitting on the ground. His account describes a narrowly
run operation that did not leave much room for error.

2382. Smith, Robert Ross. TRIUMPH IN THE PHILIPPINES.
       Washington, D.C.: Office of the Chief of Military
       History, Dept. of the Army, 1963. 756 pp.

       Using official records, especially after-action reports,
       Smith writes the history of the 8th Army's reoccupation of
       the southern Philippines. He then offers an analysis of
       the movement into Luzon by the 6th and 8th Armies.

2383. Souberman, Eugene. "Philippine Air Diary." AMER AVN HSJ,
       13 (Winter 1968), 240-256.

       The article serves as a reference source in providing
       chronological entries on the air war. There are three
       parts: commanders, units, and a fighter diary of the 17th
       Pursuit Squadron.

2384. Steinberg, Rafael. RETURN TO THE PHILIPPINES. Alexandria,
       VA: Time-Life, 1979. 208 pp.

       Steinberg provides an excellent narrative of the Allied
       return to the Philippines. Written for the general public,
       the book describes the heavy fighting and incorporates some
       interesting photos of the fierce combat.

2385. Stick, D. "Air Action at Leyte." LEATHERNECK (March
       1945).

       NE

2386. Terami-Wada, Motoe. "A Japanese Takeover of the
       Philippines." BULL AMER HIST COLL, (Manila), 13
       (January-March 1984), 31-39.

       NE

2387. Underbrink, Robert L. DESTINATION CORREGIDOR. Annapolis,
       MD: U.S. Naval Institute, 1971. 240 pp.

       Based on documents, published works, and interviews, the
       book recounts the four-month effort to provide supply

relief to MacArthur's command at Bataan and Corregidor.
Despite many heroic efforts, only three freighters and two
aircraft (one crashed on arrival) ever made it to the
American-Filipino redoubts.

2388. United States. Army Air Forces. ARMY AIR ACTION IN THE
       PHILIPPINES AND NETHERLANDS EAST INDIES, 1941-1942.
       Washington, D.C.: USAAF, 1945. 300 pp.

       This official study highlights U.S. air and naval
       weaknesses in the Pacific area before the war. MacArthur
       was unaware of these weaknesses and materiel shortages in
       1941. Moreover, according to this study, MacArthur did not
       know that Mindanao could be resupplied and reinforced.
       Unfortunately, there are no answers on the inexplicable
       loss of U.S. air resources at Clark Field. See the chapter
       entitled "A Gallant Defeat."

2389. United States. Department of the Army. Forces in the Far
       East. PHILIPPINES AIR OPERATIONS RECORD: PHASE ONE.
       Washington, D.C.: Office of the Chief of Military
       History, 1952. 71 pp.

       This Japanese surprise attack reaped unexpected success,
       according to Japanese officers who participated in the
       campaign. Their report includes statistics on the aircraft
       and units involved.

2390. Valtin, Jan. [pseud. Richard J. H. Krebes.] CHILDREN OF
       YESTERDAY. New York; Reader's Press, 1946. 429 pp.

       Here is a first-hand narrative of operations in the
       Philippines by the 24th Infantry Division. The author, a
       combat correspondent, accompanied the American forces into
       the jungle, and he gives a starkly realistic report of the
       fierce fighting.

2391. Varias, Antonio. A COMPILATION ON WORLD WAR II IN THE
       PHILIPPINES, 1941-1942. Manila, PI: Publishers
       Association of the Philippines, 1979. 328 pp.

       NE

2392. Villarin, Mariano. THE STORY OF THE DEFENDERS OF BATAAN
       AND CORREGIDOR AND THEIR CAPTIVITY. Great Neck, NY:
       Todd and Honeywell, 1986. 368 pp.

       NE

2393.   Watson, Richard L. "What Really Happened at Clark Field?"
        FLYING, 44 (February 1949), 18-20, 62-64.

        Key figures (e.g., Brereton, MacArthur, Sutherland,
        Eubank, George) disagree on who should bear responsibility
        for the disaster to U. S. air resources in the Philippines.
        The destruction of records during the war, says Watson,
        leaves a cloud of uncertainty over the issue. According to
        the author, no one knows for sure what happened in December
        1941 amidst an environment of "general confusion and bad
        luck."

2394.   Woodhall, Jeffrey. "The 26th Cavalry in the Philippines."
        ARMOR, 92 (January-February 1983), 8-16.

        Here is an account of U.S. horse soldiers and the unit's
        rearguard action in upsetting the Japanese timetable while
        U.S. and Filipino forces shifted to Bataan. Wainwright
        called the unit "the most reliable" in his command.

2395.   Wheeler, John. "Rearguard in Luzon." CAVALRY J, 52
        (March-April 1943), 5-6.

        Capt. Wheeler (U.S.A.) reports on his experiences with
        the 26th Cavalry which conducted rearguard action across
        Luzon to Bataan. See especially his account of the Battle
        of Moron.

2396.   White, William L. THEY WERE EXPENDABLE. New York:
        Harcourt, Brace, 1942. 209 pp.

        In this (immediate) contemporary report, White tells of
        Motor Torpedo Boat Squadron 3 at Cavite in the Philippines
        during the final days before the Allied defeat. The
        narrative reflects the interviews White held with four
        young officers of the group. The author calls the action
        in the Philippines "America's Little Dunkirk." The heroic,
        if vain, efforts of the unit earn his praise. The squadron
        evacuated MacArthur and some of his entourage from
        Corregidor to Mindanao. The general ordered the four
        officers to return to the United States as training
        instructors.

2397.   Winslow, W.G. BATTLING BASTARDS OF BATAAN. Davenport, FL:
        Coral Reef Publications, 1977.

        Winslow highlights the personal dimension of the
        determined Allied defense in the Philippines.

2398. Yap, D.M., ed. REMEMBER THE PHILIPPINES. Washington,
          D.C.: Capital Publishers, 1980. 192 pp.

          Here are selected articles from BATAAN MAGAZINE. The
          material addresses the sweep of Filipino history, not just
          the war years.

IV.D.1.m. Singapore

2399. Allen, Louis. SINGAPORE, 1941-1942. London:
          Davis-Poynter, 1977. 343 pp.

          Allen uses solid research in hard-to-get-at sources to
          produce a penetrating analysis of this British debacle.
          Asking who was to blame, Allen assesses the roles of key
          figures, such as Simson, Shenton Thomas, Vlieland,
          Brooke-Popham, Playfair, and Wavell. His conclusions
          spread the responsibility liberally.

2400. Attiwill, Kenneth. FORTRESS. New York: Doubleday, 1960.
          243 pp.

          Here is an initial account of the British higher direc-
          tion of the defense of Singapore. Amidst all the folly,
          errors, petty jealousies, greed and stupidity that reached
          from Singapore to the highest level in London, Attiwill
          measures out little credit to the Japanese.

2401. Barber, Noel. A SINISTER TWILIGHT: THE FALL OF SINGAPORE,
          1942. Boston: Houghton Mifflin, 1968. 364 pp.

          Barber, a correspondent and historian, tells this story
          through the experiences of selected people (e.g., the
          governor, an American nurse, the manager of a rubber
          company, a newspaper reporter, etc.). Percivall's
          sensitivity in not wanting to alarm the inhabitants by
          strengthening the fortress's defenses will (still) startle
          the reader. Barber claims to have found untapped
          documents, such as prison diaries. His direct citations,
          however, are unremarkable, but he does incorporate valuable
          primary sources. The book is well written and an
          interesting introduction to the topic.

2402. Barclay, Cyril N. "The Fall of Singapore: A Reappraisal."
          ARMY, 18 (April 1968), 44-53.

          British Brigadier Barclay argues that, with the British
          gross underestimation of the Japanese, no possible
          reinforcements could have saved Singapore.

2403.   Barclay, Glen St. John. "Singapore Strategy: The Role of
        the United States in Imperial Defense." MIL AFFS, 39
        (February 1975), 54-59.

        With the British seeking American reinforcement of
        Singapore, and with the United States keeping its main
        naval force at Pearl Harbor, Barclay asserts that no
        credible deterrent existed in the western Pacific by the
        end of 1941. Using key primary sources, he concludes that
        the success of the Singapore strategy depended on the
        commitment of commanders who had little faith in
        that strategy.

2404.   Booth, K. "Singapore 1942: Some Warnings." ARMY Q &
        DEFENCE J, 102 (January 1972), 191-200.

        Booth exposes some of the shortcomings of British
        strategy in the Far East during the inter-war years.
        According to the author, British defeatist attitudes
        translated into unpreparedness.

2405.   Callahan, Raymond. "The Illusion of Security: Singapore,
        1919-1942." J CONTEMP HIST, 9 (April 1974), 69-92.

        Bringing his broadly based research to bear, Callahan
        links the 1942 disaster to the situation accepted by the
        Coalition Government under Lloyd George after the First
        World War. The author reveals the illusion of British
        power during the interwar years and emphasizes the
        increasing British reliance on the United States,
        especially to meet the rising Japanese challenge in the Far
        East.

2406.   Callahan, Raymond. THE WORST DISASTER: THE FALL OF
        SINGAPORE. Newark, DE: University of Delaware Press,
        1977. 293 pp.

        Callahan presents a premier study of this British
        defeat. British civil and military leaders on the scene
        receive much criticism. Of special interest in this
        well-researched study is Callahan's treatment of the
        sinking of the REPULSE and PRINCE OF WALES.

2407.   Connell, Brian. RETURN OF THE TIGER. Garden City, NY:
        Doubleday, 1960. 282 pp.

        Here is a report on a 1943 raid by Australian and
        British forces under Lt. Col. Ivan Lyon against Japanese

ships near Singapore. The fact that this daring raid took
place after a long journey from Australia in a ship of
dubious seaworthiness only adds to the interest of this
exciting, well told, war story. Photos and maps enhance
the narrative.

2408. Donahue, Arthur G. LAST FLIGHT FROM SINGAPORE. New
       York: Macmillan, 1943. 169 pp.

       Here is a personal account of the final, futile attempt
to save Singapore. Donahue, an American pilot who served
with the R.A.F. in Europe, shifted to Singapore and
suffered combat wounds during the ineffectual defense of
the fortress.

2409. Falk, Stanley L. SEVENTY DAYS TO SINGAPORE. New York: G.
       P. Putnam's Sons, 1975. 301 pp.

       With the authority that stems from thorough research and
mastery of the material, Falk recounts the psychologically
devastating defeat of the fortress deemed impregnable. He
does not fail to point his finger at those responsible.

2410. Hamill, Ian. THE STRATEGIC ILLUSION: THE SINGAPORE
       STRATEGY AND THE DEFENSE OF AUSTRALIA AND NEW ZEALAND,
       1919-1942. Singapore: Singapore University Press,
       1982.

       Here is an excellent study, well researched and well
presented, of the folly of British strategic planners
between the wars. As Hamill demonstrates, the concept of
an impregnable fortress at Singapore dominated British
ideas about imperial defense schemes in the Far East for
over twenty years.

2411. Hamill, Ian. "Winston Churchill and the Singapore Naval
       Base, 1924-1929." J SEA STUD, 11 (September 1980),
       277-286.

       Hamill disclosed that Churchill not only worked to delay
the building of the base at Singapore (1924-1929) but also
disparaged the strategic considerations associated with the
project.

2412. Hunt, Leslie. "December Disaster." RAF FLYING REV, 16
       (January 1961), 26-28.

       NE

2413. Jacobs, A.E. "The Loss of REPULSE and PRINCE OF WALES,
       December 10, 1941." WARSHIP INTL, 23 (No. 1, 1986),
       12-28.

       The narrative is taken from the journal of a seaman
       aboard the REPULSE. Fighting off oil slick and sleep while
       in the water, Jacobs eventually was rescued. See
       especially his comments on anti-aircraft operations during
       the Japanese attack.

2414. Kiralfy, Alexander. "The Defense of Singapore." ASIA &
       AMERICAS, 41 (January 1941), 20-22.

       Although Kiralfy leaves open the possibility of a
       Japanese land assault on Singapore through Malaya (a
       "tedious and expensive experiment"), he believes that a
       Japanese attack would come by sea. If so, the U.S. fleet
       might be needed to aid the British defenders.

2415. Kirby, S. Woodburn. SINGAPORE: THE CHAIN OF DISASTER.
       New York: Macmillan, 1971. 270 pp.

       Here is an authoritative British interpretation of the
       disastrous losses of Singapore, Malaya, and two prize
       ships.

2416. Leasor, James. SINGAPORE: THE BATTLE THAT CHANGED THE
       WORLD. Garden City: NY: Doubleday, 1968. 325 pp.

       British blindness and illusions earn sharp critisism
       from this British professor. The book is well written and
       especially effective in its revealing profiles of leading
       personalities. Although there are few scholarly trappings,
       Leasor obviously knows his subject. The bibliography
       concentrates chiefly on published sources, but in the
       ackowledgements there is mention of interviews and
       unpublished, private sources.

2417. Low, N.I. WHEN SINGAPORE WAS SYON-TO. Singapore: Eastern
       Unversities Press, 1973. 134 pp.

       NE

2418. McIntyre, W. David. THE RISE AND FALL OF THE SINGAPORE
       NAVAL BASE, 1941-1942. London: Macmillan, 1979. 289
       pp.

       After ten years or research that includes multi-archival
       materials, the author concludes that London must bear

primary responsibility for the debacle at Singapore. Not
local conditions, he says, but protracted confusion in
London about Singapore fostered continuing problems.
McIntyre is particularly effective in dealing with the
complexities of racial relations, especially in Malaya.

2419. McIntyre, W. David. "The Strategic Significance of
      Singapore, 1917-1942: The Naval Base and the
      Commonwealth." J SEA HIST, 10 (March 1969), 69-94.

      After an exhaustive examination of the Australian and
      New Zealand archives, the author describes how a strategic
      illusion had been created.

2420. McKie, Ronald C.H. THE HEROES. New York: Harcourt,
      Brace, and World, 1961. 307 pp.

      McKie tells of two raids launched against Japanese-
      occupied Singapore from Australia. One (Jaywick) succeeded
      but the other (Rimeau) did not. The Japanese first praised
      the captives taken as "The Heroes" for their bravery, then
      executed them. It is an interesting story, well written
      and well researched.

2421. Owen, Frank. THE FALL OF SINGAPORE. London: Michael
      Joseph, 1960. 216 pp.

      In this knowledgeable analysis of the humiliating
      defeat, Owen offers a balanced view. Amidst the mistakes
      and misfortune, he also identifies examples of heroism and
      self-sacrifice.

2422. Playfair, Giles. SINGAPORE GOES OFF THE AIR. New York:
      E.P. Dutton, 1943. 273 pp.

      Through his journal, Playfair tells of his experiences
      with the Malaya Broadcasting System at the end of 1941.
      His account gives a first-hand report on conditions in
      Singapore for the last few months before the war.

2423. Sansom, Sir George. "The Story of Singapore." FOR AFFS,
      22 (January 1944), 279-297.

      Arguing that Singapore was virtually lost before the war
      began, Sansom says that the British defeat there resulted
      from a lack of machines and munitions, especially sea and
      air power. The shortages stemmed, in his view, from
      Western governments hoping that the pen was mightier than
      the sword. This British diplomat also rejects the notion

that colonialism led to the loss of Singapore. Bombs and
bullets, not ballot boxes, caused the problem.

2424. Shjinozaki, Mamoru. SYONAN: MY STORY: THE JAPANESE
       OCCUPATION OF SINGAPORE. Singapore: Asia Pacific
       Press, 1975. 123 pp.

       Here is the personal account of a Japanese officer about
       the Japanese victory and occupation at Singapore.

2425. Simson, Ivan. SINGAPORE: TOO LITTLE, TOO LATE. London:
       Leo Cooper, 1970. 165 pp.

       Here is a brief indictment against inadequate and
       mistaken British efforts to shore up the alleged fortress
       at Singapore.

2426. Smyth, Sir John. PERCIVAL AND THE TRAGEDY OF SINGAPORE.
       London: Macdonald, 1971. 304 pp.

       Here is an authoritative analysis of the British
       disaster. Smyth, a British military expert, knew Percival.
       Although Smyth treats the general with understanding, there
       is no attempt to gloss over critical British errors in the
       lack of defensive preparations at Singapore.
       Underestimation of the Japanese seems to be one of the
       chief British failings in Smyth's eyes.

2427. Sutton, Barry. JUNGLE PILOT. London: Macmillan, 1946.
       127 pp.

       Sutton retells his experiences as a pilot in the Burma
       campaign.

2428. Swinson, Arthur. DEFEAT IN MALAYA: THE FALL OF SINGAPORE.
       New York: Ballantine Books, 1970. 160 pp.

       The wartime British army officer gives his version of
       the reasons for the British defeat. Poor preparation,
       inadequate resources, and underestimation of the Japanese
       rank high on his list.

2429. Tsuji, Masanobu. SINGAPORE: THE JAPANESE VERSION.
       London: Constable, 1960. 358 pp.

       Originally published in 1951, the work is translated by
       Margaret E. Lake. Here is an unapologetic account of the
       early Japanese victories written by the chief of operations
       and planning for the 25th Japanese Army.

V.D.1.n. Wake Island

2430. Andrews, Peter. "The Defense of Wake." AMER HERITAGE, 38
       (July/August 1987), 65-80.

       Here is an account of the preparations and personalities
       involved in the defense of Wake Island. Andrews traces the
       friction between Devereaux and Cunningham as well as the
       questionable decisions of Admirals Pye and Fletcher. Of
       special interest is the author's assertion that Devereaux's
       alleged message ("send us more Japs") never occurred and
       that the story was probably invented by a Marine public
       relations specialist far from the scene.

2431. Baldwin, Hanson W. "The Saga of Wake." VA Q REV, 18
       (Summer 1942), 321-335.

       Baldwin points out that defensive preparations at Wake
       Island were not completed in December 1941. The article
       reviews these U.S. preparations, which involved 1200
       civilian laborers and about 400 Marines. Also, there is a
       summary of Wake's final radio reports, which ceased on
       December 23, 1941.

2432. Bayler, Walter L.J. LAST MAN OFF WAKE ISLAND.
       Indianapolis, IN: Bobbs-Merrill, 1943. 367 pp.

       Lt. Col. Bayler, a Marine communications officer, was
       the last American to leave Wake Island. His story includes
       reports on the battles at Wake, Midway, and Guadalcanal; he
       claims to be the only American who fought in all three.
       Cecil Cairnes serves as the "as told to" conduit.

2433. Cunningham, Winfield Scott. WAKE ISLAND COMMAND. Boston:
       Little, Brown, 1961. 300 pp.

       Cunningham, with Lydel Sims, relates his experience as
       senior naval officer at Wake Island. The book defends his
       performance and exposes the personality clash between
       Cunningham and Major James Devereaux (USMC). The author
       also includes his experience as a POW, during which time he
       twice attempted (unsucccessfully) to escape.

2434. Devereux, James P.S. THE STORY OF WAKE ISLAND.
       Philadelphia, PA: J.B. Lippincott, 1947. 252 pp.

       Devereux commanded the doomed Marine garrison which
       defended Wake Island at the start of the war. His

special vantage point enriches his commentary not only
on the ill-fated military operation but also on the
state (and spirit) of the prewar preparations to defend
the island.

2435. Graybar, Lloyd J. "American Pacific Strategy After Pearl
      Harbor: The Relief of Wake Island." PROLOGUE, 12 (Fall
      1980), 134-150.

      Incorporating interviews and archival material, Graybar
      reports that, despite the attractive ideas associated with
      a vigorous defense of Wake--for morale, for Wake's own
      value, for the chance to draw the Japanese Navy into a
      major battle--American strategists were not prepared to
      make that commitment in December 1941. Calling the
      decision to withdraw "strategically sound," the author
      notes that it was neither heroically carried out nor made
      in time to evacuate Wake's defenders.

2436. Heinl, Robert D., Jr. THE DEFENSE OF WAKE. Washington,
      D.C.: U.S. Marine Corps, 1947. 75 pp.

      This official Marine history reviews the stubborn
      defense put up by less than 450 men in December 1941.
      Toward the end of the battle, Marines annihilated a
      Japanese landing party on Wilkes. A prewar history of Wake
      Island (1586-1941) appears in the Appendix.

2437. Schultz, Duane P. WAKE ISLAND: THE HEROIC, GALLANT FIGHT.
      New York: St. Martin's Press, 1978. 247 pp.

      In this account of the defense--and loss--of Wake
      Island, Schultz generally supports the actions of the
      commander, Winfield Scott Cunningham.

2438. Werstein, Irving. WAKE: THE STORY OF A BATTLE. New York:
      Thomas Y. Crowell, 1964. 145 pp.

      Werstein describes the heroic U.S. defense for a general
      audience.

IV.D.1.o. Land Vehicles/Weapons

2439. Church, John. MILITARY VEHICLES OF WORLD WAR II. New
      York: Sterling, 1982. 160 pp.

      This well-illustrated reference includes information on
      many non-combat vehicles (some of which are
      less than familiar but necessary for wartime activities).

2440. Hogg, Ian V. THE ENCYCLOPEDIA OF INFANTRY WEAPONS OF WORLD
       WAR II. London: Bison Books, 1977. 192 pp.

       This thorough reference presents the weapons used by all
       sides in all theaters. Illustrations and photographs are
       included.

2441. Hogg, Ian V. THE GUNS OF WORLD WAR II. London: MacDonald
       and Jane's, 1976.

       Here is an encylopedic reference. Hogg provides
       information on the development of each weapon and its use
       in the war. Photographs and drawings reinforce the
       descriptions.

2442. Jeudy, J.G. and Marc Tararine. THE JEEP. n.p.: Editions
       Vilo, 1981. 272 pp.

       Here is a detailed study on the development of the jeep,
       including the use of the vehicle in the war against Japan.

2443. Marshall, S.L.A. "On Heavy Artillery: American Experience
       in Four Wars." PARAMETERS, 8 (June 1978), 2-20.

       With regard to the Pacific, Marshall argues that the
       most effective use of heavy artillery occurred in breaking
       down the walls of Intramuros during the battle for Manila.
       He reports that only one 240mm howitzer battalion went to
       the Pacific theater.

2444. Willinger, Kurt and Jean Guerney. THE AMERICAN JEEP: IN
       WAR AND PEACE. New York: Crown, 1983. 224 pp.

       This well-illustrated history traces the development of
       the jeep--and its many uses--by the U.S. Army. The authors
       provide a good deal of material on World War II.

IV.D.1.p. Japanese Army

2445. Coox, Alvin D. "Maverick General of Imperial Japan."
       ARMY, 15 (July 1965), 68-75.

       Lt. Gen. Kotoku Sato, a division commander in Buna,
       disobeyed orders to fight to the death and withdrew his
       division. His action brought him disgrace in Japan, but he
       remained convinced that his decision--Coox labels it
       "humane insubordination"--was the correct one under the
       circumstances. Sato referred to some of his superiors as

"jerks." Coox shows a sympathetic understanding for this
extraordinary man.

2446. Hayashi, Saburo with Alvin D. Coox. KOGUN: THE JAPANESE
       ARMY IN THE PACIFIC WAR. Quantico, VA: Marine Corps
       Association, 1959. 249 pp.

       During the war, Hayashi used his expertise on Soviet
       affairs in Imperial General Staff Headquarters, and at the
       end of the war he became military secretary to Minister of
       War General Korechica Anami. Without bitterness or blame,
       the book is addressed to the people of Japan. The focus of
       the book centers on the perceptions and rationale of the
       Imperial Army's highest leaders.

2447. "History of Air Defense: Japanese Antiaircraft Tactics and
       Techniques in World War II." AIR DEF, n.v.
       (July/September 1978), 37-39.

       Despite the title, this article concentrates mainly on
       questions of command and control. In general, Japanese
       anti-aircraft artillery made good use of intelligence (when
       available) but coordinated poorly above the battery level
       and had below-average capabilities at night.

2448. Ikeda, Minoru. "Anti-Aircraft Defense at Rabaul." AIR DEF
       ARTILLERY (Summer 1984), 19-22.

       Lt. Col. Ikeda served as a Japanese battery commander at
       Rabaul. In describing a typical day for his anti-aircraft
       artillery crews, he notes that air defense became the only
       mission at Rabaul. Although U.S. records indicate 435
       aircraft lost there, Ikeda says that figure is low by about
       another 355.

2449. McLean, Donald B. JAPANESE TANK TACTICS AND ANTITANK
       WEAPONS. Wickenburg, AZ: Normount Technical
       Publications, 1973. 241 pp.

       NE

2450. Merglen, Albert. "Japanese Airborne Operations in World
       War II." MIL REV, 40 (July 1960), 45-51.

       Although the Japanese gave only secondary importance to
       airborne operations, Merglen feels that the tactic could be
       valuable to defensive or offensive movements in vast areas.
       According to the author the best example of a Japanese
       airborne attack occurred at Palembang (Sumatra), February

14, 1942.

2451. Steward, Hal D. "Evolution of Japanese Cavalry." ARMORED
CAV J, (January-February 1947), 57-58.

Despite the army's emphasis on mechanized warfare,
Steward argues that the horse cavalry still has a place in
modern warfare. At the end of the war, Japan had two
operational horse cavalry brigades.

2452. United States. Department of the Army, Far East Command.
IMPERIAL GENERAL HEADQUARTERS ARMY HIGH COMMAND RECORD,
MID-1941-AUGUST, 1945. Washington, D.C.: Dept. of the
Army, 1945. 271 pp.

Here is another entry in the Japanese monograph
historical series. The Japanese Demobilization Bureau
supervised the writing of this Army history by Japanese
officers. The study explains the Army's organizational
structure and gives a valuable summary of key decisions
throughout the war. Of special interest in the description
of the general situation before the war. For example,
there are the Army's previous estimates of the United
States, British, and Dutch, as well as a report on the
assurances Japan received from Germany to expect no changes
in the status quo of NEI. See, too, the preparations made
by Japan--essentially the reinforcement of the Kwantung
Army, even after Germany attacked the Soviet Union--in
anticipation of a Soviet invasion of Manchuria.

2453. United States. War Department. JAPANESE LAND OPERATIONS.
Washington, D.C.: Military Intelligence Service, 1942.
46 pp.

Using Japanese sources, this study describes the general
progress of Japan's armed forces in 1941 and 1942. The
contemporary sources reveal the unbounded Japanese hopes
for continued successes and ultimate victory.

2454. Williams, R.C., Jr. "Jap Defensive Tactics--Attu to
Okinawa." INFANTRY J, 57 (August 1945), 28-32.

Williams traces the changes in Japanese tactics from
defense at the beach (Attu, Tarawa), to defense farther
inland (Makin), to a combination of both tactics (Saipan),
to coordinated counterattacks from a defense in depth
(Peleliu , Leyte, Iwo Jima, and Okinawa).

IV.D.1.p.i. Japanese Stragglers (ZANRYUSHA)

2455. Josephy, Alvin M., Jr. "Some Japs Surrender." INFANTRY J,
       57 (August 1945), 40-45.

       Josephy tells of American efforts to persuade Japanese
       stragglers to surrender. Of particular interest is his
       talk with Japanese POWs who convinced him that the faith
       and spirit of Bushido remain strong.

2456. Kahn, E.J., Jr. THE STRAGGLERS. New York: Random House,
       1962. 177 pp.

       For this story of the hundreds of Japanese servicemen
       who did not surrender in 1945, the author relies almost
       entirely on translations of Japanese sources and
       interpreters for his many interviews. His story of these
       stragglers (Zanryusha) centers on Masahi Ito and Bunzo
       Minkagawa, who held out for sixteen years--the straggler
       kings, up to the point of the writing of this book (other
       stragglers would surface after 1962). Kahn's description
       of how they managed to survive includes horrible accounts
       of cannibalism, especially in New Guinea, where former
       Japanese comrades took to stalking each other.

2457. Kamiko, Kiyoshi. I DIDN'T DIE ON LEYTE.

       NE

2458. ·Kishadan, Asahi. TWENTY EIGHT YEARS IN THE GUAM JUNGLE.
       Tokyo: Japan Publications, 1972. 135 pp.

       Here is the incredible tale of the struggle and survival
       of one of the emperor's most loyal soldiers. The narrative
       unfolds a study in courage, however misguided.

2459. Maruyama, Michiro. ANATAHAN. New York: Hermitage House,
       1954. 206 pp.

       Stranded on this small island in the Mariannas, Maruyama
       and his Japanese colleagues remained there from 1944 until
       1951. The food shortages and personal squabbles tended to
       relieve the boredom. As an additional source of stress,
       the only woman in the group was married to one of its
       members.

2460. Masashi, Ito. THE EMPEROR'S LAST SOLDIERS. New York:
       Coward-McCann, 1966. 191 pp.

       In a report translated by Roger Clifton, Sgt. Masashi

tells of his sixteen-year experience on Guam with two
colleagues (one of whom died). From 1944 to 1960, the
Japanese soldiers struggled to survive. During the U.S.
amphibious assault on Guam, Masashi says "a feeling grew
that we might not, after all, be going to win." From a
ragtag group of about 150 Japanese stragglers (including
only one officer, whom Masashi calls "a big noise from
Staff"), only Masashi and his two friends survived the
lengthy ordeal.

2461.   Onoda, Hiroo. "Japan Never Surrenders, She Is Still
          Fighting." JAPAN ECHO, 1 (No. 1, 1974), 73-91.

        Here is the personal account of a Japanese "straggler"
who was discovered on Lubang Island in March 1974. Of
interest is his judgment from scraps of evidence that
Japan's economic aims were being fulfilled. See, too, the
related commentary by Japanese intellectuals.

2462.   Onoda, Hiroo. NO SURRENDER: MY THIRTY-YEAR WAR. Tokyó:
          Kidansha International, 1974. 219 pp.

        2d Lt. Onoda remained on the island of Lubang
(Philippines) until 1974. Separated from his unit, he and
other stragglers divided into 3-man cells. In time,
however, he was part of the last remaining group, a 4-man
survivor unit. By 1972, he was alone. Every attempt to
contact him failed to persuade him that the war had ended.
Onoda saw every effort as an enemy ploy to get him to give
up his hope that the Japanese army would return. Finally,
a Japanese citizen found him and convinced him to
surrender. Articulate and intelligent, Onoda became a
national hero upon his return to Japan. Of interest is his
report of the situation in 1944 when he was told that it
would take 100 years of war to establish the Greater East
Asia Co-Prosperity Sphere. To illustrate the fanatical
Japanese determination to resist the enemy, a popular 1944
slogan was "one hundred million souls dying for honor"
(ICHIOKU GYOKUSAI).

2463.   Pokrass, Gregory S. "The Last Samurai." SOLDIERS, 40
          (August 1985), 34-35.

        The author, a commissioner in the Supreme Court of
Wisconsin, writes of Japanese stragglers (ZANRYUSHA) found
in 1972 (Guam), 1974 (Lubang Island), and 1975 (Morotai).
He says that, with 3,500 Japanese soldiers still
unaccounted for, Japan continues to suffer its own MIA
tragedy.

IV.D.2. AIR

  a. General Accounts

2464. Craven, Wesley Frank and James Lea Cate, eds. THE ARMY AIR
         FORCES IN WORLD WAR II. Chicago: University of Chicago
         Press, 1948-1958. 7 vols.

         Here is the official history of the Army Air Forces.
         See especially Volume 5, THE PACIFIC: MATTERHORN TO
         NAGASAKI, JUNE 1944 TO AUGUST 1945. Of special note is the
         argument that the use of the atomic bomb provided a means
         for Japanese leaders to save face in their decision to
         surrender. Volumes 6 and 7 offer useful technical and
         training information. These volumes are indispensable to
         any study of the subject. The depth of research and the
         range of interpretation are models for such projects.

2465. Francillon, Rene J. U.S. ARMY AIR FORCES IN THE PACIFIC.
         Fallbrook, CA: Aero Publishers, 1969. 96 pp.

         The book is a showcase for the encyclopedic knowledge
         of Francillon. Few can match his expertise.

2466. Futrell, Robert F. "Airpower Lessons of World War II."   AF
         & SPACE DIG, 48 (September 1965), 42-53.

         Futrell argues in general that the U.S. military
         planners never realized the full potential of airpower.

2467. Gaston, James C. PLANNING THE AMERICAN AIR WAR: FOUR MEN
         AND NINE DAYS IN 1941: AN INSIDE NARRATIVE.
         Washington, D. C.: National Defense University, GPO,
         1982. 121 pp.

         In August 1941, four AAF officers from the Air War Plans
         Division prepared the overall air strategy which was
         embodied in AWPD-1. The four men were Col. Harold George,
         Maj. Haywood Hansell, Maj. Laurence S. Kuter, and Col.
         Kenneth Walker. Notwithstanding the title, there is little
         that is new in this "inside" account.

2468. Hurley, Alfred F. and Robert C. Ehrhart, eds. AIR POWER
         AND WARFARE. Washington, D.C.: Office of Air Force
         History, 1979.   461 pp.

         Here are the proceedings of the 1978 Military History
         Symposium at the Air Force Academy. See especially the

section entitled "World War II in the Air: Different
National Experiences." Alvin D. Coox reports on the
Japanese Air Force, and John Huston offers an analysis of
Hap Arnold. See, too, the statements by Curtis LeMay and
William I. Martin.

2469. Jablonski, Edward. AIR WAR. Garden City, NY: Doubleday,
        1971-1972. 4 vols.

        This general illustrated history portrays aerial
warfare. See especially Volume I: "Terror From The Sky"
and Volume II: "Tragic Victories."

2470. Jackson, Robert. FIGHTER: THE STORY OF AIR COMBAT,
        1936-1945. New York: St. Martin's Press, 1980. 157
        pp.

        Jackson, a professor and a pilot, provides neither notes
nor bibliography, but he obviously knows his subject. What
little attention he gives to the war against Japan is
devoted to Chennault's forces in China and to carrier
operations in the Pacific.

2471. Kelsey, Benjamin S. THE DRAGON'S TEETH: THE CREATION OF
        UNITED STATES AIR POWER FOR WORLD WAR II. Washington,
        D.C.: Smithsonian Institution Press, 1982. 148 pp.

        Kelsey offers a knowledgeable summary of the air
build-up.

2472. Loosbrock, John and Richard M. Skinner, eds. THE WILD
        BLUE: THE STORY OF AMERICAN AIRPOWER. New York: G.P.
        Putnam's Sons, 1961. 620 pp.

        Most of these articles first appeared in AIR FORCE
MAGAZINE. There is much material on World War II,
including the war against Japan.

2473. McCarthy, John. "America and 'Lack of Moral Fibre' in the
        Second World War." WAR & SOC, 2 (September 1984),
        87-102.

        Researching British archival (air) records, the author,
a military historian, comes across the terms "Lacking in
Moral Fibre," "LMF," "Waverer," and "W"--all of which were
criticisms of certain British airmen who were dismissed
from service (less than 1%). He feels these terms should
never have been used by an RAF that was superbly served by
indigenous and dominion volunteers.

2474. Momyer, William. THREE WARS. Washington, D.C.: Dept. of
        the Air Force, 1978. 358 pp.

        Gen. Momyer (USAF) draws on a wealth of experience in
        aerial operations to discuss lessons learned in World War
        II, Korea, and Vietnam. Although most of his narrative on
        the Second World War deals with other theaters, some of the
        principles and tactics apply to the air war against Japan.
        See especially Momyer's views on the need for a single
        manager of all air resources in a theater.

2475. Olynyk, Frank J. USMC CREDITS FOR THE DESTRUCTION OF ENEMY
        AIRCRAFT IN AIR-TO-AIR COMBAT, WORLD WAR II. Aurora,
        OH: F.J. Olynyk, 1981. 214 pp.

        Here is a unique reference--a statistical report on one
        important element of the air war in the Pacific.

2476. Olynyk, Frank J. U.S.A.A.F. CREDITS FOR THE DESTRUCTION OF
        ENEMY AIRCRAFT IN AIR-TO-AIR COMBAT, WORLD WAR 2.
        Aurora, OH: Author, 1985. 361 pp.

2477. ------. U.S.M.C. CREDITS FOR THE DESTRUCTION OF ENEMY
        AIRCRAFT IN AIR-TO-AIR COMBAT, WORLD WAR 2. Aurora, OH:
        Author, 1981. 214 pp.

2478. ------. U.S.N. CREDITS FOR THE DESTRUCTION OF ENEMY
        AIRCRAFT IN AIR-TO-AIR COMBAT, WORLD WAR 2. Aurora, OH:
        Author, 1981. 214 pp.

        Here are valuable references for American aerial kills.
        Unlike official tallies, Olynyk discounts any enemy
        aircraft destroyed on the ground. Information is available
        by theaters of operation.

2479. Overy, R.J. THE AIR WAR, 1939-1945. New York: Stein and
        Day, 1980. 263 pp.

        Overy provides a scholarly approach to this general
        history of the air war. His emphasis is on strategy,
        tactics, training, and production. In the Far East, he
        says that effective conventional bombing had pushed Japan
        to the brink of defeat. Of interest is Overy's assessment
        of the efforts of strategic bombing, in which he
        underscores the importance of the general strategic use of
        air power for the victors.

2480. Pearl, Jack. AERIAL DOGFIGHTS OF WORLD WAR II. Derby, CT:

Monarch Books, 1962.   138 pp.

In this report, Pearl emphasizes the exploits of U.S.
pilots. In the air war against Japan, see especially his
praise for the carrier-borne air force (e.g., Air Group 15
flying off of the ESSEX).

2481. Purcell, John F. FLIGHTS TO GLORY. New York: Vanguard
       Press, 1944. 184 pp.

Purcell calls attention to heros of the air war in all
theaters. There is much material on the war against Japan.

2482. Siefring, Thomas A. U.S. AIR FORCE IN WORLD WAR II.
       Seacaucus, NJ: Chartwell Books, 1981. rev. ed. 197 pp.

With extensive photographs, Siefring summarizes the
combat exploits of the aircraft and airmen of the USAAF in
all theaters.

2483. Stanford Research Institute. IMPACT OF AIR ATTACKS IN
       WORLD WAR II. Washington, D.C.: GPO, 1953.

This general assessment includes the impact that bombing
had on Japanese economic resources and civilian morale.
This study is designed to help civil defense planning in
the United States.

2484. Sunderman, James F., ed. WORLD WAR II IN THE AIR. New
       York: Franklin Watts, 1962-1963. 2 vols.

Volume I (1962, 306 pp.) deals with the war against
Japan. Most of the stories are of the "I Was There" genre
and have been published previously. The collection offers
a realistic glimpse of the war in the air.

2485. Tanner, Doris Brinker. "We Also Served." AMER HIST ILLUS,
       20 (November 1985), 12-21, 47-49.

The author, a history professor and ex-WASP (Women
Airforce Service Pilot), remembers her flight training and
wartime experiences.

2486. Tillman, Barrett. "Age and the Fighter Ace--Or, What Was
       That About Old Pilots and Bold Pilots?" AEROSPACE H, 28
       (Summer, June 1981), 108-115.

Were there any old, bold pilots? Tillman says Yes.
Looking at U.S. aces, including those in the Pacific during

World War II, he finds all were bold but all were not
necessarily young.

2487. United States. Air Force. Office of Air Force History.
       UNITED STATES AIR FORCE CREDITS FOR THE DESTRUCTION OF
       ENEMY AIRCRAFT, WORLD WAR II. Washington, D.C.: GPO,
       1978.

       Here is the complete and official record of all
       confirmed aerial "kills" by Army Air Force personnel in all
       theaters.

2488. Whitehouse, Arthur G.J. THE YEARS OF THE WAR BIRDS.
       Garden City, NY: Doubleday, 1960. 384 pp.

       Here is a survey of aircraft and the leading airmen of
       the war in all theaters. Whitehouse stresses the human
       side of the story.

IV.D.2.b. Pacific Theater (General)

2489. Anderson, O.A. "Air War in the Pacific." AIR POWER HIST,
       4 (October 1957), 216-227.

       Major General Anderson (USAF) maintains that the United
       States entered the war with two outmoded premises: (1)
       naval surface engagements would decide the war and (2) the
       Japanese home islands would have to be invaded to ensure
       victory. He criticizes the Japanese for dispersing their
       air resources. His conclusions underscore the overriding
       importance in war of controlling the air.

2490. Frisbee, John L. "Raid on Rabaul." AF MAG, 70 (November
       1987), 112.

       Here is a brief report on the death of Maj. Raymond
       Wilkins in November 1943.

2491. Gauvreau, Emile. THE WILD BLUE YONDER: SONS OF THE
       PROPHET CARRY ON. New York: E. P. Dutton, 1945.
       389 pp.

       Here is a tribute to air power. The author argues that
       the defense of the Philippines, particularly the battles at
       Bataan and Corregidor, had been fought with outdated
       strategy. These mistakes and lessons learned, according to
       the author, convinced MacArthur of the significance of air
       power.

2492. Gilmartin, J.F. "The Air War in the Pacific." TALON, 7
       (February 1962), 15-16.

           NE

2493. Hager, Alice (Rogers). WINGS FOR THE DRAGON: THE AIR WAR
       IN ASIA. New York: Dodd, Mead, 1945. 307 pp.

           An American newswoman who arrived in C-B-I late in 1944,
       Hager describes the air war in that theater based on her
       observations and investigations. This is an excellent
       account by someone who knows her subject and her
       profession. Her report is especially good on the types of
       aircraft used and the ground support teams at the air
       bases.

2494. Hough, Donald and Elliott Arnold. BIG DISTANCE. New York:
       Duell, Sloan and Pearce, 1945. 255 pp.

           Here is a contemporary study of the development of air
       power in the Pacific. The authors make effective use of
       personal accounts and interviews with several combat
       airmen.

2495. Howard, Clive and Joe Whitley. ONE DAMNED ISLAND AFTER
       ANOTHER. Chapel Hill, NC: University of North Carolina
       Press, 1946. 403 pp.

           In this view of the air war in the Pacific, which can
       also be seen as a contemporary combat history of the 7th
       Air Force, the authors blend in the human side of the
       story. There are no explanatory notes.

2496. Leary, William M. "Writings on Asian Aviation." AEROSPACE
       H, 33 (Winter/December 1986), 242-247.

           In this historiographical review of the period covering
       World War II to the war in Vietnam, the author devotes much
       attention to the war in the Pacific.

2497. Lindley, John M. CARRIER VICTORY: THE AIR WAR IN THE
       PACIFIC. New York: Elsevier-Dutton, 1978. 184 pp.

           Here is a solid summary of the war in the air against
       Japan. Lindley highlights the unique role of corner-borne
       aircraft.

2498. Mondey, David and Lewis Nalls. USAAF AT WAR IN THE
       PACIFIC. New York: Charles Scribner's Sons, 1980.

160 pp.

With well over 200 photos, the authors provide an
excellent summary of the air war against Japan. They
stress that these USAAF accomplishments emerged despite
inadequate resources and personnel throughout the war.

2499. Philpott, Bryan. RAF COMBAT UNITS: SEAC, 1941-1945.
        London: Osprey, 1979. 48 pp.

Here is a short summary of air operations in Southeast
Asia. The title somewhat misleads the reader because the
South East Asia Command (SEAC) did not come into existence
until late 1943. After Japanese air raids against Darwin
in February-March 1942, Churchill approved the dispatch of
three squadrons of Spitfires to Australia. These aircraft,
however, did not actually take part in operations until the
following January (with the first "kill" on 6 February
1943). The author argues that British air operations near
Ceylon in early April 1942 played a role in weakening
Japanese naval-air forces for future engagements, such as
the Battle of Coral Sea. Despite some excellent
photographs and the author's obvious expertise, the book
lacks overall structure. There is, for example, little
about the substantive changes wrought by the formation of
SEAC (and the arrival of Mountbatten), and the author fails
to include an analytical assessment of the RAF's
contribution to the war in Southeast Asia. Nevertheless,
the expert commentary and the details of specific episodes,
such as C.A.C. Stone's harrowing first encounter with
Japanese Ki-27a NATE fighters and the account of two aerial
foes saluting each other, make the book a valuable
contribution to the literature of this theater.

2500. Rust, Kenn C. "They Fell Like Flies." RAF FLYING REV, 16
        (July 1961), 30-32.

        NE

2501. Sheehan, Susan. A MISSING PLANE. New York: G.P. Putnam's
        Sons, 1986. 201 pp.

On March 22, 1944, a USAAF B-24 (#42-41081) from the
Jolly Rogers 90th Bomb Group of the 5th Air Force crashed
in the Owen Stanley Range. Here is the story of the
discovery, excavation, and identification of all souls on
board thirty-eight years later. The book is divided into
three parts: (1) Recovery, (2) Identifications, and (3)
Pilot. Sheehan weaves a fascinating tale as she follows

the entire process. She adds some detective work of her
own through interviews with key people who are indirectly
related to the story. The final section describes the life
--and death--of the pilot, Robert Allred.

2502.   Stern, Robert C., comp. AIR WAR OVER THE PACIFIC. London:
        Arms and Armour, 1986. 60 pp.

        This pictorial account includes many color photos as
well as air-to-air action shots.

2503.   Taylor, Joe G. AIR SUPPLY IN THE BURMA CAMPAIGNS. Maxwell
        AFB, AL: Air University, 1957. 163 pp.

        Taylor writes authoritatively about the hazardous
operations of air resupply in Burma. The dangers of bad
weather and terrain could surpass those presented by the
enemy.

IV.D.2.c. Air Weapons/Aircraft

2504.   Anderton, David A. B-29 SUPERFORTRESS AT WAR. New York:
        Charles Scribner's Sons, 1978. 176 pp.

        An excellent collection of photos and stories solicited
(and written) by the author.

2505.   Angelucci, Enzo and Paolo Matricardi. WORLD WAR II
        AIRPLANES. Chicago: Rand-McNally, 1978. 2 vols.

        Here is a useful reference of the various types and
models of aircraft used in the war. The authors know the
material.

2506.   Bavousett, Glenn B. WORLD WAR II AIRCRAFT IN COMBAT. New
        York: Arco Press, 1976.

        Edited by Stanley M. Ulanoff, the text provides a good
deal of technical data to complement the descriptions of
the various aircraft.

2507.   Bechtel, Paul S. "The P-38, the P-39, and the F4U."
        AEROSP H, 33 (Winter/December 1986), 231-236.

        The author, an air operations officer and squadron
commander at Guadalcanal (in three separate tours),
reminisces about flying all three aircraft. Of special
interest is his report that when the air flow over a wing
of the P-38 exceeded the speed of sound, an uncontrollable

bucking of the aircraft occurred.

2508. Boyle, James M. "How the Superfortress Paced the Attack
        Against Japan." AF & SPACE DIG, 47 (December 1964),
        63-69.

        Boyle extols the contribution of the B-29's of the XXI
        Bomber Command in bringing the Japanese to their knees by
        mid-1945.

2509. Caidin, Martin. ZERO FIGHTER. New York: Ballantine
        Books, 1970. 160 pp.

        Caidin traces the original concept, testing, and
        operations of the Zero. Even impressive prewar
        demonstrations inexplicably failed to shake the
        overconfidence of American and British airmen.

2510. Cross, Roy. MILITARY AIRCRAFT, 1939-1945. Greenwich, CT:
        New York Graphic Society, 1971. 48 pp.

        Cross provides a pictorial presentation of most of the
        combat aircraft used by all sides.

2511. Devlin, Gerard M. SILENT WINGS. New York: St. Martin's
        Press, 1985. 410 pp.

        In this well-researched book, Devlin takes an interest-
        ing look at a unique group, combat glider pilots. His
        report on operations in the war against Japan include
        Burma, New Guinea (Nadzab), and Luzon. William
        Westmoreland wrote the Foreword.

2512. Gallagher, James P. "Operation SAVE-A-JACK." AMER SVN
        HSG, 18 (Summer 1973), 115-116.

        The author was a member of the 49th Fighter Group. He
        tells of his unit going to Atsugi Airfield about two months
        after the war. Some Japanese aircraft were still there,
        and some of the 49th, including Gallagher, attempted to
        restore a battered JACK. Unfortunately, he left before the
        restoration project had been completed and doesn't know the
        outcome. Photos accompany the narrative.

2513. Glines, Carroll V. and Wendell F. Mosley. THE DC-3: THE
        STORY OF A FABULOUS AIRPLANE. Philadelphia, PA: J. B.
        Lippincott, 1966. 203 pp.

        Both authors are Air Force pilots. Their narrative

traces the development and use of the DC-3 since 1936 and dwells on many tales from the war.

2514. Glines, Carroll V. and Wendell F. Moseley. GRAND OLD LADY: STORY OF THE DC-3. Cleveland, OH: Pennington Press, 1960. 250 pp.

Here is a history of the DC-3 (or the military version, C-47) presented in a collection of stories--many of which arose from the war. The two authors fly the aircraft, and they love their Gooney-Bird!

2515. Gunston, William T. AN ILLUSTRATED GUIDE TO ALLIED FIGHTERS OF WORLD WAR II. New York: Arco, 1981. 160 pp.

Gunston describes the fighter aircraft used in all theaters. Technical information is available, but the strength of this volume lies in its many drawings and photos, especially those photos which show fighters in combat action.

2516. Gunston, William T. AN ILLUSTRATED GUIDE TO BOMBERS OF WORLD WAR II. New York: Arco, 1980. 160 pp.

This volume includes a description of the strategic bombing power levied against Japanese strongholds and the home islands. The photos and drawings supplement the narrative.

2517. Gunston, William T. THE ENCYCLOPEDIA OF THE WORLD'S COMBAT AIRCRAFT. New York: Chartwell Books, 1976. 229 pp.

This general history of aviation has an extensive section on the Second World War. There is an illustration for virtually every model; some technical information is provided.

2518. Gunston, William T. COMBAT AIRCRAFT OF WORLD WAR II. New York: Bookthrift, 1978. 256 pp.

Gunston provides a report on the air resources used by both sides in all theaters. Many beautiful photos and illustrations accompany the narrative.

2519. Green, William. FAMOUS BOMBERS OF THE SECOND WORLD WAR. London: Macdonald, 1959-1960. 1st-2nd series; 2 vols.

This study covers bombers used in all theaters. For the

Pacific, see information on the B-17, B-24, and B-29.

2520.   Green, William. FAMOUS FIGHTERS OF THE SECOND WORLD WAR.
        London: Macdonald, 1947-1962. 1st-2nd series; 2 vols.

        Green writes authoritatively about these aircraft. In
        addition to his technical expertise, he offers comparisons
        among various models and describes the operational use of
        each aircraft.

2521.   Green, William. WAR PLANES OF THE SECOND WORLD WAR.
        Garden City, NY: Doubleday, 1968. 10 vols.

        Green has assembled a comprehensive reference which
        includes aircraft of both sides in all theaters.
        Illustrations and technical information supplement the
        presentation.

2522.   Green, William and F. Gordon Swanborough. U.S. ARMY AIR
        FORCES FIGHTERS. New York: Arco, 1977. 2 vols.

        Information is provided on performance characteristics
        and operational use. Some of the more useful illustrations
        include cross-sections of various models.

2523.   Gurney, Gene. B-29 STORY: THE PLANE THAT WON THE WAR.
        Greenwich, CT: Fawcett Publishers, 1963.

        Gurney extols the virtues of the superfortress. With
        obvious expertise, the author provides details of the
        aircraft's performance and operational use.

2524.   Holloway, Bruce K. "The P-40." AEROSPACE H, 25 (Fall/
        September 1978), 136-140.

        General Holloway (USAF), who logged about 300 hours in
        the P-40, discusses the strengths (e.g., armament,
        ruggedness, diving speed) and weaknesses (e.g., climate and
        altitude performance) of the aircraft. He claims that more
        Allied nations in the war flew the P-40 more than any other
        combat aircraft and that the kill ratio for Americans in
        China was 12:1.

2525.   Jablonski, Edward. FLYING FORTRESS: THE ILLUSTRATED
        BIOGRAPHY OF THE B-17s AND THE MEN WHO FLEW THEM.
        Garden City, NY: Doubleday, 1965. 362 pp.

        The photos are excellent; many are in color and show
        combat action.

2526. Knott, Richard C. BLACK CAT RAIDERS OF WORLD WAR II.
        Annapolis, MD: Nautical and Aviation Pub. Co. of
        America, 1981. 198 pp.

        Capt. Knott, a flying boat pilot, offers the combat
        stories of his comrades. The pilots saw action in all
        theaters.

2527. McDowell, Ernest R. CURTISS P-40 IN ACTION. Warren, MI:
        Squadron/Signal Publications, 1976. 56 pp.

        This is essentially a pictorial account of the
        KITTYHAWK.

2528. Makanna, Philip. GHOSTS: VINTAGE AIRCRAFT OF WORLD WAR II.
        Charlottesville, VA: Thomasson-Grant, 1987. 120 pp.

        Here is a color pictorial of the classic aircraft--all
        of which have been restored to flying condition.

2529. Mondey, David. CONCISE GUIDE TO AMERICAN AIRCRAFT OF WORLD
        WAR II. London: Hamlyn, 1981. 160 pp.

        Here is an excellent reference. There is information
        about all the U.S. aircraft, and Mondey has included
        several photos and drawings.

2530. Morrison, Wilbur H. HELLBIRDS: THE STORY OF B-29'S IN
        COMBAT. New York: Duell, Sloan and Pearce, 1960. 181
        pp.

        Curtis LeMay wrote the Foreword. Morrison is a
        knowledgeable writer on the air war. For him, the B-29
        represented the decisive factor in the war.

2531. Munson, Kenneth. AIRCRAFT OF WORLD WAR II. Garden City,
        NY: Doubleday, 1972. 2d ed. 272 pp.

        Munson describes most of the aircraft used by all the
        countries in the war. He provides much technical
        information and photographs.

2532. Munson, Kenneth. AMERICAN AIRCRAFT OF WORLD WAR II IN
        COLOR. New York: Sterling, 1982. 160 pp.

        Paintings and photographs (including some in black and
        white--despite the title) highlight this reference work.
        All of the aircraft used in the Pacific war are described.

2533. Munson, Kenneth. FIGHTERS AND BOMBERS OF WORLD WAR II.
       London: Burke's Peerage, 1981. 400 pp.

       This is a valuable compendium of the "glamorous"
       aircraft. Munson, an aviation expert, assembles
       descriptive information, including technical data, and
       numerous photographs of the various aircraft.

2534. Musciano, Walter A. CORSAIR ACES: THE BENT-WING BIRD OVER
       THE PACIFIC. New York: Arco, 1979. 136 pp.

       Here is a general description of the Pacific operations
       of the Vought F-4U. There is a separate section on the
       U.S. aces who flew the Corsair (including, but not limited
       to, Pappy Boyington).

2535. Okumiya, Masatake and Jiro Horikoshi with Martin Caidin.
       ZERO! New York: E. P. Dutton, 1956. 424 pp.

       Here is a Japanese perspective of the air war. The
       authors link the story of the development of the Zero
       fighter to accounts by participants in aerial battles. See
       especially the incredible exploit of Petty Officer Saburo
       Sakai.

2536. O'Leary, Michael. UNITED STATES NAVAL FIGHTERS OF WORLD
       WAR II IN ACTION. New York: Sterling, 1980. 160 pp.

       With many photos to complement the narrative, the author
       reports on all the carrier-borne aircraft. He includes key
       dates for highlights of the naval air war.

2537. Pimlott, John and H.P. Willmott. CLASSIC AIRCRAFT OF WORLD
       WAR II. Lincoln, NE: Bison Books, 1982. 400 pp.

       The authors give good coverage to the leading aircraft
       in the war against Japan. Some performance information is
       included with diagrams and photographs of each of the
       aircraft.

2538. Price, Alfred. THE BOMBER IN WORLD WAR II. New York:
       Charles Scribner's Sons, 150 pp.

       Within this general history, Price describes the
       important, perhaps decisive, role of these "heavies" in the
       war against Japan. Of interest is his explanation of the
       defenses mounted against the bombers.

2539. Schnapper, Morris B., ed. U.S. AVIATION IN WARTIME.
       Washington, D.C.: American Council on Public Affairs,
       1944. 203 pp.

       Here is a useful reference. The contributors evaluate
       the war performances of the Allied and Axis aircraft.

2540. Sherlock, John L. "Pacific Marauders." AMER AVN HSJ, 11
       (Fall 1966), 190-196.

       The author recounts his experiences (as told to Jay
       Sherlock) flying the new B-26s for the 70th Bomb Squadron
       of the 38th Bomb Group (Medium) early in the war. The
       plane was neither friendly nor forgiving.

2541. Sims, Edward H. FIGHTER TACTICS AND STRATEGY, 1914-1970.
       NEW YORK: Harper and Row, 1972. 266 pp.

       Using extensive interviews and official histories, Sims
       offers a knowledgeable report of aerial combat. There is
       good information on the planned (and actual) use of various
       aircraft through the years.

2542. Sinclair, William B. THE BIG BROTHERS: THE STORY OF THE
       B-29s. San Antonio, TX: Naylor, 1972. 132 pp.

       Here is a brief summary of the decisive role played by
       the strategic bombers. Sinclair credits the aircraft as
       instrumental in bringing about the defeat of Japan.

2543. Thompson, Warren. "Terror in the Dark." WINGS, 14
       (October 1984), 10-25.

       Here is an account of the P-61 Black Widow, a
       night-capable fighter, in the China Theater. Thompson
       incorporates interviews, oral histories, and photographs.

2544. Tillman, Barrett. CORSAIR: THE F4U IN WORLD WAR II AND
       KOREA. Annapolis, MD: Naval Institute Press, 1979. 219
       pp.

       Tillman's brief report incorporates many illustrations
       and technical data about the famed aircraft. His narrative
       includes a summary of the Corsair's performance in Pacific
       operations.

2545. Tillman, Barrett. THE DAUNTLESS DIVE BOMBER OF WORLD WAR
       TWO. Annapolis, MD: Naval Institute Press, 1976. 232
       pp.

Tillman describes the Douglas SBD ("Slow But Deadly")
dive bomber as a plane loved by the aviators who flew it.
The only carrier aircraft to last the entire war, the SBD
had as its primary mission search-and-strike, but it also
contributed to anti-submarine operations and performed
close air support duties.

2546.   Tillman, Barrett. HELLCAT: THE F6F IN WORLD WAR II.
        Annapolis, MD: Naval Institute Press, 1979.

        An acknowledged authority on aviation affairs, Tillman
        praises the wartime performance of the Hellcat fighter.

2547.   Tillman, Barrett. THE WILDCAT IN WW II. Annapolis, MD:
        Nautical and Aviation Publishing Company of America,
        1983.   267 pp.

        The Wildcat took part in every carrier action in the
        Pacific, from Pearl Harbor to Guadalcanal. Tillman feels
        that this Grumman F4F performed admirably in the face of
        the superior Japanese Zero.

2548.   Vader, John. PACIFIC HAWK. New York: Ballantine Books,
        1970.   160 pp.

        Vader describes Pacific operations flown by the P-40.
        Of interest are the combat photos and the performance data.

2549.   Voaden, D.J. "Nippon Gunyoke No Zenbo." ("General View of
        Nipponese Military Aircraft.") AERONAUTICS, 30 (July
        1954), 112-115.

        Voaden reports on this valuable survey by five Japanese
        editors. They provide much technical information on the
        production and performance of Japan's military aircraft.

2550.   Wagner, Ray. AMERICAN COMBAT PLANES. Garden City, NY:
        Doubleday, 1982. rev. ed. 565 pp.

        Updating the 1960 edition, Wagner describes all of the
        U.S. combat aircraft since 1908. With technical
        information, including performance data, and almost 1,500
        illustrations, Wagner has prepared a formidable reference
        work.

2551.   Weal, Elke C., comp. COMBAT AIRCRAFT OF WORLD WAR II. New
        York: Macmillan, 1977. 238 pp.

This reference describes almost 1,000 aircraft from virtually every country in the war. John Weal provided the color plates, Richard Barker contributed the line drawings and J.M. Bruce served as editorial consultant.

2552. White, William L. QUEENS DIE PROUDLY. New York: Harcourt, Brace, 1943. 273 pp.

White tells of the adventures of "The Queen," a B-17 Flying Fortress bomber. Nicknamed "The Swoose," the aircraft was under the command of pilot Frank Kurtz. The book traces the bomber and its crew from the Philippines early in the war to the South Pacific. Despite hazardous assignments, "The Swoose" made it back to the United States--one of the few "Queens" to do so. Most of the narrative quotes directly from the members of B-17 crews.

2553. Willmott, H.P. B-17 FLYING FORTRESS. London: Arms and Armour Press, 1980. 64 pp.

This pictorial history reproduces color photographs from the war. The book is part of the publisher's pictorial series on war planes.

2554. Willmott, H.P. ZERO A6M. Englewood Cliffs, NJ: Prentice-Hall, 1983.

Here is a knowledgeable assessment of the combat characteristics and performance of the famed Japanese fighter plane.

IV.D.2.d. Collective Biographies (General)

2555. Andreas, Curt. FIGHTING AIRMAN. New York: G.P. Putnam's Sons, 1966. 287 pp.

The author, a West Point graduate, provides glowing pictures of air leaders. For the war against Japan, see especially the articles on Arnold, Chennault, Doolittle, Kenney, and LeMay.

2556. Carter, P. Verrill. SIXTEEN TO FIVE. Roxbury, MA: 1945. 113 pp.

Here is the story of 16 Marines and 5 Army soldiers traveling aboard a C-47 Skytrain from New Caledonia to New Hebrides on November 23, 1943.

2557. Gage, Philip S. "Fliers and Medals of Honor." AEROSPACE

H, 30 (Winter, December 1983), 254-260.

The article includes a list of medal recipients in World
War II as well as in other wars.

2558.   George, James A. and Chris Stauder. "Remember These
        Eleven." AIRMAN, 9 (July 1965), 16-18.

        Here is an account of a Korean citizen, Hyung Duk Kim,
        arranging the burial of the only U.S. servicemen to die in
        his country during the war--the eleven-man crew of a B-24
        Liberator. The aircraft, "Lucky Lady II," crashed on an
        Island (Namhae Do) off the southern coast of Korea on
        August 7, 1945. Only ten bodies were found. Kim also
        built a monument to the crew which he completed in 1956.

2559.   Graham, Vickie M. "Peter Kouzes: Bailout Over China."
        AIRMAN, 31 (September 1987), 18.

        Kouzes bailed out of a C-46 over China on December 10,
        1944. This brief profile tells of his three-month escape
        to safety.

2560.   Hardison, Priscilla. THE SUZY-Q. Boston: Houghton
        Mifflin, 1943. 170 pp.

        The author's husband, Felix, was an aircraft commander
        in the South Pacific. Her account of the 1942 air war,
        filtered through the eyes of the crewmen of the Flying
        Fortresses, offers an indirect yet unique vantage point.

2561.   Hess, William N. THE AMERICAN ACES OF WORLD WAR II. New
        York: Arco, 1968. 64 pp.

        Here are brief profiles of America's air heroes.

2562.   Hess, William N. THE AMERICAN FIGHTER ACES ALBUM. Dallas,
        TX: Taylor, 1978.

        Photos accompany these biographical sketches of all the
        U.S. aces. Those in World War II are readily
        indentifiable.

2563.   Hess, William N. FAMOUS AIRMEN: THE ALLIED ACES OF WORLD
        WAR II. New York: Arco, 1966.

        The short sketches of the Allied aces call attention to
        the contribution of America's allies.

2564. Hess, William N. PACIFIC SWEEP. Garden City, NY:
       Doubleday, 1974. 278 pp.

       This authority on the air war turns his attention to the
       war against Japan. Hess provides a useful summary which
       highlights the heroics of individual pilots.

2565. Hirsch, Phil, ed. FIGHTING ACES. New York: Pyramid
       Books, 1965. 173 pp.

       These articles underline the aerial achievements of
       American aces. Some flew in World War II against Japan.

2566. Jackson, Robert. AIR HEROES OF WORLD WAR II. New York:
       St. Martin's Press, 1978.

       Jackson offers sixteen reports of famous aerial exploits
       by U.S. airmen.

2567. Jackson, Robert. FIGHTER PILOTS OF WORLD WAR II. New
       York: St. Martin's Press, 1976. 156 pp.

       Jackson selects fourteen fighter pilots who, he feels,
       had characteristics that set them apart from other airmen.
       From the war in the Pacific, the author chooses Frank Carey
       (Hawker Hurricane in Burma), Charles H. MacDonald (P-38
       Lightning at Leyte), and Saburo Sakai (A6M ZERO).

2568. Leiser, Edward L. "Memoirs of Pilot Elwyn H. Gibbon, the
       Mad Irishman." AMER AVN HSJ, 23 (Spring 1978), 2-18.

       Gibbon flew for China in 1937, but he returned the next
       year after clashing with (and drawing a gun on) a Chinese
       general. Leiser uses Gibbon's papers to help write the
       article. The pilot died in an airplane crash near Karachi
       in 1942.

2569. McKinley, M.R. "Butch O'Hare: Navy Ace." ALL HANDS, 63
       (April 1986), 22-23.

       Here is an account of the heroics of O'Hare who
       virtually single-handedly fended off an attack force of
       Japanese bombers near New Britain on February 20, 1942.

2570. McNally, Richard. "Walter Wyatt: Mustang Pilot." AIRMAN,
       31 (September 1987), 7.

       Wyatt, a P-51 pilot, saw action in China and Indochina.
       His experience includes being shot down and rescued by the

Chinese.

2571. Mason, Herbert M. DUEL FOR THE SKY: FIGHTER PLANES AND
        FIGHTING PILOTS OF WORLD WAR II. New York: Grosset and
        Dunlop, 1970. 148 pp.

        Mason describes some of the leading aces and unusual
        circumstances of the air war in all theaters.

2572. Messimer, Dwight R. IN THE HANDS OF FATE: THE STORY OF
        PATROL WING TEN, 8 December 1941-11 May 1942.
        Annapolis, MD: Naval Institute Press, 1985. 350 pp.

        The author, a member of the San Jose Police Department,
        uses documents and interviews with surviving members to
        tell about the only Navy aviation unit to fight the
        Japanese in the early weeks of the war. The unit first
        operated in combat out of the Philippines, then from the
        Netherlands East Indies and finally Australia. Many were
        killed after being captured at Corregidor, and the unit
        lost 66% of its aircraft in the first eight weeks. The
        book is well researched and well written.

2573. Mingos, Howard. AMERICAN HEROES OF THE WAR IN THE AIR.
        New York: Lanciar, 1943. 557 pp.

        Mingos offers short, knowledgeable passages which
        describe the background of the air war and certain events
        from the first two years. The subjects include officers
        and enlisted men from the services' air arms. The author
        provides the names and citations awarded to decorated
        aviators in all theaters.

2574. Moseley, Hugh Stephen. "CACW--An American Ace in the
        Chinese-American Composite Wing." AMER AVN HSJ, 18
        (Winter 1973), 264-268.

        The author (an M.D.) tells of Thomas Allison Reynolds,
        Jr., a U.S. pilot in CACW who was credited with 41.5 kills.
        Although Reynolds claims more, and although the official
        total exceeds that of Richard Bong, Moseley notes that 38.5
        of the 41.5 were destroyed on the ground.

2575. Olds, Robert. HELLDIVER SQUADRON. New York: Dodd, Mead,
        1944. 225 pp.

        Olds describes the exploits of Navy dive bombers,
        especially those in the Squadron 17 Helldivers. This
        contemporary narrative features the repeated attacks

against Rabaul from November 1943 to February 1944.

2576.   Oughton, Frederick.   THE ACES.   New York: G. P. Putnam's
        Sons, 1960.

        Oughton profiles the leading aviators from all theaters.

2577.   Sims, Edward H.   ACES OVER OCEANS.   Blue Ridge Summit, VA:
        Aero, 1987.   181 pp.

        Sims, himself a fighter pilot, describes some of the
        great pilots of the war.   Selecting from all theaters, he
        devotes practically all of his attention to fighter pilots.

2578.   Sims, Edward H.   AMERICAN ACES IN GREAT FIGHTER BATTLES OF
        WORLD WAR II.   New York: Harper and Brothers, 1958.
        256 pp.

        The author, a fighter pilot in the war, presents twelve
        stories about U.S. air heros.   He interviewed all twelve
        and augmented his research with official records (housed
        mainly at the Air University).   For the war against Japan,
        Sims writes about John Alison's night intercept mission in
        CBI against Japanese bombers on July 30, 1942; Bruce K.
        Holloway's CBI exploits in a P-40 Warhawk on May 15, 1943;
        John D. Landers at New Guinea in a P-40 on December 26,
        1942; Jay T. Robbins near Port Moresby (Huon Gulf) in a
        P-38 Lightning on September 4, 1943; and Charles H.
        MacDonald in a P-38 at Leyte on December 7, 1944.

2579.   Straubel, James H., ed.   AIR FORCE DIARY.   New York: Simon
        and Schuster, 1947. 492 pp.

        Here are 111 stories taken from AIR FORCE MAGAZINE.   All
        are personal accounts by USAAF personnel in all theaters.

2580.   Toliver, Raymond F. and Trevor J. Constable.   FIGHTER ACES
        OF THE U.S.A.   Fallbrook, CA: Aero Publishers, 1979.
        400 pp.

        Covering all wars from 1914 through Vietnam, the authors
        present an exhaustive report which is based on official
        U.S. Air Force records.   Their research incorporated
        extensive interviews, and their narrative is accompanied by
        hundreds of photos.

2581.   Ulanoff, Stanley M., ed.   FIGHTER PILOT.   Garden City, NY:
        Doubleday, 1962.   430 pp.

Here is a collection of personal accounts (including
letters and diary entries) by about 60 combat fighter
pilots. The contributions cover the period from the First
World War to the Korean War.

2582.   Van Vleet, Clarke. "South Pacific Saga: The Story of
         Patrol Wing Ten." NAVAL AVIATION NEWS, n.v. (February
         1977), 32-37.

         Van Vleet, a naval aviation historian, describes the
         record of the unit which flew 245 missions during the first
         three months of the war. The unit lost 41 of its 44 PBY
         Catalinas. Of interest are the exploits of Thomas Moorer
         (later admiral) who was unceremoniously dumped into the sea
         twice in one day.

2583.   Walters, Maude, ed. COMBAT IN THE AIR. New York:
         Appleton-Century, 1945. 275 pp.

         Walters presents only personal accounts by wartime
         airmen in all theaters.

2584.   Wilber, Edwin L. and E.R. Schoenholtz, eds. SILVER WINGS:
         TRUE ACTION STORIES OF THE U.S. AIR FORCE. New York:
         Appleton, 1948. 281 pp.

         This is a collection of personal narratives by
         participants in the air war in all theaters. Most of the
         selections had previously appeared in print.

2585.   Woolf, Joseph C. "Pacific Privateers: UPB-121 in World
         War II." AMER AVN HSJ , 21 (Summer 1976), 118-125.

         Patrol Bombing Squadron 121 flew the PB4Y-2 Privateer
         out of Eniwetok, Tinian, and Iwo Jima. This description of
         its operations includes art work by Bob Casey.

IV.D.2.e. Personal Accounts/Memoirs/Biographies

2586.   Anderson, Bob. "Tom McGuire, Fighter Pilot." AEROSP H, 14
         (Autumn 1967), 183-188.

         Anderson recounts the story of one of McGuire's
         missions. With 38 "kills" to his credit, McGuire died
         trying to surpass Bong's total of 40.

2587.   Anderson, Carroll R. "McGuire's Last Mission." AF MAG, 58
         (January 1975), 58-64.

This story of McGuire's ill-fated attempt to become the leading U.S. "ace" in the war comes from one of the other P-38 pilots in his outfit.

2588.   Bartek, John F. and Austin Pardue. LIFE OUT THERE. New
        York: Scribner, 1943. 117 pp.

        After surviving the ditching of Rickenbacker's Flying Fortress, Bartek spent twenty-one days on a raft in the Pacific. He credits his faith with helping pull him through this harrowing experience.

2589.   Bartsch, William H. "We Are Doomed at the Start." AMER
        AVN HSJ, 29 (Summer 1984), 141-147.

        Here is the story of Lt. Max Louk, the first aviator to be killed in the Philippines. Louk and the other pilots in the 20th Pursuit Squadron, who trained in their P-40B aircraft from May to December 1941, all knew of their bleak prospects if Japan ever attacked the Philippines. Bartsch bases his research on the letters and photos collected by the Louk family and the diary of Louk's roommate, Charles P. Gies.

2590.   Becton, F. Julian, with Joseph Morschauser III. THE SHIP
        THAT WOULD NOT DIE. Englewood Cliffs, NJ:
        Prentice-Hall, 1980. 288 pp.

        R. Adm. Becton commanded the second destroyer to bear the name LAFFEY in the war. The book incorporates his personal account of the kamikaze attacks at Okinawa.

2591.   Boeman, John. MOROTAI: A MEMOIR OF WAR. Garden City, NY:
        Doubleday, 1981. 278 pp.

        Here is a personal account of the air war aboard a B-24.

2592.   Boghosian, S. Samuel. "The One-Man Pursuit Force." AF
        MAG, 56 (September 1943), 94-98.

        The author traces the career of Lt. Boyd D. "Buzz" Wagner, the first American ace pilot in the uniform of the AAF. Wagner flew out of bases in the Philippines and, briefly, New Guinea. After returning to the United States to train pilots, Wagner died in what is so often referred to as a "routine" flight.

2593.   Braddon, Russell. NEW WINGS FOR A WARRIOR. New York:
        Rinehart, 1955. 240 pp.

Braddon, an Australian writer, tells of England's youngest group-captain in the war, Leonard Chesire. As a pilot, Chesire's exploits earned him several honors. After seeing the atomic bomb dropped on Nagasaki, Chesire converted to religion.

2594. Brown, Richard. "Singapore Mission: The Last 13th Air Force Mission of World War 2." AMER AVN HSJ, 31 (Summer 1986), 139-143.

The author was operations officer for the 68th Fighter Squadron when orders arrived on August 12, 1945, to hit Singapore. Brown scheduled himself and solicited seven volunteers to fill the eight slots. Flying their P-38s from North Borneo, Brown's flight struck shipping targets in Singapore Harbor. One pilot and aircraft were lost.

2595. Byrd, Martha H. "The War's First Hero." AMER HIST ILLUS, 13 (December 1978), 10-14.

The mythical story of Capt. Colin P. Kelly, Jr. occupies a special niche in World War II history. Mistakenly credited with sinking a Japanese battleship (HARUNA) in a suicidal maneuver with his crippled B-17 on December 10, 1941, this U.S. pilot was soon gloriously etched in the memory of many Americans. Of special interest, as Byrd knowledgeably sorts out fiction from fact about the episode, are her comparisons of the reports by Saburo Sakai (the Japanese pilot who shot down Kelly's plane) and Donald Robins (the co-pilot who bailed out with the crew on Kelly's orders).

2596. Close, Winton R. "B-29s in the CBI--A Pilot's Account." AEROSPACE H, 30 (March 1983), 6-14.

Major General Close describes his experiences flying the four-day bombing cycle: India-China-Japan-China-India. His "war stories" include the ways in which poor weather conditions and sensitive cylinder head temperatures led to some unusual in-flight practices.

2597. Corkin, Frank R. PACIFIC POSTMARK. New York: Case, Lockwood, and Brainard, 1945. 172 pp.

This book is based on Corkin's letters from aboard ship. He presents his experiences and not-always-reliable rumors.

2598. Crawford, William. GORE AND GLORY. New York: David
       McKay, 1944. 192 pp.

       Capt. Crawford (USAAF) relays his experiences as a pilot
       in the Pacific through his brother-in-law, Ted Saucier.
       The aerial adventures are exciting and well told.

2599. Dickinson, Clarence E. THE FLYING GUNS. New York:
       Charles Scribner's Sons, 1942. 196 pp.

       Lt. Dickinson (USN) relates his experiences as a naval
       pilot. The action runs from Pearl Harbor to Midway.

2600. Fosburgh, Hugh. VIEW FROM THE AIR. New York: Charles
       Scribner's Sons, 1953. 295 pp.

       After the war, Fosburgh tracked down the crew members of
       the B-24, UPSTAIRS MAID, in order to record their
       reminiscences about their experiences--at war and at
       play--in the South Pacific.

2601. Foss, Joe. JOE FOSS, FLYING MARINE. Washington, D.C.:
       Zenger, 1943. 160 pp.

       At the time this biography was published, the famed
       aviator had twenty-six aerial kills, the highest U.S. total
       thus far. The action is in the Solomons. Foss's life
       story is told to Walter Simmons.

2602. Foster, John M. HELL IN THE HEAVENS. New York: G. P.
       Putnam's Sons, 1961. 320 pp.

       Foster relates his experiences as a Marine fighter pilot
       in the Guadalcanal. The narrative covers a two-year period
       and provides an interesting glimpse of combat aerial
       operations. Foster's unit was the famed Flying Deuces
       Squadron.

2603. Frisbee, John L. "Battle Over Bougainville." AF MAG, 68
       (December 1985), 119.

       This brief article narrates the heroism of two crew
       members of a B-17 in June 1943. The two--J. R. Sarnoski
       and J. Zeamer--each earned the Medal of Honor.

2604. Fritsche, Carl H. "Liberators on the Kwai." AEROSPACE H,
       30 (Summer, June 1983), 78-91.

Fritsche, a B-29 pilot, tells the story of the aerial
bombing of the two bridges built by POWs at Kanchannaburi,
Thailand.

2605.   Galvin, John R. SALVATION FOR A DOOMED ZOOMIE. Indian
        Hills, CO: Allnut, 1983. 272 pp.

        Galvin flew Hellcats during the war. This story, as
        told to Frank Allnut, tells how a U.S. submarine rescued
        the downed Galvin from a Japanese-held island. The
        concluding section describes his religious conversion.

2606.   Omitted.

2607.   Glines, Carroll V. "Theirs Was the First." AF & SPACE
        DIG, 49 (December 1966), 88-89.

        Here is the story of a B-25 crew flying out of McChord
        Field and striking a blow against the Japanese on Christmas
        Eve, 1941. Later, the crew took part in the Doolittle
        Raid.

2608.   Graham, Garret. BONZAI NOEL! New York: Vanguard Press,
        1944. 159 pp.

        Capt. Graham (USMC) describes himself as a
        forty-five-year-old retread World War I pilot. The book
        gives an account of his experiences participating in the
        Guadalcanal campaign. The account is enlivened by his
        sense of humor and sense of perspective.

2609.   Harmon, Tom. PILOTS ALSO PRAY. New York: Thomas Y.
        Crowell, 1944. 184 pp.

        The football hero tells of his adventures as a P-38
        pilot for Chennault in China. Twice (first in South
        America and then in China) he had to make his way to safety
        after his aircraft had crashed. The book reflects Harmon's
        amateur status as a writer, but it makes interesting
        reading.

2610.   Harwood, R. Frank. "HELL'S BELLS -- Missions 19 (Tokyo)
        and 22 (Osaka): Two Memorable Incendiary Missions."
        AEROSPACE HIST, 32 (Spring/March 1985), 20-24.

        The author was a second lieutenant navigator with the
        505th Very Heavy Bomb Group on both missions. His writing
        somehow makes even the initial deployment flight from the
        United States into an exciting adventure.

2611.   Henderson, William A. "About That Bridge on the River

Kwai." AF MAG, 55 (February 1972), 42-46.

Here is the personal account from a member of the crew
on a B-24 Liberator that helped destroy the two bridges
across the Kwai-Noi branch of the Mae Klong River. Air
power, not demolition from the ground, destroyed the two
bridges (one wooden and one steel). Henderson's plane
crashed in friendly territory after this bombing run in
1945.

2612. Hynes, Samuel. FLIGHTS OF PASSAGE: REFLECTIONS OF A WORLD
      WAR II AVIATOR. Tuscon, AZ: Paul Gaudette Books, 1988.
      256 pp.

      The author, now a professor of literature, recounts his
      experiences as a Marine pilot. His humor and descriptions
      of his compatriots complement his report of combat action.

2613. Jarrel, Howard R. "I Was Forced Down in Russia." RAF
      FLYING REV, Vol. 12, 28-29, 44.

      NE

2614. Kenney, George C. DICK BONG: ACE OF ACES. New York:
      Duell, Sloan and Pearce, 1961. 116 pp.

      Kenney relays war stories about the exploits of the
      famed pilot in this book geared to the general public.

2615. Kenney, George C. THE SAGA OF PAPPY GUNN. New York:
      Duell, Sloan and Pearce, 1959. 133 pp.

      Gen. Kenney praises the aerial exploits of Paul I. Gunn
      and his contribution in designing aircraft.

2616. Lambert, John W. "Chief of the Sunsetters." AEROSPACE H,
      28 (Fall, September 1981), 182-185.

      Lambert describes Gen. Ernest M. Moore, leader of the
      7th Fighter Command. The unit flew P-51 fighter escort
      missions (very long range), including operations out of Iwo
      Jima against the Japanese home islands in 1945.

2617. Laughlin, C.H. "Ferry Flight." AMER AVN HSJ, 23 (Spring
      1978), 51-59.

      The author, a P-40 pilot credited with five "kills,"
      tells of a 20-day flight ferrying a P-40 from the Gold
      Coast to China in March 1942 and of his frustrations flying

with his slow-moving escort, a British Blenheim.

2618. Malone, Frank. "Christmas Eve, 1944." AIRMAN, 31
          (September 1987), 22.

          The author tells of his experience as a B-24 pilot
          dropping about one million Christmas card greetings from
          MacArthur on U.S. troops.

2619. Mattiace, John M. "Joe Foss at Guadalcanal." MC GAZ, 57
          (June 1973), 43-47.

          Here is the story of the beginning of the aerial combat
          career of the famed Marine ace. After his first kill on
          October 25, 1942, Foss scored fifteen more victories in the
          next twelve days and had two aircraft shot out from under
          him.

2620. Mears, Frederick. CARRIER COMBAT. Garden City, NY:
          Doubleday, Doran, 1944. 156 pp.

          The author, a naval aviator, participated in combat air
          operations at Midway and in the Solomons. His description
          of life in the Pacific follows the standard pilots' maxim
          of working hard and playing hard. Mears was killed in June
          1943.

2621. Miller, Norman. I TOOK THE SKY ROAD. New York: Dodd,
          Mead, 1945. 212 pp.

          Miller commanded a bomber squadron (109) of Liberators
          in the Central Pacific. The squadron's fame spread as the
          unit caused extensive damage to Japanese shipping. Of
          interest is Miller's descriptions of flying the first
          low-level attacks against Truk and Iwo Jima. Miller tells
          his story to Hugh Cave.

2622. Moore, Thomas. THE SKY IS MY WITNESS. New York: G.P.
          Putnam's Sons, 1943. 135 pp.

          Moore, a Marine pilot, gives a thoughtful account of his
          experiences in combat at Midway and the Solomons.

2623. Ohlinger, John F. "Incident at Foul Bay." AEROSPACE H, 23
          (Summer, June 1976), 71-74.

          Ohlinger relates his experiences as a pilot ferrying
          C-47s between Africa and China. In his opinion, Foul Bay
          in the Red Sea was an unsatisfactory air base.

624.   Park, Edwards. NANETTE. New York: W.W. Norton, 1977.
          186 pp.

          Park reports on aerial operations at New Guinea in his
          aircraft, "Nanette." Flying out of Port Moresby, Park
          describes the P-39 Airacobra that he flew as underpowered
          and unpredictable. Here is an excellent glimpse of one
          part of the air war by a participating pilot.

625.   Porter, R. Bruce and Eric Hammel. ACE! A MARINE
          NIGHT-FIGHTER PILOT IN WORLD WAR II. Pacifica, CA:
          Pacifica Press, 1985. 279 pp.

          Here is an account of Porter's experiences as a Marine
          pilot and, subsequently, as one of the few (about 2%)
          qualified night fighters. He flew the F4F Wildcat, F4U
          Corsair, and F6F Hellcat. Most of the action occurred near
          Guadalcanal. See especially the extensive description of
          his first kill and the unusual double kill at night.

626.   Reeves, Thomas C. "Tail Gunner Joe: Joseph R. McCarthy
          and the Marine Corps." WISC MAG HIST, 62 (Summer 1979),
          300-313.

          Reeves presents a balanced account which reveals that
          McCarthy performed ably in the Pacific but later indulged
          in much self-promoting publicity about his service record.

627.   Reynolds, Quentin J. 70,000 TO 1: THE STORY OF LIEUTENANT
          GORDON MANUEL. New York: Random House, 1946. 217 pp.

          Lt. Manuel (then a master sergeant) was the sole
          survivor of a B-17 downed by enemy fire on the island of
          New Britain. Rescued--and concealed--by friendly natives,
          Manuel remained on the island for nine months until
          evacuated by submarine. The adventure is well told by
          Reynolds without needless embellishment.

628.   Rickenbacker, Edward V. SEVEN CAME THROUGH. Garden City,
          NY: Doubleday, Doran, 1943. 118 pp.

          As a special consultant to Secretary of War Stimson,
          Rickenbaker toured U.S. installations around the world.
          During the tour his plane ditched in the Pacific. This
          book tells of his experience on a raft for twenty-one days
          with six crewmembers (one other had died) and four oranges.
          It is a remarkable story of self-discipline and iron will.

2629. Sakai, Saburo. "Flight to Death." RAF FLYING REV, 15
       (January 1960), 19-21.

       NE

2630. Sinclair, William Boyd. JUMP TO THE LAND OF GOD.
       Caldwell, ID: Caxton Printers, 1965.   313 pp.

       Sinclair uses his refreshing style to tell the
       adventures of an aircrew in Tibet. Much of the story is
       based on interviews with Robert E. Crozier.

2631. Sutton, Barry. JUNGLE PILOT. London: Macmillan, 1946.
       127 pp.

       Sutton retells his experiences as a pilot in the Burma
       campaign.

2632. Tillman, Barrett. "Rara Avis: The Fighter Ace as Author."
       AEROSPACE H, 33 (Fall/September 1986), 172-175.

       Here is a historiographical appraisal of the memoirs of
       American "Aces." Each one, Tillman writes, forms part of
       the documentation of a fascinating subject. Surprisingly
       few lapse into the "There I Was" syndrome.

2633. Tillman, Barrett. "A Sundowner's Adventure." AMER AVN H S
       J, 20 (Winter 1975), 274-282.

       Based on a personal interview, Tillman relates the
       adventures of H. Blake Moranville, a naval aviator ace who
       was downed in early 1945 over Indochina. After several
       weeks under detention by the French, Moranville eventually
       escaped to China.

2634. Winters, T. Hugh. SKIPPER: CONFESSIONS OF A FIGHTER
       SQUADRON COMMANDER. Mesa, AZ: Champlin Fighter Museum
       Press, 1985.   157 pp.

       The author, an aerial ace, led a squadron in Air Group
       19. The highlight of his war memoirs are the victories at
       Leyte Gulf, where three Japanese aircraft carriers
       succumbed during air strikes he helped lead.

2635. Wright, Joseph C. "Secrets of Mili." AEROSPACE H, 15
       (Autumn 1968), 52-58.

       Wright explores some of the myths associated with the

death of Capt. Clifford G. Erdman, pilot of a P-39Q, who allegedly carried out lone wolf attacks against the by-passed island of Mili. (Some stories told of a pilot actually landing on the island and taxiing about with guns blazing before taking off again.)

2636. Wyper, William W. THE YOUNGEST TIGERS IN THE SKY. Palos Verdes, CA: Wyper, 1980. 191 pp.

Here is a personal narrative of U.S. air operations in the Pacific by a participating fighter pilot.

IV.D.2.e.i. Doolittle Raid

2637. Cohen, Stan. DESTINATION TOKYO. Missoula, MT: Pictorial Histories, 1983. 120 pp.

Here is a pictorial report on the Doolittle Raid.

2638. Critchfield, John S. "The Halsey-Doolittle Tokyo Raid." SEA POWER, 14 (December 1971), 25-29.

The article concentrates on the planning of the mission and the training of the aircrews. The author singles out the contributions of Francis Low, who helped conceive the idea, and Harry L. Miller, who instructed the crews on carrier techniques.

2639. "The Doolittle Raid--Forty Years Past." AIR PROGRESS, 44 (June 1982), 44-46.

NE

2640. Funk, Arville L. "Capt. Richard E. Miller: Fort Wayne's Doolittle Raider." OLD FORT NEWS, 47 (No. 1, 1984), 3-10.

NE

2641. Funk, Arville L., ed. "The Doolittle Raid Journal of Sgt. George E. Larkin, Jr." REGIST KY HIST SOC, 83 (Spring 1985), 108-122.

Here is a diary for the thirty-day period from April 1 to May 1, 1942. Larkin served as flight engineer-gunner on Crew #10 in the Doolittle Raid. Larkin bailed out and made his way to friendly territory. Later that year he died while flying with the 11th Bomb Squadron.

2642.   Gillert, Doug. "Jimmy Doolittle: Legendary Aviator."
        AIRMAN, 31 (September 1987), 8-9.

        Here is a brief profile of Doolittle's career. In 1985,
        he was advanced to the rank of four-star general.

2643.   Glines, Carroll V. "The Day Doolittle Hit Tokyo." AF &
        SPACE DIG, 50 (April 1967), 84-88.

        Although the raid inflicted little military damage,
        Glines asserts that the real significance lies in the
        damage to the Japanese psyche by overturning the myth that
        they were protected from invasion. As a result, the
        Japanese switched to a strategy which led to
        overcommitments, such as the attack at Midway.

2644.   Glines, C.V. "Doolittle's Greatest Contributions." AF
        MAG, 68 (September 1985), 174-184.

        In this interview-article, Doolittle identifies his top
        five contributions, which include, of course, the raid
        against Tokyo.

2645.   Glines, Carroll V. DOOLITTLE'S TOKYO RAIDERS. Princeton,
        NJ: Van Nostrand, 1964. 447 pp.

        Here is a factual account of the raid. Glines says he
        was inspired to write the book by the display at the Air
        Force Academy of the eighty silver goblets which belonged
        to the raider crewmen.

2646.   Glines, Carroll V. FOUR CAME HOME. New York: Van
        Nostrand, Rinehold 1981. 226 pp.

        This account, written originally in 1966, takes yet
        another approach in Glines' continuing concentration on the
        Doolittle Raid: the eventual return of four crewmen held as
        prisoners. The research is thorough, and the narrative is
        easily read.

2647.   Glines, Carroll V. JIMMY DOOLITTLE. New York: Macmillan,
        1972. 183 pp.

        Here is a popular account of the general's life. Most
        of the emphasis is on the Tokyo raid.

2648.   Jackson, Robert. BOMBER! New York: St. Martin's Press,
        1980. 157 pp.

Jackson describes thirteen of the "most famous" bombing missions of the war. Only one of these (the Doolittle raid), in his opinion, occurred in the war against Japan.

2649. Kaplan, H.R. "Jimmy Doolittle Leaves His Calling Card." SERGEANTS, 20 (May 1982), 22-24.

NE

2650. Lawson, Ted. THIRTY SECONDS OVER TOKYO. New York: Random House, 1943. 221 pp.

Bob Considine edited this personal account by a pilot who participated in the Doolittle Raid. In addition to the raid itself, Lawson tells of the training preparation-- especially the carrier take-offs--and the harrowing aftermath. Lawson crashlanded his plane in the China Sea (just offshore) and was rescued by the Chinese. His severe wounds caused him to become a double amputee. The book is one of the best of this genre.

2651. McCullough, Bob. "Herb Macia and Travis Hoover: A Duo of Raiders." AIRMAN, 31 (September 1987), 10-11.

Here is a brief report on the adventures of two men on the Doolittle raid.

2652. Merrill, James M. TARGET TOKYO: THE HALSEY-DOOLITTLE RAID. Chicago: Rand McNally, 1964. 208 pp.

Here is a popular account of the famous raid.

2653. Mosley, Leonard. JIMMY DOOLITTLE. New York: Nelson, 1960.

Here is a readable, sympathetic biography. The raid against Japan does not dominate the book.

2654. "The Raid From Shangri-La." AIRMAN, 9 (April 1965), 32-35.

Here is a report on the Doolittle Raid which is based on an interview with Lt. Col. Carroll V. Glines (USAF). Of interest is the description of the Japanese ships sunk by the Americans in efforts to avoid detection of the U.S. naval intrusion to launch the aircraft.

2655. Sims, Jack A. "The Doolittle Raid--A Survivor's Diary." AEROSPACE H, 30 (Summer/June 1983), 92-100.

Sims served as co-pilot on crew number fourteen. The
article incorporates the appropriate entries from his
diary.

2656.   Sims, Jack A. "The Tokyo Raid." AIR POWER HIST, 4
        (October 1957), 175-185.

Here is one of the earliest published first-hand
accounts of the Doolittle mission. Sims reveals two
ironclad rules of engagement for the crews: (1) under no
condition go to Vladivostok and (2) do not bomb
non-military targets.

2657.   Sobel, Brian. "Air Assault From Shangri-La: An Aviation
        Pioneer's Early Vengeance Shocked Japan." MIL HIST, 1
        (December 1984), 8, 63-66.

Here is a summary of the Doolittle Raid. The
contemporary public announcement identified the launching
point for the attack as "Shangri-La," the Tibetan paradise
in James Hilton's prewar novel, LOST HORIZON.

2658.   Sylva, Dave. "B-25s Over Tokyo, 18 April 1942." AEROSPACE
        SAFETY, 32 (April 1976), 14-17.

Sylva gives a summary of the Doolittle Raid.

2659.   Thomas, Lowell and Edward Jablonski. DOOLITTLE: A
        BIOGRAPHY. Garden City, NY: Doubleday, 1976. 368 pp.

Here is one of the better popular accounts of the famed
general. Of special interest, of course, is the material
in the training, execution, and aftermath of the raid in
Tokyo.

IV.D.2.e.ii. Flying Tigers/China

2660.   Alison, John R. "Death of a Fighter Pilot." A F & S
        DIGEST, 47 (April 1964), 90-96.

Alison, a squadron commander and deputy group commander
under Chennault, reports on Flying Tiger pilot John
Hampshire who had seventeen air victories before his death
during a dogfight in May 1943.

2661.   Bond, Charles R., Jr. and Terry H. Anderson. A FLYING
        TIGER'S DIARY. College Station, TX: Texas A & M
        University Press, 1984. 248 pp.

Bond, who later retired from the Air Force as a major
general, joined the American Volunteer Group--the cover
organization was the Central Aircraft Manufacturing
Company (CAMCO)--in mid-1941. The diary describes life for
a pilot under Chennault during the period of Bond's
service, 1941-1942. (He left almost a double ace.)
Anderson's Introduction and Epilogue set the historical
perspective.

2662. Caidin, Martin. THE RAGGED, RUGGED WARRIORS. New York:
       E. P. Dutton, 1966. 384 pp.

Based on official reports, memoirs and interviews, this
study highlights the heroics of the American pilots who
participated in the air war in China (1937-1942). A
knowledgeable writer on aerial operations, Caidin discusses
the specific tactics introduced by Chennault. Also, the
effectiveness of the American--and other international--
pilots presented their Chinese counterparts with the
problem of losing face. While Soviet aid went directly to
Chiang Kai-shek, Caidin points out that Stalin insisted
that all Soviet forces, including their outstanding pilots,
remain under Soviet control. Of special interest is the
careful coverage Caidin devotes to the reasons for the
damage inflicted at Clark Field by China-based Japanese
planes. He is particularly critical of MacArthur's public
statement/explanation about this controversial episode.

2663. Cornelius, Wanda and Thayne Short. DING HAO: AMERICA'S
       AIR WAR IN CHINA, 1937-1945. Gretna, LA: Pelican
       Publishing Company, 1980. 502 pp.

Based on many interviews, this history of the 23d
Fighter Group in the 14th Air Force sheds light on
Chennault and his men. The authors describe the group
as "aerial guerrillas" at first but later as a "highly
specialized striking force." The strength of the work lies
in the focus on individuals in the group.

2664. Cornelius, Wanda and Thayne R. Short. "When Tigers Flew in
       China." AMER HIST ILLUS, 14 (April 1979), 40-42.

Here is a report on the work of Roy Williams (a Disney
artist and later TV mouseketeer leader) and Hank Porter in
designing a shoulder patch for the American Volunteer Group
at the request of the China Defense Supplies Office in
Washington. Their design portrayed a flying tiger. Many
unofficial versions by wildcat artists adorned AVG
aircraft. Of interest is the authors' report that both the

British and the Germans had used shark's teeth on aircraft
in the war before the AVG.

2665. Greenlaw, Olga S. THE LADY AND THE TIGERS. New York:
       E.P. Dutton, 1943. 317 pp.

       In 1941, Greenlaw was the only woman in the American
       Volunteer Group in China. Her husband served as chief of
       staff and executive officer to Chennault. This is a
       rambling, disjointed narrative, based largely on her
       personal diary. She also kept the unit's official war
       diary. Her views are made clear—especially those on
       leading personalities and on the Army's mishandling of AVG
       members after the group disbanded.

2666. Heiferman, Ronald. FLYING TIGERS: CHENNAULT IN CHINA.
       New York: Ballantine Books, 1971. 160 pp.

       This book contains good summaries of the unit's
       operations and the air war. It is not just a biographical
       sketch of the controversial leader.

2667. Holloway, Bruce K. "China As I Knew It." AF MAG, 62
       (September 1979), 112-119.

       General Holloway (USAF) gives a romantic account of his
       experiences as an observer of AVG and as a pilot in the 23d
       Fighter Group. According to the author, Chennault, despite
       his faults, was a great man.

2668. Hotz, Robert B. WITH GENERAL CHENNAULT: THE STORY OF THE
       FLYING TIGERS. New York: Coward-McCann, 1943. 276 pp.

       The author was a correspondent who visited Chennault in
       1942 and stayed to become a captain in the general's
       forces. Although the author denies that this contemporary
       story of the U.S. airmen in China is one of simple
       "heroics," he does come close to presenting exactly that
       point of view.

2669. Kay, Kenneth. "The Chinese-American Composite Wing." AF
       MAG, 59 (February 1976), 60-65.

       Created as part of Chennault's 14th Air Force, the
       Chinese American Composite Wing helped the Chinese create
       their own air force with B-25s, P-40s, and P-51s. The
       Chinese, however, kept their air resources in reserve,
       according to Kay, to fight Chinese Communists rather than
       Japanese.

2670. Kebric, Harry L. DRAGON TIGERS. New York: Vantage Press,
       1971. 137 pp.

       Here is a personal report on the activities of the
       Chinese-American Composite Wing during the Sino-Japanese
       conflict.

2671. Koenig, William. OVER THE HUMP: AIRLIFT TO CHINA. New
       York: Ballantine Books, 1972. 159 pp.

       Koenig tells two stories: (1) the Japanese blockade and
       U.S. efforts to break it and (2) the men and logistics
       management of the Air Transport Service. More important
       than the actual tonnage, says Koenig, is the visible fact
       of U.S. aid embodied in the Hump operations. That symbol
       of support may have kept China in the war, according to the
       author. Koenig criticizes Stilwell for not appreciating
       the potential of the Hump route, and he praises the
       contributions of the C-47 and C-46.

2672. Manning, Stephen O., III. "'Old Leatherface's' Bombers."
       AIRMAN, 20 (July 1976), 8-14.

       This article on the B-24 Liberator missions (308th
       Bombardment Group--Heavy) under Chennault arises chiefly
       from an interview with Col. Evans Kranidas, who served in
       the unit. Of special interest is the report that LeMay
       remembered the fire bombing of Hankow while he designed
       plans for the fire bombing of Japan.

2673. Molesworth, Carl and H. Stephens Moseley. "Fighter
       Operations of the Chinese-American Composite Wing."
       AMER AVN HSJ, 27 (Winter 1982), 242-257.

       Chennault conceived the CACW as a unit where U.S. pilots
       could supervise (and train) their Chinese counterparts.
       With excellent research and a well-written narrative, the
       article follows the wartime exploits of the combined (i.e.,
       fighter and bomber squadrons) unit.

2674. Nalty, Bernard C. TIGERS OVER ASIA. New York:
       Elsevier-Dutton, 1978. 182 pp.

       Here is a knowledgeable account of the Flying Tigers.
       Nalty is noted for his solid research and fine writing.

2675. Neilson, Raymond Perry Rodgers. AMERICANS VALIANT AND
       GLORIOUS ON EXHIBITION. New York: Grand Central Art

Galleries, 1945.   75 pp.

Here is a contemporary art collection which portrays the American Volunteer Group in China.

2676.   Pentecost, Walter E. and James J. Sloan.   "Advance of the Flying Tigers." AMER AVN H S J, 15 (Summer 1970), 137-144.

In 1941, Pentecost supervised the assembly of P-40s at Rangoon for the American Volunteer Group. Together with excellent photographs, the article includes a list of each aircraft assembled and delivered (serial number, ferry pilot, dates, etc.).

2677.   Pistole, Larry M.   A PICTORIAL HISTORY OF THE FLYING TIGERS. Orange, VA: Moss Publications, 1981.

The collection contains some unique shots of Chennault's group.

2678.   Reynolds, Quentin J.   THE AMAZING MR. DOOLITTLE. New York: Appleton-Century-Crofts, 1953.   313 pp.

Reynolds provides a popular biographical account of Gen. Jimmy Doolittle. There is a useful summary of the raid on Tokyo.

2679.   Rosholt, Malcolm L.   DAYS OF THE CHING PAO: A PHOTOGRAPHIC RECORD OF THE FLYING TIGERS--14TH AIR FORCE IN CHINA IN WORLD WAR II. Amherst, WI: Palmer Publishers, 1978. 192 pp.

Here are some excellent pictures of the Americans in action.

2680.   Schaller, Michael.   "American Air Strategy in China, 1939-1941: The Origins of Clandestine Warfare." AMER Q, 28 (Spring 1976), 3-19.

Incorporating newly declassified material, the author reveals that on at least two occasions before December 7, 1941, American officials developed plans for private citizens to make secret air attacks on Japan. Thus, Schaller argues, the tactics of clandestine U.S. intervention preceded 1941 and were not a product of the Cold War.

2681.   Schultz, Duane.   THE MAVERICK WAR: CHENNAULT AND THE

FLYING TIGERS. New York: St. Martin's Press, 1987.
335 pp.

Relying on interviews and private collections, Schultz
offers a well-written account for the general public of
Chennault and his famed tigers. An interesting epilogue
traces the postwar activities of the airmen. Of special
interest is Schultz's description of the financial
arrangements for the organization.

2682. Scott, Robert L., Jr. GOD IS MY CO-PILOT. New York:
        Charles Scribner's Sons, 1943. 277 pp.

The author, a P-40 double ace with 12 kills, commanded
Chennault's fighter group from July 1942 to January 1943.
In addition to his descriptions of fighter tactics against
Japanese aircraft, Scott's narrative traces some of the
tragic-humorous cycles of war.

2683. Shivers, Sydney P. A PICTORIAL HISTORY OF THE AMERICAN
        VOLUNTEER GROUP, FLYING TIGERS. Challenge Publications.

        NE

2684. Smith, Wilford J. "Stalking Dragons and Flying Tigers."
        AIRMAN, 6 (July 1962), 14-20.

Chennault used Chinese guerrillas and peasants for
information and an early warning system to report Japanese
movements.

2685. Sweatt, Dennis. "23rd Tactical Fighter Wing Flying
        Tigers." AEROSPACE H, 24 (Summer, June 1977), 107-111.

Here is a summary of the unit's record during the war.

2686. Taylor, Joe G. AIR INTERDICTION IN CHINA IN WORLD WAR II.
        Manhattan, KS: MA/AH, 1957. 116 pp.

Taylor is knowledgeable about aerial combat operations.
His account reveals the dimensions of the problems facing
airmen in China. See especially Taylor's analysis of the
tactics devised by Chennault.

2687. United States. Department of the Army. Forces in the Far
        East. AIR OPERATIONS IN THE CHINA AREA, JULY
        1937-AUGUST 1945. Washington, D.C.: Office of the
        Chief of Military History, 1956. 220 pp.

Each chapter covers one year in this Japanese monograph.
Some highlights reported by the Japanese officers who wrote
this study are: encountering no notable resistance in
French Indochina (Sept. 5, 1940), earning "unexpectedly
rapid" air victories at Hong Kong in 1941, building Japan's
air resources for the ICHI GO offensive in 1944, arranging
an intelligence network to trace B-29s after the super
bombers arrived in China, and summoning the entire air
strength of the China Expeditionary Force to check the
Soviets in August 1945.

2688. United States. Department of the Army. Forces in the Far
        East. AIR OPERATIONS RECORD AGAINST SOVIET RUSSIA.
        Washington, D.C.: Office of the Chief of Military
        History, 1952. 68 pp.

        This slim Japanese study reports on the activities of
        the Second Air Army. The author, a Japanese officer in
        this unit, tells of the confusion at the end of the war
        when uncoordinated movements by the Japanese Army left
        vital Japanese airfields exposed.

2689. Whelan, Russell. THE FLYING TIGERS. New York: Warner,
        1942. 160 pp.

        Here is the story of the American Volunteer Group.
        Between December 18, 1941 and July 4, 1942, the unit
        destroyed at least 286 (confirmed) enemy aircraft. The
        Central Aircraft Manufacturing Company (CAMCO) offered a
        $500 bonus for each pilot's "kill." Whelan describes the
        personalities and the combat action. Of special interest
        is Whelan's discussion of the alleged use of gas and
        bacteriological warfare by the Japanese.

2690. Zocchi, Lou. "Flying Tigers: A Campaign Survey,
        1941-1945." STRATEGY & TACTICS, 24 (1970), 16-21.

        NE

IV.D.2.e.iii. "HUMP" Operations/CBI

2691. Barnard, Jack. THE HUMP: THE GREATEST UNTOLD STORY OF THE
        WAR. London: Souvenir Press, 1960. 192 pp.

        Here is an account of the exploits of the airmen in
        C-B-I who undertook resupply missions over the notorious
        "Hump" (Himalayan Mountains) line.

2692. Billard, Tony. "Flying the Hump." TRANSLOG, 8 (March

1977), 16-18.

As a "Hump" pilot, the author gives an authoritative account of the hazards--and the accomplishments--of airlift operations over the Himalayas.

2693. Buller, H.L. ("Duffy"). "The C-46 and C-47 in CBI Operations." AEROSP HIST, 22 (Summer/June 1975), 80-83.

The author discusses his experiences flying "Hump" operations in each aircraft.

2694. CHINA AIRLIFT--THE HUMP. Poplar Bluff, MO: The Association, 1980. 596 pp.

Here is a detailed report on aerial operations to and from China.

2695. Fritz, Ricky. "Enlisted Pilots Flying the 'Hump.'" SERGEANTS, 26 (January-February 1987), 14-15.

NE

2696. Genovese, Joseph G. WE FLEW WITHOUT GUNS. Philadelphia, Pa: John C. Winston Co., 1945. 304 pp.

Genovese tells of his experiences piloting transport planes over the Hump.

2697. Great Britain. Air Ministry. WINGS OF THE PHOENIX: THE OFFICIAL STORY OF THE AIR WAR IN BURMA. London: HMSO, 1949. 143 pp.

This official history, though brief, calls attention to a little-known dimension of the difficult campaign in Burma. It is an excellent reference point.

2698. Launius, Roger D. "Flying the 'Hump.'" AIRMAN, 29 (December 1985), 15-19.

This article describes the adventures of flying the Hump, beginning with the first wartime flight on April 8, 1942, by Col. William D. Old. The author states that, since the crews had little to do except to fly, they often amassed as many as 165 hours per month (with 650 hours being the magic number for rotation back to the United States). The leadership of Brig. Gen. William H. Tunner receives special mention.

2699. McClure, Glenn E. FIRE AND FALL BACK: THE WORLD WAR "CBI"
        STORY OF "CASEY" VINCENT. Universal City, TX: Barnes
        Press, 1975. 256 pp.

        Here is an account of the air war in CBI. McClure
   relies on Vincent's diary entries (1942-1944).

2700. Rumsey, J.R.L. "Air Supply in Burma." ARMY Q, 55 (October
        1947), 33-42.

        Here is an account of air supply (a method seldom used
   before World War II) in Burma. In 1942, a few Dakotas and
   an ad hoc Royal Indian Army Service Corps provided the air
   supply service. Later, the LRPGs received their entire
   support from the air. Rumsey draws the chief lesson: if
   air superiority is assured, an army can be supplied
   effectively by air.

2701. Thorne, Bliss K. THE HUMP: THE GREAT MILITARY AIRLIFT OF
        WORLD WAR II. Philadelphia, PA: J.B. Lippincott, 1965.
        188 pp.

        The author, a pilot on "Hump" operations, calls the
   effort the first great airlift in history. In this
   personal account, Thorne describes a typical day for the
   aircrews--including an emphasis on the dangers involved.

2702. Tomlinson, Michael. THE MOST DANGEROUS MOMENT. London:
        Kimber, 1976. 205 pp.

        Here is a British account of air operations at Sri
   Lanka.

2703. Tunner, William F. OVER THE HUMP. New York: Duell, Sloan
        and Pearce, 1964. 340 pp.

        Here is an excellent report on activities of the Air
   Transport Service. Pilots braved less-than-safe flying
   conditions in order to fly into China cargo that was
   valuable to the war effort. Through interviews and a solid
   research effort, Tunner is able to bring out the human
   dimension in these dangerous aerial operations.

2704. White, Edwin L. TEN THOUSAND TONS BY CHRISTMAS. St.
        Petersburg, FL: Valkyrie Press, 1975. 2d. ed. 256 pp.

        White gives an account of aerial operations over the
   Hump. His narrative describes the hazards of this

extraordinary air delivery system.

IV.D.2.e.iv. "Black Sheep"

2705. Boyington, Gregory [pseud. Pappy Boyington.] BAA BAA,
      BLACK SHEEP. New York: Putnam, 1958. 384 pp.

      Here is a frank, opinionated, unpretentious--and
      delightful--autobiography. Boyington hardly fits the mold
      of the conservative career officer. His Marine air
      squadron (214) performed well in the Pacific.

2706. Hofrichter, Paul. "Television Brought Back Memories of WW
      II Glory for Old Corsair Pilots." MC GAZ, 63 (April
      1979), 79-83.

      "Baa, Baa, Black Sheep," the popular television series
      about "Pappy" Boyington and his men, revived memories of
      the air war in the Pacific. Often forgotten is the fact
      that Boyington fell into Japanese hands at the end of the
      war.

2707. Walton, Frank E. ONCE THEY WERE EAGLES: THE MEN OF THE
      BLACK SHEEP SQUADRON. Lexington, KT: University Press
      of Kentucky, 1986. 213 pp.

      Much of this report emerges from Walton's interviews
      with some of the surviving members of the original Black
      Sheep Squadron. Walton is a Foreign Service Officer and
      former Marine who had served with Pappy Boyington. The
      interviews revealed the brutal nature of aerial combat. Of
      interest is Walton's debunking of the "Bad Boy" myth
      attached to the unit. Finding that no pilot in the group
      had ever been charged with a court martial offense, Walton
      observes that the phony image portrayed in the popular
      television series had been deliberately encouraged by
      Boyington. There is an interesting section which sketches
      the postwar experiences of some of the Black Sheep.

IV.D.2.e.v. Marianas "Turkey Shoot"

2708. Flick, Alvin S. "The Great Marianas Turkey Shoot."
      AVIATION QTRLY, 5 (No. 3, 1979), 214-235.

      NE

2709. Miller, Thomas G., Jr. "Anatomy of an Air Battle." AMER
      AVN HSJ, 15 (Summer 1970), 115-120.

The author, a Navy carrier pilot, gives a first-hand
view of the Marianas "Turkey Shoot."

IV.D.2.e.vi. Assassination of Yamamoto

2710. Agawa, Hiroyuki. THE RELUCTANT ADMIRAL: YAMAMOTO AND THE
      IMPERIAL NAVY. Tokyo: Kodansha International, 1979.
      397 pp.

      This book, translated by John Bester, is well
      researched. Agawa suggests that, while the idea of a
      surprise attack at Pearl Harbor first evolved in Yamamoto's
      mind during April-May 1940, the Admiral may well have seen
      a similar plan in 1927-1928 which was written by Lt. Cmdr.
      Kusaka Ryunosuke, an instructor at the Kasumigaura Aviation
      Corps and at the Navy Staff College. In addition, the
      author expresses confidence that the Americans probably had
      not cracked the Japanese "HA" code. (He cites Japan's
      surprise--and bloodless--withdrawal from Kiska as the
      primary grounds for his assertion.) Despite his efforts,
      the author cannot shed further light on the question of
      which American pilot assassinated Yamamoto. The book also
      introduces Tsurushima Tsuru of Kyushu and her role in the
      Admiral's life.

2711. Omitted.

2712. Davis, Burke. GET YAMAMOTO. New York: Random House,
      1969. 231 pp.

      Davis covers the background and the details of this
      episode. Two pilots (Lanphier and Barber) separately
      claimed to have shot down a Japanese bomber, but only
      one--the one carrying Yamamoto--had fallen. None of
      the four pilots involved in the attack ever flew another
      mission in the Pacific. All departed in order to avoid
      the possibility of falling into enemy hands and disclosing
      that certain Japanese signals were being intercepted by the
      United States.

2713. Falk, Stanley L. "The Ambush of Admiral Yamamoto." NAVY,
      6 (April 1963), 32-34.

      Falk holds up the interception and destruction of
      Yamamoto's "Betty" aircraft as a classic lesson in the use
      of intelligence. He credits Lanphier with the kill.

2714. Gwynn-Jones, Terry. "In Search of Yamamoto." AIR FORCE,
      68 (April 1985), 120-125.

      Here is a report which claims to add important

information to the story of the aerial assassination of
Yamamoto. The author located the crash site of the
Japanese "Betty" bomber near Bougainville that was carrying
the Japanese leader. From his investigations Gwynn-Jones
concludes that Thomas G. Lanphier, Jr. should receive
credit for downing the aircraft. Also, this report states
that Yamamoto was killed by machine gun fire to the head
before the bomber crashed. Of interest too is the
description of the ploy by Leading Aircraftsman Ivo Riley
(an Australian) to help break the new Japanese code which
had been changed just prior to the intercept mission.

2715. Michel, Marshall. "To Kill an Admiral." AEROSPACE H, 13
      (Spring 1966), 25-29.

      In this reexamination of the death of Yamamoto, the
      author gives credit to pilot Thomas G. Lanphier, Jr. for
      the kill.

2716. Wible, John T. "The Yamamoto Mission." AMER AVN HSJ, 12
      (Fall 1967), 159-167.

      After investigating assassination of the Japanese
      leader, Wible reaches no conclusions about which U.S. pilot
      (Lanphier or Barber) should receive the credit. The
      article is marked by interviews with Barber and Mitchell
      (Lanphier's wingman) as well as a letter from Lanphier.

IV.D.2.f. Japanese Air Force

2717. Beekman, Allan. THE NIIHAU INCIDENT. Honolulu, HI:
      Heritage Press of Pacific, 1982. 126 pp.

      Here is an account of a Japanese fighter pilot,
      Shigenori Nishikaichi, who crash landed on this Hawaiian
      island and briefly terrorized the inhabitants.

2718. Coox, Alvin D. "The Rise and Fall of the Imperial Japanese
      Air Forces." AEROSP H, 27 (Summer, June 1980), 74-86.

      Before the war, the Japanese deliberately concealed
      information about their military and naval aviation. In
      his usual thorough manner, Coox points out that by 1941
      Japan's air forces ranked among the best in the world.
      (Fifty Japanese pilots became aces in 1939 against the
      Russians at Nomonhan.) Analyzing the decline of the air
      forces, Coox identifies arrogance, lack of cooperation
      between the two services, and poor use of pilots as the
      chief causes.

2719. Cortesi, Lawrence. "Requiem for the Zero." SERGEANTS, 23
       (June 1984), 23-27.

       NE

2720. D'Albas, Andrieu. DEATH OF A NAVY: JAPANESE NAVAL
       ACTION IN WORLD WAR II. New York: Devin-Adair,
       1957. 362 pp.

       Originally published in Paris in 1954, this book centers
       on the themes of fanaticism, blind loyalty, and courage.
       Presenting the Japanese perspective (based largely on
       Japanese documents and interviews with Japanese naval
       officers), the author argues that the Japanese Navy re-
       luctantly travelled the road to war but wholeheartedly
       supported the war after the decision had been made.

2721. Francillon, Rene J. JAPANESE AIRCRAFT OF THE PACIFIC WAR.
       New York: Funk and Wagnalls, 1970. 570 pp.

       With great detail, Francillon presents not only a
       compact history of Japanese aircraft during the war but
       also an examination of the Japanese aircraft industry,
       including manufacturers of airframes and engines. The book
       incorporates many excellent photographs and drawings as
       well as useful appendices.

2722. Fujita, Nobuo and Joseph D. Harrington. "I Bombed the
       U.S.A." USNIP, 87 (June 1961), 64-69.

       Warrant Officer Nobuo Fujita piloted a float-equipped
       Zero launched from a submarine. On two occasions in
       September 1942, he dropped incendiary bombs on timber lands
       in Oregon.

2723. Hirokoshi, Jrio. EAGLES OF MITSUBISHI: THE STORY OF THE
       ZERO FIGHTER. Seattle, WA: University of Washington
       Press, 1981.

       Here is a detailed evaluation of the famed aircraft.
       The author gives its history, its operational use, and
       technical specifications.

2724. Omitted.

2725. Kiralfy, Alexander. "Watch Japanese Air Power." FOR AFFS,
       23 (October 1944), 66-78.

       The author argues that the West has failed to appreciate
       the primary role assigned to air power in Japanese war

plans. Identifying air power as the key to Japanese
aggrandizement, Kiralfy warns that Japanese air resources
must be severely curtailed in the postwar era.

2726. McLean, Donald B. JAPANESE PARACHUTE TROOPS. Wickenburg,
       AZ: Normount Technical Publications, 1973. 61 pp.

       NE

2727. Mikesh, Robert C. "Japan's Little Fleet of Big American
       Bombers: Japanese-Built B-17s in World War II." AF
       SPACE DIG, 52 (August 1969), 81-85.

       Using bits and pieces in the Philippines and Java which
       the Americans had left behind, the Japanese maintained a
       "fleet" of three B-17s. (U.S. intelligence agents worried
       about the new aircraft at Tachikawa Air Base.) The fate of
       the three aircraft remains uncertain.

2728. Richards, M.C. "The Plane That Bombed America." AIR PICT,
       27 (July 1965), 242-243.

       Here is a brief report of the Japanese aircraft,
       YOKOSUKA E14Y1, code named GLEN.

2729. Richards, M.C. and Robert C. Mikesh. "Emily--Grand Old
       Lady of Japan." AIR PICT, 31 (August 1969), 280-294.

       Here is a report on the Japanese flying boat, KAWANISHI,
       H8K1 (Type 2).

2730. Sakai, Saburo. SAMURAI: THE PERSONAL STORY OF JAPAN'S
       GREATEST LIVING FIGHTER PILOT. New York: E.P. Dutton,
       1957. 383 pp.

       With the help of Martin Caidin and Fred Saito, Sakai
       recounts his war experiences which saw him become a
       legendary ace with 64 confirmed kills. He was the first
       Japanese non-comissioned officer to achieve officer rank.
       His war stories are spellbinding; see especially his report
       of finding his island home base, after being severely
       wounded, in a crippled plane with no navigational aids. By
       the end of the war, despite his war wounds, Sakai took part
       in the final aerial engagement which extended into darkness
       and saw the last U.S. B-29 shot down in the war.

2731. Scott, Robert L, Jr. DAMNED TO GLORY. New York: Charles
       Scribner's Sons. 1944. 228 pp.

Scott presents the accounts of U.S. airmen who
distinguished themselves early in the war. Most of the
stories involve combat action in the P-40.

2732.   Shershun, Carroll S. "The Man Who Downed Colin Kelly."
        AEROSPACE H, 13 (Winter 1966), 149-152.

Here is a tribute to Japanese ace Saburo Sakai, who
never lost a wingman and who accumulated sixty-four "kills"
in two hundred aerial battles.

2733.   Sims, Edward H. THE GREATEST ACES. New York: Harper and
        Row, 1967. 294 pp.

Sims gives much attention to the Second World War in
amassing these brief profiles of the leading airmen in
history.

2734.   Sims, Edward H.   GREATEST FIGHTER MISSIONS OF THE TOP NAVY
        AND MARINE ACES OF WORLD WAR II. New York: Harper,
        1962. 250 pp.

Here is an interesting collection of aerial exploits,
As a fighter pilot in the war, Sims writes with authority.

2735.   Skidmore, Hobert D. MORE LIVES THAN ONE. Boston:
        Houghton Mifflin, 1945. 265 pp.

Sgt. Skidmore (USAAF) passes on his experiences and
observations during his service with an air support group
in the South Pacific. His narrative offers a useful
description of life in the rear echelons.

2736.   Underbrink, Robert L. "The Day the Navy Caught a Zero."
        USNIP, 94 (February 1968), 136-137.

In May 1942, a Japanese pilot died while crash-landing
his Zero at Akutan in the Aleutians. Some weeks later an
American scouting party discovered the site and recovered
the first intact Zero of the war.

2737.   United States. Department of the Army. Forces in the Far
        East. AIR DEFENSE OF THE HOMELAND. Washington, D.C.:
        Office of the Chief of Military History, 1956. 91 pp.

The Japanese authors describe Japan's desperate measures
to scrape together an effective air defense force during
the war's waning moments. In August 1945, the crippled air
defenses could number only 800 fighters and bombers, 13.2

million gallons of aviation gasoline, and 2,000 special
suicide attack planes. Of special note is the drastic
cutback in planned aircraft production which was caused by
the Allied strategic bombing.

2738. United States. Department of the Army. Forces in the Far
        East. HOMELAND AIR DEFENSE: OPERATIONS RECORD.
        Washington, D.C.: Office of the Chief of Military
        History, 1952. 176 pp.

        This Japanese report incorporates material gained from
interviews with Japanese air officers. Little was done,
according to this study, before or during the early years
of the war to build up air defenses in Japan. Apparently,
Japanese air officers believed that the best defense was a
good offense. During the final days, the KETSU-GO
operation combined air and ground resources and gave a
prominent role to special suicide units. Of special
interest is the report that, after the atomic bombings,
Japanese air units could not ignore a single B-29. Also,
the officers stress that patrols were still flying when the
war ended.

2739. United States. Department of History. Forces in the Far
        East. CENTRAL PACIFIC AIR OPERATIONS RECORD.
        Washington, D.C.: Office of the Chief of Military
        History, 1953. 14 pp.

        This brief report outlines plans formulated in 1944 by
the Japanese Air Training Army for the defense of the
Philippines, Formosa and the home islands against U.S.
B-29s.

2740. "Y.U." [Ushijima, Yasushi.] "Japanese Warhawk!" AMER AVN
        H S J, 20 (Summer 1975), 89-93.

        Osamu Tagaya translated from Japanese this article which
first appeared anonymously in 1954. Upon capturing two
P-40s reasonably intact in the Philippines, the Japanese,
including the author, received help from captured U.S.
pilots and maintenance men to repair and ferry the aircraft
to Manila. The author does not know what became of the two
fighters nor does he identify any of the Americans
involved. Depending, of course, on any reader's point of
view, the story seems tilted more towards mutual respect
and the fraternal bonds of airmen than "aiding and
abetting."

IV.D.2.g. Strategic Bombing

2741. Argyle, Christopher J. "Superfortress Raids on Japan."
       AIR PICT, Pt. I: 33 (January 1971), 4-9; Pt. II: 33
       (February 1971), 64-68.

       Here are some excellent photographs of the B-29s in
       action.

2742. Birdsell, Steve. "Target: Rabaul!" AF MAG, 58 (September
       1975), 108-113.

       Birdsell highlights the accomplishments of General
       George Kenney and the 5th Air Force in October 1943. He
       addresses the controversy over the actual damage inflicted
       on Japanese shipping.

2743. Boyle, James M. "The XXI Bomber Command: A Primary Factor
       in the Defeat of Japan." AIRPOWER HIST, 21 (April
       1964), 49-53.

       Making a case for the decisive role of air power, Boyle
       claims that the B-29 bombing campaign was the most
       important single factor in (1) causing the Japanese to have
       doubts about winning the war and (2) deciding to surrender.

2744. Caidin, Martin. A TORCH TO THE ENEMY. New York:
       Ballantine Books, 1960. 160 pp.

       Here is a knowledgeable account of the fire-bombing of
       Tokyo. Caidin's perceptive narrative is accompanied by
       excellent photographs.

2745. Craig, C.A. "What's Left of Rabaul." MC GAZ, 30 (April
       1946), 3-7, 39-40.

       Craig relies on the findings of the United States
       Strategic Bombing Survey to describe how the eighty-
       thousand Japanese defenders at Rabaul deteriorated from a
       high level of efficiency to a "mole-like existence."

2746. Creekmore, Raymond. "Target: Japan." A F, 28 (January
       1945), 4-5.

       Creekmore, an artist, flew as an observer in the first
       bombing raid against Japan in late 1944. His narrative
       includes a photo of Mount Fuji. {Note: Creekmore's art
       sketches of this mission appear on pp. 32-33 of the
       February 1945 issue.}

2747.   Daniels, Gordon. "Before Hiroshima: The Bombing of Japan,
        1944-5." HIST TODAY, 32 (January 1982), 14-19.

        Daniels brings together the lethal factors, such as
        inadequate Japanese civil defense, ineffective Japanese
        military countermeasures (radar, interceptor aircraft, and
        anti-aircraft guns), and LeMay's tactics, which led to the
        devastating conventional bombing of Japan.

2748.   Daniels, Gordon, ed. A GUIDE TO THE REPORTS OF THE
        UNITED STATES STRATEGIC BOMBING SURVEY. London:
        Royal Historical Society, 1981. 115 pp.

        This summary indicates the contents and length of the
        official reports. Chapter headings used in the reports
        form the basis of Daniels' descriptions (which omit
        the exhibits and appendices). Here is a convenient
        aid for finding a treasure of information.

2749.   De Seversky, Alexander P. VICTORY THROUGH AIR POWER. New
        York: Simon and Schuster, 1942. 354 pp.

        The book and the author stirred a controversy which
        continues to the present day. What is the role of air
        power? Arguing that the United States could become the
        world's greatest power in aviation, De Seversky believes
        that air power holds the key to winning the war. He
        perhaps did not go as far in this argument as either his
        critics or his most enthusiastic supporters have since
        claimed, but his general point of view causes vigorous
        debate--a debate that was reinvigorated by the U.S.
        experience in Vietnam. Significantly, the book is
        dedicated to Billy Mitchell.

2750.   Dickens, Sir Gerald C. BOMBING AND STRATEGY: THE FALLACY
        OF TOTAL WAR. New York: Macmillan, 1949. 90 pp.

        Although Dickens concentrates on the British experience
        in Germany, his conclusions are of general interest. In
        refuting the appealing case for strategic bombing, he
        argues that the first priority in war is the destruction of
        enemy forces. For Dickens, the so-called strategic bombing
        of the enemy's homeland should occur after the first
        priority has been largely satisfied.

2751.   Edoin, Hoito. THE NIGHT TOKYO BURNED. New York: St.
        Martin's Press, 1987. 248 pp.

        Despite the title, Edoin addresses the policy devised by

LeMay of the systematic firebombing of Japan's cities
during the period March 9-August 6, 1945. Based on
interviews and government (U.S. and Japan) records, Edoin,
a journalist, concentrates on describing the bombings and
public-official reactions in both countries. Almost double
the number of Japanese perished in the firebombings as were
killed in the two atomic bombings. The author notes that
extensive international efforts have aided the atomic-
bombing victims but little has been done to assist the
firebombing victims. Of special note is Edoin's report on
class strife when refugees from the poorest classes
accepted hospitality from the middle-upper classes and saw
the relative opulence of their new surroundings. See, too,
Edoin's contention that Americans misunderstood the
character of the Japanese in hoping that bombings would
force Japan to surrender; the author believes the ordeal
made the Japanese people more determined than ever to carry
on the war.

2752. Fail, J.E.H. "RAF Heavy Bombers in the Far East." AIR
       PICT, Pt. I: 39 (February 1977), 66-69; Pt. II: 39
       (March 1977), 108-111.

       NE

2753. Graham, Vickie M. "Brother Bombadiers: Putting a Pickle in
       a Barrel." AIRMAN, 31 (September 1987), 12-13.

       Here is a brief report on the work of bombadiers aboard
       the B-29s in the Pacific. See especially the story of Bob
       Filson, who was saved--along with the rest of his
       crew--when his aircraft was able to make an emergency
       landing at the recently secured airstrip at Iwo Jima.

2754. Gurney, Gene. JOURNEY OF THE GIANTS. New York:
       Coward-McCann, 1962. 280 pp.

       Gurney writes about B-29 operations in the Pacific.
       He asserts that this aircraft made the difference in
       forcing the Japanese to surrender. His narrative
       emphasizes the role of the incendiary attacks designed by
       LeMay.

2755. Hansell, Haywood S., Jr. STRATEGIC AIR WAR AGAINST JAPAN.
       Washington, D.C.: GPO, 1983. 181 pp.

       This is the memoir of a major general who participated
       in the planning, execution and subsequent review of the
       strategic air war. The book is divided into two parts:

prelude, 1919-1943; and the strategic air war against
Japan. Much useful information appears in the Appendix.
Of special interest is Hansell's observation that the use
of the atomic bomb was intended not only to convince Japan
to cease further resistance but also to extricate the U.S.
Army from its obsession of invading Japan.

2756. Harwood, R. Frank. "Hell's Belle—Missions 19 (Tokyo) and
       22 (Osaka): Two Memorable Incendiary Missions."
       AEROSPACE H, 32 (Spring/March 1985), 20-24.

       Here is the personal account of a navigator in the 505th
       Very Heavy Bomber Group. Of the incendiary destruction,
       Harwood admits that accuracy of weapons delivery was not
       required from an altitude of seven thousand feet.

2757. Haugland, Vern. THE AAF AGAINST JAPAN. New York: Harper,
       1948. 515 pp.

       Haugland covered the war as a correspondent, and he had
       access to confidential files in Washington. His story
       comes with great detail but in a style which taxes the
       reader.

2758. Hebert, Kevin. MAXIMUM EFFORT: THE B-29'S AGAINST JAPAN.
       Manhattan, KS: Sunflower University Press, 1984.

       Here is a well-written description of the final stage of
       the strategic bombing campaign. Herbert knows the
       material!

2759. Hopkins, George E. "Bombing and the American Conscience
       During World War II." HISTORIAN, 28 (May 1966),
       451-473.

       Hopkins traces the shifting public attitudes about
       aerial bombardments, from prewar criticism to wartime
       approval. The high stakes of total warfare helped justify
       the bombing policies, according to the author.

2760. Ickle, Fred C. THE SOCIAL IMPACT OF BOMB DESTRUCTION.
       Norman, OK: Unversity of Oklahoma Press, 1960. 250 pp.

       Ickle examines the repercussions of bombing in various
       countries (e.g., Great Britain, Japan, and Germany). His
       emphasis is on the human response to the terrifying ordeal.

2761. Jackson, Robert. STORM FROM THE SKIES: THE STRATEGIC
       BOMBING OFFENSIVE, 1943-1945. London: Barker, 1974.

The author discusses the impact of strategic bombing
during the final two years of the war. Although the weight
of this study falls heavily on Germany, some of the
observations and conclusions apply to the general topic.

2762.   JAPANESE WAR MOBILIZATION AND THE PACIFIC CAMPAIGNS,
        1941-1945. Allentown, PA: Game Marketing Co., 1985.

        The book essentially summarizes the investigation of the
        U.S. Strategic Bombing Survey. There are 25 maps and 200
        tables. Of interest is the description of Japanese
        recruiting and combat replacement.

2763.   Johnsen, Frederick A. "Bombs over Brunei." AIRMAN, 30
        (December 1986), 26-28.

        Here is a description of a bombing mission, November 16,
        1944, by B-24 Liberators of the 5th and 307th Bomb Groups
        against Brunei.

2764.   Johnston, Francis J. "Ground Crew." AEROSPACE H, 25
        (Winter, December 1978), 244-252.

        The author describes his experiences in a ground crew
        for B-29s in C-B-I and Tinian.

2765.   Kennett, Lee B. A HISTORY OF STRATEGIC BOMBING. New York:
        Charles Scribner's Sons, 1982. 222 pp.

        The war against Japan plays only a small part in this
        broad history, which dates from balloon ascents in 1783.
        Kennett voices skepticism about the extravagant claims put
        forward by enthusiasts for strategic bombing.

2766.   LeMay, Curtis E. "Strategic Air Power: Destroying the
        Enemy's War Resources." AEROSPACE H, 27 (Summer, June
        1980), 9-15.

        While clarifying his role in strategic bombing
        operations, LeMay describes the main objective as hitting
        Japanese vulnerable areas. Nevertheless, he insists that
        there was no deliberate deviation from "precision" to
        "area" bombing. Japanese "cottage" industries were spread
        out, and poor weather forced the use of radar-controlled
        bombing. At the time of the atomic bombings, he says that
        he was briefing the JCS against the need to invade Japan.

2767.   MacIsaac, David. STRATEGIC BOMBING IN WORLD WAR II: THE

STORY OF THE UNITED STATES STRATEGIC BOMBING SURVEY.
New York: Garland, 1976. 231 pp.

Here is an internal history of the USSBS--how, why, and
when the survey was established and who was involved.
MacIsaac traces the origins of the survey to three
influences: (1) air operations analysts in 1943, (2) the
AAF Target Sections group in 1943-1944, and (3) the
leadership and vision of Gen. Arnold.

2768.   MacIsaac, David, ed. THE UNITED STATES STRATEGIC BOMBING
        SURVEY. New York: Garland, 1976. 10 vols.

        The collection assembles approximately 2,000 documents
        in over 3,300 pages. Volumes 7-10 deal with the war
        against Japan.

2769.   MacIsaac, David. "What the Bombing Survey Really Says."
        AF MAG, 56 (June 1973), 60-63.

        The author refutes critics, who, he says, really have in
        mind criticism of the use of air power in Vietnam, by
        arguing that the U.S. Strategic Bombing Survey praised
        Allied air attacks as "decisive" in Europe and instrumental
        in bringing Japan to defeat even before the two atomic
        bombings.

2770.   Miller, John, Jr. CARTWHEEL: THE REDUCTION OF RABAUL.
        Washington, D.C.: Office of the Chief of Military
        History, Dept., of the Army, 1959. 418 pp.

        This volume reflects the strength of the Army's official
        history series. Miller incorporates extensive research in
        analyzing the reduction of this Japanese island fortress.

2771.   Morrison, Wilbur H. POINT OF NO RETURN: THE STORY OF THE
        20TH AIR FORCE. New York: Time Books, 1979. 278 pp.

        The author is a veteran of the "Double-X" unit, which,
        he says, served as the prototype for the later Strategic
        Air Command. Morrison devotes much attention to LeMay's
        decision to switch from daylight precision bombing to
        low-level night fire raids against Japan. According to the
        author, Japanese cities accommodated much of Japan's
        industrial resources. About one-half of the targets on the
        20th Air Force's master list were located in 20 chief
        Japanese cities. Of interest is Morrison's argument that
        the bombing by the B-29s, not the Soviet entry or the
        (unnecessary) atomic bombings, caused the defeat of Japan.

Also, see his descriptions of the B-29s carrying their own
fuel on missions over the Hump into China in order to make
the return trip.

2772. Morrocco, John. THUNDER FROM ABOVE: AIR WAR, 1941-1968.
Boston: Boston Publishing Company, 1984. 192 pp.

This general survey of air power dwells mainly on
postwar events. There is some useful material, however, on
strategic bombing.

2773. Quester, George H. DETERRENCE BEFORE HIROSHIMA. New York:
John Wiley, 1966. 196 pp.

Here is an analysis of strategic bombing. Quester
devotes much attention to the moral dimension of the topic.
His narrative notes the close association between the
development of air power and the birth of modern strategy.

2774. Quester, George H. "The Impact of Strategic Air Warfare."
ARMED FORCES SOC, 4 (Winter 1978), 179-206.

Quester, a political scientist, argues that Americans
are biased by culture and analytical style against aerial
bombing (especially against non-combatants). Yet, he adds
that critics are not entirely correct in their complaints
that strategic bombing is not effective.

2775. Robertson, Bruce. "'Tiger Force': How the British Would
Have Bombed Japan in 1945." AIR PICT, 36 (October
1974), 388-391.

NE

2776. Schaffel, Kenneth. "Muir S. Fairchild: Philosopher of Air
Power." AEROSPACE H, 33 (Fall 1986), 165-171.

Tracing the highlights of Fairchild's career, Schaffel
evaluates his ideas about strategic bombing.

2777. Schaffer, Ronald. WINGS OF JUDGMENT: AMERICAN BOMBING IN
WORLD WAR II. New York: Oxford University Press, 1985.
272 pp.

Schaffer takes a close look at American perceptions of
the moral issue attached to the question of strategic
bombing. Only certain aspects of U.S. bombing are studied.
He points out that USAAF generals did not want to tarnish
the image of their service as they sought to separate

themselves from the Army after the war. Also, the author examines decision-making within groups to whom technology had given new power (e.g., scientists, mathematicians, economists, and businessmen). His conclusion is that some of these U.S. leaders were divided over the moral issue, especially on the meaning of "military necessity." Of special interest is the attention paid to the effects of fire bombing in Japan, including gathering data from insurance experts and information about the 1923 earthquake. By the end of the war, Schaffer asserts, the American people hardly noticed the moral and military revolution that had occurred.

2778. Seversky, Alexander P. de. "Victory Through Air Power." AMER MERCURY, 54 (February 1942), 135-154.

Emphasizing that new weapons call for new ideas, Seversky criticizes U.S. leaders for not understanding the importance of air power in the war. He dismisses old fashioned formulas about sea power.

2779. Sherry, Michael S. THE RISE OF AMERICAN AIR POWER: THE CREATION OF ARMAGEDDON. New Haven, CT: Yale University Press, 1987. 435 pp.

Sherry weighs the good and evil about U.S. air power. The economic destruction achieved through bombing, he feels, does not justify the human (especially civilian) costs. Of interest is the connection he draws which stresses the continuity between the nuclear age and its "conventional" antecedents. His appraisal of strategic bombing in the Second World War includes the leaders, organizations, and the methods used in air attacks. The work is well researched.

2780. Sherry, Michael. "The Slide to Total Air War." NEW REP, 185 (December 16, 1981), 20-25.

Strategists, according to Sherry, largely failed to consider any alternatives to bombing the enemy's homeland. For example, he says that no one knew or even bothered to ask how firebombing could contribute to victory. Sherry excites the controversy about the dropping of the atomic bomb, which, he claims, American leaders used because they had developed it--a decision borne of "technological fanaticism."

2781. Smith, Meldon E., Jr. "The Strategic Bombing Debate: The Second World War and Vietnam." J CONTEMP HIST, 12

(January 1977), 175-191.

Smith claims that the U.S. Stategic Bombing Survey identified strategic bombing as decisive during World War II and that the report has been misconstrued ever since it appeared. (The Vietnam experience, he says, was not a true test.) Therefore, the American public remains confused about the value of strategic bombing.

2782. Snyder, Earl A. GENERAL LEEMY'S CIRCUS: A NAVIGATOR'S STORY OF THE 20TH AIR FORCE IN WORLD WAR II. New York: Exposition Press, 1955. 175 pp.

In this interesting account, Snyder, with some humor, describes the activities and personalities of the 20th Air Force. His report yields a personal perspective on both the air war in China and the strategic bombing campaign against Japan.

2783. Spaatz, Carl. "Strategic Air Power: Fulfillment of a Concept." FOR AFFS, 24 (April 1946), 385-396.

Spaatz helped formulate strategic bombing techniques. He feels that the supreme lesson to come out of the war is that strategic air power will be the key to any future war. Of special interest is the insistence by this leading authority that strategic air power alone cannot win a war and that surface forces are essential.

2784. Wheeler, Keith. BOMBERS OVER JAPAN. Alexandria, VA: Time-Life Books, 1982. 208 pp.

Here is a popular account of the strategic bombing of the Japanese homeland. Wheeler considers these aerial operations decisive in forcing the Japanese to surrender.

2785. Wolk, Herman S. "The B-29, the A-Bomb and the Japanese Surrender." A F MAG, 58 (February 1975), 55-61.

Wolk, a distinguished military historian, examines the role of the B-29 in the bombing of Japan and the leadership of Gen. Curtis LeMay. The article is based in part on Wolk's interviews with the general.

IV.D.3. Sea
a. General

2786. Blee, Ben W. "Whodunnit?" USNIP, 108 (July 1982), 42-47.

A mystery has persisted concerning the damage inflicted on three U.S. Navy ships in the South Pacific by an unidentified source on September 15, 1942. Blee attempts to solve the mystery. In the process, his investigation uncovers the poor battle communication procedures used by the Navy.

2787. Brodie, Bernard. "The Naval Strategy of the Pacific War." INFANTRY J, 57 (August 1945), 34-39.

Brodie surveys the successes of the U.S. Navy after the first six months of the war.

2788. Creswell, John. SEA WARFARE, 1939-1945. Berkeley: University of California Press, 1967. 343 pp.

This general account, written by a British captain in the Royal Navy, surveys the war at sea in all theaters. Addressing events in the Pacific, Creswell praises the performance of American submarines and the development of amphibious warfare. See also his report on the sinking of the REPULSE and PRINCE OF WALES.

2789. Crowl, Philip A. CAMPAIGN IN THE MARIANAS. Washington, D. C.: Office of the Chief of Military History for the Dept. of the Army, 1960. 505 pp.

Crowl combines in-depth research with a felicitous style to offer an admirable official history of this campaign.

2790. Crowl, Philip A. and Edmund G. Love. SEIZURE OF THE GILBERTS AND MARSHALLS. Washington, D.C.: Office of the Chief of Military History for the Dept. of the Army, 1955. 414 pp.

This official history examines some of the final phases of the war. Of special interest are the lessons learned by both sides--in launching and in countering--about amphibious warfare.

2791. "The Death of USS EDSALL: A Gallant Fight Against Impossible Odds." SHIPMATE, 43 (April 1980), 12.

Seeking to end speculation about the fate of EDSALL, this editorial asserts that the ship sank without a trace on March 1, 1942, south of Java in the Indian Ocean. According to this report, the EDSALL was caught by Nogumo's Carrier Striking Force. See, too, the speculation by Skip Wild Harrington in ibid., (January-February 1980), 26-28.

2792.   Hart, Thomas C. "What Our Navy Learned in the Pacific."
            USNIP, 69 (January 1943), 111-117.

            In this contemporary report, the former commander of the
        Asiatic Fleet offers his frank observations about the
        situation in the Pacific. For example, he praises the work
        of U.S. submarines and Navy pilots, does not hesitate to
        criticize the mismanagement of air resources in the
        Philippines, and, somewhat surprisingly, defends the
        actions of Admiral Phillips in the debacle involving the
        REPULSE and the PRINCE OF WALES.

2793.   Hill, Harry W. OPERATIONS OF CENTRAL PACIFIC FORCES:
            GILBERT AND MARSHALL ISLANDS. Maxwell Field, AL: Air
            War College, 1947. 25 pp.

            Vice Admiral Hill (USN) gives a close explanation of
        these operations--operations in which he participated. His
        report on the lessons learned is particularly valuable.
        Examples of some lessons are: (a) carrier task forces
        could stay close to the assault area; (b) troops with
        adequate amphibious craft could be landed and supplied on
        reef-fringed atolls; (c) pre-landing bombardment could
        destroy enemy defenses; and (d) good communications were
        needed for close air support and naval gunfire. Of
        interest is Hill's description of the life guard service,
        which meant positioning submarines along air routes to save
        downed airmen.

2794.   Holbrook, Francis X. "The Road to Down Under." AEROSPACE
            H, 21 (Winter/December 1974), 225-231.

            The author outlines the prewar interest of the U.S. Navy
        in developing "stepping stones" across the Pacific which
        would provide secure lines of communication.

2795.   Hone, Thomas C. "The Similarity of Past and Present
            Standoff Threats." USNIP, 107 (September 1981),
            113-116.

            Early in the war, according to Hone, the Navy was not
        served well by its tactics during night engagements. The
        author notes much improvement after the Navy equipped every
        ship with surface radar and combat information centers.

2796.   Hough, Richard. THE LONGEST BATTLE: THE WAR AT SEA,
            1939-1945. New York: William Morrow, 1987. 371 pp.

Hough presents a readable and well-researched survey.
He integrates the first-hand accounts of many participants.
In addition to covering the major naval encounters, Hough
highlights the human side of the war at sea in all
theaters. There are short biographies of over twenty naval
leaders.

2797. Isby, David C. "'CA': Tactical Naval Warfare in the
        Pacific, 1941-1943." STRATEGY & TACTICS, 38 (1973),
        5-19.

        NE

2798. Johnson, Ellis A. and David A. Katcher. MINES AGAINST
        JAPAN. Silver Spring, MD: Naval Ordnance Laboratory,
        GPO, 1973. 313 pp.

        The authors provide much technical information in their
        report on the development, use, and effectiveness of U.S.
        Navy mines.

2799. Jones, Ken. DESTROYER SQUADRON 23. Philadelphia, PA:
        Chilton, 1959. 283 pp.

        Jones describes this unit's accomplishments in the South
        Pacific. His narrative includes a look at the leadership
        style of the unit's commanding officer, Arleigh Burke.

2800. Jones, T.M. and Ion L. Idriess. THE SILENT SERVICE.
        Sydney, Aus.: Angus and Robertson, 1952. 372 pp.

        First published in 1944, the book relates stories (in
        episodic fashion) of the ANZAC navy. Here is a good first
        look at the little-known naval force.

2801. Karig, Walter, et al. BATTLE REPORT. New York: Farrar
        and Rinehart, 1944-1949. 5 vols.

        With the official support of the Navy, Karig and his
        various colleagues have assembled a well-written, popular
        account which relies heavily on extensive interviews.

2802. Khan, Rashid Ahmad. "Strategic Role of the Indian Ocean
        During the Second World War." PAK HORIZON, 35 (No. 2,
        1982), 39-50.

        Upon surveying events of the war in the Indian Ocean,
        Khan concludes that, while the Japanese did not lose the
        war because of their failure to hold and dominate the

Indian Ocean, the outcome of the war would have been
different if they had been able to do so.

2803. King, Ernest J. THE UNITED STATES NAVY AT WAR: 1941-1945.
        Washington, D.C.: Dept. of the Navy, 1946. 312 pp.

        Here is a reprint of King's three official reports to
the secretary of the Navy. The narrative is factual and
straightforward.

2804. Lord, Walter. "Ordeal at Vella Lavella." AMER HERITAGE,
        28 (June 1977), 30-43.

        When the HELENA went down in the Solomons, not all
survivors were rescued. About 165 made their way to the
Japanese-held island of Vella Lavella. With the help of
two Coastwatchers and one missionary, the survivors evaded
the Japanese for months before finally being picked up by
the U.S. Navy.

2805. Lott, Arnold S. MOST DANGEROUS SEA: A HISTORY OF MINE
        WARFARE AND AN ACCOUNT OF U.S. NAVY MINE WARFARE
        OPERATIONS IN WORLD WAR II AND KOREA. Annapolis, MD:
        U.S. Naval Institute Press, 1959. 322 pp.

        Here is an authoritative report. The section on World
War II incoporates some excellent descriptions of U.S. mine
warfare in the Pacific. Lott is a first-rate writer.

2806. Lundstrom, John B. THE FIRST SOUTH PACIFIC CAMPAIGN:
        PACIFIC FLEET STRATEGY, DECEMBER 1941-JUNE 1942.
        Annapolis, MD: Naval Institute Press, 1976. 240 pp.

        As the U.S. Navy extended its area of responsibility
into the South Pacific, Lundstrom contends that the Pacific
Fleet sought to provoke a major engagement. Using
relatively new sources (including Japanese), the author
offers some unique insights in this strategic overview of
the first seven months of the war. For example, Nimitz,
confident not desperate, committed all available aircraft
carriers to the Coral Sea in seeking to confront the
Japanese navy. Also, Lundstrom cites the significance of
U.S. air raids against Lae and Salamaua on March 10, 1942,
which delayed Japanese plans to invade Tulagai and Port
Moresby. Of interest is the author's description of the
split in the Imperial General Headquarters over whether to
move against Midway or the New Caledonia-Fiji-Samoa area.

2807. McCandless, Bruce. "Incident in the Nanpo Shoto." USNIP,

99 (July 1973), 67-77.

The author commanded the GREGORY. He tells of his ship's rescue of three downed airmen near Iwo Jima.

2808.   McDowell, John. "The Day the USS JUNEAU Went Down." ALASKA J, (Autumn 1985), 38-43.

Only ten out of a total ship's ensemble of seven hundred survived the sinking at Guadalcanal on November 13, 1942. All five of the Sullivan brothers died in the tragedy.

2809.   McMillian, I.E. "U.S.S. NEWCOMB (DD586)--Victim of the Kamikazes." USNIP, 74 (June 1948), 682-689.

The author, who took command of the destroyer NEWCOMB in early November 1944, describes the ship being attacked near Okinawa by five aircraft. Three kamikaze planes hit the NEWCOMB, which had to be towed back to San Francisco.

2810.   Miller, Vernon J. " Major Fleet Units Lost During World War II." USNIP, 86 (January 1960), 90-101.

This valuable reference lists the names of ships lost in battle, the date, the ship's weight, the location of the encounter, and the names of the victors. No unconfirmed claims for sinkings are included.

2811.   Morison, Samuel Eliot. HISTORY OF UNITED STATES NAVAL OPERATIONS IN WORLD WAR II. Boston: Little, Brown, 1947-1962. 15 vols.

Here is a masterful piece of scholarship. The footnotes indicate the in-depth research and the primary sources (especially battle reports) that went into this study. For purposes of this guide, see volumes 3 (THE RISING SUN IN THE PACIFIC), 12 (LEYTE), 13 (THE LIBERATION OF THE PHILIPPINES) and 14 (VICTORY IN THE PACIFIC, 1945). Morison is at his best clearing the fog of war and explaining the combat action. As detailed as the volumes are, Morison slights less glamorous, but important, topics such as logistics, intelligence, and command-control arrangements. Although commissioned by the Navy, this study is not labeled an official history.

2812.   Morison, Samuel Eliot. THE TWO-OCEAN WAR: A SHORT HISTORY OF THE UNITED STATES NAVY IN THE SECOND WORLD WAR. Boston: Little, Brown, 1963. 611 pp.

Here is a popular account of the war at sea. Based on the monumental fifteen-volume history but written as a separate work, Morison describes and analyzes the naval highlights from all theaters.

2813. Morris, Frank D. "PICK OUT THE BIGGEST." Boston: Houghton, Mifflin, 1943. 132 pp.

As a correspondent aboard the light cruiser BOISE, Morris describes the action in the Solomons by the crew and the commander, Mike Moran.

2814. NAVY TIMES. OPERATION VICTORY: WINNING THE PACIFIC WAR. New York: G.P. Putnam's Sons, 1968. 192 pp.

The narrative amounts to a summary of the highlights of the naval war.

2815. Norberg, Carl. "In the Southwest Pacific With the Army's Navy." AEROSPACE H, 27 (Fall, September 1980), 163-168.

This is the personal account of service with the AAF's Air/Sea Rescue Squadron--and its 63-foot boats.

2816. Potter, E.B. and Chester W. Nimitz, eds. THE GREAT SEA WAR: THE STORY OF NAVAL ACTION IN WORLD WAR II. Englewood Cliffs, NJ: Prentice-Hall, 1960. 468 pp.

This volume is adopted from the editors' SEA POWER. Several officers contributed the articles, but the work is not an official history. Separate sections deal with the naval war in the Pacific.

2817. Potter, E.B. and Chester W. Nimitz, eds. SEA POWER: A NAVAL HISTORY. Englewood Cliffs, NJ: Prentice-Hall, 1960. 932 pp.

The contributing authors explore naval strategy, tactics, and leadership. Over 200 pages are devoted to the Second World War (and many of these to Pacific operations). Of interest is the attention given to the development of amphibious warfare in the war against Japan. In the 2d edition (1981), considerable cuts were made in the narrative.

2818. Potter, E.B. and Chester W. Nimitz, eds. TRIUMPH IN THE PACIFIC: THE NAVY'S STRUGGLE AGAINST JAPAN. Englewood Cliffs, NJ: Prentice-Hall, 1963. 186 pp.

Here is the navy's story of the war against Japan. The narrative is largely uncritical as it skips over the highlights.

2819. Pratt, Fletcher. NIGHT WORK: THE STORY OF TASK FORCE 39. New York: Henry Holt, 1946. 267 pp.

In a well-written effort, Pratt describes the combat record of the group which was organized in the Solomons. Squadron Commander A.S. Merrill earns special praise for his efforts.

2820. Sowinski, Larry, comp. ACTION IN THE PACIFIC. Annapolis, MD: Naval Institute Press, 1981. 208 pp.

Here is a collection of U.S. Navy photographs of combat action at sea and in the air against the Japanese.

2821. Tidman, Keith R. THE OPERATIONS EVALUATION GROUP: A HISTORY OF NAVAL OPERATIONS ANALYSIS. Annapolis, MD: Naval Institute Press, 1984. 359 pp.

Here is an excellent analysis of the Navy's Operations Evaluation Group. Tidman, in a well-researched, finely written analysis, traces the history of the group and its accomplishments. He is able to capture the importance of the group to the Navy's operations.

2822. United States. Department of the Army. Forces in the Far East. OUTLINE OF OPERATIONS PRIOR TO TERMINATION OF THE WAR. Washington, D.C.: Office of the Chief of Military History, 1952. 31 pp.

Based on the personal notes and recollections of officers on the Japanese Navy General Staff, this summarized conditions which prevailed at the time of the cessation of hostilities.

2823. Earle, Edward Mead, ed. MAKERS OF MODERN STRATEGY. Princeton, NJ: Princeton University Press, 1971. 553 pp.

In this excellent collection, compiled with the collaboration of Gordon A. Craig and Felix Gilbert, see especially the article by Alexander Kiralfy, "Japanese Naval Strategy." Kiralfy offers a balanced assessment without failing to measure out both praise and criticism.

2824. Winslow, W.G. THE FLEET THE GODS FORGOT: THE U.S. ASIATIC

FLEET IN WORLD WAR II. Annapolis, MD: Naval Institute
Press, 1982. 327 pp.

Here is the brief and tragic wartime story of the
Asiatic Fleet. The author experienced the three-month
battle life of the Fleet as a naval aviator aboard the
HOUSTON (flagship of the Asiatic Fleet). Later, as a POW,
he conducted interviews among the prisoners in order to
piece together other parts of the Fleet's combat
activities. Although he tries to be neutral, he fails; his
narrative is filtered through his respect and affection for
the Fleet's commander, Admiral Hart. Winslow organizes his
reports on the Fleet's operations by grouping them under
ship types.

IV.D.3.b. Personal Accounts/Memoirs/Biographies

2825. Abercrombie, Laurence A. and Fletcher Pratt. MY LIFE TO
THE DESTROYERS. NY: Henry Holt, 1945. 157 pp.

Abercrombie commanded the destroyer DRAYTON, which he
claims was the first ship to encounter the Japanese after
Pearl Harbor. The book relates his combat experiences and
describes life aboard a destroyer.

2826. Abernathy, E.P. "The PECOS Died Hard." USNIP, 95
(December 1969), 74-82.

Abernathy commanded the PECOS. The oiler maneuvered out
of Cavite for three months after the war began, but the
combined efforts of four Japanese cruisers finally sank
Abernathy's ship.

2827. Backus, Paul H. "Why Them and Not Me?" USNIP, 107
(September 1981), 48-57.

Here is a personal account of the attack at Pearl Harbor
by the signal officer aboard the OKLAHOMA.

2828. Bell, Frederick J. CONDITION RED: DESTROYER ACTION IN THE
SOUTH PACIFIC. New York: Longmans, Green, 1943. 274
pp.

Here is the personal account of the captain of an
unnamed destroyer. His experience reveals how destroyers
had become multi-purpose ships in the pacific.

2829. Casey, Robert J. TORPEDO JUNCTION: WITH THE PACIFIC FLEET
FROM PEARL HARBOR TO MIDWAY. Indianapolis, IN:

Bobbs-Merrill, 1942. 423 pp.

Correspondent Casey offers his perceptive and humorous
reports of portions of the war at sea. All the reports are
based on his first-hand observations.

2830. Divoll, Lawrence E. "LANGLEY's Last Voyage." SHIPMATE, 44
        (January-February 1981), 19-20.

The author gives a personal account of the wartime
voyages of the LANGLEY. The article includes a description
of the ship's sinking and Divoll's rescue.

2831. Exton, William. HE'S IN THE DESTROYERS NOW. New York:
        Robert M. McBride, 1944. 224 pp.

Lt. Cmdr. Exton knows his subject. His narrative
provides a good description of life aboard a destroyer.

2832. Fahey, James J. PACIFIC WAR DIARY, 1942-1945. Boston:
        Houghton Mifflin, 1963. 404 pp.

In this excellent personal account, Fahey, an enlisted
seaman aboard the MONTPELIER, provides an "American
bluejacket's point of view" of the war through his vivid
and frank diary entries on such matters as officers,
boredom, fright, kamikaze attacks, and the liberation of
the Philippines. Here is history truly from the
underside--warts and all.

2833. Gibson, Walter. THE BOAT. Boston: Houghton Mifflin,
        1953. 101 pp.

After a Japanese torpedo sank the Dutch ship (ROOSEBOOM)
he was aboard, the author spent four weeks at sea in a
lifeboat with 135 people. By the time they managed to land
at a small island, only 4 men were left. The brief volume
hardly does justice to the trauma of the ordeal.

2834. Hopkins, Harold. NICE TO HAVE YOU ABOARD. London: Allen &
        Unwin, 1964. 217 pp.

Here are the reminiscences of a Royal British Navy
liaison officer with the U.S. Navy in the Pacific. Hopkins
maintains a polite, diplomatic tone.

2835. Kauffman, Russell W. FIFTY THOUSAND HUMAN CORKS.
        Philadelphia, PA: Dorrance, 1957. 163 pp.

NE

2836. Leach, Douglas E. NOW HEAR THIS: THE MEMOIR OF A JUNIOR
       NAVAL OFFICER IN THE GREAT PACIFIC WAR. Kent, OH: Kent
       State University Press, 1987. 200 pp.

       This historian's memoir is built upon his private papers
       and official documents. Leach reports on his life in the
       Navy. In addition to the personal anecdotes, the book
       reveals some of the internal politics and rivalries that
       clog efficient management in any service.

2837. Loeffelbein, Bob. "I was There." AMER HIST ILLUS, 20
       (October 1985), 32-57.

       Here are the diary entries for June-September 1945 of a
       young seaman. He took part in the first Allied landing at
       Tokyo Bay and gives his observations of war-torn Japan. Of
       interest is his report that his and other ships in Task
       Force 31 carried many Marine stowaways who wanted to
       participate in the final invasion. Their force was en
       route from Hawaii when Japan surrendered.

2838. McKie, Ronald C.H. THE SURVIVORS. New York: W.W. Norton,
       1953. 246 pp.

       The author, an Australian correspondent, describes the
       sinking of two cruisers (the Australian PERTH and American
       HOUSTON) in the Sundra Strait on February 28, 1942. The
       narrative relies on McKie's interviews with ten of the
       survivors.

2839. Mason, Theodore C. BATTLESHIP SAILOR. Annapolis, MD:
       Naval Institute Press, 1982.

       Mason recalls his experiences as an enlisted man in the
       U.S. Navy. He was aboard the CALIFORNIA at Pearl Harbor
       during the Japanese attack.

2840. Miller, Max. IT'S TOMORROW OUT HERE. New York:
       Whittlesey House, 1945. 186 pp.

       The author, a U.S. Navy reservist, describes life on the
       liberated Pacific islands. He rambles among various
       topics, such as logistics, task forces, and gift-giving on
       Guam. The book contains excellent official Navy
       phtographs by Lt. Cmdr. Charles E. Kerlee. As he watched
       the impressions (designs?) in mud made by the footsteps of
       others, Miller felt himself "gradually going screwy."

2841.   Seaholes, Henry C. ADRIFT IN THE SOUTH PACIFIC, OR SIX
          NIGHTS IN THE CORAL SEA. Boston: W.H. Baker, 1951. 55
          pp.

          NE

2842.   Shalett, Sidney. OLD NAMELESS: THE EPIC OF A U.S.
          BATTLEWAGON. New York: Appleton-Century, 1943. 177
          pp.

          Correspondent Shalett reports on the action he observed
        while aboard a battleship near Guadalcanal.

2843.   Smart, Charles A. THE LONG WATCH. Cleveland, OH: World
          Publishing, 1968. 237 pp.

          Here is a view of the underside of life at sea. After
        enlisting in the Navy, Smart served two tours in the
        Pacific aboard three LSTs. See the account of his
        experiences in the New Guinea campaign.

2844.   Smedberg, William R. "As I Recall... 'Sink the Wasp.'"
          USNIP, 108 (July 1982), 47-49.

          Smedberg commanded the destroyer LANSDOWNE in 1942. On
        orders, his ship sank the damaged WASP--despite the
        protests of the WASP's engineer who felt he could still
        save his ship. It took five torpedoes to sink the WASP.

2845.   Stafford, Edward P. LITTLE SHIP, BIG WAR: THE SAGA OF DE
          343. New York: William Morrow, 1984. 336 pp.

          Stafford writes of his service as First Lieutenant and
        then Executive Officer of the destroyer escort ABERCROMBIE
        (DE 343). His account is based on the ship's logs and
        after action reports. He includes stories of friction
        among the crew and some of the irascible moments of the
        ship's captain. Here is a first-hand account of the damage
        inflicted by the kamikazes--and the U.S. tactics to defend
        against them. The ship played a key role at Samar in
        defending the U.S. naval forces at Leyte. Of interest is
        Stafford's explanation of the combat functions of the
        destroyer escorts.

2846.   Trumbull, Robert. THE RAFT. New York: Henry Holt, 1942.
          205 pp.

          Here is the story of three downed naval aviators who

558   MILITARY ASPECTS

     spent 34 days on a raft before reaching an inhabited
     island. Trumbull relays the adventure as told by the
     leader of the threesome.

2847. Vetter, Ernest G. DEATH WAS OUR ESCORT. Englewood Cliffs,
     NJ: Prentice-Hall, 1944. 323 pp.

     Lt. J.G. Vetter (USN) gives an account of his experieces
     in PT-boat operations near New Guinea. The nature of the
     PT mission and the relative size of the ships, he notes,
     contributed to the dangers of the assignment.

2848. Weems, George B. and F.A. Andrews. "Solomons Battle Log."
     USNIP, 88 (August 1962), 80-91.

     Ensign Weems gives his personal account of his
     perspective from on board the MCCALLA during a night
     surface gun battle near Cape Esperance in the Solomons.
     The article combines the narrative Weems wrote in a letter
     home with information added by Capt. Andrews (U.S.N.), who
     served aboard a destroyer (DUNCAN) sunk during the
     engagement.

2849. Willoughby, Malcolm F. U.S. COAST GUARD IN WORLD WAR II.
     Annapolis, MD: U.S. Naval Institute, 1958. 347 pp.

     Lt. Willoughby (USCG) describes the growth of the Coast
     Guard during the war. Readers may be surprised to learn of
     the service's activities beyond United States territorial
     waters.

2850. Wilson Sloan. VOYAGE TO SOMEWHERE. New York: Ace Books,
     1946. 256 pp.

     Sloan, a naval officer, recounts his wartime
     experiences. His narrative reveals the interplay of
     personalities.

2851. Young, Stephen Bower. "Out of the Darkness." USNIP, 91
     (December 1965), 86-94.

     Young, a mess cook aboard the OKLAHOMA, provides a
     personal account of the sinking of the ship.

IV.D.3.c. Sea Weapons/Ships
           i. General Accounts

2852. Department of the Navy, Naval History. "The U.S.S. TULSA,
     1919-1945." CHRON OKLAHOMA, 55 (Fall 1977), 259-265.

Prewar and wartime duties of the TULSA included service
with the Asiatic Fleet, inshore patrols in the Philippines,
Java, Hollandia, and Hawaii. Renamed the TACLOBAN in
December 1944, the ship was decommissioned in March 1945.

2853. Dewey, Howard. "The Ghost Ship of Kwajalein." ALL HANDS,
446 (April 1954), 18-19.

Dewey investigates the report by the crew of the USS
SUMNER near Kwajalein in March 1944 of a mysterious ship
rising out of the water and then sinking again. His best
guess is that gas pockets--perhaps from the cargo of oxygen
and acetylene cylinders--briefly supported the weight of
the sunken ship.

2854. "The Fighting 'I.'" WARSHIP INTL, 16 (No. 2, 1979),
157-161.

Here is a brief report on the aircraft carrier INTREPID,
which suffered damage in kamikaze attacks. The ship is
being converted into a museum.

2855. Griffin, Alexander R. A SHIP TO REMEMBER: THE SAGA OF THE
HORNET. New York: Howell, Soskin, 1943. 302 pp.

Here is a history of the famed aircraft carrier from
October 20, 1941, to October 26, 1942. Under skippers Marc
A. Mischer and Charles Mason, the ship participated in
significant first-year activities, such as the Doolittle
Raid, Midway, and Guadalcanal.

2856. Hanks, Robert J. "Ghost Ship of the Pacific Fleet." AMER
HIST ILLUS, 21 (October 1986), 18-21, 46-48.

Hanks tells the strange story of the ship that fought
for both sides. As the USS STEWART, the "four piper"
destroyer (DD-224) was damaged and abandoned near Java in
February 1942. About one year later, the Japanese
resurrected the ship and used it on escort duty (Imperial
Patrol Boat #102). After the war the ship fell back into
American hands intact. Used for target practice, the ship
was sunk in May 1946.

2857. Hickerson, Loren. "The LANGLEY Legacy." USNIP, Suppl.
(April 1986), 65-74.

Here is a tale of two ships named LANGLEY. The first
sank near Java. The author served aboard the second, a

light aircraft carrier. Hickerson relies on his
contemporary diary entries to report on the ship's
activities between May 1944 and June 1945.

2858. Hone, Thomas and Norman Friedman. "IOWA vs. YAMATO: The
Ultimate Gunnery Duel." USNIP, 109 (July 1983),
122-123.

In this speculative encounter, the authors feel that the
IOWA would win by using its radar and staying outside
YAMATO's firing range (at least 35,000 yards out).

2859. Kafka, Roger and Roy L. Pepperburg, eds. WARSHIPS OF THE
WORLD. New York: Cornell Maritime Press, 1947. rev.
ed. 1,167 pp.

The section on World War II describes virtually every
naval encounter. This is a comprehensive reference,
buttressed by an extensive number of photographs and useful
technical data. The editors include a list of ships lost
in the war.

2860. Messimer, Dwight R. PAWNS OF WAR: THE LOSS OF THE USS
LANGLEY AND THE USS PECOS. Annapolis, MD: Naval
Institute Press, 1983. 228 pp.

Messimer tells an interesting story, complete with
heroes and mistakes. The tragedy involved the loss of
three ships and eight hundred men in a questionable mission
across the Indian Ocean to deliver P-40s to the Allies at
Tjilatjap. The captain of the seaplane tender, LANGLEY,
later faced charges of prematurely abandoning his ship.

2861. Morris, Colton G. and Hugh B. Cave. 'FIGHTIN'EST SHIP':
THE STORY OF THE CRUISER HELENA. New York: Dodd, Mead,
1944. 192pp.

The title comes from the nickname attached to the
HELENA, which saw so much combat action. The author
narrates many of these advantures. On July 6, 1943, the
HELENA went down during an engagement in Kula Gulf.

2862. Muir, Malcolm, Jr. "Misuse of the Fast Battleship in World
War II." USNIP, 105 (February 1979), 57-62.

Although the fast battleship was eclipsed by carriers,
the attack at Pearl Harbor, and British disasters (PRINCE
OF WALES and REPULSE), Muir maintains that the fast
battleship proved it could withstand air attack, sustain

damage, and be effective. Bad luck and cautious
employment, Muir argues, detracted from general recognition
of the ship's combat effectiveness.

2863. Nalty, Bernard and Truman Strobridge. "The Saga of the
        JOSEPH T. DICKMAN." NATL DEF, Pt. I: 67 (November
        1982), 28-31; Pt. II: 67 (December 1982), 18-19, 44-45.

        This ship earned six battle stars during action in
Europe and the Pacific. Manned by a Coast Guard crew in
April 1945, the ship participated in the assault on
Okinawa. It also ferried troops from the West Coast to
Pearl Harbor in anticipation of the invasion of Japan.

2864. Roscoe, Theodore. TIN CANS: THE TRUE STORY OF THE
        FIGHTING DESTROYERS OF WORLD WAR II. New York: Bantam
        Books, 1960. 447 pp.

        With exhaustive research, Roscoe describes destroyer
operations in all theaters. His detailed report generally
praises the destroyer ships and crews.

2865. Roscoe, Theodore. UNITED STATES DESTROYER OPERATIONS IN
        WORLD WAR II. Annapolis, MD: U.S. Naval Institute,
        1953. 581 pp.

        Although not an "official" history, this book provides
information about most major, and many of the minor,
destroyer undertakings of the war. Roscoe includes
technical features and reviews the methods and techniques
of U.S. destroyer operations. In this wartime history of
the "swift, small ships," the author concludes that serious
errors were "remarkably few."

2866. Silverstone, Paul H. U.S. WARSHIPS OF WORLD WAR II.
        Garden City, NY: Doubleday, 1965. 442 pp.

        This well-illustrated introduction to the major ships
provides much technical information and descriptions of
combat operations in all theaters.

2867. Shrader, Grahame F. "USS Colorado: The 'Other'
        Battleship." USNIP, 102 (December 1976), 46-47.

        December 7, 1941, found the COLORADO delayed on the West
Coast en route to Pearl Harbor. The ship first saw combat
at Tarawa in 1943.

2868. Schreier, Konrad F. "Armament." WW II, 1 (September

1986), 12-15, 66.

Here is a brief account of the three largest battleships ever put to sea. The Japanese ships far exceeded international agreements, but none survived the war.

2869. Smith, Myron J., Jr. "Log of the 'Wee Vee': The U.S. Battleship WEST VIRGINIA." W VA HIST, Pt. I: 38 (July 1977), 291-303; Pt. II: 39 (October 1977), 3-29.

Saved by a special diplomatic bargain with Japan from being scrapped after the Washington Naval Conference, the ship went down in the attack at Pearl Harbor. Smith reports on the ship's Pacific combat service after being raised in May 1942.

2870. Smith, Myron J., Jr. "The Third INDIANA (BB-58)." INDIANA HIST BULL, Pt. I: "From Conception to the War Zone," 51 (January 1974), 3-13; Pt. II: "The Third Indiana," 51 (May 1974), 55-76; Pt. III: "From the Warzone to the Scrapheap," 51 (July 1974), 92-99.

The Navy launched the dreadnought just prior to the attack at Pearl Harbor. Smith gives a detailed account of the INDIANA's participation in Pacific operations.

2871. Williamson, John A. and William D. Lanier. "The Twelve Days of the ENGLAND." USNIP, 106 (March 1980), 76-83.

Here is the personal account of the executive officer of the ENGLAND (as told to Lanier) and the ship's successful efforts to thwart Japanese resupply shipments to Bougainville in May 1944.

IV.D.3.c.ii. Aircraft Carriers

2872. Belote, James H. and William M. Belote. TITANS OF THE SEA. New York: Harper and Row, 1975. 336 pp.

Here is an authoritative account of the evolving use of the carrier task force by both the United States and Japan.

2873. Bryan, Joseph, III. AIRCRAFT CARRIER. New York: Ballantine Books, 1954. 206 pp.

Here is a personal account by a naval officer aboard the YORKTOWN in the form of diary entries for the period January to April 1945.

2874. Clark, J.J. and Clark G. Reynolds. CARRIER ADMIRAL. New
         York: David McKay Company, 1967. 333 pp.

         J.J. Clark served aboard the YORKTOWN until his
    promotion to flag rank in February 1944. He then became
    commander of Carrier Division 13. Those under his command
    included John Roosevelt, who decided to remain on duty at
    the time of his father's death. Clark also pays close
    attention to his wartime contemporary, Admiral Halsey. For
    example, he criticizes Halsey's decisions during the
    typhoon of June 4-5, 1945. (Clark's lawyer believed Clark
    would get the blame if Halsey did not.) Here is a good
    account, complete with intra-service rivalries.

2875. Cressman, Robert J. "Carrier Strike Through Mountain
         Passage." WWII, 1 (November 1986), 34-41.

         Cressman describes the Navy's first coordinated air
    strike of the war. Navy planes hit a Japanese force off of
    Lae and Salamula (New Guinea). The damage forced the
    Japanese to halt their advance until their carriers were in
    place; this, in turn, led to the battle of the Coral Sea.

2876. Francillon, Rene J. U.S. NAVY CARRIER AIR GROUPS, PACIFIC,
         1941-1945. London: Osprey Publishing, 1978. 48 pp.

         Here is a valuable reference source.

2877. Gilbert, Price, Jr., comp. THE ESCORT CARRIERS IN ACTION.
         Atlanta, GA: Ruralist Press, 1946. 183 pp.

         Here is a pictorial account of the escort carrier force
    in the Pacific during the last year of the war.

2878. Hoehling, A.A. THE LEXINGTON GOES DOWN. Englewood Cliffs,
         NJ: Prentice-Hall, 1971. 208 pp.

         Hoehling looks at the Battle of the Coral Sea from the
    perspective of the ill-fated LEXINGTON. Of interest is his
    focus on various members of the crew.

2879. Jensen, Oliver O. CARRIER WAR. New York: Pocket Books,
         1945. 172 pp.

         Jensen chronicles U.S. carrier operations from September
    1943 to October 1944. The special focus is on Task Force
    58.

2880.   Johnston, Stanley F. THE GRIM REAPERS. New York: E. P.
        Dutton, 1943. 221 pp.

        The book is based on Johnston's newspaper series about a
        VF-10 squadron of carrier-borne bombers under the
        leadership of Cmdr. James H. Flatley.

2881.   Johnston, Stanley. QUEEN OF THE FLAT-TOPS: THE U.S.S.
        LEXINGTON AND THE CORAL SEA BATTLE. New York: E. P.
        Dutton, 1943. 280 pp.

        This is a popular, highly patriotic account.

2882.   McCracken, Kenneth D. BABY FLAT-TOP. New York: Farrar
        and Rinehart, 1944. 180 pp.

        Lt. McCracken (USN) was a navigator aboard the PRINCESS.
        Without any extraordinary experiences, he aptly describes
        life on the high seas and the role of the baby flat-tops.

2883.   McKay, Ernest A. CARRIER STRIKE FORCE: PACIFIC AIR COMBAT
        IN WORLD WAR II. New York: Julian Messner, 1981.   191
        pp.

        This survey is aimed at the general public.

2884.   Markey, Morris. WELL DONE! AN AIRCRAFT CARRIER IN BATTLE
        ACTION. New York: D. Appleton-Century Co., 1945.   223
        pp.

        The author, a correspondent, sailed aboard the ESSEX,
        and he tells of the ship's combat adventures in the
        Marianas and the Marshalls. His narrative reflects the
        excitement of participation.

2885.   Miller, Max. DAYBREAK FOR OUR CARRIER. New York:
        Whittlesey House, 1944. 184 pp.

        Here is an excellent portrait of life on board an
        aircraft carrier. The straightforward narrative contains
        little praise or mention of exceptional performances, just
        descriptions of the fulfillment of the daily routine.

2886.   Preston, Anthony. AIRCRAFT CARRIERS. London: Hamlyn,
        1979. 192 pp.

        Although this pictorial record spans the full history of
        aircraft carriers, starting with the First World War,
        Preston concentrates on the years of World War II. Preston

produced a revised (shorter) edition in 1981.

2887.   Reynolds, Clark G. "Admiral John H. Towers and the Origins
        of Strategic Flexibility in the Central Pacific
        Offensive, 1943." NAV WAR COLL REV, 40 (Spring 1987),
        28-36.

        With extensive research through private collections,
        including the Tower Papers and government records, Reynolds
        praises Towers as an excellent strategist. According to
        Reynolds, Towers' innovative ideas of carrier offensive
        operations converted the skeptical Nimitz (who was not
        personally fond of Towers).

2888.   Reynolds, Clark G. THE CARRIER WAR. Alexandria, VA:
        Time-Life Books, 1982. 176 pp.

        Reynolds presents a knowledgeable summary of the war at
        sea. Pacific operations attract most of his attention.

2889.   Reynolds, Clark G. "'SARA' in the East." USNIP, 87
        (December 1961), 74-83.

        Here is an account of the Pacific adventures of the
        carrier SARATOGA.

2890.   Reynolds, Clark G.   THE FAST CARRIERS: THE FORGING OF AN
        AIR NAVY. Huntington, NY: Krieger, 1968. 2d. ed.
        498 pp.

        With his research through official records, private
        papers, and several interviews, Reynolds examines the
        development of naval doctrine with regard to the fast
        carriers. His study reveals the debate within the Navy on
        the role of the carriers. There is an extensive discussion
        of Pacific operations.

2891.   Sears, Stephen W. CARRIER WAR IN THE PACIFIC. New York:
        American Heritage Publishing Co., 1966. 153 pp.

        Here is a brief, popular summary of carrier operations.

2892.   Sherman, Frederick C. COMBAT COMMAND: THE AMERICAN
        AIRCRAFT CARRIERS IN THE PACIFIC WAR. New York: E.P.
        Dutton, 1950. 427 pp.

        Admiral Sherman summarizes the war at sea against Japan.
        In his analysis, Sherman underlines the decisive role of
        the aircraft carrier. Of interest is his report on the

"lessons learned" in the various campaigns.

2893. Whitehouse, Arthur G.J. SQUADRONS OF THE SEA. Garden
       City, NY: Doubleday, 1962. 383 pp.

       "Arch" Whitehouse writes a detailed and knowledgeable
       history of the aircraft carrier--with special emphasis on
       World War II. The Appendix lists the carriers lost in the
       war.

2894. Winston, Robert A. AIRCRAFT CARRIER. New York: Harper
       and Brothers, 1942. 88 pp.

       Lt. Winston served as a naval aviator aboard an aircraft
       carrier. His brief (censor-shortened?) narrative generally
       describes the role of aircraft carriers in Pacific
       operations.

2895. Winston, Robert A. FIGHTING SQUADRON. New York: Holiday
       House, 1946. 182 pp.

       Here is the personal account of an aviation squadron
       Reader's experiences in Task Force 58. The combat action
       centers on the Marshalls and the Philippines. He provides
       a first-hand view of carrier operations.

IV.D.3.c.iii. Submarines

2896. Bagnasco, Erminio. SUBMARINES OF WORLD WAR TWO.
       Annapolis, MD: Naval Institute Press, 1977 ed. 256 pp.

       Originally published in 1973, this book describes about
       2,500 submarines from 18 countries. The author organizes
       his references by country and incorporates information on
       submarines, or classes, which had been laid down but never
       entered service.

2897. Baugh, Barney. "Heroes in Action Under the Sea." ALL
       HANDS, 470 (April 1956), 16-21.

       Here is a description of the activities in the Pacific
       of many submarines, including GUARDFISH, TANG, HARDER,
       BARB, BOWFIN, TRIGGER, and SEAWOLF.

2898. Blair, Clay, Jr. SILENT VICTORY: THE U.S. SUBMARINE WAR
       AGAINST JAPAN. Philadelphia, PA: J. B. Lippincott,
       1975. 2 vols.

       The author served aboard a submarine (GUARDFISH) during

the war. His well-researched account incorporates private papers, official documents, interviews, and MAGIC material. Blair traces every submarine patrol in the war, and he is especially effective in describing certain problems, such as high-level rivalries within the Navy, extensive torpedo malfunctions and flaws in basic ship design. With the first foray into the Sea of Japan in mid-1943, Blair extols the ascendacy of daring new--and young--submarine captains. The appendices are full of useful information.

2899.   Blee, Ben W. "Enemies No More." USNIP, 113 (February
        1987), 56-63.

Scoring five hits out of six torpedoes fired, the Japanese submarine I-19 sank two U.S. ships and damaged another in an unprecedented single combat sortie. I-19 was later sunk with all hands lost, but some of the original crew had not been aboard this final mission. Blee writes of a reunion arranged between American and Japanese survivors, who furnished missing details about the "5 for 6" engagement.

2900.   Boyd, Carl. "The Japanese Submarine Force and the Legacy
        of Strategic and Operational Doctrine Developed Between
        the Wars." SELECTED PAPERS FROM THE CITADEL CONFERENCE
        ON WAR AND DIPLOMACY, 1978. 27-40.

Boyd examines the operational use of Japanese submarines. He finds that prewar Japanese doctrine hampered offensive and defensive operations of the Japanese Navy. In particular, his analysis offers an explanation why the submarines were not used against vulnerable Allied shipping.

2901.   Carmer, Carl L. THE JESSE JAMES OF THE JAVA SEA. New
        York: Farrar and Rinehart, 1945. 119 pp.

In this "partially fictionalized" report, Carmer describes submarine operations in the waters near China and Java just after Pearl Harbor. He traces the activities of the submarine, USS STURGEON.

2902.   Casey, Robert J. BATTLE BELOW: THE WAR OF THE SUBMARINES.
        Indianapolis, IN: Bobbs-Merrill, 1945. 380 pp.

Casey, a war correspondent, wrote this story in 1943 with the assistance of the Navy Department. He offers no apologies for his use of superlatives in describing the work of the submariners.

2903.   Cochran, Alexander S., Jr.   "Daring to Close In."   MIL
        HIST, 2 (April 1986), 46-54.

        The article is based on an interview with Edward L.
        Beach, an authority on submarine operations.   Beach
        emphasizes that a willingness to dare was the key to much
        of the success in submarine operations.   Of interest is
        Beach's report on early operational problems for U.S.
        submarines: misfiring torpedoes, inappropriate aiming
        procedures, and circling torpedoes (which returned to hit
        the submarines from whence they came).

2904.   Cope, Harley and Walter Karig.   BATTLE SUBMERGED:
        SUBMARINE FIGHTERS OF WORLD WAR II.   New York: W. W.
        Norton, 1951.   244 pp.

        The book serves as a popular introduction to the
        subject.   The episodes selected are used to demonstrate
        the various functions of the submarine at war.

2905.   Cross, William.   CHALLENGERS OF THE DEEP: THE STORY OF
        SUBMARINES.   New York: Sloane, 1959.   258 pp.

        Here is a general overview of submarine operations in
        all theaters that appeals to the general public.

2906.   Cutter, Slade.   "We Raided the Coast of Japan."   AMER MAG,
        135 (March 1943), 26-27, 94-98.

        Lt. Cutter (USN) served as an executive officer aboard a
        submarine that sank Japanese ships in a daring attack off
        the coast of Japan.   The story, as told to Don Eddy, is
        heavily censored.

2907.   Dissette, Edward and H.C. Adamson.   GUERRILLA SUBMARINES.
        New York: Ballantine Books, 1972.   265 pp.

        Dissette commanded a submarine which brought assistance
        to guerrillas in the Philippines.   His story is of interest
        and geared to the general public.

2908.   Enright, Joseph F. and James W. Ryan.   SHINANO!   New York:
        St. Martin's Press, 1987.   250 pp.

        Enright commanded the submarine ARCHE-FISH.   SHINANO, a
        giant battleship of the YAMATO class which had been
        converted to an aircraft carrier, succumbed on its first
        day at sea to Enright's sub.

2909.   Frank, Gerald and James D. Horan. U.S.S. SEAWOLF:
             SUBMARINE RAIDER OF THE PACIFIC. New York: G.P.
             Putnan's Sons, 1945. 197 pp.

        Collaborating with J. M. Eckberg, chief radioman for
        the SEAWOLF, the authors tell the story of the outstanding
        record of this submarine. With emphasis on the relations
        among the crew members--and even their superstitions--
        Frank and Horan bring out the human dimension of sub-
        marine warfare.

2910.   Galatin, I.J. TAKE HER DEEP! Chapel Hill, NC: Algonquin,
             1987. 262 pp.

        Adm. Galatin (ret.) served as captain of the submarine
        HALIBUT. This well-written memoir captures life aboard a
        submarine, ranging from daily drudgery to the excitement of
        combat. See especially his complaints about malfunctioning
        torpedoes (until late 1943) and his account of being
        bombarded by Japanese ships in the Luzon Strait.

2911.   Goldingham, C.S. "United States Submarines in the Blockade
             of Japan in the 1939-1945 War." RUSI, Part I: 97
             (February 1952), 87-98; Part II: 97 (May 1952),
             212-222.

        Goldingham calls the blockade of Japan the most
        important single cause among the many causes contributing
        to the Japanese defeat. He says that the submarine created
        the conditions for victory and that air power exploited
        those conditions.

2912.   Grider, George. WAR FISH. Boston: Little Brown, 1958.
             282 pp.

        Here is a first-hand account of submarine operations in
        the Pacific as told to Lydel Sims. Grider captained the
        FLASHER on nine patrols. His narrative reflects the
        boredom-excitement and humor-tragedy of submarine life.

2913.   Gugliotta, Bobette. PIGBOAT 39: AN AMERICAN SUBMARINE
             GOES TO WAR. Lexington, KT: The University Press of
             Kentucky, 1984. 224 pp.

        The author is the wife of a Navy officer who had served
        on S-39 and later commanded a submarine. The book covers
        the sub's adventures from 1939 to 1942 (when the sub ran
        aground on August 14 and was destroyed). Gugliotta

interviewed many S-39 veterans for this narrative, which
includes wonderfully sensitive stories about the crew and
their loved ones. The sub was at Pearl Harbor during the
Japanese attack and saw action in the Pacific.

2914. Hashimoto, Mochitsura. SUNK: THE STORY OF THE JAPANESE
       SUBMARINE FLEET, 1941,1945. New York: Henry Holt,
       1954. 276 pp.

       Translated by E.H.M. Colegrave, the book describes the
       use of submarines by the Japanese high command. The
       author, a submarine commander, became head of the Japanese
       Imperial Navy at the end of the war. Referring to the
       submariners as "human ammunition," Hashimoto complains that
       rigid Japanese strategy deployed the submarines as a
       special attack force in the absence of careful operational
       planning. In stark contrast, the author expresses
       admiration for the performance of the U.S. submarine force.
       The appearance of the Kaitens, human torpedoes, reflected
       the desperation of the Japanese cause.

2915. Hawkins, Maxwell. TORPEDOES AWAY, SIR! OUR SUBMARINE NAVY
       IN THE PACIFIC. New York: Henry Holt, 1946. 268 pp.

       Hawkins portrays submarine life and submarine operations
       in the Pacific during the first two years of the war.

2916. Holmes, W.J. UNDERSEA VICTORY: THE INFLUENCE OF SUBMARINE
       OPERATIONS IN THE WAR IN THE PACIFIC.   Garden City, NY:
       Doubleday and Co., 1966. 505 pp.

       Holmes combines his naval experiences as a prewar
       submarine commander and highly placed intelligence officer
       during the war to present an authoritative report on
       submarine operations. In preparing this work, he analyzed
       each of the total of 4,873 attacks by United States
       submarines during the war. Because of the terms of the
       Treaty of London, Holmes apparently disagrees with the
       decision, announced on December 7, 1941, to conduct
       unrestricted submarine warfare.

2917. Lepotier, M. "Submarines in the Battle of Leyte Gulf."
       MIL REV, 30 (December 1950), 102-108.

       The author praises the close coordination between
       American submarines and surface ships in this battle, but
       he also endorses the independent command structure for
       submarines in the theater.

2918. Lockwood, Charles A. SINK 'EM ALL: SUBMARINE WARFARE IN
       THE PACIFIC. New York: E.P. Dutton, 1951. 416 pp.

       Lockwood (Vice Adm., ret.) served as overall commander
       of most of the operations he describes. He provides
       specific data about ships, personnel, and enemy tonnage
       destroyed.

2919. Lockwood, Charles A. and Hans Christian Adamson. HELLCATS
       OF THE SEA. New York: Greenberg, 1955. 335 pp.

       These expert authors describe Operation BARNEY, the
       adventurous excursion of U.S. submarines into the Sea of
       Japan. A special device guided the submarines through the
       defending mines.

2920. Lockwood, Charles A. and Hans Christian Adamson. HELL AT
       50 FATHOMS. Philadephia, PA: Chilton Books, 1962.

       The authors provide an authoritative view of wartime
       life aboard submarines.

2921. Lockwood, Charles A. and Hans Christian Adamson. THROUGH
       HELL AND DEEP WATER: THE STIRRING STORY OF THE NAVY'S
       DEADLY SUBMARINE, THE U.S.S. HARDER, UNDER THE COMMAND
       OF SAM DEALEY, DESTROYER KILLER! New York: Greenberg,
       1956. 317 pp.

       Here is a detailed report on the six sorties by the
       HARDER. Cmdr. Dealey was awarded the Congressional Medal
       of Honor posthumously. The book describes submarine
       operations in all their tediousness and terror.

2922. Lockwood, Charles A. and Hans Christian Adamson. ZOOMIES,
       SUBS, AND ZEROS. New York: Greenberg, 1956. 301 pp.

       Lockwood directed submarine operations in the Pacific
       (1943-1945), and Col. Adamson served in the USAAF. The
       book offers a view of the submarine rescue service and its
       role in the air war.

2923. Lowder, Hughston E. and Jack Scott. BATFISH: THE CHAMPION
       "SUBMARINE-KILLER" SUBMARINE OF WORLD WAR II. Englwood
       Cliffs, NJ: Prentice-Hall, 1980. 232 pp.

       Lowder served aboard the BATFISH. In three wartime
       patrols, the ship sank a total of fourteen Japanese ships,
       including three submarines in three days off the coast of
       the Philippines. Research for the book incorporates

interviews, the ship's log, and war records of both Japan
and the United States.

2924.   Lowman, David D. "The Treasure of the AWA MARU." USNIP,
          108 (August 1982), 45-48.

          On April 1, 1945, the U.S. submarine QUEENFISH sank the
          Japanese freighter AWA MARU in the Strait of Taiwan. A
          naval board of inquiry stripped Capt. Charles E. Loughlin
          of command of the QUEENFISH because the United States had
          guaranteed safe passage to the Japanese ship. Despite
          rumors, Lowman asserts that the ship carried no secret
          treasure. Loughlin received only a letter of admonition,
          and Nimitz sent a letter of reprimand to the board members.

2925.   McGivern, Charles F. "Bush Navigation in the Solomon
          Islands." USNIP, 100 (February 1974), 68-72.

          McGivern served aboard the U.S. submarine GATO.
          Hampered by poor navigational charts, McGivern describes
          how the submariners relied on unusual navigational fixes
          (e.g., a conical hill and a conspicuous palm tree) to
          complete an evacuation rendezvous mission at Teop.

2926.   Mellor, William B. SANK SAME. New York: Howell, Soskin,
          1944. 224 pp.

          Mellor gives an overview of submarine operations.

2927.   Miller, Vernon J. "An Analysis of U.S. Submarine Losses
          During World War II." WARSHIP, Pt. I: 41 (January
          1987), 52-60; Pt. II: 42 (April 1987), 118-123; Pt.
          III: 44 (October 1987), 204-209; Pt. IV: 45 (January
          1988), 45-51; Pt. V: 46 (April 1988), 48-59.

          Miller reports on every American submarine lost. He
          includes information such as the crew, captain, last
          transmission date, the cause of the loss, probable
          evidence, and analysis.

2928.   Oi, Atsushi. "Why Japan's Anti-Submarine Warfare Failed."
          USNIP, 78 (June 1952), 586-601.

          Because Japanese leaders thought primarily about
          fleet-vs.-fleet action, Oi charges that they minimized the
          importance of anti-submarine warfare. For Oi, the enemy
          blockade was crucial in the defeat of Japan.

2929.   O'Kane, Richard H. CLEAR THE BRIDGE. Chicago, IL:

Rand-McNally, 1977. 480 pp.

Here is an account of the heroic wartime voyages of the
submarine TANG by the ship's skipper. The sub ranked
highest in the Navy with 33 enemy sinkings before falling
to enemy fire. O'Kane served out the remainder of the war
as a POW, and in 1946, President Truman presented him with
the Congressional Medal of Honor.

2930.   O'Kane, Richard H. WAHOO: THE PATROLS OF AMERICA'S MOST
        FAMOUS WWII SUBMARINE. Novato, CA: Presidio, 1987. 345
        pp.

RAdm. O'Kane (ret.) served as executive officer aboard
the submarine WAHOO. He learned from the daring
innovations of the ship's commander, "Mush" Morton. One
extraordinary mission saw the WAHOO sink all four ships in
a Japanese convoy. The author moved on to captain the
submarine TANG and became the leading submariner in the
Navy with 33 sinkings. The war ended with O'Kane as a POW
after the Japanese sank the TANG. The book incorporates a
newly released official Japanese report on the sinking of
the WAHOO so that O'Kane can tell of the final voyage of
that famed sub.

2931.   Orita, Zenji. I-BOAT CAPTAIN. Canoga Park, CA: Major
        Books, 1976. 336 pp.

With the help of Joseph D. Harrington, Orita reveals
his experiences as a Japanese submarine commander.
According to Orita, the Japanese high command did not make
the most effective use of the submarine fleet.

2932.   Paine, Thomas O. "I Was a Yank on a Japanese Sub." USNIP,
        112 (September 1986), 72-78.

Paine tells of his experiences aboard Japanese
submarines giving instructions for disarmament. Taught
Japanese in the old-fashioned style, he reports that the
crews did not know what language he was speaking. One of
these submarines was I-58 which had sunk the INDIANAPOLIS.
(Paine says that the captain knew the U.S. ship had some
association with the atomic bomb.) Later, Paine commanded
a division of 7 Japanese subs and served as executive
officer of I-400--an aircraft-carrying sub to be brought to
the U.S. for study.

2933.   Perry, George Sessions and Isabel Leighton. WHERE AWAY: A
        MODERN ODYSSEY. New York: Whittlesey House, 1944. 249

pp.

The authors describe life aboard the light cruiser
MARBLEHEAD from late 1941 to mid-1942. One of the
highlights of this well-written account is the manner in
which the authors present the differing types of
personalities in the ship's complement. The ship was badly
damaged by an enemy torpedo in the Pacific on December 14,
1941, and was mistakenly reported as lost, but it managed
to limp home safely.

2934. Pratt, Fletcher. "The Torpedoes That Failed." ATLANTIC
        MON, 186 (July 1950), 25-30.

        Here is an excellent analysis of the alarming failures
of U.S. torpedoes. The reasons, Fletcher says, are
official lassitude, official reticence, false economy, and
inadequate research. Most of the problems stem from faulty
magnetic exploders of firing pins.

2935. Roscoe, Theodore. UNITED STATES SUBMARINE OPERATIONS IN
        WORLD WAR II. Annapolis, MD: U.S. Naval Institute,
        1949. 577 pp.

        This general review puts most of the emphasis on the war
against Japan. Roscoe describes the poor performance of
the submariners early in the war, and significantly, he
does not attribute all the problems to faulty equipment.
For example, he asserts that defective torpedoes did not
account for all the missed targets; some crews were simply
poor marksmen.

2936. Speer, R.T. "Let Pass Safely the AWA MARU." USNIP, 100
        (April 1974), 69-76.

        On April 1, 1945, the submarine QUEENFISH sank a
Japanese ship which was carrying supplies to POW camps in
the NEI. Earlier, the U.S. government had approved safe
passage for the ship. At his court martial, the submarine
commander, Charles E. Loughlin, enumerated mitigating
factors in the episode. (In 1961, Laughlin attained the
rank of Rear Admiral, and he feels that the incident helped
his career.

2937. Sterling, Forest J. WAKE OF THE WAHOO. Philadelphia, PA:
        Chilton, 1960. 210 pp.

        The author, a Yeoman aboard the sub WAHOO, describes
life as a combat submariner. His narrative covers the

period October 1942-September 1943. He left the ship just
before it was sunk by the Japanese. Charles A. Lockwood
wrote the Foreword.

2938.   Trumbull, Robert. SILVERSIDES. New York: Henry Holt,
        1945. 217 pp.

        Here is an interesting report on the submarine,
SILVERSIDES, and its captain, Creed Burlingame. The
submarine achieved some notable war victories against the
Japanese, accounting for about 100,000 tons of enemy
shipping destroyed or damaged. The book was written and
heavily censored in 1943, but not allowed to be published
until 1945.

2939.   Underbrink, Robert L. "Your island is moving at 20 knots!"
        USNIP, 95 (September 1969), 81-87.

        Here is the tale of the sinking of the world's largest
aircraft carrier, SHINANO, in November 1944, by the U.S.
submarine, ARCHERFISH, under the command of Joseph Enright.

2940.   United States. Department of the Army. Forces in the Far
        East. SUBMARINE OPERATIONS. Washington, D.C.: Office
        of the Chief of Military History, 1952. 5 vols.

        This lengthy report actually combines five separate
Japanese monographs which deal with submarine operations.
Of interest is the criticism of the Japanese submariner
officers about the strategic flaws in the operational use
of their vessels.

2941.   United States. Office of Strategic Services. BURMA ENEMY
        SHIPPING, OCTOBER 1943-APRIL 1944. Washington, D.C.:
        OSS, 1944. 9 pp.

        This report takes note of the increasing Allied
effectiveness, largely through submarine operations, in
reducing Japanese sea supply lines.

2942.   Voge, Richard G. "Too Much Accuracy." USNIP, 76 (March
        1950), 256-263.

        Here is an attempt by a wartime submarine captain to
bring certain mitigating circumstances (e.g., night
operations in fog, firing by radar) in the sinking of the
AWA MARU by the submarine QUEENFISH commanded by Charles E.
Loughlin.

2943. Wheeler, Keith. WAR UNDER THE PACIFIC. Alexandria, VA:
       Time-Life Books, 1980. 208 pp.

       Wheeler describes the submarine war. He incorporates
       the work of Henry H. Adams, George W. Grider and John R.
       Elting in this popular account. See the excellent
       pictorial essay.

2944. Whitehouse, Arthur G.J. SUBS AND SUBMARINERS. Garden
       City, NY: Doubleday, 1961. 335 pp.

       Here is a general history of the submarine. The author
       knows his material and provides much information about
       World War II operations.

2945. Widder, Arthur. ACTION IN SUBMARINES. New York: Harper
       and Row, 1967. 213 pp.

       Widder offers a knowledgeable summary of the development
       and history of the submarine. In this brief account, the
       author dwells on World War II.

2946. Young, Edward P. UNDERSEA PATROL. New York: McGraw-Hill,
       1953. 298 pp.

       The author, the first British reservist to command a
       submarine, recounts his combat experiences which include
       submarine operations against the Japanese.

2947. Zimmerman, Sherwood R. "Operation FORAGER." USNIP, 90
       (August 1964), 78-90.

       Ensign Zimmerman (U.S.N.) stresses the importance of the
       submarine in this operation to seize Saipan, Guam, and
       Tinian.

IV.D.3.c.iv. PT Boats

2948. Breuer, William. DEVIL BOATS: THE PT WAR AGAINST JAPAN.
       Novato, CA: Presidio Press, 1987. 229 pp.

       Here is praise for all connected with PT operations. In
       his account of the action, the author highlights the
       heroics of John F. Kennedy, John D. Bulkeley, and Arthur
       Murray Preston.

2949. Bulkley, Robert J., Jr. AT CLOSE QUARTERS: PT BOATS IN
       THE U. S. NAVY. Washington, D. C.: Naval History
       Division, 1962. 574 pp.

From MacArthur's departure from the Philippines, to bad-
weather operations in the Aleutians, to John F. Kennedy's
exploits (as narrated by Byron White), to projected
participation in the invasion of Japan, here is the
official war history of the PT boat. The author calls it
"a weapon of opportunity" designed to exceed 40 knots at
full war load. The boats could not be stored after the war
because of their light wooden construction; therefore, the
Navy kept only a few for training purposes.

2950. Cooper, Bryan. THE BATTLE OF THE TORPEDO BOATS. New York:
Stein and Day, 1969. 296 pp.

Here is a history of the use of motor torpedo boats in
all theaters of the war. Cooper also traces the
development of these boats during the 1930s. His narrative
shows how the PT boats affected the war in the Pacific.
The author gives a balanced report on John F. Kennedy's No.
109. There is no bibliography.

2951. Cooper, Bryan. PT BOATS. New York: Ballantine Books,
1970. 100 pp.

This brief survey treats the European as well as the
Pacific Theaters. There are many illustrations.

2952. Farley, Edward. PT PATROL: WARTIME ADVENTURES IN THE
PACIFIC AND THE STORY OF PTs IN WORLD WAR II. New York:
Exposition Press, 1957. 108 pp.

The author's narrative history is based principally on
personal records and the experiences of other "PT-ers."

2953. Johnson, Frank D. UNITED STATES PT-BOATS OF WORLD WAR II
IN ACTION. New York: Sterling, 1980. 159 pp.

Johnson reports on the history and development of the PT
boats. Technical data and drawings are included. In the
sections on the war against Japan, see Johnson's
descriptions of PT action in the Solomons and the
Philippines.

IV.D.3.c.v. Frogmen/UDTs

2954. Fane, Francis Douglas and Don Moore. THE NAKED WARRIORS.
New York: Appleton-Century-Crofts, 1956. 308 pp.

Heavy casualties at Tarawa led to a search for better

methods of gathering intelligence. This book examines one
result of that search: the use of underwater demolition
teams. UDTs sought information about mines and other
"static dangers." The authors underline the importance of
the UDTs at Peleliu, Leyte, and Okinawa. At the end of the
war, 3,000 UDT members were in training for the amphibious
assault on Japan.

2955. Higgins, Edward T. with Dean Phillips. WEBFOOTED WARRIORS:
       THE STORY OF A "FROGMAN" IN THE NAVY DURING WORLD WAR
       II. New York: Exposition Press, 1955. 172 pp.

       Higgins reports his experiences as a Navy frogman. The
       account explains the important role of these trained
       specialists in the seemingly endless number of amphibious
       assaults on Japanese-fortified islands.

2956. Waldron, T.J. and James Gleeson. THE FROGMEN: THE STORY
       OF THE WARTIME UNDERWATER OPERATORS. London: Evans
       Brothers, 1950. 191 pp.

       Although most of the book is devoted to the war in
       Europe, there are reports on some notable British frogmen
       operations against Japan. For example, the authors
       describe the cutting of both the Saigon-Singapore and
       Saigon-Hong Kong cables. Also, there is praise for the
       work of Leading-Seaman Magennis in Operation Struggle, in
       which frogmen helped sink the heavy cruiser TAKAO. Of
       interest is the airy advice to the frogmen: tickle any
       octopus that gets hold of you and throw dead horses in the
       water first to distract the sharks.

2957. Wright, Bruce S. THE FROGMEN OF BURMA. Toronto: Clarke,
       Irwin, 1968. 152 pp.

       Here is an account of the little-known activities of the
       British Sea Reconnaissance Unit. Lord Mountbatten wrote
       the Foreword.

IV.D.3.c.vi. INDIANAPOLIS

2958. Boyd, Carl. "Attacking the INDIANAPOLIS: A Re-Examina-
       tion." WARSHIP INT, 13 (January 1976), 15-25.

       Examining the circumstances of the sinking of the
       INDIANAPOLIS by Japanese submarine I-58, Boyd raises the
       possibility that one-man suicide subs (KAITENS) may have
       been used instead of conventional torpedoes. He calls for
       more research to resolve some of the inconsistencies that

persist.

2959.   Ethridge, Kenneth E.   "The Agony of INDIANAPOLIS."
        AMER HERITAGE, 33 (August-September 1982), 81-96.

        Ethridge interviewed many of the survivors who attended
        a 35th reunion in 1980. His narrative summarizes the
        attack and sinking of the ship as well as the terrible
        ordeal in the water (sharks, hallucinations, and
        photophobia). Of interest is the warning by Spruance about
        the dangers of the ship's top-heaviness.

2960.   Helm, Thomas. ORDEAL BY SEA. New York: Dodd, Mead, 1963.
        243 pp.

        Helm offers a general account of the tragic demise of
        the INDIANAPOLIS. The tale is well told, despite the
        restricted sources available.

2961.   Lech, Raymond B. ALL THE DROWNED SAILORS. New York:
        Stein and Day, 1982. 309 pp.

        Lech describes one of the worst disasters in U.S. naval
        history: the sinking of the INDIANAPOLIS and its tragic
        aftermath. Using documents at the Navy Historical Center,
        Lech argues that the Navy unfairly blamed the ship's
        captain, Charles B. McVay, for the disaster. In fact, the
        author feels that the Navy covered up the episode by
        censuring no one else, even though there had been some
        questionable behavior by others. Lech implies that
        ulterior motives existed to make the captain the
        scapegoat--McVay's father had once reprimanded Ernest King
        in earlier days--and the author argues that McVay remained
        guilty in the eyes of the public, despite subsequently
        winning exoneration from the Navy and having all letters of
        reprimand removed from his file. The captain committed
        suicide in 1968.

2962.   Newcomb, Richard F. ABANDON SHIP! DEATH OF THE U.S.S.
        INDIANAPOLIS. New York: Henry Holt, 1958. 305 pp.

        Using official records and interviews, Newcomb, a
        correspondent, assembles an interesting, readable account
        of the tragedy of the INDIANAPOLIS.

2963.   Mueller, Michael. "Lost at Sea." AMER HIST ILLUS, 20
        (June 1985), 28-35.

        Here is an account of the ordeal of the INDIANAPOLIS.

Mueller depends largely on material gained from interviews
with a survivor, Seaman Second Class Don McCall.

IV.D.3.c.vii. TYPHOON

2964. Adamson, Hans Christian and George F. Kosco. HALSEY'S
       TYPHOONS. New York: Crown, 1967. 239 pp.

       Here is a detailed narrative of the harrowing
experiences, including numerous deaths and extensive
damage, of Typhoon COBRA (15-20 Dec 1944) and Typhoon VIPER
(3-5 June 1945). Halsey's warnings to the 3d Fleet
emphasized the virtue of "anticipation" and the need for
ships to take precautionary measures (while they could
still maneuver).

2966. Calhoun, C. Raymond. TYPHOON: THE OTHER ENEMY.
       Annapolis, MD: Naval Institute Press, 1981. 247 pp.

       The author writes from personal experience about the 3d
Fleet and the typhoon of December 18, 1944, in the
Philippine Sea. The ship Calhoun commanded, the DEWEY,
rolled to the limit of its capacity to recover (over 75
degrees). Also, drawing on interviews, correspondence, and
recently released documents (under the Freedom of Information Act), Calhoun recounts the number of errors made by
fleet and task force leaders in preparing for and coping
with the typhoon.

2967. Nimitz, Chester W. "Letter 14CL-45." USNIP, 82 (January
       1956), 83-88.

       Nimitz wrote this letter on February 13, 1945. He
sought to set forth naval procedures when encountering a
typhoon. The occasion for the letter, of course, was the
damage inflicted by a typhoon in the Pacific on December
13, 1944. The instructions are perhaps best summarized as
giving the ship its head.

2968. Welch, Robert R. "Typhoon--1944." USNIP, 113 (January
       1987), 74-76.

       The author was aboard the DEWEY (DD-349) in the typhoon.
He describes the terrifying experience which included the
mast of the reeling DEWEY rolling to just a few feet above
the water. No one was lost, and, incredibly, waves swept
one man overboard and then back aboard.

IV.D.3.d. NAVY/U.S.M.C. AIR OPERATIONS

2969. Bedford, Al and Warren M. Bodie. "Carrier Borne." WINGS,
       17 (June 1987), 8-45.

       This interesting survey of carrier aviation carries much
       technical information, including aircraft specifications,
       and many action photographs. No citations are provided for
       the text.

2970. Bryan, Joseph, III, and Philip Reed. MISSION BEYOND
       DARKNESS. New York: Duell, Sloan, and Pearce, 1945.
       133 pp.

       The authors tell the tale of the 64 men in Air Group 16
       aboard the LEXINGTON (Mitscher's flagship for Task Force
       58). The narrative, which relies heavily on interviews of
       participants and observers, focuses on the conclusion of
       the first phase in the campaign to recapture the
       Philippines in June 1944.

2971. Buchanan, A. Russell, ed. THE NAVY'S AIR WAR: A MISSION
       COMPLETED. New York: Harper and Brothers, 1946.
       432 pp.

       Authorized by the Navy, Buchanan examines naval aviation
       during the war, including less publicized areas like train-
       ing, maintenance, and procurement. He particularly
       delineates the role of naval aviation in efforts to bring
       about the economic strangulation of Japan.

2972. De Chant, John A. DEVILBIRDS: THE STORY OF THE UNITED
       STATES MARINE CORPS AVIATION IN WORLD WAR II. New
       York: Harper and Brothers, 1947. 265 pp.

       As a war journalist, the author travelled with the
       Marines from Guadalcanal to Okinawa. He brings home the
       human side of this one part of the war effort.

2973. Doll, Thomas E. FLYING LEATHERNECKS IN WORLD WAR II.
       Fallbrook, CA: Aero Publishers, 1971. 95 pp.

       The brief narrative on Marine aviation is supplemented
       with beautiful color photographs.

2974. Hubler, Richard G. and John A. De Chant. FLYING
       LEATHERNECKS: THE COMPLETE RECORD OF MARINE CORPS
       AVIATION IN ACTION, 1941-1944. Garden City, NY:
       Doubleday, Doran, 1944. 237 pp.

These two captains (USMCR) highlight for the general
public the heroics of Marine aviators, December 1941 –
February 1944.

2975. Lundstrom, John B. THE FIRST TEAM: PACIFIC NAVAL AIR
       COMBAT FROM PEARL HARBOR TO MIDWAY. Annapolis, MD:
       Naval Institute Press, 1984.

       Lundstrom, a self-described "enthusiast" about naval
       affairs, argues that the United States had the advantage in
       tactics and leaders during the early months of the war in
       the Pacific. The account of the campaign for New Guinea is
       superb.

2976. Macintyre, Donald. WINGS OF NEPTUNE: THE STORY OF NAVAL
       AVIATION. New York: W. W. Norton, 1964. 268 pp.

       Here is an excellent report. Macintyre, a British naval
       officer and historian, writes knowledgeably about aerial
       operations in the war at sea.

2977. Miller, Nathan. THE NAVAL AIR WAR, 1939 – 1945.
       Annapolis, MD: Nautical and Aviation Publishing Co. of
       America, 1980. 232 pp.

       There is good balance here among the theaters. The
       photographs comprise an authentic representation of combat
       air operations.

2978. Morrison, Wilbur H. ABOVE AND BEYOND, 1941-1945. New
       York: St. Martin's, 1983. 314 pp.

       Here is a narrative of naval aviation in the Pacific.
       There is little that is new, but Morrison does provide a
       well-written narrative. He offers no explanatory notes and
       a woefully inadequate bibliography.

2979. Russell, James S. "Mess Treasurer of the ESSEX Class."
       USNIP, Suppl. (April 1986), 54-63.

       Here is a personal account by a naval aviator who saw
       action in the Aleutians and the Pacific.

2980. Scrivner, C.L. THE EMPIRE EXPRESS. Temple City, AZ:
       Historical Aviation Album, 1976. 56 pp.

       The author gives an account of aerial attacks against
       the Kuriles by the Navy's PV squadrons.

2981. Sherrod, Robert L.   HISTORY OF MARINE CORPS AVIATION IN
          WORLD WAR II.   Washington, D.C.:   Combat Forces Press,
          1952.   496 pp.

          Sherrod, a reporter who accompanied Marine units in the
       war, writes an operational history of the USMC air arm.
       While not an official history, he enjoyed much support from
       the Marine Corps.   Often too detailed for the general
       reader, who may become mired in unit designations and
       technical information, the book, nonetheless, reflects
       Sherrod's stated intention to write what the actual
       participants would want to know about an operation.   Marine
       aviation amounted to about 1% of the U.S. armed forces--
       with about 150,000 total personnel, including 80,000 women.
       Free of restrictions, Sherrod interviewed some 250 Marine
       pilots and incorporated Japanese sources in his account.
       The 9 air squadrons in 1939 numbered 128 by 1945.   Photos
       showing unusual combat action supplement the narrative.

2982. United States.   Navy Department.   ANTI-SHIPPING ATTACKS BY
          U.S. NAVY AIRCRAFT, NOVEMBER 1943 THROUGH MAY 1945.
          Washington, D.C.:   Navy Dept., 1946.   47 pp..

          This brief report from the Operations Evaluation Group
       in the Office of the Chief of Naval Operations provides
       statistics on the damage inflicted upon all Japanese
       vessels by American naval aviators.   The narrative comments
       on the effectiveness of the U.S. Navy's performance.

2983. United States.   Navy Department.   THE FIRST RAID ON JAPAN:
          NAVAER 50-40T-4.   Washington, D.C.:   Office of Naval
          Operations, 1947.   11 pp.

          This brief report prepared by the Office of Naval
       Operations describes the preparations, operation, and
       damage inflicted in the Navy's first air raid against the
       Japanese homeland.

2984. United States.   Navy Department.   Pacific Fleet.   ANALYSIS
          OF AIR OPERATIONS: FAST CARRIER OPERATIONS: LUZON AND
          FORMOSA.   San Francisco, CA: Pacific Fleet, 1945.   15
          pp.

          This official report of the air operations of Task Force
       38 emphasizes the unusually persistent string of bad
       weather encountered.

2985. United States.   Navy Department.   Pacific Fleet.   ANALYSIS

OF AIR OPERATIONS, FORMOSA AND NANSEI SHOTO STRIKES.
San Francisco, CA: Pacific Fleet, 1945.   17 pp.

Here is a brief summary of the carrier-borne aircraft
from Task Force 38.

2986.   United States. Navy Department. U.S. NAVAL AVIATION IN
        THE PACIFIC: A CRITICAL REVIEW. Washington, D.C.:
        Navy Dept., 1947. 56 pp.

The gist of this report seems to be an argument to
retain the U.S. Navy's air arm. Much emphasis is devoted
to explaining how naval air power not only complements
other naval forces but also contributes to control of the
sea (and large-scale land offensives). Of interest is the
conclusion that no single weapon forced Japan to
surrender; rather, the Allied victory came about through a
combination of factors.

2987.   Wolfert, Ira. TORPEDO 8. Boston: Houghton Mifflin, 1943.
        127 pp.

Here is a journalist's first-hand account of the heroics
of U.S. combat pilots at Midway. Wolfert also follows
their adventures into the South Pacific.

IV.D.3.e.   BATTLES
i.   BONINS

2988.   Head, Timothy E. and Gavan Daws. "The Bonins -- Isles of
        Contention." AMER HERITAGE, 19 (February 1968), 58-64,
        69-74.

In this historical survey of the islands, the authors
describe the fortress Chichi Jima in the Bonins which may
have been even more heavily defended than Iwo Jima. After
the war, according to the authors (who used Japanese
sources in their research), American pilots were found
killed and dismembered as victims of a cannibalistic
ritual. In 1952, Japan was awarded "residual sovereignty"
over the Bonins.

2989.   Peatross, Oscar F. "The Makin Raid." MC GAZ, 63 (November
        1979), 96-103.

The author gives a personal account of Carlson's raid on
Makin, August 17-18, 1942. Peatross includes mention of
Carlson's decision to surrender, the beheading of some U.S.
Marine prisoners by the Japanese, and the postwar trial.

2990. Y'Blood, William T.   RED SUN SETTING: THE BATTLE OF THE
          PHILIPPINE SEA. Annapolis, MD: Naval Institute Press,
          1981.   257 pp.

          In this self-described "combat narrative," the author
       focuses on the participants in the Battle of the Philippine
       Sea. The key to victory, according to Y'Blood, came on
       June 19-20, 1944, when American pilots inflicted crippling
       losses on the air resources of the Imperial Japanese Navy.
       But in his conclusion, Y'Blood calls the episode a
       "frustrating victory." He is particularly critical of
       Spruance's caution with the 5th Fleet which, in Y'Blood's
       view, cost the United States total victory. Photographs
       and battle maps accompany the narrative.

IV.D.3.e.ii. CORAL SEA

2991. "Coral Sea: The Battle and the Carrier." ALL HANDS, 518
          (March 1960), 59-63.

          Here is a convenient summary of informtion on the battle
       of the Coral Sea and the ship with the same name.

2992. Grant, Ben J. "Air Mastery in the Far East." INFANTRY J,
          57 (August 1945), 45-52.

          Grant labels the Battle of Coral Sea as the turning
       point in the struggle for air supremacy. He pictures the
       massive bombing raids as a preview to Japanese losses and
       civilian casualties (just as the Germans were suffering).

2993. "Lest We Forget." NAVY, 2 (August 1959), 29-30.

          This commemorative article marks the seventeenth
       anniversary of the Battle of Coral Sea.

2994. Millot, Bernard. THE BATTLE OF THE CORAL SEA. Annapolis,
          MD: Naval Institute Press, 1974. 166 pp.

          Millot provides a knowledgeable report on the battle.
       Twelve color plates strengthen the presentation. S.F.
       Whitley translated the work from the French.

IV.D.3.e.iii. JAVA SEA/NETHERLANDS EAST INDIES

2995. Emmanuel, Michel G. "The Java Crapshoot." SHIPMATE, 35
          (June 1972), 19-22, 24.

The author served aboard the LANGLEY which sank in the
Java Sea. Rescued by the PECOS, Emmanuel found himself
reentering the water when that ship, too, fell under enemy
attack. The tragedy of war is brought home in his account
of being among those saved by the WHIPPLE before that ship,
under threat of Japanese submarines, had to depart the area
with many American seamen still in the water.

2996. Falle, Sir Samuel. "Chivalry." USNIP, 113 (January 1987),
      86-92.

The author, aboard the ENCOUNTER in the Java Sea, saw
three ships, including his, sunk on March 1, 1942. The
survivors remained in the water eighteen hours. He
describes the unusual efforts by a Japanese destroyer to
pick up all survivors. Falle spent the rest of the war as
a POW.

2997. Pratt, John L. "Appointed in Kenari." SHIPMATE, 38
      (January-February 1975), 13-16.

Rear Adm. Pratt tells of his experiences aboard the
CHILDS, a flushdeck destroyer converted to a seaplane
tender. Early in the war, the ship went into the Java Sea
to deliver fuel to a jungle airstrip in Celebes. The
return trip (escape) created some excitement.

2998. Thomas, David A. THE BATTLE OF THE JAVA SEA. New York:
      Stein and Day, 1969. 259 pp.

Thomas describes the early naval engagements into 1942
with emphasis on Java. His account is well researched and
incorporates photos, charts, and maps.

2999. United States. Department of the Army. Forces in the Far
      East. AMBON AND TIMOR: INVASION OPERATIONS.
      Washington, D.C.: Office of the Chief of Military
      History, 1953. 23 pp.

The author, a Japanese staff officer with the Eastern
Detachment, links the operation to the planned invasion of
Java. The Japanese wanted to form a defensive line against
the expected Allied counterattack from Darwin.

3000. Van Oosten, F.C. THE BATTLE OF THE JAVA SEA, Annapolis,
      MD: Naval Institute Press, 1976. 128 pp.

Van Oosten uses official reports and interviews to

present a clear picture of this early naval encounter.

IV.D.3.e.iv. LEYTE GULF

3001. Ahlstrom, John D. "Leyte Gulf Remembered." USNIP, 110
       (August 1984), 45-53.

       Ahlstrom gives his personal views of the naval
engagement at Leyte Gulf. He participated in the battle as
an air intelligence officer aboard the baby flat-top,
PETROF BAY. Among his many observations, Ahlstrom believes
that (1) U. S. forces suffered from divided command, (2)
Kurita retired for sound reasons, and (3) Halsey seemed
justified in undertaking the famous "Bull's Run."

3002. Field, James A., Jr. THE JAPANESE AT LEYTE GULF: THE SHO
       OPERATION. Princeton: Princeton University Press,
       1947. 162 pp.

       Field presents the Japanese perspective of this key
operation--one which Japanese leaders knew would be their
last all-out chance to salvage at least part of their war
aims. According to the author, however, the close
naval-air cooperation that had characterized earlier
Japanese campaigns had largely dissipated by September
1944. Despite its brevity, the book contains sufficient
detail; despite its age, the book remains essential reading
for any serious examination of the subject.

3003. Fooks, H.E. "The Battle for Leyte Gulf." RUSI, 94
       (February 1949), 67-81.

       Here is a balanced account by an expert of the momentous
battle, which Fooks declares marked the end of the Japanese
Navy as a fighting force and cleared the way for the
surrender of Japan. A detailed list of American and
Japanese ships appears in the Appendix.

3004. Gwynn, Frederick L. "Tennyson at Leyte Gulf." PAC
       SPECTATOR, 5 (Spring 1951), 149-160.

       Ninety years apart, the Battle of Leyte Gulf and "The
Charge of the Light Brigade" occurred on the same day
(October 25--1944 and 1854). With further irony, a line
from Tennyson: "all the world wonders," appeared--and
created some confusion--in the famous telegram to Halsey.
Gwynn contrasts Tennyson's earnest motives with the
influence the poet wielded in a battle ninety years later.

3005. Halsey, William F. "The Battle for Leyte Gulf." USNIP, 78
       (May 1952), 487-495.

       Here is an attempt to justify Halsey's actions. Arguing
       that "my mission was offensive," Halsey asserts that he
       went after the greatest enemy threat, the aircraft carrier.
       The article contains implied criticism of Kincaid and
       openly points to the need for better naval coordination and
       communication.

3006. Hamilton, Andrew. "Where is Task Force Thirty-Four?"
       USNIP, 86 (October 1960), 76-80. (See also the related
       comment in ibid., 87 [1961], 110-112.)

       Incorporating official Navy reports and interviews with
       Nimitz and Halsey, Captain Hamilton (USN) tells of two
       errors in communications to Halsey during the Battle of
       Leyte Gulf. Both had to do with "padding," or deliberately
       deceptive material, that became part of the actual message
       ("All the world wonders").

3007. Hughes, Hobart. "Saga of the YMS." USNIP, 74 (January
       1948), 52-59.

       Hughes gives his account of mine-sweeping operations at
       the entrance to Leyte Gulf. Given the importance of the
       mission (which foreshadowed the Allied invasion), Hughes
       expresses surprise at encountering relatively light
       Japanese resistance.

3008. Leverett, Lee L. "The Battle of Leyte Gulf." FORUM, 110
       (December 1948), 328-334.

       The author served as a naval planner for the Leyte Gulf
       area. He feels that the lack of unity among Japanese
       commanders aided the American cause in this battle. His
       criticism, however, also extends to American leadership
       (especially "Bull's Run"), but, in his opinion, the
       Japanese naval leaders were worse.

3009. Mcintyre, Donald. LEYTE GULF: ARMADA IN THE PACIFIC. New
       York: Ballantine Books, 1970. 160 pp.

       The British naval historian writes of the beginning of
       the crucial final stage of the war at sea. For Macintyre,
       the four aircraft carriers that were sunk proved the
       decisive factor. Basil H. Liddell Hart wrote the Foreword.

3010. Potter, E. B. "Comment: 'Where Is Task Force

Thirty-Four?'" USNIP, 87 (January 1961), 110-112.

Potter offers his comments about the controversial
message sent to Halsey. The author clarifies some
information on the unfortunate choice of padding ("the
world wonders"), but he questions its significance since
the message reads the same without the padding. The
decoder for Halsey was Lt. Charles Fox, Jr.; mercifully,
the ensign who dreamed up the padding and sent the message
remains anonymous.

3011. Smith, Stanley E. THE BATTLE OF LEYTE GULF. New York:
       Belmont Books, 1961. 174 pp.

Here is a knowlegeable assessment of the crucial naval
battle which opened the door to the reoccupation of the
Philippines. Smith synthesizes his extensive research in
naval affairs. His balanced narrative does not fail to
identify those responsible for errors--and successes.

3012. Stewart, Adrian. THE BATTLE OF LEYTE GULF. New York:
       Charles Scribner's Sons, 1979. 223 pp.

Stewart follows the action closely in this kev naval
encounter.

3013. Sufrin, Mark. "Survival Cannot Be Expected." MIL HIST, 2
       (October 1985), 20-28.

Sufrin, who served in the Pacific, recounts the heroism
of the screen destroyer JOHNSTON and her commander, Ernest
Evans, at Leyte Gulf.

3014. Woodward, C. Vann. THE BATTLE FOR LEYTE GULF. New York:
       Macmillan, 1947. 244 pp.

An intelligence officer on the staff of the Chief of
Naval Operations, Woodward, a trained historian, analyzes
the largest sea battle in history. He divides the general
battle into four separate but closely related engagements.
Incorporating captured Japanese documents and interviews
with Japanese officers, Woodward breaks new ground in
presenting Japanese perspectives on the battle (e.g.,
command relationships, fleet organization, aims, losses,
and tactical decisions). This is an excellent, highly
readable account.

IV.D.3.e.v. MIDWAY

3015. Barker, A.J. MIDWAY: THE TURNING POINT. New York:
       Ballantine Books, 1971. 160 pp.

       This popular narrative is enhanced by many excellent
       photographs.

3016. Byrd, Martha H. "Six Minutes to Victory: the Battle of
       Midway." AMER HIST ILLUS, 10 (May 1975), 33-43.

       Byrd points out that even before the battle began, the
       Japanese had designated both a new commander for the island
       and a new name ("Glorious Month of June"). In her
       narrative, Byrd stresses the importance of Nimitz--through
       MAGIC--launching the resupply of Midway and the
       near-miracle of repairing the YORKTOWN just in time. There
       are excellent photos.

3017. Cagle, Malcolm W., ed. "Battle of Midway." NAVAL AVIATION
       FOUND MUSEUM, 9 (Spring 1988), 1-84.

       The entire volume is devoted to a symposium on the
       famous engagement. The sixteen articles are contributed by
       historians, military experts, and participants in the
       battle.

3018. Castillo, Edmund L. MIDWAY: BATTLE FOR THE PACIFIC. New
       York: Random House, 1968. 176 pp.

       Castillo offers a brief, uncomplicated overview of the
       battle.

3019. Coale, Griffith Baily. VICTORY AT MIDWAY. New York:
       Farrar and Rinehart, 1944. 178 pp.

       Coale served as an artist attached to the Navy. This
       volume includes his art work on the battles at Pearl Harbor
       and Midway.

3020. Cressman, Robert J. "Flight to Midway." MC GAZ, 65 (May
       1981), 73-78.

       Cressman describes an emergency flight aboard a Douglas
       R4D-1 "Skytrain" from Ewa to Midway. Intelligence sources
       had warned of an eminent attack by the Japanese.

3021. D'Andrea, Thomas M. "Marines at Midway." MC GAZ, 48
       (November 1964), 27-31.

       Here is a tribute to the Marine defenders at Midway,

especially the pilots of VMF-221.

3022.   Eller, Ernest M. "The Battle of Midway." ORDNANCE, 40
        (September-October 1955), 237-240.

        The author served on Nimitz's staff and had written the
        official Navy analysis of the battle. This article is a
        brief, useful overview which summarizes Eller's
        conclusions.

3023.   Ferrier, H.H. "Torpedo Squadron Eight, the Other Chapter."
        USNIP, 90 (October 1964), 72-76.

        Ferrier, a member of the squadron, was among the total
        of only nine survivors in the unit during the battle at
        Midway. After his aircraft (TBF-1) suffered battle damage
        and ditched in the ocean, Ferrier eventually made it back
        to Midway.

3024.   Frank, Pat and Joseph D. Harrington. RENDEZVOUS AT MIDWAY:
        USS YORKTOWN AND THE JAPANESE CARRIER FLEET. New York:
        John Day, 1967. 252 pp.

        With the help of interviews and research from available
        records, the authors provide a knowledgeable account of
        this crucial battle. See especially the forewords by Frank
        J. Fletcher and Yahachi Tenabe.

3025.   Frisbee, John L. "Marauders at Midway." AF MAG, 69 (April
        1986), 140.

        This one-page report describes the activities at Midway
        of a flight of four B-26 Marauders led by Capt. James J.
        Collins of the 69th squadron, 38th Bombardment Group. The
        pilots were not well trained in torpedo bombing--this was
        the first such mission for B-26 pilots and the last ever
        for any torpedo-armed bombers.

3026.   Fuchida, Mitsuo and Masatake Okumiya. Edited by Clarke K.
        Kawakami and Roger Pineau. MIDWAY: THE BATTLE THAT
        DOOMED JAPAN, THE JAPANESE NAVY'S STORY. Annapolis, MD:
        Naval Institute Press, 1955. 266 pp.

        There exists no better presentation in English of
        Japanese perspectives on this key battle. The telling
        point is made that the war was started by men who did not
        understand the sea and fought by men who did not understand
        the air. Forewords by Raymond A. Spruance and Nobutake

Kondo are helpful, and the editorial work is superb.

3027.   Gay, George. SOLE SURVIVOR. Naples, FL: Naples
             Ad/Graphics Services, 1979. 320 pp.

             Gay tells of his harrowing brush with death at the
        Battle of Midway and how the experience changed his life.

3028.   Heinl, Robert D., Jr. MARINES AT MIDWAY. Washington,
             D.C.: U.S. Marines Corps, 1945. 56 pp.

             Heinl singles out the role of the Marine Corps in
        developing--and defending--the base at Midway. This brief
        report calls attention to the contribution of Marine air
        power in the battle. The contributions of the other
        services are deliberately not included.

3029.   Hough, Richard. THE BATTLE OF MIDWAY. New York:
             Macmillan, 1969. 90 pp.

             Hough offers a well-written report on this crucial
        battle. His narrative emphasizes the changing nature of
        the war at sea.

3030.   Lord, Walter. INCREDIBLE VICTORY. New York: Harper and
             Row, 1967. 331 pp.

             Lord, a former member of the OSS, offers a detailed
        examination, written for the general public, of the Battle
        of Midway.

3031.   Mercer, Charles E. MIRACLE AT MIDWAY. New York: G.P.
             Putnam's Sons, 1977. 160 pp.

             Mercer offers a popular account of this key battle.

3032.   "Moment at Midway: McCluskey's Decision." USNIP, 101
             (April 1975), 64-65.

             Lt. Cmdr. Clarence McCluskey, according to this article,
        participated in the single most significant moment in the
        history of naval aviation. He located the Japanese carrier
        force near Midway.

3033.   Okumiya, Masataka and Jiro Horikoshi. MIDWAY: THE BATTLE
             THAT DOOMED JAPAN. New York: E.P. Dutton, 1955.

             Here is a Japanese perspective on this important
        battle. The authors question some of the discussion

rendered by the top naval officers involved.

3034.   Potter, E.B.   "Admiral Nimitz and the Battle of Midway."
         USNIP, 102 (July 1976), 60-68.

         Potter analyzes Nimitz's role in the encounter at
         Midway. Potter especially notes the importance of
         intelligence in this battle and praises Layton and
         Rochefort.

3035.   Powers, Thomas E.   "Incredible Midway."   USNIP, 93 (June
         1967), 64-73.

         Lt. Cmdr. Powers (U.S.N.) recounts the Battle of Midway,
         the island which he calls the "sentry of Hawaii." His
         report includes some interesting anecdotes about the antics
         of some Japanese pilots.

3036.   Prange, Gordon W.   MIRACLE AT MIDWAY.   New York:
         McGraw-Hill, 1982.   469 pp.

         Here is a report on the key battle which is presented in
         painstaking detail. There are no new revelations, but the
         research effort serves as a model. The story is complete.
         Sixteen pages of plates complement the narrative. Donald
         M. Goldstein and Katherine V. Dillon collaborated on the
         work.

3037.   Smith, Chester L.   MIDWAY, 4 JUNE 1942.   London: Regency
         Press, 1962.   67 pp.

         This slim overview is addressed to the general public.

3038.   Smith, Peter C.   THE BATTLE OF MIDWAY.   London: New
         English Library, 1976.   189 pp.

         Smith, a British writer on naval affairs, offers a
         knowledgeable assessment of this key battle.

3039.   Smith, William Ward.   MIDWAY: TURNING POINT OF THE
         PACIFIC.   New York: Thomas Y. Crowell, 1966.   174 pp.

         Vice-Admiral Smith participated in this sea engagement
         as commander of the cruiser-destroyer squadron in Task
         Force 17. Analyzing the events of the battle, Smith
         concludes that the United States was "lucky." Of interest
         is his criticism of the "inconsequential" high altitude
         bombing at sea by the USAAF in which, Smith claims, not one
         hit was made in the entire war.

3040.   "Sun Not Meant to Rise Over Island." OFFICER, 59 (March
          1983), 14-16.

          Here is a brief summary of both the battle and the ship
          named MIDWAY.

3041.   Taylor, Theodore. THE BATTLE OFF MIDWAY ISLAND. New York:
          Avon, 1981. 141 pp.

          The writer served in the war and in Korea. His
          well-written narrative describes the famous battle for a
          general audience.

3042.   Tillman, Barrett. "Dauntless Over Midway." AMER AVN H S
          J, 21 (Fall 1976), 154-167.

          Here is an article which emphasizes the importance of
          the carrier-borne SBD squadrons at the Battle of Midway.

3043.   Tuleja, Thaddeus V. CLIMAX AT MIDWAY. New York: W.W.
          Norton, 1960. 248 pp.

          Intended for the general public, this is a well-paced
          narrative of the famous battle. The author is
          knowledgeable in naval affairs.

3044.   United States. Navy Department. THE JAPANESE STORY OF THE
          BATTLE OF MIDWAY. Washington, D.C.: GPO, 1947. 68 pp.

          The Office of Naval Intelligence arranged the
          translation of this Japanese study. The narrative
          incorporates the views of planners and particpants in this
          key battle.

3045.   Wadleigh, John R. "Memories of Midway, Thirty Years Ago."
          SHIPMATE, 35 (June 1972), 3-10.

          The author served as watch officer on the bridge of the
          YORKTOWN during the famous battle. His active
          participation in the engagement ended with his rescue from
          the water by the RUSSELL. Of interest is his
          (contemporary) surprise that the crew was not kept intact
          and given another carrier to man.

3046.   Werstein, Irving. THE BATTLE OF MIDWAY. New York: Thomas
          Y. Crowell, 1961. 145 pp.

          Here is a summary of the key encounter which is

addressed to the general public.

IV.D.e.vi. PEARL HARBOR

3047. Alden, John D. "Up From Ashes--The Saga of LASSIN and
       DOWNES." USNIP, 87 (January 1961), 32-41.

       Commander Alden (USN) tells of the two destroyers
       declared lost at Pearl Harbor but subsequently salvaged.

3048. Barnhart, Michael A. "Planning the Pearl Harbor Attack: A
       Study in Military Politics." AEROSP H, 29 (Winter,
       December 1982), 246-252.

       Tracing the evolution of Japanese planning to attack
       Pearl Harbor, Barnhart shows how the international
       situation, especially the economic sanctions imposed by the
       United States, helped overcome the arguments of the plan's
       critics in Japan.

3049. Barker, A.J. PEARL HARBOR. New York: Ballantine Books,
       1969. 160 pp.

       In a well-written narrative accompanied by many
       excellent photographs, Barker identifies certain key
       factors (e.g., the prewar naval agreements, the roles of
       Yamamoto and Minoru Genda, deteriorating American-Japanese
       diplomatic negotiations) which influenced Japanese
       strategic planning. Focusing on the decision to attack
       Pearl Harbor, Barker, a retired British officer, indicates
       the careful attention to detail that went into the Japanese
       "War Plan Z."

3050. Betts, Richard K. "Surprise Despite Warning: Why Sudden
       Attacks Succeed." POL SCI Q, 95 (Winter 1980-81),
       551-572.

       Betts investigates surprise attacks (such as occurred at
       Pearl Harbor) and concludes that substantial evidence is
       usually available ahead of time for the party being
       attacked. His methodology focuses on several categories,
       including data acquisition, decision of intelligence
       experts about sounding alerts, communication lines to
       decision makers, the decision-making process, and the
       reactions of military commanders.

3051. Bonaventura, Ray and Ralph Vecchi. MONTH OF INFAMY,
       DECEMBER 1941. Culver City, CA: Venture Publications,
       1976. 144 pp.

NE

3052. Boulton, R.H. "My ol' California." USNIP, 111 (December
        1985), 134-137.

        Here is the personal amount of a senior signalman-3rd
        class aboard the CALIFORNIA. Several weeks before the
        attack at Pearl Harbor, Boulton claims that his ship
        encountered unidentified submarines. He feels (in
        retrospect) that this episode should have provided
        sufficient warning about the surprise attack. Most of the
        article, however, deals with his experiences during the
        attack. Of note is his observation that the uniform of the
        day that Sunday morning--scivey tops and white shorts--was
        never again worn because of the excessive burns suffered.

3053. Bowen, John E. "December 7, 1941: The Day the Honolulu
        Fire Department Went to War." HAWAIIAN J HIST, 13
        (1979), 126-135.

        On December 7, 1941, this civilian unit raced to Hickam
        Field to fight fires stemming from the Japanese attack.

3054. Brittin, Burdick H. "We Are Ensigns." USNIP, 92 (December
        1966), 106-109.

        The only officers on board the destroyer AYLWIN during
        the attack at Pearl Harbor were four ensigns (one of whom
        was the author). His narrative wraps around the entries he
        made in his journal at the time. The four ensigns decided
        to take the ship out to sea. This decision led, among
        other things, to the ship's captain chasing after the
        AYLWIN in a small boat and Brittin experiencing his first
        forty-seven degree roll at sea.

3055. Carpenter, Ronald H. "Admiral Mahan, 'Narrative Fidelity'
        and the Japanese Attack on Pearl Harbor." Q J SPEECH,
        72 (August 1986), 290-305.

        The author, a professor of English, integrates his
        investigation of Japanese readers of Mahan's works with
        Walter R. Fisher's concept of "Narrative Fidelity."
        Carpenter suggests that Mahan's works appealed forcefully
        to Japan's self-conceptions and guided Japanese plans for
        the attack at Pearl Harbor. For Japanese readers
        (according to Carpenter), Mahan's descriptions of England
        transposed equally well to descriptions of Japan. Of
        special note is Carpenter's observation that the reason the

Japanese did not follow-up their attacks at Pearl Harbor
may be attributed to Mahan. The admiral had stressed the
importance of protecting battleships, for each one sunk
meant a loss of at least six months in building a
replacement. Carpenter suggests that the sinking of U.S.
battleships in the attack had created in Japanese minds
several six-month delays for the Americans.

3056. Clark, Thomas B.   REMEMBER PEARL HARBOR. New York:
         Modern Age, 1942. 127 pp.

         Clark gives his eyewitness report on the Japanese
surprise attack. He makes a point of underlining the
loyalty to the United States of the Japanese-American
population in Hawaii.

3057. Cohen, Stan. EAST WIND RAIN. Missoula, MT: Pictorial
         Histories Publishing Company, 1981. 182 pp.

         Here is a pictorial account of the Japanese attack at
Pearl Harbor.

3058. DECEMBER 7: THE FIRST THIRTY HOURS. New York: A.A.
         Knopf, 1942. 229 pp.

         About fifty correspondents report from the United
States and around the world on the immediate reactions
of Americans to the attack of Pearl Harbor.

3059. De Los Santos, Anthony. "How It Happened on December 7,
         1941." NAVY, 9 (December 1966), 8-11.

         Here is a brief account of the surprise attack and the
damage inflicted at Pearl Harbor.

3060. Drake, C.B. "A Day at Pearl Harbor." MC GAZ, 49 (November
         1965), 64, 94.

         Colonel Drake (USMC) gives his personal account of the
attack at Pearl Harbor which he witnessed while aboard the
CALIFORNIA.

3061. Eldredge, Michael S. "The Other Side of the Island: USS
         UTAH at Pearl Harbor." USNIP, 102 (December 1976),
         52-54.

         The author describes the sinking of the UTAH on December
7, 1941. The ship had berthed at Ford Island in a position
usually reserved for aircraft carriers.

3062.   Emmons, Roger.   "Pearl Harbor."   MC GAZ, 28 (February
            1944), 3-8.

            In this eyewitness account, Emmons tells of the Marine
            detachment aboard the TENNESSEE. The ship took
            "astonishingly light" casualties primarily because of its
            fortuitous berthing position.

3063.   Featherman, Maurice.   "The Ship That Sank From Fright."
            USNIP, 98 (December 1972), 84-86.

            The author received an assignment to the OGLALA, but the
            minelayer sank during the attack at Pearl Harbor--even
            though the ship had not been hit directly. Apparently the
            concussion effect of an exploding bomb which landed nearby
            the OGLALA tore open her hull. The Navy raised and
            repaired the ship to sail again.

3064.   Farmer, James H. and Bruce Pruett.   "Remember Pearl
            Harbor."   AMER AVN HSJ, 20 (Fall 1975), 146-149.

            Here is an account of the quick destruction of the 14th
            Pursuit Wing at Hawaii by the Japanese attackers. The
            authors include some excellent photographs as well as a
            list of aircraft at Wheeler Field.

3065.   Fuchida, Mitsuo.   "I Led the Air Attack on Pearl Harbor."
            USNIP, 78 (September 1952), 939-952.

            Edited by Roger Pineau, this article describes the
            attack and the careful preparations made by the Japanese.
            The date chosen, Fuchida points out, was coordinated with
            the planned assault on Malaya (and favorable
            moonlight)--not just because it was a Sunday. Of special
            interest is the report on Nagumo's reasons for rejecting
            Fuchida's call for a follow-up attack at Pearl Harbor: (1)
            the first attack had inflicted all the damage hoped for,
            (2) enemy fire had been prompt despite the surprise
            achieved, (3) radio intercepts indicated that at least 50
            large U.S. aircraft were still operational--and a threat to
            the Japanese carriers, and (4) an unwillingness to have the
            Japanese carriers remain within range of land-based, enemy
            aircraft.

3066.   Fukudome, Shigeru.   "Hawaii Operations."   USNIP, 81
            (December 1955), 1315-1331.

            Vice-Admiral Fukudome (JIN) looks at the pros and cons

of the Japanese attack at Pearl Harbor. On balance, he
feels the decision to launch a surprise attack was the best
possible policy for Japan. Of interest is his tolerant
view of Nagumo's leadership during the operation.

3067. Gray, Denver D. "I Remember Pearl Harbor: A Nebraska Army
       Air Force Officer in the Pacific Theatre During World
       War II." NEBRASKA HIST, 62 (Winter 1981), 437-480.

       Gray offers reminiscences about his war career. At
Pearl Harbor, he was squadron supply officer and took
command of the unit when the two officers above him were
wounded.

3068. Hechler, Ted, Jr. "Like Swatting Bees in a Telephone
       Booth." USNIP, 106 (December 1980), 72-74.

       Here is an eyewitness report of the attack at Pearl
Harbor. Hechler was aboard the light cruiser, PHOENIX.
His account attests to the unpreparedness of American
forces that Sunday morning. For example, awnings over the
anti-aircraft guns had to be removed during the attack, and
locks on the ammunition boxes had to be hacked away.

3069. Hone, Thomas C. "The Destruction of the Battle Line at
       Pearl Harbor." USNIP, 103 (December 1977), 49-59.

       Of the five battleships sunk at Pearl Harbor, all were
hit by both torpedoes and bombs. Aided by the diagrams of
Joseph R. Beckenbach, Jr., Hone summarizes the damage—and
the human errors—that occurred during the Japanese attack.

3070. Johnson, Bobbe McKinney. "Pearl Harbor Revisited."
       SHIPMATE, 49 (December 1966), 10-12.

       The author recounts her experiences in Hawaii on
December 7, 1941. She was then the wife of a young Navy
ensign.

3071. Kraft, Carl and Nell Kraft. "USCGC TANEY: Still in
       Service 35 Years Later." USNIP, 102 (December 1976),
       50-51.

       In 1976, the Coast Guard cutter TANEY remained the only
ship still on active duty which had been in or near the
attack at Pearl Harbor. The TANEY was under way for
eighty-eight of the first ninety-eight days after the
attack.

3072.   Hatch, F.J.   "The Aleutian Campaign."   POUNDEL, Pt. I: 15
          (May 1963), 18-23; Pt. II: 15 (June 1963), 18-23.

          NE

3073.   Kaplan, H.R.   "Remembering the Day of Infamy."   SERGEANTS,
          19 (December 1981), 22-27.

          NE

3074.   Kaye, Harold S.   "Hickam Field, 7 December 1941 - The First
          U.S. Army Corps Flying Fortress (B-17D) Combat Mission
          in World War II."   AEROSPACE H, 33 (Winter, December
          1986), 218-227.

          Here is the personal account of a USAAF radioman who
          flew on the first U.S. air combat mission of the war. Kaye
          describes his success, after one aborted attempt, in
          getting airborne with pilot Brooke Allen and a makeshift
          crew shortly after the Japanese attack at Pearl Harbor. A
          second plane joined them, piloted by Blondie Saunders.
          Kaye's flight lasted from 10:30 a.m. to 6:00 p.m., but
          neither his nor the other B-17 could locate the Japanese
          carriers. As an indication of U.S. combat readiness that
          day, Kaye reports that he punctured his hand with a nail
          file trying to repair the inter-comm system, and the
          co-pilot twice left his seat (to hand deliver messages to
          other crew members because of the inoperative inter-comm)
          and both times accidentally pulled the rip cord on his
          parachute.

3075.   Layton, Edwin T.   "Rendezvous in Reverse."   USNIP, 79 (May
          1953), 478-490.

          Intelligence expert Layton recalls two magazine stories
          by Alex Hudson (the pseudonym of another intelligence
          expert, W. J. Holmes) in August 1941, in which Japanese
          submarines refueled aircraft for a surprise attack against
          the United States. Layton points out that the Japanese did
          this in reverse while preparing for a second attack on
          Pearl Harbor by flying boats ("Emilys") on May 4, 1942.
          The attack proved ineffectual, and Layton doubts that
          Holmes' imaginative stories inspired this Japanese
          operation.

3076.   Lord, Walter.   DAY OF INFAMY.   New York: Henry Holt, 1957.
          243 pp.

          This book remains one of the best popular accounts of

the attack at Pearl Harbor.

3077.   McGoran, John H. "I Remember It Well." USNIP, 105
          (December 1979), 64-66.

          Here is a personal account of the attack at Pearl Harbor
   from an officer aboard the CALIFORNIA.

3078.   McKinley, Mike. "Pearl Harbor: The Last Day of
          Innocence." ALL HANDS, 36 (December 1986), 4-7.

          Here is a brief profile of life at Pearl Harbor on
   December 6, 1941.

3079.   Merdinger, Charles J. "Under Water at Pearl Harbor."
          USNIP, 102 (December 1976), 48-49.

          The author was the junior officer aboard the NEVADA at
   Pearl Harbor. He and others remained in the ship's
   plotting room until the last possible minute before the
   NEVADA sank.

3080.   Morgan, David J. "They Were Ready." USNIP, 99 (December
          1973), 80-81.

          Morgan summarizes the wartime service of the destroyer
   WARD, which fired the first U.S. shots at Pearl Harbor and
   sank a Japanese submarine. In 1944, a kamikaze attack near
   Leyte sunk the WARD, but all the crew survived the war.

3081.   NAVY TIMES. PEARL HARBOR AND HAWAII. New York: Walker,
          1971. 184 pp.

          Here is a convenient, authoritative summary of the
   surprise attack.

3082.   Nimitz, Chester W. "Pearl Harbor Postscript." USNIP, 92
          (December 1966), 126.

          Twenty-five years after the fact, Nimitz admits that the
   damage inflicted at Pearl Harbor could have been much
   worse, especially if Nagumo had followed up his attack.

3083.   "OKLAHOMA: Up From the Mud at Pearl Harbor." USNIP, 101
          (December 1975), 46-59.

          Here is a pictorial essay of the ship which sank at
   Pearl Harbor and was raised in 1943.

3084. Parkinson, Roger. ATTACK ON PEARL HARBOUR. London:
       Wayland, 1973. 128 pp.

       Here is a brief but knowledgeable summary of the
       Japanese surprise attack.

3085. Pearl Harbor Survivors Association, Chapter No. 1,
       Indianapolis. REMEMBER PEARL HARBOR. Indianapolis, IN:
       PHSA, 1970. unpaged.

       NE

3086. PEARL HARBOR AND THE USS ARIZONA MEMORIAL. Honolulu:
       Pacific Basin Enterprises, 1977. 63 pp.

       NE

3087. Potter, Joseph. "A Handful of Pilots." AMER AVN H S J, 27
       (Winter 1982), 282-285.

       Here is an effort to praise a specific few U.S. pilots
       for their heroism during the attack at Pearl Harbor. Six
       pilots (Taylor, Welch, Brown, Sanders, Sterling, and
       Rasmussen) scored twelve air victories that day.

3088. Potter, Joseph. "A Handful of Pilots." EDUC J, 22 (Winter
       1979/80), 81-83.

       NE

3089. Prange, Gordon W. TORA! TORA! TORA! Tokyo: Reader's
       Digest, 1966. 391 pp.

       Although now somewhat outdated, Prange describes how the
       Japanese planned and executed the surprise attack at Pearl
       Harbor. Pointing out that the Japanese failed to press
       their advantage, Prange maintains that the episode served
       to unite the American people in the war effort. Prange
       interviewed virtually every participant in the battle in
       his lengthy, exhaustive research effort.

3090. Prange, Gordon W., Donald M. Goldstein, and Katherine V.
       Porter. DECEMBER 7, 1941: THE DAY THE JAPANESE ATTACKED
       PEARL HARBOR. New York: McGraw-Hill, 1988. 493 pp.

       Here is the last of the books scheduled to be taken from
       Prange's extensive (estate) holdings. Prange (37 years),
       Dillon (25 years), and Goldstein (8 years) carried out a
       prodigious research effort, including many interviews.

There are almost 70 pages of notes. The oral histories
they gathered are marked by harsh anti-Japanese rhetoric.
Items of special interest include the conclusion that
Marshall was home with his convalescing wife on December 6,
Japan's use of out-of-date maps accounts for the irregular
bombing patterns in the attack (the control tower and 2 new
hangars were neglected), and reactions of American people
in the aftermath of the attack.

3091. "A Quarter-Century Ago." USNIP, 92 (December 1966),
        110-125.

        Here is a pictorial record of the attack at Pearl
        Harbor. No credits are provided for the action
        photographs.

3092. Sakamaki, Kazuo. I ATTACKED PEARL HARBOR. New York:
        Association Press, 1949. 133 pp.

        The author piloted a midget submarine in the first hours
        of the attack at Pearl Harbor. Launched from the mother
        ship with four other midget submarines (each with two men)
        at 11:00 p.m. on December 6, Sakamaki's sub suffered
        gyrocompass-steering problems. After hours of struggling
        to control the sub, he and his partner abandoned ship.
        Captured on the beach, Sakamaki became POW #1 in the war.
        All nine of his compatriots died in this first mission. Of
        interest is his change of attitude ("spiritual eye") as a
        POW, from desiring death to hoping for reconstruction at
        the end of the war. Toru Matsumoto translated the book
        into English.

3093. Shaw, Samuel R. "Pearl Harbor, 7 December 1941." MC GAZ,
        65 (December 1981), 32-33.

        Brig. Gen. Shaw praises the work of Marine riflemen
        during the Japanese attack.

3094. Sheean, Ed. ONE SUNDAY MORNING. Norfolk Island, Aus.:
        Island Heritage, 1971. 87 pp.

        Sheehan provides an account of his experiences on the
        day that war began with Japan.

3095. Simons, R. Bentham. "Pearl Harbor As I Saw It." NAVY, 4
        (December 1961), 16-19.

        Simons relates his experience as captain of the RALEIGH
        during the attack at Pearl Harbor. He expresses pride in

the way the men of the ship responded.

3096.   Stewart, A.J.   "Those Mysterious Midgets."   USNIP, 100
         (December 1974), 54-63.

         Clarifying the role of the Japanese midget submarines at
         Pearl Harbor, Stewart accounts for four of the five subs.
         He does not discount the possibility that the Japanese
         survivor(s) of the fifth ship might still be living in
         Hawaii.

3097.   Stilwell, Paul, ed.   AIR RAID: PEARL HARBOR!   Annapolis,
         MD: Naval Institute Press, 1981. 299 pp.

         Stilwell collects an interesting collection of reports
         by people who were there on December 7, 1941.

3098.   Stone, C.S. Scott.   PEARL HARBOR: THE WAY IT WAS--DECEMBER
         7, 1941. Honolulu, HI: Island Heritage, 1977. 64 pp.

         By blending eyewitness reports into his narrative, Stone
         gives a brief report on the surprise attack. He compiles a
         list of Americans killed at Pearl Harbor that day.

3099.   Stout, Joseph A., Jr.   "U.S.S. Oklahoma, 'Minister of
         Peace.'"   CHRON OKLAHOMA, 52 (Fall 1974), 283-289.

         One of the first U.S. capital ships not dependent on
         coal, the OKLAHOMA sank during the first wave of attacks at
         Pearl Harbor. Salvaged in 1943, the ship was
         decommissioned the next year (and sank while being towed to
         the scrapheap).

3100.   Sturm, Ted R.   "Mission: War."   AIRMAN, 9 (December 1965),
         41-45.

         Here is an account of Capt. Brooke E. Allen who managed
         to get airborne in a B-17 shortly after the Japanese attack
         at Pearl Harbor. His plane and another (piloted by Capt.
         Blondie Saunders) searched fruitlessly for the Japanese
         carriers. Upon returning to Hickam Field, Allen's plane
         was almost shot down by U.S. fire. (Two Navy flying boats
         were shot down under similar circumstances.)

3101.   Sweeny, Charles.   PEARL HARBOR, n.p.: Author, 1946.   74
         pp.

         Sweeny argues that Roosevelt abused presidential powers
         in rebuking Kimmel and Short. In contrast, the author

points out, MacArthur received no official criticism for
the disastrous events in the Philippines. In subsidizing
the publication of this book, Sweeny wanted to make the
argument that Washington never provided the U.S. Fleet at
Pearl Harbor with the necessary weapons and materials.

3102.   Symonds, Craig L. "Notable Naval Books of 1981." USNIP,
        108 (January 1982), 85-88.

        This bibliographical essay touches all theaters, but
        Pearl Harbor's fortieth anniversary receives special
        attention.

3103.   Taussig, Joseph K., Jr. "I Remember Pearl Harbor." USNIP,
        98 (December 1972), 18-24.

        Then Ensign Taussig served aboard the NEVADA. His
        reminiscences associated with the attack at Pearl Harbor
        include the Japanese failure to hit other lucrative targets
        besides the ships, poor U. S. anti-aircraft fire, effective
        Japanese torpedo planes, and the unfair treatment dealt to
        Kimmel and Short.

3104.   Taylor, Blaine. "Surprise Launch at Dawn." MIL HIST, 3
        (December 1986), 42-49.

        Here is an interview with Joseph K. Taussig, Jr., about
        his experience during the attack at Pearl Harbor. Taussig
        was then an ensign on the battleship NEVADA.

3105.   Toyama, Saburo. "Lessons From the Past." USNIP, 108
        (September 1982), 62-69.

        The author tries to draw historical analogies--for
        example, Pearl Harbor and Port Arthur, Midway and Jutland,
        and Leyte and 1894--to argue we must all learn from the
        past. But what are the correct "lessons?"

3106.   Tsumoda, Jun and Kazutomi Uchida. "The Pearl Harbor
        Attack: Admiral Yamamoto's Fundamental Concept With
        Reference to Paul S. Dull's A BATTLE HISTORY OF THE
        IMPERIAL JAPANESE NAVY (1941-1945)." NAV WAR COLL REV,
        31 (Fall 1978), 83-88.

        Prompted by Dull's book, the authors elaborate on
        Yamamoto's personal opposition to drastic action against
        Anglo-American interests and his professional duty in
        planning the strike at Pearl Harbor.

3107. United States. Navy Department. Naval History Division.
       UNITED STATES SUBMARINE LOSSES, WORLD WAR II.
       Washington, D.C.: GPO, 1963. 244 pp.

       In this revised edition of the 1949 study, there is an
       additional appendix of Axis submarine losses. U.S.
       submarine crew losses were just over 3,500 total (374
       officers and 3,131 men). The narrative describes the
       submarines and the circumstances involved in the loss of
       each.

3108. Wallin, Homer N. PEARL HARBOR: WHY, HOW, FLEET SALVAGE
       AND FINAL APPRAISAL. Washington, D.C.: Navy History
       Division, Dept. of the Navy, 1968. 377 pp.

       Vice-Admiral Wallin (ret.) provides an expert report on
       the salvaging operations at Pearl Harbor. The experienced
       admiral--he commanded three naval yards and served as chief
       of the Bureau of Ships--tells his own story as fleet
       salvage officer. He includes the texts of Navy documents,
       and there are valuable additions to the official record in
       the appendices.

3109. Ward, Robert E. "The Inside Story of the Pearl Harbor
       Plan." USNIP, 77 (December 1951), 1270-1283.

       Examining the Japanese perspective, Ward traces--and
       praises--the actual planning and execution of the attack on
       Pearl Harbor.

3110. "Where Were You on December 7, 1941?" SERGEANTS, 23
       (November-December 1984), 15-18.

       NE

3111. Willmott, H.P. PEARL HARBOR. Englewood Cliffs, NJ:
       Prentice-Hall, 1983. 64 pp.

       Here is a brief treatment of the fateful event.
       Willmott surveys the differing perspectives on the Japanese
       attack.

3112. Wise, James E., Jr. "Ford Island." USNIP, 90 (October
       1964), 77-91.

       Here is an interesting pictorial essay on the "bull's
       eye" of the attack at Pearl Harbor.

IV.D.3.e.vii. PHILIPPINE SEA

3113. Byrd, Martha H. "Battle of the Phillipine Sea." AMER HIST
        ILLUS, 12 (July 1977), 20-35.

        This narrative provides colorful details about the key
battle. Byrd emphasizes the heroics of the leading pilots.

3114. Cortesi, Lawrence. PACIFIC BREAKTHROUGH. New York:
        Kensington Books, 1981. 286 pp.

        Here is a knowledgeable, popular account of the Battle
of the Philippine Sea.

3115. Danton, J. Periam. "The Battle of the Philippine Sea."
        USNIP, 71 (September 1945), 1022-1027.

        As a naval officer in an air unit in Commander Carrier
Division One, Danton offers his view on the performance of
Mitscher's Task Force 58.

3116. Dickson, W. D. THE BATTLE OF THE PHILIPPINE SEA, JUNE
        1944. London: Allan, 1975. 256 pp.

        Dickson offers a solid account of this naval clash. The
narrative is workmanlike, and he knows his material.

3117. Lockwood, Charles A. Hans Christian Adamson. BATTLES OF
        THE PHILIPPINE SEA. New York: Thomas Y. Crowell, 1967.
        229 pp.

        Lockwood commanded submarine forces of the Pacific Fleet
during the final two years of the war. The narrative
addresses the period April-October 1944, when U.S. naval
forces defeated the Japanese fleet in the Philippine Sea.

IV.D.3.e.viii. SAVO ISLAND

3118. Baker, Warren P. "The Blackest Day of the War." MC GAZ,
        68 (August 1984), 55-59.

        Baker survived the sinking of the QUINCY during the
American defeat at Savo Island in August 1942.

3119. Bell, Charles. "Shootout at Savo." AMER HIST ILLUS, 9
        (January 1975), 28-38.

        Here is an account of a naval victory by the Japanese
8th Fleet which lasted less than one hour. Bell feels that
the only positive effect of the defeat was to shake the

U.S. Navy from its complacency.

3120. Newcomb, Richard F. SAVO: THE INCREDIBLE NAVAL DEBACLE
       OFF GUADALCANAL. New York: Holt, Rinehart and Winston,
       1961. 278 pp.

       Here is a popular account of the defeat which, according
       to Newcomb, demonstrated the unpreparedness of the U.S.
       Navy. By emphasizing the lessons learned, he, by
       implication, identifies the errors committed during the
       battle.

3121. Ohmae, Toshikazu. "The Battle of Savo Island." USNIP, 83
       (December 1957), 1,263-1,278.

       Edited by Roger Pineau, here is an authoritative account
       of the Japanese perspective of the battle. The author,
       present at the battle, served on the staff of 8th Fleet
       under Admiral Gunichi Mikawa. Of interest is his report on
       the planning and the reasons behind the early retirement of
       the Japanese naval force; in addition, Mikawa appends his
       observations.

3122. Smith, Stanley E. THE BATTLE OF SAVO. New York:
       Macfadden-Bartell, 1962. 152 pp.

       The U.S. defeat at Savo receives judicious treatment in
       this brief overview. Smith points out the errors and the
       lessons learned for American naval leaders.

IV.D.3.f. AMPHIBIOUS ASSAULT PLANS AND OPERATIONS

i. GENERAL ACCOUNTS

3123. Ayling, Keith. SEMPER FIDELIS: THE U.S. MARINES IN
       ACTION. Boston: Houghton Mifflin, 1943. 194 pp.

       Ayling gives a popular contemporary account of action in
       the Solomon Islands.

3124. Barbey, Daniel. MACARTHUR'S AMPHIBIOUS NAVY: SEVENTH
       AMPHIBIOUS FORCE OPERATIONS, 1943-1945, Annapolis, MD:
       Naval Institute Press, 1969. 375 pp.

       Barbey (Vice-Adm. ret.), the commander of the Seventh
       Amphibious Force in the South West Pacific, bases his
       personal account on official documents and the notes that
       he made during the war. Observing that by December 7, 1941
       the Navy did not have a single oceangoing ship that could

run its bow onto a beach, Barbey chronicles the development
of the LCT, LST, LCI(L), LCM, and other amphibious craft in
the Pacific. His comments upon arriving in Australia
underline the deep inter-service rivalries that plagued the
war effort.

3125. Burton, Earl. BY SEA AND BY LAND: THE STORY OF OUR
        AMPHIBIOUS FORCES. New York: Whittlesey House, 1944.
        218 pp.

        According to this naval officer, everything is a "good
show" and the Japanese will get even more.

3126. Caporale, Louis G. "The Marianas." MC GAZ, 68 (June
        1984), 18-27.

        Here is a description of the largest Marine amphibious
assault, Operation FORAGER. The coordinated attacks
against Saipan, Tinian, and Guam involved two corps of
Marines. Some excellent photographs are included.

3127. Caporale, Louis G. "Prelude to Victory: The Marianas."
        MC GAZ, 68 (June 1984), 18-27.

        The assault on the Marianas was the largest in Marine
Corps history and the only one that involved two corps.
The author describes the campaign and touches on the
controversy between the two generals named Smith.

3128. "The Fighting 'I.'" WARSHIP INTL, 16 (No. 2, 1979),
        157-161.

        Here is a brief report on the aircraft carrier INTREPID,
which suffered damage in kamikaze attacks. The ship is
being converted into a museum.

3129. Godson, Susan H. VIKING OF ASSAULT: ADMIRAL JOHN LESSLIE
        HALL, JR., AND AMPHIBIOUS WARFARE. Washington, D. C.:
        University Press of America, 1982. 237 pp.

        Although the prime focus of this biography is in Europe
and the Mediterranean, Hall did go to the Pacific in late
1944 to help plan the Okinawa campaign (Operation ICEBERG)
under Adm. Turner. He also was in charge of amphibious
training for the assault on the Japanese homeland. After
Japan surrendered, Hall had orders to attack outside Tokyo
if any treachery occurred. The book is well researched and
offers a good account of the development of amphibious
techniques.

3130. Heinl, Robert D., Jr. and John A. Crown. THE MARSHALLS:
      INCREASING THE TEMPO. Washington, D.C.: U.S. Marine
      Corps, 1954. 188 pp.

      The authors write this account for the Historical Branch
      of the Marine Corps. They describe the accelerating
      progress of U.S. forces, specifically that of the Marines,
      in rolling back Japan's defensive perimeters.

3131. Isby, David C. "Island War: The U.S. Amphibious Offensive
      Against Imperial Japan, 1942 to 1945." STRATEGY &
      TACTICS, 52 (1975), 21-36.

      NE

3132. Iseley, Jeter A. and Philip A. Crowl. THE U.S. MARINES AND
      AMPHIBIOUS WAR: ITS THEORY AND ITS PRACTICE IN THE
      PACIFIC. Princeton, NJ: Princeton University Press,
      1951. 636 pp.

      Despite the commonly held prewar belief that modern
      weapons had rendered obsolete any attack against a defended
      beach, the Marines developed doctrine and techniques for
      amphibious warfare. In this examination of Pacific
      operations, the authors enjoyed complete access to battle
      plans, action reports, and interviews with participants.
      This is not an official history; in a pre-agreement with
      the publisher, the Marine Corps promised not to influence
      or interfere with the authors' work. The account is
      balanced and includes analyses of military mistakes (e.g.,
      at Guadalcanal, Tarawa, and Saipan) as well as successes
      (e.g., the near perfect assault at Iwo Jima).

3133. Josephy, Alvin M. THE LONG AND THE SHORT AND THE TALL.
      New York: A. A. Knopf, 1946. 221 pp.

      The author served as a Marine correspondent attached to
      the 3d Marine Division. His report on the unit's combat
      activities (which included amphibious assault landings at
      Guadalcanal, Guam, and Iwo Jima) incorporates portraits of
      individuals in action--many of whom never survived the war.
      See especially the transcripts of his eyewitness
      description of the landing at Guam, July 21, 1944.

3134. Ladd, James. ASSAULT FROM THE SEA, 1939-1945: THE CRAFT,
      THE LANDINGS, THE MAN. New York: Hippocrene Books,
      1976. 256 pp.

This general survey examines the various elements of
amphibious assaults in all theaters. Many illustrations
are included.

3135.   Merrifield, Robert B. "Japan's Amphibious Bid." MC GAZ,
        38 (May 1954), 40-47.

        Merrifield points out many of the flaws in Japanese
amphibious operations, but he nevertheless recognizes their
many successes.

3136.   Ogden, D.A.D. AMPHIBIOUS OPERATIONS OF ESPECIAL INTEREST
        TO THE ARMY. Ft. Belvoir, VA: Army Engineer School,
        1950. 23 pp.

        Examining some Pacific operations, Brig. Gen. Ogden
(USA) analyzes amphibious warfare doctrine and points out
two weaknesses. First, there is insufficient emphasis on
techniques of sustaining land combat once initiated after
the landing. (Navy logistical support must be continued.)
Second, differences between the organization of the Army
and Marine Corps--especially the non-divisional units of
the Army--have not been taken into consideration. In
general, Ogden underlines the importance of logistical
support, air superiority, and tactical communications.

3137.   Peyton, Green [pseud. Green Peyton Wertenbaker]. 5,000
        MILES TOWARDS TOKYO. Norman, OK: University of
        Oklahoma Press, 1945. 173 pp.

        Here is the story of the Hellcats of Air Group 60, which
took part in every important invasion from the Gilberts to
the Philippines. The author was an air combat information
officer who later served on the staff of Vice Admiral
Thomas C. Kinkaid. The air group flew off the escort
carrier SUWANNEE.

3138.   Rentz, John N. BOUGAINVILLE AND THE NORTHERN SOLOMONS.
        Washington, D.C.: Historical Section, USMC, 1948. 166
        pp.

        Rentz contributes an authoritative summary of the Marine
Corps' participation in these early encounters.

3139.   Sherrod, Robert L. ON TO WESTWARD: WAR IN THE CENTRAL
        PACIFIC. New York: Duell, Sloan and Pearce, 1945. 333
        pp.

        Sherrod makes the reader relive the amphibious

operations of the Marines. He proved an excellent observer
as he travelled with Marine combat units. His narrative
incorporates many names in his efforts to highlight the
human dimension of the war. This book covers the period
from November 1943 to April 1945.

3140.   Swan, W.N. SPEARHEADS OF INVASION. Sydney, Aus.: Angus
        and Robertson, 1953. 307 pp.

        Here is an account of some of the major invasions (e.g.,
        Arawe, Hollandia, Leyte, Lingayen Gulf, Brunei Bay,
        Balikpapan) from the perspective of the Royal Australian
        Naval Landing Ship Party (HMAS WESTRALIA). Swan gives a
        good description of the complicated organization for
        combined operations in the Pacific.

3141.   United States. Department of the Army. Forces in the Far
        East. BORNEO AREA NAVAL OPERATIONS, 1945. Washington,
        D.C.: Office of the Chief of Military History, 1952.
        7 pp.

        Here is a brief report on the deteriorating situation
        for the Japanese in the Southwest area (Tarakan Sector and
        Balikpapan Sector). The Japanese authors acknowledge that
        the fall of the Philippines jeopardized the southern areas.

3142.   United States. Navy Department. U.S. Fleet. AMPHIBIOUS
        OPERATIONS (EXCLUDING MARSHALL ISLAND OPERATIONS).
        Washington, D.C.: Navy Dept., 1944. 58 pp.

        Drawn largely from action reports, this study describes
        amphibious assaults in early 1944 against Green Island,
        Emiran, Saidor, and the Admiralty Islands. There are
        separate sections for naval gunfire, logistics, landing
        craft, and miscellaneous information.

3143.   United States. Navy Department. Pacific Fleet. AIR
        SUPPORT OF PACIFIC AMPHBIOUS OPERATIONS. San Francisco,
        CA: Pacific Fleet, 1945. 173 pp.

        Here is the story of the air support control unit in
        each of the amphibious operations. The narrative argues
        against the view that only pilots understand air power and,
        therefore, should command any joint force that
        incorporates an air arm. Some of the conclusions of the
        report are: (1) recognition of the importance of air
        power, (2) the mandatory need for positive control of each
        aircraft, (3) the weakness of having no joint doctrine for
        amphibious warfare, and (4) the need for specialized

training of pilots and air control personnel.

3144. United States. Navy Department. U.S. Fleet. AMPHIBIOUS
       OPERATIONS DURING THE PERIOD AUGUST TO DECEMBER 1943.
       Washington, D.C.: Navy Dept., 1944. 151 pp.

       This study covers all theaters. For Pacific amphibious
operations, see the reports on the Gilbert Islands, Vella
La Vella, Treasury Island, Empress Augusta Bay, Lae,
Finschhafen, Arawe, and Cape Gloucester. Each operation is
dissected by analyses of its separate parts (e.g., air
support, naval gunfire, intelligence, logistics, ship to
shore movement, landing craft, communications, and
miscellaneous topics--such as balloons and smoke).

IV.D.3.f.ii. ALEUTIANS

3146. Abbott, Collamer M. "Kiska's Dry Run." ALASKA, 49 (May
       1983), 38-40, 80-81.

       Abbott, who participated in the retaking of Kiska,
endorses the words of one of his fellow GI's (from
Alabama): "The only war Ah'm fightin' is with the
elements."

3147. Anderson, Robert. "Attu: WWII's Bloody 'Sideshow.'"
       ARMY, 33 (May 1983), 38-41.

       Here is a brief story of the amphibious assault on Attu
in May 1943.

3148. Averitte, Ruth Humphrey. COWBOY OVER KISKA. Dallas, TX:
       Avalon Press, 1945. 3 pp.

       Here is contemporary poetry--deeply felt and emotional.

3149. Blackford, Charles M., III. "Kiska Dry-Run." USNIP, 93
       (March 1967), 56-63.

       In this personal account by a commander of an LST-19,
Blackford (Coast Guard) characterizes the invasion as an
"unformed mob" following a red truck light on a destroyer
under terrible weather conditions.

3150. Carlson, William. LIFELINES THROUGH THE ARCTIC. New York:
       William Sloane Associates, 1962. 271 pp.

       This is an updated version of his wartime report on life
in a remote area of the war. His special emphasis lies in

aviation and radar warning systems.

3151. Conn, Stetson, Rose C. Engleman, and Byron Fairchild. THE
       WESTERN HEMISPHERE: GUARDING THE UNITED STATES AND ITS
       OUTPOSTS. Washington, D.C.: Office of the Chief of
       Military History, for the Dept. of the Army, 1964.

       This official Army history includes information on
       Alaska and the Aleutians. It is a well-written and
       well-researched account that remains useful.

3152. Deacon, Kenneth J. "Attu, May 1943." MIL ENGR, 59
       (January-February 1967), 25.

       Here is a brief account of the contributions of the
       engineers (e.g., landing with the shore party and
       developing supply routes on the island) in the retaking of
       Attu.

3153. "The Diary of Takahashi." USNIP, 106 (July 1980), 74-76.

       In this diary of a Japanese private on the island of
       Kiska in 1943, the diarist complains about the weather,
       expresses gratitude for the poor marksmanship of American
       bombers, and regrets having to evacuate Kiska after some of
       his comrades had died there.

3154. Ellsworth, Lyman R. GUYS ON ICE. New York: David
       McKay Company, 1952. 277 pp.

       Life at an isolated outpost in the Pribilof Islands is
       the central theme of this book. As an enlistd man,
       Ellsworth led a special detachment which had orders to
       evacuate civilians, set mines, and blow up Dutch Harbor
       if sizeable Japanese forces attacked.

3155. Ford, Corey. SHORT CUT TO TOKYO: THE BATTLE FOR THE
       ALEUTIANS. New York: Charles Scribner's Sons, 1943.
       141 pp.

       Featuring stories of the U.S. pilots, and the hazards
       they faced, Ford offers an eyewitness report on operations
       in the Aleutians.

3156. Garfield, Brian. THE THOUSAND-MILE WAR: WORLD WAR II IN
       ALASKA AND THE ALEUTIANS. Garden City, NY: Doubleday,
       1969. 351 pp.

       Garfield, a novelist, presents his first non-fiction

book. He based his research on documents concerning the
Aleutians, as well as on interviews and correspondence with
many veterans.   It is also the first full-scale history
of the fifteen-month campaign that brought the first
theater-wide American victory over Japan. The "one
thousand miles" refers to the distance between Dutch Harbor
and Attu. The narrative is well balanced, especially in
Garfield's even-handed treatment of controversial episodes
like the relief of Maj. Gen. Albert Brown, the "Battle of
the Pips," and the "invasion" of Kiska. Of interest is his
report on the various techniques used by the troops to cope
with the rugged environment.

3157.   Glines, Carroll V. "The Forgotten War in the Aleutians."
        AF & SPACE DIG, 51 (March 1968), 75-84.

        Glines summarizes events in the Aleutians, including the
Japanese attack at Dutch Harbor (a diversion for the attack
at Midway), ineffective American air attacks, the terrible
weather conditions, the U.S. invasion at Attu, and the
brilliant Japanese departure from Kiska.

3158.   Handleman, Howard. BRIDGE TO VICTORY: THE STORY OF THE
        RECONQUEST OF THE ALEUTIANS. New York: Random House,
        1943. 275 pp.

        War correspondent Handleman highlights the human
dimension of the war in the Aleutians, which he calls a
tough place to live and to fight. He witnessed the
retaking of Attu. The book is about as good as the hurried
nature of war reporting will allow. The concluding section
underlines Handleman's opinion that the Aleutians should be
used as a springboard to defeat Japan.

3159.   Hatch, F.J. "Allies in the Aleutians." AEROSPACE H, 21
        (Summer/June 1974), 70-78.

        The author maintains that the campaign set an example of
Canadian-American cooperation. Canadians worked inside an
American organization without losing their identity.

3160.   Laidlaw, Lansing. "Aleutian Experience of the 'Mad M.'"
        OREGON H Q, 80 (Spring 1979), 30-49.

        Lansing entered the Coast Guard at age forty-seven at
the start of the war and served aboard the attack transport
ARTHUR MIDDLETON ("Mad M"). He records his experiences in
the form of a diary-letter to his brother. During
1942-1943, he and his ship were in the Aleutians.

3161.   Lorelli, John A.   THE BATTLE OF THE KOMANDORSKI ISLANDS.
        Annapolis, MD: Naval Institute Press, 1984.

        Here is an authoritative account. Reporting on the
        Battle of Attu, March 27, 1943, Lorelli criticizes the
        commander of Task Force 16.6, Charles H. McMorris, for
        being overconfident, lacking aggressiveness, and failing to
        communicate to his captains the tactics to be employed.

3162.   McKay, Robert S.   "Unforgiving Struggle for Attu."   WW II,
        1 (September 1986), 16-25.

        The author descirbes the U.S. struggle against nature
        and the Japanese in this battle narrative.

3163.   McCandless, Bruce.   "The Battle of the Pips."   USNIP, 84
        (February 1958), 49-56.

        Here is a personal account of the "battle" of Kiska by
        the navigator aboard the cruiser SAN FRANCISCO. Poor
        intelligence, radar ("Pips" are targets identified by
        radar), and weather all played a role in deceiving the
        attacking Americans.

3164.   Masataka, Chihaya.   "Mysterious Withdrawal from Kiska."
        USNIP, 84 (February 1958), 31-47.

        The author blends many interviews with Japanese sources
        to describe what he calls a "perfect operation":   the
        secret Japanese withdrawal from Kiska. Poor weather caused
        seven cancellations of the evacuation, but, once
        accomplished, eighteen days passed before the Allies
        discovered the "secret."

3165.   Millsap, Ralph H.   "Skill or Luck?"   USNIP, suppl. (March
        1985), 79-87.

        On March 27, 1943, ships battled near Attu for four
        hours. Millsap served aboard one of the U. S. ships
        (RICHMOND). Although the Japanese leader, Hosogaya,
        retired unexpectedly, Millsap reports that the U. S.
        commander, McMorris, was considering doing the same thing
        at about the same time.

3166.   Morgan, Lael.   "An Artist's War in the Aleutians."   ALASKA
        J, 10 (Summer 1980), 34-39.

        The article includes the paintings and excerpts of the

account by William F. Draper, one of five naval artists in
the war. He left the Aleutians for the South West Pacific
just prior to the Battle of Attu. His portraits of the
flying tiger aircraft (the Alaskan version had a larger,
more definite tiger's head than those in China) are
particularly striking.

3167.   Pinney, Charles A. "A Military Bush Pilot on the Forgotten
        Front." AEROSPACE H, 22 (Spring/March 1975), 1-5.

        Here is the personal account of a pilot who flew
        resupply missions from Anchorage to Adak in 1942-1943.
        After only about six months of undergraduate pilot
        training, Pinney went directly to operational flying in the
        B-26. His criticism of the abominable flight conditions in
        the Aleutians is borne out by the fact that poor weather
        claimed six U.S. aircraft for every one aircraft destroyed
        by the Japanese.

3168.   Rigge, Simon. WAR IN THE OUTPOSTS. Alexandria, VA:
        Time-Life Books, 1980. 208 pp.

        Reinforced by outstanding photographs, the narrative
        describes the war in some remote areas. For the war
        against Japan, see his reports on the Aleutians ("Theater
        of Frustration") and Pacific Islands ("Guerrillas of the
        Jungle"). Of interest is the account of Maj. Harrisson's
        last battle on Borneo more than two months after the
        Japanese surrender announcement.

3169.   Stokesbury, James L. "Battle of Attu." AMER HIST ILLUS,
        14 (April 1979), 30-38.

        With excellent photographs and a well-written narrative,
        the author recounts the only major land battle fought in
        the Western Hemisphere. Of interest are his reports on
        both the personality clashes among U.S. leaders and the
        mass Japanese suicides.

3170.   Thorburn, Lois and Donaldson Thorburn. NO TUMULT, NO
        SHOUTING: THE STORM OF THE PBY. New York: Henry Holt,
        1945. 148 pp.

        Here are a reporter (later a USNR commander in the
        Pacific) and his wife describing the exploits of PBY pilots
        under difficult conditions in the Aleutians.

3171.   United States. Department of the Army. Forces in the Far
        East. ALEUTIAN NAVAL OPERATION. Washington, D.C.:

Office of the Chief of Military History, n.d. 85 pp.

Here is a report by Japanese officers of the victory and
the defeat in the Aleutions from early 1942 to early 1943.
According to the authors, the fall of Attu led to the
decision to evacuate Kiska.

3172. Webber, Bert. ALEUTIAN HEADACHE. New York: Galleon,
       Forthcoming.

       NE

IV.D.3.f.iii. ANDAMANS

3173. Srivastava, P. "In the Face of Death--The Andamans Island
       Under Japanese Occupation." INDIAN ARCH, 28 (January
       1979), 69-87.

       NE

3174. United States. Department of the Army. Forces in the Far
       East. BURMA AND ANDAMAN NAVAL OPERATIONS. Washington,
       D.C.: Office of the Chief of Military History, 1953.
       12 pp.

       The title is somewhat misleading. Here is a Japanese
       summary of the victory at Andaman.

IV.D.3.f.iv. IWO JIMA

3175. Barrett, Allen M. "I Fought at Iwo--Twice!" MC GAZ, 63
       (February 1979), 43-52.

       Lieutenant Barrett (USMC) returned to action at Iwo Jima
       after recovering from a wound he suffered there during the
       initial Marine assault.

3176. Bartlett, Tom. "The Flag Raising on Iwo Jima."
       LEATHERNECK, 68 (February 1985), 18-21.

       The author tells of the two flag-raisings that occurred
       at Iwo Jima on February 23, 1945. The first one--for
       LEATHERNECK and taken by SSGT Lou Lowery--is less well
       known.

3177. Bartley, Whitman S. IWO JIMA: AMPHIBIOUS EPIC.
       Washington, D.C.: GPO, 1954. 253 pp.

       Bartley, a Marine historian, compiles a detailed,

balanced battle report which is extremely well researched.

3178. Byrd, Martha H. "Iwo Jima." AMER HIST ILLUS, 10 (January
        1976), 4-13, 48-50.

        With excellent photos and a facile narrative, this
        article describes the determined defense of Gen.
        Kuribayashi and his forces. Of special note is Byrd's
        explanation that after the victory the U.S. built the
        largest runway in the Pacific (ten-thousand feet) at Iwo.
        By the end of the war, some 2,400 B-29s would land on that
        runway in emergency situations (far out of reach of the
        next closest U.S. airfield) that involved 27,000 airmen.

3179. Cates, C.B. "Iwo Jima." MC GAZ, 49 (November 1965), 78.

        Here is the personal account of a division commander
        (4th Marine Division) at Iwo Jima.

3180. Cochran, Alexander, S., Jr. "Firestorm Below Suribachi."
        MIL HIST, 2 (August 1985), 42-48.

        For this article, Cochran interviewed Bill Ross an
        ex-Marine sergeant who wrote a book on Iwo Jima. Ross
        describes the bloody battle, in which the adversaries
        seldom saw each other, as well worth the high human cost in
        order to gain the precious air base facilities.

3181. Dunnagan, C.G. "Iwo Jima." MC GAZ, 49 (February 1965),
        28-31.

        The author deals with the lessons learned in the famous
        battle, and he finds Marine doctrine on amphibious warfare
        to be sound.

3182. Emmons, Roger M. "Narrative of Iwo Jima." MC GAZ, 34
        (June 1950), 25-27.

        Here is a view of the battle from a Marine (automatic
        weapons) battery aboard the battleship TENNESSEE.

3183. Frank, Benis M. "The Story of a Famous Photograph: Iwo
        Jima Flag-Raising." AMER HIST ILLUS, 3 (November 1968),
        40-42.

        Frank describes the two photographs--the first by Louis
        R. Lowery (for LEATHERNECK) and the more famous one by Joe
        Rosenthal--at Iwo Jima. Only three of the six men who
        raised that flag survived the war.

3184. Gallant, T. Grady. THE FRIENDLY DEAD. Garden City, NY:
       Doubleday, 1964.

       The author landed with Regimental Combat Team 25 of the
       4th Marine Division on D-Day at Iwo Jima. He provides
       valuable information on the island's geography and the
       interlocking fortifications of the Japanese defenders. His
       narrative brings the action to the reader and provides
       vivid descriptions of Marines living--and dying--in the
       battle. On the famous flag-raising, he points out the two
       ironies that (a) it occurred fairly early in the operation
       and (b) it was one of the few less risky episodes of the
       operation.

3185. Haynes, Fred E. "Left Flank at Iwo." MC GAZ, 37 (March
       1953), 48-53.

       Here is an account of the taking of Hill 362, the key to
       Japanese defenses on Iwo Jima, by the 28th Marines of the
       5th Marine Division.

3186. Heinl, Robert D. "Target: Iwo." USNIP, 89 (July 1963),
       70-82.

       Heinl reexamines the controversy over the length of time
       allowed for the pre-invasion bombardment of Iwo Jima.
       Despite his criticism of the Navy, Heinl does present the
       reasons for the Navy's decision to shell the island for
       three days instead of the ten-day period requested by the
       Marines.

3187. Henri, Raymond. IWO JIMA: SPRINGBOARD TO FINAL VICTORY.
       New York: U.S. Camera, 1945. 95 pp.

       Here is a collection of action photographs taken during
       the epic struggle at Iwo Jima.

3188. Henri, Raymond, et. al. THE U.S. MARINES ON IWO JIMA.
       Washington, D.C.: Infantry Journal Press, 1945. 312 pp.

       Here is a contemporary account by a group of Marine
       combat correspondents and public relations officers who all
       witnessed the fierce fighting. A list of all dead and
       missing Americans in this campaign is included.

3189. Horie, Y. "Japanese Defense of Iwo Jima." MC GAZ, 36
       (February 1952), 18-27.

The author, a major in the Japanese Imperial Army, was taken prisoner at Chichi Jima. To give the Japanese view of this famous battle, Horie relies on his memory--but it is the reliable memory of someone who kept the official reports while the battle was in progress. See especially his insightful conclusions in the Appendix.

3190. Josephy, Alvin M., Jr. "Iwo Jima." AMER HERITAGE, 32 (June-July 1981), 92-102.

Here is a personal account of a Marine correspondent who witnessed the battle. Excellent photographs accompany his well-written narrative.

3191. Josephy, Alvin M., Jr. "Jungle of Stone." INFANTRY J, 57 (September 1945), 10-17.

The author recounts the dangers involved in the so-called "mopping up" operations on Iwo Jima.

3192. Leckie, Robert. THE BATTLE FOR IWO JIMA. New York: Random House, 1967. 173 pp.

The author served with the Marines in the Pacific. There are no notes or bibliography. Excellent photographs assist this fast-moving narrative.

3193. McKinnon, Donald A. "Battalion Surgeon on Iwo Jima." MC GAZ, 66 (February 1982), 28-37.

McKinnon recounts his experiences on Iwo Jima. Most of his battalion died in action. He reports that DDT spraying to counter the flies on the island led to widespread illness and diarrhea among the Americans.

3194. Matthews, Allen R. THE ASSAULT. New York: Simon and Schuster, 1947. 216 pp.

This is the diary of a Marine rifleman who spent twelve days assaulting Iwo Jima and its Japanese defenders. Before the war, Matthews was a reporter, and the diary entries reflect his skills with the pen. There is a no more chilling account of the brutal nature of warfare than that of the rifleman.

3195. Maxey, Nelson C. "Volcano Island." MC GAZ, 69 (February 1985), 44-51.

Here is a pictorial account of Marine action at Iwo

Jima.

3196. Newcomb, Richard R. IWO JIMA. New York: Holt, Rinehart
       and Winston, 1965. 338 pp.

       The author, a naval correspondent during the war, bases
       his detailed, balanced narrative on correspondence and many
       interviews with Americans and Japanese. Especially inter-
       esting are the quotations from letters sent to and from the
       doomed Japanese defenders. For example, the Japanese
       commander returned one of the last letters from his young
       daughter with his corrections on her spelling and grammar.
       With his skill as a reporter, Newcomb accompanies the
       reader through all phases of the operation (before, during,
       and after).

3197. Richardson, Robert C., Jr. PARTICIPATION IN THE IWO JIMA
       OPERATION BY THE UNITED STATES ARMY FORCES, PACIFIC
       OCEAN AREAS, FEBRUARY-MARCH 1945. n.p.: HQUSA Forces,
       Middle Pacific, 1946. 361 pp.

       This official history highlights the Army's role in the
       taking of Iwo Jima.

3198. Rosenthal, Joe and W.C. Heinz. "The Picture That Will Live
       Forever." COLLIERS, 136 (February 18, 1955), 62-67.

       Here is the personal story of the famous photograph by
       Rosenthal of the flag-raising at Iwo Jima.

3199. Ross, Bill D. IWO JIMA: LEGACY OF VALOR. New York:
       Vanguard Press, 1985. 376 pp.

       Ross, a combat correspondent at Iwo Jima, incorporates
       in his narrative many anecdotes and reports from both sides
       which remind the reader that individual human beings took
       part in this massive operation. He asserts that the
       capture of Iwo Jima saved 24,751 American crewmen who later
       made emergency landings there after bombing Japan. The
       book contains excellent photographs and no footnotes.

3200. Ross, Bill D. "Volcanic Island's Bitter Cost." W W II, 2
       (July 1987), 19-25.

       Ross served on Iwo Jima and has written extensively on
       the topic. This is a capsule narrative.

3201. Russell, Michael. IWO JIMA. New York: Ballantine Books,
       1974. 156 pp.

In a narrative supported by some excellent photos,
Russell presents a brief, readable, knowledgeable report on
the famous battle.

3202. Shershun, Carroll S. "The World's Most Costly Airstrip."
       AEROSPACE H, 14 (Winter 1967), 239-244.

       Shershun emphasizes the strategic need for a fighter
escort base at Iwo Jima to support bombers going to the
Japanese home islands. The article incorporates some of
the correspondence of the Japanese island commander, Gen.
Tadamichi Kuribayashi.

3203. Thacker, Joel D. HISTORY OF THE IWO JIMA FLAG RAISING.
       Washington, D.C.: USMC, 1951. 10 pp.

       Despite its title, this slim publication offers a
narrative of the battle as well as the circumstances of the
famous flag raising.

3204. Werts, Russell. "The Ghosts of Iwo." MC GAZ, 69 (February
       1985), 32-43.

       Here is a foxhole view of the fighting at Iwo Jima.
Werts received his baptism of fire there and describes the
action as viewed from the squad level.

3205. United States. Navy Department. Pacific Fleet. ANALYSIS
       OF AIR OPERATIONS: IWO JIMA, FEB.-MARCH 1945 AND
       SOWESPAC ACTIVITY. San Francisco, CA: Pacific Fleet,
       1945. 47 pp.

       Incorporating material gained from interviews with
Japanese POWs, this study analyses air operations at Iwo
Jima. The prisoners reported that air attacks caused few
casualties for the heavily dug-in Japanese defenders.

3206. United States. Navy Department. U.S. Fleet. AMPHIBIOUS
       OPERATIONS: CAPTURE OF IWO JIMA, 16 FEBRUARY TO 16
       MARCH 1945. Washington, D.C.: Navy Dept., 1945. 98
       pp.

       This narrative is based largely on the official Navy
reports of the various combat commanders (e.g., 5th Fleet,
Task Force 58, Amphilibious Forces, Expeditionary Troops,
etc.) Sub-topics in the book include naval gunfire, air
support, intelligence, ship to shore movement, and
logistics.

3207.   Wheeler, Richard. THE BLOODY BATTLE FOR SURIBACHI. New
            York: Thomas Y. Crowell, 1965. 148 pp.

        In this brief account, Wheeler describes the fierce
        encounter at Iwo Jima. Wheeler served with the Marines in
        the war.

3208.   Wheeler, Richard. IWO. New York: Lippincott and Crowell,
            1980. 243 pp.

        The author served at Iwo Jima as a member of the company
        that raised the flag at Mt. Suribachi. In addition to his
        experiences, Wheeler draws on Japanese sources and exten-
        sive interviews for his popular narrative. The book is
        filled with vignettes which bring home the human dimension
        of this brutal and bloody battle. Wheeler reports that the
        president vetoed suggestions to use gas attacks prior to
        the U.S. assault. There are no footnotes.

IV.D.3.f.v. KWAJALEIN

3209.   Marshall, S.L.A. ISLAND VICTORY. New York: Penguin
            Books, 1944. 213 pp.

        Here is an account of the American victory at Kwajalein.
        Gen. Marshall, an accomplished military historian, bases
        his report on several interviews with veterans of the
        battle.

3210.   Marshall, S.L.A. "The After-Action Interviews--The
            Kwajalein Experience." ARMY, 16 (September 1966),
            58-61.

        Marshall claims that the interviews after this battle
        revealed "more than had ever been learned before in the
        history of armies and war." The noted military historian
        describes his techniques, and he emphasizes the immediate
        tactical value (particularly at the company level) coming
        out of the interviews.

IV.D.3.f.vi. MAKIN ISLAND

3211.   Haughey, David W. "Carlson's Raid on Makin Island." AMER
            HIST ILLUS, 18 (October 1983), 32-41.

        Here is a careful assessment of the famous raid by two
        companies of the 2nd Raider Battalion led by Lt. Col. Evans
        Carlson. The author provides a sketch of Carlson as well

as descriptions of the successes and problems encountered
in the 1942 raid. The episode had a significant impact on
the U.S. public.

IV.D.3.f.vii. NEW BRITAIN

3212. Hough, Frank O. and J.A. Crown. THE CAMPAIGN ON NEW
        BRITAIN. Washington, D.C.: U.S. Marine Corps, 1952.
        220 pp.

        Lt. Col. Hough and Maj. Crown write the official Marine
        history of the campaign. They describe the difficulties of
        moving the marines from Australia to New Britain. Of value
        is their description of small unit tactics.

3213. Wilcox, Richard. OF MEN AND BATTLE. New York: Howell,
        Soskin, 1944. 124 pp.

        Wilcox reports on the encounter at Arawa, New Britain in
        December 1943. The narrative is complemented by the
        illustrations of David Fredenthal.

IV.D.3.f.viii. NEW GEORGIA

3214. Horton, D.C. NEW GEORGIA: PATTERNS FOR VICTORY. New
        York: Ballantine Books, 1971. 160 pp.

        Horton contrasts the local commanders on both sides in
        this campaign: the inflexible Japanese and the untrained
        U.S. novitiates (longing for the luxuries of base camp).
        He effectively places the campaign in the broad context of
        the war. There is an entire chapter on JFK and PT 109.

3215. Shaw, James C. "The Japanese Guessed Wrong at New
        Georgia." MC GAZ, 33 (December 1949), 36-42.

        Acting on unverified information, the Japanese
        commander, Adm. Koga, blundered, according to Shaw, by
        attempting to guess American intentions preceding the
        invasion at New Georgia. Koga's decisions rendered
        Japanese air and sea resources physically incapable of
        repelling the U.S. invaders.

IV.D.3.f.ix. OKINAWA

3216. Appleman, Roy, James MacGregor Burns, Russell A. Gugeler,
        and John Stevens. OKINAWA: THE LAST BATTLE.
        Washington, D. C.: Dept. of Army, Historical Division,
        1948. 529 pp.

Here is the Army's official history of Operation ICEBERG
which includes the conquest of northern Okinawa, the
capture of Ie Shima, the assaults on the Shuri defenses,
and the final stages of the enemy's last stand. The
authors were with the 10th Army. The Japanese shifted
their plan of defense from contesting the landing at the
water's edge to strong resistance around a central
fortified position. General Ushijima's 32d Army was
reduced to a mob, but just over seven thousand Japanese
defenders chose to surrender. Of particular interest is
the Americans' use of "Bait Boys," Japanese prisoners who
agreed to return and induce their comrades to surrender.
The book is indispensable.

3217. Baldwin, Hanson W. "Okinawa: Victory at the Threshold."
        MC GAZ, Part I: 34 (December 1950), 40-47. Part II:
        35 (January 1951), 42-49.

        Baldwin describes the American naval action at Okinawa
        by "the Fleet that came to stay." For three months, the
        Navy carried on extensive aerial combat and withstood
        withering kamikaze attacks.

3218. Belote, James H. and William M. Belote. TYPHOON OF STEEL.
        New York: Harper and Row, 1970. 368 pp.

        The authors analyze the campaign for Okinawa through
        both American and Japanese eyes. For the Americans, the
        ordeal served as a costly dress rehearsal for the planned
        final assault on Japan. With their expertise and extensive
        research, the authors offer an indispensable study of this
        campaign.

3219. Dodd, Joe Douglas. "Night Attack on Kunishi Ridge." MC
        GAZ, 69 (April 1985), 42-44.

        This description of part of the campaign for Okinawa
        highlights the dangers of night combat operations.

3220. Frank, Benis M. OKINAWA: CAPSTONE TO VICTORY. New
        York: Ballantine Books, 1969. 160 pp.

        Here is a popular account written by an authority on
        the subject.

3221. Frank, Benis M. OKINAWA: THE GREAT ISLAND BATTLE.
        New York: Elsevier-Dutton, 1978. 184 pp.

Frank, head of the Marine Corps oral history project,
provides an authoritative analysis of the complex
amphibious operation and the defeat of the Japanese
at Okinawa. The author is not particularly enamored
with what he calls the "blowtorch and corkscrew"
strategy adopted by the Americans.

3222. Gow, Ian. OKINAWA 1945: GATEWAY TO JAPAN. Garden City,
       NY: Doubleday, 1985. 224 pp.

The author used H. P. Willmott as a consultant in
writing this general account of the Okinawan campaign.
There are some bibliographical entries and no explanatory
notes.

3223. Kennard, Richard C. "The Fire Mission That Surprised More
       than the Enemy." MC GAZ, 69 (April 1985), 40-41.

This is a personal account by a Marine forward observer
who demonstrated uncanny accuracy while on temporary duty
with the Army on Okinawa. His former checkpoint for
gauging artillery fire with the Marines turned out to be an
actual target when he was with the Army unit. He couldn't
miss!

3224. Lott, Arnold S. BRAVE SHIP, BRAVE MEN. Indianapolis, IN:
       Bobbs-Merrill, 1964. 272 pp.

Here is a report on the destroyer AARON WARD. Lott pays
particular attention to the ship's activities in the
Okinawa campaign.

3225. Love, Edmund G. "Deception on the Shuri Line." INFANTRY,
       73 (July-August 1983), 14-20.

NE

3226. McElroy, John W. "Reaction Report." AMER NEP, 39 (October
       1979), 256-270.

McElroy, who served aboard the attack transport
MARATHON, gives a personal account of the attack on Okinawa
in April 1945. His diary-type entries contain interesting
vignettes. He is a trained historian.

3227. Morris, Morton D. OKINAWA: A TIGER BY THE TAIL. New
       York: Hawthorn Books, 1969. 238 pp.

Here is a popular account of the bloody ordeal.

3228. Nichols, Charles S., Jr. and Henry I. Shaw, Jr. OKINAWA:
         VICTORY IN THE PACIFIC. Washington, D.C.: USMC, 1955.
         332 pp.

         This official history of the final large-scale campaign
         by the Marines in the Pacific portrays the aggressive U.S.
         offense and the determined Japanese resistance. As
         amphibious tactics evolved, so did Japanese ideas about
         conducting island defenses. Here was a bloody affair that
         served as a shocking preview of what stood ahead for
         invaders of the home islands.

3229. "Okinawa 1945: The End of the Line." MC GAZ, 69 (April
         1985), 34-39.

         Here is a pictorial account of the Marines in action at
         Okinawa.

3230. Richardson, Robert C., Jr. PARTICIPATION IN THE OKINAWA
         OPERATION BY THE UNITED STATES ARMY FORCES, PACIFIC
         OCEAN AREAS, APRIL-JUNE 1945. n.p.: HQUSA Forces,
         Middle Pacific, 1946. 2 vols.

         This official report has only recently been
         declassified. Richardson is concerned primarily with the
         challenge of logistics at Okinawa.

3231. Simpson, William Penrose. ISLAND "X"--OKINAWA. West
         Hanover, MA: Christopher Publishing House, 1981. 271
         pp.

         Here is an interesting perspective on the bloody
         campaign.

3232. Soth, Lauren K. "Hacksaw Ridge on Okinawa." INF J, 57
         (August 1945), 11-14.

         Soth describes the harsh fighting, which he calls a
         shocking preview of what lay ahead for any invader of the
         Japanese homeland.

3233. Stebbins, Owen T. "Rifle Company U. S. Fortress." MC GAZ,
         57 (April 1973), 36-41.

         Here is the personal account of the ten-day battle at
         Sugar Loaf Hill on Okinawa by the commander of Company G,
         22d Marines.

3234. Taylor, Blaine. "Final Island Assault." MIL HIST, 3 (June
         1987), 42-49.

         Taylor interviews Daniel B. Brewster, a young Marine
         officer during the war--and later Senator from Maryland,
         about the Battle of Okinawa. Brewster recalls the
         suffering of the civilian population and the suicides by
         Japanese soliders who refused to surrender. Later, as a
         Marine reservist, Brewster saw action in Vietnam--as a U.S.
         senator!

3235. Werstein, Irving. OKINAWA, THE LAST ORDEAL. New York:
         Thomas Y. Crowell, 1968. 179 pp.

         Werstein provides a popular account of the final
         campaign.

IV.D.3.f.x. PALAUS

3236. Falk, Stanley L. BLOODIEST VICTORY: PALAUS. New York:
         Ballantine Books, 1974. 159 pp.

         Falk does justice to this gruesome affair.

IV.D.3.f.xi. PELELIU

3237. Gailey, Harry A. PELELIU: 1944. Annapolis, MD: Nautical
         and Aviation Publishing, 1983. 212 pp.

         Gailey reports on one of the bloodiest battles of the
         war: the invasion and reduction of Peleliu in September
         1944.

3238. Hough, Frank O. THE ASSAULT ON PELELIU. Washington, D.C.:
         U.S. Marine Corps, 1950. 209 pp.

         This official history shows the refinement of the
         techniques of amphibious assaults by the Marines--and
         island defense tactics by the Japanese.

3239. Hunt, George P. CORAL COMES HIGH. New York: Harper &
         Brothers, 1946. 147 pp.

         Hunt recalls his experiences as commander of Company K,
         3rd Battalion, 1st Marine Division, during the assault
         against Peleliu in September 1944. The casualties in his
         rifle company approached 70%. Hunt includes his drawings
         of the ordeal.

3240. Lea, Tom. PELELIU LANDING. El Paso, TX: C. Hertzog,
       1945. 34 pp.

          Here is a unique contemporary report on the bloody
       assault.

3241. "Pelelui." MC GAZ, 68 (September 1984), 14-17.

          After 6,000 USMC casualties (including 1,200 dead) and
       10,000 Japanese dead, this "forty years on" report asks if
       the gain was worth the price.

3242. Sledge, Eugene B. "Peleliu: A Neglected Battle." MC GAZ,
       Pt. I: "Defense in Depth," 63 (November 1979), 88-95;
       Pt. II: "Assault into Hell," 63 (December 1979), 28-41;
       Pt. III: "Victory at High Cost," 64 (January 1980),
       32-42.

          Here is a personal account of the horrors of this battle
       by a Marine rifleman.

3243. Sledge, E.B. WITH THE OLD BREED, AT PELELIU AND OKINAWA.
       Novato, CA: Presidio Press, 1981. 326 pp.

          Here is a first-hand account of two of the bloodiest and
       most brutal campaigns of the war.

3244. Worth, John. "Jap Barges at Peleliu." COAST ARTILL J, 88
       (March-April 1945), 29-30.

          Worth observed as Marine artillery destroyed several
       Japanese troop barges during their efforts to reinforce
       Peleliu.

IV.D.3.f.xii. SAIPAN

3245. Benson, Douglass L. "A Few Enchanted Evenings." AEROSP H,
       29 (Fall, September 1982), 186-190.

          Benson, who served with the 65th Air Services Group,
       recounts his experiences on Saipan.

3246. Hoffman, Carl W. SAIPAN: THE BEGINNING OF THE END.
       Washington, D.C.: U.S. Marine Corps, 1950. 286 pp.

          This official history for the Marine Corps is thoroughly
       researched. Hoffman describes the tenacious Japanese
       defense.

3247. McClure, Glenn E.   SAIPAN.   Universal City, TX: Emerson's,
          1978.   43 pp.

          Here is a brief report on portions of the battle.

3248. Sanders, Lawrence.   "An Incident on Saipan."   COAST
          ARTILLERY J, 90 (March-April 1947), 47-50.

          Here is a moving story of the combat deaths of two
          feuding GIs during the "mopping up" operation at Saipan.
          Earlier, one had even saved the other's life.

3249. Omitted.

3250. United States.   War Department.   SMALL UNIT ACTIONS.
          Washington, D.C.:   War Dept., 1946.   212 pp.

          Among the encounters discussed, see the narrative on
          Saipan.   This campaign saw the effective use of small units
          of the 27th Division on the Tanapag Plain.

IV.D.3.f.xiii.   TARAWA

3251. Brown, Richard G.   "Tarawa: Lest We Forget."   MC GAZ,
          64 (November 1980), 46-50.

          Citing some poor decisions and bad luck, the author
          examines the controversial--and bloody--assault at
          Tarawa on November 20, 1943.

3252. Fleming, V. Keith, Jr.   "Hurried Invasion's Grim Toll."   WW
          II, 1 (January 1987), 16-25.

          Here is an account by a Marine historian of the invasion
          of Tarawa.   The narrative emphasizes the ineffectiveness of
          naval gunfire support.   See the copies of paintings of the
          campaign.

3253. Haley, J. Frederick.   "Reconnaissance at Tarawa Atoll."   MC
          GAZ, 64 (November 1980), 51-55.

          Haley took part in a search for a native of Tarawa (Sgt.
          Joseph), who had served in the New Zealand Army in the
          First World War.   The Marines hoped that Joseph could
          provide intelligence information that would assist in the
          planning of the assault on the island.   Haley returned that
          same day to help set up a line of defense which would
          obstruct Japanese travel from north to south.

3254. Hammel, Eric M.   and John E. Lane.   "1st Battalion, 8th

Marines Lands at Tarawa." MC GAZ, 67 (November 1983), 84-91.

During this landing on November 20, 1943, the Japanese held five battalion landing teams to a standstill. The authors tell of the bloody experience of one of those battalions.

3255. Hammel, Eric M. and John E. Lane. 76 Hours: THE INVASION OF TARAWA. New York: Tower Books, 1980. 304 pp.

The authors use many interviews to describe Operation GALVANIC--the assault on Tarawa. In placing emphasis on small unit leadership, Hammel and Lane pay recognition to a significant ingredient in this U.S. victory--an ingredient that is unaccountably missing in many battle histories.

3256. Hammel, Eric M. and John E. Lane. "Third Day on Red Beach." MC GAZ, 54 (November 1970), 22-26.

Here is an account of the landing at Betio on November 23, 1943, and of the heroics of 1st Lt. Alexander Bonneyman, Jr., who was awarded posthumously the Congressional Medal of Honor.

3257. Hannah, Dick. TARAWA: THE TOUGHEST BATTLE IN MARINE CORPS HISTORY. New York: U.S. Camera Publishing, 1944. 126 pp.

Staff Sgt. Hannah (USMC) presents personal narratives and action photos of this famous battle.

3258. Jones, William K. "Tarawa: The Stinking Little Island." MC GAZ, 71 (November 1987), 30-41.

Within 76 hours, Lt. Gen. Jones (USMC) reports over 5,200 Japanese defenders (save for a few Korean prisoners) and over 900 Americans died at Betio. His account summarizes the campaign for the main island on Tarawa Atoll.

3259. Ladd, Dean. "Reliving the Battle: A Return to Tarawa." MC GAZ, 67 (November 1983), 93-98.

Ladd gives a personal account of the first seaborne assault in history launched against a heavily defended island.

3260. Lillibridge, G.D. "Not Forgetting May Be the Only Heroism of the Survivor." AMER HERITAGE, 34 (October 1983), 27-35.

Here is the personal account of a Marine lieutenant of the fighting at Tarawa. His 39-man platoon took 26 casualties.

3261. McKiernan, Patrick L. "Tarawa: The Tide That Failed." USNIP, 88 (February 1962), 38-49.

The invasion of Tarawa (November 20, 1943) depended on the tide being high enough to float LCVPs across the reefs. Although the author feels that the search for accurate data was reasonably successful, on D-Day the landing Marines were caught offshore and had to wade 400-500 yards to get ashore.

3262. Rooney, Andrew A. THE FORTUNES OF WAR: FOUR GREAT BATTLES OF WORLD WAR II. Boston: Little, Brown, 1962. 236 pp.

Three of the battles were in Europe; the fourth was Tarawa. In an interesting summary, Rooney combines a general report with stories about individual participants.

3263. Russ, Martin. LINE OF DEPARTURE: TARAWA. New York: Doubleday, 1975. 206 pp.

Here is a knowledgeable, popular account of the bloody engagement.

3264. Shapiro, Milton T. ASSAULT ON TARAWA. New York: D. McKay, 1981. 58 pp.

Here is a popular account of one of the bloodiest engagements of the war.

3265. Shaw, Henry I., Jr. TARAWA: A LEGEND IS BORN. New York: Ballantine Books, 1969. 160 pp.

The author is a Marine veteran of the war and a civilian historian for the U.S. Marine Corps. He presents an authoritative, brief analysis of this epic struggle. Excellent photographs assist Shaw's account.

3266. Shaw, H.I. "That's My Beach." MC GAZ, 62 (November 1978), 26.

Here is a portrait by Charles H. Waterhouse of the

landing at Betio Island in the Tarawa Atoll.

3267. Sherrod, Robert. "Hawk." MC GAZ, 54 (November 1970),
          27-29.

          This reprint of an April 1944 article recounts the
       heroism of 1st Lt. William Deane Hawkins, who earned the
       Congressional Medal of Honor at Tarawa. Sherrod calls
       "Hawk" the bravest man the author had seen in two years of
       war in the Pacific.

3268. Sherrod, Robert L. TARAWA: THE STORY OF A BATTLE. New
          York: Duell, Sloan and Pearce, 1944. 183 pp.

          The author, a TIME correspondent, landed with the first
       landing wave and spent three days ashore with the Marines.
       The battle marked the opening of the campaign in the
       Central Pacific and the first use of LVTs as assault
       vehicles. This is one of the best of the wartime accounts.

3269. Stockman, James R. TARAWA: THE BATTLE FOR TARAWA.
          Washington, D.C.: USMC, Historical Section, 1947.

          Here is a brief, but authoritative, summary of the
       famous battle.

3270. Wilson, Earl J., Jim G. Lucas, Samuel Shaffer, and C. Peter
          Zurlinden. BETIO BEACHHEAD. New York: G.P. Putnam's
          Sons, 1945. 160 pp.

          The four Marine authors are well qualified to tell this
       story of the battle at Tarawa: they were there. As
       participants in the bloody engagement, the authors wrote a
       realistic narrative of the Marines' performance. The book
       is geared to the general public.

3271. Wukovits, John F. "Even Hell Wouldn't Have It." AMER HIST
          ILLUS, 21 (February 1986), 38-48.

          With extensive quotations from participants he
       interviewed, Wukovits, a free-lance writer, describes the
       amphibious operation at Tarawa.

3272. Werstein, Irving. TARAWA: A BATTLE REPORT. New York:
          Thomas Y. Crowell, 1965. 146 pp.

          In this brief, popular account, Werstein emphasizes the
       tenacious Japanse defense.

IV.D.3.f.xiv. TINIAN

3273. Brown, R.J. "Maneuver Warfare at Tinian--1944." MC GAZ,
         68 (July 1984), 51-55.

        The author characterizes the calculated indirect
approach at Tinian as a classic example of Marine maneuver
warfare at its best.

3273a. Hoffman, Carl W. THE SEIZURE OF TINIAN. Washington, D.C.:
         U.S. Marine Corps, 1951. 169 pp.

        Hoffman, in the USMC Historical Division, writes the
official Marine history of this epic campaign. His work
integrates primary records and many interviews as well as
maps and photographs.

IV.D.3.f.xv. TRUK

3274. Cortesi, Lawrence. PACIFIC HELLFIRE. New York: Kensington
         Books, 1983. 240 pp.

        Cortesi offers a readable report on the naval-air
encounters in the Carolines, especially at Truk.

3275. Lindemann, Klaus P. HAILSTORM OVER TRUK LAGOON. Hong
         Kong: Maruzen Investment, 1982.

        NE

3276. Tillman, Barrett. "Hellcats Over Truk." USNIP, 103 (March
         1977), 63-71.

        Here is a description of an air attack, led by "Killer"
Kane, by carrier-borne Grumman F6F-3 Hellcats against Truk
in February 1944.

IV.D.3.g. BRITISH NAVY

3277. Bartlett, Merrill and Robert William Love, Jr.
         "Anglo-American Naval Diplomacy and the British Pacific
         Fleet, 1942-1945." AMER NEP, (July 1982), 203-216.

        The authors, historians at the Naval Academy, trace the
guarded relations between the two navies. Americans were
reluctant to become deeply involved in the Indian Ocean,
and Admiral King opposed any combined Anglo-American
operations. The turning point came, according to the
authors, in late 1943 (with the success of the ESSEX-class

carrier building program in the United States), when
Americans no longer sought British assistance.

3278. Brown, David. CARRIER OPERATIONS IN WORLD WAR II. Vol. I:
       THE ROYAL NAVY. Vol. II: THE PACIFIC NAVIES, DECEMBER
       1941-FEBRURAY 1943. Annapolis, MD: Naval Institute
       Press, 1974.

       Volume Two of this revised edition describes the Royal
       Navy's role in the Pacific--under the watchful eye of
       Admiral King and his colleagues.

3279. Calnan, Denis. "The Suamarez and the Haguro." USNIP, 94
       (October 1968), 147-150.

       This confrontation in the Strait of Malacca between the
       Japanese heavy cruiser and a British destroyer flotilla
       on May 15-16, 1945, was the last major surface action
       fought by the Royal Navy in the war. The author describes
       the action as a classic model of a torpedo attack at night
       by destroyers.

3280. Grenfell, Russell. MAIN FLEET TO SINGAPORE. London: Faber
       & Faber, 1951. 238 pp.

       The author, a British naval captain in planning, fills
       the book with an unhappy tone. Displeased that the British
       never redeemed the sinking of the REPULSE and PRINCE OF
       WALES, Grenfall calls the episode a turning point in world
       history which marked the end of an epoch: British
       pre-eminence as a sea power. He criticizes Churchill and
       Roosevelt for their roles in this debacle.

3281. Hicken, Victor. "UNDINE and the Airman." AEROSPACE H, 26
       (Spring, March 1979), 40-44.

       In March 1945, Lt. Willard Parker (USN) ditched his
       Corsair aircraft near Okinawa and was rescued by the
       British ship, UNDINE. Parker kept a diary while en route
       to the Philippines aboard the ship. He later died in a
       flight accident.

3282. Horan, H.E. "Sinking the HAGURO." USNIP, 86 (January
       1960), 39-44.

       Rear Admiral Horan, chief of the Naval Staff, New
       Zealand, describes how five British destroyers caught and
       sunk the heavy cruiser HAGURO.

3283.   Kemp, Peter.   ALMS FOR OBLIVION.   London: Cassell, 1961.
            189 pp.

            Kemp describes his adventures as a British naval officer
        in Thailand, Indochina, and the Netherlands East Indies.
        He has an interesting story to tell.

3284.   Kemp, Peter.   KEY TO VICTORY: THE TRIUMPH OF BRITISH
            SEAPOWER IN WORLD WAR II.   Boston: Little, Brown, 1957.
            383 pp.

            By researching records closed at the time, Kemp writes
        this one-volume history with the approval of the Admiralty.
        There is very, very little on the war against Japan.   Lt.
        Cmdr. Kemp was an archivist and historian at the Admiralty
        at the time.

3285.   Marder, Arthur.   OLD FRIENDS, NEW ENEMIES.   New York:
            Oxford University Press, 1981.

            The author is knowledgeable on the topic and writes of
        strategic illusions that beset the Royal British Navy
        before the war.   Analyzing the period 1936-1941, Marder
        demonstrates in particular how the naval leadership
        overestimated its ability to defend the far reaches of the
        British Empire and underestimated the Imperial Japanese
        Navy.

3286.   Tomlinson, H.M.   MALAY WATERS.   London: Hodder and
            Stoughton, 1950.   199 pp.

            The author tells of the ships and men of the Straits
        Steamship company in the struggle against the Japanese.
        The Malayan coasting ships, however, all eventually escaped
        or were sunk.

3287.   Winton, John.   THE FORGOTTEN FLEET: THE BRITISH NAVY IN
            THE PACIFIC, 1944-1945.   New York: Coward-McCann, 1970.
            433 pp.

            Using official histories and many interviews, Winton
        reports on the activities of the East Indies Fleet and the
        British Pacific Fleet.   His narrative unfolds the
        development of amphibious operations and the efforts of the
        British to create secure supply lines to the fleets.
        Despite American resistance, the British, especially
        Churchill, were determined to reestablish an imperial
        presence in the Far East before the end of the war.   The
        book helps correct a neglected subject in the literature of

the war.

3288. Winton, John. SINK THE HAGURO! THE LAST DESTROYER ACTION
       OF THE SECOND WORLD WAR. London: Seeley, Service,
       1979. 182 pp.

       Winton gives a well-researched account of this final
       naval encounter, which occurred in the Strait of Malacca.
       Lord Mountbatten wrote the Foreword. Winton, a British
       military writer, explains the activities of the Royal
       British Navy in detail.

IV.D.3.h. SOVIET NAVY

3289. Khametov, M. "The Pacific Fleet in the War Against Japan."
       SOVIET MIL REV, 8 (August 1975), 6-8.

       The article arises from an interview with Admiral Semyon
       Zakharov, a member of the military council of the Soviet
       Pacific Fleet. The admiral describes the amphibious
       landings in the Manchurian campaign. He stresses the
       importance of the combat experience in Europe to the
       success of the landings in Manchuria.

3290. Lemieux, C.P. "L-16 Sinking--'No Mistake, Just Dirty
       Work.'" USNIP, 89 (June 1963), 118-120.

       Here are the comments and criticisms of a Soviet admiral
       who complains about an article by George M. Lowry on the
       sinking of a Soviet submarine (L-16). The Soviet position,
       unlike Lowry's, is that a U.S. submarine sunk L-16.

3291. Lowry, George M. "L-16--Mystery No Longer." USNIP, 88
       (January 1962), 114-116.

       Lowry suggests that the Soviet submarine L-16 lost in
       October 1942 was sunk by a Japanese submarine--even though
       Japan and the Soviet Union were not at war. He says that
       at the time the Soviets blamed an internal explosion for
       the loss of L-16.

3292. Zakharov, Semyon. "The Pacific Fleet in the War Against
       Japan." SOVIET MIL REV (August 1975), 6-8.

       The article adopts an interview format with Admiral
       Zakharov. His report stresses the surprise blows and
       amphibious assaults of the Soviet Pacific Fleet, despite
       its numerical inferiority to the Japanese Navy.

IV.D.3.i. JAPANESE NAVY

3293. Drake, Hal. "Attack the U.S. With a 5-inch Gun!" NAVY,
       11 (June 1968), 30-35.

       For this article, Drake interviewed Nubukiyo Nambu, who
       shelled the United States mainland from his submarine in
       early 1942. Although the Japanese attacker missed the
       oilfields near Santa Barbara, he did escape unscathed--and
       managed to strike two U.S. ships during his exit.

3294. Dull, Paul S. A BATTLE HISTORY OF THE IMPERIAL JAPANESE
       NAVY, 1941-1945. Annapolis, MD: Naval Institute
       Press, 1978. 402 pp.

       Dull integrates extensive research through Japanese
       official sources in this excellent analysis of the im-
       portant naval (surface) battles of the war. He conducts
       a close examination of key decisions by Japanese leaders.

3295. Evans, David C., ed. THE JAPANESE NAVY IN WORLD WAR II.
       Annapolis, MD: Naval Institute Press, 1986. 400 pp.

       Here are reports and observations by leading Japanese
       naval officers. The collection offers a valuable
       analytical review of the Japanese perspective.

3296. Francillon, Rene J. JAPANESE CARRIER AIR GROUPS,
       1941-1945. London: Osprey Publishing, 1979. 48 pp.

       Here is a synopsis of operations involving the carrier
       air groups of the Japanese Imperial Navy. Francillon
       points out that in 1941, the relative naval air strengths
       of Japan (501 aircraft) and the United States (512
       aircraft) were in rough approximation. Moreover, many
       Japanese airmen had gained combat experience in China.
       Japan sought a decisive engagement with the United States
       and suffered grievous losses, especially among air crews,
       at Midway. The book contains excellent photographs and
       much detailed information. Two new aircraft--NAKAJIMA and
       AICHI--reached the production stage too late to make a
       difference in the war.

3297. Genda, Minoru. "Tactical Planning in the Imperial Japanese
       Navy." NAV WAR COLL REV, 22 (October 1969), 45-50.

       The author explains the evolution from the concept of
       forcing a decisive battle with battleships to one of
       carrier airstrikes at long ranges. General Genda (then

admiral) advocated carrier operations and helped plan the
attack at Pearl Harbor.

3298. Goldingham, C.S. "Japanese Submarines in the Second World
       War." RUSI, 96 (February 1951), 93-100.

       The Japanese committed a fundamental error, according to
       the author, in failing to devise plans for disrupting enemy
       supply lines. Moreover, the Japanese ignored urgings from
       the Germans, until too late, to exploit the advantages of
       submarine warfare. Japan's submarine service eventually
       became a suicide force.

3299. Great Britain. Admiralty. GERMAN, ITALIAN AND JAPANESE
       U-BOAT CASUALTIES DURING THE WAR. London: HMSO, 1946.
       35 pp.

       Incorporating many tables of statistics, this report
       demonstrates the progressively effective anti-submarine
       measures by the Allies.

3300. Hara, Tameichi with Fred Saito and Roger Pineau. JAPANESE
       DESTROYER CAPTAIN. New York: Ballantine Books, 1961.
       312 pp.

       This excellent account by Capt. Hara describes the naval
       war from a Japanese perspective. Saito and Pineau ensure
       that the book can be read easily.

3301. Howarth, Stephen. THE FIGHTING SHIPS OF THE RISING SUN:
       THE IMPERIAL JAPANESE NAVY, 1895-1945. New York:
       Atheneum, 1983.

       The material on World War II is extensive. Photographs,
       technical data, and descriptions about the operational use
       of various classes complement the narrative. Howarth
       writes knowledgeably about his subject.

3302. Ito, Masanori and Roger Pineau. THE END OF THE IMPERIAL
       JAPANESE NAVY. New York: W.W. Norton, 1962. 240 pp.

       The work, originally published in Japan in 1956, is
       translated by Pineau and Andrew Y. Kuroda. Ito provides an
       excellent short history which highlights the views of
       leading Japanese navalists. Ito agrees with postwar
       criticism in Japan that the Navy should not have yielded to
       the narrow-minded Army in the decision for war. In his
       authoritative commentary, see especially the emphasis on
       the Battle of Leyte Gulf and the poor use of Japanese

submarines. The Appendix includes a list of Japanese
warships.

3303. THE JAPANESE NAVY IN WORLD WAR II. Annapolis, MD: U.S.
       Naval Institute Press, 1969. 147 pp.

       Most of these articles, written by Japanese Naval and
       Air officers, appeared in the U. S. NAVAL INSTITUTE
       PROCEEDINGS between 1952 and 1958. Raymond G. O'Connor
       wrote the Introduction. The articles address the period
       from Pearl Harbor to the sinking of the YAMATO. Here is an
       authoritative collection which presents Japanese
       perspectives.

3304. Kiyooka, Chiyono (Sugimoto). BUT THE SHIPS ARE SAILING--
       SAILING. Tokyo: Hokuse Press, 1959. 238 pp.

       Here is a personal account which reveals the views of a
       Japanese sailor.

3305. Kiralfy, Alexander. "Why Japan's Fleet Avoids Action."
       FOR AFFS, 22 (October 1943), 45-58.

       Kiralfy maintains that, unlike the American and British
       emphasis on the navy, the Japanese historically have used
       their naval resources as a "floating wing" of the army.
       The United Nations, according to the author, must be ready
       to keep peace in the Pacific after the war with land, air,
       and amphibious forces rather than just naval forces.

3306. Layton, Edwin T. "24 SENTAI--Japan's Commerce Raiders."
       USNIP, 102 (June 1976), 53-61.

       Layton, an intelligence expert, describes how two
       Japanese ships, part of the force (24 SENTAI) designed to
       attack American lines of communication, narrowly missed
       detecting the task forces under Halsey and Fletcher en
       route to attack the Gilberts and Marshalls.

3307. Mitsuru, Yoshida. REQUIEM FOR THE BATTLESHIP YAMATO.
       Seattle, WA: University of Washington Press, 1985. 152
       pp.

       Here is a report on the fortunes--and worse--of the
       giant warship. Richard H. Minear translated the work.

3308. Morss, Strafford. "IOWA vs. YAMATO--Another View."
       WARSHIP INTL, 23 (No. 2, 1986), 118-135.

The author speculates on the outcome of this imaginary
duel. He sees a draw with both ships so damaged that they
would be unfit for the rest of the war.

3309. O'Connor, Raymond G., ed. THE JAPANESE NAVY IN WORLD WAR
        II. Annapolis, MD: Naval Institute Press, 1986. 2d ed.
        568 pp.

        David C. Evans has edited the second edition. The
volume presents the views of former Japanese naval
officers. O'Connor's original version appeared in 1970.

3310. Reynolds, Clark G. "Submarine Attacks on the Pacific
        Coast, 1942." PAC HR, 33 (May 1962), 183-193.

        Using archival materials and interrogations of Japanese
officers, Reynolds reports on three 1942 attacks by
Japanese submarines against the U.S. mainland. In
February, I-17, commanded by Nishino, and in August and
September, I-25, commanded by Tagami, sought to blow up
U.S. oil storage tanks in California and Oregon. I-25
twice launched a single Zero that dropped incendiary bombs
in Oregon.

3311. Spurr, Russell. A GLORIOUS WAY TO DIE: THE KAMIKAZE
        MISSION OF THE BATTLESHIP YAMOTO, APRIL 1945. New York:
        New Market Press, 1981. 341 pp.

        The author served in the Royal Indian Navy during the
war and later became a correspondent. His account
describes the last attack by the YAMOTO, the largest
battleship ever built. Commissioned in 1941, just as the
Japanese use of carriers at Pearl Harbor indicated the
obsolescence of battleships, the YAMOTO made a suicidal run
at Okinawa, according to Spurr, to save the honor of the
Imperial Japanese Navy by showing that not just the Army
was defending Okinawa. Successive waves of U.S. carrier
aircraft sunk the giant ship. Although Spurr claims to
have used U.S. and Japanese documents, the bibliography
(there are no notes) appears weighted with published
sources.

3312. Tanabe, Yahachi with Joseph D. Harrington. "I Sank the
        YORKTOWN at Midway." USNIP, 89 (May 1963),
        58-65.
        Here is the personal account of the commander of I-168
and his orders to attack that particular U.S. carrier at
Midway.

3313. Thomas, David A. JAPAN'S WAR AT SEA: PEARL HARBOR TO THE
          CORAL SEA. London: A. Deutsch, 1978. 222 pp.

          Here is a well-researched, well-written account of the
          early stages of the war. Thomas presents the Japanese
          perspective of the naval engagements. The book has an
          excellent bibliography.

3314. Thornton, Tim. "Air Power: The Sinking of IJN Battleship
          MUSASHI." WARSHIP, 45 (January 1988), 27-33.

          On October 24, 1944, the large battleship was placed in
          a highly vulnerable situation. Discovered and assaulted by
          U.S. aircraft, the MUSASHI sank after the fifth wave of
          attacks. Despite faults in the ship's design, Thornton
          maintains that the MUSASHI's defenses performed as well as
          could be expected.

3314a. Thornton, Tim. "YAMATO: The Achilles Heel." WARSHIP, 41
          (January 1987), 2-8.

          Here is a discussion of the flaws in the design of the
          big ship, particularly the vulnerability of YAMATO's
          underwater defenses.

3315. Torisu, Kennosuke. "Japanese Submarine Tactics." USNIP,
          87 (February 1961), 78-83.

          The author served as operations staff officer of the
          Japanese Sixth Fleet. He piles praise upon Japanese
          submarine exploits and, in fact, the article carries an
          editorial note which warns that discrepancies exist for
          some of the author's claims.

3316. United States. Department of the Army. Far East Command.
          THE IMPERIAL JAPANESE NAVY IN WORLD WAR II. Tokyo: Far
          East Command, 1952. 279 pp.

          In addition to a naval history, here is a graphic
          presentation of the Japanese naval organization. Prepared
          by the Military History Section in Far East Command's
          Headquarters, the study includes a listing of all ships,
          combatant and non-combatant, lost or damaged in the war.

3317. United States. Joint Army-Navy Assessment Committee.
          JAPANESE NAVAL AND MERCHANT MARINE SHIPPING LOSSES
          DURING WORLD WAR II BY ALL CAUSES. Washington, D.C.:
          GPO, 1947.

This official report indicates the dimensions of the war damage inflicted by Allied attacks on Japanese vessels. The non-combat damage appears higher than normal. Of special interest in determining the war's outcome is the ruinous damage inflicted on Japan's merchant fleet.

3318. Watts, Anthony J. JAPANESE WARSHIPS OF WORLD WAR II. Garden City, NY: Doubleday, 1967. 400 pp.

Watts provides an authoritative report on Japan's combat fleet in the war. He gives technical information about the ships as well as their wartime performances.

3319. Watts, Anthony J. and Brian G. Gordon. THE IMPERIAL JAPANESE NAVY. Garden City, NY: Doubleday, 1971. 529 pp.

Here is a detailed survey, well-written, of Japan's naval history. The authors point out strengths and weaknesses of the navy's performance in the Second World War. Of interest is the material on the origins and use of the human torpedoes (KAITEN).

3320. Webber, Bert. IMPERIAL DRAGON FISH. Medford, OR: Webb Research Group, 1980.

Webber reports on combat activities of some Japanese submarines. See especially his accounts of Japanese probing along the Pacific coast of Canada and the United States.

IV.E. UNIT HISTORIES
        1. GENERAL

3321. United States Adjutant-General's Office, Administrative Services Division. LIST OF UNOFFICIAL UNIT HISTORIES AND UNIT ASSOCIATIONS. Washington, D.C.: GPO, 1947. 91 pp.

3322. United States Army. COMBAT DIVISIONS OF WORLD WAR II. Washington, D.C.: ARMY TIMES, 1946. 96 pp.

This compilation by the Army incorporates diverse information about the units (e.g., nicknames, important dates, commanding officers, insignia, shoulder patches, awards, and commendations).

3323. Dornbusch, C.E., comp. HISTORIES OF AMERICAN ARMY UNITS, WORLD WARS I AND II AND KOREAN CONFLICT, WITH SOME

EARLIER HISTORIES. Washington, D.C.: Dept. of the Army,
1956. 310 pp.

3324. Dornbusch, C.E., comp. HISTORIES PERSONAL NARRATIVES
UNITED STATES ARMY: A CHECKLIST. Cornwallville, NY:
Hope Farm Press, 1967. [2742 items.]

3325. Dornbusch, C.E., comp. UNIT HISTORIES OF THE UNITED STATES
AIR FORCES INCLUDING PRIVATELY PRINTED PERSONAL
NARRATIVES. Hampton Bays, NY: Hampton Books, 1958.

2. NAMED UNITS

AMERICAL DIVISION

3326. Cronin, Francis D. UNDER THE SOUTHERN CROSS: THE SAGA OF
THE AMERICAL DIVISION. Washington, D.C.: Combat Forces
Press, 1951. 444 pp.

AUSTRALIAN COMMANDO SQUADRONS

3327. Bottrell, Arthur Edwin E. CAMEOS OF COMMANDOS: MEMORIES OF
EIGHT AUSTRALIAN COMMANDO SQUADRONS IN NEW GUINEA AND
QUEENSLAND. Daw Park, S.A.: Author, 1971. 309 pp.

AVIATION HISTORY UNIT

3328. Buchanan, A.R., ed. THE NAVY'S AIR WAR; A MISSION
COMPLETED. New York: Harper, 1946. 432 pp.

EASTERN AIR COMMAND

3329. Allied Forces, Eastern Air Command. BURMA AIR VICTORY.
Calcutta, India: Indian Press, 1945.

3330. Omitted.

3331. Unit. EASTERN INDIA AIR DEPOT, INDIA-BURMA AIR SERVICE
COMMAND. Calcutta, India: Calcutta Phototype, 1945.

ENGINEERS, CORPS OF

3332. Coll, Blanch D., Jean E. Keith, and Herbert H. Rosenthal.
THE CORPS OF ENGINEERS: TROOPS AND EQUIPMENT.
Washington, D.C.: Office of the Chief of Military
History, Dept. of the Army, 1958. 622 pp.

3333. Dod, Karl Christian. THE CORPS OF ENGINEERS. Washington,

D.C.: GPO, 1966.   759 pp.

PHOTO INTELLIGENCE

3334. Babington-Smith, Constance.   AIR SPY: THE STORY OF PHOTO
       INTELLIGENCE IN WORLD WAR II.   New York: Harper, 1957.
       266 pp.

SERVICE NEWSPAPERS

3335. Anglo, Michael.   SERVICE NEWSPAPERS OF THE SECOND WORLD
       WAR.   London: Jupiter, 1977.   138 pp.

WAC DETACHMENT, FAR EAST AIR FORCE

3336. Unit.   WACS AND WINGS: THIS BOOK IS PUBLISHED IN AN EFFORT
       TO KEEP ALIVE AND VIVID OUR OVERSEAS EXPERIENCES.
       Manila, PI: 955 Top. Engineers, 1945.   171 pp.

WOMEN'S AUXILIARY SERVICE (BURMA)

3337. Allied Forces, SEAC, Women's Auxiliary Service (Burma).
       THE WASBIES: THE STORY OF THE WOMEN'S AUXILIARY SERVICE
       (BURMA).   London: War Facts Press, 1946.   79 pp.

3. UNITS--NAVAL SHIPS

ARKANSAS

3338. Unit.   U.S.S. ARKANSAS PACIFIC WAR DIARY.   n.p.: Unit,
       1945.   110 pp.

BELLEAU WOOD

3339. Alexander, John W., ed.   "FLIGHT QUARTERS": THE WAR STORY
       OF THE U.S.S. BELLEAU WOOD.   Los Angeles, CA:
       Cole-Holmquist Press, 1946.   192 pp.

BOUNTIFUL

3340. Morris, Jack Clayton.   THE U.S.S. BOUNTIFUL (AH-9) IN THE
       PACIFIC.   [no information available.]   55 pp.

CABOT

3341. Hudson, J. Ed.   THE HISTORY OF THE U.S.S. CABOT (CVL-28): A
       FAST CARRIER IN WORLD WAR II.   Hickory, NC: Author,

1986. 178 pp.

CHENANGO

3342. Unit. THE CHENANIGAN VICTORY EDITION, 1942-1945. Los
Angeles, CA: Kater, 1945. 64 pp.

COLUMBIA

3343. Unit. BATTLE RECORD AND HISTORY OF U.S.S. COLUMBIA,
1942-1945. Baltimore, MD: Horn-Shafer, 1946. 88 pp.

ESSEX

3344. Unit. SAGA OF THE ESSEX. Baton Rouge, LA: Army and Navy
Pictorial, 1946. 141 pp.

HIGHLANDS

3345. Oelschlager, Don L. and S.W. Tuell. THE STORY OF U.S.S.
HIGHLANDS. Santa Monica, CA: Unit, 1946. 35 pp.

IOWA

3346. Regan, Steven D. "'The Mighty I': The USS IOWA Story."
PALIMPSEST, 64 (March-April 1983), 45-57.

LADY

3347. Unit. "This We Remember." U.S. LADY, 10 (July-August
1965), 7-16.

LEXINGTON

3348. Steichen, Edward. THE BLUE GHOST: A PHOTOGRAPHIC LOG AND
PERSONAL NARRATIVE OF THE AIRCRAFT CARRIER U.S.S.
LEXINGTON IN COMBAT OPERATION. New York: Harcourt,
Brace, 1947. 150 pp.

LOUISVILLE

3349. Unit. MAN OF WAR: LOG OF THE UNITED STATES HEAVY CRUISER
LOUISVILLE. Philadelphia, PA: Dunlap, 1946. 212 pp.

MINNEAPOLIS

3350. Luey, Allen T. and H.P. Bruvold. THE "MINNIE"; OR THE WAR
CRUISE OF THE U.S.S. MINNEAPOLIS. Elkhart, IN: 1946.

126 pp.

O'BARNNON

3351.   Horan, James D. ACTION TONIGHT: THE STORY OF THE DESTROYER
        O'BARNNON IN THE PACIFIC. New York: G.P. Putnam, 1945.
        171 pp.

PENSACOLA

3352.   Unit. A HISTORY OF THE U.S.S. PENSACOLA, WITH EMPHASIS ON
        THE YEARS SHE SERVED IN THE PACIFIC AGAINST THE JAPANESE
        DURING WORLD WAR II. San Francisco, CA: Phillips and
        Van Orden, 1946. 108 pp. (Pictorial.)

PONDERA

3353.   Unit. U.S.S. PONDERA (APA-191). San Diego, CA: Frye and
        Smith, 1946. 115 pp.

SAN JUAN

3354.   Hines, Eugene G. THE PANTHER STRIKES: A HISTORY OF THE
        U.S.S. SAN JUAN (CL-54). n.p.: 1946. Unpaged.

SARATOGA

3355.   Richards, Benjamin J. SARA, THE STORY OF THE U.S.S.
        SARATOGA. n.p.: 1945. 173 pp.

SAVO ISLAND

3356.   Benton, Brantford B., ed. BATTLE BABY: A PICTORIAL HISTORY
        OF THE ESCORT CARRIER U.S.S. SAVO ISLAND (CVE 78), BORN
        FEBRUARY 3, 1944, AT ASTORIA, OREGON, LIVED, FOUGHT AND
        RAISED HELL UNTIL V-J DAY. SHE WILL NEVER DIE! Baton
        Rouge, LA: Army and Navy Publishing, 1946. 132 pp.

SEAWOLF

3357.   Frank, Gerold and James D. Horan. U.S.S. SEAWOLF:
        SUBMARINE RAIDER OF THE PACIFIC. New York: G.P. Putnam,
        1945. 197 pp.

SHANNON

3358.   Noyes, John H. SAGA SHANNON: THE STORY OF THE SHANNON (DM
        25) IN ACTION, 1944-1945. Brooklyn, NY: 1948. 80 pp.

TANG

3359. O'Kane, Richard H. CLEAR THE BRIDGE!: THE WAR PATROLS OF
        THE U.S.S. TANG. Chicago, IL: Rand-McNally, 1977. 480
        pp.

VINCENNES

3360. Dorris, Donald H. A LOG OF THE VINCENNES. 1947.

WASHINGTON

3361. Baker, R.W., ed. HISTORY OF THE U.S.S. WASHINGTON,
        1941-1946. New York: Kelly, 1946. 116 pp.

WASP

3362. Ferris, James S., ed. THE AIRCRAFT CARRIER U.S.S. WASP,
        CV-18. Boston, George E. Crosby Co., 1946. 105 pp.

3363. Unit. PREP CHARLIE: A HISTORY OF THE PEREGRINATIONS OF OUR
        FIGHTING LADY U.S.S. WASP WHILE MOTHERING AIR GROUP
        EIGHTY-ONE. New York: WASP and Air Group 81, 1945. 206
        pp.

WEST VIRGINIA

3364. Smith, Myron J., Jr. MOUNTAINEER BATTLEWAGON: U.S.S. WEST
        VIRGINIA (BB-48). Missoula, MT: Pictorial Histories
        Publishing, 1982. 48 pp.

YORKTOWN

3365. Brandt, Robert L. INTO THE WIND: U.S.S. YORKTOWN, WORLD
        WAR II. n.p.: 1946. 160 pp.

3366. Cressman, Robert J. THAT GALLANT SHIP: U.S.S. YORKTOWN
        (CV-5).

3367. Reynolds, Clark G. THE FIGHTING LADY: THE NEW YORKTOWN IN
        THE PACIFIC WAR. Missoula, MT: Pictorial Histories
        Publishing, 1986. 355 pp.

4. NUMBERED UNITS

1st AIR COMMANDO GROUP

3368. Prather, Russell E. EASY INTO BURMA. Dayton, OH:
        Prather, 1977. 91 pp.

1st CAVALRY DIVISION

3369. Wright, Bertram C., comp. THE 1st CAVALRY DIVISION IN
       WORLD WAR II. Tokyo: Toppan, 1947. 245 pp.

3370. Moerler, William T., comp. SOUVENIR BATTLE DIARY. Tokyo:
       1945. 24 pp.

3371. Stewart, Harold D. THE FIRST WAS FIRST. Manila, PI:
       Santo Tomas University Press, 1945. 18 pp.

3372. United States. War Department, Historical Division. THE
       ADMIRALTIES: OPERATIONS OF THE 1st CAVALRY DIVISION.
       Washington, D.C.: GPO, 1946. 151 pp.

1st MARINE DIVISION

3373. Stockman, James R. THE FIRST MARINE DIVISION ON OKINAWA.
       Washington, D. C.: Historical Division, USMC, 1946.

3374. McMillan, George. THE OLD BREED: A HISTORY OF THE FIRST
       MARINE DIVISION IN WORLD WAR II. Washington, D.C.:
       Infantry Journal Press, 1949. 490 pp.

2d ENGINEER SPECIAL BRIGADE

3375. 2d Engineer Special Brigade. HISTORY OF THE SECOND
       ENGINEER SPECIAL BRIGADE, U.S. ARMY, WORLD WAR II.
       Harrisburg, PA: Telegraph Press, 1946. 272 pp.

2d MARINE DIVISION

3376. Johnston, Richard W. FOLLOW ME! THE STORY OF THE SECOND
       MARINE DIVISION IN WORLD WAR II. Toronto: Random House
       of Canada, 1948.

3d AMPHIBIOUS FORCE

3377. United States. Pacific Fleet. THIRD AMPHIBIOUS FORCE:
       COMMAND HISTORY: SOUTH PACIFIC. Washington, D.C.:
       Dept. of the Navy, 1946. 39 pp.

3d ATTACK GROUP

3378. Martin, Charles P., Frederick L. Newmeyer, Jr., Edward
          Mandell, and Harold A. Larsen. THE REAPER'S HARVEST:
          THE STORY OF THE THIRD ATTACK GROUP. Sydney, Aus.:
          Halstead Press, 1945. 120 pp.

3d INFANTRY DIVISION

3379. Taggert, Donald G., ed. HISTORY OF THE THIRD INFANTRY
          DIVISION IN WORLD WAR II. Washington, D.C.: Infantry
          Journal Press, 1947. 574 pp.

4th GENERAL HOSPITAL

3380. FOURTH GENERAL HOSPITAL, UNITED STATES ARMY, 1942-1945.
          Melbourne, Aus.: McLaren, 1945. 59 pp. (Pictorial.)

4th MARINE DIVISION

3381. Proehl, Carl W., ed. THE 4th MARINE DIVISION IN WORLD WAR
          II. Washington, D.C.: Infantry Journal Press, 1947.
          237 pp.

3382. Stott, Frederic A. SAIPAN UNDER FIRE. Andover, MA: 1945.
          26 pp. (1st Battalion, 24 Marines.)

5th AIR FORCE

3383. Birdsall, Steve. FLYING BUCCANEERS: THE ILLUSTRATED STORY
          OF KENNEY'S FIFTH AIR FORCE. New York: 1977. 312 pp.

3384. Bozung, Jack H., ed. THE 5th OVER THE SOUTHWEST PACIFIC.
          Los Angeles, CA: AAF Publications, 1947. 40 pp.

3385. DOWN UNDER SOUTH-WEST PACIFIC AREA. Sydney, Aus.: Angus
          and Robertson, 1945.

3386. "Forgotten Fifth." AERO ALBUM, 5 (No. 2, 1972), 23-25.

3387. Public Information Office and 34th Statistical Control
          Unit. THE FIFTH AIR FORCE IN JAPAN AND KOREA. Nagoya,
          Japan: n.p., 1946. 74 pp.

3388. RABAUL, 2 NOVEMBER 1943, FIFTH AIR FORCE, U.S.A.A.F.

Washington, D.C.: GPO, 1944. 12 pp.

3389. Rust, Kenn C. FIFTH AIR FORCE STORY. Temple City, CA: Historical Aviation Album Publications, 1973. 64 pp.

3390. Stafford, Gene B. ACES OF THE SOUTHWEST PACIFIC. Warren, MI: Squadron/Signal Publications, 1977. 64 pp.

3391. Stinton, Russell L., comp. THE MENACE FROM MORESBY: A PICTORIAL HISTORY OF THE FIFTH AIR FORCE IN WORLD WAR II. San Angelo, TX: Newsfoto, 1950. 109 1.

3392. United States Army Air Forces, Historical Office. HUON PENINSULA CAMPAIGN, OCTOBER 1943 TO FEBRUARY 1944. Washington, D. C.: HQ USAAF, 1947. 280 pp.

3393. United States Army Air Forces, 5th Air Force. THE LUZON PLAN. Luzon, PI: 5th Air Force, 1945. 43 pp.

3394. United States Strategic Bombing Survey. THE FIFTH AIR FORCE IN THE WAR AGAINST JAPAN. Washington, D. C.: GPO, 1947. 114 pp.

3395. Wistrand, R.B. PACIFIC SWEEP. Sydney, Aus.: F.H. Johnston, 1945. 112 pp. (Pictorial.)

5th BOMBARDMENT GROUP, 13th AIR FORCE

3396. Davis, Fred L., Harold Armstrong, and Lt. Mander. THE STORY OF THE FIFTH BOMBARDMENT GROUP (HEAVY). Raleigh, NC: Hillsborough House, 1946.

6th AIR REPAIR UNIT (FLOATING)

3397. THE BUCCANEER, 6th A.R.U.F. Tokyo: Toppan, 1946. 144 pp.

6th ARMORED DIVISION

3398. Hofman, George F. THE SUPER SIXTH: HISTORY OF THE 6th ARMORED DIVISION IN WORLD WAR II AND ITS POST-WAR ASSOCIATION. Louisville, KT: 6th Armored Division Association, 1975. 512 pp.

3399. Omitted.

6th ARMY

3400. Fourteenth Corps, Assistant Chief of Staff, G-2, 6th Army.
      JAPANESE DEFENSE OF CITIES, AS EXEMPLIFIED BY THE BATTLE
      OF MANILA. Manila, PI: 6th Army, 1945. 26 pp.

3401. Niles, Gibson. THE OPERATIONS OF THE ALAMO SCOUTS. Ft.
      Riley, KS: Ground General School, 1949. 23 pp.
      (Reconnaissance Units.)

3402. Pershall, William R. ENEMY ORDER OF BATTLE IN SIXTH ARMY,
      S.W.P.A. Ft. Riley, KS: Ground General School, 1949,
      13 pp.

3403. REPORT OF THE OCCUPATION OF JAPAN: SIXTH UNITED STATES
      ARMY, 22 SEPTEMBER 1945-30 NOVEMBER 1945. n.p.: 1945.
      99 folios.

3404. Schmidt, James N., ed. THE SIXTH ARMY IN ACTION: A PHOTO
      HISTORY, JANUARY 1943-JUNE 1945. Kyoto, Japan: 8th
      Information and Historical Service, 1945. 68 pp.

3405. Sixth Army. THE SIXTH ARMY, HISTORY, MISSION, BIOGRAPHIES
      OF COMMANDERS, DECORATIONS, AWARDS AND CHRONOLOGY. San
      Francisco, CA: Presidio, 1954.

3406. Sixth Army. SIXTH UNITED STATES ARMY REPORT OF THE LEYTE
      OPERATION, 17 OCTOBER 1944-25 DECEMBER 1944. n.p.:
      1945. 282 pp.

3407. Sixth Army. SIXTH UNITED STATES ARMY REPORT OF THE LUZON
      CAMPAIGN, 9 JUNE 1945-30 JUNE 1945. n.p.: 1945. 4
      vols.

3408. Smith, Robert Ross. THE APPROACH TO THE PHILIPPINES.
      Washington, D.C.: Office of the Chief of Military
      History, Dept. of the Army, 1953. 623 pp.

6th INFANTRY DIVISION

3408a. Public Relations Section, 6th Infantry Division. THE 6th
       INFANTRY DIVISION IN WORLD WAR II, 1939-1945.
       Washington, D.C.: Infantry Journal Press, 1947.
       179 pp.

SIXTH MARINE DIVISION

3409. Stockman, James R. THE SIXTH MARINE DIVISION. Washington,
      D.C.: Historical Division, USMC, 1946. 19 pp.

SIXTH RANGER INFANTRY BATTALION

3410. Mucci, H.H. "Rescue at Cabantuan By the 6th Ranger
        Infantry Battalion." INFANTRY J (April 1945), 15-19.

JOINT TASK FORCE SEVEN

3411. White, Clarence H., ed. OPERATION SANDSTONE: THE STORY OF
        JOINT TASK FORCE SEVEN. Washington, D. C.: Infantry
        Journal Press, 1949. 104 pp.

SEVENTH AIR FORCE

3412. United States Army Air Forces, Historical Office.
        OPERATIONAL HISTORY OF THE SEVENTH AIR FORCE, 6 NOVEMBER
        1943 TO 31 JULY 1944. Washington, D. C.: HQ USAAF,
        1945. 248 pp.

SEVENTH AMPHIBIOUS FORCE

3413. United States Navy. 7th Amphibious Force. SEVENTH
        AMPHIBIOUS FORCE, COMMAND HISTORY, 10 JANUARY 1943-23
        DECEMBER 1945. n.p.: 1945. 208 pp.

SEVENTH FIGHTER COMMAND

3414. United States Army Air Forces, Statistical Control Section.
        VII FIGHTER COMMAND ON IWO JIMA: A STATISTICAL SUMMARY.
        Washington, D. C.: USAAF, 1945. 78 pp.

SEVENTH INFANTRY DIVISION

3415. Carroll, E.D. BAYONET: A HISTORY OF THE 7TH INFANTRY
        DIVISION. Tokyo: Toppan, 1951. 50 pp.

3416. Love, Edmund G. THE HOURGLASS: A HISTORY OF THE 7th
        INFANTRY DIVISION IN WORLD WAR II. Washington, D. C.:
        Infantry Journal Press, 1950. 506 pp.

3417. Marshall, S.L.A. ISLAND VICTORY: THE BATTLE OF KWAJALEIN
        ATOLL. Washington, D. C.: Infantry Journal Press,
        1945. 117 pp.

3418. Seventh Infantry Division. 7th INFANTRY DIVISION OPERATION
         REPORT: RYUKUS CAMPAIGN. Washington, D. C.: Dept. of
         the Army, 1945. 106 pp.

EIGHTH ARMY

3419. Eighth Army. THE AMPHIBIOUS EIGHTH. n.p.: AG Printing
         Plant, 1946. 64 pp.

3420. Eighth Army. EIGHTH U.S. ARMY IN JAPAN, 30 AUGUST 1945-1
         MAY 1946. Tokyo: 8th Army Printing Plant, 1946. 11
         pp.

3421. Eighth Army, Commander. REPORTS OF THE COMMANDING GENERAL,
         8th ARMY. Tokyo: Eighth Army, 1945.

3422. Eighth Army, G-3 Section. UP TO NOW! EIGHTH U.S. ARMY.
         Tokyo: Boonjudo Printing Works, 1947. 54 pp.

EIGHTH CAVALRY REGIMENT

3423. Eighth Cavalry Regiment. AMPHIB AT IWO. n.p.: 1945.
         9 pp.

EIGHTH PHOTO SQUADRON

3424. Olsen, Harlan H., ed. THE DIARY OF 8th PHOTO SQUADRON.
         New York: AD Press, 1945. 217 pp.

NINTH ANTI-AIRCRAFT ARTILLERY MISSILE BATTALION

3425. THE HISTORY OF THE NINTH AAA MISSILE BATTALION. San
         Francisco: Unit, 1954.

NINTH FIGHTER SQUADRON

3426. Wandrey, Ralph Henry. FIGHTER PILOT. Mason City, IA:
         Stoyles Press, 1950. 82 pp.

3427. ------. PHOTO HISTORY OF THE 9th FIGHTER SQUADRON, THE
         FLYING KNIGHTS. Sydney, Aus.: Angus and Robertson,
         1944. 85 pp.

NINTH MARINES

3428. Hendrix, Gene. SEMPER FI! THE STORY OF THE NINTH MARINES.
         1959.

VF-9M, MARINE SQUADRON NINE

3429. Barrow, Jess C. WORLD WAR II MARINE FIGHTING SQUADRON
         NINE. Blue Ridge Summit, PA: Tab Books, 1981.

FIGHTER SQUADRON TEN (NAVY)

3430. Johnston, Stanley. GRIM REAPERS. New York: E. P. Dutton,
         1943. 221 pp.

3431. Mersky, Peter B. THE GRIM REAPERS: FIGHTING SQUADRON TEN
         IN WORLD WAR II. Mesa, AZ: Champlin. Fighter Museum
         Press, 1986. 131 pp.

PT SQUADRON TEN

3432. Cave, Hugh B. LONG WERE THE NIGHTS: THE SAGA OF PT
         SQUADRON "X" IN THE SOLOMONS. New York: Dodd, Mead,
         1943. 220 pp.

TENTH AIR FORCE

3433. Rust, Kenn C. TENTH AIR FORCE STORY . . . IN WORLD WAR II.
         Temple City, CA: Historical Aviation Album, 1980. 64
         pp.

3434. United States Army Air Forces, Historical Division. THE
         TENTH AIR FORCE, 1942. Washington, D. C.: USAAF, 1944.
         177 pp.

TENTH MARINES

3435. Buckner, David N. A BRIEF HISTORY OF THE TENTH MARINES.
         Washington, D. C.: USMC, Historical Division, 1981.
         131 pp.

ELEVENTH AIRBORNE DIVISION

3436.   ELEVENTH AIRBORNE DIVISION.   Atlanta, GA: Albert Love
        Enterprises, 1944.   58 1.

3437.   Flanagan, Edward M., Jr.   THE ANGELS: A HISTORY OF THE
        11th AIRBORNE DIVISION, 1943-1946.   Washington, D. C.:
        Infantry Journal Press, 1948.   176 pp.

ELEVENTH BOMBARDMENT GROUP (HEAVY)

3438.   Cleveland, W.M.   PLANES' NAMES.   Portsmouth, NH: Author,
        1977.   100 pp.

3439.   United States Army Air Forces, Office of Assistant Chief of
        Air Staff, Intelligence.   PACIFIC COUNTERBLOW: THE 11th
        BOMBARDMENT GROUP AND THE 67th FIGHTER SQUADRON IN THE
        BATTLE FOR GUADALCANAL: AN INTERIM REPORT.   Washington,
        D. C.:   GPO, 1945.

ELEVENTH BOMBARDMENT SQUADRON (MEDIUM)

3440.   THE RECORD: THE ELEVENTH BOMBARDMENT SQUADRON (M).
        Richmond: 1945.   103 pp.

ELEVENTH CORPS

3441.   Eleventh Corps, Historical Section.   HISTORY OF XI CORPS,
        15 JUNE 1942-15 MARCH 1946.   n.p.:   1946.   124 pp.

3442.   Kutcher, Milton M., ed.   PARADISE PARADE.   Tokyo: Shyubido
        Printing, 1949.   39 pp.

TWELFTH BOMB GROUP

3443.   Wilson, Robert Earl.   THE EARTHQUAKERS, OVERSEAS HISTORY OF
        THE 12th BOMB GROUP.   Tacoma, WA: Dammeier Printing,
        1947.   147 pp.

THIRTEENTH AIR FORCE

3444.   Lippincott, Benjamin E., ed.   FROM FIJI THROUGH THE
        PHILIPPINES WITH THE THIRTEENTH AIR FORCE.   San Angelo,
        TX: Newsfoto Publishing, 1948.   192 pp.

3445.   Rust, Kenn C. and Dana Bell. THIRTEENTH AIR FORCE
        STORY--IN WORLD WAR II. Temple City, CA: Historical
        Aviation Album, 1981.

3446.   United States Army Air Forces, Historical Office. THE
        THIRTEENTH AIR FORCE, MARCH-OCTOBER 1943. Washington,
        D.C.: HQAAF, 1946. 331 pp.

3447.   United States Strategic Bombing Survey, Military Analysis
        Division. THE 13th AIR FORCE IN THE WAR AGAINST JAPAN.
        Washington, D.C.: GPO, 1946.

THIRTEENTH BOMBER COMMAND

3448.   THE STORY OF THE XIII BOMBER COMMAND AT WORK, JANUARY,
        1943-JULY, 1944. n.p.: 1944. 160 pp.

THIRTEENTH BATTALION

3449.   Leonard, Herman M. BURMA MISSION: COMPANY "D," 13th MTN.
        MED. BN. Allentown, PA: 1946. 66 pp.

THIRTEENTH TROOP CARRIER SQUADRON

3450.   Yeomans, William C. et al., eds. TWO YEARS C/O POSTMASTER:
        A PICTORIAL ESSAY. Sydney, Aus.: John Sands, 1946. 46
        pp.

FOURTEENTH AIR FORCE

3451.   Rust, Kenn C. and Stephen Muth. FOURTEENTH AIR FORCE STORY
        IN WORLD WAR II. Temple City, CA: Historical Aviation
        Album, 1977. 64 pp.

3452.   United States Army Air Forces, 14th Air Force. AN
        ORIENTATION BOOKLET AND UNITED STATES MILITARY PERSONNEL
        IN CHINA: BACKGROUND OF THE WAR IN THE AIR, 1943-1944.
        Washington, D.C.: GPO, 1945. 89 pp.

FOURTEENTH ANTIAIRCRAFT COMMAND

3453.   HISTORY OF THE HEADQUARTERS, 14th ANTIAIRCRAFT COMMAND.
        APO San Francisco: Dept. of the Army, 1950. 268 pp.

FOURTEENTH ARMY

3454. Cooper, Raymond. "B" COMPANY, 9th BATTALION, THE BORDER
       REGIMENT, 48 BRIGADE, 17 INDIAN (LIGHT) DIVISION, IV
       CORPS, 14th ARMY, SOUTH EAST ASIA COMMAND. London:
       Dobson, 1978. 152 pp.

FOURTEENTH CORPS

3455. Miller, John. GUADALCANAL: THE FIRST OFFENSIVE.
       Washington, D.C.: Dept. of the Army, 1949. 413 pp.

FIFTEENTH AIR FORCE

3456. Rust, Kenn C. FIFTEENTH AIR FORCE STORY . . . IN WORLD WAR
       II. Temple City, CA: Historical Aviation Album, 1976.
       64 pp.

FIFTEENTH FIGHTER GROUP

3457. Lambert, John W. THE LONE CAMPAIGN. Manhattan, KS:
       Sunflower University Press, 1982. 186 pp.

RADIO COUNTERMEASURES, DIVISION FIFTEEN

3458. Association of Old Crows. RADIO COUNTERMEASURES RCM: A
       BRIEF LOOK AT NDRC DIVISION 15's IMPACT ON RADIO
       COUNTERMEASURES (RCM) ACTIVITIES DURING THE SECOND WORLD
       WAR. Nashua, NH: The Association, 1981.

SEVENTEENTH FIGHTER SQUADRON

3459. Vail, Richard M., ed. STRIKE: THE STORY OF THE FIGHTING
       17th. Sydney, Aus.: Jackson & O'Sullivan, 1945.
       244 pp.

SEVENTEENTH INFANTRY REGIMENT

3460. United States Army, Military Intelligence Division. THE
       CAPTURE OF ATTU. Washington, D.C.: Infantry Journal
       Press, 1944. 144 pp.

SEVENTEENTH PHOTO RECONNAISSANCE SQUADRON

3461. Olsen, Leonard and George A. Shiffert, eds. 17th PHOTO
       RECONNAISSANCE SQUADRON. Los Angeles, CA: Brown and de
       Haven, 1946. 127 pp.

EIGHTEENTH CONSTRUCTION BATTALION

3462. United States Navy. THE ODYSSEY EIGHTEENTH U.S. NAVAL
       CONSTRUCTION BATTALION. San Francisco, CA: 1946. 94
       pp.

NINETEENTH BOMBARDMENT GROUP (VH)

3463. THE HISTORY OF THE 19th BOMBARDMENT GROUP (VH). Union
       City, IN: 1947. 26 folios.

AIR GROUP TWENTY

3464. AIR GROUP 20: AN UNOFFICIAL PORTRAYAL OF CARRIER AIR GROUP
       TWENTY, U.S. PACIFIC FLEET, FROM COMMISSIONING TO
       COMPLETION OF COMBAT CRUISE, 1943-1945. n.p.: 1949.
       84 pp.

TWENTIETH AIR FORCE

3465. Bozung, Jack H., ed. THE 20th OVER JAPAN. Los Angeles,
       CA: AAF Publication, 1946. 40 pp.

3466. MEMORIAL ALBUM, DEDICATED TO THE BOYS OF THE 20th AIR
       FORCE. Los Angeles, CA: Economy Typesetting, 1951.
       134 pp.

3467. Office of Information Services, HQ AAF. HIGHLIGHTS OF THE
       20th AIR FORCE. New York: 1945. 9 pp.

3468. Rust, Kenn C. TWENTIETH AIR FORCE STORY. Temple City, CA:
       Historical Aviation Album, 1979. 64 pp.

TWENTIETH CORPS

3469. THE XX CORPS: ITS HISTORY AND SERVICE IN WORLD WAR II.
       Osaka, Japan: Mainichi, 1951. 406 pp.

TWENTY-SECOND BOMB GROUP

3470.   Brosius, J.W., Jr., ed. THE MARAUDER: A BOOK OF THE 22nd
        BOMB GROUP. Sydney, Aus.: Halstead Press, 1944.
        120 pp.

TWENTY-THIRD FIGHTER GROUP

3471.   Muth, Steve. "23d Fighter Group." AERO ALBUM, 5 (No. 3,
        1972), 2-11.

3472.   United States Air Force, Historical Studies. A BRIEF
        HISTORY OF THE TWENTY-THIRD FIGHTER GROUP: 1941-1955.
        Maxwell AFB, AL: USAF, 1956.

TWENTY-FOURTH INFANTRY DIVISION

3473.   Koons, William B., ed. THE TWENTY-FOURTH INFANTRY
        DIVISION: A BRIEF HISTORY. Kyoto, Japan: Benrido,
        1947. 103 pp.

3474.   Krebs, R.J.H. [pseud. Jan Valtin]. CHILDREN OF YESTERDAY.
        New York: Reader's Press, 1946. 429 pp.

TWENTY-FIFTH CONSTRUCTION BATTALION

3475.   United States Navy, 25th Construction Battalion. PACIFIC
        DIARY. n.p.: Whelan, 1946. 125 pp.

TWENTY-FIFTH DIVISION

3476.   Karolevitz, Robert F. THE TWENTY-FIFTH DIVISION AND WORLD
        WAR II. Baton Rouge, LA: Army & Navy Publishing, 1946.
        207 pp.

3477.   Rutherford, William de Jarnette. 165 DAYS: A STORY OF THE
        25th DIVISION ON LUZON. Manila, PI: 1945. 175 pp.

TWENTY-SIXTH CAVALRY PHILIPPINE SCOUTS

3478.   Chandler, William E. "The 26th Cavalry (PS) Battles to
        Glory." ARMORED CAV J, 56 (March-August 1947), 3 Parts.

3479. Lee, Clark. "The Fighting 26th." In: Karl Detzer, ed.
        THE ARMY READER. Indianapolis, IN: Bobbs-Merrill,
        1943. 469 pp.

TWENTY-SEVENTH AIR DEPOT GROUP

3480. Miles, Charles T., ed. A HISTORY OF THE 27th AIR DEPOT
        GROUP. Sydney, Aus.:   S. T. Leigh, 1945.

TWENTY-SEVENTH ENGINEER CONSTRUCTION BATTALION

3481. GOING HARD: HISTORY OF OVERSEAS WAR SERVICE OF 27th
        ENGINEER CONSTRUCTION BATTALION, DECEMBER 1943-OCTOBER
        1945. Tokyo: 1946. 101 pp.

TWENTY-SEVENTH INFANTRY DIVISION

3482. Love, Edmund G. THE 27th INFANTRY DIVISION IN WORLD WAR
        II. Washington, D.C.:   Infantry Journal Press, 1949.
        685 pp.

TWENTY-SEVENTH TROOP CARRIER SQUADRON

3483. Burwell, Lewis C. "SCRAPBOOK": A PICTORIAL AND HISTORICAL
        RECORD OF THE DEEDS, EXPLOITS, ADVENTURES, TRAVELS, AND
        LIFE OF THE TWENTY-SEVENTH TROOP CARRIER SQUADRON FOR
        THE YEAR 1944. Charlotte, NC: Lassiter Press, 1947.
        130 pp.

THIRTY-FIRST INFANTRY DIVISION

3484. HISTORY OF THE 31st INFANTRY DIVISION IN TRAINING AND IN
        COMBAT, 1940-1945. Baton Rouge, LA: Army & Navy
        Publishing, 1946. 188 pp.

THIRTY-SECOND INFANTRY DIVISION

3485. Blakely, Harold Whittle. THE 32d INFANTRY DIVISION IN
        WORLD WAR II. Madison, WI: 32d Inf. Div. History
        Commission, 1957. 435 pp.

3486. Carlisle, John M. RED ARROW MEN: STORIES ABOUT THE 32d

DIVISION ON THE VILLA VERDE. Detroit, MI:
Arnold-Powers, 1945. 215 pp.

3487. Pokrass, Gregory S. "The Red Arrow Division in New
Guinea." MILWAUKEE HIST, 6 (Autumn 1983), 83-91.

3488. 32d Infantry Division. 13,000 HOURS: COMBAT HISTORY OF
THE 32d INFANTRY DIVISION, WORLD WAR II. Manila, PI:
1945. 30 pp.

THIRTY-THIRD INFANTRY DIVISION

3489. 33d Inf. Div. Historical Committee. THE GOLDEN CROSS: A
HISTORY OF THE 33d INFANTRY DIVISION IN WORLD WAR II.
Washington, D.C.: Infantry Journal Press, 1948.
404 pp.

THIRTY-FOURTH CONSTRUCTION BATTALION

3490. Trice, Frasia Davis. THIRTY-FOURTH UNITED STATES NAVAL
CONSTRUCTION BATTALION. Arlington, VA: L.M. Marx,
1946. 81 pp.

THIRTY-FIFTH PHOTO TECH UNIT

3491. THIRTY-FIFTH PHOTO TECH UNIT. n.p.: 1945. 35 pp.

THIRTY-SEVENTH INFANTRY DIVISION

3492. Frankel, Stanley A. THE 37th INFANTRY DIVISION IN WORLD
WAR II. Washington, D.C.: Infantry Journal Press,
1948. 398 pp.

THIRTY-EIGHTH BOMBARDMENT GROUP

3493. Henry, John. A HISTORY OF THE 38TH BOMBARDMENT GROUP.
Manhattan, KS: MA/AH, 1978.

THIRTY-EIGHTH INFANTRY DIVISION

3494. Hodge, Peyton et al. 38th INFANTRY DIVISION: "AVENGERS OF
BATAAN." Atlanta, GA: Albert Love Enterprises, 1947.
187 pp.

FORTIETH ANTI-AIRCRAFT ARTILLERY BRIGADE

3495.   ON TARGET WITH THE AMERICAN AND AUSTRALIAN ANTI-AIRCRAFT
        BRIGADE IN NEW GUINEA. Sydney, Aus.: Angus &
        Robertson, 1943. 171 pp.

FORTIETH BOMBARDMENT GROUP

3496.   Eustis, Lawrence B., ed. 40th BOMBARDMENT GROUP. San
        Angelo, TX: Newsfoto, 1946. 141 pp. (Pictorial.)

FORTIETH INFANTRY DIVISION

3497.   40th INFANTRY DIVISION: THE YEARS OF WORLD WAR II, 7
        DECEMBER 1941-7 APRIL 1946. Baton Rouge, LA: Army &
        Navy Publishing, 1947. 180 pp.

3498.   HISTORY OF THE 40th INFANTRY DIVISION IN THE PHILIPPINES.
        n.p.: 657th Engineer Topographic Battalion, 1945.
        58 pp.

FORTY-FIRST INFANTRY DIVISION

3499.   McCartney, William F. THE JUNGLEERS: A HISTORY OF THE
        41st INFANTRY DIVISION. Washington, D.C.: Infantry
        Journal Press, 1948. 221 pp.

FORTY-SECOND BOMBARDMENT GROUP

3500.   Smith, Paul T. THE PACIFIC CRUSADERS. Reseda, CA: Mojave
        Books, 1980.

FORTY-SECOND GENERAL HOSPITAL

3501.   THE 42d GENERAL HOSPITAL IN WORLD WAR II. Brisbane, Aus.:
        Truth & Sportsman, 1944. 116 pp.

FORTY-THIRD INFANTRY DIVISION

3502.   Zimmer, Joseph E. THE HISTORY OF THE 43d INFANTRY
        DIVISION, 1941-1945. Baton Rouge, LA: Army & Navy

Publishing, 1946. 86 pp.

FORTY-FOURTH AIR SERVICE GROUP

3503. THE 44th AIR SERVICE GROUP IN INDIA, 1944-1945. n.p.:
       1945. 29 pp.

FORTY-FIFTH GENERAL HOSPITAL

3504. Brashear, Alton D. FROM LEE TO BARI: THE HISTORY OF THE
       FORTY-FIFTH GENERAL HOSPITAL, 1940-1945. Richmond:
       Whittet and Shipperson, 1957. 468 pp.

FORTY-FIFTH INFANTRY DIVISION

3505. Owens, Oscar Lee. A HISTORY OF THE SECOND WORLD WAR: A
       REMEMBRANCE, AN APPRECIATION, AND A MEMORIAL, WITH A
       HISTORICAL SKETCH OF THE FORTY-FIFTH INFANTRY DIVISION.
       Oklahoma City, OK: Victory Publishing, 1946.

FORTY-SEVENTH CONSTRUCTION BATTALION

3506. 47, OUR RECORD: A HISTORY OF THE FORTY-SEVENTH ENGINEER
       CONSTRUCTION BATTALION. Okinawa: Unit, 1945-1946. 2
       vols.

FIFTIETH CONSTRUCTION BATTALION

3507. 50th Construction Battalion. THE FIFTIETH SEABEES. San
       Francisco: Unit, 1945. 108 pp.

FIFTY-THIRD ENGINEER REGIMENT

3508. Amory, Robert, ed. SURF AND SAND: THE SAGA OF THE 53rd
       ENGINEER BOAT AND SHORE REGIMENT AND 1461st ENGINEER
       MAINTENANCE COMPANY, 1942-1945. Andover, MA: 1947.
       408 pp.

FIFTY-FOURTH AIR SERVICE GROUP

3509. Bondurant, John F. THE 54th AIR SERVICE GROUP. New York:
       Kerner Printing, 1976.

FIFTY-FOURTH GENERAL HOSPITAL

3510.   Schaefer, Philip A., ed. 54th IN REVIEW, 1943-1945: A
        RESUME OF THE ACTIVITIES OF THE 54th GENERAL HOSPITAL.
        Tokyo: Dai Nippon, 1945. 54 l.

FIFTY-FOURTH TROOP CARRIER WING

3511.   Jacobson, Richard S. MORESBY TO MANILA VIA TROOP CARRIER.
        Sydney, Aus.: Angus and Robertson, 1945. 278 pp.

FIFTY-SEVENTH CONSTRUCTION BATTALION

3512.   Brodd, Lawrence J., ed. SOPAC SAGA: 57th SEABEES,
        1942-1945. Arlington, VA: L. M. Marx, 1946. 182 pp.

FIFTY-SEVENTH TROOP CARRIER SQUADRON

3513.   Pennock, H. and James M. Healey, eds. SAGA OF THE BISCUIT
        BOMBER. Sydney, Aus.: Halstead Press, 1945. 131 pp.

TASK FORCE 57

3514.   Smith, Peter C. TASK FORCE 57: THE BRITISH PACIFIC FLEET,
        1944-1945. London: Purnell, 1969.

FIFTY-NINTH ANTI-AIRCRAFT ARTILLERY BRIGADE

3515.   Foor, R.H. THE ANTIAIRCRAFT ALBUM OF A.P.O. 244. Los
        Angeles, CA: Times-Mirror, 1945. 22 pp.

SIXTY-FIRST SERVICE SQUADRON

3516.   Morrow, James E. A HISTORICAL RECORD OF DAYS SPENT IN THE
        SOUTH WEST PACIFIC AREA. Ottumwa: Messenger Printing,
        1946. 120 pp.

SIXTY-THIRD INFANTRY DIVISION

3517.   63rd Infantry Division, I & E Section. THIS IS CORREGIDOR!

n.p.: Unit, 1945. 4 l.

SIXTY-FOURTH TROOP CARRIER SQUADRON

3518. 64th T.C. SQ. JUNGLE AIR FORCE. Sydney, Aus.: Waite &
      Bull, 1945. 88 pp.

SIXTY-SEVENTH TROOP CARRIER SQUADRON

3519. Birdzell, Bill C. SKY TRAIN: ADVENTURES OF A TROOP
      CARRIER SQUADRON, FEBRUARY 10, 1943 - AUGUST 10, 1944.
      Sydney, Aus.: Angus and Robertson, 1945. 217 pp.

SIXTY-NINTH COAST ARTILLERY REGIMENT

3520. A NARRATIVE HISTORY OF THE SIXTY-NINTH COAST ARTILLERY
      REGIMENT. Saipan: Unit, 1946. 31 folios.

SIXTY-NINTH ENGINEER REGIMENT

3521. SIXTY-NINTH OVERSEAS, MCMXLII-MCMXLV. Seoul, Korea: 69th
      Engineers, 1945. 24 l.

SEVENTY-THIRD BOMB WING

3522. Davis, Joseph T., ed. THE STORY OF THE 73rd: THE
      UNOFFICIAL HISTORY OF THE 73rd BOMB WING. San Angelo,
      TX: Newsfoto Publishing, 1946. 101 pp.

SEVENTY-SEVENTH INFANTRY DIVISION

3523. Becker, Marshall O. OPERATIONS OF THE 77th INFANTRY
      DIVISION. Ft. Benning, GA: Infantry School, 1948.
      31 pp.

3524. Meyers, Max, ed. OURS TO HOLD IT HIGH: THE HISTORY OF THE
      77th INFANTRY DIVISION IN WORLD WAR II, BY MEN WHO WERE
      THERE. Washington, D.C.: Infantry Journal Press, 1947.
      585 pp.

3525. United States. War Department. General Staff. GUAM:
      OPERATIONS OF THE 77th DIVISION, 21 JULY-10 AUGUST 1944.
      Washington, D.C.: War Dept., 1946. 136 pp.

SEVENTY-EIGHTH INFANTRY DIVISION

3526. United States Army. 78th DIVISION, LIGHTNING. Washington,
       D.C.: Infantry Journal Press, 1973. 301 pp.

EIGHTY-FIRST AIR DEPOT GROUP

3527. Wiesenfeld, W., ed. 81st AIR DEPOT GROUP, 1943-1944.
       Sydney, Aus.: S.T. Leigh, 1944. 204 pp.

EIGHTY-FIRST INFANTRY DIVISION

3528. 81st Wildcat Division, Historical Committee. THE 81st
       INFANTRY WILDCAT DIVISION IN WORLD WAR II. Washington,
       D.C.: Infantry Journal Press, 1948. 324 pp.

CARRIER AIR GROUP 86

3529. Camp, Robert, Jr., ed. CARRIER AIR GROUP 86. n.p.: Unit,
       1946. 280 pp.

EIGHTY-NINTH BOMBARDMENT SQUADRON (LIGHT)

3530. Houha, William F. and Conrad S. Stuntz, eds. ALTITUDE
       MINIMUM: 89th BOMBARDMENT SQUADRON (LIGHT), SOUTHWEST
       PACIFIC. Sydney, Aus.: Angus and Robertson, 1945. 150
       pp.

NINETIETH BOMBARDMENT GROUP (HEAVY)

3531. Alcorn, John S. "The Jolly Rogers at Iron Range and Port
       Moresby." AMER AVN HSJ, 17 (Fall 1972), 178-183.

3532. Segal, Jules F. THE BEST DAMN HEAVY BOMBER UNIT IN THE
       WORLD: THE JOLLY ROGERS, SOUTHWEST PACIFIC, 1942-1944.
       Sydney, Aus.: John Sands, 1944. 112 pp.

NINETIETH INFANTRY DIVISION

3533. McConahey, William M. BATTALION SURGEON. Rochester, MN:
       1966. 201 pp.

NINETY-FIRST FIELD HOSPITAL

3534. Childress, Louise. MABUHAY. Niigata: Aoki Printing,
          1945. 4 pp.

NINETY-FOURTH CONSTRUCTION BATTALION

3535. United States Navy. 94th Construction Battalion. PACIFIC
          DUTY, 94th, AN OFFICIAL STORY OF THE WORK AND TRAVELS OF
          THE 94th NAVAL CONSTRUCTION BATTALION IN TRAINING AND IN
          THE PACIFIC OCEAN AREAS, MAY 1943-JULY 1945. n.p.:
          Unit, 1945. 155 pp.

NINETY-SIXTH INFANTRY DIVISION

3536. Davidson, Orlando R., J. Carl Willems, and Joseph A. Kahl,
          eds. THE DEADEYES. Washington, D.C.: Infantry Journal
          Press, 1947. 310 pp.

NINETY-NINTH INFANTRY BATTALION

3537. Bergen, Howard R. HISTORY OF THE 99th INFANTRY BATTALION.
          n.p.: E. Moestue, 1956. 85 pp.

ONE HUNDREDTH INFANTRY DIVISION

3538. Tanaka, Chester. GO FOR BROKE. Richmond, CA: JACP, 1982.
          172 pp.

PATROL BOMBING SQUADRON 106

3539. Hastings, Robert P. PRIVATEER IN THE COCONUT NAVY. Los
          Angeles, CA: Author, 1946. 105 pp.

3540. Smith, Frank F. "VPB-106: The Wolverators." AERO ALBUM,
          5 (No. 4, 1972), 2-7.

PATROL BOMBING SQUADRON 109

3541. Steele, Theodore M., ed. A PICTORIAL RECORD OF THE COMBAT.
          DUTY OF PATROL BOMBING SQUADRON ONE HUNDRED NINE IN THE

WESTERN PACIFIC, 20 APRIL 1945-15 AUGUST 1945. New
York: General Offset, 1946. Unpaged.

FLEET HOSPITAL 115

3542. Fleet Hospital 115. FLEET HOSPITAL 115, GUAM.
Philadelphia, PA: G. Fein, 1945. 136 pp.

ONE HUNDRED TWENTY-THIRD INFANTRY REGIMENT

3543. Carlson, Stan W., ed. A PICTORIAL HISTORY OF THE 123d
INFANTRY REGIMENT. Minneapolis, MN: Author, 1946.
240 pp.

126 INFANTRY REGIMENT

3544. Modendorp, Alfred. THE MARCH AND OPERATIONS OF ANTITANK
AND CANNON COMPANIES, 126th INFANTRY (32d INFANTRY
DIVISION). Ft. Riley, KS: Ground General School, 1949.
15 pp.

3545. Mohl, John L. OPERATIONS OF A SPECIAL PATROL FROM UNITS OF
THE 2d BATTALION, 126th INFANTRY (32d INFANTRY
DIVISION). Ft. Riley, KS: Ground General School, 1949.
19 pp.

145 INFANTRY REGIMENT

3546. Girardeau, Marvin D. DRAGONS PENINSULA. New York:
Vantage Press, 1967. 141 pp.

148 INFANTRY REGIMENT

3547. Cauthorn, Jesse. 3rd BATTALION, 148th INFANTRY ACTION ON
LUZON. n.p.: Author, 1945. 14 sketches.

158 INFANTRY REGIMENT

3548. Lancaster, Roy. 40th ANNIVERSARY MOBILIZATION OF THE
BUSHMASTERS. Detroit, MI: Lancaster, 1980. 48 l.

3549. ------. THE STORY OF THE BUSHMASTERS. Detroit, MI:
Lancaster, 1945. 48 l.

160 INFANTRY REGIMENT

3550. McCreedy, William Ward. SUNBURST SAGA: A STORY OF THE
       160th INFANTRY REGIMENT. Louisville, KT: Bishop's
       Press, 1947. 214 pp.

161 INFANTRY REGIMENT

3551. Unit. THE STORY OF THE 161st INFANTRY: "THE GOLDEN GATE
       IN FORTY EIGHT." New Caledonia: Unit, 1944. 105 pp.

166 AAA GUN BATTALION

3552. Unit. HISTORY OF THE 166th ANTIAIRCRAFT ARTILLERY GUN
       BATTALION. n.p.: Unit, 1945. 58 pp.

194 TANK BATTALION

3553. Miller, Ernest Brumaghim. BATAAN UNCENSORED. Long
       Prairie, MN: Hart Publishers, 1949. 403 pp.

233 ENGINEER COMBAT BATTALION

3554. Weaver, Victor E. THE 233rd ENGINEER COMBAT BATTALION,
       1943-1945. Washington, D.C.: Infantry Journal Press,
       1947. 160 pp.

305 INFANTRY REGIMENT

3555. 305 Infantry Regiment. SECOND TO NONE! Washington, D. C.:
       Infantry Journal Press, 1949. 255 pp.

307 BOMBARDMENT GROUP

3556. Harvey, Gordon and Eugene K. Hamilton, eds. WE'LL SAY
       GOODBYE: STORY OF THE 307th BOMBARDMENT GROUP (HV),
       13th ARMY AIR FORCES, SOUTH AND SOUTHWEST PACIFIC.
       Sydney, Aus.: F. H. Johnston, 1945. 106 pp.

308 BOMBARDMENT WING

3557. Herring, Robert R., ed. FROM DOBODURA TO OKINAWA: HISTORY
       OF THE 308th BOMBARDMENT WING. San Angelo, TX:
       Newsfoto Publishing, 1946. 98 pp.

312 BOMBARDMENT GROUP

3558. Sturzebecker, Russell L. THE ROARIN' 20'S: A HISTORY OF
       THE 312 BOMBARDMENT GROUP, U.S. ARMY AIR FORCE, WORLD
       WAR II. West Chester, PA: Author, 1976. 301 pp.

319 BOMB GROUP

3559. Corey, Wilfred G. BOMBS ON THE TARGET, 319th BOMB GROUP
       OPERATIONAL HISTORY. Okinawa: 948 Engr. Avn. Topo.
       Co., 1945. 130 pp.

319 HEAVY BOMBARDMENT SQUADRON

3560. Unit. ASTERPERIOUS: 319 HEAVY BOMBARDMENT SQUADRON IN THE
       SOUTH-WEST PACIFIC AREA. Sydney, Aus.: Angus &
       Robertson, 1944. 62 pp.

311 HEAVY BOMBARDMENT SQUADRON

3561. Unit. BOMBS AWAY. Sydney, Aus.: John Sands, 1944. 48
       pp.

330 ENGINEER REGIMENT

3562. Unit. 330th ENGINEER REGT. UNIT HISTORY. Ledo Base,
       Burma: Unit, 1945. 44 folios.

THREE HUNDRED FORTIETH ENGINEER REGIMENT

3563. Unit. 340th ENGINEERS IN THE PACIFIC. Milwaukee, WI:
       Hammersmith-Kortmeyer, 1946. 84 l.

THREE HUNDRED FORTY-SECOND FIGHTER SQUADRON

3564. Russo, Frank G. 342d FIGHTER SQUADRON. Jacksonville, FL:
       Douglas Printing, 1945. 125 pp.

THREE HUNDRED FORTY-SECOND INFANTRY

3565. 342d Infantry, Information and Education Office. A
NARRATIVE HISTORY. Manila, PI: Unit, 1945. 14 folios.

THREE HUNDRED FORTY-SEVENTH FIGHTER GROUP

3566. Ferguson, Robert L. GUADALCANAL--THE ISLAND OF FIRE,
REFLECTIONS OF THE 347th FIGHTER GROUP. Blue Ridge
Summit, PA: Aero, 1987. 456 pp.

THREE HUNDRED FIFTIETH BOMBARDMENT SQUADRON (H)

3567. Sheridan, Jack Walrath. THEY NEVER HAD IT SO GOOD: THE
PERSONAL AND UNOFFICIAL HISTORY OF THE 350th BOMBARDMENT
SQUADRON (H), 100th BOMBARDMENT GROUP (H), USAAF,
1942-1945. San Francisco, CA: Stark-Raith Printing,
1946. 165 pp.

THREE HUNDRED SEVENTY-FOURTH INFANTRY DIVISION

3568. Frankel, Stanley A. THE 374th INFANTRY DIVISION IN WORLD
WAR II. Washington, D.C.: Infantry Journal Press,
1945. 408 pp.

THREE HUNDRED EIGHTY-THIRD ANTI-AIRCRAFT ARTILLERY BATTALION

3569. Bullard, Oral. THE HOT COOP. Waterloo, IA: Author, 1950.
111 pp.

THREE HUNDRED EIGHTY-SEVENTH INFANTRY REGIMENT

3570. Schambs, Paul A., ed. 387th INFANTRY: THE GLOBETROTTERS.
Tokyo: Dai Nippon, 1946. 129 pp.

FOUR HUNDREDTH BOMBARDMENT SQUADRON

3571. Markham, Floyd A. THE BLACK PIRATES, 1942-4. Sydney,
Aus.: John Sands, 1944. 96 pp.

FOUR HUNDRED ELEVENTH ENGINEER BATTALION

3572. Zufelt, Edwin J.H. THE ODYSSEY OF THE 411 ENGINEER BASE
         SHOP BATTALION, 1943-1944. Sheboygan, WI: Diamond
         Print, 1946. 85 pp. (Pictorial.)

FOUR HUNDRED THIRTEENTH FIGHTER GROUP

3573. Tyler, Parker R. FROM SEATTLE TO IE SHIMA WITH THE 413th
         FIGHTER GROUP (SE). Ie Shima: Unit, 1945. 30 pp.

FOUR HUNDRED SEVENTEENTH BOMB GROUP

3574. Green, Eugene L., Paul A. Keane, and Lewis E. Callanan,
         Jr., eds. THE SLAY LANCER: 417th BOMB GROUP. Sydney,
         Aus.: John Sands, 1946. 114 pp.

FOUR HUNDRED FORTY-SECOND REGIMENT

3575. Sakamoto, Lawrence H. HAWAII'S OWN: PICTURE STORY OF THE
         442nd REGIMENT, 100th BATTALION AND INTERPRETERS.
         Honolulu, HI: Honolulu Lithograph, 1946. 103 pp.

FOUR HUNDRED FORTY-THIRD TROOP CARRIER GROUP

3576. BACK LOAD, FEBRUARY 1943-JUNE 1944, 443rd TROOP CARRIER
         GROUP, NEW GUINEA. Sydney, Aus.: Halstead Press, 1945.
         247 pp.

FOUR HUNDRED SIXTY-SECOND BOMBARDMENT GROUP

3577. Oliver, Philip G. HELLBIRD WAR BOOK. n.p.: A. F.
         Kalberger, 1945.

FOUR HUNDRED SIXTY-FIFTH FIGHTER SQUADRON

3578. Saffern, Eugene L. THE JUG. Ashland, OR: Ashland
         Printing, 1946. 72 pp.

FOUR HUNDRED SEVENTY-FOURTH FIGHTER GROUP

3579. Barrett, Joseph P. THE MAVERICK OUTFIT. n.p.: Author,

1966. 140 pp.

FOUR HUNDRED SEVENTY-FIFTH FIGHTER GROUP

3580. Unit. SATAN'S ANGELS: 475th FIGHTER GROUP. Sydney, Aus.:
        Angus and Robertson, 1946. 150 pp.

FOUR HUNDRED NINETY-FOURTH BOMB GROUP

3581. Williams, Jack J. 494th GROUP HISTORY. Philadelphia, PA:
        W.T. Peck, 1947. 147 pp.

FOUR HUNDRED NINETY-SEVENTH BOMB GROUP

3582. Goforth, Pat E., ed. THE LONG HAUL, STORY OF THE 497th
        BOMB GROUP (VH). San Angelo, TX: Newsfoto, 1946, 124
        pp. (Pictorial.)

FOUR HUNDRED NINETY-NINTH BOMB GROUP

3583. Burkett, Prentiss. THE UNOFFICIAL HISTORY OF THE 499th
        BOMB GROUP (VH). Temple City, CA: Historical Aviation
        Album, 1981. 55 pp.

FIVE HUNDREDTH BOMB GROUP

3584. McClure, Glenn E., ed. AN UNOFFICIAL HISTORY OF THE 500th
        BOMB GROUP. Riverside, CA: Roubidoux Printing, 1946.
        100 pp.

FIVE HUNDRED THIRD COMBAT PARACHUTE TEAM

3585. COMBAT OVER CORREGIDOR. n.p.: Unit, 1945. 131 pp.

3586. Raff, Edson Duncan. WE JUMPED TO FIGHT. New York: Eagle
        Books, 1944. 207 pp.

3587. Templeman, Harold. THE RETURN TO CORREGIDOR. New York:
        Strand Press, 1945. 35 1.

FIVE HUNDRED NINTH COMPOSITE GROUP

3588. Ossip, Jerome J. 509th PICTORIAL ALBUM. Chicago, IL:
          Rogers Printing, 1946. 56 pp.

FIVE HUNDRED ELEVENTH PARACHUTE INFANTRY REGIMENT

3589. Faulkner, Lyman S. THE OPERATIONS OF THE 511th PARACHUTE
          INFANTRY REGIMENT. Ft. Riley, KS: Ground General
          School, 1949. 20 pp.

FIVE HUNDRED THIRTEENTH ANTIAIRCRAFT ARTILLERY GUN BATTALION

3590. Unit. 513th IN RETROSPECT: A HISTORICAL RECORD OF THE
          513th ANTIAIRCRAFT ARTILLERY GUN BATTALION. Manila, PI:
          Unit, 1945. 37 1.

FIVE HUNDRED THIRTEENTH BOMBARDMENT SQUADRON

3591. Thomas, Rowan T. BORN IN BATTLE: ROUND THE WORLD
          ADVENTURES OF THE 513th BOMBARDMENT SQUADRON.
          Philadelphia, PA: John C. Winston, 1944.

FIVE HUNDRED THIRTIETH ENGINEER COMPANY

3592. Unit. HISTORY OF THE 530th ENGINEER LIGHT PONTOON COMPANY.
          n.p.: Unit, 1945. 68 1.

FIVE HUNDRED THIRTY-THIRD ENGINEER REGIMENT

3593. Amory, Robert, Jr. and Reuben M. Waterman, eds. SURF AND
          SAND: THE SAGA OF THE 533d ENGINEER BOAT AND SHORE
          REGIMENT AND 1461st ENGINEER MAINTENANCE COMPANY,
          1942-1945. Andover, MA: Andover Press, 1947. 408 pp.

FIVE HUNDRED THIRTY-FOURTH REGIMENT

3594. 534th Boat and Shore Regiment. BOTTOMS UP: THE STORY OF A
          BOAT BATTALION. Nagoya, Japan: Hishigen Printing,
          1946. 37 pp.

FIVE HUNDRED FIFTY-SIXTH ENGINEER BATTALION

3595. Best, Walter E. BATTALION HISTORY: 556th ENGINEER HV.

PON. BATTALION. Tokyo: Toppan Printing, 1945. 32
folios.

607 AIR SQUADRON

3596. Holmes, J. Gordon. "Auxiliaries in the Far East: No. 607
Squadron's Exploits in India and Burma." AIR PICT, 36
(February 1974), 60-61.

SIX HUNDRED ELEVENTH QUARTERMASTER GRAVES REGISTRATION COMPANY

3597. Shomon, Joseph J. CROSSES IN THE WIND. New York:
Stratford House, 1948. 191 pp.

SIX HUNDRED FORTY-EIGHTH ENGINEER TOPOGRAPHIC BATTALION

3598. Unit. STORY OF THE 648th ENGINEER TOPOGRAPHIC BATTALION.
Manila, PI: Unit, 1945. 250 pp.

SEVEN HUNDREDTH MILITARY POLICE COMPANY

3599. 700th MILITARY POLICE COMPANY. Calcutta, India: ESCO
Press, 1945. 9 1.

SEVEN HUNDRED TWENTY-SIXTH BATTALION

3600. Unit. 726th AMPHIBIAN TRACTOR BATTALION: UNIT HISTORY.
Okinawa: Unit, 1945. 18 folios.

EIGHT HUNDRED FIRST ENGINEER AVIATION BATTALION

3601. Unit. 801st ENGR. AV. BN. HISTORY, 1943-1945. Okinawa:
Reproduction Section, 928th Engr. Avn. Regt., 1945. 59
pp.

EIGHT HUNDRED NINTH ENGINEER BATTALION

3602. Shaver, William, ed. A HISTORY OF THE 809th ENGINEER
BATTALION (Heavy Construction). Guam: Navy Dept.-PPO,
1958.

EIGHT HUNDRED SEVENTY-THIRD BOMBARDMENT SQUADRON

3603. Kroesen, Paul, ed. THE 873rd BOMB SQUADRON PRESENTS
      SUPERFORT SAGA: HISTORY OF THE FIRST AND FINEST B-29
      SQUADRON IN THE MARIANAS ISLANDS. Westminster, CA:
      West Orange County Publishing, 1946. 96 pp.

EIGHT HUNDRED EIGHTY-FIFTH BOMBARDMENT SQUADRON

3604. MacCloskey, Monro. SECRET AIR MISSIONS. New York:
      Richard Rosen Press, 1966.

1190 ENGINEER BASE DEPOT

3605. Posey, John T. A UNIT HISTORY: 1190 ENGINEER BASE DEPOT.
      Tokyo: Dai Nippon, 1946. 45 pp.

1281 ENGINEERS

3606. Wallace, William N., ed. MEMOIRS OF THE 1281st ENGINEERS.
      Manila, PI: Manila Daily Press, 1946. 30 pp.

1333 ENGINEERS

3607. Unit. 1333d ENGINEER REGIMENT: EUROPE AND WEST PACIFIC.
      n.p.: Unit, 1945. 7 folios.

1629 ENGINEER CONSTRUCTION BATTALION

3608. Meinke, Robert D., ed. HISTORY OF 1629th ENGINEER
      CONSTRUCTION BATTALION. n.p.: Unit, 1945. 26 1.

3609. United States Army Corps of Engineers. 1629th Construction
      Battalion. ENGINEERING IN THE PACIFIC THEATER WITH THE
      1629th ENGINEER CONSTRUCTION BATTALION. n.p.: Dept. of
      the Army, 1946. 52 pp.

1876 ENGINEER AVIATION BATTALION

3610. PADDOCK, Robert H. A HISTORY OF THE 1876th ENGINEER
      AVIATION BATTALION. Madison, WI: 1947. 147 pp.

1880 ENGINEER AVIATION BATTALION

3611. Rowley, Charles R., ed. SITUATION CBI: THE STORY OF THE
        1880th ENGINEER AVIATION BATTALION IN WORLD WAR II,
        MARCH 1943-DECEMBER 1945. New York: Ziff-Davis
        Publishing, 1946. 237 pp.

1887 ENGINEER AVIATION BATTALION

3612. Unit. THE 1887th ENGINEER AVIATION BATTALION. n.p.:
        927th Engr. Avn. Regt., 1945. 80 pp.

2273 ANTI-AIRCRAFT ARTILLERY COMMAND

3613. Unit. HAWAIIAN ANTIAIRCRAFT ARTILLERY COMMAND SCRAPBOOK.
        Honolulu, HI: Paradise of the Pacific, 1945. 16 l.

2771 ENGINEERS

3614. Unit. WE WENT OVERSEAS. Manila, PI: Unit, 1945. 34 pp.

2773 ENGINEERS

3615. Unit. BRIBANILA ODYSSEY, 1943-1945. n.p.: Unit, 1945.
        69 pp.

5307 COMPOSITE UNIT (PROVISIONAL) [REORGANIZED AUGUST 10, 1944, AS 475 INFANTRY REGIMENT]

3616. Jones, John M. WAR DIARY OF THE 5307th COMPOSITE UNIT
        (PROVISIONAL).

3617. Ogburn, Charlton. THE MARAUDERS. New York: Harper and
        Brothers, 1956. 307 pp.

3618. Stone, James H. "The Marauders and the Microbes."
        INFANTRY J (March 1949), 4-11.

3619. War Department. Historical Division. MERRILL'S MARAUDERS.
        Washington, D.C.: GPO, 1945. 117 pp.

5332 PROVISIONAL BRIGADE [124 CAVALRY REGIMENT AND 475 INFANTRY
      REGIMENT]

3620. Randolph, John H.   MARSMEN IN BURMA. Houston, TX: Author,
       1946. 229 pp.

IV.F. THE SECRET WAR

       1. ESPIONAGE/INTELLIGENCE/CRYPTOGRAPHY (MAGIC)

3621. Allen, Louis. "Japanese Intelligence Systems." J CONTEMP
       HIST, 22 (October 1987), 547-562.

       Allen offers some corrective to what he feels is an
       exaggerated present-day view that Japanese intelligence was
       inferior in most respects to Allied intelligence. He does
       point out, however, that the Japanese budget allocations
       for intelligence averaged about 37% of total military
       spending. His thorough research incorporates Japanese
       sources, especially government documents.

3622. Allied Forces, South West Pacific Area. THE EXPLOITATION
       OF JAPANESE DOCUMENTS. Melbourne, Aus.: Allied Forces,
       SWPA, 1944. 70 pp.

       Here is much praise for the Allied Translator and
       Interpreter Section and its accomplishments.

3623. Bratzell, John F. and Leslie B. Rout, Jr. "Once More:
       Pearl Harbor, Microdots and J. Edgar Hoover." AMER HR,
       88 (October 1983), 953-960.

       Here is a collection of correspondence which relates to
       the criticism of the FBI by the two professors. A letter
       from the FBI argues that the agency sent information
       uncovered from TRICYCLE to army and navy intelligence
       officers. A rejoinder from the two professors refutes this
       contention and maintains the information that was passed
       along was too general to be of any value (e.g., little
       about the questionnaire on Pearl Harbor was included). See
       also the letter from John F. Toland which describes his
       tribulations and frustrations in trying to obtain records
       from the FBI.

3624. Bratzell, John F. and Leslie B. Rout, Jr. "Pearl Harbor,
       Microdots and J. Edgar Hoover." AMER HR, 87 (December
       1982), 1342-1351.

       Using materials released through the Freedom of
       Information Act, the authors report that Hoover withheld
       from the president important prewar information obtained

from the British double agent, TRICYCLE. When talking with Roosevelt, the FBI chief dwelled on the way his agency uncovered a secret microdot (which in fact was voluntarily revealed ahead of time to the FBI), while little of the actual intelligence information, such as a questionnaire seeking detailed data about Pearl Harbor, ever got out of the FBI (let alone reach the president) according to the authors. The article criticizes Hoover's judgment and points out not only inter-agency rivalries within the U.S. government but also poor Anglo-American relations in intelligence (especially between the FBI and MI-6) before the war.

3625. Brugioni, Dino A. "Naval Photo Intel in WWII." USNIP, 113 (June 1987), 45-51.

The author, a CIA expert on the subject, reviews how photo intelligence work contributed to the war effort. Much of the material addresses the Pacific war.

3626. Clark, Ronald. THE MAN WHO BROKE PURPLE. Boston: Little, Brown, 1977.

Here is the story of the behind-the-scenes intelligence work of Col. William F. Friedman. This expert in cryptography helped lead the counter-intelligence attack against Japanese communications.

3627. Cochran, Alexander, Jr. MAGIC DIPLOMATIC SUMMARIES: A CHRONOLOGICAL FINDING AID. New York: Garland, 1982. 160 pp.

A comprehensive research tool, this book lists—by originator and recipient, by subject, and by date of intercept—every daily summary of this precious intelligence information.

3628. Deakin, F. W. and G. R. Storry. THE CASE OF RICHARD SORGE. New York: Harper and Row, 1966. 373 pp.

This excellent work by two British historians cuts through much of the emotion associated with the controversial case. Sorge, a German journalist who was wounded in World War I, worked for the Fourth Bureau of the Red Army. He lived in Tokyo (amidst influential circles) from September 1933 until his arrest in October 1941. Despite Sorge's reliable espionage—he warned, for example, that Germany would attack the Soviet Union and that Japan would not—his information, according to the authors, seems

largely to have been ignored in Moscow. The book contains
a perceptive summary of the international repercussions of
the case.

3629.   Drea, Edward J. "Missing Attentions: Japanese
          Intelligence and the Soviet Invasion of Manchuria." MIL
          AFFS, 48 (April 1984), 66-73.

The Kwantung Army lacked adequate
intelligence.
Drea relates how the Soviet offensive caught the
Japanese unawares. The Kwantung Army lacked adequate
intelligence.

3630.   Farago, Ladislas. THE BROKEN SEAL. New York: Bantam
          Books, 1968 ed. 464 pp.

The author, who served in the Office of Naval
Intelligence during the war, links the development of U.S.
code-breaking activities with the questions surrounding the
surprise attack at Pearl Harbor. Some of the revelations
offered by Farago include Yardley (of "Black Chamber" fame)
selling secrets to Japan, the contribution of "Miss Aggie"
in the breaking of a Japanese admiral's code, and the
non-existence of a "winds code" message. Roosevelt,
according to the author, was not given enough MAGIC
material to form accurate assessments. There are no
villains here, but there are many fools and incompetents in
Farago's interpretation--the book should be read with
caution. A special postscript to this edition announces
that no earlier conclusions have been altered from the
original (1967) version.

3631.   Farago, Ladislas. BURN AFTER READING. New York: Pinnacle
          Books, 1961. 319 pp.

Although concerned largely with other theaters, Farago
describes espionage activities in the war, including
clandestine operations and the theatrics/heroics of leading
personalities. Topics covered which address the war
against Japan are the Sorge ring, the Japanese spy ring in
the United States, U.S. counter-espionage activities,
Donovan and the OSS, and Zacharias' role in influencing the
surrender of Japan. The author's service in naval
intelligence allowed him to play a part in the planning and
psychological warfare of radio broadcasts by Zacharias.

3632.   Fujiwara, Iwaich. F KIKAN! JAPANESE ARMY INTELLIGENCE IN
          SOUTHEAST ASIA DURING WORLD WAR II. London: Heinemann
          Educational, 1983. 338 pp.

The author was a Japanese army officer who wrote these memoirs shortly after the war. Japanese historian Akashi Yoji translated the material.

3633. Gilman, William. THE SPY TRAP. New York: Bartholemew House, 1944. 185 pp.

Gilman, a reporter, writes of some activities of the secret service in Japan.

3634. Haldane, Robert A. THE HIDDEN WAR. New York: St. Martin's Press, 1978. 224 pp.

This book explores some aspects of espionage and cryptography in the war. Haldane, a former British intelligence officer (Home Defense Committee), concentrates most of his attention on Europe. There are, however, separate chapters on the Sorge spy ring and MAGIC (which nonetheless rely heavily on secondary sources). Haldane feels that newly revealed information about the breakthroughs in cryptography may require a rewriting of the history of the war.

3635. Harris, Ruth R. "The 'Magic' Leak of 1941 and Japanese-American Relations." PAC HR, 50 (February 1981), 77-96.

Harris reports that, in May 1941, a German official told a Japanese counterpart that the United States had broken some of Japan's codes. In trying to trace the U.S. leak, she notes that American intelligence services, concerned over lax White House security, actually denied the White House access to MAGIC information from May to November 1941. Of interest is her conclusion that MAGIC, while valuable, had certain limitations.

3636. Hicks, Clifford B. "Tales From the Black Chambers." AMER HERITAGE, 24 (April 1973), 56-61, 95.

There is much information on cryptology here, but little pertains to World War II.

3637. Hinsley, F.H., E.E. Thomas, C.F.G. Ranson, and R.C. Knight. BRITISH INTELLIGENCE IN THE SECOND WORLD WAR. Cambridge, UK: Cambridge University Press, 1979-. 3 vols.

The series is the official history of British intelligence in the war. Most of the attention is on the

war against Germany and Italy, but there is some material
pertinent to this project. The volumes fuel the growing
debate on whether the history of the war needs to be
rewritten.

3638.   Holmes, W.J.   DOUBLE-EDGED SECRETS: U.S. NAVAL
        INTELLIGENCE OPERATIONS IN THE PACIFIC DURING WORLD WAR
        II.   Annapolis, MD: Naval Institute Press, 1979.   232
        pp.

        Holmes worked with the combat intelligence unit in
        Hawaii after having been recalled to active duty in June
        1941.   He offers extremely useful information about the
        intertwining of intelligence and operations.   His informed
        opinions open new perspectives on many diverse subjects,
        such as Kimmel, Turner, Nimitz, Halsey, navy politics, the
        INDIANAPOLIS, and even the Communications Act of 1934.

3639.   Hoover, J. Edgar.   "The Enemy's Masterpiece of Espionage."
        READER'S DIG, 48 (April 1946), 1-17.

        The FBI director boasts of finding a secret microdot,
        which contained important intelligence information, being
        carried by a young "playboy" traveler from the Balkans.
        The article mentions nothing specifically about Pearl
        Harbor (the information on the microdot was a Japanese
        questionnaire about activities there), nor does it indicate
        that the "playboy" was actually the double agent "TRICYCLE"
        (whom the British sent to Hoover and whose cover was nearly
        blown by bungling FBI agents).

3640.   Horner, D.M.   "Special Intelligence in the South West
        Pacific Area in World War II."   AUS OUTLOOK, 32
        (December 1978), 310-327.

        Major Horner (Royal Australian Infantry) integrates
        ULTRA revelations with SWPA operations.   His research
        includes archival materials and private collections,
        especially the Blamey Papers.   The article attributes much
        of the Allied successes in SWPA to cryptoanalysis.   Of
        interest is an example of an ULTRA message in the Appendix.

3641.   Hyde, H. Montgomery.   ROOM 3603:   THE STORY OF THE BRITISH
        INTELLIGENCE CENTER IN NEW YORK DURING WORLD WAR II.
        New York: Farrar, Strauss, 1962.   257 pp.

        The main attention is on the war against Germany and
        Italy. The one chapter on Asia focuses on the role of
        Velvalee Dickinson.   She ran a doll shop in New York City

and was the only agent in the United States who continued
conveying intelligence to Japan after the attack at Pearl
Harbor. The author served in Sir William Stephenson's
organization and used Stephenson's papers in preparing this
study. Of interest is Hyde's revelation that Stephenson
learned directly from Roosevelt (through the president's
son, James) of the U.S. decision not to present the
original proposal for a modus vivendi to Japan on November
26, 1941.

3642. Ind, Allison. ALLIED INTELLIGENCE BUREAU: OUR SECRET
        WEAPON IN THE WAR AGAINST JAPAN. New York: David
        McKay, 1958. 305 pp.

        Ind served in Charles Willoughby's G-2 (Intelligence)
        Section of MacArthur's General Headquarters. He assembles
        an interesting collection of anecdotes and personalities.

3643. "Japanese Naval Intelligence." ONI REV, 1 (July 1946),
        36-40.

        NE

3644. Johns, Philip. WITHIN TWO CLOAKS. London: Kimber, 1979.
        216 pp.

        The author served as head of the British Secret
        Intelligence Service station in Portugal during the war.
        He received the report from Popov (TRICYCLE), via the
        infamous microdot, about German requests in August 1941 for
        information on Pearl Harbor. Johns downplays the
        significance of the episode and points out that TRICYCLE
        was still regarded with suspicion by the British in 1941.

3645. Johnson, Chalmers. AN INSTANCE OF TREASON: OZAKI HOTSUMI
        AND THE SORGE SPY RING. Stanford, CA: Stanford
        University Press, 1964. 278 pp.

        This reliable report is based largely on Japanese
        sources. Johnson explores the Japanese connections in the
        famed Sorge spy activities on behalf of the Soviet Union.

3646. Kahn, David. THE CODE-BREAKERS: THE STORY OF SECRET
        WRITING. New York: Macmillan, 1967. 1164 pp.

        Kahn, a journalist and amateur cryptologist, gives an
        overview of the history of writing in code. There is a
        large section devoted to the war; see especially Kahn's
        description of John F. Kennedy's adventures and the

assassination of Yamamoto. Kahn generally portrays the
code war in the Pacific in terms of U.S. successes and
Japanese incompetence (trusting too much their native
language). Drawing connections among music, math, and
cryptoanalysis, Kahn argues that cryptology provided the
most important source of secret intelligence in World War
II and helped shorten the war.

3647.   Kahn, David. "Code Breaking in World Wars I and II." HIST
        J, 23 (September 1980), 617-639.

        In this useful summary, Kahn corrects errors in his
        book, THE CODEBREAKERS. He claims that the PURPLE solution
        did not help much in the Pacific war because diplomats
        played a minor role. PURPLE, however, did prove valuable
        in the European war, according to Kahn, as a source in
        revealing Hitler's plans.

3648.   Kahn, David. "Cryptology and the Origins of Spread
        Spectrum." IEE SPECTRUM, 21 (September 1984), 70-80.

        This article reveals the development by mid-1943 of an
        unbreakable scrambler (SIGSALY) for secure communications
        between Roosevelt and Churchill. Earlier versions of the
        scrambler insured a certain amount of privacy but could not
        withstand determined, studied attacks (which is why
        Marshall would not use one on December 7, 1941).

3649.   Kahn, David. "World War II History: The Biggest Hole."
        MIL AFFS, 39 (April 1975), 74-76.

        Although concerned primarily with the war in Europe,
        this article, in calling for more work on intelligence
        operations, has some relevance to the war against Japan.

3650.   Kirkpatrick, Lyman B., Jr. CAPTAINS WITHOUT EYES:
        INTELLIGENCE FAILURES IN WORLD WAR II. New York:
        Macmillan, 1969. 303 pp.

        The author, a CIA and former Army intelligence officer,
        discusses mainly European affairs. His only reference to
        the war in the Pacific addresses the attack at Pearl
        Harbor. He criticizes U.S. inefficiency and organizational
        deficiencies.

3651.   Kluckhohn, Frank. "Heidelberg to Madrid--The Story of
        General Willoughby." REPORTER, 7 (August 19, 1952),
        25-30.

Here is a critical account of Willoughby's career. The
author observed the general's work in intelligence and
calls it sound, but Kluckhohn does not minimize the
miscalculations by Willoughby that other observers have
identified. Of special interest are the passages about the
secret historical project of MacArthur's command and
Willoughby's feuds with Whitney and Thorpe.

3652. Layton, Edwin T. "AND I WAS THERE." New York: William
       Morrow, 1985. 596 pp.

Here is the posthumous memoir of the intelligence
officer for the U.S. Pacific Fleet. Roger Pineau and John
Costello completed the project after Layton's death.
Layton provided daily intelligence reports directly to
Nimitz. The author credits the unsung work of Joseph J.
Rochefort who helped the United States win the Battle of
Midway by breaking a key Japanese code. The book reveals
much of the inner workings of naval intelligence in the
Pacific.

3653. Lewin, Ronald. THE AMERICAN MAGIC: CODES, CIPHERS AND THE
       DEFEAT OF JAPAN. New York: Penguin Books, 1983. 332
       pp.

Lewin offers a well-researched, well-written view of
the way Americans penetrated Japanese codes. Analyzing the
two major controversies from the beginning and end of the
war, Lewin feels that (a) leadership in Washington did not
have sufficient information to foresee precisely the threat
to Pearl Harbor, but Kimmel and Short, while not receiving
the important information that was available, do bear some
responsibility for Hawaii's unpreparedness; and (b) the dec
(MAGIC revelations, for instance, never indicated internal
divisions within Japan) but appears based in part on the
desire to impress the Soviet Union (MAGIC revealed the
aggressive intentions harbored in Moscow). Lewin sharply
criticizes the obsessive concern with security in
Washington that blocked the development of a realistic
organization for disseminating effectively the important
information gleaned from MAGIC.

3654. Lewin, Ronald. THE OTHER ULTRA. London: Hutchinson,
       1982. 332 pp.

Lewin has written authoritatively about Ultra in Europe.
In this book he turns his expert attention to the use of
the "other Ultra" in the war against Japan.

3655. Lewin, Ronald. "A Signal-Intelligence War." J CONTEMP
       HIST, 16 (July 1981), 501-512.

       Lewin maintains that signal-intelligence is the dominant
       theme of the war, so sweeping in fact that the revelations
       concerning SIGINT make necessary the rewriting of the
       history of the war.

3656. London. Imperial War Museum. BIBLIOGRAPHY OF ESPIONAGE
       AND TREASON IN WORLD WAR I AND II. London: Imperial
       War Museum, 1955. 21 pp.

       This reference is interesting but contains little on the
       war against Japan.

3657. MacDonald, Elizabeth P. UNDERCOVER GIRL. New York:
       Macmillan, 1947. 305 pp.

       The author was working as a correspondent in 1943 when
       she joined the Morale Operations Branch of the OSS in China
       and Southeast Asia. The book is well written and contains
       much humor. MacDonald complains that the Morale Operations
       staff was always moving and taking the phones with them.
       Her work in subversive morale activities acquainted her
       with novel devices such as phosphorous-coated foxes, snake-
       call whistles and Indonesian love curry. She recalls the
       need for a special decoding team to read the handwriting of
       OSS Chief William Donovan.

3658. McLachlin, Donald. ROOM 39: A STUDY IN NAVAL
       INTELLIGENCE. New York: Atheneum, 1968. 438 pp.

       The author served on the wartime staff of the British
       Director of Naval Intelligence. Incorporating a variety of
       sources, McLachlin discusses the policies and procedures of
       British Intelligence operations.

3659. THE "MAGIC" BACKGROUND OF PEARL HARBOR. Washington, D. C.:
       GPO, 1978. 5 vols.

       Here is an extensive amount of material gained through
       MAGIC prior to the start of the war. The intercepted
       Japanese messages contribute to the continuing debate about
       U.S. policies and the origins of the war.

3660. Masterman, John C. THE DOUBLE CROSS SYSTEM IN THE WAR OF
       1939-1945. New Haven, CT: Yale University Press, 1972.
       203 pp.

The book reproduces a secret report that Masterman compiled as a member of MI5. The permission of the Prime Minister was required to publish this material. Although most of the report deals with the war against Germany (and British efforts to convert German spies into double agents), there is some information about TRICYCLE, a British-controlled agent who in August 1941 discovered some information about Pearl Harbor. Retrospect, however, may have induced Masterman to exaggerate the importance of this episode.

3661. Mathams, R.J. SUB ROSA: MEMOIRS OF AN AUSTRALIAN
      INTELLIGENCE ANALYST. Winchester, MA: Allen & Unwin,
      1983.

      NE

3662. Merillat, Herbert Christian. "The 'Ultra Weapon' at
      Guadalcanal." MC GAZ, 66 (September 1982), 44-49.

      The author concludes that the ULTRA intelligence information was not vital to the victory at Guadalcanal but did help. Interestingly, Merillat asserts that Vandegrift, who was outside the Ultra distribution channels, learned through an accidental slip in security about the forthcoming Japanese attack.

3663. Mersky, Peter. "My Dad Made Models." USNIP, 113 (June
      1987), 51-53.

      The author describes how his father contributed to the war effort by building recognition models (mock ups) for U.S. bomber pilots who were preparing for the final invasion of Japan. The article includes directions on how to construct these models.

3664. Phillips, Claire and Myron B. Goldsmith. MANILA ESCAPE.
      Portland, OR: Binfords and Mort, 1947. 226 pp.

      Phillips, the notorious "HIGHPOCKETS," operated a nightclub in Manila for Japanese officers. Arranging false papers and feeding information to the guerrillas, the author flirted with disaster and admits to taking needless risks. Some of the tales stretch the limits of credibility.

3665. Popov, Dusko. SPY-COUNTERSPY. London: Weidenfeld and
      Nicholson, 1974. 278 pp.

In this autobiography of the double (British-German)
agent, TRICYCLE, Popov tells how the Germans pressed him
for information about the U.S. naval facility at Pearl
Harbor. Using microdots to transmit the information, the
author reports on his clash with J. Edgar Hoover. Perhaps
retrospect and the events of December 7, 1941, have caused
the significance of this episode to be exaggerated.

3666. Prange, Gordon W., Donald M. Goldstein, and Katherine V.
       Dillon. TARGET TOKYO: THE STORY OF THE SORGE SPY RING.
       New York: McGraw-Hill, 1984. 595 pp.

       With excellent portrayals of the leading personalities,
       the authors compose a detailed account of the sensational
       spy story.

3667. READER'S DIGEST. SECRETS AND SPIES: BEHIND-THE-SCENES
       STORIES OF WORLD WAR II. Pleasantville, NY: Reader's
       Digest Association, 1964. 576 pp.

       For articles on the war against Japan in this
       interesting collection, see especially John G. Hubbell,
       "The Great Manila Bay Silver Operation," and Thomas M.
       Johnson, "Joey's Quiet War."

3668. Russell, Francis. THE SECRET WAR. Alexandria, VA:
       Time-Life Books, 1981. 208 pp.

       Here is a popular account of the successes and failures
       in cryptography during the war.

3669. Sayers, Michael and Albert E. Kahn. SABOTAGE! THE SECRET
       WAR AGAINST AMERICA. New York: Harper, 1942. 266 pp.

       The two reporters uncover methods and plans of enemy
       agents operating in the United States.

3670. Seth, Ronald. SECRET SERVANTS. New York: Farrar, Strauss
       and Cudahy, 1957. 278 pp.

       Seth presents a history of Japanese espionage. Of
       interest is the material relating to preparations for the
       attack at Pearl Harbor.

3671. Singer, Kurt D. SPIES AND TRAITORS OF WORLD WAR II. New
       York: Prentice-Hall, 1945. 295 pp.

       Here is an interesting, well-written summary of selected
       spy stories. See especially the report on the Kuehn family

and their signals to Japan on the eve of the war.

3672. Singer, Kurt D. SPY STORIES FROM ASIA. New York: W.
       Funk, 1955. 336 pp.

       Singer narrows his focus and updates his previous work
       on the general subject. Not all the stories are taken from
       World War II, but all make interesting reading.

3672a. Spector, Ronald H., ed. LISTENING TO THE ENEMY.
       Wilmington, DE: Scholarly Resources, 1987. 368 pp.

       Here is an excellent collection of documents which touch on
       the role of intelligence work in communications. The
       collection is devoted entirely to the war against Japan.
       Spector highlights the impact of intelligence discoveries
       on military operations.

3673. Stanley, Roy M., II. WORLD WAR II PHOTO INTELLIGENCE. New
       York: Charles Scribner's Sons, 1981. 374 pp.

       Col. Stanley (USAF) served in photo intelligence. He
       describes the skills and techniques needed to obtain and
       analyze photo intelligence. With over 500 photos, he
       presents a unique view of the war. Reference information
       on units and aircraft appears in the Appendix.

3674. Thorpe, Elliott R. EAST WIND, RAIN: THE INTIMATE ACCOUNT
       OF AN INTELLIGENCE OFFICER IN THE PACIFIC, 1939-1949.
       Boston: Gambit, 1969. 307 pp.

       Thorpe claims that he notified Washington in "very early
       December" 1941 about forthcoming Japanese attacks in
       Hawaii, the Philippines, Malaya, and Thailand. His sources
       were Dutch cryptanalysts in Java who had intercepted
       Japanese diplomatic messages. Despite this important point
       in a continuing controversy, and despite the implications
       of the title (the term "East Wind, Rain" forms a keystone
       in this historical debate), Thorpe devotes only a few
       pages--with very little explanation--to the
       intelligence-gathering process immediately prior to the
       attack at Pearl Harbor. The remaining portions of the
       book, which touch on the war and his experiences as
       assistant chief of staff, G-2, USAFFE, reveal Thorpe's
       anecdotes and opinions.

3675. United States. Army Air Forces. IMPACT. New York: James
       Parton, 1984. 8 vols.

Here are reproductions of a confidential intelligence magazine, IMPACT. Thirty of the issues cover the period from April 1943 to September 1945. There are almost 4,000 photographs, most of which are black and white.

3676. United States. Congress. House of Representatives.
        HEARINGS ON AMERICAN ASPECTS OF THE RICHARD SORGE SPY
        CASE. Washington, D.C.: GPO, 1951.

The testimony provides some new, mostly peripheral, information about German-Japanese-Russian intelligence work before the war.

3677. Van Der Rhoer, Edward. DEADLY MAGIC; A PERSONAL ACCOUNT
        OF COMMUNICATIONS INTELLIGENCE IN WORLD WAR II IN THE
        PACIFIC. New York: Charles Scribner's Sons, 1978. 194
        pp.

Here is a first-hand report on the workings--and the effectiveness--of the cryptologists in the war against Japan. The author's revelations open a previously hidden (and therefore unappreciated) list of war heroes: those, like Van Der Rhoer, in intelligence, who intercepted and analyzed enemy signals.

3678. Wallace, David, comp. THE MAGIC DOCUMENTS: SUMMARIES AND
        TRANSCRIPTS OF THE TOP-SECRET DIPLOMATIC COMMUNICATIONS
        OF JAPAN, 1938-1945: A SUBJECT AND NAME INDEX.
        Frederick, MD: University Publications of America,
        1982.

Here is a useful aid for wading through the voluminous amount of material that was intercepted through MAGIC. Wallace's work helps the researcher to separate the germane from the clutter.

3679. Wasserman, Benno. "The Failure of Intelligence
        Prediction." POL STUD, 8 (June 1960), 156-169.

Wasserman seeks to develop a theoretical model that will analyze why intelligence sometimes fails to predict foreseeable events. Accepting the commonly held notion that Pearl Harbor was an intelligence failure because of faulty evaluation rather than lack of available information, the author emphasizes the importance of evaluating intelligence from foreign countries in terms of how they view the situation. For him, a first step to success lies in the honest recognition of policy and intelligence shortcomings.

3680. West, Nigel. A THREAD OF DECEIT: ESPIONAGE MYTHS OF WORLD
       WAR II. New York: Random House, 1985. 166 pp.

       The author is a military historian who has written on
       the British secret service and security service. This book
       includes material on the roles of Sir John Masterman and
       the British agent TRICYCLE with regard to intelligence
       information on the Japanese attack at Pearl Harbor.
       Explicitly reflecting John Toland's contention that
       Roosevelt knew beforehand about the attack, West claims
       that the whole microdot episode involving British double
       agent Dusko Popov is overblown because of the distortions
       of retrospect.

3681. Wilhelm, Maria. THE MAN WHO WATCHED THE RISING SUN. New
       York: Franklin Watts, 1967. 238 pp.

       Here is a profile of Ellis M. Zacharias. Wilhelm
       describes the activities of Zacharias and his colleagues in
       Navy intelligence trying to interpret--and divine?--
       Japanese intentions. There is a useful explanation of
       MAGIC and its invaluable revelations.

3682. Williams, Robert C. KLAUS FUCHS, ATOM SPY. Cambridge, MA:
       Harvard University Press, 1987. 267 pp.

       Williams describes the extent of the Soviet spy network
       that sought to gain control of British Intelligence. Of
       interest are Fuch's activities at Los Alamos and Harwell.

3683. Willoughby, Charles A. SHANGHAI CONSPIRACY: THE SORGE SPY
       RING. New York: E.P. Dutton, 1952.

       Gen. Willoughby, a trained historian, reports on the
       Soviet-inspired espionage scheme in Japan. Writing in the
       midst of the Cold War, Willoughby seems to overemphasize
       the nefarious implications of international Soviet
       espionage.

3684. Winks, Robin W. CLOAK AND GOWN: SCHOLARS IN THE SECRET
       WAR, 1939-1961. New York: William Morrow, 1987. 607
       pp.

       Here is a close examination of the ethical issues which
       surround the academic community's association with
       government intelligence agencies. A Yale professor, Winks
       establishes the close connection between Yale scholars and
       the OSS (later CIA). His study is particularly effective

in identifying the wartime work of academics in the
Research and Analysis Branch of the OSS. It is ironic that
at the same time these R & A memoranda have been used
extensively by scholars researching the war, growing voices
in academia have criticized such unholy alliances with the
government. Of interest is Winks' insistence that the
wartime scholars performed their services with only the
best of intentions.

3685. Yardley, Herbert O. THE CHINESE BLACK CHAMBER. Boston:
        Houghton Mifflin, 1983. 225 pp.

        From 1938 to 1940, the author performed intelligence
        services for the Chinese government. Yardley, an American
        expert in cryptology, had been instrumental in establishing
        highly secret U.S. activities in the field ("the Black
        Chamber") shortly after the First World War. This
        personal account reveals his achievements and frustrations
        with the Chinese.

3686. Zacharias, Ellis M. SECRET MISSIONS: THE STORY OF AN
        INTELLIGENCE OFFICER. New York: G.P. Putnam's Sons,
        1947. 433 pp.

        Zacharias describes his wartime activities for Navy
        intelligence. Of special interest are his accounts of the
        start and end of the war with Japan. With important
        contacts in Japan, especially among naval officers,
        Zacharias played a role in hastening the surrender of
        Japan. His broadcasts, which provided certain reassurances
        about the limits of unconditional surrender, received
        attention at the highest levels in Tokyo. The book
        contains a useful account of the development of the U.S.
        Navy's intelligence organization during the war.

IV.F.2. Special Operations

3687. Cady, John F. CONTACTS WITH BURMA, 1935-1949: A PERSONAL
        ACCOUNT. Athens, OH: Ohio University Press, 1983. 117
        pp.

        Cady has a long and close connection with Burma—as a
        history teacher in Rangoon and as a specialist for the OSS
        and the State Department. He claims that his support for
        indigenous aspirations eventually caused him to fall from
        grace (and resign) at the State Department.

3688. Cruickshank, Charles. SOE IN THE FAR EAST. Oxford:
        Oxford University Press, 1983. 285 pp.

With access to government documents (some of which
remain closed), the author traces in detail the development
of the British Special Operations Executive in the Far
East.

3689.   Dunlop, Richard. BEHIND JAPANESE LINES: WITH THE OSS IN
          BURMA. Chicago: Rand-McNally, 1979. 448 pp.

Dunlop spent three years in Burma with OSS Detachment
101. The unit, which included loyal natives such as the
Kachin headhunters, engaged in espionage and guerrilla
warfare. Their enemies included weretigers as well as
Japanese. Many of the men he describes seem to take on
superhuman qualities. "Wild Bill" Donovan--complete with
lethal "L" pill--went behind the lines to see 101 at work.
Of interest is Dunlop's account of the unit arranging the
bombing of the jail at Lashio to kill suffering (tortured)
comrades.

3690.   Gilchrist, Sir Andrew. BANGKOK TOP SECRET. London:
          Hutchinson, 1970. 231 pp.

Gilchrist provides a personal account of his experiences
with the secret Force 196 in Siam.

3691.   Harrington, Joseph D. YANKEE SAMURAI: THE SECRET ROLE OF
          NISEI IN AMERICA'S PACIFIC VICTORY. Detroit, MI:
          Pettigrew Enterprises, 1979. 383 pp.

Here is a story about Japanese-American language
specialists who played an important role in the Pacific war
even though they rarely fired a shot in anger. The author
argues that the NISEI suffered unfair treatment, and some
justification for his criticism may be found in the
promotion records up to 1945. The book lacks a clear
organization and frequently lapses into mere anecdotal
"asides" drawn from various dates and locations. There is
some useful/interesting material, such as the NISEI
manufacturing "captured battleflags" and posing with their
comrades as "captured enemy soldiers," but the author's
strong feelings about the topic interfere with his
presentation.

3692.   Harrisson, Tom. WORLD WITHIN. London: Cresset Press,
          1959. 349 pp.

The author describes his work in Borneo with a secret
(British-Australian-Dutch) unit. His narrative focuses on

his life with the Kelabit people deep in the interior.

3693. Peers, William R. and Dean Brelis. BEHIND THE BURMA ROAD.
Boston: Little, Brown, 1963. 246 pp.

Maj. Gen. Peers commanded OSS Detachment 101; Brelis, a
novelist, served in that unit. Their report describes the
unit's activities: conducting guerrilla operations behind
enemy lines, gathering intelligence throughout Burma, and
rescuing downed Allied airmen.

3694. Reit, Seymour. MASQUERADE: THE AMAZING CAMOUFLAGE
DECEPTIONS OF WORLD WAR II. New York: New American
Library, 1980. 263 pp.

Here are some fascinating and ingenious devices and
deceptions. Most of the material, however, is taken from
the European Theater.

3695. Trenowden, Ian. OPERATIONS MOST SECRET: SOE--THE MALAYAN
THEATRE. London: Kimber, 1978. 231 pp.

Here is a knowledgeable report on the secret work of SOE
in Southeast Asia. Unfortunately, the unexpected surrender
of Japan did not enable some of these activities to come to
fruition. Of special interest is the attitude of
Mountbatten about these special operations.

3696. Yoseloff, Thomas. [pseud. Thomas Young.] DOGS FOR
DEMOCRACY: THE STORY OF AMERICA'S CANINE HEROES IN THE
GLOBAL WAR. New York: B. Ackerman, 1944.

NE

IV.F.2.a. Coastwatchers

3697. Andresen, Andy. [On Coastwatchers.] PAC ISLANDS MONTHLY
(January 1944).

NE

3698. Baird, Leonard J., Benjamin Katz, John D. Sweeney, and John
L. Chew. "Nights to Remember." SHIPMATE, 38
(July-August 1975), 25-26.

The central theme in these four related stories is the
role of the Coastwatchers. Baird and Chew survived the
sinking of the HELENA on July 6, 1943. Sweeney helped pick
up some of the survivors, and Katz participated in the

rescue of some survivor-fugitives on the Japanese-held
island of Vella Lavella.

3699. Bowers, Richard H. "Bougainville Rendezvous." USNIP, 78
        (July 1952), 763-768.

        In this personal account, Bowers tells how his submarine
rescued Coastwatchers being chased by Japanese troops. In
his account of this mission, the author describes several
other unanticipated passengers coming aboard too!

3700. Dalrymple-Hay, Ken. Pt. I: "Unhappy Story of Singapore in
        the Solomons." PAC ISLANDS MONTHLY, 42 (July 1971),
        53-55. Pt. II: "Behind the Japanese Lines on Wartime
        Guadalcanal." Ibid., 42 (August 1971), 71-77.

        Here is a posthumous personal account of a Coastwatcher.
The author, a manager of a rubber plantation on Guadalcanal
when the war broke out, eventually took to the hills to
become a Coastwatcher. Of interest is his claim that the
Battle of Tenaru was influenced by his warnings. He took a
commission (RANVR) so that he would not be shot as a spy if
he were captured.

3701. Evans, Reg. [On Coastwatchers.] PAC ISLANDS MONTHLY
        (January 1961).

        NE

3702. Feldt, Eric A. THE COASTWATCHERS. New York: Oxford
        University Press, 1946. 264 pp.

        Feldt describes a small group which he helped organize
to report enemy ship movements in parts of Australia and
New Guinea, Papua, and the Solomons. Despite the author's
eforts, the Coastwatchers (code named FERDINAND) have not
received the attention they deserve.

3703. Hoagland, Beth. "Personality." WWII, 1 (July 1986),
        12-14, 58-60.

        Here is a profile of Coastwatcher Franklin Nash (U.S.
Army corporal) on Kolombangara in the Solomons.

3704. Horton, D.C. FIRE OVER THE ISLANDS. Sydney, Aus:. Reed,
        1970.

        Here is an excellent report, as yet unpublished in the
United States, on the Coastwatchers of the Solomons.

Horton has accumulated much information, including some
interview material, on these rugged individuals.

3705. Lord, Walter. LONELY VIGIL: COASTWATCHERS OF THE
        SOLOMONS. New York: Viking, 1977. 272 pp.

        The Coastwatch Service originated in the years following
the First World War. In 1939, Eric Feldt began organizing
and strengthening this network. With the code name
"FERDINAND" (no fighting, just watching and reporting), the
Coastwatchers, according to Lord, helped save Guadalcanal.
The author tells of the colorful figures--Ken Hay (who,
with an Electrolux refrigerator on Gold Ridge, insisted
that his butter always be served on ice), Reg Evans (who
was instrumental in rescuing John F. Kennedy and his crew),
and even a Coastwatching family (husband, wife, and baby
son)-- and their courageous activities. Lord makes clear
that, between the Coastwatchers and the Japanese troops,
downed enemy airmen could not expect to enjoy the
protections of the Geneva Convention. The book benefits
from the assistance and reports of former Coastwatchers.

3706. Murray, Mary. HUNTED. Adelaide, Aus.: Rigby, 1967. 240
        pp.

        Here is the personal account of one of the famed
Coastwatchers. Murray performed her service on the island
of New Ireland.

3707. Whipple, Chandler. CODE WORD FERDINAND. New York: G.P.
        Putnam's Sons, 1971. 160 pp.

        Here is a popular account of the accomplishments of the
famed Coastwatchers in the Solomons.

3708. Wright, Malcolm. IF I DIE. Melbourne, Aus.: Lansdowne,
        1965.

        Here is a personal account by one of the famed
Coastwatchers. The narrative is of interest as an
authoritative description of not only the dangers of the
job but also the colorful personalities who did the job.

IV.F.2.b. SACO/China

3709. Caldwell, Oliver J. A SECRET WAR: AMERICANS IN CHINA,
        1944-1945. Carbondale, IL: Southern Illinois
        University Press, 1972. 218 pp.

The author spent one year in western China attached to
the OSS. His sympathies flowed first to and then away from
Chiang Kai-shek, but Caldwell says he never supported the
Chinese Communists. In late 1944, according to the author,
the United States could have encouraged centrist democrats
to form a new government in China. The book follows
Caldwell's experiences as a double agent (U.S. and Tai Li's
secret police) and then a triple agent (to help the three
secret societies, TRIAD). The documentation is sparse.

3710.   Miles, Milton E. A DIFFERENT KIND OF WAR. Garden City,
          NY: Doubleday, 1967. 629 pp.

Miles and the U.S. Navy helped create the Sino-American
Cooperative Organization (SACO), combined guerrilla forces
in China. The story of this so-called "Rice Paddy Navy" is
taken from a manuscript written by Miles before he died.
Miles describes the obstruction of SACO's activities by the
U.S. Army, the State Department, and the O.S.S. because of
his loose association with the notorious head of the secret
police, Tai Li. In addition, he complains that
misunderstanding of the Chinese Communists by American
leaders contributed to the postwar disaster in China. Of
special interest is his report of how the U.S. Navy became
involved in the China Theater. Apparently, after Pearl
Harbor the Chinese offered guerrillas to work with the U.S.
Army; when the Army refused, the Chinese received a more
cordial welcome to their offer from the U.S. Navy.

3711.   Schaller, Michael. "SACO! The United States Navy's Secret
          War in China." PAC HR, 44 (November 1975), 527-553.

Schaller tells of the military aid, training, and
political support to the Nationalist government in China by
the U.S. Navy's secret operations group, the Sino-American
Cooperation Association (SACO). By exposing the work of
the organization, Schaller concludes that U.S. involvement
in Chinese politics was much greater than previously
thought. Of interest is the author's analysis of why SACO
proved a bitter experience for the Chinese Communists.

3712.   Stratton, Roy O. THE ARMY-NAVY GAME. Falmouth, MA:
          Volta, 1977. 264 pp.

In this well-researched report on the Sino-American
Cooperation Organization (SACO), Stratton calls his work a
case study in how not to conduct inter-service and
international relations. He started his investigation with
questions about the U.S. Navy setting up bases in the Gobi

Desert, northern India, and along the China Coast. Only
Milton Miles knew the full story, according to Stratton.
The author traces Miles' secret plans and clandestine
contacts (including Gen. Tai Li, the head of the Chinese
secret service) in building up SACO, which encompassed
everything from gathering routine weather-geographical
information to reporting enemy movements and rescuing
downed aircrews. Stratton calls attention to the
effectiveness of SACO operations.

3713.   Stratton, Roy O. SACO, THE RICE PADDY NAVY.
         Pleasantville, NY: C.S. Palmer Publishing Co., 1950.
         408 pp.

         Here is one of the first accounts of SACO and its
         activities in China. Milton Miles played a key role in the
         development of this organization. He convinced Admiral
         King of the usefulness of such a group, and by May 1942,
         Miles was in China getting the project started.

IV.F.3.   Commando Operations (General)

3714.   Ladd, James. COMMANDOS AND RANGERS OF WORLD WAR II. New
         York: St. Martin's Press, 1978. 288 pp.

         Here is a broad description of commando-ranger
         activities in all theaters. See especially the material on
         these British and U.S. forces in the Burma campaign.

3715.   Thomas, David. "The Importance of Commando Operations in
         Modern Warfare, 1939-1982." J CONTEMP HIST, 18 (October
         1983), 689-717.

         With regard to the war against Japan, Thomas says that
         the British commando organization had to rise from the
         disorganization of the defeat in Burma. He concludes that
         the importance of these commando units has been
         overestimated in the postwar years and that the chief
         lessons have escaped present-day senior officers.

IV.G.   Resistance/Collaboration
1.   General

3716.   Brown, Robert M. V. and Donald Permenter. "I SOLEMNLY
         SWEAR": THE STORY OF A G.I. NAMED BROWN. New York:
         Vantage Press, 1957. 203 pp.

         Brown gives an account of his close association with
         Sgt. John David Proovo, who was later tried for treason and

collaboration. The tone throughout is extremely defensive.

3717.   Conroy, F. Hilary. "Thoughts on Collaboration." PEACE +
        CHANGE, 1 (Fall 1972), 43-46.

        Conroy argues that the term collaboration as used in
        Europe did not have the same connotations in Asia,
        principally because of the colonial context. Asian leaders
        who aided Japan thought of themselves as "nationalist
        politicos," not traitors. For Conroy, these included
        people like Wang Ching-Wei, Jose Laurel, Subhas Chandra
        Bose, and Achmed Sukarno. Conroy takes special note of the
        fact that only one internee--"Tokyo Rose"-- was convicted
        as a collaborator.

3718.   Nurick, Lester and Roger W. Barrett. "Legality of
        Guerrilla Forces Under the Laws of War." AMER J INTL
        LAW, 40 (July 1946), 563-583.

        The authors, serving in the U.S. Army's Judge Advocate
        General's office, can find no consistent precedents that
        define, identify, or recognize military forces that claim
        to be operating in behalf of a legitimate government.
        Consequently, they argue that the legal status of
        resistance movements must be examined on a case-by-case
        base.

3719.   Ride, Edwin. BAAG: HONG KONG RESISTANCE, 1942-1945.
        Oxford: Oxford University Press, 1981. 347 pp.

        Here is a detailed report on the activities of the
        British Secret Service's underground resistance in Hong
        Kong. "BAAG" identifies the British Army Aid Group in the
        Japanese-occupied colony.

3720.   Trainin, I.P. "Questions of Guerrilla Warfare in the Law
        of War." AMER J INTL LAW, 40 (July 1946), 534-562.

        Originally published in Russian (and directed to
        European affairs), this article directs attention to the
        role of the resistance in supporting the general principles
        of democracy and self-determination. Guerrilla warfare,
        the author says, is a form of people's war and, therefore,
        a just and legal war.

IV.G.2. Philippine Islands

3721.   Abaya, Hernando J. BETRAYAL IN THE PHILIPPINES. New York:

Wynn, 1946. 272 pp.

This Filipino author reveals his strong liberal
sentiment. Unable or unwilling to offer evidence to
substantiate his charges, Abaya makes sweeping accusations
of widespread collaboration in the Philippines. This book
generated some controversy at the time but is now of
limited value.

3722. Allied Forces, South West Pacific Area. GUERRILLA
        RESISTANCE MOVEMENTS IN THE PHILIPPINES. Melbourne,
        Aus.: Allied Press, SWPA, 1945. 143 pp.

Here is a laudatory piece of cotton in which everyone
did a "good show."

3723. Ancheta, Celedonio A. "Josefa Llanes Escoda and Her Agents
        in World War II." PHILIPPINE HIST ASSOC: HIST BULL, 12
        (Nos. 1-4, 1968), 267-274.

NE

3724. Aurillo, Francisco, Sr. "The Leyte Guerrilla Movement."
        LEYTE-SAMAR STUD, 17 (No. 2, 1983), 135-153.

Here is an assessment of the guerrilla personalities and
their work. When the Leyte Provisional Regiment under Lt.
Col. Theodore Cornell surrendered to the Japanese, many
Filipinos in the unit fled to continue the resistance.
Aurillo mentions many of the these guerrillas, including
their differences. He particularly praises the efforts of
the Women's Auxiliary Service and the importance of
underground papers (e.g., Voice of the People, the Bugle,
KARATUNG, and Pioneer).

3725. Baclagon, Uldarico S. FILIPINO HEROES OF WORLD WAR II.
        Manila, PI: Argo, 1980. 344 pp.

The knowledgeable author extends praise to the Filipinos
who served with distinction against the Japanese.

3726. Baclagon, Uldarico S. THE PHILIPPINE RESISTANCE MOVEMENT
        AGAINST JAPAN, 10 DECEMBER 1941-14 JUNE 1945. Manila,
        PI: Munoz Press, 1966. 538 pp.

Here is a good overview of the resistance. Baclagon
examines the regional activities of various units.
Especially valuable is his treatment of the Hukbalahap,
which draws heavily on the account of an early Huk leader,

Luis M. Taruc.

3727. Baclagon, Uldarico S. THEY SERVED WITH HONOR. Quezon
       City, PI: DM Press, 1965. 304 pp.

       Col. Backlagon writes of Filipino heroes of the
       resistance.

3728. Bell, H. Roy (Mrs.). TRAILS TO FREEDOM. Dumaguete, PI:
       Silliman University, 1958. 64 pp.

       Mrs. Bell recounts the troubles she and her husband
       encountered in keeping up their morale while hiding from
       the Japanese. Also in this pamphlet is her husband's
       report on the guerrilla movement on Negros Island and the
       contribution of Silliman University to the war effort.

3729. Blackburn, Donald. "War Within a War." CONFLICT, 7 (No. 2,
       1987), 129-153

       Blackburn recounts his experiences in building a
       military organization and command structure while serving
       three years with the Filipino resistance. He describes his
       guerilla unit's improvised supply lines, jungle
       communications, interaction with the natives, combat
       operations, psychological warfare, and the preparations for
       the invasion of the returning Allied forces.

3730. Clarke, Hugh V. LAST STOP NAGASAKI. Winchester, MA: G.
       Allen & Unwin, 1984. 135 pp.

       Clarke provides an account of his experiences as an
       Australian POW in Japan.

3731. Cruz, Roman A. THE HERO WHO WAS "NOT." Kalibo, PI: 1969.

       NE

3732. Doromal, Jose D., ed. THE WAR IN PANAY: A DOCUMENTARY
       HISTORY OF THE RESISTANCE MOVEMENT IN PANAY DURING WORLD
       WAR II. Manila: Diamond Historical Publications, 1952.
       313 pp.

       The collection offers useful information on the
       guerrilla organizations--and efforts--in Panay.

3733. Dyess, William E. THE DYESS STORY. New York: G. P.
       Putnam's Sons, 1944. 182 pp.

This book captured public attention when it appeared.
Dyess gives a first-hand account of the surrender at Bataan
and the infamous Death March. As a POW at Davio, he
managed to escape to Australia with eleven others. His
report, especially the accent on Japanese brutality, was
among the first of such accounts to be made public. Dyess
died in a 1944 air training accident.

3734.   Haggerty, J. Edward. GUERRILLA PADRE IN MINDANAO. New
        York: Longmans, Green, 1946. 257 pp.

Here is the personal story of an American Catholic
priest in the Philippines who decided to stay even after
the Japanese occupation. The narrative centers on his
assistance to the guerrilla forces. He describes the daily
drudgery as well as the excitement.

3735.   Hall, E.R. "Bon." THE BURMA-THAILAND RAILWAY OF DEATH.
        Armadale, Victoria, Aus.: Graphic Books, 1981. 295 pp.

The Australian author gives a lengthy report on his
experiences as a POW working on the notorious railway. The
horrible conditions and the personal suffering, no matter
how often told, continue to hold the reader's interest.

3736.   Harkins, Philip. BLACKBURN'S HEADHUNTERS. New York: W.
        W. Norton and Co., 1955. 336 pp.

This book is based on the experiences of First
Lieutenant Donald Blackburn as a guerrilla in the
Philippines. Blackburn and a few other Americans escaped
through Japanese lines and thereafter operated mainly in
the Cagayan Valley with the assistance of the fierce
Igorots (reputed to be headhunters). Apart from its
considerable value as a commentary on guerrilla operations,
the book provides a view of life among the tribes in remote
areas of the Philippines (including the dominant influence
of animal sacrifice ceremonies).

3737.   Hart, Donn V. "Filipino Resistance on Negros, 1942-1945."
        J SEA HIST, 5 (March 1964), 101-125.

Hart provides an excellent survey of the literature in
this bibliographic essay.

3738.   Hawkins, Jack. NEVER SAY DIE. Philadelphia, PA:
        Dorrance, 1961. 196 pp.

This Marine officer recounts his escape from the

Japanese in the Philippines and his experience with the
guerrilla forces.

3739. Hunt, Ray C. and Bernard Norling. BEHIND JAPANESE LINES.
       Lexington, KT: University Press of Kentucky, 1986. 258
       pp.

       Hunt, a USAAF sergeant, tells of his escape during the
       Death March from Bataan. After natives helped restore his
       health, Hunt took part in guerrilla activities.

3740. Ingham, Travis. RENDEZVOUS BY SUBMARINE: THE STORY OF
       CHARLES PARSONS AND THE GUERRILLA SOLDIERS IN THE
       PHILIPPINES. Garden City, NY: Doubleday, Doran, 1945.
       255 pp.

       This tribute to Parsons contains some needless puffery.
       His record in providing leadership, planning, and
       organization to the resistance forces stands on its own
       merits. Carlos P. Romulo says as much in the Foreword.

3741. James W. "Guerrilla." LEATHERNECK (January 1945).

       NE

3742. Kalaw, Maximo M. "Filipino Opposition to the Japanese."
       PAC AFFS, 18 (December 1945), 340-345.

       The author, a Filipino professor and member of Osmena's
       War Cabinet, describes briefly the organization and
       character of the guerrilla resistance. Calling the
       resistance a "spontaneous protest" by the common man, he
       notes that tactics used against the Japanese were similar
       to those Filipinos had used earlier in the century against
       Americans.

3743. Keats, John. THEY FOUGHT ALONE. Philadelphia, PA: J. B.
       Lippincott, 1963. 425 pp.

       This is a highly imaginative war biography of Wendell
       Fertig. With the U.S. Army engineers on Mindanao, he led
       Filipino guerrilla forces after the U.S. surrender. Keats
       provides excellent descriptions of the Philippines.

3744. Lear, Elmer. THE JAPANESE OCCUPATION OF THE PHILIPPINES:
       LEYTE, 1941-1945. Ithaca, NY: Cornell Univeristy,
       1961.

       Here is an excellent study of one segment of guerrilla

operations in the Philippines.

3745. Lichauco, Marcial P. "DEAR MOTHER PUTNAM": A DIARY OF THE
       WAR IN THE PHILIPPINES. Washington, D.C.: 1949. 219
       pp.

       The author tells of the aid he and his wife provided to
       the guerrillas. This is one of the best accounts of life
       under the Japanese occupation.

3746. Manikan, Gamaliel L. GUERRILLA WARFARE ON PANAY ISLAND IN
       THE PHILIPPINES. Quezon City, PI: Bustamante Press,
       1977. 756 pp.

       NE

3747. Marquez, Adalia. BLOOD ON THE RISING SUN. New York:
       DeTanko Publishers, 1957. 253 pp.

       The author served in the resistance as part of
       MacArthur's Counter-Intelligence Corps. Her narrative
       describes life in Manila under the Japanese occupation.

3748. Mellnick, Stephen M. PHILIPPINE DIARY, 1939-1945. New
       York: Van Nostrand Reinhold, 1969. 316 pp.

       Here is the personal account of an artillery officer who
       participated in both the defense and recapture of the
       Philippine Islands. Mellnick commanded a battery of scouts
       and was captured at Corregidor. After his escape, he
       provided one of the first eyewitness reports on conditions
       in the Philippines and Japanese treatment of their
       prisoners. From intelligence work in Australia, Mellnick
       returned to the Philippines to participate in guerrilla
       operations. He served as an American representative at the
       independence ceremonies in the Philippines on July 4, 1946.

3749. Nuval, Leonardo Q. NE'ER SHALL INVADERS. Quezon City, PI:
       Diliman, 1972. 172 pp.

       Here is a narrative which describes the Filipino
       resistance against the Japanese.

3750. Panlilo, Yay. THE CRUCIBLE: AN AUTOBIOGRAPHY. New York:
       Macmillan, 1950. 348 pp.

       In this unusual story, the author, a Filipino
       newspaperwoman, tells of her life in the resistance with
       Marking's guerrillas. "Marking" was, in fact, Marcos V.

Agustin. The author and Marking fell in love, and the two
guerrillas married.

3751. Philmus, Harriette. BRAVE GIRLS: THE STORY OF GIRL SCOUTS
       AND GIRL GUIDES IN THE UNDERGROUND. New York: Girl
       Scouts National Organization, 1947. 115 pp.

       This collection includes the story of Josefa Escoda, who
was killed (with her husband) after being caught smuggling
medicine to American POWs in the Philippines.

3752. St. John, Joseph F. LEYTE CALLING. New York: Vanguard
       Press, 1945. 220 pp.

       The author was with the 14th Bombardment Group in the
first Flying Fortresses that arrived in the Philippines.
When the war began, he soon evacuated Clark Field for
Mindanao. His account describes how he was stranded at
Mindanao and covers his experiences with guerrilla forces
until the Allied return in 1944. In telling his story to
Howard Handleman, Lt. St. John (USAAF) perpetuates the myth
of Colin Kelly crashing his aircraft into a Japanese ship.
Although Kelly was in his unit, St. John probably never
knew the real story of Kelly's death.

3753. Sanchez, Jorge A. "Guerrilla Warfare in Luzon." ARMORED
       CAV J, 56 (July-August 1947), 26-29.

       By mid-1943, over a dozen guerrilla bands operated
independently of each other on Luzon. The U.S. Sixth Army
extended recognition only to those guerrillas who were
attached to U.S. Army units. Sanchez feels that much
injustice arose because of this policy.

3754. Segura, Manuel F. TABUNAN. Cebu City, PI: Segura
       Publications, 1975. 354 pp.

       The title is taken from the name of the headquarters for
the Cebu guerrillas. The author, a colonel in the
resistance, includes many quotations from observers who
attest to the fierceness and effectiveness of these
guerrillas. The book contains some excellent photos. See
especially Segura's tale of the capture of a Japanese
admiral who held all the plans for the Japanese defense of
the Philippines.

3755. Spencer, Louise Reid. GUERRILLA WIFE. New York: Thomas
       Y. Crowell, 1945. 209 pp.

Spencer, the Canadian wife of a U.S. mining engineer on
the island of Masbate in the Philippines, lived two years
in the hills of Panay Island hiding from the Japanese. She
describes the rigors of her ordeal and the effective
resistance of the loyal natives. In early 1944, a
submarine evacuated her to Australia.

3756.   Steinberg, David. "Jose P. Laurel: A 'Collaborator'
        Misunderstood." J ASIAN STUD, 24 (August 1965),
        651-665.

        Maintaining that misunderstanding about Laurel's role
        arose because of confusion Laurel created after the war,
        Steinberg portrays Laurel's wartime presidency as one of
        voluntary collaboration as a means of national survival for
        the Philippines. Describing him as neither a puppet nor a
        martyr, Steinberg presents a balanced assessment which
        includes key mistakes by Laurel.

3757.   Steinberg, David Joel. PHILIPPINE COLLABORATION IN WORLD
        WAR II. Ann Arbor, MI: University of Michigan Press,
        1967. 244 pp.

        Steinberg tackles a controversial subject in analyzing
        Filipino wartime collaboration. His focus is the struggle
        for survival of the elite, conservative class.

3758.   Taylor, Joe G. "American Support of Guerrillas on Cebu."
        MIL AFFS, 23 (Fall 1959), 149-152.

        Taylor describes how the Thirteenth Air Force aided
        guerrillas in the Philippines. By March 1945, five
        Guerrilla Air Support Teams were operational.

3759.   Vellut, J.L. "Foreign Relations of the Philippines,
        1943-1945." J SEA HIST, 5 (March 1964), 126-142.

        The author uses the term "ambiguity" to characterize the
        policies of Laurel's government. Integrating contemporary
        reports and newspaper accounts, Vellut describes the
        preoccupation with emancipation ("Asia for Asians") and the
        limited scope of international intercourse (Japan and
        friends) available to Laurel.

3760.   Villamor, Jesus A. THEY NEVER SURRENDERED: A TRUE STORY
        OF RESISTANCE IN WORLD WAR II. Quezon City, PI: Vera-
        Reyes, 1982. 335 pp.

        The author, a U.S. citizen, expresses anger at what he

considers cavalier treatment accorded to Filipinos who
fought with Americans in the resistance in the Philippines.
Selected to return to the Philippines in January 1943 as
the representative of the Allied Intelligence Bureau,
Villamor and his Planet Party worked to organize American
and Filipino guerrillas in a country-wide net. Of interest
is his criticism of Courtney Whitney who opposed Villamor's
efforts to unify the resistance forces. The author
departed the Philippines in October 1943 to brief MacArthur
in Australia and Quezon in the United States on the
situation. Claiming to incorporate secret documents from
the archives in St. Louis, Villamor's story appears here as
told to Gerald S. Snyder.

3761.   Volckmann, Russell W. WE REMAINED: THREE YEARS BEHIND THE
        ENEMY LINES IN THE PHILIPPINES. New York: W.W. Norton,
        1954. 244 pp.

        The author was intelligence officer for the 11th
        Division at Bataan when the time came to surrender to the
        Japanese. Obtaining permission from Gen. Brougher,
        Volckmann and Don Blackburn escaped through Japanese lines
        to northern Luzon and joined the resistance. The
        well-written account describes the development--and
        achievements--of the guerrilla force. The resistance
        organization, USAFIP, Nathan Luzon, took as their motto:
        "We Remained."

3762.   Willoughby, Charles A., ed. THE GUERRILLA RESISTANCE
        MOVEMENT IN THE PHILIPPINES, 1941-1945. New York:
        Vantage Press, 1945. 702 pp.

        This contemporary collection relies on Willoughby's
        distant observations from Australia. He presents the texts
        of reports from Filipino guerrillas and translations of
        captured Japanese documents.

3763.   Wise, William. SECRET MISSION TO THE PHILIPPINES: THE
        STORY OF "SPYRON" AND THE AMERICAN-FILIPINO GUERRILLAS
        OF WORLD WAR II. New York: E.P. Dutton, 1968. 160 pp.

        In this popular account, Wise concentrates almost
        exclusively on the activities of Chick Parsons in the
        Filipino resistance.

3764.   Wolfert, Ira. AMERICAN GUERRILLA IN THE PHILIPPINES. New
        York: Simon and Schuster, 1945. 301 pp.

        Wolfert, a war correspondent, tells the story of Iliff

David Richardson (Lt., USN). When the war began,
Richardson was serving on a torpedo boat (Squadron 3) in
the Philippines. With the Japanese victorious sweep, and
with his efforts to escape foiled, Richardson returned to
Leyte. He joined the resistance and became chief of staff
to Col. Ruperto Kangleon. The book describes Richardson's
guerrilla adventures--and even includes a love story.

3765. Yay, Colonel. [pseud. Yay Panlilo.] THE CRUCIBLE: AN
        AUTOBIOGRAPHY. New York: Macmillan, 1950. 348 pp.

        The author, a Filipino reporter (born in the United
        States), became associated with the resistance.
        Eventually she married the famed guerrilla leader,
        "MARKING" (Marcus V. Agustin).

IV.G.3. Thailand (Siam)

3766. Clifton, Paul. "Escape from Siam." RAF FLYING R, 9
        (March 1954), 21-23, 32.

        Clifton was on board a Liberator which crash-landed
        in Thailand. The OSS and the Free Thais helped the
        survivors of the crash out of the country.

3767. Moss, William S. A WAR OF SHADOWS. London: Boardman,
        1952. 240 pp.

        Although Moss, a British secret agent, spent much of his
        service in the war against Germany, he saw some action in
        Thailand. His narrative gives a good description of the
        Thai people, the rise of nationalist fervor in Southeast
        Asia, and the communist influence in that region.

3768. Smith, Nicol and Thomas B. Clark. INTO SIAM, UNDERGROUND
        KINGDOM. Indianapolis, IN: Bobbs-Merrill, 1946. 315
        pp.

        Here is a well-written account of a group of Free Thais,
        educated in the United States and trained by the OSS, who
        secretly returned to their country. Smith and Clark tell
        of their preparations and clandestine operations.

IV.H. Logistics/Technical Support in the War Against Japan

3769. Ballantine, Duncan S. U.S. NAVAL LOGISTICS IN THE SECOND
        WORLD WAR. Princeton, NJ: Princeton University Press,
        1947. 308 pp.

Ballantine provides an excellent overview. His
treatment of logistical problems across the distances of
the Pacific is particularly effective.

3770. Bowman, Waldo G., et al. BULLDOZERS COME FIRST: THE STORY
OF U.S. WAR CONSTRUCTION IN FOREIGN LANDS. New York:
McGraw-Hill, 1944. 278 pp.

Among this collection of laudatory stories are two which
deal with the Pacific: H.W. Richardson on Alaska-Aleutians
and N.A. Bowers on Pacific Ocean areas.

3771. Carse, Robert. LIFELINE: THE SHIPS AND MEN OF OUR
MERCHANT MARINE AT WAR. New York: Morrow, 1944. 189
pp.

Carse tells of the heroic deeds of these men as they
travel in troubled waters.

3772. Carter, Worrall Reed. BEANS, BULLETS, AND BLACK OIL: THE
STORY OF FLEET LOGISTICS AFLOAT IN THE PACIFIC DURING
WORLD WAR II. Washington, D.C.: Government Printing
Office, 1953. 482 pp.

Carter stresses the importance of both shore bases and
the mobile floating bases for the logistical support of the
Navy. He points out that support operations in the Central
Pacific differed from those in the South Pacific because
the relatively small land areas usually meant available
space for only a runway and the accompanying garrison.
Consequently, logistical support in the Central Pacific
remained primarily afloat. The author assumed
responsibility for organizing Service Squadron Ten, which
was commissioned in early 1944. Overall, Carter examines
the growth of the Navy's logistical support from its scant
prewar attention to a fleet of almost one thousand ships by
1945. The book contains excellent photographs and charts.

3773. Castillo, Edmund L. THE SEABEES OF WORLD WAR II. New
York: Random House, 1963. 190 pp.

Combined with excellent Navy photographs, the text
describes the work of the naval construction batallions in
the Pacific. Castillo particularly highlights the work of
the Bobcats at Bora-Bora and the Sixth Batallion at
Guadalcanal.

3774. Cave, Hugh B. WE BUILD, WE FIGHT. New York: Harper and
Brothers, 1944. 122 pp.

Rather than undertake a complete history, Cave selects certain episodes to indicate the value of the Seabees.

3775. Coakley, Robert W. and Richard M. Leighton. GLOBAL LOGISTICS AND STRATEGY, 1943-1945. Washington, D. C.: Office of the Chief of Military History, for the Dept. of the Army, 1968. 889 pp.

The authors researched this official history for the Army with meticulous care. It remains the premier work on the topic. (See also the companion volume listed under Leighton and Coakley.)

3776. Contractors Pacific Naval Air Bases. A REPORT TO RETURNED CPNAB PRISONER OF WAR HEROES AND THEIR DEPENDENTS. Boisie, ID: CPNAB, 1945. 51 pp.

This brief account highlights the CPNAB achievements.

3777. Crump, Irving. OUR TANKER FLEET. New York: Dodd, Mead, 1952. 244 pp.

Crump offers a general history of the ships that carried liquid cargo. These ships were instrumental in Pacific operations through their servicing of the naval battle forces.

3778. Donahue, Ralph J. READY ON THE RIGHT: THE TRUE STORY OF A NATURALIST SEABEE. Kansas City, MO: Smith Printing, 1946. 194 pp.

Donahue, a self-proclaimed naturalist, tells of his vocational and avocational pursuits during his Pacific travels. His narrative includes his trips to Kodiak, Oahu, Eniwetok, Guam, and Okinawa.

3779. Elliott, Peter. ALLIED ESCORT SHIPS OF WORLD WAR II: A COMPLETE SURVEY. Annapolis, MD: Naval Institute Press, 1977. 575 pp.

This book appeals to the specialists. Elliott, who served in the British Royal Navy, sets forth detailed information on Allied corvettes, frigates, and destroyer escorts that were built during the war (1939-1945). The technical information for each ship (about 2,000 are cited) includes design, weapons carried, and operations.

3780. Ellis, Christopher. MILITARY TRANSPORT OF WORLD WAR II.

New York: Macmillan, 1971. 177 pp.

Ellis presents information on transport vehicles used in all theaters by both sides. Many illustrations are included.

3781.   Franzwa, Gregory M. LEGACY: THE SVERDRUP STORY. St. Louis, MO: Sverdrup Corporation, 1978. 286 pp.

This borders on hagiography. The book is unexceptional save for the assertion that Truman, shortly after assuming the presidency, asked Sverdrup to take over as secretary of war. Franzwa claims that Sverdrup declined because he did not want to be giving orders to MacArthur—orders which Sverdrup knew MacArthur would ignore.

3782.   Franzwa, Gregory M. and William J. Ely. LEIF SVERDRUP. Gerald, MO: The Patrice Press, 1980. 387 pp.

MacArthur called Sverdrup "the engineer soldier at his best." The authors assert that the war in the Pacific essentially became a struggle for airstrips, and, therefore, engineers played a key role. This is a highly favorable account.

3783.   Heavey, William F. DOWN RAMP! THE STORY OF THE ARMY AMPHIBIAN ENGINEERS. Washington, DC: Infantry Journal Press, 1947. 272 pp.

Here is an excellent source of information about little-known specialists. The Army amphibian engineers played an important part in the assault landings. Heavey describes operations and identifies key personalties.

3784.   Huie, William Bradford. FROM OMAHA TO OKINAWA: THE STORY OF THE SEABEES. New York: E.P. Dutton, 1945. 322 pp.

This 257-page text is buttressed by 65 pages of photographs (many of which are appearing in public for the first time). The author served in the Navy with the Seabees and later travelled with them as a correspondent. Complete with "Seabee slang," this narrative portrays the seabees as a crazy bunch of guys who accomplished their mission.

3785.   Leighton, Richard M. and Coakley, Robert, W. GLOBAL LOGISTICS AND STRATEGY, 1940-1943. Washington, D. C.: Office of the Chief of Military History, for the Dept. of the Army, 1955. 780 pp.

        This official history of the Army's logistical
operations includes prewar preparations and plans as well
as discussions of the early years of the war. Although the
study touches on the various theaters, the main thrust
remains fixed in Washington. (See also the companion
volume listed under Coakley and Leighton.)

3786. McCoy, Samuel D. NOR DEATH DISMAY. New York: Macmillan,
        1944. 248 pp.

        Here is a report on the activities of the Merchant
Marine. McCoy includes rosters of personnel and ships.

3787. Masterson, James R. UNITED STATES ARMY TRANSPORTATION IN
        THE SOUTHWEST PACIFIC AREA, 1941-1947. Washington,
        D.C.: Transportation Unit Historical Division,
        Department of the Army, 1949.

        Here is the official history of the regional
transportation service. The peculiar features of the
Southwest Pacific presented unusual wartime challenges.

3788. Quick, Richard W. "Pacific Theater in World War II:
        Challenges to Air Logistics." AF J LOGIST, 10 (Spring
        1986), 2-6.

        Here is a report of air operations over the Hump and the
activities of XX Bomber Command. Quick describes the
difficulties of logistical support from the United States
for these all-important activities.

3789. Riesenberg, Felix. SEA WAR. New York: Rinehart, 1956.
        320 pp.

        Here is the wartime history of the U.S. Merchant Marine.
The author, an officer who served in the Maritime Service
during the war, offers a study in undiluted praise.

3790. Rogers, C.A. "Quartermaster Corps in the South Pacific
        During World War II." QUARTERMASTER R, 32 (September-
        October 1952), 128-144.

        Until September 1942, most American units received
support directly from the continental United States. After
that date, a new organization, the Services of Supply South
Pacific Area (SOSSPA) supported American forces from
Auckland, New Zealand. Rogers provides a lengthy summary
of SOSSPA activities. His main criticism falls on the lack

of a central planning branch.

3791. Spight, Edwin L. and Jeanne L. Spight. EAGLES OF THE
      PACIFIC. Temple City, CA: Historical Aviation Album,
      1980. 224 pp.

      Here is the story of CONSAIRWAYS. Edwin Spight was a
      pilot for the Air Transport Service. The book contains his
      reminiscences and provides information on ATS operations
      across the Pacific.

3792. Stauffer, Alvin P. THE QUARTERMASTER CORPS: OPERATIONS IN
      THE WAR AGAINST JAPAN. Washington, D.C.: Office of the
      Chief of Military History, Dept. of the Army, 1956. 358
      pp.

      Part of the U.S. Army in World War II series, this
      volume sheds light on a little-known ingredient of the
      winning team. Stauffer incorporates much statistical
      information on the contribution of the Quartermaster Corps.

3793. Terret, Dulany. THE SIGNAL CORPS: THE EMERGENCY (TO
      DECEMBER 1941). Washington, D.C.: Office of the Chief
      of Military History, Dept. of the Army, 1956. 383 pp.

      In this official history, Terret explains the
      preparations, including development and delivery of radar
      and other signal equipment, as the U.S. Army increased the
      tempo of its training for combat readiness.

3794. Thompson, Clary, ed. UNSUNG HEROES! YOUR SERVICE FORCES
      IN ACTION: A PHOTOGRAPHIC EPIC OF ARMY SERVICE FORCE
      OPERATIONS IN WORLD WAR II. New York: Wise, 1949. 385
      pp.

      This interesting collection surveys ASF operations in
      all theaters.

3795. Thompson, George R. and Dixie R. Harris. THE OUTCOME
      (MID-1943 THROUGH 1945). Washington, D.C.: Office of
      the Chief of Military History, Dept. of the Army, 1966.
      693 pp.

      The authors provide a blend of operational and
      administrative histories in this official study of the
      Signal Corps in the war.

3796. Thompson, George R., Pauline M. Oakes, and Dulany Terret.
      THE TEST (DECEMBER 1941 TO JULY 1943). Washington,

D.C.: Office of the Chief of Military History, Dept. of
the Army, 1957. 621 pp.

The authors focus on combat operations of the Signal
Corps in all theaters. Of special interest is the
description of the last moments at Corregidor---with a
soldier (Irving Strobing) sending farewells to his family
and Chief Warrant Officer Robert L. Scearce confirming the
destruction of cipher strips in the final message.

3797. Thomson, Harry C. and Lida Mayo. PROCUREMENT AND SUPPLY.
        Washington, D.C.: Office of the Chief of Military
        History, Dept. of the Army, 1960. 504 pp.

This is the official history of the Army's Ordnance
Department. The authors report on the manufacture,
storage, and distribution of munitions throughout all
theaters.

3798. United States. Army Air Forces. ADMINISTRATIVE HISTORY OF
        THE FERRYING COMMAND, 29 MAY 1941-30 JUNE 1942.
        Washington, D.C.: USAAF, 1945. 170pp.

The USAAF Historical Office sets forth the
organizational development of the Ferrying Command prior to
its redesignation as Air Transport Command. The book
contains a discussion of the decision leading to the
formation of the Ferrying Command in May 1941 as well as
the organization's relationship with other USAAF and UN
agencies. Of interest is the rapid expansion of domestic
and overseas activities, especially in the Pacific.

3799. United States. Army Air Forces. AIRWAY TO INDIA. New
        York: Air Transport Command, 1945.

Edited by Lt. Joseph B. Roberts, Jr., this study traces
ATC operations between Africa and India. Long crew hours
and hazardous conditions (e.g., bad weather and mountainous
terrain) challenged the airmen.

3800. United States. Navy Department. Air Transport Service.
        THE ROLE OF THE NAVAL AIR TRANSPORT SERVICE IN THE
        PACIFIC WAR. Washington, D.C.: GPO, 1945.

Here is an official report on the wartime performance of
NATS. The great distances across the Pacific placed heavy
demands on the transport service.

3801. Van Deurs, George. "The SEGI Man." USNIP, 84 (October

1958), 56-61.

Here is the story of Cmdr. Bill Painter and the search
for a landing field close to Munda. After selecting Segi,
Painter and his men built the airstrip.

3802. Wardlow, Chester. MOVEMENTS, TRAINING AND SUPPLY.
Washington, D.C.: Office of the Chief of Military
History, Dept. of the Army, 1956. 564 pp.

Here is an official report on the development of the
movement of men and materiel to the overseas theaters.

3803. Wardlow, Chester. THE TRANSPORTATION CORPS:
RESPONSIBILITIES, ORGANIZATION AND OPERATIONS.
Washington, D.C.: Office of the Chief of Military
History, Dept. of the Army, 1951. 454 pp.

This official account traces the wartime history of the
Transportation Corps. Wardlow is particularly effective in
identifying the problems that arose and (for the most part)
the solutions that emerged in ensuring the flow of troops
and equipment to the global fronts.

3804. Woodbury, David O. BUILDERS FOR BATTLE: HOW THE PACIFIC
NAVAL BASES WERE CONSTRUCTED. New York: E.P. Dutton,
1946. 415 pp.

Here is the story of an important program: the
six-billion dollar construction of Pacific naval air bases.
This ambitious project began in 1939 as a result of the
Hepburn report. The author chooses to omit the human
dimension--the debates and personality clashes--that
accompanied the construction of the bases (e.g., Pearl
Harbor, Midway, Wake, Palmyra, Alaska, Aleutians, Johnston,
and Guam). His narrative emphasizes the speedy
accomplishments in overcoming natural and man-made
obstacles. See the introductory statement by Admiral B.
Moreel.

IV.I. Medical Aspects

3805. Allen, Ted. THE SCALPEL, THE SWORD: THE STORY OF DR.
NORMAN BETHUNE. Boston: Little, Brown, 1952. 336 pp.

NE

3806. Beebe, Gilbert W. and John W. Appel. VARIATION IN
PSYCHOLOGICAL TOLERANCE TO GROUND COMBAT IN WORLD WAR

II. Washington, D.C.: National Academy of Science,
1958. 280 pp.

NE

3807. Beebe, Gilbert W. and Michael E. DeBakey. BATTLE
CASUALTIES: INCIDENCE, MORTALITY, AND LOGISTIC
CONSIDERATIONS. Springfield, IL: Thomas, 1952. 277
pp.

NE

3808. Blasingame, Wyatt. MEDICAL CORPS HEROES OF WORLD WAR II.
New York: Random House, 1969. 176 pp.

Blasingame, obviously familiar with his subject,
compiles a formidable catalogue of medical corps heroes in
all theaters. The book suffers from a lack of footnotes
and bibliography.

3809. Omitted.

3810. Davis, Dorothy. "I Nursed at Santo Tomas, Manila." AMER J
NURSING, 44 (January 1944), 29-30.

Davis spent twenty-one months (from January 1942 to her
repatriation when she became ill) as a civilian nurse at
Santo Tomas. This contemporary article was one of the
first reports available to the American people of wartime
conditions in the Philippines.

3811. Doherty, William B. and D.D. Runes, eds. REHABILITATION OF
THE WAR INJURED. New York: Philosophical Library,
1943. 684 pp.

Most of this collection had been published previously in
medical journals. The varieties of treatment indicate the
extent of the progress made in just the first years of the
war.

3812. Flikke, Julia O. NURSES IN ACTION. Philadelphia, PA: J.
B. Lippincott, 1943. 239 pp.

This narrative-history extols the exploits of the
nurses. Some sections describe the courage of the nurses
in the Philippines down to the 1942 surrender at
Corregidor.

3813. Flowers, Wilfred S. A SURGEON IN CHINA. London: Carey
Press, 1946. 52 pp.

Flowers gives a brief description of his experiences as a surgeon with a British Red Cross unit in China.

3814.   Fox, Monroe, L. BLIND ADVENTURE. Philadelphia, PA: J. B. Lippincott, 1946. 205 pp.

The author is a seaman who, in February 1945, was blinded in combat in the Pacific. The story focuses on his subsequent treatment and personal development.

3815.   Griffin, Alexander R. OUT OF CARNAGE. New York: Howell, Soskin, 1945. 327 pp.

Griffin presents a series of articles on the practice of medicine during the war. The emphasis is on new developments and techniques.

3816.   Hamilton, Thomas. SOLDIER SURGEON IN MALAYA. Sydney, Aus.: Angus & Robertson, 1957. 218 pp.

Here are the war memoirs of an Australian surgeon.

3817.   Hardison, Irene. A NIGHTINGALE IN THE JUNGLE. Philadelphia, PA: Dorrance, 1954. 133 pp.

Hardison gives a personal account of her experiences as a medic in Burma. She conveys a sense of making do with what was available.

3818.   Hill, Justina H. SILENT ENEMIES. New York: G.P. Putnam, 1942. 266 pp.

This book tells the story of diseases in the war and the efforts to bring them under control. The author, a bacteriologist, offers a special section on jungle diseases.

3819.   Hill, Reuben L. FAMILIES UNDER STRESS. New York: Harper, 1950. 443 pp.

Hill studied 135 Iowa families in compiling this report on wartime stress. His research concentrated on the psychological trauma of separation because of the war.

3820.   Howard, Richard A. 999 SURVIVED. Maxwell AFB, Al: Arctic, Desert, Tropic Information Center, Air University, 1953. 60 pp.

This report analyzes survival experiences of American

servicemen in the Southwest Pacific. There is a critique
of wartime survival training.

3821. Jones, Edgar L. "The Wounded Still Fight." ATLANTIC MON,
178 (December 1946), 84-90.

The journal's special correspondent in the Pacific
describes the dilemmas faced by wounded servicemen whom he
interviewed. Those with less serious wounds face a wait of
over one year for corrective ("cosmetic") surgery. Those
severely wounded, however, are given immediate discharges
after short-term treatment and left to fend for themselves
with the U.S. Veterans Administration.

3822. Mackenzie, Dewitt. MEN WITHOUT GUNS. Philadelphia, PA:
Blakiston, 1946. 47 pp.

Here is the art work (118 pieces) of 12 artists who were
attached to the medical corps. The subject material comes
from front and rear echelons in all theaters.

3823. Maisel, Albert Q. THE WOUNDED GET BACK. New York:
Harcourt, Brace, 1944. 230 pp.

The author spent six months observing the care given to
wounded U.S. servicemen. Maisel is not trained in
medicine, but his report reassures Americans on the home
front about the quality of the medical treatment in Pacific
hospitals and hospital ships.

3824. Menninger, William C. PSYCHIATRY IN A TROUBLED WORLD. New
York: Macmillan, 1948. 636 pp.

Here is a psychiatric study of the effects of combat
experience. Menninger discusses the long-term
ramifications and the support services available for
veterans.

3825. Moyer, William L. "Last Ship Out of Manila." AMER HIST
ILLUS, 20 (May 1985), 34-39.

Here is a tale about the hospital ship MACTAN under
Capt. Julian Tamayo which sailed on a medical mission of
mercy from the Philippines to Australia. The ship departed
Manila on December 31, 1941, with 224 wounded (including
134 Americans) after the Swiss Red Cross had searched for
contraband. It arrived in Darwin (January 13, 1942) and
Sydney (January 27). Not all of the patient-passengers
survived the trip.

3826.   Newcomb, Ellsworth. BRAVE NURSE: TRUE STORIES OF HEROISM.
        New York: Appleton-Century, 1945. 176 pp.

        Here are contemporary portraits of U.S. nurses, both in
        combat and in rear echelons, in all theaters.

3827.   Page, Robert C. AIR COMMANDO DOC. New York: Ackerman,
        1946. 186 pp.

        Lt. Col. Page organized a medical unit to penetrate
        enemy lines in Burma via gliders. The medics supported
        pilots who were performing secret missions. The story is
        told to Alfred Aiken.

3828.   Parsons, Robert P. MOB 3: A NAVAL HOSPITAL IN A SOUTH SEA
        JUNGLE. Indianapolis, IN: Bobbs-Merrill, 1945. 248
        pp.

        As a naval captain and physician, Parsons reports on his
        command of an island medical unit. Wartime censorship
        prevented him from identifying the exact location. His
        account includes descriptions of native life and culture.

3829.   Powell, Lyle S. A SURGEON IN WARTIME CHINA. Lawrence, KS:
        University of Kansas Press, 1946. 233 pp.

        Dr. Powell (M.D.) describes his experiences under
        less-than-optimal conditions. Of interest are his
        improvisations and techniques to make do with what he had
        available.

3830.   Reister, Frank A., ed. MEDICAL STATISTICS IN WORLD WAR II.
        Washington, D.C.: GPO, 1975. 1,215 pp.

        Part of the U.S. Army in World War II series, the volume
        incorporates research through millions of medical records.
        The Army's Medical Department categorizes the combat
        injuries and deaths by nature and by casual factors. This
        statistical reference forms a comprehensive guide to a
        significant aspect of the war.

3831.   Rogers, Lindsay. GUERRILLA SURGEON. Garden City, NY:
        Doubleday, 1957. 280 pp.

        NE

3832.   Seagrave, Gordon S. BURMA SURGEON. New York: W.W.
        Norton, 1943. 295 pp.

Seagrave, an American medical missionary in Burma, accompanied Stilwell on the famous "walk-out" evacuation. The author had lived in Burma for twenty years. His story forms one of the truly remarkable contemporary accounts of the war.

3833. Seagrave, Gordon S. BURMA SURGEON RETURNS. New York: W.W. Norton, 1946. 268 pp.

In this sequel, Seagrave describes the reorganization in India of his medical group and their return to Burma. The author makes no secret of his admiration for Stilwell.

3834. Sharon, Henrietta B. IT'S GOOD TO BE ALIVE. New York: Dodd, Mead, 1945. 150 pp.

Here is a report on rehabilitation treatment available to U.S. veterans.

3836. Steere, Edward and Thayer M. Boardman. FINAL DISPOSITION OF WORLD WAR II DEAD, 1945-1951. Washington, D.C.: Historical Branch, Office of Quartermaster General, 1957. 710 pp.

Here is a detailed report on a necessary chore for a nation at war.

3837. Stone, James H. ed. CRISIS FLEETING: ORIGINAL REPORTS ON MILITARY MEDICINE IN INDIA AND BURMA IN THE SECOND WORLD WAR. Washington, D.C.: GPO, 1969. 423 pp.

Although the narratives in these reports are hardly lively, the collection does offer excellent information on an important dimension of the war.

3838. Taliaferro, William H., ed. MEDICINE AND THE WAR. Chicago: University of Chicago Press, 1974. 193 pp.

The editor assembles lectures by faculty at the University of Chicago. This highly technical information is addressed to a knowledgeable audience. See especially the material on malaria and other tropical diseases.

3839. Thumm, Helen M. "Aides Trained at Army Hospitals in the Philippines." AMER J NURSING, 45 (July 1945), 533-554.

Lt. Thumm (A.N.C.) started the nurse's aide program in the Philippines. The article sets forth the training and duties of the civilian women volunteers.

3840. United States. Navy Department. THE HISTORY OF THE
        MEDICAL DEPARTMENT OF THE U.S. NAVY IN WORLD WAR II.
        Washington, D.C.: GPO, 1950-. 3 vols.

        This on-going series provides the official history of
        the organization, administration, and operation of the
        Navy's Medical Department, which included the Marine Corps.
        Volume III incorporates material on diseases.

3841. Walker, Arthur E. and Seymour Jackson. A FOLLOW-UP STUDY
        OF HEAD WOUNDS IN WORLD WAR II. Washington, D.C.: GPO,
        1961. 202 pp.

        Here is an authoritative study of the medical treatment
        for those serious wounds. The array of statistics and the
        medical terminology make the narrative difficult to follow.

3842. Wees, Marshall P. KING-DOCTOR OF ULITHI. New York:
        Macmillan, 1950. 128 pp.

        During the war, Dr. Wees went to Ulithi (in the
        Carolines) to help fight an epidemic of yaws. His efforts
        were successful, and the grateful natives selected Wees as
        their second king. Wees's account is told to Rev. Francis
        Beauchesne Thornton.

3843. Wheeler, Keith. WE ARE THE WOUNDED. New York: E.P.
        Dutton, 1945. 224 pp.

        An American war correspondent, Wheeler was wounded while
        covering the action at Iwo Jima. In this first-hand
        report, he describes the medical care made available at the
        front and in the rear echelons. See, too, the account of
        his recovery.

IV.J. Science and Technology

1. General Accounts

3844. Becker, Lawrence C. "Is Science Moral?" ZYGON, 3
        (September 1968), 335-342.

        The author, a professor of philosophy, argues against
        divorcing science from the scientists. He insists that
        science is not morally neutral.

3845. Crowther, James G. and Richard Whiddington. SCIENCE AT

WAR. New York: Philosophical Library, 1948. 185 pp.

As members of a project officially sponsored through the British Cabinet's Scientific Advisory Committee, the authors provide a useful overview that is easily read despite the presence of much technical information. See especially the material on radar and the British perspective on the development of the atomic bomb.

3846.   Eggleston, Wilfred. SCIENTISTS AT WAR. Toronto: Oxford University Press, 1950. 291 pp.

The role of Canadian scientists in the war is not generally recognized. Eggleston, in focusing on that role, concludes that, although considerable, the contribution of the Canadian scientists was simply a part of the overall war effort--an effort dominated by U.S. and British scientists.

3847.   Ford, Brian J. ALLIED SECRET WEAPONS: THE WAR OF SCIENCE. New York: Ballantine Books, 1971. 160 pp.

NE

3848.   Jones, R.V. THE WIZARD WAR: BRITISH SCIENTIFIC INTELLIGENCE, 1939-1945. New York: Coward, McCann, and Geoghegan, 1978. 556 pp.

Jones served as one of the leading British scientists in the war. Although his work centered on the war against Germany, the book contains much general information about the "scientific front." Illustrations and the appendices support Jones's narrative.

3849.   Slocum, Winthrop. "Japan's Technical Secrets." CANADIAN ARMY J, 4 (April 1950), 56-66.

In 1946, an American naval technical mission went to Japan to obtain information on scientific research done during the war. The Japanese did little such research outside of army-navy circles. Slocum believes that the Japanese copied existing information in order to catch up (not because of a lack of ability). Projects of special interest identified in the report include submarines for specialized purposes, unusual types of torpedoes, underwater ambulatory kamikaze packets, medical work, and geological inquiries.

3850.   Smith, Alice Kimball. A PERIL AND A HOPE: THE SCIENTISTS'

MOVEMENT IN AMERICA, 1945-1947. Chicago: University of
Chicago Press, 1965. 591 pp.

Smith writes authoritatively about the so-called golden
age in American science. In analyzing the divisions--and
the achievements--among the U.S. scientists, the author has
produced a masterpiece.

3851. Thiesmeyer, Lincoln R. and John R. Burchard. COMBAT
SCIENTISTS. Boston: Little, Brown, 1947. 412 pp.

NE

IV.J.2. Special Weapons

a. Scientific Development of the Atomic Bomb

3852. AMERICAN HERITAGE, Editors of. THE HISTORY OF THE ATOMIC
BOMB. New York: American Heritage, 1968. 150 pp.

With Michael Blow as a consultant, this popular account
traces the story from the first nuclear fission experiment
to the use of the two atomic bombs against Japan.

3853. Anderson, Herbert L. "Early Days of the Chain Reaction."
SCIENCE PUBLIC AFFS, 29 (April 1973), 8-12.

The author was a member of the team that arranged the
first nuclear chain reaction. As a graduate student,
Anderson first learned of nuclear fission from Bohr and
Fermi. After a site for the experiment was secured through
Compton's approval to use facilities at the University of
Chicago, the fateful event occurred in 1942.

3854. Anderson, Herbert L. Part I: "The Legacy of Fermi and
Szilard." BULL ATOMIC SCI, 30 (September 1974), 56-62.
Part II: "Fermi, Szilard and Trinity." BULL ATOMIC
SCI, 30 (October 1974), 40-47.

The author helped build the first atomic pile which
resulted in the first self-sustaining or controlled nuclear
reaction December 2, 1942, at the University of Chicago.
He recalls working with Fermi and Szilard at Columbia
University, Chicago, and Los Alamos.

3855. Badash, Lawrence, Elizabeth Hodes, and Adolph Tiddens.
"Nuclear Fission: Reaction to the Discovery in 1939."
AMER PHILOS SOC PROC, 130 (June 1986), 196-231.

The three historians look at worldwide reaction to the
discovery. They specifically examine two questions.
First, why did the discovery come as a surprise? (Despite
intensive literature on harnessing atomic energy, the 1939
discovery overturned established models of nuclear
disintegration and the logic against chain reactions.)
Second, why did the discovery generate little moral or
ethical introspection? (Although they arbitrarily set
their definitions, the authors feel that 1939 was too early
for moral and ethical opposition, which emerged in 1942 and
later.) The sources used include private collections,
interviews, and questionnaires to participants in 1939 (37
responded from a total of 70).

3856. Badash, Lawrence, Joseph O. Hirschfelder, and Herbert P.
       Broida, eds. REMINISCENCES OF LOS ALAMOS, 1943-1945.
       Dordrecht, Holland: D. Reidel, 1980. 188 pp.

       Scientists provide first-hand accounts of the problems
       and triumphs of the Manhattan Project.

3857. Bainbridge, Kenneth T. Part I: "Prelude to Trinity."
       BULL ATOMIC SCI, 31 (April 1975), 42-46. Part II: "A
       Foul and Awesome Display." BULL ATOMIC SCI, 31 (May
       1975), 40-46.

       Bainbridge, who built the first cyclotron at Harvard,
       played a major role in the test at Los Alamos.

3858. Baldwin, Ralph B. THE DEADLY FUZE: SECRET WEAPON OF WORLD
       WAR II. Novato, CA: Presidio Press, 1980.

       Baldwin, an engineer in the office of Scientific
       Research and Development, was instrumental in developing
       the radio-controlled proximity fuze. The weapon played a
       key role in defending the U.S. Pacific Fleet from enemy air
       attacks.

3859. Baxter, James P. SCIENTISTS AGAINST TIME. Boston:
       Little, Brown, 1946. 473 pp.

       In this official history of the Office of Scientific
       Research and Development, the author has written one of the
       best studies of the contribution scientists made to the war
       effort of the United States. Baxter, president of Williams
       College at the time, provides not only an administrative
       history but also the story of the weapons produced in the
       war. See especially his perspective on the development of
       the atomic bomb.

3860.   Bernstein, Barton J.   "Oppenheimer and the Radioactive
            Poison Plan." TECH REV, 88 (May-June 1985), 14-18.

        In a letter to Enrico Fermi on May 25, 1943, Oppenheimer
        considered the possibility of poisoning 500,000 enemy with
        radiologically contaminated food. Although nothing came of
        the project, Bernstein includes present-day reactions from
        some scientists who worked on the Manhattan Project.

3861.   Bess, Michael.   "Leo Szilard: Scientist, Activist,
            Visionary." BULL ATOMIC SCI, 41 (December 1985), 11-18.

        Bess focuses on the moral issues involved in Szilard's
        work. The scientist foresaw the escalating arms race
        between the United States and the Soviet Union.

3862.   Brown, Bahngrell W.   "Who Ever Heard of John Johnston?"
            SOUTHERN Q, 15 (October 1976), 89-95.

        The author, a geology professor, tells of a Yale
        professor in the 1920s who wrote about atomic energy.
        Acknowledging the important role of intuition in science,
        Brown characterizes scientific genius as a combination of
        the real world, data, and fantasy.

3863.   Campbell, J.W.   THE ATOMIC STORY. New York: Henry Holt,
            1947.

        Here is a popular account of the development of the
        atomic bomb.

3864.   Cave Brown, Anthony and Charles B. MacDonald, eds. THE
            SECRET HISTORY OF THE ATOMIC BOMB. New York: Dial
            Press, 1977. 582 pp.

        The documents presented are unexceptional and stem
        mainly from the declassified history of the Manhattan
        Engineer District. There is material on the scientific
        developments, the selection of personnel, the site for
        research and development, and the use of the atomic bomb.
        Technical information is included.

3865.   Church, Peggy Pond.   THE HOUSE AT OTOWI BRIDGE.
            Albuquerque, NM: University of New Mexico Press, 1960.
            149 pp.

        Here is the story of Edith Warner at Los Alamos.
        Illustrations by Lonnie Fox Boyd complement the narrative.

3866.   Clarfield, Gerard H. and William M. Wiscek. NUCLEAR
        AMERICA: MILITARY AND CIVILIAN NUCLEAR POWER IN THE
        UNITED STATES, 1940-1980. New York: Harper & Row, 1984.
        518 pp.

        This narrative by two historians begins with the
        development of the atomic bomb, including material on the
        Yalta and Potsdam Conferences. Relying heavily on
        secondary works, the authors make clear their opposition to
        the nuclear arms race.

3867.   Clark, Ronald W. THE BIRTH OF THE BOMB. New York:
        Horizon Press, 1961. 209 pp.

        Clark, relying on interviews with British participants,
        describes the British role in the development of the atomic
        bomb. An interesting feature of this study is the
        author's argument that British scientists had realized
        progress on this project prior to merging their efforts
        with those of their U.S. counterparts.

3868.   Coleman, Earl E. "The 'Smyth Report': A Descriptive
        Checklist." PRINCETON LIB CHRON, 37 (Spring 1976),
        204-218.

        Coleman describes the various versions of this
        "official" report--and the various publishers involved in
        its public appearance.

3869.   Compton, Arthur H. ATOMIC QUEST: A PERSONAL NARRATIVE.
        New York: Oxford University Press, 1956.

        In these memoirs, Compton, a self-avowed Christian,
        grapples with the moral dilemma presented by his
        involvement in developing the atomic bomb. This
        retrospective anguish is exacerbated not only by the
        present arms race but also by his approval of the use of
        the atomic bomb in 1945. See especially (a) his account of
        his role in making facilities at the University of Chicago
        available for the first nuclear chain reaction in 1939 and
        (b) his treatment of an alleged 1945 questionnaire
        concerning the decision to use the Atomic Bomb (in this
        regard, Kenneth Davis, in EXPERIENCE OF WAR, indirectly
        counters Compton's version by publishing the text of the
        alleged questionnaire).

3870.   Conant, James B. MY SEVERAL LIVES: MEMOIRS OF A SOCIAL
        INVENTOR. New York: Harper & Row, 1970. 701 pp.

Conant favored the development and wartime use of the
atomic bomb, and these memoirs reveal his regret that the
weapon was not ready sooner than mid-1945. Conant opposed,
however, the development of the hydrogen bomb.

3871. Omitted.

3872. Davis, Nuell Pharr. LAWRENCE AND OPPENHEIMER. New York:
       Da Capo, 1968. 384 pp.

Here is a review of the lives of two men perhaps most
responsible for developing the atomic bomb.

3873. Day, Samuel H., Jr. "How We Learned to Love the Bomb: The
       American Scientists Put Conscience on Hold."
       PROGRESSIVE, 48 (July 1984), 26-28.

Day presents the dubious proposition that those who
unlocked the secrets of atomic power should have known how
best to use it.

3874. Fermi, Laura. ILLUSTRIOUS IMMIGRANTS: THE INTELLECTUAL
       MIGRATION FROM EUROPE, 1930-1940. Chicago, IL:
       University of Chicago Press, 1968. 440 pp.

Fermi identifies the escape routes as well as the
organizations and individuals who aided the flight of the
European intellectuals. Of special interest to this
project are the scientists who later became involved in the
development of the atomic bomb.

3875. Fermi, Laura. THE STORY OF ATOMIC ENERGY. New York:
       Random House, 1961. 194 pp.

Here is an excellent popular account of the development
of the atomic bomb. Fermi writes of this subject with
special authority.

3876. Fisher, Phyllis. LOS ALAMOS EXPERIENCE. Tokyo: Kodansha
       International, 1985. 266 pp.

The book is largely made up of Fisher's contemporary
letters to her husband, a scientist working on the
Manhattan Project. She also includes her retrospective
views which make interesting reading.

3877. Fitch, Val L. "The View From the Bottom." BULL ATOMIC
       SCI, 31 (February 1975), 43-46.

Fitch, a physics professor at Princeton when he wrote

this article, offers the perspective of an enlisted man in
the Special Engineering Detachment at Los Alamos. Selected
for duty with the special unit because of his undergraduate
preparation, Fitch received from the Army technical
training for the Manhattan Project.

3878. Fleming, Donald and Bernard Bailyn, eds. THE INTELLECTUAL
      MIGRATION: EUROPE AND AMERICA, 1930-1960. Cambridge,
      MA: Harvard University Press, 1969.

      See the essay by Charles Weiner, "A New Site for the
      Seminary: The Refugees and American Physics in the
      Thirties" (pp. 190-234).

3879. Frisch, Otto R. "How It All Began." PHYSICS TODAY, 20
      (November 1967), 43-48.

      Frisch, who was the first person to observe energy
      liberated in the fission of a single uranium nucleus,
      traces the background of the discovery of fission.
      Pointing out that the scientific centers in Europe did
      little work in nuclear physics during the 1930s and that
      scientists had not developed an appreciation for the
      concept of team research, Frisch shows how luck and "good
      solid chemistry" eventually led scientists to important
      discoveries in the field. Frisch worked at Los Alamos.

3880. Frisch, Otto R. "Somebody Turned the Sun On With a
      Switch." BULL ATOMIC SCI, 30 (April 1974), 13-18.

      Frisch describes his experiences at Los Alamos as a
      "free lance consultant."

3881. Frisch, Otto. WHAT LITTLE I REMEMBER. Cambridge, Eng.:
      Cambridge University Press, 1979.

      Frisch's memoirs cover his participation in the
      scientific development of the atomic bomb.

3882. Gigon, Fernand. FORMULA FOR DEATH. London: Wingate,
      1958. 223 pp.

      This work is translated from the original French version
      by Constantine Fitzgibbon. Gigon describes the scientific
      work of the physicists in developing the atomic bomb. His
      narrative reaches beyond 1945 to include research and
      development of the hydrogen bomb.

3883. Goodchild, Peter J. ROBERT OPPENHEIMER: SHATTERER OF

WORLDS. Boston: Houghton Mifflin, 1981. 301 pp.

There is much information on the postwar years in this
biography, which includes files and several interviews.
Focusing on the man as opposed to the scientist, Goodchild
finds no evidence of association with communists after
early 1942. Of interest is the description of the
psychological depression some of the Manhattan scientists
suffered after the two atomic bombings.

3884.   Goudsmit, Samuel A.   ALSOS.   New York: Henry Schuman,
        1947.   259 pp.

Here is an interesting report on ALSOS, a military-
scientific group which in 1944 sought to get information in
Europe about the progress the Germans were making on the
development of an atomic bomb.

3885.   Gowing, Margaret.   BRITAIN AND ATOMIC ENERGY, 1939-1945.
        London: St. Martin's 1964.

Although now somewhat outdated, Gowing offers one of the
best British perspectives on the development of the atomic
bomb. It remains useful despite the subsequent opening of
many new primary sources.

3886.   Gowing, Margaret.   "Reflections on Atomic Energy History."
        BULL ATOMIC SCI, 35 (March 1979), 51-54.

While Szilard succeeded in getting American scientists
not to publish their work out of concern for security,
similar efforts failed during 1939 and 1940 in England and
France, largely because of the attitude of the French
scientists. The wartime secrecy, according to the author,
allowed for quick, difficult, but sound decisions.

3887.   Groom, A.S.R.   "United States-Allied Relations and the
        Atomic Bomb in the Second World War."   WORLD POL, 15
        (October 1962), 123-137.

This is a review article, but Groom also incorporates an
extended synthesis of Anglo-American relations with respect
to the atomic bomb.

3888.   Groueff, Stephane.   MANHATTAN PROJECT: THE UNTOLD STORY OF
        THE MAKING OF THE ATOMIC BOMB.   Boston: Little Brown,
        1967.   372 pp.

The author, a U.S. correspondent, carefully presents

each step of the development of the atomic bomb. Starting
with the appointment of Gen. Groves in 1942, Groueff
emphasizes the technical developments and scientific
breakthroughs.

3889. Groves, Leslie R. NOW IT CAN BE TOLD: THE STORY OF THE
        MANHATTAN PROJECT. New York: Harper and Row, 1962.
        464 pp.

        Here is an indispensable account by the man who headed
        the project. His story can also be viewed as an
        administrative history.

3890. Groves, Leslie R. "Some Recollections of July 16, 1945."
        BULL ATOMIC SCI, 26 (June 1970), 21-27.

        The head of the Manhattan Project recounts some of the
        important decisions, such as site selection, use of the
        gun-type bomb, and conditions for the test. Groves
        reaffirms that the top priority of the entire project,
        putting a prompt end to the war, never changed.

3891. Gruber, Carol S. "Manhattan Project Maverick: The Case of
        Leo Szilard." PROLOGUE, 15 (Summer 1983), 73-87.

        Supported by research through Szilard's papers and
        interviews with scientists from the Manhattan Project,
        Gruber focuses on contemporary matters beyond the science
        and technology of making an atomic bomb, such as the making
        of policy and concern over a future arms race. In this
        prize-winning essay, the author shows how Szilard moved
        outside of military channels to present his views to high
        government officials. Szilard believed that scientists
        bore a heavy responsibility for their work, and he never
        again worked for an official agency of the federal
        government.

3892. Hacker, Barton C. THE DRAGON'S TAIL: RADIATION SAFETY IN
        THE MANHATTAN PROJECT, 1942-1946. Berkeley, CA:
        University of California Press, 1987. 258 pp.

        Hacker provides a close look at radiation protection
        standards in the earliest phase of the atomic age. As
        Hacker shows, the dangers of radiation fall-out were
        unappreciated in the concentrated drive to develop--and
        use--the atomic bomb.

3893. Hawkins, David. MANHATTAN DISTRICT HISTORY: PROJECT Y, THE
        LOS ALAMOS PROJECT. Los Alamos, NM: University of

California and U.S. Atomic Energy Commission, 1961. 2
vols.

This official history was written originally in 1946-47
but not released until 1961. Volume I, by Hawkins, deals
with the inception of the project. Volume II, by Edith C.
Truslow and Ralph Carlisle Smith, examines the period
August 1945 to December 1946.

3894. Hershberg, James G. "James B. Conant and the Atomic Bomb."
        J STRAT STUD, 8 (March 1985), 78-92.

In an imperfect world, and in wartime, the ends can
sometimes justify the means, according to Conant. The
author traces Conant's role in advocating the use of the
atomic bomb against Japan. Conant, however, certainly did
not want an arms race in time of peace, and he fretted
about Soviet-American relations in the postwar era.

3895. Hewett, Richard, G. and Oscar E. Anderson, Jr. THE NEW
        WORLD, 1939-1946: A HISTORY OF THE UNITED STATES ATOMIC
        ENERGY COMMISSION. University Park, PA: Pennsylvania
        State University Press, 1962. 766 pp. (vol. I.)

The first volume of this official history examines the
origins, development, and use of the atomic bomb. Here is
administrative history at its best. Using classified
documents, the authors discuss the political and scientific
problems that beset the Manhattan Project.

3896. Holloway, Davis. "Entering the Nuclear Arms Race: The
        Soviet Decision to Build the Atomic Bomb, 1939-45." SOC
        STUD SCI, 11 (May 1981), 159-197.

Holloway, a political scientist, presents a detailed
account of Soviet scientific decisions during the period
from December 1938 (the discovery of nuclear fission in
Berlin) to August 1945 (the Soviet decision to launch an
all-out scientific effort to develop an atomic bomb).
Warning that this is a working paper (which avoids the task
of evaluating problematical Soviet sources), the author
cites three major Soviet decisions: (1) in 1940 Soviet
scientists decided not to ask the government for funds to
accelerate their research; (2) in 1942, Stalin approved a
small-scale effort when he learned of German, British, and
American work in progress; and (3) in August 1945, Stalin
wanted to break the U.S. nuclear monopoly as soon as
possible. Points of interest include Russian scientists
taking note of the "dogs that did not bark" in

international scientific journals; evidence by Shtemenko
that at Potsdam, Stalin knew little about the U.S. atomic
bomb; and the exclusion of Soviet military leaders from all
these decisions. There is extensive research through
Russian-language sources.

3897. Jackman, Jarrell J. and Carla M. Borden, eds. THE MUSES
        FLEE HITLER: CULTURAL TRANSFER AND ADAPTATION, 1930-
        1945. Washington, D.C.: Smithsonian, 1983. 347 pp.

        Here is an excellent collection of articles which deal
        with the migration of the intellectuals. For this project,
        see especially the articles by Gerald Holton on the
        physicists (pp. 169-188) and Nathan Reingold on the
        mathematicians (pp. 205-234).

3898. Jette, Eleanor. INSIDE BOX 1663. LOS ALAMOS, NM: Los
        Alamos Historical Society, 1977. 132 pp.

        Here is a view of the Manhattan Project from the
        perspective of the wife of one of the scientists.

3899. Jones, Vincent C. MANHATTAN: THE ARMY AND THE ATOMIC
        BOMB. Washington, D. C.: GPO, 1985. 660 pp.

        Part of the Army's special studies on World War II, this
        volume focuses on the administrative framework of the
        Manhattan Project. During the early phase of the project
        (1939-1942), the Army played a small part, but, as Jones
        points out, after Gen. Groves assumed the lead, the Army's
        involvement rose dramatically. The book is extremely well
        researched.

3900. Jungk, Robert. BRIGHTER THAN A THOUSAND SUNS. New York:
        Harcourt, Brace, and World, 1958. 369 pp.

        This work, translated by James Cleugh, presents the
        personal stories of scientists who helped develop the
        atomic bomb. Of interest are their reactions to the
        TRINITY test.

3901. Kevles, Daniel. THE PHYSICISTS: THE HISTORY OF A
        SCIENTIFIC COMMUNITY IN MODERN AMERICA. Cambridge, MA:
        Harvard University Press, 1987. 489 pp.

        Originally published in 1977, this edition (with a new
        Preface) traces in detail the development of this special
        science in the United States. Of foremost concern for this
        project, if correct, is the material on the breakthroughs

and research leading to the atomic bomb.

3902. Kistiakowsky, George B. "Trinity--A Reminiscence." BULL
       ATOMIC SCI, 36 (June 1980), 19-22.

       This reminiscence incorporates not only the author's
       contribution in developing the atomic bomb but also a
       report on the internecine feuding among the scientists
       working on the project.

3903. Knebel, Fletcher and Charles W. Bailey. "The Fight Over
       the Atomic Bomb." LOOK, 37 (August 13, 1963), 19-23.

       Based on research through the Manhattan Project files,
       the authors point out that Truman was denied access to the
       petitions of scientists opposed to the use of the atomic
       bomb. Of interest is the role of Leo Szilard in
       confronting Gen. Groves.

3904. Kragh, Helge. "The Fine Structure of Hydrogen and the
       Gross Structure of the Physics Community, 1916-1926."
       HIST STUD PHYSICAL SCI, 15 (No. 2, 1985), 67-125.

       In this detailed study, the author describes the
       development of new ideas in physics, especially the work
       (and controversies created by) Arnold Sommerfeld.

3905. Kramish, Arnold. THE GRIFFIN. Boston: Houghton Mifflin,
       1986. 294 pp.

       Kramish tells the story of Paul Rosbaud, a German
       science editor. Rosbaud, code-named The Griffin, relayed
       information about German scientific activities, especially
       research to develop an atomic bomb, through an elaborate
       network (inside Germany and Norway) to the British.
       Interestingly, the British never told the Americans of
       Rosbaud's conclusion that the Germans would not be able to
       develop an atomic weapon.

3906. Lamont, Lansing. DAY OF TRINITY. New York: Atheneum,
       1965. 333 pp.

       Based on the oral histories of many of the participants,
       Lamont presents a unique perspective on the TRINITY test,
       July 16, 1945.

3907. Lang, Daniel. EARLY TALES OF THE ATOMIC AGE. Garden City,
       NY: Doubleday, 1948. 223 pp.

Here are stories about the development of the atomic
bomb. They first appeared in the NEW YORKER.

3908. Lapp, Ralph E. ATOMS AND PEOPLE. New York: Harper, 1956.

This popular account summarizes the history of atomic
power. See the material relating to the development of the
atomic bomb.

3909. Lathrop, Judith M., comp. "The Oppenheimer Years." LOS
ALAMOS SCI, 4 (Winter/Spring 1983), 6-25.

Here is an interesting collection of documents on
Project Y, selected from the Los Alamos Archives and Report
Library. Lathrop presents some contemporary views of
intellectual giants such as Szilard, Fermi,
and...Groves(?). See especially Oppenheimer's request for
a salary reduction.

3910. Laurence, William L. DAWN OVER ZERO: THE STORY OF THE
ATOMIC BOMB. New York: A.A. Knopf, 1946. 274 pp.

Laurence, a science reporter assigned to the Manhattan
Project, offers a primer on atomic power for the general
public. His assignment included reporting not only on the
development of the atomic bomb but also on its use. He was
on board the aircraft that dropped the weapon on Nagasaki.
Here is an important contemporary source.

3911. Laurence, William L. MEN AND ATOMS. New York: Simon and
Schuster, 1959. 302 pp.

Here is a knowledgeable summary of the discovery, uses,
and future of atomic power.

3912. Levin, Bob. "The Dawn of the Nuclear Age." MACLEAN'S, 98
(July 22, 1985), 18-21.

Here is a short survey of the development and use of the
atomic bomb.

3913. Lewis, Richard D. and Jane Wilson, eds. ALAMOGORDO PLUS
TWENTY-FIVE YEARS. New York: Viking, 1971.

The articles provide a retrospective look at the events
and people associated with the development of the atomic
bomb. The Manhattan Project lives!

3914. McDaniel, Boyce. "A Physicist at Los Alamos." BULL ATOMIC

SCI, 30 (October 1974), 39-43.

Here is the personal account of a young Ph.D. at Los
Alamos who had been a protege of Robert Bacher. McDaniel
describes the development of the first plutonium,
implosive-type bomb.

3915. Malisoff, William Marias. "On the Non-Existence of the
        Atomic Secret." PHILOS SCIENCE, 13 (January 1946), 1-2.

Arguing that the atomic secret is not ours to keep or
share (and that "atomic" is a misnomer for "nuclear"), the
author distinguishes between the invention of the atomic
bomb and the unsolved secret of the nucleus. To obtain the
latter, he says, will require international cooperative
efforts.

3916. Mandelbaum, Michael. THE NUCLEAR REVOLUTION: INTERNATIONAL
        POLITICS BEFORE AND AFTER HIROSHIMA. New York:
        Cambridge University Press, 1981. 283 pp.

Mandelbaum sets the development of the atomic bomb
within an international context. The book is well written
and solidly researched.

3917. Manley, J.H. "Assembling the Wartime Labs." BULL ATOMIC
        SCI, 30 (May 1974), 42-47.

After working under Arthur Compton both in the
metallurgical laboratory and in weapons development, the
author helped Oppenheimer assemble the staff and develop
the facilities at Los Alamos. He feels that no major
developments in nuclear science (as opposed to nuclear
technology) occurred at Los Alamos because everyone there
concentrated on practical problems.

3918. Nichols, K.D. THE ROAD TO TRINITY. New York: William
        Morrow, 1987.

Gen. Nichols (USA) participated in the planning,
development, and use of the atomic bomb. Later, his
service included administrative work in the Atomic Energy
Commission. Here is a unique perspective from a man whose
wartime career integrated key elements of the atomic
project.

3919. Peierls, Rudolf. "Reflections of a British Participant."
        BULL ATOMIC SCI, 41 (August 1985), 27-29.

Peierls, a British physicist at Los Alamos from mid-1944
to the end of the war, never dreamed that the atomic bomb
would be used against a city without warning. He had
always assumed that an international demonstration would be
arranged.

3920.   Pringle, Peter and James Spigelman. THE NUCLEAR BARONS.
        London: Sphere Books, 1981. 578 pp.

Here is an exhaustive analysis of the development of the
atomic bomb. The authors highlight the British
perspective.

3921.   Purcell, John F. THE BEST KEPT SECRET. New York:
        Vanguard Press, 1963. 188 pp.

Although now outdated, the book gives a convenient
summary of the highlights in the development and use of the
atomic bomb.

3922.   Rabi, I.I. MY LIFE AND TIMES AS A PHYSICIST. Claremont,
        CA: Claremont College, 1960. 55 pp.

Here is a first-hand report on the development of the
atomic bomb. Rabi was one of the few Manhattan scientists
to raise with Oppenheimer the implications of atomic
weapons for national policy. According to Rabi, the two
men discussed the necessity for nuclear arms control.

3923.   Rhodes, Richard. "'I Am Become Death...': The Agony of J.
        Robert Oppenheimer." AMER HERITAGE, 28 (October 1977),
        70-83.

The author, a journalist, takes a sentimental look at
what he calls the "tortured life" of Oppenheimer.

3924.   Rhodes, Richard. THE MAKING OF THE ATOMIC BOMB. New York:
        Simon and Schuster, 1986. 886 pp.

The author, a professional writer, describes the
scientific, human, and political development of the atomic
bomb over a period that dates back to the turn of the
century. In this prize-winning book, Rhodes presents
science as the "preeminent transnational community." His
research is extensive and includes material from interviews
and private collections. Of interest is his treatment of
Szilard's first conceptualization of a nuclear chain
reaction while walking near London's Russell Square.

3925.   Rider, Robin E.   "Alarm and Opportunity: Emigration of
        Mathematicians and Physicists to Britain and the United
        States, 1933-1945."   HIST STUD PHYSICAL SCI, 15 (No. 1,
        1984), 107-176.

        Rider includes a listing of scientist-emigres during the
        period 1933-1945. According to the author, the metaphor of
        saturation (at U.S. research and teaching posts) turned out
        to be misleading.

3926.   Rotblat, Joseph.   "Leaving the Bomb Project."   BULL ATOMIC
        SCI, 41 (August 1985), 16-19.

        Rotblatt worked on the Manhattan Project but left in
        disillusionment. He says his reasons were: (1) the end of
        the fear that Germany would be the first to develop the
        atomic bomb, (2) his fear of the start of an arms race, (3)
        Gen. Groves told him that the atomic bomb would be used to
        influence the Soviet Union, and (4) his lack of control
        over his work. He concludes the article by observing that
        morality is abandoned when war begins.

3927.   Savage, John and Barbara Storms.   REACH TO THE UNKNOWN.
        Los Alamos, NM: University of California and U.S.
        Atomic Energy Commission, 1965. 46 pp.

        Here is an authoritative report on the Trinity test in
        July 1945. Leaders of the Manhattan Project made clear
        that the atomic bomb had to be tested before any military
        use of the weapon could be considered. Of interest is the
        careful attention paid to collecting the Trinity data.

3928.   Schlegel, Richard.   "Quantum Physics and the Divine
        Postulate."   ZYGON, 14 (June 1979), 163-185.

        The author, a physics professor, feels there is a close
        association between physics and theology. Changes in
        physics, he argues, will be accompanied by parallel changes
        in theology.

3929.   Sembower, John F.   "Democracy and Science Fused by the
        Atomic Bomb."   ANTIOCH REV, 5 (Winter 1945-46), 493-500.

        Calling attention to the usual criticisms leveled
        against democratic governments by totalitarian regimes, the
        author finds it remarkable that the atomic bomb could be
        developed during wartime while Allied scientists adhered to
        established norms of democratic institutions.

3930.   Sherwin, Martin J. A WORLD DESTROYED: THE ATOMIC BOMB AND
        THE GRAND ALLIANCE. New York: Alfred A. Knopf, 1975.
        315 pp.

        Incorporating extensive research through primary
        sources, many of which have only recently been released,
        Sherwin analyzes the tensions during the war between
        advocates of postwar international control of atomic energy
        and those who preferred to retain an Anglo-American atomic
        monopoly as a means of gaining postwar diplomatic leverage.
        Specifically, Niels Bohr led the former group, and Sherwin
        places Roosevelt and Churchill at the head of the latter.
        The author argues that Truman, far from breaking with
        Roosevelt's policies on this subject, faithfully adhered to
        them. Criticizing the decision to use the atomic bomb,
        Sherwin clearly sympathizes with the "international"
        approach--the road not taken.

3931.   Smith, Alice Kimball and Charles Weiner, eds. ROBERT
        OPPENHEIMER: LETTERS AND RECOLLECTIONS. Cambridge, MA:
        Harvard University Press, 1980. 376 pp.

        This collection is indispensable to any study of this
        complex, gifted individual.

3932.   Smith, Alice Kimball. "The Elusive Dr. Szilard."
        HARPER'S, 221 (July 1960), 77-86.

        Here is an informal picture of Szilard--warm and
        friendly.

3933.   Smith, Alice Kimball. "Los Alamos: Forces In An Age."
        BULL ATOMIC SCI, 26 (June 1970), 15-20.

        In this description of the scientific work at Los Alamos
        in developing the atomic bomb, Smith avoids the
        ever-present issue of moral guilt.

3934.   Smith, Datus C., Jr. "The Publishing History of the 'Smyth
        Report.'" PRINCETON LIB CHRON, 27 (Spring 1976),
        191-203.

        The author had been the contemporary director of
        Princeton University Press. His narrative follows the
        report as it made its way into print with total sales of
        126,741 (before expiring in 1973).

3935.   Smyth, Henry DeWolf. ATOMIC ENERGY FOR MILITARY PURPOSES;
        THE OFFICIAL REPORT ON THE DEVELOPMENT OF THE ATOMIC

BOMB UNDER THE AUSPICES OF THE U.S. GOVERNMENT,
1940-1945. Princeton, NJ: Princeton University Press,
1945. 264 pp.

Here is an excellent account of the development of the
atomic bomb. Smyth provides technical explanations without
lapsing into scientific jargon. This contemporary work
remains a useful introduction to the topic.

3936. Smyth, H.D. "The 'Smyth Report.'" PRINCETON LIB CHRON, 37
       (Spring 1976), 173-189.

The author says that in 1944 he was asked to write a
report of the Manhattan Project for public use. His
teaching and consulting responsibilities forced him to work
only part-time on the project. This article, written
largely in 1947, provides details about the official
report.

3937. Steiner, Arthur. "Baptism of the Atomic Scientists." BULL
       ATOMIC SCI, 31 (February 1975), 21-28.

Analyzing the fate of the Franck Report, Steiner, a
political scientist, argues that the document (1) provoked
the only serious formal discussion on a possibly non-lethal
demonstration of the atomic bomb, and (2) helped promote
the decision to reveal the existence of the weapon to the
Soviet Union. Generalizing from this episode, the author
points out that similar problems persist for scientific
advisers to policy makers.

3938. Strauss, Lewis L. MEN AND DECISIONS. Garden City, NY:
       Doubleday, 1962. 468 pp.

Admiral Strauss was special assistant to Navy Secretary
Forrestal. His position gave him access to high-level
information, especially on the atomic bomb. Strauss
presents the text of the dissenting opinion by Ralph Bard
against the use of the bomb. There is also the text of a
letter from Einstein to Roosevelt on Szilard's concern
about the widening gulf separating the scientists from the
policy makers.

3939. Sutherland, Don S. "Mary Helen Gosnell: Women's Airforce
       Service Pilot." AIRMAN, 31 (September 1987), 15.

Gosnell's duties included ferrying supplies and
personnel for the Manhattan Project.

3940. Szasz, Ferenc M. THE DAY THE SUN ROSE TWICE: THE STORY OF
          THE TRINITY SITE NUCLEAR EXPLOSION, JULY 16, 1945.
          Albuquerque, NM: University of New Mexico Press, 1984.

          Here is an authoritative report on the critical test of
          the atomic bomb. Szasz describes the painstaking
          preparations for TRINITY. Also of interest is the pre-test
          speculation among the scientists about the improbable
          circumstances that might occur.

3941. Szilard, Gertrud Weiss and Bernard T. Feld, eds. THE
          COLLECTED WORKS OF LEO SZILARD. Cambridge, MA: MIT
          Press, 1972. 2 vols.

          Szilard's writings and correspondence provide insight
          into his views about the atomic bomb. An acknowledged
          leader in the scientific community, Szilard played a key
          role in shaping attitudes about the decision to use the
          weapon against Japan. Of special interest are the concerns
          he voiced about removing the scientists from policy-making
          circles in Washington.

3942. Szilard, Gertrud Weiss and Spencer R. Weart. LEO SZILARD:
          HIS VERSION OF THE FACTS. Cambridge, MA: MIT Press,
          1978. 259 pp.

          His widow and a scientific colleague combine to offer an
          explanation of their understanding of Szilard's views. The
          authors trace his shifting ideas about the atomic bomb and
          the role of the scientific community. Of interest is the
          story of Einstein selecting the longer of two drafts
          written by Szilard for a letter to Roosevelt. For the
          scientist, development of the atomic bomb meant that the
          world would have to live under one government. See, too,
          the description of Szilard's disappointment at having
          Byrnes speak of both the need to impress Moscow and to
          justify the money spent on the Manhattan Project.

3943. United States. Scientific Laboratory. Los Alamos, New
          Mexico. THE EFFECTS OF ATOMIC WEAPONS. New York:
          McGraw-Hill, 1950. 456 pp.

          Here is a highly technical report. Some of the jargon
          makes for difficult reading. See especially the sections
          on scientific, engineering, and medical effects.

3944. Wattenberg, Albert. "The Building of the First Chain
          Reaction Pile." BULL ATOMIC SCI, 30 (June 1974), 51-57.

Wattenberg discusses his role in helping to arrange the first nuclear chain reaction. From 1943 to the end of the war, Wattenberg bore responsibility for making all the neutron sources used as standards for the Manhattan Project.

3945. Wattenberg, Albert. "December 2, 1942: The Event and the People." BULL ATOMIC SCI, 38 (December 1982), 22-32.

Here is the reminiscence of a participant about the first self-sustaining nuclear chain reaction. The author, one of the young physicists present at the University of Chicago that day, had studied at Columbia University under Fermi and other leaders in the field.

3946. Weart, Spencer R. "Scientists With a Secret." PHYSICS TODAY, 29 (February 1976), 23-30.

Basing his account on interviews and private papers, Weart writes of the self-imposed censorship of U.S. scientists (without the participation of the government) in 1939 about a nuclear chain reaction. Szilard and other scientists were confident that such an event was possible.

3947. Weisskopf, Victor F. "Looking Back at Los Alamos." BULL ATOMIC SCI, 41 (August 1985), 20-22.

The author served as a group leader at Los Alamos. Feeling, as he does, that the achievement of the Manhattan Project has been the (unintended) cause of the postwar world's tragic predicament, Weisskopf charges the scientific community with the responsibility to work to reduce these present difficulties.

3948. Weisskopf, Victor F. "A Memorial to Oppenheimer: The Los Alamos Years." PHYSICS TODAY, 20 (October 1967), 39-42.

The author, a Manhattan Project scientist, reports that no other man commanded as much respect from his colleagues there as did Oppenheimer.

3949. Weltman, John J. "Trinity: The Weapons Scientists and the Nuclear Age." SAIS REV, 5 (Summer-Fall 1985), 29-39.

Insisting that blame or praise should go to the authors of policy instead of the scientists, Weltman argues that policy determines technology and not, as is commonly believed, the other way around. When good physics points

to a radical transformation of human affairs, he says,
morale is at its highest for the scientific community; such
was the case during the war.

3950.   Wheeler, John A.   "Mechanism of Fission."   PHYSICS TODAY,
20 (November 1967), 49-52.

Wheeler, one of the first American scientists to
concentrate on nuclear fission, discusses early
developments and leading personalities in the field.
Wartime breakthroughs led to postwar research in the
"collective" model of the nucleus.

3951.   Wilson, Jane, ed.   ALL IN OUR TIME.   Chicago, IL: Bulletin
of Atomic Scientists, 1975.   236 pp.

Here are the reminiscences of twelve nuclear pioneer
physicists about their participation in the development of
the atomic bomb.   All were then relatively junior,
assisting the giants, and are now distinguished scientific
leaders.   The twelve are Abelson, Alvarez, Anderson,
Bainbridge, de Hoffmann, Fitch, Frisch, Kamen, Manley,
McDaniel, Wattenberg, and Wilson.

3952.   Wilson, Robert R.   "Niels Bohr and the Young Scientists."
BULL ATOMIC SCI, 41 (August 1985), 23-26.

The author, a young scientist at Los Alamos, unabashedly
praises Bohr.

3953.   Wilson, Robert R.   "A Recruit for Los Alamos."   BULL ATOMIC
SCI, 31 (March 1975), 41-47.

In this amusing memoir, Wilson discusses how Oppenheimer
recruited him to Los Alamos from Princeton, the schemes to
remove cyclotrons from Harvard, and the failure of his
isotron project.

3954.   Wyden, Peter.   DAY ONE: BEFORE HIROSHIMA AND AFTER.   New
York: Simon and Schuster, 1984.   413 pp.

Wyden, a professional writer, narrates the story of the
creation and use of the atomic bomb.   Interviews with U.S.
scientists and Japanese survivors, as well as recently
opened official documents, form the basis of his account,
which he calls integrated history (scientific, political,
military, moral, and human).   The paucity of citations is
disconcerting, especially in light of the synthesis he has
produced.   The author regrets that the idea of an

international demonstration/warning never merited serious
consideration. According to Wyden, Hiroshima, by 1945, had
ceased to be a military target and the docks nearby were no
longer shipping Japanese troops. Of special interest is
Wyden's treatment of Japanese atomic research (led by
Yoshio Nishina) and that of the Soviets (under Igor "The
Beard" Kurchatov and aided by master spy Klaus Fuchs) as
well as the proposal by Lewis L. Strauss to drop the bomb
in the Nikko forest near Tokyo (where the resultant damage
to the cryptomeria trees would provide a convenient measure
of the power of the new weapon). The book contains some
excellent photos. Despite occasional lapses into
simplistic criticisms of the use of the bomb--Wyden writes,
for example, of the desire to "use the Japanese as living
guinea pigs for Oppenheimer's bomb"--the book offers a good
introduction to the topic for the general public,
especially for those readers not familiar with the
properties of heavy water.

3955. Yass, Marion. HIROSHIMA. New York: G.P. Putnam's Sons,
        1972. 128 pp.

Reviewing the debate about the momentous decision, Yass
argues that the use of the atomic bomb became a moral issue
only after the fact. There is a good summary of the
scientific breakthroughs in developing the weapon. Of
interest is the description of guarded cooperation on the
project between British and Americans.

IV.J.2.b. **THE DECISION/USE OF THE ATOMIC BOMB**

3956. Akira, Kouchi. THE PARACHUTE IN THE SKY OVER HIROSHIMA.
        1985.

The atomic bomb is portrayed as a weapon of racists
that was developed to punish America's yellow-skinned
enemy.

3957. Amrine, Michael. THE GREAT DECISION: THE SECRET HISTORY
        OF THE ATOMIC BOMB. New York: G. P. Putnam's Sons,
        1959. 251 pp.

This book unfolds the story of events which culminated
in the decision to use the atomic bomb against Japan. The
author is particularly critical of the warning announcement
to Japan, the selection of targets, and the dropping of the
second atomic bomb. His sympathetic treatment of the
Franck report is intended to demonstrate that scientific

experts are capable of sound political thinking.

3958. Anders, Gunther with Claude Eatherly. BURNING CONSCIENCE.
       New York: Monthly Review Press, 1962. 139 pp.

       Here is an absorbing story of Eatherly's personal
       problems which he attributes, in large part, to his
       association with the atomic bombing of Japan.

3959. Ashworth, Frederick L. "Dropping the Atomic Bomb on
       Nagasaki." USNIP, 84 (January 1958), 12-17.

       Ashworth flew on the mission to Nagasaki as a personal
       representative of General Groves. One of the chief values
       of this personal account lies in the description of
       mounting circumstances during the flight which eliminated
       the crew's option of returning without dropping the bomb.

3960. Baker, Paul R., ed. THE ATOMIC BOMB: THE GREAT DECISION.
       Hinsdale, IL: Dryden Press, 1976 ed. 193 pp.

       The revised edition of this excellent introduction to
       the topic incorporates new historiographical
       interpretations. Baker's bibliographic essay is
       first-rate. The book is part of Dryden's noted "American
       Problems Studies."

3961. Baldwin, Paul. "The Ending of World War II." AEROSP H, 23
       (Fall, September 1976), 136-139.

       The author, a trained physicist and radar observer, flew
       in P-61's as a night fighter observer in the Philippines.
       He predicted in 1937 that atomic energy would be used by
       1944 (probably by Hitler). His comments reflect the awe
       contemporaries felt upon learning of the destructive power
       of the atomic bomb.

3962. Omitted.

3963. BAREFOOT GEN. San Francisco: Educomics, n.d.

       NE

3964. Barnouw, Erik. "The Hiroshima-Nagasaki Footage: A Report."
       HIST J FILM RADIO TV, 2 (March 1982), 91-100.

       NE

3965. Batchelder, Robert C. THE IRREVERSIBLE DECISION,
       1939-1950. Boston: Houghton Mifflin, 1962. 306 pp.

The author, a minister and mathematician, examines the moral implications of the use of the atomic bomb. In his analysis, Batchelder feels that the atomic bombs probably saved lives in the long run. Yet, he argues that an act must be judged on objective moral standards. Evil means, he writes, are never sanctioned. Thus, with the decision to use the bomb being "morally compromised," Batchelder criticizes American decision-makers for failing to maintain both a commitment to moral principle and a realistic calculation of consequences.

3966. "Before Hiroshima." BULL ATOMIC SCI, 1 (May 1, 1946), 1-4, 16.

This article includes the text of the Franck Report, June 11, 1945. This "Report to the Secretary of War" calls the use of the atomic bomb against Japan "inadvisable."

3967. Bennett, Raul C. "An Interview with Brig Gen Paul W. Tibbets" COMBAT CREW, 37 (October 1987), 22-25.

Most of this interview deals with Tibbets' wartime activities prior to his selection for special training to drop the atomic bomb.

3968. Bennett, Raul C. "Training for the Mission to Hiroshima." COMBAT CREW, 37 (August 1987), 4-6

The author, a USAF pilot, describes the preparation for "Special Bombing Mission 13," the dropping of "Little Boy" on Hiroshima. Col. Tibbets arranged to have many combat veterans placed in the new 509th composite bomb group. Initially, the unit trained over U.S. western deserts, but, to train navigators in gauging the rate of closure over water, the unit later practiced bombing runs over Cuba. Of interest is the calculation that the aircraft required a 159-degree turn after releasing the bomb in order to fly tangent to the shock circle. To do so, Tibbets had to hold the aircraft in a 50 or 55-degree bank turn for 48 seconds.

3969. Bernstein, Barton J. "The Atomic Bomb and American Foreign Policy, 1941-1945: An Historiographical Controversy." PEACE & CHANGE, 2 (Spring 1974), 1-16.

Sorting through the "limited, sometimes ambiguous evidence," Bernstein presents an excellent survey and analysis of writings about the use of the atomic bomb. He suggests that the opposing writers seem to be on different wavelengths and, because of the moral values involved, will probably never reach a consensus.

3970. Bernstein, Barton J. "The Challenges and Dangers of
        Nuclear Weapons: Foreign Policy and Strategy,
        1941-1978." MD HISTORIAN, 9 (Spring 1978), 73-99.

        Bernstein asserts that, although the use of the atomic
        bomb carried certain bonuses, such as inflicting
        retribution on Japan and making the Soviets more tractable
        in the postwar era, the United States would have used the
        atomic bomb anyway--even if the Japanese had been
        Caucasians. With his extensive research on the subject,
        the author maintains that the first atomic bombing helped
        speed the Japanese surrender, but the second was
        unnecessary. By October 1945, he states, twenty urban
        Soviet targets had been selected. Throughout this survey,
        Bernstein argues that the people should not abrogate
        decision-making to politicians and generals.

3971. Bernstein, Barton J. "The Dropping of the A-Bomb: How
        Decisions Are Made When a Nation Is at War." CENTER
        MAG, 16 (March-April 1983), 7-15.

        Bernstein sheds light on the difficult dilemma facing
        U.S. leaders in mid-1945.

3972. Bernstein, Barton J. "Hiroshima's Hidden Victims."
        INQUIRY, 2 (August 6 and 20, 1979), 9-11.

        After careful and considered analysis of the research
        sources available, Bernstein concludes that, despite
        official disavowals, American POW's died in the atomic
        bombing of Hiroshima. He calls for more evidence so that
        the definite number of U.S. casualties can be ascertained.
        Of special interest is his assertion that Japanese
        officials linked the deaths of nine other American POWs
        (not in Hiroshima) with the casualty figures of Hiroshima
        to conceal war atrocities in so-called "medical"
        experiments.

3973. Bernstein, Barton J. HIROSHIMA AND NAGASAKI RECONSIDERED:
        THE ATOMIC BOMBINGS OF JAPAN AND THE ORIGINS OF THE COLD
        WAR, 1941-1945. Morristown, NJ: General Learning
        Press, 1975. 31 pp.

        This pamphlet, part of the publisher's "University
        Programs Modular Studies," centers on the role of the
        scientists in the Manhattan Project and how the atomic bomb
        contributed to the onset of the Cold War. Bernstein, who

has written extensively on this subject, not only criticizes Roosevelt's excessive secrecy and his exclusion of the Soviet Union from the scientific development of the weapon but also faults Truman and Byrnes for failing to use the atomic bomb to reshape the postwar world.

3974. Bernstein, Barton J. "Hiroshima Reconsidered--Thirty Years Later." FOR SERVICE J, 52 (August 1975), 8-13, 32-33.

The author brings formidable research to this review of the decision to use the atomic bomb. Observing that U.S. leaders felt no moral or political reason to avoid dropping the bomb on Japan (and citing the expected influence on the Soviet Union as subtle confirmation for those officials of that decision), Bernstein argues that American leaders reflected the consensus of the American people in 1945.

3975. Bernstein, Barton J. "A Postwar Myth: 500,000 U.S. Lives Saved." BULL ATOMIC SCI, 42 (June/July 1986), 38-40.

Bernstein claims that no wartime evidence suggests that any U.S. official or planner believed the invasion of Japan would cost one-half million lives. Instead, the claim seems to have emerged from postwar writings. Available archival (contemporary) sources, according to Bernstein, all contain estimates which range close to a total of 50,000 U.S. casualties. He feels that his conclusions raise new questions about the use of the two atomic bombs.

3976. Bernstein, Barton J. "The Quest for Security: American Foreign Policy and International Control of Atomic Energy, 1942-1946." J AMER HIST, 60 (March 1974), 1,003-1,044.

Bernstein focuses on the role of the atomic bomb in the origins of the Cold War. Pointing out that both Roosevelt and Truman were less than forthright with the Soviet Union about the development of the new weapon, the author argues that the belated U.S. plan for international control of atomic weapons was rejected by the Soviets, who felt that Americans would continue to hold a nuclear monopoly. The United States rejected the Soviet plan to destroy all nuclear weapons because of insufficient provisions for inspection and verification. Thus, the stalemate in 1945 and 1946, for Bernstein, reflected the mutual mistrust of the two powers. The article incorporates extensive research, especially through private collections.

3977. Bernstein, Barton J. "Roosevelt, Truman, and the Atomic

Bomb: A Reinterpretation." POL SCI Q, 90 (Spring 1975), 23-69.

In a carefully worded, well-researched analysis, Bernstein assesses some of the significant dimensions of the decision to use the atomic bomb. Without overstating his arguments, he places that fateful decision in the broader context of Soviet-American relations, the origins of the Cold War, and U.S. policies--less cautious, more demanding, and more optimistic because of the nuclear monopoly--in the postwar era.

3978.   Bernstein, Barton J. "Shatterer of Worlds: Hiroshima and Nagasaki." BULL ATOMIC SCI, 31 (December 1975), 12-22.

This article is less carefully presented than some of Bernstein's other work on this subject. He argues that U.S. leaders had come to a state of moral insensitivity by 1945. Also, according to Bernstein, the use of the atomic bomb contributed to the origins of the Cold War by instilling American leaders with overconfidence in atomic diplomacy.

3979.   Bernstein, Barton J. "The Uneasy Alliance: Roosevelt, Churchill, and the Atomic Bomb, 1940-1945." WESTERN POL Q, 29 (June 1976), 202-230.

Here is an examination of how Roosevelt and Churchill not only defined the Anglo-American relationship on atomic energy but also tried to arrange a nuclear monopoly for their two countries.

3980.   Bernstein, Barton J. "Unravelling a Mystery: American POWs Killed at Hiroshima." FOR SERVICE J, 56 (October 1979), 17-19, 40.

Bernstein's thorough investigations have led him to conclude that at least eleven and perhaps as many as twenty-three American POW's were in Hiroshima on August 6, 1945. Although lacking direct proof, he infers that the United States government continues to cover up the episode.

3981.   Besse, Janet and Harold D. Lasswell. "Our Columnists on the A-Bomb." WORLD POL, 3 (October 1950), 72-87.

The authors studied what fourteen of the leading American columnists wrote about the atomic bomb over a three-year period. Opinions differ about the role of

syndicated columnists in shaping public opinion, but the
authors feel that, at least on this subject, the columnists
reflected the wide-ranging views of the American people.

3982. Boller, Paul F., Jr. "Hiroshima and the American Left:
       August 1945." INT SOC SCI REV, 57 (Winter 1982), 13-28.

       The author, a historian, finds that those American
       leftists who were friendliest to Stalinist Russia generally
       supported not only the use of the atomic bomb but also a
       harsh unconditional surrender policy. On the other hand,
       anti-Stalinist liberals and radicals opposed the use of the
       atomic bomb and the imposition of a harsh peace. Boller
       admits that "ideological correctness" in these complex
       issues proved difficult to maintain. His study is based on
       a survey of some intellectual journals of the day that were
       reputed to reflect leftist views.

3983. Buck, Pearl S. "The Bomb--Did We Have to Drop It?"
       READER'S DIG, 75 (August 1959), 111-115.

       Buck bases her article on an interview with Dr.
       Arthur H. Compton. The scientist voted at the time to
       use the atomic bomb and still believes that decision,
       including the second bomb, saved many lives. According
       to Compton, the use of the two bombs made it possible for
       Japan to surrender with honor.

3984. Buckley, William F., Jr. "Hiroshima And All That."
       NATL REV, 37 (September 30, 1985), 54-55.

       Decrying the "pacifist tendentiousness" in the
       debate about the use of the atomic bomb, Buckley insists
       that Washington should never agree ahead of time not to
       use atomic weapons.

3985. Bungei, Shunju Senshi Kenkyukai. THE DAY MAN LOST
       HIROSHIMA, 6 AUGUST 1945. Tokyo: Kodansha
       International, 1972. 312 pp.

       The Pacific War Research Society (in Palo Alto)
       sponsored this study of the first atomic bombing. Of
       special interest is the wide range of reactions from the
       survivors who were interviewed.

3986. Bunichiro Sano et al, eds. HIROSHIMA-NAGASAKI DOCUMENT
       1961. Tokyo: Japan Council Against Atomic and Hydrogen
       Bombs, 1961.

NE

3987. Cary, Otis. "Secret Documents: Atomic Bomb Targeting--
       Myths and Realities." Japan Q, 26 (October-December
       1979), 506-514.

       Quoting at length from many important documents, Cary
       demonstrates that the process of target selection was
       far from a random affair.

3988. Cary, Otis. "The Sparing of Kyoto--Mr. Stimson's 'Pet
       City.'" JAPAN Q, 22 (October-December 1975), 337-347.

       Kyoto had been bombed seven times during the war. In
       a fascinating display of detective work, Cary concludes
       that Stimson acted alone in removing Kyoto from the list
       of possible targets for the atomic bomb.

3989. Chinnock, Frank W. NAGASAKI: THE FORGOTTEN BOMB.
       Cleveland, OH: World, 1969. 305 pp.

       This professional writer/editor adds touching human
       profiles to his solid research.

3990. Clark, Ian. NUCLEAR PAST, NUCLEAR PRESENT: HIROSHIMA,
       NAGASAKI, AND CONTEMPORARY STRATEGY. Boulder, CO:
       Westview Press, 1985. 146 pp.

       Clark takes issue with the traditional arguments
       advanced in support of using the atomic bomb against Japan.
       He feels that similar erroneous and confused thinking about
       nuclear war exists today.

3991. Coerr, Eleanor. SADAKO AND THE THOUSAND PAPER CRANES. New
       York: G. P. Putnam's Sons, 1977. 64 pp.

       Sadako, a two-year old girl at Hiroshima in August 1945,
       died ten years later of leukemia. According to a Japanese
       legend, she began making good luck cranes out of paper.
       The legend holds that an ailing person will be cured by
       making 1,000 such cranes. Sadako made 644 before she died.
       Japanese children still make paper cranes in her honor, and
       a memorial to Sadako stands in the Hiroshima Peace Park.

3992. Committee for the Compilation of Materials on Damage Caused
       by the Atomic Bomb in Hiroshima and Nagasaki.
       Translated by Eisei Ishikawa and David L. Swain.
       HIROSHIMA AND NAGASAKI: THE PHYSICAL, MEDICAL, AND
       SOCIAL EFFECTS OF THE ATOMIC BOMBINGS. New York: Basic

Books, 1981. 706 pp.

This group of scientists conducted exhaustive research.
The report is divided into four parts: (1) physical aspects
of destruction, (2) injury to the human body, (3) the
impact on society and daily life, and (4) toward the
abolition of nuclear arms. The book is indispensable to
any serious study of the use of the atomic bomb against
Japan.

3993. Compton, Karl. "If the Atomic Bomb Had Not Been Used."
ATLANTIC MON, 178 (December 1946), 54-56.

Compton argues that the use of the atomic bomb saved
hundreds of thousands, perhaps millions, of lives. He
bases his claim on his participation in the Manhattan
Project, his first-hand knowledge of the work of
MacArthur's planning staff in Manila preparing the final
invasion, the interrogations of Japanese soldiers after the
war that there would be no surrender to enemy invaders, and
MacArthur's frequent postwar statements about the need for
one million U.S. troops over ten years to defeat Japanese
guerrillas. The author notes that MacArthur's planners had
estimated 50,000 American casualties with several times
that number of Japanese casualties just to establish the
initial beachhead on Kyushu.

3994. Cotter, Donald R. "How World War II Really Ended." NAT
REV, 37 (August 23, 1985), 22-25.

Cotter, the director of a policy research center,
concocts fanciful headlines for his "what if" history of
the end of the war. His fictional scenario includes a
fizzled demonstration of the atomic bomb, two years of
bloody fighting in the Japanese home islands, American
troop withdrawals from Europe, the control of Europe by
the Soviet Union, the abandonment of the United States by
its allies, and the final peace terms dictated by the
Soviet Union. Are there any questions about the actual
use of the atomic bomb in August 1945?

3995. Davidson, James West and Mark H. Lytle. AFTER THE FACT:
THE ART OF HISTORICAL DETECTION. New York: A. A.
Knopf, 1982. 400 pp.

The two historians describe methods of investigation in
what they call the "apprentice approach" to history. Among
their case studies is "The Decision to Drop the Bomb" (pp.
320-355). Pointing out that the scientific field during

the 1930s mirrored trends in American culture toward
organization and bureaucracy, the authors shed light on the
use of the atomic bomb by adapting Graham Allison's work on
the essence of the decision-making process. Their analysis
concentrates on three influences: national character
analysis, organizational processes, and internal
institutional processes. This well-written essay clarifies
much of the confusion that clouds this controversial
subject.

3996.   "The Decision to Drop the Atomic Bomb on Hiroshima." EDUC
        J, 20 (Fall 1977), 39-41.

        NE

3997.   De Seversky, Alexander P.   "Atomic Bomb Hysteria."
        READER'S DIG, 48 (February 1946), 121-126.

        The author, an air power enthusiast and special
        consultant to Stimson, argues that the effects of the
        atomic bombings have been wildly exaggerated. The damage,
        according to de Seversky, was "overwhelmingly incendiary,
        with comparatively little structural damage to
        noninflammable targets."

3998.   Dower, John W.   "Art, Children and the Bomb." BULL CON
        ASIAN SCHOL, 16 (April-June 1984), 33-39.

        Dower observes that children seem to understand that art
        can be a constructive medium to come to grips with the two
        atomic bombings. The art in BAREFOOT GEN by Nakazawa is
        particularly recommended by Dower as a vivid and engrossing
        introduction to the unimaginable experience of surviving an
        atomic attack.

3999.   Eggleston, Noel C.   "Role Playing: The Atomic Bomb and the
        End of World War II." TEACHING HIST: J METHODS, 3 (No.
        2, 1978), 52-58.

        NE

4000.   Enderlin, Lee. "Greatest of All Invasions." MIL HIST, 2
        (August 1985), 28-33.

        The author, a free-lance writer, describes the plans to
        invade the Japanese home islands. In assessing the
        estimated losses, he accepts the one-million figure
        projected for U.S. casualties, 500,000 for the British, and
        possibly ten million for the Japanese. There are no

citations.

4001. Evans, Medford. THE SECRET WAR FOR THE ATOMIC BOMB.
         Chicago: Regnery, 1953. 302 pp.

         Here is a spirited defense of the decision to use the
       atomic bomb. Evans' argument includes a reproach to
       critics of that decision.

4002. Fairlie, Henry. "The Press: Ban the Bombast." NEW REP,
         193 (September 2, 1985), 12-14.

         Fairlie complains about the anti-American strains and
       the overindulgence by the press in marking the fortieth
       anniversary of the two atomic bombings. He quotes a line
       from Dylan Thomas: "After the first death, there is no
       other."

4003. Finney, John W. HIROSHIMA PLUS TWENTY. New York: 1965.

         NE

4004. Fogelman, Edwin, ed. HIROSHIMA: THE DECISION TO USE THE
         A-BOMB. New York: Charles Scribener's Sons, 1964.
         125 pp.

         The collection, part of a research anthology series,
       offers different perspectives on this fateful decision.

4005. Forsberg, Franklin S. "Atomic Bomb Away." READER'S DIG,
         56 (January 1950), 107-110.

         Here is an account of the first atomic bombing mission.
       The author dwells on the various charms and talismans
       brought aboard the aircraft.

4006. Freedman, Lawrence. "The Strategy of Hiroshima." J STRAT
         STUD, 1 (May 1978), 76-97.

         The author, associated with the Royal Institute of
       International Affairs, seeks to follow the thought
       processes of American officials which led to the
       operational use of the bomb. He finds that while the
       leaders wanted to emphasize the shock value of the atomic
       bomb and to set it apart from conventional bombs, there was
       no conscious effort either to intimidate the Soviet Union
       or to gain experimental value from the dropping of the
       bomb. Also, the use of the second bomb, according to
       Freedman, required no separate decision. The article

squarely addresses many of the controversial issues which surround this complex subject.

4007.   Feis, Herbert.   THE ATOMIC BOMB AND THE END OF WORLD WAR
        II.   Princeton, NJ: Princeton University Press, 1966
        rev. ed.   213 pp.

        Originally published in 1961 under the title JAPAN
        SUBDUED, the book covers the events leading to the end of
        the war.   Feis carefully treats the complex issues
        surrounding the decision to drop the atomic bomb but
        concludes that its use was justified.   The subject receives
        scholarly treatment in his hands.

4008.   Feis, Herbert.   "The Secret That Traveled to Potsdam."   FOR
        AFFS, 38 (January 1960), 300-317.

        Feis speculates on how the secret--the pending first
        test of the atomic bomb--affected the conference.   He feels
        that the secret buttressed Anglo-American determination not
        only to be firm in dealing with the Russians but also to
        further the aims of the San Francisco Conference.   The
        article includes the full text of the report to Stimson on
        July 18, 1945, by Groves about the test.

4009.   Frisch, David H.   "Scientists and the Decision to Bomb
        Japan."   BULL ATOMIC SCI, 26 (June 1970), 107-115.

        The author was a graduate student who worked at Los
        Alamos.   Investigating the reason why scientists did not
        press for alternatives to using the atomic bomb against
        Japan, Frisch suggests two explanations: (1) the
        compartmentalization of information and (2) the perception
        that one person had little chance of affecting the outcome
        of a problem.

4010.   Fussell, Paul.   "Hiroshima: A Soldier's View."   NEW REP,
        185 (August 22 & 29, 1981), 26-30.

        In the debate over the use of the atomic bomb, Fussell
        asserts that   experience and theory clash.   According to
        the author, one's experience--especially if that experience
        included first-hand knowledge of an infantry
        assault--shapes one's position on this question.   Fussell
        learned of the atomic bombings when preparing in a European
        staging area for the planned invasion of Honshu; he remains
        thankful that the two bombs helped end the war.

4011.   Geddes, Donald P., ed.   THE ATOMIC AGE OPENS.   New York:

1945. 251 pp.

This is probably the first book published on the use of
the atomic bomb. It appeared within days after Hiroshima
and Nagasaki. Geddes assembles a collection of statements
by world leaders and media reports on the startling
displays of this new power.

4012. Giacomelli, Raffael. THE ATOM BOMB AND MASS DESTRUCTION.
Rome, Italy: Editoriale Aeronautico, 1947. 51 pp.

The book is made up of nine articles by Giacomelli which
appeared in LA TRIBUNA in 1946. He tries to gain some
understanding of the new weapon.

4013. Gilbert, James. "Memorializing the Bomb." RADICAL HIST
REV, 34 (January 1986), 101-104.

Gilbert feels we need to publicize the controversial
nature of the decision to drop the atomic bomb. A
"dispassionate" museum exhibit about the wartime use of the
bomb touched off the author's emotional reaction.

4014. Giovannitti, Len and Fred Freed. THE DECISION TO DROP THE
BOMB. New York: Coward-McCann, 1965. 348 pp.

The narrative covers the period from Roosevelt's death
to the end of the war. In evaluating the events and
influences which led to the fateful decision, the authors
present a balanced perspective. The arguments presented by
contemporary opponents of the dropping of the atomic bomb
on Japan are given full play, but they are set by the
authors within the context of the overwhelming opinion to
use the new weapon. Statements by key figures about the
use of the atomic bomb are provided in the appendix.

4015. Glazier, Kenneth M., Jr. "The Decision to Use Atomic
Weapons Against Hiroshima and Nagasaki." PUBLIC POLICY,
18 (Summer 1970), 463-516.

Two key points emerge in this article about the
decision: (1) it was made during a time of transition in
the presidency and (2) it was made in secrecy. The
administrative-bureaucratic process, according to Glazier,
accepted the use of the atomic bomb as a given; nor did
Truman seek military advice for this military decision.
The author is critical of the lack of long-range planning
in the new administration.

4016.   Great Britain. British Mission to Japan. REPORT: THE
        EFFECTS OF THE ATOMIC BOMBS AT HIROSHIMA AND NAGASAKI.
        London: HMSO, 1946.

        This official report includes economic information as
        well as scientific data.

4017.   Harper, John L. "Henry Stimson and the Origin of America's
        Attachment to Atomic Weapons." SAIS REV, 5
        (Summer-Fall, 1985), 17-28.

        In this reflective, speculative essay, Harper suggests
        that the atomic bomb had "tutemic qualities." Stimson's
        postwar explanation, the author writes, failed to explain
        why U.S. leaders preferred to end the war in that
        particular way. Harper also addresses the lingering
        controversies of why the second bomb was dropped and why
        the Potsdam Declaration made no direct mention of either
        the bomb or the status of the emperor. For Harper, the
        omissions in the Potsdam statement may have been deliberate
        so as not to jeopardize the use of the bomb. Perhaps, the
        author observes, the use of the bomb will serve as a
        warning against future general wars.

4018.   Harper, Stephen. MIRACLE OF DELIVERANCE: THE CASE FOR THE
        BOMBING OF HIROSHIMA AND NAGASAKI. New York: Stein and
        Day, 1986.   224 pp.

        Stoutly maintaining that Japan's capacity to wage war in
        August 1945 remained strong, the author defends the use of
        the atomic bomb. His case rests on the "bottom line":   the
        atomic bombings helped end the war and aborted the need for
        an invasion which would have cost many lives. Harper, a
        correspondent, also argues from one British point of view
        that Mountbatten's Operation ZIPPER (an invasion into the
        Port Swettenham-Port Dickson area by SEAC forces) not only
        would have been costly but also might well have been
        defeated.

4019.   Harris, Jonathon. HIROSHIMA: A STUDY IN SCIENCE, POLITICS,
        AND THE ETHICS OF WAR. Menlo Park, CA: Addison-Wesley,
        1970. 77 pp.

        Harris takes a moral-religious perspective in
        interpreting the use of the atomic bomb.

4020.   Hazzard, Shirley. "A Writer Reflects." BULL ATOMIC SCI, 38
        (March 1982), 43-44.

The author, an Australian writer, protests the use of the atomic bombs in 1945.

4021. Hersey, John. HIROSHIMA. New York: A.A. Knopf, 1981.
       117 pp.

       This publication is a reissue of the original 1946 edition. Hersey follows the traumatic fortunes of six survivors of the first atomic bombing. The book remains a classic long after the event. It is essential reading on the subject.

4022. Hikins, James. "The Rhetoric of 'Unconditional Surrender' and the Decision to Drop the Atomic Bomb." Q J SPEECH, 69 (November 1983), 379-400.

       The author, a speech professor, contends that the rhetoric of unconditional surrender unnecessarily constrained U.S. policy makers and probably accounted for these leaders resorting to the use of the atomic bomb. His arguments about the foreclosure of certain policy options which would have terminated the war "weeks or even months earlier" require more elaboration and supporting evidence. Ironically, he says, Truman's speech accepting the Japanese surrender misled most Americans into believing that the goal of unconditional surrender had been achieved.

4023. Hirschfield, Burt. A CLOUD OVER HIROSHIMA. New York: Julian Messner, 1967. 191 pp.

       The story of the first atomic bombing is well told for a general readership.

4024. Horder, Mervyn. "If No Atom Bomb?" BLACKWOOD, 318 (August 1975), 110-115.

       Lord Horder served on Mountbatten's SEAC staff and in the occupation of Japan. He confirms that the invasion would have been a most difficult task if the atomic bombs had not been available.

4025. Hoshima, Tsutomu. "The Inheritance of Hiroshima." BULL ATOMIC SCI, 42 (June/July 1986), 37-38.

       The author, a Japanese editorial writer, focuses on present-day Hiroshima and the shadow of August 6, 1945.

4026. Huie, William Bradford. THE HIROSHIMA PILOT. New York: G.P. Putnam, 1964. 318 pp.

Claude Etherly flew the advance weather plane over
Hiroshima and signalled the "all-clear" for the first
atomic bombing. With extensive interviews and research,
Huie explodes many of the myths surrounding Etherly.

4027.   Japan. National Prepatory Committee. A CALL FROM
        HIBAKUSHA OF HIROSHIMA AND NAGASAKI. Elmsford, NY:
        Pergamom, 1979.

        Here are the proceedings of an international symposium
        in 1977 on the damage and after-effects of the two atomic
        bombings.

4028.   Johnsen, Julia E., comp. THE ATOMIC BOMB. New York: H.
        W. Wilson, 1946. 335 pp.

        The articles address many questions related to the
        atomic bomb, such as its development, social implications
        and its effect on international relations. Of special
        interest are the discussions of government support for
        scientific research and development, civilian control of
        the military, and international sharing of the technology
        of atomic power. Johnsen adds a chronology of the
        development of the weapon.

4029.   Johnson, Leon J. "The First Atomic Bombardier."
        NAVIGATOR, 32 (Spring 1985), 16-18.

        Here is a profile of Thomas Ferebee, whom Col. Tibbetts
        selected as the navigator for the historic mission which
        dropped the first atomic bomb on Japan. Ferebee designed a
        special headrest over the bombsight to hold the
        bombardier's head in the same position during each bombing
        run and thus reduce the probability of error. During
        training, the crews used a 300-foot circular target zone.

4030.   Jones, Edgar L. "Japan's Secret Weapon." ATLANTIC MON,
        176 (July 1945), 44-47.

        After observing the determined defenses of Iwo Jima and
        Okinawa by the Japanese, this U.S. war correspondent
        predicts a bitter struggle in any invasion of Japan. Jones
        feels that the enemy's secret weapon is a willingness to
        die rather than surrender.

4031.   Jones, John P. "Target--Hiroshima!" AIRPOWER HIST, 9
        (April 1962), 112-116.

Here is an account of the accomplishments of the 20th
Combat Mapping Squadron, from New Guinea to the Japanese
homeland.

4032. Kamata, Sadao and Stephen Salaff. "The Atomic Bomb and the
       Citizens of Nagasaki." BULL CON ASIAN SCHOL, 14
       (April-June 1982), 38-50.

Kamata (a Japanese science professor) and Salaff (a
Canadian writer and mathematician) feel that neither atomic
bomb was necessary to end the war. The article describes
not only the impediments within Japan that hindered the
recovery of survivors but also the political activism of
the survivors since 1945.

4033. Kane, Thomas and Richard M. Weiler. "Truman and the A-Bomb
       Decision: A Response to J.M. Williams." SPEAKER &
       GAVEL, 16 (Fall 1978), 3-12.

The authors, professors of oral communication and
speech, argue that Williams inaccurately portrayed Truman
as abdicating his responsibility as a decision-maker.
According to the authors, Williams made at least 28 errors
(either in citing sources or in offering incomplete
quotations), and her description of the "rhetoric of
incrementalism" is vague and confusing.

4034. Knebel, Fletcher and Charles W. Bailey. NO HIGH GROUND:
       THE INSIDE STORY OF THE MEN WHO PLANNED AND DROPPED THE
       FIRST ATOMIC BOMB. New York: Harper and Row, 1961.
       272 pp.

Granted special permission to use government files on
the Manhattan Project, the two correspondents write a
detailed account of the development and use of the atomic
bomb. They pay particular attention to the human
dimension. See especially their report on the
disagreements between Szilard and Gen. Groves and on the
shielding of Truman from the scientists opposed to dropping
the weapon on Japan.

4035. Kurzman, Dan. DAY OF THE BOMB: COUNTDOWN TO HIROSHIMA.
       New York: McGraw-Hill, 1986. 546 pp.

An ex-foreign correspondent, Kurzman recounts events
that led to the decision to drop the atomic bomb on
Hiroshima. His solid research includes interviews with
people such as 2d Lt. Thomas C. Cartwright (a POW at
Hiroshima), Seiko Ogawa (disfigured in the bombing), and

Deak Parsons (who loved the Navy but was disappointed by
his country with regard to J. Robert Oppenheimer). From
another interview--this with a hometown friend of
Truman--the author claims to have discovered new evidence
that Truman knew about the development of the atomic bomb
before succeeding to the presidency. Truman told this
friend that Roosevelt had revealed the existence of the
Manhattan Project to the Vice President. A strength of the
book is the author's concentration on the major
personalities involved in this momentous project.

4036.   Laver, Ross.   "The Two Days That Changed the World."
        MACLEAN'S, 98 (July 22, 1985), 16-17.

        Laver points out how little was known at the time of the
        consequences of using the atomic bomb.

4037.   Leigh, Michael.   "Is There a Revisionist Thesis on the
        Origins of the Cold War?"   POL SCI Q, 89 (March 1974),
        101-116.

        Leigh answers his question in the negative. His
        investigation identifies differences among the so-called
        revisionists. The article has a particularly helpful
        section on the decision to use the atomic bomb.

4038.   Leighton, Alexander H.   "That Day at Hiroshima."   ATLANTIC
        MON, 178 (October 1946), 85-97.

        The author recounts his experiences in Japan as part of
        the U.S. Strategic Bombing Survey. In his interviews, he
        found very few Japanese citizens inclined to put guilt on
        the Americans. Of note is the observation of the mayor of
        a nearby town about the victims: "Everybody looked alike."

4039.   Levine, Alan J.   "Dropping the A-Bomb in Retrospect."   ASIA
        PROFILE, 14 (August 1986), 315-325.

        Rejecting the idea that the atomic bomb was used to
        impress the Soviet Union, the author, a free-lance writer,
        argues that the Strategic Bombing Survey (despite being
        frequently quoted out of context) did assert that the
        atomic bombings shortened the war. Of interest is his
        observation that, although Truman was wrong in thinking
        that an invasion was necessary to save lives, the number of
        lives at stake was still just as high as the president had
        imagined. By this, Levine is referring to what he calls an
        imminent famine in Southeast Asia.

4040.   Lifton, Betty Jean. A PLACE CALLED HIROSHIMA. Tokyo:
        Kodansha International, 1985. 151 pp.

        The author reports on what the atomic bomb did to the
        city. She also describes the postwar changes that have
        taken place in the city. The book includes photos by Elkoh
        Hosoe.

4041.   Lifton, Robert Jay. "On Death and Death Symbolism: The
        Hiroshima Disaster." PSYCHIATRY, 27 (August 1964),
        191-210.

        Having done extensive research (especially interviews)
        in Japan, Lifton examines how the atomic bomb survivors
        encounted death at a variety of psychological levels. He
        argues that the existence of nuclear weapons impairs
        psychological processes and our ability to deal with those
        weapons.

4042.   Lifton, Robert Jay. DEATH IN LIFE: SURVIVORS OF
        HIROSHIMA. New York: Random House, 1967. 594 pp.

        Lifton describes his approach to the survivors as
        "psychoanalytic" and "psychoformative." The title is taken
        from his view that in the atomic bombing, life and death
        were out of phase with one another.

4043.   Lifton, Robert Jay. "The Psychological Effects of the
        Atomic Bomb in Hiroshima: The Theme of Death."
        DAEDALUS, 92 (Summer 1963), 462-497.

        Lifton analyzes the dramatic psychological shift from
        normal existence to an overwhelming encounter with death.
        His investigation draws on two years of research in Japan,
        including several interviews with survivors.

4044.   Littell, Robert. "What the Atom Bomb Would Do To Us."
        READER'S DIG, 48 (May 1946), 125-128.

        The author takes issue with the assertion by de Seversky
        that the effects of the two atomic bombings have been
        wildly exaggerated.

4045.   Loebs, Bruce D. "Nagasaki: The Decision and the Mistake."
        RENDEZVOUS, 7 (Spring 1972), 53-69.

        The author, a professor of rhetoric and public address,
        argues that the dropping of the second atomic bomb was
        unnecessary. The second bombing changed no one's views,

according to Loebs. He disputes Truman's claim about
ordering the second bombing while aboard the AUGUSTA. By
not waiting for the full impact of the first bombing to
work through Japan, Loebs feels that the United States lost
moral stature.

4046. Luft, John and W.M. Wheeler. "Reaction to John Hersey's
       'Hiroshima.'" J SOCIAL PSYC, 28 (August 1948), 135-140.

       The authors analyzed three hundred thirty-nine pieces of
mail which Hersey received during the first two weeks after
the NEW YORKER published "Hiroshima" on August 31, 1946.
According to the authors, ninety percent approved the
publication of the story, and, in general, the
correspondents revealed a sophisticated understanding of
the issues involved.

4047. MacDonald, Dwight. "The Bomb." POLITICS, 2 (1945).

       NE

4048. McMillan, George. THE INVASION OF JAPAN. New York:
       Random House, 1983.

       McMillan served with the 1st Marine Division during the
war. His unit was set to participate in the planned
invasion of Japan. That stark fact tends to color his
discussion of whether or not the United States should have
used the atomic bomb.

4049. Maddox, Robert J. "Atomic Diplomacy: A Study in Creative
       Writing." J AMER HIST, 59 (March 1973), 925-934.

       The author investigates the citations of the so-called
revisionist historians and accuses them of unscholarly
methods, errors, and deliberate distortions. He questions
whether the history profession has abdicated its
responsibilities in embracing uncritically the work of
these historians with regard to the decision to use the
atomic bomb.

4050. Maier, Charles S. "Revisionism and the Interpretation of
       Cold War Origins." PERSPECTIVES AMER HIST, 4 (1970),
       311-347.

       Maier shows that the revisionists are divided among
themselves, particularly on U.S. motives behind the use of
the atomic bomb. Here is a sensible journey through the
literature. The author avoids the harsh rhetoric, value

systems, and a priori judgments that cloud the Cold War
historiography so as to ask questions of (not to attack)
all sides of the issue.

4051.   Marx, Joseph L. NAGASAKI: THE NECESSARY BOMB? New York:
        Macmillan, 1971. 239 pp.

        The conclusion here is that the second atomic bombing
        was necessary. Marx argues that the bombing at Nagasaki
        provided the Emperor with a means to convince the Military
        to end the war and provided the militarists with a
        face-saving way out of the war. Denying that the
        motivation behind the atomic bombings was racist, Marx
        believes that no credible international demonstration could
        have been arranged. Also, according to the author, many
        Japanese refused to believe the reports of the devastation
        at Hiroshima. The book has no bibliography.

4052.   Marx, Joseph L. SEVEN HOURS TO ZERO. New York: G. P.
        Putnam's Sons, 1967. 256 pp.

        This is a report on the crew of the ENOLA GAY. Marx
        tries to get behind the myths and rumors which surround
        this unique group of twelve men and others who were
        associated with the first atomic attack. He finds among
        these people an overwhelming sense of doing the right
        thing. The crew felt that way at the time, and the feeling
        persists.

4053.   Merton, Thomas. ORIGINAL CHILD BOMB: POINTS FOR
        MEDITATION TO BE SCRATCHED ON THE WALLS OF A CAVE. New
        York: New Directions, 1962. Unpaged.

        Merton gives a summary of the development and use of the
        atomic bomb. The title comes from the original Japanese
        references to the bomb as the first of its kind. Some
        sections represent the imagined wall writings of the last
        human.

4054.   Messer, Robert L. "New Evidence on Truman's Decision."
        BULL ATOMIC SCI, 41 (August 1985), 50-56.

        Seeking to clarify Truman's role in the decision to use
        the atomic bomb, Messer raises anew the idea that limiting
        Soviet expansion in Asia was a motivating factor for the
        President. The article incorporates new evidence based on
        Truman's private journal and his 1945 correspondence.

4055.   Miles, Rufus. "The Strange Myth of Half a Million Lives

Saved." INT SECURITY, 10 (Fall 1985), 121-140.

The author, a retired government officer, argues that
though the traditional rationale for using the atomic bomb
(i.e., saving at least 500,000 U.S. lives) has flaws, the
weapon's use still might have been necessary.
Nevertheless, American leaders should have seriously
explored alternatives to dropping the bomb, including a
negotiated settlement, intensified conventional bombing and
blockade until November 1, 1945, and a November attack on
southern Kyushu. Using second-hand reports of U.S.
military planning documents, Miles believes that American
casualties would not exceed 20,000 on Kyushu and 250,000 on
Honshu.

4056. Mitchell, Greg. "Forgotten Bomb, Forgotten City."
       PROGRESSIVE, 49 (August 1985), 27-32.

In calling attention to the second atomic bombing,
Mitchell describes the blow at Nagasaki as the first strike
in the battle to control the postwar world. Of special
interest is the story of Kenshi Hirata, who suffered in
both atomic bombings.

4057. Mitchell, Jared. "Survivors of a Nuclear Age." MAC-
       LEAN'S, 98 (July 22, 1985), 22-25.

The author looks at Hiroshima and Nagasaki forty years
after the atomic bombings.

4058. Miura, Kazue. SURVIVAL AT 500 METERS IN HIROSHIMA. Osaka,
       Japan: Osaka Women's Section, Osaka Association of
       A-Bomb Victims, 1979.

Here is a gripping account by a survivor of the first
atomic attack. The shadow of the experience followed her
thoughout her life. She expresses guilt about having one
stillborn child and unease about her anemic daughter (Miura
bore a boy as well) now married with children of her own.
The author died of stomach cancer shorty after this book
appeared.

4059. Moll, Kenneth L. "The Birth of the A-Bomb--and the
       Aftermath." AF SPACE DIG, 48 (August 1965), 29-36.

Moll summarizes the development and use of the atomic
bomb. He defends the decision to drop the bomb on Japan.

4060. Morrison, Roy D., II. "Albert Einstein: The

Methodological Unity Underlying Science and Religion."
ZYGON, 14 (September 1979), 255-266.

The author, a professor of philosophical theology,
argues that attention should be given to Einstein's
religious-theological reflections as well as his scientific
work. This account of Einstein's world view provides
useful background on the dilemma surrounding the use of the
atomic bomb.

4061. Morton, Louis. "The Atomic Bomb and the Japanese
Surrender." MC GAZ, 43 (February 1959), 20-28.

Morton views the two atomic bombings as part of a
sequence which led to the surrender of Japan, but he does
not feel that the Truman administration used the atomic
bomb to influence the Soviet Union. Nevertheless, in this
article, Morton identifies a strong predisposition to use
the atomic bomb once it had been developed. Without the
weapon, he says, the continuing aerial bombardment and
seaborne blockade probably would have forced the Japanese
to surrender.

4062. Morton, Louis. "The Decision to Use the Atomic Bomb." FOR
AFFS, 35 (January 1957), 334-353.

Here is a superb analysis of the developments leading to
the fateful decision. Morton casts doubt upon the
allegation that U.S. leaders used the bomb to forestall
Soviet intervention, and he can not say for sure if the
bombs were necessary to force the Japanese decision to
surrender.

4063. Nagai, Takashi. THE BELLS OF NAGASAKI. New York: Harper
and Row, 1984. 118 pp.

Originally published in Japan in 1949, the book has been
translated by William Johnston. The author was a nuclear
physicist at Nagasaki who survived the atomic bombing.
Although he supported the war, after the destructioon of
his city, he spent the rest of his life writing and working
for peace. He had been bed-ridden prior to the atomic
attack; later, he contracted leukemia and died in 1951.
Amidst the gory details, the book provides a valuable
eyewitness account by a trained observer. The city bells
still ring for peace.

4064. Nagai, Takashi. WE OF NAGASAKI. New York: Duell, Sloan
and Pearce, 1951. 189 pp.

The author tells the stories of eight survivors,
including three children, of the atomic bombing who were
relatives or neighbors of Dr. Nagai. All, like Nagai, were
Catholic. Nagai portrays the best and worst of human
nature in these tales of generosity and self-interest.
Ichiro Shirato and Herbert B.L. Silverman translated the
work.

4065. Nagasaki Prefecture, Hibakusha Teachers Association. IN
        THE SKY OVER NAGASAKI. Wilmington, OH: Wilmington
        College, 1977.

        Here is a powerful and emotional report which focuses on
        the human response to the second atomic bomb and on the
        suffering it caused. Like many similar works, especially
        emanating from Japan, the book makes no effort to examine
        larger issues, such as the origins of the war or the
        rationale behind the use of the atomic bomb. This is by
        design, not necessarily a weakness, and works such as this
        can be accepted for that very reason.

4066. Nufer, Harold F. "The Evolution of Frag Orders: World War
        II to Vietnam." AEROSPACE H, 33 (Summer/June 1986),
        105-113.

        Here is a report on the bureaucratic evolution of the
        field order from 2-3 pages to a much lengthier document.
        Of special interest is the material on the two atomic
        bombing missions (CENTERBOARD STRIKE 1 and 2).

4067. Oxford, Edward. "The Flight That Changed the World." AMER
        HIST ILLUS, 20 (September 1985), 12-19, 49.

        Here is a description, adorned with related details, of
        the atomic bombing mission against Hiroshima. Some of the
        details include Tibbets selecting his B-29 from the bomber
        plant in Omaha, a back-up B-29 waiting at Iwo Jima prepared
        for an emergency switch of the weapon, cyanide capsules
        carried by the crew, and the electrolytic action of the
        bomb in Tibbets' silver-lead dental fillings.

4068. Pacific War Research Society. THE DAY MAN LOST:
        HIROSHIMA, 6 AUGUST 1945. Tokyo: Kodansha
        International, 1972. 312 pp.

        This study provides some information about the
        development of the atomic bomb and includes new
        revelations--more suggestive than definitive--on Japanese

nuclear experiments conducted during the war. Examining
the Japanese perspective, the book reveals the human side
as well as historical details.

4069.   Ramsey, Norman F. "August 1945: The B-29 Flight Logs."
          BULL ATOMIC SCI, 38 (December 1982), 33-35.

          Here is an excerpt from a 1945 report by Ramsey
        ("History of Project A"). The article presents the actual
        flight logs of both atomic bombing missions.

4070.   Reynolds, Barbara. "Hiroshima/Nagasaki." PEACE & CHANGE,
          5 (Spring 1978), 45-47.

          The author, associated with the Hiroshima/Nagasaki
        Memorial Collection in Wilmington College, reports on her
        1977 journey to the two Japanese cities.

4071.   Rothermel, John E. HIROSHIMA AND NAGASAKI FROM GOD'S POINT
          OF VIEW. New York: Carlton, 1971.

          NE

4072.   Ryerson, Andre. "The Cult of Hiroshima." COMMENTARY, 80
          (October 1985), 36-40.

          The author, a writer and artist, feels that the victims
        of Japanese aggression have been forgotten as revisionists
        assess the use of the atomic bomb out of context through
        "selective amnesia."

4073.   Sadao, Asada. "Japanese Perceptions of the A-Bomb
          Decision, 1945-1980," in Joe E. Dixon, ed. THE AMERICAN
          MILITARY AND THE FAR EAST. Washington, D.C.: GPO,
          1980.

          In reviewing the literature, Asada emphasizes that the
        war and the use of the atomic bombs "dehumanized victor and
        vanquished alike."

4074.   Sano, Bunichiro, ed. HIROSHIMA-NAGASAKI, DOCUMENT 1961.
          Tokyo: Japan Council Against Atomic and Hydrogen Bombs,
          1961.

          NE

4075.   Sbrega, John J. "The Japanese Surrender: Some Unintended
          Consequences in Southeast Asia." ASIAN AFFS, 7
          (September/October 1979), 45-63.

Using interviews, private collections, and archival
sources, Sbrega points out that the unanticipated Japanese
surrender created a political vacuum in Southeast Asia.
The sudden demands for occupation forces throughout the
region, he says, exceeded the capacity of already strained
Allied resources. Thus, indigenous political associations
with leftist tendencies, in most cases armed and under the
spell of the rhetoric of autonomy, remained outside Allied
control.

4076.   Schoenberger, Walter S. DECISION OF DESTINY. Athens, OH:
        Ohio University Press, 1969. 330 pp.

The author analyzes the domestic and international
context in which Truman decided to use the atomic bomb.
Although Truman in some ways was captive to the
scientific-military momentum gained in developing the
atomic bomb, Schoenberger emphasizes that the president
never entertained seriously any alternative to dropping the
weapon on Japan. Of interest is the author's criticism of
the policy of unconditional surrender. Also, Schoenberger
claims that the decision reflected not only certain
characteristics of the U.S. political system (e.g., a
complicated administrative apparatus, the irrelevant method
of selecting vice presidential candidates, and the lack of
preparation for a vice president to assume the presidency)
but also the bankruptcy of the nation-state system.

4077.   Schwartz, Robert. "Atomic Bomb Away." READER'S DIG, 56
        (January 1950), 107-110.

Here is a glimpse of the human side of the Enola Gay's
fateful mission.

4078.   Schweitz, Robert E. "The Great A-Bomber Myth." A N A F
        REG, 80 (November 28, 1959), 13-14.

Schweitz corrects the several myths and misconceptions
which have plagued the crew of the Enola Gay.

4079.   Sherry, Michael S. "Was 1945 a Break in History?" BULL
        ATOMIC SCI, 43 (July/August 1987), 12-15.

Outlining continuities between events before and after
the atomic bombings, Sherry writes that momentous actions
are often the result of slow accretions, thoughtless
assumptions, confused bureaucratic pressures, and
incremental initiatives.

4080.   Sherwin, Martin J.   "The Atomic Bomb As History: An Essay
        Reviewed."   WISC MAG HIST, 53 (Winter 1969-70), 128-134.

        Here is a historiographical review.   Sherwin raises
        important questions for further study.

4081.   Sherwin, Martin Jay.   "The Atomic Bomb and the Origins of
        the Cold War: U.S. Atomic-Energy Policy and Diplomacy,
        1941-45."   AMER HR, 78 (October 1973), 945-968.

        Sherwin asks two key questions: (1) did diplomatic
        considerations about postwar Soviet behavior influence
        Roosevelt's atomic-energy policies and (2) what effect did
        the atomic legacy have on Truman's atomic-energy policies?
        Of interest is Sherwin's suggestion that historians have
        exaggerated Roosevelt's confidence and perhaps, too, his
        commitment to amiable postwar relations with the Soviets.
        The article is well researched and calls attention to U.S.
        contributions to the origins of the Cold War.

4082.   Sherwin, Martin J.   "How Well They Meant."   BULL ATOMIC
        SCI, 41 (August 1985), 9-15.

        According to Sherwin, "scientific greatness" in the
        research and development of the atomic bomb gave way to the
        "political folly" of its use.

4083.   Sherwin, Martin J.   "Old Issues in New Editions."   BULL
        ATOMIC SCI, 41 (December 1985), 40-45.

        This review article focuses on the reissue of three
        books: John Hersey's HIROSHIMA, Gar Alperovitz's ATOMIC
        DIPLOMACY, and John Major's THE OPPENHEIMER HEARINGS.

4084.   Sigal, Leon V.   "Bureaucratic Politics and Tactical Use of
        Committees: The Interim Committee and the Decision to
        Drop the Atomic Bomb."   POLITY, 10 (Spring 1978),
        326-364.

        Sigal integrates archival material with published works
        to call attention to "bureaucratic politics."   Arguing that
        historians ("orthodox" and "revisionist") have missed this
        important maneuvering, Sigal says that the Interim
        Committee became part of the bureaucratic strategy of a few
        senior American officials in the War Department and the
        Manhattan Project who wanted to use the atomic bomb and
        head off opposition from certain scientists.

4085.   Skipper, Debbie. "Nagasaki: The City of Suffering."
        AMERICA, 145 (December 5, 1981), 355-357.

        Incorporating many interviews, the author looks at the
        survivors (HIBAKUSHA) of the second atomic bombing. There
        are no footnotes.

4086.   Solomon, Joan. THE ATOMIC BOMB. New York: Basil
        Blackwell, 1986.

        NE

4087.   Steinberg, Rafael. POSTSCRIPT HIROSHIMA. New York:
        Random House, 1966. 120 pp.

        The author, a correspondent in the Far East, travelled
        to Hiroshima after the war. In his interviews with the
        inhabitants, Steinberg found mixed views about the war and
        the use of the atomic bomb.

4088.   Steiner, Jesse F. "Japanese Attitudes and Problems of
        Peace." AMER SOC REV, 10 (April 1945), 288-299.

        Steiner points out the difficulties of measuring public
        opinion in Japan, but he feels certain that the policy of
        unconditional surrender will prolong the war. For the
        people of Japan, he writes, surrender would be unthinkable
        until all resources were exhausted.

4089.   Stimson, Henry L. "The Decision to Use the Atomic Bomb."
        HARPER'S MAG, 197 (February 1947), 97-107.

        Here is the classic statement in defense of the use of
        the atomic bomb. The secretary of war accepts the Potsdam
        statement as a warning which Japan rejected as "unworthy of
        public notice." The U.S. goal behind this decision and the
        decision to return the emperor, he writes, was to end the
        war by avoiding the horrifying casualties forecast for any
        invasion of Japan. The world must never have another war,
        he concludes.

4090.   Tadatoshi, Akiba. "Message From Hiroshima." JAPAN Q, 34
        (October-December 1987), 385-391.

        The author, a math professor, describes a project he
        helped start to bring foreign correspondents to Hiroshima.
        His narrative complains that Americans in general have not
        reevaluated their position on the righteousness of the two
        atomic bombings. His dream is the abolition of all nuclear

weapons. Of interest is his refutation of Lifton's theory
that survivors (HIBAKUSHA) feel guilty for being alive.

4091. Teller, Edward. THE LEGACY OF HIROSHIMA. Garden City, NY:
        Doubleday, 1962.

        The famed physicist argues that, although the atomic
        bomb should have been developed, the United States
        government should have warned Japan of its destructive
        power. An international demonstration, he says, could then
        have been followed with an ultimatum.

4092. Thomas, Gordon and Max Morgan-Witts. ENOLA GAY. New York:
        Stein and Day, 1977. 327 pp.

        Here is a detailed look at the selection and training of
        the aircrew that would deliver the first atomic bomb
        against Japan. The authors concentrate on the human side
        of the story as the crew, armed with cyanide pills and
        lucky cigarette boxes, embarked on its fateful flight. Of
        interest is the shock wave of the bomb being mistaken by
        the crew for Japanese anti-aircraft fire.

4093. Tibbets, Paul W. "Training the 509th for Hiroshima." AF
        MAG, 56 (August 1973), 49-55.

        The head of this special air group describes the
        difficult standards set for the training of the air crews.
        He reveals that security checks turned up some amazing
        evidence and that the entire Manhattan project had "camps"
        to detain those deemed security risks.

4094. "Training Camp for the Atomic Age: Wendover Field."
        AEROSPACE H, 20 (March 1973), 137-139.

        Col. Tibbets selected the Utah site for the training of
        the aircrews of the 509th Composite Group in dropping the
        atomic bomb. There was little activity at Wendover Field
        once the unit departed in 1945.

4095. United States. Atomic Energy Commission. IN THE MATTER OF
        J. ROBERT OPPENHEIMER. Washington, D.C.: GPO, 1954.

        Here is the transcript of the hearing which occurred
        before the agency's Personnel Security Board. Some of the
        testimony pertains to the Manhattan Project.

4096. United States. Department of the Army. The Manhattan
        Engineer District. THE ATOMIC BOMBINGS OF HIROSHIMA AND

NAGASAKI. Washington, D.C.: GPO, 1957. 43 pp.

Here is a brief report on the highlights of the two
fateful missions.

4097. United States. Department of the Army. The Manhattan
      Engineer District. PHOTOGRAPHS OF THE ATOMIC BOMBINGS
      OF HIROSHIMA AND NAGASAKI. Washington, D.C.: Dept. of
      the Army, 1945. 101 plates.

      The collection includes aerial and ground photographs.
      Although there is no general narrative or introduction,
      each photo is identified in a brief caption.

4098. Villa, Brian Loring. "A Confusion of Signals: James
      Franck, the Chicago Scientists, and Early Efforts to
      Stop the Bomb." BULL ATOMIC SCI, 31 (December 1975),
      36-42.

      In April 1945, Franck wrote a memorandum which
      sanctioned the use of the atomic bomb. He reversed this
      position in his report a few months later.

4099. Walzer, Michael and Paul Fussell. "An Exchange on
      Hiroshima: on the Moral Calculus of the Bomb." NEW
      REP, 185 (September 23, 1981), 13-14.

      Here is a brief debate which seems to turn on
      generational differences.

4100. Warren, Shields. "Hiroshima and Nagasaki Thirty Years
      After." PROC AMER PHIL SOC, 121 (April 29, 1977),
      97-99.

      The author, a consulting pathologist to the Cancer
      Research Institute, discusses radiation studies conducted
      at the two cities in 1945, 1946, 1947, and 1975. The 1950
      census in Japan identified over two hundred eighty thousand
      survivors of the two atomic bombings.

4101. "Was A-Bomb on Japan a Mistake?" US NEWS WORLD REP, 49
      (August 19, 1960), 62-76.

      Fifteen years after the fact, several Americans who held
      prominent positions in August 1945 voice their misgivings
      about the use of the atomic bomb. The article contains
      interviews with James F. Byrnes, Lewis L. Strauss, Leo
      Szilard, Edward Teller, and Ralph Bard.

4102. Williams, J.M. "Truman and the A-Bomb Decision: The
       Rhetoric of Incrementalism." SPEAKER & GAVEL, 15
       (Summer 1978), 71-79

       The author is a professor of media studies who
specializes in presidential rhetoric. Relying on published
secondary accounts, she argues that Truman's "passive
acquiescence" contributed to an incrementalism "too
formidable to halt" which, in turn, led to the decision to
drop the atomic bomb. Her thesis remains more suggestive
than irrefutable.

4103. Wilson, Robert R. "The Conscience of a Physicist." BULL
       ATOMIC SCI, 26 (June 1970), 30-34.

       Maintaining that moral considerations were lost in the
Manhattan Project, Wilson warns of the ease with which
scientists overrated their position in the political
structure. He worked on an isotron, but he admits that the
decision not to select his project eased his conscience.

4104. Winnacker, Rudolph A. "The Debate About Hiroshima," MIL
       AFFS, 11 (Spring 1947), 25-30.

       The author, an Army historian, essentially reviews and
applauds Stimson's article (HARPER'S MAG) defending the use
of the atomic bomb. The use of the bombs, for the author,
was a "grim necessity."

4105. Yakushevsky, A. "How the Atomic Blackmail Began." SOVIET
       MIL REV, n.v. (August 1980), 47-49.

       The author argues that the United States use of the
atomic bomb against civilians was a political act against
the Soviet Union rather than a military act against Japan.

4106. Yavenditti, Michael J. "The American People and the Use of
       Atomic Bombs on Japan: the 1940s." HISTORIAN, 36
       (February 1974), 224-247.

       Based on extensive research, Yavenditti traces the
reasons for widespread public approval of the atomic
bombings (e.g., it ended the brutal war, one could admire
it as a technical achievement). He finds that critics,
especially Catholic writers who universally condemned the
use of the atomic bomb, could not rouse public indignation.

4107. Yavenditti, Michael J. "John Hersey and the American
       Conscience: The Reception of 'Hiroshima.'" PAC HR, 43

(February 1974), 24-49.

Until Hersey's article "Survival" appeared in 1946,
Yavenditti writes, Americans were not aroused about the use
of the atomic bomb. In 1945, for example, 85% of the
American people approved the atomic bombings. Hersey
pricked the American conscience. In a letter to the
author, Hersey said that the understated article proved
more effective than a public scream of outrage.

IV.J.2.b.i. Personal Accounts

4108. Agawa, Hiroyuki. DEVIL'S HERITAGE. Tokyo: Kokuseido
        Press, 1957.

        Here is an account of suffering inflicted by the atomic
        bomb.

4109. Akizuki, Tatsuichiro. NAGASAKI 1945. London: Quartet
        Books, 1981. 159 pp.

        Here is an eyewitness account of the second atomic
        bombing. The personal narrative is translated by Keiichi
        Nagata.

4110. Bruin, Janet and Stephen Salaff. "August 1945: Memoirs
        of the Survivors." PROGRESSIVE, 45 (August 1981), 39.

        This brief article highlights the experiences of three
        women survivors and indicates the value of the Women's
        Section of the Osaka Association of A-Bomb Victims.

4111. Bruin, Janet and Stephen Salaff. "Never Again! Women
        Hibakusha in Osaka." BULL CON ASIAN SCHOL, 12
        (October-December 1980), 20-25.

        Here is a description of the origins (September 1967)
        and work of the Women's Section Osaka Association of A-Bomb
        victims. The authors include excerpts from the life
        histories of the women.

4112. Bruin, Janet and Stephen Salaff. "The Organization of
        Women Atomic Bomb Victims in Osaka." FEMINIST STUD, 7
        (Spring 1981), 5-18.

        The authors describe the problems of survivors of the
        atomic bombings (HIBAKUSHA), especially the women's
        "feelings of loss, shame, anger, guilt, and fear." The
        Osaka Association assisted male and female survivors and

their offspring (NISEI HIBAKUSHA).

4113.   "Fifteen Years Later--The Men Who Bombed Hiroshima."
        CORONET, 48 (August 1960), 76-96.

        The article pieces together separate dictaphone recorded
        interviews with the crew members. At the time, no one on
        the crew regretted participating in the mission; later,
        some had second thoughts. This publication helped put to
        rest the myth that all of the crew members were in mental
        hospitals. Of interest is the information that, without
        the crew's knowledge, a disc recorder was carried on the
        flight by Beser--the only man to go on both atomic bombing
        missions.

4114.   Franklin, George. "August 6, 1981--A Survivor of Hiroshima
        Writes to His Son." COEVOL Q, No. 39 (Fall 1983), 59.

        The author, who lost his son, wife, and his sight at
        Hiroshima, writes a poignant letter about his son's lost
        future.

4115.   Fussell, Paul. THANK GOD FOR THE ATOM BOMB. New York:
        Summit, 1988. 298 pp.

        The book offers a series of Fussell's essays on various
        topics which were written during the period 1945-1982. He
        served as a second lieutenant platoon leader in Europe. At
        war's end, he and his unit were awaiting transportation to
        participate in the invasion of Japan. Reflecting on the
        likelihood of heavy casualties in that considerable
        undertaking, Fussell is thankful for the use of the atomic
        bomb and the end of the war. He feels that postwar critics
        of the use of the atomic bomb misunderstand the
        contemporary situation.

4116.   Hachiya, Michihiko. HIROSHIMA DIARY. Chapel Hill, NC:
        University of North Carolina Press, 1955. 256 pp.

        Here is the journal (August 6 - September 30, 1945) of a
        Japanese doctor who was the bed-ridden director of
        Hiroshima Communications Hospital. Wounded in the atomic
        bombing, Hachiya records the first shocking hours in
        Hiroshima after the attack. On August 15, he turned on his
        radio expecting to learn of an enemy invasion rather than
        Japan's surrender. When a U.S. officer told him to sue his
        country, the doctor found the advice incomprehensible. He
        does, however, write, "If one thinks of the past and
        future, he will find matters for reconsideration." The

journal is translated by Warner Wells, M.D., who had been a
surgical consultant to the Atomic Bomb Casualty Commission.

4117.   Hiroshima. Jogakuin High School, Department of English,
            ed. SUMMER CLOUD. Tokyo: San-Yu-Sha, 1950.

        The English Department presents the experiences of
students and staff at this girls' high school during the
atomic bombing of Hiroshima. Even in retrospect, the
writers clearly recall that vivid experience.

4118.   Japan Broadcasting Corporation. UNFORGETTABLE FIRE:
            PICTURES DRAWN BY ATOMIC BOMB SURVIVORS. New York:
            Pantheon Books, 1977. 111 pp.

        All the scenes were drawn about thirty years after the
fact, but the traumatic experience remains seared in the
memory of these survivors. As the accompanying narratives
make clear, the details have not been forgotten.

4119.   Jungk, Robert. CHILDREN OF THE ASHES: THE STORY OF A
            REBIRTH. New York: Harcourt, Brace and World, 1959.
            317 pp.

        Translated by Christine Fitzgibbon, the book reports on
individuals who survived atomic bombing. In a unique twist
to projects of this kind, Jungk asks survivors what they
have done after the war to justify their survival. (Does
he mean "good fortune"?)

4120.   Kawai, Michi. SLIDING DOORS. Tokyo: Kaisen-Jo-Gaku-En,
            1950. 201 pp.

        NE

4121.   Lewis, Robert A. "How We Dropped the Bomb." POP SCI, 171
            (August 1957), 71-75, 209-210.

        Lewis, a pilot on board with Tibbets, tells his story to
Eliot Tozer about the flight of the ENOLA GAY (call sign:
"Dimples One Two"). Of interest is his report that four
B-29s had crashed on the Tinian runway the same week of
their mission.

4122.   Maruki, Toshi. HIROSHIMA NO PIKA. New York: Lothrop,
            Lee, Shepard Books, 1980. 48 l.

        This book contains powerful art work (and accompanying
narrative) based on true incidents in the first atomic

bombing. In concentrating on this human dimension, Maruki makes no effort to discover the reasons for the atomic attack. This is an emotional record-response to unparalleled suffering visited upon human beings; the book does not venture into detached, objective analysis.

4123. Miller, Merle and Abe Spitzer. WE DROPPED THE A-BOMB. New York: Crowell, 1946. 152 pp.

Spitzer was the radio man on the crew of the GREAT ARTISTE in both atomic bombing missions. He expresses his horror at the destructive power of the weapon. His story is told to Merle Miller.

4124. Osada, Arata, ed. CHILDREN OF THE A-BOMB. New York: G. P. Putnam's Sons, 1959. 256 pp.

The editor has collected the contemporary thoughts of the children-survivors of Hiroshima about the atomic bombing. The 60-odd articles are refreshingly untinted by political ideology. Osada served as president of Hiroshima University from 1945 to 1951. Jean Dan and Ruth Sieben-Morgen translated the book. The book first appeared in Japan in 1951. A new version, CHILDREN OF HIROSHIMA (Tokyo: Publishing Committee for "Children of Hiroshima, 1980. 335 pp.), incorporates 105 such accounts drawn from Osada's total collection of nearly 1200. The articles are arranged in ascending order of each child's grade level at the time.

4125. Seldon, Kyoko, ed. "Children of Nagasaki." BULL CON ASIAN SCHOL, 18 (July 1986), 32-38.

Here are seven accounts of the atomic bombing of Nagasaki by elementary and junior high school students who survived the ordeal. The students were ages 4-10 in August 1945.

4126. Siemes, John A., S.J. "Hiroshima -- August 6, 1945." BULL ATOMIC SCI, 1 (May 15,1946), 2-6.

Here is a first-hand report of the atomic bombing. Siemes and his associates tried to aid the survivors but were completely overwhelmed.

4127. Siemes, John A., S.J. "Hiroshima: Eyewitness." SAT REV LIT, 29 (May 11, 1946), 24-25, 40-44.

Father Siemes taught philosophy at Tokyo's Catholic

University. In this eyewitness account, he describes his
efforts to help the suffering victims. On the moral
question of the use of the bomb, Father Siemes feels that
the crux of the matter lies in whether or not total war is
justifiable.

4128. Siomes, P. HE WAS THERE--HIROSHIMA. Upland, CA: Piequet
       Press, 1985. 95 pp.

       NE

4129. Takemi, Taro. "Remembrance of the War and the Bomb." J
       AMER MED ASSOC, 250 (August 5, 1983), 618-619.

       The author was the only physician studying nuclear
       physics at the Institute of Physical and Chemical
       Researches in Tokyo. He reported on the first atomic
       bombing to Count Makino who, in turn, immediately went to
       see the emperor. Of interest is Takemi's first-hand
       account of a conversation in 1942 between Makino and Grew
       (just before Grew's departure). Makino said that (1) the
       emperor system was essential to Japan, (2) the U.S. should
       refrain from bombing Kyoto and Nara, and (3) the Japanese
       would lose the war--especially if they reaped early
       victories.

4130. Tibbets, Paul W., Jr. THE TIBBETS STORY. New York: Stein
       and Day, 1978. 316 pp.

       With the help of Clair Stebbins and Harry Franken,
       Tibbets gives an autobiographical account that, of course,
       focuses on his association with the atomic bombing of
       Hiroshima. Of interest is his report of the formation and
       the training of the select aircrews in the program.

4131. Trumbull, Robert. NINE WHO SURVIVED HIROSHIMA AND
       NAGASAKI. New York: E.P. Dutton, 1957. 148 pp.

       Trumbull, a war correspondent, tells the stories of nine
       Japanese men who lived through the atomic bombings. His
       focus is on man helping man--and the futility of these
       frail efforts in juxtaposition to the enormous power of the
       atom.

IV.J.2.b.ii. Medical Aspects

4132. Alvarez, Robert. "Radiation Standards and A-Bomb
       Survivors." BULL ATOMIC SCI, 40 (October 1984), 26-28.

Ironically, according to Alvarez, studies have added
uncertainties about the risks of radiation. In 1981, after
thirty years of investigation, the U.S. Department of
Energy suggested that radiation doses may have been much
lower than previously thought. The author calls for more
study through an independent peer review process rather
than having the scientific community rely on government
reports.

4133. Atomic Bomb Casualty Commission. GENERAL REPORT.
      Washington, D.C.: National Research Council, 1947.
      112 pp.

      Austen M. Brues and his associates have amassed a
      formidable array of statistics and topical reports. See
      especially the work of Dr. Masao Tsuzuki, "Report on the
      Medical Studies of the Effects of the Atomic Bomb."

4134. Averilla, Liebow. ENCOUNTER WITH DISASTER: A MEDICAL DIARY
      OF HIROSHIMA, 1945. New York: W.W. Norton, 1985. 209
      pp.

      This report on the emergency medical service includes
      valuable perspectives on social as well as physiological
      aspects of the first atomic bombing.

4135. Barker, Rodney. THE HIROSHIMA MAIDENS. New York: Viking,
      1985. 240 pp.

      The author, a journalist, narrates the story of three of
      the "Hiroshima Maidens." Victims of the first atomic
      bombings, the women came to America for medical assistance
      in 1955, largely through the work of Norman Cousins.
      Barker's family had served as host for one of the women.

4136. Block, Melvin A. and Masao Tsuzuki. "Observations on Burn
      Scars Sustained by Atomic Bomb Survivors: A Preliminary
      Study." AMER J SURGERY, 75 (March 1948), 417-434.

      Citing the lack of detailed studies of a large group,
      Captain Block (USA) and Dr. Tsuzuki investigated the
      effects of the atomic bomb. Among the conventional bombing/
      burn victims, the authors discovered a high incidence of
      scar keloid and hypertrophic scar formation but not an
      unusual incidence among the survivors of the atomic
      bombings. The authors call for more study and point out
      the many contributing factors in the etiology of keloids.

4137. Brill, A. Bertrand, Masanobu Tomonaga, and Robert M.

Heyssel. "Leukemia in Man Following Exposure to
Ionizing Radiation." ANNALS INTERNAL MED, 56 (April
1962), 590-609.

The physician-authors summarize the findings of studies
of the victims at Hiroshima and Nagasaki. The risk of
leukemia continued for fourteen years, and there is
insufficient evidence to predict future trends of the
incidence of leukemia among the survivors of the two
bombings.

4138. Hiroshima Gembaku Shogal Kenkyuka. PHYSICAL AND MEDICAL
EFFECTS OF THE ATOMIC BOMB IN HIROSHIMA. Tokyo:
Maruzen, 1958. 117 pp.

This study is prepared by the Hiroshima Research Group
of the Atomic Bomb Casualty Commission. Although brief,
the report indicates the broad dimensions of the subject.

4139. Hollingsworth, Dorothy W., Howard B. Hamilton, Hideya
Tamagaki, and Gilbert W. Beebe. "Thyroid Disease: A
Study in Hiroshima, Japan." MEDICINE, 42 (January
1963), 47-71.

These three medical doctors and a Ph.D. in statistics
(Beebe) undertook this investigation to determine whether
occurrence of thyroid disease is related to single, whole
body exposure to ionization radiation. From July 1958 to
October 1959, the authors studied 5,553 subjects in the
prefecture of Hiroshima. Of the 168 thyroid abnormalities
discovered, 152 were female. The most frequent problem
encountered was simple non-toxic goiter. The authors,
associated with the Atomic Bomb Casualty Commission, call
for more work on their work--the first study in goiter.
The Bibliography includes 168 sources.

4140. Hollingsworth, J.W. "Delayed Radiation Effects in
Survivors of the Atomic Bombings." NEW ENG J MED, 263
(September 8, 1960), 481-487.

Hollingsworth, a Yale professor and former chief of the
Medical Service of the Atomic Bomb Casualty Commission,
feels that the fate of the survivors of the atomic bombings
plays an important role in assessing the perils of
radiation. He summarizes the findings of the 1947-1949
investigation in Japan under general categories, such as
genetics, leukemia, cataracts, carcinoma, growth and
development of children, microcephaly in children, aging
acceleration, and general medical effects in adults.

4141. Liebow, Averill A. ENCOUNTER WITH DISASTER: A MEDICAL
      DIARY OF HIROSHIMA, 1945. New York: W.W. Norton, 1970.
      209 pp.

      The author served as an Army medical officer on the U.S.
      team organized by Col. Ashby W. Oughterson to work with
      Japanese medical investigators after the war. The diary
      entries (September 18 - December 6, 1945) trace the origins
      and proceedings of the Joint Commission for the
      Investigation of the Effects of the Atomic Bomb in Japan.
      There is much technical information. Stark photographs are
      included. Of interest is Liebow's observation that,
      because the U.S. surgeon general was not forewarned about
      the atomic bombings, no American medical team was ready to
      conduct investigations immediately after Japan surrendered.

4142. Neel, James V., Gilbert W. Beebe, and Robert W. Miller.
      "Delayed Biomedical Effects of the Bombs." BULL ATOMIC
      SCI, 41 (August 1985), 72-75.

      Even after forty years of studying the survivors of the
      atomic bombings, the scientist-authors claim that the
      findings remain inconclusive.

4143. Neel, James V. and W.O. Schull. THE EFFECT OF EXPOSURE TO
      THE ATOMIC BOMB ON PREGNANCY TERMINATION IN HIROSHIMA
      AND NAGASAKI. Washington, D.C.: GPO, 1956.

      This study, sponsored by the National Research Council
      of the National Academy of Sciences, uncovers genetic
      problems that appear traceable to the atomic bombings. The
      two scientists call for more study on this connection.

4144. Neel, James V. and William J. Schull. "Radiation and Sex
      Ratio in Man." SCIENCE, 128 (August 15, 1958), 343-348.

      Analyzing the data concerning the children of survivors
      of the atomic bombings, the authors find genetic problems
      which are sex-linked. The significant changes in the
      sex-ratio of the offspring are to be expected, say Neel and
      Schull, after undue exposure to mutagenic influences (such
      as an atomic bombing).

4145. Nussbaum, Rudi H. "Survivor Studies and Radiation
      Standards." BULL ATOMIC SCI, 41 (August 1985), 68-71.

      Nussbaum suggests that the early studies of survivors to
      determine tolerable levels of radiation exposure may have

greatly underestimated the problem.

4146. Oughterson, Ashley W. and Shields Warren, eds. MEDICAL
        EFFECTS OF THE ATOMIC BOMB IN JAPAN. New York:
        McGraw-Hill, 1956. 477 pp.

        The two doctors have assembled an ambitious array of
        technical data in assessing the medical effects of the
        atomic bombings. The study is arranged by
        medical-scientific topic. Although the short-term
        problems were fairly recognizable, the long-term
        dimensions (even in 1956) remained uncharted.

4147. Prentice, Ross L. and Donovan J. Thompson, eds. ATOMIC
        BOMB SURVIVOR DATA: UTILIZATION AND ANALYSIS.
        Philadelphia, PA: Society for Individual and Applied
        Mathematics, 1984. 289 pp.

        From data on radiation and the various dosages suffered
        by survivors of the atomic bombings, these scientists
        assess the health risks involved.

4148. Salaff, Stephen. "Medical Care for Atomic Bomb Victims in
        the United States." BULL CON ASIAN SCHOL, 12
        (January-March, 1980), 69-71.

        The author, a Canadian writer and mathematician, briefly
        traces the attempts to provide medical assistance to
        survivors of the atomic bombings who live in the United
        States--about 370,000. To avoid far-reaching precedents,
        Salaff observes, the State and Defense Departments have
        blocked congressional efforts to make the aid available.

4149. Schonberger, Howard. "People's Art As History: Hiroshima
        Survivors and the Atomic Bomb." JAPAN INTERPRETER, 12
        (Winter 1978), 44-53.

        The world has remained largely ignorant of the
        survivors, the author writes, and their drawings or other
        artistic creations should be included in the historical
        analysis of the atomic bomb.

4150. Shigematsu, Itsuzo and Abraham Kagan, eds. CANCER IN
        ATOMIC BOMB SURVIVORS. New York: Plenum, 1986. 196 pp.

        This collection offers a variety of knowledgeable
        assessments. Even after forty years however, many of the
        conclusions remain qualified and tentative. See especially
        the material on radiation-induced tumors.

4151. Socolow, Edward L., A. Hashizume, S. Neriishi, and R.
       Niitani. "Thyroid Carcinoma in Man After Exposure to
       Ionizing Radiation: A Summary of the Findings in
       Hiroshima and Nagasaki." NEW ENG J MED, 268 (February
       21, 1963), 406-410.

       Analyzing data obtained in a three-year study of some
       nineteen thousand survivors (including biopsies for about
       half that total) by the Atomic Bomb Casualty Commission,
       the four doctors find that thyroid carcinoma becomes
       significantly more prevalent because of such high levels of
       exposure.

4152. Stricker, Raphael B. and Charles A. Linker. "Acute
       Lymphoblastic Leukemia With Monosomy 7 in a Hiroshima
       Survivor 37 Years After the Bomb." J AMER MED ASSOC,
       250 (August 5, 1983), 640-641.

       The two M.D.s acknowledge that the occurrence of a
       single case in 1982 must be used with caution, but they
       believe that the unusual chromosonal deletion of ALL
       suggests a link to the atomic bombing.

4153. Thompson, Donovan J., ed. UNITED STATES-JAPAN JOINT
       WORKSHOP FOR REASSESSMENT OF ATOMIC BOMB RADIATION IN
       HIROSHIMA AND NAGASAKI. Hiroshima: Radiation Effects
       Research Foundation, 1983. 224 pp.

       This workshop, held February 16-17, 1983, at Nagasaki,
       centered on radiation dosimetry as part of these continuing
       joint study ventures.

4154. United States. Department of the Army. Combat
       Developments Command. MILITARY, POLITICAL AND
       PSYCHOLOGICAL IMPLICATIONS OF MASSIVE POPULATION
       CASUALTIES IN HISTORY. Ft. Belvoir, VA: Dept. of the
       Army, 1965. 4 vols.

       This study, prepared by noted historians (e.g., T.N.
       Dupuy, S.L.A. Marshall, S.R. Spard, W.A. Foley, R.
       Sunderland, R. Ropp) in the Historical Evaluation and
       Research Organization (HERO), points out that, except for
       the threat of retaliation, belligerents are rarely
       inhibited from inflicting mass casualties on noncombative
       populations. Such attacks, the authors argue, do
       accomplish wartime objectives but leave a legacy of hatred
       and resentment.

4155. Watanage, Susumu. "On the Incidence of Leukemias in
           Hiroshima During the Past Fifteen Years From 1946-1960."
           J RADIATION RES, 2 (September 1961), 131-140.

           In a comprehensive survey of survivors within 5 miles of
       the hypocenter, the author concludes that the incidence of
       leukemia is higher for this exposed population ("remarkably
       higher" acute form than chronic form) than for non-exposed
       Japanese. Dr. Watanabe, at the Research Institute for
       Nuclear Medicine and Biology at Hiroshima University, feels
       that the ABCC report overlooked "induced radioactivity"
       from the atomic bombings.

4156. Wells, Warner and Neal Tsukifuji. "Scars Remaining in
           Atomic Bomb Survivors." SURGEY, GYNECOLOGY, &
           OBSTETRICS, 95 (August 1952), 129-141.

           Studying 90 survivors in 1946-1947 and re-examining 63
       of these in 1951, the two doctors find no peculiar effects
       of the atomic bombings in the scar keloids.

4157. Yavenditti, Michael J. "The Hiroshima Maidens and American
           Benevolence in the 1950s." MID-AMERICA, 64 (April-July
           1982), 21-39.

           The author feels that the episode stemmed from an
       American guilt complex and symbolized the healing of the
       war.

IV.J.2.c. Postwar ("Atomic Diplomacy"/Nuclear Testing)

4158. Allen, James S. ATOMIC IMPERIALISM: THE STATE, MONOPOLY
           AND THE BOMB. New York: International Publishers, 1952.
           288 pp.

           Allen is critical of the U.S. arms buildup, which, he
       feels, not only reinforces American imperialism but also
       directly threatens the Soviet Union.

4159. Alperovitz, Gar. ATOMIC DIPLOMACY, HIROSHIMA, AND POTSDAM:
           THE USE OF THE ATOMIC BOMB AND THE AMERICAN
           CONFRONTATION WITH SOVIET POWER. New York: Penguin,
           1965. 317 pp.

           The author argues that Truman abandoned Roosevelt's
       policy of cooperation and launched instead new foreign
       policy initiatives which aimed at reducing Soviet influence
       (especially in Europe). Much of Truman's tough stance,
       according to Alperovitz, can be traced to the progress made

by the United States in developing the atomic bomb.
Calling for more research on American motives for using the
bomb, the author believes that American officials gave no
serious consideration to not using the atomic bomb. He
contends that the weapons were not needed to defeat the
Japanese who were already badly beaten. His carefully
drawn conclusions go no further than this, but, without
saying so directly, Alperovitz implies that more research
may tie American motives for using the atomic bomb to the
desire to influence (or threaten) the Soviet Union. An
expanded and updated version appeared in 1985 (New York:
Elisabeth Sifton. 427 pp.) without any appreciable changes
in the basic conclusions.

4160. Alperovitz, Gar. "More on Atomic Diplomacy." BULL ATOMIC
          SCI, 41 (December 1985), 35-39.

          While calling for more research, and inserting important
caveats, Alperovitz cites new evidence which indicates not
only that Truman decided definitely in the spring of 1945
to use the atomic bomb but also that the President hoped
that the bomb would intimidate the Soviet Union. The
author argues that, despite general impressions,
influential Americans--Eisenhower, Leahy, Ralph Bard,
McCloy, Grew and even Stimson--opposed the use of the
atomic bomb.

4161. Blackett, P.M.S. FEAR, WAR AND THE BOMB: MILITARY AND
          POLITICAL CONSEQUENCES OF ATOMIC ENERGY. New York:
          Whittlesey House, 1949. 244 pp.

          This British author was among the first to argue that
American leaders used the atomic bomb not only to prevent
the entry of the Soviet Union but also, in the immediate
postwar era, to intimidate the Russians.

4162. Botti, Timothy J. THE FORGING OF THE ANGLO-AMERICAN
          NUCLEAR ALLIANCE, 1945-1958. Westport, CT: Greenwood,
          1987. 274 pp.

          Botti calls the development of this nuclear partnership
"the long wait." What had seemed such a promising
beginning in understandings reached by Churchill and
Roosevelt took inordinately long to come to fruition. The
author raises questions about Anglo-American relations
being rooted in cooperation or competition. The book is
well researched.

4163. Boyer, Paul. BY THE BOMB'S EARLY LIGHT: AMERICAN

THOUGHT AND CULTURE AT THE DAWN OF THE ATOMIC AGE. New
York: Pantheon Books, 1985. 440 pp.

In a pioneering work, Boyer examines the impact of the
atomic bomb on American culture at the dawn of the nuclear
age. He uses many examples from contemporary sources to
show how the atomic weapons quickly became embedded in
American thought and society. He ranges from the silly (a
1945 magazine publicized one movie starlet as an "Anatomic
Bomb") to the serious (the growing movement for a "World
Government"). Especially valuable are his insights about
the role of the atomic scientists in explaining their
discoveries to the American people. The author includes
only a short note on his sources.

4164.   Boyer, Paul. "The Cloud Over the Culture." NEW REP, 193
        (August 12, 1985), 26-32.

        Boyer, a noted historian, argues that the American
        people have failed to come to terms with the actual use of
        the atomic bomb in the war. Hiroshima and Nagasaki have
        been taken out of the American conscience, according to
        Boyer.

4165.   Brown, Harrison S. MUST DESTRUCTION BE OUR DESTINY? New
        York: Simon and Schuster, 1946. 158 pp.

        The author, a U.S. scientist who worked on the Manhattan
        Project, advocates the control of atomic energy. His great
        concern stems directly from his first-hand knowledge of the
        destructive power of atomic weapons and the devastation
        visited upon Hiroshima and Nagasaki.

4166.   Gormly, James L. "The Washington Declaration and the 'Poor
        Relation': Anglo-American Atomic Diplomacy, 1945-1946."
        DIP HIST, 8 (Summer 1984), 125-143.

        The author argues that London was unable to convince
        Washington to share scientific information about nuclear
        weapons. According to Gormly, American leaders sought to
        maintain U.S. nuclear superiority through such devices as
        delaying tactics and false promises to the British.

4167.   Graybar, Lloyd J. "The 1946 Atomic Bomb Tests: Atomic
        Diplomacy or Bureaucratic Infighting?" J AMER HIST, 72
        (March 1986), 888-907.

        With extensive research, Graybar examines the many sides
        of Operation Crossroads--the atomic tests at Bikini--which

forms part of the debate on atomic diplomacy and the
origins of the Cold War. The author, however, finds more
controversy within inter-service rivalries and U.S.
domestic politics. Only Byrnes and Wallace among Truman's
cabinet, he says, worried about the consequences of
international testing.

4168. Greenwood, John T. "The Atomic Bomb -- Early Air Force
        Thinking and the Strategic Air Force, August 1945-March
        1946." AEROSPACE HIST, 34 (Fall/September 1987),
        158-166.

        Relying firmly on archival records, Greenwood, a
        military historian, shows how the USAAF incorporated the
        atomic bomb into doctrine. He highlights an important
        study headed by Carl Spaatz which concluded that the atomic
        bomb did not alter basic concepts of the strategic air
        offensive. The wartime experience and the key role of
        strategic bombing dominated the thinking of AAF leaders--
        who had only peripheral involvement with the development of
        the bomb. A separate atomic strike force was created
        (without the word "atomic") in the unit's designation: the
        58th Bomb Wing, made up of the 40th, 444th, and 509th
        groups.

4169. Hammond, Thomas T. "'Atomic Diplomacy' Revisited." ORBIS,
        19 (Winter 1976), 1403-1428.

        Hammond examines the "thesis" of Gar Alperovitz (not
        necessarily his "scholarship"). Pointing out that the book
        appeared at a time when Americans were inclined to
        criticize U.S. foreign policy, the author questions
        Alperovitz's thesis and (despite the disclaimer)
        scholarship. Hammond concludes by calling the work "a
        beautiful theory being murdered by a gang of brutal facts."

4170. Haskins, Caryl P. "Atomic Energy and American Foreign
        Policy." FOR AFFS, 24 (July 1946), 591-609.

        Summarizing the general scientific work in the
        development of the atomic bomb, Haskins warns that the
        secret will not remain hidden. His arguments support the
        case for international control (even if some national
        sovereignty had to be surrendered) and for outlawing the
        stockpiling of nuclear weapons. He states that "the race
        is between education and disaster."

4171. Herken, Gregg. THE WINNING WEAPON: THE ATOMIC BOMB IN THE
        COLD WAR, 1945-1950. New York: A.A. Knoff, 1980. 425

pp.

After Hiroshima and Nagasaki, Herken says, atomic
weapons became a "colossal reality." His thesis is that
atomic diplomacy--how to use this winning weapon--in the
period embracing the end of the war and immediately
thereafter gave Americans a "false sense of security and
power." For Herken, the attempts to pin diplomacy to the
broad implications of atomic power proved an illusion for
the United States. The research and the analysis are
outstanding.

4172. Hines, Neal O. PROVING GROUND. Seattle, WA: University of
       Washington Press, 1962. 366 pp.

       Here is an analysis of governmental radiobiological
       studies conducted in the Pacific during the period
       1946-1961 in connection with atomic testing.

4173. Monin, S. "Why Did the Soviet Union Make an Atomic Bomb?"
       SOVIET MIL REV, n.v. (August 1986), 42-44.

       Without saying anything about wartime Soviet research,
       the author insists that Anglo-American hostility prompted
       Moscow to undertake the development of an atomic bomb.

4174. Possony, Stefan T. "The Atomic Bomb." REV POL, 8 (April
       1946), 147-167.

       The author, a writer on military affairs, considers what
       should be done now that the atomic bomb exists. Although
       he proposes a military union--beyond a military pact--he
       has no immediate solution about the new weapon.

4175. Potichny, Peter J. and Jane P. Shapiro, eds. FROM COLD WAR
       TO DETENTE. New York: Praeger, 1976. 223 pp.

       See especially in this collection of essays on foreign
       policy: Thomas Hammond, "Did the United States Use Atomic
       Diplomacy Against Russia in 1945?" Hammond remains
       unconvinced.

4176. Weart, Spencer R. "The Heyday of Myth and Cliche." BULL
       ATOMIC SCI, 41 (August 1985), 38-44.

       Weart believes that myths and cliches about "hidden
       forces of the universe" have derailed sensible thinking
       about atomic energy.

4177.   Weisgall, Jonathan M. "Micronesia and the Nuclear Pacific
        Since Hiroshima." SAIS REV, 5 (Summer-Fall 1985),
        41-55.

        The author is a lawyer who represents the people of
        Bikini atoll. He traces the interconnection between
        Micronesia and the development and use of nuclear weapons.

4178.   Williams, Robert E. "Christian Realism and 'The Bomb':
        Reinhold Niebuhr on the Dilemmas of the Nuclear Age." J
        CHURCH & STATE, 28 (Spring 1986), 289-304.

        The author, a political scientist, argues that Niebuhr
        calls into question previous teachings that the triumph of
        science should be a main goal for a society. The nuclear
        dilemma centers on the capacity for good and evil. In his
        critique of liberalism through a "Christian realism,"
        Neibuhr, according to the author, became a leader in the
        realist school of political science.

IV.J.2.d. Japan's Attempt to Develop an Atomic Bomb

4179.   Dower, John W. "Science, Society, and the Japanese
        Atomic-Bomb Project During World War II." BULL CON
        ASIAN SCHOL, 10 (April-June 1978), 41-54.

        Dower describes the wartime work on a uranium bomb as
        "virtually meaningless." What little was done, he says,
        came at the initiative of the military, the project at
        Kyoto--ironically the city spared by Stimson from a list of
        potential atomic bomb targets--never got to the
        experimental stage, according to the author.

4180.   Herken, Gregg. "'A Most Deadly Illusion': The Atomic
        Secret and American Nuclear Weapons Policy, 1945-1950."
        PAC HR, 49 (February 1980), 51-76.

        Herken feels that American policy on the atomic bomb was
        based on the dangerous illusion that the U.S. could retain
        a monopoly of resources and knowledge. According to
        Herken, this illusion nurtured a false sense of security.

4181.   Shapley, Deborah. "Nuclear Weapons History: Japan's
        Wartime Bomb Projects Revealed." SCIENCE, 199 (January
        13, 1978), 152-157.

        Here is a report that Japanese scientists led by Yoshio
        Nishina worked on building an atomic bomb during the war.
        For evidence, the author cites two official Japanese

histories (1970, n.a., The History of Science and
Technology in Japan, vol. 13; and 1973, Tetu Hirosige's
social history of science), a worker's diary (by Masa
Takeuchi), an unconfirmed account in an article by Yoichi
Yamamoto, and two independent U.S. studies (Herbert F.
York, Jr. and Charles Weiner). In 1945, Shapley writes,
the Japanese lacked the necessary organization and
resources (especially the uranium) to complete their task,
but she argues that the extent of military-scientific
cooperation indicates that Japan would not hesitate to use
an atomic weapon if it had been available.

4182. Wilcox, Robert K. JAPAN'S SECRET WAR. New York: William
        Morrow, 1985. 236 pp.

        In what could become a significant area of investigation
about the war (with far-reaching implications), Wilcox
concludes that Japanese scientists had solved the
theoretical and manufacturing problems of producing an
atomic bomb. In fact, he writes, the Japanese had embarked
on steps to build an atomic bomb just as the war was
ending. According to Wilcox, on August 12, 1945, the
Japanese conducted an atomic test explosion near Hungnan,
in northern Korea. Also, the author claims that the
Japanese were operating a uranium ore processing facility
in the Hungnan area. Despite an extensive bibliography,
Wilcox warns that information about their secret project is
difficult to obtain because of the Japanese wanting to
distance themselves from the topic and contemporary
Americans wanting to prevent this scientific information
from getting to the Soviets. Much of the author's research
emerged through declassified U.S. documents and interviews
with Japanese scientists (and members of the support
staff). Of interest is his statement that Spanish
espionage kept Japanese intelligence informed about the
progress of atomic research in the United States.

IV.J.2.e. Japanese Balloon-Bombs

4183. Bauman, Richard. "When Japan Bombed California."
        SERGEANTS, 23 (February 1984), 30-31.

        NE

4184. Conley, Cornelius W. "The Great Japanese Balloon
        Offensive." AIR U REV, 19 (January-February 1968),
        68-83.

        The Japanese Military Scientific Laboratory began

research in 1933 on the military value of balloons but
discontinued the project. In an interview with the author,
the Japanese general who resurrected the balloon research
denies any intention to use the balloons for dropping
chemical/biological weapons or transporting enemy agents
(as American officials feared). The purpose of the
balloons was to carry incendiary devices to North America.

4185. Frankoski, Joseph P. "The Silent Bombers." AIR DEF MAG,
       n.v. (April-June 1976), 34-36.

       In 1944 the Japanese began launching balloon-carried
       bombs against North America. Lt. Col. Frankoski (USAF),
       however, asserts that the balloons (about 9,300 total)
       inflicted little damage.

4186. Hidagi, Yasushi. "Attack Against the U. S. Heartland."
       AEROSPACE H, 27 (Summer, June 1981), 87-93.

       Beginning in November 1944, the Japanese launched over
       nine-thousand balloons with incendiary bombs ("FU-GO"
       weapon) aimed at the United States. Maj. Gen. Hidagi wrote
       an official report on this effort immediately after the
       war. He estimates that only about ten percent actually
       landed in the United States. The incendiary bombs would
       have caused more damage during the summer months, Hidagi
       claims, but the Japanese launched most of the balloons
       during the winter to take advantage of the prevailing
       winds. Although American officials expressed concern about
       biological warfare devices being placed in the balloons,
       the author denies any Japanese intention to do so.

4187. Johnson, Randall A. "Japanese Balloons Bombed the West."
       PAC NORTHWESTERNER, 20 (No. 3, 1976), 33-43.

       NE

4188. Larsen, Lawrence H. "War Balloons Over the Prairie: The
       Japanese Invasion of South Dakota." S DAKOTA HIST, 9
       (No. 2, 1979), 103-115.

       NE

4189. Mikesh, Robert C. JAPAN'S WORLD WAR II BALLOON BOMB
       ATTACKS ON NORTH AMERICA. Washington, D. C.:
       Smithsonian Institution Press, 1973. 85 pp.

       Here is a report, based mainly on Air Force records, on
       one of the strangest episodes of the war. In reprisal for

the Doolittle Raid, Japan designed, developed, and launched
balloon-bombs which were intended to soar across the
Pacific and drop their destructive payloads on the
continental United States. The first of about 9,000 total
such weapons was launched on November 3, 1944. Mikesh
concludes that the project was an "interesting experiment"
but a "military failure."

4190. Mikesh, Robert C. "The World's First Intercontinental
        Missiles--Japan's Balloon Bombs in World War II." AF
        SPACE DIG, 51 (April 1968), 158-162.

        Conceived in 1933, the "FU-GO" weapon fit Japanese plans
        for revenge after the Doolittle Raid. The author feels
        that the balloon-bombs might have produced a serious threat
        to the United States had the Japanese opted for chemical or
        biological warfare payloads instead of incendiary devices.

4191. Miller, Don. "When Japan Bombed Oregon." ARMY, 32
        (February 1982), 63-65.

        Miller surveys the actual damage inflicted by the
        Japanese balloon-bombs. In May 1945, five children and one
        adult died on Gearhart Mountain in Oregon--the only deaths
        in the war in the continental United States attributable
        directly to enemy action. The last balloon to drop was at
        Idaho Falls, Idaho, on August 9, 1945.

4192. Prioli, Carmine A. "The FU-GO Project." AMER HERITAGE, 33
        (April-May 1982), 89-92.

        The author, a professor of English, describes the
        balloon weapon project launched by Japan. Although U.S.
        censorship effectively squashed public reports about the
        balloons, Prioli says that the hardships of war, not
        uncertainty about the results, caused Japan to abandon the
        project. There is no evidence that any of the balloons
        contained harmful bacteria--as U.S. officials feared. Of
        special interest is his report that one balloon almost
        caused the shutdown of the reactors turning out radioactive
        uranium at the Hanford Engineering Works in the state of
        Washington. On March 10, 1945, the plant's safety
        mechanism engaged when a Japanese balloon became entangled
        in electrical wires.

4193. Reynolds, Clark G. "Attack of the Paper Balloons."
        AIRPOWER HIST, 12 (April 1965), 51-55.

        Based on classified naval records, this article examines

the Japanese balloon attacks launched against the
continental United States. He says that the
balloon-weapons, while potentially harmful, could not have
appreciably affected the situation that existed in
1944-1945.

4194. Webber, Bert. "The Bombing of North America." AMER HIST
        ILLUS, 11 (December 1976), 30-38.

        Building on the research of Cornelius W. Conley (who
        gave his papers to Webber), the author traces over 350
        incidents, including 13 in the postwar years, of Japanese
        balloon bombings of North America. Although he affirms
        that the voluntary U.S. censorship was effective, the
        author points out that B-29 bombings disrupted the
        transport of hydrogen which contributed to the end of the
        balloon launchings.

4195. Webber, Bert. RETALIATION: JAPANESE ATTACKS AND ALLIED
        COUNTERMEASURES ON THE PACIFIC COAST IN WORLD WAR II.
        Corvallis, OR: Oregon State University Press, 1975.
        178 pp.

        With the advantage of the files of the long, painstaking
        research done by Cornelius W. Conley, Webber provides a
        detailed account of the Japanese balloon attacks against
        the United States. The Japanese motives in launching the
        unusual project stemmed from the desire to gain retaliation
        for the Doolittle Raid on Tokyo. Webber traces the
        development of the weapon and offers reports on the small
        number of the weapons that actually reached North America.
        The balloon-bombs inflicted negligible damage. Of interest
        is the description of the not entirely successful U.S.
        efforts to censure reports about the weapon.

4196. Webber, Bert. SILENT SIEGE: JAPANESE ATTACKS AGAINST
        NORTH AMERICA IN WORLD WAR II. Fairfield, WA: Ye
        Galleon Press, 1984.

        Webber expands his work on the Japanese balloon attacks
        to include more information about isolated and ineffectual
        Japanese probes on the West Coast.

4197. Wilbur, W.H. "Those Japanese Balloons." READER'S DIG, 57
        (August 1950), 23-26.

        Wilbur worked on U.S. defenses against the balloons.
        Despite the belittling of the balloons by many Americans,
        he describes the concept as a significant development in

the art of war. About one thousand balloons reached the
North American continent. Each cost about eight hundred
dollars, and each contained three or four bombs (one
incendiary and the rest thirty-two pound fragmentation
anti-personnel).

4198. Zahl, Harold A. "The Secret Everyone Knew." SIGNAL, 24
       (April 1970), 39-43.

       Here is an account of the self-imposed censorship in the
       U.S. concerning the Japanese balloon-bombs--despite
       widespread public knowledge of the weapons. Zahl, a radar
       expert, was a member of a team that inspected one of the
       first balloon landing sites.

IV.J.2.f. Japanese Kamikazes/Kaitens/Fukuryu

4199. Barker, A.J. SUICIDE WEAPON. New York: Ballantine Books,
       1971. 160 pp.

       Barker, a retired British officer, describes the
       suicidal attacks conducted by individual Japanese airmen
       and seamen. The many photographs in the book attest to the
       damage inflicted in these attacks.

4200. Carrison, D.J. "Death Rode the Divine Wind." MC GAZ,
       39 (July 1955), 40-46.

       Discussing the extensive damage inflicted by the
       kamikazes, Carrison feels that the only defense against
       these attacks lay in "providence, speed, and good gunnery."

4201. Inoguchi, Rikihei and Tadashi Nakajima. "The Kamikaze
       Attack Corps." USNIP, 79 (September 1953), 933-945.

       The authors trace the origins and development of the
       kamikaze attack ("the most diabolical tactic of war the
       world has ever seen"). News of early kamikaze successes
       spread quickly and inspired other Japanese to volunteer for
       the missions.

4202. Inoguchi, Rikihei, Tadashi Nakajima, and Roger Pineau.
       DIVINE WIND: JAPAN'S KAMIKAZE FORCE IN WORLD WAR II.
       Annapolis, MD: U.S. Naval Institute Press, 1959. 240
       pp.

       The two Japanese authors served with the Naval Special
       Attack Force from the inception to the end of the Kamikaze
       Corps. Pineau translated the work. In all, over four

thousand Japanese volunteered for the program. As the
narrative makes clear, however, this was not a spontaneous
act of momentary enthusiasm. Many months passed before
some were called, and the volunteers, upholding the
traditional Japanese belief in "life through death," wanted
to die for the great cause of their country. The authors
take care to refute criticism in Japan that volunteers were
used to protect the professional soldiers. Of interest is
the final chapter, which presents excerpts of the last
letters home from these pilots.

4203.   "Japanese Davy Jones." ALL HANDS, No. 361 (March 1947),
        14-15.

        Here is a U.S. naval report on Japanese wartime plans to
dispatch underwater suicide troops, equipped with hand-held
mines, against invading vessels. Elaborate preparations,
such as underwater foxholes and bunkers, were in place at
the time of the Japanese surrender. Each troop in theory
was considered a combat naval vessel and wore an ensign.

4204.   "Japan's Undersea Suicide Troops." WARSHIP INTL, 10 (No.
        3, 1973), 266-269.

        Based on an official Navy report in 1947 by Capt. C.G.
Grimes, the article describes Japanese plans for underwater
suicide troopers (FUKURYU). Each of these volunteers would
have a mine-mounted ram stick to blow up enemy ships,
especially landing craft, associated with the invasion of
the homeland. Underwater pillboxes, foxholes, and a
communications system were developed as integral parts of
the concept.

4205.   Kuwahara, Yasuo and Gordon T. Allred, KAMIKAZE. New York:
        Ballantine Books, 1957. 187 pp.

        The Japanese author describes his involvement with the
controversial kamikaze program. The book offers the
Japanese perspective on the suicidal missions.

4206.   Larteguy, Jean, ed. THE SUN GOES DOWN: LAST LETTERS FROM
        JAPANESE SUICIDE-PILOTS AND SOLDIERS. London: New
        English Library, 1975. 127 pp.

        Nora Wydenbruck translated the work from French. The
proud, peaceful tone of these letters is striking. Most of
these last letters to loved ones were written by
individuals who expressed pride in making the extreme
sacrifice for the emperor and the homeland. It is a

touching collection.

4207. Millot, Benard. DIVINE THUNDER: THE LIFE AND DEATH OF THE
       KAMIKAZES. New York: McCall Publishing, 1971. 243 pp.

       The work is translated from the French by Lowell Bair.
       Millot tells of the concept of suicide as it fits the
       Japanese heritage. Affirming his fundamental opposition to
       the subject, Millot traces the development of wartime
       kamiaze operations (by airmen and seamen) from the initial
       discussions on October 19, 1944 by Vice-Admiral Takijiro
       Onishi, commander of the First Air Fleet, to the final days
       of the war. The original concept called for only a
       temporary effort, and this, according to Millot, was, in
       part, why the project attracted so many volunteers.
       Despite his self-avowed opposition, the author writes with
       a sympathy that is unsettling to the reader, especially
       when he describes the kamikazes as an "extraordinary
       spiritual phenomenon" and a lesson in "purity" and "human
       grandeur."

4208. Monsarrat, John. ANGEL ON THE YARDARM: THE BEGINNINGS OF
       FLEET RADAR DEFENSE AND THE KAMIKAZE THREAT. Newport,
       RI: Naval War College, 1985. 188 pp.

       Part of the Naval War College's historical monograph
       series, this personal account focuses on the efforts of the
       LANGLEY (CVL-27) to cope with the fanatical Japanese in air
       attacks.

4209. Nagatsuka, Ryuj. I WAS A KAMIKAZE. New York: Macmillan,
       1972. 212 pp.

       The author describes his life as a cadet and air force
       pilot. The call for kamikazes received an enthusiastic
       response without coercion or brainwashing. By negating the
       value of life, Nagatsuka says that he and his fellow
       volunteers sought a meaning and justification for death.
       His must have been a rare experience in that he returned
       from not one but two suicide missions. Poor weather caused
       him to return from the first attempt (June 29, 1945);
       wounds sustained in an aerial battle forced him to land in
       the second (August 12, 1945). Of interest is his admission
       that, upon entering the Air Force, he received authentic
       briefings of the war situation since he was no longer a
       civilian from whom much must be hidden. Nina Rootes
       re-translated the work from the French.

4210. O'Neill, Richard. SUICIDE SQUADS, W.W. II. New York: St.
       Martin's Press, 1982. 296 pp.

       O'Neill describes ingenious destructive devices and
       special units that appeared during the war. His account
       examines Japanese kamikazes and midget submarines.

4211. Pineau, Roger. "Spirit of the Divine Wind." USNIP, 84
       (November 1958), 23-29.

       Pineau explores the origins and development of the
       Kamikaze Corps. Of special interest is his report on the
       damage inflicted by the kamikaze attacks.

4212. "The Suicide Blade." RAF FLYING REV, 16 (June 1961),
       40-41.

       NE

4213. United States. Navy Department. Pacific Fleet.
       INFORMATION ON AND COMMENTS CONCERNING SUICIDE ATTACK
       PLANES. San Francisco, CA: Pac Fleet, 1945. 174 pp.

       This report incorporates several recommendations
       compiled and endorsed by Adm. R.K. Turner in combatting
       kamikaze attacks. These common-sense items include early
       detection, maximum volume of gunfire by all anti-aircraft
       weapons, and the need to maintain the highest possible
       speeds. The damage caused by the kamikazes, according to
       this report, was more extensive than popularly believed.

4214. United States. Navy Department. U.S. Fleet. ANTIAIRCRAFT
       ACTION SUMMARY: SUICIDE ATTACKS. Washington, D.C.:
       Navy Dept., 1945. 76 pp.

       This report covers the period October 1944-January 1945.
       Emphasizing the point that these suicide air attacks were
       not new--fanatics had carried out such attacks since the
       early days of this war--the narrative cautions U.S.
       personnel not to expect a shortage of Japanese kamikaze
       pilots as long as the attacks continue to be successful.
       Readers are warned that, from the Japanese perspective, the
       kamikazes were a "profitable tactic."

4215. United States. Navy Department. U.S. Fleet. RADAR
       PICKETS AND METHODS OF COMBATING SUICIDE ATTACKS OFF
       OKINAWA. Washington, D.C.: Navy Dept., 1945. 42 pp.

       Drawn largely from battle experience reports, this study

surveys a range of opinions on how to counter the
kamikazes. The recommended use of the pickets included
providing early warning and fighter direction, offering
some anti-aircraft fire, and rescuing downed U.S. airmen
(350 miles off the coast of Japan).

4216. Vogel, Bertram. "Who Were the Kamikaze?" USNIP, 73 (July
        1947), 832-837.

        After interrogating Japanese POWs, the author is able to
provide important information about the kamikaze pilots.

4217. Warner, Denis and Peggy Warner. THE SACRED WARRIORS:
        JAPAN'S SUICIDE LEGIONS. New York: Van Nostrand
        Reinhold, 1982. 370 pp.

        Here is a well-written account of the motivations and
cultural background of the Japanese soldiers who willingly
sacrificed their lives for the emperor. Their letters and
poems clearly reveal that these Japanese embraced a
contentment and serenity in the fate they had chosen. The
book is a useful introduction to this complex Japanese
phenomenon.

4218. Williams, Gordon B. "Encounter With the Divine Wind."
        SHIPMATE, 51 (March 1988), 13-15.

        The author commanded the one-stack destroyer STERETT.
He describes the kamikaze attacks against his ship in April
1945. Of interest is his expression of gratitude in
hearing of the two atomic bombings--at a time his ship was
undergoing battle damage repairs.

4219. Yokoi, Toshiyuki with Roger Pineau. "Kamikazes and the
        Okinawa Campaign." USNIP, 80 (May 1954), 505-513.

        Admiral Yokoi was chief of staff to the 5th Fleet when
the Kamikaze force was being formed. Although not
originally planned as a large-scale or continuing
operation, the authors report that enthusiasm, heroism, and
misleading damage reports caused the continuation of the
kamikaze tactic. Special emphasis is given to the campaign
in Okinawa. Yokoi acknowledges the shame of this "mistaken
way of command."

4220. Yokota, Yutaka and Joseph D. Harrington. "Kaiten ...
        Japan's Human Torpedoes." USNIP, 88 (January 1962),
        55-68.

The oxygen-fueled, "Long Lance" torpedo was an effective
weapon for the Japanese--then they added a pilot. Yokota
draws from a rare experience; not once but three times, he
sailed off on suicide Kaiten missions, but each time the
mission had to be aborted. He and Harrington combine to
describe Kaiten operations during the war.

4221. Yokota, Yutaka and Joseph D. Harrington. THE KAITEN
        WEAPON. New York: Ballantine Books, 1962. 255 pp.

Here is a knowledgeable report on Japan's maritime
version of the suicide unit. These underwater manned bombs
were designed for head-on collision with enemy ships. Of
interest are the descriptions of the contentment of the
sea-going volunteers with their fate.

IV.J.2.g. Bats

4222. Feist, Joe Michael. "Bats Away." AMER HERITAGE, 33
        (April-May 1982), 93-96.

Soon after Pearl Harbor, Lytle S. Adams conceived the
idea of attaching incendiary bombs to bats. He was able to
put his idea before Roosevelt, and the Army began testing
the concept (at first with 3-5 grams of explosives, later
15-18 grams). After the Army gave up on the idea, the Navy
began its own tests. It all came to nothing, and Feist
estimates the entire project wasted about two million
dollars.

IV.J.2.h. Biological/Chemical Warfare

4223. Bernstein, Barton J. "Why We Didn't Use Poison Gas in
        World War II." AMER HERITAGE, 36 (Aug-Sept 1985),
        40-46.

If the war had dragged on, Bernstein argues, Truman
might have come under growing pressure to use gas against
the Japanese. Although Roosevelt firmly resisted all such
proposals, Bernstein questions whether Truman would have
been as firm, especially, as Bernstein points out, the
"costly struggle was eroding American repugnance to gas."
According to the author, a number of U.S. leaders--McCloy,
MacArthur, Marshall, and Stilwell--showed sympathy with the
recommendation of the Chemical Warfare Service to use gas
in the tough island campaigns, especially after Iwo Jima
and with the grim prospects associated with the invasion of
the Japanese home islands. Hull, Leahy, Arnold, Knox and
top naval leaders remained firmly opposed to the use of

gas. Stimson preferred to say nothing publicly in order to
foster doubt in the enemy's mind. Bernstein advances three
reasons why the United States did not use gas: (1) the
damage to U.S. prestige would not be worth the gain, (2)
the use of gas, while helpful, was not necessary, and (3)
Roosevelt had publicly pledged that the U.S. would not use
gas in the war. Nevertheless, Bernstein leaves open the
possibilities that the U.S. might have used gas if things
had begun to get difficult at the end of the war.

4224.   Condon, Jane and Nancy Faber. "An Author Accuses the
        Japanese of Horrifying Medical Experiments on World War
        II POWs." PEOPLE, 17 (January 11, 1982), 107-108.

        This popular article publicizes the findings of John
Powell about medical experiments conducted under Gen. Shiro
Ishii. The authors make clear that the U.S. government has
offered a detailed denial of Powell's allegations.

4225.   Gomer, Robert, John W. Powell, and Bert V.A. Roling.
        "Japan's Biological Weapons, 1930-1945." BULL ATOMIC
        SCI, 37 (October 1981), 43-53.

        The authors offer perspectives on the shocking reports
of Japanese biological experimentations on thousands of
Chinese, Russian, Manchurian, and American prisoners. The
experiments include prolonged exposure to x-rays,
transfusions using horse blood, vivisections, and massive
doses of diseases (e.g., plague, typhus, dysenteries, gas
gangrene, typhoid, hemorrhagic fever, cholera, anthrax,
tularemia, smallpox, tsutsugamushi, and glanders.) The
Japanese scientists, leg by Gen. Ishii, all lived out their
natural lives. According to the authors, the U.S. was
willing to grant immunity to them in order to gain
information "at a fraction of the original cost."

4226.   Harris, Robert and Jeremy Paxman. A HIGHER FORM OF
        KILLING: THE SECRET STORY OF CHEMICAL AND BIOLOGICAL
        WARFARE. New York: Hill and Wang, 1982.

        Using newly declassified documents and private British
papers, the authors present a sobering account of the dark
side of the war. It is one thing, however, to plan
comprehensively for certain contingencies and quite another
to formulate concrete policies. The authors confuse these
two different worlds.

4227.   "Japan's Biological Weapons: 1930-1945--An Update." BULL
        ATOMIC SCI, 38 (October 1982), 62.

This brief report states that the Japanese government has admitted the existence of Unit 731. The United States government, meanwhile, continues to offer no comment on the assertion that Japanese personnel in Unit 731 had received immunity for the alleged war crimes. Accusations persist that the Japanese conducted biological experiments on American, British, Dutch, and Australian POWs, as well as Chinese, Russian, and Korean prisoners.

4228. Jones, R.V. and J.M. Lewis. "Churchill's Anthrax Bombs: A Debate." BULL ATOMIC SCI, 43 (November 1987), 42-45.

Jones (head of Scientific Intelligence) and Lewis (a political research consultant) criticize Barton Bernstein's allegations (ibid., January/February 1987) about Churchill's willingness to use biological warfare. Their article includes a rebuttal by Bernstein who still believes that Churchill did not feel constrained to use anthrax bombs.

4229. Kamen, Martin D. RADIANT SCIENCE, DARK POLITICS: A MEMOIR OF THE NUCLEAR AGE. Berkely, CA: University of California Press, 1985. 348 pp.

Kamen's account sheds light on developments in the field of biochemistry. His conclusions about the postwar era call into question the government's scientific policies.

4230. Kleber, Brooks E. and Dale Birdsall. THE CHEMICAL WARFARE SERVICE: CHEMICALS IN ACTION. Washington, D.C.: Office of the Chief of Military History, Dept. of the Army, 1965. 673 pp.

The authors write on the wartime history not only of the combat use (and plans) of chemicals but also of the organization and operation of the Chemical Warfare Service.

4231. MATERIALS OF THE TRIAL OF FORMER SERVICEMEN OF THE JAPANESE ARMY CHARGED WITH MANUFACTURING AND EMPLOYING BACTERIOLOGICAL WEAPONS. Moscow: Foreign Languages Publishing House, 1950.

Twelve Japanese soldiers stood trial at Khabarovsk, December 25-29, 1949. This Soviet report in the proceedings includes written evidence by two defendants (Kawashima and Karasawa) about their Japanese unit conducting bacteriological experiments on humans.

4232.   McGill, Peter. "A Coverup for a Death Camp." MACLEAN'S,
            98 (May 20, 1985), 32.

            Here is a brief summary of Japanese Unit 731, which
        engaged in bacteriological warfare experiments on POWs.
        The U.S. government extended immunity to the unit after the
        war, supposedly because the unit's data were deemed vital
        to U.S. security. Some of today's prominent Japanese
        physicians and researchers served in this unit.

4233.   Van Courtland Moon, John Ellis. "Chemical Weapons and
            Deterrence: The World War II Experience." INTL
            SECURITY, 8 (Spring 1984), 3-35.

            Here is an excellent survey of both the European and
        Pacific theaters. Moon includes a discussion of Japanese
        preparations for chemical warfare, and he feels that the
        Japanese probably used these weapons in China. According
        to the author, Americans discussed (and rejected) waging
        chemical warfare on at least two occasions: after the
        heavy losses at Tarawa and on planning for the final
        invasion of Japan.

4234.   Newman, Barclay M. JAPAN'S SECRET WEAPON. New York:
            Current, 1944. 223 pp.

            Based on flimsy evidence, Newman asserts that Japan has
        bacteriological weapons ready for use as soon as the
        protective antidote is ready. The author, serving in the
        U.S. Public Health Service, makes an unpersuasive
        presentation.

4235.   Powell, John W. "The Gap Between the Natural and the
            Social Sciences Sometimes Leaves the Public Poorly
            Informed." BULL CONCERNED ASIAN SCHOLARS, 18
            (July-September 1986), 39-42.

            Powell feels that a recent scientific report on Epidemic
        Hemorrhagic Fever (EHF) would have been more comprehensive
        had the scientists linked the EHF, which broke out in Korea
        during the Korean War and persists to the present day, to
        the work of Japanese army scientists during the Second
        World War in culturing songo fever. Unfortunately, Powell
        draws only a tenuous connection, based on inference,
        between EHF and his own excellent research on Japanese
        experimentation in biological warfare. Perhaps natural and
        social scientists can cooperate in solving these questions.

4236.   Powell, John W. "Japan's Biological Weapons, 1930-1945: A

Hidden Chapter in History." BULL ATOMIC SCI, 37
(October 1981), 44-52.

Largely through the Freedom of Information Act, Powell
has obtained documents concerning the biological warfare
unit of the Japanese army (Unit 731). Located near Harbin,
the unit, according to Powell, accounted for some three
thousand deaths (Chinese, Russian, and Koreans) in its
experiments. He charges that the U.S. government aided in
covering up information about the unit in order to secure
exclusive possession of Japanese expertise in germ warfare.
At least two other Japanese units--Tama Detachment in
Nanjing and Unit 100 near Changchun--may have undertaken
similar "research." In addition, Powell recounts alleged
incidents of biological warfare waged by the Japanese in
China.

4237. Powell, John W. "Japan's Germ Warfare: The U.S. Cover-Up
of a War Crime." BULL CON ASIAN SCHOL, 12
(October-December 1980), 2-17.

The author, a former editor of CHINA WEEKLY REVIEW,
criticizes Washington's double standard in covering up
Japanese biological warfare experiments in order to gain
the benefits of the knowledge gained by Japanese Unit 731
under Dr. Ishii Shiro. Beginning in 1931, the Japanese
continued until August 1945 the tests which claimed the
lives of over 3,000 human guinea pigs. Powell suggests
that the CIA, Smithsonian, and National Academy of Sciences
may have some links to this story.

4238. Rosebury, Theodore. PEACE OR PESTILENCE. New York:
McGraw-Hill, 1949. 218 pp.

The author, an American bacteriologist, raises questions
about Japan's use of germ warfare.

4239. Omitted.

4240. Yamada, Otozo. MATERIALS ON THE TRIAL OF FORMER SERVICEMEN

OF THE JAPANESE ARMY CHARGED WITH MANUFACTURING AND
EMPLOYING BACTERIOLOGICAL WEAPONS. Moscow: Foreign
Language Publishing House, 1950.   534 pp.

NE

V. RELIGIOUS ASPECTS OF THE WAR AGAINST JAPAN

A. GENERAL

4241. Carmer, Carl L., ed. WAR AGAINST GOD. New York: Henry
        Holt, 1943. 261 pp.

        This collection of essays focuses on the question of
        whether or not the Japanese and the Germans are at war with
        Christianity. Hovering over this volume is the troublesome
        and complex issue of aligning national interests with God's
        interests.

4242. Dennis, Clyde H., THESE LIVE ON: THE BEST OF TRUE STORIES
        UNVEILING THE POWER AND PRESENCE OF GOD IN WORLD WAR II.
        Chicago: Good Books, 1945. 204 pp.

        These selections, taken from all theaters, reflect a
        powerful religious theme.

4243. Klemm, Edwin O. UPON REQUEST: GOD IN ACTION, THE AMAZING
        PART IN THE HISTORY: UNITED STATES AND CHINA. Saginaw,
        MI: Author, 1971.

        In this brief report on Sino-American relations during
        the war, Klemm emphasizes the importance of divine
        inspiration--and intervention.

4244. "In Matters of War and Peace." CHRISTIANITY TODAY, 24
        (November 21, 1980), 14-15.

        Although not directly related to the war against Japan,
        this editorial argues that (a) total pacifism is
        unrealistic (and unbiblical) and (b) certain
        qualities--honor, truth, justice, freedom,
        righteousness--are more valuable than life itself.

807

4245. Smylie, Robert F. "A Presbyterian Witness on War and
       Peace: An Historical Interpretation." J PRESBYTERIAN
       HIST, 59 (Winter 1981), 498-516.

       The author explores the Presbyterian Church's response
       to the war (also Korea and Vietnam). The case for the
       necessity for World War II gained cautious acceptance.

V.B. CHURCHES/MISSIONARY WORK/CHAPLAINS (GENERAL)/CONSCIENTIOUS OBJECTORS

4246. Abrams, Ray H. PREACHERS PRESENT ARMS. Scottdale, PA:
       Herald Press, 1969. 330 pp.

       Here is a survey of some of the activities of American
       churches and clergy in the two world wars as well as in
       Vietnam.

4247. Adams, Jennie Clare. THE HILLS DID NOT IMPRISON HER. New
       York: Women's American Foreign Baptist Mission Society,
       1947. 48 pp.

       Here is a personal account by an American missionary in
       the Philippines during the war. The book seems more a
       commentary on a remarkable woman than a valuable resource
       on the war.

4248. Corbett, Charles H. "Christian Missions in the New China."
       FE SURVEY, 13 (March 8, 1944), 40-43.

       The author, an officer of the Associated Board for
       Christian Colleges in China, praises (exaggerates?) the
       benefits and the changed attitudes associated with the end
       of extraterritoriality privileges by the West.

4249. Ekirch, Arthur A., Jr. " A Political Prisoner in Wartime."
       PEACE & CHANGE, 12 (No. 1/2, 1987), 77-92.

       Here is a personal account by the noted historian of his
       experiences as a conscientious objector in the Civilian
       Public Service during the war. In his mind, Ekirch
       believed himself to be a political prisoner and Roosevelt
       to be his "personal jailer." He describes the difficulties
       his wife faced, the support he received from Merle Curti
       (his professor at Columbia), and the complaints against him
       to the Selective Service from relatives. After the war,
       Hofstra University gave him a teaching job and assured
       Ekirch that his CO status was of no concern.

4250.   Forgy, Howell M. AND PASS THE AMMUNITION. New York:
          D. Appleton-Century, 1944. 242 pp.

          The author recounts his experiences as a chaplain
          aboard the NEW ORLEANS. He uttered the famous phrase
          ("Praise the Lord and pass the ammunition") during the
          attack at Pearl Harbor (but he did not man a gun as alleged
          in the popular song based on the incident).

4251.   Frillman, Paul and Graham Peck. CHINA: THE REMEMBERED
          LIFE. Boston: Houghton Mifflin, 1968. 291 pp.

          Frillman, as a prewar missionary, lived among the
          Chinese people and spoke their language. Later, he served
          as chaplain to the American Volunteer Group, as a G.I., and
          as a postwar representative of the State Department in
          China. Illustrated by Peck, the book concentrates on
          Frillman's experiences. Of special interest is the
          material concerning Indochina.

4252.   Hamilton, Esther Terger. AMBASSADOR IN BONDS. East
          Stroudsburg, PA: Pinebrook, 1946. 264 pp.

          The author recounts her life as a Baptist missionary in
          the Philippines--and as an internee during the Japanese
          occupation.

4253.   Hurford, Grace Gibberd. "Missionary Service in China." J
          CANADIAN CHURCH HIST SOC, 19 (Nos. 3/4, 1977), 177-181.

          NE

4254.   Jenkins, Burris A. FATHER MEANY AND THE FIGHTING 69th.
          New York: Fell, 1944. 61 pp.

          This brief book recounts the experience of a chaplain
          who was wounded at Makin Island.

4255.   McGoey, John H. NOR SCRIP, NOR SHOES. Boston, MA:
          Atlantic Monthly Press, 1959. 280 pp.

          Father McGoey, a Canadian Catholic priest, writes about
          his experiences and observations in China during the war
          and immediately thereafter.

4256.   McMillan, Archibald M. FOR CHRIST IN CHINA. Nashville,
          TN: Broadman Press, 1948. 141 pp.

          Here is a first-hand account by a Baptist missionary in

China during the war.

4257.   McRoberts, Duncan. PLEADING CHINA. Grand Rapids, MI:
        Zondervan, 1946. 141 pp.

        The author gives a personal account of his evangelist
        crusade in China.

4258.   Monaghan, Forbes. UNDER THE RED SUN: A LETTER FROM
        MANILA. New York: McMullen, 1946. 279 pp.

        The author, a Jesuit priest and professor of philosophy
        in the Philippines, remained in that country from 1941
        through the return of the Allies to Manila. From his
        unique perspective, Fr. Monaghan emphasizes the important
        wartime contribution of the Filipino people.

4259.   Runbeck, Margaret Lee. THE GREAT ANSWER. Boston, Houghton
        Mifflin, 1944. 238 pp.

        NE

4260.   Sisters of Our Lady of the Sacred Heart. RED GREW THE
        HARVEST. Sydney, Aus.: 1947. 185 pp.

        Here is an interesting account of the missionary work of
        this Catholic order of nuns in Oceania during the war.
        The sisters give personal accounts of their activities and
        accomplishments.

4261.   Society for the Propagation of the Faith. THE PRIEST GOES
        TO WAR: A PICTORIAL OUTLINE OF THE WORK OF THE CATHOLIC
        CHAPLAINS IN THE SECOND WORLD WAR. New York: Society
        for the Propagation of the Faith, 1946. 128 pp.

        This brief photographic account covers all theaters.
        One motive behind the publication of this book is to show
        the diverse roles that the priests performed in the war.

4262.   Tennien, Mark A. CHUNGKING LISTENING POST. New York:
        Creative Age Press, 1945. 201 pp.

        The author, a Maryknoll priest, served for almost four
        years as a banker and liaison for 1,500 Catholic
        missionaries in wartime China. His unique position enables
        him to give a good description of the Chinese people at
        war.

4263.   THROUGH TOIL AND TRIBULATION: MISSIONARY EXPERIENCES IN

CHINA DURING THE WAR OF 1937-1945 TOLD BY THE
MISSIONARIES, London: Carey Press, 1947. 208 pp.

Here is an interesting anthology of personal accounts by
missionaries who served in China. Their reports tell much
about life in China during the war.

4264. United States. Department of the Army. Chaplain Section.
HISTORY OF CHAPLAINS' ACTIVITIES IN THE PACIFIC. n.p.:
AFPAC, 1946. 543 pp.

This official account surveys the activities of the Army
chaplains throughout the war against Japan.

4265. Van Dusen, Henry P. THEY FOUND THE CHURCH THERE: THE
ARMED FORCES DISCOVER CHRISTIAN MISSIONS. New York:
Charles Scribner's Sons, 1945. 148 pp.

The author makes the telling point that missionaries had
preceded the soldiers into the remote areas of Asia and
would remain long after the armed troops had withdrawn.

4266. Wells, Ronald A., ed. THE WARS OF AMERICA: CHRISTIAN
VIEWS. Grand Rapids, MI: Eerdmans, 1981. 239 pp.

NE

4267. Wilson, Roger C. QUAKER RELIEF. London: Allen and Unwin,
1952. 373 pp.

Here is an account of the relief work around the world
of the Quakers during the period 1940 to 1948.

V.C. MEMOIRS AND BIOGRAPHIES

4268. Amoury, Daisy. FATHER CYCLONE. New York: Julian Messner,
1958. 253 pp.

Amoury, a correspondent, offers a glowing tribute to
Lawrence E. Lynch, a chaplain in the South Pacific and
Okinawa. The author uses private papers and some
interviews to portray her interesting subject. Father
Lynch died while ministering to his "charges."

4269. Clare, Thomas H. LOOKIN' EASTWARD: A G. I. SALAAM TO
INDIA. New York: Macmillan, 1945. 322 pp.

Clare, Army chaplain with the 341st Bombardment Group in
India, enjoyed close relationships with the men he served.

This posthumous account of his experiences is based on
letters he wrote to his wife Irma.

4270. Farris, Marvin. DO IT AGAIN. . . WAS IT LUCK OR PRAYER?
        Fort Worth, TX: Branch-Smith, 1969. 185 pp.

        In this story of what he calls "the dark months" of the
        war in the Pacific, Farris emphasizes the spiritual aspects
        of his experience.

4271. Go Puan Seng. THE HOUR HAD COME: HOW FAITH BROUGHT US
        THROUGH PERIL. Grand Rapids, MI: Douma Publishers,
        1958. 228 pp.

        The Chinese author published a newspaper in the
        Philippines before the war. The book recounts his
        experiences while he hid from the Japanese during the
        occupation. He states that his Christian faith pulled him
        through the ordeal.

4272. Lynip, G. Louise, ed. ON GOOD GROUND: MISSIONARY STORIES
        FROM THE PHILIPPINES. Grand Rapid, MI: Eerdmans, 1946.
        149 pp.

        Here is a collection of reports, some of which dwell on
        the experiences of American missionaries just prior to and
        during the war in the Philippines.

4273. Morris, David E. CHINA CHANGED MY MIND. London: Cassell,
        1948. 202 pp.

        Here is the personal account of a driver for a Quaker
        ambulance unit on the Burma Road. During his two-year
        stint and while observing conditions in Southwest China,
        Morris switched from pacifist to soldier. It is an
        unusual, readable war tale.

4274. Norris, Ronald. THE PASSIONISTS IN CHINA. n.p.: 1942.
        78 pp.

        Rev. Norris tells of his experiences as a missionary in
        China.

4275. O'Callahan, Joseph T., S.J. I WAS CHAPLAIN ON THE FRANKLIN.
        New York: Macmillan, 1956. 153 pp.

        Fr. O'Callahan received the Congressional Medal of
        Honor for helping wounded crew members aboard the
        FRANKLIN. On March 19, 1945, the aircraft carrier was

badly damaged during a kamikaze assault. He modestly
downplays his role and praises his shipmates' efforts to
save the ship.

4276. Sato, Tasuku and Mark Tennien. I REMEMBER FLORES. New
       York: Farrar, Strauss and Cudahy, 1957,   129 pp.

       Sato, a Japanese naval officer, was stationed at Flores
Island in the NEI. He met Tennien, a Maryknoll priest,
there.   The book tells of their discussions and Sato's
eventual conversion to Catholicism.

4277. Tower, H.H. FIGHTING THE DEVIL WITH THE MARINES.
       Philadelphia, PA: Dorrance, 1945. 172 pp.

       The author, a Navy chaplain, spent almost three years
with the Marines in the Pacific.

4278. Willard, W. Wyeth. THE LEATHERNECKS COME THROUGH. New
       York: Fleming H. Revell, 1944. 224 pp.

       Here is a unique perspective on the campaigns to take
the Solomons and the Gilberts. The author served as a
Protestant chaplain with the Marines in the engagements
from Guadalcanal to Tarawa. Neither a "pass the
ammunition" type of personality nor one of the boys,
Willard writes that he tried to remain true to his calling,
both in spirit and in deed. The stories that he tells
about individual Marines underscores heroism and humor. Of
special interest is his report on not wearing the Geneva
cross, which, to him, was of no use in the face of Japanese
brutal disregard of such international markings for
non-combatants.

4279. Whittaker, James C. WE THOUGHT WE HEARD THE ANGELS SING.
       New York: E.P. Dutton, 1943. 139 pp.

       The author was co-pilot of a plane carrying Eddie
Rickenbaker. The plane ditched at sea. The story of their
21-day odyssey adrift in a raft, for Whittaker, is one of
newly found religious faith which pulled him through the
ordeal.

VI. SOCIAL AND CULTURAL ASPECTS OF THE WAR AGAINST JAPAN

A. THE ARTS AND THE WAR AGAINST JAPAN

1. GENERAL

4280. Almaraz, Felix Diaz, Jr. "The Little Theater in the Atomic
Age: Amateur Dramatics in Los Alamos, New Mexico,
1943-1946." J WEST, 17 (April 1978), 72-82.

Here is the story of the theatrical group which helped
meet the social and cultural needs of those associated with
the Manhattan Project. Beginning in late 1943, local
performers acted in small auditoriums for local audiences,
and their efforts earned artistic and financial success.

4281. Black, Gregory D. "Keys of the Kingdom: Entertainment and
Propaganda." S ATL Q, 75 (Autumn 1976), 434-446.

With careful research through primary (archival) and
secondary sources, Black describes the propaganda maneuvers
of the OWI. Elmer Davis believed that entertainment served
as an effective propaganda tool (largely because of an
unsuspecting public). As a case study, Black exposes the
calculated reworking of the script of the 1944 movie, "Keys
of the Kingdom," to promote a favorable image of China, one
of the "Big Four." The author asserts that about five
hundred films which appeared during the war carried some
form of propaganda message.

4282. Meserve, Walter J. and Ruth I. Meserve. "The Stage History
of ROAR CHINA!: Documentary Drama as Propaganda."
THEATRE SURVEY, 21 (May 1980), 1-13.

This overview traces the writing and the popularization
of the play by Sergei Mikhailovich Tretiakov. Of interest
is the changing nature of the villain for the Soviets:
Japan during the war and imperialism in the postwar era.

815

4283.   Shulimson, Jack. "Maurice Evans, Shakespeare and the U.S.
        Navy." J POP CUL, 10 (Fall 1976), 255-266.

        Criticized (by chaplains) for the sex-oriented humor of
        his entertainment, Evans set out (with Judith Anderson) to
        present MACBETH to the military audiences. The success of
        the production led to performances of other Shakespearean
        works.

4284.   Supreme Commander for the Allied Powers. Civil Information
        and Education Section. POST-WAR STATUS OF MUSEUMS IN
        JAPAN. Tokyo: SCAP, 1946. 14 pp.

        This special report, which includes descriptions of the
        war damage inflicted upon Japanese museums, was prepared by
        SCAP's Cultural Resources Research Unit.

4285.   Williams, Annabelle R. OPERATION GREASE-PAINT. Hollywood,
        CA: House-Warven, 1951. 240 pp.

        NE

4286.   Wooley, Sir Charles L. A RECORD OF THE WORK DONE BY THE
        MILITARY AUTHORITIES FOR THE PROTECTION OF THE TREASURES
        OF ART AND HISTORY IN WAR AREAS. London: HMSO, 1947.
        71 pp.

        NE

4287.   THE WORLD WARS REMEMBERED. Dublin, NH: Yankee, 1979.
        190 pp.

        NE

VI.A.2. ART

4288.   Abbott Laboratories. THE ABBOTT COLLECTION: PAINTINGS OF
        NAVAL AVIATION. Chicago: Abbott, 1944. 16 pp.

        A contemporary collection which includes aircraft the
        U.S. Navy used in combat.

4289.   Baldwin, Hanson W., ed. THE NAVY AT WAR. New York:
        Morrow, 1943. 160 pp.

        Baldwin introduces the art work of fine artists whom the
        Navy selected to portray various naval branches in combat.

4290. Benton, Thomas Hart. THE YEAR OF PERIL. North Chicago,
         IL: Abbott Laboratories, 1942. 4 leaves.

         Here are six color plates by the famed artist.

4291. Chrysler Corporation. SIGNIFICANT WAR SCENES BY
         BATTLEFRONT ARTISTS, 1941-1945. Detroit: Chrysler
         Corporation, 1951. 32 pp.

         The book contains memorable scenes by sixteen artists
         from around the world.

4292. Crane, Aimee, ed. ART IN THE ARMED FORCES. New York:
         Charles Scribner's Sons, 1944. 232 pp.

         Here is a collection of art created by men and women in
         the U.S. armed forces. The work is of uneven quality but
         holds popular appeal.

4293. Crane, Aimee, ed. G. I. SKETCH BOOK. New York: Penguin
         Books, 1944. 136 pp.

         Crane presents art work on the war by men and women in
         uniform. Not all are serious; not all depict actual
         combat.

4294. Crane, Aimee, ed. MARINES AT WAR. New York: Charles
         Scribner's Sons, 1943. 128 pp.

         Here are the water colorings and drawings of nineteen
         artists which portray the U.S. Marines at Guadalcanal.

4295. Emanual, Cedric. SOUTHWEST PACIFIC SKETCHBOOK. Englewood
         Cliffs, NJ: Prentice-Hall, 1946. 56 pp.

         Emanuel, an Australian air defense officer, portrays
         life behind the front lines. His artwork includes sketches
         of island natives.

4296. Greening, C. Ross. NOT AS BRIEFED. St. Paul, MN: Brown &
         Bigelow, 1945. 51 plates.

         Greening designed a special bombsight for Doolittle and
         piloted a B-25 on the Doolittle Raid. Later, he fell
         prisoner to the Germans. These striking plates provide a
         genuine "feel" for the air war.

4297. Hammond, Mason. "'Remembrance of Things Past': The
         Protection and Preservation of Monuments, Works of Art,

Libraries, and Archives during and after World War II."
PROC MASS HIST SOC, 92 (1980), 84-99.

The article surveys efforts at protection and
preservation during the war, including efforts in occupied
areas.

4298. Larkin, Oliver W. ART AND LIFE IN AMERICA. New York:
Holt Rinehart, 1960. rev. ed.

This excellent survey of American society and the arts
contains chapters on Roosevelt, the war, and the postwar
era that are noteworthy.

4299. LIFE. ART EXHIBITION BY MEN OF THE ARMED FORCES, SPONSORED
BY LIFE. Chicago: Time, 1942. 3 1.

Here is a catalogue of 117 contributor-artists.

4300. LIFE. WAR ART: A CATALOGUE OF PAINTINGS DONE ON THE WAR
FRONTS BY AMERICAN ARTISTS FOR LIFE. Chicago: Time,
1943. 35 pp.

Here are excellent contemporary perspectives on the war
in all theaters.

4301. Misselwitz, Henry Francis. JAPAN COMMITS HARA-KIRI. San
Mateo, CA: D.M. Paulson, 1945. 151 pp.

Misselwitz offers a contemporary sketchbook of Japan's
defeat as drawn from the first-hand observations of
Misselwitz.

4302. Phillips, Christopher. STEICHEN AT WAR. New York: Harry
N. Abrams Publishers, 1981. 256 pp.

Phillips reports on the work of Edward Steichen and the
Navy Photographic Unit. The book presents black and white
photographs from all theaters.

4303. "No More War: An Art Essay." FEMINIST STUD, 7 (Spring
1981), 76-88.

Josephine Withers provides the introduction to this
general collection. Artist Mine Okubo ("Citizen 13660")
and photographer Dorthea Lange deal with the
Japanese-American experience.

4304. Rorimer, James J. SURVIVAL: THE SALVAGE AND PROTECTION OF

ART IN WAR. New York: Abelard Press, 1950. 91 pp.

NE

4305.   Steinberg, Saul. ALL IN LINE. New York: Duell, Sloan and
        Pearce, 1945. 120 pp.

        Lt. Steinberg (USNR) presents his sketchwork and humor
        about the war in China. Some of his wartime work appeared
        in the NEW YORKER.

4306.   United States. Department of the Treasury. War Finance
        Division. THE ARMY AT WAR: A GRAPHIC RECORD BY
        AMERICAN ARTISTS. Washignton D.C.: GPO, 1944. 44 pp.

        Here is a catalogue of the war art created by American
        artists. Some of the artists were under special commission
        to various governmental agencies.

VI.A.3. FILM

4307.   Bartlett, Tom. "John Wayne and 'The Sands of Iwo Jima.'"
        LEATHERNECK, 68 (February 1985), 38-39.

        This famous movie was one of three Marine roles in
        Wayne's career.

4308.   Basinger, Janine. THE WORLD WAR II COMBAT FILM: ANATOMY
        OF A GENRE. New York: Columbia University Press, 1986.
        373 pp.

        This book presents a study of the films themselves, not
        the techniques of film making, or audiences, or the indi-
        viduals involved. After grappling with the definition of
        genre, Basinger concludes that (a) World War II gave birth
        to the isolation of a story pattern which became known as a
        combat genre (which later fit Korea and Vietnam) and
        (b) the combat film genre did not exist before 1941
        (despite the existence of war films). The bibliography is
        less than exhaustive, but there is a valuable annotated
        filmography. The author excludes foreign films.

4309.   Barsam, Richard Meran. "'This is America': Documentaries
        for Theaters, 1942-1951." CINEMA J, 12 (Fall 1972),
        22-38.

        Basing his study on interviews and correspondence,
        Barsam examines the film work of Frederic Ullman, Jr.
        Guided by his enthusiastic optimism for the United States,

Ullman made 112 films about America at war and the
American way. The propaganda effects of the series
touched many American film-goers. Barsam attaches a
complete list of these films.

4310.   Black, Gregory D. and Clayton R. Koppes. "OWI Goes to the
        Movies: The Bureau of Intelligence's Criticism of
        Hollywood, 1942-43." PROLOGUE, 6 (Spring 1974), 44-59.

        OWI officials, according to the authors, grew concerned
that Hollywood was not taking the war seriously. It took
some time to gather film statements on behalf of the Four
Freedoms and the United Nations. The authors, however,
emphasize that the very diversity of the films made during
the war years served to reflect the freedom enjoyed in the
United States.

4311.   Black, Gregory D. and Clayton R. Koppes. "OWI Goes to the
        Movies." FOR SERVICE J, 51 (August 1974), 18-23, 29-30.

        The authors regret the "OWI-inspired sermonette"
approach by the Bureau of Intelligence of OWI which sought
to influence artistic expressions for propaganda purposes.

4312.   Dick, Bernard F. THE STAR-SPANGLED SCREEN: THE AMERICAN
        WORLD WAR II FILM. Lexington, KT: University of
        Kentucky Press, 1985. 294 pp.

        The book reflects both the author's encyclopedic
knowledge of films and his easy familiarity with the
history and technical production of each film. Drawing
on film-industry sources, such as production files and
screenplay manuscripts, Dick reviews various phases of
the interpretations on film of the global conflict. His
analysis of the film versions of the war against Japan
underlines a shift from the contemporary-early postwar
years, when racial epithets abounded (with the notable
exception of the work of Dalton Trumbo), to the postwar
revisionism, when the characters played by Sessue
Hayakawa elicited more sympathy from American audiences
and films like "Tora! Tora! Tora!" and "Farewell to
Manzanar" overshadowed the earlier racial stereotypes.

4313.   Farmer, Patrick A. "Moss Hart and WINGED VICTORY: The
        Mind of 1943 America." S SPEECH COMM J, 49 (Winter
        1984), 187-197.

        Farmer argues that this play, written and directed by
Hart, reflected the American people's widespread support

for the war.

4314.   Suid, Lawrence. GUTS AND GLORY: GREAT AMERICAN WAR MOVIES.
        Reading, MA: Addison-Wesley, 1978. 357 pp.

        See especially Suid's essay on "The Sands of Iwo Jima,"
        "Twelve O'Clock High," and "Battleground." Suid writes
        almost as much about military history as about films.

4315.   Hughes, William. "The Propagandist's Art." FILM & HIST, 4
        (September 1974), 11-15.

        Examining the series "Films of Persuasion" and the
        subject of propaganda in the films of World War II, Hughes
        concludes that style deteriorated quickly into cliche.
        There are no footnotes.

4316.   Jacobs, Lewis. "WWII and the American Film." CINEMA J, 7
        (Winter 1967-68), 1-21.

        Jacobs observes that in 1940-1941 Hollywood began moving
        from escapist films to mirror Roosevelt's concern about
        dangers abroad. During the war, he writes, film served as
        a "potent instrument of national policy," shaping American
        political-social-military attitudes and promoting U.S. war
        aims.

4317.   Jarvie, I. "Fanning the Flames: Anti-American Reactions to
        'Objective Burma' (1945)." HIST J FILM RADIO TV, 1
        (October 1981), 117-137.

        NE

4318.   Jones, Ken D. and Arthur F. McClure. HOLLYWOOD AT WAR:
        THE AMERICAN MOTION PICTURE AND WORLD WAR II. New York:
        Castle Books, 1973. 320 pp.

        This reference work incorporates introductory essays
        with encyclopedic information about each film (e.g., casts,
        directors, studios, release dates, etc.). See especially
        the section on films about espionage.

4319.   Kane, Kathryn. VISIONS OF WAR: HOLLYWOOD COMBAT FILMS OF
        WORLD WAR II. Ann Arbor, MI: U.M.I. Research Press,
        1982. 174 pp.

        The volume is part of the series, "Studies in Cinema,"
        under the general editorship of Diane M. Kirkpatrick. Kane
        draws attention to the similarities of what she calls a

film group, or genre, of combat films. Of the 24 films she
selects for analysis in this grouping, 19 deal with the war
against Japan (a war she calls America's own war). Her
criteria for selecting these films are: (a) the plot
involves uniformed soldiers fighting a uniformed enemy, (b)
the film was made in America, and (c) each was a feature
film. Her analysis examines the themes, setting, character
development, and plots of each film.

4320. Koppes, Clayton R. and Gregory D. Black. HOLLYWOOD GOES TO
        WAR: HOW POLITICS, PROFITS, AND PROPAGANDA SHAPED WORLD
        WAR II MOVIES. New York: Free Press, 1987. 374 pp.

        This is a well-written, well-researched account of these
films, many of which touched on the war against Japan.

4321. Koppes, Clayton R. and Gregory D. Black. "What to Show the
        World: Office of War Information and Hollywood,
        1942-1945." J AMER HIST, 64 (June 1977), 87-105.

        Using chiefly unpublished sources, the two historians
examine the interaction between OWI and Hollywood. OWI
liberals, the authors argue, gained unprecedented control
over the content of American motion pictures (thereby
undermining the very principles being fought for in the
war).

4322. Manvell, Roger. FILMS AND THE SECOND WORLD WAR. South
        Brunswick, NJ: A. S. Barnes, 1974.

        Here is an excellent survey which is international in
scope.

4323. Meerse, David E. "To Reassure a Nation: Hollywood
        Presents World War II." FILM & HIST, 6 (December 1976),
        79-91.

        The author, a history professor, incorporates extensive
research to describe Hollywood's tangible contributions to
the war effort (e.g., "film people" serving in the armed
services and the work of Frank Capra, William Wyler, and
Louis Hayward). The wartime films, Meerse writes,
reinforced American beliefs and reassured the nation.

4324. Morella, Joe, Edward Z. Epstein, and John Griggs. THE
        FILMS OF WORLD WAR II. Secaucus, NJ: The Citadel
        Press, 1973.

        Here is a reference work which incorporates almost 100

films. The subjects include prewar international relations
as well as combat against Japan.

4325. Murphy, William T. "John Ford and the Wartime
        Documentary." FILM & HIST, 6 (February 1976), 1-8.

        The author is in charge of the Motion Picture Division
        at the National Archives. Analyzing two of Ford's
        documentaries ("Battle of Midway" and "December 7th"),
        Murphy argues that each manipulates rather than informs.

4326. Nieuwenhof, Frans. "Japanese Film Propaganda in World War
        II: Indonesia and Australia." HIST J FILM RADIO TV, 4
        (October 1984), 161-177.

        NE

4327. Oehling, Richard A. "Hollywood and the Image of the
        Oriental, 1910-1950." FILM & HIST, Pt. I: 8 (May
        1978), 33-41; Pt. II: 8 (September 1978), 59-67.

        The author shows that Hollywood stays persistently to
        the stereotype of the diabolical Oriental villain.

4328. Rubin, Steven Jay. COMBAT FILMS: AMERICAN REALISM,
        1945-1970. Jefferson, NC: McFarland, 1981.

        The author examines the development and production of
        selected war films. See the material on "Bridge on the
        River Kwai."

4329. Shindler, Colin. HOLLYWOOD GOES TO WAR: FILMS AND
        AMERICAN SOCIETY, 1939-1952. Boston: Routledge and
        Kegan Paul, 1979. 152 pp.

        This well-written and well-researched book portrays U.S.
        war films and sets them within the context of American
        society.

4330. Short, K.R.M. FILM AND RADIO PROPAGANDA IN WORLD WAR II:
        A GLOBAL PERSPECTIVE. Knoxville, TN: University of
        Tennessee Press, 1983. 341 pp.

        Short uses exhaustive research to portray the techniques
        and psychological ploys of the various combatants.

4331. Steele, Richard W. "'The Greatest Gangster Move Ever
        Filmed': Prelude to War." PROLOGUE, 11 (Winter 1979),
        221-235.

Using archival sources, Steele analyzes the public's acceptance of the Army's propaganda. The central theme, he says, played to the well-known gangster motif of good-vs.-evil (a theme extended to the postwar era against the Soviets).

4332.   Suid, Lawrence. "The Sands of Iwo Jima, the United States Marines, and the Screen Image of John Wayne." FILM & HIST, 8 (May 1978), 25-32.

Here is a report on the making of the famous film. Suid interviewed Wayne as well as Edmund Grainger (producer-director). The film became a classic, Suid points out, despite discrepancies and inaccuracies.

VI.B.   HUMOR

4333.   Bairnsfather, Bruce. NO "KIDDIN"! New York: G. P. Putnam's Sons, 1945. 112 pp.

The cartoons feature a biting, penetrating perspective on the war.

4334.   Brown, Joe E. YOUR KIDS AND MINE. Garden City, NY: Doubleday, 1944. 192 pp.

The great comedian relates stories of his entertainment tour in a sensitive and humorous vein. His story takes on tragic overtones with his loss of a son in the war.

4335.   Davidson, William, ed. TALL TALES THEY TELL IN THE SERVICES.
New York: Thomas Y. Crowell, 1943. 75 pp.

Here is a collection of humorous war stories, not all of which are from the Second World War.

4336.   Harris, Jack M. SOME FUNNY THINGS HAPPENED DURING WORLD WAR II. Sacramento, CA: Custom Publishing, 1986. 286 pp.

Harris offers personal accounts of wartime experiences that are laced with humor.

4337.   Hersey, Harold B., ed. G.I. LAUGHS. New York: Sheridan House, 1944. 255 pp.

This collection of humor comes straight from the

servicemen, setting it apart from other works in this
category. A sequel--MORE G.I. LAUGHS (256 pp.)--appeared
later the same year.

4338. Lewis, Warfield, ed. FIGHTING WORDS. Philadelphia, PA:
       J.B. Lippincott, 1944. 330 pp.

       Lewis collects humorous stories and cartoons created by
members of the U.S. armed forces in all theaters.

4339. Lewis, D.B. Wyndham, ed. I CAN'T HELP LAUGHING: AN
       ANTHOLOGY OF WARTIME HUMOR. London: L. Drummond, 1942.
       128 pp.

       Here is an excellent collection of war stories--the
happy variety.

4340. Nielson, Lou, ed. G.I. JOKES. New York: 1945. 190 pp.

       Nielson draws together a collection of jokes and
cartoons that appeared for the most part in Army or Navy
sources. The subject material comes from all theaters.

4341. Olday, John. THE MARCH TO DEATH. London: Freedom Press,
       1943. 79 pp.

       NE

4342. Osborn, Robert C. WAR IS NO DAMN GOOD! New York:
       Doubleday, Doran, 1946. 96 pp.

       Here is humor with an anti-war sting. The
author/artist/cartoonist served in the U.S. Navy.

4343. Phillips, Harry I. PRIVATE PURKEY IN LOVE AND WAR. New
       York: Harper and Brothers, 1942. 150 pp.

       In this humorous account, the confused private reports
his experiences in letters home.

4344. Schacht, Alexander. GI HAD FUN. New York: G.P. Putnam's
       Sons, 1945. 136 pp.

       Collaborating with Murray Goodman, Schacht, one of
baseball's clown princes, tells of his travels throughout
the theaters, including the South Pacific. He confesses
that the U.S. servicemen knew more baseball history and
statistics than he did!

4345. Stevens, Bob. THERE I WAS... FLAT ON MY BACK. Fallbrook
        CA: Aero Publishers, 1975. 224 pp.

        Stevens and his art work appeared regularly in AIR FORCE
        MAGAZINE. Not all the cartoons and humor on aviation
        affairs apply to World War II, but his contributions
        reflect a delightful perspective.

4346. IT'S A TOUGH WAR. Garden City, NY: Garden City Publishing
        Co., 1943. 96 pp.

        Here is a collection of cartoons about the war (in all
        theaters).

4347. Wuest, Karl A. THEY TOLD IT TO THE CHAPLAIN. New York:
        Vantage Press, 1953. 138 pp.

              NE

VI.C. **MUSIC**

4348. Hopkins, Anthony, ed. SONGS FROM THE FRONT AND REAR.
        Edmonton, Alberta: Hurtig, 1979. 192 pp.

        Here are the songs of Canadian servicemen in World War
        II. Hopkins gives the historical background of each song,
        which he groups into subject categories. There are no
        expletives deleted!

4349. Leitch, Michael. GREAT SONGS OF WORLD WAR II. New York:
        Wise Publications, 1975. 181 pp.

        Although the emphasis is on Europe, Leitch assembles an
        interesting collection.

4350. Mathias, Frank F. G.I. JIVE: AN ARMY BANDSMAN IN WORLD
        WAR II. Lexington, KT: University Press of Kentucky,
        1982.

        In this autobiographical account, Mathias tells of his
        musical duties in the war. While in the Philippines, he
        took great delight in "blowing the dust of war out of their
        souls."

4351. Mohrmann, G.P. and F. Eugene Scott. "Popular Music and
        World War II: The Rhetoric of Continuation." Q J
        SPEECH, 62 (April 1976), 145-156.

        The authors view the war songs as rhetorical artifacts

of society. According to the authors, the attack at Pearl
Harbor stimulated a militant tone in American popular
songs, including racist denigrations of the enemy.
Nevertheless, noting that few war songs reached the popular
charts during the war, the authors conclude that the
popular song is not an effective vehicle for propaganda in
the United States.

4352. Palmer, Edgar A., ed. G.I. SONGS. New York: Sherman
House, 1944. 253 pp.

This collection, written by people in uniform,
encompasses a broad spectrum of attitudes and emotions.

4353. Posselt, Eric. G.I. SONGS. New York: Sheridan House,
1944. 253 pp.

Here is a contemporary collection of the famous--and
infamous -- war songs.

4354. Tawa, Nicholas E. SERENADING THE RELUCTANT EAGLE:
AMERICAN MUSICAL LIFE, 1925-1945. New York: Schirmer
Books, 1984. 261 pp.

Tawa argues that the composers and music mirrored U.S.
society during the period under review. His narrative
addresses the social premises of the war.

VI.D. LITERATURE

1. GENERAL

4355. Gunn, Edward M. UNWELCOME MUSE: CHINESE LITERATURE:
SHANGHAI AND PEKING, 1937-1945. New York: Columbia
University Press, 1980. 320 pp.

This well-written report gives a comprehensive analysis
of wartime literature in occupied China.

4356. Irwin, Leonard B., comp. GUIDE TO HISTORICAL FICTION.
Brooklawn, NJ: McKinley, 1971. 255 pp.

The annotated entries are arranged chronologically.
Sub-sections, such as "juvenile," facilitate the location
of specific citations. There is a separate section for
World War II.

4357. Lundberg, David. "The American Literature of War: The
Civil War, World War I and World War II." AMER Q, 36

(No. 3, 1984), 373-388.

Arguing that war provides the source of an important body of American literature, the author, in focusing on World War II, identifies three major literary themes: (a) the acceptance of violence and inhumane acts, (b) the military as a microcosm of American society, and (c) the absurdity of war.

4358. MacDonald, Charles B. "Novels of World War II: The First Round." MIL AFFS, 13 (Spring 1949), 42-46.

Although the author disputes some narrow military points, he is generally impressed by the contemporary novels--especially with the work of authors who participated in combat.

4359. Mandelbaum, Michael. "The Political Lessons of Two World War II Novels: A Review Essay." POL SCI Q, 94 (Fall 1979), 515-522.

Mandelbaum, a professor of government, analyzes a "hybrid literary genre," a combination of fiction and history, which appears in Herman Wouk's two novels: THE WINDS OF WAR (1971) and WAR AND REMEMBRANCE (1978).

4360. Rosenberg, Emily S. "Decoding the Values of an Age: The Use of Novels in the Study of American Foreign Relations." HIST TEACHER, 11 (May 1978), 353-359.

The author argues that the novels "elucidate widespread values" and reflect the cultural milieu. She suggests that incorporating novels in the teaching of history helps combat the problem of anachronistic judgments by students.

4361. Waldmeir, Joseph J. AMERICAN NOVELS OF THE SECOND WORLD WAR. Paris: Mouton, 1969. 180 pp.

Narrowing the list of about 250 war novels by Americans in print by 1969, Waldmeir focuses on the ideological aspects of the novels. His examination of causes and consequences of the war reveals authors supporting the general proposition that laudable objectives justified the bloodshed and the inhumanity. Waldmeir, however, analyzes these selected works, not as ideology, but as literature.

4362. Wermuth, Anthony L. "Novels of World War II: Fire For Effect." MIL REV, 35 (August 1955), 18-25.

With the exception of CAINE MUTINY, Wermuth is not impressed with the fiction dealing with the war. He particularly decries the "tub-thumping" lack of effort to delineate the perspectives of the opposing sides and the work of certain authors who present their petty grievances based on their limited experience in the military.

VI.D.2. FICTIONAL ACCOUNTS

4363. Agawa, Hiroyuki. DEVIL'S HERITAGE. Tokyo: Hokuseido Press, 1957. 247 pp.

4364. Ageton, Arthur A. THE JUNGLE SEAS. 1954. 339 pp.

4365. Ahmad, Murad. LIFE AT THE POINT OF A SWORD. 1956.

4366. Aistron, Jack, ed. BUGLE BLAST: AN ANTHOLOGY FROM THE SERVICES. London: Allen and Unwin, 1943.

4367. Anderson, Kenneth. SHADOWS UNDER THE MIDNIGHT SUN. Grand Rapids, MI: Zondervan, 1943. 247 pp.

4368. Andreev, Veseling. GUERILLA STORIES AND POEMS. Sofia: Sofia Press, 1969. 263 pp.

4369. Andrews, Laurie. DEADLY PATROL. New York: D. McKay, 1947.

4370. Anthony, Evelyn. VOICES ON THE WIND. Thorndike, ME: Thorndike Press, 1985.

4371. Appel, Benjamin. WE WERE THERE AT THE BATTLE FOR BATAAN. New York: Grosset and Dunlap, 1957. 178 pp.

4372. Arnold, Elliott. THE COMMANDOS. New York: Duell, Sloan and Pearce, 1942. 300 pp.

4373. Asada, Teruhiko. THE NIGHT OF A THOUSAND SUICIDES. New York: St. Martin's Press, 1972. 125 pp.

4374. Atchison, Carroll J. MESSENGER FROM WAKE ISLAND. Houston, TX: Curtain Printers, 1942. 23 pp. (Play.)

4375. Baker, Richard M. THE REVOLT OF ZENGO TAKAKUWA. New York: Farrar, Strauss and Cudahy, 1962. 279 pp.

4376. Ballard, J.G. EMPIRE OF THE SUN. New York: Simon and Schuster, 1984. 279 pp.

4377. Bancroft, Bernard N. BREAD UPON THE WATERS: THE SPIRITUAL
      BATTLE OF TWO GI's IN THE PHILIPPINES IN WORLD WAR II.
      New York: Exposition Press, 1959. 85 pp.

4378. Bartlett, Norman. ISLAND VICTORY. Sydney, Aus.: Angus
      and Robertson, 1955. 166 pp.

4379. Bass, Ronald. THE EMERALD ILLUSIONS. New York: William
      Morrow, 1984. 298 pp.

4380. Bassett, James. HARM'S WAY. New York: Signet Books,
      1962. 446 pp.

4381. Bassett, Ronald. THE TIN FISH RUN. London: Macmillan,
      1977. 264 pp.

4382. Bates, Herbert E. THE CRUISE OF THE BREADWINNER. Boston:
      Little, Brown, 1947. 112 pp.

4383. --------. THE JACARANDA TREE. Boston: Little, Brown,
      1949. 299 pp.

4384. --------. THE PURPLE PLAIN. Boston: Little, Brown, 1947.
      308 pp.

4385. Baxter, Walter. LOOK DOWN IN MERCY. London: Heinemann,
      1951. 288 pp.

4386. Beach, Edward L. RUN SILENT, RUN DEEP. New York: Holt,
      1955. 364 pp.

4387. Bechtel, John. PERLA OF THE WALLED CITY. 1946.

4388. Bergamini, David. THE FLEET IN THE WINDOW. New York:
      Simon and Schuster, 1961. 331 pp.

4389. Blunden, Godfrey. THE TIME OF THE ASSASSINS.
      Philadelphia, PA: J. B. Lippincott, 1952. 375 pp.

4390. Bonham, Frank. WAR BENEATH THE SEA. New York: Thomas Y.
      Crowell, 1962. 263 pp.

4391. Boulle, Pierre. THE BRIDGE ON THE RIVER KWAI. New York:
      Vanguard Press, 1954. 174 pp.

4392. Bowman, Peter. BEACH RED. New York: Random House, 1945.
      122 pp.

4393. Bowen, R. Sidney. DAVE DAWSON WITH THE FLYING TIGERS. New

York: Crown Publishers, 1942.

4394. --------. DAVE DAWSON AT GUADALCANAL.

4395. --------. DAVE DAWSON WITH THE PACIFIC FLEET.

4396. --------. DAVE DAWSON AT SINGAPORE.

4397. --------. DAVE DAWSON AT TRUK.

4398. --------. RED RANDALL IN BURMA.

4399. Bowen, Vernon. THE EMPEROR'S WHITE HORSES. New York: D.
       McKay, 1956. 147 pp.

4400. Braddon, Russell. THE NAKED ISLAND. London: T. Werner
       Laurie, 1951. 266 pp.

4401. Brochman, Elizabeth. WHAT'S THE MATTER GIRL. New York:
       Harper & Row, 1980. 121 pp.

4402. Brophy, John. SPEARHEAD. New York: Harper Brothers,
       1943. 277 pp.

4403. --------. TARGET ISLAND. New York: Harper Brothers,
       1944. 184 pp.

4404. Brown, Eugene. THE LOCUST FIRE. New York: Doubleday,
       1957. 191 pp.

4405. Brown, Harry. A SOUND OF HUNTING. New York: A. A. Knopf,
       1946. 176 pp. (Play.)

4406. Buck, Pearl. THE PROMISE. New York: John Day, 1943. 248
       pp.

4407. --------. DRAGON SEED. New York: John Day, 1942.
       378 pp.

4408. Buenafe, Manuel E., ed. THE VOICE OF THE VETERAN. Manila,
       PI: Philippines Educational Promotions, 1971. 113 pp.

4409. Callison, Brian. THE JUDAS SHIP. New York: E. P. Dutton,
       1978. 192 pp.

4410. Chamales, Tom. NEVER SO FEW. New York: Charles
       Scribner's Sons, 1957. 499 pp.

4411. Chamberlain, William. COMBAT STORIES OF WORLD WAR II AND

KOREA. New York: John Day, 1962. 255 pp.

4412. --------. MORE COMBAT STORIES OF WORLD WAR II AND KOREA.
      New York: John Day, 1964. 253 pp.

4413. Chambliss, William C. BOOMERANG. Boston: Houghton
      Mifflin, 1944. 87 pp.

4414. Charyn, Jerome. AMERICAN SCRAPBOOK. New York: Viking,
      1969.

4415. Chin, Kee Onn. SILENT ARMY. New York: Longmans, Green,
      1953. 259 pp.

4416. Clagett, John. THE SLOT. New York: Crown, 1958.

4417. Clark, Hugh. THE TUB. Brisbane, Aus: 1963.

4418. Cleary, Jon. THE LONG PURSUIT. New York: William Morrow,
      1967.

4419. Clifford, Frances. A BATTLE IS FOUGHT TO BE WON. New
      York: Coward McCann, 1961. 189 pp.

4420. Clive, John. THE LAST LIBERATOR. New York: Delacorte
      Press, 1980. 276 pp.

4421. Cochrell, Boyd. THE BARREN BEACHES OF HELL. New York:
      Holt, 1959. 379 pp.

4422. Coleman, William L. ("Lonnie"). SHIP'S COMPANY. Boston:
      Little, Brown, 1955. 229 pp.

4423. Colina, Edward J. HOUR OF THE DREADNOUGHTS IN THE PACIFIC
      WAR. Cincinnati, OH: Develle Publishing, 1983. 526
      pp.

4424. Collins, Larry. FALL FROM GRACE. New York: Simon and
      Schuster, 1985. 437 pp.

4425. Collison, Thomas, ed. THIS WINGED WORLD: AN ANTHOLOGY OF
      AVIATION FICTION. New York: Coward-McCann, 1943.
      520 pp.

4426. Cook, Canfield. SPRINGBOARD TO TOKYO. New York: Grosset
      and Dunlap, 1943. 210 pp.

4427. --------. WINGS OVER JAPAN. New York: Grosset and
      Dunlap, 1944. 215 pp.

4428.   Cox, Theodore St. John. CALL ME MAC. Boston: W. H.
        Baker, 1948.   30 pp. [Play.]

4429.   Cozzens, James Gould. GUARD OF HONOR. New York: Harcourt
        Brace, 1948. 631 pp.

4430.   Crockett, Lucy H. THE MAGNIFICENT BASTARDS. New York:
        Farrar, Strauss and Young, 1954. 296 pp.

4431.   Davis, Paxton. TWO SOLDIERS. New York: Simon and
        Schuster, 1956. 183 pp.

4432.   Denham, Elizabeth. I LOOKED RIGHT. London: Cassell,
        1956. 191 pp.

4433.   Dibner, Martin. THE ADMIRAL. New York: Doubleday, 1967.
        453 pp.

4433a. --------. DEEP SIX. New York: Doubleday, 1953.

4434.   Dickson, Stan. THE COPPERHEAD. New York: Greenwich,
        1959. 77 pp.

4435.   Ditton, Thom. WE SAILED AT DAWN. Boston: Christopher,
        1955. 201 pp.

4436.   Divine, A.D. THE KING OF FASSARAI. New York: Macmillan,
        1950. 296 pp.

4437.   Doan-Vinh-Thai. ANCESTRAL VOICES: RECOLLECTIONS OF
        CHUNGKING, AUGUST-DECEMBER, 1943. London: Collins,
        1956. 192 pp.

4438.   Dodson, Kenneth. AWAY ALL BOATS. Boston: Little, Brown,
        1954.

4439.   Dorling, H. Taprell. WHITE ENSIGNS. New York: G. P.
        Putnam's Sons, 1943. 280 pp.

4440.   Dunsany, Lord. GUERRILLA. London: W. Heinemann, 1944.
        175 pp.

4441.   Fabricus, Johan. NIGHT OVER JAVA. New York: Greenberg,
        1946. 168 pp.

4442.   Fenton, Charles A., ed. THE BEST SHORT STORIES OF WORLD
        WAR II. New York: Viking, 1957. 428 pp.

4443. Ferguson, John A. TERROR ON THE ISLAND. New York:
       Vanguard Press, 1942. 301 pp.

4444. Ferry, Charles. RASPBERRY ONE. Boston: Houghton Mifflin,
       1983. 232 pp.

4445. Fleming, Thomas. TIME AND TIDE. New York: Simon and
       Schuster, 1987. 734 pp.

4446. Follett, James. THE WOTAN WARHEAD. New York: Stein and
       Day, 1979. 201 pp.

4447. Forbes, Gordon. GOODBYE TO SOME. New York: W. W. Norton,
       1961. 288 pp.

4448. Forrest, David. THE LAST BLUE SEA. London: Heinemann,
       1959. 271 pp.

4449. Fruto, Ligaya Victorio. ONE RAINBOW FOR THE DURATION.
       Honolulu, HI: Rainbow Publishers, 1976. 312 pp.

4450. Gale, Bob. 1941. New York: Ballantine Books, 1979. 112
       pp.

4451. Garth, David. THE WATCH ON THE BRIDGE. New York: G. P.
       Putnam's Sons, 1959. 320 pp.

4452. Gifford, Lee. PIECES OF THE GAME. Greenwich, CT:
       Fawcett, 1960. 176 pp.

4453. Gillespie, Jane. SIDE EFFECTS. London: R. Hale, 1983.
       176 pp.

4454. Gilpatric, Guy. MR. GLENCANNON IGNORES THE WAR. New York:
       E. P. Dutton, 1944. 157 pp.

4455. Glemser, Bernard. RADAR COMMANDOS: A STORY OF WORLD WAR
       II. Philadelphia, PA: Winston, 1953. 180 pp.

4456. Goodman, Mitchell. THE END OF IT. New York: Signet
       Books, 1980.

4457. Goodson, Felix E. SWEET SALT. Rutland, VT: C. E. Tuttle
       Co., 1976. 295 pp.

4458. Graham, Burton. UNTIL THIS DAY. Melbourne, Aus.:
       Robertson and Mullens, 1944. 26 pp.

4459. Gray, J. Glenn. THE WARRIORS. New York: Harcourt, Brace,

1959. 242 pp.

4460. Greener, Leslie. NO TIME TO LOOK BACK. New York: 1950.

4461. Gregg, Martin. DHOW PATROL. London: R. Hale, 1984. 208
        pp.

4462. Gwaltney, Francis Irby. THE DAY THE CENTURY ENDED. New
        York: Rinehart, 1955. 312 pp.

4463. Haislip, Harvey. ESCAPE FROM JAVA. New York: Doubleday,
        1962. 334 pp.

4464. Hall, James N. LOST ISLAND. Garden City, NY: Sun Dial
        Press, 1945. 212 pp.

4465. Hall, Willis. THE LONG, THE SHORT AND THE TALL. London:
        Heinemann, 1959. 104 pp.

4466. Halm, Agnes K. PACIFIC PATROL. New York: Vantage, 1954.
        304 pp.

4467. Hanley, Gerald. SEE YOU IN YASUKUNI. New York: World
        Publishing, 1970. 224 pp.

4468. Hannon, James J. NASAKENAI--WE ARE FORESAKEN. San Diego,
        CA: Grossmont Press, 1977. 155 pp.

4469. Hardy, William M. THE SHIP THEY CALLED THE FAT LADY. New
        York: Dodd, Mead, 1969. 250 pp.

4470. Hart, Moss. WINGED VICTORY. New York: Random House,
        1943. 201 pp.

4471. Heatter, Basil. THE DIM VIEW. New York: Signet Books,
        1946. 256 pp.

4472. Heggen, Thomas. MR. ROBERTS. Boston: Houghton Mifflin,
        1946. 221 pp.

4473. Herber, William. TOMORROW TO LIVE. New York:
        Coward-McCann, 1957. 317 pp.

4474. Hetherington, John A. THE WINDS ARE STILL. Melbourne,
        Aus.: Georgian House, 1947. 285 pp.

4475. Holmes, Wilfred J. [pseud. Alec Hudson.] OPEN FIRE! New
        York: Macmillan, 1942. 303 pp.

4476.   _____ . RENDEZVOUS. New York: Macmillan, 1942. 94 pp.

4477. Homewood, Harry. FINAL HARBOR. 1980.

4478. Hooker, John. THE BUSH SOLDIERS. New York: Viking, 1984.
       438 pp.

4479. Horan, James D. ACTION TONIGHT. New York: G. P. Putnam's
       Sons, 1945. 171 pp.

4480. Hough, Donald. CAMELEPHAMOOSE. New York: Duell, Sloan
       and Pearce, 1946. 209 pp.

4481. Hubler, Richard. MAN IN THE SKY. New York: Duell, Sloan
       and Pearce, 1956. 407 pp.

4482. Huie, William Bradford. THE HERO OF IWO JIMA AND OTHER
       STORIES. New York: Signet Books.

4483. Hunt, Howard. EAST OF FAREWELL. New York: A. A. Knopf,
       1942. 270 pp.

4484. Hursley, Frank and Doris Hursley. ATOMIC BOMBS. Syracuse,
       NY: Syracuse University Press, 1945. 67 pp.

4485. Ibuse, Masuji. BLACK RAIN. New York: Bantam Books, 1985.

4486. Icenhower, Joseph B. SUBMARINE RENDEZVOUS: PACIFIC
       ADVENTURES IN WORLD WAR II. Philadelphia, PA: Winston,
       1957. 182 pp.

4487. Irving, Clifford. THE ANGEL OF ZIN. New York: Stein and
       Day, 1984. 306 pp.

4488. Jackson, Robert. TARGET TOBRUK. London: Barker, 1979.
       167 pp.

4489. Jones, James. FROM HERE TO ETERNITY. New York: Charles
       Scribner's Sons, 1951.

4490.   _____ . THIN RED LINE. New York: Charles Scribner's
       Sons, 1962.

4491. Jones, Peter G. WAR AND THE NOVELIST. Columbia, MO:
       University of Missouri Press, 1976.

4492. Jordan, Humfrey. THIS ISLAND DEMANDS. London: Houghton
       and Stoughon, 1941. 320 pp.

4493.   Kantor, MacKinlay. DON'T TOUCH ME. New York: Random
          House, 1951. 243 pp.

4494.   Karaka, Dosoo Framjee and G.N. Acharya, comps. WAR PROSE.
          Bombay, India: Thacker, 1944.

4495.   Kauffman, Ray F. THE COCONUT WIRELESS. New York:
          Macmillan, 1948. 202 pp.

4496.   Kehoe, Karon. CITY IN THE SUN. New York: Dodd, Mead,
          1946. 269 pp.

4497.   Killens, John O. AND THEN WE HEARD THE THUNDER. New York:
          A. A. Knopf, 1963. 485 pp.

4498.   Kilpatrick, Washington Irving. GOD MADE ME CRY. 1948.

4499.   Kinross, James. THE PIKE IN THE REEDS. London: Murray,
          1956. 296 pp.

4500.   Klein, Holger, John Flower, and Eric Homberger, eds. THE
          SECOND WORLD WAR IN FICTION. London: Macmillan, 1984.
          249 pp.

4501.   Kogawa, Joy. OBASAN. Boston: David R. Godine, 1982.

4502.   Kolitz, Zvi. THE TIGER BENEATH THE SKIN: STORIES AND
          PARABLES OF THE YEARS OF DEATH. New York: Creative Age
          Press, 1947. 172 pp.

4503.   Kuniczak, W.S. THE MARCH. New York: Doubleday, 1979.
          824 pp.

4504.   Lambert, Eric. HIROSHIMA REEF. New York: W. W. Norton,
          1967. 249 pp.

4505.   Lamott, Kenneth. THE STOCKADE. Boston: Little, Brown,
          1952.

4506.   Lampell, Millard. THE LONG WAY HOME. New York: Julian
          Messner, 1946. 174 pp.

4507.   Lea, Tom. A GRIZZLY FROM THE CORAL SEA. El Paso, TX: C.
          Hertzog Printers, 1944. 32 pp.

4508.   Leckie, Robert. MARINES! New York: Bantam, 1960. 150
          pp.

4509.   Leopold, Chester. FOOL'S PARADISE. New York: Doubleday,

1980. 276 pp.

4510. Levin, Dan. MASK OF GLORY. New York: Whittlesey House,
       1948. 278 pp.

4511. Loomis, Edward. END OF A WAR. New York: Ballantine,
       1958. 245 pp.

4512. Lou, Chi-kuei. THE FIVE HEROES OF WOLF'S TEETH MOUNTAIN.
       Peking, PRC: Foreign Language Press, 1977. 36 pp.

4513. MacCuish, David. DO NOT GO GENTLE. Garden City, NY:
       Doubleday, 1960.

4514. McInerney, Carl R. ("Ted"). POM-POM: A NOVEL OF THE
       SOUTHWEST PACIFIC. New York: Stratford House, 1949.
       258 pp.

4515. MacLean, Alistair. SOUTH BY JAVA HEAD. Garden City, NY:
       Doubleday, 1958. 319 pp.

4516. McSwigan, Marie. JUAN OF MANILA. New York: E. P. Dutton,
       1947. 152 pp.

4517. Mailer, Norman. THE NAKED AND THE DEAD. New York:
       Rinehart, 1948.

4518. Maltz, Albert. A TALE OF ONE JANUARY. London: Calder and
       Boyars, 1966. 158 pp.

4519. Mason, Richard. THE WIND CANNOT READ. Leicester, Eng.:
       Ulverscroft, 1976. 571 pp.

4520. Matthews, Allen R. THE ASSAULT. New York: Simon and
       Schuster, 1947. 216 pp.

4521. Maugham, Somerset. THE HOUR BEFORE DAWN. New York:
       Doubleday, Doran, 1942. 307 pp.

4522. Means, Florence Crannell. THE MOVED-OUTERS. Boston:
       Houghton Mifflin, 1945. 154 pp.

4523. Mercer, Charles E. PACIFIC. New York: Simon and
       Schuster, 1981. 334 pp.

4524. Michener, James. TALES OF THE SOUTH PACIFIC. New York:
       Macmillan, 1947. 413 pp.

4525. Miller, Merle. ISLAND 49. New York: Thomas Y. Crowell,

1945,   186 pp.

4526.   Misola, Agustin T. ANGELS IN BATAAN. New York: U. S.
        Carlton Press, 1980.   524 pp. (This work appeared under
        different titles: THE BRIDGE TO CHINA, MY HEART IS
        FORGIVING, and PORTRAIT OF YESTERDAY.)

4527.   Montgomery, R.G. [pseud. Al Avery.] A YANKEE FLIER IN THE
        SOUTH PACIFIC. New York: Grosset and Dunlap, 1943.
        208 pp.

4528.   Morrill, George P. DARK SEA RUNNING. New York:
        McGraw-Hill, 1959.   211 pp.

4529.   Moss, Sidney. THY MEN SHALL FALL. Chicago: Ziff-Davis,
        1948.   351 pp.

4530.   Myrer, Anton. THE BIG WAR. New York: Bantam, 1957.   423
        pp.

4531.   Neser, James M. THE DEAD ARE HAPPIER. 1958.

4532.   Noma, Hiroshi. ZONE OF EMPTINESS. Cleveland, OH: World
        Publishing, 1950.   317 pp.

4533.   Norway, N.S. [pseud. Nevile Shute.] MOST SECRET. New
        York: William Morrow, 1945.   310 pp.

4534.   O'Brine, Manning. PALE MOON RISING. New York: St.
        Martin's Press, 1977.   255 pp.

4535.   Oe, Kenzaburo, ed. THE CRAZY IRIS AND OTHER STORIES OF THE
        ATOMIC AFTERMATH. New York: Grove Press, 1985.   204
        pp.

4536.   Oldfield, Barney. OPERATION NARCISSUS. New York: Pandick
        Press, 1978.   429 pp.

4537.   Olsen, Robert I. and David Porter. TORPEDOES AWAY! New
        York: Dodd, Mead, 1957.   247 pp.

4538.   Ooka, Shohei. FIRES ON THE PLAIN. London: Panther, 1968.
        204 pp.

4539.   Oxford, James. THE NIGHT OF THE FALCON. New York: St.
        Martin's Press, 1981.   206 pp.

4540.   Patrick, John. THE HASTY HEART. New York: Dramatists
        Play Service, 1945.

4541. Paul, Louis. THIS IS MY BROTHER. New York: Crown, 1943.
      166 pp.

4542. Perna, Albert F. THE GLIDER GLADIATORS. Freeman, SD:
      Pine Hill Press, 1970. 383 pp.

4543. Piercy, Marge. GONE TO SOLDIERS. New York: Summit Books,
      1987. 703 pp.

4544. Pratt, Rex K. YOU TELL MY SON. New York: Signet Books,
      1958.

4545. Pronzini, Bill and Martin H. Greenberg, eds. A TREASURY OF
      WORLD WAR II STORIES. New York: Bonanza Books, 1985.
      755 pp.

4546. Rayner, Denys A. THE ENEMY BELOW. London: Collins, 1956.
      191 pp.

4547. --------. THE LONG HAUL. New York: McGraw-Hill, 1960.
      194 pp.

4548. Redding, Jack and Thor Smith. WAKE OF GLORY.
      Indianapolis, IN: Bobbs-Merrill, 1945. 268 pp.

4549. Reynolds, Quentin. THE MAN WHO WOULDN'T TALK. New York:
      Random House, 1953. 214 pp.

4550. Robinson, Derek. KRAMER'S WAR. New York: Viking Press,
      1977. 319 pp.

4551. Rollins, Kelly. FIGHTER PILOTS. Boston: Little, Brown,
      1981. 308 pp.

4552. Rusholt, Malcolm. DOG SUGAR EIGHT: A NOVEL OF THE
      FOURTEENTH AIR FORCE FLYING TIGERS IN CHINA IN WORLD WAR
      II. Rosholt, WI: Rosholt House, 1977. 216 pp.

4553. Ruttle, Lee. THE PRIVATE WAR OF DR. YAMADA. San
      Francisco, CA: San Francisco Book Co., 1978. 245 pp.

4554. Ryan, Patrick. HOW I WON THE WAR. 1964. 274 pp.

4555. Savage, Junes A. THE BLONDE HEATHEN, NORTHEAST OF BORNEO:
      A STORY OF INTRIGUE, MURDER, AND ESPIONAGE. San
      Antonio, TX: Naylor, 1951. 266 pp.

4556. Schevill, James E. THE ARENA OF ANTS. Providence: Copper

Beech Press, 1977. 271 pp.

4557. Scott, Douglas. THE GIFT OF ARTEMUS. London: Secker and
        Warburg, 1979. 381 pp.

4558. --------. THE SPOILS OF WAR. New York: Coward, McCann
        and Geohegan, 1978. 286 pp.

4559. Seldon, K Yoko, ed. "Hayashi Kyoko's 'Two Grave Markers':
        A Translation." BULL CON ASIAN SCHOLARS, 18
        (January/March 1986), 23-35.

4560. Shaw, Irwin. THE YOUNG LIONS. 1948.

4561. Shohei, Ooka. FIRES ON THE PLAIN.

4562. Siegelberg, Mark. THE FACE OF PEARL HARBOUR. Melbourne,
        Aus.: The View Publishing, 1943. 53 pp.

4563. Simpson, Colin. SIX FROM BORNEO. Sydney, Aus.:
        Australian Broadcasting Commission, 1945. 26 pp.

4564. Simonds, Peter. DAVID AND MAX. Nashville, TN: Aurora,
        1977. 265 pp.

4565. Skidmore, Hobert D. VALLEY OF THE SKY. Boston: Houghton
        Mifflin, 1944. 169 pp..

4566. Slaughter, Frank G. BATTLE SURGEON. Garden City, NY:
        Doubleday, Doran, 1944. 265 pp.

4567. Smith, Henry T. THE LAST CAMPAIGN. New York: Walker,
        1985. 191 pp.

4568. Sneider, Vern. THE TEAHOUSE OF THE AUGUST MOON. New York:
        G. P. Putnam, 1951. 221 pp.

4569. Sparrow, Gerald. THE GOLDEN ORCHID. London: Jarrolds,
        1963. 208 pp.

4570. Stanley, John B. WHISPER FLIGHT: ADVENTURES OF LT. BOB
        HILTON, ENGINEER, ON A SPECIAL GLIDER MISSION IN BURMA.
        New York: Dodd, Mead, 1945. 210 pp.

4571. Stein, Gertrude. MRS. REYNOLDS. New York: Sun and Moon
        Press, 1987 ed.

4572. Strachey, John. THE FRONTIERS. New York: Random House,
        1952. 250 pp.

4573. Stuart, Donald. CRANK BACK ON ROLLER. Melbourne, Aus.:
         Georgian House, 1979. 230 pp.

4574. Sutton, Felix. WE WERE THERE AT PEARL HARBOR. New York:
         Grosset and Dunlap, 1957. 177 pp.

4575. Sykes, Christopher. A SONG OF A SHIRT. London: D.
         Verschoyle, 1953. 144 pp.

4576. Tanner, Janet. ORIENTAL HOTEL. New York: St. Martin's
         Press, 1984. 447 pp.

4577. Tasaki, Hanama. LONG THE IMPERIAL WAY. Boston: Houghton
         Mifflin, 1950. 372 pp.

4578. Taylor, Geoff. THE HOUR OF THE OCTOPUS. Richmond, Aus.:
         Hutchinson of Australia, 1978. 159 pp.

4579. Taylor, Ward. ROLL BACK THE SKY. New York: Holt, 1956.

4580. Tibbetts, Albert B., comp. SALUTE TO THE BRAVE: STORIES
         OF WORLD WAR II. Boston: Little, Brown, 1960. 274 pp.

4581. Toland, John. OCCUPATION. New York: Doubleday, 1987.
         453 pp.

4582. A TREASURY OF WORLD WAR II STORIES. New York: Bonanza
         Books, 1985. 755 pp.

4583. Tregaskis, Richard W. STRONGER THAN FEAR. New York:
         Random House, 1945. 144 pp.

4584. Tute, Warren. THE CRUISER. New York: Ballantine Books,
         1956. 342 pp.

4585. --------. THE ROCK. New York: W. Sloane Associates,
         1959. 378 pp.

4586. Uris, Leon, BATTLE CRY. New York: G. P. Putnam & Sons,
         1953.

4587. Van Der Haas, Henrietta. VICTORIOUS ISLAND. New York:
         Harcourt, Brace, 1947. 193 pp.

4588. Vidal, Gore. WASHINGTON, D.C. 1967.

4589. --------. WILLIWAW. New York: E. P. Dutton, 1946. 222
         pp.

4590. Wallner, Cathryn J. WITNESS TO WAR: A THEMATIC GUIDE TO
       YOUNG ADULT LITERATURE ON WORLD WAR II. Metuchen, NJ:
       Scarecrow Press, 1982.

4591. Walsh, Jeffrey. AMERICAN WAR LITERATURE, 1914 TO VIETNAM.
       New York: St. Martin's Press, 1982. 218 pp.

4592. Watkins, Yoko Kawashima. SO FAR FROM THEE BAMBOO GROVE.
       New York: Lothrop, Lee and Shepard, 1986. 183 pp.

4593. Waugh, Evelyn. THE END OF THE BATTLE. Boston: Little,
       Brown, 1961. 319 pp.

4594. --------. MEN AT ARMS. Boston: Little, Brown, 1952.
       342 pp.

4595. --------. OFFICERS AND GENTLEMEN. Boston: Little, Brown,
       1955. 339 pp.

4596. --------. UNCONDITIONAL SURRENDER. Boston: Little,
       Brown, 1961. 239 pp.

4597. White, Barbara A. LADY LEATHERNECK. New York: Dodd, Mead
       & Co., 1945. 180 pp.

4598. White, Theodore. MOUNTAIN ROAD. New York: Sloane, 1958.

4599. Wilder, Robert. MR. G. STRINGS ALONG. New York: G. P.
       Putnam's Sons, 1944. 217 pp.

4600. Wilson, Sloan. PACIFIC INTERLUDE. New York: Arbor House,
       1982. 317 pp.

4601. Wingate, John. GO DEEP. New York: St. Martin's Press,
       1985. 191 pp.

4602. Wolfert, Ira. AN ACT OF LOVE. New York: Simon and
       Schuster, 1948. 577 pp.

4603. Wood, Christopher. NORTH TO RABAUL. New York: Arbor
       House, 1979. 275 pp.

4604. Wouk, Herman. CAINE MUTINY. Garden City, NY: Doubleday,
       1951. 494 pp.

4605. --------. WAR AND REMEMBRANCE. Boston: Little, Brown,
       1978. 1042 pp.

4606. --------. THE WINDS OF WAR. Boston: Little, Brown, 1971.
       888 pp.

4607. Wynd, Oswald. BLACK FOUNTAINS. Garden City, NY:
       Doubleday, 1947. 374 pp.

4608. --------. THE BLAZING AIR. New Haven, CT: Tricknor and
       Fields, 1981. 311 pp.

4609. Young, Robert F. "Divine Wind," MAG FANTASY SCI FICTION,
       66 (April 1984), 8-24.

VI.D.3. POETRY

4610. Adams, Marie. LIFE WITHOUT LIPSTICK. Bellevue, WA:
       National Headquarters, American Ex-POWs.

4611. Bulosan, Carlos. VOICE OF BATAAN. New York:
       Coward-McCann, 1944. 28 pp.

4612. Brown, Charles. BARS FROM BILIBAD PRISON. 129 pp.

4613. Burt, Maxwell S. WAR SONGS. New York: Charles Scribner's
       Sons, 1942. 46 pp.

4614. Clarke, George H., ed. THE NEW TREASURY OF WAR POETRY.
       Boston: Houghton Mifflin, 1943. 285 pp.

4615. Currey, Ralph N. POETS OF THE 1939-1945 WAR. London, UK:
       Longmans Green, 1960. 48 pp.; rev. ed. 1967. 52 pp.

4616. Davidman, Joy, ed. SONGS AND BATTLE CRIES OF A WORLD AT
       WAR. New York: Dial Press, 1943. 395 pp.

4617. Dawless, Smith. THE LEDO ROAD AND OTHER VERSES FROM
       CHINA-BURMA-INDIA. Washington, D.C.: Enterprise
       Services, 1946.

4618. Derby, Richard. VALOR ON THE PACIFIC. Glen Head, NY: J.
       H. Knight, 1943.

4619. Everson, William. EASTWARD THE ARMIES: SELECTED POEMS
       1939-1942 THAT PRESENT THE POET'S PACIFIST POSITION
       THROUGH THE SECOND WORLD WAR. Torrance, CA: Labyrinth
       Editions, 1980. 52 pp.

4620. Gardner, Brian, ed. THE TERRIBLE RAIN: THE WAR POETS,
       1939-1945. London, UK: Methuen, 1966. 227 pp.

4621. Hamilton, Ian, ed. THE POETRY OF WAR, 1939-45. London,
       UK: Alan Ross, 1965. 173 pp.

4622. Harvey, Eleanor T.M. SONNETS FROM CAPTIVITY AND OTHER
       POEMS. Philadelphia, PA: Dorrance, 1949. 70 pp.

4623. Hays, Robert W. PACIFIC PARODIES. Clinton, SC: Jacob's
       Press, 1947. 57 pp.

4624. Henderson, Daniel, John Kieran, and Grantland Rice, eds.
       REVEILLE: WAR POEMS BY MEMBERS OF OUR ARMED FORCES.
       New York: A. S. Barnes, 1943. 254 pp.

4625. Kearton, Mira. SOLDIER FROM BATAAN. Philadelphia, PA:
       Dorrance, 1945. 122 pp.

4626. Ledward, Patricia and Colin Strang, eds. POEMS OF THIS
       WAR. New York: Macmillan, 1942. 99 pp.

4627. Lee, Amy Freeman. REMEMBER PEARL HARBOR. New York: Fine
       Editions Press, 1943. 34 pp.

4628. Lee, Henry G. NOTHING BUT PRAISE. Culver City, CA:
       Murray and Gee, 1948. 93 pp.

4629. Lewis, Alun. RAIDERS' DAWN. New York: Macmillan, 1943.
       43 pp.

4630. McCall, James E. SANTO TOMAS INTERNMENT CAMP: S.T.I.C. IN
       VERSE AND REVERSE. Lincoln, NB: Woodruff, 1945. 146
       pp.

4631. McGovern, James P. POEMS OF WORLD WAR II. Bethesda, MD:
       Bethesda-Chevy Chase, Post 105, 1945. 16 pp.

4632. Matthews, Courtland W. ALEUTIAN INTERVAL. Seattle, WA:
       Frank McCaffery, 1950. 61 pp.

4633. Rukeyser, Muriel. WAKE ISLAND. Garden City, NY:
       Doubleday, Doran, 1942. 16 pp.

4634. Stork, Charles W. NAVPAC. New York: Bookman Associates,
       1952. 79 pp.

4635. Williams, Oscar, ed. WAR POETS: AN ANTHOLOGY OF THE WAR
       POETRY OF THE 20TH CENTURY. New York: John Day, 1945.

VI.E   INTELLECTUAL/EDUCATIONAL ASPECTS

4636. Furnivall, John S. EDUCATIONAL PROGRESS IN S.E. ASIA.
       London: Institute of Pacific Relations, 1943.

       Furnivall links educational progress in the region to
postwar planning for the status of dependent peoples.

4637. Gleason, Philip. "World War II and the Development of
       American Studies." AMER Q, 36 (No. 3, 1984), 343-358.

       Gleason argues that the war enhanced American studies by
giving new visibility and respectability to research into
American civilization and the American national character.

4638. Harrer, Heinrich. SEVEN YEARS IN TIBET. New York: Dutton,
       1954. 314 pp.

       The author, an Austrian mountaineer, was interned in
India in 1939. Eventually he escaped to Tibet, where he
lived in contentment--for a time he tutored the Dalai
Lama--until the Chinese Communists arrived. At times the
modest tone of these memoirs lends a certain charm to the
book, but the self-effacement can be overdone.

4639. Jackson, Carl T. "The Influence of Asia Upon American
       Thought: A Bibliographic Essay." AMER STUD INT, 22
       (April 1984), 3-31.

       Here is a useful overview of the literature. The author
concludes that Asia had an important impact in such areas
as general surveys, intellectual and literary achievements,
philosophy, and religion.

4640. McGill, Peter. "A Cease Fire in Words of War." MACLEAN'S,
       95 (August 9, 1982), 22.

       Here is a brief report on the treatment of the war in
present-day Japanese school textbooks.

4641. NEW TOOLS FOR LEARNING ABOUT WARS AND POSTWAR PROBLEMS: A
       GUIDE TO FILMS, PAMPHLETS AND RECORDINGS FOR TEACHERS,
       SPEAKERS, AND DISCUSSION LEADERS. New York: New Tools
       for Learning, 1943.

       NE

4642. Ninkovich, Frank A. "Cultural Relations and American China
       Policy, 1942-1945." PAC HR, 49 (August 1980), 471-498.

In 1942, the State Department launched a cultural relations policy for China that was not intended as political. The author argues that the fallacies of this U.S. cultural policy highlighted Sino-American differences. American officials believed that culture was simply the final barrier to the triumph of human reason, according to the author, and that, by the process of acculturation in China, problems, such as Sino-Japanese rivalry, would take care of themselves in the new, democratic China.

4643. United Nations. Information Organization. London. ALLIED PLAN FOR EDUCATION: THE STORY OF THE CONFERENCE OF ALLIED MINISTERS OF EDUCATION. London: HMSO, 1945. 38 pp.

Here is a report on the proceedings of the Allied conference on education. The participants promise to give great emphasis to education as part of the U.N. relief and reconstruction activities in the postwar era.

4644. United States. Office of Education. EDUCATION UNDER ENEMY OCCUPATION. Washington, D.C.: Federal Security Agency, 1945. 71 pp.

Although this report concentrates on education in occupied China, there is some material on Japanese policies elsewhere in the Pacific.

VI.F. REPORTING THE WAR

4645. Abend, Hallett. RECONQUEST: ITS RESULTS AND RESPONSIBILITIES. Garden City, NY: Doubleday, 1946. 305 pp.

Abend reports his observations while fresh from a trip, sponsored by the War Department for some correspondents, to areas liberated from the Axis enemies. The sections on Asia, which is the focus of his knowledge and experience, are the most useful.

4646. Alcott, Carroll. MY WAR WITH JAPAN. New York: Henry Holt, 1943. 368 pp.

Alcott, a correspondent-radio commentator with over fifteen years' experience in Asia, sets forth his observations of the trouble caused throughout Asia by Japan--trouble that ranged from overzealous propaganda to extensive involvement in the traffic of illegal commodities. He had long been convinced that the Japanese

harbored aggressive designs, and he tried to use his
reports to warn of these designs. His basic conclusion is
that Japan must be destroyed.

4647. Associated Press. REPORTING TO REMEMBER: UNFORGETTABLE
        STORIES AND PICTURES OF WORLD WAR II BY CORRESPONDENTS
        OF THE ASSOCIATED PRESS. New York: Associated Press,
        1945. 71 pp.

        The grandiose subtitle notwithstanding, this
        contemporary collection is of varied quality.

4648. Baldwin, Hanson W. "Solomons Action." MC GAZ, 49
        (November 1965), 75-77.

        This article is a reprint of one of Baldwin's
        contemporary newspaper reports in 1942.

4649. Baldwin, Hanson W. "Solomons Action Develops into Battle
        for South Pacific." MC GAZ, 56 (August 1972), 42-44.

        In this reprint of one of his 1942 newspaper reports,
        Baldwin describes his observations of the confusion during
        the early stage of the battle.

4650. Beldon, Jack. STILL TIME TO DIE. Philadelphia:
        Blakiston, 1944. 322 pp.

        This book is a showcase for Beldon's perceptive views as
        a war correspondent in Asia and Europe. His interesting
        tales and portraits of individuals (at varying levels of
        influence) flow from his first-hand observations.

4651. Brown, Cecil. SUEZ TO SINGAPORE. New York: Random House,
        1942. 556 pp.

        Here is the eyewitness report of a CBS broadcaster who
        travelled throughout Europe and Asia from April 1940 to
        March 1942. Brown witnessed the fall of Singapore and then
        made his way to Australia before returning to the United
        States. His criticism of the British leadership at
        Singapore underscores Brown's feeling that the disaster
        could have been averted. Of special interest is his report
        of the sinking of the REPULSE and the PRINCE OF WALES;
        Brown actually was a participant on this ill-fated voyage.

4652. Burns, Eugene. THEN THERE WAS ONE. New York: Harcourt
        Brace, 1944. 179 pp.

Burns, a correspondent, spent some time aboard the
ENTERPRISE during the first year of the war. This is his
eyewitness account of the performance of the crew and the
ship.

4653. Button, Bole. "Deadline at Ie Shima." SOLDIERS,
       38 (April 1983), 16-18.

Button tells of the death of Ernie Pyle on April 18,
1945.

4654. Cant, Gilbert. WAR ON JAPAN. New York: American Council,
       IPR, 1945. 64 pp.

Here is a brief report by an informed author on the
progress of the war.

4655. Carey, Arch. THE WAR YEARS AT SHANGHAI, 1941-45-48. New
       York: Vantage Press, 1967. 339 pp.

Carey, an astute observer, describes his
experiences--and the wartime situation in China--during his
stay in Shanghai.

4656. Carroll, Gordon, ed. HISTORY IN THE WRITING. New York:
       Duell, Sloan, and Pearce, 1945. 401 pp.

Carroll edits the eyewitness war reports filed by the
correspondents of TIME, LIFE, and FORTUNE. Arranged
chronologically (1941-1944), most of these reports are
among the best of their kind. Beldon and Sherrod are
particularly good on the war against Japan.

4657. Cohn, David L. THIS IS THE STORY. Boston: Houghton
       Mifflin, 1947. 563 pp.

Here is Cohn's record of his trip in 1944-1945 to
Europe, the Mediterranean, and the Far East (India, Burma,
and China). He offers his views, based largely on his
first-hand reports, in a well-written style.

4658. Columbia Broadcasting System. FROM PEARL HARBOR INTO
       TOKYO: THE STORY AS TOLD BY WAR CORRESPONDENTS ON THE
       AIR. New York: CBS, 1945. 312 pp.

These verbatim reports offer unique and first-hand
perspectives. Paul Hollister and Robert Strunsky edited
the collection.

4659. Congdon, Don, ed. COMBAT, PACIFIC THEATER, WORLD WAR II.
       New York: Dell, 1959. 382 pp.

       Here is an excellent collection of contemporary reports
       on the war. See especially the work of William Dyess on
       the Death March and Hanson Baldwin on the battle at Leyte
       Gulf.

4660. Curie, Eve. JOURNEY AMONG WARRIORS. Garden City, NY:
       Doubleday and Doran, 1943. 501 pp.

       This French biographer and writer tells of her global
       travels during the war, including trips to India and China.
       She talked with Asian leaders as well as common citizens.
       Her report assesses the war situation in China, and she
       does not hesitate to comment on the lack of offensive
       spirit by Chinese forces. In addition, Curie recognizes
       the enormous impact emerging nationalism will play on
       postwar affairs in India.

4661. Custer, Joe James. THROUGH THE PERILOUS NIGHT. New York:
       Macmillan, 1944. 243 pp.

       Custer, a sports writer, became a war correspondent when
       he found himself caught in the attack at Pearl Harbor. He
       was aboard the cruiser ASTORIA and continued his combat
       reporting until the ship sank at Savo (where he was
       wounded). His experiences hold the reader's interest.

4662. Dos Passos, John. TOUR OF DUTY. Boston: Houghton
       Mifflin, 1946. 336 pp.

       The memoir-report contains some useful material on the
       war against Japan. See especially his interviews with
       newly-released internees.

4663. Driscoll, Joseph. WAR DISCOVERS ALASKA. Philadelphia: J.
       B. Lippincott, 1943. 352 pp.

       As a correspondent who travelled extensively during the
       war, Driscoll reports on his visit to Alaska. He pays
       particular attention to economic, social, and geographical
       conditions.

4664. Duffett, W.E., A.R. Hicks, and G.R. Parkin. INDIA TODAY.
       New York: John Day, 1942. 173 pp.

       The three Canadian writers describe the political situation

in contemporary India. This attention is fixed on the
general context of Indian nationalism.

4665.   Eskelund, Karl. MY CHINESE WIFE. Garden City, NY:
        Doubleday, 1945. 247 pp.

        Correspondent Eskelund reminisces about his experiences.

4666.   Gallagher, O'Dowd. ACTION IN THE EAST. Garden City, NY:
        Doubleday, Doran, 1942. 300 pp.

        The author, a South African reporter, went on the
        fateful mission of the REPULSE and PRINCE OF WALES and
        spent two hours in the water awaiting rescue. He also was
        in Singapore when that fortress fell, and he travelled
        throughout war-torn Burma. His observations and
        experiences not only hold attention but also criticize the
        lack of preparation and British leadership before the war.

4667.   Gervasi, Frank H. WAR HAS SEVEN FACES. Garden City, NY:
        Doubleday, Doran, 1942. 296 pp.

        The author, a U.S. reporter, tells of his global travels
        in 1941, including visits to India, Thailand, and the
        Philippines. The report contains perceptive comments as
        well as his first-hand observations.

4668.   Gilman, William. OUR HIDDEN FRONT. New York: Reynal &
        Hitchcock, 1944. 266 pp.

        This narrative comes from notes the author kept during
        his travels as a correspondent in Alaska. Instead of
        wasting the men and materials in Alaska by allowing them to
        just sit there, Gilman argues that Alaska should be the
        springboard for the invasion of Japan. His experiences and
        observations provide a useful view of wartime Alaska.

4669.   Goette, John A. JAPAN FIGHTS FOR ASIA. New York:
        Harcourt Brace, 1943. 248 pp.

        Correspondent Goette traveled with the Japanese Army in
        China before the U.S. entry into the war. Prior to 1941,
        he tried unsuccessfully to warn Americans of Japanese
        aggressive designs in Asia. His narrative describes the
        Japanese methods he witnessed in a "Know Your Enemy"
        report.

4670.   Gramling, Oliver, et al. FREE MEN ARE FIGHTING: THE STORY
        OF WORLD WAR II. New York: Farrar and Rinehart, 1942.

488 pp.

Here is a collection of reports by Associated Press
correspondents from all theaters of the war.

4671. Hailey, Foster. PACIFIC BATTLE LINE. New York:
Macmillan, 1944. 405 pp.

Hailey, a U.S. correspondent, gives his eyewitness
report on the first two years of the war in the Pacific.
In addition to the battles, the author is particularly
adept at bringing the war down to the personal level. Thus
we have vignettes of pilot Butch O'Hare taking on nine
enemy aircraft singlehandedly (shooting down 5 and
crippling a 6th); Col. Ted Wyman making defensive
preparations--and being criticized for cutting down
night-blooming cereus; and the G.I. who called himself a
Christian Scientist and wanted to go to San Francisco to
cure his bad back.

4672. Hodson, James L. WAR IN THE SUN. New York: Dial Press,
1943. 449 pp.

Hodson, a British correspondent, travelled throughout
the Far East (and elsewhere) in 1941-1942. Not all his
reports are based on first-hand observations, but much of
the book stems from his diary.

4673. Hollister, Paul and Robert Strunsky, eds. FROM PEARL
HARBOR TO TOKYO: THE STORY AS TOLD BY WAR
CORRESPONDENTS ON THE AIR. New York: Columbia
Broadcasting System, 1945. 315 pp.

The contemporary collection is of uneven quality but
provides an example of broadcast reporting in the war.

4674. Homer, Joy. DAWN WATCH IN CHINA. Boston: Houghton
Mifflin, 1941. 340 pp.

The author, a journalist, reports on wartime conditions
in China before the entry of the United States into the
war. Of interest is the material on the Chinese
Communists.

4675. Ingersoll, Ralph M. ACTION ON ALL FRONTS. New York:
Harper & Brothers, 1942. 330 pp.

Ingersoll, editor of PM, gives a personal account of the
war on all fronts. His eyewitness reports stem from his

global travels during 1941. In Asia, he visited the
Philippines, Malaysia, and China.

4676. Joseph, Franklin H. FAR EAST REPORT. Boston: Christopher
      Publications, 1946. 96 pp.

      Maj. Joseph reports on the war damage he saw during his
      travels in 1945.

4677. Lee, Clark G. THEY CALL IT PACIFIC. New York: Viking,
      1943. 374 pp.

      The author, a reporter with extensive experience in
      Asia, gives his eyewitness report on the war as it extended
      into the Solomons. In November, 1941, the Japanese warned
      Lee to leave Shanghai, and he went to the Philippines just
      in time to witness the first Japanese bombings. His
      travels helped him construct an excellent account of the
      ill-fated defense of the Philippines. This is one of the
      best "contemporary correspondent" reports.

4678. Lucas, Jim G. COMBAT CORRESPONDENT. New York: Reynal and
      Hitchcock, 1944. 210 pp.

      Lt. Lucas provides a contemporary account of his
      experiences and observations as a Marine combat
      correspondent in the Pacific. He covered many of the most
      brutal engagements.

4679. Mazzeno, Laurence W. "Getting the Word to Willie and Joe."
      MIL REV, 67 (August 1987), 69-82.

      Here is a description of the efforts of Army Command
      Information to keep the troops informed. These efforts
      were not entirely free of propaganda.

4680. Moats, Alice-Leon. BLIND DATE WITH MARS. New York:
      Doubleday, 1943. 486 pp.

      As a correspondent for Colliers, Moats travelled
      extensively, including through much of Asia, from 1940 to
      1942. The book takes a light-hearted look at her
      experiences.

4681. Mead, James M. TELL THE FOLKS BACK HOME. New York:
      Appleton-Century, 1944. 298 pp.

      The Senator (Dem., N.Y.) presents the diary entries
      concerning his global trip with four of his colleagues for

about two months in mid-1943. He particularly emphasizes
his contacts and visits with U.S. servicemen. Of special
note is the furor created in London by the remarks of the
five touring senators which criticized British colonial
policies. Mead did not know it at the time, but only the
tactful intercession of Harry Hopkins persuaded an irate
Churchill not to create an international incident over the
episode.

4682. Norton-Taylor, Duncan. WITH MY HEART IN MY MOUTH. New
        York: Coward-McCann, 1944. 167 pp.

        As a writer for TIME, Norton-Taylor traveled to the
        Pacific in 1943. His report provides an excellent
        description for Americans back home of the war in the
        Pacific.

4683. O'Sheel, Patrick and Gene Cook, eds. SEMPER FIDELIS: THE
        U.S. MARINES IN THE PACIFIC, 1942-1945. New York:
        William Sloane Associates, 1947. 360 pp.

        These stories by Marine combat correspondents are
        arranged to cover key areas and campaigns as well as types
        of combat. Given the circumstances, the articles are
        surprisingly well written.

4684. Overseas Press Club of America. DEADLINE DELAYED. New
        York: E.P. Dutton, 1947. 311 pp.

        Here are over twenty original stories by overseas U.S.
        correspondents concerning the war on all fronts.

4685. Perry, Glen C.H. "DEAR BART": WASHINGTON VIEWS OF WORLD
        WAR II. Westport, CT: Greenwood Press, 1982. 341 pp.

        Perry and Phelps Adams directed the Washington bureau of
        the NEW YORK SUN. Their access to background information
        from public figures (e.g., Marshall and King) and their
        perspective of life in Washington provided material for
        memoranda and correspondence to the paper's city editor,
        Edmond P. Bartnett. In this book, Perry offers a selection
        from this wartime material. See especially their writings
        about the fighting qualities of the Japanese soldier, the
        atomic bomb, the Japanese surrender, and the great and
        not-so-great personalities.

4686. Raleigh, John M. PACIFIC BLACKOUT. New York: Dodd, Mead,
        1943. 244 pp.

As a CBS correspondent, Raleigh was in Java when the war started. His story indicates the tough attitude of Japanese in the Netherlands East Indies before the war. Here is a useful report on the contemporary situation in the NEI. Of interest is his description of the eruption in October 1941 of the volcano Smeru which lasted for three weeks. Raleigh evacuated Java on Gen. Lewis Brereton's airplane to Australia. The book includes Raleigh's observations on the wartime situation in Australia.

4687. Randau, Carl and Leane Zugsmith. THE SETTING SUN OF JAPAN. New York: Random House, 1942. 342 pp.

The married couple, both reporters, travelled throughout Asia, especially Japan, on the eve of the war. They describe the situation in China, the Philippines, Malaya, Singapore, NEI, Australia, and Hawaii, as well as in Japan. Of interest is their belief that the Japanese fostered the illusion of being mired in China.

4688. Riess, Curtis, ed. THEY WERE THERE: THE STORY OF WORLD WAR II AND HOW IT CAME ABOUT BY AMERICA'S FOREMOST CORRESPONDENTS. Garden City, NY: Garden City Publishing, 1945. 714 pp.

The stories by the U.S. correspondents underscore the dangers of their civilian occupation. For purposes of this guide, see especially the articles by Melville Jacoby, Henry C. Wolfe, Wilfrid Fleisher, Hugh Byas, Agnes Smedley, and John Hersey. The editor offers biographical sketches of the contributors.

4689. Ross, Bill D. "Ernie Pyle." W W II, 1 (November 1986). 10, 62-66.

Here is a sympathetic portrait. Ross excuses some of Pyle's columns which did not compare the fighting in the Pacific favorably to that in Europe on the grounds that Pyle resented his assignment to the Pacific. Only reluctantly did Pyle go to Okinawa--his last assignment.

4690. Sheean, Vincent. THIS HOUSE DIVIDED AGAINST THIS HOUSE. New York: Random House, 1946. 420 pp.

Sheean includes a report on his brief trip to India and China. His narrative describes the first B-29 operations against the Japanese. Of interest is his critical analysis of the Versailles Treaty.

4691. Stowe, Leland. THEY SHALL NOT SLEEP. New York: A.A.
          Knopf, 1944. 399 pp.

          Stowe, a correspondent, bases his report on notes he
       took while traveling through China, Burma and India in 1941
       and 1942. The book is marked by Stowe's observations and
       opinions frankly stated.

4692. Treanor, Thomas C. ONE DAMN THING AFTER ANOTHER. Garden
          City, NY: Doubleday, 1944. 294 pp.

          Here is the personal account of a reporter who traveled
       to all theaters, including China and India, during a
       21-month period. Much humor enlivens the narrative as he
       tells of his experiences and the incidents he observed.

4693. "V-J Day." A F, 38 (September 1955), 43-50.

          Here is a composite of the work of the journal's staff
       staff correspondents during the war.

4694. Wheeler, Keith. THE PACIFIC IS MY BEAT. New York: E.P.
          Dutton, 1943. 383 pp.

          Wheeler, a newspaperman, accompanied American troops in
       combat against the Japanese from Pearl Harbor to early
       1943. See especially his report from the Aleutians.

4695. White, Osmar. GREEN ARMOR. Sydney, Aus.: Angus and
          Robertson, 1945. 288 pp.

          The author, a New Zealand reporter, describes his
       experiences accompanying combat forces in New Guinea and
       the Solomons. His narrative reflects contemporary
       attitudes about not only the Japanese enemy but also the
       island natives.

4696. Wolfert, Ira. BATTLE FOR THE SOLOMONS. Boston: Houghton
          Mifflin, 1943. 200 pp.

          Wolfert, a war correspondent, draws on his daily journal
       entries to provide a running account of the 1942 struggle
       in the Solomons. Here is a contemporary report in the most
       literal sense.

VI.F.1. CENSORSHIP

4697. Fleming, Thomas. "The Big Leak." AMER HERITAGE, 38
         (December 1987), 64-71.

         Here is a report on the publication of the secret war
         plan RAINBOW 5 by reporter Chelsey Manly, December 4, 1941,
         in the CHICAGO TRIBUNE. Although the source of the leak
         was never found, Fleming speculates that Roosevelt may well
         have arranged it as part of his complex maneuvers in late
         1941.

4698. Frank, Larry J. "The United States Navy v. the Chicago
         Tribune." HISTORIAN, 42 (No. 2, 1980), 284-303.

         On June 7, 1942, Stanley Johnston wrote an article in
         the Chicago newspaper which indicated that the United
         States, through counterintelligence activities, had broken
         Japanese codes and had forewarning of Japanese activities.
         Although in the ensuing litigation a grand jury failed to
         indict either Johnston or the TRIBUNE, Frank points out the
         irony that the episode led to more government censorship
         through more restrictive interpretations of the First
         Amendment. The author criticizes Johnston and the
         newspaper for their irresponsible disclosure.

4699. Goren, Dina. "Communication Intelligence and the Freedom
         of the Press." J CONTEMP HIST, 16 (October 1981),
         663-690.

         This detailed account is bolstered with excellent
         research. Goren analyzes the controversy over the
         publication on June 7, 1942, of an article in the CHICAGO
         TRIBUNE (which also appeared in the New York DAILY NEWS and
         the Washington TIMES-HERALD) that the United States had
         broken the Japanese naval code. Of interest is the fact
         that the government's Bureau of Censorship and a grand jury
         dropped the matter. Navy Secretary Knox, however,
         continued to pursue the case against reporter Stanley
         Johnston (who claimed his chief source was the publication
         JANE'S FIGHTING SHIPS).

4700. Johnson, Charles W. and Charles O. Jackson. CITY BEHIND A
         FENCE: OAK RIDGE, TENNESSEE, 1942-1946. Knoxville, TN:
         University of Tennessee Press, 1981. 248 pp.

         Here is a glimpse of life for the city's inhabitants in
         the secret scientific project. Based on interviews and
         official records, the authors present a unique social
         history in that fences and armed guards ensured the
         relative isolation of Oak Ridge.

4701.   Knight, Mary Lamar. "The Secret War of Censors vs. Spies."
             READER'S DIG, 48 (March 1946), 79-83.

        The author, a wartime censor, describes the thousands of
        codes and ciphers discovered in wartime correspondence.
        She feels that the two most successful efforts of the
        censors had to do with exorcising references to the
        development of the atomic bomb and the Japanese
        balloon-bombs.

4702.   Mitchell, Richard H. CENSORSHIP IN IMPERIAL JAPAN.
             Princeton, NJ: Princeton University Press, 1983.   424
             pp.

        Mitchell provides a first-rate survey of the subject
        from the Meiji Era through the end of the war.

4703.   Potts, E. Daniel and Annette Potts. "American Newsmen and
             Australian Wartime Propaganda and Censorship,
             1940-1942." HIST STUD, 21 (October 1985), 565-575.

        The article indicates the irony of one part of the
        Australian government working hard to get news about
        Australia into print in the United States while another
        part made it difficult for U.S. correspondents to do their
        job. The authors describe the censorship imposed about
        labor strikes, the Australia First Movement, and laws
        preventing the militia from serving outside the country.
        By January 1943, they point out, almost all talented U.S.
        correspondents had left Australia--driven out, they say, by
        the poor state of one of the Four Freedoms.

4704.   Richstad, Jim. THE PRESS UNDER MARTIAL LAW: THE HAWAIIAN
             EXPERIENCE. Lexington, KT: Association for Education
             in Journalism, 1970. 41 pp.

        This brief report describes the forms of censorship
        imposed on the press in Hawaii during the war. Unlike the
        48 states, Hawaii remained under martial law.

VI.G. DEMOGRAPHIC ASPECTS/UNITED STATES HOME FRONT/UNITED NATIONS COALITION

4705.   Allen, Gwenfread E. HAWAII'S WAR YEARS, 1941-1945.
             Honolulu: University of Hawaii Press, 1950. 418 pp.

        In a carefully documented narrative, Allen traces the
        effect of the war in Hawaii. With extensive research in

the Hawaii War Records Depository, she pays particular
attention to civilian life (see especially the chapter
entitled "Social Upheaval").

4706. Blake, Alfred E. [pseud. Al Ethelred Blakely.] CONVOY TO
       INDIA. Brooklyn, NY: Trilon Press, 1953, 214 pp.

       Here is an account of American blacks entering the
       Pacific war zone.

4707. Blum, John Morton. "United Against: American Culture and
       Society During World War II." PROC MIL HIST SYMPOSIUM,
       10 (October 1982), 5-15, 233.

       NE

4708. Buck, Pearl S. AMERICAN UNITY AND ASIA. New York: The
       John Day Company, 1942. 140 pp.

       This series of articles gives testimony to Buck's
       continuing efforts to provide education about Asia. Her
       protests against racial bigotry reinforce her arguments
       that United States unity is essential to the war effort.

4709. Carey, Otis. WAR WASTED ASIA: LETTERS, 1945-1946. Tokyo:
       Kodansha International, 1975. 322 pp.

       NE

4710. Cornell University. THE IMPACT OF THE WAR ON AMERICA.
       Ithaca, NY: Cornell University Press, 1942. 159 pp.

       In early 1942, six Cornell professors delivered
       lectures on the war. Of particular interest are the
       lectures by C.W. Kiewiet on the United States and the
       British Empire, Knight Biggerstaff on American policy
       in the Far East, and Herbert W. Briggs on a postwar
       international organization.

4711. Catlin, George E.G. et al, comps. ABOVE ALL NATIONS. New
       York: Harper and Row, 1949. 189 pp.

       This collection of essays addresses some of the moral
       aspects of the war. Touching on more than two hundred
       episodes or statements which emerged from all theaters, the
       accent is heavy on the pacifist perspective.

4712. Costello, John. VIRTUE UNDER FIRE. Boston: Little,
       Brown, 1985. 309 pp.

With extensive research, including many interviews and
recently declassified government documents, Costello looks
at the impact of the war on the sexual attitudes of the
American people. For purposes of this project, see the
personal account of Tokyo Rose.

4713. DeBenedetti, Charles. "The American Peace Movement and
        Asia, 1941-1961." PAC HR, 50 (May 1981), 192-214.

The author, a noted scholar in this field, identifies
three groups in the U.S. peace movement: (1) pacifists and
war resisters, (2) social progressives, and (3)
internationalists seeking firmer forms of global order.
During the war, he says, the three groups maintained a
facade of harmony. Moreover, with regard to U.S. policy in
Asia, DeBenedetti argues that the peace groups acted as the
loyal opposition.

4714. DeBenedetti, Charles. "The American Peace Movement and the
        National Security State, 1941-1971." WORLD AFFS, 141
        (Fall 1978), 118-129.

The author has written extensively on this general
subject. The article incorporates his analysis of the
reactions of American pacifists to the attack at Pearl
Harbor and the U. S. entry into the war.

4715. Dennis, Peter. TROUBLED DAYS OF PEACE: MOUNTBATTEN AND
        SOUTH EAST ASIA COMMAND, 1945-1946. New York: St.
        Martin's Press, 1987. 270 pp.

Here is a well-researched report on the enormous
difficulties that faced SEAC at war's end. For example,
about one million Japanese troops had to be disarmed and
repatriated; moreover, 100,000 POWs and civilian internees
required careful attention. A critical shortage of food
threatened to devastate much of Southeast Asia. Dennis
chronicles Mountbatten's prompt and decisive actions in
coping with the crisis. Of interest is SEAC's use of armed
Japanese soldiers to help with the policing duties.

4716. Dower, John W. WAR WITHOUT MERCY: RACE AND POWER IN THE
        PACIFIC WAR. New York: Pantheon Books, 1986. 399pp.

Moving past official documents and battle reports,
Dower analyzes cultural reflections (in movies, songs,
cartoons, and popular writings) of virulent racism on
both sides. His thorough research and balanced per-

spectives enrich the penetrating insights he brings to
this work. For example, a wartime report by the Japanese
government has recently surfaced; it envisioned a new
order for the postwar work led by the Yamato race. For
Dower, the war words (propaganda) on both sides were
racist words. Although the early Japanese victories
spawned a "superman" myth among alarmed Westerners, Dower
argues that "superman" and "subhuman" (an anti-Japanese
epithet used by General Sir Thomas Blarney) had the
common feature of being "nonhuman." With considerable
irony, he shows how race hatred contributed to poor
military planning—and merciless fighting. The book
suffers some exaggerations (the term "turkey shoot"
has early American origins and does not necessarily
demean the Japanese as animals; the use of the term
"Japs," rather than a slur, was viewed by Churchill—
not the best role model for nonracist thinking—as too
familiar), but Dower has made a major contribution.

4717. Ellis, Albert F. MID-PACIFIC OUTPOSTS. Auckland, NZ:
        Brown and Stewart, 1946. 303 pp.

        Ellis provides a description of the people, climate, and
        cultures of Oceana.

4718. Gardner, Brian. THE YEAR THAT CHANGED THE WORLD: 1945.
        New York: Coward-McCann, 1964. 356 pp.

        Gardner offers a well-written narrative of the final
        year of the war. His reporting of the major events in all
        theaters is supplemented with references to social-cultural
        events in the West. Gardner is no social analyst, but his
        narrative of 1945 makes for enjoyable reading.

4719. Goodman, Jack, ed. WHILE YOU WERE GONE. New York: Simon
        and Schuster, 1946. 625 pp.

        Goodman assembles an excellent collection as a report on
        wartime life in the United States. See especially the
        article by Carey McWilliams on the treatment of racial
        minorities (including the Japanese-Americans).

4720. Klestadt, Albert. THE SEA WAS KIND. New York: David
        McKay, 1961. 208 pp.

        This is the story of a young German refugee who made his
        way from the Japanese-occupied Philippines to Australia.
        Klesdadt recontructed diary notes he made at the time.
        Troubles with the boat and his companions (natives of Moro

Island) helped lengthen his adventure to over a year
(December 1941–December 1942).

4721. Lardner, John. SOUTHWEST PASSAGE: THE YANKS IN THE
       PACIFIC. Philadelphia, PA: J.B. Lippincott, 1943.
       302 pp.

       An American correspondent in Australia and New Guinea,
       Lardner describes the general feelings of Australians and
       Americans towards each other. He is particularly adept at
       explaining Australia and its people to an American
       audience.

4722. Lasker, Bruno. ASIA ON THE MOVE. New York: Henry Holt,
       1945. 207 pp.

       This contemporary study explores population migrations
       and resettlements in East Asia. Lasker views the wartime
       experience as an integral part of a continuing historical
       process.

4723. Lasker, Bruno. PEOPLES OF SOUTHEAST ASIA. New York: A.A.
       Knopf, 1944. 288 pp.

       In a study sponsored by the Institute of Pacific
       Relations, the author describes economic–political–social
       conditions in Malaya, Indonesia, and the Philippines. The
       book serves its intended purpose of shaping the debate over
       the postwar era.

4724. Lawry, John. THE CROSS OF LORRAINE IN THE SOUTH PACIFIC:
       AUSTRALIA AND THE FREE FRENCH MOVEMENT, 1940–1942.
       Canberra, Aus.: Journal of Pacific History, 1982.
       142 pp.

       During the early years of the war (1940–1943), the
       author served as an assistant to the Australian
       representative in New Caledonia. He describes the
       Australian contribution as the New Caledonians rallied to
       the Free French cause.

4725. Lingeman, Richard R. DON'T YOU KNOW THERE'S A WAR ON? New
       York G.P. Putnam's Sons, 1970. 495 pp.

       This history of the home front is well researched and
       easy to read. The author claims that, by late 1941, U.S.
       public opinion favored aid to China and Britain and
       supported the embargo against Japan. With regard to the
       relocation of Japanese–Americans, Lingeman points out that

certain Americans felt patriotic in saying "No Japs wanted
here." Moreover, he warns that this detention established
a dangerous precedent in American society.

4726. Lorimer, Frank, "Population Trends in the Orient." FOR
       AFFS, 23 (July 1945), 668-674.

       Calling for further study on the topic, the author
       suggests that only higher standards of living and
       democratic mass movements will cause the transition to
       controlled reproduction.

4727. MacDonald, Alexander W. REVOLT IN PARADISE: THE SOCIAL
       REVOLUTION IN HAWAII AFTER PEARL HARBOR. Brattleboro,
       VT: Stephen Daye Press, 1944. 288 pp.

       MacDonald outlines the profound social changes in Hawaii
       during the war. There is a summary of historical events in
       the islands since 1820.

4728. Monnett, John R., Lester Cole, and Jack C. Cleland. HARBOR
       DEFENSES OF LOS ANGELES, HDLA, IN WORLD WAR II. Los
       Angeles, 1946. 32 pp.

       This brief report indicates the contemporary anxiety
       about the Japanese threat to the West Coast in the
       aftermath of Pearl Harbor.

4729. Montagu, M.F. Ashley. "Racism, the Bomb and the World's
       People." ASIA & AMERICAS, 46 (December 1946), 533-535.

       One of the good things about the war, according to the
       author, is the heightened awareness of Asia in the United
       States. He describes the dangers of racism and the atomic
       bomb in an age of excessive nationalism and power politics.

4730. Moore, John Hammond. OVER-SEXED, OVER-PAID, AND OVER HERE:
       AMERICANS IN AUSTRALIA, 1941-1945. St. Lucia, Aus.:
       University of Queensland Press, 1981. 303 pp.

       Moore describes some of the effects, mainly social, of
       stationary American soldiers in Australia. There were
       happy times and times of trouble. The book takes on a
       demanding load as topics range from music to diet to race
       relations to organized labor. This is a useful beginning;
       much remains to be done.

4731. Pei, Mario A. WHAT LANGUAGES ARE OUR SOLDIERS UP AGAINST?
       New York: S.F. Vanni, 1944. 32 pp.

NE

4732. Polenberg, Richard. WAR AND SOCIETY: THE UNITED STATES,
        1941-1945. Philadelphia, PA: J.B. Lippincott, 1972.
        298 pp.

        In this excellent study of the home front, see
        especially the analysis of the education policy for
        Japanese-Americans. Denying any resemblance to Nazi
        concentration camps, Polenberg writes that the WRA tried to
        follow a generous and humane policy. According to the
        author, the evacuation policy did not rise from evil
        intentions but, nonetheless, was shaped by public opinion
        and military necessity.

4733. Porteus, Stanley D. AND BLOW NOT THE TRUMPET: A PRELUDE
        TO PERIL. Palo Alto, CA: Pacific Books, 1947. 304 pp.

        Describing the Hawaiian perspective, Porteus tells of
        Hawaii's contributions to national defense. The author, a
        psychologist, reports on the immediate reactions of
        civilians to the surprise attack at Pearl Harbor. Here is
        a useful contemporary source. Blame is spread
        extensively--and thinly--for the disaster.

4734. Potts, E. Daniel and Annette Potts. YANKS DOWN UNDER,
        1941-45. New York: Oxford University Press, 1985. 455
        pp.

        Here is an excellent history of Australian perspectives
        on the American presence. The social changes are well
        researched and well presented.

4735. Rollins, Alfred B., Jr., ed. DEPRESSION, RECOVERY AND WAR:
        1929-1945. New York: McGraw-Hill, 1966. 404 pp.

        Rollins finds the "roots of contemporary life" contained
        in these fateful years. Most of the documentary material
        is well known by now, but some of the selections,
        especially the war poetry of e.e. cummings, continue to
        hold interest. The volume is part of the "Documentary
        History of American Life" series edited by David Donald.

4736. Saunders, Kay. "Conflict Between the American and
        Australian Governments Over the Introduction of Black
        American Servicemen into Australia During World War II."
        AUS J POL HIST, 32 (No. 2, 1987), 39-46.

Like no other issue in Australia, Saunders says, the policy of racial exclusiveness brought on internal bipartisan agreement and a major quarrel with the United States. Australian acquiescence in accepting American black (segregated) units reflected its junior status in the partnership with the United States.

4737. Selth, Andrew. "Race and Resistance in Burma, 1942-1945." MOD ASIAN STUD, 20 (July 1986), 483-507.

Selth maintains that Burma was wracked by racial antagonisms that became political divisions. The war years, according to the author, saw a hardening of the split between the majority Burmans and the minority hill people.

4738. Winkler, Allan M. HOME FRONT U.S.A.: AMERICA DURING WORLD WAR II. Arlington Heights, IL: Harlan Davidson, 1986. 115 pp.

Here is both an enlightened synthesis and interpretive essay about the domestic scene. Of special interest is Winkler's analysis of the dislocations of the war. For example, the Japanese-American evacuees are placed in the context of "Outsiders and Ethnic Groups." According to Winkler, the Japanese-Americans lost as much as $400 million in income and property losses.

4739. Zeitzer, Glen and Charles F. Howlett. "Political Versus Religious Pacifism: The Peace Now Movement of 1943." HISTORIAN, 48 (May 1986), 375-393.

Using private collections, including the papers of the Peace Now Movement, the authors trace the activities of the movement, which advocated a negotiated settlement rather than a victor's peace. Other U.S. peace groups rejected the Peace Now Movement, according to the authors, because of certain personnel and its political (not religious) base.

VI.G.1. TREATMENT OF JAPANESE MINORITIES

a. United States Policies and Procedures (Evacuation and Relocation Camps)

4740. Adamic, Louis. FOREIGN-BORN AMERICANS AND THE WAR. New York: American Committee for the Protection of Foreign-Born, 1943. 22 pp.

The book includes a brief mention of Japan-born Americans.

4741. Adams, Ansel. BORN FREE AND EQUAL. New York: U.S. Camera, 1944. 44 pp.

Here are photos of life in the relocation centers.

4742. Aleutian/Pribilof Islands Association. THE ALEUT RELOCATION AND INTERNMENT DURING WORLD WAR II: A PRELIMINARY EXAMINATION. Anchorage, AK: The Association, 1981.

NE

4743. Alexandre, Maurice. "Wartime Control of Japanese-Americans: The NISEI—A Casualty of World War II." CORNELL LAW Q, 28 (June 1943), 385-413.

The author sets as his purpose the exploration of the constitutional validity of the curfew, exclusion, detention, and other regulations affecting the Japanese-Americans. His lengthy brief finds that the restrictions are a proper exercise of the war power of Congress (Public Law 503). While the restrictions are "not pleasant" for the Japanese-Americans, according to Alexandre, the government cannot gamble with national interests or the lives or U.S. servicemen.

4744. Ano, Masaharu. "Loyal Linguists: Nisei of World War II: Learned Japanese in Minnesota." MINNESOTA HIST, 45 (Fall 1977), 273-287.

Ano tells of the Military Intelligence Language School, where English-speaking NISEI learned the Japanese language. According to Ano, the school, located in Minnesota, provided a vehicle for 5,500 NISEI to show their loyalty to the United States. Many ISSEI opposed this project because the NISEI students would be fighting against the homeland rather than in Europe. The author, who surveyed many graduates of the school, calls this a story of trust and confidence amidst the unhappy general background of exclusion and discrimination.

4745. Arrington, Leonard J. THE PRICE OF PREJUDICE: THE JAPANESE-AMERICAN RELOCATION CENTER IN UTAH DURING WORLD WAR II. Logan, UT: The Faculty Association, 1962. 48 pp.

This book reproduces a lecture given by Arrington, a professor of economics. He describes the wretched life for the inhabitants of the camp located near Topaz Mountain ("Jewel of the Desert").

4746.   Bailey, Paul. CITY IN THE SUN: THE JAPANESE CONCENTRATION CAMP AT POSTON, ARIZONA. Los Angeles: Western Lore Press, 1971. 222 pp.

NE

4747.   Omitted.

4748.   Baldwin, Roger. "Japanese-Americans and the Law." ASIA & AMERICAS, 42 (September 1942), 518-519.

The author, then contemporary director of ACLU, argues that racism and hysterical wartime intolerance have contributed to a new concept of quasi-martial law. Baldwin believes that the concept is unconstitutional, and he points out that, although five groups were named in General DeWitt's order, only the Japanese-Americans have been removed from their homes. In questioning the military necessity of the removals, Baldwin expresses surprise that American public opinion is not disturbed by these actions.

4749.   Ballif, Ariel S. "Reactions to Laborers from Relocation Centers." SOCIOLOGY & SOC RES, 29 (September-October 1944), 40-45.

Ballif, a sociology professor, studies the harvesting of fruit and root crops by 680 Japanese and Japanese-Americans. The investigation is based on a survey of the 43 farmers who employed all these harvesters. Ballif found that wages seemed fair, employers were satisfied, and both groups were brought closer together.

4750.   Barnhart, Edward N. comp. JAPANESE AMERICAN EVACUATION AND RESETTLEMENT: CATALOG OF MATERIAL IN THE GENERAL LIBRARY. Berkeley, CA: University of California Press, 1958. 177 pp.

The two major sources listed here are (1) materials on the study led by Dorothy S. Thomas and (2) War Relocation Authority records (the library is one of the depositories for WRA). No published material is cited. Barnhart listed the materials by chronology and by source/origin. See especially the diaries and reports of the evacuees.

4751.   Barnhart, Edward N. "The Individual Exclusion of Japanese
          Americans in World War II." PAC HR, 29 (May 1960),
          111-130.

              In December 1944, the policy of mass exclusion ended.
          The Army then screened each evacuee, and some 5,000,
          including 2,500 U.S. citizens, were barred from returning
          to the West Coast until after Japan surrendered. Although
          particularly harsh on the Army's Western Defense Command,
          Barhhart argues that the screening process was as flawed
          as the entire episode of evacuation.

4752.   Barnhart, Edwin N., Jacobus tenBroek, and Floyd W. Matson.
          PREJUDICE, WAR, AND THE CONSTITUTION. Berkeley, CA:
          University of California Press, 1954. 408 pp.

          Here is a sympathetic study of the relocation. Upon
          examining the background, chronology, and legal aspects of
          relocation, the authors stoutly defend the policy. Their
          detailed study includes experiences on both the national
          and local levels.

4753.   Beardon, Russell. "The False Rumor of Tuesday: Arkansas's
          Internment of Japanese-Americans." ARKANSAS H Q,
          41(Winter 1982), 327-339.

              Beardon, a history teacher, tells of the two camps in
          Arkansas of the total of ten relocation centers in the
          country. His narrative describes limited self-government
          in the camps but a great degree of self-discipline.
          According to the author, the "No-No" controversy, which
          surrounded the loyalty questionnaire, was the only troubled
          period of the war at the two camps. The title arises from
          a premature surrender announcement. Of special interest is
          the reluctance of many evacuees to leave the camps and face
          new challenges in unfriendly environments.

4754.   Biddle, Francis. IN BRIEF AUTHORITY. Garden City, NY:
          Doubleday, 1962.

          Biddle sheds light on the role of the Justice Department
          (in which he served) and the internment of the
          Japanese-Americans.

4755.   Bloom, Leonard. "Familial Adjustments of Japanese-Americans
          to Relocation: First Phase." AMER SOC REV, 8 (October
          1943), 551-560.

          As part of his pioneering contemporary studies on the

relocation experience, Bloom concentrates in this article
on the inter-generational conflict among Japanese-American
families.

4756.   Bloom, Leonard. "Familial Problems and Japanese Removal."
        RES STUD STATE COLL WASH, 11 (March 1943), 21-26.

        Bloom began this study of Japanese-American families at
        the time of the declaration of war. His examination of the
        internal adjustment within a minority group developed into
        an analysis of the evacuation. At first, the evacuation
        experience strengthened family solidarity, but later, the
        dominant pattern shifted to idleness and individualization.
        Bloom points out that the Japanese-American family, if not
        destroyed by the experience, will be very different after
        the war. Of interest is his description of parents
        speaking Japanese to each other and children speaking
        English among themselves but pidgin Japanese to their
        parents.

4757.   Bloom, Leonard. "Prisonization and the WRA Camps." PROC
        PAC SOCIOLOGICAL SOCIETY, (1943), 29-34.

        NE

4758.   Bloom, Leonard. "Transitional Adjustments of Japanese
        American Families to Relocation." AMER SOC R, 12 (April
        1947), 201-209.

        After analyzing the relocation experiences of three
        thousand families, Bloom continues his study on their
        postwar resettlement. He finds that many
        Japanese-Americans had to live in conditions even worse
        than that of the camps. His primary focus is on the
        splintering of family solidarity.

4758a. Bloom, Leonard and Ruth Riemer. REMOVAL AND RETURN.
        Berkeley, CA: University of California Press, 1949.
        259 pp.

        The authors call attention to the economic-sociological
        effects of the war on Japanese-Americans from Los Angeles.
        In particular, sociologists Bloom and Riemer concentrate on
        the place held by the Japanese-Americans in the West Coast
        economy before the evacuation. The losses suffered are
        difficult to replace, the authors say, because of legal
        obstacles encountered in lodging claims. [See also studies
        on this general subject under Leonard Broom.]

4759.   Bogardus, Emory S. "Culture Conflicts in Relocation
        Centers." SOCIOLOGY SOC RES, 27 (May-June 1943),
        381-390.

        The author, a sociology professor, uses interviews and
        reports from each of the ten relocation centers in this
        study of cultural conflicts within the Japanese-American
        sub-groups. He identifies five categories in his study:
        (1) ISSEI-NISEI; (2) KIBEI as a sub-group of NISEI; (3)
        sub-groups of KIBEI, based on their various ages when they
        visited Japan; (4) HANSEI (half-generation) and non-HANSEI;
        and (5) rural-urban differences, based on type of economic
        occupation and years of residency in the United States. Of
        interest is this contemporary defense of the WRA (acting
        "intelligently"), and the author's observation that early
        releases of "loyal Americans" were relieving pressures in
        the camps.

4760.   Bogardus, Emory S. "Relocation Centers as Planned
        Communities." SOCIOLOGY SOC RES, 28 (Jan-Feb 1944),
        218-234.

        With each of the ten relocation centers recently
        completing its first year of existence, this contemporary
        study suggests that the activities of each camp be
        considered in terms of a planned community. Sociologist
        Bogardus looks at life in the centers through selected
        topics, including housing, food, work, business, education,
        religion, welfare, citizenship, and plans for resettlement.
        He concludes that the administrations of the camps are
        open-minded, progressive, and "in general have worthily
        represented the American and democratic spirit for which
        our country is fighting."

4761.   Bosworth, Allan R. AMERICA'S CONCENTRATION CAMPS. New
        York: W. W. Norton, 1967. 283 pp.

        Bosworth, a naval officer, narrates the plight of the
        Japanese-Americans. These people, according to the author,
        suffered a devastating violation of civil rights on a
        massive scale. In his view, the original policy mistake
        was exacerbated through prejudice, greed, and hysteria.

4762.   Broom, Leonard and John I. Kitsuke. THE MANAGED CASUALTY:
        THE JAPANESE-AMERICAN FAMILY IN WORLD WAR II. Berkeley,
        CA: University of California Press, 1956. 226 pp.

        This study analyzes the impact of the war experience on
        the Japanese-American family. The two sociologists draw

general conclusions from their detailed examination of ten
such families. Broom, who changed his name from Bloom,
carries on the work he had helped formulate on the economic
impact of the war (with Ruth Riemer in REMOVAL AND RETURN).

4763. Broom, Leonard and John I. Kitsuse. "The Validation of
        Acculturation: A Condition to Ethnic Assimilation."
        AMER ANTHROP, 57 (February 1955), 44-48.

        In this case study of the Japanese-Americans, the
        authors analyze such concepts as acculturation, access
        to the dominant segment of society, and stress in inter-
        ethnic situations.

4764. Omitted.

4765. Brown, G. Gordon. "War Relocation Authority Gila River
        Project: Rivers Arizona Community Analysis Section. APP
        ANTHROP, 4 (Fall 1945), 1-49.

        Here is the final report for the Gila River center,
        which closed November 10, 1945. This thorough report
        identifies weaknesses as well as strengths. Brown is
        especially critical of the poor communication (liaison)
        arrangements not only between Washington and the centers
        but also within each center.

4766. Burkhardt, William R. "Institutional Barriers,
        Marginality, and Adaptation Among the American-Japanese
        Mixed Bloods in Japan." J ASIAN STUD, 42 (May 1983),
        519-544.

        Burkhardt describes the discrimination (according to
        race, class, and family background) and the barriers
        (education, employment, marriage, and legal status)
        which the American-Japanese mixed-blood group encountered
        in Japan. Black-Japanese were especially victimized.
        Reactions varied among the mixed bloods, and only a few
        were integrated into Japanese society.

4767. "Business in Evacuation Centers." BUS WEEK, No. 672 (July
        18, 1942), 19-21.

        This editorial looks at the evacuation camps as a
        business enterprise. The camps became self-supporting but
        no profits were allowed for private activities. Cash and
        coupons were used to pay employees, and, according to the
        article, the co-op projects, such as the one at Manzanar,
        carried implications for the postwar era. This
        contemporary review affirms that the great majority of the
        evacuees were "essentially American."

4768.   Caruso, Samuel T. "After Pearl Harbor: Arizona's Response
        to the Gila River Relocation Center." J ARIZONA HIST,
        14 (No. 4, 1973), 335-346.

        NE

4769.   Chleboun, William and Don DeNevi. THE WESTCOAST GOES TO
        WAR. San Diego, CA: Howell-North, 1983.

        NE

4770.   Christgau, John. "Collins versus the World: The Fight to
        Restore Citizenship to Japanese-American Renunciants of
        World War II." PAC HR, 54 (February 1985), 1-32.

        Here is an account of the work of attorney Wayne Collins
        in arranging to have U.S. citizenship restored to
        Japanese-American renunciants. Focusing on the case of
        Tadayasu Abo, the author highlights Collins' argument that
        renunciation under detention was unconstitutional.

4771.   Christgau, John. "ENEMIES": WORLD WAR II ALIEN
        INTERNMENT. Ames, IW: Iowa State University Press,
        1985. 187 pp.

        Christgau takes his stories from the Enemy Alien
        Internment Program which imprisoned over 31,000 enemy
        aliens, including about 5,000 Japanese-Americans who
        renounced their U.S. citizenship. Based on interviews,
        diaries, and correspondence, the author emphasizes
        the human dimension of those interred at Ft. Lincoln
        in Bismarck, ND. Underlining the key role of Attorney
        Wayne Collins in litigation which extended to 1968,
        Christgau believes that the renunciations stemmed from
        three major sources: (1) anger at having to relocate,
        (2) militant peer pressure of the Hokoku organization,
        and (3) fear of postwar resettlement in hostile
        communities.

4772.   Chuman, Frank F. THE BAMBOO PEOPLE: THE LAW AND JAPANESE-
        AMERICANS. Del Mar, CA: Author, 1976. 386 pp.

        NE

4773.   Collins, Donald E. NATIVE AMERICAN ALIENS: DISLOYALTY
        AND THE RENUNCIATION OF CITIZENSHIP BY JAPANESE
        AMERICANS DURING WORLD WAR II. Westport, CT: Greenwood,
        1985. 218 pp.

Over 5,500 Japanese-Americans renounced their U.S.
citizenship, the author maintains, not because of disloyalty but through their sense of injustice. This
well-researched book addresses a neglected area in the
unhappy wartime experience of Japanese-Americans.

4774.   Colorado River War Relocation Center, Bureau of Socio-
        logical Research. "The Japanese Family in America."
        ANNALS AMER ACAD POL SOC SCI, 229 (September 1943),
        150-156.

        This official report identifies the many sources of
        stress which the war imposed upon Japanese families. The
        conclusion points out that the Japanese-Americans must be
        given something to earn their loyalty.

4775.   Colorado River War Relocation Center, Bureau of Socio-
        logical Research. "The Psychiatric Approach in Problems
        of Community Management." AMER J PSYCHIATRY, 100
        (November 1943), 328-333.

        Here is an official study of the declared purpose of
        attempting to make a community. Although confessing that
        the project was not "entirely" successful, the reporters
        take heart from the lessons learned. Their contemporary
        tone is overly optimistic.

4776.   Conrat, Maisie and Richard Conrat, comps. EXECUTIVE
        ORDER 9066: THE INTERNMENT OF 110,000 JAPANESE
        AMERICANS. Los Angeles, CA: California Historical
        Society, 1972. 120 pp.

        The Conrats assemble a collection of black and white
        photographs (taken mainly from the War Relocation
        Authority archives) which provide stark glimpses of the
        relocation experience.

4777.   Council on Foreign Relations. THE POSTWAR SETTLEMENT OF
        PROPERTY RIGHTS. New York: Council on Foreign
        Relations, 1945. 78 pp.

        Here is the text of a contemporary memorandum by the
        Council which examines the question of restitution or
        indemnification of property confiscated or destroyed during
        the war. Given the popular wartime sentiment on this
        subject, the memo is a model of moderation.

4778.   Culley, John H. "Relocation of Japanese Americans: The

Hawaiian Experience." A F LAW REV, 24 (No. 2, 1984),
176-183.

Here is a sharp contrast to the heavy-handed racism on
the West Coast. In Hawaii, military leaders, FBI agents,
and influential (non-Japanese) businessmen defended the
rights of the Japanese-American population and fostered a
tolerant climate. Culley particularly emphasizes the
contribution of Short's successor, Lt. Gen. Delos C.
Emmons. Another significant point, according to the
author, lies in the fact that the JCS rather than the
Department of the Interior supervised the treatment of the
Japanese-Americans because Hawaii was under martial law.

4779. Culley, John H. "Trouble at the Lordsburg Internment
        Camp." NEW MEX HIST REV, 60 (July 1985), 225-248.

Disputes over work rules and the controversial
trial-acquittal of two guards (accused of murdering two
interns under strange circumstances) at Lordsburg raises
questions in Culley's mind about the ability of the Army to
maintain war relocation camps.

4780. Culley, John H. "World War II and a Western Town: The
        Internment of the Japanese Railroad Workers of Clovis,
        New Mexico." WESTERN H Q, 13 (January 1982), 43-61.

In this prize-winning article, Culley, a history
teacher, had access to records of the Santa Fe Railroad.
Describing the emotions of the local population (to the war
and to the fact that the New Mexico National Guard had
surrendered at Bataan) and the realistic attitude of Santa
Fe Railroad officials (unwilling to counter local
sentiment), the author traces the evacuation of some 34
Japanese aliens and Japanese-Americans (U.S. citizens).
None returned to Clovis after the war. The article is
marked by its firm foundation in primary sources.

4781. Daniels, Roger. CONCENTRATION CAMPS U.S.A.: JAPANESE
        AMERICANS AND WORLD WAR II. New York: Holt, Rinehart
        and Winston, 1971. 188 pp.

Daniels examines the legal issues as well as the
sociological impact of the wartime relocation of
Japanese-Americans. His evaluations of the advisers
who suggested the policy--people like Stimson, McCloy,
General DeWitt, Earl Warren, and Tom C. Clark--are
particularly effective. The book should be included
in any examination of this controversial subject.

4782. Daniels, Roger. THE DECISION TO RELOCATE THE JAPANESE
      AMERICANS. Philadelphia, PA: J.B. Lippincott, 1975.
      150 pp.

      Daniels examines--and criticizes--the decision. It was
      not, he maintains, a military necessity. Moreover, Daniels
      questions the constitutionality of the treatment meted out
      to the Japanese-Americans.

4783. Daniels, Roger. "Decisions to Relocate the North American
      Japanese: Another Look." PAC HR, 51 (February 1982),
      71-77.

      Daniels finds that U.S. and Canadian evacuation policies
      were not unrelated. Although joint discussions did take
      place, Daniels can make no causal link to the actual
      policies adopted by each government.

4784. Daniels, Roger. THE POLITICS OF PREJUDICE. Berkeley, CA:
      University of California Press, 1978. 2nd ed. 165 pp.

      Here is a biting criticism of the decisions and policies of
      the U.S. government with regard to the Japanese-Americans.

4785. Daniels, Roger, Sandra C. Taylor, and Harry H. L. Kitano,
      eds. JAPANESE AMERICANS: FROM RELOCATION TO REDRESS.
      Salt Lake City, UT: University of Utah Press, 1986.
      216 pp.

      Most of this book is made up of papers read at a 1983
      conference in Salt Lake City. The collection represents
      one of the most complete accounts of the Japanese-American
      experience in World War II. Some of the principal
      contributers are G. K. Hirabayashi, who brought litigation
      to the Supreme Court in 1943 against the U.S. government,
      H. Kitano on psychological effects, J. J. Culley on the
      Santa Fe camp and T. Kashima on mistreatment of the
      evacuees. The editors organize the contributions into
      topical categories (e.g., Prewar, Life in Camps, Redress
      Questions, etc.) and provide a chronology of
      Japanese-American history from 1868 to 1945.

4786. Danovitch, Sylvia E. "The Past Recaptured? The
      Photographic Record of the Internment of
      Japanese-Americans." PROLOGUE, 12 (Summer 1980),
      91-103.

      The author, a professional photographer and graduate

student in history, examined 12,500 photos by the WRA (most
by Dorthea Lange) of the internment camps. She criticizes
most of the collection for making life in the camps appear
too normal, but she admits that these photos may indicate
why strikes and rebellions were rare. Pointing out that
the WRA photos provide affective information that aids
understanding, Danovitch concludes, "We committed a grave
error, but we were civilized."

4787. Davis, Daniel S. BEHIND BARBED WIRE: THE IMPRISONMENT
       OF JAPANESE AMERICANS DURING WORLD WAR II. New York:
       E.P. Dutton, 1982. 166 pp.

       Davis makes no attempt to present a balanced assessment
       of the relocation or the context within which it occurred.
       The book must be read with caution.

4788. "A Demand of History." PROGRESSIVE, 47 (AUGUST 1983), 12.

       This brief editorial calls for Americans to accept
       responsibility for the denial of the civil liberties of the
       Japanese-Americans during the war.

4789. Dembitz, Nanette. "Racial Discrimination and the Military
       Judgment: The Supreme Court's Korematsu and Endo
       Decisions." COLUMBIA LAW REV, 45 (March 1945), 175-239.

       Employing 267 footnotes, Dembitz discusses the two cases
       in which race was the sole consideration. She criticizes
       the Supreme Court's decisions in both cases and emphasizes
       the need for judicial review of the decisions and actions
       of military commanders in civilian areas.

4790. DeWitt, John. D. FINAL REPORT: JAPANESE EVACUATION FROM
       THE WEST COAST, 1942. Washington, D. C.: GPO, 1943.
       618 pp.

       Lt. Gen. DeWitt gives his assessment of the evacuation
       of Japanese-Americans and their families from the West
       Coast. He, of course, was instrumental in the decision to
       remove these people as security threats. Was it really a
       military necessity?

4791. Drinnon, Richard. "Jap Camps." INQUIRY, 4 (April 27,
       1981), 28-31.

       Charging that racism laced the Roosevelt administration,
       Drinnon finds that liberals who directed the relocation
       camps received sympathetic understanding from most civil

libertarians.

4792.   Drinnon, Richard. KINDLY KEEPER: DILLON S. MYER AND
        AMERICA'S CONCENTRATION CAMPS. Berkeley, CA:
        University of California Press, 1987.   384 pp.

        Drinnon criticizes Myer's performance as head of the
        WRA. The author points out that Myer understood little
        about the history and culture of the Japanese-Americans.

4793.   Eaton, Allen H. BEAUTY BEHIND BARBED WIRE: THE ARTS OF
        THE JAPANESE IN OUR WAR RELOCATION CAMPS. New York:
        Harper and Brothers, 1952.

        Eaton presents the work of the evacuees. The artists
        reveal a range of emotions about their situation, the war,
        and the United States.

4794.   Eisenhower, Milton. THE PRESIDENT IS CALLING. Garden
        City, NY: Doubleday, 1974.   598 pp.

        This memoir includes some material on the origins of the
        War Relocation Authority.

4795.   Embree, John F. "Dealing With Japanese-Americans." APP
        ANTHROP, 2 (January-March 1943), 37-41.

        Embree examines some behavioral patterns of the
        evacuees. He calls special attention to the role of the
        older ISSEI group.

4796.   Embree, John F. "Resistance to Freedom: An Administrative
        Problem." APP ANTHROP, 2 (September 1943), 10-14.

        Embree discusses the surprising resistance of
        Japanese-American internees against being released from the
        WRA camps.

4797.   Fairman, Charles. "The Law of Martial Rule and the
        National Emergency." HARVARD LAW REV, 55 (June 1942),
        1253-1302.

        With 193 footnotes, the author offers a stout defense
        for the government's decision to evacuate the Japanese-
        Americans. His argument turns on what he calls the
        reasonable assumption that enough disloyalty existed among
        the Japanese-Americans to justify the "inconvenience" (not
        a punishment). It may be of interest that, at the time of
        writing, Fairman was a law professor on the West Coast

(Stanford University).

4798. Fine, Sidney. "Mr. Justice Murphy and the Hirabayashi
       Case." PAC HR, 33 (May 1964), 195-209.

       Relying on Murphy's papers, Fine reports that Justice
       Frank Murphy concurred only reluctantly in the Hirabayashi
       case (which avoided judgment on the constitutionality of
       the evacuation of Japanese-Americans). Later, in the
       Korematsu case, however, Murphy decided against the
       unconstitutionality and the racism inherent in the
       evacuation policy.

4799. Fisher, Anne R. EXILE OF A RACE. Seattle, WA: F & T
       Publishers, 1965. 245 pp.

       Here is a biting indictment of the "forcible removal and
       imprisonment by the Army" of the Japanese-Americans.

4800. Fisher, Galen M. "Japanese Evacuation From the Pacific
       Coast." FE SURVEY, 11 (June 29, 1942), 145-150.

       This contemporary report is mildly favorable (or at
       least sympathetic) to the government's policy of
       relocation. Fisher feels the Four Freedoms should guide
       the implementation of the policy.

4801. Foote, Caleb. OUTCASTS!: THE STORY OF AMERICA'S TREATMENT
       OF HER JAPANESE-AMERICAN MINORITY. New York: Fellowship
       of Reconciliation, 1943. 24 pp.

       Here is a contemporary view which criticizes the
       government's policy of evacuation.

4802. Freeman, Harrop A. "GENESIS, EXODUS, and LEVITICUS:
       Genealogy, Evacuation and the Law." CORNELL LAW Q, 28
       (June 1943), 414-458.

       The evacuation can not be defended, according to the
       author. Criticizing those who want to remove "protrusions
       from the streamlined war machine," Freeman offers a
       reminder that the war is being fought, in part, to protect
       civil liberties.

4803. Friedlander, E.J. "Freedom of Press Behind Barbed Wire:
       Paul Yokota and the Jerome Relocation Center Newspaper."
       ARK H Q, 44 (Winter 1985), 303-313.

       The author, a professor of journalism, praises the

benign central administration at Jerome and the absence of
overt censorship concerning the newspaper. He also
expresses admiration for the editorial work of Yakota and
Shiramizu in presenting a thorough, balanced newspaper.

4804. Friedson, Anthony. "No More Farewells: An Interview With
       Jeanne and John Houston." BIOGRAPHY, 7 (Winter 1984),
       50-73.

       The co-authors of the "non-fiction novel" FAREWELL TO
MANZANAR wrote the book with the intention of educating the
American people about the relocation of Japanese-Americans.
Jeanne Wakatsuki (Houston) and her family suffered through
the relocation experience.

4805. Fukuhara, Henry. PORTFOLIO OF 50 SCENES OF THE RELOCATION
       CENTERS. New York: Plantin Press, 1944. 50 plates.

       The contemporary art represents a critical response to
the policy of relocating the Japanese-Americans.

4806. Gerken, Edna A. "Health Education in a War Relocation
       Project." AMER J PUBLIC HEALTH, 33 (April 1943),
       357-361.

       The author, a public health official, helped organize
community services at the Colorado River Center in Poston,
Arizona. The information she provided on health education
extinguished many groundless fears and rumors.

4807. Gesensway, Deborah and Mindy Roseman. BEYOND WORDS: IMAGES
       FROM AMERICA'S CONCENTRATION CAMPS. Ithaca, NY: Cornell
       University Press, 1987. 176 pp.

       The authors searched out survivors of the evacuation and
taped their interviews. The book centers on 75 newly
discovered art pieces by internees about life in the camps.

4808. Girdner, Audrie and Anne Loftis. THE GREAT BETRAYAL: THE
       EVACUATION OF THE JAPANESE-AMERICANS DURING WORLD WAR
       II. New York: Macmillan, 1969. 562 pp.

       Bolstering their extensive research with materials
gained from interviews and the private papers of evacuees,
the authors highlight the human dimension of this sorrowful
tale. Many stories about individuals help to give specific
information about general, impersonal policies. One
evacuee said, "If we had only one Joe DiMaggio it would
never have happened." The authors strive for objectivity

but are clearly sympathetic to the plight of the Japanese-
Americans. Their conclusion is that the whole episode
amounted to "an aberration and a warning."

4809. Grodzins, Morton. AMERICANS BETRAYED: POLITICS AND THE
      JAPANESE EVACUATION. Chicago: University of Chicago
      Press, 1949. 445 pp.

      The author, a staff member of the Japanese Evacuation
      and Relocation Study, examines the decision, the manner in
      which the decision was carried out, and the policy-making
      process which produced the decision. Pointing to a gap in
      the federal system which encourages regional interests,
      Grodzins argues that there was no high-level critical
      review of the suggestion to evacuate the Japanese-
      Americans. That suggestion, according to the author,
      stemmed from self-serving economic and political groups.
      Also, once military control is granted, Grodzins warns,
      democratic procedures dissolve, particularly the protection
      of civil liberties. For him, a dangerous constitutional
      precedent has been set. Like many works in this highly
      emotional topic, the book lacks balance.

4810. Hansen, Arthur A. "Cultural Politics in the Gila
      Relocation Center, 1942-1943." ARIZONA W, 27 (Winter
      1985), 327-362.

      NE

4811. Hansen, Arthur A. and David A. Hacker. "The Manzanar Riot:
      An Ethnic Perspective." AMERASIA J, 2 (Fall 1974),
      112-157.

      Taking issue with the standard interpretation about
      merely curious onlookers, the authors report that the
      trouble stemmed from the mounting discontent among the
      internees. With exhaustive research, the authors analyze
      the disturbance in terms of heightened ethnic
      consciousness.

4812. Hansen, Asael T. "Community Analysis at Heart Mountain."
      APP ANTHROP, 5 (Summer 1946), 15-25.

      This is the final report for the federal government on
      Heart Mountain Center in Wyoming. Hansen, who served
      almost two years as chief analyst, draws modest conclusions
      about the mixed results of the work at Heart Mountain.
      While assistance from Washington was generally supportive,
      Hansen complains that government relations with the

center's staff were decidedly cool.

4813.   Hata, Donald and Nadine Ishitani Hata.   JAPANESE-AMERICANS
         AND WORLD WAR II.   St. Louis, MO: Forum Press, 1975.   16
         pp.

         NE

4814.   Hohri, William M.   REPAIRING AMERICA: AN ACCOUNT OF THE
         MOVEMENT FOR JAPANESE-AMERICAN REDRESS.   Pullman, WA:
         Washington State University Press, 1987.

         This study traces the accelerating, ever-growing
         movement.   Despite some early setbacks, the movement seems
         to be gaining the attention--and the sympathy--of the
         nation.

4815.   Hosokawa, Bill.   JACL: IN QUEST OF JUSTICE.   New York:
         William Morrow, 1982.   383 pp.

         Relying heavily on JACL records and many interviews,
         Hosokawa, a reporter, ties the League's work to the legal
         aftermath of the wartime relocation.

4816.   Hosokawa, Bill.   NISEI: THE QUIET AMERICANS.   New York:
         William Morrow, 1970.   522 pp.

         The author studies the second generation Americans of
         Japanese descent.   His discussion of the wartime evacuation
         takes him to motives such as greed and racism.   Hosokawa, a
         reporter, had been an evacuee.

4817.   Ichioka, Yuji.   THE ISSEI: THE WORLD OF THE FIRST
         GENERATION JAPANESE IMMIGRANTS, 1885-1924.   New York:
         The Free Press, 1988.   336 pp.

         Here is an analysis of the problems and prejudices that
         met these first-generation immigrants.   Ichioka's report
         clarifies the unusual wartime evacuation policies invoked.

4818.   Iiyama, Patty.   "American Concentration Camps: Racism and
         Japanese-Americans During World War II."   INT SOCIALIST
         REV, 34 (April 1973), 24-33.

         The author is a political activist whose parents were
         interned at Topaz, Utah.   Her analytical framework hinges
         on the racism of the American people and the imperial
         economic ambitions of the American ruling class.   For her,
         the evacuation experience represents a logical outgrowth of

a consistent policy of racism--with a firm economic
base--against Asians in the United States. The use of the
atomic bomb and the war in Vietnam are other examples of
this persistent racism, according to the author. In this
pattern, she also criticizes the FBI's arrests of ISSEI
leaders and the sacrificial use of the NISSEI 442nd Combat
Team (which suffered 314% casualties over its original
strength).

4819. An Intelligence Officer. [pseud.] "The Japanese in
        America: The Problem and the Solution." HARPER'S MAG,
        185 (October 1942), 489-497.

        The author proposes a graduated system of segregation.
        The solution, he feels, lies in managing the issue on an
        individual basis rather than by large groups or by race.

4820. Irons, Peter. JUSTICE AT WAR. New York: Oxford
        University Press, 1983. 407 pp.

        Irons is a legal activist seeking to reverse criminal
        convictions of Japanese-Americans which arose from the
        wartime relocation. In fact, he is a participating
        attorney in some of these cases. Despite his strong
        conviction that a grave injustice occurred, Irons tries to
        offer a balanced presentation. His report of the various
        court cases is excellent, as is his account of the
        evolution of the decision to relocate the
        Japanese-Americans.

4821. Izumi, Kiyotaka. "The Japanese-American Evacuation of
        1942." J ASIAN AFRICAN STUD, 17 (July & October 1982),
        266-275.

        The author identifies two preconditions which made the
        evacuation possible: (1) the racial prejudice of white
        Americans and (2) the administration's conviction that the
        evacuation justified a breach of the Constitution. Izumi
        calls for more evidence to validate his theory that
        Roosevelt used the evacuation to justify the official
        reports about Japanese-American fifth-column activities in
        the attack at Pearl Harbor.

4822. Jackman, Norman R. "Collective Protest in Relocation
        Centers." AMER J SOCIOLOGY, 63 (November 1957),
        264-272.

        After examining over one hundred incidents, Jackman
        concludes that protests in the centers stemmed from the

communication process. A failure in communications (closed
channels), he says, left no arena for rational
consideration of issues. His research identifies a direct
correlation between the level of incidents and centers with
open or closed channels of communication.

4823. Japanese American Citizens League. THE CASE FOR THE NISEI.
      Salt Lake City, UT: JACL, 1945.   143 pp.

      The Japanese-American group presents a contemporary
      defense of these U.S. citizens, second-generation Japanese
      who were born in the United States.

4824. Japanese American Citizens League. THEY WORK FOR VICTORY:
      THE STORY OF JAPANESE AMERICANS AND THE WAR EFFORT.
      Salt Lake City, UT: JACL, 1945.

      Most of this spirited defense is centered on the
      Japanese-Americans in uniform.

4825. James, Thomas.   "The Education of Japanese Americans at
      Tule Lake, 1942-1946."   PAC HR, 61 (February 1987),
      25-58.

      The WRA arranged limited social services, like education
      and recreation, in all evacuation camps. Concentrating on
      Tule Lake, James points out that education became a focus
      of controversy in the camp--a camp already badly divided by
      the "loyalty" (questionnaire) issue. James shows how
      internees split over the idea of promoting "Japan"
      (privately) or the "United States" in the educational
      program. The article is marked by solid research through
      government records and interviews.

4826. James, Thomas.   EXILE WITHIN: THE SCHOOLING OF JAPANESE
      AMERICANS, 1942-1945.   Cambridge, MA: Harvard University
      Press, 1987.   212 pp.

      Using private collections, WRA records, and other
      archival materials, James, a professor of education,
      explores how the perennial conflicts of Japanese-Americans
      took on heightened meaning in the camps. Specifically, he
      examines the experiences of about 30,000 students and their
      teachers in the camps' schools. According to James,
      parents and school officials, despite many differences,
      agreed on the need to develop the youth of the camps, but
      contrary to their fears the experience solidified the
      youth and contributed to the loosening of control by the
      parents and officials. Of interest is the author's

conclusion that the students emerged from the war as one of
the better educated groups in America, prepared for the
postwar economic boom and able to find niches beyond their
reach in prewar America.

4827.   Kashima, Tetsuden. "Japanese-American Internees Return,
        1945 to 1955: Readjustment and Social Amnesia."
        PHYLON, 41 (Summer 1981), 107-115.

        The author identifies this period as one of crisis
        rather than transition. Deploring the social amnesia which
        arose during the ten years after the war, he argues that
        Japanese-Americans must be more vocal about their wartime
        relocation experience.

4828.   Kirtland, John C. THE RELOCATION AND INTERNMENT OF THE
        ALEUT PEOPLE DURING WORLD WAR II: A CASE IN LAW AND
        EQUITY FOR COMPENSATION. Anchorage, AK:
        Aleutian/Pribiloff Islands Association, 1981. 27 pp.

        Here is a sympathetic discussion of a little-known
        aspect of the relocation policy.

4829.   Kitagawa, Daisuke. ISSEI AND NISSEI: THE INTERNMENT
        YEARS. New York: Seabury Press, 1967. 174 pp.

        The author is an American Episcopal clergyman who was
        born in Japan. During his internment, Kitagawa acted not
        only as a chaplain to the internees but also as a field
        representative for his church and the government. In this
        view from within, he describes life inside a relocation
        camp. Of interest is his analysis of the changing
        attitudes of the Japanese-Americans about the United States
        and about themselves.

4830.   Kitano, Harry H.L. JAPANESE-AMERICANS: THE EVOLUTION OF A
        SUBCULTURE. Englewood Cliffs, NJ: Prentice-Hall, 1969.
        186 pp.

        Kitano traces the interethnic contact and conflict of
        the Japanese-Americans in the United States. In his
        opinion, the Japanese-Americans came to the wrong country
        and wrong state at the wrong time. Their skin color,
        religion, and ethnic heritage, all worked against them.

4831.   Kitano, Harry H.L. RACE RELATIONS. Englewood Cliffs, NJ:
        Prentice-Hall, 1985. 3d ed. 286 pp.

        Within this indictment of U.S. racism, see the material

on the relocation of Japanese-Americans during the war.

4832. Kitano, Harry H. L. and Roger Daniels. AMERICAN RACISM.
       Englewood Cliffs, NJ: Prentice-Hall, 1970.

       The authors present a critique of racist elements in
       U.S. society. They include a discussion which criticizes
       the wartime relocation of Japanese-Americans. The anti-
       Asian sentiment, they feel, is not restricted to the West
       Coast. It could happen again, according to the authors.

4833. Kodachi, Zuigaku. "Portland Assembly Center: Diary of
       Saku Tumita." OREGON H Q, 81 (Summer 1980), 149-171.

       The diary entries cover the period May 5-August 17,
       1942. Saku wrote the diary while waiting with her husband
       and two children for relocation from Portland. They
       eventually went to Minidoka, Idaho. The article includes
       excellent annotations and footnotes. Janet Cormack edited
       the article, and Jan Heikkala provided the translation.

4834. Kumamoto, Bob. "The Search for Spies: American
       Counterintelligence and the Japanese American Community,
       1931-1942." AMERASIA J, 6 (Fall 1979), 45-75.

       The author, a graduate student in history, uses archival
       records and FBI files to report on this melancholy story of
       the roundups of suspected saboteurs and spies. Most of
       those Japanese Americans arrested--Hoover said each had
       been on a list prepared before the war--were not released
       to WRA camps and remained in detention for the duration of
       the war. According to the author, the "ABC" selected
       classifications ("A" for known to be dangerous; "B" for not
       fully investigated but potentially dangerous; and "C" for
       pro-Japanese inclinations) and the evacuation of the
       general Japanese American population amounted to an assault
       on Japanese culture.

4835. Leighton, Alexander H. THE GOVERNING OF MEN: GENERAL
       PRINCIPLES AND RECOMMENDATIONS BASED ON EXPERIENCES AT A
       JAPANESE RELOCATION CAMP. Princeton, NJ: Princeton
       University Press, 1945. 404 pp.

       Leighton, director of the Bureau of Sociological
       Research, reports on the work of the social scientists,
       sponsored by the Bureau, who studied the relocation centers
       and advised the administrative staffs. Specifically,
       Leighton focuses on the Colorado River War Relocation
       Center at Poston, Arizona. His report deals with the early

disturbances that led to a strike by the evacuees. He
emphasizes the different administrative personalities
(people-centered, organization-centered, stereotype-
centered) that influenced the situation at Poston.

4836.   Libby, Justin H. "Anti-Japanese Sentiment in the Pacific
        Northwest: Senator Schwellenbach and Congressman Coffee
        Attempt to Embargo Japan, 1937-1941." MID-AMERICA, 58
        (October 1976), 167-174.

        Both politicians, Democrats from the state of
        Washington, opposed U.S. passivity in this period and
        regularly urged retaliatory legislation against Japan. For
        the most part, their efforts failed, but they helped call
        attention to Japan's behavior. The 1940 and 1941 measures
        embodied the extreme position taken by the two men in 1937.

4837.   Lind, Andrew W. HAWAII'S JAPANESE: AN EXPERIMENT IN
        DEMOCRACY. Princeton, NJ: Princeton University Press,
        1946. 264 pp.

        This study refutes the idea of fifth-column activities
        by the Japanese in Hawaii. Lind underscores the
        contemporary affirmations of local officials and national
        officials (e.g., Stimson and J.E. Hoover) about the loyalty
        of these people. According to the author, approximately
        one percent (981) of the adult Japanese population in
        Hawaii were sent to camps on the mainland. (Less than 500
        more were held on suspicion in Hawaii.)

4838.   Littell, Norman M. MY ROOSEVELT YEARS. Seattle, WA:
        University of Washington Press, 1987. 422 pp.

        Littell served as assistant attorney general in charge
        of the Lands Division (1939-1944). His diary entries
        provide an inside view on the relocation of
        Japanese-Americans, but he did not participate directly in
        it. Jonathan Dembo edited the work. See, too, some of the
        passages concerning the attack at Pearl Harbor.

4839.   Luomala, Katharine. "California Takes Back Its Japanese
        Evacuees: The Readjustment of California to the
        Japanese Evacuees." APP ANTHROP, 5 (Summer 1946),
        25-39.

        The author, who worked for WRA, examines the reactions
        in central California to the return of about sixty thousand
        evacuees. She finds that the reactions were mixed and that
        the whole issue remained plagued by stereotypes.

4840. Luomala, Katharine. "Community Analysis Outside the
           Centers--A War Relocation Experience." APP ANTHROP, 6
           (Winter 1947), 25-31.

           The author identifies some of the problems of the
       analysts working in communities outside the relocating
       centers. Most did a fine job, she says, and administrators
       needed their services.

4841. Luomala, Katharine. "Research and Records of the War
           Relocation Authority." APP ANTHROP, 7 (Winter 1948),
           23-32.

           Calling for more study--and less emotion (wartime
       hysteria)--the author hopes that the lessons of the WRA
       experience will not have to be learned by Americans one
       nationality at a time. The article includes an excellent
       description of the WRA records.

4842. McAfee, Ward M. "America's Two Japanese-American Policies
           During World War II." S CALIF Q, 69 (Summer 1987),
           151-164.

               NE

4843. McWilliams, Carey. BROTHERS UNDER THE SKIN. Boston:
           Little Brown, 1943.

           The collection strikes against wartime racism in the
       United States. See especially the article "Our Japanese
       Hostages" (pp. 147-175).

4844. McWilliams, Carey. "Moving the West Coast Japanese."
           HARPER'S MAG, 185 (September 1942), 359-369.

           The author asserts that the relocation has been
       accomplished "on time, without mishap, and with virtually
       no friction." Denying any notion of "concentration camps,"
       he feels that the relocation can be successful if the
       government treats Japanese-Americans fairly and
       race-baiters are ignored. The article provides a
       contemporary view of the relocation by a thoughtful social
       commentator.

4845. McWilliams, Carey. PREJUDICE: JAPANESE-AMERICANS: SYMBOL
           OF RACIAL INTOLERANCE. Boston: Little Brown, 1944.

           Here is a stinging indictment of the government's policy

of evacuating the Japanese-Americans.

4846.   Martin, Ralph G.   BOY FROM NEBRASKA: THE STORY OF BEN
        KUROKI.   New York: Harper, 1946.   208 pp.

        Martin reports the efforts of Ben Kuroki, of
        Japanese-American descent, to enter the Army.   Kuroki
        indicates that the prejudice he faced in the Army was
        something he never had encountered in his home state of
        Nebraska.   As an aircrew member, Kuroki flew on a total of
        nearly 60 missions.

4847.   Masumoto, Davis Mas.   COUNTRY VOICES: THE ORAL HISTORY OF A
        JAPANESE-AMERICAN FAMILY FARM COMMUNITY.   Del Ray, CA:
        Inaka Countryside Publications, 1987.   240 pp.

        Using material gained from interviews and private
        collections, Masumoto traces three generations of family
        histories (wrapped around the war years) for the
        Japanese-Americans at Del Ray, California.

4848.   Matsumoto, Toru.   BEYOND PREJUDICE: A STORY OF THE CHURCH
        AND JAPANESE AMERICANS.   New York: Friendship Press,
        1946.   145 pp.

        Here is a report on the work of Christian groups--Home
        Mission Council of North America, Foreign Missions
        Conference of North America, and Federal Council of
        Churches of Christ in America--bringing some aid to the
        Japanese-American evacuees.

4849.   Means, Florence C.   THE MOVED-OUTERS.   Boston: Houghton
        Mifflin, 1945.

        Here is a report on the children of the
        Japanese-American evacuees.

4850.   Mitson, Betty E.   "Looking Back in Anguish: Oral History of
        Japanese-American Evacuation."   ORAL HIST REV (1974),
        24-51.

        Mitson stresses the importance of oral history.   Her
        work is particularly valuable for research on the
        relocation experiences.

4851.   Modell, John.   THE ECONOMICS AND POLITICS OF RACIAL
        ACCOMMODATION: THE JAPANESE OF LOS ANGELES, 1900-1942.
        Urbana, IL: University of Illinois Press, 1977.

This broad survey includes much material on the
circumstances of Japanese-Americans just before the war.
Modell's well-researched study of this local population
indicates the extent of the sacrifices made by the total
group of West Coast evacuees.

4852.   Modell, John. "The Japanese American Family: A
         Perspective for Future Investigations." PAC HR, 37
         (February 1968), 67-81.

         Arguing that life in America posed challenges but not
overwhelming obstacles for Japanese Americans, Modell
emphasizes the key role of the family as a support base.
The article traces the shift in values for the ISSEI.

4853.   Mondello, Salvatore. "The Integration of Japanese Baptists
         in American Society." FOUNDATIONS, 20 (July-September
         1977), 254-263.

         Commenting on this successful resettlement--and the
contrast with the exclusionists and jingoists--Mondello
claims that the Baptist community on the West Coast
reflected "Christian beliefs, democratic traditions, and
cosmopolitan heritage."

4854.   Miyamoto, S. Frank. "The Forced Evacuation of the Japanese
         Minority During World War II." J SOC ISSUES, 29 (No. 2,
         1973), 11-31.

         By examining three general causes of the relocation
policy--collective disposition (antagonism towards
immigrants and the special conditions on the West Coast),
situational factors (the suspicion that all Japanese were
treacherous), and collective interaction (the main elements
which led to the policy of evacuation)--the author
concludes that after the attack at Pearl Harbor the
probability of harsh action against Japanese-Americans was
extremely high.

4855.   Myer, Dillon S. UPROOTED AMERICANS: THE JAPANESE
         AMERICANS AND THE WAR RELOCATION AUTHORITY DURING WORLD
         WAR II. Tucson, AZ: University of Arizona Press, 1971.
         360 pp.

         Myer reflects on his experience as director of the War
Relocation Authority. Calling attention to the "rampant
emotions and hysteria" of the times, Myer, nonetheless,
concludes that "in spite of mistakes the results have
generally been good." Myer makes clear his belief that

selective evacuation of certain Japanese-Americans in
military areas may have been justified but the mass
evacuations never should have been approved. Of interest
is his praise of the actions and attitudes of most of the
NISEI.

4856.   Myer, Dillon S. "The WRA Says 'Thirty.'" NEW REP, 112
             (June 25, 1945), 867-868.

         The WRA leader writes that the agency is working itself
out of business. The three years of WRA's existence, he
says, shows that the policy was bad for the country and bad
for the evacuees. Myer charges that the War Department
blocked long-standing (2 years?) plans by WRA to return the
evacuees to a normal life. He admits being surprised by
the general refusal of the evacuees to resettle on the West
Coast.

4857.   Naske, Claus-M. "The Relocation of Alaska's Japanese
             Residents." PAC NWQ, 74 (July 1983), 124-132.

         The Japanese-American population in Alaska exceeded two
hundred. Most ended up in a relocation camp in Idaho.
Naske tells this story after researching through private
papers, public documents, newspapers, and personal
interviews.

4858.   National Japanese American Student Relocation Council.
             FROM CAMP TO COLLEGE: THE STORY OF THE JAPANESE
             AMERICAN STUDENT RELOCATION. Philadelphia, PA: NJASRC,
             1945. 12 pp.

             NE

4859.   Nelson, Douglas W. HEART MOUTAIN: THE HISTORY OF AN
             AMERICAN CONCENTRATION CAMP. Madison, WI: State
             Historical Society, for the University of Wisconsin,
             1976.

         The author sharply criticizes the policy of relocation.
His general description of life at Heart Mountain is
enlivened by the discussion of the controversy over the
loyalty questionnaire.

4860.   Nicholson, Herbert V. and Margaret Wilke. COMFORT ALL WHO
             MOURN: THE LIFE STORY OF HERBERT AND MADELINE
             NICHOLSON. Fresno, CA: Bookmates International, 1982.

             Here is a warm account of assistance rendered by a

Quaker couple to a segment of the Japanese-American population.

4861. Oakie, John H. "Japanese in the United States." FE SURVEY, 11 (January 26, 1942), 23-26.

Giving key statistics and describing the conditions of the Japanese population, Oakie generally defends the treatment they are receiving. In this pre-evacuation period, Oakie quotes the Committee on Fair Play for Citizens and Aliens of Japanese Ancestry: "The American tradition of fair play has been observed."

4862. O'Brien, Robert W. THE COLLEGE NISEI. Palo Alto, CA: Pacific Books, 1949. 165 pp.

The author, a professor of sociology, writes only of those NISEI who attended college. Before the war, members of this generation, according to the author, had adjusted well to American academic life. The outbreak of the war, however, caused them anxiety about their status within the Japanese-American community. O'Brien describes their life in the relocation camps as ambivalence laced with indifference. On one hand, the NISEI worried about going stale inside the camps; on the other hand, they feared caucasian renunciation outside the camps. Upon leaving the camps to go to college, the NISEI were surprised to be well received. O'Brien makes clear that the NISEI proved their loyalty to the United States.

4863. O'Brien, Robert W. "Selective Dispersion as a Factor in the Solution of the NISEI Problem." SOCIAL FORCES, 23 (December 1944), 140-147.

In this study of the impact of American culture on the NISEI, O'Brien offers an analysis of the period 1931-1944. For the future, he offers two suggestions to Japanese-Americans: take advantage of opportunities in higher education and do not return en masse to the segregated communities.

4864. Oda, James. HEROIC STRUGGLES OF JAPANESE AMERICANS: PARTISAN FIGHTING FROM AMERICA'S CONCENTRATION CAMPS. Los Angeles, CA: Author, 1980. 277 pp.

The author--a KIBEI--was in his late twenties when the war began. Despite his anti-military feelings, he served in the armed forces. The book reveals the troubled times experienced by Oda, both in the war and in his attempts to

tell his story. He wrote parts of this book at the time
(or by 1948).

4865. Ogburn, William F., ed. AMERICAN SOCIETY IN WARTIME.
       Chicago: University of Chicago Press, 1943.

       Here is a contemporary collection that focuses on
various aspects of the home front. See especially the
essay by Robert Redfield, "The Japanese-Americans."

4866. Okamura, Raymond. "'The Great White Father': Dillon Myer
       and Internal Colonialism." AMERASIA J, 13 (No. 2,
       1986-87), 155-160.

       Here is a stinging indictment of Myer and "putrid" U.S.
racism for the massive violations of human and civil
rights.

4867. Okihiro, Gary Y. "Japanese Resistance in America's
       Concentration Camps: A Re-evaluation." AMERASIA J, 2
       (Fall 1973), 20-34.

       The author feels that historians have minimized the
importance of the underlying layer of resistance by
Japanese-Americans to white control. His research includes
memoirs and unpublished (or unfamiliar) sources.

4868. Okimoto, Daniel. AMERICAN IN DISGUISE. New York: John
       Weatherhill, 1971.

       Here is a personal account of the prejudice and harsh
policies inflicted upon the Japanese-Americans.

4869. Okubo, Mine. CITIZEN 13660. New York: Columbia
       University Press, 1946. 209 pp.

       Okubo describes her disturbing experiences as a young
Japanese-American evacuee.

4870. Opler, Marvin K. "A 'Sumo' Tournament at Lake Tule
       Center." AMER ANTHROP, 47 (January-March 1945),
       134-139.

       Here is a detailed description of this one part of
Japanese culture. The event took place June 10, 1944.

4871. Osaka, Mary Reiko. "Japanese Americans and Central
       European Jews: A Comparison of Post-War Reparation
       Problems." HASTINGS INTL COMP LAW REV, 5 (Fall 1981),

211-234.

Osaka seems to align these two cases of "racially-based
deprivation of liberty." Her narrative emphasizes one
overwhelming similarity about the wrongs committed: the
basis for redress should be on moral grounds and not depend
on legal obligations. The United States government, she
says, should act accordingly and provide reparations to the
Japanese Americans.

4872.   Pauley, Edwin W.   REPORT ON THE JAPANESE REPARATIONS TO THE
        PRESIDENT OF THE UNITED STATES, NOVEMBER 1945-APRIL
        1946. Washington, D.C.: GPO, 1946. 271 pp.

        Ambassador Pauley served as Truman's personal
representative on reparations. Calling for verification of
the information provided by Japan, he argues that
reparations are necessary, especially from Japan's
industrial resources, in order to eliminate the war-making
potential of the Japanese. A lengthy list of data on
Japanese industries and assets is appended. Of interest is
Pauley's recommendation against "any program of recurring
reparations over a term of years" as self-defeating.

4873.   Polner, Murray. "Wartime Relocation: A Tangible Gesture:
        Compensation for the Japanese." COMMONWEAL, 108
        (October 23, 1981), 581-583.

        Here is an argument for some "tangible gesture" to help
rectify the mistaken policy of wartime relocation.

4874.   "The Problem of Student Nurses of Japanese Ancestry." AMER
        J NURSING, 43 (October 1943), 895-896.

        This contemporary report calls for careful study to
solve the problem of training Japanese-American student
nurses. Only about twenty nursing schools accept students
of Japanese ancestry, and very few (84 of 371) such
applicants have been placed, despite the efforts of the War
Relocation Authority and the National Nursing Council.

4875.   Provinse, John H. and Solon T. Kimball. "Building New
        Communities During War Time." AMER SOC REV, 11 (August
        1946), 396-410.

        Provinse (Dept. of Interior) and Kimball (sociology
professor) examine external and internal pressures on the
development of evacuee communities. Specifically, the
authors examine two key issues: (1) the absence of an

economic base and (2) dependence on bureaucracy and
political maneuverings. Leonard Bloom provides some
helpful concluding observations.

4876. Renne, Lois O. OUR DAY OF EMPIRE: WAR AND THE EXILE OF
      JAPANESE AMERICANS. Glasgow: Strickland Press, 1954.
      24 pp.

      NE

4877. Rostow, Eugene V. "The Japanese-American Cases -- A
      Disaster." YALE LAW J, 54 (June 1945), 489-533.

      Here is a severe criticism of the evacuation policy
      ("hasty, unnecessary and mistaken"). In what Rostow calls
      a terrible precedent, he points out that the courts for the
      first time seriously weakened a basic civil right, habeus
      corpus.

4878. Rostow, Eugene. "Our Worst Wartime Mistake." HARPER'S
      MAG, 191 (September 1945), 193-201.

      Rostow excoriates the treatment of Japanese-Americans.
      Calling the policy a "tragic and dangerous mistake" and a
      terrible precedent, Rostow argues that the Supreme Court
      should reverse the policy and provide for a generous
      financial indemnity.

4879. Sawada, Mitziko. "After the Camps: Seabrook Farms, New
      Jersey, and the Resettlement of Japanese Americans,
      1944-47." AMERASIA J, 13 (No. 2, 1986-87), 117-136.

      This article examines Seabrook Farm's most prosperous
      years, when Japanese-Americans were recruited from what the
      author calls concentration camps to meet a critical labor
      shortage. Sawada discusses the impact of 2,000 Japanese-
      Americans brought to southern New Jersey. Although many
      volunteered to stay there after the war, Sawada maintains
      that these decisions merely reflected the limited options
      available to the Japanese-Americans.

4880. Schlenker, Gerald. "The Internment of the Japanese of San
      Diego County During the Second World War." J SAN DIEGO
      HIST, 18 (No. 1, 1972), 1-9.

      NE

4881. Schwartz, Harvey. "A Union Combats Racism: The ILWU's
      Japanese-American 'Stockton Incident' of 1945." S CAL

Q, 62 (Summer 1980), 161-176.

Despite a long-held reputation for tolerance and non-discrimination, Local 6 (Stockton) of the International Longshoremen's and Warehousemen's Union, in May 1945, refused to work with Japanese-Americans who were recently released from a WRA camp. Strong pressure from the Union leadership eventually forced Local 6 to change its policy of resistance.

4882. Sheridan, Peter B. "Should Compensation Be Given to Japanese-Americans Relocated During World War II?" CONG RES SERV REV, 5 (March 1984), 11-13.

In the aftermath of the 1983 congressional report PERSONAL JUSTICE DENIED, Sheridan surveys the arguments of both sides on the question of compensation.

4883. Shibutani, Tamotsu. THE DERELICTS OF COMPANY K. Berkeley, CA: University of California Press, 1978. 455 pp.

One unit did not uphold the high standards of NISEI conduct during the war. Company K never entered a combat zone and had a poor record of insubordination, absenteeism, and internal violence. The author, a sociologist, goes behind the reputation to tell the story from the point of view of the participants. According to Shibutani, the soldiers in Company K felt that their interests were not being served. The book is a long-delayed publication of field notes made by the author in 1947. See the glossary of slang, pidgin, and other unusual forms of communication.

4884. Shimada, Noriko. "The Resettlement Process of the Japanese-Americans, 1942-1952." AMER REV (Tokyo), 19 (1985), 236-237.

NE

4885. Sims, Peter C. "'A Fearless, Patriotic, Clean-Cut Stand': Idaho's Governor Clark and Japanese-American Relocation in World War II." PAC NWQ, 70 (April 1979), 75-81.

Gov. Chase Clark advocated "detention" and "armed guards" for the Japanese-Americans. Sims, examining private papers, finds no evidence Clark took this popular stand for political gain.

4886. Sims, Robert C. "The Japanese-American Experience in Idaho." IDAHO YESTERDAYS, 22 (January 1978), 2-10.

NE

4887.   Slackman, Michael. "The Orange Race: George S. Patton
        Jr.'s Japanese-American Hostage Plan." BIOGRAPHY, 7
        (Winter 1984), 1-49.

        As chief of Army Intelligence in Hawaii (1935-37),
        Patton devised a plan in the event of war with Japan to
        make hostages of over one hundred Japanese-Americans and
        Japanese aliens. Slackman discovered the plan, which
        reveals Patton's prejudices and political naivete, in the
        National Archives. The author appends the full text of the
        plan, which lists the names and occupations of the proposed
        hostages.

4888.   Smith, Bradford. AMERICANS FROM JAPAN. Philadelphia, PA:
        J.B. Lippincott, 1948. 409 pp.

        NE

4889.   Smith, Cornelius C., Jr. "A Hell of a Christmas." USNIP,
        94 (December 1968), 63-71.

        Here is the journal/diary of a Marine at Pearl Harbor
        during December 1941. While worrying about the loyalty of
        Japanese-Americans, Smith participated in the search of
        Monana Canyon for spies.

4890.   Smith, Elmer R. "The Japanese in Utah." UTAH HUMANITIES
        R, Pt. I: 2 (April 1948), 129-144; Pt. II: 2 (July
        1948), 208-230.

        Smith deals with the psychological-sociological-cultural
        influences in the adjustments of Japanese and non-Japanese
        in Utah to the relocation. Although Smith states that the
        history of Utah is one of toleration and integration, he
        notes that discrimination--primarily economic, not social--
        does still exist in Utah.

4891.   Smith, Elmer R. "Resettlement of Japanese-Americans." FE
        SURVEY (May 18, 1949), 117-118.

        The author was a community analyst for WRA. The article
        describes the difficulties of postwar resettlement, but the
        author concludes that most Americans are indifferent to the
        return of the Japanese-Americans.

4892.   Smith, Geoffrey S. "Doing Justice: Relocation and Equity in Public Policy." PUBLIC HIST, 6 (Summer 1984), 83-88.

Here is a historiographical appraisal of the debate
about the evacuation of Japanese-Americans. The author
accepts the characterization of a "grave injustice" done,
and he takes particular issue with the continuing defense
of the policy by John McCloy.

4893.   Spicer, Edward H., Asael T. Hansen, Katherine Luomala, and
        Marvin K. Opler. IMPOUNDED PEOPLE: JAPANESE-AMERICANS
        IN THE RELOCATION CENTERS. Tucson, AZ: University of
        Arizona Press, 1969. 342 pp.

        The authors served as community analysts for WRA. All
        four are anthropologists with professional interest in
        planned, administrated communities. This edition is a
        reprint, with little change, of the 1946 report to WRA.
        The report is divided into four sections: "Moving In,"
        "Being Sorted," "Settling Down," and "Getting Out." The
        experts conclude, "The centers were incapable of being
        anything except undesirable places in which to live." From
        the outset, according to the authors, the top WRA officials
        viewed the relocation camps as places to be eliminated.

4894.   Spicer, Edward H. "The Use of Social Scientists By the War
        Relocation Authority." APP ANTHROP, 5 (Spring 1946),
        16-36.

        Here is a report by a social scientist who served on the
        staff of Alexander H. Leighton at the Colorado River Center
        in Poston, Arizona. Spicer explains the functions and the
        potential value (not always realized) of community
        analysis.

4895.   Spickard, Paul R. "Injustice Compounded: Amerasians and
        Non-Japanese-Americans in World War II Concentration
        Camps." J ETHNIC HIST, 5 (Spring 1986), 5-22.

        Using largely unpublished sources, Spickard focuses on
        the spouses of Japanese-Americans and the children of mixed
        parentage who were sent to the camps. Despite pressure
        from Dillon Myer and Eleanor Roosevelt to make the policy
        more liberal, the author cites bureaucratic bungling,
        twisted racism, and petty cruelty in the treatment of these
        internees. Although the option to leave the camps became
        available in 1943, many chose to stay (some out of fear of
        encountering hostility from fellow Americans).

4895a. Spickard, Paul R. "The Nisei Assume Power: The Japanese

American Citizens League, 1941-1942." PAC HR, 52 (May 1983), 147-174.

The author, a historian, argues that NISEI leadership was replacing the ISSEI before the war. Tracing some differences between the two generations, Spickard describes how the emerging NISEI took advantage of opportunities presented in 1941-1942.

4896.   Sprague, Claire D. "Till You Come Back." PAC HISTORIAN, 24 (Summer 1980), 192-195.

The author taught at a grammar school in San Joaquin Valley. Eighty (Japanese-American) students in the school were relocated, and their letters to Sprague describe life in the assembly centers. Perhaps not surprisingly, none of these grammar-school students questioned the evacuation policy, but neither is there criticism of living conditions at the centers.

4897.   Stang, Alan. "Relocation Guilt Trip." AMER OPINION, Pt. I: 26 (February 1983), 41-54; Pt. II: 26 (March 1983), 43-54.

Americans love to feel guilty, says Stang, who denounces the "crippling delusions" of American liberals. Particularly annoyed by what he calls the lies of present-day "revolutionaries and freeloaders," Stang says that he started his research believing that the relocation had been an evil experience. His findings led him to a contrary conclusion, and now Stang is crusading against the "myths" of the relocation.

4898.   Stebbins, Robert A. "Formalization: Notes on a Theory of the Rise and Change of Social Norms." INTL J CONTEMP SOCIAL, 11 (2/3, 1974), 105-119.

NE

4899.   Sue, Stanley and Harry H.L. Kitano. "Stereotypes as a Measure of Success." J SOC ISSUES, 29 (No. 2, 1973), 83-98.

The authors review the history of stereotypical thinking in the United States about Japanese-and Chinese-Americans. The war reversed the positive trends of the Twentieth Century up to 1941, but today, according to the authors, those groups carry highly successful images.

4900. Suzuki, Lester E. MINISTRY IN THE ASSEMBLY AND RELOCATION
          CENTERS OF WORLD WAR II. Berkeley, CA: Yardbird
          Publishing, 1979.

          Here is a detailed listing of the religious support
       provided for the Japanese-American evacuees.

4901. Suzuki, Peter T. "Anthropologists in the Wartime Camps for
          Japanese Americans: A Documentary Study." DIALECTICAL
          ANTHROP, 6 (August 1981), 23-60.

          The author, a wartime internee, mounts a devastating
       attack against the WRA anthropologists. Drawing on
       extensive research in the National Archives, Suzuki
       maintains that the anthropologists were too preoccupied
       with policy analysis instead of cultural studies.

4902. Suzuki, Peter T. "A Retrospective Analysis of a Wartime
          National Character Study." DIALECTICAL ANTHROP, 5 (May
          1980), 33-46.

          Criticizing wartime national character studies by
       anthropologists (especially Gorer, LaBarre and Benedict),
       Suzuki dismisses what he calls "anthropology in the service
       of ideology" and lambasts an intellectually inadequate
       attempt to discredit the persecuted Japanese internees.

4903. Tajiri, Larry. "Democracy Corrects Its Own Mistakes."
          ASIA & AMERICAS, 43 (April 1943), 213-216.

          The author, editor of the JACL's PACIFIC CITIZEN, argues
       with sincerity that the United States government in the
       midst of the war was correcting its mistake of evacuating
       the Japanese-Americans. Of interest is his suggestion that
       the Manzanar incident showed both the existence of an
       Axis-minded minority in the camp and the active promotion
       of democracy by most of the residents.

4904. Tanaka, Richard K. AMERICA ON TRIAL. New York: Carlton
          Press, 1987. 176 pp.

          Tanaka issues a bitter critique of the evacuation policy
       imposed upon Japanese-Americans.

4905. Tani, Henry. "The Nisei Since Pearl Harbor." PAC
          SPECTATOR, 1 (Spring 1947), 203-213.

          Hoping that the unhappy--and expensive ($250 million)
       --experience of relocation could be the prelude to a better

day, Tani finds that the resettlement process is going
reasonably well. Many Japanese-Americans are not only
settling in the Midwest and the East but also finding jobs
commensurate with their education and training.

4906.   Taylor, Sandra C. "The Federal Reserve Bank and the
        Relocation of the Japanese in 1942." PUBLIC HIST, 5
        (Winter 1983), 9-30.

        Federal Reserve field agents tried to assist the
        evacuees in disposing of their property, but Taylor finds
        fault with some of their procedures. Drawing on interviews
        and solid archival research, the author criticizes the
        Federal Reserve policies as "hastily devised,
        ill-conceived, and procedurally sloppy."

4907.   Taylor, Sandra C. "Japanese Americans and Keetley Farms:
        Utah's Relocation Camp." UTAH HQ, 54 (Fall 1986),
        328-344.

        The author describes the success of the Keetly
        settlement as a voluntary relocation site (in the vicinity
        of Camp Topaz). Highlighting the key roles of Fred Wada
        and Major George Fisher, Taylor shows how the
        self-contained Japanese community gained gradual
        acceptance. At war's end, she reports, about 67% of the
        Japanese at Keetley returned to the West Coast.

4908.   tenBroek, Jacobus, Edward N. Barnhart, and Floyd W. Matson.
        PREJUDICE, WAR AND THE CONSTITUTION: CAUSES AND
        CONSEQUENCES OF THE EVACUATION OF THE JAPANESE AMERICANS
        IN WORLD WAR II. Berkeley, CA: University of
        California Press, 1954. 408 pp.

        This study is part of a project started in early 1942 by
        Charles Aiken and Dorothy Thomas. The book explores racial
        prejudice on the United States, particularly anti-Asian
        sentiment on the West Coast--its historical origins,
        political characteristics and legal implications. The
        authors deny that any "military necessity" required the
        relocation of Japanese-Americans, but, they maintain, the
        government's decision arose out of "folly, not of knavery."
        Gen. DeWitt, for example, acted out of false beliefs,
        according to the authors. Arguing that the perceived
        requirements of total war permitted the erosion of
        constitutional safeguards, the authors conclude that the
        evacuation was "a great and evil blotch" on U.S. history.

4909.   Thomas, Norman. "Dark Day for Liberals." CHRISTIAN CENT,

59 (July 29, 1942), 929-931.

Thomas lodges an eloquent complaint against the
trespassing of the civil liberties of Japanese-Americans by
the U.S. government.

4910. Thomas, Norman. DEMOCRACY AND JAPANESE-AMERICANS. New
        York: Post War World Council, 1942.

Thomas criticizes the prejudice and unconstitutional
behavior that the American people and their government
visited upon the Japanese-Americans.

4911. Thomas, Dorothy, Charles Kinchi, and James Sakoda. THE
        SALVAGE. Berkeley, CA: University of California Press.
        1952. 637 pp.

In this short-term study, the authors argue that the
social status of the Japanese-Americans, at least
temporarily, improved through the resettlement process. Of
interest is their study of the NISEI who resisted pressures
to renounce their U.S. citizenship and left the camps
before the war's end to resettle in non-coastal U.S.
regions. The volume is part of a major contemporary
sociological study of the evacuation which Thomas helped
direct.

4912. Thomas, Dorothy and Richard S. Nishimoto. THE SPOILAGE.
        Berkeley, CA: University of California Press, 1946.
        388 pp.

The origins of this ambitious study began in 1942. The
premise of this major effort centered on an
interdisciplinary approach which included sociology, social
anthropology, political science, social psychology, and
economics. The research team made a close study of three
relocation centers and visited five of the other seven
centers. Their reference to "spoilage" is to the short-run
view of the effects of evacuation and detention. Of
interest is the study of the steps whereby some NISEI in
the centers renounced their U.S. citizenship. Also, the
authors carefully set forth the reactions of the
Japanese-American evacuees.

4913. Thomas, Dorothy Swaine. "Some Social Aspects of Japanese
        American Demography." PROC AMER PHILOS SOC, 94 (October
        1950), 459-480.

The noted sociologist analyzes immigration of Japanese

to the United States during the Twentieth Century, the WRA, and the resettlement. Of interest is her report that "detention" had originally been seen as a transitory phase between evacuation and resettlement, but the WRA shifted to planning a way of life for the Japanese-Americans behind barbed wire.

4914.   Trager, James G. "Haunting Echoes of the Last Round-Up: '9066' Revisited." PERSPECTIVES, 12 (Summer 1980), 8-15.

Trager reviews the human and financial loss to the Japanese-American community as a result of the wartime relocations and detentions.

4915.   Uchida, Yoshiko. "Topaz, City of Dust." UTAH H Q, 48 (Summer 1980), 234-243.

Ms. Uchida lived for eight months in the Japanese resettlement camp in the Sevier Desert (Topaz, UT). Her article provides a vivid account of daily life in the camp.

4916.   United States. Commission on Wartime Relocation and Internment of Civilians. PERSONAL JUSTICE DENIED. Washington, D.C.: GPO, 1982. 467 pp.

During the second half of 1981, the commission conducted hearings, which gathered testimony from 750 witnesses, and an extensive staff research effort. The group concluded that Executive Order 9066 was shaped not on military necessity (as alleged) but on more venal matters, such as race prejudice, war hysteria, poor political leadership, and widespread ignorance about Japanese-Americans. Although the study rejects the use of the term "concentration camps," the commission argues that a "grave injustice" had been committed. See, too, the discussion (criticism) of the detention of the Aleuts in southeast Alaskan camps. Of special interest is the outraged reaction of John J. McCloy, who continues to defend the evacuation policy.

4917.   United States Commission on Wartime Relocation-Internment of Civilians. "Right of Passage: The Commission's Hearings 1981." AMERASIA J, 8 (Fall/Winter 1981), 55-105.

Here is a collection of selected testimony from the commission's hearings during August 1984 in Los Angeles and San Francisco. According to the editorial preface, the

selections "demonstrate overwhelmingly" the "massive
injustice" of the evacuation. See especially the poem
"Breaking Silences" by Janice Mirikitani.

4918.   United States. Congress. House of Representatives.
Committee on the Judiciary. JAPANESE-AMERICAN
EVALUATION CLAIMS (HEARINGS). Washington, D.C.: GPO,
1956.

These hearings uncovered a broad division among the
American people about the justice of the wartime
evacuation. The number of critics seems to be on the rise.
The claims put forward indicate some dimensions of the
hardships inflicted by Executive Order 9066.

4919.   United States. Department of the Army. Western Defense
Command and Fourth Army. FINAL REPORT: JAPANESE
EVACUATION FROM THE WEST COAST, 1942. Washington,
D.C.: GPO, 1943.

Apparently, as far as the Western Defense Command was
concerned, the completion of the actual evacuations marked
the end of the exercise. Here is the offical version of
the forced withdrawals from the West Coast.

4920.   United States. Department of the Interior. COMMUNITY
GOVERNMENT IN WAR RELOCATION CENTERS. Washington, D.C.:
GPO.

NE

4921.   United States. Department of the Interior. PEOPLE IN
MOTION: THE POST WAR ADJUSTMENT OF THE EVACUATED
JAPANESE-AMERICANS. Washington, D.C.: GPO, 1947.

NE

4922.   United States. Department of the Interior. WRA--A STORY
OF HUMAN CONSERVATION. Washington, D.C.: GPO.

NE

4923.   United States. War Relocation Authority, ADMINISTRATIVE
HIGHLIGHTS OF THE WRA PROGRAM. Washington, D.C.: GPO,
1946. 82 pp.

Here is an embellished chronology which summarizes the
major points of the WRA wartime performance.

4924. United States, War Relocation Authority. THE EVACUATED
      PEOPLE: A QUANTITATIVE DESCRIPTION. Washington, D.C.:
      GPO, 1946. 200 pp.

      Here is a description, based on official statistics, of
      the evacuated people, including information on some Aleuts
      as well as the Japanese-Americans.

4925. United States. War Relocation Authority. NISEI IN
      UNIFORM. Washington, D.C.: GPO, 1944. 24 pp.

      Here is a pictorial presentation used by WRA for
      propaganda purposes.

4926. United States. War Relocation Authority. WRA: A STORY OF
      HUMAN CONSERVATION. Washington, D.C.: GPO, 1946. 212
      pp.

      This official report presents a stout defense of WRA
      goals and activities.

4927. Van Horne, Winston A., ed. ETHNICITY AND WAR. Milwaukee,
      WI: University of Milwaukee System, 1984. 172 pp.

      See especially in this interesting collection the
      article by Lane Ryo Hirabayashi and James A. Hirabayashi,
      "A Reconsideration of the United States Military's Role in
      the Violation of Japanese-American Citizenship Rights."

4928. Walls, Thomas K. THE JAPANESE TEXANS. Austin, TX:
      University of Texas Press, 1987. 354 pp.

      Here is an economic-social history of Japanese-Americans
      living in Texas that focuses on the World War II era.
      Walls uses private papers, contemporary newspapers, and
      interviews in this popular account. Of interest is his
      description of the internment camps in Texas during the war
      for Japanese-Americans, Japanese-Latin Americans, and
      German-Americans.

4929. "War Relocation Projects." AMER J NURSING, 43 (January
      1943), 61-63.

      This contemporary account traces the problems in
      establishing adequate nursing staffs at the relocation
      centers.

4930. Wax, Rosalie Hankey. DOING FIELDWORK: WARNINGS AND
      ADVICE. Chicago: University of Chicago Press. 1971.

395 pp.

Wax gives a personal account of her work at Tule Lake
with the evacuation and resettlement study directed by
Dorothy S. Thomas. The author frankly admits her mistakes
and naivete as a field researcher. First, Wax says, she
too zealously acted as defender of the oppressed; then,
she swung to an opposite extreme and became a staunch
"antifanatic." Eventually, Wax left the Tule Lake camp and
the WRA project.

4931. Wax, Rosalie H. "In and Out of the Tule Lake Segregation
Center: Japanese Internment in the West, 1942-1945."
MONTANA, 37 (Spring 1987), 12-25.

NE

4932. Weglyn, Michi and Betty F. Mitson, eds. VALIANT ODYSSEY:
HERBERT NICHOLSON IN AND OUT OF AMERICA'S CONCENTRATION
CAMPS. Upland, CA: Bruhn's Printing, 1978.

NE

4933. White, G. Edward. "The Unacknowledged Lesson: Earl Warren
and the Japanese Relocation Controversy." VA Q REV, 55
(Autumn 1979), 613-629.

White was a law clerk for Warren during the time (1971)
the Chief Justice wrote his memoirs. According to White,
during the war Warren not only held stereotyped views of
Asians but also voiced strong concerns about civil defense.
Although Warren strongly supported the relocation of
American-Japanese, he acknowledged regret for doing so in
his memoirs (published posthumously in 1977).

4934. Wilson, Robert A. and Bill Hosokawa. EAST TO AMERICA. New
York: William Morrow, 1980. 351 pp.

Here is a history of the Japanese in the United States.
See especially the description of the wartime evacuation.

4935. Wollenberg, Charles. "Schools Behind Barbed Wire." CALIF
H Q, 55 (Fall 1976), 210-217.

Based largely on published sources, Wollenberg describes
the public schools set up by the War Relocation Authority.
Because California Att. Gen. Earl Warren did not officially
recognize them, the schools came under federal control.
Instruction purposefully centered on "American ideals,

institutions, and practices." With well over twenty-five
thousand total students, the schools, according to
Wollenberg, produced graduates who seemed to assimilate
readily to American society outside WRA control.

4936. Yatsushiro, Toshio, Iwao Oshino, and Yoshiharu Matsumoto.
      "The Japanese-American Looks at Resettlement." PUB OPIN
      Q, 8 (Summer 1944), 188-201.

      The authors, trained social scientists working with OWI,
      survey Japanese-Americans at the Poston Relocation Center
      in Arizona. Uncovering mixed views about any plan for
      resettlement (especially about assimilating through
      dispersal in the United States), the authors argue that the
      resettlement process presents a test for the basic
      principles of American democracy and must be well thought
      out--unlike the hasty evacuation.

4937. Zeller, William D. AN EDUCATIONAL DRAMA: THE EDUCATIONAL
      PROGRAM PROVIDED THE JAPANESE-AMERICANS DURING THE
      RELOCATION PERIOD, 1942-1945. New York: American Press,
      1969.

          NE

VI.G.1.a.i. PERSONAL ACCOUNTS

4938. Blicksilver, Edith. "The Japanese-American Woman, the
      Second World War, and the Relocation Camp Experience."
      WOMEN STUDIES INT FORUM, 5 (No. 3-4, 1982), 351-353.

      The article centers on the poem "Lullabye" by Janice
      Mirikitani who, thirty years later, challenges her
      Japanese-American mother for docily entering a relocation
      camp.

4939. Omitted.

4940. Embrey, Sue Kunitomi et al. MANZANAR MARTYR: AN INTERVIEW
      WITH HARRY Y. VENO. Fullerton, CA: Oral History
      Porgram, California State University, 1986. 225 pp.

      Here is a first-hand description of life--and sorrow--in
      the evacuation camp. Time has not diminished the pain.

4941. Eschmann, Ron. "Minidoka: Christmas in Confinement."
       AIRMAN, 30 (December 1986), 34-36.

       This article is based on interviews with George
       Yashihara, a 9-year old resident of the Minidoka, Idaho
       Relocation Center and presently chief of personnel for
       Pacific Information Systems Division at Hickam AFB, Hawaii.
       There are detailed descriptions of the physical layout of
       the camp and the grim daily routine for the internees.
       Yashihara and his family lost their land (a 38-acre farm in
       Oregon) and some personal belongings.

4942. Hansen, Arthur A. and Betty E. Mitson, eds. VOICES LONG
       SILENT. Fullerton, CA: California State University
       Press, 1974. 216 pp.

       The collection is taken from the Fullerton Oral History
       program. Japanese-Americans describe their experiences as
       wartime internees.

4943. Ishigo, Estelle. LONE HEART MOUNTAIN. Los Angeles, CA:
       Anderson, Ritchie and Simon, 1972. 104 pp.

       Here is a personal reflection on life at the Heart
       Mountain camp in Wyoming for Japanese-American evacuees.

4944. Maeda, Laura. "Life at Minidoka: A Personal History of
       the Japanese-American Relocation." PAC HISTORIAN, 20
       (Winter 1976), 379-387.

       The author found life at the relocation camp in Idaho
       much different from her home in Portland, Oregon. From her
       writing it is clear that the bitter experience of
       relocation still lives inside of her.

4945. Masaoka, Mike Masaru with Bill Hosokawa. THEY CALL ME
       MOSES MASAOKA: AN AMERICAN SAGA. New York: William
       Morrow, 1987. 383 pp.

       Masaoka, an activist with the JACL, tells of the wartime
       relocation and JACL activities. Of interest is the report
       on JACL's work after the war in seeking to remove
       immigration restrictions against Asians and to ease
       naturalization requirements.

4946. Modell, John, ed. THE KIKUCHI DIARY: CHRONICLE FROM AN
       AMERICAN CONCENTRATION CAMP. Urbana, IL: University of
       Illinois Press, 1973. 258 pp.

When the war began, Charles Kikuchi was a twenty-six
year-old graduate student in social welfare at the
University of California. His diary covers the period of
December 7, 1941 - September 1942. The entries reveal the
breaking down of traditional Japanese ways inside the
relocation camp (Gila River, Arizona), especially between
the children (NISEI) and the older generation (ISSEI).
Modell maintains a balance between contemporary official
views of the relocation and the critical attitude of
today's perspective. Of interest is Kikuchi's explanation
of the role of the associated farmers in California, a
group which actively promoted the policy of relocation.
Also, Modell describes the NISEI characteristic of DAI-KON
ASHII (legs shaped like Japanese white radishes) which
became part of the cruel stereotype (e.g., buck teeth and
glasses) of Japanese people.

4947.   Ochikubo, Clark. "My Grandfather and the Relocation."
        SENIOR SCHOLASTIC, 113 (May 15, 1981), 8-10.

Here is a prize-winning essay by a California high
school senior about the harsh experiences of Dr. George
Ochikubo and his family. Based on the dentist's oral
history, the account is limited to only his first-hand
knowledge of the evacuation experience.

4948.   Okamura, Raymond Y. "The American Concentration Camps: A
        Cover-Up Through Euphemistic Terminology." J ETHNIC
        STUD, 10 (Fall 1982), 95-109.

Severely criticizing the polite nomenclature of
"evacuation-relocation," Okamura states that the literature
of the incarceration of Japanese-Americans is flawed by
such euphemisms. The author spent three years at the Gila
River camp in Arizona, and he remains puzzled that the
euphemistic terminology persists to the present day.

4949.   Sone, Monica I. NISEI DAUGHTER. Boston: Little, Brown,
        1953.   238 pp.

Here is an autobiographical account which portrays the
dislocation and the havoc visited upon Japanese-Americans
by the evacuation.

4950.   Takashima, Shizuye. A CHILD IN PRISON CAMP. New York:
        William Morrow, 1974.   63 pp.

This personal account, which first appeared in 1971

(Plattsburg, NY: Tundra Books), tells of a
Japanese-Canadian girl's experiences with her family at the
internment camp in New Denver, B.C. They remained there
for three years.

4951. Tateishi, John. AND JUSTICE FOR ALL: AN ORAL HISTORY OF
      THE JAPANESE AMERICAN DETENTION CAMPS. New York:
      Random House, 1984. 260 pp.

      The author, an evacuee at age 3, is a professor of
      literature and National Redress Director of the Japanese
      American Citizens League. His narrative, based on recorded
      interviews with 30 evacuees, underlines the human, deeply
      personal terms of what he calls the "false imprisonment."
      The stories come from most of the camps as well as the
      NISEI unit in Europe (442d Regimental Combat Team). There
      is nothing, however, on the Military Intelligence Service
      in the Pacific Theater. The book lacks an index and a
      bibliography.

4952. Tsuchida, William Shinji. WEAR IT PROUDLY. Berkeley, CA:
      University of California Press, 1947. 147 pp.

      Here are the letters written by a NISEI soldier--a
      medical aid--to his family between September 1944 and July
      1945. Despite the prejudice and mistreatment endured by
      Japanese-Americans, the themes of pride and patriotism
      surface in this correspondence.

4953. Uchida Yoshiko. DESERT EXILE: THE UPROOTING OF A JAPANESE
      AMERICAN FAMILY. Seattle, WA: University of Washington
      Press, 1982. 154 pp.

      The author was a student at the University of California
      when the war started. She and her family were evacuated
      from their California home and eventually became internees
      at Camp Topaz in Utah's Sevier Desert. The book is
      especially effective in describing the daily life and
      challenges of the internees: the weather and bureaucrats
      and frustration that had to be endured. Accepted at Smith
      College in 1943, Uchida left Topaz in 1943. Of interest is
      her report on the confusion and the humiliation of the
      family's evacuation--burning personal papers, neighbors
      taking flowers from the garden, and her father being
      detained for five months before rejoining the family.

4954. Weglyn, Michi. YEARS OF INFAMY: THE UNTOLD STORY OF
      AMERICA'S CONCENTRATION CAMPS. New York: William
      Morrow, 1976. 351 pp.

In this stark report, the author, a teen-aged evacuee,
combines research from government documents with her
wartime experience to describe the physical and
psychological ordeal of the evacuation process. Her
narrative incorporates some frank assessments about
prominent figures. U.S. Attorney General Biddle, for
example, is portrayed as not being forceful enough to
oppose the evacuation. Weglyn praises the work of Karl P.
Bendetson in building a legal case in defense of the
Japanese-Americans. See, too, her account of the prewar
report on Japanese-American loyalty which Curtis B. Munson
submitted to the State Department.

4955. Yamashita, Shonin. IT HAD TO BE SO. San Diego, CA:
        Author, 1976. 39 l.

        The author describes the personal ordeal of evacuation.
        Of interest is the view expressed that, despite the
        difficulties of the experience, the Japanese-Americans may
        have been saved even more trouble by being evacuated. In
        arriving at this unorthodox view, Yamashita feels that the
        mixture of war hysteria and the already existing racial
        prejudice on the West Coast would have meant disaster for
        the Japanese-Americans.

VI.G.1.a.ii. CONDITIONS IN HAWAII

4956. Anthony, J. Garner. HAWAII UNDER ARMY RULE. Honolulu, HI:
        University of Hawaii Press, 1975. 203 pp.

        Here is a well-researched, well-written account of
        martial law during the war. See especially the material on
        the treatment of Japanese and Japanese-Americans--a group
        that seemed to fare better under the military than did
        their counterparts on the mainland. The author served as
        attorney general in Hawaii during the war.

4957. Omitted.

4958. Horlings, Albert. "Hawaii's 150,000 Japanese." NATION, 155
        (July 25, 1942), 69-71.

        This contemporary account criticizes American policy for
        gambling that the Japanese population in Hawaii is loyal to
        the United States. The author calls for a congressional
        investigation on possible fifth-column activities.

4959. Horlings, Albert. "Reply to Ige." NATION, 155 (August
        1942), 140.

Responding to criticism of his position, Horlings reiterates his doubts about the loyalty of the Japanese in Hawaii. Since making decisions about individuals within such a large group would prove too cumbersome, he argues that mass evacuation provides the fairest and most efficient way to treat them.

4960. Omitted.

4961. Ige, Thomas H. "Reply to A. Horlings." NATION, 155 (August 8, 1942), 120.

The author, a Hawaiian-born Japanese, criticizes Horling's call for mass relocation of all Japanese in Hawaii. Ige asks for only a chance to serve the United States.

4962. Murphy, Thomas D. AMBASSADORS IN ARMS. Honolulu, HI: University of Hawaii Press, 1954. 315 pp.

Murphy describes the exploits of the 100th Infantry Battalion in Italy. The unit was composed of NISEI from Hawaii.

4963. Ogawa, Dennis. KODOMO NO TAME NI: FOR THE SAKE OF THE CHILDREN: THE JAPANESE AMERICAN EXPERIENCE IN HAWAII. Honolulu, HI: University of Hawaii Press, 1978.

The experiences described in this account contrast sharply with the ragged-edged prejudices encountered by Japanese-Americans on the West Coast.

4964. Rademaker, John A. and James T. Lane. THESE ARE AMERICANS: THE JAPANESE AMERICANS IN HAWAII IN WORLD WAR II. Palo Alto, CA: Pacific Books, 1951. 278 pp.

Here is a description of the contribution of Japanese Americans in Hawaii to the war effort. The book affirms the loyalty of these Americans.

VI.G.1.b. CANADIAN POLICIES AND PROCEDURES

4965. Adachi, Ken. THE ENEMY THAT NEVER WAS. Buffalo, NY: Books Canada, 1976. 456 pp.

In this personal but scholarly account, Adachi chronicles the unfair treatment and the prejudice endured by Canadian-Japanese.

4966. Broadfoot, Barry. YEARS OF SORROW, YEARS OF SHAME: THE STORY OF THE JAPANESE CANADIANS IN WORLD WAR II.

Toronto: Doubleday, 1977. 370 pp.

Incorporating material gained through extensive
interviews with the people involved, Broadfoot focuses on
the little-known experiences of the Japanese-Canadians. In
some respects, he argues, these people suffered even more
hardships than the Japanese-Americans.

4967. Canada. Department of Labour. TWO REPORTS ON JAPANESE
CANADIANS IN WORLD WAR II. New York: Arno Press, 1978.
84 pp.

This reprint of two contemporary reports relates the
administration of the wartime internments (1942-1944) and
the process of resettlement (1944-1946). The Japanese-
Canadian population exceeded 23,000, virtually all of whom
lived in British Columbia.

4968. Carter, David John. BEHIND CANADIAN BARBED WIRE: ALIEN,
REFUGEE, AND PRISONER OF WAR CAMPS IN CANADA, 1914-1946.
Calgary, Can.: Tumbleweed Press, 1980. 334 pp.

NE

4969. Daniels, Roger. "Chinese and Japanese in North America:
The Canadian and American Experiences Compared." CAN
REV AMER STUD, 17 (Summer 1986), 173-187.

Daniels finds quite similar actions and procedures
against Japanese in the U.S. and Canada. The policy of
forced evacuation in the U.S. was ending in 1944, but,
according to Daniels, no Japanese-Canadian returned to the
western coastal area until 1949. In contrast to the
degradation of the Japanese, Daniels notes improvement in
the conditions and status of the Chinese populations in
both countries--especially in statutory improvements in
immigration restriction and citizenship.

4970. Ferguson, Ted. A WHITE MAN'S COUNTRY. Toronto:
Doubleday, 1975.

NE

4971. Hughes, David R. and Evelyn Kallen. THE ANATOMY OF RACISM:
CANADIAN DIMENSIONS. Buffalo, NY: Books Canada, 1974.
240 pp.

The authors' purpose is to provide the background of the
struggle for human rights in Canada. Their tone is

critical as they review the experiences of various ethnic
groups in Canadian society. See especially their
presentation on Japanese-Canadians.

4972. Omitted.

4973. Iwaasa, David B. "The Japanese in Southern Alberta,
         1941-1945." ALBERTA HIST, 24 (No. 3, 1976), 5-19.

         NE

4974. Laviolette, Forrest E. "The Canadian-Japanese: A New
         Look." PAC AFFS, 50 (January 1977), 107-111.

         The author applauds the emerging revelations about the
         discrimination against Canadian-Japanese during the war.
         Laviolette admits that in his report in 1948 he could not
         tell the full story.

4975. Laviolett, Forrest E. THE CANADIAN-JAPANESE AND WORLD WAR
         II: A SOCIOLOGICAL AND PSYCHOLOGICAL ACCOUNT. Toronto:
         University of Toronto Press, 1948. 332 pp.

         The book is issued under the auspices of the Canadian
         Institute of International Affairs and the Institute of
         Pacific Relations. The author reports in a straight
         forward manner on the official policy and treatment of the
         Canadian-Japanese. [Note: About 30 years later, Laviolett
         admitted (in PACIFIC AFFAIRS) that he could not tell the
         full story in 1948 of the prejudice and unfair treatment
         inflicted upon the Japanese-Canadians.]

4976. LaViolette, Forrest E. "Japanese Evacuation in Canada."
         FE SURVEY, 11 (July 29, 1942), 163-167.

         After surveying the problems and costs of the
         evacuation, the author agrees that military necessity did
         justify the policy.

4977. LaViolette, Forrest E. "Two Years of Japanese Evacuation
         in Canada." FE SURVEY, 13 (May 31, 1944), 93-100.

         Here is a report that the resettlement process was
         proceeding at a slow pace. Noting the impasse between
         Canadian-Japanese attitudes and governmental policy, the
         author calls for more liberalization of the policy.

4978. Lee, Carol F. "The Road to Enfranchisement: Chinese and
         Japanese in British Columbia." BC STUDIES, 30 (1976),
         44-76.

NE

4979.   Makabe, Tomoko. "Canadian Evacuation and Nisei Identity."
         PHYLON, 41 (Summer 1980), 116-125.

         The wartime treatment of the Canadian-Japanese can be
         viewed as more severe than in the United States. (It
         started earlier and ended later.) Canada's official
         policies were dispersal during the war and mass
         deportations after the war. Some were not permitted back
         to the British Columbia coastal area until 1949. Makabe
         contends that the Canadian-Japanese are making conscious
         efforts to repress the entire experience.

4980.   Palmer, Howard. "Patterns of Racism: Attitudes Towards
         Chinese and Japanese in Alberta, 1920-1950." HISTOIRE
         SOCIALE, 13 (May 1980), 137-160.

         With a relatively small population of Chinese and
         Japanese, Alberta wielded little influence on policy,
         according to the author. Rather, Palmer says, British
         Columbia with far larger populations shaped the policies of
         legal restrictions and removal to Alberta. The acceptance
         of the Chinese, he argues, shows that racism was not the
         only factor motivating Alberta's rejection of the Japanese.

4981.   Patton, Janice. THE EXODUS OF THE JAPANESE. Toronto:
         McClelland and Stewart, 1973. 47 pp.

         NE

4982.   Roy, Patricia E. "The Soldiers Canada Didn't Want: Her
         Chinese and Japanese Citizens." CANADIAN HR, 59
         (September 1978), 341-358.

         Making extensive use of government documents, the
         author, a history professor, analyzes how racial prejudice
         (politicians supported it, the army feared it) delayed
         valuable contributions to the war effort by Chinese and
         Japanese citizens.

4983.   Sunahara, Ann Gomer. THE POLITICS OF RACISM. Toronto:
         James Lorimer, 1981.

         Based on wide-ranging research, including newly released
         government documents, Sunahara offers an excellent account
         of the prejudice and mistreatment inflicted upon the
         Japanese-Canadians.

VI.G.1.b.i. PERSONAL ACCOUNTS

4984. Adachi, Ken. THE ENEMY THAT NEVER WAS. Buffalo, NY: Books
       Canada, 1976. 456 pp.

       In a well-researched, documented account, the author
       traces the history of the ugly racism and unfair treatment
       encountered by Canadian-Japanese (from the first
       immigrants). This is a personal but scholarly objective
       report by someone who experienced the internment,
       expulsion, and resettlement policies during the war.

4985. Nakano, Takeo Ujo. WITHIN THE BARBED WIRE FENCE: A
       JAPANESE MAN'S ACCOUNT OF HIS INTERNMENT IN CANADA.
       Seattle, WA: University of Washington Press, 1981.

       Through his poems and diary entries, Nakano gives a good
       description of the hardships of his internment.

4986. Takashima, Shizuye. A CHILD IN PRISON CAMP. New York:
       William Morrow, 1974. 63 pp.

       This personal account, which first appeared in 1971
       (Plattsburg, NY: Tundra Books), tells of a
       Japanese-Canadian girl's experiences with her family at the
       internment camp in New Denver, B.C. They remained there
       for three years.

VI.G.1.c. PERUVIAN POLICIES AND PROCEDURES

4987. Barnhart, Edward N. "Japanese Internees From Peru." PAC
       HR, 31 (May 1962), 169-178.

       In the name of internal security, Peru evacuated one
       thousand Japanese (plus their families) in 1943-1944.
       Barnhart traces the pressures of prejudice and war to
       discover that only a few ever remained in the United
       States or Peru. Virtually all of these people were
       deported after the war to Japan.

4988. Gardiner, C. Harvey. PAWNS IN A TRIANGLE OF HATE.
       Seattle, WA: University of Washington Press, 1981.
       222 pp.

       Gardiner presents one of the first accounts of the 1,800
       Japanese people taken from Peru and interned in the United
       States. The research is thorough and grounded in primary
       sources. The unhappy experience continued for these people
       after the war when very few ever returned to Peru. The

author effectively examines the dual perspective of the
impersonal policies of governments and the personal stories
of powerless individuals. His conclusions reveal the
pressure tactics of the U.S. Government on Peru and the
overall responsibility of Roosevelt and President Manuel
Prado of Peru.

4989.   Gerbi, Antonello. "The Japanese in Peru." ASIA &
          AMERICAS, 43 (January 1943), 43-46.

In this wartime report, the author, an Italian economist
who lives in Peru, describes the well-organized
Japanese-Peruvian population (20-25,000). Coastal
landowners in Peru encouraged Japanese immigration to
obtain a source of cheap labor. Public opinion in Peru,
however, is overwhelmingly anti-Japanese.

4990.   Emmerson, John K. "Japanese and Americans in Peru,
          1942-1943." FOR SERV J, 54 (May 1977), 40-47, 56.

Because of his proficiency in the Japanese language, the
author, a Foreign Service officer, served in Peru by
reading the intercepted mail of the Japanese population.
He traces the unhappy experiences of the approximately one
thousand Japanese who were sent from Peru to wartime
internment in the United States and then to postwar "exile"
in Japan.

4991.   Seoane, Manuel. "The Japanese Are Still in Peru." ASIA &
          AMERICAS, 43 (December 1943), 674-676.

The author is described as a Peruvian revolutionary in
exile (Chile). He describes with disapproval the Japanese
penetration of Peru where anti-Japanese laws are not being
enforced.

4992.   White, John W. "Japan's Amazon Dream." ASIA & AMERICAS,
          43 (October 1943), 580-583.

The author, a U.S. correspondent in Chile, writes of a
secret, well-trained Japanese army positioned in Peru to
carry out Tokyo's plan to seize the Amazon Basin as part of
its design for world conquest.

VI.G.2. UNITED STATES DEMOBILIZATION

4993.   Garza, Hedda. "Bring the Boys Home!" AMER HIST ILLUS, 20
          (June, 1985), 36-41.

The author, a free-lance writer, reports on the
disgruntled American servicemen in the Far East and their
spontaneous postwar movement to bring about wholesale
rotations back to the United States. Morale plummeted
after V-J Day, and led to demonstrations (e.g., Christmas
Day 1945 in Manila) for an accelerated schedule of
replacements.

4994. Ballard, Jack Stokes. THE SHOCK OF PEACE: MILITARY AND
       ECONOMIC DEMOBILIZATION AFTER WORLD WAR II. Lanham, MD:
       University Press of America, 1983. 270 pp.

The author explores the means by which the United States
prepared for peace. The unexpected suddenness of the
Japanese surrender provided a sense of urgency to this
planning process.

4995. Banks, C. "Rock Morale." MC GAZ, 30 (February 1946),
       29-31.

"Rock" is the generic name for the postwar occupation
garrisons on Pacific islands. The author warns of flagging
morale among these garrisons, because while Marines
tolerated deprivations during the war, they are no longer
willing to do so.

4996. United States. Office of War Mobilization and
       Reconversion. THE ROAD TO TOKYO AND BEYOND.
       Washington, D.C.: GPO, 1945. 63 pp.

This report summarizes the achievements of the office in
amassing the United States armed forces that proved so
valuable in winning the war. Of interest is the framework
presented for the demobilization of that massive force.

VI.H. MILITARY GOVERNMENT

4997. Embree, John F. "Military Government in Saipan and
       Tinian." APP ANTHROP, 5 (Winter 1946), 1-39.

This article is the text of a report Embree wrote for
the Office of War Information. He surveys the attitudes of
the Japanese population in occupied areas at the end of the
war. In general, these grief-stricken Japanese had
difficulty accepting the surrender announcement from Tokyo.

4998. Holborn, Hajo. AMERICAN MILITARY GOVERNMENT: ITS
       ORGANIZATION AND POLICIES. Washington, D. C.: Infantry
       Journal Press, 1947. 243 pp.

Holborn, a noted historian who served in the OSS,
provides an analysis of the planning for the military
governments of the various enemy territories. One chapter
and some excellent material in the appendices are devoted
to the war against Japan.

4999.   Israel, Fred L. "Military Justice in Hawaii." PAC HR, 36
        (August 1967), 243-267.

Within three hours after the Japanese attack at Pearl
Harbor, the author notes, territorial Governor Joseph B.
Poindexter imposed martial law in Hawaii. Israel critiques
the Army's disregard for the safeguards which had been
established in the Supreme Court's decision in EX PARTE
MILLIGAN. The postwar DUNCAN case, which reaffirmed
MILLIGAN, he says, came too late.

5000.   Weeks, Charles J., Jr. "The United States Occupation of
        Tonga, 1942-1945: The Social and Economic Impact." PAC
        HR, 56 (August 1987), 399-426.

The article portrays British acquiescence in flagrant
violations of Tongan rights by U.S. servicemen. See, for
example, Weeks' account of the so-called "Great Cigarette
Raid." Tongans were eager to absorb American culture, but,
he feels, the U.S. wartime occupation accelerated some of
the present-day problems in Tonga (e.g., overpopulation,
debt, and dependency). Of special interest is the author's
description of Queen Salote.

VI.I. CIVIL AFFAIRS

1. RED CROSS

5001.   Campbell, Alfred S. GUADALCANAL ROUND-TRIP. Lambertville,
        NJ: Author, 1945. 112 pp.

Here is the personal account by a field director for the
American Red Cross of his experience in the Southwest
Pacific.

5002.   Ellis, Jean M. FACE POWDER AND GUNPOWDER. Toronto:
        Saunders, 1947. 229 pp.

NE

5003.   Korson, George G. AT HIS SIDE: THE STORY OF THE AMERICAN
        RED CROSS OVERSEAS IN WORLD WAR II. New York: Coward-

McCann, 1945. 322 pp.

See especially the report on Red Cross activities in the
Philippines.

5004. International Committee of the Red Cross. REPORT ON THE
       ACTIVITY OF THE INTERNATIONAL COMMITTEE OF THE RED CROSS
       FOR THE INDEMNIFICATION OF FORMER ALLIED PRISONERS OF
       WAR IN JAPANESE HANDS. Geneva: International Committee
       of the Red Cross, 1971. 39 pp.

       This special project supplements the three-volume report
       on the wartime activities of the Red Cross which was
       published in 1948. In Article Sixteen of the 1951 peace
       treaty, Japan agreed to transfer assets to the
       International Committee of the Red Cross for the payment of
       these indemnities. With the lengthy delays since 1951,
       however, many payments went instead to family survivors of
       the POWs. This account describes the problems in
       collecting the funds and in compiling a list of claimants.
       Only military POWs were eligible, not civilian internees,
       merchant marines, or irregular (guerrilla) forces. Two
       rounds of payments (1956 and 1962) provided a ridiculously
       low POW individual share (under $40 total).

5005. McClure, Robert B. THE RED CROSS AT WORK IN CHINA.
       Sheffield, Eng: Sheffield Newspapers, 1943. 48 pp.

       In letters home, McClure describes his war work with the
       Red Cross. The letters give a glimpse of the ravages of
       the war in China.

5006. Red Cross. REPORT OF THE INTERNATIONAL COMMITTEE OF THE
       RED CROSS ON ITS ACTIVITIES DURING THE SECOND WORLD WAR,
       SEPTEMBER 1, 1939 - JUNE 30, 1947. Geneva, Switz.:
       International Red Cross, 1948. 3 vols.

       This comprehensive report covers all of the Red Cross
       activities. In the Far East, the humanitarian work of the
       organization included aid to evacuees, internees, and
       refugees. See especially the Red Cross efforts to ease the
       dislocations at the end of the war.

VI.I.2. RELIEF

5007. Davidson, Walter. FIVE YEARS OF SERVICE IN AID OF THE
       PHILIPPINE PEOPLE EMERGING FROM THE RAVAGES OF THE GREAT
       WAR IN THE PACIFIC: FINAL REPORT, 1944-1949.
       Washington, D. C.: Philippine War Relief, 1949. 27 1.

Davidson, secretary and executive director of Philippine
War Relief, Inc., offers a brief, uncritical review of the
corporation's activities in the Philippines.

5008. United Nations. Education, Scientific, and Cultural
       Organization. THE BOOK OF NEEDS OF FIFTEEN
       WAR-DEVASTATED COUNTRIES IN EDUCATION, SCIENCE AND
       CULTURE. Paris: UNESCO, 1947.

       With a heavy emphasis on Europe, this survey sets out an
       ambitious agenda for postwar recovery. See especially the
       report on the needs of China.

5009. United Nations. Relief and Rehabilitation Administration.
       IN THE WAKE OF THE ARMIES. Washington, D.C.:
       U.N.R.R.A., 1946. 13 nos.

       This contemporary survey at war's end outlines the
       enormous tasks facing the relief and recovery effort.

5010. United Nations. Relief and Rehabilitation Administration.
       U.N.R.R.A.: THE HISTORY OF THE UNITED NATIONS RELIEF
       AND REHABILITATION ADMINISTRATION. New York: Columbia
       University Press, 1950. 3 vols.

       Prepared by a special staff of the U.N.R.R.A.'s chief
       historian, and directed by George Woodbridge, this
       organizational history sets forth in great detail the work
       of U.N.R.R.A. in Europe and Asia.

VI.J. JAPAN AND FRIENDS

5011. "Altering History: 'winners write the history books.'"
       SENIOR SCHOLASTIC, 115 (October 15, 1982), 27.

       This brief editorial charges the current Japanese
       Ministry of Education with glossing over the history of the
       war in school texts used in Japan. For example, the
       revised texts now refer to "military advances" rather than
       aggression and invasion, and terrible atrocities have
       become "unfortunate incidents."

5012. Bache, Carol. PARADOX ISLE. New York: Knopf, 1943. 183
       pp.

       By December 1941, the author had lived in Japan for
       fourteen years and worked for the intelligence section of
       the General Staff. The book, which presents her personal

observations, is a collation of stories about the social
life and customs in Japan.

5013. Bain, H. Foster. "Japan's Power of Resistance." FOR AFFS,
        22 (April 1944), 424-432.

        Speculating on the wartime situation in Japan, Bain
        points to some severe shortages, especially in manpower and
        shipping.

5014. Benedict, Ruth. THE CHRYSANTHEMUM AND THE SWORD. Boston:
        Houghton, Mifflin, 1946. 324 pp.

        This study, sponsored by the Office of War Information,
        examines Japanese assumptions about the conduct of life by
        offering insights on religious-economic-political-social
        aspects within Japan. Benedict, a distinguished
        sociologist-anthropologist, shows how culture contributed
        to the Japanese war effort. The book is weakened somewhat
        by the fact that she had never been to Japan and by her
        overgeneralizations about national character.

5015. Byas, Hugh. THE JAPANESE ENEMY: HIS POWER AND HIS
        VULNERABILITY. New York: Knopf, 1942. 107 pp.

        With his extensive first-hand knowledge of Japan, this
        American reporter predicts a long hard war. Byas tries to
        rely solely on objective facts in order to strip away myths
        surrounding the Japanese people.

5016. Chamberlain, William Henry. "Who Are These Japanese."
        AMER MERCURY, 54 (February 1942), 155-164.

        The author, a correspondent in Japan for four years
        prior to the war, describes the Japanese (peaceful at
        home, violent abroad) and the role of the Emperor.
        Chamberlain warns that the West has misjudged the
        Japanese and that they will not surrender readily.

5017. Caulfield, Genevive. KINGDOM WITHIN. New York: Harper
        and Row, 1960. 278 pp.

        Here is the autobiography of a woman who founded schools
        for the blind in Japan. Blind herself, Caulfield survived
        the war and the ordeal of internment.

5018. Coleman, Homer J. "Bushido." INFANTRY J, 57 (September
        1945), 36.

In this brief article, Coleman characterizes Bushido, the
psychological framework for every Japanese soldier, as
"gross barbarism."

5019. De Weerd, Harvey A. "Japan Explains the War." INFANTRY J,
       57 (August 1945), 6-10.

Focusing on the attempts by the Japanese government to
explain the war to its people, the author dismisses these
efforts as "childish and third rate." The official tone
shifted from one of arrogance to appeals for sacrifice.

5020. Embree, John F. "Applied Anthropology and Its Relationship
       to Anthropology." AMER ANTHROP, 47 (October-December
       1945), 635-637.

In this brief article, Embree calls for recognition of
the difference between science and applied science. He is
particularly upset by the so-called national character
studies done for the government during the war. For him,
such studies, especially those on Japan, offer false
rationalizations about being a "true science" and smack of
racism.

5021. Embree, John F. "A Note on Ethnocentrism in Anthropology."
       AMER ANTHROP, 52 (July-September 1950), 430-432.

Embree argues that assertions about the need for
objectivity before the war were accepted as truisms, but,
during the war, governmental studies on national character
trampled those truisms. Scoffing at "ingenious theories"
that traced the alleged Japanese penchant for war to toilet
training and food habits, Embree warns that anthropologists
are losing touch with their own field through
ethnocentrism.

5022. Embree, John F. "Standardized Error and Japanese
       Character: A Note on Political Interpretation." WORLD
       POL, 2 (No. 3, 1950), 439-443.

Embree criticizes the "character structure"
interpretations which are seized, especially by
non-anthropologists, apparently to fill a social need to
denounce the Japanese. Thus, he warns, the errors in these
studies are becoming standardized. Embree questions the
validity of using culture patterns which determine
individual behavior as an explanation for national and
international developments.

5023. Garon, Sheldon M. "State and Religion in Imperial Japan."
       J JAPANESE STUD 12 (Summer 1986), 273-302.

       The author, a history professor, uses Japanese sources
       to dispute the notion that the imperial system is the
       source of all values. According to Garon, a popular new
       religious movement arose in Japan during the inter-war
       years. He calls attention to the efforts by the Japanese
       government to suppress this movement in 1937 to control
       "dangerous thought."

5024. Goldston, Robert C. PEARL HARBOR: DECEMBER 7, 1941. New
       York: Franklin Watts, 1972. 90 pp.

       This condensed, popular version races through Japanese
       history from 660 B.C. to 1945. Despite the title, the
       material on Pearl Harbor is sparse.

5025. Gorer, Geoffrey. "The Occupation of Enemy Territory: The
       Special Case of Japan." PUB OPIN Q, 7 (Winter
       1943),567-9.

       The author, a British anthropologist at the Yale
       Institute of Human Relations, warns that, because of
       Japanese culture, the Allies will have difficulty
       influencing Japan to become a cooperative, democratic
       member of the family of nations.

5026. Gorer, Geoffrey. "Themes in Japanese Culture." TRANS ACAD
       SCI, 5 (February 1943), 106-124.

       Although he does not know the Japanese language and has
       never been to Japan, Gorer offers a view of Japanese
       culture through "fairly rigid theoretical formulations."
       He attempts to construct for the first time a unified
       theory of social science, integrating social anthropology,
       psychoanalysis, and stimulus-response psychology. Taking
       as one of his basic assumptions that human behavior is
       learned, the author focuses on a questionnaire about child
       training. Three general themes emerging from his study
       identify learning patterns associated with (1) the
       gastro-intestinal tract, (2) parents, and (3) control of
       one's own body as well as "social and inanimate
       environment."

5027. Guillan, Robert. I SAW TOKYO BURNING: AN EYEWITNESS
       NARRATIVE FROM PEARL HARBOR TO HIROSHIMA. Garden City,
       NY: Doubleday, 1981. 298 pp.

Guillan, a French journalist, lived in Japan during the
war. He tries to capture the perspective of the average
citizen. Originally published in 1946, the book is
translated by William Byron.

5028. Hall, Basil. "The Mind and the Sword." ARMY Q DEF J, 90
       (April 1965), 69-76.

This article stresses the importance of the sword to the
Japanese as a symbol of man and his bravery. Hall sides
with Slim who disagreed with MacArthur's orders against the
"archaic" practice of accepting swords at surrender
ceremonies.

5029. Haring, Douglas. BLOOD ON THE RISING SUN. Philadelphia,
       PA: Macrae-Smith, 1943. 239 pp.

After having lived over seven years as a missionary in
Japan (during the period 1917-1926), the author turned to a
career in anthropology. Haring believes that there is an
absence of moral feeling in Japan, and he particularly
attacks the ideas embodied in KODO (the Imperial Way) and
SHINTO. According to the author, the Japanese are bent in
nothing less than a design for world conquest. Japanese-
language sources are incorporated in this unique view of
Japan.

5030. Havens, Thomas R.H. VALLEY OF DARKNESS: THE JAPANESE
       PEOPLE AND WORLD WAR TWO. New York: W.W. Norton, 1978.
       280 pp.

Tracing the start of the war for Japan to the Marco Polo
Bridge, Havens portrays the endurance of the Japanese
community, which remained united until the war ended. This
social-urban history concentrates chiefly on the women,
children, and elderly. The research is admirable and
springs from many Japanese-language sources. ("Respect
Imperial Rescripts" proclaims one rousing propaganda
poster.) Here is a well-conceived research project that
points the way to further study.

5031. Havens, Thomas R.H. "Women and War in Japan, 1937-1945."
       AMER HR, 80 (October 1975), 913-934.

In this analysis of the implications of the war for
Japanese women, Havens focuses on three key forces: natural
mobilization, patriarchal attitudes, and hardships imposed
by a war economy.

5032. Hill, Max. "Behind the Jap Front." AMER MAG, 135 (January
       1943), 116-119.

       The author, a correspondent in Tokyo, was interned until
       being deported in June 1942. The article includes his
       observations about Japan's war economy and the role of the
       emperor. He provides the somber warning: "The Japanese
       diet literally starves a white man."

5033. Johnson, Sheila K. AMERICAN ATTITUDES TOWARD JAPAN,
       1941-1975. Washington, D.C.: American Enterprise
       Institute for Public Policy, 1975. 114 pp.

       Under the sponsorship of the Hoover Institution, Johnson
       presents a discussion of the national characteristics of
       the Japanese people and the shifting perspectives of U.S.
       public opinion.

5034. Johnston, Bruce F., Mosaburo Hosoda, and Yoshio Kusumi.
       JAPANESE FOOD MANAGEMENT IN WORLD WAR II. Stanford, CA:
       Stanford University Press, 1953. 283 pp.

       This report reveals not only the dire situation
       confronting the Japanese but also the resolute discipline
       with which they faced the situation.

5035. Kato, Masuo. THE LOST WAR: A JAPANESE REPORTER'S INSIDE
       STORY. New York: A. A. Knopf, 1946. 264 pp.

       Educated in the United States, Kato was in Washington as
       a Japanese reporter during the 1941 negotiations. Although
       he claims to have opposed going to war with the United
       States, Kato provides an objective account of the Japanese
       perspective without apology or regret.

5036. Keene, Donald. "The Barren Years: Japanese War
       Literature." MONUM NIPPON, 33 (Spring 1978), 67-112.

       Keene, a professor of Japanese literature, characterizes
       the large body of wartime literature in Japan as
       unimpressive. His examination of some typical examples
       also leads him to conclude that the war years mark the
       distinction between the modern and contemporary ages in
       Japanese literature.

5037. Keene, Donald. "Japanese Writers and the Greater East Asia
       War." J ASIAN STUD, 23 (February 1964), 209-225.

       Keene presents a survey of Japanese literature during

the war years. With four exceptions (and they maintained discrete silence), Japanese authors, according to Keene, wrote in support of the war effort, at least in the early years of the war. Keene makes the point that many of the authors were prominent public figures who came under pressure to support the government policies.

5038. Kiyooka, Chiyono (Sugimoto). BUT THE SHIPS ARE SAILING--SAILING. Tokyo: Hokuseido Press, 1959. 338 pp.

NE

5039. Kranzler, David. JAPANESE, NAZIS, AND JEWS: THE JEWISH REFUGEE COMMUNITY OF SHANGHAI, 1938-1945. New York: Yeshiva University Press, 1976. 644 pp.

This well-researched report reveals a little-known aspect of the war in China. As Kranzler demonstrates, the Japanese occupiers, taking a cue from the Nazis, were not lenient to the Jewish community.

5040. LaBarre, Weston. "Some Observations on Character Structure in the Orient." PSYCHIATRY, 8 (August 1945), 319-342.

The author, a former WRA community analyst at Camp Topaz, believes that the American tendency to deny or ignore cultural differences contributes to U.S. naivete in diplomacy. His focus is on the unique life history of each person in shaping their character. Americans, he says, differ from Japanese, whom he calls the most compulsive people in the world (e.g., ceremonious, secretive, sadomasochistic, etc.). The author also offers self-described value judgments on political and military events. This article must be read with caution.

5041. Leighton, Alexander H. HUMAN RELATIONS IN A CHANGING WORLD. New York: E.P. Dutton, 1949. 354 pp.

The author, a sociologist and a doctor of medicine and psychiatry, integrates a social scientist approach in a comparative analysis of Japan. During the war Leighton evaluated the collective mentality of the Japanese people. In this postwar study, he uses improved data to test and critique his earlier reports for U.S. officials.

5042. Lindesmith, Alfred and Anselm L. Strauss. "A Critique of Culture-Personality Writings." AMER SOCIOLOGICAL REV, 15 (October 1950), 587-600.

The two anthropologists criticize the work of LaBarre,
Mead, Benedict, and others as ineffectual attempts to
salvage the theory of infantile determinism. According to
the authors, these writers have confused fact with
interpretation; the effects of infant experience remain
undemonstrated.

5043. MacIsaac, David, ed. THE MILITARY AND SOCIETY.
       Washington, D.C.: Office of Air Force History, 1974.
       164 pp.

       Among the proceedings of the Fifth Military History
       Symposium at the Air Force Academy, October 5-6, 1972, see
       especially the article by Alvin D. Coox, "Chrysanthemum and
       Star in Modern Japan" (pp. 37-60). Coox deftly chronicles
       the splintering of national unity in Japan and the growing
       mistrust that separated the civilian from the soldier.

5044. Minear, Richard H. "Cross-Cultural Perception and World
       War II: American Japanists and their Images of Japan."
       INTL STUD Q, 24 (December 1980), 555-580.

       The article examines the writings of six prominent
       Japanists (Benedict, Reischauer, Fahs, Embree, and Mears),
       and the relationship (sometimes changing) between their
       views of Japan and of the United States. The author says
       that the 1940s represented a crucial decade in the
       development of U.S. studies on Japan.

5045. Minear, Richard H. "The Wartime Studies of Japanese
       National Character." JAPAN INTERPRETER, 13 (Summer
       1980), 36-59.

       The author, a history professor, sharply criticizes the
       wartime work of anthropologists, especially Benedict,
       Gorer, and LaBarre. Attacking the concept of national
       character in promoting misunderstanding, Minear notes some
       of the ludicrous evidence used by those who claimed to
       identify a fatal flaw in Japanese character.

5046. Morris, Ivan, ed. JAPAN, 1931-1945. Lexington, MA: D.C.
       Heath, 1963. 77 pp.

       As part of the noted D.C. Heath "Problems" series, this
       collection explores the dimensions of militarism and
       Fascism in wartime Japan.

5047. Morris, John. "Tokyo Since Pearl Harbor." HARPER'S MAG,

188 (February 1944), 271-283.

The author, a British professor, lived and taught in
Tokyo in 1941 under the sponsorship of the Japanese Foreign
Office. His descriptions of life in wartime Japan include
the rationing of food and restrictions on the movement of
foreigners. Although he was not interned before his
repatriation, Morris was watched carefully. Of interest is
his view that Japanese military leaders launched their
attacks without the approval or knowledge of the
government.

5048. Morris, John. TRAVELLER FROM TOKYO. New York: Sheridan
       House, 1944. 253 pp.

The author, a British professor of English in Japan
(1938 - July 1942), offers a perceptive analysis of
Japanese culture and thought. Joseph C. Grew wrote the
Foreword.

5049. Morrison, Ian. OUR JAPANESE FOE. New York: G.P. Putnam's
       Sons, 1944. 129 pp.

Morrison, a British correspondent, lived several years
in Asia. His knowledgeable descriptions of Japan and the
Japanese people focus especially on economic problems.

5050. Olds, C. Burnell. "Education for Conquest: the Japanese
       Way." FOR AFFS, 21 (October 1942), 34-43.

Asserting that the ideals of a culture emerge from the
educational process, Olds points to Japan's educational
emphasis on its glorious mission in Asia and the world.

5051. Olds, C. Burnell. "Japan Harnesses Religion in the
       National Service." FOR AFFS, 21 (April 1943), 535-547.

In this contemporary account, Olds describes religion as
the key instrument of national policy in Japan.

5052. Olds, C. Burnell. "Potentialities of Japanese Liberalism."
       FOR AFFS, 22 (April 1944), 433-443.

Looking beyond the sadistic cruelty of the Japanese
military, Olds emphasizes how the Japanese people have a
love of beauty and a "passionate fondness" for children.
For him, militarism is the real enemy, not the common
people of Japan.

5053. Sansom, Sir George. "Liberalism in Japan." FOR AFFS, 19 (April 1941), 551-560.

This expert on Japan advises that the idea of liberalism in Japan in the Western sense (e.g., belief in democratic processes and anti-militarism) is erroneous. Also, he points out that, without active discontent in Japan, the West should expect no reactions of public opinion by the Japanese people.

5054. Seeman, Bernard. "Life in Japan Today." AMER MERCURY, 61 (July 1945), 7-15.

The author, a correspondent and OWI consultant, describes the food, clothing, housing, and coal shortages in Japan. Basing his report on information from inside Japan, Seeman warns, too, of the growing "suicide psychology" to resist invaders.

5055. Shillony, Ben-Ami. "Universities and Students in Wartime Japan." J ASIAN STUD, 45 (August 1986), 769-787.

Incorporating many Japanese-language sources, the author finds that patriotic idealism, including kamikaze volunteers, among the students remained strong to the end. Despite repressive tactics by the government against the left, however, he argues that wartime changes accelerated the prewar process of modernization.

5056. Silberman, Bernard S., ed. JAPANESE CHARACTER AND CULTURE. Tucson, AZ: University of Arizona Press, 1962.

Here is a valuable collection. See especially the articles by Geoffrey Gorer, "Themes in Japanese Culture" (pp. 308-324); Fred Kerlinger, "Behavior and Personality in Japan: A Critique of Three Studies of Japanese Personalities" (pp. 400-413); and Weston La Barre, "Some Observations on Character Structure in the Orient: The Japanese" (pp. 325-359). These three authors swim in unsure waters as they attempt to assess the national character of the Japanese.

5057. Terasaki, Gwen. BRIDGE TO THE SUN. Chapel Hill, NC: University of North Carolina Press, 1957. 260 pp.

In 1931, the author married a Japanese diplomat and thereafter lived in Japan and China. The book gives a good description of life in wartime Japan. She and her daughter eventually came to the United States. A sub-plot of the

book is the enduring love between her and her husband (who
died in 1950).

5058. Tsurumi, Shunsuke. A CULTURAL HISTORY OF POSTWAR JAPAN,
        1945-1980. London: Routledge and Kegan Paul, 1987. 174
        pp.

        The book reproduces lectures at McGill University by the
        Japanese philosopher. Although much of his attention falls
        beyond the immediate postwar years and turns to pop
        culture, see Tsurumi's analysis of Japanese public opinion
        on the war crimes trials.

5059. Tsurumi, Shunsuke. AN INTELLECTUAL HISTORY OF WARTIME
        JAPAN, 1931-1945. New York: KPI, 1986. 136 pp.

        The author, a Japanese philosopher, sets forth the
        pressures put upon Japanese intellectuals to support
        nationalist aims. The liberals were especially pressed for
        their ideological conversion (TENKO), according to Tsurumi.
        Many succumbed, but of special interest in this book is the
        material relating to the anti-war sentiments and activities
        inside Japan.

5060. United States. Army Air Forces. MISSION ACCOMPLISHED.
        Washington, D.C.: GPO, 1946. 110 pp.

        Here is a report on the interrogations of Japanese
        military, civilian, and industrial leaders. The
        interviewees, for the most part, were cooperative. Of
        interest is their identification of Saipan as the turning
        point and the decisive effect of the strategic bombing
        campaign by the B-29s.

5061. United States. Office of Strategic Services. CONDITIONS
        IN TOKYO AFTER DECEMBER 7, 1941. Washington, D.C.:
        OSS, 1942. 9 pp.

        Based largely on newspaper reports, this OSS report
        describes the high morale in the capital city.

5062. United States. Office of Strategic Services. INFORMATION
        GATHERED ON THE S.S. GRIPSHOLM. Washington, D.C.: OSS,
        1942. 19 pp.

        Here is a valuable summary of first-hand observations of
        Japan during the early months of the war. The ship
        returned the U.S. noncombatants in August 1942.

5063. United States. Office of Strategic Services. THE JAPANESE
           EMPEROR AND THE WAR. Washington, D.C.: OSS, 1944. 3
           pp.

       Written at a time when American officials were debating
       the announced war aim of unconditional surrender, this
       brief report describes the relative non-involvement of the
       emperor in Japan's march to war and its subsequent
       direction.

5064. United States. Office of Strategic Services. MORALE AND
           SOCIAL CONDITIONS IN JAPAN AND OCCUPIED AREAS AS
           REPORTED BY AMERICAN REPATRIATES. Washington, D.C.:
           OSS, 1944. 63 pp.

       Many of these reports came from U.S. repatriates early
       in the war. By 1944, their observations were not current.
       Reports from more recent observers are not numerous enough
       to provide a reliable analysis.

5065. United States. War Department. JAPANESE RECRUITMENT AND
           REPLACEMENT SYSTEM. Washington, D.C.: Military
           Intelligence Division, 1945. 366 pp.

       The General Staff's Military Intelligence Division
       provided this detailed report on the current status of
       enemy forces and capabilities. The origins of the study
       emerged from the concern in the War Department about the
       costs of an invasion of the Japanese home islands.

5066. Vining, Elizabeth Gray. QUIET PILGRIMMAGE. Philadelphia,
           PA: J.B. Lippincott, 1970. 410 pp.

       Here is the autobiography of the woman selected to tutor
       the crown prince of Japan. She calls her experience a
       "modern and international variation on the Cinderella
       story."

5067. Watkins, Floyd C. "Even His Name Will Die: The Last Days
           of Paul Nobuo Tatsuguchi." J ETHNIC STUD, 3 (Winter
           1976), 37-48.

       Here is a report on a diary (or second-hand versions) of
       a Japanese army doctor at Attu in 1943. The diarist wrote
       little about the Japanese cause, but he confided his
       willingness to die for the emperor. Watkins incorporates
       some postwar information about the diarist's family.

5068. Women's Division, SOKA GAKKAI. WOMEN AGAINST WAR. Tokyo:

Kodansha International, 1986. 247 pp.

Here are oral histories of the war by 40 Japanese women
which begin in 1937 and extend into the postwar years. The
testimony indicates not only the suffering inflicted on the
Japanese people by the war effort and the war damage but
also the prejudice that the women of Japan had to endure.
The women offer a view of wartime Japanese society that
rarely surfaces. Richard L. Gage translated the work.

VI.K. PRISONERS OF WAR

5069. Adams, Geoffrey P. NO TIME FOR GEISHAS. London: Cooper,
       1973. 217 pp.

       NE

5070. American Ex-POW, Inc. National Medical Research Committee.
       THE JAPANESE STORY. Marshfield, WI: American Ex-POW,
       Inc., 1979. 83 pp.

       NE

5071. Bailey, Ronald. PRISONERS OF WAR. Alexandria, VA:
       Time-Life, 1981. 208 pp.

       Part of the Time-Life series on the war, this volume is
       a popularly written account which is designed for the
       general public. The statistics and camp listings help to
       make the book a useful reference tool.

5072. Barker, A.J. BEHIND BARBED WIRE. London: Universe Books,
       1974. 249 pp.

       The British historian takes a general look at the stages
       of the POW experience from capture through repatriation.
       Some of the material relates directly to the Second World
       War. This book was published in the United States under
       the title PRISONERS OF WAR.

5073. Beaumont, Joan. "Rank, Privilege, and Prisoners of War."
       WAR & SOC, 1 (May 1983), 67-94.

       The author, a social science lecturer in Australia,
       shows how the POW experience in the war led to four new
       Geneva conventions in 1949. Her thorough research enables
       her to examine closely the rights of POW officers and
       actual wartime practices.

5074. Boatner, Haydon L. "Asian Teeth Are Needed for Geneva
          Conventions--We Must Protect Future POWs." ARMY, 24
          (January 1974), 27-30.

          Major General Boatner (USA) served with Stilwell and
          commanded POW's in the Korean War. He maintains that the
          Geneva Conventions, which have not protected Americans in
          three wars, reflect Western values that hold no validity in
          Asia.

5075. Byrd, Martha H. "Captured By the Americans." AMER HIST
          ILLUS, 11 (February 1977), 24-35.

          This article describes the POW camps in the United
          States for captured Japanese, German, and Italian troops.
          Of 1,800 escapes, Byrd writes, only 31 lasted longer than 2
          weeks. She explores the difficulties involved in operating
          these POW camps.

5076. Caffrey, Kate. OUT IN THE MIDDAY SUN. New York: Stein
          and Day, 1973. 312 pp.

          This is one of the few studies which examines not only
          the fall of Singapore but also the fate thereafter of the
          prisoners in Japanese hands. One interesting feature is
          her attention to linguistic development among the
          prisoners.

5077. Carr-Gregg, Charlotte. JAPANESE PRISONERS OF WAR IN
          REVOLT. New York: St. Martin's Press, 1978. 225 pp.

          Here is a well-researched report on two incidents of
          revolt by Japanese POWs: one at Coura, Australia; the other
          at Featherston, New Zealand.

5078. Chunn, Calvin E., ed. OF RICE AND MEN: THE STORY OF
          AMERICANS UNDER THE RISING SUN. Los Angeles, CA:
          Veterans Publishing Co., 1946. 230 pp.

          Here is a collection of stories about American POWs
          which, even in retrospect, evokes powerful emotions.

5079. Cohen, Bernard M. and Maurice Z. Cooper. A FOLLOW-UP STUDY
          OF WORLD WAR II PRISONERS OF WAR. Washington, D. C.:
          GPO, 1954. 81 pp.

          Cohen (Ph.D.) and Cooper (M.D.) are with the Division of
          Medical Science in the National Research Council. Their
          follow-up is more suggestive than definitive. As it is

apparent that the end of the war did not mark the end of difficulties for POWs, the authors call for more research on this neglected topic.

5080. Cornfeld, B.A. "Escape From Corregidor." ALL HANDS, 63 (January 1986), 6-15.

Here is an account of the escape by two officers and sixteen crewmen (from the minesweeper QUAIL) after the surrender of Corregidor. They escaped in a 36-foot open motor launch in a 31-day, island-hopping adventure. Of interest is their report of firing continuing at Corregidor some 48 hours after the surrender.

5081. Dancocks, Daniel G. IN ENEMY HANDS: CANADIAN PRISONERS OF WAR. St. Edmonton, Alberta: Hurtig, 1983. 303 pp.

Over 150 POWs told their stories in this wide-ranging collection. It is the first such volume of its kind. Some of the Canadians surrendered at Hong Kong. All who fell into Japanese hands came to know the brutality of some of their captors. The stories are interesting, and Dancocks' skill assures their readability.

5082. Flory, William E.S. PRISONERS OF WAR: A STUDY IN THE DEVELOPMENT OF INTERNATIONAL LAW. Washington, D.C.: American Council on Public Affairs, 1942.

Although not directly related to the war against Japan, this study frames the legal background to the postwar charges of Japanese mistreatment of POWs.

5083. Garrett, Richard. P.O.W. Devon, Eng.: David and Charles, 1982. 240 pp.

The author, himself a POW in Africa during the war, surveys the plight of prisoners from the Hundred Years War to Vietnam. The narrative is filled with anecdotes and escape stories. See especially the chapter on the brutal treatment by Japanese captors.

5084. Hammond, Robert B. BONDSERVANTS OF THE JAPANESE. San Pedro, CA: Sheffield Press, 1943. 89 pp.

NE

5085. Hargreaves, R. "Bushido and Barbed Wire." ARMY Q, 14 (April 1947), 82-90.

The article centers on the secret POW journal of Maj. D. Russell-Roberts. Despite some terrible ordeals, such as the mass terrorism at Selerang in September 1942 and the forceful Japanese pressures to coerce the POWs into signing "non-escape forms," the spirit of the POWs remained generally high.

5086.   Holloway, Bruce K. "Escape From Hanoi: An Incident of World War II." LAURELS, 55 (Spring 1984), 7-12.

The article centers on Holloway's interview (as operations officer of the 23d Fighter Group) of Pierre Pouyade, a captain in the French Air Force. After being caught by the Japanese in Indochina, Pouyade towed targets for Japanese gunnery practice until his escape in October 1942. The French captain flew northward across the border in a Potez 5, a 1926 biplane, with bedsheets displayed to indicate his surrender.

5087.   Imonti, Felix. "Soldier's Story." AMER HERITAGE, 34 (December 1982), 108-110.

The author presents the reminiscences of a Japanese soldier named Ebina who fought at Bataan. Given the difficult fighting and the heavy casualties, Ebina expresses no remorse for the way the Japanese treated U.S. POWs. In fact, he feels Japanese guards did the very sick POWs a favor by shooting them. The rigors of the Death March, for him, merely indicated the hard life in the Japanese Army.

5088.   Jackson, Robert. WHEN FREEDOM CALLS. London: Barker, 1973.

These stories of POW escapes are devoted primarily to the war in Europe.

5089.   Janson, Dorothy. "Prisoners of War and the YMCA." BULL AMER HIST COLL (Manila), 10 (April-June 1982), 16-24.

NE

5090.   Jinbo, Nobuhiko. DAWN OF THE PHILIPPINES.

NE. Reportedly, the author, a Japanese colonel, claims that he received orders to kill all the prisoners at Bataan. This account is of dubious authenticity.

5091.   Junghans, Earl A. "Wake's POWs." USNIP, 109 (February

1983), 43-50.

Here is the reminiscence of the postwar commander of Wake
Island. All ninety-eight U.S. prisoners taken by Admiral
Sakaibara perished before the end of the war. Despite
Japanese excuses, all ninety-eight were murdered. The
Allies executed Sakaibara in 1947.

5092. Kerr, E. Bartlett. SURRENDER AND SURVIVAL: THE EXPERIENCE
OF AMERICAN POWs IN THE PACIFIC, 1941-1945. New York:
William Morrow, 1985. 356 pp.

As an Army historian whose father died as a POW under
the Japanese, Kerr carries a unique perspective to this
study. About 40% of the 25,000 Americans taken prisoner
died in captivity. Looking at all the POW situations
across the Pacific, Kerr provides a sensitive, relatively
objective narrative that is well researched. There is not
only an excellent bibliography but also a helpful
discussion of the aftermath, which describes the postwar
penalties handed out for war crimes.

5093. Krammer, Arnold. "Japanese Prisoners of War in America."
PAC HR, 52 (February 1983), 67-91.

Using unpublished sources, especially governmental
records, Krammer reports on the treatment of 5,424 Japanese
POWs in the United States. Most of these prisoners,
involuntarily taken, were processed through Angel Island,
California, and one of two interrogation centers (near D.C.
and San Francisco). Of interest is Krammer's description
of the Japanese-American interrogators who graduated from
special language school in Minnesota. The prisoners then
went to one of several POW camps, and Krammer tells of life
in these camps. Most were sent home immediately after the
war.

5094. Krammer, Arnold, comp. PUBLIC ADMINISTRATION OF PRISONER
OF WAR CAMPS IN AMERICA SINCE THE REVOLUTIONARY WAR.
Monticello, IL: Vance Bibliographies, 1980. 19 pp.

See the bibliographical entries for World War II. The
material concerning Japanese POWs is sparse.

5095. MacKenzie, Kenneth P. OPERATION RANGOON JAIL. C. Johnson,
1954. 201 pp.

Here is a report on medical treatment available to the
POWs.

5096. Magener, Rolf. PRISONERS' BLUFF. New York: E. P. Dutton,
        1955. 250 pp.

        Here is a report on the escape of Germans from a British
        camp in India. Upon making their way to Japanese lines in
        Burma, the escapees were almost executed as spies. Basil
        Credighton translated the work from the German.

5097. Mason, Wayne. PRISONERS OF WAR. Wellington, NZ: Dept. of
        Internal Affairs, 1954. 546 pp.

        Here is an exhaustive official report on New Zealand's
        prisoners of war. A detailed listing is provided.

5098. Myers, Hugh H. PRISONER OF WAR, WORLD WAR II. Portland,
        OR: Metropolitan Press, 1965. 200 pp.

        Myers examines the plight of prisoners of war. His
        report is especially critical of conditions--facilities and
        treatment--imposed on prisoners by the Japanese.

5099. Nelson, Hank. "'The Nips Are Going for the Parker': The
        Prisoners Face Freedom." WAR & SOC, 3 (September 1985),
        127-143.

        The author, a history professor, writes of the delays in
        freeing the Australian POWs. MacArthur's orders to wait
        for the general surrender on September 2 and the apparent
        lethargy of "Linger Longer Louis" Mountbatten are severely
        criticized. "Parker" is an Australian term for surrender.

5100. Pelletier, Lawrence L., Jr. "Chronic Strongyloidiasis in
        World War II Far East Ex-Prisoners of War." AMER J TROP
        MED HYGIENE, 33 (January 1984), 55-61.

        Almost forty percent of this group suffer from this
        infection, which carries symptoms including indigestion;
        abdominal pain; heartburn; pruritusani; diarrhea; and
        urticarial creeping skin eruption on the abdomen, buttocks,
        and thighs. Dr. Pelletier notes that the use of
        thiabendazole has produced clinical cure in ninety-three
        percent of the cases treated--despite some side
        effects--and he recommends that physicians treating members
        of this group look for strongyloidiosis.

5101. Pluth, Edward J. "Prisoner of War Employment in Minnesota
        During World War II." 44 (Winter 1975), 290-303.

With excellent research, especially through unpublished
documents and records, Pluth examines the POW experience in
Minnesota. Only a small percentage of the five thousand
POWs were Japanese. The author describes the local
opposition to using POW contract labor on the farms.
Eventually the disputants reached accommodation about the
POWs.

5102. Pounder, Thomas. DEATH CAMPS OF THE RIVER KWAI. Cornwall,
        Eng.: United Writers Publishers, 1977.

        Pounder tells of the suffering and brutal treatment
        inflicted by the Japanese upon their captives who toiled on
        the Siamese-Burmese railway.

5103. Richardson, Walter K. "Prisoners of War as Instruments of
        Foreign Policy." NAV WAR COLL REV, 23 (September 1970),
        47-64.

        In this brief general survey, there is a section devoted
        to World War II and the Pacific. Richardson relies
        (perhaps overly so) on social-cultural differences among
        Japanese captors to explain his arguments.

5104. Rundell, Walter, Jr. "Paying the POW in World War II."
        MIL AFFS, 22 (Fall 1958), 121-134.

        Here is an account of the international agreements which
        regulated the payment of POWs. Separate categories exist
        for normal salary, wages for labor services performed, and
        compensation for inhumane treatment.

5105. Schacht, Kenneth G. "Reflections on the Code of Conduct."
        USNIP, 108 (April 1982), 34-38.

        The author, an ex-POW under the Japanese, points out
        defects in the code as revealed in his experiences. He
        particularly identifies the problems of POW leadership and
        cohesiveness.

5106. Sharp, John Charles. IN JAPANESE HANDS: A LIST OF BOOKS
        DEALING WITH PRISONER OF WAR AND INTERNMENT CAMPS IN THE
        FAR EAST, 1941-1945, WITH A SUPPLEMENTAL LIST OF OTHER
        WORKS WRITTEN IN PRISON CAMPS. Birmingham: 1952. 2d
        supplement, 1953; 3d supplement, 1954.

        NE

5107. Sheya, Mel. PACIFIC PANDEMONIUM. Salt Lake City, UT:

Western Hotel Register Co., 1950. 96 pp.

In this personal account, Sheya tells of his experiences with the 4th Marine Regiment in the Philippines when the war began. The narrative includes his experiences at Corregidor and as a POW in the Philippines, Japan, and Manchuria.

5108. Smith, Dean A. and Michael F.A. Woodruff. DEFICIENCY DISEASES IN JAPANESE PRISON CAMPS. London: HMSO, 1951. 214 pp.

In this official history, the authors concentrate on Malaya and Singapore, but their observations and findings seem applicable to most of the other Japanese camps. Both the quantity and quality of the POW diet under the Japanese were woefully inadequate.

5109. Sommers, Stan, comp. THE JAPANESE STORY. Marshfield, WI: National Medical Research Commission, Ex-POW Inc., 1979. 83 pp.

Here is a medical report on the damage inflicted by the Japanese upon U.S. prisoners. Almost forty years after the fact, the atrocities continue to horrify the reader.

5110. Stahl, Alfred J. HOW WE TOOK IT: VIGNETTES OF JAPANESE INTERNMENT CAMPS IN THE PHILIPPINES. New York: Author, 1945. 118 pp.

Stahl tells of the vicious Japanese treatment of the internees. Despite the uneven literary quality, the book holds value as a contribution to the literature of the topic. See, too, the cartoons by "Jigger" Jay.

5111. Tavris, Carol. "The Valor of Women." VOGUE, 173 (August 1983), 198.

Here is a column about the eighty-one women who were POWs under the Japanese--and are all but invisible in the history of the war.

5112. Thomas, Elbert D. AMERICAN PRISONERS OF WAR IN THE FAR EAST. Washington, D.C.: GPO, 1944. 3 pp.

Utah Senator Thomas reports in information obtained in hearings about Japanese treatment of U.S. POWs.

5113. United States. Department of the Army. Forces in the

Western Pacific. AMERICAN AND ALLIED PERSONNEL
RECOVERED FROM JAPANESE PRISONS. Manila, PI: Dept. of
the Army, 1945. 51 1.

Here is a pictorial report of the liberation of the POWs
and internees. The photographs reveal the shocking
condition of some of the POWs.

5114. United States. Office of Strategic Services. FACTORS
UNDERLYING JAPANESE TREATMENT OF PRISONERS. Washington,
D.C.: OSS, 1944. 2 1.

Here is some unfounded speculation on why some Japanese
troops behaved so brutally against their captives.

5115. Urwin, Gregory. "THE ROAD BACK FROM WAKE ISLAND." AMER
HIST ILLUS, Pt. I: 15 (December 1980), 16-23; Pt. II:
(Janaury 1981), 43-49.

Here is the story of 2d Lt. John F. Kinney (USMC) who
fell prisoner at Wake. Taken to China, he and four other
prisoners escaped in May 1945. They were rescued by the
Chinese Communists and moved into Nationalist then American
hands. Urwin interviewed Kinney and other survivors.

5116. Valentine, Douglas. THE HOTEL TACLOBAN. Westport, CT:
Lawrence Hill, 1984. 175 pp.

The author's father fell captive to the Japanese at New
Guinea--the only one spared in his patrol--and was shipped
to the Philippines. At the POW camp in Tacloban, Valentine
was the only American among about 165 British and
Australians. He apparently became something of a maverick
and seems to have been involved in a conspiracy that ended
with the murder of senior Allied officers. The author
charges that the U.S. Army has covered up this episode by
altering his father's official records (including his
medical files).

5117. VO, Carl La. "Footprints in the Sand." USNIP, 112
(January 1986), 84-88.

Based on interviews with some survivors, VO tells of the
crew of the U.S. submarine SCULPIN. Captured in November
1943, the crew eventually ended up in a secret camp in
Japan and were not officially registered as POWs.

5118. Vromans, A.G. A LIST OF BOOKS ON PRISONERS OF WAR AND
INTERNMENT CAMPS IN THE FAR EAST DURING THE SECOND WORLD

WAR. Amsterdam, Neth. 25 pp.

NE

5119. Williams, Eric E., ed. GREAT ESCAPE STORIES. New York:
      R.M. McBride, 1959. 256 pp.

      NE

5120. Yutang, Lin. "A Talk With Japanese Prisoners." ASIA &
      AMERICAS, 44 (November 1944), 484-487.

      The author, a contributing editor of this journal,
      visited POW camps. His report emphasizes the truculent
      attitude of the Japanese pilots (some of whom have been
      prisoners since 1937). Of interest is the use of few
      guards by the Chinese who rely instead on the PAOCHIA--an
      intelligence/communications network among the people to
      detect any escapees.

VI.K.1. PERSONAL ACCOUNTS

5121. Abraham, Abie. GHOST OF BATAAN SPEAKS. New York:
      Vantage, 1971. 244 pp.

      Here is the personal account of a master sergeant in the
      31st Infantry. He endured the Death March and various
      Japanese prison camps.

5122. Aida, Yuj. PRISONER OF THE BRITISH: A JAPANESE SOLDIER'S
      EXPERIENCES IN BURMA. London: Cresset, 1966. 202 pp.

      Here is the personal account of a Japanese soldier taken
      prisoner by British forces. The book is translated by Hide
      Ishiguro and Louis Allen.

5123. Bank, Bertram. BACK FROM THE LIVING DEAD. Tuscaloosa, AL:
      Author, 1945. 108 pp.

      Here is the personal account of a survivor of the Death
      March and almost three full years of captivity under the
      Japanese.

5124. Ashton, Paul L. BATAAN DIARY. Santa Barbara, CA: Author,
      1984. 463 pp.

      Captain Ashton, an Army surgeon at Bataan, fell prisoner
      to the Japanese. His narrative-diary is intended to
      represent the experiences of his many compatriots. He

wrote this book to fulfill a promise to his fellow
prisoners.

5125. Bertram, James M. BENEATH THE SHADOW. New York: The John
       Day Co., 1948. 308 pp.

       Bertram, a New Zealander, tells of his suffering for
       four years as a POW after his capture at Hong Kong. In the
       postwar years, he served as a civilian official for New
       Zealand in the occupation of Japan.

5126. Blair, Joan and Clay Blair, Jr. RETURN FROM THE RIVER
       KWAI. New York: Simon and Schuster, 1979. 338 pp.

       Using interviews and other primary source material, the
       Blairs chronicle the ordeal of the POWs who built the now-
       famous bridge and then had their ship sunk by U.S.
       submarines while en route to Japan.

5127. Bloom, Freddy. DEAR PHILLIP: A DIARY OF CAPTIVITY,
       CHANGI, 1942-1945. London: Bodley Head, 1980. 157 pp.

       Here is a personal account of the indignities and
       hardships endured under Japanese captors after the fall of
       Singapore.

5128. Bodine, Roy L. NO PLACE FOR KINDNESS: THE PRISONER OF WAR
       DIARY OF ROY L. BODINE. Fort Sam Houston, TX: Fort Sam
       Houston Museum, 1983. 52 pp.

       The diarist spent over three years as a POW, but,
       because his earlier papers were lost, this book begins in
       late October 1944. Dr. Bodine, a major in the Army Dental
       Corps, describes in vivid details his observations of the
       medical effects on his fellow prisoners of poor diet,
       inadequate living conditions, and negligent treatment. He
       tells of the "Red Cross Bombing" in the days immediately
       following the Japanese surrender when supplies dropped from
       United States aircraft in fifty-gallon oil drums caused
       unintended damage.

5129. Boulle, Pierre. MY OWN RIVER KWAI. New York: Vanguard
       Press, 1966. 214 pp.

       When the war broke out, Boulle was working as an
       engineer on a Malayan rubber plantation. After going to
       serve the war effort in Indochina and China, he was
       captured in 1942. His escape in 1944 led him to Calcutta
       where he spent the rest of the war. These memoirs are

especially good in describing the prewar situation in
Indochina (1940-1941), including the friction between
Indochina and Siam. Boulle, of course, wrote "The Bridge
on the River Kwai."

5130. Bowles, George. "Surviving the Death March." MIL HIST, 3
      (February 1986), 42-49.

      The article takes the format of an interview with Wayne
      W. Dominick, Jr. (Spec. 4th Class, AAF), who was taken
      prisoner in the Philippines. Dominick tells of his ordeal
      as a POW, routinely "roughed up" and aboard a hell ship for
      62 days en route to a POW camp in Japan. Of interest is
      his report that all Bataan prisoners were promoted one
      grade on the day of their capture.

5131. Boyle, Martin. YANKS DON'T CRY. New York: Bernard Geis
      Associates, 1963. 249 pp.

      In brutally frank language, Boyle tells of his suffering
      and trials as a U.S. Marine POW under the Japanese.

5132. Braddon, Russell. JAPAN AGAINST THE WORLD, 1941-2041. New
      York: Stein and Day, 1983. 252 pp.

      Braddon, an Australian writer, tells of his experiences
      as a POW under the Japanese in Malaya. Despite the ordeal,
      he is able to keep his sense of humor. The story line of a
      one-hundred year war for supremacy is intended to serve as
      a warning to the West to remain ever vigilant about Japan.

5133. Braddon, Russell. NAKED ISLAND. Garden City, NY:
      Doubleday, 1953. 286 pp.

      This is a well-written account of Braddon's experiences
      as a POW. A fellow prisoner, Ronald Searle, provides
      accompanying illustrations. Although Braddon, a
      professional author, writes with good grace and humor, he
      confesses to his continuing hatred for the Japanese.

5134. Brougher, William Edward. SOUTH TO BATAAN, NORTH TO
      MUKDEN. Athens, GA: University of Georgia Press, 1971.
      207 pp.

      Brig. Gen. Brougher (U.S.A.) kept a secret diary after
      his capture by the Japanese in the Philippines. Some of
      the entries were lost during his moves to different camps;
      this book begins on January 1, 1943 and continues until his
      liberation at the end of the war. Of special value is his

retrospective account of the prewar preparations (and lack
thereof) for the defense of the Philippines.

5135.   Bush, Lewis W. THE ROAD TO INAMURA. Rutland, VT: C.E.
        Tuttle, 1972. 238 pp.

        Here is a personal account by a POW under the Japanese.
        Almost as a by-product, Bush provides some interesting
        material on Japanese social life.

5136.   Cates, Tressa R. THE DRAINPIPE DIARY. New York: Vantage
        Press, 1957. 273 pp.

        Cates offers the personal account of the ordeal of being
        a POW under the Japanese.

5137.   Coleman, John S. BATAAN AND BEYOND. College Station, TX:
        Texas A & M University Press, 1978. 224 pp.

        Here is the personal account of a POW who was taken
        prisoner early in the war during the Japanese victory in
        the Philippines. His experiences reveal the brutal,
        unsympathetic treatment the Japanese inflicted on their
        captives.

5138.   Davis, W.L. "The Bridges on the River Kwai." AEROSP H, 20
        (Spring, March 1973), 7-9.

        Davis served in the Royal Norfolk Regiment-5th Battalion.
        Captured in January 1942, he labored on the two bridges
        built to span the Kwai. Davis witnessed the destruction of
        both bridges by U. S. B-24s. On one bombing raid, errant
        bombs fell into the camp and killed seventeen POWs.
        J. T. Sweet edited the account by Davis.

5139.   Domantay, Pat. MY TERRIBLE DAYS AND SURVIVAL IN WORLD WAR
        II. New York: Vantage Press, 1972. 78 pp.

        Domantay's account describes the suffering of a POW
        under the Japanese in the Philippines.

5140.   Doward, Jan S. THE SEVENTH ESCAPE. Mountain View, CA:
        Pacific Press, 1968. 119 pp.

        NE

5141.   Downer, S.F., ed. RAGGLE TAGGLE. Aldershot, Eng.: Gale
        and Polden, 1947.

Here is a collection of stories and articles that appeared in the POW journal at Formosa in 1944.

5142.   Dunn, Benjamin. THE BAMBOO EXPRESS. Chicago: Adams Press, 1979. 204 pp.

NE

5143.   Eads, Lyle W. SURVIVAL AMIDST THE ASHES. Winona, MN: Apollo Books, 1985. 191 pp.

The author had enlisted in the Navy and was serving in Guam when the war began. Captured in the Japanese victory over the island, Eads spent the rest of the war at Zentsuji prison camp in Japan. Eads claims that the book is based on true episodes, but his use of fictitious names weakens the historical value of his work. Nevertheless, the author presents a chilling account of life in a prisoner of war camp, including sharp psychological swings and squabbling among the prisoners. Of particular interest is the decision by some prisoners driven by their hunger to eat rice which they knew had been unintentionally laced with rat poison.

5144.   Feuer, A.B., ed. BILIBAD DIARY: THE SECRET NOTEBOOKS OF COMMANDER THOMAS HAYES. Hamden, CT: Shoe String Press, 1987. 262 pp.

Hayes, taken prisoner by the Japanese, was kept in the Manila prison. The diary makes clear the poor conditions--created by both the facility and the Japanese--that had to be endured. Hayes kept the secret diary against regulations and at great peril.

5145.   Fili, William J. OF LICE AND MEN. Philadelphia, PA: Dorrance, 1973.

NE

5146.   Fillmore, Clyde. PRISONER OF WAR. Quanah, TX: Nortex, 1974. 152 pp.

Fillmore writes a moving account of his experience as a POW under the Japanese.

5147.   Fitzgerald, Earl A., ed. VOICES IN THE NIGHT: MESSAGES FROM PRISONERS OF WAR IN THE SOUTH PACIFIC, 1942-1945. Bellingham, WA: Pioneer Printing, 1948. 203 pp.

The collection deserves widespread distribution even
today. The pain-filled, highly personal commentaries still
evoke emotional responses.

5148. Fletcher-Cooke, John. THE EMPEROR'S GUEST, 1942-1945.
       London: Hutchinson, 1971.

       Here is the memoir of a British POW under the Japanese.

5149. Fortier, Malcolm V. THE LIFE OF A P.O.W. UNDER THE
       JAPANESE IN CARICATURE. Spokane, WA: C. W. Hill, 1946.
       150 pp.

       Col. Fortier offers sketchings he drew from his POW
       experiences in the Philippines. There is humor in these
       cartoons, but a sense of the ordeal is present. The book
       includes a roster of 2,300 POWs.

5150. Gaskill, Robert C. GUESTS OF THE SON OF HEAVEN. New York:
       Vantage, 1976. 138 pp.

       Gaskill recounts his experiences as a POW in the
       Philippines.

5151. Goodman, Julien M. M.D. P.O.W. New York: Exposition
       Press, 1972. 218 pp.

       The author, a medical doctor, discusses his experiences
       as a POW in the Philippines. He describes the misery and
       horrid conditions at Camp O'Donnell, Cabanatuan, and
       Caloocan.

5152. Gordon, Ernest. "It Happened on the River Kwai." READER'S
       DIG, 76 (June 1960), 59-64.

       Here is a prisoner's account (as told to Clarence W.
       Hall) of the horrors of working on the "Railway of Death."
       In particular, Gordon praises the efforts of two corporals
       (Denis Moore and a man named Miller) in spreading a spirit
       of cooperation and love among the prisoners. After the
       war, many of the POWs became teachers, physicians, and
       social workers.

5153. Gordon, Ernest. THROUGH THE VALLEY OF THE KWAI. New York:
       Harper and Row, 1962. 257 pp.

       Gordon, a British officer, endured four years as a POW
       under the Japanese. He attributes his survival to the
       strength of his newly found religious faith. He later

wrote a similar work entitled MIRACLE ON THE RIVER KWAI
(London: Collins, 1973).

5154. Guirey, E.L. and H.C. Nixon. LAUGHTER IN HELL. Caldwell,
        ID: Caston Printers, 1954. 256 pp.

        The two Marines, Lt. Guirey and Tech. Sgt. Nixon, tell
        the story of their POW experiences at Osaka and Tsuruga
        under the Japanese. Their look on the bright side does not
        entirely disguise the suffering of the ordeal. The story
        appears as told to Stephen Marek.

5155. Omitted.

5156. Grashio, Samuel C. and Bernard Norling. RETURN TO FREEDOM:
        THE WAR MEMOIRS OF COL. SAMUEL C. GRASHIO USAF (RET.).
        Tulsa, OK: MCN Press, 1982. 178 pp.

        Grashio survived the Death March and later escaped (with
        nine other Americans and two Filipinos) from the Japanese.
        He remained as a guerrilla in Mindanao for a time before
        leaving the Philippines. Grashio feels that news of their
        escape should have been released rather than suppressed,
        because Japanese authorities might then have corrected the
        harsh treatment being inflicted on the prisoners of war.

5157. Harrison, Kenneth. THE BRAVE JAPANESE. San Francisco, CA:
        Tri-Ocean Books, 1967. 280 pp.

        Harrison, an Australian sergeant, exhibits commendable
        understanding in telling of his ordeal as a POW in several
        locations (Malaya, Singapore, Thailand, and Japan).
        Nevertheless, his narrative describes the brutal conduct of
        his Japanese captors.

5158. Howell, John Benjamin. 42 MONTHS OF HELL. Muskogee, OK:
        Hoffman Printing, 1970. 54 pp.

        Howell survived the Death March from Bataan and Japanese
        prison camps in the Philippines and Japan. This is the
        tale of a wretched experience with a melancholy epilogue.

5159. James, D. Clayton, ed. SOUTH TO BATAAN, NORTH TO MUKDEN:
        THE PRISON DIARY OF BRIGADIER GENERAL W. E. BROUGHER.
        Athens, GA: University of Georgia Press, 1971. 207 PP.

        Brougher commanded the 11th Division of the Philippine
        Army. The editor's excellent introduction surveys
        Brougher's combat record and experiences until the
        surviving diary pages begin in 1943. General Harold K.
        Johnson, a POW under the Japanese and later the Army's

Chief of Staff, introduces the book and observes that the
Brougher diaries reflect the more favorable end of the POW
spectrum (despite the hardships the general suffered). In
his occasional moods of depression, Brougher questions
prewar American policies and preparedness.

5160. Johnson, Leland E. I WAS PRISONER OF THE JAPS. Los
        Angeles, CA: Author, 1947, 144 pp.

        Johnson, a pentacostal minister, tells of his experience
as an internee at Baguio.

5161. Keith, Agnes Newton. "Proudery and Arrogance." ATLANTIC
        MON, 179 (January 1947), 29-38.

        The title comes from a description of the British by the
Japanese. The author describes her experiences and those
of her husband and young son as internees under the
Japanese in North Borneo. Both Japanese brutality and the
Japanese quality of mercy were shown to her, according to
this narrative.

5162. Keith, Agnes Newton. "White Man Returns." ATLANTIC MON,
        182 (October 1948), 39-48.

        The author, an American wife of a British citizen,
describes her family's return (after more than three years
as internees during the war) in 1947 to North Borneo.

5163. Keith, Billy. DAYS OF ANGUISH, DAYS OF HOPE. Garden City,
        NY: Doubleday, 1972. 216 pp.

        Here is the double-tragic story of a chaplain taken
prisoner in the Philippines. After surviving the ordeal of
captivity at war's end, Keith found that his wife had
remarried.

5164. Kent Hughes, Wilfred S. SLAVES OF THE SAMURAI. Melbourne,
        Aus.: Oxford University Press, 1946. 296 pp.

        The author presents his experiences as an Australian POW
for 3 years and 7 months under the Japanese. See
especially the selections of his poetry.

5165. Kephart, Rodney. WAKE, WAR AND WAITING. New York:
        Exposition Press, 1950. 84 pp.

        Captured at Wake Island, Kephart reveals his wartime

experiences as a POW. The brevity of his report does not
do justice to the ordeal.

5166. Kinvig, Clifford. DEATH RAILWAY. New York: Ballantine
Books, 1973. 159 pp.

The author worked on the notorious Burma-Siam Railroad
as a prisoner of the Japanese.

5167. Lawton, Manny. SOME SURVIVED. Chapel Hill, NC: Algonquin
Books, 1984. 295 pp.

Lawton tells of his experiences as a POW after
surrendering at Bataan. See especially the horrific tale
of his survival aboard one of the Japanese "Hell Ships," in
which about three-quarters of his comrades perished. It is
a tale of self-discipline and an iron will to survive.

5168. Levering, Robert W. HORROR TREK: A TRUE STORY OF BATAAN.
THE DEATH MARCH AND THREE AND ONE-HALF YEARS IN JAPANESE
PRISON CAMPS. Dayton, OH: Horstman Printing, 1948.
233 pp.

The author, a civil engineer, describes in vivid detail
the difficulties of his long ordeal in the Philippines.

5169. McCormac, Charles. YOU'LL DIE IN SINGAPORE. New York: E.
P. Dutton, 1955. 189 pp.

This readable POW account ends happily, with the author
escaping into the Malayan jungle and finally reaching safe
haven in Australia.

5170. McCoy, Melvyn H. and Stephen M. Mellnick. TEN ESCAPE FROM
TOJO. New York: Farrar and Rinehart, 1944. 106 pp.

The authors give their account to Willbourn Kelly. In
describing the harsh treatment against POWs in the
Philippines by the Japanese, the authors claim that their
reporting is restricted to first-hand knowledge. After
their escape, the authors joined with Filipino guerrilla
forces. It is a chilling account.

5171. McCracken, Alan. VERY SOON NOW, JOE. New York: Hobson
Book Press, 1947. 186 pp.

Here is McCracken's account of his trials as a POW under
the Japanese.

5172. McDougall, William H. BY EASTERN WINDOWS. New York:
       Charles Scribner's Sons, 1949. 349 pp.

       The author spent three years as a POW in Sumatra. He
       manages to maintain a charitable tone despite the brutal
       hardships inflicted by his captors.

5173. McDougall, William H. SIX BELLS OFF JAVA: A NARRATIVE OF
       ONE MAN'S PRIVATE MIRACLE. New York: Charles
       Scribner's Sons, 1948. 222 pp.

       This American reporter escaped from Shanghai when Japan
       declared war on the United States. The ship, however, that
       was taking him to Australia sank, and he fell captive to
       the Japanese. With his gift of effective writing,
       McDougall describes his adventures and his ordeal as a
       captive in Sumatra.

5174. Moody, Samuel B. and Maury Allen. REPRIEVE FROM HELL. New
       York: Pageant Press, 1961. 213 pp.

       Here is Moody's account of his experiences as a
       non-commissioned officer in the Philippines. After being
       taken prisoner, he was subsequently sent to Japan. Moody
       testified at the war crimes trial. There is much G.I.
       lingo.

5175. Morin, Relman. CIRCUIT OF CONQUEST. New York: A.A.
       Knopf, 1943. 361 pp.

       Morin, a U.S. reporter, spent three years in Japan prior
       to the war. Just before hostilities erupted, he went to
       Indochina. He was caught there, imprisoned, and finally
       repatriated. The book not only presents his account of the
       experience but also provides a good look at Japanese
       society on the edge of war with the United States.

5176. Nason, Joseph G. and Robert Lawrence Hold. HORIO YOU NEXT
       DIE. Carlsbad, CA: Pacific Rim Press, 1987. 264 pp.

       Nason was shot down on his first combat mission over
       Rabaul. Conditions were particularly bad for POWs there.
       Only 6 of the 63 Allied POWs at Rabaul survived the war.
       Of special interest is the description of another of the
       survivors, Pappy Boyington.

5177. Nash, David. "Those Wonderful Naval Aviators." USNIP, 87
       (May 1961), 84-87.

Nash, a POW in the Philippines, was aboard a transport ship that U.S. naval aviators sunk--and he was happy about it!

5178. Newman, Samuel A. HOW TO SURVIVE AS A PRISONER OF WAR. Philadelphia, PA: Franklin, 1970. 183 pp.

Newman's advice is based on personal experience with the Japanese.

5179. Nolan, Liam. SMALL MAN OF NANTAKI. New York: E.P. Dutton, 1966.

This account by a POW praises the adventures of a Japanese man who risked his life to provide aid to the enemy POWs.

5180. Nussbaum, Chaim. CHAPLAIN ON THE RIVER KWAI: STORY OF A PRISONER OF WAR. New York: Shapolsky Publishers, 1987. 328 pp.

Taken captive at Java, Nussbaum kept a secret diary during his ordeal, which also included stops at Singapore and Thailand. He promoted cultural activities among the POWs (e.g., a cultural magazine), and he established a prison synagogue. Illustrations are provided by a fellow POW, Ronald Searle.

5181. O'Leary, Cedrick P. A SHAMROCK UP A BAMBOO TREE: THE STORY OF EIGHT YEARS BEHIND THE 8-BALL IN SHANGHAI, 1941-49. New York: Exposition Press, 1956. 235 pp.

Here is a colorful account of O'Leary's experiences. For much of this period, he suffered as a POW. Despite the ordeal, he manages to maintain a sense of humor.

5182. Oliver, William P., Jr. DIARY OF WILLIAM P. OLIVER, JR., A PRISONER OF THE JAPANESE IN THE PHILIPPINE ISLANDS. Cedar Rapids, IA: Torch Press, 1947. 72 pp.

The diary covers the period April 30, 1942-June 21, 1944. Suffering separate sicknesses, Oliver claims that the Japanese fed him better than had the U.S. quarter-master. The secretly recorded document survived the war but its author did not. Oliver died when the Japanese transport ship he was aboard fell victim to U.S. torpedos. His recorded observations provide a description of life as a POW in the Philippines.

5183. Parkin, Ray. OUT OF THE SMOKE. New York: William Morrow,
       1960. 310 pp.

       Parkin wrote this account during the more than three
       years that he spent in various Japanese prison camps. An
       artist and quartermaster aboard the Australian cruiser
       PERTH. Returning from the Battle of Java Sea, and carrying
       some American survivors from the U.S.S. HOUSTON, the ship
       was sunk by the Japanese in Sundra Strait. Parking was the
       last man to leave the PERTH, directed to do so by the
       captain who went down with his ship. A collection of 49
       Australian and American survivors managed to reach a small
       island. Rigging a sail to an abandoned lifeboat, ten of
       the group, including the author, decided to try to sail to
       Australia. When their vessel was put in at Tjilatjap, the
       group fell captive to the Japanese. Almost as an
       anticlimax, Parking toiled on the notorious Burma-Siamese
       Railway.

5184. Pavillard, Stanley S. BAMBOO DOCTOR. New York: St.
       Martin's Press, 1960. 206 pp.

       Pavillard reports on medical and sanitary conditions
       during his captivity under the Japanese.

5185. Philpot, Oliver. "Morale in a Prison Camp." AIR U Q REV,
       6 (Spring 1953), 55-62.

       Although Philpot was imprisoned by the Germans (and
       escaped), this article is of general interest on the
       subject of prisoners of war. For example, he describes
       positive and negative influences on the general morale of a
       POW.

5186. Pohlman, Max Edward and Edward Francis Ritter, Jr.
       "Observations on Vitamin Deficiencies in An Eye, Ear,
       Nose and Throat Clinic of a Japanese Prison Hospital."
       AMER J OPHTHALMOLOGY, 35 (February 1952), 228-230.

       The authors treated U.S. POWs in Manila's Bilibad
       prison. This excellent, well-written article notes the
       dramatic response proper food and vitamin therapy produced.
       (Ritter was killed by U.S. attackers while aboard an
       unmarked Japanese ship.)

5187. Poweleit, Alvin C. USAFFE, THE LOYAL AMERICANS AND
       FAITHFUL FILIPINOS: A SAGA OF ATROCITIES PERPETUATED
       DURING THE FALL OF THE PHILIPPINES, THE BATAAN DEATH
       MARCH, AND JAPANESE IMPRISONMENT AND SURVIVAL. n.p.:

Author, 1975. 182 pp.

Virtually every page of this book indicates the deeply emotional response of the author to his ordeal.

5188. Priestwood, Gwen. THROUGH JAPANESE BARBED WIRE. New York: Appleton-Century, 1943. 197 pp.

Here is the escape account of a British woman who had been interned at Hong Kong by the conquering Japanese. In a light-hearted vein, she describes her thousand-mile flight to a safe haven in China with an Englishman who also escaped from the Japanese.

5189. Proulx, Benjamin A. UNDERGROUND FROM HONG KONG. New York: E.P. Dutton, 1943. 214 pp.

Having lived as a stockholder more than twenty years in Hong Kong by 1941, the author volunteered for service. Here is his description of his adventures in battle, his capture, and his escape from the Japanese.

5190. Quinn, Michael A. LOVE LETTERS TO MIKE. New York: Vantage Press, 1977. 331 pp.

Quinn spent forty months as a prisoner of the Japanese, from April 9, 1942, to September 17, 1945. His lengthy narrative describes in detail the challenges of that experience.

5191. Rawlings, Leo. AND THE DAWN CAME UP LIKE THUNDER. Harpenden, Eng.: Rawlings Chapman Publications, 1972. 160 pp.

Rawlings gives a personal report on the disastrous British defeat at Malaya and his chilling experiences as a POW.

5192. Reynolds, Robert. OF RICE AND MEN. Philadelphia, PA: Dorrance, 1947. 186 pp.

Reynolds reveals his experiences at Bataan, on the Death March, and in varous Japanese prison camps. Unlike some such accounts, he confines his narrative to first-hand evidence.

5193. Robinson, Frank and E.R. "Bon" Hall. THROUGH HELL AND BOMB BLAST. Waverley, Tasmania: 1982.

The colorful Australian "Bon" Hall, gives a memorable
account of his captivity under the Japanese. Of special
interest is his report on a fellow Australian prisoner,
Peter McGrath-Kerr, at Nagasaki.

5194. Searle, Ronald. TO THE KWAI AND BACK. Atlantic Monthly
        Press, 1986. 192 pp.

        Here are the war drawings of Searle (an art student)
        during his years as a POW. A brief narrative accompanies
        the art work.

5195. Shimel, J. "32 Months a Jap Prisoner." LEATHERNECK (May
        1945).

        NE

5196. Simson, I. "Education Extraordinary: A Story of Prisoners
        of War in the Far East." ARMY Q DEF J, 86 (April 1963),
        63-69.

        The author draws on his experiences as a POW to
        emphasize the importance of formal study and other
        educational opportunities ("Changi University") while in
        such difficult circumstances.

5197. Skidmore, Ian: ESCAPE FROM SINGAPORE, 1942. New York:
        Charles Scribner's Sons, 1974. 198 pp.

        Skidmore, a British soldier, chronicles his journey from
        Singapore to safety (evading the conquering Japanese). In
        Great Britain, the book was published in 1973 under the
        title ESCAPE FROM THE RISING SUN.

5198. Smith, C.D. QUENTIN REYNOLDS' OFFICIALLY DEAD. New York:
        Random House, 1945. 244 pp.

        Here is the story, pieced together by Quentin Reynolds,
        of Cmdr. C.D. Smith, captain of the gunboat WAKE on the
        Yangtse River. Captured by the Japanese, Smith escaped and
        made his way some 700 miles to safe haven in China.

5199. Smith, Stanley E. THIRTEEN AGAINST THE RISING SUN. New
        York: Belmont Books, 1961. 140 pp.

        NE

5200. Stellingwerff, J. FAT MAN IN NAGASAKI. Franeker, Wever,
        1980. 159 pp.

NE

5201.   Stewart, Sidney. GIVE US THIS DAY. New York: W.W.
        Norton, 1956. 254 pp.

        The author was taken prisoner at Bataan. His narrative
        is filled with the terrible details, frankly described, of
        captivity under the Japanese. Moved from camp to camp and
        a survivor of the horrible hell ship transportation to
        Japan, Stewart, astonishingly, reports on his ordeal with
        toleration and an absence of bitterness.

5202.   Taylor, Vince. CABANATUAN: JAPANESE DEATH CAMP. Maco, TX:
        Texian Press, 1985. 208 pp.

        Taylor recounts his ill treatment at the hands of the
        Japanese in this special POW camp in the Philippines.

5203.   Tharp, Mel. "The Nightmare of Bataan." SERGEANTS, 23 (May
        1984), 24-25.

        NE

5204.   Tinker, Frank. "Yup, it hurts." MC GAZ, 54 (May 1970),
        47-50.

        Tinker, a wartime prisoner, relates the terrible
        treatment endured by a fellow POW, "Pappy" Boyington.
        According to Tinker, Boyinton was a model prisoner, not the
        rebel and hell raiser portrayed in the media.

5205.   Vance, John R. DOOMED GARRISON--THE PHILIPPINES (A POW
        STORY). Ashland, OR: Cascade House, 1974. 248 pp.

        The author served as principal disbursing officer from
        the U.S. Army in the Philippines. Before the surrender to
        the Japanese, he was in charge of two million pesos in
        currency. As a POW, he was moved from Bilibad to Tarlac to
        Taiwan (where he stayed with Wainwright, Percival and other
        VIPs) and to Mukden. At war's end, Americans took over the
        camp in Manchuria after a couple of Russian soldiers had
        appeared and announced news of Japan's surrender. Vance
        writes that a short time later substantial Soviet forces
        arrived and the commander could not believe that the former
        Japanese guards (now prisoners) were still alive.

5206.   Van Der Post, Laurens. THE PRISONER AND THE BOMB. New

York: William Morrow, 1971. 152 pp.

The book appeared in England under the title THE NIGHT
OF THE NEW MOON in 1970. Col. van der Post, a British
Afrikaaner, was a POW in Java. The book generally
describes what he calls "my own private little world
underneath my mosquito net." Through a reliable source he
discovered that Field Marshal Terauchi had prepared orders
to kill all POWs and internees under him (200,000-400,000?)
on the date that the Allies launched an invasion of
Southeast Asia. After the war the author learned that
Mountbatten had scheduled the invasion for September 6,
1945. Faced with this three-week reprieve, van der Post is
amazed at what he considers the "one-sided thinking" which
condemns the use of the atomic bomb. He had secreted a
cache of rocks to fight off his would-be exterminators
whenever they came for him. Of interest is his report that
POWs suffered more at the hands of their Korean guards than
under the Japanese. He writes that the "proxy" destruction
of animals and furniture by the guards invariably
foreshadowed imminent violent treatment of the POWs.

5207. Warner, Lavinia and John Sandilands. WOMEN BEYOND THE
        WIRE. London: Joseph, 1982. 289 pp.

Here is a report on conditions of British prisoners
under the Japanese in Malaya and Indonesia.

5208. Weinstein, Alfred A. BARBED-WIRE SURGEON. New York:
        Macmillan, 1948. 310 pp.

The author served as a surgeon in the Army Medical Corps
in Manila and Bataan. Weinstein then practiced medicine
for his fellow prisoners while in the Philippines and
Japan. In addition to his medical reports, he tells of the
human strengths and weaknesses in coping with the
challenges of captivity under the Japanese.

5209. Whitcomb, Edgar D. ESCAPE FROM CORREGIDOR. Chicago:
        Henry Regnery, 1958. 274 pp.

When the war began, the author was serving as a
navigator with the 19th Bombardment Group in the
Philippines. He enjoyed the unique experience of escaping
twice from the Japanese after being taken prisoner.
Finally, under a civilian disguise, Whitcomb was
repatriated. He later returned to the Philippines with the
liberating Allied forces.

5210.   Whitney, Hans. GUEST OF THE FALLEN SUN: IN THE
         PRISONER-OF-WAR CAMPS IN JAPAN AND CHINA. New York:
         Exposition Press, 1951. 69 pp.

         Whitney's writings of his POW ordeal are edited by Dan
         Sterling.

5211.   Wilkinson, John D. SKETCHES OF A P.O.W. IN KOREA.
         Melbourne, Aus.: Wilke and Co., 1945. 36 pp.

         Wilkinson, taken prisoner at Singapore and subsequently
         transferred by the Japanese to Korea, presents the drawings
         and art work he created during his captivity. The art
         underscores the emotions and suffering of the prisoners.

5212.   Yamamoto, Tomomi. FOUR YEARS IN HELL. Tokyo: Asian,
         1952. 300 pp.

         The author survived four years as a prisoner in the
         Soviet Union. His account of the ordeal is remarkably
         similar to those of U.S. prisoners under the Japanese.

VI.K.2. CIVILIAN INTERNEES

5213.   Abkhazi, Peggy. THE CURIOUS CAGE: A SHANGHAI JOURNAL.
         Victoria, B.C.: Sono Nis Press, 1981. 143 pp.

         The author, an Englishwoman who enjoyed a high standard
         of living in prewar Shangai, kept a daily journal from
         December 8, 1941, to--and through--her internment. The
         journal, edited by S. W. Jackman, remains an important
         contemporary account.

5214.   Argall, Phyllis. MY LIFE WITH THE ENEMY. New York:
         Macmillan, 1944. 290 pp.

         Here is the personal account of a Canadian woman who
         lived in Japan for twenty-six years as a missionary,
         educator, and reporter. In fact, her anti-Axis writings
         led to her arrest and imprisonment in 1942. Through the
         help of Joseph Grew, Argall was repatriated aboard the
         GRIPSHOLM. Her critical views run against extreme Japanese
         militarists, as opposed to the Japanese people.

5215.   Bartter, George. FRANCES CROSBY BARTTER, AUGUST 23,
         1879-JUNE 13, 1946: A MEMOIR OF FOUR YEARS. Boston:
         Merrymount Press, 1946. 12 pp.

         The author extols the work of his late wife, who was

interned during the war at Baguio (Philippines).

5216.   Bloom, Lynn Z.   "The Diary As Pop Culture."   J POP CULT, 9
        (Spring 1976), 794-807.

        Bloom argues that diaries comprise an important element
        of historical study.   As an example, she identifies the
        types of information (e.g., food, recreation, organization
        and hierarchy of the interns) available in the diary of a
        civilian intern in the Philippines, Natalie Crouter.
        (Bloom edited the publication of this diary.)

5217.   Bloom, Lynn Z.   "Till Death Do Us Part: Men's and Women's
        Interpretations of Wartime Internment."   WOMEN'S STUD
        INTL FORUM, 10 (No. 1, 1987), 75-83.

        NE

5218.   Booker, Edna Lee.   FLIGHT FROM CHINA.   New York: Macmillan
        Company, 1945.   236 pp.

        The author, a foreign correspondent, collaborates with
        her husband, John S. Potter, to recount their war
        experiences.   The family had lived in Shanghai for over
        twenty years prior to the 1940 evacuation of Edna and her
        daughter.   John, a Shanghai businessman, remained under
        Japanese internment from 1940 until his repatriation in
        December 1943.   Their story includes vivid examples of the
        daily insults and boorish behavior of certain elements of
        the Japanese forces in China.

5219.   Brines, Russell.   UNTIL THEY EAT STONES.   Philadelphia:
        J.B. Lippincott, 1944.   340 pp.

        As a correspondent, Brines observed the brutality of
        Japanese militarism.   He actually lived with Japanese
        troops during the battle at Nomonhan in 1939.   After
        covering part of the story of occupied Asia, he (and his
        family) suffered the indignities of internment by the
        Japanese until being repatriated.   Here is a valuable
        contemporary account by someone who knows his material and
        writes well.

5220.   Bryant, Alice Franklin.   THE SUN WAS DARKENED.   Boston:
        Chapman and Grimes, 1947.   262 pp.

        Bryant describes her experiences at Negros as she, her
        husband, and her daughter attempted to hide from the
        Japanese.   Eventually the family was captured and interned

in the Philippines. With a keenly observant eye, she
examines the differing reactions of various interns to
their plight.

5221. Chapman, James and Ethel Chapman. ESCAPE TO THE HILLS.
       Lancaster, PA: The Jaques Cattell Press, 1947. 247 pp.

       James Chapman, an entomologist from Harvard, had been
       teaching at Silliman in the Philippines since 1916. When
       the war broke out, he and his wife chose not to surrender
       to the Japanese. Instead, they lived at Camp Lookout until
       Wainwright's defeat and then moved into the mountains.
       They comment about their satisfactory diet in the mountains
       (and even had the good fortune to observe the rare aenictus
       ants). The Japanese captured them in November 1943, and
       the couple spent the rest of the war in the Santo Tomas
       Internment Camp.

5222. Corbett, P. Scott. QUIET PASSAGES: THE EXCHANGE OF
       CIVILIANS BETWEEN THE UNITED STATES AND JAPAN DURING THE
       SECOND WORLD WAR. Kent, OH: Kent State University
       Press, 1987. 242 pp.

       The author traces the activities of the State
       Department's "Special Division" in arranging two exchanges
       with Japan. Of interest is the linkage formed by Corbett
       between these exchanges and the evacuation of
       Japanese-Americans in the United States. Praising the work
       of James H. Keeley, the author reveals that Keeley elicited
       an admission from a U.S. submarine commander who realized
       beforehand that his sub was about to attack a Japanese
       hospital ship (actually carrying American POWs). The
       article is well researched and well written.

5223. Crouter, Natalie. "Forbidden Diary." AMER HERITAGE, 30
       (April/May 1979), 78-95.

       Accompanied by sketches from Daphne Bird, Crouter
       provides excerpts of the secret diary she kept as an
       internee under the Japanese in the Philippines.

5224. Crouter, Natalie. FORBIDDEN DIARY: A RECORD OF WARTIME
       INTERNMENT. New York: Burt Franklin and Co., 1980.
       546 pp.

       Lynn Z. Bloom edited the diary of Mrs. Crouter, who,
       together with her husband, daughter, and son, spent the war
       as internees in the Philippines. The book, an abridgment
       of the entire wartime diary, describes the relatively mild

captivity at Camp Holmes. (Despite the undeniable
hardships at Camp Holmes, a shocked Crouter got her first
look at the skeletal military prisoners on February 5,
1945, and she exclaimed, "THERE was starvation....") In
addition to portraying the daily "rage and feeling of
helplessness," the diary traces the development of the
camp's government including its sexist, discriminatory
base. Here is an important contribution.

5225.   Deutsch, Helen E. GOD WAS WITH ME IN A JAPANESE
        CONCENTRATION CAMP. Miami, FL: Author, 1945. 28 pp.

        Deutsch reveals the religious influence on her trying
        experiences under the Japanese.

5226.   Dew, Given. PRISONER OF THE JAPS. New York: A.A. Knopf,
        1943. 309 pp.

        Dew, a U.S. reporter in Hong Kong, witnessed the
        Japanese victory there. The Japanese interned Dew for six
        months before repatriating her. The book details the
        horrors of the Japanese captors.

5227.   Edwards, B.F. "Los Banos Internment Camp: Escape and
        Liberation." BULL AMER HIST COLL, (Manila), 13
        (April-June 1985), 60-68.

        NE

5228.   Emmens, Robert G. GUESTS OF THE KREMLIN. New York:
        Macmillan, 1949. 291 pp.

        Col. Emmens (USAAF) flew as a co-pilot on one of the
        crews in the Doolittle mission. His aircraft made a forced
        landing in the Soviet Union. International law required
        that the crew be interned by the Soviets. Over a year
        later a secret arrangement enabled the crew to "escape" to
        Iran. Stalin, however, apparently demanded that the crew
        be used in the European theater. The narrative is
        straightforward and refreshingly restrained.

5229.   Gilkey, Langdon. SHANTUNG COMPOUND: THE STORY OF MEN AND
        WOMEN UNDER PRESSURE. New York: Harper and Row, 1966.
        242 pp.

        The author, a professor at Yenching University, was
        interned by the Japanese. His story of the captivity--and
        of his fellow prisoners--emphasizes the psychological
        stress as well as the physical ordeal. Gilkey credits his

religious impluse for his survival, and it is this
perspective that prompts him to discuss the challenges that
captivity inflicted on human values.

5230. Gunnison, Royal Arch. SO SORRY, NO PEACE. New York:
       Viking, 1944. 272 pp.

       Correspondent Gunnison and his wife spent twenty-two
       months in Japanese intern camps. Their life--particularly
       the hardships they endured--under the Japanese in the
       Philippines and China comes through with surprising
       objectivity. Both were repatriated aboard the GRIPSHOLM in
       late 1943.

5231. Hahn, Emily. "Kato." NEW YORKER, 59 (December 12, 1983),
       50-60.

       Here is a touching story which shows the human side of
       the war. Hahn, her baby daughter, and her sisters lived in
       Hong Kong during the early part of the war, while the
       Japanese held her British husband captive. A Japanese
       lieutenant named Kato helped Hahn until she and her baby
       left on an exchange ship. Thirty-seven years later,
       circumstances brought Kato and Hahn together for a visit.

5232. Hartendorp, A.V.H. THE SANTO TOMAS STORY. New York:
       McGraw-Hill, 1964. 447 pp.

       Hartendorp, the editor of PHILIPPINE MAGAZINE when the
       war broke out, became the secret camp historian at Santo
       Tomas with the aid and encouragement of the
       internees--often at great risk. His observations and
       descriptions help to make this a valuable source on the
       Santo Tomas internment camp.

5233. Hill, Max. EXCHANGE SHIP. New York: Farrar and Rinehart,
       1942. 312 pp.

       The author, an Associated Press correspondent in Tokyo,
       was interned by the Japanese when the war began. As a
       passenger involved in the first U.S.-Japanese exchange of
       non-combatants (using the ships ASAMA MARU and GRIPSHOLM),
       Hill tells of the trip home. His fellow passengers
       provided him with good material. Of interest is his
       description of his treatment as an intern.

5234. Hind, R. Renton. SPIRITS UNBROKEN. San Francisco, CA:
       John Howell, 1947. 291 pp.

The author spent over three years (December
1941-February 1945) as a civilian internee in the
Philippines. His account shows how Japanese guards
alternated between strict and moderate enforcement of the
rules. Hind tries to be objective, yet realistic, about
the experience.

5235.   Keith, Agnes Newton. THREE CAME HOME. Boston: Little,
        Brown, 1947. 317 pp.

Keith wrote secretly of her experience as an intern with
her young son (and her husband in a separate camp) under
the Japanese in Borneo. She uses the label "prisoner"
instead of internee because the Japanese conducted the camp
according to POW rules. Identifying the greatest enemy as
hope deferred, Keith feels that the women were bound
together by the belief that they could not surrender to
their hatreds. Their captivity lasted from January 1942 to
September 1945. The camp commandant, Col. Suga, took his
own life while awaiting trial after the surrender.

5236.   Leffelaar, Hendrik L. THROUGH A HARSH DAWN: A BOY GROWS
        UP IN A JAPANESE PRISON CAMP. Barre, MA: Barre
        Publishing, 1963. 246 pp.

The author, a member of an influential Dutch family in
Sumatra, spent the war years in Japanese internment camps.
At different times both he and his father kept secret
journals of their experiences and life in the camps.

5237.   Lin, Ch'iu-mei. SOLD FOR SILVER. Cleveland, OH: World
        Publishers, 1959. 252 pp.

Here is the autobiography of a Chinese woman who was
sold into slavery in Singapore as a young girl.
Eventually, she escaped to a Methodist mission and later
became a nurse. When Singapore fell to the Japanese, Lin
began a horrifying period in her life. After the war, she
remained a nurse in Singapore.

5238.   Long, Frances. HALF A WORLD AWAY: FROM BOARDING SCHOOL TO
        JAP PRISON. New York: Farrar and Rinehart, 1943. 243
        pp.

The author grew up in Shanghai, where her father served
as secretary to the Consular Body. After attending
boarding school in England, she returned to Shanghai. Her
engagement to an American naval ensign led her to the
Philippines. When war broke out, Long became a civilian

intern. Surviving some unsettling experiences, Long was
repatriated aboard the GRIPSHOLM. This contemporary
account finds the author as a much-sought speaker because
of her "escape" from the Japanese.

5239. Lucas, Celia. PRISONERS OF SANTO TOMAS. London: Cooper,
        1975. 220 pp.

        This account of the civilian internees is based largely
        on the secret diaries of Isla Corfield.

5240. Meyer, Elizabeth Thomas. "Teenager Internee at Santo
        Tomas." BULL AMER HIST COLL (Manila), 14 (January-March
        1986), 7-31.

        NE

5241. Moule, William R. GOD'S ARMS AROUND US. New York:
        Vantage, 1960. 399 pp.

        Here is the personal account of an American miner and
        his family in the Philippines. When the war broke out,
        they fled to Baguio but were eventually captured and
        interned. Moule stresses the importance of religious faith
        in surviving the ordeal.

5242. Mydans, Carl. MORE THAN MEETS THE EYE. New Harper and
        Row, 1959. 319 pp.

        The LIFE photographer and his wife, Shelley, were in the
        Philippines when the war started. He tells of their
        internment at Santo Tomas and their repatriation.

5243. Mydans, Carl and Shelley Smith Mydans. "Tomorrow We Will
        Be Free," in Gordon Carroll, ed. HISTORY IN THE
        WRITING. New York: Duell, Sloan and Pearce, 1945. 413
        pp.

        The married partners report on their experiences as
        civilian internees in the Philippines. Carl is a
        professional photographer. As their story reveals, the
        couple had plenty of exposure to Japanese brutality before
        their repatriation.

5244. Ogle, Mary. WORTH THE PRICE. Washington, D. C.: Review
        and Herald Publishing Assoc., 1958. 319 pp.

        Ogle, a missionary in the Philippines, became an
        internee at Camp Holmes in Baguio. Avoiding what she

calls "unhappy experiences," Ogle offers instead a view
of internment life at the camp.

5245. Petillo, Carol M, ed. THE ORDEAL OF ELIZABETH VAUGHAN: A
        WARTIME DIARY OF THE PHILIPPINES. Athens, GA:
        University of Georgia Press, 1985. 312 pp.

        Trained as a sociologist, Vaughan served as a uniquely
        competent observer of life in captivity under the Japanese.
        She and her two children survived their ordeal as civilian
        internees. The family was living in the Philippines when
        the war began. Vaughan's husband happened to be away on
        December 7, 1941, and he joined the U.S. Army. (He died
        while a POW in 1942--after surviving the Bataan Death
        March.) Among her perceptive oberservations, see Vaughan's
        comments about the medical needs of the camp (Santo Tomas)
        and the horrifying executions by the Japanese. The book
        makes a contribution to history and sociology.

5246. Rubens, Doris. BREAD AND RICE. New York: Thurston
        Macauley, 1947. 235 pp.

        The author, a professor and news broadcaster in the
        Philippines, escaped into the hills with her husband (Ron
        Johnston) when the Japanese began occupying the country.
        Her narrative describes life with the natives and guerrilla
        activities. After about eighteen months, she surrendered
        and remained interned until being liberated by the 11th
        Airborne and Filipino guerrillas.

5247. Sneed, Bessie. CAPTURED BY THE JAPANESE. Denver, CO:
        Bradford-Robinson, 1946. 108 pp.

        The author was living in the Philippines, married to an
        American in the mining business, when the war bagan. Taken
        by the Japanese as a civilian internee, Sneed recounts her
        experiences.

5248. Stevens, Frederick H. SANTO TOMAS INTERNMENT CAMP,
        1942-1945. New York: Stratford House, 1946. 569 pp.

        Here is an excellent reference source. Stevens writes a
        history of the camp which incorporates diverse topics such
        as culture, education, medicine, and recreation. In
        addition, he presents a roster of internees at the camp.

5249. Strong, Herman E. A RINGSIDE SEAT TO WAR. New York:
        Vintage, 1965. 115 pp.

Strong's "ringside seat" was located in the Santo Tomas internment camp. His narrative traces his experiences under the Japanese.

5250. Thomas, Susie M. MORE THAN CONQUERORS THROUGH HIM THAT LOVED US. Newton, KS: United Printing, 1970. 104 pp.

Thomas offers a personal account of her missionary work in the Philippines and her internment under the Japanese.

5251. United States. Congress. Senate. Committee on the Judiciary. RELIEF FOR AMERICAN CITIZENS CAPTURED AND INTERNED BY THE JAPANESE. Washington, D.C.: GPO, 1947. 107 pp.

The hearings on this topic provide some important information about not only Japanese policies but also the extraordinary situations of some U.S. citizens (civilians).

5252. Vaughan, Elizabeth H. COMMUNITY UNDER STRESS: AN INTERNMENT CAMP CULTURE. Princeton, NJ: Princeton University Press, 1949. 160 pp.

The book originally appeared as a Ph.D dissertation at the University of North Carolina. Vaughan had received some training in sociology before the war—and her internment in the Philippines. A keen observer of group behavior, Vaughan reports on the collective reactions of the internees at the camp.

5253. White, Marcy C. I WAS THERE...WHEN IT HAPPENED IN CHINA. Nashville, TN: Abingdon-Cokesbury Press, 1947. 123 pp.

The author suffered as a civilian internee under the Japanese. Her account uncovers the brutal behavior of some of the Japanese conquerors.

5254. Witthoff, Evelyn M. and Geraldine V. Chappell. THREE YEARS' INTERNMENT IN SANTO TOMAS. Kansas City, MO: Beacon Hill Press, 1950. 62 pp.

NE

5255. Omitted.

VI.L. MEMOIRS AND BIOGRAPHIES

5256. Harrison, Earl G. AMERICANS OF FOREIGN BIRTH IN THE WAR PROGRAM FOR VICTORY. New York: American Committee for the Protection of Foreign Born, 1942. 23 pp.

Congressman Harrison speaks of the accomplishments of
these Americans and the aims of the movement at a time when
civil liberties of foreign-born Americans are under fire.
The pamphlet includes a special message of support from
President Roosevelt.

5257. Hunt, Michael H. "Pearl Buck--Popular Expert on China,
        1931-1949." MOD CHINA, 3 (January 1977), 33-64.

Hunt feels that Buck's influence stemmed chiefly from
THE GOOD EARTH, which, he says, shaped the American image
of China more than any other contemporary work. The
article traces her shifting feelings: increasingly
favorable to the Chinese Communists, uncertain about Chiang
Kai-shek, and disillusioned about U.S. foreign policies in
Asia.

5258. Sevareid, Eric A. NOT SO WILD A DREAM. New York: A.A.
        Knopf, 1946. 516 pp.

In this autobiography, Sevareid recounts his adventures
as a war correspondent. See especially his escape and
evasion of the Japanese after parachuting from a doomed
aircraft. See, too, his keen insights about the
Kuomintang. A new edition in 1976 carries an updated
Introduction.

5259. Thomas, Harry J. THE FIRST LADY OF CHINA. New York:
        International Business Machines Corp., 1943.

Here is a glowing report on Madame Chiang's visit to the
United States in 1943.

Appendixes

AERO ALBUM
AERONAUTICS
AEROSPACE HISTORIAN
AEROSPACE SAFETY
AIR DEFENSE ARTILLERY
AIR DEFENSE MAGAZINE
AIR FORCE
AIR FORCE JOURNAL OF LOGISTICS
AIR FORCE LAW REVIEW
AIR FORCE MAGAZINE
AIRMAN
AIR POWER HISTORIAN
AIR PROGRESS
AIR UNIVERSITY (QUARTERLY)
    REVIEW
ALASKA
ALASKA JOURNAL
ALBERTA HISTORY
ALL HANDS
AMERASIA
AMERASIA JOURNAL
AMERICA
AMERICAN ANTHROPOLOGIST
AMERICAN AVIATION HISTORICAL
    SOCIETY JOURNAL
AMERICAN BAR ASSOCIATION
    JOURNAL
AMERICAN HERITAGE
AMERICAN HISTORICAL REVIEW
AMERICAN HISTORY ILLUSTRATED
AMERICAN JOURNAL OF
    INTERNATIONAL LAW
AMERICAN JOURNAL OF NURSING
AMERICAN JOURNAL OF
    OPHTHALMOLOGY
AMERICAN JOURNAL OF PSYCHIATRY
AMERICAN JOURNAL OF PUBLIC
    HEALTH
AMERICAN JOURNAL OF SURGERY
AMERICAN JOURNAL OF TROPICAL
    MEDICINE AND HYGIENE
AMERICAN MAGAZINE
AMERICAN MERCURY

AMERICAN NEPTUNE
AMERICAN OPINION
AMERICAN PERSPECTIVES
AMERICAN PHILOSOPHICAL SOCIETY
    TRANSACTIONS
AMERICAN QUARTERLY
AMERICAN REVIEW
AMERICAN SOCIOLOGICAL REVIEW
AMERICAN STUDIES
AMERICAN STUDIES INTERNATIONAL
ANNALS OF INTERNAL MEDICINE
ANNALS OF THE AMERICAN ACADEMY
    OF POLITICAL AND SOCIAL
    SCIENCE
ANTIOCH REVIEW
APPLIED ANTHROPOLOGY
ARIZONA WEST
ARKANSAS HISTORICAL QUARTERLY
ARMED FORCES JOURNAL
    INTERNATIONAL
ARMED FORCES AND SOCIETY
ARMOR
ARMORED CAVALRY JOURNAL
ARMY
ARMY INFORMATION DIGEST
ARMY MAGAZINE
ARMY QUARTERLY (DEFENCE
    JOURNAL)
ASIA AND PACIFIC COMMUNITY
ASIA AND THE AMERICAS
ASIAN AFFAIRS
ASIAN AFFAIRS (LONDON)
ASIAN PROFILE
ASIAN SURVEY
ASIAN THOUGHT AND SOCIETY
ASSEMBLY
ATLANTIC MONTHLY
AUSTRALIAN ECONOMIC HISTORY
    REVIEW
AUSTRALIAN JOURNAL OF POLITICS
    AND HISTORY
AUSTRALIAN OUTLOOK
AVIATION QUARTERLY

INDONESIA
INFANTRY
INFANTRY JOURNAL
INQUIRY
INTERNATIONAL AFFAIRS (LONDON)
INTERNATIONAL AFFAIRS (MOSCOW)
INTERNATIONAL CONCILIATION
INTERNATIONAL HISTORY REVIEW
INTERNATIONAL JOURNAL OF
    CONTEMPORARY SOCIETY
INTERNATIONAL RELATIONS
INTERNATIONAL REVIEW OF SOCIAL
    HISTORY
INTERNATIONAL SECURITY
INTERNATIONAL SOCIAL SCIENCE
    REVIEW
INTERNATIONAL SOCIALIST REVIEW
INTERNATIONAL STUDIES QUARTERLY
ITIHAS

JAPAN ECHO
JAPAN INTERPRETER
JAPAN QUARTERLY
JOINT PERSPECTIVES
JOURNAL OF ABNORMAL AND SOCIAL
    PSYCHOLOGY
JOURNAL OF AMERICAN HISTORY
JOURNAL OF THE AMERICAN MEDICAL
    ASSOCIATION
JOURNAL OF AMERICAN STUDIES
JOURNAL OF ARIZONA HISTORY
JOURNAL OF ASIAN AND AFRICAN
    STUDIES
JOURNAL OF ASIAN HISTORY
JOURNAL OF ASIAN STUDIES
JOURNAL OF THE BAR ASSOCIATION
    OF WASHINGTON, D.C.
JOURNAL OF THE CANADIAN CHURCH
    HISTORY SOCIETY
JOURNAL OF CHURCH AND STATE
JOURNAL OF CONTEMPORARY HISTORY
JOURNAL OF ETHNIC STUDIES
JOURNAL OF EUROPEAN STUDIES
JOURNAL OF INDIAN HISTORY
JOURNAL OF IMPERIAL AND
    COMMONWEALTH HISTORY
JOURNAL OF INTERNATIONAL
    STUDIES
JOURNAL OF JAPANESE STUDIES

JOURNAL OF LIBERTARIAN STUDIES
JOURNAL OF LIBRARY HISTORY
JOURNAL OF MODERN HISTORY
JOURNAL OF PEACE RESEARCH
JOURNAL OF POPULAR CULTURE
JOURNAL OF PRESBYTERIAN HISTORY
JOURNAL OF RADIATION RESEARCH
JOURNAL OF RESOLUTION STUDIES
JOURNAL OF SAN DIEGO HISTORY
JOURNAL OF THE SIAM SOCIETY
JOURNAL OF SOCIAL ISSUES
JOURNAL OF SOCIAL PSYCHOLOGY
JOURNAL OF SOUTHEAST ASIAN
    HISTORY
JOURNAL OF SOUTHEAST ASIAN
    STUDIES
JOURNAL OF SOUTHERN HISTORY
JOURNAL OF STRATEGIC STUDIES
JOURNAL OF THE WEST
JOURNALISM QUARTERLY

LABOR TODAY
LAURELS
LEATHERNECK
LEYTE-SAMAR STUDIES
LIBERTY
LIBRARY OF CONGRESS INFORMATION
    BULLETIN
LIFE
LOOK
LOS ALAMOS SCIENCE
LOUISIANA BAR JOURNAL

MACLEAN'S
MARINE CORPS GAZETTE
MARYLAND HISTORIAN
MEDICINE
MICHIGAN ACADEMICIAN
MICROFORM REVIEW
MID-AMERICA
MIDWAY
MILITARY AFFAIRS
MILITARY ENGINEER
MILITARY HISTORY
MILITARY LAW REVIEW
MILITARY REVIEW
MILLENIUM
MILWAUKEE HISTORY
MINNESOTA HISTORY

MISSISSIPPI VALLEY HISTORICAL
    REVIEW
MODERN AGE
MODERN ASIAN STUDIES
MODERN CHINA
MONUMENTA NIPPONICA
NATION
NATIONAL DEFENSE
NATIONAL REVIEW
NAVAL AVIATION FOUNDATION
    MUSEUM
NAVAL AVIATION NEWS
NAVAL REVIEW
NAVAL WAR COLLEGE FORUM
NAVAL WAR COLLEGE REVIEW
NAVIGATOR
NAVY
NEBRASKA HISTORY
NEVADA HISTORICAL SOCIETY
    QUARTERLY
NEW ENGLAND JOURNAL OF MEDICINE
NEW MEXICO HISTORICAL REVIEW
NEW REPUBLIC
NEW STATESMAN
NEW YORKER

OFFICER, THE
OHIO HISTORY
OLD FORT NEWS
ONI REVIEW
ORACLE
ORAL HISTORY REVIEW
ORBIS
ORDNANCE
OREGON HISTORICAL QUARTERLY
OSIRIS

PACIFIC AFFAIRS
PACIFIC HISTORIAN
PACIFIC HISTORICAL REVIEW
PACIFIC NORTHWEST QUARTERLY
PACIFIC NORTHWESTERNER
PACIFIC SPECTATOR
PACIFIC STUDIES
PAKISTAN HORIZON
PARAMETERS
PEACE AND CHANGE
PEOPLE
PERSPECTIVES

PERSPECTIVES IN AMERICAN
    HISTORY
PHILIPPINE STUDIES
PHILIPPINES HISTORY ASSOCIATION
PHILOSOPHY OF SCIENCE
PHYLON
PHYSICS TODAY
POLITICAL SCIENCE QUARTERLY
POLITICAL STUDIES
POLITY
POPULAR SCIENCE
PRESIDENTIAL STUDIES QUARTERLY
PRINCETON LIBRARIAN
PRINCETON UNIVERSITY LIBRARY
    CHRONICLE
PROCEEDINGS OF THE AMERICAN
    PHILOSOPHICAL SOCIETY
PROCEEDINGS OF THE CONFERENCE
    ON WAR AND DIPLOMACY, THE
    CITADEL
PROCEEDINGS OF THE
    MASSACHUSETTS HISTORICAL
    SOCIETY
PROCEEDINGS OF THE PACIFIC
    SOCIOLOGY ASSOCIATION
PROGRESSIVE
PROLOGUE
PSYCHIATRY
PUBLIC HISTORIAN
PUBLIC OPINION QUARTERLY
PUBLIC POLICY

QUARTERLY JOURNAL OF SPEECH
QUARTERLY REVIEW OF HISTORICAL
    STUDIES
QUARTERMASTER REVIEW

RACE AND CLASS
RADICAL HISTORY REVIEW
READER'S DIGEST
RECORDS OF THE AMERICAN
    CATHOLIC HISTORICAL
    SOCIETY OF PHILADELPHIA
REGISTER OF THE KENTUCKY
    HISTORICAL SOCIETY
RENDEZVOUS
REPORTER
RESEARCH STUDIES OF THE STATE
    COLLEGE OF WASHINGTON

REVIEW OF INTERNATIONAL STUDIES
REVIEW OF POLITICS
ROYAL AIR FORCES QUARTERLY
ROYAL UNITED SERVICE INSTITUTE
    (FOR DEFENCE STUDIES)
    JOURNAL
SAIS REVIEW
SATURDAY REVIEW
SATURDAY REVIEW OF LITERATURE
SCHOOL LIBRARY JOURNAL
SCIENCE
SCIENCE AND PUBLIC AFFAIRS
SCIENCE AND SOCIETY
SEA POWER
SENIOR SCHOLASTIC
SERGEANTS
SHIPMATE
SIGNAL
SOCIAL FORCES
SOCIAL HISTORY
SOCIAL RESEARCH
SOCIAL STUDIES OF SCIENCE
SOCIOLOGY AND SOCIAL RESEARCH
SOLDIERS
SOUTH ATLANTIC QUARTERLY
SOUTH DAKOTA HISTORY
SOUTH EAST ASIA
SOUTHEAST ASIA: AN
    INTERNATIONAL QUARTERLY
SOUTH EAST ASIAN CHRONICLE
SOUTHERN CALIFORNIA QUARTERLY
SOUTHERN HISTORY
SOUTHERN QUARTERLY
SOUTHERN SPEECH COMMUNICATION
    JOURNAL
SOVIET MILITARY REVIEW
SOVIET STUDIES IN HISTORY
SPEAKER AND GAVEL
STRATEGIC REVIEW
STRATEGY AND TACTICS
STUDIES IN COMPARATIVE
    COMMUNISM
SURGERY, GYNECOLOGY AND
    OBSTETRICS
SURVEY

TEACHING HISTORY
TECHNOLOGY REVIEW
THEATRE SURVEY

TOWSON STATE JOURNAL OF
    INTERNATIONAL AFFAIRS
TRANSACTIONS OF THE GROTIUS
    SOCIETY
TRANSACTIONS OF THE NEW YORK
    ACADEMY OF SCIENCES
TRANSLOG

UNITED NATIONS REVIEW
UNITED NATIONS WORLD
UNITED SERVICE INSTITUTION OF
    INDIA JOURNAL
U.S. NEWS AND WORLD REPORT
UNITED STATES ARMY MILITARY
    HISTORY RESEARCH
    COLLECTION
UNITED STATES NAVAL INSTITUTE
    PROCEEDINGS
UNIVERSITY OF KANSAS CITY LAW
    REVIEW
UTAH HISTORICAL QUARTERLY
UTAH HUMANITIES REVIEW

VIETNAM FORUM
VIRGINIA MAGAZINE OF HISTORY
    AND BIOGRAPHY
VIRGINIA QUARTERLY REVIEW
VIRGINIA SOCIAL SCIENCE JOURNAL
VOGUE

WAR AND SOCIETY
WARSHIP
WARSHIP INTERNATIONAL
WEST GEORGIA COLLECTION STUDIES
    IN SOCIAL SCIENCE
WEST VIRGINIA HISTORY
WESTERN HUMANITIES REVIEW
WESTERN POLITICAL QUARTERLY
WINGS
WISCONSIN LAW REVIEW
WISCONSIN MAGAZINE OF HISTORY
WOMAN, THE
WOMEN STUDIES INTERNATIONAL
    FORUM
WORLD AFFAIRS
WORLD POLITICS
WORLD WAR II
WYOMING LAW JOURNAL

YALE LAW REVIEW

ZYGON

APPENDIX B:
ABBREVIATIONS

ABDACOM   AMERICAN-BRITISH-DUTCH-AUSTRALIAN COMMAND

ATS   AIR TRANSPORT SERVICE

BAAG   BRITISH ARMY AID GROUP

CBI   CHINA-BURMA-INDIA THEATER

CPNAB   CONTRACTORS PACIFIC NAVAL AIR BASES

FEA   FOREIGN ECONOMIC ADMINISTRATION

GPO   GOVERNMENT PRINTING OFFICE

HMSO   HIS/HER MAJESTY'S STATIONERY OFFICE

IMTFE   INTERNATIONAL MILITARY TRIBUNAL FOR THE FAR EAST

IPR   INSTITUTE OF PACIFIC RELATIONS

JACL   JAPANESE AMERICAN CITIZENS LEAGUE

KMT   KUOMINTANG

LRPG   LONG RANGE PENETRATION GROUP

NATS   NAVY AIR TRANSPORT SERVICE

NE   NOT EVALUATED

OCMH   OFFICE OF THE CHIEF OF MILITARY HISTORY

OSS   OFFICE OF STRATEGIC SERVICES

OWI   OFFICE OF WAR INFORMATION

RIIA   ROYAL INSTITUTE OF INTERNATIONAL AFFAIRS

ROC   REPUBLIC OF CHINA

SACO   SINO-AMERICAN COOPERATIVE ORGANIZATION

SACSEA   SUPREME ALLIED COMMANDER, SOUTH EAST ASIA

SEAC   SOUTH EAST ASIA COMMAND

WRA   WAR RELOCATION AUTHORITY

APPENDIX C:
JAPANESE-AMERICAN RELOCATION CENTERS

ARIZONA
    GILA RIVER
    POSTON

ARKANSAS
    JEROME
    ROHWER

CALIFORNIA
    MANZANAR
    TULE LAKE

COLORADO
    GRANADA

IDAHO
    MINIDOKA

UTAH
    CAMP TOPAZ

WYOMING
    HEART MOUNTAIN

APPENDIX D:
CHRONOLOGY

1940

14 January   Admiral Mitsumasa Yonai forms a new cabinet in Japan.

30 March   Chinese puppet government under Wang Chung-wei is established at Nanking.

18 July   Britain closes the Burma Road.

4 September   Secretary of State Cordell Hull warns Japan against aggressive action in Indochina.

22 September   Japan and Vichy France conclude an agreement allowing Japanese forces use of air and maintenance bases.

22 September   Japanese forces move into Indochina.

26 September   Roosevelt announces an embargo on exports of scrap iron and steel to all countries outside the Western Hemisphere except Britain.

27 September   Japan, Germany, and Italy conclude the Tripartate Pact which calls for material aid if one of them is attacked over the next ten years.

8 October   Japanese Ambassador Kensuke Horinouchi describes U.S. embargo on scrap iron and steel as an "unfriendly act."

18 October   Britain reopens the Burma Road.

1941

27 January– 29 March	Secret American-British staff conversations (ABC-1) evolve strategy of "Europe First."
11 March	Congress passes Lend-Lease Act.
13 April	Japan and Soviet Union reach agreement on a treaty of neutrality.
21-27 April	U.S., British, and Dutch staff officers meet at Singapore to plan combined operations against further Japanese aggression.
24 July	Japan launches occupation of southern Indochina with permission of French Vichy government.
25 July	Roosevelt administration freezes Japanese assets in U.S. and halts all trade with Japan.
26 July	MacArthur is recalled to active service as commander of U.S. forces in the Far East.
9-12 August	Roosevelt and Churchill meet at Placentia Bay and issue Atlantic Charter.
September	First members of American Volunteer Group arrive at Rangoon to begin training at Toungoo.
18 October	Lt. Gen. Hideki Tojo becomes Prime Minister of Japan after Japanese Cabinet under Prince Fumimaro Konoye resigns.
5 November	Japan sends special envoy (Saburo Kurusu) to Washington to join Ambassador Kichisaburo Nomura in discussing U.S.-Japanese relations with Cordell Hull. The Japanese Imperial General Headquarters issues war plans for attacks against American, British, and Dutch possessions to be launched if the diplomatic negotiations in Washington failed.
20 November	Japanese envoys present list of demands to Hull.
26 November	Cordell Hull withdraws proposed modus vivendi and, instead, gives the Japanese a strongly worded statement of the U.S. position on American-Japanese relations.

7 December   Japanese planes attack Pearl Harbor. Japan also
                  attacks Malaya, Midway, Philippines, and Hong
                  Kong. Japan declares war on U.S. and Great
                  Britain.

8 December   U.S. and Britain declare war on Japan.

10 December   Five waves of attacking Japanese aircraft sink the
                  British battleship PRINCE OF WALES and cruiser
                  REPULSE.

11 December   Germany and Italy join their Tripartate Pact
                  partner in declaring war on the U.S. Congress
                  declares war on Germany and Italy.

22 December   The special commission chaired by Associate
                  Justice Owen J. Roberts, U.S. Supreme Court,
                  begins its hearings about the responsibility for
                  the disaster at Pearl Harbor.

22 December   Japanese forces land in the Philippines.

23 December   The last radio report is sent by the besieged
                  Americans at Wake Island.

25 December   Japan conquers Hong Kong.

1942

2 January   Gen. Sir Archibald Wavell is named commander of
                  American-British-Dutch-Australian forces in the
                  Far East (ABDACOM).

2 January   MacArthur and the army of the Philippines fall
                  back to Bataan peninsula as Japanese forces enter
                  Manila.

11 January   Japan invades the Netherlands East Indies.

21-26 January   Japan seizes Balikpapan.

24 January   Roberts Commission reports on its inquiry into
                  responsibility for the disaster at Pearl Harbor.

29 January   U.S. Attorney General Francis Biddle identifies
                  certain strategic areas on West Coast and orders
                  all enemy aliens removed from those areas.

31 January   British imperial forces withdraw from Malaya to
                  Singapore and destroy causeway connecting the
                  island to the mainland.

6 February   Japanese capture oil facilities in Borneo.

15 February   Singapore (Gen. Percival) surrenders to Yamashita.

19 February   Roosevelt signs Executive Order No. 9066 which
                  authorizes evacuation of all people within
                  designated military areas.

23 February   Japanese submarine shells oil refinery near Santa
                  Barbara, California.

24 February   British imperial forces in Burma withdraw from
                  Rangoon.

25 February   ABDACOM under the command of Gen. Wavell ceases to
                  exist.

27 February–   U.S. suffers naval losses in the Battle of the
1 March   Java Sea.

2 March   Gen. John L. DeWitt creates military areas in
                  parts of Washington, Oregon, California, and
                  Arizona. All people of Japanese blood will be
                  removed from these areas.

6 March   Japan conquers Batavia, the capital of the
                  Netherlands East Indies.

8 March   Japanese forces land at Lae and Salamua in New
                  Guinea.

10 March   Batavia falls to the Japanese.

10 March   Lt. Gen. Joseph W. Stilwell is appointed chief of
                  staff of Allied armies in the China Theater.

17 March   MacArthur arrives in Australia after having been
                  ordered to leave the Philippines.

18 March   Roosevelt signs Executive Order 9102 which
                  establishes War Relocation Authority to aid
                  evacuees. Milton S. Eisenhower is appointed
                  director.

22 March	First large group of Japanese aliens and U.S. (Japanese-American) citizens move from Los Angeles to Manzanar Assembly Center.
9 April	Bataan peninsula is taken by Japanese. American and Filipino prisoners suffer "Death March." Wainwright withdraws to island of Corregidor.
18 April	Tokyo is bombed in Doolittle Raid.
6 May	Wainwright surrenders Corregidor.
8-9 May	American naval forces score victory in the Battle of Coral Sea.
4-6 June	Japan suffers defeat in the Battle of Midway.
3-21 June	Japanese forces occupy Attu and Kiska in the Aleutians.
17 June	Dillon S. Myer becomes new director of WRA.
21 June	Oregon coastal area is shelled by Japanese submarine.
7 August	U.S. Marines land at Guadalcanal.
10 August	Japanese navy sinks three U.S. cruisers near Savo Island.
1 September	Tojo takes over as Foreign Minister after the resignation of Shigenori Togo.
3 September	Lt. Gen. George C. Kenney, head of Allied air forces, makes 5th Air Force a separate command.
7 September	Japanese forces are defeated in the Milne Bay sector.
11-12 October	U.S. naval forces earn victory at the Battle of Cape Esperance.
18 October	Adm. Halsey succeeds Adm. Ghormley as Commander, South Pacific Area.
26-27 October	Ten Japanese vessels are sunk or damaged during the Battle of Santa Cruz.
16 November	The Buna campaign begins.

29 November   Lt. Gen. Robert L. Eichelberger receives orders to
                   leave the training site at Rockhampton, Australia
                   and report to New Guinea. MacArthur allegedly
                   tells him to take Buna or die.

1 December   Airlift operations to China are taken from
                   Stilwell's control and put under Air Transport
                   Command.

3 December   Scientists arrange the first self-sustaining,
                   controlled nuclear reaction at the University of
                   Chicago.

                                   1943

14-24 January   Roosevelt and Churchill meet at Casablanca. They
                   issue call for "unconditional surrender" as a
                   chief war aim.

23 January   Eichelberger's forces take Buna.

9 February   Japanese forces evacuate Guadalcanal.

18 February   Wingate's first Long Range Penetration Group (77th
                   Indian Brigade) begins operations. The two-month
                   operation carries psychological importance, but
                   the LRPG suffered heavy losses.

2-4 March   Battle of Bismarck Sea ends in major U.S. victory.

26 March   During the Battle of the Komandorski Islands,
                   Japanese cautiousness prevents a possible major
                   victory.

18 April   U.S. pilots intercept and shoot down the Japanese
                   aircraft carrying Adm. Yamamoto at Bougainville.
                   Credit for this air victory is generally given to
                   Thomas G. Lanphier, Jr.

30 May   U.S. forces reclaim Attu.

11-24 August   Roosevelt and Churchill meet at Quebec and
                   announce creation of the new South East Asia
                   command under Mountbatten (SACSEA).

15 August   U.S. and Canadian forces launch assault on Kiska

but discover that the Japanese had secretly
abandoned the island. Allied losses in this
operation were slight, especially in light of the
fact that about 10,000 Japanese troops were lost!
(Kiska, qu'est-que c'est?)

11 October   "Disloyal" evacuees are segregated at Tule Lake
                    Center in California.

2 November   Decisive U.S. naval victory in the Battle of
                    Empress Augusta Bay enables Allies to cut supply
                    lines to Rabaul.

4 November   Riots at Tule Lake Center causes Army to take
                    control.

20 November   U.S. forces land on Tarawa and Makin in the
                    Gilbert Islands.

22 November   U.S. forces suffer heavy losses but win important
                    victories at Tarawa and Makin.

22-26 November   Roosevelt, Churchill, and Chiang Kai-shek meet in
                    Cairo and announce intention to reduce the
                    Japanese empire.

25 November   In the Battle of Cape St. George, U.S. naval
                    forces sink 3 Japanese ships and suffer no losses.

27 November-   Roosevelt and Churchill meet Stalin at Teheran.
  4 December   Stalin provides assurances that the Soviet Union
                    will enter the war against Japan after Germany is
                    defeated.

21 December   Stilwell launches campaign in northern Burma.

                                    1944

2 February   U.S. Marines land at Manur and Kwajalein--the
                    first Allied occupation of prewar Japanese
                    territory.

21 February   Tojo becomes chief of the army.

22 February-   The U.S. Navy conducts a special investigation led
  15 June   by Adm. Thomas C. Hart about the responsibility

for the disaster at Pearl Harbor.

1 March	U.S. forces invade Admiralty Islands.
22 March	Japanese forces enter India and head for Imphal.
22 April	MacArthur directs U.S. attack on Hollandia.
17 May	Allies open air route to China with their victory at Myitkyina in northern Burma. (Myitkyina, however, is not secured until 3 August 1944.)
16 June	U.S. B-29s bomb southern Japan (Kyushu).
19-20 June	Battle of the Philippine Sea is fought entirely by carrier-based aircraft.
20 June	American forces invade Marianas.
9 July	U.S. Marines gain control of Saipan.
17 July	U.S. naval ships bombard Guam in preparation for an assault to reclaim the island.
18-19 July	Gen. Yoshijiro Umezu succeeds Tojo as chief of the General Staff. Tojo's cabinet resigns, and Emperor Hirohito asks Gen. Kuniaka Koiso to form a new cabinet.
20 July–20 October	The Army Pearl Harbor Board led by Lt. Gen. George Grunert investigates responsibility for the debacle at Pearl Harbor.
24 July–19 October	Adm. Orin G. Murfin presides over an investigation by a special Navy Court of Inquiry into the responsibility for the defeat at Pearl Harbor.
26 July	Roosevelt, MacArthur, Nimitz, and Leahy meet at Pearl Harbor to discuss strategy in the Pacific.
14-16 September	Col. Carter W. Clarke (U.S.A.) holds hearings for the U.S. Army on the circumstances during the attack at Pearl Harbor.
15-17 September	U.S. Marines land at Peleliu.
17 September	U.S. 14th Air Force in China abandons air base at Kweilin.

20 September	Americans win control of Anguar Island (Carolines).
1 October	Japanese offensive in China moves through Kwangsi Province.
19 October	U.S. forces land in the Philippines (east coast of Leyte Island).
23 October	MacArthur and President Osmena establish government at Tacloban, Leyte (temporary capital).
23–26 October	U.S. naval forces win significant victory in battle for Leyte Gulf (the last and largest naval battle of the war).
28 October	Stilwell is recalled and replaced by Wedemeyer.
3 November	Japan begins balloon-bomb campaign aimed at continental United States. Over 9,000 are launched during the next ten months.
7 November	Roosevelt defeats Dewey in bid for fourth term.
13 November	14th Air Force withdraws from air base at Liuchow.
23 November	Lt. Col. Henry C. Clausen, JAGD, begins his special investigation for the U.S. Army about responsibility for the disaster at Pearl Harbor.
24 November	B-29s bomb Tokyo.
26 November	14th Air Force abandons base at Nanning.
15 December	U.S. forces land at Mindoro Island (PI).
15–20 December	Typhoon COBRA strikes the U.S. 3rd Fleet in the Philippine Sea. The typhoon caused the loss of three destroyers, severe damage to 9 ships, lesser damage to 19 other ships, the loss of 790 officers and men, and severe injuries to 80 others.
17 December	War Department revokes West Coast exclusion orders as of 2 January 1945.

1945

9 January	MacArthur's 6th Army lands at Lingayen Gulf on Luzon.
28 January	First convoy of trucks reaches China from India across Ledo Road (renamed for Stilwell).
5 February	U.S. forces enter Manila and begin 3-week struggle to oust the Japanese defenders.
7-12 February	Big Three meet at Yalta.
8 February	Alger Hiss plays key role in agreement on territorial trusteeship. Only certain limited categories of colonies and dependent areas will be brought under international supervision.
19 February	U.S. Marines land at Iwo Jima.
23 February	Famous photograph of flag-raising at Iwo Jima is taken by Joe Rosenthal. Earlier photo by Lou Lowery receives far less attention.
9 March	Japan coup seizes control of French Indochina.
10 March	A Japanese balloon-bomb becomes emeshed in the electrical wiring of the Hanford Engineering Works in the state of Washington, trips the plant's safety mechanism, and almost causes a shutdown of the reactor turning out radioactive uranium.
1 April	U.S. forces invade Okinawa.
5 April	Admiral Suzuki replaces Koiso as Prime Minister and forms a new Cabinet. Soviet Union denounces neutrality pact with Japan.
6 April	Giant Japanese battleship YAMATO is sunk by U.S. aircraft near Okinawa.
12 April	President Roosevelt dies at Warm Springs, Georgia.
25 April	Conference of the United Nations begins in San Francisco.
May	Five children and one adult die while investigating a downed Japanese balloon-bomb on Gearhart Mountain in Oregon.

15 May– 11 July	VADM H. Kent Hewitt heads a special naval inquiry into the circumstances surrounding the disaster at Pearl Harbor.
26 May	U.S. aircraft inflict fire bombing on Tokyo.
3–5 June	Typhoon VIPER strikes U.S. ships of the 3rd Fleet in Okinawan waters. The toll of the storm included 6 lives lost, 4 injured, 33 ships damaged, 76 planes destroyed, and 16 planes damaged.
18 June	Lt. Gen. Simon Bolivar Buckner, Jr., commander of all Allied forces on Okinawa, is killed while observing "mopping up" operations.
21 June	U.S. claims victory at Okinawa.
26 June	Representatives of 50 nations sign World Security Charter at the San Francisco Conference.
27 June	U.S. forces claim victory at Luzon.
1 July	MacArthur directs invasion of Balikpapan (Borneo).
4 July	MacArthur announces the liberation of the entire Philippine Islands.
5 July	Gen. Spaatz assumes command of Strategic Air Forces in the Pacific.
13 July– 4 August	Col. Carter W. Clarke (U.S.A.) completes his inquiry on the attack at Pearl Harbor.
16 July	"Trinity" test of atomic bomb at Alamogordo, New Mexico is successful.
17 July– 2 August	Truman, Stalin, and Churchill (later Attlee) meet at Potsdam Conference. Truman reveals to Stalin the existence of a new and powerful weapon.
21 July	Big Three at Potsdam will call on Japan to surrender or face total destruction.
29 July	Japan rejects Potsdam Declaration.
30 July	The INDIANAPOLIS sank within 12 minutes after being attacked by a Japanese submarine (I-58). The ship was en route to Leyte after delivering a

component of the atomic bomb at Tinian. Rescue operations began late (2 August) because of a misunderstanding of the ship movement report system and continued until 8 August. Only 316 of the crew of 1199 survived the ordeal.

6 August   Truman announces atomic bombing of Hiroshima.

8 August   Soviet Union declares war on Japan, and Soviet forces move into Manchuria.

9 August   Second atomic bomb is dropped on Nagasaki.

9 August   Last Japanese balloon-bomb to arrive in continental United States lands near Idaho Falls, Idaho.

10 August   Soviet forces invade Korea and southern Sakhalin Island.

10-11 August   Rogue Japanese officers stage unsuccessful attempt to thwart surrender announcement by the emperor.

14 August   Emperor Hirohito broadcasts surrender announcement. Sino-Soviet treaty is signed.

17 August   Achmed Sukarno and Mohammed Hatta proclaim independence of Republic of Indonesia.

19 August   Japanese emissaries arrive at Manila to receive instructions from MacArthur.

23 August   Truman halts all Lend-Lease shipments.

29 August   Truman makes public investigations by army and navy boards of inquiry on the disaster at Pearl Harbor.

30 August   MacArthur lands at Atsugi air base in Japan.

2 September   MacArthur supervises surrender proceedings aboard the battleship MISSOURI in Tokyo Bay. Ho Chi Minh proclaims the Republic of Vietnam.

9 September   Mountbatten supervises surrender ceremonies at Singapore.

12 September   Lt. Col. Henry C. Clausen completes his special investigation for the U.S. Army on Pearl Harbor.

30 September   U.S. Marines land in Hopei and Shantung to prevent
                   armed confrontation between Nationalists and
                   Chinese Communists.
24 October   United Nations Organization is officially
                   established as 29 countries ratify its charter.

15 November-   A joint congressional committee chaired by Sen.
15 July 1946   Alben W. Barkley (D., Kent.) investigates the
                   question of responsibility for the disaster at
                   Pearl Harbor.

Cleveland, W.M., 3438
Clifford, Frances, 4419
Clifford, Nicholas R., 504
Clifton, Paul, 3766
Clive, John, 4420
Close, Winton R., 2596
Clubb, O. Edmund, 1186
Clymer, Kenton J., 1410
Coakley, Robert W., 362, 3775, 3785
Coale, Griffith Baily, 3019
Coble, Parks M., Jr., 1187
Cochran, Alexander S., Jr., 2903, 3180, 3627
Cochran, Thomas C., 168
Cochrane, Robert B., 249
Cochrell, Boyd, 4421
Coerr, Eleanor, 3991
Coffer, Thomas M., 1810
Coffey, Thomas M., 1639, 1770
Coffman, Edward M., 1817
Coggins, Jack, 2167
Cohen, Bernard, 1327, 5079
Cohen, Eliot A., 1395
Cohen, Jerome B., 1495-1496
Cohen, Stan, 2637, 3057
Cohen, Theodore, 1259
Cohen, Warren I., 367-368, 750, 1188, 1314, 2100
Cohn, David L., 4657
Cole, Wayne S., 391-394, 505
Colegrove, Kenneth W., 897
Coleman, Earl E., 3868
Coleman, Homer J., 5018
Coleman, John S., 5137
Coleman, William L. ("Lonnie"), 4422
Coletta, Paulo E., 54
Colina, Edward J., 4423
Coll, Blanch D., 3332
Collier, Basil, 169, 1640-1641
Collier, Richard, 170, 395
COLLIER'S MAGAZINE, 274
Collins, Donald E., 4773
Collins, Larry, 4424
Collins, Maurice, 2033
Collison, Thomas, 4425
Colorado River War Relocation Center, 4774-4775

Columbia Broadcasting System, 4658
Colville, John, 749, 1260, 1328
Commager, Henry Steele, 171
Committee for the Compilation of Materials on Damage Caused By the Atomic Bomb in Hiroshima and Nagasaki, 3992
Compton, Arthur H., 3869
Compton, Karl, 3993
COMPTON'S ENCYCLOPEDIA, 275
Comyns-Carr, A.S., 1598-1599
Conant, James B., 3870
Condon, Jane, 4224
Confesor, Thomas, 751
Congdon, Don, 1750, 4659
Congressional Quarterly Service, 1315
Conley, Cornelius W., 4184
Conn, Stetson, 3151
Connell, Brian, 2407
Conrat, Maisie, 4776
Conrat, Richard, 4776
Conroy, F. Hilary, 506-508, 2101-2102, 3717
Conroy, Robert, 2291
Considine, Bob, 1818-1819
Constable, Trevor J., 2580
Contractors Pacific Naval Air Bases, 3776
Cook, Canfield, 4426-4427
Cook, Charles O., Jr., 1964, 2168, 2292
Cook, Gene, 4683
Cooper, Bryan, 2950-2951
Cooper, Dennis Glen, 1642
Cooper, Maurice Z., 5079
Cooper, Raymond, 3454
Coox, Alvin D., 26, 353, 355, 361, 509-512, 1025, 1108, 1643, 1958, 2103, 2445-2446, 2718
Coox, Alan C., 1958
Cope, Harley, 2904
Corbett, Charles H., 4248
Corbett, P. Scott, 5222
Corey, Wilfred G., 3559
Corkin, Frank R., 2597